Copyediting: Christine Thillen

Text and Cover Design: Lois Stanfield,
  LightSource Images

Composition: Carlisle Communications, Ltd.

Index: Schroeder Indexing Services

Cover image: Tom Pressly, REFLECTIONS
  OF JUSTICE
acrylic, 48″ × 36″, West Art and the Law 1983
Photo courtesy of West Publishing Corp.
Eagan, Minnesota
Photo credits appear after Index

WEST'S COMMITMENT TO THE ENVIRONMENT
In 1906, West Publishing Company began recycling materials left over from the production of books. This began a tradition of efficient and responsible use of resources. Today, up to 95 percent of our legal books and 70 percent of our college and school texts are printed on recycled, acid-free stock. West also recycles nearly 22 million pounds of scrap paper annually—the equivalent of 181,717 trees. Since the 1960s, West has devised ways to capture and recycle waste inks, solvents, oils, and vapors created in the printing process. We also recycle plastics of all kinds, wood, glass, corrugated cardboard, and batteries, and have eliminated the use of Styrofoam book packaging. We at West are proud of the longevity and the scope of our commitment to the environment.

Production, Prepress, Printing and Binding by West Publishing Company.

Explanatory Note
The authors have attempted to present the general principles of criminal law in this textbook. However, because of the variance in state statutes and court decisions from state to state, it is recommended that students and officers consult with their legal advisors before assuming that principles of law applicable in other states exist in their state.

Library of Congress Cataloging-in-Publication Data
Scheb, John M. (John Malcolm), 1926-
   Criminal law and procedure / John M. Scheb, John M. Scheb II. —
2nd ed.
     p.   cm.
   Includes index.
   ISBN 0-314-02765-3
   1. Criminal law—United States.   2. Criminal procedure—United States.   I. Title.
KF9219.S35   1994
345.73—dc20
[347.305]   93-34757
                                              CIP

CRIMINAL LAW AND PROCEDURE

SECOND EDITION

JOHN M. SCHEB, J.D., LL.M.
Judge, Florida Court of Appeal, Second District (Ret.)
Adjunct Professor, Stetson University, College of Law

JOHN M. SCHEB II, Ph.D.
Associate Professor of Political Science
University of Tennessee, Knoxville

West Publishing Company
Minneapolis/St. Paul   New York   Los Angeles   San Francisco

DEDICATED TO
JOHN M. SCHEB III
(Born April 2, 1992)

About The Authors

John M. Scheb was born in Orlando, Florida in 1926. He entered the practice of law in 1950. He served as municipal judge in Sarasota, Florida from 1957 to 1959. From 1959 to 1970, he served as City Attorney for the city of Sarasota. In 1974, he was appointed to the Florida District Court of Appeal, 2nd district, a position he held until his retirement in 1992. Judge Scheb is now an adjunct professor at Stetson University College of Law in St. Petersburg. He holds the B.A. from Florida Southern College, the J.D. from the University of Florida, and the LL.M. from the University of Virginia.

John M. Scheb II was born in Sarasota, Florida in 1955. He attended the University of Florida from 1974 to 1982, receiving the B.A., M.A., and Ph.D. in political science. He is now Associate Professor and Director of Graduate Studies in the Department of Political Science at the University of Tennessee, Knoxville. Professor Scheb is coauthor, with Otis H. Stephens, Jr., of *American Constitutional Law* (West Publishing Co., 1993).

CONTENTS

Chapter 7. Crimes Against Property and Habitation 167

Chapter 8. Offenses Against Public Morality 203

Chapter 17. The Criminal Trial

Chapter 18. Sentencing and Punishment

PREFACE

This textbook is designed for courses in American criminal law and procedure. It is intended to furnish students in criminology, criminal justice, pre-law, and paralegal programs a concise yet comprehensive introduction to the substantive and procedural criminal law. The book is also an appropriate reference for the criminal justice professional who needs to better understand the legal environment in which he or she must function.

The criminal law is constantly evolving, reflecting the rapid pace of change in our dynamic society. In this second edition of *Criminal Law and Procedure*, we have tried to capture some of the important developments in the criminal law that have taken place in the five years since the first edition was published. For example, the problem of "hate speech" is examined in Chapter 3, "Constitutional Limitations on the Prohibition of Criminal Conduct." The new crime of "stalking" is dealt with in Chapter 6, "Offenses Against Persons." In Chapter 6 we have also expanded the discussion of suicide, which has emerged recently as a serious social and legal issue. "Carjacking," computer theft, and credit card fraud, all of which pose new challenges to law enforcement, are discussed in Chapter 7, "Crimes Against Property and Habitation."

We have also added two new chapters to Part II, "The Substantive Criminal Law." Chapter 9, "Drug and Alcohol Offenses," reflects the widespread contemporary concern over the adverse effects of drug and alcohol abuse on society. Chapter 10, "Offenses Against Public Health and the Environment," reflects society's increasing concern for the natural environment.

In addition to addressing new concerns in criminal justice, this edition provides a more complete description of the criminal law. To this end, we have added Part IV, entitled "Specialized Topics in Criminal Law and Procedure." Part IV includes two totally new chapters: Chapter 20, "Juvenile Justice" and Chapter 21, "The Military Justice System." While these chapters address important topics in the administration of justice, they are placed in a separate section of the book because we recognize that some instructors will not address these matters in an introductory criminal law course.

In revising the text, we have tried to respond to suggestions and criticisms we have received over the last five years. Reflecting two of the more frequent suggestions, we have: (1) increased the number of "Cases in Point" that are interspersed throughout the chapter essays; and (2) have shortened the length of the edited cases that appear at the end of each chapter. To make these cases more intelligible to students, we have added a brief comment at the beginning of each case to give the reader a sense of what the case is about.

We would like to thank the following individuals who read and commented on parts of the manuscript: Lynn M. Leonard, a former staff attorney for the Florida Second District Court of Appeal; Charlie Ann Scott, an attorney in Sarasota, Florida; Cynthia S. Barry, an attorney in Bradenton, Florida; Lt. Col. Lawrence Klepetko, U.S. Air Force Reserve (J.A.G.); Marguerite L. Robinson, a senior at Stetson University College of Law; and Hon. Lee E. Haworth, Judge, 12th Judicial Circuit, State of Florida.

We would also like to thank Naina Bowen and Debra McCauley, secretaries in the Department of Political Science, University of Tennessee, Knoxville, for their tireless work in word processing edited cases and other parts of the manuscript. Additionally, we wish to express our gratitude to Loretta Maxwell, Eric Davis, and John Shanks, graduate students at the University of Tennessee, for their assistance in research and/or proofreading. It is difficult to imagine how the project could have been completed on schedule without their assistance.

Much of the credit for this book belongs to the staff at West Publishing Company who provided excellent assistance and support throughout the project. We would especially like to thank our editor, Joan Gill, her executive assistant, Becky Stovall, and our production editor, Poh Lin Khoo. Working with these professionals made the task of producing a textbook infinitely easier and more pleasant.

Finally, we would like to thank our wives, Mary Burns Scheb and Sherilyn Claytor Scheb, for their patience and support, without which the project could not have been undertaken, much less completed.

We hope this book is useful to students and teachers of criminal law. Naturally, we assume full responsibility for any errors contained herein.

John M. Scheb
John M. Scheb II
November 1, 1993

REVIEWERS AND AFFILIATIONS

Jerry C. Armor, Calhoun Community College, Decatur, AL

Sherry Biddinger-Gregg, Indiana State University, Terre Haute, IN

Elaine Cohen, Broward Community College, Fort Lauderdale, FL

Paul Falzone, California State University-Sacramento, Sacramento, CA

Barbara May, Montgomery County Community College, Telford, PA

Robert W. Peetz, Midland College, Midland, TX

Bob Plesha, Lakewood Community College, St. Paul, MN

Chet Zerlin, Miami-Dade Community College, Coral Gables, FL

CRIMINAL LAW AND PROCEDURE

SECOND EDITION

PART

I

INTRODUCTION TO THE CRIMINAL JUSTICE SYSTEM

CHAPTER 1

FUNDAMENTALS OF CRIME, LAW, AND PUNISHMENT

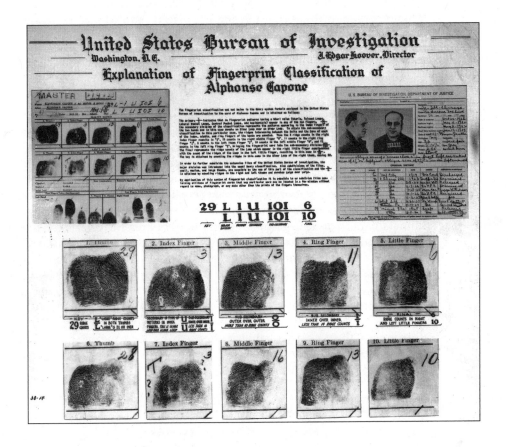

CHAPTER OUTLINE

INTRODUCTION

The fundamental problem facing any society is how to control the actions of individuals that threaten the life, liberty, and property of other individuals as well as society's collective interests in order, peace, safety, and decency. Societies have developed a number of informal means of achieving this control, including family structures, social norms, and religious precepts. On the other hand, law is a formal means of achieving social control. In general, law can be defined as a body of rules prescribed and enforced by government for the regulation and protection of society. Criminal law is that branch of the law that prohibits certain forms of conduct and imposes penalties on those who engage in prohibited behavior.

WHAT IS A CRIME?

Every crime involves a wrongful act (*actus reus*) specifically prohibited by the criminal law. For example, in the crime of battery, the *actus reus* consists in the striking or offensive touching of another person. Even the failure to take action can be considered a wrongful act, if the law imposes a duty to take action in a certain situation. For example, in many jurisdictions, one who fails to report an instance of child abuse to the proper authorities may be guilty of an offense.

In most cases the law requires that the wrongful act be accompanied by criminal intent (*mens rea*). Criminal intent does not refer to one's motive or reason for acting, but merely to one's having formed a mental purpose to act. To convict a person of a crime, it is not necessary to know *why* a person committed a crime. It is only necessary to show that the individual intentionally committed a prohibited act. An unintentional act is usually not a crime, although, as we will discover, there are exceptions to this principle. Moreover, in certain instances, one may be held criminally responsible irrespective of intent. Crimes of this latter nature are classified as strict liability offenses. A good example of a strict liability offense is selling liquor to a minor. (Strict liability offenses and elements of crimes generally are discussed in Chapter 4.)

Nullen Crimen, Nulla Poena, Sine Lege

A person cannot be convicted of a crime unless he or she committed a specific offense against a law that provides for a penalty. This principle is expressed in the maxim *nullen crimen, nulla poena, sine lege*, a Latin phrase that means "there is no crime, there is no punishment, without law." A related principle of American law is the proscription of *ex post facto* laws. Under the United States Constitution (Article I, Sections 9 and 10), an act cannot be made a crime retroactively. To be criminal, an act must be illegal at the time it was committed.

Felonies and Misdemeanors

Criminal law distinguishes between serious crimes, known as felonies, and less serious offenses, called misdemeanors. Generally speaking, felonies are offenses

FORM 1. COMPLAINT—SUMMONS FOR
MISDEMEANOR OR PETTY
MISDEMEANOR

STATE OF MINNESOTA DISTRICT COURT
COUNTY OF _____ _____ JUDICIAL DISTRICT

_____ ,)   COMPLAINT—SUMMONS
   Plaintiff,)   FOR
vs.   )   MISDEMEANOR OR
)   PETTY MISDEMEANOR
_____ ,)
   Defendant.)   District Court File No. _____

COMPLAINT

The Complainant being duly sworn, makes complaint to the above-named Court and states that Complainant believes there is probable cause to believe that the above-named Defendant committed the offense described below. The Complainant states that the following facts established PROBABLE CAUSE:

The above facts constitute Complainant's basis for believing that the above-named Defendant, on the ___ day of _____, 19 ___ at _____ ,
                     (location)
in the above-named County, committed the following described

OFFENSE

Charge: _____ in violation of Section: _____

(description)

THEREFORE, Complainant requests that the Defendant, subject to bail or conditions of release where applicable,

(1) be arrested or that other lawful steps be taken to obtain the Defendant's appearance in court; or

(2) be detained, if already in custody, pending further proceedings; and that the Defendant otherwise be dealt with according to law.

_____
(Name of Complainant)
Complainant

Being duly authorized to prosecute the offense charged, _____ hereby approves this   (Prosecuting Attorney)

Complaint.

_____
(Prosecuting Attorney)
Name:
Attorney License No.:
Title:
Address:
Telephone No.:

FINDING OF PROBABLE CAUSE

From the above sworn facts, and any supporting affidavits or supplemental sworn testimony, I, the Issuing Officer, have determined that probable cause exists to support, subject to bail or conditions of release where applicable, Defendant's arrest or other lawful steps to be taken to obtain Defendant's appearance in Court, or Defendant's detention, if already in custody, pending further proceedings. The Defendant is therefore charged with the above-stated offense.

SUMMONS

THEREFORE YOU, THE ABOVE-NAMED DEFENDANT, ARE HEREBY SUMMONED to appear on the ___ day of _____, 19 ___, at ___ o'clock ___ m., before the above-named Court at

_____
(Room Number)   (Place)   (Address)
to answer this complaint.

IF YOU FAIL TO APPEAR in response to this Summons, a warrant for your arrest may be issued.

This Complaint—Summons was sworn to, subscribed before, and issued by the undersigned authorized Issuing Officer this ___ day of _____, 19 .

_____
Issuing Officer*

Sworn testimony has been given before the Issuing Officer by the following witnesses:

*The name and title of the Issuing Officer should be printed or stamped following the Issuing Officer's signature.
[Effective for criminal actions commenced or arrests made after 12 o'clock midnight January 1, 1990.]

FIGURE 1.1 A Form for Filing a Criminal Complaint. Source: *Minnesota Rules of Court, State and Federal, 1991.* (West Publishing Co., 1991), p. 216.

THE ELEMENTS OF A CRIME

Normally, the following elements must be present to constitute a crime:

1. Actus reus, *or wrongful act.* There must be some specific act of commission or omission by the accused. Unlike the religious concept of sin, a crime must involve more than evil thoughts.
2. Mens rea, *or guilty mind.* Generally speaking, an act cannot be regarded as criminal unless accompanied by an intention to commit the prohibited act. Thus a person who was insane at the time of committing an offense cannot be held criminally liable for his or her actions.
3. *Concurrence of action and intent.* Society does not punish a person for merely entertaining an evil intention, nor for committing an un-

avoidable act. Rather, for a crime to occur, there must be a concurrence between the *actus reus* and *mens rea.*

4. *Harm.* To constitute a crime, an act must cause harm to a legally recognized interest such as an individual's person, property or reputation, or societal interests in order, safety, peace, morality, and health.
5. *Causation.* There must be a causal relationship between the act and the harm suffered. Thus, for example, if Bunny Burns stabs Jimmy Johnson and the latter soon dies from a pre-existing disease, Bunny Burns would not ordinarily be found guilty of murder. Of course, she could be found guilty of a lesser felony such as mayhem or aggravated assault.

for which the offender can be imprisoned for more than one year; misdemeanors carry jail terms of less than one year. Common examples of felonies include murder, rape, kidnapping, arson, assault with a deadly weapon, robbery, and grand larceny. Typical misdemeanors include petit theft, simple assault and battery, public drunkenness, disorderly conduct, prostitution, gambling, and various motor vehicle infractions.

Crime: An Injury Against Society

Our legal system regards crimes not merely as wrongs against particular victims but as offenses against the entire community. Indeed, there does not have to be an individual victim for there to be a crime. For example, it is a crime to possess cocaine, even though it is unlikely that a particular individual will claim to have been victimized by another person's use of the drug. It is a crime because society, through its governing institutions, has made a collective judgment that cocaine use is inimical to the public welfare.

Because crime is an injury against society, it is government, as society's legal representative, that brings charges against persons accused of committing crimes. In the United States, we have a federal system, that is, a division of power and responsibility between the national and state governments. Both the national government and the states enact their own criminal laws. Thus both the national and state governments may prosecute persons accused of crimes. The national government initiates a prosecution when a federal (national) law has been violated; a state brings charges against someone who is believed to have violated one of its laws.

The Role of the Crime Victim

Because the government prosecutes criminals on behalf of society, the victim of a crime is not a party to the criminal prosecution. By filing a complaint with a law enforcement agency, a victim initiates the process that leads to prosecution, but once the prosecution begins, the victim's participation is primarily that of being a witness. Quite often victims feel lost in the shuffle of the criminal process. They sometimes feel that the system is insensitive or even hostile to their interests in seeing justice done. As we shall see, some states are now taking steps to address victims' concerns (see "The Rights of Crime Victims" in Chapter 18). But fundamentally, the victim is a secondary player in the criminal justice system. The principal parties in a criminal case are the prosecution (i.e., the government) and the defendant (i.e., the accused person). There are situations, however, in which the victim may have another remedy—a civil suit to recover damages for losses or injuries suffered.

CIVIL AND CRIMINAL LAW

The criminal law is not the only body of law that regulates the conduct of individuals. The civil law provides remedies for essentially private wrongs, offenses in which the state has a less direct interest. Most civil wrongs are classified as breaches of contract or torts. A breach of contract occurs when a party to a contract violates the terms of the agreement. A tort, on the other hand, is a wrongful act that does not violate any enforceable agreement but that nevertheless violates a legal right of the injured party. Common examples of torts include wrongful death, intentional or negligent infliction of personal injury, wrongful destruction of property, trespass, and defamation of character. As noted earlier, a crime normally entails intentional conduct. A driver who accidentally hits and kills another person with his or her car would not necessarily be guilty of a crime, depending on the circumstances (see discussions of manslaughter and vehicular homicide, Chapter 6). If the accident resulted from the driver's negligence, he or she would have committed the tort of wrongful death, and would be subject to a civil suit for damages.

The criminal and the civil law often overlap. Thus, conduct that constitutes a crime may also involve a tort. For example, suppose Randy Wrecker intentionally damages a house belonging to Harvey Homeowner. Wrecker's act may well result in both criminal and civil actions being brought against him. Wrecker may be prosecuted by the state for the crime of willful destruction of property and also may be sued by Homeowner for the tort of wrongful destruction of property. The state would be seeking to punish Wrecker for his antisocial conduct, whereas Homeowner would be seeking compensation for the damage to his property. The criminal case would be designated *State v. Wrecker* (or *People v. Wrecker*, or even *Commonwealth v. Wrecker*, depending on the state); the civil suit would be styled *Homeowner v. Wrecker*.

CONSTITUTIONAL LIMITATIONS

Under our system of government, the prohibitions of the criminal and civil law are subject to limitations contained in the federal and state constitutions. Thus the First Amendment to the U.S. Constitution prohibits government from using the civil or criminal law to abridge freedom of speech. For example, the United States Supreme Court has interpreted the First Amendment to limit the ability of public officials to sue their critics for the torts of libel and slander. *New York Times v. Sullivan*, 376 U.S. 254, 84 S.Ct. 710, 11 L.Ed.2d 686 (1964). In the criminal law context, the Supreme Court has said that one cannot be punished merely for advocating violence unless there is "imminent lawless action." *Brandenburg v. Ohio*, 395 U.S. 444, 89 S.Ct. 1827, 23 L.Ed.2d 430 (1969). The First Amendment also has important implications for the crimes of obscenity and indecency.

Other important constitutional principles limit the authority of government to define certain conduct as criminal. Among them is the right of privacy, which relates to abortion and a wide range of sexual conduct that traditionally was defined as criminal. We discuss these limitations in some detail in Chapter 3.

SUBSTANTIVE AND PROCEDURAL CRIMINAL LAW

As we have noted, there can be no prosecution, and no punishment, except as provided by law. Our criminal law prescribes both substantive and procedural rules governing the everyday operation of the criminal justice system. Substantive criminal law prohibits certain forms of conduct by defining crimes and establishing the parameters of penalties. Procedural criminal law regulates the enforcement of the substantive law, the determination of guilt, and the punishment of those found guilty of crimes. For example, while substantive law makes the possession of heroin a crime, the procedural law regulates the police search and seizure that produce the incriminating evidence. The substantive law makes premeditated murder a crime; the procedural law determines the procedures to be observed at trial and, if a conviction results, at sentencing.

THE ORIGINS AND SOURCES OF THE CRIMINAL LAW

Many antisocial acts classified as crimes have their origin in the norms of primitive societies. Certain types of behavior have been universally condemned by mankind since ancient times. Acts such as murder, rape, robbery, and arson are considered *mala in se*, or inherent wrongs. Other acts that the modern criminal law regards as offenses are merely *mala prohibita;* they are offenses only because they are so defined by the law. Many so-called victimless crimes, such as possession of marijuana or gambling, are generally not regarded as offensive to universal principles of morality. Rather, they are wrong simply because the law declares them wrong. In the case of *mala prohibita* offenses, the legislature has reached a judgment that certain conduct, while not contrary to universal moral principles, is nevertheless incompatible with the public good.

Development of Law in the Western World

There is a general consensus that law developed in Western civilization as leaders began formalizing and enforcing customs that had evolved among their peoples. Eventually, informal norms and customs came to be formalized as codes of law. The Code of Hammurabi regulated conduct in ancient Babylonia some two thousand years before Christ. In the seventh century B.C., Draco developed a very strict code of laws for the Athenian city-states. Even today, one hears strict rules or penalties characterized as being "Draconian." These developments influenced the Romans in their development of the Twelve Tables in the fifth century B.C. And, of course, long before the time of Jesus, the Hebrews had developed very elaborate substantive and procedural laws.

In the first century A.D., the Code of Justinian was promulgated throughout the Roman Empire. The Code of Justinian became very influential in determining the evolution of law on the European continent. The Napoleonic Code, promulgated under Napoleon Bonaparte in 1804 as a codification of all the civil and criminal laws of France, was based in large part on the Code of Justinian. The Napoleonic Code became a model for a uniform system of law for the nations of Western Europe. It is for this reason that the legal systems of Western Europe are often said to be "Roman law" systems. Roman law systems are based on the primacy of statutes enacted by the legislature. These statutes are integrated into a comprehensive code designed to be applied by the courts with a minimum of judicial interpretation.

Development of the English Common Law

American criminal law is derived largely from the English common law, which dates from the eleventh century. Prior to the Normal Conquest of 1066, English law was a patchwork of local laws and customs, often applied by feudal courts. William the Conqueror, the first Norman king of England, dispatched royal judges who traveled the country settling disputes based on the common customs of the people (hence the term *common law*). By 1300 the decisions of the royal judges were being recorded to serve as precedents to guide judges in future similar cases. The common-law doctrine of following precedent, known as *stare decisis,* remains an important component of both the English and American legal systems. As the centuries passed, coherent principles of law and definitions of crimes emerged from the decisions of the judges. Thus, in contrast to Roman law systems, which are based on legal codes, the common law developed primarily through judicial decisions.

By 1600, the common-law judges had defined the crimes of murder, manslaughter, mayhem, robbery, burglary, arson, larceny, rape, suicide, and sodomy as felonies. They had also begun to develop a number of lesser offenses known as misdemeanors. In contrast to the criminal law that was developing on the continent, England developed trial by jury and trained barristers to argue cases on an adversarial basis. A "barrister" is a lawyer permitted to cross the "bar" in the courtroom that separates the bench from the spectators. Thus, in England, a barrister is a trial lawyer. Although we do not use the term *barrister* in the United States, we do refer to licensed attorneys as having been "admitted to the bar."

As representative government developed in England, the dominance of the common-law courts diminished. Parliament came to play a significant role in the formation of the criminal law by adopting statutes that revised and supplemented the common law. However, the adversarial system of justice continued and the basic English felonies remain today defined essentially as they were by the common-law judges centuries ago.

Development of the American Criminal Law

Our criminal laws came basically from the common law as it existed at the time that America proclaimed its independence from England in 1776. After independence, the new American states adopted the English common law to the extent that it did not conflict with the new state and federal constitutions. However, the federal government did not adopt the common law of crimes. From the outset, federal crimes were defined by statutes passed by Congress. Of the fifty states in the Union, Louisiana is the only one whose legal system is not based ultimately on the common law. Rather, it is based primarily on the Napoleonic Code.

The new American judges and lawyers were greatly aided by *Blackstone's Commentaries*, published in 1769, in which Sir William Blackstone, a professor at Oxford, codified the principles of the common law. Blackstone's seminal effort was a noble undertaking, but it had the effect of demystifying English law. Consequently, Blackstone's encyclopedic treatment of the law was less than popular among English barristers, who by this time had developed a close fraternity and took great pride in offering their services to "discover the law." In America, however, *Blackstone's Commentaries* became something of a "legal bible."

As the American nation developed, most common-law definitions of crimes were superseded by legislatively defined offenses in the form of statutes. These criminal statutes, or codes, for the most part retain the offenses defined by the common law. However, criminal statutes and codes often go far beyond the common law in prohibiting offenses that are *mala prohibita*. Criminal offenses can also be defined by regulatory agencies where such authority has been specifically delegated by Congress or a state legislature. When authorized by state constitutions or acts of state legislatures, cities and counties may adopt ordinances that define certain criminal violations.

Although the majority of states have abolished all, or nearly all, common-law crimes, and replaced them by statutorily defined offenses, the common law remains a valuable source of interpretation. This is because legislatures frequently use terms known to the common law without defining such terms. For example, in proscribing burglary, the legislature may use the term *curtilage* without defining it. In such an instance, a court would look to the common law, which defined the term to mean "an enclosed space surrounding a dwelling."

The Model Penal Code (MPC)

The American Law Institute (ALI) is an organization of distinguished judges, lawyers, and academics who have a strong professional interest in drafting model codes of laws. In 1962, after a decade of work that produced several tentative drafts, the ALI published its Proposed Official Draft of the Model Penal Code (MPC). The MPC consists of general provisions concerning criminal liability, sentences, defenses, and definitions of specific crimes. The MPC is not law; rather, it is designed to serve as a model code of criminal law for all states. It has had a significant impact on legislative drafting of criminal statutes, particularly during the 1970s when the majority of the states accomplished substantial reforms in their criminal codes. Additionally, the MPC has been influential in judicial interpretation of criminal statutes and doctrines, thereby making a contribution to the continuing development of the decisional law. In this text, we illustrate many principles of law by representative statutes from federal and state jurisdictions; however, in some instances where the MPC is particularly influential, the reader will find references to specific provisions of the MPC.

Sources of Procedural Law

The procedural criminal law is promulgated both by legislative bodies, through enactment of statutes, and by the courts, through judicial decisions and the development of rules of court procedure. The U.S. Supreme Court prescribes rules of procedure for the federal courts. Generally, the highest court of each state, usually called the state supreme court, is empowered to promulgate rules of procedure for all the courts of that state.

In addition to the common law, statutes, regulations, and ordinances, the federal and state constitutions contribute to the body of substantive and procedural law. The U.S. Constitution, for example, defines the crime of treason. U.S. Const. Art. III, Sec. 3. The Constitution has much to say about criminal procedure, most notably as it relates to search and seizure, U.S. Const. Amend. IV, the protection against compulsory self-incrimination, U.S. Const. Amend. V, the right to counsel, U.S. Const. Amend. VI, and the right to trial by an impartial jury, U.S. Const. Amend. VI. Of course, the responsibility for "fleshing out" the general principles of criminal procedure contained in the federal and state constitutions rests primarily with the courts by deciding specific cases presented to them. Also, through the adoption of statutes, the Congress and the state legislatures provide additional details in this area.

Due Process of Law

By far the broadest, and probably the most important, constitutional principle relating to criminal procedure is found in the due process clauses of the Fifth and Fourteenth Amendments to the Constitution. The same principle can be found in some provision of every state constitution. Reflecting a legacy that can be traced to the Magna Charta (1215), such provisions forbid the government from taking a person's life, liberty, or property, whether as punishment for a crime or any other reason, without due process of law. Due process refers to those procedural safeguards necessary to assure the fundamental fairness of a legal proceeding. Many essential elements of due process are found in the Bill of Rights of the Constitution (e.g., the right to a trial by an impartial jury, the right to counsel, and the freedom from unreasonable searches and seizures).

Other important due process protections are not specifically mentioned in the Constitution. For example, it is fundamental that in a criminal case the defendant is presumed innocent, and the prosecution must establish the defendant's guilt beyond a reasonable doubt. *In re Winship*, 397 U.S. 358, 90 S.Ct. 1068, 25 L.Ed.2d 368 (1970). While no one seriously challenges the reasonable doubt standard as an essential element of due process, other traditional characteristics of criminal trials, such as the twelve-member jury and the requirement of a unanimous verdict finding the defendant guilty of a crime are not always viewed as necessary elements of constitutional due process. *Williams v. Florida*, 399 U.S. 78, 90 S.Ct. 1893, 26 L.Ed.2d 446 (1970); *Apodaca v. Oregon*, 406 U.S. 404, 92 S.Ct. 1628, 32 L.Ed.2d 184 (1972). Consequently these traditional elements of criminal procedure have been modified in a number of states.

CRIMINAL PUNISHMENT

During the colonial period of American history, and indeed well into the nineteenth century, the death penalty was often inflicted for a variety of felonies including rape, arson, and horse theft. Likewise, such corporal punishments as flogging or being placed in a pillory were common. Now that officially sanctioned corporal punishment is no longer administered to those convicted of crimes in this country, criminal sanctions entail one or more of the following:

1. **The death penalty.** Although the Supreme Court's decision in *Furman v. Georgia*, 408 U.S. 238, 92 S.Ct. 2726, 33 L.Ed.2d 346 (1972), temporarily halted the imposition of the death penalty, capital punishment returned in 1977 when the state of Utah placed convicted murderer Gary Gilmore in front of a firing squad. Since then, the administration of the death penalty has become more common. Currently, thirty-six states as well as the federal government have statutes providing for capital punishment, either by electrocution, the gas chamber, the firing squad, or by lethal injection. The Supreme Court has held that the death penalty is a legitimate punishment, but only for the crime of murder. *Coker v. Georgia*, 433 U.S. 584, 97 S.Ct. 2861, 53 L.Ed.2d 982 (1977). Although the public largely supports the death penalty for the crime of premeditated murder, the penalty remains controversial among criminologists. The evidence to support the hypothesis that capital punishment is a general deterrent to murder seems tenuous at best.

2. **Incarceration.** This is the conventional mode of punishment prescribed for those convicted of felonies. Under federal and state law, felonies are classified by their seriousness, and convicted felons may be imprisoned for periods ranging from one year to life. Incarceration is usually available as a punishment for those convicted of the more serious misdemeanors, but for only up to one year in most jurisdictions. While it was originally thought to be an effective means of rehabilitation, most criminologists now view incarceration simply as a means of isolating those persons who pose a serious threat to society. The U.S. Department of Justice reported that the number of inmates in federal and state prisons reached an all-time high in 1992, with 883,593 persons incarcerated. Indeed, prison populations grew approximately 150 percent between 1980 and 1992. This tremendous increase reflects the fact that during the 1980s federal and state sentencing laws were amended to increase the length of prison terms given to convicted felons. Unfortunately, many prisons are now seriously overcrowded to the point that courts must limit the number of inmates that can be confined.

3. **Monetary fines.** Fines are by far the most common punishment for those convicted of misdemeanors. Felons are likewise often subject to fines in addition to, or instead of, incarceration. Usually, the law allows the sentencing judge to impose a fine, a jail term, or some combination of the two. A number of felonies, especially serious economic crimes, now carry very heavy fines. For example, violations of federal banking and securities laws are punishable by fines running into the millions of dollars.

4. **Community service.** This sanction is becoming more attractive as a punishment for less serious crimes, especially for juveniles and first-time offenders. Community service is generally regarded as a more meaningful sanction than the imposition of a fine. It is also viewed as less likely than incarceration to promote future criminal behavior. The theory underlying community service is that an offender will become aware of his or her

obligations to the community and how his or her criminal conduct violated those obligations.

5. **Probation.** This alternative to incarceration is common for first-time offenders, except in cases involving the most serious crimes. Probation is usually conditioned on restrictions on the probationer's everyday conduct. Arguably, it has the advantage of placing the individual in the supervision of the government while keeping him or her away from the possibly crime-inducing environment of the prison. Unfortunately, the success of probation has often been hindered by inadequate staffing, resulting in inadequate supervision of probationers.

6. **Loss of civil rights.** Federal and state statutes deprive convicted felons of certain rights, most notably the right to vote and to hold public office. In recent years, however, the courts have held that incarcerated criminals do retain certain fundamental constitutional rights, such as the right to freely exercise their religious beliefs. *Cruz v. Beto*, 405 U.S. 319, 92 S.Ct. 1079, 31 L.Ed.2d 263 (1972). Even where courts have recognized the constitutional rights of prisoners, they have generally restricted the scope of these rights in light of the overriding necessity for security and discipline in the prison environment. *Bell v. Wolfish*, 441 U.S. 520, 99 S.Ct. 1861, 60 L.Ed.2d 447 (1979).

Sentencing Persons Convicted of Crimes

Sentencing takes place after the accused has been convicted of a crime. Sentences for particular crimes are spelled out in the statutes, although typically these statutes allow for considerable discretion on the part of the judge or jury imposing the sentence. In an effort to reduce disparities in sentencing, the federal government and some states have developed sentencing guidelines, a subject discussed in Chapters 2 and 18.

WHY DO PEOPLE COMMIT CRIMES?

For centuries it was widely believed that people who committed crimes were "touched by the devil." In modern times, we tend not to ascribe criminal behavior to metaphysical causes but to factors that can be observed, examined, and explained. The science of criminology is devoted to identifying the causes and effects of criminal behavior. Criminology is far from a merely academic concern—our understanding of the causes of criminal behavior affect the policies we follow in attempting to prevent and control crime.

In the nineteenth century, criminologists like Cesare Lombroso (1835–1909) began to examine crime as a biologically based phenomenon, arguing that some people are "born criminal types." Most contemporary criminologists reject such biological models of crime in favor of theories that stress environmental factors. Today most criminologists would concede that there are multiple causes of crime.

Fundamentally, it must be recognized that the existence of crime is a function of the criminal law itself, for, by definition, there can be no crime without criminal law. As more forms of conduct have become prohibited by law, the incidence of crime has increased. Currently, the federal government defines more than 2,800 distinct criminal offenses; the number of offenses designated by state and local governments is even greater. Much behavior not traditionally regarded as criminal has been incorporated into modern criminal codes. For example, numerous federal and state laws now criminalize actions that threaten the natural environment and the public health (see Chapter 10). Consequently, the traditional concept of what constitutes a crime has been greatly expanded.

Undoubtedly, the overwhelming majority of Americans regard themselves as law-abiding citizens. Yet many of these people routinely commit crimes they do not regard as morally wrong, such as underreporting their income for tax purposes, smoking marijuana, betting on football games, or speeding on interstate highways. Many so-called upperworld crimes are regarded by their perpetrators simply as shrewd business practices (e.g., consumer fraud, insider trading in stocks, price fixing, or violations of health and safety regulations).

Criminologists have focused most of their attention on why people commit crimes that are *mala in se*, such as offenses against persons like murder, rape, robbery, and aggravated assault. Of lesser magnitude are the crimes against property such as grand larceny, burglary, forgery, and fraud. Criminologists have also examined why some people are much more likely than others to commit these economic crimes.

As noted, *mala in se* offenses like murder, rape, mayhem, burglary, robbery, and arson have existed from the very outset of human experience. Some would say that such behavior flows from human nature itself. But the prevalence of crime in modern society requires more explanation than unfavorable characterizations of human nature. Social scientists have, not surprisingly, placed great emphasis on sociological, economic, and political factors. Many have stressed the decline of religion and the nuclear family as agents of socialization, the alienation of the individual from an impersonal mass society, and the emergence of huge cities that provide subcultures conducive to crime and frequent opportunities to commit crimes. Others have pointed to the lessening of criminal penalties and the increased restrictions placed on law enforcement by courts. Still others have cited the existence of massive unemployment and poverty in a society that has so much wealth and that places so much importance on individual affluence. In dealing with a phenomenon as complex as crime, most social scientists agree that all these hypotheses are quite plausible.

Criminals as Rational Actors

During the Age of Enlightenment, the Italian criminologist Cesare Beccaria (1738–1794) argued that crimes are rational acts committed by rational individuals who believe that the benefits of committing a crime outweigh the disadvantages of doing so. The widespread belief in the deterrent effect of punishment is based on this rationalistic view of criminal behavior. If criminals are rational actors who calculate the costs and benefits of their actions, then making punishment swift, certain, and severe ought to deter people from committing crimes. Of course, the constitutional requirement of due process and the constitutional prohibition against "cruel and unusual punishments" militate against swift, certain, and severe punishment. Moreover, it is doubtful that all or even most criminals rationally assess the costs and benefits of their acts. Certainly crimes of passion, which are impulsive acts of violence committed by people whose emotions have run away with them, are by definition not rational acts. But it is also difficult to understand how the numerous rapes, assaults, kidnappings, child molestations, and homicides that occur today are the result of rational thought by rational people, even if these crimes are carefully planned. Nevertheless, most people believe that, to the extent that criminal conduct is rational, crime would be lessened by strengthening law enforcement agencies, removing impediments to police investigations, expediting trials, limiting appeals, and enhancing criminal penalties. Clearly, the American public is apprehensive about crime and tends to support all of these strategies. Of course, the courts of law owe their primary allegiance to the Constitution, not to public opinion.

THE SERIOUSNESS OF THE CURRENT CRIME PROBLEM

While crime is generally perceived as having worsened over the last three decades, it is very difficult to know exactly the scope of the problem. Since the 1930s the Federal Bureau of Investigation (FBI) has published the Uniform Crime Reports (UCR). These are based on standardized definitions of certain key "index crimes" reported to state and federal law enforcement agencies. With the exception of theft, these index crimes do not include misdemeanor offenses. Moreover, the actual occurrence of crime exceeds reported crime by an unknown margin that probably varies markedly across jurisdictions. It is well known that people in large cities are much less likely to report crimes than are residents of suburbia or small towns. Similarly, reportage probably varies according to the nature and severity of crimes. For example, the victims of rape, embarrassed by what has happened to them and reluctant to experience the difficulties of a criminal trial, often let their attacks go unreported. Victims of motor vehicle theft, on the other hand, are very likely to report their misfortunes since there is little stigma attached to being a victim of theft and it is often necessary to report losses to secure reimbursement from insurance companies. Consequently, the UCR gives us a very fuzzy picture of the incidence of crime in America.

More accurate and useful than the Uniform Crime Reports are victimization surveys in which representative samples of people are asked whether they have been the targets of criminal activity. The victimization studies done by the Bureau of the Census under sponsorship of the Law Enforcement Assistance Administration (LEAA) in the 1970s revealed that the actual incidence of crime far surpassed that reported to the FBI. These victimization studies also revealed much about the demographics of crime victimization in America. Except for rape and purse snatching, men tend to be victims of both violent and economic crime more frequently than do women. Young people also tend to be disproportionately victimized, as do African Americans and other ethnic and racial minorities. However, it must be recognized that, given the pervasiveness and degree of randomness of crime, no one is exempt from potential victimization. In 1987, the U.S. Department of Justice released a report predicting that five out of six twelve-year-olds would be the victims or intended victims of crimes during their lifetimes.

TABLE 1.1   Criminal Victimizations, 1991

Type of Crime	Number of Victimizations	% Change 1990–1991
Personal crimes	19,414,500	+2.3
Violent	6,427,480	+7.0
Theft	12,991,880	+0.1
Household crimes	15,640,490	+1.4
Larceny	8,601,820	+3.6
Burglary	5,092,570	−1.1
Motor vehicle theft	1,947,850	−1.0
TOTAL	35,054,040	+1.9

Source: U.S. Department of Justice, Bureau of Justice Statistics, *National Update* (July 1992), p. 4.

While crime is certainly more prevalent in America today than it was thirty years ago, victimization studies conducted by the Department of Justice show a significant decline in violent crime over the last decade. According to the 1991 National Crime Victimization Survey, the rate of "violent victimizations" (rape, robbery, and assault) declined from approximately 35 per 1,000 people in 1981 to around 31 per 1,000 in 1991. On the other hand, violent victimizations rose 7 percent between 1990 and 1991, perhaps signaling a reversal of the trend. The National Crime Victimization Survey found that 23.7 percent of the nation's households experienced some form of criminal victimization in 1991. Clearly, crime remains a serious social, legal, and political problem for this country.

Conclusion

One of the more tragic aspects of the crime problem is that many Americans are losing faith in the ability of their government to protect them from criminals. Indeed, in some areas of the country victims are unlikely even to report crimes to the police. Some victims are unwilling to endure the difficulties of being a witness. Others simply believe that the perpetrator will not be apprehended, or if so, will not be punished.

Our state and federal governments are severely constrained both by legalities and practicalities in their efforts to fight crime. Not only is the specter of "a cop on every corner" distasteful to most Americans, it is well nigh impossible to achieve even with unlimited public resources, let alone in this age of fiscal retrenchment.

Obviously, one of the most serious problems currently facing law enforcement is the massive importation of illegal drugs into this country. How many personnel, aircraft, and ships would it take to stem the flow of cocaine, heroin, and marijuana across our borders? Are we willing, indeed are we able, to commit such massive resources to the fight against drug smuggling?

Currently, the nation's prison system is filled beyond its capacity, yet the public is demanding that more convicted criminals be incarcerated and for longer periods of time. Yet the public appears unwilling to provide the revenues needed to build the additional prisons necessary to house these inmates.

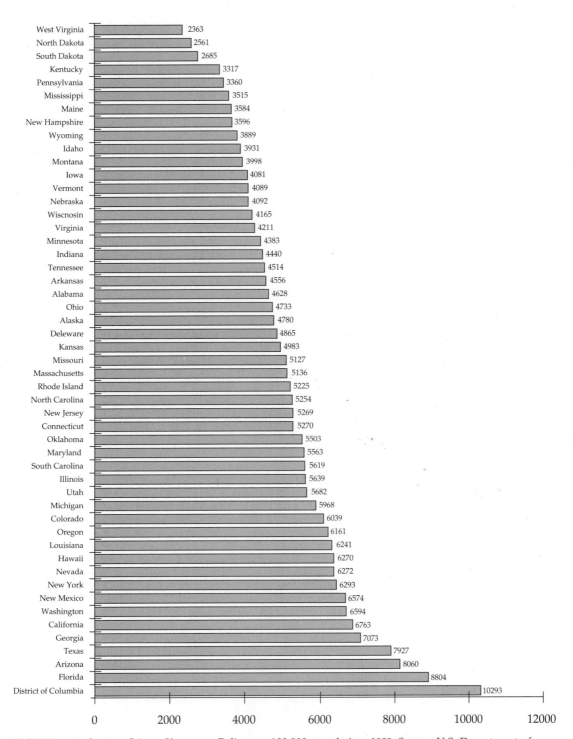

FIGURE 1.2 Serious Crimes Known to Police per 100,000 population, 1989. Source: U.S. Department of Commerce, Bureau of the Census, 1990.

Finally, society must confront the problem of the constitutional limitations on crime definition and law enforcement. Judges do have considerable discretion in interpreting the commands of the state and federal constitutions. Yet, if these documents are to be viable protections of our cherished liberties, we must accept the fact that they place significant constraints on our efforts to control crime. For instance, to what degree is the public willing to allow the constitutional protection against unreasonable searches and seizures to be eroded? To what degree are we willing to sacrifice our constitutionally protected privacy and liberty in order to speed up the ferreting out of crime? Perhaps this is the fundamental question of criminal law and procedure in a society that prides itself in preserving the rights of the individual.

QUESTIONS FOR THOUGHT AND DISCUSSION

1. What are the chief distinctions between the civil and criminal law, and why do they often overlap?

2. To what extent is the English common law significant in contemporary American criminal law?

3. What is the essential difference between the substantive and procedural criminal law? Can you give examples of each?

4. How does the U.S. Constitution affect the ability of a legislature to define certain conduct as criminal?

5. What social, economic, and psychological factors cause individuals to commit serious crimes?

6. In what ways does the prevalence of illegal drug use contribute to the crime problem? Would crimes such as burglary, larceny, robbery, and murder diminish in frequency if drugs like heroin and cocaine were legalized?

7. Why is it difficult to obtain a clear statistical picture of crime in the United States? What suggestions would you offer to expedite a more accurate assessment of crime in America?

8. What means of punishment for criminal offenses exist in your state? Is capital punishment available for persons convicted of first-degree murder? Which punishments, if any, do you think are most effective in controlling crime in your state?

THE ORGANIZATION OF THE CRIMINAL JUSTICE SYSTEM

INTRODUCTION

In every modern country, criminal justice is a complicated process involving a plethora of agencies and officials. In the United States, criminal justice is particularly complex, due largely to the existence of federalism, the constitutional division of authority between the national and state governments. Under this scheme of federalism, the national government operates one criminal justice system for the purpose of enforcing the criminal statutes adopted by Congress; each of the fifty states has its own justice system for enforcing its own criminal laws. As a result of this structural complexity, it is difficult to provide a coherent overview of criminal justice in America. Each system is to some extent unique, in terms of both substantive and procedural law. Yet there are a number of similarities: All fifty-one criminal justice systems in the United States involve law enforcement agencies, prosecutors, defense attorneys, courts of law, and corrections agencies. All follow certain general procedures beginning with arrest and, in some cases, ending in punishment. Finally, all systems are subject to the limitations of the United States Constitution, as interpreted by the United States Supreme Court.

LAW ENFORCEMENT AGENCIES

Law enforcement agencies are charged with the task of enforcing the criminal law. They have the power to investigate suspected criminal activity, to arrest suspected criminals, and to detain arrestees until their cases come before the appropriate courts of law. We expect law enforcement agencies not only to arrest those suspected of crimes but also to take steps to prevent crimes from occurring. In the United States there are nearly forty thousand federal, state, and local agencies involved in law enforcement and crime prevention.

At the national level, the Federal Bureau of Investigation is the primary agency empowered to investigate violations of federal criminal laws. Located in the Department of Justice, the FBI is by far the most powerful of the federal law enforcement agencies, with broad powers to enforce all of the many criminal laws adopted by the Congress. The FBI currently employs more than 25,000 people, including nearly eleven thousand agents spread out over fifty-six field offices in the United States and twenty-one foreign offices. Its annual budget exceeds 2.3 billion dollars. The FBI uses the most sophisticated methods in crime prevention and investigation.

In addition to the FBI, a number of federal agencies have law enforcement authority in specific areas. Among them are the Bureau of Alcohol, Tobacco, and Firearms; the Drug Enforcement Administration; the Customs Service; the Immigration and Naturalization Service; the Bureau of Postal Inspection; and the Secret Service.

Many states have their own counterparts to the FBI. Similarly, every state has a number of state agencies responsible for enforcing specific areas of the law, ranging from laws governing traffic safety to laws governing agricultural importation, from casino gambling to the dispensing of alcoholic beverages.

At the local level, we find both county and municipal law enforcement agencies. Nearly every county in America has a sheriff. In most states, sheriffs are elected to office and exercise broad powers as the chief law enforcement officers of their respective counties. In some areas, particularly the urban Northeast, many of the powers traditionally exercised by sheriffs have been assumed by state or metropolitan police forces. However, in the rest of the country, especially in the rural areas, sheriffs (and their deputies) are the principal law enforcement agents at the county level. More than twenty thousand cities and towns have police departments. Local police are charged with enforcing the criminal laws of their states, as well as of their municipalities. Although the county sheriff usually has jurisdiction within the municipalities of the county, generally he or she concentrates enforcement efforts on those areas outside municipal boundaries.

In addition to providing law enforcement in the strictest sense of the term, local law enforcement agencies are heavily involved in order maintenance or "keeping the peace," hence the term *peace officers*. Often, keeping the peace involves more discretion than merely applying the criminal law.

PROSECUTORIAL AGENCIES

While law enforcement agencies are the "gatekeepers" of the criminal justice system, prosecutors are central to the administration of criminal justice. They determine whether to bring charges against suspected criminals. They have enormous discretion, not only in determining whether to prosecute but also in determining what charges to file. Moreover, prosecutors frequently set the tone for plea bargaining and have a powerful voice in determining the severity of sanctions imposed on persons convicted of crimes. Accordingly, prosecutors play a crucial role in the criminal justice system.

The chief prosecutor at the federal level is the Attorney General, who is the head of the Department of Justice. Below the Attorney General are a number of United States Attorneys, each responsible for a specific geographical area of the country. The United States Attorneys in turn have a number of assistants who handle most of the day-to-day criminal cases brought by the federal government. The Attorney General and the United States Attorneys are appointed by the president, subject to the consent of the Senate. The assistant U.S. Attorneys are federal civil service employees.

In addition to the regular federal prosecutors, Congress has provided for the appointment of special prosecutors (or "independent counsel") in cases involving alleged misconduct by high government officials. By far the most infamous such case was "Watergate," which resulted in the convictions of several high-ranking officials and the resignation of a president. But there have been several cases where, under congressional direction, a special prosecutor has been appointed. One of the more dramatic instances was the Iranian arms scandal of 1986. There, a special prosecutor was assigned to investigate shipments of arms to Iran and subsequent diversion of profits from the arms sales to rebel forces in Nicaragua.

Each state likewise has its own attorney general and a number of assistant attorneys, plus a number of district or state's attorneys at the local level.

Generally speaking, local prosecutors are elected for set terms of office. In most states local prosecutors act autonomously and possess broad discretionary powers.

Cities and counties also have their own attorneys. These attorneys sometimes prosecute violations of city and county ordinances, but increasingly their function is limited to representing their cities or counties in civil suits and giving legal advice to local councils and officials. These city and county attorneys are generally appointed by the governing bodies they represent.

DEFENSE ATTORNEYS

It is axiomatic in American criminal law that individuals accused of any crime, no matter how minor the offense, have the right to employ counsel for their defense. U.S. Const. Amend. VI. Beginning in the 1960s, the United States Supreme Court greatly expanded the right to counsel by requiring states to provide attorneys to indigent defendants. *Gideon v. Wainwright*, 372 U.S. 335, 83 S.Ct. 792, 9 L.Ed.2d 799 (1963); *Argersinger v. Hamlin*, 407 U.S. 25, 92 S.Ct. 2006, 32 L.Ed.2d 530 (1972). In some states an indigent person who requests counsel at public expense has an attorney from the private bar appointed to represent him or her. Many states, however, have chosen to handle the problem of indigent defense by establishing public defender's offices. Like public prosecutors, public defenders are generally elected to set terms of office.

THE COURTS

Courts of law are the centerpieces of the federal and state criminal justice systems. It is their responsibility to determine both the factual basis and legal sufficiency of criminal charges and to insure that criminal defendants are provided due process of law.

Basically, there are two kinds of courts: trial and appellate courts. Trial courts conduct criminal trials and various pretrial and posttrial proceedings. Appellate courts hear appeals from the decisions of the trial courts. While trial courts are primarily concerned with ascertaining facts, determining guilt or innocence and imposing punishments, appellate courts are primarily concerned with matters of law. Appellate courts serve both to correct legal errors made by trial courts and to develop law when new legal questions arise.

Jurisdiction

The first question facing a court in any criminal prosecution is that of jurisdiction, the legal authority to hear and decide the case. A court must have jurisdiction, over both the subject matter of a case and the parties to a case, before it may proceed to adjudicate that controversy. The jurisdiction of the federal courts is determined both by the language of Article III of the Constitution and by statutes enacted by Congress. The jurisdiction of the state courts is determined by the respective state constitutions and statutes. Essentially, the federal courts adjudicate criminal cases where defendants are charged with violating federal criminal laws; state courts adjudicate alleged violations of state laws.

The Federal Court System

Article III of the U.S. Constitution provides that "The judicial Power of the United States shall be vested in one supreme Court, and in such inferior Courts as the Congress may from time to time ordain and establish." Under this authority Congress has created the federal court system comprising a number of trial and appellate tribunals. These courts handle prosecutions for violations of federal statutes. In addition, federal courts sometimes review convictions from state courts where defendants raise issues arising under the U.S. Constitution.

Federal District Courts   The principal trial court in the federal system is the United States District Court. There are district courts in ninety-four federal judicial districts around the country. A criminal trial in the district court is presided over by a judge appointed for life by the president with the consent of the Senate. Pretrial proceedings in the district courts and trials of misdemeanors are often handled by federal magistrates, who are appointed by federal district judges.

The district courts were created by an act of Congress in 1789. Since then, Congress has created specialized courts to handle specific kinds of cases (e.g., the United States Court of International Trade and the United States Claims Court).

The United States Courts of Appeals   The intermediate appellate courts in the federal system are the United States Courts of Appeals (also known as circuit courts). Twelve geographical circuits (and one "federal circuit") cover the United States and its possessions. Figure 2.1 indicates the geographical distribution of the circuit courts. The circuit courts hear both criminal and civil appeals from the district courts and from "quasi-judicial" tribunals in the independent regulatory agencies. Generally, decisions of the courts of appeals are rendered by panels of three judges who vote either to affirm or to reverse the lower court decisions under review. There is a procedure by which the circuit courts provide *en banc* hearings, where all judges assigned to the court participate in a decision. Like their counterparts in the district courts, federal appeals court judges are appointed to life terms by the president with the consent of the Senate.

Military Tribunals   Crimes committed by persons in military service are prosecuted in proceedings before courts-martial, with appeals decided by the Court of Military Appeals in Washington, D.C. Only under conditions of martial law do military tribunals have the authority to try civilians. *Ex parte Milligan*, 71 U.S. (4 Wall.) 2, 18 L.Ed.281 (1866). Article 1, Section 8 of the U.S. Constitution grants Congress the authority to regulate the armed forces. Under this authority, Congress has enacted the Uniform Code of Military Justice (UCMJ), 10 U.S.C.A. §§ 801–940. The UCMJ gives courts-martial jurisdiction to try all offenses under the code committed by military personnel. Notwithstanding this grant of authority, the United States Supreme Court held in 1969 that military jurisdiction

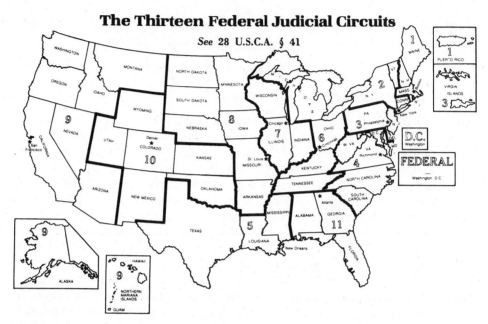

FIGURE 2.1   The Federal Judicial Circuits. Source: *Federal Reporter*, 2d Series (West Publishing Co.).

was limited to offenses that were service connected. *O'Callahan v. Parker*, 395 U.S. 258, 89 S.Ct. 1683, 23 L.Ed.2d 291 (1969). The *O'Callahan* decision had the effect of greatly narrowing military jurisdiction over offenses committed by servicepersons. In 1987 the Court, in a 5–4 decision, overruled *O'Callahan* and said that military jurisdiction depends solely on whether an accused is a military member. *Solorio v. United States*, 483 U.S. 435, 107 S.Ct. 2924, 97 L.Ed.2d 364 (1987). Thus courts-martial may now try all offenses committed by service persons in violation of the UCMJ.

Decisions of courts-martial are reviewed by military courts of review in each branch of the armed forces. In specified instances appeals are heard by the United States Court of Military Appeals. The Court of Military Appeals is staffed by civilian judges who are appointed to fifteen-year terms by the president with the consent of the Senate. (For further discussion of the military justice system, see Chapter 21.)

The United States Supreme Court.   The highest appellate court in the federal judicial system is the U.S. Supreme Court. The Supreme Court has jurisdiction to review, either on appeal or by writ of *certiorari*, all the decisions of the lower federal courts and many of the decisions of the highest state courts. Naturally, the Supreme Court is able to review only a very small percentage of the numerous criminal cases decided by lower courts.

The Supreme Court is staffed by nine justices who, like district and circuit judges, are appointed for life. These nine individuals have the final word in

JURISDICTION OVER CRIMES COMMITTED ON INDIAN RESERVATIONS

Article I, Section 8 of the U.S. Constitution mentions Indian tribes as being subject to Congressional legislation. Congress has provided that federal courts have jurisdiction over specified offenses committed by Native Americans on Indian reservations. 18 U.S.C.A. § 1153. At the same time, Congress has permitted certain states to exercise jurisdiction over such offenses. 18 U.S.C.A. § 1162. Furthermore, offenses committed by one native American against another on a reservation are generally subject to the jurisdiction of tribal courts, unless the crime charged has been expressly made subject to federal jurisdiction. *Keeble v. United States*, 412 U.S. 205, 93 S.Ct. 1993, 36 L.Ed.2d 844 (1973).

Courts of the state where an Indian reservation is located, not federal courts, have jurisdiction over crimes on the reservation where the offense is perpetrated by a non-Indian against a non-Indian, but non-Indian defendants charged with committing a crime on a reservation are subject to federal jurisdiction if the victim was a member of the tribe. *United States v. Antelope*, 430 U.S. 641, 97 S.Ct. 1395, 51 L.Ed.2d 701 (1977).

determining what the U.S. Constitution requires, permits, and prohibits in the areas of law enforcement, prosecution, adjudication, and punishment. The Supreme Court also promulgates procedural rules for the lower federal courts to follow in both criminal and civil cases.

State Court Systems

Each state has its own independent judicial system. These courts handle more than 90 percent of criminal prosecutions in the United States. State judicial systems are characterized by enormous variation in structure, but every state has one or more levels of trial courts and at least one appellate court. Some states, like North Carolina, have adopted tidy, streamlined court systems (see fig. 2.2). Other states' court systems are extremely complex, as is the case in Texas (see fig. 2.3). In complexity, most states fall somewhere between the two extremes.

STAGES IN THE CRIMINAL PROCESS

Certain basic procedural steps are common to all criminal prosecutions, although specific procedures vary greatly among jurisdictions. As cases move through the system from arrest through adjudication and, in many instances, toward the imposition of punishment, there is considerable attrition. Of any one hundred felony arrests, perhaps as few as twenty-five will result in convictions. This "sieve effect" occurs for a number of reasons, including insufficient evidence, police misconduct, procedural errors, and the transfer of young offenders to juvenile courts.

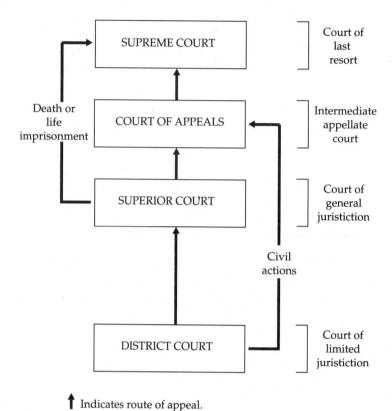

↑ Indicates route of appeal.

FIGURE 2.2 North Carolina Court System. Source: U.S. Department of Justice/ National Center for State Courts.

Search and Seizure

Search and seizure normally occur prior to arrest. Searches are directed at locating evidence of crime; seizures occur when searches are fruitful. Like all activities of law enforcement, search and seizure is subject to constitutional limitations. The Fourth Amendment to the U.S. Constitution, enforceable against the states through the due process clause of the Fourteenth Amendment, explicitly protects citizens from unreasonable searches and seizures. *Mapp v. Ohio,* 367 U.S. 643, 81 S.Ct. 1684, 6 L.Ed.2d 1081 (1961). The Supreme Court has interpreted this protection as requiring law enforcement officers to have specific grounds for conducting searches, either "probable cause" or the less stringent standard of "reasonable suspicion." *Terry v. Ohio,* 392 U.S. 1, 88 S.Ct. 1868, 20 L.Ed.2d 889 (1968). Furthermore, the Court has held that officers must obtain warrants authorizing searches unless "exigent circumstances" make it impossible to obtain a warrant and also preserve evidence of crime. *Carroll v. United States,* 267 U.S. 132, 45 S.Ct. 280, 69 L.Ed. 543 (1925). There are several well-defined types of searches, each subject to a distinct set of constitutional rules. The limited investigatory stop, the "stop-and-frisk," the border search, the search incident to a lawful arrest, and electronic eavesdropping are examples of types of searches that have been addressed by the courts.

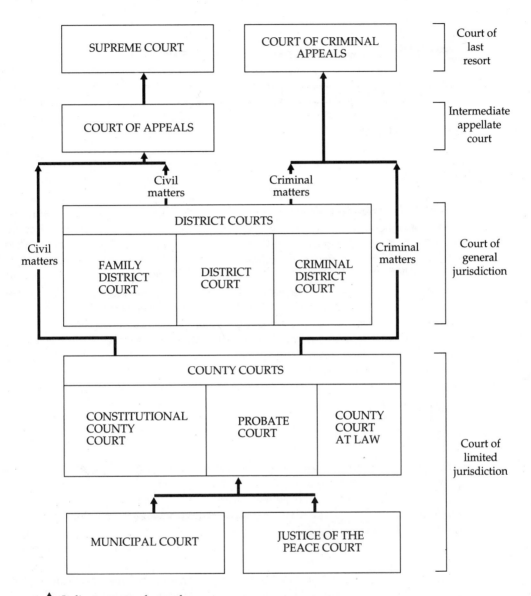

FIGURE 2.3 The Texas Court System. Source: U.S. Department of Justice/National Center for State Courts.

To enforce the protections of the Fourth Amendment, the Supreme Court has fashioned a broad "exclusionary rule" that bars the fruits of illegal searches and seizures from being used as evidence in criminal trials. *Weeks v. United States,* 232 U.S. 383, 34 S.Ct. 341, 58 L.Ed. 652 (1914); *Mapp v. Ohio,* 367 U.S. 643, 81 S.Ct. 1684, 6 L.Ed.2d 1081 (1961). Recent decisions by the Court have narrowed somewhat the scope of this exclusionary rule. See, for example, *United States v. Leon,* 468 U.S. 897, 104 S.Ct. 3405, 82 L.Ed.2d 677 (1984). Nevertheless, because it excludes from many cases evidence that is both reliable and probative, the exclusionary rule remains controversial.

Arrest and Interrogation

Arrest consists of taking into custody a person suspected of having committed a crime. Arrests can be made on the basis of warrants issued by magistrates or indictments handed down by grand juries. More commonly, arrests are made by police who observe commission of a crime or have probable cause to believe a crime has been committed, but face exigent circumstances that prevent them from obtaining an arrest warrant. When an officer restricts a person from leaving the officer's presence or formally places that person under arrest, a number of constitutional protections come into play. These include the well-known *Miranda* warnings given to suspects in custody advising them of their constitutional rights. *Miranda v. Arizona*, 384 U.S. 436, 86 S.Ct. 1602, 16 L.Ed.2d 694 (1966).

The investigative tool of police interrogation takes many forms—from direct questioning to the use of subtle psychological techniques. Subject to narrow exceptions, custodial interrogation is not permitted until the suspect has been issued the *Miranda* warnings and has either waived those rights or has obtained counsel. A Fifth Amendment analogue of the Fourth Amendment exclusionary rule requires that confessions obtained by police through custodial interrogation must be excluded from evidence unless they meet these constitutional criteria. *Miranda v. Arizona*, 384 U.S. 436, 86 S.Ct. 1602, 16 L.Ed.2d 694 (1966).

An individual arrested for a minor misdemeanor is generally released from police custody and ordered to appear in court at a later date to answer the charge. If the arrest is for a major misdemeanor or felony, the individual is usually held in custody pending an initial appearance before a judge or magistrate.

Initial Appearance

Under the Constitution, a person accused of a crime has the right to a "speedy and public trial." U.S. Const., Amend. 6. This includes the right to be brought before a judge to be formally apprised of the charges. In addition to reading the charges, the judge at the first appearance attempts to ascertain whether the defendant is represented by an attorney. If not, and the defendant is indigent, the judge generally appoints counsel. Finally, the judge determines whether the accused is to be released from custody pending further proceedings. A defendant who merits pretrial release can be released either on bail or on his or her own recognizance. In deciding whether to grant pretrial release, and whether to require that the defendant post a bond to assure the court the defendant will appear to answer the charges, a judge must weigh the seriousness of the alleged crime as well as the defendant's prior record and ties to the community.

Summary Trials for Minor Offenses

In the case of minor misdemeanors, including many traffic violations, trials are often held in a summary fashion without the use of a jury, usually at the defendant's first appearance in court. The U.S. Supreme Court has held that a jury trial is not constitutionally required unless the defendant is subject to incarceration for more than six months. *Duncan v. Louisiana*, 391 U.S. 145, 88 S.Ct. 1444, 20 L.Ed.2d 491 (1968). In such cases, we might question whether the traditional presumption of innocence applies. In a summary trial the charges are read, the defendant is asked to plead to the charges, and a verdict is reached, often within a few minutes. In most such cases, defendants do in fact plead guilty, but even when they protest innocence, they are seldom accquitted. This is largely because judges are much more inclined to take the word of the arresting officer over that of the accused, and rarely are there any additional witnesses. Although a person charged with any criminal offense has the right to retain counsel to represent him or her at a summary proceeding, most defendants charged with minor misdemeanors are not represented by counsel. A principal reason is the expense of retaining a lawyer. The Supreme Court has said that indigent persons do not have a right to counsel at public expense unless they are actually sentenced to more than six months in jail. *Scott v. Illinois*, 440 U.S. 367, 99 S.Ct. 1158, 59 L.Ed.2d 383 (1979).

The Grand Jury

According to the Constitution, "no person shall be held to answer for a capital, or other infamous crime, unless on a presentment of indictment of a Grand Jury ..." U.S. Const. Amend. 5. The grand jury, not to be confused with the trial jury, is a body that considers evidence obtained by the prosecutor in order to determine whether there is probable cause to hold a trial. As a mechanism designed to prevent unwarranted prosecutions, the grand jury dates back to twelfth-century England.

Each federal judicial district maintains a grand jury. These grand juries comprise twenty-three jurors. Grand juries are also maintained in many state jurisdictions, although the Supreme Court has held that states are not required to use grand juries in charging criminal defendants. *Hurtado v. California*, 110 U.S. 516, 4 S.Ct. 111, 28 L.Ed. 232 (1884).

Grand jury proceedings are typically closed to the public. The prosecutor appears before the grand jury with a series of cases he has built against various defendants. Witnesses are called and physical evidence is presented. If the grand jury believes that a given case is substantial, it hands down an indictment, or "true bill." In the overwhelming majority of cases, grand juries hand down indictments against persons as requested by prosecutors, leading some to question the utility of the grand jury procedure as a means of guarding against arbitrary or unwarranted prosecution.

The Preliminary Hearing

About half of the states, especially those that entered the Union more recently, have dispensed with the ancient institution of the grand jury. They have opted instead for charging defendants in a fashion that is less cumbersome and arguably more protective of the innocent. Under the more modern approach, the prosecutor files an accusatorial document called an "information" containing the charge against the accused. A preliminary hearing is then held in which a judge or magistrate must determine whether there is probable cause to hold the defendant for trial. At the preliminary hearing, the prosecutor presents physical evidence and testimony designed to persuade the judge that probable cause exists. The defense attorney, whose client is also usually present, generally exercises the right to cross-examine the prosecution's witnesses. In addition, the defense may, but seldom does, present evidence on behalf of the defendant at that time.

A number of states, for example, Tennessee and Georgia, use the grand jury mechanism, supplemented by an optional preliminary hearing. This hybrid model provides a double check against the possibility of unwarranted prosecution.

Arraignment

The arraignment is the first appearance of the defendant before the court that has the authority to conduct a trial. At this stage the defendant must plead to the charges that have been brought. The defendant has four options: (1) to plead guilty, in which case guilt will be pronounced and a date set for sentencing; (2) to plead not guilty, in which case a trial date will be set; (3) to plead *nolo contendere,* or no contest, which is tantamount to a plea of guilty; (4) to remain silent, in which case the court enters a plea of not guilty on behalf of the accused.

Plea Bargaining

Only a small proportion (perhaps 5 percent) of felony cases ever reach the trial stage. Many cases are dropped by the prosecutor for lack of evidence. Some cases may be dropped due to obvious police misconduct. Others are dismissed by judges at preliminary hearings, usually for similar reasons. Of the cases that reach the arraignment stage, only about 10 percent result in trials. In the other 90 percent, defendants enter pleas of guilty, often in exchange for concessions from the prosecution. To avoid trial, which is characterized by both delay and uncertainty, the prosecutor often attempts to persuade the defendant to plead guilty, either by reducing the number or severity of charges, or by promising not to seek the maximum penalty allowed by law. This controversial practice is known as plea bargaining.

Under a plea bargain, a charge of possession of cocaine with intent to distribute may be reduced to simple possession. First-degree murder, which may carry a death sentence, might be reduced to second-degree murder, which carries a term of imprisonment. A series of misdemeanor charges stemming from an altercation in a bar might be reduced to single charge of disorderly conduct.

The U.S. Supreme Court has upheld the practice of plea bargaining against claims that it violates the due process clauses of the Fifth and Fourteenth Amendments. *Brady v. United States,* 397 U.S. 742, 90 S.Ct. 1463, 25 L.Ed.2d 747 (1970); *North Carolina v. Alford,* 400 U.S. 25, 91 S.Ct. 160, 27 L.Ed.2d 162 (1970). However, because there is always a danger of coerced guilty pleas, especially when defendants are ignorant of the law, it is the judge's responsibility to ascertain whether the defendant's guilty plea is voluntarily and knowingly entered. *Boykin v. Alabama,* 395 U.S. 238, 89 S.Ct. 1709, 23 L.Ed.2d 274 (1969).

Pretrial Motions

Typically, a number of pretrial motions are available to both the defense and prosecution in a criminal case. Of particular importance are these motions:

- To dismiss the charges against the accused
- To inspect evidence in the hands of the prosecution
- To suppress evidence because of alleged illegalities in gathering it
- To change the venue of a trial in order to protect the accused from prejudicial pretrial publicity
- To obtain a continuance (postponement) of the trial
- To inspect the minutes of grand jury proceedings
- To ask for psychiatric evaluation of the accused
- For closure of pretrial proceedings (again, to protect the right of the accused to a fair trial)

Jury Selection

The Supreme Court has held that defendants in both state and federal prosecutions have the right to a jury trial if they are subject to more than six months incarceration. *Duncan v. Louisiana*, 391 U.S. 145, 88 S.Ct. 1444, 20 L.Ed.2d 491 (1968). Potential trial jurors (venirepersons) are selected typically, but not universally, from the rolls of registered voters. The actual process of jury selection, known as *voir dire*, consists of questioning potential jurors to determine their suitability for jury duty. In the federal courts, *voir dire* is conducted primarily by the judge; in the states, it is typically conducted by the attorneys for both sides. In all jurisdictions, attorneys may challenge jurors they find to be unsuitable. Attorneys may exercise a limited number of peremptory challenges, which are generally granted as a matter of course. However, peremptory challenges may not be based solely on the race of a prospective juror. *Batson v. Kentucky*, 476 U.S. 79, 106 S.Ct. 1712, 90 L.Ed.2d 69 (1986). Unlike peremptory challenges, challenges for cause must be supported by reasons acceptable to the court. There is, however, considerable discretion in the court's allowance of such challenges. While peremptory challenges are limited in number, there is no set limit to the number of challenges for cause.

Trial Procedures and Adjudication

The criminal trial is a formal and complex adversarial encounter between the government and the accused. The trial is governed by rules of evidence and procedure that are designed to develop the case in an orderly fashion and assist the fact finder (judge or jury) in reaching the correct result. After opening statements by counsel, the prosecution, through the introduction of testimony and physical evidence, attempts to prove the guilt of the accused beyond a reasonable doubt. The purpose of the defense is to create reasonable doubt about the government's case. In some cases the defense relies solely on cross-examination of the prosecution's witnesses to establish doubt. In most cases, the defense introduces evidence to contradict the evidence against the defendant or to discredit the government's witnesses. Witnesses called by each side are subject to cross-examination, and physical evidence is subject to inspection and challenge. During closing arguments counsel attempt to persuade juries of the merits of their positions. Following this, the trial judge instructs the jury on the relevant points of law and the jurors' responsibilities in reaching a verdict. Where a jury returns a verdict of guilty, defense counsel frequently moves the court for a new trial or other relief.

Sentencing

After the guilt of the accused has been determined, sentence is imposed by the court. Very often, a separate court appearance is scheduled to allow for a presentence investigation before imposing sentence. In imposing sentences, judges generally must follow statutory requirements governing the type and severity of sentence for particular crimes. Types of sentences include probation, incarceration, work release, monetary fines, community service, and, of course, death. Different statutory approaches govern the length of prison sentences that courts may impose. Indeterminate sentencing occurs when individuals are incarcerated for periods of time to be determined by correctional agencies. Determinate sentencing occurs when statutes specify prison terms for particular crimes. In most jurisdictions, judges are able to impose particular sentences within broad parameters defined by statutes. In recent years, we have witnessed two trends away from broad judicial discretion in the area of sentencing. First is the tendency for legislatures to require imposition of flat or mandatory sentences. Second, some juridictions have developed sentencing guidelines to address the problem of sentencing disparity.

Congress enacted the Sentencing Reform Act of 1984 to "provide certainty and fairness in meeting the purposes of sentencing, avoiding unwarranted sentencing disparities among defendants with similar records who have been found guilty of similar criminal conduct while maintaining sufficient flexibility to permit individualized sentences also warranted by mitigating or aggravating factors. . . ." 28 U.S.C.A. § 992(b)(1)(B). Where unusual circumstances exist, federal appellate courts have permitted district courts to exercise wide discretion in determining upward or downward departures from the recommended sentences.

Even before the federal government adopted sentencing guidelines, Minnesota, in 1980—followed by a few other states—adopted its own guidelines through legislation. The experience of these states, along with that of the federal courts, has over the past few years given impetus to a number of state efforts in enacting similar guidelines.

Appeal and Discretionary Review

Federal law and the laws of every state provide those convicted of crimes a limited right to appeal their convictions to higher tribunals. Appellate courts generally confine their review of convictions to legal, as distinct from factual, issues. While appellate courts review the legal sufficiency of evidence, they do not attempt to second-guess the factual determinations of trial judges and juries. Rather, appellate courts review such procedural issues as denial of fair trial, denial of counsel, admission of illegal evidence, and improper jury instructions.

Appellate courts focus on errors of consequence, often overlooking so-called harmless errors.

When convictions are upheld on appeal, defendants may petition higher appellate courts for further review. Such review is available at the discretion of the higher court. The Supreme Court receives thousands of petitions each year from defendants whose convictions have been affirmed by the United States Courts of Appeals or the highest appellate tribunals of the states. Naturally, the Supreme Court is able to review only the small percentage of these cases that present important issues of law.

Postconviction Relief

A person who has been convicted of a crime, has exhausted all normal appellate remedies, and is confined to prison may still challenge his or her conviction, sentence, or conditions of confinement by filing a petition for a writ of *habeas corpus*. *Habeas corpus* is an ancient common-law device that permits judges to review the legality of someone's confinement. In modern American criminal procedure, *habeas corpus* has become a way for prisoners who have exhausted all other avenues of appeal to obtain judicial review. A federal prisoner petitions the appropriate federal district court for *habeas corpus* relief. Under most state statutes, state prisoners may file *habeas corpus* petitions or other similar petitions for postconviction relief with the appropriate state courts.

Under federal law, a state prisoner may petition a federal district court for *habeas corpus relief* if he or she wishes to raise federal constitutional issues, for example, the alleged denial of the Sixth Amendment right to be represented by counsel. The power of federal courts to issue *habeas corpus* in state cases can be traced to an act of Congress adopted just after the Civil War. See *Ex parte McCardle*, 74 U.S. (7 Wall.) 506, 19 L.Ed. 264 (1869).

There is no statutory limit to the number of federal *habeas corpus* petitions a prisoner may file; in several cases, prisoners have brought numerous petitions requiring many years to resolve. The denial or grant of *habeas corpus* relief by a federal district court is subject to appeal in the U.S. Court of Appeals. The circuit court's ruling is subject to review by the Supreme Court on a discretionary basis. Thus it can take several years to finally resolve one federal *habeas corpus* petition, especially if the petition raises difficult constitutional claims where the law is not yet fully settled. If a state prisoner were permitted to raise each of many issues in separate federal *habeas corpus* petitions, it could take decades to resolve all of the claims. It is for this reason that the Supreme Court has moved recently to require prisoners to raise all claims in their first *habeas corpus* petition. The Court has said that, unless there are exceptional circumstances, failure to do so constitutes an abuse of the writ of *habeas corpus*. *McCleskey v. Zant*, 499 U.S. 467, 111 S.Ct. 1454, 113 L.Ed.2d 517 (1991).

THE CORRECTIONS SYSTEM

As with courts, there is a federal corrections system and fifty separate state corrections systems. Each of these systems is responsible for supervising those persons sentenced to prison by courts of law. Originally, prisons were conceived as a place for criminals to reflect on their misdeeds and repent, hence the term *penitentiary*. In the twentieth century, the emphasis has been on rehabilitation through psychological and sociopsychological methods. Unfortunately, these efforts have been less than successful. Ironically, prisons appear to "criminalize" individuals more than rehabilitate them. Inmates are exposed to an insular society with norms of conduct antithetical to those of civil society. As "total institutions," prisons do not encourage individuals to behave responsibly; furthermore, prisons provide an excellent opportunity for spreading of criminal techniques. It is probably unrealistic to expect rehabilitation programs to succeed in such an environment. Today, prisons are generally regarded as little more than a way to punish and isolate those persons deemed unfit to live in civil society.

The federal and state prison systems are currently undergoing a crisis. There is simply not enough space to house inmates. The public continues to demand stiffer sentences for convicted felons, but legislators (and taxpayers) are often unwilling to pay the price of constructing more prisons. In many state prisons, cells originally designed for one or two inmates now house three or four prisoners.

In many instances federal courts have ordered prison officials to reduce overcrowding so as to comply with the federal constitutional prohibition against "cruel and unusual punishments." U.S. Const. Amend. 8. Aside from the threat of federal judicial intervention, overcrowded prisons are more likely to produce inmate violence and even riots.

In addition to prisons, corrections systems include agencies that supervise probation, parole, community service, and other forms of alternative sentences (see Chapter 18). With burgeoning prison populations, these alternatives to incarceration are assuming more importance and consuming more resources, especially at the state level.

CONCLUSION

The American system of criminal justice is an extremely complicated one. The primary reason for this complexity is the principle of federalism, which refers to the division of political and legal authority in this country among one national government and fifty state governments. The national government and each of the fifty states has its own criminal laws, as well as its own law enforcement agencies, prosecutors, courts, and prison systems. No two systems are exactly alike. Indeed, there is tremendous variation from one jurisdiction to the next, both in terms of the substantive criminal law and the practices and procedures used by the various components of the criminal process. Yet, despite their substantive and procedural differences, all jurisdictions share two basic goals: to protect society from crime and, at the same time, to protect the rights of the individual suspected of having committed an offense. Much of the conflict and inefficiency inherent in our criminal justice system stems from the need to balance these two competing objectives.

QUESTIONS FOR THOUGHT AND DISCUSSION

1. How does the concept of federalism complicate the criminal justice process in the United States?

2. What provisions of the United States Constitution protect a defendant at the following stages of the criminal process?
   a. A pre-arrest police search of the suspect's home designed to seize incriminating evidence
   b. A police interrogation of the suspect at the station house
   c. A magistrate's determination whether to grant pretrial release to a person arrested on a felony charge
   d. A judge's determination whether to appoint an attorney for a defendant who claims to be too poor to afford a lawyer
   e. A prosecutor's decision whether to file a formal accusation or information charging the defendant with one or more felonies
   f. A trial judge's determination to accept the defendant's plea of guilty at arraignment
   g. A judge's determination of the nature and extent of punishment to be imposed on a convicted felon

3. Compare and contrast the functions of trial and appellate courts in deciding criminal cases. How are they similar? How are they different?

4. How would you account for the recent trend toward curtailing judicial discretion in criminal sentencing?

PART II

THE SUBSTANTIVE CRIMINAL LAW

CHAPTER 3

CONSTITUTIONAL LIMITATIONS ON THE PROHIBITION OF CRIMINAL CONDUCT

INTRODUCTION

Under a parliamentary system, such as those in Great Britain, Italy, Japan, and most of the world's democracies, the statutes enacted by the legislature are by definition the supreme law of the land. There is no overarching authority, except for the will of the people expressed through the ballot box, to limit exercises of legislative power. In the wake of the American Revolution, the founders were as wary of a parliamentary system as they were of a monarchy. The framers of the Constitution understood that unbridled power to make and enforce criminal prohibitions constitutes a serious threat to liberty. Thus, they framed a Constitution that delimits the power of Congress and state legislatures to enact criminal statutes. For example, Article III, Section 3 provides that the crime of treason against the United States "shall consist only in levying War against them, or in adhering to their Enemies, giving them Aid and Comfort." By circumscribing the crime of treason, the framers sought to prohibit the federal government from using the offense to punish political dissenters. Incidentally, treason is the only crime actually defined in the Constitution; all other crimes are defined by the common law, state and federal statutes, or both.

The Importance of Judicial Review

Constitutional limits on the enactment and enforcement of criminal statutes do not depend for their vitality only upon the voluntary compliance of legislators, prosecutors, and police officers. Under the doctrine of judicial review, courts are empowered to declare null and void laws that violate constitutional principles. In a landmark decision in 1803, the Supreme Court first asserted the power to invalidate legislation that is in conflict with the Constitution. *Marbury v. Madison,* 5 U.S. (1 Cranch) 137, 2 L.Ed. 60 (1803). Speaking for the Court in *Marbury,* Chief Justice John Marshall said, "It is emphatically the province and duty of the judicial department to say what the law is." 5 U.S. (1 Cranch) at 177, 2 L.Ed. at 175. Although the power of judicial review is generally associated with the Supreme Court, all courts of record, whether state or federal, may exercise the power to strike down unconstitutional legislation. It is doubtful whether constitutional limitations on governmental power would be meaningful in the absence of judicial review.

Unconstitutional *"Per Se"* and Unconstitutional *"As Applied"*

Throughout this textbook, we will be discussing constitutional limitations on the criminal justice system. Many of these principles are procedural in nature, imposing restrictions and obligations on law enforcement, prosecution, adjudication, and sentencing. In this chapter we are concerned only with those constitutional provisions that place limits on the substantive criminal law, both in the types of laws that legislatures are barred from enacting and the situations in which police and prosecutors are barred from enforcing existing statutes.

A statute may be declared unconstitutional on its face, in that it inherently trenches on some constitutionally protected liberty or exceeds the constitutional powers of government. Alternatively, a law that is facially valid, such as an ordinance prohibiting disorderly conduct, may be declared unconstitutional as applied if it is enforced in a way that impermissibly restricts or punishes the exercise of constitutional rights.

BILLS OF ATTAINDER AND *EX POST FACTO* LAWS

Two historic abuses of the English Parliament that the Framers of the Constitution sought to correct were bills of attainder and *ex post facto* laws. A bill of attainder is a legislative act inflicting punishment on an individual, or a group of easily identifiable individuals. *United States v. Brown*, 381 U.S. 437, 85 S.Ct. 1707, 14 L.Ed.2d 484 (1965). Laws of this character are antithetical to the basic principle that a person accused of wrongdoing is entitled to a fair trial in a court of law.

An *ex post facto* law is one that retroactively (1) makes an innocent act illegal; (2) increases the punishment for a criminal act; or (3) decreases the standard of proof required to convict a defendant of a crime. *Calder v. Bull*, 3 U.S. (3 Dall.) 386, 1 L.Ed. 648 (1798). Because the essence of the *ex post facto* law is retroactivity, it is flatly inconsistent with the principle of legality, which holds that individuals are entitled to know in advance if particular contemplated conduct is illegal.

Article I, Section 9 of the Constitution prohibits the Congress from adopting bills of attainder and *ex post facto* laws. Article I, Section 10 extends these same prohibitions to the state legislatures. These categorical injunctions probably account for the fact that there have been relatively few judicial decisions striking down laws on these grounds.

THE BILL OF RIGHTS

While the original Constitution contained few express limitations on legislative power, the Bill of Rights added several important constraints on the Congress. For criminal law, the most significant of these are the First Amendment freedoms of expression, religion, and assembly; the Second Amendment protection of "the right to keep and bear arms"; the Fifth Amendment Due Process Clause; the Eighth Amendment Cruel and Unusual Punishments Clause; and the Ninth Amendment guarantee of "rights retained by the people."

Although legislation is normally presumed by courts to be constitutional, the Supreme Court has recognized that "there may be narrower scope for the operation of the presumption of constitutionality when legislation appears on its face to be within a specific prohibition of the Constitution, such as those of the first ten amendments." *United States v. Carolene Products Co.*, 304 U.S. 144, 151 n. 4, 58 S.Ct. 778, 783 n. 4, 82 L.Ed. 1234, 1241, n. 4 (1938). Effectively, this means that government must carry the burden of proving that its enactment does not offend the Constitution.

Application of the Bill of Rights to State and Local Laws

The Bill of Rights begins with the injunction that "*Congress* shall make no law . . ." [emphasis added]. Unlike certain provisions in the original, unamended

Constitution, the Bill of Rights makes no mention of limitations on the state and local governments. Throughout much of the nineteenth century, the Bill of Rights was viewed as imposing limitations only on the Congress, having no effect on state legislatures or local governing bodies. The Supreme Court officially adopted this view in a landmark decision in 1833. *Barron v. Baltimore,* 32 U.S. (7 Pet.) 243, 8 L.Ed. 672 (1833). Under this interpretation of the Bill of Rights, citizens had to look to their state constitutions and state courts for protection against state and local actions that infringed on their rights and liberties.

The ratification of the Fourteenth Amendment in 1868 provided a justification for extending the scope of the Bill of Rights to apply against the states. Section 1 of the Fourteenth Amendment enjoins the states from depriving "any person of life, liberty, or property, without due process of law." It also prohibits states from adopting laws that "abridge the privileges and immunities of citizens of the United States."

In a series of decisions, the Supreme Court has held that the Due Process Clause of the Fourteenth Amendment makes enforceable against the states those provisions of the Bill of Rights that are "implicit in the concept of ordered liberty." *Palko v. Connecticut,* 302 U.S. 319, 58 S.Ct. 149, 82 L.Ed. 288 (1937). This doctrine of "selective incorporation" has been employed by the Court to enforce the procedural guarantees of the Bill of Rights in state criminal prosecutions. For example, in *Wolf v. Colorado,* 338 U.S. 25, 69 S.Ct. 1359, 93 L.Ed. 1782 (1949), the Court said that the Fourth Amendment protection against unreasonable searches and seizures is applicable to state and local, as well as federal, law enforcement authorities. Similarly, in *Duncan v. Louisiana,* 391 U.S. 145, 88 S.Ct. 1444, 20 L.Ed.2d 491 (1968), the Court held that the Fourteenth Amendment requires states to observe the jury trial requirement of the Sixth Amendment.

In addition to incorporating the procedural protections of the Bill of Rights into the Fourteenth Amendment, the Court has extended the substantive limitations of the Bill of Rights to the states. In 1925 the Supreme Court recognized that the First Amendment protections of free speech and free press applied to state as well as federal laws. *Gitlow v. New York,* 268 U.S. 652, 45 S.Ct. 625, 69 L.Ed. 1138 (1925). Likewise, in 1934 the Court said that the First Amendment guarantee of free exercise of religion is enforceable against state and local governments. *Hamilton v. Regents of the University of California,* 293 U.S. 245, 55 S.Ct. 197, 79 L.Ed. 343 (1934).

Since the process of selective incorporation began in 1897, (see *Chicago, Burlington and Quincy R.R. v. Chicago,* 166 U.S. 226, 17 S.Ct. 581, 41 L.Ed. 979 (1897)), the Court has incorporated virtually all the provisions of the Bill of Rights into the Fourteenth Amendment, making them applicable to the state and local governments. The Federal Constitution, and in particular the Bill of Rights, now stands as a barrier to the enactment or enforcement of unreasonable or oppressive criminal laws, whether they are enacted by Congress, a state legislature, or a local governing body.

THE FIRST AMENDMENT FREEDOM OF EXPRESSION

Perhaps the most treasured of our liberties, and the rights most essential to maintaining a democratic polity, are the First Amendment freedoms of speech and press. Often, freedom of speech and freedom of the press are referred to jointly as freedom of expression. Although the concept of free expression is fundamental to our democratic society, the Supreme Court has said that the First Amendment has "never been thought to give absolute protection to every individual to speak whenever or wherever he pleases, or to use any form of address in any circumstances that he chooses." *Cohen v. California*, 403 U.S. 15, 19, 91 S.Ct. 1780, 1785, 29 L.Ed.2d 284, 290 (1971). The task of the courts, of course, is to strike a reasonable balance between the right of expression and the legitimate interests of society in maintaining security, order, peace, safety, and decency. In what has become a classic phrase, Justice Oliver Wendell Holmes, Jr., observed that the "most stringent protection of free speech would not protect a man in falsely shouting fire in a theater, and causing a panic." *Schenck v. United States*, 249 U.S. 47, 51, 39 S.Ct 247, 249, 63 L.Ed. 470, 473 (1919). Moreover, the Supreme Court has said that certain types of speech are so inherently lacking in value as not to merit any First Amendment protection.

> There are certain well defined and narrowly limited classes of speech, the prevention and punishment of which have never been thought to raise any constitutional problem. These include the lewd and obscene, the profane, the libelous, and the insulting or "fighting" words—those which by their very utterance inflict injury or tend to incite an immediate breach of the peace. It has been well observed that such utterances are no essential part of any exposition of ideas, and are of such slight social value as a step to truth that any benefit that may be derived from them is clearly outweighed by the social interest in order and morality. *Chaplinsky v. New Hampshire*, 315 U.S. 568, 571, 62 S.Ct 766, 769, 86 L.Ed. 1031, 1035 (1942).

Advocacy of Unlawful Conduct

One of the most basic and perplexing problems posed by the First Amendment is whether speech advocating unlawful conduct may itself be made unlawful. The Supreme Court first encountered this problem in *Schenck v. United States, supra,* where an official of the Socialist Party appealed from a conviction under the Espionage Act of 1917, 40 Stat. at L. 217, 219. Charles T. Schenck had been convicted of participating in a conspiracy to cause insubordination in the military services and to obstruct military recruitment at a time when the United States was at war. The "conspiracy" consisted of activities surrounding the mailing of a leaflet to draftees urging them to resist induction into the military. The Supreme Court upheld Schenck's conviction, saying that

> the question in every case is whether the words used are used in such circumstances and are of such a nature as to create clear and present danger that they will bring about the substantive evils that Congress has a right to prevent. It is a question of proximity and degree. When a nation is at war many things that might be said in time of peace are such a hindrance to its effort that their utterance will not be endured so long as men fight, and that no court could regard them as protected by any constitutional right. 249 U.S. at 52, 39 S.Ct. at 249, 63 L.Ed. at 473.

The Supreme Court first invoked the "clear and present danger" doctrine to reverse a criminal conviction in a case involving a Georgia man who had been prosecuted under a state law prohibiting "any attempt, by persuasion or otherwise" to incite insurrection. *Herndon v. Lowry*, 301 U.S. 242, 57 S.Ct. 732, 81

L.Ed. 1066 (1937). Since then, the doctrine has been used by state and federal courts to reverse numerous convictions where persons have been prosecuted for merely advocating illegal acts.

The modern Supreme Court has refined the clear and present danger doctrine so that public advocacy may be prohibited only in situations when there is "imminent lawless action." *Brandenburg v. Ohio,* 395 U.S. 444, 89 S.Ct 1827, 23 L.Ed.2d 430 (1969). Today, it is questionable whether the courts would uphold a conviction in circumstances similar to those in the *Schenck* case. The courts would most likely find that mailing a leaflet or standing on a street corner urging resistance to the draft—activities that were fairly common during the Vietnam War—are not fraught with "imminent lawless action" and therefore do not constitute a clear and present danger.

Symbolic Speech and Expressive Conduct

Freedom of expression is a broad concept embracing speech, publication, performances, and demonstrations. Even the wearing of symbols is considered to be constitutionally protected "symbolic speech." *Tinker v. Des Moines Independent Community School District,* 393 U.S. 503, 89 S.Ct. 733, 21 L.Ed.2d 731 (1969). The Supreme Court has recognized a wide variety of conduct as possessing "sufficient communicative elements to bring the First Amendment to play." *Texas v. Johnson,* 491 U.S. 397, 404, 109 S.Ct. 2533, 2539, 105 L.Ed.2d 342, 353 (1989). The Court has accorded First Amendment protection to, among other things, "sit-ins" by blacks to protest racial segregation, *Brown v. Louisiana,* 383 U.S. 131, 86 S.Ct. 719, 15 L.Ed.2d 637 (1966); the wearing of American military uniforms by civilians to protest the Vietnam War, *Schacht v. United States,* 398 U.S. 58, 90 S.Ct. 1555, 26 L.Ed.2d 44 (1970); and "picketing" over a variety of issues, *Amalgamated Food Employees Union v. Logan Valley Plaza, Inc.,* 391 U.S. 308, 88 S.Ct. 1601, 20 L.Ed.2d 603 (1968).

Without question, the most controversial applications of the concept of expressive conduct have been the Supreme Court's decisions holding that the public burning of the American flag is protected by the First Amendment. In *Texas v. Johnson, supra,* the Court invalidated a Texas statute banning flag desecration. Gregory Johnson had been arrested after he publicly burned an American Flag outside the Republican National Convention in Dallas in 1984. The Supreme Court's decision to reverse Johnson's conviction and strike down the Texas law resulted in a firestorm of public criticism of the Court as well as the enactment of a new federal statute. The Flag Protection Act of 1989, amending 18 U.S.C.A. § 700, imposed criminal penalties on anyone who knowingly "mutilates, defaces, physically defiles, burns, maintains upon the floor or ground, or tramples upon" the American flag. In *United States v. Eichman,* 496 U.S. 310, 110 S.Ct. 2404, 110 L.Ed.2d 287 (1990), the Supreme Court invalidated this federal statute as well, saying that "punishing desecration of the flag dilutes the very freedom that makes this emblem so revered, and worth revering." 496 U.S. at 319, 110 S.Ct. at 2410, 110 L.Ed.2d at 296.

"Fighting Words" and Threats to Public Order

One type of expression that sometimes transgresses the criminal law is public speech that threatens the public peace and order. The Supreme Court has said that no one would have the hardihood to suggest that the principle of freedom of speech sanctions incitement to riot... When clear and present danger of riot, disorder, interference with traffic upon the public streets, or other immediate threat to public safety, peace, or order appears, the power of the State to prevent and punish is obvious. *Cantwell v. Connecticut,* 310 U.S. 296, 308, 60 S.Ct. 900, 905, 84 L.Ed. 1213, 1220 (1940).

At the same time, government "may not unduly suppress free communication of views . . . under the guise of conserving desirable conditions." *Cantwell v. Connecticut, supra.* Again, the problem for courts is to strike a reasonable balance between legitimate competing interests in the context of the particular facts in the case at hand.

In *Feiner v. New York,* 340 U.S. 315, 71 S.Ct. 303, 95 L.Ed. 295 (1951), the Supreme Court upheld a disorderly conduct conviction stemming from an incident in which a street-corner speaker excited a hostile crowd by insulting President Truman and the mayor of New York. Writing for the Court, Chief Justice Vinson noted that "It is one thing to say that the police cannot be used as an instrument for the suppression of unpopular views and another thing to say that, when as here the speaker passes the bounds of argument or persuasion and undertakes incitement to riot, they are powerless to prevent a breach of the peace." 340 U.S. at 321, 71 S.Ct. at 306, 95 L.Ed. at 300.

As noted previously, the Supreme Court has held that so-called fighting words are unprotected by the Constitution. *Chaplinsky v. New Hampshire, supra.* Fighting words are "those personally abusive epithets which, when addressed to the ordinary citizen, are, as a matter of common knowledge, inherently likely to provoke violent reaction." *Cohen v. California,* 403 U.S. at 20, 91 S.Ct. at 1785, 29 L.Ed.2d at 291.

"Hate Speech"

Would a public cross-burning by the Ku Klux Klan in a black neighborhood qualify as fighting words, or would it be considered expressive conduct protected by the First Amendment? What about the display of swastikas by Nazis parading through the streets of a predominantly Jewish city? Would police be justified in these instances to make arrests for incitement to riot? These questions became more than hypothetical during the 1980s, when the country witnessed a resurgence of racist organizations, and cities and states countered with laws proscribing "hate speech." One such law, a St. Paul, Minnesota, ordinance, provided:

> Whoever places on public or private property a symbol, object, appellation, characterization or graffiti, including, but not limited to, a burning cross or Nazi swastika, which one knows or has reasonable grounds to know arouses anger, alarm or resentment in others on the basis of race, color, creed, religion or gender commits disorderly conduct and shall be guilty of a misdemeanor.

In *R.A.V. v. St. Paul,* 505 U.S. ___ , 112 S.Ct. 2538, 120 L.Ed.2d 305 (1992), the Supreme Court declared this ordinance unconstitutional in the context of a criminal prosecution of a white teenager who burned a cross on the front lawn of a black family's home. Lest the public be tempted to conclude that the Supreme Court condoned racially motivated cross-burnings, the Court stated:

> Let there be no mistake about our belief that burning a cross in someone's front yard is reprehensible. But St. Paul has sufficient means at its disposal to prevent such

behavior without adding the First Amendment to the fire. 505 U.S. at ___ , 112 S.Ct. at 2550, 120 L.Ed.2d at 326.

Obscenity

Traditionally, state and local governments have proscribed speech, pictures, films, and performances regarded as obscene, generally classifying these as misdemeanor offenses. Despite challenges to the constitutionality of such obscenity laws, the Supreme Court has held that obscenity is beyond the pale of the First Amendment, and thus subject to criminal prosecution. *Roth v. United States*, 354 U.S. 476, 77 S.Ct. 1304, 1 L.Ed.2d 1498 (1957).

The problem for the legislatures, police, prosecutors and courts is to determine what is obscene and therefore unprotected by the First Amendment. The Supreme Court has held that for expression to be obscene, it must (1) appeal to a prurient interest in sex; (2) depict sexual conduct in a patently offensive way; and (3) lack serious literary, artistic, political or scientific value. *Miller v. California*, 413 U.S. 15, 93 S.Ct 2607, 37 L.Ed.2d 419 (1973). Despite this test, arguably, the concept of obscenity remains somewhat vague. Yet the Supreme Court has made it clear that obscenity refers only to "hard-core" pornography. *Jenkins v. Georgia*, 418 U.S. 153, 94 S.Ct. 2750, 41 L.Ed.2d 642 (1974). (The "intractable obscenity problem," as it has been called, is dealt with more fully in Chapter 8.)

Nude Dancing

Every state has a prohibition against indecent exposure. Generally, these statutes are applied in situations where individuals expose themselves in public or private to unwilling viewers. But what if the exposure takes place by mutual consent, such as in a night club that features nude dancing? The Supreme Court has recognized that this form of entertainment is entitled to First Amendment

---

CASE IN POINT

OBSCENITY

Billy Jenkins managed a movie theater in Albany, Georgia, in which the film "Carnal Knowledge" was being shown. The film, which starred Jack Nicholson, Candice Bergen, Art Garfunkel, and Ann-Margret, appeared on many critics' "Ten Best" lists for 1971. On January 13, 1972, local law enforcement officers entered the theater, pursuant to a warrant, and seized the film. Jenkins was later convicted of distributing obscene material and was fined $750 and sentenced to 12 months probation. By a divided vote, the Georgia Supreme Court affirmed the conviction. On appeal, the United States Supreme Court reversed Jenkins' conviction, holding that "Carnal Knowledge" simply was not hard-core pornography and was thus protected under the First Amendment standards delineated in *Miller v. California*.

Jenkins v. Georgia, 418 U.S. 153, 94 S.Ct. 2750, 41 L.Ed.2d 642 (1974).

protection under certain circumstances, but has also expressed a willingness to uphold reasonable regulations, especially involving establishments that serve alcoholic beverages. *Doran v. Salem Inn,* 422 U.S. 922, 95 S.Ct. 2561, 45 L.Ed.2d 648 (1975). In *Barnes v. Glen Theatre, Inc.,* 501 U.S. ___ , 111 S.Ct. 2456, 115 L.Ed.2d 504 (1991), the Court upheld an Indiana statute requiring that night club dancers wear "pasties" and "G-strings" when they dance. In an opinion expressing the view of three justices, Chief Justice Rehnquist observed that

> the governmental interest served . . . is societal disapproval of nudity in public places among strangers. The statutory prohibition is not a means to some greater end, but an end in itself. It is without cavil that the public indecency statute is "narrowly tailored"; Indiana's requirement that the dancers wear at least pasties and a G-string is modest, and the bare minimum necessary to achieve the state's purpose. 501 U.S. at ___ , 111 S.Ct. at 2463, 115 L.Ed.2d at 515.

Profanity

Although in *Chaplinsky v. New Hampshire, supra,* the Supreme Court specifically enumerated profanity as being among those categories of speech so lacking in value as not to merit First Amendment protection, this view no longer prevails. In *Cohen v. California, supra,* the Supreme Court invalidated the "offensive conduct" conviction of a man who entered a courthouse wearing a jacket emblazoned with the slogan "Fuck the Draft." Writing for the Court, Justice Harlan opined that

> the state has no right to cleanse public debate to the point where it is grammatically palatable to the most squeamish among us. Yet no readily ascertainable general principle exists for stopping short of that result if we were to affirm the judgment below. For, while the particular four-letter-word being litigated here is perhaps more distasteful than others of its genre, it is nevertheless often true that one man's vulgarity is another's lyric. Indeed, we think it is largely because government officials cannot make principled distinctions in this area that the Constitution leaves matters of taste and style so largely to the individual. 403 U.S. at 25, 91 S.Ct. at 1788, 29 L.Ed.2d at 294.

Notwithstanding the Supreme Court's decision in *Cohen v. California,* most states and many cities retain laws proscribing profanity. These laws are seldom enforced and even more rarely challenged in court.

FREEDOM OF ASSEMBLY

The First Amendment specifically protects the "right of the people peaceably to assemble." Yet, as we have seen, one of the most important purposes of the criminal law is to maintain public peace and order. Sometimes these values come into conflict, as in the civil rights struggle of the 1960s, when public demonstrations became an important part of a powerful political movement. See, for example, *Cox v. Louisiana,* 379 U.S. 559, 85 S.Ct. 476, 13 L.Ed.2d 487 (1965); *Adderley v. Florida,* 385 U.S. 39, 87 S.Ct. 242, 17 L.Ed.2d 149 (1966); *Walker v. City of Birmingham,* 388 U.S. 307, 87 S.Ct. 1824, 18 L.Ed.2d 1210 (1967).

In one classic case, *Edwards v. South Carolina,* 372 U.S. 229, 83 S.Ct. 680, 9 L.Ed.2d 697 (1963), the Supreme Court reversed the breach-of-the-peace convictions of 187 black citizens who were arrested after they refused to disperse a peaceful civil rights demonstration on the grounds of the state capitol. The Court, per Justice Stewart, found that the "circumstances in this case reflect an exercise of . . . constitutional rights in their most pristine and classic form." 372 U.S. at 235, 83 S.Ct. at 683, 9 L.Ed.2d at 702.

As the *Edwards* decision indicates, governments may not ban assemblies in the public forum as long as they are peaceful and do not impede the operations of government or the activities of other citizens. Yet, in order to promote the interests of safety, order and peace, governments may impose reasonable time, place, and manner regulations on public assemblies. The character of a given place and the pattern of its normal activities determine the type of time, place, and manner regulations that the courts consider reasonable. *Grayned v. City of Rockford,* 408 U.S. 104, 92 S.Ct. 2294, 33 L.Ed.2d 222 (1972). For example, a restriction against the use of sound amplifiers in close proximity to a courthouse or library might well be judged reasonable, while a ban on "picketing" on the steps of the same buildings would not. In imposing time, place, and manner regulations, governments must be careful not to deprive demonstrations or protests of their essential content by imposing excessive or unnecessarily burdensome regulations. *United States v. Grace,* 461 U.S. 171, 103 S.Ct. 1702, 75 L.Ed.2d 736 (1983).

FREE EXERCISE OF RELIGION

The value of freedom of religion is so deeply rooted in American culture that rarely have legislatures sought to impinge directly on that right. Yet from time to time lawmakers have sought to prevent certain unpopular religious groups from proselytizing. The Supreme Court has been quick to invalidate such efforts. In one leading case, the Court struck down a state statute that made it a misdemeanor for any person to solicit door-to-door for religious or philanthropic reasons without prior approval from local officials, who were authorized to make determinations as to whether solicitors represented bona fide religions. The law was successfully challenged by a member of the Jehovah's Witnesses sect who was prosecuted for engaging in door-to-door proselytizing without a permit. *Cantwell v. Connecticut, supra.*

Much more problematic are government attempts to enforce criminal statutes designed to protect the public health, safety, and welfare against religious practices deemed inimical to these interests. Does the right to freely exercise one's religion permit one to violate an otherwise valid criminal statute? In 1878, the Supreme Court answered this question in the negative by upholding the prosecution of a polygamist. *Reynolds v. United States,* 98 U.S. (8 Otto) 145, 25 L.Ed. 244 (1878). More recently, however, the Supreme Court granted to members of the Old Order Amish sect an exemption to the Wisconsin compulsory education law. The Court found that the law significantly interfered with the Amish way of life and thus violated their right to freely exercise their religion. *Wisconsin v. Yoder,* 406 U.S. 205, 92 S.Ct. 1526, 32 L.Ed.2d 15 (1972).

CASE IN POINT

FREE EXERCISE OF RELIGION

Douglas Clifford was convicted of driving without a license, as required by Washington law, 46.20.021. On appeal, he claimed that the state requirement that he obtain a license violated his right to free exercise of religion in that "to accept the licensing requirements of the State is to put the State on a footing equal or superior to God, absolutely contrary to my convictions." The Washington Court of Appeals, Division 3, affirmed the conviction. Although accepting the sincerity of Clifford's religious objections to the law, the court sustained the constitutionality of the statute as applied. The court observed that "the licensing statute serves a compelling state interest in law enforcement as well as a compelling state interest in highway safety." The court further observed that "any exemption to the licensing requirement carved out for religious reasons . . . would eventually be requested by a potentially unlimited number of members of their religious community."

State v. Clifford, 787 P.2d 575 (Wash. App. 1990).

Unusual Religious Practices

Several state courts have decided cases arising from unusual forms of worship. The Tennessee Supreme Court upheld the validity of a statute making it a crime to handle poisonous snakes in religious ceremonies against the claim that the law violated the right to free exercise of religion guaranteed by the state constitution. *Harden v. State,* 216 S.W.2d 708 (Tenn. 1949).

In a decision that cuts the other way, the California Supreme Court reversed the convictions of several members of the Native American Church for possession of peyote. *People v. Woody,* 394 P.2d 813 (Cal. 1964). In the court's view, the sacramental use of peyote was central to the worship of the Native American Church, and thus protected by the First Amendment. Similarly, an Oklahoma appellate court recognized the right of members of the Native American Church to use peyote in religious rituals. *State v. Whitehorn,* 561 P.2d 539 (Okl. Crim. App. 1977). Yet the appellate court cautioned against the nonsacramental use of the drug, which would still be subject to criminal prosecution.

In 1990, the U.S. Supreme Court held that the sacramental use of peyote by members of the Native American Church was *not* protected by the Free Exercise Clause of the First Amendment. *Employment Division v. Smith,* 494 U.S. 872, 110 S.Ct. 1595, 108 L.Ed.2d 876 (1990). This decision by the Nation's highest court means that state courts that have granted such protection may wish to reconsider their positions. However, in our federal system, state courts are free to provide greater levels of protection to individual rights under the terms of their state constitutions than those provided by the federal constitution.

Refusal of Medical Treatment

One of the more troubling and tragic situations in which the Free Exercise Clause potentially comes into conflict with the criminal law involves the refusal of medical treatment. Certain religious groups, such the Christian Scientists, believe that physical healing is to be achieved through spiritual power. Thus, when faced with an illness or injury, they are likely to refuse medical treatment. Other groups, such as the Jehovah's Witnesses, believe that blood transfusions are specifically enjoined by Scripture.

The courts have recognized the right of a competent adult to refuse medical treatment on religious grounds, even if the refusal results in death. See, for example, *In re Estate of Brooks*, 205 N.E.2d 435 (Ill. 1965); *In re Milton*, 505 N.E.2d 255 (Ohio 1987). It is another matter entirely when parents refuse to allow medical treatment for their children. The Supreme Court has recognized that

> parents may be free to become martyrs themselves. But it does not follow that they are free in identical circumstances, to make martyrs of their children before they have reached the age of full legal discretion when they can make that choice for themselves. *Prince v. Massachusetts*, 321 U.S. 158, 170, 64 S.Ct. 438, 444, 88 L.Ed. 645, 654 (1944).

Accordingly, courts seldom allow freedom of religion as a defense to a criminal charge stemming from a situation in which parents refused to seek or allow medical treatment for their children. In one recent case, a member of the Christian Scientist faith was prosecuted for involuntary manslaughter after failing to seek medical treatment of her daughter's meningitis, which turned out to be fatal. The California Supreme Court rejected the defendant's free exercise of religion defense, saying that "parents have *no* right to free exercise of religion at the price of a child's life." *Walker v. Superior Court*, 763 P.2d 852 (Cal. 1988).

The Right to Keep and Bear Arms

There are numerous criminal prohibitions—at the federal, state, and local levels—against the sale, possession, and use of certain types of firearms. "Gun

---

CASE IN POINT

Free Exercise of Religion

After receiving a number of complaints about the practice of animal sacrifice associated with the Santeria religion, the city of Hialeah, Florida adopted an ordinance making it an offense to "unnecessarily kill, torment, torture, or mutilate an animal in a public or private ritual or ceremony not for the primary purpose of food consumption." Practitioners of Santeria sued to challenge the constitutionality of the ordinance. On June 11, 1993, the United States Supreme Court unanimously declared the ordinance unconstitutional. Writing for the Court, Justice Anthony Kennedy observed that "the laws in question were enacted by officials who did not understand, failed to perceive, or chose to ignore the fact that their official actions violated the Nation's essential commitment to religious freedom."

Church of the Lukumi Babula Aye, Inc. v. City of Hialeah, 508 U.S. ___ , 113 S.Ct. 2217, 124 L.Ed.2d 472 (1993).

control" laws are seen by many as antithetical to the "right to keep and bear arms." The Second Amendment to the U.S. Constitution provides:

> A well regulated Militia, being necessary to the security of a free state, the right of the people to keep and bear arms shall not be infringed.

In *United States v. Miller*, 307 U.S. 174, 59 S.Ct. 816, 83 L.Ed 1206 (1939), the Supreme Court upheld a federal law criminalizing the interstate shipment of sawed-off shotguns, saying that "the right to keep and bear arms" had to be interpreted in relation to the "well regulated militia." The Court concluded that possession of sawed-off shotguns had no reasonable relationship to serving in the militia. In recently reaffirming *Miller*, the Court said that "the Second Amendment guarantees no right to keep and bear a firearm that does not have some reasonable relationship to the preservation or efficiency of a well regulated militia." *Lewis v. United States*, 445 U.S. 55, 65 n.8, 100 S.Ct. 915, 921 n.8, 63 L.Ed.2d 198, 209 n.8 (1980). Like the federal constitution, many state constitutions contain language dealing with the right to keep and bear arms. Yet state courts tend to give wide latitude to state and local gun control laws.

THE DOCTRINES OF VAGUENESS AND OVERBREADTH

The Fifth Amendment to the U.S. Constitution provides that "no person . . . shall be deprived of life, liberty or property without due process of law." The two fundamental aspects of due process are "fair notice" and "fair hearing." The principle of fair notice implies that a person has a right to know whether particular contemplated conduct is illegal. The Supreme Court has emphatically stated, "No one may be required at peril of life, liberty or property to speculate as to the meaning of penal statutes." *Lanzetta v. New Jersey*, 306 U.S. 451, 453, 59 S.Ct. 618, 619, 83 L.Ed. 888, 890 (1939). A criminal law that is excessively vague in its proscriptions offends this principle, and is thus invalid under the Due Process Clause of the Fifth or Fourteenth Amendments (depending on whether it is a *federal* or *state* statute). However, we must realize that the vagueness doctrine is "designed more to limit the discretion of police and prosecutors than to ensure that statutes are intelligible to persons pondering criminal activity." *United States v. White*, 882 F.2d 250, 252 (7th Cir. 1989). Accordingly, the Supreme Court has held that the requisite specificity of criminal statutes may be achieved through judicial interpretation. *Rose v. Locke*, 423 U.S. 48, 96 S.Ct. 243, 46 L.Ed.2d 185 (1975). As interpreted by the Seventh Circuit Court of Appeals in *United States v. White*, "provided that conduct is of a sort widely known among the lay public to be criminal. . . , a person is not entitled to clear notice that the conduct violates a *particular* criminal statute." [emphasis in original] *United States v. White, supra* at 252.

In a landmark decision, the Supreme Court struck down a Jacksonville, Florida, ordinance that prohibited various forms of vagrancy including loitering and "prowling by auto." *Papachristou v. Jacksonville*, 405 U.S. 156, 92 S.Ct. 839, 31 L.Ed.2d 110 (1972). Writing for the Court in *Papachristou*, Justice Douglas objected to the "unfettered discretion" the ordinance placed in the hands of the police, allowing for "arbitrary and discriminatory enforcement of the law." (For further discussion of the vagueness doctrine as it relates to the crimes of vagrancy and loitering, see Chapter 11.)

C A S E I N P O I N T

THE RIGHT TO KEEP AND BEAR ARMS

Part I, Article 2-a of the New Hampshire Constitution provides: "All persons have the right to keep and bear arms in defense of themselves, their families, their property and the state." At the same time, a New Hampshire statute proscribes possession of firearms by convicted felons. RSA 159:3. Scott Smith, who was convicted in the Rockingham Superior Court of being a felon in possession of a firearm, challenged the constitutionality of the statute. The New Hampshire Supreme Court affirmed the conviction and sustained the validity of the statute, saying, "the State constitutional right to keep and bear arms is not absolute and may be subject to restriction and regulation. . . . The governmental interest served by the statute, protection of human life and property, is patently significant."

State v. Smith, 571 A.2d 279, 281 (N.H. 1990).

Closely related to the concept of vagueness, the doctrine of overbreadth was developed exclusively in the context of the First Amendment. It is concerned with the precision of a criminal law that potentially infringes on First Amendment freedoms. Thus a law that forbids people from congregating on the street and engaging in speech that is "annoying" to passersby is overbroad. *Coates v. City of Cincinnati*, 402 U.S. 611, 91 S.Ct. 1686, 29 L.Ed.2d 214 (1971). The overbreadth of the law may permit police to make arrests for constitutionally protected conduct, such as political speech, as well as unprotected activity, such as fighting words.

The doctrine of overbreadth enables a person to contest the legality of a law imposing restrictions on First Amendment freedoms even when he or she has not been charged with violating the law. It also permits the person being prosecuted to challenge the facial constitutionality of the law, even though his or her actions might not be constitutionally protected, on the ground that the law might be applied in the future against activities protected by the First Amendment. This controversial doctrine was designed to bring to the courts' attention laws that have a "chilling effect" on the exercise of First Amendment rights.

In the 1980s, the Supreme Court appeared to be retreating somewhat from the overbreadth doctrine. In *New York v. Ferber*, 458 U.S. 747, 102 S.Ct. 3348, 73 L.Ed.2d 1113 (1982), for example, the Court rejected an overbreadth challenge to a child pornography statute that criminalized child pornography well beyond the legal test of obscenity delineated in *Miller v. California, supra*. Although expressing concern that the statute might possibly be applied to punish constitutionally protected artistic expression, the Court concluded that the law was not "substantially overbroad" and that impermissible applications of the statute should be addressed on a case-by-case basis. According to the *Ferber* Court, a statute should not be invalidated for overbreadth if its legitimate reach "dwarfs its arguably impermissible applications." 458 U.S. at 773, 102 S.Ct. at 3363, 73 L.Ed.2d at 1133.

THE PROHIBITION AGAINST CRUEL AND UNUSUAL PUNISHMENTS

The Eighth Amendment prohibits the imposition of "cruel and unusual punishments." This principle applies both to the procedures by which criminal sentences are imposed, *Furman v. Georgia*, 408 U.S. 238, 92 S.Ct. 2726, 33 L.Ed.2d 346 (1972), and to the substantive laws that define punishments. For example, in *Coker v. Georgia*, 433 U.S. 584, 97 S.Ct. 2861, 53 L.Ed.2d 982 (1977), the Supreme Court invalidated a provision of a state death penalty law that allowed capital punishment in cases of rape. Writing for the plurality, Justice White concluded that "the death penalty, which is 'unique in its severity and its irrevocability,'is an excessive penalty for the rapist who, as such, does not take human life." 433 U.S. at 598, 97 S.Ct. at 2869, 53 L.Ed.2d at 993. Generally, however, in Eighth Amendment cases, the Supreme Court does not rule on the validity of a statute, but rather confines its inquiry to the constitutionality of a particular sentence. For example, in *Solem v. Helm*, 463 U.S. 277, 103 S.Ct. 3001, 77 L.Ed.2d. 637 (1983), the Supreme Court vacated a life sentence without possibility of parole imposed under a state habitual offender law. The Court found that life imprisonment without parole was significantly disproportionate to the defendant's crimes, all of which were nonviolent in nature.

On occasion, the Eighth Amendment has even been employed to limit the definition of crimes. In *Robinson v. California*, 370 U.S. 660, 82 S.Ct. 1417, 8 L.Ed.2d 758 (1962), the Supreme Court, relying on the Cruel and Unusual Punishments Clause, struck down a state law that made it a crime for a person to be "addicted to the use of narcotics." The Court found it unacceptable that an individual could be punished merely for a "status" without regard to any specific criminal conduct. In effect, the Court "constitutionalized" the traditional requirement that a crime involve a specific *actus reus*.

CASE IN POINT

THE VAGUENESS DOCTRINE

Dan D. Robinson was convicted of failing to "securely confine or restrain a vicious dog," an offense under Ohio R.C. § 955.22(D)(1).Under 955.11(A)(4)(a)(iii), a "vicious dog" included any dog that belonged to "a breed that is commonly known as a pit bull dog." On appeal, Robinson challenged the law as excessively vague in that it failed to define the meaning of *pit bull*. An Ohio appellate court rejected the challenge, saying that although the statute lacked a specific definition, "mathematical certainty is not always essential to constitutionality." The court concluded that the statute "refers to those animals which display the physical characteristics generally conforming to the various standards normally associated with pit bulls."

State v. Robinson, 541 N.E. 2d 1092, 1097 (Ohio App. 1989).

THE CONSTITUTIONAL RIGHT OF PRIVACY

Although there is no mention of "privacy" in the text of the Constitution, the Supreme Court has held that a sphere of intimate personal conduct is immune from legislative interference. In its first explicit recognition of this "meta-textual" constitutional right, *Griswold v. Connecticut*, 381 U.S. 479, 85 S.Ct. 1678, 14 L.Ed.2d 510 (1965), the Court relied in part on the Ninth Amendment, which provides that:

> The enumeration in the Constitution, of certain rights, shall not be construed to deny or disparage others retained by the people.

In the *Griswold* case, the Supreme Court invalidated as applied to married couples a state law proscribing the use of birth control devices. In *Eisenstadt v. Baird*, 405 U.S. 438, 92 S.Ct. 1029, 31 L.Ed.2d 349 (1972), the Court extended the principle to protect single individuals from a similar anti-contraception statute. Writing for the Court in *Eisenstadt*, Justice Brennan stated that the right of privacy is "the right of the individual, married or single, to be free from unwarranted governmental intrusion into matters so fundamentally affecting a person as the decision whether or not to beget a child." 405 U.S. at 453, 92 S.Ct. at 1038, 31 L.Ed.2d at 362.

Abortion

The Supreme Court's *Griswold* and *Eisenstadt* decisions paved the way for its landmark abortion decision in *Roe v. Wade*, 410 U.S. 113, 93 S.Ct. 705, 35 L.Ed.2d 147 (1973). In *Roe*, per Justice Blackmun, the Court held that the right of privacy was broad enough to include a woman's decision to terminate her pregnancy. This 7–2 decision invalidated the Texas antiabortion statute, and rendered unenforceable similar laws in most states. The essential holding in *Roe v. Wade* was reaffirmed by the Supreme Court in 1992, albeit by a 5–4 vote. *Planned Parenthood v. Casey*, 505 U.S. ___, 112 S. Ct. 2791, 120 L.Ed.2d 674. The shrinking Supreme Court majority favoring the constitutional right to abortion and the continuing "pro-life" and "pro-choice" demonstrations around the country attest to the extremely controversial nature of the right to abortion. (The abortion issue is discussed more thoroughly in Chapter 8.)

Sexual Conduct

In 1986, the Supreme Court declined to extend the right of privacy to protect homosexual conduct between consenting adults. In *Bowers v. Hardwick*, 478 U.S. 186, 106 S.Ct. 2841, 92 L.Ed.2d 140 (1986), the Court upheld a Georgia statute making sodomy a crime. However, the Court did not address the question of whether the state could enforce its sodomy law against private heterosexual activity between consenting adults. Under a strict interpretation of the right of privacy, sexual relations between consenting adults would not be subject to governmental prohibition. Such a principle could, of course, invalidate long-standing (and still fairly prevalent, if seldom enforced) proscriptions against sodomy, adultery, fornication, and seduction. It might also raise serious questions as to the validity of statutes proscribing incest, bigamy, and prostitution, which are nearly universal among the American states (see Chapter 8).

The Right to Die

As we noted previously in the context of free exercise of religion, courts have held that competent adults have the right to refuse medical treatment in some circumstances. It is now well-established that a competent adult with a terminal illness has the right to refuse medical treatment that would unnaturally prolong his or her life. See, for example, *Satz v. Perlmutter,* 379 So.2d 359 (Fla. 1980). Under certain circumstances courts have allowed the family of a comatose individual to direct removal of extraordinary means of life support. See, for example, *In re Quinlan,* 355 A.2d 647 (N.J. 1976), cert. denied, 429 U.S. 922, 97 S.Ct. 319, 50 L.Ed.2d 289 (1976).

The so-called right to die, if extended beyond the right of a terminally ill person to refuse artificial means of life support, runs headlong into criminal prohibitions against suicide and, potentially, homicide. As yet, courts have been unwilling to extend the right of privacy this far. For example, in *Gilbert v. State,* 487 So.2d 1185 (Fla.App. 1986), a Florida appeals court rejected Roswell Gilbert's "euthanasia" defense to the charge that he committed premeditated murder against his wife, who suffered from osteoporosis and Alzheimer's disease (see Chapter 6).

EQUAL PROTECTION OF THE LAWS

The Fourteenth Amendment of the U.S. Constitution forbids states from denying persons "equal protection of the laws." The Due Process Clause of the Fifth Amendment has been interpreted to impose a similar prohibition on the federal government. *Bolling v. Sharpe,* 347 U.S. 497, 74 S.Ct. 693, 98 L.Ed. 884 (1954). Most state constitutions contain similar requirements. On occasion, the concept of equal protection has been used to challenge the validity of criminal statutes. For example, in *Loving v. Virginia,* 388 U.S. 1, 87 S.Ct. 1817, 18 L.Ed.2d 1010 (1967), the Supreme Court relied on the Equal Protection Clause of the Fourteenth Amendment in striking down a state statute that criminalized interracial marriage. The effect of *Loving* was that any law that criminalized conduct solely on the basis of the race of the parties was rendered null and void. In *Eisenstadt v. Baird, supra,* the Court invoked the Equal Protection Clause in striking a Massachusetts law that criminalized the use of birth control devices by single persons, but not by married couples. And in *Craig v. Boren,* 429 U.S. 190, 97 S.Ct. 451, 50 L.Ed.2d 397 (1976), the Court invalidated an Oklahoma law that forbade the sale of beer containing 3.2 percent alcohol to females under the age of eighteen and males under the age of twenty-one. The Court concluded that the state lacked a sufficient justification for discriminating between the sexes in the availability of the contested beverage.

STANDARDS OF JUDICIAL REVIEW

At a minimum, a criminal law that touches on constitutionally protected interests must be "rationally related to furthering a legitimate government interest." *Massachusetts Board of Retirement v. Murgia*, 427 U.S. 307, 96 S.Ct. 2562, 49 L.Ed.2d 520 (1976). For example, a state law that makes it a crime for a person to perform surgery without a license is obviously a rational means of advancing the state's legitimate interests in public health and safety. Thus, even though the law deprives lay persons of their right to make contracts freely, and discriminates against those unable to obtain a license, there is little doubt it would withstand judicial review under the "rational basis test."

Criminal laws that infringe "fundamental rights" such as First Amendment freedoms are judged by a more stringent standard of review. Such laws are subject to "strict judicial scrutiny," which means, in effect, that they are presumed to be unconstitutional. To survive judicial review, government must show that the challenged law furthers a compelling government interest. *Shapiro v. Thompson*, 394 U.S. 618, 89 S.Ct. 1322, 22 L.Ed.2d 600 (1969). This is a heavy burden for the government to carry. Consequently, many laws subjected to strict judicial scrutiny are declared unconstitutional. However, the application of strict scrutiny is not necessarily equivalent to a declaration of unconstitutionality. For example, in *New York v. Ferber, supra*, the Supreme Court upheld a child pornography law that impinged on the First Amendment freedom of expression because, in the view of the Court, the law served a compelling interest in protecting children from the abuse typically associated with the pornography industry.

THE IMPORTANCE OF STATE CONSTITUTIONS

Under our federal system of government, the highest court of each state possesses the authority to interpret with finality its state constitution and statutes. A decision by a state court is not subject to review by the United States Supreme Court, except insofar as the state law on which it is based is being challenged as a violation of the federal constitution and/or statutes. Since every state constitution contains language protecting individual rights and liberties, many state court decisions implicate both state and federal constitutional provisions. Under the relevant language of their constitutions and statutes, state courts are free to recognize greater (but not lesser) protections of individual rights than are provided by the U.S. Constitution as interpreted by the federal courts. As a result of the increased conservatism of the federal judiciary, and in particular the Supreme Court, over the last decade, there has been a resurgence of interest in state constitutional law as it relates to civil rights and liberties.

In *Michigan v. Long*, 463 U.S. 1032, 1040, 103 S.Ct. 3469, 3476, 77 L.Ed.2d 1201, 1214 (1983), the U.S. Supreme Court said that "when a state court decision fairly appears to rest primarily on federal law, or to be interwoven with the federal law, and when the adequacy and independence of any possible state law ground is not clear from the face of the opinion, we will accept as the most reasonable explanation that the state court decided the case the way it did because it believed that federal law required it to do so." However, the Court also indicated that "if the state court decision indicates clearly and expressly that it is alternatively based on bona fide separate, adequate, and independent grounds, we, of course, will not undertake to review the decision." 463 U.S. at 1041, 103 S.Ct. at 3476, 77 L.Ed.2d at 1214 (1983).

Michigan v. Long effectively invited the state courts to consider the parallel provisions of their state constitutions independently. Some state courts have accepted the invitation. For example, in *In re T.W.*, 551 So.2d 1186 (Fla. 1989), the Florida Supreme Court struck down as a violation of the right of privacy a statute that required parental consent in cases where minors sought abortions. The constitutionality of a similar law had been upheld on federal grounds by the U.S. Supreme Court in *Planned Parenthood v. Ashcroft*, 462 U.S. 476, 103 S.Ct. 2517, 76 L.Ed.2d 733 (1983). In *T.W.*, the Florida Supreme Court made it clear that it was basing its decision on an amendment to the Florida Constitution that (unlike the federal constitution) explicitly protects the right of privacy. Similarly, in *State v. Kam*, 748 P.2d 372 (Hawaii 1988), the Hawaii Supreme Court adopted an interpretation of its state constitution that affords considerably broader protection to pornography than that provided by the U.S. Constitution. Finally, in *Williams v. City of Fort Worth*, 782 S.W.2d 290 (Tex. 1989), a Texas appellate court struck down as a violation of the state equal rights amendment a city ordinance prohibiting females, but not males, from publicly exposing their breasts! These decisions, and many others like them, mean that a person interested in constitutional limitations on the prohibition of criminal conduct must not ignore the provisions of state constitutions that parallel the U. S. Constitution.

CONCLUSION

The constitutional limitations discussed in this chapter have a direct bearing on the legislative definition of crimes, especially with respect to offenses against public morality (discussed in Chapter 8) and offenses against public order (discussed in Chapter 11). The well-established power of judicial review sustains both the constitutional rights of the individual and the rule of law. These rights and principles impose serious constraints on the definition of criminal conduct and the enforcement of the criminal law.

QUESTIONS FOR THOUGHT AND DISCUSSION

1. Can you think of a hypothetical example of a bill of attainder? What about an *ex post facto* law?

2. Is it possible for the criminal law to define the crime of obscenity, precisely enough to avoid the "vice of vagueness" or the problem of overbreadth?

3. Can a municipality enforce an ordinance totally banning religious organizations from canvassing neighborhoods in search of new members? What about an ordinance that prohibits such canvassing between the hours of 8 P.M. and 8 A.M.?

4. Should the constitutional right of privacy invalidate criminal statutes that proscribe homosexual conduct between consenting adults?

5. Would the constitutional right of privacy provide a defense to a charge of possession of obscene materials where videotapes were viewed only by the defendant in the privacy of his or her home?

6. John Masters, a licensed psychotherapist, has been charged with violating a new state statute making it a crime for "any licensed psychologist, psychiatrist, or psychotherapist to have sexual intercourse with a patient during the existence of the professional relationship." Masters is challenging the constitutionality of the statute on two principal grounds: (a) that it intrudes on his right of privacy; and (b) that it violates the Equal Protection Clause of the Fourteenth Amendment in that it fails to apply the same prohibition to other health-care professionals. Do you think Masters is likely to prevail in his challenge to the statute? If you were a judge faced with these constitutional questions, how would you be inclined to rule? What additional information would you need to render your decision?

7. Could a father who, without judicial approval, unplugs the respirator sustaining the breathing of his comatose, terminally ill child be prosecuted for murder?

8. Would a law making it an offense for a person to carry prescription medicine in other than the original labeled container meet the rational basis test?

9. How does the doctrine of judicial review affect the power of a state legislature to define criminal conduct? Would the constitutional limitations on legislative power be as stringent without the power of courts to declare laws unconstitutional?

A NOTE ON READING AND BRIEFING CASES

Beginning with this chapter, each chapter in this book includes a number of excerpted decisions by appellate courts. We have chosen these decisions to illustrate some of the important concepts and principles described in the chapters. Some instructors may wish to have their students "brief" some or all of these cases. Whether or not the instructor assigns it, students may find briefing cases useful in learning material and preparing for examinations.

A case brief is simply a summary of a court decision, usually in outline format. Typically, a case brief contains the following elements:

1. The name of the case, the court deciding the case, and the date of the decision
2. The essential facts of the case
3. The key issue(s) of law involved (or those applicable to a point of law being considered)
4. The holding of the court
5. A brief summary of the court's opinion, especially as it relates to the key issue(s) in the case
6. Summaries of concurring and dissenting opinions, if any

Students may also wish to make a note of any questions or comments they have at the end of the brief.

CASES

BRANDENBURG V. OHIO

Supreme Court of the United States, 1969.
395 U.S. 444, 89 S. Ct. 1827, 23 L.Ed.2d 430.

[In this landmark case, the U.S. Supreme Court considers whether, and under what circumstances, the advocacy of unlawful conduct is protected by the First Amendment.]

PER CURIAM.

The appellant, a leader of a Ku Klux Klan group, was convicted under the Ohio Criminal Syndicalism statute for "advocat[ing] . . . the duty, necessity, or propriety of crime, sabotage, violence, or unlawful methods of terrorism as a means of accomplishing industrial or political reform" and for "voluntarily assembl[ing] with any society, group, or assemblage of persons formed to teach or advocate the doctrines of criminal syndicalism." . . . He was fined $1,000 and sentenced to one to 10 years' imprisonment. The appellant challenged the constitutionality of the criminal syndicalism statute under the First and Fourteenth Amendments to the United States Constitution, but the intermediate appellate court of Ohio affirmed his conviction without opinion. The Supreme Court of Ohio dismissed his appeal, sua sponte, "for the reason that no substantial constitutional question exists herein." It did not file an opinion or explain its conclusions. Appeal was taken to this Court, and we noted probable jurisdiction. . . .

The record shows that a man, identified at trial as the appellant, telephoned an announcer-reporter on the staff of a Cincinnati television station and invited him to come to a Ku Klux Klan "rally" to be held at a farm in Hamilton County. With the cooperation of the organizers, the reporter and a cameraman attended the meeting and filmed the events. Portions of the films were later broadcast on the local station and on a national network.

The prosecution's case rested on the films and on testimony identifying the appellant as the person who communicated with the reporter and who spoke at the rally. The State also introduced into evidence several articles appearing in the film, including a pistol, a rifle, a shotgun, ammunition, a Bible, and a red hood worn by the speaker in the films.

One film showed 12 hooded figures, some of whom carried firearms. They were gathered around a large wooden cross, which they burned. No one was present other than the participants and the newsmen who made the film. Most of the words uttered during the scene were incomprehensible when the film was projected, but scattered phrases could be understood that were derogatory of Negroes and, in one instance, of Jews. Another scene on the same film showed the appellant, in Klan regalia, making a speech. The speech, in full, was as follows:

"This is an organizers' meeting. We have had quite a few members here today which are—we have hundreds, hundreds of members throughout the State of Ohio. I can quote from a newspaper clipping from the Columbus, Ohio, Dispatch, five weeks ago Sunday morning. The Klan has more members in the State of Ohio than does any other organization. We're not a revengent organization, but if our President, our Congress, our Supreme Court, continues to suppress the white, Caucasian race, it's possible that there might have to be some revengeance taken.

"We are marching on Congress July the Fourth, four hundred thousand strong. From there we are dividing into two groups, one group to march on St. Augustine, Florida, the other group to march into Mississippi. Thank you."

The second film showed six hooded figures, one of whom, later identified as the appellant, repeated a speech very similar to that recorded on the first film. The reference to the possibility of "revengeance" was omitted, and one sentence was added: "Personally, I believe the nigger should be returned to Africa, the Jew returned to Israel." Though some of the figures in the films carried weapons, the speaker did not.

The Ohio Criminal Syndicalism Statute was enacted in 1919. From 1917 to 1920, identical or quite similar laws were adopted by 20 States and two territories. In 1927, this Court sustained the constitutionality of California's Criminal Syndicalism Act, the test of which is quite similar to that of the laws of Ohio. . . . The Court upheld the statute on the ground that, without more, "advocating" violent means to effect political and economic change involves such danger to the security of the State that the State may outlaw it. But [this view] has been thoroughly discredited by later decisions. . . . These later decisions have fashioned the principle that the constitutional guarantees of free speech and free press do not permit a State to forbid advocacy . . . [unless it] is directed to inciting or producing imminent lawless action and is likely to incite or produce such action. As we said in Noto v. United States, "the mere abstract teaching . . . of the moral propriety or even moral necessity for a resort to force and violence, is not the same as preparing a group for violent action and steeling it to such action." A statute which fails to draw this distinction impermissibly intrudes upon the freedoms guaranteed by the First and Fourteenth Amendments. It sweeps within its condemnation speech which our Constitution has immunized from governmental control. . . .

Measured by this test, Ohio's Criminal Syndicalism Act cannot be sustained. The Act punishes persons who "advocate or teach the duty, necessity, or propriety" of violence "as a means of accomplishing industrial or political reform"; or who publish or circulate or display any book or paper containing such advocacy; or who "justify" the commission of violent acts "with intent to exemplify, spread or advocate the propriety of the doctrines of criminal syndicalism"; or who "voluntarily assemble" with a group formed "to teach or advocate the doctrines of criminal syndicalism." Neither the indictment nor the trial judge's instructions to the jury in any way refined the statute's bald definition of the crime in terms of mere advocacy not distinguished from incitement to imminent lawless action.

Accordingly, we are here confronted with a statute which, by its own words and as applied, purports to punish mere advocacy and to forbid, on pain of criminal punishment, assembly with others merely to advocate the described type of action. Such a statute falls within the condemnation of the First and Fourteenth Amendments. The contrary teaching of Whitney v. California [1927] . . . cannot be supported and that decision is therefore overruled.

Reversed.

Mr. Justice BLACK, concurring . . .

Mr. Justice DOUGLAS, concurring . . .

Miller v. California
Supreme Court of the United States, 1973.
413 U.S. 15, 93 S. Ct. 2607, 37 L.Ed.2d 419.

[In this case the U.S. Supreme Court articulates a three-part test for determining what is obscene.]

Mr. Chief Justice BURGER delivered the opinion of the Court.

This is one of a group of "obscenity-pornography" cases being reviewed by the Court in a reexamination of standards enunciated in earlier cases involving what Mr. Justice Harlan called "the intractable obscenity problem." . . . Appellant conducted a mass mailing campaign to advertise the said illustrated books, euphemistically called "adult" material. After a jury trial, he was convicted of violating California Penal Code 311.2(a), a misdemeanor, by knowingly distributing obscene matter, and the Appellate Department, Superior Court California, County of Orange, summarily affirmed the judgment without opinion Appellant's conviction was specifically based on his conduct in causing unsolicited advertising brochures to be sent through the mail in an envelope addressed to a restaurant in Newport Beach, California. The envelope was opened by the manager of the restaurant and his mother. They had not requested brochures; they complained to the police.

The brochures advertise four books entitled "Intercourse," "Man-Woman," "Sex Orgies Illustrated," and "An Illustrated History of Pornography," and a film entitled "Marital Intercourse." While the brochures contain some descriptive printed material, primarily they consist of pictures and drawings very explicitly depicting men and women in groups of two or more engaging in a variety of sexual activities, with genitals often prominently displayed.

I

This case involves the application of a State's criminal obscenity statute to a situation in which sexually explicit materials have been thrust by aggressive sales action upon unwilling recipients who had in no way indicated any desire to receive such materials. This Court has recognized that the States have a legitimate interest in prohibiting dissemination or exhibition of obscene material when the mode of dissemination carries with it a significant danger of offending the sensibilities of unwilling recipients or of exposure to juveniles. . . . It is in this context that we are called on to define the standards which must be used to identify obscene material that a State may regulate without infringing the First Amendment as applicable to the States through the Fourteenth Amendment. . .

II

This much has been categorically settled by the Court, that obscene material is unprotected by the First Amendment. . . . "The First and Fourteenth Amendments have never been treated as absolutes." . . . We acknowledge, however, the inherent dangers of undertaking to regulate any form of expression. State statutes designed to regulate obscene materials must be carefully limited. . . . As a result, we now confine the permissible scope of such regulation to works which depict or describe sexual conduct. That conduct must be specifically defined by the applicable state law, as written or authoritatively construed. A state office must also be limited to works which, taken as a whole, appeal to the prurient interest in sex, which portray sexual conduct in a patently offensive way, and which, taken as a whole, do not have serious literary, artistic, political, or scientific value.

The basic guidelines for the trier of fact must be: (a) whether "the average person, applying contemporary community standards" would find that the work, taken as a whole, appeals to the prurient interest, . . . (b) whether the work depicts or describes, in a patently offensive way, sexual conduct specifically defined by the applicable state law, and (c) whether the work, taken as a whole, lacks serious literary, artistic, political, or scientific value. We do not adopt as a constitutional standard the "utterly without redeeming social value" test of Memoirs v. Massachusetts; . . . that concept has never commanded the adherence of more than three Justices at one time. . . . If a state law that regulates obscene material is thus limited, as written or construed, the First Amendment values applicable to the States through the Fourteenth Amendment are adequately protected by the ultimate power of appellate courts to conduct an independent review of constitutional claims when necessary. . . .

We emphasize that it is not our function to propose regulatory schemes for the States. That must await their concrete legislative efforts. it is possible, however, to give a few plain examples of what a state statute could define for regulation under the second part (b) of the standard announced in this opinion supra:

(a) Patently offensive representations or descriptions of ultimate sexual acts, normal or perverted, actual or simulated.

(b) Patently offensive representations or descriptions of masturbation, excretory functions, and lewd exhibition of the genitals.

Sex and nudity may not be exploited without limit by films or pictures exhibited or sold in places of public accommodation any more than live sex and nudity can be exhibited or sold without limit in such public places. At a minimum, prurient, patently offensive depiction or description of sexual conduct must have serious literary, artistic, political, or scientific value to merit First Amendment protection. . . .

Under the holdings announced today, no one will be subject to prosecution for the sale or exposure of obscene materials unless these materials depict or describe patently offensive "hard core" sexual conduct specifically defined by the regulating state law, as written or construed. We are satisfied that these specific prerequisites will provide fair notice to a dealer in such materials that his public and commercial activities may bring prosecution. . . .

It is certainly true that the absence, since Roth, of a single majority view of this Court as to proper standards for testing obscenity has placed a strain on both state and federal courts. But today, for the first time since Roth was decided in 1957, a majority of this Court has agreed on concrete guidelines to isolate "hard core" pornography from expression protected by the First Amendment. . . .

This may not be an easy road, free from difficulty. But no amount of "fatigue" should lead us to adopt a convenient "institutional" rationale—an absolutist, "anything goes" view of the First Amendment— because it will lighten our burdens. "Such an abnegation of judicial supervision in this field would be inconsistent with our duty to uphold the constitutional guarantees." . . . Nor should we remedy "tension between state and federal courts" by arbitrarily depriving the States of a power reserved to them under the Constitution, a power which they have enjoyed and exercised continuously from before the adoption of the First Amendment to this day. . . .

III

Under a national Constitution, fundamental First Amendment limitations on the powers of the States do not vary from community to community, but this does not mean that there are, or should or can be, fixed, uniform national standards of precisely what appeals to the "prurient interest" or is "patently offensive." These are essentially questions of fact, and our nation is simply too big and too diverse for this Court to reasonably expect that such standards could be articulated for all 50 States in a single formulation, even assuming the prerequisite consensus exists. When triers of fact are asked to decide whether "the average person, applying contemporary community standards" would consider certain materials "prurient," it would be unrealistic to require that the answer be based on some abstract formulation. The adversary system, with lay jurors as the usual ultimate factfinders in criminal prosecution, has historically permitted triers-of-fact to draw

on the standards of their community, guided always by limiting instructions on the law. To require a State to structure obscenity proceedings around evidence of a national community standard" would be an exercise in futility. . . .

It is neither realistic nor constitutionally sound to read the First Amendment as requiring that the people of Maine or Mississippi accept public depiction of conduct found tolerable in Las Vegas, or New York City. People in different States vary in their tastes and attitudes, and this diversity is not to be strangled by the absolutism of imposed uniformity.

IV

The dissenting Justices sound the alarm of repression. But, in our view, to equate the free and robust exchange of ideas and political debate with commercial exploitation of obscene material demeans the grand conception of the First Amendment and its high purposes in the historic struggle for freedom. It is a "misuse of the great guarantees of free speech and free press." . . . The First Amendment protects works which, taken as a whole, have serious literary, artistic, political or scientific value, regardless of whether the government or a majority of the people approve the ideas these works represent. "The protection given speech and press was fashioned to assure unfettered interchange of ideas for the bringing about of political and social changes desired by the people." . . . But the public portrayal of hard core sexual conduct for its own sake, and for the ensuing commercial gain, is a different matter.

One can concede that the "sexual revolution" of recent years may have had useful byproducts in striking layers of prudery from a subject long irrationally kept from needed ventilation. But it does not follow that no regulation of patently offensive "hard core" materials is needed or permissible; civilized people do not allow unregulated access to heroin because it is a derivative of medicinal morphine.

Vacated and remanded.

Mr. Justice DOUGLAS, dissenting.
. . . Today the Court retreats from the earlier formulations of the constitutional test and undertakes to make new definitions. This effort, like the earlier

ones, is earnest and well-intentioned. The difficulty is that we do not deal with constitutional terms, since "obscenity" is not mentioned in the Constitution or Bill of Rights. And the First Amendment makes no such exception from "the press" which it undertakes to protect nor, as I have said on other occasions, is an exception necessarily implied, for there was no recognized exception to the free press at the time the Bill of Rights was adopted which treated "obscene" publications differently from other types of papers, magazines, and books. So there are no constitutional guidelines for deciding what is and what is not "obscene." The Court is at large because we deal with tastes and standards of literature. What shocks me may be sustenance for my neighbor. What causes one person to boil up in rage over one pamphlet or movie may reflect only his neurosis, not shared by others. We deal here with problems of censorship which, if adopted, should be done by constitutional amendment after full debate by the people. . . .

. . . The idea that the First Amendment permits government to ban publications that are "offensive" to some people puts an ominous gloss on freedom of the press. That test would make it possible to ban any paper or any journal or magazine in some benighted place. The First Amendment was designed "to invite dispute," to induce "a condition of

unrest," to "create dissatisfactions with conditions as they are," and even to stir "people to anger." The idea that the First Amendment permits punishment for ideas that are "offensive" to the particular judge or jury sitting in judgment is astounding. No greater leveler of speech or literature has ever been designed. To give the power to the censor, as we do today, is to make a sharp and radical break with the traditions of a free society. The First Amendment was not fashioned as a vehicle for dispensing tranquilizers to the people. Its prime function was to keep debate open to "offensive" as well as to "staid" people. The tendency throughout history has been to subdue the individual and to exalt the power of government. The use of the standard "offensive" gives authority to government that cuts the very vitals out of the First Amendment. As is intimated by the Court's opinion, the materials before us may be garbage. But so is much of what is said in political campaigns, in the daily press, on TV or over the radio. By reason of the First Amendment—and solely because of it—speakers and publishers have not been threatened or subdued because their thoughts and ideas may be "offensive" to some. . . .

Mr. Justice BRENNAN, with whom Mr. Justice STEWART and Mr. Justice MARSHALL join, dissenting. . . .

COATES V. CINCINNATI
Supreme Court of the United States, 1971
402 U.S. 611, 91 S. Ct. 1686, 29 L.Ed.2d 214.

[Here the U.S. Supreme Court applies the vagueness and overbreadth doctrines to a local ordinance.]

Mr. Justice STEWART delivered the opinion of the Court.
A Cincinnati, Ohio, ordinance makes it a criminal offense for "three or more persons to assemble . . . on any of the sidewalks . . . and there conduct themselves in a manner annoying to persons passing by . . . ." The issue before us is whether this ordinance is unconstitutional on its face.

The appellants were convicted of violating the ordinance, and the convictions were ultimately affirmed by a closely divided vote in the Supreme Court of Ohio, upholding the constitutional validity of the ordinance. . . . An appeal from that judgment was brought here and we noted probable jurisdiction. . . . The record brought before the reviewing courts tells us no more than that the appellant Coates was a student involved in a demonstration and the other appellants were pickets involved in a labor dispute. For throughout this litigation it has been the appellants' position that the ordinance on its face violates the First and Fourteenth Amendments of the Constitution. . . .

In rejecting this claim and affirming the convictions the Ohio Supreme Court did not give the ordinance any construction at variance with the apparent plain import of its language. The court simply stated:

> The ordinance prohibits, inter alia, "conduct . . . annoying to persons passing by." The word "annoying" is a widely used and well understood word; it is not necessary to guess its meaning. "Annoying" is the present participle of the transitive verb "annoy" which means to trouble, to vex, to impede, to incommode, to provoke, to harass or to irritate.

We conclude . . . that the ordinance "clearly and precisely delineates its reach in words of common understanding. It is a "precise and narrowly drawn regulatory statute [ordinance] evincing a legislative judgment that certain specific conduct be . . . proscribed.' " . . .

Beyond this, the only construction put upon the ordinance by the state court was its unexplained conclusion that "the standard of conduct which it specifies is not dependent upon each complainant's sensitivity." . . . But the court did not indicate upon whose sensitivity a violation does depend—the sensitivity of the judge or jury, the sensitivity of the arresting officer, or the sensitivity of a hypothetical reasonable man.

We are thus relegated, at best, to the words of the ordinance itself. If three or more people meet together on a sidewalk or street corner, they must conduct themselves so as not to annoy any police officer or other person who should happen to pass by. In our opinion this ordinance is unconstitutionally vague because it subjects the exercise of the right of assembly to an unascertainable standard, and unconstitutionally broad because it authorizes the punishment of constitutionally protected conduct.

Conduct that annoys some people does not annoy others. Thus, the ordinance is vague, not in the sense that it requires a person to conform his conduct to an imprecise but comprehensible normative standard, but rather in the sense that no standard of conduct is specified at all. As a result, "men of common intelligence must necessarily guess at its meaning.". . .

It is said that the ordinance is broad enough to encompass many types of conduct clearly within the city's constitutional power to prohibit. And so, indeed, it is. The city is free to prevent people from blocking sidewalks, obstructing traffic, littering streets, committing assaults, or engaging in countless other forms of antisocial conduct. It can do so through the enactment and enforcement of ordinances directed with reasonable specificity toward the conduct to be prohibited. . . . It cannot constitutionally do so through the enactment and enforcement of an ordinance whose violation may entirely depend upon whether or not a policeman is annoyed.

But the vice of the ordinance lies not alone in its violation of the due process standard of vagueness. The ordinance also violates the constitutional right of free assembly and association. Our decisions establish that mere public intolerance or animosity cannot be the basis for abridgement of these constitutional freedoms. . . . The First and Fourteenth Amendments do not permit a State to make criminal the exercise of the right of assembly simply because its exercise may be "annoying" to some people. If this were not the rule, the right of the people to gather in public places for social or political purposes would be continually subject to summary suspension through the good-faith enforcement of a prohibition against annoying conduct. And such a prohibition, in addition, contains an obvious invitation to discriminatory enforcement against those whose association together is "annoying" because their ideas, their lifestyle, or their physical appearance is resented by the majority of their fellow citizens.

The ordinance before us makes a crime out of what under the Constitution cannot be a crime. It is aimed directly at activity protected by the Constitution. We need not lament that we do not have before us the details of the conduct found to be annoying. It is the ordinance on its face that sets the standard of conduct and warns against transgression. The details of the offense could no more serve to validate this ordinance than could the details of an offense charged under an ordinance suspending unconditionally the right of assembly and free speech. The judgment is reversed.

Mr. Justice BLACK. . . .

Mr. Justice WHITE, with whom the Chief Justice and Mr. Justice BLACKMUN join, dissenting.

The claim in this case, in part, is that the Cincinnati ordinance is so vague that it may not constitutionally be applied to any conduct. But the ordinance prohibits persons from assembling with others and "conduct[ing] themselves in a manner annoying to persons passing by . . . ." . . . Any man of average comprehension should know that some kinds of conduct, such as assault or blocking passage on the street, will annoy others and are clearly covered by the "annoying conduct" standard of the ordinance. It would be frivolous to say that these and many other kinds of conduct are not within the foreseeable reach of the law.

It is possible that a whole range of other acts, defined with unconstitutional imprecision, is forbidden by the ordinance. But as a general rule, when a criminal charge is based on conduct constitutionally subject to proscription and clearly forbidden by a statute, it is no defense that the law would be unconstitutionally vague if applied to other behavior. Such a statute is not vague on its face. It may be vague as applied in some circumstances, but ruling on such a challenge obviously requires knowledge of the conduct with which a defendant is charged. . . .

Our cases, however, recognize a different approach where the statute at issue purports to regulate or proscribe rights of speech or press protected by the First Amendment. . . . Although a statute maybe neither vague, overbroad, nor otherwise invalid as applied to the conduct charged against a particu-lar defendant, he is permitted to raise its vagueness or unconstitutional overbreadth as applied to others. And if the law is found deficient in one of these respects, it may not be applied to him either, until and unless a satisfactory limiting construction is placed on the statute. . . . The statute, in effect, is stricken down on its face. This result is deemed justified since the otherwise continued existence of the statute in unnarrowed form would tend to suppress constitutionally protected rights. . . .

Even accepting the overbreadth doctrine with respect to statutes clearly reaching speech, the Cincinnati ordinance does not purport to bar or regulate speech as such. It prohibits persons from assembling "conduct[ing]" themselves in a manner annoying to other persons. Even if the assembled defendants in this case were demonstrating and picketing, we have long recognized that picketing is not solely a communicative endeavor and has aspects which the State is entitled to regulate even though there is incidental impact on speech. . . .

In the case before us, I would deal with the Cincinnati ordinance as we would with the ordinary criminal statute. The ordinance clearly reaches certain conduct but may be illegally vague with respect to other conduct. The statute is not infirm on its face and since we have no information from this record as to what conduct was charged against these defendants, we are in no position to judge the statute as applied. That the ordinance may confer wide discretion in a wide range of circumstances is irrelevant when we may be dealing with conduct at its core.

I would therefore affirm the judgment of the Ohio Supreme Court.

GRISWOLD V. CONNECTICUT
Supreme Court of the United States, 1965.
381 U.S. 479, 85 S. Ct. 1678, 14 L.Ed.2d 510.

[In this case, the U.S. Supreme Court reviews a state law making it a crime, even for married couples, to use birth control devices.]

Mr. Justice DOUGLAS delivered the opinion of the Court.

Appellant Griswold is Executive Director of the Planned Parenthood League of Connecticut. Appellant Buxton is a licensed physician and a professor at the Yale Medical School who served as Medical Director for the League at its Center in New Haven—a center open and operating from November 1 to November 10, 1961, when appellants were arrested.

They gave information, instruction and medical advice to married persons as to the means of preventing conception. They examined the wife and prescribed the best contraceptive device or material for her use. Fees were usually charged, although some couples were serviced free. . . .

The appellants were found guilty as accessories and fined $100 each, against the claim that the accessory statute as so applied violated the Fourteenth Amendment. The Appellate Division of the Circuit Court affirmed. The Supreme Court of Errors affirmed that judgment. . . .

. . . We do not sit as a super-legislature to determine the wisdom, need and propriety of laws that touch economic problems, business affairs, or social conditions. This law, however, operates directly on an intimate relation of husband and wife and their physician's role in one aspect of that relation.

The association of people is not mentioned in the Constitution nor in the Bill of Rights. The right to educate a child in a school of the parents' choice—whether public or private or parochial—is also not mentioned. Nor is the right to study any particular subject or any foreign language. Yet the First Amendment has been construed to include certain of those rights.

[Previous] . . . cases suggest that specific guarantees in the Bill of Rights have penumbras, formed by emanations from those guarantees that help give them life and substance. Various guarantees create zones of privacy. The right of association continued in the penumbra of the First Amendment is one, as we have seen. The Third Amendment in its prohibition against the quartering of soldiers "in any house" in time of peace without the consent of the owner is another facet of that privacy. The Fourth Amendment explicitly affirms the "right of the people to be secure in their persons, houses, papers, and effects, against unreasonable searches and seizures." The Fifth Amendment in its Self-Incrimination Clause enables the citizen to create a zone of privacy which government may not force him to surrender to his detriment. The Ninth Amendment provides: "The enumeration in the Constitution, of certain rights, shall not be construed to deny or disparage others retained by the people." The Fourth and Fifth Amendments were described in Boyd v. United States . . . as protection

against all governmental invasions "of the sanctity of a man's home and the privacies of life." We recently referred in Mapp v. Ohio . . . to the Fourth Amendment as creating a "right to privacy, no less important than any other right carefully and particularly reserved to the people." . . .

We have had many controversies over these penumbral rights of "privacy and repose." . . . These cases bear witness that the right of privacy which presses for recognition here is a legitimate one.

The present case, then, concerns a relationship lying within the zone of privacy created by several fundamental constitutional guarantees. And it concerns a law which, in forbidding the use of contraceptives rather than regulating their manufacture or sale, seeks to achieve its goals by means having a maximum destructive impact upon that relationship. Such a law cannot stand in light of the familiar principle, so often applied by this Court, that a "governmental purpose to control or prevent activities constitutionally subject to state regulation may not be achieved by means which sweep unnecessarily broadly and thereby invade the area of protected freedoms." . . . Would we allow the police to search the sacred precincts of marital bedrooms for telltale signs of the use of contraceptives? The very idea is repulsive to the notions of privacy surrounding the marriage relationship. . . .

Mr. Justice GOLDBERG, whom the Chief Justice and Mr. Justice BRENNAN join, concurring.

. . . Although the Constitution does not speak in so many words of the right of privacy in marriage, I cannot believe that it offers these fundamental rights no protection. The fact that no particular provision of the Constitution explicitly forbids the State from disrupting the traditional relation of the family—a relation as old and as fundamental as our entire civilization—surely does not show that the Government was meant to have the power to do so. Rather, as the Ninth Amendment expressly recognizes, there are fundamental personal rights such as this one, which are protected from abridgment by the Government though not specifically mentioned in the Constitution. . . .

Although the Connecticut birth control law obviously encroaches upon a fundamental personal liberty, the State does not show that the law serves any "subordinating [state] interest which is compelling" or that it is "necessary . . . to the accomplishment of a permissible state policy." The State, at most, argues that there is some rational relation between this statute and what is admittedly a legitimate subject of state concern—the discouraging of extra-marital relations. It says that preventing the use of birth-control devices by married persons helps prevent the indulgence by some in such extra-marital relations. The rationality of this justification is dubious, particularly in light of the admitted widespread availability to all persons in the State of Connecticut, unmarried as well as married, of birth-control devices for the prevention of disease, as distinguished from the prevention of conception. . . . But, in any event, it is clear that the state interest in safeguarding marital fidelity can be served by a more discriminately tailored statute, which does not, like the present one, sweep unnecessarily broadly, reaching far beyond the evil sought to be dealt with and intruding upon the privacy of all married couples. . . .

"Adultery, homosexuality and the like are sexual intimacies which the State forbids . . . but the intimacy of husband and wife is necessarily an essential and accepted feature of the institution of marriage, an institution which the State not only must allow, but which always and in every age it has fostered and protected. It is one thing when the State exerts its power either to forbid extra-marital sexuality . . . or to say who may marry, but it is quite another when, having acknowledged a marriage and the intimacies inherent in it, it undertakes to regulate by means of the criminal law the details of that intimacy." . . .

In sum, I believe that the right of privacy in the marital relation is fundamental and basic—a personal right "retained by the people" within the meaning of the Ninth Amendment. Connecticut cannot constitutionally abridge this fundamental right, which is protected by the Fourteenth Amendment . . . [The] convictions must therefore be reversed.

Mr. Justice HARLAN, concurring in the judgment. . . .

Mr. Justice WHITE, concurring in the judgment. . . .

Mr. Justice BLACK, with whom Mr. Justice STEWART joins, dissenting.

. . . I get nowhere in this case by talk about a constitutional "right of privacy" as an emanation from one or more constitutional provisions. I like my privacy as well as the next one, but I am nevertheless compelled to admit that government has a right to invade it unless prohibited by some specific constitutional provision. For these reasons I cannot agree with the Court's judgment and the reasons it gives for holding this Connecticut law unconstitutional. . . .

I realize that many good and able men have eloquently spoken and written, sometimes in rhapsodical strains, about the duty of this Court to keep the Constitution in tune with the times. The idea is that the Constitution must be changed from time to time and that this Court is charged with a duty to make those changes. For myself, I must with all deference reject that philosophy. The Constitution makers knew the need for change and provided for it. Amendments suggested by the people's elected representatives can be submitted to the people or their selected agents for ratification. That method of change was good for our Fathers, and being somewhat old-fashioned I must add it is good enough for me. . . .

Mr. Justice STEWART, whom Mr. Justice BLACK joins, dissenting.

Since 1879 Connecticut has had on its books a law which forbids the use of contraceptives by anyone. I think this is an uncommonly silly law. As a practical matter, the law is obviously unenforceable, except in the oblique context of the present case. As a philosophical matter, I believe the use of contraceptives in the relationship of marriage should be left to personal and private choice, based upon each individual's moral, ethical, and religious beliefs. As a matter of social policy, I think professional counsel about methods of birth control should be available to all, so that each individual's choice can be meaningfully made. But we are not asked in this case to say whether we think this law is unwise, or even asinine. We are asked to hold that it violates the United States Constitution. And that I cannot do. . . .

CHAPTER 4

ELEMENTS OF CRIMES; PARTIES TO CRIMES

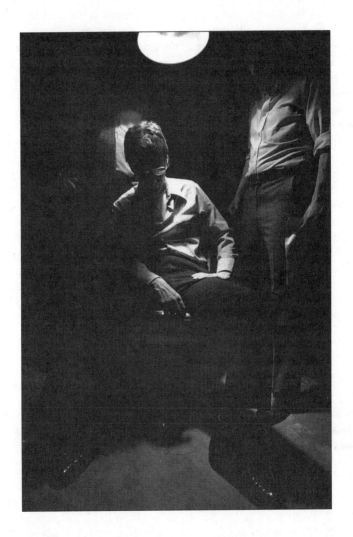

CHAPTER OUTLINE

Introduction
What Constitutes a Criminal
  Act or Omission?
The Nature of Criminal Intent
Parties to a Crime
Conclusion

Cases
Morissette v. United States
State v. Ferguson
State v. Starks

INTRODUCTION

As we explained in Chapter 1, the essential elements of a crime are a physical act, often referred to as the *actus reus* (wrongful act) and the intent or state of mind, frequently called the *mens rea* (guilty mind). To establish that a defendant is guilty of a crime, the prosecution must prove the defendant committed some legally proscribed act or failed to act when the law required certain action. It is also essential to prove that such act or failure to act occurred with a simultaneous criminal intent. It would be contrary to our common-law heritage to punish someone who accidentally or unwittingly committed an act without any intent to commit a crime. Likewise, a person cannot be punished for a mere intention, however wrongful that intention may be. Certain regulatory and public welfare offenses are classified as strict liability crimes and are exceptions to the common-law concept of requiring proof of a defendant's criminal intent. They came into prominence during the Industrial Revolution and today they form a significant part of the substantive criminal law.

In addition to the basic requirement of establishing a physical act and intent, in some instances the prosecution must establish that certain circumstances existed at the time the act was committed. For example, in the trial of a homicide offense, the prosecution must prove a causal relationship between the defendant's act and the victim's death. Also, in some sexual battery offenses the prosecution must establish that the defendant's acts occurred without the victim's consent.

The terms commonly used in modern criminal law (such as felony, misdemeanor, principal, and accessory) are derived from the common law. An understanding of their history leads to a better understanding of their function in contemporary American criminal law and procedure in federal and state court systems.

WHAT CONSTITUTES A CRIMINAL ACT OR OMISSION?

To fulfill the requirements of the criminal law, the actor must willfully commit a proscribed physical act or intentionally fail to act where the law requires a person to act. Courts have generally held that some outward manifestation of voluntary conduct must occur to constitute the required physical act. Consider two hypothetical examples:

- A enters B's house or strikes B. A has quite obviously committed an "act."
- A hands B a glass of liquid to be given to C. Unknown to B, A added poison to the glass of liquid before handing it to B. B gives the liquid to C, who drinks it and dies. Here A has acted through B, an innocent agent; thus A has committed the "act."

Even a person's failure to act can satisfy the requirements of a physical act in the criminal law. Remember that to be guilty of a crime for failure to act, there must have been a legal duty to act in the first place. Such a duty can arise in one of three ways: (1) by relationship of the actor to the victim, for example, a parent-child or husband-wife; (2) by a statutory duty; or (3) by contract between the actor and the victim. Consider these examples:

- A, an expert swimmer, is lying on the beach when he sees a young girl, unrelated to him, struggling to stay afloat and crying for help. A disregards her cries and she drowns. Is A criminally liable? The answer is no, for although we may agree that A had a strong moral obligation to attempt to save the child, there was no legal obligation that he do so. If, on the other hand, A was the child's parent or guardian, or a lifeguard on duty, then A's omission to act would most likely qualify as a criminal act.
- B receives an annual income of $50,000 from operation of her business. She fails to file a federal income tax return as required by the laws of the United States. Is B's omission a criminal act? Clearly it is, for she has violated a statutory obligation, the breach of which is punishable by law.
- C, a surgeon, undertakes to perform an operation on a patient for a fee. Before completing the operation, C decides to cease his efforts. As a result of such inattention, the patient dies. Would C's failure to complete what he undertook professionally qualify as an act within the meaning of the criminal law? Yes, because C had a contractual relationship with his patient.

Finally, we must realize that the requisite criminal act or omission must be voluntarily accomplished by the actor. The rationale for the requirement of a voluntary act is simple: Only those persons whose acts result from free choice should be criminally punished. Most acts are voluntary. For example, when you raise your hand it is considered a voluntary act, but when your hand moves as a result of a muscle spasm, it is not a voluntary act. Likewise, movements

---

CASE IN POINT

THE *ACTUS REUS* REQUIREMENT

Law officers found two whiskey stills and all the paraphernalia for making liquor on the defendant's land. Seeing no activity, they drove away. As they did, they met a car driven by the defendant heading toward the property. The car contained a quantity of sugar and other indicators of the illegal activity the officers suspected. The defendant committed no act of making liquor in the presence of the officers, but on the basis of what they observed, they arrested the defendant and he was convicted of making liquor unlawfully.

On appeal, the South Carolina Supreme Court reversed the conviction, observing, "the evidence overwhelmingly tends to show an intention to manufacture liquor. . . But intent alone, not coupled with some overt act . . . is not cognizable by the court. [T]he act must always amount to more than mere preparation, and move directly toward the commission of the crime." Citing respectable textbook authority, the court explained that the law does not concern itself with mere guilty intention, unconnected with any overt act.

State v. Quick, 19 S.E.2d 101 (S.C. 1942)

committed by a person who is unconscious, or acts by someone having an epileptic fit or sleepwalking are not regarded as voluntary acts. On the other hand, a driver who takes sleeping pills before beginning to operate an automobile and then falls asleep at the wheel would generally be held criminally responsible for a traffic accident, because the driver voluntarily committed the act of taking the pills.

Possession as a Criminal Act

In certain crimes possession alone is the wrongful act. For example, in the offense of carrying a concealed weapon, possession of the weapon concealed from ordinary observation is the wrongful act. Likewise, possession of contraband such as illegal drugs or untaxed liquors constitutes the wrongful act element of certain offenses.

There are two classes of possession: actual and constructive. Actual possession exists when a person has something under his or her direct physical control. Examples of actual possession are when an item is on your person or within your reach or located in a place where you alone have access. Constructive possession, on the other hand, is a more difficult concept because it is based on a legal fiction. A person who has the power and intention to control something either directly or through another person is said to be in constructive possession. The exact meaning of these terms is usually determined by the context of the situation. The difficulty is exacerbated when two or more persons are in joint possession of the premises or vehicle where an object is found. Consider the following examples:

- A and B rent and jointly share an apartment. A police search yields contraband drugs found on the coffee table in the living room used by both A and B. Can both be charged with possession of the contraband? They probably can: Possession by both A and B can be inferred, since the drugs are in plain view and located in a place to which both have access.
- Under the same circumstances of a shared apartment, drugs are found in a privately owned, closed container in a dresser drawer where only A keeps clothing and valuables. Since B has no access to this area, the law does not infer that B has constructive possession of the contents in the drawer. Of course, there may be circumstances under which the prosecution could prove that B actually had rights to the drugs, knowledge of their whereabouts, and access to them. Then the prosecution could establish that B was in constructive possession of the contraband.

Status as a Criminal Act

"Status" refers to a person's state of being, and ordinarily the state cannot criminalize a person's status. This principle was highlighted by the U.S. Supreme Court in *Robinson v. California*, 370 U.S. 660, 666–667, 82 S.Ct. 1417, 1420; 8 L.Ed.2d 758, 762–763, (1962), where the Court, in declaring unconstitutional a California statute that made it an offense for a person "to be addicted to the use of narcotics," states that we deal with a statute which makes the "status" of narcotic addiction a criminal offense, for which the offender may be prosecuted "at any time before he reforms.". . . We hold that a state law which imprisons a person thus afflicted as a criminal, even though he has never touched any narcotic drug within the State or been guilty of any irregular behavior there, inflicts a cruel and unusual punishment in violation of the Fourteenth Amendment.

The issue of when a criminal statute proscribes status, as opposed to conduct, can be very close. This is illustrated by the Supreme Court's decision in *Powell v. Texas*, 392 U.S. 514, 88 S.Ct. 2145, 20 L.Ed.2d 1254 (1968). Powell was a chronic alcoholic who was convicted of being drunk in public. Four justices held that defendant Powell was punished for being in a public place on a particular occasion while intoxicated, and not for his status as a chronic alcoholic. A fifth justice concurred in affirming Powell's conviction. As you study Chapter 11 concerning offenses against public order and safety, consider whether a statute that makes it a crime to be a vagrant offends the principle that a person's status cannot be criminalized.

THE NATURE OF CRIMINAL INTENT

The common law developed the doctrine that there should be no crime without a *mens rea* or "guilty mind." This element is customarily referred to as the criminal intent and, as noted, to constitute a crime there must be a concurrence of the *actus reus* or "act requirement" with a person's criminal intent. See, for example, *People v. Leckner*, 500 N.E.2d 721 (Ill. App. 1986). "Strict liability" offenses discussed in a later topic are an exception to this principle.

Criminal intent must be distinguished from motive. To obtain a conviction, a prosecutor must establish the defendant's criminal intent, but not necessarily the defendant's motive for committing a crime. A person's motive often equates with an impulse, an incentive, or a reason for certain behavior, and proof of one's motive may assist in establishing criminal intent. To illustrate, if the prosecution relies on circumstantial evidence to establish the defendant's guilt in a homicide case, the fact that the defendant had vowed "to get even" with the victim may be a relevant factor in the proof. Yet the failure to establish a defendant's motive is not material to proof of guilt, because the law prohibits criminal acts, not bad motives. Moreover, good motives do not exonerate you from a crime. Thus, a person who steals food simply to give it to a poor hungry family is probably well-motivated in doing so. Nevertheless, such a person would be guilty of a crime because of his or her act and intent.

The basic reason the law requires proof of a criminal intent as well as an act or omission is to distinguish those acts or omissions that occur accidentally from those committed by a person with a "guilty mind." As the court observed in *In re Hayes*, 442 P.2d 366, 369 (Cal. 1968), "an essential element of every orthodox crime is a wrongful or blameworthy mental state of some kind."

General and Specific Intent

Traditionally, courts distinguish the intent requirement of various crimes by describing them as requiring either "general" or "specific" intent. General intent is the intent presumed from the act the defendant commits. It refers to an actor's physical conduct in the sense that the actor intends the consequences of his or her voluntary actions.

For example, a person who fires a pistol at another is presumed to have intended either to kill or at least to injure the victim. Where a crime requires only proof of a general intent, the fact finder (i.e., the judge or jury) may infer the defendant's intent from the mere act itself. Thus, the prosecution does not have to prove that the defendant had any specific intent when the act was committed. An Indiana appellate court recently explained the concept of general intent quite well: "General intent exists when from the circumstances the prohibited result may reasonably be expected to follow from the offender's voluntary act, irrespective of a subjective desire to have accomplished such result." *Myers v. State*, 422 N.E.2d 745, 750 (Ind. App. 1981).

Criminal statutes that prohibit particular voluntary acts are generally classified as "general intent" statutes. See *State v. Poss*, 298 N.W.2d 80 (S.D. 1980). Statutory words such as *willfully* or *intentionally* generally indicate that the offender must only have intended to do the act and not to accomplish any particular result. To illustrate: A statute that makes it arson for a person to willfully and unlawfully damage by fire any dwelling defines a general intent crime. See *Linehan v. State*, 476 So.2d 1262 (Fla. 1985).

A specific-intent crime, on the other hand, is one in which the actor intends a particular result. Thus, a crime that requires a specific intent prohibits an act done with an intent beyond that which ordinarily accompanies an act. Again, in the context of the crime of arson, if the statute read that it was an offense for any person "willfully and with the intent to injure or defraud the insurance company to set fire to any building," then the prosecution would be required to prove that the defendant had the specific intent to injure or defraud the insurance company when the proscribed act was perpetrated.

Assume State X charged a defendant with burglary of a dwelling under a statute defining the offense as "the unauthorized entry of a dwelling by a person with the intent to commit theft therein." Three basic elements must be established to convict the defendant. First, the state must prove the defendant made an unauthorized entry. Second, it must prove that the entry was into a dwelling house. Finally, it must establish that the defendant made such unauthorized entry with the intent to commit a theft therein. Because the statute defines a specific-intent crime, the state must prove that the defendant intended certain definite consequences to follow an entry into the dwelling, that is, to commit a theft. Intent, of course, is a state of mind. Nevertheless, it can be (and almost always is) inferred from the defendant's actions and surrounding circumstances. Therefore, if some of the dwelling owner's property had been moved and other items left in disarray, the inference would be that the defendant who made an unauthorized entry intended to commit theft from the dwelling. And this would be true whether the defendant did in fact commit a theft within the dwelling.

The Model Penal Code Approach to Intent

The Model Penal Code (MPC) was drafted in 1962 by the American Law Institute, an organization composed of prominent lawyers, judges, and academics. The MPC is not law, but it represents a modern criminal code greatly influencing the reform of criminal statutes in the majority of states. The MPC rejects the common-law terms for intent and instead proposes four states of mind: purposeful; knowing; reckless; and negligent. It defines a purposeful act as one taken with an intent to cause a particular result, while a knowing act is one taken when the result is practically certain to occur, although causing that result is not the purpose for doing the act. The MPC defines a reckless act as one taken in disregard of a substantial risk and a negligent act as one taken by a person who fails to perceive the substantial risk of harm that may result from it. M.P.C. § 2.02.

The MPC classification of culpability is analytical, and each category is clearly defined, whereas over the years the common-law classifications of specific and general intent have become subject to considerable variations in court decisions in various jurisdictions. Nevertheless, in reading cases, you will find that most courts cling to the common-law classifications of specific and general intent. Two reasons come to mind: First, the law is traditional and based on precedent; and second, most appellate court judges probably completed their legal education before the MPC classification became well known. In any event, you should be familiar with both the common-law and MPC classifications.

The Doctrine of Transferred Intent

When a person intends to commit one criminal act but accomplishes another, the law implies that the necessary criminal intent for the second wrongful act is present. For example, if A aims a gun at B intending to kill B but misses and kills C instead, A's intent to kill B is transferred to C, the victim. This is the doctrine of transferred intent, in which the defendant's original intent is transferred from one against whom it was directed to the one who suffered the consequences. The doctrine does not require one fact to be presumed based upon finding of another fact. Rather, under this concept it becomes immaterial whether the accused intended to injure a person who is actually harmed. If the accused acted with the required intent toward someone, that intent suffices as the required element of intent for the crime charged. *State v. Locklear,* 415 S.E.2d 726 (N.C. 1992).

The concept of the doctrine of transferred intent is designed to hold a person who is committing a dangerous illegal act responsible for the consequences to the innocent victim. The doctrine is most frequently applied in homicide cases, even though some courts have had difficulty justifying its application where no actual intent to kill a third party is evidenced. Yet, application of the doctrine seems to achieve just results and, perhaps more importantly from the viewpoint of the prosecution, it obviates the need to establish that it was predictable A's actions directed against B would result in injury to C, an innocent victim. Of course, the actor must have had a criminal intent in the first place. Thus, if a parent lawfully administering punishment to a child accidentally strikes an innocent bystander, there is no criminal intent to transfer.

The Importance of Determining the Intent Required

It is essential to determine whether a particular offense is a general-intent or a specific-intent crime. First, the intent requirement determines the proof required of the prosecution. Second, in certain crimes the intent required determines whether particular defenses are available to the defendant.

The "Strict Liability" Offenses

While common-law crimes consist of a criminal act or omission known as the *actus reus* and the mental element known as the *mens rea,* legislative bodies have the power to dispense with the necessity for the mental element and authorize punishment of particular acts without regard to the intent of the actor. At this point, acquaintance with two terms becomes important. *Mala in se* offenses are "wrongs in themselves," while *mala prohibita* refers to "offenses deemed wrong by statute." In the common-law felonies of murder, rape, robbery, larceny, etc., the proscribed conduct is considered *mala in se,* and the intent is deemed inherent in the offense. This is true even if the statute now proscribing such criminal conduct fails to specify intent as an element of the offense. On the other hand, many criminal statutes proscribe conduct not deemed criminal at common law, and these offenses are generally classified as *mala prohibita.* Statutes of this type generally proscribe commission or omission of acts through neglect and do not require proof of criminal intent.

These *mala prohibita* offenses are commonly referred to as strict liability offenses. For the most part, they include "regulatory" or "public welfare" types of offenses often tailored to address unique problems created by the Industrial Revolution and present-day technology. Some of the earliest examples of strict liability are seen in cases involving sale of liquor and adulterated milk. See, for example, *Barnes v. State,* 19 Conn. 398 (1849); *Commonwealth v. Boynton,* 84 Mass. (2 Allen) 160 (1861). Examples of strict liability offenses today include traffic regulations, food and drug laws, and laws prohibiting the sale of liquor and cigarettes to minors. Today, strict liability offenses constitute a substantial part of the criminal law.

In *Morissette v. United States,* 342 U.S. 246, 255–256, 72 S.Ct. 240, 246, 96 L.Ed. 288, 296–297 (1952), the Supreme Court commented on strict liability offenses and observed:

> These [public welfare offenses] do not fit neatly into any of such accepted classifications of common-law offenses. . . . While such offenses do not threaten the security of the state ... they may be regarded as offenses against its authority, for their occurrence impairs the efficiency of controls deemed essential to the social order as presently constituted. In this respect, whatever the intent of the violator, the injury is the same, and the consequences are injurious or not according to fortuity. Hence, legislation applicable to such offenses, as a matter of policy, does not specify intent as a necessary element. The accused, if he does not will the violation, usually is in a position to prevent it with no more care than society might reasonably expect and no more exertion than it might reasonably exact from one who assumed his responsibilities. Also, penalties commonly are relatively small, and conviction does no grave damage to an offender's reputation. Under such considerations, courts have turned to construing statutes and regulations which make no mention of intent as dispensing with it and holding that the guilty act alone makes out the crime.

The definition of *mala prohibita* as referring to acts not essentially involving moral wrong can be deceptive. For example, having consensual sexual relations with a minor is generally considered a strict liability offense, and the offender can be held criminally responsible even if the minor claims to be and has the appearance of an adult. Of course, in this instance the offender's conduct would clearly be termed a moral wrong as well as a criminal offense.

In the chapters that follow, note that as penalties for statutory offenses become heavier, courts are reluctant to dispense with proof of intent. This is true in environmental crimes (Chapter 10) and in some serious motor vehicle violations. For example, many state courts have addressed the issue of whether proof of a criminal intent is necessary to convict of the statutory crime of driving with a revoked or suspended license. In *Jeffcoat v. State*, 639 P.2d 308 (Alaska App. 1982), the Alaska Court of Appeals held that even though the statute is silent, the element of *mens rea* must be read into it by implication. Several other state courts agree. On the other hand, in *State v. Antonsen*, 525 A.2d 1048 (Me.1987), the Supreme Court of Maine held that such a statute does not require proof of a culpable mental state, thereby aligning that state with the courts in several other states.

PARTIES TO A CRIME

Historically, the common law classified parties to crimes as either principals or accessories. Principals were persons whose conduct involved direct participation in a crime; accessories were accomplices or those who gave aid and comfort to principals.

Common law had three categories of crimes: treason, felonies, and misdemeanors. The highest-ranked crime under the English common law was treason. Treason consisted of killing the monarch or the monarch's high ministers or giving aid and comfort to the enemies of the Crown. Under the common law, all parties involved in a crime of treason were considered principals.

Given the history of the English monarchy, the American colonists were understandably conscious of the potential for abuse in enforcing the common law for treason. Thus, the framers of the Constitution provided that "Treason against the United States, shall consist only in levying war against them, or in adhering to their Enemies, giving them Aid and Comfort." U.S. Const. Art. 3, Sec. 3. Moreover, to emphasize the need to protect citizens from the abusive power of government, the framers also provided that "No Person shall be convicted of Treason unless on the Testimony of two Witnesses to the same overt Act, or on Confession in open Court." U.S. Const. Art. 3, Sec. 3.

The common law classified crimes other than treason as felonies and misdemeanors. Felonies were very serious crimes: At times, a person found guilty of a felony could be deprived of all worldly possessions and suffer either death or lengthy imprisonment. Because of the serious nature of felonious conduct, and because all persons involved might not be equally guilty, the common law developed a number of technical distinctions among the various participants. To comprehend present criminal law regarding participants in a crime, a basic knowledge of the common-law scheme is essential.

At common law, a person directly involved in committing a felony was classified as a principal; a person whose conduct did not involve direct participation was classified as an accessory. Principals were further classified by the degree of their participation. A person who directly or through the acts of an innocent agent actually committed the crime was a principal in the first degree. A principal in the second degree was a person not directly involved but actually

---

CASE IN POINT

THE *MENS REA* REQUIREMENT

The defendant was convicted under a statute that made it an offense to fondle or caress the body of a child under sixteen years "with the intent to gratify the sexual desires or appetites of the offending person or . . . to frighten or excite such child." On appeal, the Indiana Supreme Court noted that the strongest evidence in favor of the prosecution was that both the defendant's daughters admitted that during playfulness the father touched and came in contact with one of his daughter's breasts. There was, however, no evidence that this was done with the intent to gratify the sexual desires of the defendant or to frighten the child.

In reversing the defendant's conviction the court observed: "A crime has two components—an evil intent coupled with an overt act. The act alone does not constitute the crime unless it is done with a specific intent declared unlawful by the statute in this state. . . There must also be proved beyond a reasonable doubt, the specific intent at the time of touching to gratify sexual desires or to frighten the child as stated in the statute."

Markiton v. State, 139 N.E.2d 440 (Ind. 1957).

---

or constructively present at the commission of the crime who aided and abetted the perpetrator. The concept of actual presence is self-explanatory; however, the concept of constructive presence requires further explanation. To be constructively present, you must be sufficiently close to render assistance to the perpetrator. For example, if a man led a woman's escort away from her so that another man could sexually attack the woman, the man who led the escort away would probably be constructively present at the crime and would be classified as a principal in the second degree because he was aiding and abetting a crime. To aid and abet another in the commission of a crime means to assent to an act or to lend countenance or approval, either by active participation in it or by encouraging it in some other manner. *State v. Myers,* 158 N.W.2d 717 (Iowa 1968).

An accessory at common law was classified as either an accessory before or after the fact. An accessory before the fact procured or counseled another to commit a felony, but was not actually or constructively present at the commission of the offense. An accessory after the fact knowingly assisted or gave aid or comfort to a person who had committed a felony.

Because misdemeanors were far less serious than felonies, the common law found no necessity to distinguish between participants. As in the case of treason, all participants in misdemeanor offenses were regarded as principals.

Accessories to felonies were not regarded as being as culpable as the principals, so they were punished less severely at common law. Moreover, the common law gave accessories some significant technical advantages. A party had to be charged as a principal or as an accessory, and a principal had to be tried first. If the principal was found not guilty, the accessory could not be tried for the offense.

The Modern American Approach

Federal law stipulates that "Whoever commits an offense against the United States or aids, abets, counsels, commands, induces, or procures its commission, is punishable as a principal." 18 U.S.C.A. § 2(a). The federal statute reflects the law of most of the states insofar as it abolishes the distinction between principals and accessories before the fact.

The trend in American criminal law has been to abolish both the substantive and procedural distinctions between principals and accessories before the fact. As early as 1872, California enacted a statute defining principals as "all persons concerned in the commission of a crime, whether it be felony or misdemeanor, and whether they directly commit the act constituting the offense, or aid and abet in its commission, or, not being present, have advised and encouraged its commission." West's Ann. Cal. Penal Code § 31. As explained by the Supreme Court of Appeals of West Virginia in *State v. Fortner,* 387 S.E.2d 812, 822 (W.Va. 1989):

> Being an accessory before the fact or a principal in the second degree is not, of itself, a separate crime, but is a basis for finding liability for the underlying crime.... In essence, evidence of such complicity simply establishes an alternative theory of criminal liability, i.e., another way of committing the underlying substantive offense.

Even though the common-law distinction between principals and accessories before the fact has been largely abolished, the concept of accessory after the fact as a separate offense has been retained by many jurisdictions. Modern statutes view an accessory after the fact as less culpable than someone who plans, assists, or commits a crime. Thus, statutes generally define accessory after the fact as a separate offense and provide for a less severe punishment.

CASE IN POINT

AIDING AND ABETTING

Both Walter Godinez and Julio Montes were indicted for murder, attempted armed robbery, and armed violence. Montes' case was tried separately before a judge. The evidence revealed that Eduardo Soto was shot to death on April 28, 1986, in Chicago, Illinois. Montes confessed that Walter Godinez attempted to rob Soto and shot him while the defendant Montes acted as a lookout. Montes was convicted.

On appeal, Montes argued several points, including his contention that the evidence failed to establish his guilt on the basis of accountability. The court rejected his contention, stating that "the defendant said that he knew that Godinez intended to rob Soto two days before the shooting and again on the night of the shooting. On both occasions he agreed to act as lookout; and he knew that Godinez was armed with a revolver. Acting as a lookout is an act aiding and abetting the commission of the offense."

People v. Montes, 549 N.E.2d 700, 707 (Ill. App. 1989).

Under the law of most states, a lawful conviction as an accessory after the fact requires proof that the defendant knew that a felony had been committed by the person aided or assisted. The gist of being an accessory after the fact lies essentially in obstructing justice, and a person is guilty when he or she knows that an offense has been committed and receives, relieves, comforts, or assists the offender in order to hinder his or her apprehension, trial, or punishment. *United States v. Barlow,* 470 F.2d 1245 (D.C. Cir. 1972). Federal law, however, does not distinguish whether the person assisted has committed a felony or a misdemeanor. 18 U.S.C.A. § 3.

Because of a wife's duty at common law to obey her husband, a woman who gave aid and comfort to her husband was exempt from the law governing accessories after the fact. While this exemption no longer prevails, some state statutes exempt spouses and other classes of relatives from penalty for being accessories after the fact. For example, Florida law prevents the prosecution as an accessory after the fact of any person standing in the relation of husband or wife, parent or grandparent, child or grandchild, brother or sister, either by blood or marriage. West's Fla. Stat. Ann. § 777.03.

CONCLUSION

The concepts discussed in this chapter are basic to an understanding of the criminal law in the United States. At this stage, such fundamental concepts as the *actus reus* and the *mens rea* seem abstract; however, they will become more concrete as we relate them to the various offenses discussed in later chapters.

Common-law crimes were considered *mala in se* or wrongs in themselves and required proof of a general or specific intent. In contrast, many modern statutory offenses are classified as *mala prohibita,* simply because a legislative body has classified them as such wrongs.

The elements of crimes will be of continuing relevance throughout the text. In contrast, the background concerning the designation of parties to crimes is largely of historical importance. The trend in modern criminal law is to treat as principals all parties to crimes, whether perpetrators or accomplices. This approach may be debatable but society has found it necessary, and this principle is firmly ingrained in modern criminal law.

QUESTIONS FOR THOUGHT AND DISCUSSION

1. Distinguish between the concepts of motive and intent in the criminal law. Can you cite an instance where a person would be guilty of a crime despite his or her good motives?

2. Does the proliferation of strict liability crimes offend the basic principles of criminal liability outlined in Chapter 1?

3. Should the criminal law punish a person whose mere carelessness, as opposed to willfulness, causes harm to another?

4. Is there a justification for the criminal law not punishing a person for failing to act when there is a clear moral duty to act?

5. Has the moral integrity of the criminal law been jeopardized by the increasing number of offenses for which a person can be convicted without proof of any criminal intent?

6. What justifies the criminal law making mere possession of contraband articles illegal? Would this rationale extend to criminalizing the mere possession of such innocent items as a screwdriver, pliers, or ice pick that could be used to commit burglary?

7. Why is the common-law doctrine distinguishing between principals and accessories before the fact of diminished importance in contemporary criminal law?

8. Is it fair to assess the same degree of fault and impose the same punishment on an accomplice as on a perpetrator?

9. Is there a valid reason to exempt close family relatives from punishment as accessories after the fact to felonious conduct?

10. I. N. Mate, a prisoner in a state institution, was visited by his long-time friend, Sol Toolmaker. Mate had previously told Toolmaker how much he wanted to escape from the prison. So on this occasion, Toolmaker brought Mate two small saws. Mate hid the saws in a place where he thought they would not be found by the prison guards, but the guards promptly discovered and confiscated the saws. The warden turned this evidence over to prison's legal counsel with a request that charges be prepared against Mate for attempting to escape from prison. Assuming Mate intended to escape from prison, did his conduct constitute a criminal act?

11. A.H., a juvenile, was adjudged delinquent on the basis that he became a principal by having aided and abetted O.M., another juvenile, in committing a robbery. The victim, Ms. Turista, was seated on a bench waiting for the bus when the two young males (A.H. and O.M.) approached. O.M. began to struggle with Ms. Turista and grabbed her purse. A.H. stood by, doing nothing during the incident. The two juveniles then ran away together. At the adjudicatory hearing, the detaining officer testified that A.H. agreed to discuss the matter with officers because "he said he didn't do anything wrong." On appeal, A.H. contends that his adjudication of delinquency based on his being an aider and abettor was in error because there was no evidence that he intended to participate or that he assisted in any way in committing the robbery. Do you think A.H.'s conduct made him a principal in the robbery? If you were an appellate judge, on the basis of this scenario, would you vote to overturn A.H.'s adjudication of delinquency?

CASES

MORISSETTE V. UNITED STATES

Supreme Court of the United States, 1952.
342 U.S. 246, 72 S.Ct. 240, 96 L.Ed. 288.

[In this case the U.S. Supreme Court rules that where the intent of the accused is an ingredient of the offense charged, its existence may not be presumed but must be proved by the evidence.]

Mr. Justice JACKSON delivered the opinion of the Court.

. . . On a large tract of uninhabited and untilled land in a wooded and sparsely populated area of Michigan, the government established a practice bombing range over which the Air Force dropped simulated bombs at ground targets. These bombs consisted of a metal cylinder about 40 inches long and eight inches across, filled with sand and enough black powder to cause a smoke puff by which the strike could be located. At various places the range signs read "Danger—Keep Out—Bombing Range." Nevertheless, the range was known as good deer country and was extensively hunted.

Spent bomb casings were cleared from the targets and thrown into piles "so that they will be out of the way." They were not stacked or piled in any order but were dumped in heaps, some of which had been accumulating for four years or upwards, were exposed to the weather and rusting away.

Morissette, in December of 1948, went hunting in this area but did not get a deer. He thought to meet expenses of the trip by salvaging some of these casings. He loaded three tons of them on his truck and took them to a nearby farm, where they were flattened by driving a tractor over them. After expending this labor and trucking them to market in Flint, he realized $84.

Morissette, by occupation, is a fruit stand operator in summer and a trucker and scrap iron collector in winter. An honorably discharged veteran of World War II, he enjoys a good name among his neighbors and has no blemish on his record more disreputable than a conviction for reckless driving.

The loading, crushing and transporting of these casings were all in broad daylight, in full view of passers-by, without the slightest effort at conceal-

ment. When an investigation was started, Morissette voluntarily, promptly and candidly told the whole story to the authorities, saying that he had no intention of stealing but thought the property was abandoned, unwanted and considered of no value to the government. He was indicted, however, on the charge that he "did unlawfully, wilfully and knowingly steal and convert" property of the United States of the value of $84, in violation of 18 U.S.C. § 641. . . . Morissette was convicted and sentenced to imprisonment for two months or to pay a fine of $200. The Court of Appeals affirmed, one judge dissenting.

On his trial, Morissette, as he had at all times told investigating officers, testified that from appearances he believed the casings were cast-off and abandoned, that he did not intend to steal the property, and took it with no wrongful or criminal intent. The trial court, however, was unimpressed, and . . . refused to submit or to allow counsel to argue to the jury whether Morissette acted with innocent intention. It charged:

"And I instruct you that if you believe the testimony of the government in this case, he intended to take it. . . . He had no right to take this property. [A]nd it is no defense to claim that it was abandoned, because it was on private property. . . . And I instruct you to this effect: That if this young man took this property (and he says he did), without any permission (he says he did), that was on the property of the United States Government (he says it was), that it was of the value of one cent or more (and evidently it was), that he is guilty of the offense charged here. If you believe the government, he is guilty. . . . The question on intent is whether or not he intended to take the property. He says he did. Therefore, if you believe either side, he is guilty."

Petitioner's counsel contended, "But the taking must have been with a felonious intent." The court ruled, however, "That is presumed by his own act."

The Court of Appeals suggested that "greater restraint in expression should have been exercised," but affirmed the conviction because "[a]s we have interpreted the statute, appellant was guilty of its violation beyond a shadow of doubt, as evidenced even by his own admissions." Its construction of the statute is that it creates several separate and distinct offenses, one being knowing conversion of government property. The court ruled that this particular offense requires no element of criminal intent. This conclusion was thought to be required by the failure of Congress to express such a requisite.

... Stealing, larceny, and its variants and equivalents, were among the earliest offenses known to the law that existed before legislation; they are invasions of rights of property which stir a sense of insecurity in the whole community and arouse public demand for retribution, the penalty is high and, when a sufficient amount is involved, the infamy is that of a felony, which, says Maitland, is " . . . as bad a word as you can give to man or thing." State courts of last resort, on whom fall the heaviest burden of interpreting criminal law in this country, have consistently retained the requirement of intent in larceny-type offenses. If any state has deviated, the exception has neither been called to our attention nor disclosed by our research.

Congress, therefore, omitted any express prescription of criminal intent from the enactment before us in the light of an unbroken course of judicial decision in all constituent states of the Union holding intent inherent in this class of offense, even when not expressed in a statute. Congressional silence as to mental elements in an act merely adopting into federal statutory law a concept of crime already so well defined in common law and statutory interpretation by the states [does not mean that intent is not required as an element of the crime]. Nor do exhaustive studies of state-court cases disclose any well-considered decisions applying the doctrine of crime without any intent to such enacted common-law offenses.

The government asks us by a feat of construction radically to change the weights and balances in the scales of justice. The purpose and obvious effect of doing away with the requirement of a guilty intent is to ease the prosecution's path to conviction, to strip the defendant of such benefit as he derived at common law from innocence of evil purpose, and to circumscribe the freedom heretofore allowed juries. Such a manifest impairment of the immunities of the individual should not be extended to common-law crimes on judicial initiative. . . .

We hold that mere omission from § 641 of any mention of intent will not be construed as eliminating that element from the crimes denounced. . . .

Congress has been alert to what often is a decisive function of some mental element in crime. It has seen fit to prescribe that an evil state of mind, described variously in one or more such terms as "intentional," "willful," "knowing," "fraudulent" or "malicious," will make criminal an otherwise indifferent act, or increase the degree of the offense of its punishment. Also, it has at times required a specific intent of purpose which will require some specialized knowledge or design for some evil beyond the common-law intent to do injury. . . . In view of the care that has been bestowed upon the subject, it is significant that we have not found, nor has our attention been directed to, any instance in which Congress has expressly eliminated the mental element from a crime taken over from the common law.

The section with which we are here concerned was enacted in 1948, as a consolidation of four former sections of Title 18. . . . We find no other purpose in the 1948 re-enactment than to collect from scattered sources crimes so kindred as to belong in one category. Not one of these had been interpreted to be a crime without intention and no purpose to differentiate between them in the matter of intent is disclosed. No inference that some were and some were not crimes of intention can be drawn from any difference in classification or punishment. . . . [E]ach is, at its least, a misdemeanor, and if the amount involved is $100 or more each is a felony. If one crime without intent has been smuggled into a section whose dominant offenses do require intent, it was put in ill-fitting and compromising company. The government apparently did not believe that conversion stood so alone when it drew this one-count indictment to charge that Morissette "did unlawfully, willfully and knowingly steal and convert to his own use."

Congress, by the language of this section, has been at pains to incriminate only "knowing" conversions. But, at common law, there are unwitting acts which constitute conversions. In the civil tort, except for recovery of exemplary damages, the defendant's knowledge, intent, motive, mistake, and good faith are generally irrelevant. If one takes property which turns out to belong to another, his innocent intent will not shield him from making restitution or indemnity, for his well-meaning may not be allowed to deprive another of his own.

Had the statute applied to conversions without qualification, it would have made crimes of all unwitting, inadvertent and unintended conversions. Knowledge, of course, is not identical with intent and may not have been the most apt words of limitation. But knowing conversion requires more than knowledge that defendant was taking the property into his possession. He must have had knowledge of the facts, though not necessarily the law, that made the taking a conversion. In the case before us, whether the mental element that Congress required be spoken of as knowledge or as intent, would not seem to alter its bearing on guilt. For it is not apparent how Morissette could have knowingly or intentionally converted property that he did not know could be converted, as would be the case if it was in fact abandoned or if he truly believed it to be abandoned and unwanted property.

It is said, and at first blush the claim has plausibility, that, if we construe the statute to require a mental element as part of criminal conversion, it becomes a meaningless duplication of the offense of stealing, and that conversion can be given meaning only by interpreting it to disregard intention. But here again a broader view of the evolution of these crimes throws a different light on the legislation. . . .

The purpose which we here attribute to Congress parallels that of codifiers of common law in England and in the states and demonstrates that the serious problem in drafting such a statute is to avoid gaps and loopholes between offenses. It is significant that the English and state codifiers have tried to cover the same type of conduct that we are suggesting as the purpose of Congress here, without, however, department from the common-law tradition that these are crimes of intendment.

We find no grounds for inferring any affirmative instruction from Congress to eliminate intent from any offense with which this defendant was charged.

As we read the record, this case was tried on the theory that even if criminal intent were essential its presence (i) should be decided by the court (ii) as a presumption of law, apparently conclusive, (iii) predicated upon the isolated act of taking rather than upon all of the circumstances. In each of these respects we believe the trial court was in error. . . .

Reversed.

STATE V. FERGUSON
Supreme Court of South Carolina, 1990.
302 S.C. 269, 395 S.E.2d 182.

[In this case the South Carolina Supreme Court considers whether the distribution of cocaine is a strict liability offense and, if not, whether the trial court's jury instruction to the contrary constitutes a reversible error.]

TOAL, Justice:
On November 3, 1988, deputy sheriff Douglas Pernell of Dillon County phoned an individual known as the "Fatman" (an unidentified co-conspirator with the appellant) concerning the receipt of bribes in exchange for illegal police protection. The "Fatman" told Pernell that Ferguson (a.k.a. "Dino") would deliver the bribe monies. Pernell then spoke with Ferguson, who informed Pernell that he needed more time to come up with the requisite amount of money and that Pernell should come back later. Implicitly, Ferguson then changed his mind and offered to bring Pernell $250.00 in cash and a quantity of cocaine instead of the usual $500.00 cash amount.

Ferguson met with Pernell approximately ten minutes later at a post office, bringing him a shoe polish box containing $250.00 and a bag of cocaine. Two . . . officers witnessed the transaction. Upon giving Pernell the box, Ferguson said, "It's all there.". . .

Ferguson argues that the trial court committed two charging errors warranting reversal. He complains that, as to both the bribery offense and the distribution of cocaine offense, the trial court failed to properly charge the jury on the required criminal intent, or mental state of the defendant. Ferguson bases his arguments on the basic premise in criminal law that ordinarily, in order to establish criminal liability, a criminal intent of some form is required. This premise is rooted in the maxim *actus non facit reum nisi mens sit rea.* For example, the mental state required to be proven by the State for a particular crime might be purpose (intent), knowledge, recklessness, or criminal negligence. Of course, the legislature, if it so chooses, may make an act or omission a crime regardless of fault. . . . These crimes are referred to commonly as "strict liability" offenses. Whether an offense is a strict liability offense, and if not, what kind of criminal intent is required to satisfactorily show a commission of that offense, are questions of legislative intent. . . .

As for the bribery charge, we simply disagree with Ferguson's contention. The trial court charged the jury, in pertinent part:

> Thirdly, the defendant is charged with violating a statute which reads 'whoever corruptly gives to any officer, including police officers, any gift, or gratuity with the intent to influence such officer's act or judgment on any matter which is pending before him shall be guilty of an offense.' Corruptly, when used in that statute, simply means dishonestly. It means an effort to procure dishonest activities of the person to whom the gratuity or gift is offered to get him to fail to perform his duties in whatever office he is holding and whatever duty he is required to exercise. . . .

We hold that the jury was adequately instructed as to the mental state required for the bribery offense.

We agree that the trial court committed error, however, in ruling, in effect, that there is no mental state required for the offense of distribution of cocaine. We held in *State v. American Agricultural Chem. Co.*, 118 S.C. 333, 337, 110 S.E. 800 (1922) that:

> In offenses at common law, and under statutes which do not disclose a contrary legislative purpose, to constitute a crime, the act must be accompanied by a criminal intent, or by such negligence or indifference to duty or to consequences as is regarded by the law as equivalent to a criminal intent.

A reading of the entire statutory scheme convinces us that the legislature intended to place a mental state requirement in the offense contained in S.C. Code Ann. § 44–53–370(a) (1985).

Having held that the legislature did not intend this serious offense to be a strict liability crime, we now turn to what kind of mental state is required to be proven in order to show a violation of § 44–53–370(a). We are guided in this decision by our ruling in *State v. Freeland*, 106 S.C. 220, 91 S.E. 3 (1916). In *Freeland*, the alleged offense was illicit possession of cocaine. No mental state requirement was mentioned in the statute. The trial court instructed the jury that, if the defendant did not know that she had cocaine in her possession, she should be acquitted. This Court held, regarding an attack on this charge:

> [t]he instruction was really too favorable to defendant, in that it did not eliminate the possibility of willful or negligent want of knowledge. If she was culpably ignorant of the fact, her ignorance would not excuse her. . . .

The instant case is therefore controlled, in our view, by *Freeland*. Hence, the State must show that a given defendant was at least criminally negligent when he/she manufactured, distributed, or dispensed a controlled substance in order to prove a violation of § 44–53–370(a).

Nevertheless, although we find error, we hold that such was harmless in this case, in light of the overwhelming evidence that Ferguson was well aware that he was distributing cocaine. *State v. Mitchell*, 286 S.C. 572, 336 S.E.2d 150 (1985). For instance, Ferguson specifically told Pernell, "I've got $250.00 and the white stuff" when setting up their rendezvous at the post office. . . . Ten minutes later, Ferguson then delivered a shoe polish box to Pernell at the post office containing $250 cash and a quantity of cocaine with $250 written on it. Under these circumstances, it strains credulity past the breaking point to adhere to Ferguson's theory that he was just an honest delivery man with no knowledge or reason to know he was distributing cocaine.

Accordingly, the judgment of the lower court is AFFIRMED.

GREGORY, C.J. and HARWELL, CHANDLER, and FINNEY, J.J., concur.

State v. Starks
Supreme Court of Kansas, 1991.
249 Kan. 516, 820 P.2d 1243.

[In this case the Kansas Supreme Court considers whether there is sufficient evidence to support charges of possession of marijuana with intent to sell within 1,000 feet of an elementary or secondary school and conspiracy to sell marijuana.]

SIX, Judge.

This criminal case arises from a "reverse sting" drug operation. The case concerns the determination of probable cause during a preliminary hearing.

The State Appeals the preliminary hearing order of dismissal. . . .

The trial court, at the conclusion of the preliminary hearing, dismissed the charges against defendant Terry L. Starks and Ricky L. Casey for possession of marijuana with intent to sell within 1,000 feet of an elementary or secondary school (K.S.A. 1990 Supp. 65–4127b[e]) and against Starks for conspiracy to sell marijuana (K.S.A. 21–3302 and K.S.A. 1990 Supp. 65–4127b).

We disagree with the disposition of the intent to sell charge. We agree that the dismissal of the conspiracy charge against Starks was proper.

Facts

Starks, Casey, and Jon A. Heter were charged with possession of marijuana with intent to sell within 1,000 feet of an elementary or secondary school (count I) and conspiracy to sell marijuana (count II). Their arrests were the result of a "reverse sting" operation conducted by the Reno County Drug Enforcement Unit and the Kansas Bureau of Investigation (KBI). A reverse sting occurs when law enforcement officials sell drugs to individuals who seek to purchase a large quantity for resale. Once the drugs are purchased from the undercover agent, the purchasers are arrested for drug possession, often with intent to sell.

The reverse sting, in the present case, began when a confidential informant told a sheriff's detective that Heter wanted to purchase a large quantity of marijuana. The KBI agreed to supply the marijuana. Special Agent Atteberry was sent to Hutchinson to act as an undercover agent.

Atteberry and a confidential informant arranged a meeting with Heter at a Hutchinson motel. According to Atteberry, Heter and a drug connection originally planned to purchase five kilos of marijuana for the price of a quarter pound of cocaine and $1,500. Heter told Atteberry that he did not know if the connection could obtain the cocaine. Heter agreed with Atteberry to buy five kilos of marijuana for $7,500 ($1,500 per kilo). Heter then left to show the connection a sample of the marijuana, stating he would return in 15 minutes with the money to complete the transaction. He did not return. Atteberry later learned that Heter believed that there were undercover police around the motel.

Atteberry met with Heter at Heter's residence the following day. They agreed to complete the transaction that evening at the residence, which was located 96 feet from Liberty Middle School.

Atteberry's Testimony

The State relied heavily on Atteberry's testimony. Atteberry testified that Heter stated the connection did not have a driver's license; consequently, another individual would drive the connection to Heter's residence. According to Heter, a vehicle would pull all the way to the back of a neighbor's driveway on the east, and the connection would bring $9,000 to exchange for the marijuana. The connection did not want to meet Atteberry.

The complex arrangements among Heter, the connection, and the driver were related by Atteberry. Heter planned on paying Atteberry $7,500 for five kilos of marijuana; however, the connection was told the price was $9,000. Heter wanted Atteberry to return $1,500 to him after the connection left. Heter and his connection intended to deceive the driver regarding the quantity of marijuana purchased. Atteberry testified:

"Earlier, one of our conversations that Mr. Heter asked how much five kilos of marijuana weighed, and I replied eleven pounds. He believed it to be ten pounds. His deal with his connection was for ten pounds of marijuana for $9,000, so his intentions, what he stated was that he was going to cut one of the bricks in half and keep the one pound and him and his connection was going to meet later and split that one pound, but the connection did not want the driver of the vehicle to know that they were splitting the one pound up."

Atteberry also related Heter's statements regarding the driver's involvement:

"He stated that, that as I stated earlier, that Heter replied that he was charging his buddy a little bit more and that they're in it together on this, the driver and the connection. He says, I'm trying to make a little off it, 'cause he stated he was selling, Heter was selling the marijuana to his connection for $9,000, and at that time the connection was selling some of this marijuana to the driver of the car."

Atteberry testified that: (1) Heter stated his connection was leaving for Texas the following day to sell the marijuana; (2) Heter intended to sell some of the marijuana to make money to fix up his car; and (3) marijuana was currently selling for $60 per quarter ounce or $200 per ounce in the Hutchinson area.

The Reverse Sting

While Atteberry, Heter, and the informant waited for the connection to arrive, Atteberry brought in five kilos of marijuana. Heter picked out one of the kilos, cut it in half, and placed one half kilo under his chair. The remaining four and one-half kilos were placed next to the chair.

A brown Maverick, announced by its noisy muffler, pulled into the neighbor's driveway on the east side of Heter's residence. Heter went to the rear of the residence and returned to the living room carrying a large wad of money clutched with both fists. Heter and Atteberry began counting the money. The $9,000 cash pile had a strong odor of marijuana.

Law enforcement officers, listening to the conversation over the informant's body transmitter, moved in when they heard the money being counted. Heter was in the living room. A KBI agent testified that he observed a subject, identified as Casey, attempt to exit the back door of the residence. The agent illuminated Casey with a flashlight and ordered him into the house. Casey ran to the basement. Later, Casey informed the police officers that he was told

to go to the basement and that he did not know what was going on. Casey had no driver's license.

Starks was slumped down low behind the wheel in the Maverick when apprehended.

After being Mirandized, Heter agreed to talk to the police. According to police, Heter stated that he had spoken with Casey about the $9,000 and about buying the five kilos of marijuana. Casey came to Heter's residence, brought $9,000, and the transaction took place. Heter claimed he was just the "middle man."

Starks, after being Mirandized, also agreed to talk to the police. According to police, Starks stated he (1) had no knowledge of any drug transaction; (2) was Casey's friend; (3) had been called by Casey and asked for a ride; (4) picked up Casey and took him to Heter's residence at Casey's direction; (5) did not know Heter; and (6) did not notice Casey carry anything into the residence.

Heter, Casey, and Starks did not testify at the preliminary hearing. Neither Casey's nor Starks' names were mentioned by Heter before the arrest.

The State admitted that neither Casey nor Starks actually possessed the marijuana. The State argued that Casey and Starks aided and abetted Heter's possession of marijuana with intent to sell and was criminally responsible under K.S.A. 1990 Supp. 21–3205.

The trial court bound Heter over for trial on both count I (possession with intent to sell) and count II (conspiracy to sell). Casey was bound over for trial on count II. The trial court dismissed count I against Casey and Counts I and II against Starks. The State then dismissed count II against Casey.

Probable Cause

If, from the evidence presented at the preliminary hearing, it appears that a crime has been committed and there is probable cause to believe the defendant committed the crime, the magistrate shall bind the defendant over for trial. . . .

Count I—Possession of Marijuana With Intent to Sell

The State argues that the trial court erred when it found insufficient evidence to establish probable cause that Starks and Casey aided and abetted Heter in possessing the marijuana with intent to sell.

Starks argues that he did not know Heter and did not have any idea of the transaction among Heter, Casey, and Atteberry. . . .

The evidence presented at the preliminary hearing was sufficient to establish probable cause that Starks and Casey aided and abetted Heter in possessing the marijuana with intent to sell within 1,000 feet of an elementary or secondary school.

The distance of 96 feet from Heter's residence to Liberty Middle School is not contested.

K.S.A. 1990 Supp. 21–3205(1) provides that a person is criminally responsible for a crime committed by another if the person charged intentionally aids, abets, advises, hires, counsels, or procures the other to commit the crime. Mere association with the person who commits the crime or mere presence in the vicinity is insufficient to establish guilt as an aider and abettor. However, when a person knowingly associates with an unlawful venture and participates in a way which indicates the person is willfully furthering the success of the venture, there is sufficient evidence of guilt to go to the jury. . . .

Starks stated to the police officer that he: (1) simply gave Casey a ride to Heter's residence; (2) did not know Casey and Heter were conducting a drug transaction; and (3) did not see Casey carry anything into the residence.

Casey stated to police that he was told to go down in the basement and that he did not know what was going on.

In contrast, Atteberry testified that Heter told him the driver and the connection were "in it together." According to Heter, Casey planned to sell some of the marijuana to Starks. Casey and Heter did not want Starks to know that they were purchasing 11 pounds rather than 10 pounds. Atteberry also testified that Casey brought the money into Heter's house in a large wad that smelled of marijuana. In addition, Atteberry testified Heter (1) told Atteberry he was selling the marijuana to Casey for $1,500 more than Heter paid; and (2) planned to sell his portion of the split one pound in order to have money to fix his car.

The KBI agent testified that Starks was slumped down in the car seat and that Casey attempted to flee the residence.

There is a conflict between the statements of Starks and Casey, and the testimony of Atteberry. Looking at all the evidence, viewed in the light most favorable to the prosecution, the evidence is sufficient to cause a person of ordinary prudence and caution to entertain a reasonable belief that Starks and Casey willfully furthered the success of Heter's possession of the marijuana with intent to sell. The jury could find that Casey knowingly provided the money necessary for Heter to possess the marijuana with intent to sell and that Starks knowingly provided the transportation.

Count II—Conspiracy to Sell Marijuana

K.S.A. 21–3302(1) provides: "A conspiracy is an agreement with another person to commit a crime or to assist to commit a crime. No person may be convicted of conspiracy unless an overt act in furtherance of such conspiracy is alleged and proved to have been committed by him or by a co-conspirator."

The State contends that the trial court improperly weighed the evidence, finding it "too thin" to bind Starks over on count II. The State argues that Atteberry's testimony provides sufficient evidence that Starks was involved in the agreement between Casey and Heter to sell marijuana. Starks counters that the evidence was insufficient to support a finding of probable cause that Starks was involved in the agreement.

A review of the evidence indicates that Starks did not enter into an agreement to sell marijuana.

Atteberry testified that Heter told him Starks and Casey were in it together. Starks planned on purchasing some of the marijuana from Casey. There was no testimony concerning either the quantity Starks intended to purchase or what Starks intended to do with the marijuana after the purchase. There was no testimony that Starks knew what Casey intended to do with the marijuana. The only evidence of an agreement involving Starks relates to his intention to purchase an unknown quantity from Casey. The evidence is not sufficient to establish probable cause of an agreement to sell marijuana.

We affirm the trial court's dismissal of the count II charge against Starks for conspiracy to sell marijuana (K.S.A. 21–3302 and K.S.A. 1990 Supp. 65–4127b).

We reverse the trial court's dismissal of the count I charges against Starks and Casey for possession of marijuana with intent to sell within 1,000 feet of an elementary or secondary school (K.S.A. 1990 Supp. 65–4127b[e]).

Affirmed in part and reversed in part. . . .

INCHOATE OFFENSES

CHAPTER OUTLINE

Cases

INTRODUCTION

The word *inchoate* means underdeveloped or unripened. Thus, an inchoate offense is one involving activities or steps preparatory to the completion of a crime. There are three such offenses: attempt, solicitation, and conspiracy. Although preparatory to commission of other offenses, they are separate and distinct crimes. During the 1800s each was recognized as a misdemeanor at common law; however, this was too late to become a part of the common law under the reception statutes adopted by most new American states. Most American jurisdictions now define these offenses by statute, frequently classifying them as felonies.

Why Criminalize Preparatory Conduct?

Inchoate offenses were originally created by the courts in response to the need to prevent commission of serious crimes. The development of the law in this area has been primarily through the courts. Frequently the courts have found difficulty in determining when mere noncriminal activity has reached the stage of criminal conduct. Yet, by recognizing an actor's design toward commission of an offense, the law permits police to apprehend dangerous persons who have not yet accomplished their criminal objectives. Consequently, by making certain preparatory conduct illegal, the law gives law enforcement officers an opportunity to terminate such conduct at an early stage.

ATTEMPT

Of these inchoate crimes, attempt is probably the most frequently charged. "Attempt," of course, means an effort to accomplish a particular purpose. A criminal attempt consists of an intent to commit a specific offense and an act that constitutes a substantial step toward the commission of that offense. *People v. Tuczynski,* 378 N.E.2d 1200 (Ill. App. 1978). Thus, as explained in an early New York opinion, whether an attempt to commit a crime has been made depends on both the actor's mind and conduct. *People v. Moran,* 25 N.E. 412 (N.Y. 1890).

No particular federal statute proscribes the offense of attempt. In general, federal courts have recognized the requisite elements of attempt as (1) an intent to engage in criminal conduct, and (2) the performance of an act that constitutes a substantial step toward the completion of the substantive offense. See *United States v. Manley,* 632 F.2d 978 (2d Cir. 1980), *cert. denied,* 449 U.S. 1112, 101 S. Ct. 922, 66 L.Ed.2d 841 (1981).

State penal codes often specifically provide for attempts to commit the most serious crimes such as murder. The remaining offenses are then covered by a general attempt statute. A typical statute that covers all attempts provides "Whoever attempts to commit an offense prohibited by law and in such attempt does any act toward the commission of such an offense, but fails in the perpetration or is intercepted or prevented in the execution of the same, commits the offense of criminal attempt." West's Fla. Stat. Ann. § 777.04(1). The requirement of an act contemplates an act that constitutes a substantial step toward commission of an offense. While the quoted statute makes no distinction between felony or misdemeanor offenses, statutes in some states limit the crime of attempt to attempts to commit felonies or certain specified crimes.

The Requisite Criminal Intent

To find a defendant guilty of the crime of attempt, most courts require the prosecution to prove that the defendant had a specific intent to commit the intended offense, frequently referred to as the "target crime." Most courts reason that one cannot attempt to do something without first forming the specific intent to accomplish that particular act. See, for example, *Thacker v. Commonwealth*, 114 S.E. 504 (Va. 1922). The rationale for this majority view seems to be that an attempt involves the concept of intended consequences by the actor. One state supreme court disagrees on whether specific intent is always required. In 1983, the Florida Supreme Court found it illogical to require proof of a specific intent for the successful prosecution of an attempt to commit a crime when the target crime only required proof of a general intent. *Gentry v. State*, 437 So.2d 1097 (Fla. 1983). Under this view the prosecution must prove a specific intent to convict a defendant of an attempted premeditated murder, a specific-intent crime. On the other hand, it would only have to prove the defendant had a general intent to commit an attempted battery, a general-intent crime. As pointed out in Chapter 4, a general intent is usually inferable from the actor's conduct and the surrounding circumstances. In any event, it seems that courts should require proof of at least the type of intent that must be established in prosecuting the target crime.

What Constitutes a Substantial Step toward Commission of a Substantive Offense?

As noted earlier, the "act" element in the crime of attempt requires an act that constitutes a substantial step toward the commission of an offense. The Model Penal Code distinguishes preparatory conduct from an attempt by allowing conviction for the crime of attempt, where the actor engages in "an act or omission constituting a substantial step in a course of conduct planned to culminate in the commission of the crime." M.P.C. § 5.01. Federal courts follow this test. *United States v. Mandujano*, 499 F.2d 370, 376 (5th Cir. 1974), cert. denied, 419 U.S. 1114, 95 S.Ct. 792, 42 L.Ed.2d 812 (1975).

Many state statutes also include the term *substantial* in defining the act requirement. Where they do not, courts usually imply that the act must constitute a substantial step toward commission of a substantive offense. In either instance, it becomes necessary to distinguish between mere preparatory acts of planning or arranging means to commit a crime and those acts that constitute a direct movement toward commission of an offense. The question is: How close must that act be to accomplishment of the intended crime? Appellate courts have taken various approaches to determining what constitutes such a substantial step. This issue frequently turns on the specific factual situation involved. An early, and demanding, test held that an actor must have engaged in the "last proximate act necessary to accomplish the intended crime," but most courts have now rejected that test. See, for example, *People v. Parrish*, 197 P.2d 804, 806 (Cal. App. 1948). Some courts apply a more realistic test that holds that the actor's conduct must be "within dangerous proximity to success." New York courts have summed it up in a practical manner, opining simply that an accused's conduct must be "very near" to the completion of the intended crime. *People v. Mahboubian*, 544 N.Y.S. 2d 769 (N.Y. 1989).

Attempts in Relation to Substantive Crimes

Generally, when a criminal act completes a substantive crime, the attempt usually merges into the target offense. The actor is then guilty of the substantive crime, rather than merely an attempt to commit it. Thus, a person who is successful in an attempt to commit murder is guilty of murder.

The Model Penal Code proposes that an accused who "purposely engages in conduct which would constitute the crime if the attendant circumstances were as he believed them to be" is guilty of an attempt. M.P.C. § 5.01(1)(a). While many state statutes track this Model Penal Code language, it may be debatable whether the law should pursue a conviction for an attempt to commit a crime that is legally impossible to commit.

Moreover, there can be no attempt to commit certain crimes because some substantive offenses by definition embrace an attempt. To illustrate, take the statutory crime of uttering a forged instrument. This offense is usually defined as

---

CASE IN POINT

A JUDICIAL CONSTRUCTION OF "SUBSTANTIAL STEP"

Defendant, Mark Molasky, was charged with attempted murder of Ellis and Ellen Denos. At Molasky's trial the evidence revealed that while he was imprisoned for various sexual offenses, the Denoses sought to adopt Molasky's son. Molasky opposed their action, and while the Denoses were in the process of adoption, he had a conversation with Ricky Holt, a fellow inmate, concerning payment, time, and manner in which Holt was to kill Ellis and Ellen Denos. Molasky was convicted of second-degree murder and appealed, arguing the evidence was insufficient to establish that he was guilty. The Missouri Supreme Court pointed out that the Missouri statute on general attempts was patterned after Section 5.01 of the Model Penal Code, and before a defendant could be guilty of an attempt it must be established that the defendant's actions constituted a "substantial step" toward the target crime. The court found that the evidence disclosed a solicitation by Molasky, but it was not accompanied by other corroborating action to indicate a seriousness of purpose. There was no payment of money or furnishing Holt with a picture or other identification of the potential victims. The court observed that "given factually different circumstances, a solicitation could support an attempt charge. Here, however, this burden has not been met."

State v. Molasky, 765 S.W.2d 597, 602 (Mo. 1989).

CASE IN POINT

THE LAW OF ATTEMPT

Defendant was found guilty of attempting to escape from prison. He appealed, contending that the state failed to prove beyond a reasonable doubt that he had committed an overt act as required by law. He characterized his actions as preparatory steps indicative only of an intention to attempt an escape. The Supreme Judicial Court of Maine rejected his contention and affirmed his conviction. "[T]here was undisputed evidence that a dummy was found in defendant's cell; that defendant was in an unauthorized area attempting to conceal his presence; and that a rope ladder was found in a paper bag close to where he was concealed. [Defendant] had gone far beyond the preparation stage."

State v. Charbonneau, 374 A.2d 321, 322 (Me. 1977).

---

including an attempt to pass a forged instrument to someone to obtain something of value. Therefore, one who makes such an attempt would be guilty of uttering a forged instrument, not merely an attempt to do so. In effect, the attempt is subsumed by the very definition of the substantive crime. Needless to say, it would be redundant to charge someone with attempting to attempt to commit a given crime.

Defenses to the Crime of Attempt

Generally, a defendant cannot be found guilty of attempt if it is legally impossible to commit the offense attempted. For example, a man who assaults a mannequin dressed as a woman would not be guilty of attempted rape. Yet, this example must be distinguished from similar situations. A person who fires a pistol at another's shadow, believing it to be an intended victim, could be prosecuted for attempted homicide. Likewise, a woman who picks another's pocket intending to steal money may be found guilty of attempted theft, even if the victim's pocket is empty. In these instances courts have said that although it was factually impossible to commit the crime, it was legally possible to do so. Admittedly, the distinction is a close one.

New York law currently provides that it is no defense to a prosecution for attempt that the crime charged to have been attempted was factually or legally impossible to commit, if it could have been committed had the circumstances been what the defendant believed them to be. N.Y. McKinney's Penal Law § 110.10. The trend is toward finding an attempt to commit a crime in instances where the actor's intent has been frustrated merely because of some factor unknown at the time. Thus, if the accused believed a victim was alive when shooting at the victim, an attempt to kill a dead person constitutes an attempt under New York law. *People v. Dlugash,* 363 N.E.2d 1155 (N.Y. 1977).

Some jurisdictions have laws providing that it is a defense to the crime of attempt if the defendant abandons an attempt to commit an offense or otherwise prevents its consummation. See, for example, Vernon's Tex. Ann. Penal Code §

15.04(a). If recognized as a defense, abandonment must be wholly voluntary. It cannot be the result of any outside cause like the appearance of the police on the scene. See, for example, *People v. Walker*, 191 P.2d 10 (Cal. 1948) (en banc), *aff'd on rehearing*, 201 P.2d 6 (1948), *cert. denied*, 336 U.S. 940, 69 S. Ct. 744, 93 L.Ed. 1098 (1949).

SOLICITATION

By the 1800s, the common law specified that a person who counseled, incited, or solicited another to commit either a felony or a misdemeanor involving breach of the peace committed the offense of solicitation. A person was guilty of solicitation even if the crime counseled, incited, or solicited was not committed. *State v. Blechman*, 50 A.2d 152 (N.J. 1946).

The offense of solicitation is now defined by statute in most American jurisdictions. The statutory definition in Illinois is typical: "A person commits solicitation when, with intent that an offense be committed, other than first-degree murder, he commands, encourages, or requests another to commit the offense." Illinois S.H.A. 720 ILCS 5/8–1. The gist of the offense remains the solicitation, so the offender may be found guilty irrespective of whether the solicited crime is ever committed.

Some statutes stipulate that the crime solicited must either be a felony or fall within a certain class of offenses. See, for example, Vernon's Tex. Penal Code Ann. § 15.03(a). In contrast, the Model Penal Code takes the position that solicitation of any offense is a crime. M.P.C. § 5.02.

Commission of the crime of solicitation does not require direct solicitation of another; it may be perpetrated through an intermediary. In *State v. Cotton*, 790 P.2d 1050 (N.M. App. 1990), the court reversed a defendant's conviction of criminal solicitation because there was no evidence that the defendant ever communicated the solicitation to the person he intended to solicit to commit a crime. The court, however, recognized that solicitation could be perpetrated through an intermediary and offered the following example:

> If A solicits B in turn to solicit C to commit a felony, A would be liable even where he did not directly contact C because A's solicitation of B itself involves the commission of the offense. Where the intended solicitation is not in fact communicated to an intended intermediary or to the person sought to be solicited, the offense of solicitation is incomplete; although such evidence may support, in proper cases, a charge of attempted criminal solicitation. 790 P.2d at 1055.

In contrast, the Model Penal Code states that "It is immaterial . . . that the actor fails to communicate with the person he solicits to commit a crime if his conduct was designed to effect such communication." M.P.C. § 5.02(2).

The Requisite Criminal Intent

The language of statutes making solicitation a crime may not seem to require the prosecution to establish the defendant's specific intent. Most courts, however, hold that to commit solicitation the solicitor must have specifically intended to induce or entice the person solicited to commit the target offense. See, for example, *Kimbrough v. State,* 544 So.2d 177 (Ala. Crim. App. 1989). The prosecution should at least establish that the actor who solicits someone to commit a crime had the requisite intent for the crime solicited.

The Rationale for Making Solicitation a Crime

In explaining why its penal code makes solicitation an offense, a California appellate court offered two reasons: first, to protect individuals from being exposed to inducement to commit or join in the commission of crime; and second, to prevent solicitation from resulting in the commission of the crime solicited. *People v. Cook,* 199 Cal.Rptr. 269 (Cal. App. 1984).

Most students of the criminal law would concede that solicitation should be a criminal offense. But, you might ask, is it more serious than the inchoate crime of attempt? The Tennessee Supreme Court has suggested that it is not, stating: "There is not the same degree of heinousness in solicitation as in attempts, nor is solicitation as likely to result in a completed crime, there not being the same dangerous proximity to success as found in attempts." *Gervin v. State,* 371 S.W.2d 449, 451 (Tenn. 1963). In taking the contrary point of view, the Connecticut Supreme Court said:

> The solicitation to another to [commit] a crime is as a rule far more dangerous to society than the attempt to commit the same crime. For the solicitation has behind it an evil purpose, coupled with the pressure of a stronger intellect upon the weak and criminally inclined. *State v. Schleifer,* 121 A. 805, 809 (Conn. 1923).

Solicitation Distinguished from Other Inchoate Crimes

The offenses of solicitation and attempt are different crimes, analytically distinct in their elements. Although each is an inchoate offense, solicitation is complete when the request or enticement to complete the intended offense is made; and it is immaterial if the solicitee agrees, if the offense is carried out, or if no steps were taken toward consummation of the offense. Mere solicitation is generally not sufficient to constitute an attempt, because attempt requires proof of an overt act to commit the intended criminal act. This principle was succinctly explained by the Idaho Supreme Court when it said: "The solicitation of another, assuming neither the solicitor or solicitee proximately acts toward the crime's commission cannot be held for an attempt." *State v. Otto,* 629 P.2d 646, 650 (Idaho 1981).

Solicitation is distinguished from conspiracy because while solicitation requires an enticement, conspiracy requires an agreement. Sometimes a solicitation may result in a conspiracy, and some courts have looked upon the offense as "an offer to enter into a conspiracy." See, for example, *Commonwealth v. Carey,* 439 A.2d 151, 155 (Pa. Super. 1981).

Defenses to the Crime of Solicitation

Generally, the fact that the solicitor countermands the solicitation or the fact that it was impossible for the person solicited to commit the crime are not defenses to

---

C A S E I N P O I N T

The Law of Solicitation

Defendant Roger Gardner, an alleged contract killer, subcontracted the killing of Alvin Blum to a man named Tim McDonald for a fee of $10,000. Gardner met with McDonald and gave him some expense money, a gun, and ammunition. In talking with McDonald, Gardner said that he (Gardner) would first kill a man named Hollander, and if this did not create the desired result then McDonald would be directed to kill Blum. Gardner's attempts were foiled when he was arrested and charged with solicitation to murder. It turned out that McDonald was a police informant whose assistance led to Gardner's arrest. On appeal, Gardner argued that he did not commit the crime of solicitation because he did not actually direct McDonald to proceed with the murder of Blum or pay him all of the money he had promised. In affirming Gardner's conviction the Maryland Court of Appeals said:

> What Gardner fails to take into account is that the crime of solicitation was committed when he asked McDonald to commit the murder. Neither a final direction to proceed nor fulfillment of conditions precedent (paying of the money) was required. The gist of the offense is incitement. [W]e agree that the crime of solicitation was committed.

Gardner v. State, 408 A.2d 1317, 1322 (Md. 1979).

---

a charge of solicitation. However, in some states, it is a defense if the defendant can affirmatively establish that after soliciting another person to commit an offense, the defendant prevented commission of the crime under circumstances manifesting a complete and voluntary renunciation of his or her criminal purpose. The Model Penal Code provides that it is a defense to a charge of solicitation if there has been a timely, complete, and voluntary renunciation of the accused's criminal purpose. M.P.C. § 5.02 (3). Some states have adopted this position. See, for example, Ky. Rev. Stat. § 506.020.

Conspiracy

At common law, conspiracy consisted of an agreement by two or more persons to accomplish a criminal act or to use unlawful means to accomplish a noncriminal objective. The gist of the offense was the unlawful agreement between the parties, and no overt act was required. *State v. Carbone,* 91 A. 2d 571 (N.J. 1952).

Today the offense of conspiracy is generally defined by statute in all jurisdictions. Most state laws define the elements of the offense along the lines of the common law. Typically, the Florida law states: "Whoever agrees, conspires, combines, or confederates with another person or persons to commit any offense commits the offense of criminal conspiracy." West's Fla. Stat. Ann. § 777.04(3). On the other hand, federal law (with some exceptions) requires an overt act in a conspiracy to commit an offense or defraud the United States. 18 U.S.C.A. § 371.

A number of states also require proof of an overt act in order to convict someone for conspiracy. Texas law, for example, provides: "A person commits criminal conspiracy if, with intent that a felony be committed, (1) he agrees with one or more persons they or one or more of them engage in conduct that would constitute the offense, and (2) he or one or more of them performs an overt act in pursuance of the agreement." Vernon's Tex. Penal Code Ann. § 15.02(a). Note that the Texas statute also requires an intent that a felony be committed, whereas in most states it is only necessary to prove an intent to commit a criminal offense.

Because of the variations encountered in statutory language, in reviewing any statute defining conspiracy it is necessary to determine at the outset (1) the type of the offense or unlawful activity the statute proscribes, and (2) whether it requires proof of an overt act in furtherance of the parties' agreement.

Why the Offense of Conspiracy? The Perceived Danger of Group Action

Why is conspiracy considered an offense distinct from the substantive offense the conspirators agree to commit? Perhaps one of the most cogent responses to this question was articulated by the late U.S. Supreme Court Justice Felix Frankfurter. In *Callanan v. United States,* 364 U.S. 587, 593–594, 81 S.Ct. 321, 325, 5 L.Ed.2d 312, 317 (1961), the late justice observed:

> Concerted action both increases the likelihood that the criminal object will be successfully attained and decreases the probability that the individuals involved will depart from their path of criminality. Group association for criminal purposes often, if not normally, makes possible the attainment of ends more complex than those which one criminal could accomplish . . . . Combination in crime makes more likely the commission of crimes unrelated to the original purpose for which the group was formed. In sum, the danger which a conspiracy generates is not confined to the substantive offense which is the immediate aim of the enterprise.

The Required Act and Intent in Conspiracy

In general, the *actus reus* of the crime of conspiracy is the unlawful agreement. Where an overt act is required, such act need not be a substantial movement toward the target offense. For example, in California, where the law requires an overt act, the courts have said that an overt act tending to effect a conspiracy may merely be a part of preliminary arrangements for commission of the ultimate crime. *People v. Buono,* 12 Cal. Rptr. 604 (Cal. App. 1961). In fact, a single act such as a telephone conversation arranging a meeting has been held to be sufficient proof of an overt act. *United States v. Civella,* 648 F.2d 1167 (8th Cir. 1981), *cert. denied,* 454 U.S. 867, 102 S. Ct. 330, 70 L.Ed.2d 168 (1981).

Statutes frequently fail to encompass the intent requirement in the offense of conspiracy. This difficulty is compounded by failure of the courts to clearly define the intent required for a conviction. In general, the prosecution must prove that a defendant intended to further the unlawful object of the conspiracy, and such intent must exist in the minds of at least two of the parties to the alleged conspiracy. *People v. Cohn*, 193 N.E. 150 (Ill. 1934). Many courts refer to the crime as requiring a specific intent. See, for example, *People v. Marsh*, 376 P.2d 300 (Cal. 1962). As previously noted with respect to attempts, such intent may be inferable from the conduct of the parties and the surrounding circumstances. While many federal court decisions have not required proof of a specific intent, the U.S. Supreme Court has said that in federal prosecutions there must be proof of at least the criminal intent necessary for the requirements of the substantive offense. *United States v. Feola*, 420 U.S. 671, 95 S. Ct. 1255, 43 L.Ed.2d 541 (1975).

Some Common Misconceptions about the Crime of Conspiracy

Contrary to some popular views, the participants in a conspiracy need not even know or see one another as long as they otherwise participate in common deeds.

CASE IN POINT

CONSPIRACY TO DELIVER CONTROLLED SUBSTANCES

In a non-jury trial, Brian Smith was found guilty of conspiracy to deliver lysergic acid diethylamide (LSD). On appeal, he argued that the evidence was insufficient to support his conviction because there was no proof beyond a reasonable doubt (1) that he agreed to engage in delivery of LSD, and (2) that he intended that it be delivered. The appellate court rejected both contentions and affirmed Smith's conviction.

On February 16, 1988, Corporal Cook, working undercover, agreed to purchase fifty doses of LSD from Bruce Erickson at a park in the City of Snohomish, Washington. Erickson asked Smith for a ride to go there, ostensibly to meet David Hensler (who owed Smith $600, a sum Smith very much wanted to collect). When Smith and Erickson arrived in Smith's vehicle, the officer approached the car and asked Erickson if he had LSD. When Erickson produced a bag of LSD, the officer asked Smith if he had tried it. Smith replied "he was going to college . . . and couldn't afford to get messed up, but that his wife had taken some of it, and . . . 'it really [messed] her up.'" At that point Corporal Cook agreed to purchase the LSD, handed the money to Erickson, and arrested both Smith and Erickson.

In affirming Smith's conviction, the appellate court first pointed out that "a formal agreement is not necessary to the formation of a conspiracy." Then the court observed that although Smith's primary purpose in giving Erickson a ride to the park was to meet Hensler, his secondary purpose was to assist in delivering LSD. In finding the evidence sufficient to show that Smith intended to assist Erickson, the court opined, "there was evidence not only of knowledge of Erickson's unlawful purpose, but an agreement to assist with the plan by providing the necessary transportation . . . Here there were two overt acts: first, that Smith drove Erickson to Snohomish knowing, according to Corporal Cook, Erickson's purpose for the trip; and second, that Smith provided encouragement for the sale by assuring the officer of the potency of the drug . . . We hold that there is sufficient evidence to convince a rational trier of fact beyond a reasonable doubt that Smith agreed to transport Erickson to Snohomish for the common purpose of delivering LSD."

State v. Smith, 828 P.2d 654, 656, 657 (Wash. App. 1992).

The essence of the offense is the mutual agreement of the parties to the conspiracy, not the acts done to accomplish its object. Moreover, the agreement need not be explicit. In fact, it seldom is. In most instances, the agreement is implied from the acts of the parties and the circumstances surrounding their activities. Furthermore, all the conspirators do not have to join in the conspiracy at the same time.

Conspiracy Distinguished from Aiding and Abetting and Attempt

As noted in Chapter 4, aiding and abetting someone in the commission of a crime makes a person either a principal or an accessory before the fact. Conspiracy is a separate offense and must be distinguished from aiding and abetting. Conspiracy involves proof of an agreement between two or more persons, an element often present, but not essential, in proving that a defendant aided and abetted a crime. On the other hand, aiding and abetting requires some actual participation. *Shedd v. State*, 87 So.2d 898 (Miss. 1956), *cert. denied*, 352 U.S. 944, 77 S. Ct. 262, 1 L.Ed. 2d 237 (1956). Conspiracy differs from the crime of attempt in that it focuses on intent, whereas attempt places more emphasis on the defendant's actions.

Spousal Conspiracies

Because the common law regarded a husband and wife as one person for most purposes, a husband and wife could not be guilty of conspiring with one another. Since the trend of the law in recent years has been to recognize the separate identities of the spouses, there appears to be no valid reason to continue the common-law approach. See, for example, *People v. Pierce*, 395 P.2d 893 (Cal. 1964).

Conspiracy Does Not Merge into the Target Offense

Conspiracy is regarded as a separate and distinct crime; therefore, it usually does not merge into the target offense. As the New Jersey Supreme Court has pointed out, a conspiracy may be an evil in itself, independent of any other evil it seeks to accomplish. *State v. Lennon*, 70 A.2d 154 (N.J. 1949). A pragmatic consideration is that by not merging conspiracy into the target offense, the law can more effectively deter efforts of organized crime.

The Range of Conspiracies in Our Society

The range of conspiracies cuts across socioeconomic classes in society. Traditionally, state prosecutions for conspiracy have been directed at criminal offenses such as homicide, arson, perjury, kidnapping, and various offenses against property. In recent years an increasing number of both state and federal conspiracy prosecutions have been related to illicit drug trafficking. In addition to the large number of narcotics violations, federal prosecutions include a variety of conspiracies not found under state laws. Among these are customs violations, counterfeiting of currency, copyright violations, mail fraud, lotteries, and violations of antitrust laws and laws governing interstate commerce and other areas of federal regulation. Recently, a number of federal prosecutions have involved conspiracies to deprive persons of their civil rights or equal protection of the law.

Defenses to the Charge of Conspiracy

Where a statute requires proof of an overt act as an element of the crime, an alleged conspirator may defend by showing withdrawal from the conspiracy before commencement of such an act. Where an overt act is not required, a more difficult issue is presented. In some states, statutes specifically provide for the defense of withdrawal and renunciation. As an illustration, Missouri law specifies: "No one shall be convicted of conspiracy if, after conspiring to commit the offense, he prevented the accomplishment of the objectives of the conspiracy under circumstances manifesting a renunciation of his criminal purpose." Vernon's Mo. Ann. Stat. § 564.016(5)(1).

In the absence of statutory authority, courts have been reluctant to approve a person's withdrawal as a defense. One of the difficulties in approving withdrawal as a defense is that even though a conspirator withdraws, the criminal objective of the conspiracy may proceed. Therefore, it seems reasonable to require that a person who would rely on such defense not only renounce any criminal purpose but also take the necessary steps to thwart the objective of the conspiracy. To accomplish this result, the conspirator would probably have to notify law enforcement authorities of the pertinent details of the conspiracy. In any event, if an accused is allowed to offer such a defense, the defendant has the burden of establishing his or her withdrawal from the conspiracy.

Entrapment, a defense to be examined in Chapter 13, may under some circumstances be a defense to conspiracy. *Stripling v. State,* 349 So. 2d 187 (Fla. App. 1977), *cert. denied,* 359 So. 2d 1220 (Fla. 1978).

The *Pinkerton* Rule; Wharton's Rule

In *Pinkerton v. United States,* 328 U.S. 640, 66 S.Ct. 1180, 90 L.Ed 1489 (1946), Pinkerton was charged with conspiring with his brother for tax evasion, including some offenses allegedly committed by his brother during times that Pinkerton was incarcerated. The trial court instructed the jury that it could find Pinkerton guilty if it found he was a party to a conspiracy and that the offenses were in furtherance of the conspiracy. Pinkerton was convicted and upon review the U.S. Supreme Court upheld his conviction, stating that a member of a conspiracy is liable for all offenses committed in furtherance of the conspiracy. The Court did indicate that a different result may occur if the offenses were not reasonably foreseeable as a natural consequence of the unlawful agreement of the conspirators. This has come to be known as the "*Pinkerton* Rule." It is based on the theory that conspirators are agents of each other, and just as a principal is bound by the acts of his agents within the scope of the agency relationship, so is a conspirator bound by the acts of his co-conspirators. *United States v. Troop,* 890 F.2d 1393 (7th Cir. 1989). Obviously, the doctrine has broad implications, and not all courts have accepted it.

Another legal doctrine, Wharton's Rule, is named after Francis Wharton, a well-known commentator on criminal law. The Rule is an exception to the principle that a conspiracy and the target crime do not merge. Wharton's Rule holds that two people cannot conspire to commit a crime such as adultery, incest, or bigamy since these offenses require only two participants. The rationale is that, unlike the usual conspiracy, which is often like a wheel with many spokes, the offenses named do not endanger the public generally. Wharton's Rule has been applied in many state and federal courts, but it has its limitations. In holding the rule inapplicable to various federal gambling offenses under the Organized Crime Control Act of 1970, the Supreme Court pointed out that the rule itself is simply an aid to determination of legislative intent and must defer to a discernible legislative judgment. *Iannelli v. United States*, 420 U.S. 770, 786, 95 S.Ct. 1284, 1294, 43 L.Ed.2d 616, 628 (1975).

Some Unique Aspects of the Offense of Conspiracy

The courts regard conspiracy as a partnership in crime, and view each conspirator as an agent of the others. It follows that each will be held responsible for the acts of the others within the context of their common design. *Commonwealth v. Thomas*, 189 A.2d 255 (Pa. 1963), *cert. denied*, 375 U.S. 856, 84 S.Ct. 118, 11 L.Ed.2d 83 (1963). This principle permits an exception to the rule of evidence that ordinarily excludes hearsay statements from being used in a trial over the defendant's objection. Indeed, statements by a co-conspirator in furtherance of the conspiracy made during the pendency of the conspiracy may be admitted into evidence. Statements that have been found to be "in furtherance of" the conspiracy include statements to inform other conspirators of the activities or status of the conspiracy and those identifying other conspirators. Federal courts have upheld the use of statements as to the sources or purchaser of controlled substances. See, for example, *United States v. Patton*, 594 F.2d 444 (5th Cir. 1979). Before receiving this type of evidence, a court must receive independent evidence that a conspiracy has been committed. In some instances courts receive the hearsay evidence subject to it being tied into the offense by independent evidence of the conspiracy. Court procedures in this area are very technical evidentiary matters. A principal problem is for the court to determine the scope of the conspiracy and the inception of the conspirator's participation.

The Supreme Court of Hawaii properly characterized the judicial approach to conspiracy when it stated:

> In the eyes of the law conspirators are one man, they breathe one breath, they speak one voice, they wield one arm, and the law says that the acts, words, and declarations of each, while in the pursuit of the common design, are the words and declarations of all. *Territory v. Goto*, 27 Hawaii 65 (1923).

Courts have held that once formed, a conspiracy continues to exist until consummated, abandoned, or otherwise terminated by some affirmative act. *Cline v. State*, 319 S.W.2d 227 (Tenn. 1958).

These unique aspects are significant. They assist the prosecution in proof of cases that otherwise might be unprovable. Perhaps the law has established these exceptions in recognition of the difficulties of prosecuting persons involved in conspiracies, which are generally formed in secret.

C A S E   I N   P O I N T

FIRST AMENDMENT CONCERNS
IN A CONSPIRACY PROSECUTION

American involvement in the Vietnam conflict and the attendant military draft engendered considerable controversy in the 1960s. Dr. Benjamin Spock, the well-known "baby doctor," and several others were convicted of conspiracy to counsel registrants to resist the military draft. In reversing his conviction, the United States Court of Appeals for the First Circuit observed that while Spock was one of the drafters of a call to resist duties imposed by the Military Selective Service Act of 1967, "his speech was limited to a condemnation of the war and the draft, and lacked any words or content of counseling." Thus, the court concluded that Spock's actions lacked the clear character necessary to imply specific intent under the strict standards of the First Amendment.

United States v. Spock, 416 F.2d 165 (1st Cir. 1969).

Criticism of the Conspiracy Laws

There has been an increased tendency in recent years to prosecute defendants for conspiracies as well as target crimes. The offense of conspiracy is a potent weapon in the hands of the prosecutors, particularly in coping with the problem of organized crime. But since the intent requirement and the form of agreement required are somewhat imprecise, some commentators have criticized the offense and the activities of certain prosecutors, particularly where an overt act is not required. The most basic criticism is that prosecutors, judges, and juries are given too wide a latitude in finding a defendant guilty because a conspiracy is easier to prove than specific criminal acts. Additionally, some critics argue that conspiracy prosecutions chill or effectively abolish First Amendment rights of free expression.

CONCLUSION

Inchoate offenses often pose substantial problems for law enforcement agencies, courts, and legislative bodies. Police and courts often have great difficulty determining the stage at which an act tends toward commission of a crime so as to qualify as criminal attempt. There remains controversy whether it should be a criminal offense to solicit another person to commit a crime, irrespective of whether the solicited offense is a felony or a misdemeanor. Conspiracy too is problematic. Some statutes extend criminal liability beyond legislatively defined crimes to include injuries to the public health and morals, making the offense of conspiracy vulnerable to the criticism that the law is converting civil wrongs into criminal conduct.

Despite the problems associated with inchoate offenses, there remains strong support for criminalizing conduct directed toward future injuries to society. Criminalizing preparatory conduct permits the timely intervention of law enforcement agencies to restrain dangerous persons and prevent intended crimes.

QUESTIONS FOR THOUGHT AND DISCUSSION

1. What is the justification for criminalizing attempt, solicitation, and conspiracy? *inchoate offenses*

2. How does the criminal law distinguish between mere preparatory conduct and the overt act required for a criminal attempt? Can you think of a situation in which preparatory conduct would not constitute a criminal attempt?

3. Should it be a defense to a charge of attempt that the accused voluntarily abandoned the attempt?

4. Would impotency be a legitimate defense to a charge of attempted rape?

5. What is the rationale for making solicitation a crime even where a solicitor's requests are completely unheeded?

6. Which do you think poses a more serious threat to society: an attempt or a solicitation to commit murder? Why?

7. Should statutes defining conspiracy require proof of an overt act in furtherance of the conspirators' agreement? Why or why not?

8. Given the First Amendment protections of freedom of expression and association, can members of a revolutionary political organization be prosecuted for conspiring to overthrow the government of the United States?

9. Would a person who offers a bribe to someone believed to be a juror, but who is not a juror, be guilty under a statute making it an offense to offer bribes to jurors?

10. What is the evil the offense of conspiracy is designed to combat?

11. Leo Lothario was having an affair with Lucy Slarom, a woman separated from her husband, Joe. One night while Lothario and Lucy were playing tennis in her backyard, Joe appeared on the scene. Lothario demanded he leave, but Joe declined and sat in one of the yard chairs. Lothario went to the garage, picked up a rifle, pointed it at Joe, and from a distance of approximately seventy-five feet, fired a shot in the direction of Joe. The bullet missed Joe by about eighteen inches. Lothario explained to the police that he was simply trying to scare Lucy's estranged husband so he would not bother her. On the strength of these facts, do you think there is a basis to charge Lothario with attempted murder?

12. John and Jane were running a student loan "scam." They were convicted of soliciting several students to make false applications in exchange for a "cut" of the loan proceeds and also for aiding and abetting those same students in making false applications for loans. On appeal, they argue that the solicitation charges merged into their convictions for aiding and abetting the making of the false applications. The state responds that John and Jane were guilty of both crimes because the solicitation offenses were completed before John and Jane assisted the students in making the false applications. How should the appellate court rule on this appeal? Why?

CASES

BUCKLEW V. STATE

Supreme Court of Mississippi, 1968.
206 So.2d 200.

[This case deals with an attempt to commit a crime.]

ROGERS, Justice:

This is an appeal from a judgement of conviction of attempted embezzlement from the Circuit Court of Jones County, Mississippi, wherein the mayor of the City of Laurel was fined in the amount of $816.05. The testimony in this case shows that sometime in the summer of 1965 Henry Bucklew, the mayor of Laurel, Mississippi, called a representative of Kelly-Lowe Dodge, Inc., an automobile repair shop, advised them that he had a jeep which belonged to the Pest Control Department of the City of Laurel, and asked whether or not they could repair it. Kelly-Lowe Dodge, Inc., repaired the jeep and purchased tires and chains for it. The repair bill, including labor and parts, amounted to $816.05.

Kelly-Lowe submitted its bill by mail to the City of Laurel on November 25, 1965. When the clerk saw the bill he recognized that it was not an obligation of the city and took it to the mayor. The mayor advised the clerk that he would "take care of it." Some time later, John Jacobs, who was in charge of what is known as the Pest Control Department of the City of Laurel, was requested by the mayor to sign the bill which had been submitted by Kelly-Lowe. In the meantime, the city clerk had requested a copy of this bill from the repair shop "for the files" of the City of Laurel. Later, the mayor was indicted by the grand jury of Jones County for the crime of an attempt to commit embezzlement. The bill for repairs to the jeep was never finally submitted to the city for payment by the mayor or anyone else. The testimony shows that the city clerk had an understanding with the mayor and city commissioners that before bills could be paid by the city it was necessary for the heads of the various departments to approve the payment before they were submitted to the clerk for payment. Thereafter, the mayor or commissioner to whom the bill had been referred would indicate his approval of the bill by signing his name to the approval sheet attached to the bill.

The city clerk would then prepare a check in the payment of the amount indicated and return it to the mayor for his signature. Before the check could be cashed it required the signature of the clerk. In the absence of the mayor it was necessary for one of the commissioners to sign checks with the clerk before they could be paid.

The testimony showing the approval of Mr. Jacobs by affixing his signature on the bill is the only testimony showing the intention of the mayor after the bill had been turned over to him by the clerk, except that an auditor testified that the mayor told him that he approved the bill by mistake. The original bill was not offered in evidence.

The defendant, Henry Bucklew, was indicted under section 2122, Mississippi Code 1942 Annotated (1956).

When the State had concluded its testimony, the defendant made a motion to exclude the evidence offered on behalf of the State and requested the court to direct the jury to find the defendant not guilty, for the reason that the State had not shown that the defendant had committed an overt act toward the commission of the crime of embezzlement as charged in the indictment. The court overruled this motion and defendant rested his case, without introducing testimony in his behalf and without having testified in his own defense. The issue is, therefore, clearly defined: Did the State show that the defendant committed an overt act in an attempt to commit the crime of embezzlement?

Under the general law it has been pointed out that an attempt to commit a crime consists of three elements: (1) an intent to commit a particular crime; (2) a direct ineffectual act done toward its commission; and (3) the failure to consummate its commission. . . . Our statutory law requires proof of an overt act in order to sustain a conviction of an attempt to commit a crime.

The pertinent part of section 2017, Mississippi Code 1942 Annotated (1956), is as follows:

Every person who shall design and endeavor to commit an offense, and shall do any overt act

toward the commission thereof, but shall fail therein, or shall be prevented from committing the same, on conviction thereof, . . .

This Court is in accord with the general law as to the essential elements of the crime of "attempt to commit a crime." We have held that the law requires that the State establish criminal *intent* as an element to the crime of attempt "to commit a crime.". . .

We have also held that there must be an *overt act* done toward the commission of the crime in order to establish the crime of "attempt to commit a crime.". . .

We have no trouble with the third element, since the Legislature has provided for this element by enactment of section 2018, Mississippi Code 1942 Annotated (1956). This law prevents prosecution for the "attempt to commit an offense, when it shall appear that the crime intended or the offense attempted was perpetrated. . . ."

We have held that the mere intention to commit a crime is not punishable. . . . The intention must therefore be coupled with an overt act. But, what is meant by the requirement that the State prove "an overt act"? . . .

In *Williams v. State,* 209 Miss. 902, 48 So.2d 598 (1950), the defendant was convicted of attempting to commit larceny by the "pigeon dropping" game. The Court there said:

> The necessary elements of an attempt are the intent to commit, and the overt act toward its commission. . . . The rule is well recognized that "whenever the design of a person to commit crime is clearly shown, slight acts done in furtherance of this design will constitute an attempt.". . .

In that case, however, the testimony showed that the various acts of preparation had been concluded and that the defendant then went to the place to receive the money. This Court held that this was a sufficient overt act to establish an attempt.

In the case of *Stokes v. State,* 92 Miss. 415, 46 So. 627 (1908), this Court pointed out that where one attempted to procure another to kill a third party, and in furtherance of his design took a gun, loaded it and went with the party to a point where the killing was to occur, but was arrested, his act was sufficient to establish an attempt to commit a crime.

The records in the foregoing cases indicate that the defendants had reached a point in the proceedings to commit a crime beyond mere preparation, so that they had actually begun to commit the alleged crime. In *Williams* the defendant had done everything necessary to commit a crime except receive the money, and in *Stokes* the defendant had performed his part in the crime of murder and there was nothing left for him to do in furtherance of the crime.

In *State v. Lindsey,* 202 Miss. 896, 32 So.2d 876 (1947), this Court held that stalking, chasing and running after the prosecuting witness, in a lonesome and secluded place in the country was not a sufficient overt act on which to base a charge of attempt to "forcibly ravish her." In that case we said:

> The gravamen of the offense of an attempt to commit a crime is fixed by the statutory requirement that the defendant must do an overt act toward the commission thereof and be prevented from its consumation. . . .

It is contended by the State in the instant case that the appellant, defendant in the court below, accomplished the required overt act by having the department head of the Pest Control Department sign the bill submitted by Kelly-Lowe Dodge, Inc. An examination of the testimony in this case, however, shows that if all the State attempted to prove was true, the acts done by the defendant were mere acts in preparation to the submission of the bill to the clerk for payment. The testimony shows that it was necessary for the mayor to sign the bill before submitting it to the clerk for payment, and the proof shows that the mayor did not submit the bill to the clerk for payment. Moreover, there is nothing in the record to show that there was any extraneous cause that prevented the mayor from attempting to collect the amount due to the automobile company. Moreover, the record shows that the mayor told the auditor that the bill had been signed through a mistake. Therefore, if the mayor had intended to defraud the City, the record shows that he had abandoned his purpose before attempting to collect the funds from the city treasury. . . .

From the foregoing facts, and our study of the law in this case, we have come to the conclusion that the proof here shown does not sustain the charge of "an attempt to embezzle" funds from the City of Laurel by the appellant.

We pause to point out that the law, like religion, holds out a promise to those who would commit crime and sin that if they voluntarily resist temptation so as to recant and desist before attempting to carry into effect their evil purpose, they will not be held accountable for mere evil intent. On the other hand, facts such as we have in this case prove the rule that those in high places should not only avoid wrongdoing, but should avoid the appearance of evil, because, although the law will not punish for mere evil intent, public opinion will convict and will certainly condemn.

Inasmuch as the law does not punish for the mere appearance of evil, we conclude that the testimony in this case does not establish an attempt to commit a crime, for the reason that it does not show an *overt act* on the part of the appellant to commit the crime charged, before it is shown that he abandoned his alleged purpose. We are, therefore, constrained to hold that the judgement of the trial court must be reversed, and the appellant, Henry Bucklew, discharged.

Judgment reversed and appellant discharged.

ETHRIDGE, C.J., and JONES, Inzer and SMITH, JJ., concur.

STATE V. KEEN
North Carolina Court of Appeals, 1975.
214 S.E.2d 242.

[This case deals with solicitation.]

Defendant was charged in a bill of indictment with soliciting Blaine Bacon and Ben Wade to kill and murder Susan Page Keen, wife of defendant.

Evidence for the State is summarized as follows. Blaine Bacon first saw Patrick Alan Keen, the defendant, on the afternoon of 12 September 1973. Defendant brought his Volkswagen bus into Bacon's garage to be repaired. Bacon examined the vehicle, told defendant that he did not have the necessary parts, and suggested that defendant return the next day. Defendant returned the next day and Bacon proceeded to repair the vehicle. Defendant asked Bacon if he knew "someone with few scruples and in need of some money." Defendant replied that he wanted his wife killed so that he could collect the proceeds from an insurance policy in her name. He agreed to pay Bacon $5,000.00 from the proceeds of policy.

Defendant told Bacon the death of his wife must occur before 1 October since that was the expiration date of her life insurance policy. At the close of the conversation Bacon asked the defendant to give him a few days to consider the proposition and to contact him the following Monday.

Defendant had purchased a $100,000.00 policy on his wife's life dated 1 July 1973, and was the named beneficiary. Defendant paid the quarterly premium for the months of July, August, and September but did not pay the premium due 1 October 1973, and the policy lapsed on 31 October.

Bacon immediately attempted to contact several law enforcement officers with whom he had become acquainted when he had worked as an informer or undercover agent. He finally reached a U.S. Treasury agent and informed him of what defendant had said. The agent advised him to keep in contact. Bacon's actions thereafter were generally directed by law enforcement officers. On Friday, the defendant again visited Bacon, told him of the urgency of the time factor, and sought a definite answer as to whether Bacon would kill Mrs. Keen. Defendant informed Bacon that she was in Fayetteville and said he could go there and "blow her brains out." Bacon again told the defendant to wait until Monday for an answer.

The following Monday afternoon, defendant met Bacon at his garage. Ben Wade, an agent of the State Bureau of Investigation, was concealed in Bacon's rear office so that he could overhear their conversation. At this meeting defendant again stressed the importance of time and asked Bacon when he was going to kill Mrs. Keen. Bacon replied that accidents were not his style but that he had discussed the matter with a friend who was a professional killer. Bacon told the defendant that his friend was an expert at making deaths appear accidental and that he would be in Asheville the following Friday. On Wednesday defendant visited Bacon again. The two established Friday morning as their meeting time, and defendant was asked to bring a picture of his wife.

On that Friday the two men drove in defendant's van to a motel in Asheville. They went to a room where Wade, posing as a professional killer, was waiting. A wireless transmitter was taped to Wade's back for the purpose of recording the conversation. Tapes of the conversation were introduced at trial for the purpose of corroboration.

At the motel defendant told Wade that his wife was in Fayetteville and gave him her address. He also gave him a photograph and physical description of her. He told Wade that his wife's death must appear accidental and must occur prior to the cancellation of her life insurance policy on the first of October. Defendant volunteered to raise the fee for the killing to $6,000.00 and the method of payment was discussed. With respect to "front money," defendant said that he had no cash but did have a motorcycle, a Volkswagen bus, and a five-acre tract of land to which titles could be signed over to Bacon who, in turn, could transfer them to Wade. Wade replied that he wanted the titles transferred that day and instructed defendant to put the vehicles in Bacon's name and the property in Wade's name. He told defendant he would wait at the motel until 2:30 that afternoon.

At the conclusion of the conversation, defendant left the room. Police immediately placed him under arrest. Upon being arrested defendant replied, "Oh my God how did you find out about it so fast?"

Defendant testified, in substance, as follows. He did not originally intend to have his wife killed but Bacon implanted the idea in his mind. After he and Bacon discussed the life insurance policy in Mrs. Keen's name, Bacon suggested that defendant "knock her off" and collect on the policy. Bacon volunteered to kill Mrs. Keen for $5,000.00. When Bacon telephoned and told him that his friend had

arrived, defendant indicated to Bacon that he wanted to call off the thing and did not care to visit Bacon's friend. Bacon responded that his friend had come all the way to Asheville, would be very upset if defendant did not at least talk with him and might seek vengeance on defendant. Defendant, although he had no intention of following through with the plan, proceeded to the motel in order to talk the other men out of it. He was frightened and answered Wade's questions because of his fear.

The jury found defendant guilty and judgment was entered imposing a sentence of confinement of not less than five nor more than ten years. . . .

VAUGHN, Judge.

In support of his contention that the court should have granted his motion for judgment of nonsuit, defendant argues that the State's own evidence shows that: " . . . the defendant was (1) entrapped and (2) that there was the interposition of a resisting will thereby making the commission of a crime impossible."

We hold that defendant's contentions on entrapment were properly submitted to the jury with instructions from the court which were correct in law and manifestly fair to defendant.

Defendant argues that there could have been no completion of the crime since all parties with whom he spoke were connected with law enforcement. The answer is that the interposition of a resisting will, by a law enforcement officer or anyone else, between the solicitation and the proposed felony is of no consequence. This is so "because the solicitation was complete before the resisting will of another had refused its assent and cooperation.". . . Defendant was not charged with the crime of conspiracy, a crime which was not completed because of the failure of Bacon, in fact, to concur in defendant's scheme to murder defendant's wife. The crime of solicitation to commit a felony is complete with the solicitation even though there could never have been an acquiescence in the scheme by the one solicited.

Defendant also contends that his conviction of solicitation to commit murder cannot be punished by imprisonment for more than two years. We concede that the applicable statute . . . and the reported cases leave some lack of certainty as to what crimes may be designated and punished as "infamous.". . . It appears, nevertheless, to be settled that conspiracy to murder is an infamous offense and punishable as a felony. . . .

The crime of which defendant was convicted is but one step away from conspiracy to murder—and that step is not one defendant could have taken. If Bacon had concurred in defendant's scheme to murder the latter's wife, the conspiracy would have been complete. Bacon's rejection of defendant's atrocious scheme does not render defendant's conduct any less "infamous" than it would have been if his offer had been accepted. We hold that the punishment imposed does not exceed that authorized by law.

We have considered the other contentions made in defendant's brief and find them to be without merit.

No error.

MARTIN and ARNOLD, JJ., concur

GOMEZ V. PEOPLE
Colorado Supreme Court, 1963.
381 P.2d 816.

[This case involves conspiracy to commit larceny.]

MCWILLIAMS, Justice.

Joyce Gomez and Roberta Taylor were jointly tried and convicted by a jury of conspiring on November 1, 1960, to commit the crime of larceny from the person of one Edward Cook. By the present writ of error Gomez alone seeks reversal of the judgment and sentence entered pursuant to the verdict of the jury.

The only assignment of error pertains to the sufficiency of the evidence, Gomez contending that the trial court erred in refusing to direct a verdict in her favor and, a fortiori, that the evidence does not support the subsequent determination by the jury that she is guilty of the crime of conspiracy. From a careful review of the record we conclude that her contention is without merit. However, inasmuch as the legal sufficiency of the evidence has been challenged, it becomes necessary to review the record before us in some detail in order to give meaning to our conclusion that here is evidence to support the verdict.

The evidence adduced by the People established the following:

1. That Cook, a locomotive engineer, got off work at about midnight on November 1, 1960, and he was going via automobile from the roundhouse at 40th Avenue and Williams Street in Denver to his home in southwest Denver when he encountered Gomez and Taylor at 26th Avenue and Welton Street;

2. That Cook at this time had approximately $340 in his wallet, $75 of which was secreted in an inside compartment of the wallet, the balance of the currency being in the wallet proper;

3. That Cook had this comparatively large amount of money on his person because this was his pay day, and he had cashed his pay check, getting "paid in ten dollar bills";

4. That while Cook was stopped for a traffic light at 26th Avenue and Welton Street, Gomez and Taylor with no invitation opened the right-hand door of his car and proceeded to deposit themselves on the front seat;

5. That Gomez, who was seated immediately next to Cook, asked or "ordered" him to drive on, stating: "Help us out; this girl's [Taylor's] husband is going to kill her," and that one of the two women stated that Taylor's husband was armed with a gun;

6. That Cook promptly proceeded to drive for several blocks, but when he got over his "surprise" stopped the car and ordered the two women to leave his car;

7. That the two refused to leave, whereupon Cook got out of his car, went around it and opened the right-hand door, and with only little difficulty succeeded in getting Taylor out of the automobile;

8. That with his back turned to Taylor he then proceeded to forcibly evict Gomez from his car, that she initially resisted, but after considerable

struggle he was able to pull her out of his car by the coat collar;

9. That about this time he realized for the first time that his wallet which he carried in his left rear trousers pocket was missing;

10. That Gomez and Taylor then broke and ran, whereupon he gave hot pursuit, and after a four-to-five-block chase espied the two crouching down on the floor of the front seat of an abandoned automobile;

11. That he opened the left-hand front door of this auto and saw Taylor and Gomez "down on the floor board attempting to hide";

12. That as he was in the act of pulling Taylor out of the car as the police arrived, whereupon Gomez got out of the front door on the right-hand side of the vehicle, crying "rape";

13. That a subsequent search of this auto by the police revealed 26 ten-dollar bills under the front seat in such a position that they could not have been accidently "dropped there," because they were a foot or so back under the seat;

14. That search of Cook's automobile by the police thereafter disclosed that his wallet was "pushed down in the crack on the [front] seat quite a ways"; and

15. That though Cook's wallet still contained the $75 hidden in the inside compartment, the remainder of his currency was missing.

The foregoing resume demonstrates quite clearly to us that the trial court did not commit error in submitting the case to the jury, and that actually there is ample evidence to support the jury's verdict.

True, there was evidence to the contrary. Although Taylor elected not to testify, Gomez did testify in her own behalf, and her testimony was radically different from that of Cook in virtually all particulars, as under the circumstances might well be expected. However, no good purpose would be served by detailing Gomez's testimony, as it did no more than create a conflict in the evidence and thereby pose a disputed issue of fact properly to be resolved by the jury. . . . There being competent evidence, both of a direct and circumstantial nature, to support the jury's determination, we are not at liberty to set it aside.

In support of the general proposition that a conspiracy "need not be proved directly, but may be inferred by the jury from the facts proved." . . .

The judgement is affirmed.

FRANTZ, C.J. and DAY, J., concur.

CHAPTER 6

OFFENSES AGAINST PERSONS

CHAPTER OUTLINE

INTRODUCTION

Every civilized society attempts to protect its people from injury or death at the hands of wrongdoers. Imposing criminal sanctions is society's way of protecting human life from those whose conduct it cannot tolerate. As the English common law developed, the judges created offenses to protect individuals from conduct that society concluded was wrongful and injurious. These basic offenses as defined by English common law were inherited by the American colonists. Since then, many social changes have occurred in America, and federal and state statutes have redefined many of these offenses and have created new ones. In this chapter, we examine the common-law crimes against persons and discuss their statutory development in the United States. We also explore some representative statutes defining present-day offenses against persons.

THE COMMON-LAW BACKGROUND

By the time of the English colonization in America, the common law had identified four groups of offenses against persons. These consisted of: (1) the assaultive crimes, that is, assault, battery, and mayhem; (2) the homicidal crimes of murder, manslaughter, and suicide; (3) sexual offenses of rape, sodomy, and abortion; and (4) the offenses known as false imprisonment and kidnapping. Murder, manslaughter, rape, sodomy, and suicide were common-law felonies; the remaining offenses named were classified as misdemeanors.

THE AMERICAN DEVELOPMENT

Early substantive criminal law in America was essentially a continuation of the English common law of crimes. By the 1800s, however, America's quest for representative government and its penchant for definiteness and certainty, combined with the standards of written constitutions, resulted in legislative definition of crimes. Defining offenses against persons became primarily a state rather than a federal legislative function, and the new states basically followed the common-law themes with variations deemed necessary in the new social and political environment.

   As the United States became urbanized, more densely populated, and increasingly mobile, the areas of conduct statutorily defined as criminal offenses against persons required revision and, in many instances, an enlargement. Under modern statutes, assault and battery have been classified according to their seriousness, the character of the victim, and the environment in which these crimes are committed. Homicidal offenses, too, have been divided into classifications of murder and manslaughter based on the degree of the offender's culpability, and a new offense of vehicular homicide has been created to cope with the dangers inherent in motor vehicle traffic. At early common law, suicide was punished by causing the forfeiture of the decedent's goods and chattels to the king. See *State v. Willis*, 121 S.E.2d 854 (N.C. 1961). Suicide statutes are now designed primarily to punish those who would attempt or assist in self-destruction.

In recent years, contemporary moral standards have caused the offense of rape to be expanded into a more comprehensive offense of sexual battery, with new emphasis on the victim's age and vulnerability. At the same time, enforcement of laws proscribing sodomy has declined, and abortion, a common-law crime, has become a woman's constitutional right. Finally, while the offense of false imprisonment is essentially the same as at common law, the crime of kidnapping serves a much different role in American society than it did under the English common law.

Assault and Battery

Assault and battery, while commonly referred to together, were separate offenses at common law. An assault was basically an attempted battery consisting of an offer to do bodily harm to another by using force and violence; a battery was a completed or consummated assault. *State v. Maier*, 99 A.2d 21 (N.J. 1953). Although an actual touching was not required, words alone did not constitute an assault. *Herrington v. State*, 172 So. 129 (Miss. 1937). The common law made no distinction between classes or degrees of assault and battery but dealt with aggravated cases more severely.

Modern Statutory Development

Today all jurisdictions make assault an offense, and most make battery a crime as well. Assault is usually defined by statute, as is battery. Sometimes the term *assault and battery* is used to indicate one offense. Simple assaults and batteries generally remain misdemeanors, while those perpetrated against public officers (e.g., fire and police personnel) are frequently classified as felonies. Legislatures commonly classify as felonies more egregious assaultive conduct as aggravated assault, aggravated battery, and assault with intent to commit other serious crimes.

The California Penal Code defines an assault as "an unlawful attempt, coupled with a present ability, to commit a violent injury on the person of another." West's Ann. Cal. Penal Code § 240. It imposes increased penalties for an assault committed upon a person engaged in performing the duties of a peace officer, fire fighter, lifeguard, process server, paramedic, physician, or nurse, West's Ann. Cal. Penal Code § 241(b); and, like most states, makes it a felony to commit an assault with a deadly weapon or with force likely to produce great bodily injury. West's Ann. Cal. Penal Code § 245. Many states classify this latter offense as aggravated assault. For example, under Florida law, a person who commits an assault with a deadly weapon without intent to kill or an assault with an intent to commit a felony is guilty of aggravated assault, a felony offense. West's Fla. Stat. Ann. § 784.021.

Again, the California Penal Code defines as battery "any willful and unlawful use of force or violence upon the person or another." West's Ann. Cal.

Penal Code § 242. The code also specifies increased punishment for batteries committed against specific classes of officers, West's Ann. Cal. Penal Code § 243; against transportation personnel, West's Ann. Cal. Penal Code § 243.3; or when committed on school property, West's Ann. Cal. Penal Code § 243.2. Consistent with its handling of aggravated assaults, Florida law classifies a battery resulting in great bodily harm, permanent disability, or permanent disfigurement, or one committed with a deadly weapon as an aggravated battery, an even more serious felony than aggravated assault. West's Fla. Stat. Ann. § 784.045.

While most assault and battery prosecutions occur under state laws, the federal government also has a role in this area. Federal statutes proscribe assault within the maritime and territorial jurisdiction of the United States. 18 U.S.C.A. § 113. Federal courts have held that the statute covers the entire range of assaults, *United States v. Eades*, 615 F.2d 617 (4th Cir. 1980), *cert. denied*, 450 U.S. 1001, 101 S. Ct. 1709, 68 L.Ed.2d 203 (1981), and that the word *assault* includes acts that would constitute batteries under most state laws. *United States v. Chaussee*, 536 F.2d 637 (7th Cir. 1976). Additional federal statutes proscribe assaults on federal officers engaged in the performance of official duties, 18 U.S.C.A. § 111, and assaults of foreign diplomatic and other official personnel. 18 U.S.C.A. § 112.

Common Illustrations of Assault and Battery

Statutory definitions vary, but under most statutes a simple assault would include a threat to strike someone with the fist, or a missed punch. Firing a shot in the direction of a person, throwing a rock at someone but not hitting them, or threatening someone with a weapon would probably all qualify as aggravated assault.

A battery, on the other hand, involves some physical contact with the victim. Some common illustrations of a simple battery would include hitting or pushing someone, a male hugging and kissing a female—or even an offensive touching, if against her will—using excessive force in breaking up a fight, intentionally tripping another individual, or using excessive force (by a parent or teacher) in disciplining a child. The acts referred to as constituting aggravated assault, if completed, would most likely be prosecuted as aggravated batteries.

A frequently litigated issue in prosecutions for aggravated assault and aggravated battery is whether the instrument used by the defendant is a dangerous weapon capable of producing death or great bodily harm. Throwing someone out of a window, or using an air pistol, a hammer, a club, or an ice pick—and under some circumstances, even the fist—have been found to qualify. Courts generally reason that the test is not whether great bodily harm resulted, but whether the instrument used was capable of producing such harm.

The Burden of the Prosecution

The proof required to establish assaultive offenses is dependent on the statutory language of the offense. However, to convict a defendant of simple assault or battery, the prosecution generally need only prove the act and the defendant's general, but not specific, intent. In aggravated assault and aggravated battery prosecutions, courts have arrived at different interpretations of the intent requirement, but usually proof of the defendant's general intent is sufficient. In contrast, if a defendant is prosecuted for committing an assault or battery "with the intent to do great bodily harm" or "with the intent to commit a specific felony, e.g., murder," courts usually require the prosecution to prove the defendant's specific intent to accomplish those results.

Defenses to Charges of Assault and Battery

Many forms of conduct involving intentional use of physical force do not constitute batteries. In many instances there is an express or implied consent of the person against whom the physical force is exerted. Reasonableness is the test applied in sports contests and friendly physical encounters. Everyday examples include such contact sports as football, in which the participants obviously consent to forceful bodily contact. The physician who performs surgery with consent of the patient provides another example of physical contact that, if properly applied, does not constitute a battery. Reasonableness is also the test applied to interpersonal relationships. Thus, while a person may imply consent to a friendly kiss or caress, seldom could a person imply consent to an act of violence, even when done under the guise of affection. A teacher may discipline a pupil, and a police officer or prison guard may use reasonable force to effect an arrest or preserve order. Often the degree of force used by teachers, police officers, and correction officials is regulated by statutory law, and an excessive use of force may constitute a battery. See *State v. Mendoza*, 258 N.W.2d 260 (Wis. 1977). Likewise, parents and guardians and those standing *in loco parentis* have a right to impose reasonable punishment when disciplining a child, but must take into consideration the child's age, health, size, and all other relevant circumstances. Parents who inflict injury on a child or who impose excessive punishment may be guilty of committing a simple or even an aggravated battery. *State v. Thorpe*, 429 A.2d 785 (R.I. 1981). They may also be subject to prosecution under modern statutes proscribing child abuse.

A person charged with battery may defend by showing that the touching or hitting was unintentional, that the physical force used was reasonable, or that the action was taken in self-defense. Self-defense is subject to qualifications, as explained in Chapter 13. Defenses applicable to the offense of battery generally apply as well to a charge of assault. The theory is that a person who fails to make physical contact with another can defend on the same basis of reasonableness or self-defense as a person who successfully commits a battery.

A Variation in Criminal Offenses: The New Crime of Stalking

By the end of the 1980s, police and legislators were receiving complaints from victims and their families and friends that persons were being continually harassed by conduct consisting of continued surveillance and threats, often with the intent to cause a person targeted to reasonably fear for his or her safety. Law enforcement officers refer to this type of behavior as "stalking." Many prosecutors felt that the traditional protections of the criminal law were not always sufficient to protect victims from the needless torment caused by this conduct, and they urged legislators to adopt appropriate statutes to combat the problem.

California enacted a stalking law in 1991, and by 1993 a majority of the states had enacted laws making stalking a crime. These laws often stipulate that to be

> ## CASE IN POINT
>
> ## Assault With a Deadly Weapon
>
> Rasor, a police officer, stopped a vehicle and attempted to arrest the driver, Jackson, for driving while intoxicated. As he did, a fight broke out between the officer and Jackson. At that point the defendant, Lloyd Gary, a passenger in Jackson's car, approached the two combatants, removed the officer's pistol, and pointed it at Rasor and Jackson.
>
> Gary was convicted of assault with a deadly weapon. On appeal, he argued that the trial judge erred in not directing the jury to return a verdict of not guilty because the evidence showed no attempt to commit a physical injury. The Arizona Supreme Court rejected Gary's argument, saying "The pointing of a gun may constitute 'an assault' . . . and it is not necessary to show in addition that there was an intent to do physical harm to the victim."
>
> *State v. Gary,* 543 P.2d 782, 783 (Ariz. 1975).

guilty of the offense a person must willfully, maliciously, and repeatedly follow or harass another and make a credible threat against that person. The Illinois statute is one of the toughest new laws against stalking. Chapter 38 of the Criminal Code was amended, making it a felony to stalk and a more serious felony to be guilty of aggravated stalking, and now provides:

§ 12–7.3

(a) A person commits stalking when he or she transmits to another person a threat with the intent to place that person in reasonable apprehension of death, bodily harm, sexual assault, confinement or restraint, and in furtherance of the threat knowingly does any one or more of the following acts on at least 2 separate occasions:

(1) follows the person, other than within the residence of the defendant;

(2) places the person under surveillance by remaining present outside his or her school, place of employment, vehicle, other place occupied by the person, or residence other than the residence of the defendant.

§ 12–7.4

(a) A person commits aggravated stalking when he or she, in conjunction with committing the offense of stalking, also does any of the following:

(1) causes bodily harm to the victim;

(2) confines or restrains the victim; or

(3) violates a temporary restraining order, an order of protection, or an injunction prohibiting the behavior described in . . . [the Domestic Violence Act of 1986].

Stalking laws have been criticized as being excessively vague. It remains to be seen how stalking statutes will be construed by the courts and whether challenges to their constitutionality will prevail. As the number of prosecutions under these new laws increases, judicial activity in this area is likely.

MAYHEM

At common law, mayhem consisted of willfully and maliciously injuring another so as to render the victim less able in fighting, either in self-defense or in ability to annoy an adversary. To obtain a conviction for mayhem, it was only necessary to establish that the act was committed with a general intent. *Terrell v. State*, 8 S.W. 212 (Tenn. 1888). The crime of mayhem has been extended to include injuries that disfigure a person. Most states only require proof of a general intent that may be presumed from the offender's act of maiming the victim. Some, however, require proof of the actor's specific intent to maim or disfigure the victim.

Two appellate decisions illustrate the applicability of mayhem statutes. In Texas, a man who found his wife committing an act of adultery cut off her paramour's sex organ with a razor. The defendant was found guilty of mayhem under a Texas statute, and his conviction was affirmed on appeal. *Sensobaugh v. State*, 244 S.W. 379 (Tex. Crim. App. 1922). In another instance, a defendant deliberately struck another man, and as a result of the battery the victim lost his eye. The defendant's conviction under a New Mexico penal statute was affirmed on appeal. *State v. Hatley*, 384 P.2d 252 (N.M. 1963).

California statutes classify mayhem in two categories: basic and aggravated. The statute defining mayhem states:

> Every person who unlawfully and maliciously deprives a human being of a member of his body, or disables, disfigures, or renders it useless, or cuts or disables the tongue, or puts out an eye, or slits the nose, ear, or lip, is guilty of mayhem. West's Ann. Cal. Penal Code § 203.

While mayhem appears to be a general-intent offense, aggravated mayhem is a specific-intent crime because Section 205 refers to the intent to do some further act such as "to permanently disable the victim," or to achieve some additional consequences beyond the act of mayhem. West's Ann. Cal. Penal Code § 205; *People v. Daniels*, 537 P.2d 1232 (Cal. 1975).

In *People v. Ferrell*, 267 Cal. Rptr. 283 (Cal. App. 1990), the defendant was a stranger to the victim. Yet, she came looking for her by name at the address furnished her by a friend from jail. When the defendant approached the victim, she knocked the phone from the victim's hand and shot her in the neck. Defendant's conviction for aggravated mayhem was upheld by the appellate court, which concluded the jury could reasonably have inferred that the defendant intended both to kill the victim, and if she did not die, to disable her permanently.

Mayhem statutes are less common today because many of the acts formerly prosecuted under laws proscribing mayhem are now prosecuted as other statutory crimes (e.g., aggravated battery and attempted murder).

HOMICIDE

The word *homicide* means the taking of the life of one human being by another. The English common law recognized both criminal and noncriminal homicides. Criminal homicide embraced the crimes of murder and manslaughter; noncriminal homicide included those killings of humans deemed either justifiable or excusable. The killing of a human being was common factor in all classes of homicide; however, the state of mind of the perpetrator was significant in determining whether an offense had been committed, and if so, the category of that offense.

At common law, murder was the unlawful killing of one person by another with "malice aforethought." The required malice could be either express or implied. *State v. Robinson*, 78 So. 933 (La. 1918). There were no degrees of murder.

Manslaughter at common law was the unlawful killing of one human being by another when no malice was involved. *State v. Boston*, 11 N.W.2d 407 (Iowa 1943). There were two categories: voluntary and involuntary. *People v. Richardson*, 293 N.W.2d 332 (Mich. 1980). Voluntary manslaughter consisted of an intentional, unlawful killing that occurred in the heat of passion due to some adequate provocation. *Cottrell v. Commonwealth*, 111 S.W.2d 445 (Ky. 1937). Involuntary manslaughter was the unintentional killing of another by gross, or wanton negligence of the accused. *People v. Campbell*, 212 N.W. 97 (Mich. 1927). Simply stated, the difference between the two was that the former was intentional while the latter was unintentional. *Wiley v. State*, 170 P. 869 (Ariz. 1918).

At common law, homicide was justifiable if performed by the command or permission of the law; it could be excusable if it occurred through accident or when committed for necessary self-protection. *State v. Brown*, 126 A.2d 161 (N.J. 1956).

The American Approach to Homicide

With some variations, the basic scheme of common-law homicide has been carried over into the statutory law of American jurisdictions. Most states, however, classify murder as either first or second degree. Murder in the first degree is usually defined as requiring either *malice aforethought* or *premeditation*. Second-degree murder commonly requires proof that the accused was guilty of *imminently dangerous* or *outrageous* conduct, albeit not malicious in the common-law sense of malice aforethought.

All states make manslaughter a crime, although some statutes abolish the distinction between voluntary and involuntary manslaughter. Moreover, modern statutes extend the offense of manslaughter to embrace a person's responsibility for death resulting from an omission to act where the law imposes such a requirement.

Modern criminal codes generally provide that it is justifiable homicide for one to take another's life by authority of the law (e.g., an executioner performing a duty). It is usually considered excusable homicide if death results from the inadvertent taking of another's life when the actor is not guilty of criminal negligence (e.g., death occurring from an unavoidable traffic accident).

The overwhelming majority of homicide prosecutions are brought under state laws. However, federal statutes provide jurisdiction over the killing of certain officers and employees of the United States engaged in performance of their official duties, 18 U.S.C.A. § 1114, as well as certain foreign officials, 18 U.S.C.A. § 1116. Federal statutes classify criminal homicide as murder in the first degree, felony murder, and manslaughter. 18 U.S.C.A. § 1111–1112.

First-Degree Murder.   The California Penal Code illustrates a modern statutory approach to homicide. It defines murder as the "unlawful killing of a human being, or a fetus, with malice aforethought" but stipulates that death of the fetus is not murder when an abortion is performed with the mother's consent. West's Ann. Cal. Penal Code § 187. The malice required by the code may be either express or implied. When a deliberate intention is manifested to take a person's life unlawfully the malice is considered express; it may be implied when no considerable provocation appears or under other circumstances indicating malice. West's Ann. Cal. Penal Code § 188.

In defining degrees of murder, the California code states:

> All murder which is perpetrated by means of a destructive device or explosive, knowing use of ammunition designed primarily to penetrate metal or armor, poison, lying in wait, torture, or by any other kind of wilful, deliberate, and premeditated killing, or which is committed in the perpetration of, or attempt to perpetrate, arson, rape, robbery, burglary, mayhem . . . is murder of the first degree; and all other kinds of murder are of the second degree. West's Ann. Cal. Penal Code § 189.

The penalties in California and other jurisdictions for first-degree murder are the most severe, with decreasing penalties provided for second-degree murder and manslaughter.

First-degree murder is the highest classification of homicide. It contemplates a true "intent to kill" and usually requires proof of either malice aforethought or premeditation. Thus, to obtain a conviction, the prosecution must establish the defendant's specific intent to take another's life.

The California Supreme Court has said that "when a defendant with a wanton disregard for human life, does an act that involves a high degree of probability that it will result in death, he acts with malice aforethought." Moreover, the court opined that "willful, deliberate, and premeditated" as used in the statute indicates its intent to require as an essential element of first-degree murder substantially more reflection "than the mere amount of thought necessary to form the intention to kill." *People v. Cruz*, 605 P.2d 830, 834 (Cal. 1980). The Pennsylvania Supreme Court has defined malice aforethought more elaborately, saying it is "not only a particular ill will, but a hardness of heart, cruelty, recklessness of consequences, and a mind regardless of social duty." *Commonwealth v. Buzard*, 76 A.2d 394, 396 (Pa. 1950) (citing *Commonwealth v. Drum*, 58 Pa. 9 (1868)). Such malice may be expressed or may be implied from the circumstances under which a homicidal act is performed.

Many jurisdictions define first-degree murder in terms of the "premeditated intent" of the offender. Florida, for example, classifies a homicide as a first-degree murder if the unlawful killing of a human being is "perpetrated from a premeditated design to effect the death of the person killed or any human being." West's Fla. Stat. Ann. § 782.04.

Initially, you may think of a premeditated act as requiring a lengthy period of deliberation. Indeed, dictionaries commonly define *premeditation* as a conscious and deliberate preplanning over a period of time. Judicial decisions defining premeditation, however, emphasize that although it requires thought before-hand, no particular length of time is required. The length of time necessary to deliberate, or to form a specific intent to kill, need only be time enough to form the required intent before the killing. It matters not how short that time may be, *State v. Davis*, 260 A.2d 587 (Conn. 1969), *vac'd. in part*, 408 U.S. 935, 92 S. Ct. 2856, 33 L.Ed. 2d 750 (1972), as long as the process of premeditation occurs at any point before the killing. See, for example, *State v. Corn*, 278 S.E. 2d 221(N.C. 1981).

The prosecution may establish either malice aforethought or premeditation by a variety of evidentiary facts and circumstances. These include threats, quarrels, and expressions of ill will, as well as the nature of the weapon used, the presence or absence of adequate provocation, previous difficulties between the parties, the manner in which the homicide was committed, the nature of the wound inflicted, and the manner in which it was inflicted.

Felony Murder.   The common law developed a doctrine that where an accused was engaged in the commission of a felony and a homicide occurred, the felonious act was regarded as a substitute for the proof of malice aforethought required to find the defendant guilty of murder. Thus, it became felony murder where an accused unintentionally killed a human being while committing, or attempting to commit, such common-law felonies as burglary, arson, rape, or robbery. The theory was that if a killing resulted, even though unintentional or accidental, the required malice was carried over from the original felony. Consequently, the felon would be found guilty of murder.

Although of dubious ancestry, the felony murder doctrine has been incorporated into most criminal codes in the United States. See *People v. Aaron*, 229 N.W.2d 304 (Mich. 1980). With the proliferation of crimes classified as felonies, legislatures have generally limited its applicability to felonies involving violence or posing great threat to life or limb (e.g., rape, robbery, kidnaping, arson, and burglary). See, for example, West's Ann. Cal. Penal Code § 189. Recently some have sought to equate certain

---

C A S E   I N   P O I N T

FIRST-DEGREE MURDER: EVIDENCE OF PREMEDITATION

Defendant Phillip Lee Young suggested to his two companions that they rob and kill John Cooke in order to obtain money to buy liquor. After the three men used a ruse to gain entry to Cooke's house, Young stabbed Cooke twice in the chest, and one of the companions stabbed the victim several times in the back. Cooke died as a result of the injuries.

A jury found Young guilty of first-degree murder and he appealed. After explaining that first-degree murder is the unlawful killing of a person with malice and with premeditation and deliberation, the North Carolina Supreme Court rejected Young's contention that the evidence was insufficient to support a conviction.

State v. Young, 325 S.E.2d 181 (N.C. 1985).

felonious drug offenses with violent felonies. Some statutes even provide for degrees of felony murder depending on the seriousness of the felony attempted or perpetrated by the accused, and whether the accused is present at the scene when the killing occurs. See, for example, West's Fla. Stat. Ann. § 782.04.

Felony murder statutes have produced much litigation in the criminal courts. Some of the questions raised include

- Can a felon who perpetrates an offense be guilty of felony murder where the victim of the intended offense kills a co-felon?
- Should the felon committing a crime such as robbery be guilty of felony murder if a police officer mistakenly kills the felon's intended victim?
- Can a felon be guilty of felony murder when a co-felon accidentally kills a bystander or a police officer?

Most courts have held that the doctrine of felony murder does not extend to a killing stemming from the commission of the felony if it is directly attributable to the act of someone other than the defendant or those actively participating with the defendant in the unlawful enterprise. Nevertheless, courts have arrived at different solutions to these and other problems of felony murder laws.

Perhaps questions such as these led the Michigan Supreme Court in 1980 to abrogate the felony murder doctrine. After commenting on how its prior decisions had already significantly restricted the doctrine, the court concluded that the rule that substitutes the intent to commit the underlying felony for the malice element of murder had to be abolished. Its abrogation of the doctrine does not make irrelevant the fact that a death occurred in the course of a felony. Rather, the court noted that a jury can properly infer malice from evidence that a defendant intentionally set in motion a force likely to cause death or great bodily harm. Michigan juries, however, are no longer required to find malice if they are satisfied from all the evidence that it does not exist. *People v. Aaron,* 299 N.W.2d 304 (Mich. 1980).

A cogent argument can be made that the felony murder rule violates the basic requirement of moral culpability in the criminal law. Moreover, critics of the doctrine point out that under the early common law, conviction of a felony was punishable by death. Consequently, they note, when a death occurred in the commission of a felony and the accused was guilty of felony murder, no additional consequences resulted. Not so today, because no felony except for murder committed under aggravating circumstances is punishable by death. Nevertheless, the felony murder doctrine is well established in most jurisdictions. With legislatures perceiving the need to take a "hard line" on crime, it is doubtful that many will be motivated to repeal felony murder statutes. Courts, therefore, will most likely become increasingly conscious of the need to strictly interpret such statutes. Observing that it is the commission of a specified felony that supplants the requirement of premeditation for first-degree murder, the Florida Supreme Court declared that for the felon to be guilty of felony murder there must be some causal connection between the homicide and the underlying felony. *Bryant v. State,* 412 So.2d 347 (Fla. 1982).

Second-Degree Murder. In many jurisdictions second-degree murder is a residual classification applied to unlawful homicides not evidenced by malice aforethought or premeditation, not occurring in conjunction with other felonies, and not falling within the statutory definition of manslaughter. See, for example, West's Ann. Cal. Penal Code § 189. More commonly, second-degree murder is defined in terms of the defendant having a "depraved mind or heart." Florida statutes define second-degree murder as a killing "perpetrated by any act imminently dangerous to another and evincing a depraved mind regardless of human life, although without any premeditated design to effect the death of any particular individual." West's Fla. Stat. Ann. § 782.04. Florida courts have said that an act is imminently dangerous to another and evinces a depraved mind if a person of ordinary judgment would know it is reasonably certain to kill or cause serious bodily injury to another and is done from ill will, hatred, spite, or an evil intent, so as to indicate an indifference to human life. See, for example, *Marasa v. State,* 394 So.2d 544 (Fla. App. 1981). Second-degree murder is a general-intent crime. *Gentry v. State,* 437 So.2d 1097 (Fla. 1983).

In practice, convictions for second-degree murder often reflect a "jury pardon." A classic example is when the state prosecutes a defendant for first-degree murder and the jury determines that the circumstances surrounding the killing do not show malice aforethought, premeditation, or are simply not sufficient to justify the penalty, often death. In such an instance a jury sometimes returns a verdict for the lesser offense of second-degree murder, always a noncapital felony. We might generalize that second-degree murder convictions often occur when a jury is convinced the defendant acted recklessly or even outrageously, but with no intent to take the victim's life.

Manslaughter.   As noted, there were two classes of manslaughter at common law: voluntary and involuntary. California, like many states, preserves that distinction and defines manslaughter as the "unlawful killing of a human being without malice." It enumerates three categories: voluntary, involuntary, and vehicular. Voluntary manslaughter refers to instances where death of the victim occurs upon a sudden quarrel or in the heat of passion. Involuntary manslaughter is where a death occurs from the commission of a lawful act that might produce death, in an unlawful manner, or without due caution and circumspection. The third category, vehicular homicide, involves death resulting from the perpetrator driving a vehicle while in the commission of an unlawful act not amounting to a felony, and with gross negligence, or driving a vehicle in the commission of a lawful act that might produce death in an unlawful manner, and with gross negligence. West's Ann. Cal. Penal Code § 192.

Many other states define manslaughter without categorizing it as voluntary or involuntary. Still other state legislatures have defined manslaughter by degrees. New York law, for example, provides that a person who recklessly causes the death of another person, or commits an unlawful abortional act on a female that causes her death, or a person who intentionally causes or aids another to commit suicide commits manslaughter in the second degree. McKinney's N.Y. Penal Law § 125.15. However, a person who inflicts certain intentional serious injuries that cause death of another under circumstances that do not constitute murder may be guilty of the more serious offense of manslaughter in the first degree if he or she (1) acts under influence of extreme emotional

---

C A S E   I N   P O I N T

SECOND-DEGREE MURDER:
EVIDENCE OF DEPRAVED INDIFFERENCE

The state charged a fifteen-and-a-half-year-old boy with murder in the second degree under Section 125.25(2) of the New York—McKinney's Penal Law, which provides: "A person is guilty of murder in the second degree when: . . . (2) Under circumstances evincing a depraved indifference to human life, he recklessly engages in conduct which creates a grave risk of death to another person, and thereby causes the death of another person." The evidence at trial revealed the defendant loaded a mix of "live" and "dummy" shells at random into the magazine of a 12-gauge shotgun and then pumped a shell into the firing chamber, not knowing whether it was a "dummy" or "live" round. He next raised the gun to his shoulder and pointing it directly at the victim exclaimed, "Let's play Polish roulette," and asked, "Who is first?" Then the defendant pulled the trigger, discharging a live round into a thirteen-year-old victim's chest, resulting in the eventual death of the victim.

On appeal, the court first distinguished the crime of second-degree murder by depraved indifference from manslaughter, by saying that it must be shown that the actor's reckless conduct is imminently dangerous and presents a grave risk of death, whereas in manslaughter the conduct need only present the lesser "substantial risk" of death. Then pointing out that the defendant had an intense interest in and a detailed knowledge of weapons and analogizing the incident to a macabre game of chance, the New York Court of Appeals held the evidence was legally sufficient to support the defendant's conviction of second-degree murder.

People v. Roe, 542 N.E.2d 610 (N.Y. 1989).

---

disturbance, or (2) commits an unlawful abortional act that causes the death of a female pregnant for more than twenty-four weeks unless it is an abortional act deemed justifiable by statutory exceptions. McKinney's N.Y. Penal Law § 125.20.

Irrespective of whether a statute classifies manslaughter as voluntary, involuntary, or by degree, certain situations generally fall within the definition of the offense. Common examples include a death resulting from mutual combat, or killing someone by use of excessive force while defending yourself or a family member or acting in defense of your property.

The intent that must be established to obtain a conviction of manslaughter may depend on the nature of the charge. To establish voluntary manslaughter, the prosecution may have to establish the defendant's specific intent. On the other hand, in a prosecution for involuntary manslaughter, the defendant's intent need only be general and may be inferred from the defendant's act and surrounding circumstances.

Often a charge of involuntary manslaughter is based on allegations of criminal negligence. A highly publicized example of this arose from a tragic accident occurring in the film industry. In 1982, some Hollywood moviemakers shooting a scene for the movie "The Twilight Zone" used a helicopter that

---

CASE IN POINT

SPOUSAL ADULTERY NOT AVAILABLE TO REDUCE MURDER OF FORMER COHABITANT TO MANSLAUGHTER

David McCarthy was convicted of the murder of Adrianne Neal, with whom he had enjoyed a long-standing romantic relationship. McCarthy and Neal never married, but cohabited for several years and even had two children out of wedlock. Eventually Neal terminated the relationship, and she and the children moved to their own apartment. Several months later, McCarthy entered the apartment and discovered Neal in bed with another man. McCarthy shot both of them, but only Neal died. At trial, McCarthy's defense counsel sought to obtain a conviction for the lesser offense of manslaughter on the ground that McCarthy was acting under serious provocation as a result of "spousal adultery." Counsel requested that the jury be instructed on voluntary manslaughter in addition to murder. The trial judge denied the request, reasoning that the absence of a marital relationship precluded the use of such an instruction.

On appeal, the Illinois Supreme Court upheld the defendant's conviction. The court refused to enlarge the concept of spousal adultery as a basis for considering a lesser degree of homicide to include a relationship between former co-habitants which had effectively ended.

People v. McCarthy, 547 N.E.2d 459 (Ill. 1989).

---

crashed on the set, decapitating an actor and a child and crushing another child. The state prosecuted the director and four of his associates for involuntary manslaughter, claiming they were guilty of criminal negligence. The defendants argued that the tragic deaths resulted from an unforeseeable accident. The media reported in May 1987, after a dramatic five-month trial, that a jury found them all not guilty.

Provocation frequently comes into play in the trial of manslaughter cases. Provocation that would cause a reasonable person to lose control may be sufficient to convert an otherwise intentional killing of another to manslaughter. Mere words, however gross or insulting, are not sufficient to constitute provocation. Rather, to reduce a homicide from murder to manslaughter, it must generally be shown that there was sufficient provocation to excite in the defendant's mind such anger, rage, or terror as would obscure an ordinary person's reasoning and render the person incapable of cool reflection. *Hardin v. State,* 404 N.E.2d 1354 (Ind. 1980). A classic example: discovering one's spouse in an act of adultery with significant sexual contact taking place. See, for example, *Tripp v. State,* 374 A.2d 384 (Md. App. 1977).

Modern statutes often define manslaughter as consisting of the negligent performance of a legal duty or the doing of a lawful act in an unlawful manner. In addition to the more common instances, courts have upheld manslaughter convictions under such statutes for death occurring because of criminal negligence of medical practitioners or because of parental failure to provide medical

---

CASE IN POINT

MANSLAUGHTER BY CULPABLE NEGLIGENCE

William Burge and Juanita Calloway became involved in an argument over the fact that Calloway was apparently sleeping with one of her sons. When Calloway displayed a knife, Burge pulled a gun that he carried to kill snakes that lurked in the walls of his house. Burge pointed the gun at Calloway and cocked it. Burge then pushed Calloway in an attempt to get her into his car. When he did, Calloway's hand hit the gun and it went off, severely wounding Calloway. While driving her to the hospital, Burge ran out of gas and called an ambulance. Calloway died en route to the hospital.

Despite his plea of self-defense, a jury found Burge guilty of manslaughter by culpable negligence. In affirming the conviction, the Mississippi Supreme Court rejected the defendant's contentions of self-defense and excusable and justifiable homicide. The court observed that the jury could reasonably have determined that although the victim was holding a knife the defendant was not in danger of great personal injury.

Burge v. State, 472 So.2d 392 (Miss. 1985).

---

attention or adequate nourishment for their children. See, for example, *People v. Ogg*, 182 N.W.2d 570 (Mich. App. 1970). The California Supreme Court held that a parent of a seriously ill child who makes only provision for prayer may be guilty of such criminal negligence as to justify finding the parent guilty of involuntary manslaughter or child endangerment. *Walker v. Superior Court*, 763 P.2d 852 (Cal. 1988), *cert. denied*, 491 U.S. 905, 109 S.Ct. 3186, 105 L.Ed.2d 695 (1989).

Vehicular Homicide. The carnage on American highways has caused many states to enact statutes making vehicular homicide a specific felony, rather than opting to rely on prosecutors charging a defendant with manslaughter for causing a traffic death. The Florida statute is typical and reads:

> "Vehicular homicide" is the killing of a human being by the operation of a motor vehicle by another in a reckless manner likely to cause the death of, or great bodily harm to, another. West's Fla. Stat. Ann. § 782.071.

The Florida Supreme Court has said that in enacting the statute the legislature created a separate offense with a lesser standard of proof than is required for conviction under the state's manslaughter statute. Thus, the statute enables the prosecution to secure a conviction where the state is unable to meet the level of proof otherwise required in establishing manslaughter. Therefore, the court said the state could charge a defendant with manslaughter for operating a motor vehicle in a culpably negligent manner that causes the death of a human being or could proceed under vehicular homicide, a lesser included offense. *State v. Young*, 371 So.2d 1029 (Fla. 1979).

Justifiable and Excusable Homicide.   As in most jurisdictions, California classifies nonculpable homicide as excusable or justifiable. It is excusable when committed by accident or misfortune or in doing any other lawful act by lawful means, with usual and ordinary caution, and without any unlawful intent. It may also be excusable when committed in the heat of passion, or on sudden and sufficient provocation, or on sudden combat where no dangerous weapon is used and the killing is not done in a cruel or unusual manner. West's Ann. Cal. Penal Code § 195.

Examples of excusable homicide include killing someone when resisting attempts to murder or inflict great bodily injury upon a person; or when in defense of a person's home under certain circumstances; or in some instances of self-defense where there is a reasonable ground to apprehend imminent danger of great bodily harm to a person's self or spouse, parent, or child. See West's Ann Cal. Penal Code §§ 196–197; *People v. Collins*, 11 Cal.Rptr. 504 (Cal. App. 1961).

When death is inflicted by public officers in obedience to a court judgment or in discharge of certain other legal duties, or when necessarily committed in apprehending felons, homicide is considered justifiable. West's Ann. Cal. Penal Code § 196; *People v. Young*, 29 Cal.Rptr. 595 (Cal. App. 1963).

A New Concern in the Law of Homicide.   Another area of contemporary concern has resulted from technological advances in medicine that have enabled physicians to use sophisticated life-support systems to prolong life for indefinite periods. In a landmark case involving Karen Quinlan, the New Jersey Supreme Court in 1976 reviewed the request of Karen's parents to remove the life-support systems sustaining the life of their daughter, who lay in a comatose state with no reasonable medical probability of regaining a sapient existence. The court said

---

CASE IN POINT

VEHICULAR HOMICIDE:
CRIMINAL LIABILITY FOR SECOND ACCIDENT

On the evening of February 14, 1987, Gary Dawson was a passenger in a car driven by Richard Peaslee, Jr., on a snow-packed, icy road in Maine. As a result of Peaslee's intentional "fishtailing," the car went out of control and overturned, throwing Dawson onto the road. Dawson, unable to move, lay on the road where he was run over by another vehicle several minutes later. Dawson died before help arrived on the scene. A jury found Peaslee guilty of vehicular manslaughter, and he appealed.

In affirming Peaslee's conviction, the Maine Supreme Court rejected his contention that he was not criminally responsible for the second accident. "The separate accidents were not independent of each other," said the court, "because Dawson would not have been lying immobile on the road in the path of the other car were it not for Peaslee's conduct." Moreover, the court concluded that "[w]hether Dawson was killed by the first or second impact makes no difference."

State v. Peaslee, 571 A.2d 825 (Me. 1990).

that withdrawal of such life-support systems, under the circumstances, would not constitute a criminal homicide. *In re Quinlan*, 355 A.2d 647 (N.J. 1976).

A significant body of decisional law is now developing on the issue of when life-sustaining measures should be initiated and when they may be removed. Generally, a competent adult who is terminally ill may decide to forgo such extraordinary measures or may order such measures discontinued. There are, however, varying judicial opinions as to when, under what circumstances, and by whom discontinuance may be ordered for minors and incompetents. Statutes in several states now address many of the problems in this area; yet, there is no statutory or judicial consensus on the procedures to effectuate discontinuance. Moreover, the issue of whether removal of life supports extends to discontinuance of hydration and nourishment as well as respirators and similar life-prolonging devices has only recently surfaced. These problems involve moral, ethical, and religious concerns that must be considered in the development of any viable policy in this area by legislators and judges. Courts have been cautious not to allow criminal prosecutions where life-sustaining medical procedures have been discontinued in good faith based on competent medical advice and consent of a competent patient and the patient's family. See, for example, *Barber v. Superior Court*, 195 Cal.Rptr. 484 (Cal. App. 1983).

Prosecutorial Burdens in Homicide Cases

To obtain a conviction in a homicide case, the prosecution must carry a number of burdens.

Requirement That Victim Was "Alive" before Homicidal Act.   By definition, a criminal homicide consists of someone taking another person's life. It follows that before the accused can be found guilty of a homicidal crime, the prosecution must establish that the victim was alive before the accused's criminal act. In most instances this is not too difficult, but it can present a real problem. Consider, for example, the killing of a fetus. Under common law a child was not considered born until the umbilical cord had been severed, and the child's circulation became independent of its mother.

In the highly publicized case of *Keeler v. Superior Court*, 470 P.2d 617 (Cal. 1970), the California Supreme Court held that in enacting its homicide statute, the legislature intended it to have the settled common-law meaning that to be the subject of homicide a fetus must be "born alive." Consequently, the court overturned a murder conviction where the defendant stomped on a pregnant woman's abdomen, thereby causing the death of her fetus. As a result, California amended section 187 of its penal code that defines murder to include the present language, "the unlawful killing of a human being, *or a fetus*, with malice aforethought [emphasis added]."

Absent legislative reform, most courts today would probably follow the view taken by the California court prior to the legislative amendment to section 187.

The **Corpus Delicti** *Requirement.*   In addition to establishing that a human being was alive before a killing took place, the prosecution must always establish the *corpus delicti*, or body of the crime. The *corpus delicti* consists of the fact that a human being is dead and that the death was caused by the criminal act or agency of another person. *State v. Feuillerat*, 292 N.W.2d 326 (S.D. 1980). Some argue that the *corpus delicti* requirement is simply a technicality that impedes the search for truth. Others contend that by requiring some independent evidence to link a defendant to the crime charged ensures that no one is convicted based on a mistake or fabricated confession. As of now, the rule is firmly implanted in American law. To prove the *corpus delicti*, the prosecution must show by either direct or circumstantial evidence, independent of the accused's statements, that the victim died as a result of a criminal act. Usually, the victim's body is available for medical examination and a physician can testify as to the cause of death. If the deceased's body is not recovered *and* the victim's death cannot be determined to have resulted from a criminal act, a conviction cannot be lawfully obtained. Consider the case of *Ex parte Flodstrom*, 277 P.2d 101 (Cal. 1954). There, it could not be determined if a baby died from the mother's alleged homicidal act or whether death occurred as a result of natural causes. Consequently, since there was no evidence available to establish the *corpus delicti*, the appellate court discharged the accused mother from custody on the ground that she was being held to answer charges of murder without probable cause.

The "Proximate Cause" of the Victim's Death.   To hold a defendant responsible for the death of a victim, the prosecution must establish that the victim's death was "proximately caused" by the defendant. This means that the victim's death must have been the natural and probable consequence of the defendant's unlawful conduct. See *Hamrick v. People*, 624 P.2d 1320 (Colo. 1981).

Where A shoots or physically beats B, or A pushes B out of a window or overboard from a boat, or A administers poison to B, medical evidence can usually establish the cause of the victim's death. Killings, however, can be accomplished in hundreds of ways. For example, death may be precipitated by fright or shock or by other means not involving physical contact with the victim. The accused's acts or omissions need not be the immediate cause of the victim's death as long as the death results naturally from the accused's conduct. *State v. Leopold*, 147 A. 118 (Conn. 1929).

Some situations present perplexing issues for medical experts and courts. For example, a defendant fired a shot into the water about six feet from a boat occupied by two boys. When a second shot struck nearer to the boat than the first, one of the boys leaped out of the boat into the water. The boat capsized with the remaining boy in it. Both boys drowned. The defendant argued that he could not be guilty of causing the death of the boy who drowned when the boat overturned. The Tennessee Supreme Court rejected his contention and upheld the defendant's conviction for involuntary manslaughter, concluding that it was his shots, not the act of the boy who caused the boat to capsize, that caused the decedent's death. *Letner v. State*, 299 S.W. 1049 (Tenn. 1927).

In another instance, a wife who had been severely beaten by her husband in the past was impelled by fear of another beating at his hands to jump from a moving automobile. She died from injuries sustained. Her husband was charged with her murder and was found guilty of the lesser offense of manslaughter. On appeal, the Florida Supreme Court upheld the conviction. *Whaley v. State*, 26 So.2d 656 (Fla. 1946).

When Death Occurs.   Just as it is necessary to determine that a homicide victim was alive before the injury that caused death, it is also necessary to establish that death has, in fact, occurred. In most instances, the classic definition will suffice: Death occurs when the heart stops beating and respiration ends. However, technological advances have rendered this definition obsolete as the sole means of determining when death occurs. Many state legislatures have now adopted a definition of "brain death" that specifies that irreversible cessation of total brain functions constitutes death. In other instances, courts have adopted the new definition. See, for example, *In re Bowman*, 617 P.2d 731 (Wash. 1980). In November 1992, the Florida Supreme Court held that an encephalic newborn whose heart was beating and who was breathing was not considered "brain dead" for purposes of an organ donation. *In re: T.A.C.P.*, 609 So.2d 588 (Fla. 1992).

The "One Year and a Day" Rule.   Another obstacle to the prosecution of homicide cases can be the common-law "one year and a day" rule. Under this ancient common-law doctrine, if more than a year and a day intervened between the injury inflicted by the accused and the victim's death, the person who caused the injury could not be held criminally responsible for the victim's death. *State v. Moore*, 199 So. 661 (La. 1940). This inflexible rule has been continued because of uncertainties of medical science in establishing the cause of a victim's death after a lengthy period had elapsed.

In this age of advancing medical technology, the "one year and a day" rule has little relevance and has been rejected or revised either by statute or judicial decision in many jurisdictions. The California Penal Code now states: "To make the killing either murder or manslaughter, it is requisite that the party die within three years and a day after the stroke received or the cause of death administered." West's Ann. Cal. Penal Code § 194. Other jurisdictions have abrogated the rule by judicial fiat. In that vein, the North Carolina Supreme Court recently observed that for a court to remain oblivious to advances in medical science when considering whether to apply an ancient common-law rule would be "folly." *State v. Hefler*, 310 S.E.2d 310 (N.C. 1984). Nevertheless, where such temporal requirements have not been abrogated, the prosecution must establish that the victim's death occurred within the prescribed common-law or statutory period.

This is another instance where the rationale for the strict common-law rule no longer exists. The sophistication of modern medicine leaves little reason for continued adherence to the common-law rule. In light of widespread criticism of the "year and a day" rule, legislatures should either adopt a statute along the lines of the California enactment or just abolish the rule. Increasingly, legislatures have recognized the obsolescence of the "year and a day" rule. Florida did so in 1988; Georgia in 1991.

Defenses to Homicidal Crimes

Defendants charged with murder or manslaughter frequently plead either self-defense or insanity. These defenses are discussed in detail in Chapter 13. Where an accused defends against a charge of manslaughter, the "heat of passion" defense discussed earlier may be available in some instances, as would be the defense of reasonable care or accidental killing in others.

SUICIDE

The early English common law defined the offense of suicide as the intentional taking of a person's life by self-destruction. Suicide was not only regarded as being contrary to nature, it was looked upon as an offense against the biblical commandment, "Thou shalt not kill." Suicide was a species of felony punishable by forfeiture of the decedent's goods and chattels because it deprived the king of one of his subjects. *May v. Pennell*, 64 A. 885 (Me. 1906).

In the United States, the thrust of statutory criminal law has been to make it an offense to cause or aid another person to commit suicide. As of 1993, a majority of the states had laws making assisted suicide a crime. New York law provides that a person is guilty of manslaughter in the second degree if he or she "intentionally causes or aids another person to commit suicide." McKinney's N.Y. Penal Law § 125.15. In Texas, a person who, with intent to promote or assist in the commission of suicide, aids or attempts to aid another to commit suicide is guilty of a misdemeanor. If the actor's conduct causes a suicide or an attempted suicide that results in serious bodily injury, the offense becomes a felony. Vernon's Tex. Penal Code Ann. § 22.08.

The Michigan Experience

Michigan, and several other states, had no laws against assisted suicide. This was dramatized on June 4, 1990, when a fifty-four-year-old woman suffering from Alzheimer's disease took her life by pressing a button that injected a lethal substance into her system through use of a suicide machine developed by Dr. Jack Kevorkian, a retired Michigan pathologist. Murder charges filed against the doctor were dismissed on the ground that Michigan had no law against assisted suicide and the prosecutors failed to show that the doctor tripped the device used to effect the death.

After several additional instances of assisted suicide of terminally ill patients, the Michigan legislature enacted and the governor on December 16, 1992, signed a bill banning assisted suicide. The new law took effect on April 1, 1993, and set a fifteen-month period to allow the legislature to address the problem in more depth. The new law provides a four-year prison sentence and $2,000 fine for violators. On August 17, 1993, Dr. Kevorkian was arraigned on charges of violating the new law for assisting in the suicide of a man suffering from Lou Gehrig's disease. Kevorkian attacked the Michigan law as being unconstitutional.

Competing Values in Suicide Laws

Laws against assisted suicide bring into play significant policy issues and require legislatures to carefully balance competing claims of individual liberty, ethics, and the interest of society. Some proponents of allowing assisted suicide argue that it simply enables a person who has a rational capacity to make a choice. Those who reject this view urge that the state has an interest in the preservation of life, and that some individuals may die needlessly as a result of misdiagnosis. Moreover, they argue that allowing assisted suicide leads to an indifference to the value of life.

SEXUAL BATTERY

There are early biblical accounts of the offense of rape; however, the law of rape, as it exists today, has its roots in the early English common law. It was a felony for a male to have unlawful carnal knowledge (i.e., sexual intercourse) of a female by force and against her will. This is usually referred to as "common-law rape" or "forcible rape." In later stages of the English law, it became a statutory offense for a man to have carnal knowledge of a female child under ten years of age with or without the child's consent. This latter offense came to be known as "statutory rape." See *State v. Keturokis*, 276 N.W. 600 (Iowa 1937).

The common-law offenses required penetration, however slight, of the female's sexual organ by the male sexual organ; no emission of seed was required. At common law, there was a conclusive presumption that a male under age fourteen could not commit the crime of rape. *Foster v. Commonwealth*, 31 S.E. 503 (Va. 1898).

Common-law rape contemplated unlawful intercourse; therefore, a husband could not be guilty of raping his wife. Although this so-called marital exception is of somewhat dubious judicial origin, it is generally credited to the writings of Sir Matthew Hale, who served as Lord Chief Justice in England from 1671 to 1676. Of course, in egregious cases the husband could be charged with assault or battery of his wife. Furthermore, a husband or even another woman could be charged as an aider or abettor if he or she assisted or procured another man to rape his wife.

In March 1991, England's Court of Appeal dismissed an appeal by a man who was convicted of an attempted rape of his estranged wife. In delivering the opinion of the five-judge court, the Lord Chief Justice observed that a rapist remains a rapist irrespective of his relationship with his victim, and that the centuries-old legal doctrine that a husband could not be guilty of raping his wife no longer represented the law considering the position of a wife in contemporary society.

The American Approach

The new American states followed the common-law scheme in statutorily defining rape; however, two principal changes occurred. First, many states explicitly rejected the common-law presumption that males under age fourteen could not commit the offense. Second, legislatures in most states made consensual intercourse with a young female an offense if the female was younger than sixteen or eighteen, rather than ten. Some, however, added the qualification that the female must have been "of previous chaste character." See, for example, West's Fla. Stat. Ann. § 794.05. A female of previous chaste character is generally defined as one who has not previously voluntarily indulged in sexual intercourse outside of marriage.

American courts divided on the intent required for a defendant to be guilty of rape. Some held that no intent other than that evidenced by the doing of the act of intercourse was needed. See, for example, *Walden v. State*, 156 S.W.2d 385 (Tenn. 1941). Others required proof of the defendant's specific intent. See, for example, *Thomas v. State*, 95 P.2d 658 (Okl. Crim. App. 1939).

Courts in American jurisdictions struggled with the requirements of "force" and "consent" in the law of forcible rape. When focusing on these elements some judges instructed juries that "in order for the defendant to be found guilty of rape, you must find that the woman resisted to her utmost." Later cases recognized that it was not necessary for a female victim to resist to the utmost; rather, the degree of resistance came to be regarded as a relative matter dependent on all the circumstances surrounding the incident. Yet, courts continued to recognize that resistance generally had to be more than a mere negative verbal response by a female.

All courts recognized that to constitute common-law rape, sexual intercourse had to be without the female's consent. It was presumed, however, that there could be no consent by a woman who was asleep, unconscious, or mentally incapable. Moreover, consent obtained by fraud or impersonation or through pretext was invalid. Thus, if a man impersonated a woman's husband and caused her to submit to sexual intercourse, he would be guilty of rape. Likewise, a physician who had intercourse with female patients who were not conscious of the nature of the doctor's acts because of the treatments being administered, was properly found guilty of rape. *People v. Minkowski*, 23 Cal.Rptr. 92 (Cal. App. 1962).

In contrast to common-law rape, the elements of force and consent were irrelevant in statutory rape because the purpose of these statutes was to protect young women from all acts of sexual intercourse. See, for example, *State v. Horton*, 39 S.E.2d 222 (S.C. 1946). Some jurisdictions allowed a man to defend against a charge of statutory rape on the basis that he was mistaken about the female's age; others held a defendant strictly liable even if he made a good faith and reasonable inquiry to determine the victim's age. This latter concept of a "strict liability" offense was discussed in Chapter 4. A California law making statutory rape a crime was challenged on the basis of gender discrimination, since only males could be prosecuted for the offense. The United States Supreme Court rejected the challenge. *Michael M. v. Superior Court*, 450 U.S. 464, 101 S. Ct. 1200, 67 L.Ed.2d 437 (1981).

While most jurisdictions held that the prosecution could obtain a conviction in a rape case based on the uncorroborated testimony of the victim, many courts instructed juries to the effect that "a charge of rape is easily made by a woman and difficult to refute by a man," a statement also attributed to England's Lord Hale. Consequently, when the complainant was the only witness who testified to the act, juries were frequently admonished to "rigidly scrutinize" the victim's testimony. Furthermore, in rape prosecutions it became common for courts to admit evidence of the female complainant's general reputation for sexual immorality and to allow inquiry concerning her prior specific sexual acts. This latter practice probably accounts for the fact that in all too many instances rape became an unreported crime. Indeed, many women came to believe that they were being denied the protection of the law and at the same time were made to feel guilty for having been raped.

Reform in the American Law of Rape

During the late 1970s and the 1980s, protests led to a number of statutory and judicial reforms in the law of rape. Initially, many such protests were by women's groups who complained of traumatic encounters between female victims and police, prosecutors, defense attorneys, and courts. In all too many instances, they contended, a female rape victim was degraded and made to feel ashamed for the assault she suffered. As societal awareness increased, significant changes in the law were accomplished. Before examining a modern criminal code proscribing sexual offenses, you should become aware of the more significant legislative and judicial reforms in this area.

A Gender-Neutral Offense.   The offense of sexual battery has evolved from the crime of rape and is now frequently defined by statute in gender-neutral terms. These new statutes embrace all types of sexual impositions and do not limit the offense to the common-law concept of vaginal rape of a female. Instead, they proscribe anal, oral, or vaginal penetrations by a sex organ or by another object, excepting acts performed for *bona fide* medical purposes. The offender and victim may be of either sex. As we will explain under gender-neutral statutes in a later section, in appropriate circumstances a husband may be charged with rape of his wife.

Classification of Offenders.   The trend of the newer statutes has been to divide the offense of sexual battery into various classifications. Thus, sexual contacts other than intercourse are proscribed. Punishment varies according to the type of sexual conduct or contact, the character and extent of force used, and the age and vulnerability of the victim. Those who commit sexual batteries against the helpless, and those who take advantage of their position of familial or supervisory authority, can be singled out for special punishment. These reforms have achieved more just results in punishing offenders. Furthermore, proper classification of offenses has led to convictions where merited by the evidence.

Rape Shield Laws.   One of the most significant legal reforms concerning rape has been the enactment of "rape shield laws" by a majority of the states. In a prosecution for rape (or sexual battery), these laws preclude presentation of evidence of a victim's prior sexual activity with anyone other than the defendant. Even where the defendant seeks to introduce evidence of prior relations with a victim, some statutes require such evidence to be first presented to the court *in camera* for a determination as to whether the evidence of the defendant's prior relationship with the victim is relevant to the victim's consent.

By 1993 most states had enacted rape shield laws based on the theory that a victim's prior sexual activity does not prove whether the victim has been violated in the instance for which the defendant stands accused. Thus, in *State v. Madsen*, 772 S.W.2d 656 (Mo. 1989), the Missouri Supreme Court held that neither evidence of a victim having a "live-in" boyfriend or having two illegitimate children was relevant in a prosecution for rape. But can a female victim offer testimony of a prior rape to explain her conduct in failing to resist an attacker? In *Raines v. State*, 382 S.E.2d 738 (Ga. App. 1989), the appellate court found this to be appropriate.

In interpreting the applicability of rape shield laws to some unusual factual situations, courts have faced some difficult judgments. In a Massachusetts decision, the court ruled that a defendant charged with rape should have been allowed to question the complainant as to whether she had sexual intercourse with anyone else on the night of the attack. The court concluded that such evidence would not constitute an attack on the complainant's credibility. Rather, the court held that such evidence tended to support the defendant's theory that someone else had attacked the complainant and that she had wrongly accused him. *Commonwealth v. Fitzgerald*, 590 N.E.2d 1151 (Mass. 1992).

A Virginia appellate court ruled that evidence that a victim did not report the alleged rape until a month after the incident, when she learned that she had contracted gonorrhea, was admissible to show ill will of the complainant. The court found that such evidence did not relate to sexual conduct of the victim and was therefore not barred by the Virginia rape shield statute. *Evans v. Commonwealth*, 415 S.E.2d 851 (Va. App. 1992).

The Resistance Requirement. Significant judicial reforms have also occurred. For example, courts no longer insist that a woman must "resist to the utmost" in order to establish that her sexual privacy has been violated. This is consistent with the advice of law enforcement officers who frequently caution women that violent resistance to a rapist's attack may result in the victim's serious injury or death. In considering whether a victim's resistance has been overcome, courts find it appropriate to consider several factors. The extent of the offender's force and violence remains important. So, too, is the psychological and emotional stress of a female victim whose sensibilities are outraged by fear of violation of her bodily integrity. See, for example, *State v. Studham*, 572 P.2d 700 (Utah 1977).

Testimony of Victims. Courts have also come to realize that there is no unique reason to single out the testimony of a sexual battery victim and instruct juries that it deserves more scrutiny than the testimony of other crime victims. See, for example, *Marr v. State*, 494 So.2d 1139 (Fla. 1986). The low conviction rate for persons accused of rape belies the need for special scrutiny for the uncorroborated testimony of a rape victim. In fact, data compiled by the Federal Bureau of Investigation revealed that of the FBI's four violent crimes (murder, forcible rape, robbery, and aggravated assault), rape has the highest rate of acquittal or dismissal. See *People v. Rincon-Pineda*, 538 P.2d 247 (Cal. 1975).

A Modern Statutory Treatment of Sexual Offenses

Michigan has modern, comprehensive laws that classify criminal sexual conduct by various degrees, depending on whether it involves sexual penetration or sexual contact with another person as well as other factors. It defines "sexual penetration" as sexual intercourse, cunnilingus, fellatio, anal intercourse, or any other intrusion, however slight, of any part of a person's body or of any object into the genital or anal openings of another person's body; but emission of seed is not required. "Sexual contact" is defined as including the intentional touching of the victim's intimate parts or the intentional touching of the clothing covering the immediate area of the victim's intimate parts, if that intentional touching can reasonably be construed as being for the purpose of sexual arousal or gratification. Mich. Comp. Laws Ann. § 750.520a(k)(l).

Section 520(b) deals with first-degree criminal sexual conduct and provides:

1. A person is guilty of criminal sexual conduct in the first degree if he or she engages in *sexual penetration* with another person and if any of the following circumstances exists:

(a) That other person is under 13 years of age.

(b) That other person is at least 13 but less than 16 years of age and any of the following:

    (i) The actor is a member of the same household as the victim.

    (ii) The actor is related to the victim by blood or affinity to the fourth degree.

    (iii) The actor is in a position of authority over the victim and used this authority to coerce the victim to submit.

(c) Sexual penetration occurs under circumstances involving the commission of any other felony.

(d) The actor is aided or abetted by 1 or more other persons and either of the following circumstances exists:

    (i) The actor knows or has reason to know that the victim is mentally incapable, mentally incapacitated, or physically helpless.

    (ii) The actor uses force or coercion to accomplish the sexual penetration. Force or coercion includes but is not limited to any of the circumstances listed in subdivision (f)(i) to (v).

(e) The actor is armed with a weapon or any article used or fashioned in a manner to lead the victim to reasonably believe it to be a weapon.

(f) The actor causes personal injury to the victim and force or coercion is used to accomplish sexual penetration. Force or coercion includes but is not limited to any of the following circumstances:

    (i) When the actor overcomes the victim through the actual application of physical force or physical violence.

    (ii) When the actor coerces the victim to submit by threatening to use force or violence on the victim, and the victim believes that the actor has the present ability to execute these threats.

    (iii) When the actor coerces the victim to submit by threatening to retaliate in the future against the victim, or any other person, and the victim believes that the actor has the ability to execute this threat. As used in this subdivision, "to retaliate" includes threats of physical punishment, kidnapping, or extortion.

    (iv) When the actor engages in the medical treatment or examination of the victim in a manner or for purposes which are medically recognized as unethical or unacceptable.

    (v) When the actor, through concealment or by the element of surprise, is able to overcome the victim.

(g) The actor causes personal injury to the victim, and the actor knows or has reason to know that the victim is mentally incapable, mentally incapacitated, or physically helpless.

(h) The other person is mentally incapable, mentally disabled, mentally incapacitated, or physically helpless, and any of the following:

    (i) The actor is related to the victim by blood or affinity to the fourth degree.

    (ii) The actor is in a position of authority over the victim and uses this authority to coerce the victim to submit.

2. Criminal sexual conduct in the first degree is a felony of the first-degree. . . . Mich. Comp. Laws Ann. § 520(b).

Second-degree criminal sexual conduct follows substantially along the lines of the preceding section, but instead of penetration it makes *sexual contact* with a victim's intimate parts unlawful. Violation is a second-degree felony. Mich. Comp. Laws Ann. § 750.520(c).

Third-degree criminal sexual conduct includes two of the same elements as a first-degree offense (i.e., penetration and use of force or coercion), but does not include the element that the defendant was aided and/or abetted in the act by one or more persons. Mich. Comp. Laws Ann. § 750.520(d).

Fourth-degree criminal sexual conduct involves sexual *contact* with another person involving force or coercion, or where the actor knows or has reason to know that the victim is mentally incapable, mentally incapacitated, or physically helpless, or the victim is under jurisdiction of the department of corrections and the actor is associated with that department. It is a serious misdemeanor. Mich. Comp. Laws Ann. § 750(e).

Note that the Michigan law makes no distinction as to the sex of the actor or victim. It broadly defines sexual penetration and sexual contact and divides the offense of criminal sexual conduct into degrees considering the conduct of the actor and the vulnerability of the victim. Thus, it embodies many of the changes that are reforming the law of rape in the United States.

The Trend to Eliminate the Marital Exception

As noted, Lord Hale, the famous English jurist of the seventeenth century, wrote that a husband could not be guilty of the rape of his wife. A wife, he explained, had given herself in marriage to her husband. It was as simple as that. To support this rationale the common-law courts offered such reasons as (1) the wife is a chattel belonging to her husband; (2) a husband and wife are "one" and obviously a husband cannot rape himself; and (3) by marriage the wife irrevocably consents to intercourse with her husband on a continuing basis.

Whatever value this principle had in seventeenth-century England, its justification is no longer viable in contemporary American society. Despite the fact that the rationale for it is outmoded, until recently "Hale's Rule" was universally accepted by American courts.

By the 1980s the so-called marital exception rule began to erode. In 1981, the New Jersey Supreme Court held that the state's rape statute that used language "any person who has carnal knowledge of a woman forcibly against her will" did not except from its operation a husband who was living apart from his wife. *State v. Smith*, 426 A.2d 38 (N.J. 1981). One justice who concurred in the result would have gone even further:

> Whatever may have been common law rule in seventeenth century England in the time of Sir Matthew Hale, it never was the law of this State that there was a marital exemption from the law of rape and that a husband could not be guilty of the rape of his wife. 426 A.2d at 47 (Sullivan, J. concurring).

By the beginning of the 1990s about half of the states had either abrogated or modified the marital exception. Some states created a new offense of "spousal rape" carrying lesser penalties than the traditional rape statutes. See, for example, Ariz. Rev. Stat. § 13–1406.01. Some criticize this approach as tending to minimize spousal rape. In 1990, Louisiana made rape a gender-neutral offense by redefining it as "the act of anal or vaginal sexual intercourse with a male or female person committed without the person's lawful consent." Oklahoma continued to define rape as "an act of sexual intercourse involving vaginal or anal penetration accomplished with a male or female *who is not the spouse of the perpetrator.* Okl. Stat. Ann. Tit. 21, § 1111(b)(4). A few states will allow prosecution of a husband for rape of his wife only if the wife has filed for divorce or other termination of their legal relationship and the couple are living apart.

Pending adoption of gender-neutral sexual battery statutes, some courts are addressing challenges to traditional rape statutes on constitutional grounds. In *People v. Liberta,* 474 N.E.2d 567 (N.Y. 1984), New York's highest court rejected such traditional rationales for the marital exception as implied consent and "wife as property." The court termed the notion of implied consent as "irrational and absurd" and emphasized that a married woman should have the same right to bodily autonomy as a single woman. It dismissed any idea of the wife being property of the husband because the state recognizes that wives and husbands are separate legal entities. In rejecting any distinction between marital and nonmarital rape, appellate courts in other states have relied on constitutional arguments similar to those expounded by the New York court. See, for example, *Shunn v. State,* 742 P.2d 775 (Wyo. 1987).

Reform in this area is not without problems. There is considerable apprehension that any criminalization of sexual acts within a marriage may lead to threats and unfounded charges by unhappy wives. Some argue that prosecution of a husband for rape may make reconciliation of marital differences impossible. Furthermore, they contend proof of guilt will be difficult to obtain because of the usual lack of corroborating evidence of the incident. Be that as it may, marriage in contemporary society is looked upon as a partnership, and neither spouse should be legally permitted to commit a sexual battery or any other offense against the other spouse. In light of prevailing values, a marriage contract should not be deemed a license to enforce sex on demand by a forcible encounter with one's spouse. The solution lies primarily with legislative bodies. At a minimum, statutes should be amended to provide there is no marital exception between husbands and wives who live separate and apart by agreement or judicial decree.

Prosecutorial Burdens

As in all criminal cases, the prosecution must prove the *corpus delicti,* that is, the fact that the crime has been committed. Proof that an act of sexual intercourse has taken place with the victim is usually sufficient in a rape case. Additionally, in a statutory rape case, proof must be offered of the age of the female, and in some instances, age of the male. In sexual battery prosecutions, proof of the defendant's general intent is usually sufficient, absent a statute requiring proof of specific intent.

One of the common problems in sexual battery prosecutions is the lack of independent eyewitness testimony. Consequently, it frequently becomes the victim's word against the defendant's word. Thus, police and prosecutors place paramount importance on a "fresh complaint" by a victim. Preservation of semen, photographs of bruises, torn clothing, and even pubic hairs become valuable evidence to corroborate a victim's testimony. Seldom is the credibility of a complaining witness as vital as in sexual battery prosecutions. To appear in court and testify concerning a sexual assault is a traumatic experience for a victim of sexual assault. This is particularly true for young children. To assist youngsters,

---

CASE IN POINT

DOES ASKING ONE'S ATTACKER TO WEAR A CONDOM CONSTITUTE CONSENT?

In May 1993, in Travis County, Texas, Joel Valdez, a 28-year-old defendant who was charged with rape, claimed that the female with whom he admittedly had sexual intercourse had asked him to wear a condom. Valdez testified that he complied with the woman's request, and that accordingly they were simply "making love." But the 26-year-old complainant explained that she pleaded with her attacker to wear a condom only to protect herself from AIDS. The jury in Austin, Texas found Valdez guilty of rape, implicitly finding that asking the attacker to wear a condom does not constitute consent to sexual intercourse.

---

many courts permit them to illustrate their testimony through the use of anatomically detailed dolls. See *State v. Lee*, 459 N.E.2d 910 (Ohio App. 1983).

Rape Trauma Syndrome

In 1974, the term *rape trauma syndrome* was coined by psychiatrists to describe a recurring pattern of physical and emotional symptoms experienced by rape victims. Since then prosecutors have sought to introduce expert testimony at rape trials to establish that a victim's symptoms are consistent with that of the syndrome. This type of evidence has particular relevance to prosecutions where the defendant claims consent of the victim as a defense. On review of convictions, appellate courts have disagreed on whether such evidence is admissible. The Kansas Supreme Court allowed the introduction of psychiatric testimony that a rape victim suffered from rape trauma syndrome, noting that such expert evidence is relevant where the defendant claims consent. *State v. Marks*, 647 P.2d 1292 (Kan. 1982). The supreme courts in Montana and Arizona have reached a similar conclusion. *State v. Liddell*, 685 P.2d 918 (Mont. 1984); *State v. Huey*, 699 P.2d 1290 (Ariz. 1985). An Ohio appellate court held that such expert psychiatric testimony is admissible where its value outweighs its prejudicial impact. The court noted that expert opinion of this type assists laypersons in interpreting reactions of a victim, especially in child rape cases. *State v. Whitman*, 475 N.E.2d 486 (Ohio App. 1984).

There is respectable judicial authority to the contrary. In 1982, the Minnesota Supreme Court ruled that the rape trauma syndrome is not a fact-finding tool but rather a therapeutic tool and that admission of expert testimony on the subject at a rape trial is erroneous. *State v. Saldana*, 324 N.W.2d 227 (Minn. 1982). Several other appellate courts have held that expert testimony concerning the syndrome is not admissible to prove that a rape in fact occurred. For example, in *People v. Pullins*, 378 N.W.2d 502 (Mich. App. 1985), the court held evidence of rape trauma syndrome inadmissible to establish that a rape in fact occurred. This came the year after the Missouri Supreme Court in *State v. Taylor*, 663 S.W.2d 235

(Mo. 1984), concluded that such testimony was beyond that proper basis of expert opinion. The subject remains controversial and there is much to be written yet.

New York's highest court recently concluded that the scientific community has now generally accepted that rape is a highly traumatic event that triggers the onset of certain identifiable symptoms. The court agreed that expert testimony of the rape trauma syndrome may be admitted to aid the jury's understanding of the victim's behavior after the assault. Nevertheless, the court observed that identifiable symptoms in rape victims do not indicate whether an incident did or did not occur; thus trial judges cannot allow such testimony to be introduced for such purpose. *People v. Taylor,* 552 N.E.2d 131 (N.Y. 1990).

Can a defendant charged with rape introduce expert testimony concerning the rape trauma syndrome to establish that a rape did not occur? In *Henson v. State,* 535 N.E.2d 1189 (Ind. 1989), the defense presented a witness who testified to seeing the victim dancing and drinking at a bar on the evening after the alleged rape. The defense then sought to introduce expert testimony on the subject, but the trial judge would not allow it. The state supreme court ruled that the testimony must be permitted because it would be unfair to allow the prosecution to present expert testimony on rape trauma syndrome but deny a defendant the same opportunity.

Defenses to Charges of Sexual Battery

Beyond a general denial of the charges, the most common defense asserted in a rape case is that the victim consented. For consent to be a defense, it must be voluntarily given before the sexual act. As pointed out previously, the defense of consent is not available where the victim is unconscious, asleep, or mentally deficient.

The defense of consent would not be valid in a case of voluntary sexual battery (i.e., statutory rape), since persons under a certain age are legally incapable of consent. Moreover, it is usually not a defense to a charge of voluntary sexual battery that the defendant believed that the victim was above the prohibited age. Most courts hold this to be true even if the victim's age or appearance was misrepresented by the victim. If the statute under which the defendant is being prosecuted for voluntary sexual battery requires proof of the victim's prior chastity, then proof of the victim's unchastity is a defense.

Impotency (i.e., the inability to engage in sexual intercourse) can be asserted as a defense to a charge of rape. The majority of cases where the defense of impotency is asserted involve charges against young males and men who have reached an advanced age. This defense, however, is seldom successful.

Finally, if the statute under which the defendant is prosecuted requires proof of a specific intent, the defendant may show an inability to form such intent due to voluntary intoxication (see Chapter 13).

SODOMY

Consensual sodomy is not a crime against a person, but in the jurisdictions that retain this offense, it is considered an offense against morality (for further discussion, see Chapter 8). Nonconsensual sodomy, on the other hand, is very definitely a crime against a person, falling under the category of rape or sexual battery.

ABORTION

Abortion has been legally defined as the willful bringing about of the miscarriage of a pregnant woman. It was a common-law misdemeanor for a woman who was "quick" with child to have an abortion. The stage of being quick referred to the point during a woman's pregnancy when the fetus stirred in the womb.

Most American jurisdictions adopted statutes along the lines of the common law in proscribing abortion. There was a tendency, however, to spell out that an abortion was justified if physicians found it essential to save the mother's life. More liberal statutes allowed abortions to be performed when one or two physicians advised it was necessary to prevent serious injury to the mother. By 1970 a few states had even repealed criminal penalties for abortions where they were performed under medical supervision in the very early stages of a woman's pregnancy.

The 1960s and 1970s, a period of liberalized views on sexual practices, witnessed a clamor for liberalization of abortion laws. But before significant reforms occurred in the States, the U.S. Supreme Court entertained a challenge to the constitutionality of a Texas law that permitted abortion only on medical advice that it was necessary to save the mother's life. In a landmark 7–2 decision in 1973, the Court in *Roe v. Wade,* 410 U.S. 113, 93 S. Ct. 705, 35 L.Ed.2d 147 (1973), held that a fetus was not a "person" within the meaning of the Fourteenth Amendment to the United States Constitution. Therefore, the fetus was not entitled to the constitutional protection of the law granted persons. The Court then extended its views on privacy by holding that a woman's personal right of privacy was involved in the decision whether to abort a fetus. The Court's decision had the effect of invalidating most state laws proscribing or regulating abortions. A decision whether to abort during the first trimester of a pregnancy, the Court said, was a matter between the woman and her physician without state regulation. After the first trimester, procedures for abortion could be regulated when "necessarily related to maternal health." In the final trimester, when the fetus has become "viable," the state may prohibit abortion except "when it is necessary, in appropriate medical judgment, to preserve the life or health of the mother."

The controversial issue of abortion has philosophical, religious, ethical, medical, and political dimensions. As part of the national debate, Congress in the early 1980s considered but rejected a constitutional amendment to restrict abortions. A more conservative Supreme Court has modified *Roe* to allow states greater leeway in regulating abortions in such areas as waiting periods and required counseling. In the wake of one of these decisions, *Planned Parenthood v. Casey,* 505 U.S. ____ , 112 S.Ct. 2791, 120 L.Ed.2d 674 (1992), supporters of abortion rights clamored for Congress to adopt a statute that would codify the holding in *Roe v. Wade.* Upon assuming office, President Clinton issued an executive order eliminating a number of restrictions on abortion counseling in federally funded clinics that had been imposed by the prior administration.

CHILD ABUSE

During the 1980s complaints of child abuse increased dramatically. Many cases involve commission of assault, battery (or aggravated categories thereof), or some category of sexual assault or sexual battery. Nevertheless, with the rise of neglect, abuse, and violence against children, many states have enacted specific child abuse laws to cover a broader range of abusive behavior.

McKinney's New York Penal Law § 260.10(1) provides:

> A person is guilty of endangering the welfare of a child when: He knowingly acts in a manner likely to be injurious to the physical, mental or moral welfare of a child less than seventeen years old or directs or authorizes such child to engage in an occupation involving a substantial risk of danger to his life or health.

Statutes now commonly require medical professionals and social workers to report instances of suspected child abuse to the enforcement authorities. When such cases of child abuse reach the courts, they often involve legal issues as to whether parents, social workers, and others who discuss these matters with an abused child are to be permitted to testify in court concerning communications with the child. Moreover, expert testimony of physicians, psychologists, and social workers is often relied upon to explain a child's sometimes curious behavior that may grow out of certain types of abuse.

The widespread drug problem has led to prosecutions of women for child abuse where during pregnancy the mothers-to-be ingested cocaine and demonstrable medical effects were present in their children at birth. Courts have generally declined to hold that such action constitutes child abuse. See e.g., *State v. Gethers*, 585 So.2d 1140 (Fla. App. 1991); *State v. Gray*, 584 N.E. 2d 710 (Ohio 1992).

SPOUSE ABUSE; ABUSE OF THE ELDERLY

Legislatures and courts have also been giving increased attention to the problem of spouse abuse and abuse of the elderly. Many of these abuses constitute criminal violations of traditional statutes previously discussed; however, laws have been enacted in many states to provide for issuance of court injunctions to protect spouses from domestic violence and provide for arrest of those who violate these orders. In other instances legislatures have provided for enhanced penalties for those who commit crimes of violence against elderly persons.

FALSE IMPRISONMENT AND KIDNAPPING

In recognition of the need to protect an individual's freedom of movement, the common law developed two misdemeanor offenses: false imprisonment and kidnapping. False imprisonment consisted of confining someone against the person's will, while kidnapping involved forcibly abducting and taking a person to another country. See *Smith v. State*, 23 N.W. 879 (Wis. 1885).

The Statutory Offense of False Imprisonment

Not all states have adopted statutes making false imprisonment an offense. Those that have generally classify it as a misdemeanor and define it much as did the common law. Typically, the Texas statute states: "A person commits an offense if he intentionally and knowingly restrains another person." Vernon's Tex. Penal Code Ann. § 20.02(a). Texas law declares the offense to be a misdemeanor but provides that if the offender recklessly exposes the victim to a substantial risk of serious bodily injury it becomes a felony. Vernon's Tex. Penal Code Ann. § 20.02(c). Usually, a prosecution for false imprisonment only requires proof of a defendant's general intent, although this depends on the particular statute.

Some Common Scenarios of False Imprisonment.   Four hypothetical situations illustrate the crime of false imprisonment:

- A police officer takes a person into custody under an unlawful arrest.
- A prison warden fails to release a prisoner who has served his or her term.
- A storekeeper detains a customer when the storekeeper has a hunch the customer has shoplifted but has no reasonable basis for such suspicion.
- An overzealous male suitor refuses to allow his female companion to leave his apartment without yielding to his sexual demands.

False Imprisonment Not a Commonly Charged Offense.   In recent years false imprisonment has not been a commonly charged offense. Three reasons chiefly account for this:

- Serious charges involving restraint of a person frequently reveal elements constituting the statutory offense of kidnapping.
- Persons claiming to have been falsely imprisoned often seek to recover damages in a civil suit, rather than press criminal charges.
- Upon close investigation many restraints undoubtedly are determined to have been imposed based on authority, or at least a reasonable belief that there was authority to have restrained the complaining party.

Modern Statutory Treatment of Kidnapping

Unlike false imprisonment, the crime of kidnapping is a serious felony universally proscribed by state and federal jurisdictions. It plays a far greater role in our society than it did at common law.

Under modern legislation it is not necessary, as it was at common law, that the victim of kidnapping be taken to another country. The elements of the crime are necessarily dependent on the precise wording of the statute in a particular jurisdiction, but in general, to constitute kidnapping there must be an unlawful taking and forcible carrying away (sometimes called "asportation") of a victim without that person's consent. Intimidation and coercion can substitute for the required force, and even where consent has been given, it must have been voluntarily given by a person who has the capacity to consent. Therefore, young children and incompetent persons cannot legally consent to an act of asportation.

Some states classify kidnapping as either simple kidnapping or kidnapping for ransom. Others classify the offense by degrees. In New York, kidnapping in the second degree is a felony that merely involves the abduction of another person. McKinney's N.Y. Penal Code § 135.20. Kidnapping in the first degree is a more serious felony, and the statute proscribing it states:

A person is guilty of kidnapping in the first degree when he abducts another person and when:

1. His intent is to compel a third person to pay or deliver money or property as ransom, or to engage in other particular conduct, or to refrain from engaging in particular conduct; or

2. He restrains the person abducted for a period of more than twelve hours with intent to:

   (a) Inflict physical injury upon him or violate or abuse him sexually; or
   (b) Accomplish or advance the commission of a felony; or
   (c) Terrorize him or a third person; or
   (d) Interfere with the performance of a governmental or political function; or

3. The person abducted dies during the abduction or before he is able to return or to be returned to safety. McKinney's N.Y. Penal Code § 135.25.

The Requirement of "Asportation" in Kidnapping.   The asportation or movement of the victim distinguishes the crime of kidnapping from the offense of false imprisonment. One of the more commonly litigated issues in kidnapping prosecutions concerns the extent of movement of the victim required to meet this element of the crime. In recent years courts have tended to limit the scope of kidnapping statutes by deciding that the required movement of a victim must be something more than that inherent in or incidental to the commission of another felony. The proliferation of court decisions on this subject may be the result of the tendency of prosecutors to levy multiple charges against a criminal defendant for conduct arising out of a single criminal episode.

When is the offender's movement of a victim in conjunction with an independent offense such as assault, rape, or robbery sufficient to constitute an independent offense of kidnapping? If the movement is merely incidental to a crime and does not involve an additional significant risk to the victim, courts generally will not sustain a conviction for kidnapping in addition to the other offense. Recent appellate court decisions are instructive. In 1978, the New Hampshire Supreme Court held that a defendant was properly convicted as an accomplice of a defendant who forced a woman into a car and drove her to an apartment where the principal defendant assaulted her. *State v. Goodwin*, 395 A.2d 1234 (N.H. 1978). In the same vein, two years later, the North Carolina Supreme Court sustained a kidnapping conviction where a handyman forced a woman off the street and into her home for purposes of sexually assaulting her. *State v. Adams*, 264 S.E.2d 46 (N.C. 1980).

Two 1983 appellate court decisions addressed the problem, expounding a somewhat different approach. The Florida Supreme Court held that the statutory requirement of "confining, abducting, or imprisoning another person . . . with intent to commit or facilitate commission of any felony" does not include movement

---

CASE IN POINT

RAPE AND KIDNAPPING:
REQUIRED RESISTANCE IN FACE OF THREATS

Late one night after leaving work, a woman responded to a request by two men to assist them in getting their car off the road. When she began to leave both men grabbed her, ordered her into the back seat of the car, and threatened to kill her unless she cooperated. The men told her that they had escaped from prison and were holding her as a hostage. They then drove their victim to a tent, disrobed her, and forced her to submit to sexual acts with each of them. When they drove her back to her car the next morning, they told her that they would kill her if she reported the incident to the police.

The defendants were convicted of rape, kidnapping, and several other offenses. On appeal, they argued that the victim had cooperated in their endeavors, hence they were not guilty of either rape or kidnapping. The Indiana Supreme Court rejected their contentions and explained that the resistance necessary to protect against sexual attack is dependent on all circumstances. Further, the court noted that a victim need not physically resist after being confronted with threats and being in fear of injury.

Ballard v. State, 385 N.E.2d 1126 (Ind. 1979).

---

or confinement that is inconsequential or inherent in the nature of the felony. *Faison v. State*, 426 So.2d 963 (Fla. 1983). In applying this rationale a California appellate court held that moving a robber's victim across a room or from one room to another was an insufficient movement to meet the requirement for kidnapping. *People v. John*, 197 Cal. Rptr.340 (Cal. App. 1983).

Federal Kidnapping Laws. Perhaps the most notorious kidnapping to have occurred in the United States was the abduction of the infant son of Charles A. Lindbergh, the "Lone Eagle" who, in 1927, made the first nonstop solo flight across the Atlantic Ocean. The Lindbergh baby was abducted from the family home in New Jersey in 1932. Bruno Richard Hauptman was convicted of the crime after a spectacular trial and was executed in 1936. The Lindbergh kidnapping led to a demand for federal laws to enable the Federal Bureau of Investigation to become involved in the apprehension of kidnappers. This, in turn, led to sweeping changes in state and federal laws on kidnapping. The Federal Kidnapping Act, commonly called the Lindbergh Law, provides:

> Whoever unlawfully seizes, confines, inveigles, decoys, kidnaps, abducts, or carries away and holds for ransom or reward or otherwise any person, except in the case of a minor by a parent thereof . . . shall be punished by imprisonment. . . . 18 U.S.C.A. § 1201(a).

Subsection (b) of the statute raises a presumption that if the kidnapped victim is not returned within twenty-four hours after the taking, then the defendant did, in fact, take the victim across state lines. This presumption effectively allows the federal government to bring federal agents into the investigation of an alleged kidnapping promptly.

A recent federal statute makes hostage taking an offense, 18 U.S.C.A. § 1203, while other federal statutes make it a crime to knowingly receive, possess, or dispose of any money or property that has been delivered as ransom for a victim of a kidnapping, 18 U.S.C.A. § 1202, or for a bank robber to avoid apprehension by forcing someone to accompany him. 18 U.S.C.A. § 2113(e).

Defenses to Charges of False Imprisonment and Kidnapping

It is not false imprisonment for a person to detain another under authority of the law. Thus, an officer, or even a private citizen, who makes a lawful arrest or a jailer who detains a prisoner lawfully committed to custody are not guilty of an offense. Likewise, a parent who reasonably disciplines a child or a teacher who reasonably restrains a pupil would not be guilty of false imprisonment.

Consent, also, can be a defense to false imprisonment or kidnapping. Of course, the consent must not have been induced by threat, coercion, or misrepresentation and must have been given by a person competent to give consent. A person who relies on consent as a defense has the burden of establishing the validity of such consent.

The Problem of Child-Snatching

In recent years marital disputes have given rise to many serious problems concerning the custody of children of divorced or separated parents. The term *child-snatching* is now commonly applied to situations in which one parent deliberately retains or conceals a child from the other parent. The problem has resulted partly from the ability of one parent to seize a child from the custodial parent, travel to another state, and petition the court in the latter state for custody of the child. This activity is now being curbed by several approaches:

- In many states trial judges include a provision in a divorce judgment requiring court approval to remove a child from the state where the divorce is granted. Violation may subject the offending party to being held in contempt of court, or in some states, to be prosecuted for a felony.
- The Uniform Child Custody Jurisdiction Act (UCCJA), proposed in 1968 and now in force in all fifty states, generally continues jurisdiction for custody in the home or resident state of the child. Cooperation between the courts in the different states is becoming increasingly effective in preventing "judge shopping."
- The majority of states have made child-snatching a felony, thereby subjecting violators to extradition for prosecution in the state where the offense occurs.
- The Parental Kidnapping Prevention Act (PKPA), 28 U.S.C.A. § 1738A, enacted by Congress in 1980 addresses the problem of interstate child abduction.
- Federal and state governments, as well as religious and civic organizations and the media, have initiated programs for identifying children and for collecting and disseminating information on missing children.

CONCLUSION

Crimes against persons usually result in either death or injury to the victim. Victims of violent personal crimes who survive often suffer emotional and psychological damage, as well as physical injury. Additionally, offenses resulting in death or injury frequently have long-lasting social and economic effects on the victim. Consider the economic plight of a family in which a working parent is disabled by a penniless assailant; or the strains imposed on a marital union in which the young bride was sexually assaulted or kidnapped and ravished as a teenager.

Over the centuries the assaultive, homicidal, sexual, and detention crimes have been a stable base for prosecuting those whose antisocial conduct offended the basic norms of civilized people. Yet, society changes and laws must change to cope with the needs of a dynamic society.

Many searching questions must be examined in respect to offenses against persons. For example: Is it justifiable to find a thief guilty of murder simply because a co-felon kills a victim during commission of the theft? Should the marital exception in the law of rape be eliminated to make it possible to charge a husband with raping his wife? If so, must the courts employ different standards of determining the elements of consent and force? Are there other biases against female victims of sexual assault that must be addressed? By whom: legislatures or the courts? Is there any solution to end the divisive struggle over legalized abortion? Is the defendant who moves a victim during commission of a felony likely to be pressured into pleading guilty to a charge to avoid a threatened prosecution for kidnapping the victim?

Indeed, offenses against persons are the crimes from which people probably suffer the most direct consequences. Understandably, the prosecution of serious offenders attracts more public interest than other actions in the criminal justice system.

As you study succeeding chapters discussing the procedural aspects of the criminal law, consider not only the rights of the defendant, but also the rights of society and the rights of the victims of crimes.

QUESTIONS FOR THOUGHT AND DISCUSSION

1. What are the essential differences between the offenses of assault and battery under modern statutes?

2. Shortly before midnight, a man is driving through a residential area in an attempt to get his wife, who is in labor, to the hospital. The posted speed limit is 30 MPH, but the anxious husband is driving 50 MPH. In a dark area, the car strikes and kills a ten-year-old boy who is playing in the middle of the street. Can the driver be convicted of (a) manslaughter or (b) vehicular homicide?

3. Is it legitimate for a jury to find a defendant guilty of manslaughter in a case where there is evidence of premeditation, simply because members of the jury feel that the defendant was somewhat justified in taking the life of the victim?

4. How can the prosecution establish the *corpus delicti* in a murder case when the body of the victim cannot be found?

5. Given the scope of the constitutional right of privacy discussed in Chapter 3, how can a state make it a crime for a person to attempt suicide or to aid another in such an attempt?

6. Why has the common-law doctrine of felony murder become controversial among courts and legal scholars in recent years?

7. Can a state make it a crime to kill a viable fetus, notwithstanding the Supreme Court's decision in *Roe v. Wade?*

8. A male who has been diagnosed with acquired immune deficiency syndrome (AIDS) engages in sexual intercourse with a female. He does not inform the female that he has AIDS. As a result, the female contracts AIDS and dies from the disease some two years later. Under the laws of your state, could the male be convicted of a homicidal act?

9. What interests does the law seek to protect in proscribing (a) forcible rape; (b) statutory rape?

10. Which statutory and judicial reforms of the 1970s and 1980s in the law of rape were the most significant from the standpoint of a female victim? Why?

11. Is there any justification for courts to continue following "Hale's Rule" that creates a "marital exception" in the law of rape?

12. A store manager observes Lucy Grabit stuffing a pair of nylon hose into her purse before going through the check-out counter in a supermarket. The manager detains her and promptly directs his employee to call the police. Is the store manager guilty of false imprisonment? Why?

13. Several college freshmen enter the dean's private office and remain there for several hours. They refuse to let the dean leave until he yields to their demands to allow unrestricted visitation in all dormitories. Under contemporary criminal statutes what offense, if any, have the students committed? Explain.

14. Defendant was convicted of battery under a statute that provides: "A person commits a battery when he either intentionally or knowingly, and without legal justification, makes physical contact of an insulting or provoking nature with an individual." The evidence disclosed that one morning the male defendant picked up a female friend whom he had invited to have breakfast with him. En route to the restaurant he unbuttoned her blouse, placed his hand on her breast, and after she removed his hand and asked him to stop, he again placed his hand on her breast. On appeal, the defendant argues that his conviction should be reversed because his acts were not insulting, there was no struggle, and the female did not testify that she was traumatized or disturbed by his acts. Moreover, he points out that the evidence disclosed that after the incident the female complainant remained with him and accompanied him to a restaurant where they had breakfast together. Should the appellate court reverse this conviction on the ground that the evidence is insufficient? Why or Why not?

15. Defendant and her husband have two sons, ages 5 and 3. Without notifying her husband, she left the family home with both children at a time when no court proceedings were pending concerning either their marriage or custody of their children. Two weeks later, and without the wife's knowledge, the husband

obtained a court order granting him custody of the two children. An arrest warrant was eventually issued for the wife and she was arrested in another state and brought back to her home state, where she now faces prosecution under a statute that provides: "Whoever, being a relative of a child . . . without lawful authority, holds or intends to hold such a child permanently or for a protracted period, or takes or entices a child from his lawful custodian . . . shall be guilty of a felony." The wife's attorney stipulates that the facts are correct as stated, but contends the wife cannot be convicted of parental kidnapping under the quoted statute. What result do you think should occur? Why?

16. A nineteen-year-old woman returns home from an evening at the beach. She tells her mother that she has been raped and sodomized by an attacker she doesn't know. Some hours later, the woman identifies her attacker to her mother, and they notify the police. At trial the prosecution seeks to admit testimony of the rape trauma syndrome to explain the victim's reticence in promptly identifying her attacker. The defense objects. Should the court allow expert testimony on this subject to explain the reactions of the female victim in the hours following her attack and to explain why she may initially have been unwilling to report the defendant who attacked her? Why or why not?

C A S E S

STATE V. TOWERS
Supreme Court of Maine, 1973.
304 A.2d 75.

[This case involves the offense of aggravated assault and battery.]

WERNICK, Justice.

Defendant has appealed from a judgment of the Superior Court (Penobscot County) embodying his conviction, on October 15, 1971, of the offense of assault and battery, high and aggravated in degree. . . .

Evidence produced at the trial, jury-waived, warranted the following factual conclusions.

Defendant had visited a friend's house to return a car bed. The complaining witness, a thirteen year old girl, was in the house "babysitting" for a child two years of age and an infant of six months. She had known defendant as a neighbor for approximately half a year, and in all of her prior contacts with him he had always acted toward her as a gentleman. Defendant and the complaining witness engaged in conversation for about fifteen minutes. Then, while complainant was holding the six months old infant, who was crying, under her right arm, defendant took hold of her and kissed her on the cheek and lips. She immediately asked him "to leave me alone," but defendant continued to hold her and proceeded to touch her breasts and place one of his hands between her legs in contact with her "private part" from outside her clothing. The complainant told defendant to "stop," whereupon defendant did stop and with the remark to complainant: "Don't tell anybody," he left the house. The complainant did not mention the incident until the following morning, almost twenty-four hours later, when she told her mother. The complainant waited because when she had returned home, she found that "everybody was around."

Defendant's single contention on appeal is that, within the legal meaning of "high and aggravated,"

the finding of an aggravated degree of assault and battery may not here stand as a matter of law. Defendant points to the fleeting nature of the incident insofar as he ceased his actions upon the second request by complainant. He further mentions that there were no physical injuries inflicted and maintains that the psychological impact upon the girl must have been minimal since she waited almost twenty-four hours before she reported what had transpired.

In *State v. Bey*, 161 Me. 23, 206 A. 2d 413 (1965) this Court observed that assault and battery may become "high and aggravated in nature" by the presence of "circumstances of aggravation, such as . . . great disparity between the ages and physical conditions of the parties, a difference in the sexes, indecent liberties or familiarities with a female, the purposeful infliction of shame and disgrace, . . ." . . .

State v. Rand, 156 Me. 81, 161 A. 2d 852 (1960) involved a factual situation so remarkably similar to the instant case that, for purposes of the appropriate application of controlling legal principles, the cases must be held indistinguishable. Sustaining a conviction of assault and battery, high and aggravated in nature, we said in *Rand*: "What intention could the respondent have had other than an evil intention to indulge his own lustful desires? By his indecent acts he violated the person and dignity of the child in a manner abhorrent to society." . . .

Under the combined import of *State v. Bey* and *State v. Rand* the present adjudication that defendant had committed an assault and battery, high and aggravated in degree was legally warranted.

The entry is:

Appeal denied.

FURR V. STATE
Supreme Court of Arkansas, 1992.
308 Ark. 41, 822 S.W.2d 380.

[In this case the Arkansas Supreme Court considers the sufficiency of evidence to sustain a conviction for first-degree murder.]

NEWBERN, Justice.

The appellant, Jesse Robert Furr, was convicted of murder in the first degree and sentenced to life imprisonment in connection with the shooting death of his stepmother, Ruth Furr. He argues the Trial Court erred by refusing to direct a verdict in his favor because there was insufficient evidence that he possessed the necessary purposeful mental state. We affirm the conviction.

Furr lived with his father and stepmother near Huntsville. On the day the killing occurred, Furr got off work at 12:30 P.M., went home, and began drinking beer. His father and stepmother, and others present, were also drinking. Eventually, everyone except Furr and his stepmother left the house.

According to Furr's testimony, the two began discussing the family's financial problems, and he told his stepmother, "Well, if you ain't got no money, why don't you get rid of some of these guns?" He picked up a .22 caliber pistol, cocked it, and began pointing it around the room. Furr testified his finger accidentally hit the trigger, the gun went off, and the bullet struck his stepmother who was standing some five feet away from him at the kitchen sink.

Furr testified that after the shooting he saw that his stepmother was not breathing and he panicked. He took some money, two pistols, and his stepmother's truck and left for Midland, Texas, where his mother lived. He testified he was afraid to call the police because he was on parole for a burglary committed in Texas and knew he could not possess any weapons.

Furr was apprehended in Texas and brought back to Arkansas. After being advised of his rights, Furr admitted his responsibility for the shooting but stated it was an accident. The sheriff testified Furr told him he had been drinking the day of the shooting and had a "buzz." He further told the officer "[I] was acting crazy with a .22 caliber revolver, pointing it around," and "I pointed it at her

and touched the trigger and it went off." Furr first told the sheriff he was standing across the room from his stepmother when the gun went off, but later said, "I could have been closer than I previously said."

Chief medical examiner, Dr. Fanny Malak, testified the victim was shot once behind the left ear, and the bullet traveled down towards the right ear and entered the brain. A large amount of gunpowder residue was found inside and outside the wound. An autopsy revealed multiple fractures of the skull. According to Dr. Malak, gases had entered and expanded inside the brain leading to increased pressure there. The pressure caused a crack in the roof of the victim's left eye, and the eye was visibly swollen and discolored as a result. Based on the gunpowder residue inside the wound and the multiple fractures of the skull, Dr. Malak inferred that the gun had touched the victim's scalp when fired.

The jury was instructed on premeditated and deliberated capital murder and the lesser included offenses of murder in the first degree, murder in the second degree, and manslaughter.

Murder in the first degree is purposely causing the death of another person. Ark. Code Ann. § 5–10–102(a)(2) (Supp. 1001). "A person acts purposely with respect to his conduct or a result thereof when it is his conscious object to engage in conduct of that nature or to cause such a result." Ark. Code. Ann. § 5–2–202(1) (1987).

On appeal from denial of a directed verdict, this Court reviews the evidence in the light most favorable to the appellee, in this case the State, and affirms if there is any substantial evidence to support the conviction. . . . Evidence is substantial if it is of sufficient force and character to compel reasonable minds to reach a conclusion, passing beyond suspicion and conjecture. . . .

Intent is seldom capable of proof by direct evidence and must usually be inferred from the circumstances surrounding the killing. . . . The intent necessary for first degree murder may be inferred from the type of weapon used, the manner of its use, and the nature, extent, and location of the wounds. . . .

The evidence with respect to Furr's purposeful mental state at the time of the crime, viewed in the light most favorable to the State, was substantial. From Dr. Malak's expert testimony that the gun used in the shooting was fired at close, or point blank, range the inference could easily be drawn that it was the purpose of the person firing to kill the victim. One is presumed to intend the natural and probable consequences of one's act. . . . The jury was free to determine the weight to be given the expert testimony, and they could reject or accept all or any part of it they believed to be true. . . .

The State also presented evidence that Furr stole some money, a truck, and two guns from his stepmother after the shooting and then fled the scene.

Furr testified he had no intent to return the money or the guns. A jury could reasonably conclude from this evidence that Furr purposely killed his stepmother for financial reasons.

Furr claimed his finger accidentally hit the trigger, and the gun went off, but the trier of fact is not required to believe the testimony of any witness. This is especially true when the witness is the accused. . . .

We find the evidence supporting the conviction to have been substantial. The record of trial has been examined for error in accordance with our Rule 11(f), and we have found no errors prejudicial to Furr.

Affirmed.

MANUEL V. STATE
District Court of Appeal of Florida, Second District, 1977.
344 So.2d 1317.

[This case deals with second-degree murder.]

OTT, Judge.

Appellant was convicted of second-degree murder. We reverse and remand for the imposition of a sentence of manslaughter for reasons hereinafter stated.

On the night of March 26, 1976, Robert Jackson, 10, was playing with Wendell Elliott, 13, in the vicinity of Janie Mae Hayes' house. The house fronted on Ohio Street in Lake Wales. The boys were playing "chase"—a game which rewards silence and stealth. They were playing so quietly and the night was so dark that a woman sitting on a nearby porch was unaware of their presence.

Earlier that night, Louise Manuel, wife of the appellant, had come to Ms. Hayes' house and accused a lodger, Ella Mae Kindrick, of having an affair with her husband. An argument ensued, after which Mrs. Manuel left the area.

The appellant was in a bar when he heard that his wife had been involved in a tiff. He obtained his .32 caliber pistol and began walking down Ohio Street toward the Hayes house. Upon reaching the area in front of the Dunlap house—two doors from the Hayes house—Manuel stopped walking when he saw Ella Mae Kindrick on the Dunlap front porch. He said to her, "Who's doing this to my wife?" . . . "Who's that messing with my wife?" He then fired a single shot into the ground.

After firing the first shot, Manuel proceeded to a lightpost (the light was broken) in front of the house between the Dunlap and Hayes houses. At this point, Wendell Elliott, having heard the shot, ran from the rear of the Hayes house to a point about three feet from Manuel. Once there, Wendell called for Robert, but received no answer. The record contains no indication that Wendell attempted to warn Manuel that Robert was in the area.

About three minutes after firing the first shot, Manuel fired another shot. According to Ms. Kindrick, from her vantage point on the Dunlap porch she could not tell exactly in which direction Manuel had pointed the pistol when he fired the second shot. On direct examination, Wendell Elliott testified that he could not tell at what, if anything, Manuel was aiming. On cross-examination, however, Wendell testified that the gun was pointed in the general direction of an area on the far side of Ms. Hayes' front yard where a trash barrel and other garbage containers were located. Nothing in his testimony indicated he could actually see the trash barrel and other garbage containers. Nothing in his testimony indicated he knew where Robert Jackson was at the time the second shot was fired.

The deputy sheriff who took Manuel into custody testified that Manuel asked about Jackson's condition and stated that he had not intended to hit the boy and was sorry about it. According to this deputy, Manuel did not indicate whether or not he knew the boy was in the area, but did say that "he knew he hit the boy when he shot" and that "the boy got in the way."

The testimony was uncontradicted that Ohio Street was very badly lit, especially in the area where the boys were playing. A police photographer who arrived soon after the shooting testified that one could not see where to walk without a flashlight.

The record is somewhat sparse with regard to Manuel's mental state. The deputy who took Manuel into custody testified that Manuel stated that "he had got his pistol to try to protect his wife, stop the fight, keep anybody from hurting her."

The statute governing murder in the second degree, Section 782.04(2), Florida Statutes, provides in relevant part:

> The unlawful killing of a human being, when perpetrated by any act imminently dangerous to another and evincing a depraved mind regardless of human life, although without any premeditated design to effect the death of any particular individual, shall be murder in the second degree.

The Florida Standard Jury Instruction for murder in the second degree provides as follows:

> An act is one imminently dangerous to another and evincing a depraved mind regardless of human life if it is an act (or a series of acts) which
>
> 1. a person of ordinary judgment would know is reasonably certain to kill or do serious bodily injury to another;
> 2. is done from ill will, hatred, spite or an evil intent, and

> 3. is of such a nature that the act itself indicates an indifference to human life.

Number 2 above amounts to what is frequently termed malice. The depravity of mind required in second degree murder has been equated with malice in the commonly understood sense of ill will, hatred, spite or evil intent. . . .

Within the category of second degree murder there exist varying gradations of cases. The reason for this is that some acts are simply more depraved than others. For example, in *Weaver v. State*, 220 So.2d 53 (Fla. 2d DCA 1969), the court found the evidence to overwhelmingly support a finding of malice. In *Weaver*, the victim was a police officer. He was responding to the scene of a domestic dispute at the Weaver household. When Weaver resisted the officer's illegal attempt to enter his home, the officer maced Weaver. Weaver then disarmed the police officer, pursued him, ignored the officer's pleas for mercy, expended all the bullets in his gun in shooting the officer in the back and made an immediate res gestae exclamation acknowledging the killing. The court found these facts furnished more than a sufficient basis for a finding of the requisite depravity of mind. . . .

Another "strong" case is that of *Grissom v. State*, 237 So.2d 57 (Fla. 3d DCA 1970). In *Grissom*, the defendant, a junior high school student, was disciplined by a teacher for a rule violation. Upon being disciplined, the defendant threatened to return and kill the teacher. A short time later he did return armed with a handgun and fired two shots at the teacher, wounding but not killing him. While fleeing the building after shooting the teacher, he fired one shot up a stairway in the school building. That shot struck and killed a student standing on the stairs.

Second degree murder convictions were also upheld in cases involving the pointing of a weapon at a vital area of the body before the weapon discharged. In *Edwards v. State*, 302 So.2d 479 (Fla. 3d DCA 1974), the court found that the act of the defendant in pointing his gun at the victim's head, waiting until the victim had taken three steps backward, and then firing the gun, to be both depraved and imminently dangerous. See *State v. Bryan*, 287 So.2d 73 (Fla. 1973).

In *Hines v. State*, 227 So.2d 334 (Fla. 1st DCA 1969), the defendant had pointed a shotgun at the head of the deceased. The defendant stated that he "had a gun" and that she (the deceased) "should go out . . . and act like a squirrel and if he killed her . . . it wouldn't be no accident." The gun discharged striking the deceased in the face and killing her. The court found that even if it accepted the defendant's contention that the gun had fired upon closing the breach that such an act committed while a gun is purposely pointed at the head of another from a very short distance certainly implied malice.

The instant case contrasts with the "pointed gun" cases in that Manuel pointed his gun in a direction (toward the garbage area) where one would think a shot could not result in harm to any person. In addition, the lack of any substantial evidence of malevolence directed toward any person strongly suggests to this court that Manuel's conduct, while certainly culpable and inexcusable, falls far short of malice.

The statute governing manslaughter, Section 782.07, Florida Statutes, provides in relevant part:

The killing of a human being by the . . . culpable negligence of another, without lawful justification . . . shall be deemed manslaughter.

The Florida Standard Jury Instruction for manslaughter defines culpable negligence as follows:

Culpable negligence is negligence of a gross and flagrant nature and consists of more than a mere failure to use ordinary care. Culpable negligence is consciously doing an act or following a course of conduct which any reasonable person would know would likely result in death or great bodily injury to some other person, even though done without the intent to injure any person but with utter disregard for the safety of another.

In *Savage v. State*, 152 Fla. 367, 11 So.2d 778, 779 (1943), the court defined culpable negligence as that conduct which showed a

. . . gross and flagrant character, evincing reckless disregard of human life or of the safety of persons exposed to its dangerous effects; or that entire want of care which would raise the presumption of indifference to consequences; or such wantonness or recklessness or grossly careless disregard of the safety and welfare of the public, or that

reckless indifference to the rights of others, which is equivalent to an intentional violation of them.

In the manslaughter area, one distinct line of cases involves accidental shootings in which manslaughter convictions were not upheld. As with the second degree murder cases, these "accident" cases are not all alike; some illustrate more serious and reprehensible conduct than do others. . . . [A] . . . "totally accidental" case was that of *Walsingham v. State*, 272 So. 2d 215 (Fla. 2d DCA 1973). There, the defendant was holding a rifle on his lap in his bedroom while examining it. The rifle accidentally discharged. The bullet passed through a door and a wall and eventually struck one of defendant's children, killing him. . . .

Two other "accident" cases, a bit stronger on the facts, were *Parker v. State*, 318 So.2d 502 (Fla. 1st DCA 1975), and *Sharp v. State*, 120 So.2d 206 (Fla. 2d DCA 1960). In *Parker*, the defendant was "fooling around" by waving his pistol around in the cab of a moving truck. At one point, he waved the pistol past the decedent's head when it went off. The fact that the defendant had the hammer positioned in the safety notch and believed the gun would not fire was considered an important factor.

In *Sharp*, the defendant intentionally pointed a loaded shotgun in the direction of a crowd for the purpose of restoring order. He then stumbled and the gun fired accidently, killing a man. An important factor in the defendant's not being convicted was his bad leg which apparently precipitated the stumbling and resultant firing of the gun.

One step beyond the "accident" cases are those in which the actual shooting was certainly accidental, but the act fits within the culpable negligence standard. In *Williams v. State*, 336 So. 2d 1261 (Fla. 1st DCA 1976), a conviction for manslaughter was upheld. In that case there had been a bar fracas in which the appellant had been involved. During a lull in the fighting a vehicle in which the victim was riding arrived at the bar. When the driver of the vehicle pulled a shotgun out of his trunk the appellant—observing this—took his shotgun out of his truck and held it pointed toward the ground. As he shifted his grasp the shotgun discharged.

In *McBride v. State*, 191 So.2d 70 (Fla. 1st DCA 1966), a conviction for manslaughter was also upheld. The court found that the defendant "needlessly [had] on his person a deadly weapon which he brandished ... in a careless and reckless manner." The court stated that the defendant "set the stage for the tragedy which ultimately followed (an accidental shooting) even though he may have had [no] intention of killing the decedent." ...

It is submitted that the facts in the instant case, although clearly indicating more culpable conduct than the facts of the non-manslaughter "accident" cases, supra, are not sufficient to warrant a conviction for second degree murder. Rather, if the *McBride* or *Williams* facts do not fall within second degree murder, i.e., they do not make out a prima facie case

of a depraved mind, then it is inescapable that the facts in the instant case fall far short of second degree murder. In the instant case there was no evidence that the appellant either observed the victim or had any notice (actual or constructive) of his possible presence.

Thus, the noiseless playing of the victim, the inky blackness of the night and the lack of demonstrated ill will on the part of the appellant point more toward culpable negligence than the evincing of a depraved mind regardless of human life.

REVERSED and REMANDED.

HOBSON, Acting C. J., and SCHEB, J., concur.

COMMONWEALTH V. GRAVES
Superior Court of Pennsylvania, 1983.
310 Pa. Super, 184, 456 A.2d 561.

[This case involves the crime of third-degree murder.]

VAN der VOORT, Judge:
A jury found appellant guilty of third degree murder for the death of Lynette Weston, age 10, and of first degree murder for the death of Lloyd Weston, age 10, and recommended a death sentence on the first degree murder conviction. . . .

. . . [A]ppellant argues . . . that all of the evidence of guilt presented in this case is circumstantial and insufficient to prove beyond a reasonable doubt that he is the individual who committed these two homicides.

Initially, we note that circumstantial evidence may be sufficient to establish, beyond a reasonable doubt a crime, and that the accused was responsible for the crime. . . . Here, the Commonwealth's evidence established the following.

The appellant had been caring for the victims on the night when they were strangled to death. At 4:45 A.M., Daniel Anderson left the Weston home, leaving appellant alone with the children. At 7:10 A.M., the victims were discovered dead by their mother; appellant was not on the premises. No one else had been seen entering the house between 4:45 A.M. and 7:10 A.M. After several calls, appellant was advised of

the children's deaths. He claimed that he was forced to leave the house. A sample of appellant's pubic hair was found to be consistent with a hair found on the female victim. A bathrobe which appellant had been wearing earlier contained blood stains, consistent with the type of the female victim and inconsistent with appellant's type. Dried blood was found under the finger nails of the female victim (its type was not determinable); fresh scratches were found on appellant's upper body. Such scratches did not match appellant's girl friend's nails and she denied having made them. Scratch marks found on the male victim were consistent with the characteristics of appellant's finger nails.

We find that the evidence was sufficient beyond a reasonable doubt to show that appellant was responsible for the death of the two young victims. We must also inquire whether the Commonwealth proved the requisite intent for the killing of Lynette Weston . . . and for the premeditated killing of Lloyd Weston. . . .

The evidence, as it differs between the two deaths does not appear to support the different verdicts: murder in the third degree (Lynette) and murder in the first degree (Lloyd). A jury's verdict in a criminal case will not be set aside merely because it appears to be inconsistent with another verdict of the jurors. So long as the challenged verdict is supported by the evidence we will not on review delve into the thought process of the jury. . . .

Murder of the third degree has been defined as "an unlawful killing with malice expressed or implied, but absent any specific intent to take a life." . . . As to the death of Lynette Weston we find no need to expound on the facts already given; they clearly show the existence of malice.

The conviction for murder of the first degree for the death of Lloyd Weston requires a little more discussion. The trial court . . . found the fact that the victim had been manually strangled to death raised a presumption that the murder was both intentional and malicious. Appellant argues that the verdict was based on conjecture that the killing occurred to "silence a witness" who viewed the first crime.

Where there is no direct or concrete evidence of a specific intent to kill the fact-finder must look to the act itself and all the surrounding circumstances. . . . It is the law of this Commonwealth that premeditation and deliberation may be found where there is a conscious effort to cause death; this design can be formed in a very short time. . . . Where a deadly force is knowingly applied by a defendant to his victim, the intent to kill may be as evident as if the defendant had verbally announced his intent. . . . *[Commonwealth v.] Meredith* offers special guidance to this case; there the defendant was convicted of the beating death of a two and one half (2 ½) year old child. On appeal, it was held that the number and severity of blows, the size and age of the victim permitted a finding that a deadly force had been applied to a vital part of the body and allowed the jury to infer an intent to kill. Likewise here, we believe the jury was entitled to find, where a ten year old child is strangled to death, the specific intent to kill required for a conviction for first degree murder.

Judgment of sentence affirmed.

STATE V. STUDHAM
Supreme Court of Utah, 1977.
572 P.2d 700.

[This case deals with the crime of rape.]

CROCKETT, Justice:
Defendant, Clyde Lloyd Studham, appeals from a jury conviction of rape. . . .

The prosecutrix, Janis _____, had lived with defendant in a meretricious relationship beginning in November, 1972. A son, Chad _____ , was born on September 14, 1973. The relationship between Janis and the defendant had terminated in December of 1974 and the defendant was under a court order not to annoy or visit her.

At approximately 4:00 A.M. on the morning of March 5, 1976, Janis was awakened at her apartment by a knocking and ringing of her doorbell. Defendant, who had been drinking, was at the door and he said he wanted to talk to her, but she refused to let him in. He kicked the door open and entered; and he remained in the apartment for about two hours, during which there was some kissing and amorous advances.

The prosecutrix testified that in his efforts to force sexual intercourse upon her defendant threatened her, pinned her to the floor during a struggle, put his hand over her mouth so that she had difficulty breathing, and forced intercourse upon her against her will. She did not scream or attempt to run from her apartment, which she said was due to its futility and the fact that her young son was asleep in the adjoining room.

After the defendant left, she called her mother, who reported the incident to the police. Deputy Lester Newren of the Salt Lake County Sheriff's office came to investigate. Janis's only visible injuries were a bruised face and cut lip; and there were blood stains on her bathrobe. Pursuant to his questioning and investigation, he took the prosecutrix to St. Mark's Hospital where she was examined by Dr. John Corkrey. Later in the day the defendant was arrested and charged with this offense.

Defendant's argument that the evidence is not sufficient to prove his guilt beyond a reasonable doubt is: that it rests almost solely upon her own self-interested testimony; that it is inherently improbable and inconsistent because, though she claims force, and denies consent, she did not scream, or try to escape from the apartment even though during the time he was there she had opportunity to do so.

Most crimes are committed in such secrecy as can be effected; and that is particularly so of this type of offense. Therefore, the question of guilt or innocence often depends upon the weighing of the credibility of the victim against that of the accused. Accordingly, the rule is that if there is nothing so inherently incredible about the victim's story that reasonable minds would reject it, a conviction may rest upon her testimony alone.

In regard to the failure of the victim to make an outcry, this is to be said: Whether an outcry was made, or should have been made, depends upon how practical and effective it might have been. It is evidence which may be received and it is one of the circumstances to be considered as bearing upon the critical issue of consent. But mere failure to make such an outcry does not render a conviction unsupportable.

The essential element in rape is the forcing of intercourse upon a woman "without her consent" and "against her will." It is sometimes said that those terms mean essentially the same thing, but this is not true because such an act might occur in circumstances which would be "without her consent" but which would not necessarily involve overcoming her will and her resistance, both of which must be proved. In that regard there has often been much preoccupation with and stress placed upon the matter of the physical confrontation between the accused and the victim; and it has sometimes been said that she "must resist to the utmost" or other expressions of that import. But that view no longer obtains. Even though it is necessary that the rape be against the victim's will, manifest by a determined effort on her part to resist, it is not necessary that it

be shown that she engaged in any heroics which subjected her to great brutality or that she suffered or risked serious wounds or injuries.

What we think is a sounder view recognizes that the bruising and terrorizing of the senses and sensibilities can be just as real and just as wrong as the beating and bruising of the flesh; and that the law should afford a woman protection, not only from physical violence, but from having her feelings and sensibilities outraged by force or fear in violation of what she is entitled to regard and protect as the integrity of her person. Accordingly, in determining whether the victim's will and resistance were overcome, it is appropriate to consider that this may be accomplished by either physical force and violence, or by psychological or emotional stress imposed upon her, or by a combination of them. As to the degree of resistance required: The victim need do not more than her age and her strength of body and mind make it reasonable for her to do under the circumstances to resist. In this case there is a reasonable basis in the evidence upon which the jury could believe beyond a reasonable doubt that that test was met.

In urging that the court committed error in refusing to instruct the jury that rape is easy to charge and difficult to defend against, defendant asserts that it was particularly applicable here because, in addition to the lack of corroboration, and their prior difficulties, there existed the possibility of malice behind the charge. We are aware that such an instruction in abstract terms and not focused upon the particular evidence in the case has been given without it being prejudicial error. Nevertheless, such an instruction is not looked upon with favor since it is in the nature of a directive to the jury as to how they should evaluate evidence, rather than a statement of law. Under our procedure the judging of the evidence should be left exclusively to the jury and the trial judge should neither comment thereon nor give any indication as to what he may or may not think as to the quality of the evidence. In any event, we see no reason to believe that the failure to give such an instruction in this case was error. . . .

Affirmed. No cost awarded.

STATE V. ROTHENBERG

Supreme Court of Connecticut, 1985.
195 Conn. 253, 487 A.2d 545.

[This case examines the sufficiency of the evidence to support Rothenberg's conviction for sexual assault and unlawful restraint.]

PETERS, Chief Justice.

... After a trial to the court, the defendant was found guilty ... and judgment was rendered accordingly. The defendant appeals from the judgment against him.

The trial court reasonably found the following facts. The defendant and the complainant met at a bar in Southbury during the early morning hours of August 23, 1981. The complainant recognized the defendant as someone she had met there previously. They danced. The defendant asked the complainant to accompany him to a party at a friend's condominium in Woodbury. Somewhat reluctantly, the complainant agreed and drove to the condominium in her own car.

When the couple arrived at the condominium, it appeared to be empty. In fact, however, the two bedrooms, although their doors were closed, were occupied throughout the events that then transpired. The owner of the condominium was in one bedroom and two guests were in the other.

After a brief tour of the condominium, the complainant and the defendant sat on a couch in the living room. They kissed and the defendant gave the fully clothed complainant a back rub. The complainant, at the defendant's request, gave him a back rub while he was clad only in his undershorts.

The complainant then told the defendant that she wanted to leave, but he told her that she could not go. On the pretext of wanting to use the bathroom, the complainant ran to and partially opened the front door of the condominium. The defendant closed the door and forcibly prevented her from leaving by holding her arms. The complainant could not persuade the defendant to let her leave the condominium but was allowed to use the bathroom, where she remained for approximately thirty minutes until she looked for a way to escape or a weapon. During this time, the defendant alternately promised that he would let the complainant leave and threatened to wake up his friend to join the harassment of the complainant if she did not leave the bathroom.

As the complainant emerged from the bathroom, the defendant took her by the arms and pulled her, struggling, to the living room couch. Fearing injury if she were to resist further, the complainant then submitted. The defendant sexually assaulted the complainant several times before finally releasing her.

The unseen occupants of the bedrooms in the condominium remained there throughout the night. One did not hear either the defendant or the complainant at all. The others heard sounds of conversation when the defendant and complainant first entered the condominium, but soon thereafter fell asleep and heard nothing further.

The defendant does not deny the occurrence of the sexual activity but contends that the state failed to prove that it was anything other than consensual. ...

The defendant claims that the evidence adduced at trial to support his conviction was insufficient in two respects. First, the defendant argues that the complainant's testimony that the defendant restrained and sexually assaulted her was unbelievable as a matter of law in light of the totality of the evidence at the trial. Second, the defendant claims that the evidence showed that he lacked the criminal intent necessary to a finding of guilt. We find neither assertion persuasive.

... [T]he defendant claims that the complainant's account of the events at the condominium is fatally undermined by the evidence given by the occupants of the bedrooms. The complainant testified that the defendant had "slammed" the front door during her escape attempt and had "yelled" at her while she was in the bathroom. The other people in the condominium testified that they had heard nothing beyond normal conversation and had slept throughout the incident. According to the defendant, the juxtaposition of this evidence necessarily validates his contention that the complainant's continued presence in the condominium and participation in the sexual activity was consensual.

The defendant's argument fails to recognize that, in determining the credibility of witnesses, the trier of the facts may properly believe all or part of the testimony of a witness.... The contours of the determination of credibility are uniquely shaped by the trial court and are not reviewable on appeal. "The trier of the facts determines with finality the credibility of witnesses and the weight to be accorded their testimony."... The trial court could have believed the complainant's testimony that the defendant prevented her from leaving, and forcibly imposed himself upon her, without giving significant weight to her account of how loudly the defendant spoke or how noisily he closed the door. Alternatively, the court could have disbelieved the testimony of the occupants of the bedrooms. Viewing the evidence, as we must, in the light most favorable to sustaining the judgment of the trial court, ... we conclude that the trial court could reasonably have found that the evidence established the defendant's guilt beyond a reasonable doubt....

The defendant's second claim of insufficiency of the evidence relies upon the trial court's own finding that the complainant's conduct was ill-advised and subject to misconstruction. The trial court did find that the complainant "committed a serious error in judgment when she accompanied the defendant, a young man whom she knew only slightly, to an unknown location, where she really had no idea what might confront her. And once there, she compounded her error in judgment by her voluntary conduct in engaging in intimate physical contact with the defendant, who was almost completely unclothed. In the Court's view, this was a foolhardy act of very poor judgment that was subject to misinterpretation by a young man, such as the defendant, as indicative of a willingness to engage in more explicit sexual conduct. I am satisfied in my own mind that this is essentially what happened. The defendant did misconstrue the complainant's conduct and concluded that she would, in fact, be a willing participant in further sexual activity." According to the defendant, this finding proves that he was mistaken about the complainant's consent and therefore lacked the mental state necessary to commit the charged offenses.

This argument would be compelling had the trial court's opinion ended where the defendant's quota-

tion stops. The trial court went on, however, to find that "[w]hen the complainant sought to withdraw from the situation, a situation that was developing beyond her expectations, the defendant was unwilling to permit her to do so. And he thereafter forced his attentions on the complainant and compelled her to engage in sexual intercourse against her will. The defendant failed to recognize that consensual sexual relations are one thing, forced sexual intercourse is something altogether different. The term 'consensual sexual relations' means full consent, and that clearly implies that a party should always be free to decline to go beyond a certain point. This the complainant tried to do. The defendant refused to honor this decision of the complainant and permit her to leave. For this he must be and is found guilty of both offenses as charged in the information." The trial court's finding in its totality makes it clear that the complainant's unambiguous request to leave the condominium disabused the defendant of any misinterpretation of her wishes. The defendant's conduct thereafter was knowingly coercive. A temporary misunderstanding about consent does not give irreversible license to compel sexual intercourse. There was ample evidence to support the trial court's finding and the defendant's conviction.

The defendant's second claim of error is that the trial court should have excluded testimony about his prior sexual history, just as the court upheld objections to similar questions asked of the complainant on her cross-examination. Under General Statutes Section 54-861, evidence of the sexual history of a sexual assault victim is now admissible only in clearly and narrowly defined circumstances established in a separate hearing. The defendant urges us to hold that the policy represented by that statute is as applicable to defendants as it is to complaining witnesses. In either case, he maintains, the prejudicial effect of evidence of prior sexual conduct, in the absence of special circumstances, far outweighs its probative value.

The defendant questions the admissibility of evidence concerning his prior activities at the Southbury bar and his prior visits to the condominium with other women whom he had met at that bar. Although the defendant objected at trial to the admission of this testimony, he did not then advance the reasoning upon which he now relies. In the main, his objections were devoid of any specific grounds. On the one occasion when a special objection was taken, the defendant's proferred grounds were that the challenged question was beyond the scope of cross-examination and argumentative. In response to that claim, the trial court noted that the evidence was admissible because it was relevant to the defendant's credibility, motive and intent. . . .

On this record, it would be improper to find error. We recognize that the defendant's argument has much to commend it; especially in light of the recent enactment of General Statutes Section 54–86f. . . . We therefore agree that defendants, like sex crime victims, should be shielded from unnecessarily prejudicial evidence of their prior sexual conduct. Appellate review of evidentiary rulings of the trial court is, however, limited to the specific legal issue raised by the objection of trial counsel. . . . The purpose of requiring trial counsel to object properly is not merely formal but serves the important function of alerting the trial court to error while there is time to correct it without ordering a retrial. . . . In the absence of an objection in the trial court on the grounds of prejudice, we find no error in the admission of the challenged evidence. . . .

STATE v. SNIDER
Court of Appeal of Iowa, 1991.
479 N.W.2d 622.

[In this case the Iowa Court of Appeals considers whether there is sufficient evidence to support the defendant's conviction for false imprisonment.]

SACKETT, Judge.

. . . Iowa Code section 710.7 (1989), False Imprisonment, states:

A person commits false imprisonment when, having no reasonable belief that the person has any right or authority to do so, the person intentionally confines another against the other's will. A person is confined when the person's freedom to move about is substantially restricted by force, threat or deception.

The facts, taking the evidence in light most favorable to the verdict, are the defendant had been drinking for a considerable period in a bar where the victim worked as a bartender. The defendant and the victim were the last people in the bar when the victim told the defendant her boyfriend was coming. She asked the defendant to finish his drink so she could close the bar. The defendant went behind the bar, grabbed the victim by the arms, took her from behind the bar and pushed her about ten feet to a pool table. Once at the pool table, he pushed her backward against the table and held her against her will for no more than fifteen minutes. He then left the bar. Her boyfriend arrived two minutes later and called the police. The defendant was arrested.

The essential elements of false imprisonment are (1) detention or restraint against one's will, and (2) the unlawfulness of such detention or restraint. . . .

The term *confines or removes* in defining kidnapping under section 710.1 requires no minimum period of confinement or distance of removal, but does require more than the confinement or removal that is an inherent incident of commission of the crime. . . .

Section 710.7 specifies a person is confined when the person's freedom to move about is substantially restricted. The words *substantially restricted* do not appear in the kidnapping statute. . . .

We first look to whether the period of confinement or distance of removal exceeded that which would normally be incidental to an assault. . . . To do so, we assess whether the confinement or removal was significantly independent from the assault because it either (1) substantially increased the risk of harm to the victim, (2) lessened the risk of detection, or (3) significantly facilitated the defendant's escape following the assault.

Holding the victim against the pool table did not lessen defendant's risk of detection or facilitate his escape. The defendant had been at the bar for some time. He was known by the victim. The bar area where the victim was held was open to the public. The victim had told the defendant her boyfriend was coming to help her close up. Consequently, the longer the defendant stayed in the bar and held the victim down, the more likely he would be detected.

A pivotal question is whether holding the victim against the pool table substantially increased her risk of harm. The victim was harmed by the assault. The defendant was convicted of assault. He has not appealed that conviction. The State has the burden to show the confinement or movement was not merely incidental to the assault. . . . In *[State v.] Rich*, 305 N.W.2d at 745, the court determined a defendant's movement of a victim a short distance from a mall into a restroom was not in and of itself sufficient confinement or removal within the meaning of Iowa Code section 710.1. The factors that raised the defendant's actions to a removal and confinement in Rich, are not present here. The facts of this case do not show the victim's freedom was substantially restricted. We reverse the conviction for false imprisonment.

REVERSED AND DISMISSED.

All judges concur except HABHAB and DONIELSON, JJ., who dissent.

HABHAB, Judge (dissenting).

I respectfully dissent from the majority's reversal and dismissal of Snider's conviction for false imprisonment. I believe the evidence was sufficient to generate a jury question on the issue. . . .

Forcible confinement for almost fifteen minutes is not merely incidental to the initial assault. Additionally, the facts show the confinement was separate from the assault. . . . The confinement itself was substantial. . . . Unlike the majority, I do not find the confinement against the victim's will merged into the assault charge. I believe both offenses were separate.

The evidence supports submission of both assault and false imprisonment charges to the jury. I would find the trial court did not err in denying the motion for directed verdict on the false imprisonment charge.

I would affirm.

DONIELSON, J., joins this dissent.

CHAPTER

CRIMES AGAINST PROPERTY AND HABITATION

CHAPTER OUTLINE

Introduction
The Common-Law
  Background
The Basic Common-Law
  Property Offenses Dealing
  with Theft
The Modern Approach to
  Theft Offenses
The Offense of Robbery
Forgery and Uttering a Forged
  Instrument
Worthless Checks; Credit Card
  Fraud

Habitation Offenses
Malicious Mischief
Extortion
Defenses to Crimes Involving
  Property
Conclusion

INTRODUCTION

Private property is a basic tenet of American law. In the early history of the new America, property interests beyond raw land were often meager, consisting primarily of those possessions necessary for survival. Dwellings for most people were modest. At that time, enforcement of the law was largely dependent on "self-help." As the new nation developed, property interests became a vital part of the American economy, and professional law enforcement became the rule and not the exception. The public law recognized the need to deter people from infringing on the property interests of others and to punish transgressors. In today's affluent society and with the rapid technological advances of the past few decades, crimes against property have assumed even greater significance. In this chapter we examine the background of basic common-law property and habitation offenses and provide a sampling of the present-day statutory crimes in this area.

THE COMMON-LAW BACKGROUND

When the common law emerged, England was an agrarian country with relatively little commercial activity. Possession of private property was an important concept; but beyond the right to occupy a dwelling, property interests of most people consisted largely of what the law refers to as "tangible" property (i.e., such things as animals, cooking implements, and tools). The "intangible" property interests that are often referred to legally as "choses in action" (e.g., stocks, bonds, notes, and other evidences of wealth of such great economic importance in contemporary society), were either nonexistent or of little significance.

The common-law offenses involving property reflect the environment in which they matured. It was a very serious offense for someone to permanently deprive another of the possession of personal property, whether through stealth or through force, violence, or intimidation. Thus larceny and robbery were felonies, yet it was of far less consequence to cheat someone by the use of false tokens or false weights and measures. When it came to such breaches of ethics as misrepresentations and violations of trust, the common law generally left victims to their civil remedies. This view gave rise to such early maxims as *caveat emptor,* meaning "let the buyer beware." Since commercial transactions were not a major concern, forgery remained a misdemeanor. Likewise, extortion and malicious mischief were also misdemeanors, because the conduct involved in these offenses did not qualify for the severe punishment meted out for felonies. Finally, offenses concerning the rights of landholders were dealt with largely through the civil law.

THE BASIC COMMON-LAW PROPERTY OFFENSES
DEALING WITH THEFT

The early common law recognized two offenses dealing with theft: larceny and receiving stolen property. The theft offenses of "false pretenses" and embezzlement were created by statutes passed by the English Parliament.

Larceny

The basic common-law offense against infringement of another's personal property was larceny, the crime from which all other property offenses developed. Larceny was a felony that consisted of (1) the wrongful taking and carrying away of (2) the personal property of another (3) with the intent to permanently deprive the other person of the property. *State v. Griffin,* 79 S.E.2d 230 (N.C. 1953). Many terms used in reference to larceny are not commonly used today. The taking was called the "caption," the carrying away, the "asportation," and the personal property had to have a "corporeal" (i.e., a physical) existence. The wrongful act of taking was described as a "trespass," while the intent to permanently deprive the victim of the property was known as the *"animus furundi."*

To constitute common-law larceny, the taking had to be a deprivation of the owner's or possessor's interest in personal property. Real estate and the property attached to it were not subject to larceny; neither were trees nor crops wrongfully severed from the land. But, if the owner of property had already severed crops and a thief carried them away, it was larceny because the thief was carrying away personal property rather than merely infringing on the owner's real property. *State v. Collins,* 199 S.E. 303 (S.C. 1938).

These distinctions are difficult to appreciate today, but they were significant in the development of the common law, where wrongs concerning a person's land gave rise to chiefly civil, as opposed to criminal, remedies. Also, at common law, anyone wrongfully deprived of possession of personal property was entitled to recover damages based on the tort (civil wrong) of conversion. Thus, there was overlap between the crime of larceny and the tort of conversion.

As the common law developed, personal property consisted largely of tools, household items, and domestic animals. Items such as promissory notes were not subject to larceny because they represented intangible legal rights; coins and bills were, because they had a physical existence.

A taking by a person who had a lawful right to possession was not larceny. As we will discuss later, this led Parliament to enact the crime of embezzlement. Since the property had to be taken from another, a co-owner or partner did not commit larceny by taking jointly owned property. *State v. Kusnick,* 15 N.E. 481 (Ohio 1888). Nor did a spouse commit larceny by taking the other spouse's property, because at common law spouses were considered one. *State v. Phillips,* 97 N.E. 976 (Ohio 1912).

To find an accused guilty of larceny, it was necessary to prove that the taker carried the property away. This was required to show termination of the owner's right of possession and possession by the wrongdoer. *Driggers v. State,* 118 So. 20 (Fla. 1928). This element was usually satisfied by even a slight removal of the property. *State v. Williams,* 97 S.W. 562 (Mo. 1906). It was also essential to prove the taker's intent to permanently deprive the owner of the property. See *Hubbard v. State,* 41 So.2d 1 (Miss. 1949). A person could not be convicted for just borrowing or using property under a reasonable belief of a right of possession. Consequently, a man who temporarily took another's horse would not be guilty of larceny because there was no intent to permanently deprive the owner of the horse. See *In re Mutchler,* 40 P. 283 (Kan. 1895). Furthermore, had a man taken a horse that reasonably appeared to be the taker's own, the taker would likely have been acting under a *bona fide* mistake of fact, hence not guilty of larceny. Yet, a person who secured possession of goods through trickery could be found guilty of larceny if there was proof that the trickster intended to deprive the owner of the goods. *Murchison v. State,* 26 So.2d 622 (Ala. App. 1946).

Receiving Stolen Property

The common-law offense of receiving stolen property was a misdemeanor consisting of knowingly receiving possession and control of personal property belonging to another with the intent to permanently deprive the owner of possession of such property. See *Engster v. State,* 10 N.W. 453 (Neb. 1881). In contrast, the crime of larceny was a common-law felony, except where property of a very minor value was involved. *People v. Burke,* 145 N.E. 164 (Ill. 1924).

False Pretenses and Embezzlement

Many technical and often subtle distinctions developed in the common-law crime of larceny. Perhaps one reason for this was the reluctance of courts to find a thief guilty of larceny since the penalty at early common law was death. As commerce became more significant in England, the crime of larceny was not adequate either to deal with those who obtained financial advantage through false pretenses, or to deter or punish servants who fraudulently appropriated property that rightfully came into their possession. Consequently, by the late 1700s, the English Parliament created two supplemental misdemeanor offenses:

CASE IN POINT

RECEIVING STOLEN PROPERTY: SUFFICIENT EVIDENCE TO CONVICT

Defendent Lynn Belt was convicted of receiving stolen property in violation of Utah Code Ann. 76–6–408(1) (Supp. 1989), which makes it a crime for a person to receive property of another "knowing that it has been stolen or believing that it probably has been stolen. . . . with a purpose to deprive the owner thereof." Belt appealed, contending the evidence was legally insufficient to support his conviction.

The evidence revealed the defendant purchased videocassette recorders from Sgt. Illsley of the Metro Major Felony Unit during an undercover operation involving purchase and sale of stolen property. Defendant met Illsley at an empty parking lot, where Illsley offered the new recorders to the defendant at a very low price, explaining that the store name and serial numbers had been cut off. Defendant replied, "I don't want to hear about the serial number or store names—just do our business." Illsley testified that at one point the defendant said, "I wish you wouldn't cut the serial numbers off. That makes it look hot." The Court of Appeals of Utah held that the evidence was sufficient for the jury to have found that the defendant believed the goods he purchased were stolen and affirmed Belt's conviction.

State v. Belt, 780 P.2d 1271 (Utah App. 1989).

false pretenses and embezzlement. The offense of false pretenses came into being in 1757, 30 Geo. 2, ch. 24, before the American Revolution. The offense thereby became a part of the common law of those states that adopted it with the statutory modifications made by Parliament prior to the American Revolution. See *State v. McMahon*, 140 A. 359 (R.I. 1928). Embezzlement, on the other hand, did not become a statutory crime until 1799, 39 Geo. 3, ch. 85, too late to become part of the common law adopted by the new American states. By subsequent enactments, Parliament broadened the scope of embezzlement.

False pretenses (actually "obtaining property by false pretenses") was usually directed at a seller who obtained someone else's property by (1) the accused obtaining wares or merchandise of another (2) by false pretenses and (3) with the intent to cheat or defraud the other person. *State v. Tower*, 251 P. 401 (Kan. 1926). Parliament's enactment of the offense of false pretenses during the industrial revolution represented an important development in the English law of crimes. Since false pretenses became an offense just prior to the American Revolution, few English decisions became a part of the common law adopted by the new American states. Yet the English law in this area influenced American legislation and judicial decisions.

In contrast to larceny, embezzlement occurred where an accused who had lawful possession of another's property (e.g., a servant or employee) wrongfully appropriated the property. *Murchison v. State*, 26 So.2d 622 (Ala. App. 1946). A series of enactments by the English Parliament brought not only servants and employees, but also brokers, bankers, lawyers, and trustees within the scope of embezzlement. Thus, an embezzlement occurred when someone occupying a position of trust converted another's property to his or her own use, *State v. Griffin*, 79 S.E.2d 230 (N.C. 1953), whereas larceny required proof of a wrongful taking and carrying away of the personal property of another. Nevertheless, to convict a defendant of embezzlement, it was necessary to prove that the accused intended to defraud the victim. *People v. Hurst*, 28 N.W. 838 (Mich. 1886).

THE MODERN APPROACH TO THEFT OFFENSES

A review of the various technical distinctions that developed in the common-law offenses of larceny, receiving stolen property, false pretenses, and the early statutory offense of embezzlement makes it obvious that significant reforms were needed. A redefinition of these basic property offenses was required to cope with the various aspects of theft in American society. Modern theft ranges from the theft of vehicles, shoplifting, and looting to such sophisticated forms of theft as credit card frauds, various scams, theft of trade secrets, and computer-related crimes. Indeed, theft is a nationwide problem that must be dealt with by both state and federal authorities.

Federal Approaches

Congress has enacted a series of statutes comprehensively proscribing theft and embezzlement. The first, 18 U.S.C.A. § 641, provides:

CASE IN POINT

LARCENY COMMITTED THROUGH A PHONY NIGHT-DEPOSIT BOX

A Massachusetts jury convicted Brian Donovan and Robert Grant of larceny. Evidence introduced at trial showed that they had constructed a phony night-deposit box and attached it to the wall of a bank building. The box was constructed of heavy-gauge steel just like a real depository. Seven depositors lost an estimated $37,000 by making deposits to the phony box. Although the phony box was never recovered, a witness testified that he overheard defendants in a bar talking about the phony deposit box as "a helluva'n idea." Another witness stated that Grant had admitted to her that he had robbed a bank using a phony deposit box. On appeal, the Massachusetts Supreme Court rejected defendants' contentions that certain testimony had been improperly admitted into evidence and that the evidence produced at trial was legally insufficient to prove the crime of larceny.

Commonwealth v. Donovan, 478 N.E.2d 727 (Mass. 1985).

Whoever embezzles, steals, purloins, or knowingly converts to his use or the use of another, or without authority, sells, conveys or disposes of any record, voucher, money, or thing of value of the United States or any department or agency thereof, or any property made or being made under contract for the United States or any department or agency thereof; or

Whoever receives, conceals, or retains the same with intent to convert it to his use or gain, knowing it to have been embezzled, stolen, purloined or converted;

Shall be fined. . . .

The purpose of 18 U.S.C.A. § 641 is to place in one part of the criminal code crimes so kindred as to belong in one category. The Supreme Court has said that despite the failure of Congress to have expressly included the common-law intent requirement for larceny, Section 641 should not be construed to eliminate that intent requirement from the statute. The statute has been held to apply not only to larceny and embezzlement but also to all instances in which a person may obtain wrongful advantage from another's property. *Morissette v. United States*, 342 U.S. 246, 72 S. Ct. 240, 96 L.Ed. 288 (1952). Another federal statute provides penalties for embezzling or unlawfully taking the contents of any vehicle moving in interstate commerce. 18 U.S.C.A. § 659. Federal appellate courts have characterized the intent requirements under this statute as the intent to appropriate or convert the property of the owner. Furthermore, the federal appellate courts have said that a simultaneous intent to return the property or make restitution does not make the offense any less embezzlement. See, for example, *United States v. Waronek*, 582 F.2d 1158 (7th Cir. 1978).

A variety of other federal statutes concern embezzlement and theft by public officers or employees of the United States and custodians of federal funds, bank examiners, and bank officers and employees. See 18 U.S.C.A. §§ 641–665.

State Approaches

All states have enacted statutes expanding the common-law concept of larceny to include all types of tangible and intangible property. Historically, the states maintained numerous statutes basically adopting the concepts of common-law larceny, receiving stolen property, false pretenses, and embezzlement. As new problems developed, legislative bodies attempted to fill in the gaps by creating new offenses. As a result, numerous statutory offenses proscribing various forms of stealing and dishonest dealings were enacted. Often these statutes have been confusing; in some instances, they have been contradictory.

In recent years many states have replaced their various statutes with a consolidated theft statute that proscribes stealing in very broad terms. These new statutes make it unlawful for a person to commit any of the common-law offenses mentioned as well as other crimes, and they scale penalties based on the amount and character of the property stolen.

Florida, for example, passed the Florida Anti-Fencing Act in 1977. Despite its narrow title, the new act defines theft as including all of the common-law offenses, a number of former statutory offenses, possession of property with altered or removed identifying features, and dealing in stolen property (i.e., fencing). West's Fla. Stat. Ann. § 812.012–037. The law says that:

> A person commits theft if he knowingly obtains or uses, or endeavors to obtain or to use, the property of another with intent to, either temporarily or permanently:
> (a) Deprive the other person of a right to the property or a benefit therefrom.
> (b) Appropriate the property to his own use or to the use of any person not entitled thereto. West's Fla. Stat. Ann. § 812.014(1).

Under the simplified, yet comprehensive, theft statute, the phrase "obtains or uses" replaces the old common-law requirements of "taking and carrying away" with any manner of (a) taking or exercising control over property; (b) making any unauthorized use, disposition, or transfer of property; (c) obtaining property by fraud, willful misrepresentation of a future act, or false promise; (d) by conduct previously known as stealing, larceny, purloining, abstracting, embezzlement, misapplication, misappropriation, conversion, obtaining money or property by false pretense, fraud, or deception; or (e) other conduct similar in nature. West's Fla. Stat. Ann. § 812.012 (2). "Property of another" is generally construed to mean that the victim either owned or had a right to custody of the property taken. See *R. C. v. State*, 481 So.2d 14 (Fla. App. 1985).

As in other modern statutes, the Florida statute defining theft includes tangible as well as intangible property. The seriousness of the offense is categorized by the value or type of property stolen. Grand theft in the first degree, the most serious felony, involves stealing property valued at $100,000 or more, while grand theft in the second degree, a somewhat less serious felony, involves theft of property valued at $20,000 or more, but less than $100,000. It is grand theft of the third degree and a lesser felony if the property stolen is either valued at $300 or more, but less than $20,000 or if the property falls into any of the following classes: a will, codicil, or other testamentary instrument; a firearm; a motor vehicle; livestock; a fire extinguisher; 2,000 pieces or more of citrus fruit; or property taken from an identified construction site. West's Fla. Stat. Ann. §

812.014 (2)(a)(b)(c). Note the emphasis placed not only on the value of items stolen and their character but also on the importance of local economic interests. Except for the specified articles, theft of property having a value under $300 is petit theft, a misdemeanor, but a person who commits petit theft and who has previously been convicted two or more times commits a felony of the third degree. West's Fla. Stat. Ann. § 812.014(2)(d). West's Fla. Stat. Ann. § 812.014(2)(d).

Theft remains a specific-intent crime, but like many of the newer theft statutes, the Florida statute simply refers to "the intent to deprive." According to the Florida Supreme Court, this simply means the "intent to steal" and *not* the intent to *permanently* deprive the owner of the property. *State v. Dunmann*, 427 So. 2d 166 (Fla. 1983). In *Dunmann*, the court also held that the enactment of the omnibus theft statute (§ 812.012 *et seq.*) by implication repealed Florida's so-called joyriding statute. Additionally, the court has ruled that because the definition of theft contained in this statute includes an *endeavor* to commit theft, the crime is fully proved when an attempt, along with the requisite intent, is established. *State v. Sykes*, 434 So.2d 325 (Fla. 1983) (see Chapter 5).

Computer Crime: New Offenses to Cope with High-Tech Crime

Once the use of computers became common in today's society, they soon became tools employed by criminals to commit a variety of offenses. Indeed, the pervasiveness of computers poses some unique challenges to law enforcement agencies and prosecutors. Most computer crimes violate laws defining theft, fraud, embezzlement, etc. at the state level and often, mail fraud at the federal level. Nevertheless, starting with Florida in 1978, nearly every state has adopted some form of laws specifically defining computer crimes. These laws define such terms as *access, computer program, computer software, data base, computer hacking, financial instrument,* and other terms used in modern computer parlance, and address such activities as computer manipulation, theft of intellectual property, telecommunications crimes, and software piracy. They also create such offenses as computer fraud, computer trespass, and theft of computer services.

Section 18.2–152.3 of the Virginia Computer Crimes Act provides:

> Any person who uses a computer or computer network without authority and with the intent to:
> 1. Obtain property or services by false pretenses;
> 2. Embezzle or commit larceny; or
> 3. Convert the property of another shall be guilty of the crime of computer fraud.

Depending on the value of property or services actually obtained, the offense is either a felony or a serious misdemeanor. Additional Virginia statutes make computer trespass, invasion of privacy by computer, and theft of computer services offenses.

A Unique Prosecutorial Burden in Theft Offenses

Except where statutorily specified articles are stolen, theft offenses are usually classified as grand or petit theft based on the value of goods stolen. Usually

---

C A S E   I N   P O I N T

UNAUTHORIZED ACCESSING A VOICE MAIL BOX VIOLATES A STATE STATUTE PROHIBITING UNLAWFUL USE OF A COMPUTER

Defendant, Andrea M. Gerulis, was convicted in a bench trial of two counts of unlawful use of a computer and two counts of violating a statute that criminalized intentionally obtaining various electronic services "available only for compensation" by deception, unauthorized connection, etc. Defendant was ordered to make restitution. The evidence before the trial court revealed that the defendant deposited and retrieved information from voice mailboxes (VMBs) of a hospital and a telephone message company without authority from either to do so. By altering passwords she thereby prevented authorized users from using their VMBs. The defendant appealed, contending the evidence was insufficient to sustain her convictions.

The appellate court found that VMBs are high speed data processing devices that perform memory functions and therefore are "computers" within the meaning of the statute, and the defendant's disruption of normal use of the VMBs violated the statute. The court then addressed the defendant's convictions for theft of services. The court observed that the prosecution had charged the defendant under a statute that makes it an offense if a person "intentionally obtains services for himself or for another which he knows are available only for compensation." Because the evidence revealed that the VMBs the defendant accessed were provided by the hopsital and message company without charge for their employees, the court found that the defendant's mere intent to obtain free services did not violate that statute. Accordingly, the court affirmed the defendant's convictions for unlawful use of a computer, reversed her convictions for theft of services, and remanded the case to the trial court to modify the restitution order imposed as defendant's sentence.

Commonwaelth v. Gerulis, 616 A.2d 686 (Pa. Super. 1992).

---

grand theft is a felony. Therefore, the prosecution must establish the value of goods or services stolen. The determining factor is generally the market value at the time and in the locality of the theft. *State v. Kimbel*, 620 P.2d 515 (Utah 1980). This may be shown by proof of the original market cost, the manner in which the property stolen has been used, and its general condition and quality. *Negron v. State*, 306 So.2d 104 (Fla. 1974). Judges customarily instruct juries that if the value of the property cannot be ascertained, they must find the value to be less than that required for grand theft. But consider the theft of a credit card. Holders of these cards usually have set credit limits available to them on proper signature. Therefore, a credit card has no market value in lawful channels for a third person. In *Miller v. People*, 566 P.2d 1059 (Colo. 1977), the Colorado Supreme Court held that the amount that could be purchased on the stolen card in the "illegitimate" market could be considered in determining whether a defendant was guilty of felony theft.

In any event, proof of value is very important in a theft case because it can often mean the difference between the defendant being convicted of a misdemeanor or a felony, or even of a felony of various degrees.

THE OFFENSE OF ROBBERY

At common law, robbery was a felony that consisted of (1) a taking of another's personal property of value (2) from the other person's possession or presence (3) by force or placing the person in fear and (4) with the intent to permanently deprive the other person of that property. *Houston v. Commonwealth,* 12 S.E. 385 (Va. 1890). In reality, robbery was an aggravated form of larceny where the taking was accomplished by force or threats of force with the same specific-intent requirement as in common-law larceny. To constitute robbery, the violence or intimidation had to overcome the victim's resistance and precede or accompany the actual taking of property. *State v. Parker,* 170 S.W. 1121 (Mo. 1914). Property in the victim's dwelling or vicinity was regarded as being in the victim's possession. See *Hill v. State,* 60 N.W. 916 (Neb. 1894). To illustrate a significant difference between larceny and robbery: A person who spirited a man's wallet from his pocket would be guilty of larceny, but if the victim resisted and the thief took the wallet by force or violence, the offense constituted robbery.

Statutory Approaches to Robbery

In some respects robbery is an offense against the person, because it usually involves an assault or battery. See, for example, *State v. Shoemake,* 618 P.2d 1201 (Kan. 1980). Yet it involves a taking of property also and is generally classified as an offense against property.

A federal statute makes it an offense to take, or attempt to take, by force and violence or intimidation from the person or presence of another, any property or money belonging to or in the care of a bank, credit union, or savings and loan association. 18 U.S.C.A. § 2113(a).

Federal jurisdiction is established where the bank is a federally chartered institution or where its deposits are federally insured. *United States v. Harris,* 530 F.2d 576 (4th Cir. 1976). The statutory offense varies from the common-law crime of robbery in that the government need only establish the defendant's general intent. *United States v. Klare,* 545 F.2d 93 (9th Cir. 1976), *cert. denied,* 431 U.S. 905, 97 S. Ct. 1699, 52 L.Ed.2d 390 (1977).

Robbery is an offense in every state. Many states have enacted statutes simply defining it as did the common law, a practice sometimes referred to as codifying the common law. Other states classify robbery according to degree, with the seriousness of the offense usually based on whether the assailant is armed, the degree of force used, and, in some instances, on the vulnerability of the victim. The value of the property taken does not usually affect the degree of the crime of robbery, as it does that of theft.

The Colorado Criminal Code provides a good illustration of classification of robbery offenses: "A person who knowingly takes anything of value from the person or presence of another by the use of force, threats, or intimidation commits robbery." West's Colo. Rev. Stat. Ann. § 18–4–301(1). This is "simple robbery" in contrast to the statutory offense of "aggravated robbery." The Colorado statute further provides:

(1) A person who commits robbery is guilty of aggravated robbery if during the act of robbery or immediate flight therefrom:

   (a) He is armed with a deadly weapon with intent, if resisted, to kill, maim, or wound the person robbed or any other person; or

   (b) He knowingly wounds or strikes the person robbed or any other person with a deadly weapon or by the use of force, threats, or intimidation with a deadly weapon knowingly puts the person robbed or any other person in reasonable fear of death or bodily injury; or

   (c) He has present a confederate, aiding or abetting the perpetration of the robbery, armed with a deadly weapon, with the intent, either on the part of the defendant or confederate, if resistance is offered, to kill, maim, or wound the person robbed or any other person, or by the use of force, threats, or intimidation puts the person robbed or any other person in reasonable fear of death or bodily injury. West's Colo. Rev. Stat. Ann. § 18–4–302.

Under Colorado law, robbery of the elderly or handicapped is punishable the same as the offense of aggravated robbery. West's Colo. Rev. Stat. Ann. § 18–4–304.

The Colorado Supreme Court has said that the gist of the crime of robbery under the Colorado statutes is "the putting in fear and taking of property of another by force or intimidation." *People v. Small*, 493 P.2d 15 (Colo. 1972). Aggravated robbery is distinguished from simple robbery by the fact that an accomplice or confederate is armed with a dangerous weapon with intent, if resisted, to maim, wound, or kill. The court said that simple and aggravated robbery are but two degrees of the same offense. *Atwood v. People*, 489 P.2d 1305 (Colo. 1971). The intent the prosecution is required to prove is simply the perpetrator's intent to force the victim to give up something of value. *People v. Bridges*, 612 P.2d 1110 (Colo. 1980). Property is taken from the "presence of another" under Colorado law when it is so within the victim's reach, inspection, or observation that he or she would be able to retain control over the property but for the force, threats, or intimidation directed by the perpetrator. *People v. Bartowsheski*, 661 P.2d 235 (Colo. 1983).

The Temporal Relationship of Force to the Taking

Is it essential that the element of violence or intimidation occur before or at the same time as the taking of the victim's property? State appellate courts are divided on this issue, often based on the specific statutory language. Note that the Colorado statute in addressing aggravated robbery includes the language "if during the act of robbery or immediate flight therefrom." The Colorado Supreme Court has said that force used in robbery need not occur simultaneously with the taking. *People v. Bartowsheski*, 661 P.2d 235 (Colo. 1983). Other courts have agreed. In *Hermann v. State*, 123 So.2d 846 (Miss. 1960), a defendant, after stealthily obtaining gasoline, made a getaway from a filling station by pointing a deadly weapon at the attendant. The attendant stuck his hand through the window of the vehicle but was pushed away by the offender. The Mississippi Supreme Court held that this act of pushing the victim away constituted the force element of robbery. Again, in *People v. Kennedy*, 294 N.E.2d 788 (Ill. App. 1973), the court held that while the taking may be without force, the offense is robbery if the departure with the property is accomplished by the use of force.

In 1986, the Florida Supreme Court held that defendants who used force while fleeing a retail store after committing theft in the store could not be convicted of robbery. The court followed the traditional common-law view that the use of force must occur before or at the same time as the taking of property. *Royal v. State*, 490 So.2d 44 (Fla. 1986). The state legislature promptly amended the statutory definition of robbery to add that "an act shall be deemed in the course of committing the robbery *if it occurs in an attempt to commit robbery or in flight after the attempt or commission.*" [emphasis added] West's Fla.Stat. Ann. § 812.13(3)(b).

A New Statutory Offense: Carjacking

Recognizing the serious threat that forcible auto theft poses to persons and their motor vehicles, and after a nationwide spree of "carjacking," Congress enacted

---

CASE IN POINT

ARMED ROBBERY: IS AN UNLOADED GUN A "DANGEROUS WEAPON"?

On the morning of July 26, 1984, Lamont Julius McLaughlin and a companion, both wearing masks, entered a bank in Baltimore. McLaughlin brandished a handgun and told those in the bank to put up their hands and not to move. While McLaughlin held the gun, his companion leaped over the counter and stuffed several thousand dollars into a brown paper bag. Police officers were waiting outside and promptly arrested the pair. It was then determined that McLaughlin's gun was not loaded.

McLaughlin was found guilty in federal court of bank robbery "by the use of a dangerous weapon." 18 U.S.C.A. § 2113(d). On appeal, McLaughlin argued that his unloaded gun did not qualify as a "dangerous weapon" under the federal bank robbery statute. The United States Supreme Court rejected the argument and upheld McLaughlin's conviction. The court said:

> Three reasons, each independently sufficient, support the conclusion that an unloaded gun is a "dangerous weapon." First, a gun is an article that is typically and characteristically dangerous; the use for which it is manufactured and sold is a dangerous one, and the law reasonably may presume that such an article is always dangerous even though it may not be armed at a particular time or place. In addition, the display of a gun instills fear in the average citizen; as a consequence, it creates an immediate danger that a violent response will ensue. Finally, a gun can cause harm when used as a bludgeon. 476 U.S. at 18.

McLaughlin v. United States, 476 U.S. 16, 106 S. Ct. 1677, 90 L.Ed.2d 15 (1986).

the Anti-Car Theft Act of 1992. Included in the new law is a section (to be codified as 18 U.S.C.A. § 2119) imposing severe penalties for anyone who "takes a motor vehicle that has been transported, shipped, or received in interstate or foreign commerce from the person or presence of another by force and violence or by intimidation, or attempt to do so."

The first trial under the new federal law was held in February, 1993, in the United States District Court in Orlando, Florida. Three young males were accused of stealing two vehicles and committing execution-style slayings of two young men and injuring a third in Central Florida in November 1992. The prosecution argued that the defendants committed the carjacking offense by stealing a car involved in interstate commerce, doing it by force, and using a firearm. Defense lawyers, on the other hand, argued that while the defendants may be guilty of some offenses under state law, they were not guilty of violating the new federal law on armed carjacking involving violence. A fourth defendant pleaded guilty and testified against the other three. After deliberating for six hours, a jury found the defendants guilty of conspiracy, two counts of armed carjacking involving death, and two counts of using a firearm during a felony. In April 1993, the three defendants were sentenced to life terms, plus 25 years. After their sentences were imposed in federal court, state prosecutors said they would prosecute the three for first-degree murder and seek the death penalty.

FORGERY AND UTTERING A FORGED INSTRUMENT

Blackstone defined common-law forgery as "the fraudulent making or alteration of a writing to the prejudice of another man's right." *State v. Murphy*, 24 A. 473 (R.I. 1892). The early cases reveal that such writings as wills, receipts, and physicians' certificates were subject to forgery. To convict a defendant of forgery under common law, it was essential to establish the accused's intent to defraud. *Levinson v. United States*, 47 F.2d 470 (6th Cir. 1931). Uttering a forged instrument was also a common-law offense, but one separate and distinct from forgery. *Utter*, a term of art synonymous with publishing, serves to distinguish the actual forgery from the act of passing a forged instrument to someone. See *State v. Singh*, 419 P.2d 403 (Ariz. App. 1966). As an indication of the lesser importance of commercial matters in early English society, the common law classified both forgery and uttering a forged instrument as misdemeanors. *State v. Murphy*, 24 A. 473 (R.I. 1892).

Statutory Expansion of Forgery Offenses

Unlike the common law, federal and state statutes generally classify forgery as a felony. Reflecting the importance of written and printed documentation in our modern economy, statutes in all American jurisdictions have extended the crime of forgery to almost every type of public or private legal instrument.

Federal Statutes.   Under Federal law "[w]hoever, with intent to defraud, falsely makes, forges, counterfeits, or alters any obligation or other security of the United States" commits the crime of forgery. 18 U.S.C.A. § 471. Federal courts have stated that the manifest purpose of these laws is to protect all currency and obligations of the United States, *United States v. LeMon*, 622 F.2d 1022 (10th Cir. 1980), and that the prosecution must prove not only the passing, but also the defendant's "intent to pass the bad money." *United States v. Lorenzo*, 570 F.2d 294, 299 (9th Cir. 1978).

A number of other federal statutes relate to forgery and the counterfeiting of stamps, money orders, public records, and court documents. See 18 U.S.C.A. §§ 472–509. Additionally, many prosecutions are brought under 18 U.S.C.A. § 495, which makes it unlawful to forge and utter forged United States Treasury checks. To convict someone under this statute, the government must establish the defendant's specific fraudulent intent. *United States v. Sullivan*, 406 F.2d 180 (2d Cir. 1969).

State Statutes.   Most states have substantially adopted the common-law definition of forgery, but have expanded the number of instruments that can be forged to include a lengthy list of public and private documents. For example, the Arizona Criminal Code makes forgery a felony and provides that

> A. A person commits forgery if, with intent to defraud, such person:
> 1. Falsely makes, completes or alters a written instrument; or
> 2. Knowingly possesses a forged instrument; or
> 3. Offers or presents, whether accepted or not, a forged instrument or one which contains false information.
> Ariz. Rev. Stat. § 13–2002.

Under this section, the offenses of forgery and uttering have been coupled under the term *forgery*, but the distinction as separate offenses must still be observed since the elements of the offenses are not the same and the proof required may differ. *State v. Reyes*, 458 P.2d 960 (Ariz. 1969). Thus under Arizona law the crime of forgery has three elements: (1) signing the name of another person; (2) intending to defraud; and (3) knowing that there is no authority to sign. *State v. Nettz*, 560 P.2d 814 (Ariz. App. 1977). Uttering, on the other hand, is the passing or publishing of a false, altered, or counterfeited paper or document. *State v. Reyes*, 458 P.2d 960 (Ariz. 1969). Proof of the intent to defraud is essential to obtain a conviction of forgery, *State v. Maxwell*, 445 P.2d 837 (Ariz. 1968), but such intent may be inferred from circumstances in which the false instrument is executed or issued. *State v. Gomez*, 553 P.2d 1233 (Ariz. App. 1976). Note that based on the wording of the statute proscribing forgery, a conviction of "attempt to pass" is a conviction of forgery, not of an attempt. *Ponds v. State*, 438 P.2d 423 (Ariz. App. 1968) (see Chapter 5).

Common Examples of Forgery and Uttering a Forged Instrument.   Among the more common examples of forgery in our contemporary society are

- Signing another's name to an application for a driver's license
- Printing bogus tickets to a concert or sports event
- Signing another's name to a check on his or her bank account without authority
- Altering the amount of a check or note
- Signing another's name without authority to a certificate transferring shares of stock

- Signing a deed transferring someone's real estate
- Making an unauthorized change in the legal description of property being conveyed under a deed
- Altering the grades or credits on a college transcript

Uttering a forged instrument commonly occurs when a person knowingly delivers a forged check to someone in exchange for cash or merchandise, or knowingly sells bogus tickets for an event to others, or submits a deed with forged signatures for official recording.

Falsification of computerized records such as college credits and financial records poses new challenges to laws proscribing forgery. The increasing use of computers gives rise to the need for new applications of statutes proscribing forgery and uttering a forged instrument.

WORTHLESS CHECKS; CREDIT CARD FRAUD

As commercial banking developed, the passing of "bad checks" became a serious problem. A person who writes a worthless check on his or her bank account does not commit a forgery. In early cases some courts referred to issuance of checks without funds in the bank as use of a "false token." These cases were prosecuted under statutes making it unlawful to use false pretenses to obtain property. See, for example, *People v. Donaldson*, 11 P. 681 (Cal. 1886).

States have now enacted a variety of statutes making it unlawful to issue checks with insufficient funds to cover payment. Earlier statutes often provided that in order to be guilty of false pretenses for issuing a worthless check, a person had to fraudulently obtain goods. This proved to be an impracticable method to control issuance of checks by depositors who misgauged their checking account balances. The widespread use of commercial and personal banking led legislatures to create "worthless check" statutes to cope with the problem. These statutes usually classify such an offense as a misdemeanor, and legislatures have increasingly opted to allow offenders to make restitution of losses caused by worthless checks.

For example, the Texas law that makes issuance of bad checks a misdemeanor stipulates

(a) A person commits an offense if he issues or passes a check or similar sight order for the payment of money knowing that the issuer does not have sufficient funds in or on deposit with the bank or other drawee for the payment in full of the check or order as well as all other checks or orders outstanding at the time of issuance. Vernon's Tex. Penal Code Ann., § 32.41(a).

The Texas Penal Code presumes the issuer knows that there are insufficient funds if he or she had no account with the bank or other drawee when the check was issued, or if payment is refused by the bank on presentation within thirty days after issue and the person who wrote the check failed to pay the holder in full within ten days after receiving notice of such refusal. Vernon's Tex. Penal Code Ann., § 32.41(b)(1–2). A person charged with an offense under Section 32.41 is permitted to make restitution under certain conditions. Vernon's Tex. Penal Code Ann., § 32.41(e).

CASE IN POINT

FORGERY

The state prosecuted defendant Donald E. Hicks for forgery. At trial the evidence revealed that on August 4, 1984, defendant Hicks went to see Edmond Brown to make a payment on a debt. Hicks told Brown that he could pay him $100 on his debt if Brown could cash a two-party check for him. Hicks presented Brown with a check for $349 made out to Hicks on the account of Gott, Young, and Bogle, P.A., a Wichita law firm. The check was signed "Gott Young." The defendant told Brown that the check was a partial payment of a settlement of a claim stemming from an automobile accident. Hicks assured Brown that the check was good and endorsed it over to him. Brown accepted the check and returned $249 to Hicks. When the check was returned by the bank, Brown contacted the law firm. He was told that there was no one by the name of "Gott Young" at the firm, and that the firm had never represented Hicks. He further learned that some twenty-five checks from the firm's petty cash account were missing. Hicks was found guilty by a jury and his conviction was affirmed on appeal.

State v. Hicks, 714 P.2d 105 (Kan. App. 1986).

Credit Card Fraud

A credit card is issued to a named individual to provide its holder with a line of credit so that purchases may conveniently be made on credit. The person to whom the card is issued assumes the obligation to pay for goods or services delivered or rendered to that person or to the authorized bearer of the card. As previously noted, a person who makes a purchase through use of a stolen or otherwise fraudulently obtained credit card may be found guilty of theft under most modern larceny and theft statutes. Credit cards, however, are now in such widespread use that many states have enacted laws creating specific offenses for their improper use.

Pennsylvania has enacted such a statute, which is similar to Section 224.6 of the Model Penal Code:

Section 4106. Credit cards
(a) Offense defined—A person commits an offense if he:
  (1) uses a credit card for the purpose of obtaining property or service with knowledge that:
    (i)   the card is stolen, forged or fictitious;
    (ii) the card belongs to another person who has not authorized its use;
    (iii) the card has been revoked or canceled; or
    (iv) for any other reason his use of the card is unauthorized by the issuer or the person to whom issued; or
  (2) makes, sells, gives, or otherwise transfers to another, or offers or advertises, or aids and abets any other person to use a credit card with the knowledge or reason to believe that it will be used to obtain property or services without payment of the lawful charges therefor; or

(3) publishes a credit card or code of an existing, canceled, revoked, expired, or nonexistent credit card, or the numbering or coding which is employed in the issuance of credit cards, with knowledge or reason to believe that it will be used to avoid the payment for any property or services. Purdon's Penn. Stat. Ann. § 4106(a).

Section 4106(c) of the above statute makes violation either a third-degree felony, a misdemeanor, or a summary offense, depending on the value of the property or service illegally secured or sought to be secured. Section 4106(d) provides that it is a defense if the actor can prove the intent and ability to meet all obligations to the issuer arising out of his or her use of the credit card.

HABITATION OFFENSES

Two felonies developed at common law reflect the value of privacy and the need to protect the security of a person's dwelling. The offenses of burglary and arson gave credence to the old English saying, "A man's home is his castle." These offenses were created to protect not only the dwelling house but also the buildings within the "curtilage," an enclosed area around the dwelling that typically included the cookhouse and other outbuildings. In England the enclosure had to be by a stone fence or wall; however, this custom has not been established in the United States. *State v. Bugg*, 72 P. 236 (Kan. 1903).

Both burglary and arson became felonies in the United States. Modern statutes have greatly broadened the scope of the common-law crimes of burglary and arson and extended the protection of the criminal law far beyond the traditional concept of offenses against habitation. Nevertheless, to understand their historic development it is helpful to classify them as offenses against habitation.

Burglary at Common Law

According to Blackstone, common-law burglary consisted of (1) breaking and entering of (2) a dwelling of another (3) during the nighttime (4) with intent to commit a felony therein. *State v. Ward*, 86 So. 552 (La. 1920). The "breaking" at common law could be either "actual" or "constructive." An actual breaking could be merely technical such as pushing open a door or opening a window. See *Cooper v. State*, 90 So. 693 (Fla. 1922). An entry gained through fraud or deception was considered a "constructive" breaking. *Commonwealth v. Lowrey*, 32 N.E. 940 (Mass. 1893). Even the slightest entry was deemed sufficient; for instance, a hand, a foot, or even a finger within the dwelling was regarded as a sufficient entry. See *Commonwealth v. Glover*, 111 Mass. 395 (1873). Proof of the defendant's intent to commit a felony was essential: A breaking and entering did not constitute burglary at common law unless the perpetrator had a specific intent to commit a felony (e.g., murder, rape, or larceny); it was not necessary, however, to prove that any felony was committed. *Hayes v. Commonwealth*, 188 S.W. 415 (Ky. 1916). *Dwelling* was defined as the house or place of habitation used by the occupier or member of the family "as a place to sleep in." See *Ex parte Vincent*, 26 Ala. 145

(1855). Finally, to constitute burglary at common law it was essential that the offense be committed at nighttime, generally defined as the period between sunset and sunrise. *Bowser v. State*, 110 A. 854 (Md. 1920).

Statutory Revisions of Burglary

Many states have enacted statutes proscribing breaking and entering, thereby placing a new label on the common-law crime of burglary. At a minimum these statutes expand the offense of burglary beyond dwelling houses and eliminate the requirement that the offense take place in the nighttime. Most retain the common-law requirement that the accused break and enter with intent to commit a felony. Many states, however, have also included the language "or theft." Even where the offense is still labeled burglary, legislatures have made significant changes in the common-law definition. In addition to eliminating the nighttime requirement, they have broadened the offense to include buildings and structures of all types. Today, most criminal codes include vehicles, aircraft, and vessels either in the definition of burglary or by a separate statute. Finally, modern statutes frequently provide that a person who enters a structure with consent, but who remains therein with intent to commit a felony, may be found guilty of burglary notwithstanding an original lawful entry. An example of this would be someone intentionally remaining in a department store intending to commit an offense therein after the store closes for the day.

Michigan law illustrates a modern statutory approach and specifies:

> Any person who shall break and enter with intent to commit any felony, or any larceny therein, any tent, hotel, office, store, shop, warehouse, barn, granary, factory or other building, structure, boat or ship, railroad car or any private apartment in any of such buildings or any unoccupied dwelling house, shall be guilty of a felony. Mich. Comp. Laws Ann. § 750.110.

The Michigan statute states that if the dwelling is occupied, the offender shall be punished more severely. Mich. Comp. Laws Ann. § 750.110. Another Michigan statute makes it an offense for a person to enter without breaking into any of the structures or vehicles enumerated in the breaking and entering statute. Mich. Comp. Laws Ann. § 750.111.

Possession of Burglar's Tools

Michigan, like most states, makes possession of burglar's tools a felony if the possessor has the intent to use the tools for burglarious purposes. Michigan law provides:

> Any person who shall knowingly have in his possession any nitroglycerine, or other explosive, thermite, engine, machine, tool or implement, device, chemical or substance, adapted and designed for cutting or burning through, forcing or breaking open any building, room, vault, safe or other depository, in order to steal therefrom any money or other property, knowing the same to be adapted and designed for the purpose aforesaid, with intent to use or employ the same for the purpose aforesaid, shall be guilty of a felony. Mich. Comp. Laws Ann. § 750.116.

CASE IN POINT

EVIDENCE SUFFICIENT TO ESTABLISH BURGLARY

On the morning of October 18, 1981, Philadelphia police were called to Cramer's Kiddy Shop. Entering the store, they heard footsteps on the roof. They went up to the second floor, where they discovered a two-foot hole in a wall with access to the roof. One of the officers went through the hole and found himself covered with plaster dust. He then observed two males climbing down an exterior wall. One of them was apprehended. His hands were dirty and his clothes were covered with plaster dust. In the alley behind the store, police located several items of children's clothing that had been taken from the store along with a crowbar. Patrick Carpenter, who was apprehended, was found guilty of burglary and other offenses. On appeal, Carpenter argued that the evidence was insufficient to warrant a conviction for burglary. The appellate court rejected the contention and upheld defendant's conviction.

Commonwealth v. Carpenter, 479 A.2d 603 (Pa. Super. 1984).

Many years ago, the Michigan Supreme Court emphasized that to obtain a conviction the state must prove the accused knowingly had possession of burglar's tools, knew the tools could be used for a criminal purpose, and intended to use them for such purpose. *People v. Jefferson,* 126 N.W. 829 (Mich. 1910).

Arson at Common Law

Like burglary, arson was a felony at common law designed to protect the security of the dwelling place. The crime consisted of (1) the willful and malicious burning (2) of a dwelling (3) of another. *State v. Long,* 90 S.E.2d 739 (N.C. 1956). There was no requirement that the dwelling be destroyed or even that it be damaged to a significant degree. In fact, a mere charring was sufficient, *People v. Oliff,* 197 N.E. 777 (Ill. 1935), but scorching or smoke damage did not constitute arson at common law. *Woolsey v. State,* 17 S.W. 546 (Tex. 1891). The common law defined the term *dwelling* as in burglary. Consequently, the burning of buildings within the curtilage constituted arson.

The language "willful and malicious" makes it appear that arson was a specific-intent crime, but it was not. Rather, the term *malice* was construed to mean deliberately and without justification or excuse. *State v. Pisano,* 141 A. 660 (Conn. 1928). The common law regarded arson as a general-intent crime with the required malice being presumed from an intentional burning of someone's dwelling. However, it was not arson at common law to set fire to one's own home. *State v. Young,* 36 So. 19 (Ala. 1904). Yet, some early English cases indicate that under circumstances where burning one's own house posed a danger to others that "houseburning" was a misdemeanor offense.

CASE IN POINT

PROVING THE CRIME OF ARSON

Early on the morning of September 23, 1981, a fire destroyed a log cabin belonging to Henry Xavier Kennedy. Investigators determined the fire was incendiary in origin. A hot plate with its switch in the "on" position was found in the most heavily burned area of the cabin. Investigators also determined that kerosene poured around the area of the hot plate had accelerated the fire.

Five days before the fire, Kennedy had renewed a $40,000 insurance policy on the cabin. Evidence was also presented that Kennedy's building business was slow. Kennedy introduced evidence of an alibi from midnight until 4:00 A.M. Although the fire was reported at 3:42 A.M., investigators testified that the incendiary device could have been set before midnight.

Kennedy was convicted of arson and his conviction was upheld on appeal.

Kennedy v. State, 323 S.E.2d 169 (Ga. App. 1984).

Statutory Revision of Arson

Modern statutes have extended the offense of arson to include the intentional burning of buildings, structures, and vehicles of all types. Frequently, this even includes a person's own property. A number of states have enacted statutes that provide that use of explosives to damage a structure constitutes arson. As in burglary, the modern offense of arson is designed to protect many forms of property. Therefore, arson can no longer be considered strictly a habitation offense. By categorizing arson, legislatures can make appropriate distinctions and provide penalties accordingly.

Michigan law embraces four categories of arson. One section provides:

> Any person who wilfully or maliciously burns any dwelling house, either occupied or unoccupied, or the contents thereof, whether owned by himself or another, or any building within the curtilage of such dwelling house, or the contents thereof, shall be guilty of a felony. Mich. Comp. Laws Ann. § 750.72.

Section 750.73 makes it a lesser felony for anyone to willfully or maliciously burn any building or other real property, or contents thereof, while Section 750.74 makes it a misdemeanor to willfully and maliciously burn personal property worth less than $50 and a felony if the value is greater. In contrast to Michigan, many state statutes broaden the scope of the offense by referring to "damage caused by fire" rather than "burning." And in contrast to the common law, under many modern statutes proof of damage by smoke or scorching is sufficient to constitute arson. See, for example, *State v. McVeigh,* 516 P.2d 918 (Kan. 1973).

The Michigan Compiled Laws also address insurance fraud and provide:

> Any person who shall wilfully burn any building or personal property which shall be at the time insured against loss or damage by fire with intent to injure and defraud the insurer, whether such person be the owner of the property or not, shall be guilty of a felony. Mich. Comp. Laws Ann. § 750.75.

For a fire to be "wilfully" set by the accused requires that the defendant commit such act stubbornly and for an unlawful purpose. Mere proof of carelessness or accident is not sufficient to establish guilt. *People v. McCarty,* 6 N.W.2d 919 (Mich. 1942). Most jurisdictions have enacted statutes making it a crime to burn any property with the intent to defraud an insurance company, usually requiring the prosecution to prove the defendant's specific intent to defraud.

MALICIOUS MISCHIEF

A mere trespass to land or personal property was not a crime at common law unless it was committed forcibly or maliciously. *State v. Wheeler,* 3 Vt. 344 (1830). It was however, a common-law misdemeanor called "malicious mischief" for a person to damage another's real or personal property. *State v. Watts,* 2 S.W. 342 (Ark. 1866). Modern statutes usually define the offense much as did the common law, often referring to the offense as "vandalism" and imposing penalties based on the extent of damage inflicted on the victim's property. For example, the California Penal Code states:

> (a) Every person who maliciously (1) defaces with paint or any other liquid, (2) damages or (3) destroys any real or personal property not his or her own, in cases otherwise than those specified by state law, is guilty of vandalism. West's Ann. Cal. Penal Code § 594.

The California statute sets the penalty based on the amount of defacement, damage, or destruction.

EXTORTION

In describing common-law extortion, Blackstone said it was "the taking by color of an office of money or other thing of value, that is not due, before it is due, or more than is due." See *State v. Cooper,* 113 S.W. 1048 (Tenn. 1908). Under most modern statutes extortion has been extended beyond acts by public officers.

The California law provides:

> Extortion is the obtaining of property from another, with his consent, or the obtaining of an official act of a public officer, induced by a wrongful use of force or fear, or under color of official right. West's Ann. Cal. Penal Code § 518.

It further stipulates:

> Fear, such as will constitute extortion, may be induced by a threat, either:
> 1. To do an unlawful injury to the person or property of the individual threatened or of a third person; or,
> 2. To accuse the individual threatened, or any relative of his, or member of his family, of any crime; or,
> 3. To expose, or to impute to him or them any deformity, disgrace or crime, or,
> 4. To expose any secret affecting him or them. West's Ann. Cal. Penal Code § 519.

In many instances the statutory offense of extortion has become synonymous with the common understanding of "blackmail." In fact, a federal statute, 18 U.S.C.A. §§ 875–876, that forbids sending extortion threats by mail is sometimes called "the blackmail statute."

Defenses to Crimes Involving Property

The common-law offenses of larceny and robbery were specific-intent crimes. This intent requirement has been carried over in statutes proscribing theft, either comprehensively or in various descriptive crimes, but the intent requirement in modern robbery statutes varies. Therefore, in a prosecution for theft a defendant may raise the defense of mistake of fact, but this does not necessarily follow when defending a charge of robbery (see Chapter 13). This means that a defendant who took items of property from another person in the good-faith belief that they belonged to the taker may have a defense. A classic example: Sherry leaves a coat on a coat rack and later Mary does also. The jackets are similar and Sherry mistakenly walks away with Mary's jacket. The problem becomes more acute if Mary has left a wallet in her jacket with hundreds of dollars of currency in it. These mistakes happen and furnish the justification for requiring the prosecution to prove a defendant's specific intent in theft offenses. Have you ever opened the door of a car like yours in a shopping center parking lot, thinking the car was your own?

In some theft prosecutions, mistake of law has been held to be a defense. This is limited to situations where there are exceedingly technical questions concerning ownership rights (see Chapter 13).

In a prosecution for forgery, an accused can defend by proving that he or she was authorized to sign another's name. Since forgery is a specific-intent crime, a mistake of fact can constitute a defense (see Chapter 13).

Burglary is generally a specific-intent crime. Thus, a mistake of fact can constitute a defense. For example, an intoxicated person who enters a "row-house" identical to his or her own may have a defense. And, of course, the requirement that the prosecution prove "an intent to commit a felony" would make it difficult to prove that a person who took refuge from a storm on the porch of an unoccupied dwelling did so with intent to commit a felony therein (see Chapter 13). Arson, on the other hand, is usually a general-intent crime. This imposes a limitation on defenses beyond consent, in which a person intentionally commits the proscribed acts. Since statutes proscribing the commission of arson with the intent to defraud an insurer usually require proof of the defendant's specific intent to defraud, the lack of such intent can be shown in defense.

Conclusion

Most statutory property crimes parallel the basic common-law scheme, but have been broadened to meet the demands of our changing society. While the common-law crimes against property and habitation provide a good starting point for legislating against offenses involving property, there is a need for continuing statutory revision to consolidate the laws proscribing certain property offenses that have proliferated over the years.

Statutes that proscribe various forms of theft and forgery need to be updated, particularly in light of computer and credit card crimes, which increasingly create serious problems in both the public and private sectors. Definitions must be reviewed to assure adequate protection against those who willfully take computer data or access computer systems without authority. Consumers are no longer willing to acquiesce in outmoded doctrines such as *caveat emptor*. Thus, laws concerning representations made in commercial transactions assume a role of importance in today's society. Consumer fraud, intentional false advertising, credit card fraud, and a variety of other scams need to be specifically proscribed or included in omnibus definitions of theft and forgery statutes.

The laws proscribing burglary and arson must protect more than homes. These offenses pose serious threats to lives and property, regardless of whether they are committed in a residential or business property, whether the structure involved is private or public, and whether it is a vehicle, vessel, building, or other structure. These offenses have moved from being crimes against habitation to being crimes against property. Modern statutes tend to make these offenses crimes against persons as well. With the almost universal dependence on insurance to protect against casualty losses, the need for a close look at statutes proscribing insurance fraud is also essential.

QUESTIONS FOR THOUGHT AND DISCUSSION

1. A. H. Hacker is a skilled computer operator at a business office. Through stealthful operation of his computer, he successfully obtains a list of names and addresses of a competitor's customers without the knowledge or consent of the competitor. For what offense would Hacker most likely be prosecuted in your state?

2. What advantages do you see in a state adopting a comprehensive theft statute?

3. Lefty Lightfingers steals a ham with a price tag of $19.50 from the meat counter in a supermarket. As he leaves the store, he is approached by a security guard. Lightfingers injures the security guard in his attempts to leave with the ham he has stolen. In your state, would Lightfingers be charged with petit theft, grand theft, or robbery? Explain.

4. Should the offense of forgery be divided into degrees based on the importance of the forged documents? If so, what criteria would you propose for the various degrees of the crime?

5. Sally Spendthrift has an established bank account at a local bank. She gives a check to a merchant for purchase of a new stereo. Her bank returns the check to the merchant because Ms. Spendthrift's account has insufficient funds to cover payment. Do you think Ms. Spendthrift should face criminal charges or simply be required to compensate the bank and anyone who suffered a loss?

6. Considering the various types of structures protected by burglary statutes, how would you classify burglary from the standpoint of ranking the most serious categories to the least serious categories?

7. Is it more important for theft offenses than robbery to be classified as specific-intent crimes? Why?

8. What provisions would you include in a model statute making arson a crime? Would you provide for separate degrees of the offense?

9. Give some examples of actions that would probably fall within the conduct proscribed by (a) extortion and (b) vandalism or malicious mischief statutes.

10. What offense would a person commit who destroyed or damaged data in someone's computer? If a person electronically accessed another's computer without permission, would this constitute a criminal offense?

CASES

STATE V. RICHARD
Supreme Court of Nebraska, 1984.
216 Neb. 832, 346 N.W.2d 399.

[This case deals with the offense of shoplifting.]

PER CURIAM.
Defendant was convicted in the county court for Scotts Bluff County of violation of Scottsbluff city ordinance § 13–201, which provided in part: "It is hereby declared unlawful for any person within the city to steal any money, goods or chattels of any kind whatever." Defendant appealed to the district court, in which his conviction and fine of $100 were affirmed. Defendant appeals to this court. For the reasons hereinafter stated we reverse and dismiss.

The evidence on behalf of the State showed that defendant entered Alexander's Super Market on March 25, 1983, between 7 and 8 A.M. He examined the bacon displayed for sale, picked up a 1-pound package, and walked by the meat counter. Alexander's meat manager followed defendant, and by demonstration at trial showed that defendant thrust his hand into his coat, went toward the express lane, and "didn't have the bacon [in his hand] anymore." The meat manager told the checker to call "service 50," which indicated that "shoplifting" was going on.

Other Alexander employees then came up, and the meat manager saw nothing further. On cross-examination the meat manager testified that he followed and watched defendant "[b]ecause he looked suspicious, in that when he picked up the bacon he moved his head from side to side."

The manager of Alexander's testified that he responded to the "service 50" call and first saw defendant halfway down one of the aisles, approached him and talked to him about the bacon, and defendant took the pound of bacon from his coat. The bacon was priced at $1.89. This witness could not remember whether defendant told him that he was going to pay for the bacon, but did remember that defendant handed the bacon to the witness and walked out of the store after the confrontation.

A Scottsbluff policeman testified that the manager of the store told the police officer that defendant told them he was going to pay for the bacon, gave the bacon back, informed the store personnel that "they were not going to hold him for the police," and left.

Defendant testified that he had examined different types of bacon, selected one pound, did not put it in his coat, was stopped by the store personnel, showed them his wallet with "seventy-some" dollars in it, offered to pay, and when that offer was refused told the store personnel that he was not trying to steal the bacon; and said "either you're going to take my money or . . . I'm going to walk back, . . . I'm going to put it down, I'm going to walk out of here."

It is clear from the evidence considered in the light most favorable to the State that the bacon was not removed from the store by defendant. Counsel for the parties agree that to constitute the crime of "stealing" there must be a taking and "asportation" with intent to steal. The State contends that in a self-service store, "The elements of a taking and asportation are satisfied where the evidence shows that the property was taken from the owner and was concealed or put in a convenient place for removal. The fact that the possession was brief or that the person was detected before the goods could be removed from the owner's premises is immaterial." . . .

We cannot agree. With the changes in merchandising and the enactment of new and different statutes affecting a shopper's conduct, we have gone beyond the law cited by the State that to take an article feloniously is accomplished by simply laying hold of, grasping, or seizing it *animo furandi,* with the hands or otherwise, and that the very least removal of it by the thief from the place where found is an asportation or carrying away. . . . To constitute larceny the object stolen must be removed from the premises of the owner, with intent to steal, before the larceny is complete. In so stating we reiterate what we said in *State v. Hauck,* 190 Neb. 534, 537, 209 N.W.2d 580, 583 (1973): "The determination of what constitutes a taking and carrying away of property with the intent to permanently deprive the owner of possession and whether that taking is with or without the consent of the owner involves issues of intent which are often difficult of determination. Where merchandise in a store is involved, those issues are vitally affected if the store is operated on a self-service basis. The cases appear to be in agreement that in a self-service store, where customers select and pick up articles to be paid for at the checkout counter, the mere picking up of an article in the display area does not constitute asportation." . . . In *Durphy v. United States*, 235 A.2d 326, 327 (D.C. 1967), the court stated that "the normal procedure in this type of market is for customers to circulate through the sales area, taking from the shelves any items they wish to buy but not paying for their selections until they pass through the check-out counter. . . . The fact that appellant placed the goods in a shopping bag provided no valid reason for the trial court to infer a criminal intent or a possession clearly adverse to the interest of the store."

Our holding is not to be read that defendant's conduct might not have warranted conviction on other charges, such as attempted stealing (Neb. Rev. Stat. § 28–201 (Reissue 1979), or violation of Neb. Rev. Stat. § 28–551.01(1) (Cum. Supp. 1982), which provides that a person commits the crime of theft by shoplifting when, with intent to appropriate property without paying for it, he "(a) Conceals or takes possession of the goods or merchandise of any store or retail establishment."

In this difficult area of the law regarding self-service stores, precision in charging and proving offenses will result in clarity in determining what conduct is, or is not, criminal.

Reversed and dismissed.

JONES v. COMMONWEALTH
Court of Appeals of Virginia, 1992.
13 Va. App. 566, 414 S.E.2d 193.

[In this case the Virginia Court of Appeals considers the sufficiency of the evidence to support the appellant's conviction for robbery.]

BRAY, Judge.

Jerry Earl Jones (defendant) was convicted in a jury trial of robbery and sentenced in accordance with the verdict to twenty years imprisonment. He contends that the evidence was insufficient to sustain the verdict. We disagree and affirm the conviction.

The evidence disclosed that, on the morning of March 17, 1989, Deputy John Stanton (Stanton) of the Williamsburg Sheriff's Department was transporting defendant from the "Richmond Penitentiary" to Williamsburg. Defendant was manacled in "leg chains and . . . a waist chain that ha[d] a handcuff attached to each side." Stanton was the operator of the "unmarked" vehicle, defendant was seated in the rear and no "divider" separated the two.

In route, defendant suddenly stated, "Sheriff, don't make me blow your damn brains out." Stanton was "startled" and "scared" and "jerked" his "head to the right to see what was going on." He observed defendant with "an object . . . something metal that appeared to be the barrel of a pistol," which Stanton "assumed it was." The vehicle was then travelling "approximately 65 [mph]," and Stanton lost control for "10 or 15 seconds," until it came to rest in the grassy median.

Stanton immediately began to "look and feel for [his] gun," which was missing and had been "in [his] holster at the time . . . the car went out of control." Unarmed, the deputy "was fearful for [his] life" and, when defendant demanded that Stanton "get the car back on the road," he "decided . . . that [he] wasn't going with" defendant. In an effort to "wreck" the car and "bail out," Stanton "cut . . . toward the guardrail" and "jumped out on the grass." Defendant, however, "got to the wheel and got it straightened out" and escaped in the vehicle.

The car was discovered in downtown Richmond later the same day with its two radio antennae and several hubcaps removed and in the truck. A "fake gun" was found on the rear seat. Defendant was arrested shortly thereafter on a Richmond street and Stanton's stolen pistol was found in the "waistband" of his trousers. He was indicted on March 20, 1989. . . .

. . . When the sufficiency of the evidence is challenged on appeal, it is well established that we must view the evidence in the light most favorable to the Commonwealth, granting to it all reasonable inferences fairly deducible therefrom. The conviction will be disturbed only if plainly wrong or without evidence to support it. . . .

The elements of robbery, a common law offense in Virginia, include a "taking, with intent to steal, of the personal property of another, from his person or in his presence, against his will, by violence or intimidation" which precedes or is "concomitant with the taking." . . .

Defendant threatened Stanton's life while brandishing an object which appeared to be a weapon. As a result, Stanton was fearful and surrendered the vehicle to defendant. Defendant then escaped with both the automobile and Stanton's pistol, apparently taken by defendant while Stanton was in extremity. These circumstances amply support a robbery conviction.

Accordingly, the judgment of conviction is affirmed.

STATE V. GOMEZ

Court of Appeals of Arizona, 1976.
27 Ariz. App. 248, 553 P.2d 1233.

[This case involves the crimes of forgery and embezzlement.]

KRUCKER, Judge.

This is an appeal from convictions of forgery, A.R.S. 13–421, and theft by embezzlement, A.R.S. 13–682, and concurrent sentences thereon of not less than eight nor more than ten years on the forgery charge and not less than eight nor more than ten years on the embezzlement charge. . . .

The pertinent facts are as follows. On June 3, 1975, Emma Cisneros purchased a 1964 Volkswagen van bus from one Chris Powers. A certificate of title was conveyed to Ms. Cisneros and testimony revealed that Gerald Wager, a notary public, notarized the signature of Chris Powers, which assigned the title to Ms. Cisneros.

The record reflects that Ms. Cisneros came in contact with appellant, Bobby Gomez, while dining at the Coronado Inn in Nogales on the evening of June 7, 1975. Appellant expressed interest in purchasing the 1964 VW microbus for $500, predicated upon a one-hour test drive. Ms. Cisneros agreed and when appellant failed to return after one and a half

hours, she left the restaurant. For the next three months she was unsuccessful in her attempts to locate either the vehicle or appellant.

On September 17, 1975, Ms. Cisneros observed her VW microbus at the Diaz Garage in Nogales, Arizona. Mr. Diaz, a mechanic, testified that in mid-June, 1975, the vehicle was delivered for repairs to his garage in Mexico by Mr. Rodolfo Gomez, appellant's uncle. Although the record is not completely clear, apparently at a later date Diaz contacted Gomez to inform him that the repairs were complete. Diaz was directed to bring the microbus to the garage in Nogales, Arizona, which was owned by his uncle. The vehicle was delivered at noon on September 17, 1975.

After observing the microbus, Ms. Cisneros removed the ignition keys and told Mr. Diaz to send the person who claimed the van to her office at the Wager Insurance Agency in Nogales, Arizona. That same day appellant appeared at the Wager Insurance Agency to pick up the keys to the vehicle. Upon Ms. Cisneros' refusal to give up the keys, appellant left the agency but later returned with the certificate of title. Claiming that he did not want to have anything else to do with the car, Gomez gave the title to Ms. Cisneros.

The name and address of Ms. Cisneros had been removed from the certificate and replaced with the name and address of Bobby Gomez. Testimony revealed that the document was on the sun visor of the microbus when it was loaned to appellant on June 7, 1975.

On October 22, 1975, a preliminary hearing was held in the Santa Cruz County Justice Court. On January 14, 1976, verdicts of guilty were returned against appellant after a trial by jury on the aforementioned counts. . . .

Sufficiency of the Evidence

Appellant's . . . contention on appeal is that the State failed to present sufficient evidence to convict him of the crime of forgery. A.R.S. 13–421 (A) (1). Specifically, he complains that there was no showing that he actually did forge his name upon the document in question or of the requisite intent to defraud.

We have held that intent to defraud is an essential element of forgery. . . . However, intent to defraud may be, and often must be, inferred from the circumstances in which the false instrument is executed or issued. . . .

We do not require direct evidence of appellant physically obscuring or obliterating Ms. Cisneros' name and address with liquid paper and inserting his own. To do so would place a virtually impossible burden on the State. It is not within the best interests of justice to grant a special status to covert activities by rendering immune from prosecution those individuals performing actions outside the public view.

In the case at bench, a certificate of title was transferred to Ms. Cisneros and the signature of the transferor, Chris Powers, was notarized. Ms. Cisneros testified that the title was inside the microbus when appellant took the vehicle on June 7, 1975. She further testified that she next saw this document on September 17, 1975, when appellant produced it from his wallet at her place of work and returned it to her.

Her name and address, which has appeared on the document, were replaced by that of appellant.

We have no difficulty in concluding that the circumstances of the disappearance and recovery of the vehicle, along with appellant's physical possession of the altered document, provided sufficient evidence to support the jury's determination that appellant altered the document with intent to defraud or aided and abetted the alteration with the same intent.

Appellant also contends that the State never showed "that the appellant ever embezzled anything" in violation of A.R.S. 13–682. We have stated that the gist of the crime of embezzlement is a breach of trust. . . . The elements necessary to establish embezzlement are a trust relation, possession or control of property by virtue of the trust relation, and a fraudulent appropriation of the property to a use or purpose not in the due and lawful execution of the trust. . . .

We believe there is ample evidence to support appellant's conviction of embezzlement. The record reflects that during a discussion of the possibility of appellant's purchase of Ms. Cisneros' VW microbus, appellant requested possession and control of the vehicle for the purpose of a test drive and stated that he would return "in about an hour or so." Ms. Cisneros waited for approximately one and a half hours before leaving the restaurant where she had met appellant. From early June until the discovery of the van in mid-September she attempted to locate both appellant and the vehicle.

The foregoing certainly reflects that possession and control of the microbus was entrusted to appellant for the express and limited purpose of a one-hour test drive as a condition of purchase. The vehicle was never returned and at no time did appellant tender payment for it or notify Ms. Cisneros of its whereabouts. Instead, from June 7 until its discovery on September 17, the microbus was apparently converted to appellant's own use. . . . The requisite intent is inferred from the circumstances. . . .

Affirmed.

STATE V. FELDT

Supreme Court of Montana, 1989.
239 Mont. 398, 781 P.2d 255.

[Charles Matthew Feldt was convicted of burglary and theft and was sentenced to concurrent five-year prison terms for each offense. In this case the Montana Supreme Court considers an appeal of the burglary conviction.]

SHEEHY, Justice.

... The issue on appeal is stated as follows: (1) Whether the trial court erred in finding that the defendant entered his employer's premises "unlawfully," thereby committing burglary under 45–6–204(1), MCA.

On the morning of April 27, 1987, the manager of T.C. Foods, a convenience store in Great Falls, Montana, was called to the store by the morning clerk. Upon arrival, the manager found a set of keys in the door, subsequently determined to have been issued to defendant, Feldt, an employee at T.C. Foods. The manager discovered $1,459 was missing from the safe. In addition, the manager found a note posted on the cash register which stated, "I know you trusted me, but I couldn't handle it at home. I am sorry. If you want, you can try and get the money out of my car or bike. Chuck."

On April 28, 1987, the defendant turned himself in to the Great Falls police department. He gave the police a bag containing $1,219 at the time of his surrender. He confessed to entering the store after hours by means of his keys, taking the money and leaving the note on the cash register.

At trial, the manager testified that all employees were given keys to the store and access to the store safe. The defendant testified that he was required to open and close the store and he was permitted access to the store's safe. According to both the manager and the defendant, the manager allowed employees to enter the store after business hours for any proper purposes. The evidence fails to disclose, from the State or from the defendant, that when the store key was delivered to Feldt, any limitation, written or oral, was placed upon his use of it, or upon his access to the safe. ...

Section 45–6–204(1), MCA, defines burglary as follows:

"A person commits the offense of burglary if he knowingly enters or remains unlawfully in an occupied structure with the purpose to commit an offense therein. . . ."

"Enters or remains unlawfully" is defined in 45–6–201, MCA, which reads in pertinent part:

"A person enters or remains unlawfully . . . when he is not licensed, invited, or otherwise privileged to do so."

This Court in *State v. Starkweather* . . . [1931] held that an entry made by one who is licensed or privileged to be on the premises is not unlawful under the burglary statute. The Court in *Starkweather* stated: "There is no breaking in or entering a house or room and therefore, no burglary, if the person who enters has a right to do so." . . . To constitute a burglary the nature of the entry must itself be a trespass. . . .

This Court in *Starkweather* focused on whether there was a limitation upon the defendant's right to enter a pool hall. In *Starkweather*, the Court found no limitation on the defendant's right to enter the pool hall. This case turns on the same issue, that is whether there is any limitation on Feldt's right to enter T.C. Foods. The defendant Feldt was given permission to enter T.C. Foods where he was employed. As an employee of T.C. Foods, the manager gave Feldt a set of keys to enter the store and provided Feldt with access to the safe. In issuing the keys, the manager provided Feldt with authority to enter the premises at any time. The record reveals no limitations to the defendant's right to enter the store. However, the manager did testify at trial that Feldt could only enter the store after it was closed for proper purposes. Despite the manager's testimony, Feldt could enter T.C. Foods at any time day or night.

Under this Court's holding in *Starkweather*, and 45–6–204 and 45–6–201, MCA, the defendant can not be convicted of burglary. He lawfully entered the building after closing hours with keys provided by the manager of T.C. Foods. Feldt did not trespass when he entered T.C. Foods. His keys granted him authority to enter T.C. Foods after hours.

The State argues that Feldt abused his privilege to enter T.C. Foods after hours, when he entered for the improper purpose to steal the money from the safe. The State further contends that Feldt's improper entry into T.C. Foods after hours transforms his original permissible entry into a trespass that can form the basis of a burglary charge.... While Feldt acted improperly in taking the money from the safe, his entry into T.C. Foods was authorized by management. Feldt was properly charged and convicted for theft, but the State failed to meet the "unlawful entry" element of the burglary statute and this Court's previous holding under *Starkweather.*

Finally, the State argues that the requirement of a trespassory entry under *Starkweather* is no longer accurate under the new burglary statute. We find little merit in the State's argument, since the Criminal Code Commission specifically endorsed the Court's holding in *Starkweather* in rewriting the burglary statute....

The defendant had access to T.C. Foods and did not "enter or remain unlawfully" as defined in 45–6–201, MCA. Since there was no unlawful entry, the defendant's actions do not constitute a burglary as defined in 45–6–204, MCA. We reverse the burglary conviction. The theft conviction was not appealed. The sentence imposed upon Feldt for the District Court is modified to strike therefrom the penalty assessed for burglary, and as modified, the sentence is affirmed.

HARRISON, WEBER, and HUNT, JJ., concur.

GULBRANDSON, Justice, dissenting.

I respectfully dissent. The trial judge ... found [that] T.C. Foods store was closed for business when the defendant entered said store and took the money. Defendant did not have permission to enter the store at that time and he did not have permission to take the money.

In my view, there is sufficient evidence in the record to affirm the conviction for burglary. The manager of T.C. Foods store had personally hired the defendant and knew the defendant's work schedule. At trial, the manager testified as follows:

Q. Now, the Defendant, Charles Matthew Feldt, even though he is an employee of your store, did he have your permission to enter the store after hours?

A. No.

Q. And, if the Defendant was not working a shift on Sunday night before you arrive at the store Monday morning, then technically, isn't it correct, if at all, that an employee in his position would not have permission to go back and turn the coffee off or anything like that?

A. Right.

Q. Because he wouldn't have been working that shift, isn't that my understanding?

A. Yes.

Q. So, he really can't have any permission at all to go into the T.C. Foods between the times you closed on Sunday and you opened on Monday, isn't that my understanding of it?

A. Yes.

Q. He didn't have permission to go into the store for any purpose such as turning the alarm on, or turning the coffee off, maybe to lock a door, things like that. Isn't that my understanding of the situation?

A. Yes.

Testimony at trial established that the defendant had not worked on the Sunday preceding the incident, and he was not scheduled to work Monday, the day of the incident. The defendant testified personally as follows:

Q. Now you had nobody's permission to go into the store at that time; isn't that correct?

A. Not at that time.

The foregoing testimony, in my view, supports the trial judge's finding that defendant did not have permission to enter the store at that time. The record as a whole supports the trial judge's verdict that the defendant was guilty of burglary....

McDONOUGH, J., concurs.

TURNAGE, Chief Justice, concurring....

FOX V. STATE

Court of Appeals of Indiana, 1979.
179 Ind. App. 267, 384 N.E.2d 1159.

[This case deals with the crime of arson.]

SHIELDS, Judge.

Appellants were tried by a jury and convicted of first degree arson.... The statute under which appellants were charged and convicted is I.C. 35–16–1–1, which provides, in pertinent part:

Any person who wilfully and maliciously sets fire to or burns or causes the setting of fire to or burning of ... any kitchen, shop, barn, stable, garage or other outhouse, or other building that is part or parcel of any dwelling house ...

Although no Indiana case has defined the phrase "part or parcel of any dwelling house," many other jurisdictions have done so. At common law, an outhouse which was a "parcel of" a dwelling house was one "used in connection therewith and situated within the curtilage." ...

"Curtilage" has been defined as:

... the space of ground adjoining the dwelling house used in connection therewith in the conduct of family affairs and for carrying on domestic purposes, usually including the buildings occupied in connection with the dwelling house. It is the propinquity to a dwelling and the use in connection with it for family purposes which is to be regarded....

As the authorities indicate, it is the proximity to the dwelling and the use in connection therewith for family purposes and the carrying on of domestic employment that are of major importance in determining whether an area or building is to be considered within the "curtilage" (i.e., part or parcel) of the dwelling house. This comports with the view that first degree arson is an offense against the security of habitation, rather than property....

In the case at bar, the evidence viewed most favorably to the State shows that the burned building was a barn that had been converted into a combination garage-work area-recreation room. The building, located 80 to 100 feet from the dwelling house, was insulated and panelled and housed a furnace, telephone, and stereo. The Mowerys (owners of the property) often kept vehicles in the building, and Mr. Mowery also had a work area in the building. The building had been used on several occasions for parties and the Mowery's daughter and her friends often used the building to play music and dance.

The usage of the building as an addition to their dwelling house, i.e., "for family purposes and the carrying on of domestic employment," and its proximity to the dwelling house, persuade us that it was within the "curtilage," i.e., that the building burned was "part or parcel" of the Mowery dwelling house....

Appellants challenge the sufficiency of the evidence to establish their identity as the perpetrators of the arson at Mowerys' building. When reviewing the sufficiency of the evidence, this Court considers the evidence most favorable to the verdict together with all reasonable inferences which may be drawn from that evidence. If there is substantial evidence of probative value to support each element of the offense, the judgment will be affirmed.... Furthermore, this Court does not judge the credibility of witnesses nor weigh the evidence....

In the case at bar, the evidence most favorable to the state reveals that the five appellants were seen together from approximately 2:30 to 3:00 A.M. visiting several bars in Marion, Grant County, Indiana, and driving a dirty, goldish-green 1968 Oldsmobile, registered to [defendant] Fox, which reportedly had "extremely loud mufflers." The appellants were imbibing in spirits at the Swing Bar when, somewhere around 3:00 A.M., Marion police officers were called to the bar twice to quell disturbances and, on the later occasion, also to close the bar. On the former occasion the bar was surrounded by police and [defendant] York was heard to say, "Isn't there some kind of charge against police harassment?" During this first visit Captain Mowery (Mowery), the owner of the property that was burned, "broke up" what appeared to be a verbal confrontation between Fox and another patron. As Fox was walking back to his table he stated "That's cool, Mowery. That's cool." During the second police visit to the bar, after Mowery announced that the bar was closed, Fox leaned over as he passed Mowery on the way out and said, "I'll see you later, Mowery," following which a verbal exchange of words occurred between Fox and Mowery. About the same time this confrontation occurred, [defendant] Havens said, "F_____ the pigs. We don't have to listen to this s_____ . Let's get out of here."

While the Swing Bar was being closed, Officer Ellis, en route back to his squad car, noticed suspicious-looking tools on the rear floor board of Fox's Oldsmobile. Mowery, upon being informed of these tools, ordered the vehicle to be kept under surveillance. Appellants left the Swing Bar and proceeded to the Kewpie Bar. While at the Kewpie Bar, [defendant] Perry left the table where all five appellants had been sitting, came back a few minutes later and stated, "Everything's okay. They're scattered." Fox then said, "Well, let's go then," telling an inquirer who was asking to go with them, ". . . we are just going to take care of a little business." After departing from the Kewpie Bar, appellants stopped at Stoller's Tavern and purchased a fifth of whiskey and six 6 oz. (sic) bottles of Coca Cola. Appellants were last seen, prior to the fire at Mowery's, parking the Oldsmobile behind a house in Marion at about 3:25 A.M., at which time surveillance of the vehicle was withdrawn. The vehicle was gone when Officer Stevens checked back at 3:50 A.M.

Carol Mowery (wife of Captain Mowery) was awakened by the dog's barking sometime between 3:30 and 4:00 A.M. After hearing a car idling for some time, she went downstairs and looked out the window and saw two people in a car parked by the barn and three others milling about by the barn. Immediately thereafter she saw flames shoot out of the cab of the stake-bed truck parked outside, next to the barn. She then saw the subjects get into the car and drive off. Some minutes later she called the police (testimony revealed that the call was received at 4:12 A.M.) and her brother-in-law, Clifford Mowery, who was a fireman. In a matter of minutes Clifford arrived and went out to the barn with Mrs. Mowery where they discovered that, in addition to the truck being on fire, the floor mat of the Corvette

parked inside the barn and a wall and part of the ceiling of the barn were also aflame. Mrs. Mowery could not identify or describe any of the persons she saw except to say that she assumed they were males by the way they were dressed, and that one of them was very tall and large. She described the car she saw parked beside the barn as a dirty, greenish-gold Oldsmobile which had a noisy exhaust.

After the fire, the greenish-gold Oldsmobile was observed driving through Van Buren, Grant County, Indiana, which is located approximately seven miles east of Mowery's house. Marshall Marley and Officer Campbell pursued the vehicle and stopped it approximately three-fourths of a mile east of Van Buren at about 5:27 A.M. They arrested the occupants of the car, [defendants] Perry, Kapp, and Havens, on a preliminary charge of arson. The automobile was impounded. Mrs. Mowery later identified it as the car she saw by the barn the morning of the fire when an officer took her to a garage where it was parked with "several cars . . . and some trucks and stuff."

Deputy Sheriff Cook pursued a gold, 1967 Buick through Marion sometime between 4:00 and 4:45 A.M. The Buick was subsequently found to have been stolen from Van Buren sometime earlier that night. Cook identified [defendants] Fox and York as the individuals who abandoned the vehicle and fled on foot.

Sheriff Ash, while looking around the burned area, found a 7 oz. (sic) coke bottle which smelled as if it had contained whiskey or alcohol. He further observed a bootprint in the snow beside the barn. Kapp's boots were subsequently brought to the scene and an impression of one of them was made in the snow beside this print. Photographs of the bootprint, as well as Kapp's boots, were admitted into evidence and the similarities were pointed out by the Sheriff. There was no evidence as to the presence of any inflammables on the scene. Fireman Mowery testified that in his opinion the fires were not accidental.

Assuming, arguendo, that this evidence is sufficient to prove that appellants were the five individuals Mrs. Mowery observed at the scene, there is still a link missing in the chain of circumstantial evidence which the State has woven around appellants: that is who were the two individuals Mrs. Mowery observed that remained in the car, and were these two individuals accessories to the commission of the arson? The State has proven that two individuals remained in the car while three other individuals were perpetrating the crime. Thus, in order to sustain the convictions of these two individuals, it must be shown that they were accessories to the arson.

The general rule is that mere presence at the scene of the crime is not sufficient to allow an inference of participation. . . . However, we acknowledge that presence, coupled with other circumstances, may be sufficient. Thus, evidence of companionship with one engaged in a crime, a course of conduct before and after the offense, and failure to oppose the crime when imposed with a duty to do so, without active participation in the commission of the crime, are circumstances which may be considered in determining whether aiding and abetting may be inferred. . . . However, an inference from such evidence, to be reasonable, must be coupled with evidence of knowledge or evidence from which knowledge may be reasonably inferred, that the criminal conduct is contemplated, in progress or completed.

Thus, the State must show that the ones alleged to aid or abet were aware of and consented to the activity condemned by law, . . . although it need not necessarily prove a pre-conceived plan. . . . In the case at bar, there was no evidence that could show the two individuals in the car had any knowledge that the arson was planned or committed. There was no evidence of their location in the car, or of any motion by them. While the testimony relating to the appellants' activities in the Kewpie Bar might indicate a criminal design in the making, can one infer from this evidence that they were scheming to commit an arson? This may raise a suspicion that appellants may have known of a criminal design to commit an arson, however, mere suspicion that appellants were aware of a criminal design is not enough. . . . The evidence adduced at trial is insufficient to sustain the convictions of the two individuals who were inside the car while the arson was being committed.

This leads to a further problem, being the lack of evidence indicating which of the appellants were inside the car. The only evidence indicating which of the appellants were outside the car was Kapp's bootprint found at the scene. The evidence is, therefore, sufficient to sustain Kapp's conviction as a principal.

With respect to the other four appellants, however, we must reach a different result. Because there is insufficient evidence to sustain the convictions of the two individuals that were inside the car, and since there is no evidence indicating who those individuals were, how can we, as an appellate court, pick and choose which of the four remaining appellants were inside that car? The answer is: We cannot. It is fundamental to our system of law that guilt is individual. . . . Here, that means there must be sufficient evidence to support a finding, as to each appellant, that he was either a principal or an accessory to the arson as charged. The evidence was insufficient in this regard; thus, we are constrained to hold that the evidence was not sufficient to sustain the convictions of Fox, Havens, York, and Perry. . . .

Next, we consider Kapp's argument that the evidence is insufficient to establish a willful and malicious burning. Kapp properly cites *Ellis v. State,* (1969) 252 Ind. 472, 250 N.E.2d 364, as authority for the proposition that the law of Indiana presumes that a fire accidentally resulted from some providential cause, rather than from a criminal cause, unless the evidence proves otherwise. We do not agree, however, that the evidence was insufficient to overcome the State's burden of proving that the fire was not the result of natural causes.

As the Supreme Court noted in *Ellis,* there is rarely direct evidence of the actual lighting of a fire by an arsonist; rather, the evidence of arson is usually circumstantial. Such evidence is often of a negative character; that is, the criminal agency is shown by the absence of circumstances, conditions, and surroundings indicating that the fire resulted from an accidental cause. . . .

In the instant case, three persons were observed milling about a building late at night on property where they had no right to be. Immediately after one individual was observed standing beside it, flames shot out of the stake-bed truck. Furthermore, fires were subsequently discovered in two other separate locations. All this evidence, taken together, supports the inference that the fires were set "wilfully and maliciously." . . .

MILLER, J., concurs with opinion. [omitted.]
BUCHANAN, C. J., dissents with opinion. [omitted.]

State v. Tonnisen

Superior Court of New Jersey, Appellate Division, 1966.
92 N.J. Super. 452, 224 A.2d 21.

[This case involves the offense of malicious mischief.]

The opinion of the court was delivered by SULLIVAN, S.J.A.D.

After a trial by jury, defendant was convicted of malicious mischief. The statute involved is N.J.S. 2A:122–1, N.J.S.A., which provides:

Any person who willfully or maliciously destroys, damages, injures or spoils any real or personal property of another, either of a public or private nature, for which no punishment is otherwise provided by statute, is guilty of a misdemeanor.

The State produced evidence that the employees of the Peter J. Schweitzer Plant were on strike and some of the employees were on a picket line across the entrance to the plant. Defendant was one of the employees at or near the plant entrance at the time of the incident in question.

A tank trailer truck loaded with caustic soda arrived at the plant entrance but was blocked by the pickets. A police officer on duty proceeded to clear a path for the truck through the picket line. Defendant was then seen by the officer and other persons to go over to the side of the truck and stick his hand in between the tractor and the trailer. When he withdrew his hand there was grease on it. The officer attempted to tell the driver "to hold it" but before his warning could be heard, the tractor pulled ahead and separated from the trailer which fell down on the road causing the bottom of the tank to crack and the contents thereof to begin to leak out on the road. Examination of the vehicle showed that the safety mechanism of the coupling between the tractor and trailer had been pulled. The dollar amount of the damage resulting from the incident was not shown by the State.

Defendant, who testified in his own defense, denied that he had put his hand "anywheres in the vicinity of the coupling between the truck and the trailer."

On this appeal defendant argues that the State failed to prove criminal willfullness or malice on defendant's part. We disagree. These elements are rarely if ever susceptible of direct proof. In the usual case they are inferred from the totality of the State's case. Here we find ample credible evidence from which a jury could have found that beyond a reasonable doubt defendant pulled the safety mechanism and did so willfully or maliciously within the intent of the statute. . . .

Affirmed.

CHAPTER 8

OFFENSES AGAINST PUBLIC MORALITY

INTRODUCTION

In this chapter we discuss a number of crimes traditionally classified as offenses against public morality. Many deal with sexual conduct—fornication and adultery, seduction, incest, bigamy, sodomy, prostitution, indecent exposure—and in a sense, obscenity and profanity. In this chapter we also examine gambling offenses. Offenses involving alcohol and drugs, while they may be viewed as crimes against morality, can also be seen as offenses against the public order and safety. Accordingly, they are dealt with in Chapter 9.

The Common-Law Background

The common law of crimes developed largely because of society's demands for security of persons and property, the need to maintain public order, and the judges' perceptions of society's concepts of morality. Many ideas of morality were based on the Bible and church doctrine; others were simply the product of the shared experiences of the people. These concepts became the foundation for the criminal laws in this country in the prerevolutionary days, when early settlers tended to equate sin with crime. Later, as legislative bodies defined crimes, the statutes more closely reflected the moral standards of the new American society. Eventually, the equation of crime with sin gave way to a more secular approach to crime.

Religious Influences

The contemporary criminal law still reflects to a great extent the morality of the Bible and church doctrine. In fact, it has been said that organized religion is the greatest single moral force in our society. Conflicts sometimes surface because this pluralistic nation has a constitutional prohibition against the establishment of religion and a guarantee of the free exercise thereof. Therefore, questions arise concerning whether a law with a religious origin can be enforced without offending these basic constitutional guarantees. The short answer is that most criminal laws that proscribe behavior forbidden by the Bible have also been found to serve a recognized secular purpose. Obviously, certain moral principles must be enforced for the protection of society. No one suggests that murder should not be regarded as criminal simply because of the biblical injunction, "Thou shall not kill." Historically, some of our ancestors imposed severe criminal sanctions for taking the name of the Lord in vain. Yet, few today who regard such an act as a serious sin would support criminal sanctions for violation of this commandment.

Is Morality a Legitimate Basis for Legislation?

An essential characteristic of a sovereign state is "police power," the power to legislate in pursuit of public health, safety, welfare, and morality. More than a century ago the United States Supreme Court assumed that regulation of morality was among the purposes of government when it stated:

Whatever differences of opinion may exist as to the extent and boundaries of the police power, and however difficult it may be to render a satisfactory definition of it, there seems to be no doubt that it does extend to . . . the preservation of good order and the public morals. *Boston Beer Co. v. Massachusetts*, 97 U.S. (7 Otto) 25, 33, 24 L.Ed. 989 (1878).

Constitutional Limitations

In the United States, legislative bodies have broad authority to define conduct as criminal and to set the punishment to be meted out to violators. Of course, there are restrictions. As noted in Chapter 3, the U.S. Constitution and the constitutions of every state impose limitations on government efforts to criminalize certain forms of conduct. For example, in *Griswold v. Connecticut*, 381 U.S. 479, 85 S.Ct. 1678, 14 L.Ed.2d 510 (1965), the U.S. Supreme Court struck down a state law that made it a crime for all persons, even married couples, to use birth control devices. The Court said that the law violated the right of privacy that inheres in the Bill of Rights and is imposed on the states via the Fourteenth Amendment. Some would argue that this right of privacy ought to be interpreted to prohibit government from "legislating morality" altogether. The Supreme Court, however, has never accepted this view. Writing for the Court in *Bowers v. Hardwick*, 478 U.S. 186, 106 S.Ct. 2841, 92 L.Ed.2d 140 (1986), Justice Byron White observed that "the law . . . is constantly based on notions of morality, and if all laws representing essentially moral choices are to be invalidated . . ., the courts will be very busy indeed." 478 U.S. at 196, 106 S.Ct. at 2846, 92 L.Ed. at 149.

Police Power and the Social Consensus

It has long been assumed that legislative bodies have the authority to criminalize conduct they determine to be contrary to the health, safety, and morals of the people, as long as such prohibitions do not infringe rights protected by the state and federal constitutions. The problem is primarily one of legislative perception of the standards that society requires and is willing to accept. Historically, enforcement of the criminal law has largely depended on community acceptance of certain conduct being forbidden by law. But public opinion about law changes. A societal consensus resulted in a constitutional amendment in 1919 prohibiting the sale of intoxicating liquors. It proved unworkable, and after a strong consensus developed to repeal prohibition, the amendment was repealed in 1933. See U.S. Const. Amendments XVIII & XXI.

Today, there are varying attitudes as to whether certain forms of conduct should be illegal. For example, public opinion is divided on the need for laws making it a crime to engage in certain forms of gambling. Consequently, the criminal prohibitions against gambling vary considerably throughout the United States. Since the sexual revolution of the 1960s there has been an erosion of the consensus supporting laws prohibiting sexual activities between consenting adults. This decline in consensus has led many legislatures to revise their criminal codes to remove prohibitions against certain sexual conduct. As in the case of gambling laws, statutes governing sexual conduct now vary from state to state.

CRIMINAL PROHIBITIONS ON SEXUAL CONDUCT

Debate concerning offenses against public morality usually centers primarily on the statutory prohibitions against fornication, adultery, seduction, sodomy, prostitution, and, to a lesser degree, incest. Many people today believe that such behavior is, or at least ought to be, private in character and thus beyond the reach of the criminal law. In contrast, many still subscribe to the classical conservative view that such prohibitions are necessary to maintain a proper moral climate.

Fornication and Adultery

Fornication is sexual intercourse between unmarried persons. Adultery is generally defined as sexual intercourse between a male and female, at least one of whom is married to someone else. Fornication and adultery were regarded as offenses against morality and were punishable in the ecclesiastical courts in England. Neither was a common-law crime unless committed openly. In such instances the act was prosecuted as a public nuisance. *Richey v. State*, 87 N.E. 1032 (Ind. 1909). While these offenses have a biblical basis, there is a threefold legal rationale for proscribing such conduct: (1) to avoid disharmony in family relationships; (2) to prevent illegitimate births; and (3) to prevent the spread of sexually transmitted diseases.

Minnesota law addresses the subject of sex crimes in the traditional manner. Its criminal code provides: "When any man and single woman have sexual intercourse with each other, each is guilty of fornication, which is a misdemeanor." Minn. Stat. Ann. § 609.34. The Minnesota Supreme Court has said that the term *fornication* has a definite, well-understood meaning, and a single clandestine act of intercourse constitutes fornication in the usual acceptation of the term. *State v. Gieseke*, 147 N.W. 663 (Minn. 1914). In respect to adultery, a Minnesota statute provides: "When a married woman has sexual intercourse with a man other than her husband, whether married or not, both are guilty of adultery." Minn. Stat. Ann. § 609.36(1). The statute, however, stipulates that it is a defense to violation thereof "if the marital status of the woman was not known to the defendant at the time of the act of adultery." Minn. Stat. Ann. § 609.36(3).

These offenses, especially fornication, are rarely prosecuted today. Violations may be widespread, but they generally occur under the most private of circumstances. Consequently, complaints about these sexual encounters are seldom reported to the authorities. Furthermore, where the conduct is the subject of a complaint by a participant, it may fall under the classification of sexual battery offenses (see Chapter 6).

Seduction

Seduction was not a crime at a common law; hence, it exists only by statute. *Young v. Young*, 184 So. 187 (Ala. 1938). Statutes defining seduction vary somewhat, but in general the essence of the offense is that a male obtains sexual intercourse with a virtuous female on the unfulfilled promise of marriage. Many states have repealed their seduction statutes. Where such laws still exist, they generally provide that the female victim must be of previous chaste character

---

CASE IN POINT

SEDUCTION

A young man in Kentucky maintained that he was willing to marry the woman he seduced, but his parents would not consent so he could not secure a license. He was convicted of seduction, and he appealed. The appellate court upheld his conviction and sentence but was willing to give him another chance. The court directed the local judge to inform the defendant that he would be permitted to obtain a license without his parents' consent. The court then ruled: "If, upon such advice, the accused renews his statement of willingness to marry, the court will order that consent of the accused's parents be dispensed with, and that upon the marriage the judgment of conviction be suspended. Otherwise, the conviction will stand."

Combs v. Commonwealth, 283 S.W. 2d 714, 715 (Ky. 1955).

(i.e., one who has not voluntarily lost her virginity outside the bonds of wedlock), and that the male's promise to marry must be absolute and precede the act of intercourse. *State v. Wells,* 188 S.E. 326 (N.C. 1936). Statutes often stipulate that the offense can be committed only by a male of marriageable age. See, for example, *State v. Creed,* 88 S.E. 511 (N.C. 1916).

Today criminal prosecutions for seduction are rare. Historically, they served a significant role in persuading a recalcitrant suitor to marry the woman he seduced or face criminal proceedings.

Incest

Incest is sexual intercourse within or outside the bonds of marriage between persons related within certain prohibited degrees. *Haller v. State,* 232 S.W. 2d 829 (Ark. 1950). Incest was not a crime at common law but was punishable by the ecclesiastical courts. *State v. Tucker,* 93 N.E. 3 (Ind. 1910).

There are strong religious and moral taboos against incest. Furthermore, it has been almost universally believed that incest not only disrupts family relationships but also leads to genetically defective offspring. For these reasons, all states prohibit marriage or sexual relations between certain close relatives.

In *State v. Tucker,* the Indiana Supreme Court explained the background of incest as an offense in the United States by stating:

> [I]ncest has been forbidden to some extent by general custom, from the earliest times, and by peoples very little advanced in civilization. It is generally agreed that marriages between persons in the direct lineal line of consanguinity, and also between brother and sister, are unlawful as against the law of nature, independent of any church canon or statutory prohibition. This inflexible rule arises from the institution of the family, the basis of civilized society; and, the rights, duties, habits, and affections, flowing from that relation. Family intermarriage and domestic licentiousness would inevitably confuse parental filial duties and affections, and corrupt the moral sentiments of mankind. *State v. Tucker,* 93 N.E. 3 (Ind. 1910).

Statutes that prohibit intermarriage or sexual relations between persons within certain degrees of kinship usually refer to relationship by consanguinity (i.e., blood relationships). Typically, Florida law provides:

> Whoever knowingly marries or has sexual intercourse with a person to whom he is related by lineal consanguinity, or a brother, sister, uncle, aunt, nephew, or niece, commits incest, which constitutes a felony of the third degree. West's Fla. Stat. Ann. § 826.04.

Statutes do not usually distinguish between relationships of half-blood and full-blood. Some, however, go further than the Florida statute and classify close relationships between persons related by affinity (i.e., marriage), as well as relationships by the blood line, as incestuous. For example, Section 22–22–19.1 of the South Dakota Codified Laws provides: "Any person, fourteen years of age or older, who knowingly engages in sexual contact with another person, other than his spouse, if that person is under the age of twenty-one and is within the degree of consanguinity or affinity within which marriages are by the laws of this state declared void ... is guilty of a felony."

To prove incest, the prosecution is usually only required to prove the defendant's knowledge of the relationship; the act of sexual intercourse in violation of the statute then satisfies the intent requirement.

Bigamy

Like most sexual offenses, bigamy was originally a canonical offense punishable by the ecclesiastical courts in England; later it became a common-law offense. See *People v. Martin*, 205 P. 121 (Cal. 1922). All American jurisdictions prohibit bigamy (i.e., marriage between two persons when one is already legally married to another). Usually these statutes require the prosecution to prove that the defendant had knowledge of the prior marital status of the person whom he or she married. Since everyone is presumed to know the consequences of his or her acts, no further intent need be shown.

Before the turn of the century, arguments were advanced that polygamy—the practice of one person being married to several spouses at the same time—was a religious practice protected by the First Amendment. These contentions were soundly rejected by the United States Supreme Court when it held that a religious belief cannot be made a justification for commission of an overt act made criminal by the state. *Reynolds v. United States*, 98 U.S. (8 Otto) 145, 25 L.Ed. 244 (1878).

Sodomy

The word *sodomy* is derived from the biblical account of Sodom, the city that was destroyed because of its vices. Sodomy consists of committing acts that were once commonly referred to as "crimes against nature." Sodomy was originally an ecclesiastical offense, but became a felony in the later stages of the common law. In his *Commentaries on the Laws of England*, Blackstone described sodomy as an offense "the very mention of which is a disgrace to human nature" and "a crime not fit to be named." In general, the offense includes oral and/or anal sex between humans and sexual intercourse between humans and animals (the latter is often termed "bestiality"). Until 1961, all states had statutes outlawing sodomy.

Today, less than half the states retain this offense, and enforcement is rare. When a person is prosecuted for sodomy, it is generally as an incident to a charge of rape or sexual battery. When sodomy is nonconsensual, it is considered a crime against a person, not as an offense against morality.

In the mid-1980s, sodomy became the subject of public discussion when a federal appeals court in Georgia struck down that state's sodomy law on the ground that it violated the constitutional right of privacy. The decision came in a civil case brought by an adult male who was arrested (but not prosecuted) for committing sodomy with another adult male in the privacy of his bedroom. In a 5–4 decision, the U.S. Supreme Court overturned the ruling and upheld Georgia's sodomy law. *Bowers v. Hardwick*, 478 U.S. 186, 106 S.Ct. 2841, 92 L.Ed.2d 140 (1986). Writing for the Court in *Hardwick*, Justice White concluded that the Constitution did not confer "a fundamental right to homosexuals to engage in acts of consensual sodomy." 478 U.S. at 192, 106 S.Ct. at 2844, 92 L.Ed.2d at 146. Dissenting, Justice Blackmun, joined by three other members of the Court, insisted that the case was not about the right to engage in homosexual sodomy, but, rather, about "the right to be let alone." 478 U.S. at 199, 106 S.Ct. at 2848, 92 L.Ed.2d at 151. Indeed, the Court's decision left open the question of whether sodomy laws would be enforceable against acts of heterosexual sodomy, whether within or without the bounds of marriage.

As an apparent moral statement, the *Hardwick* decision engendered considerable controversy. But the impact of the decision has been, and will continue to be, quite limited. First, as just noted, many jurisdictions have repealed their prohibitions against sodomy. Second, because most acts of sodomy are performed in private by consenting adults, they tend to be beyond the effective reach of the criminal law.

As noted in Chapter 3, a state constitution may afford more protection to its citizens than does the federal constitution. A recent judicial opinion based on the right of privacy illustrates this point. The Texas Court of Appeals held that the Texas statute criminalizing private sexual relations between consenting adults of the same sex violated the right of privacy guaranteed by the Texas Constitution. The court rejected the state's contention that the law implemented public morality, and further observed that there was no indication that the legislature intended the statute to be a disease-prevention measure. *State v. Morales*, 826 S.W.2d 201 (Tex. Cr. App. 1992).

Kentucky's sodomy statute makes it an offense for persons of the same sex to have consensual oral or anal sex. Observing that, "We need not sympathize, agree with, or even understand the sexual preference of homosexuals in order to recognize their right to equal treatment before the bar of criminal justice," the Kentucky Supreme Court also struck down the sodomy law on the ground that it violated privacy provisions of its state constitution. The court recognized the U.S. Supreme Court's decision in *Bowers v. Hardwick*, but noted that in *Bowers* the Supreme Court did not address the issue of equal protection because, unlike the Kentucky statute, the Georgia law before it applied to both heterosexual and homosexual sodomy. *Wasson v. State*, 842 S.W. 2d 487 (Ky. 1992).

Prostitution

Although prostitution was not a crime at common law, *Commonwealth v. King*, 372 N.E.2d 196 (Mass. 1977), statutes proscribing prostitution have been part of the

---

CASE IN POINT

Invalidity of Sodomy Law Under the New York Constitution

Ronald Onofre was charged with violating New York's consensual sodomy statute. Before his trial, Onofre moved for a dismissal of the indictment on the ground that enforcement of the statute invaded his constitutional right to privacy. After the motion was denied, Onofre admitted to having had "deviate sexual intercourse" with another male and was convicted. On appeal, the Appellate Division reversed the conviction and declared the sodomy law unconstitutional. The New York Court of Appeals affirmed, saying that the constitutional right of privacy included the freedom "to seek sexual gratification from what at least once was commonly regarded as 'deviant' conduct, so long as the decisions [to engage in such conduct] are voluntarily made by adults. . . ."

People v. Onofre, 415 N.E.2d 936, 940 (N.Y. 1980).

---

laws directed against public immorality since the early history of the United States. A prostitute is a person who indulges in indiscriminate sexual activity for hire. Today prostitution is illegal in all states except Nevada, where it exists by local option in some counties, although it is strictly regulated by law. See Nev. Rev. Stat. 201.380, 201.430, 201.440. Historically, statutes prohibiting prostitution have been directed at females who have sexual intercourse with males for compensation, but in recent years, as prostitution by males has increased, enforcement has come to be directed at males as well.

Previously, enforcement was directed almost exclusively at the prostitute. Newer statutes, however, provide for conviction of customers as well as prostitutes. This is appropriate because all participants in an offense should share the responsibility for their acts. Indeed, if the statutes are not so construed, they may be vulnerable to constitutional attack as a denial of equal protection of the law.

Lawmakers have officially deplored the existence of prostitution, and law enforcement authorities have long linked the activity with vice, narcotics offenses, and the exploitation of women. In addition to making prostitution an offense, most states make it an offense to solicit for a prostitute or to live off the earnings of a person engaged in prostitution. Statutes also commonly declare brothels and houses of prostitution as public nuisances.

Texas statutes provide that a person who offers or agrees to engage, or engages in sexual conduct for a fee, or who solicits another in a public place to engage in such conduct commits the misdemeanor offense of prostitution. Vernon's Tex. Penal Code Ann. § 43.02. Texas also makes promotion of prostitution a misdemeanor offense, Vernon's Tex. Penal Code Ann. §§ 43.03–43.04, and makes it a serious felony for a person to cause another by force, threat, or fraud to commit prostitution or to cause by any means a person younger than seventeen years to commit prostitution. Vernon's Tex. Penal Code Ann. § 43.05.

Prostitution has been dealt with primarily at the state and local level, but the federal government has also shown an interest in coping with the problem. The Mann Act, 18 U.S.C.A. § 2421 *et seq.*, prohibits interstate transportation of an individual for purposes of prostitution or with the intent to compel an individual to become a prostitute or to engage in any other immoral practice. The Supreme Court has held that the act applies to transporting persons for immoral purposes even if commercial vice is not involved. *Cleveland v. United States*, 329 U.S. 14, 67 S. Ct. 13, 91 L.Ed. 12 (1946).

Criticism of Laws Regulating Sexual Conduct

Considerable criticism is leveled at laws that proscribe sexual conduct between consenting adults. Those who advocate the repeal of statutes making fornication, adultery, and seduction crimes argue that sexual conduct between consenting adults is essentially a matter of private moral concern. They believe such behavior should be left to the discretion of the participants. Furthermore, they contend that the resources needed to fight serious crime should not be wasted in attempts to apprehend violators of sexual mores. Moreover, they argue that since laws against these activities are largely unenforced, they lend themselves to charges of arbitrary enforcement against persons whose lifestyles are socially unacceptable. Finally, many critics contend that the very fact that these laws are not enforced breeds disrespect and encourages violation of laws that society regards as essential.

There is considerably less support for repeal of laws forbidding incest. Some who do advocate the repeal of these laws advance the same arguments as for decriminalizing fornication, adultery, and seduction. Additionally, many who see incest as a genuine concern urge that government should approach the problem through counseling and by furnishing psychiatric assistance to transgressors, rather than making incest a penal offense.

TABLE 8.1 PROSTITUTION ARRESTS IN THE UNITED STATES, 1990, BY AGE AND SEX

Age	Arrests	Percent*
Under 18	1281	1%
18–24	26,262	29%
25–29	25,875	28%
30–34	18,981	21%
35–39	9,703	11%
40–64	8,496	9%
65 and over	495	1%
Sex	**Arrests**	**Percent***
Male	32,770	36%
Female	58,323	64%
Total	**91,093**	**100%**

Note: Percentages have been rounded to nearest whole number.
Source: *Sourcebook of Criminal Justice Statistics 1991*, U.S. Department of Justice, Bureau of Justice Statistics, Washington, D.C.: USGPO, 1992.

Those who oppose the prostitution laws now extant in the United States point to the fact that the so-called oldest profession has survived many centuries of condemnation and yet exists as a cultural institution. Thus, they argue, it fulfills a socially desirable function because it furnishes an outlet for certain sexual impulses and tends to lessen the incidence of forcible sexual attacks on women. In addition to the need to conserve scarce resources to fight serious crime and the futility of trying to eradicate an ingrained institution, reformers contend that legalization of prostitution would lead to needed regulation. This, they point out, could provide for medical inspections to diminish the spread of sexually transmitted diseases. Finally, many critics of the present laws concerning prostitution contend that legalization would allow the police to wrest control of this activity from the grips of organized crime, and prohibit more effectively many of the vices that now accompany prostitution.

Bigamy and polygamy are still practiced in some areas. Given the fact that such marriages are considered null and void, some argue criminalizing such conduct is unnecessary. There is, however, no great movement to abolish such laws, and, in truth, any such effort would probably be to little avail.

The Prognosis for Reform

The repeal of laws prohibiting fornication is not a priority item for legislators. However, when criminal codes are revised, such laws often disappear. In our monogamous society, laws proscribing adultery will most likely remain as a public statement on morality, but for the reasons indicated, they will be largely unenforced. Seduction has been for the most part relegated to civil suits for breach of promise to marry, but even this type of action has been outlawed in many jurisdictions.

The practice of incest among those related by consanguinity is widely condemned in Western civilization, and laws forbidding it will undoubtedly remain. There is an area for limited reform. As noted, certain statutes forbid marriage among certain persons related by affinity. To the extent that incest statutes prohibit such practices as a brother marrying his deceased brother's wife, a change would be inoffensive to most and welcomed by many. In some cultures, such a practice is regarded as an obligation.

Monogamy is an ingrained institution in contemporary American culture, and it seems safe to predict that scattered efforts to revise laws prohibiting bigamy will continue to fall on deaf ears of legislators.

The prognosis on prostitution is a difficult one. One certainty is that increasingly, buyers as well as sellers of sexual services will be prosecuted. Despite the cries for reform, any decriminalization of prostitution will most likely be in selected locations only, and will confine activities to prescribed areas. The inherent privacy of the scene of offenses makes it very difficult to apprehend prostitutes and their customers. Therefore, enforcement is better directed to prosecution of those who are the procurers of prostitutes and solicitors for their services and not merely to those who render their services.

INDECENT EXPOSURE

At common law, it was a misdemeanor for persons to intentionally expose their "private parts" in a public place. *Noblett v. Commonwealth*, 72 S.E. 2d 241 (Va.

1952). Today, statutes and local ordinances in most jurisdictions make it a misdemeanor to expose one's private parts to the view of another under offensive circumstances. A number of state courts have upheld laws criminalizing indecent exposure against a variety of constitutional challenges. See, for example, *Keller v. State,* 738 P. 2d 186 (Okl. Crim. App. 1987), *cert. denied,* 484 U.S. 940, 108 S. Ct. 323, 98 L.Ed.2d 351 (1987); *State v. Ludwig,* 468 So.2d 1151 (La. 1985). Such laws, however, have been generally interpreted not to prohibit public exposure of the buttocks. See, for example, *Duvallon v. District of Columbia,* 515 A.2d 724 (D.C. App. 1986).

Frequently the offense of indecent exposure is termed "lewd and lascivious conduct." Because a person may expose himself or herself either accidentally or of necessity, laws generally provide that indecent exposure must be done willfully and in an offensive manner. See, for example, *People v. Randall,* 711 P.2d 689 (Colo. 1985). Often statutes require that offensive exposure must be in the "presence" of another person. Interpreting the term *presence,* the Florida Supreme Court has ruled that the term "encompasses sensory awareness as well as physical proximity." Consequently, the court reversed the conviction of a man who admitted to masturbating in the presence of his thirteen-month-old child. In the court's view, the child did not have "sensory awareness" of the act in question. *State v. Werner,* 609 So.2d 585 (Fla. 1992).

Nude Dancing in Places of Public Accommodation

Is nude dancing for entertainment in a bar or theater a form of indecent exposure? Or is it a form of expression protected by the First Amendment? In *Barnes v. Glen Theatre,* 501 U.S. ___ , 111 S.Ct. 2456, 115 L.Ed.2d 504 (1991), the U.S. Supreme Court upheld an Indiana law that prohibited totally nude dancing. Writing for a plurality of justices, Chief Justice Rehnquist observed that "the governmental interest served by the text of the prohibition is societal disapproval of nudity in public places and among strangers." 501 U.S. at ___ , 111 S.Ct. at 2463, 115 L.Ed.2d at 515. In Rehnquist's view, "Indiana's requirement that the dancers wear at least pasties and a G-string is modest, and the bare minimum necessary to achieve the state's purpose." 501 U.S. at ___ , 111 S.Ct. at 2463, 115 L.Ed.2d at 515.

C A S E   I N   P O I N T

INDECENT EXPOSURE

A man exposing himself in a second-story apartment in New Orleans was seen from below by persons in the apartment parking lot. He was prosecuted for indecent exposure under a statute that had been interpreted as criminalizing indecent exposure if it was viewable from any location open to the public. In upholding his conviction, the Louisiana Supreme Court noted that the parking lot from which the victims observed the man exposing himself was not enclosed, nor was it posted as private property, and was open to any visitors to the apartment complex.

State v. Clark, 372 So.2d 1218 (La. 1979).

Nudity and Seminudity on Public Beaches

Historically, public nudity has been taboo in Western societies. Yet only a few states have imposed outright bans. Many states maintain that public nudity on beaches and other recreational areas violates laws proscribing lewd and lascivious conduct or indecent exposure. For example, in Florida, where public beaches are popular attractions, signs are commonly posted notifying beachgoers that nude sunbathing is a violation of Florida Statute Section 877.03. Actually, that law prohibits "such acts as are of a nature to corrupt the public morals, or outrage the sense of public decency, or affect the peace and quiet of persons who may witness them." Arrests under this provision are not common, and the Florida appellate courts have yet to address the question of whether this section actually prohibits nude sunbathing. Meanwhile, Miami Beach and other Florida cities that attract large numbers of tourists have set aside specified areas where topless or nude sunbathing is permitted. Currently some local governing bodies in Florida are debating whether abbreviated types of beach attire, such as "thong bikinis," should be permitted on public beaches. Whether nude sunbathing should be permitted in public areas is moving to the forefront as such organizations as the American Sunbathing Association seek to expand recreational opportunities for those who perceive current societal restrictions on nudity as excessively repressive.

OBSCENITY

At common law, vulgar and obscene language and indecent public exhibitions were considered public nuisances, punishable as misdemeanors. See *State v. Miller*, 112 S.E.2d 472 (W. Va. 1960). Historically, federal and state governments in the United States passed laws banning various forms of obscenity. By the late 1800s, Congress had made it an offense to mail any "obscene, lewd or lascivious paper or writing" and provided that the word *obscene* should be given fully as broad a significance as it had at common law. *Knowles v. United States*, 170 F. 409 (8th Cir. 1909). The states also passed laws making sale or distribution of obscene materials a crime. Typically, Section 6567 of the Connecticut General Statutes (1949 Revision) provided that "Buying, selling, giving or showing any obscene, indecent or impure book, paper or picture is a crime." Likewise, most municipalities adopted ordinances proscribing various forms of obscenity.

Statutes and ordinances making obscenity an offense seldom defined it. Thus, they were vulnerable to contentions that they were vague and did not provide an ascertainable standard of guilt. As questions arose, the courts tended to define obscenity as sexual or erotic speech or conduct. The word *obscene* came to mean something offensive to the senses, that is, repulsive, disgusting, foul, or filthy. See *Williams v. State*, 94 So. 882 (Miss. 1923).

The Emerging Constitutional Standards

As mass communications developed, laws banning obscene speech, materials, and performances became subject to scrutiny under the First Amendment. The Supreme Court's first direct encounter with regulating obscenity came in *Roth v.*

United States, 354 U.S. 476, 77 S.Ct. 1304, 1 L.Ed.2d 1498 (1957). Roth was found guilty of sending erotic materials through the mail, and his conviction was affirmed on appeal. The Supreme Court granted review and announced that the dispositive issue was "whether obscenity is utterance within the area of protected speech and press." The Court held that obscenity was not constitutionally protected; rather, the Court viewed it as "utterly without redeeming social importance." After observing that "sex and obscenity are not synonymous," Justice Brennan, writing for the Court, said the test for determining obscenity was "whether to the average person applying contemporary community standards, the dominant theme of the material taken as a whole, appeals to the prurient interest."

By the late 1950s, there was a flood of erotic materials on the market. Whether particular materials were obscene had become an increasingly important issue. *Roth* effectively made the definition of obscenity a matter of federal constitutional law. It also evidenced the Court's concern for First Amendment freedoms and for protecting the free flow of expression from local interpretations of what constituted obscenity. Because of the problems in determining whether materials were obscene under the *Roth* standards, law enforcement officers experienced great difficulty in enforcing obscenity laws.

From 1957 to 1973, the Supreme Court granted review of a number of lower court decisions determining that particular books, plays, and movies were obscene, often explicating due process guidelines to be followed by lower courts in determining what constitutes obscenity. During this period the Court found the French film, "The Lovers," not to be obscene, and implied that national standards would govern in determining whether materials were obscene. There Justice Stewart, in expressing the view that obscenity is limited to "hard-core pornography," made his oft-quoted remark on obscenity, "I know it when I see it." *Jacobellis v. Ohio,* 378 U.S. 184, 197, 84 S. Ct. 1676, 1683, 12 L.Ed.2d 793 (1964) (Stewart, J. concurring).

As the 1970s approached, observers speculated that the Supreme Court was taking a more liberal approach. In *Stanley v. Georgia,* 394 U.S. 557, 89 S. Ct. 1243, 22 L.Ed.2d 542 (1969), the Court reviewed a defendant's conviction for violating a statute making knowing possession of obscene materials a crime. In *Stanley,* the police had seized materials (which the Court assumed to be obscene) from the defendant's home. In reversing the defendant's conviction, the Court held that "the State may no more prohibit mere possession of obscene matter on the ground that it may lead to antisocial conduct than it may prohibit possession of chemistry books on the ground that they may lead to the manufacture of homemade spirits." *Stanley,* 394 U.S. at 567, 89 S.Ct. at 1248, 22 L.Ed.2d at 551. Some read *Stanley* as an indication the Court was relaxing its standards on regulating obscenity. They were mistaken.

The Intractable Obscenity Problem

When the Supreme Court decided the seminal case of *Miller v. California,* 413 U.S. 15, 93 S.Ct. 2607, 37 L.Ed.2d 419 (1973), it referred to it as "one of a group of 'obscenity-pornography' cases" involving what Justice Harlan has called "the 'intractable obscenity problem'." 413 U.S. at 16, 93 S. Ct. at 2610, 37 L.Ed.2d at 426.

In *Miller,* the defendant had mailed unsolicited material containing explicit sexual drawings in violation of a California law. A jury found him guilty and an appellate court upheld the judgment without opinion. At the outset, Chief Justice Burger reiterated that obscene materials were unprotected by the Constitution. Then the Court made two revisions in its interpretations in *Roth.* First, the Court defined *community* in order to permit local juries to base their judgments on local and not national standards. Then the Court redefined the standards for determining obscenity, saying that the

> basic guidelines for the trier of fact must be: (1) whether "the average person, applying contemporary community standards" would find that the work, taken as a whole, appeals to the prurient interest; (b) whether the work depicts or describes, in a patently offensive way, sexual conduct specifically defined by the applicable state law; and (c) whether the work, taken as a whole, lacks serious literary, artistic, political, or scientific value. 413 U.S. at 24, 93 S.Ct. 2614, 37 L.Ed.2d at 431.

Finally, the Court expressly rejected any requirement that the challenged materials be found to be "utterly without redeeming social importance." 413 U.S. at 24, 93 S.Ct. at 2614, 37 L.Ed.2d at 431.

The Court gave examples of "patently offensive" by saying it meant "representations or descriptions of ultimate sexual acts, normal or perverted, actual or simulated . . . representations or descriptions of masturbation, excretory functions, and lewd exhibition of genitals." 413 U.S. at 25, 93 S.Ct. at 2615, 327 L.Ed.2d at 431. The Court made it clear that no one would be subject to prosecution unless the materials alleged to be obscene described patently offensive "hard-core" sexual conduct.

In a companion case, *Paris Adult Theatre I v. Slaton,* 413 U.S. 49, 93 S.Ct. 2628, 37 L.Ed.2d 446 (1973), the Court observed that the states have a right to "maintain a decent society" and may challenge obscene material even if it is shown only to consenting adults.

These decisions indicated an increasing concern over the issue of obscenity and allowed local juries to make judgments based on more explicit standards. They also tended to eliminate the practice of using expert witnesses to testify on such issues as contemporary community standards and whether materials were "utterly without redeeming social value."

Significant Post-*Miller* Developments

Miller may have clarified the tests for obscenity, but it did not satisfy those who sought to ban pornographic materials. For example, "Carnal Knowledge," a very successful movie in the early 1970s, was held not obscene under the *Miller* test. There were scenes in which "ultimate sexual acts" were understood to be taking place; however, the camera did not focus on the bodies of the actors nor was there any exhibition of genitals during such scenes. The Court said that the film was not a "portrayal of hard core sexual conduct for its own sake, and for the ensuing commercial gain" and did not depict sexual conduct in a patently offensive way. *Jenkins v. Georgia,* 418 U.S. 153, 161, 94 S. Ct. 2750, 2755, 41 L.Ed.2d 642, 650 (1974).

The 1980s witnessed two significant developments in the laws concerning obscenity. First, in *New York v. Ferber,* 458 U.S. 747, 102 S.Ct. 3348, 73 L.Ed.2d 1113

(1982), a unanimous Supreme Court held that child pornography, like obscenity, is unprotected by the First Amendment to the Constitution. The Court upheld a New York law prohibiting persons from distributing materials that depict children engaging in lewd sex. The Court found such laws valid even if the material does not appeal to the prurient interest of the average person and is not portrayed in a patently offensive manner. The Court found a compelling state interest in protecting the well-being of children and perceived no value in permitting performances and photo reproductions of children engaged in lewd sexual conduct.

The second significant development was a refinement of the Court's decision in *Miller*. In *Pope v. Illinois*, 481 U.S. 497, 107 S.Ct. 1918, 95 L.Ed.2d 439 (1987), the Court said that application of "contemporary community standards" is appropriate in evaluating the first two prongs of the *Miller* test for obscenity, that is, the work's appeal to the prurient interest and its patent offensiveness. However, the Court concluded that the third prong concerning the work's value cannot be tested by "community standards." The Court said the third prong must be determined on an objective basis, with the proper inquiry being

> not whether an ordinary member of any given community would find serious literary, artistic, political, or scientific value in allegedly obscene material, but whether a reasonable person would find such value in the material, taken as a whole. 481 U.S. at 500, 107 S.Ct. at 1921, 95 L.Ed.2d at 445.

State and Local Regulation of Obscenity

States, of course, may interpret their own constitutions to allow greater freedom of expression than is allowed under the current federal constitutional interpretations. In that vein, in 1987 the Oregon Supreme Court said:

> In this state any person can write, print, read, say, show or sell anything to a consenting adult even though that expression may be generally or universally condemned as "obscene." *State v. Henry*, 732 P.2d 9, 18 (Or. 1987).

Some states classify violations of their obscenity statutes by degree. For example, in New York, a person is guilty of obscenity in the third degree when, knowing its content and character, he or she:

1. Promotes, or possesses with intent to promote, any obscene material; or
2. Produces, presents or directs an obscene performance or participates in a portion thereof which is obscene or which contributes to its obscenity. McKinney's N.Y. Penal Law § 235.05.

A person is guilty of obscenity in the second degree "when he commits the crime of obscenity in the third degree ... and has been previously convicted of obscenity in the third degree." McKinney's N.Y. Penal Law § 235.06. A person is guilty of obscenity in the first degree "when, knowing its content and character, he wholesale promotes or possesses with intent to wholesale promote, any obscene material." McKinney's N.Y. Penal Law § 235.07. New York law makes third-degree obscenity a misdemeanor, while second- or first-degree obscenity is a felony.

States generally set higher penalties for exposing juveniles to pictures or shows where obscenity or even pornography is involved. In New York, disseminating indecent material to minors is a felony. McKinney's N.Y. Penal Law § 235.22.

Defenses to Charges of Obscenity

New York law provides a defense for those charged with obscenity if they can establish that the allegedly obscene material was disseminated to or performed for an audience of persons having scientific, educational, governmental, or other similar justification for possessing or viewing the material. McKinney's N.Y. Penal Law § 235.15. Moreover, it is a defense for disseminating indecent material to minors if the defendant had reasonable cause to believe that the minor involved was seventeen years old or older and exhibited official documentation to the defendant to establish that fact. McKinney's N.Y. Penal Law § 235.22. This latter provision was undoubtedly inserted to protect theater personnel from conviction on a strict liability basis.

Problems of Enforcement

Police and prosecutors often experience difficulty in determining what is to be considered obscene based on "contemporary community standards." Juries in most instances now determine the issue of obscenity simply by reviewing the material. As a result, it is not unusual for a given work to be determined obscene by a jury in one locality and not obscene by another jury in a different locality. For example, the rock musical stage production, "Hair," was found not to be obscene by a federal court in Georgia. *Southeastern Promotions, Ltd. v. Atlanta,* 334 F.Supp. 634 (N.D. Ga. 1971). The following year, it was found to be obscene by another federal court in Tennessee, but this decision was reversed by the Supreme Court. *Southeastern Promotions, Inc. v. Conrad,* 341 F.Supp. 465 (E.D. Tenn. 1972), *aff'd.,* 486 F.2d 894 (6th Cir. 1973), *rev'd.,* 420 U.S. 546, 95 S.Ct. 1239, 43 L.Ed.2d 448 (1975).

Legal problems incident to searches and seizures of allegedly obscene materials can be very technical. Since books, movies, and even live performances are presumptively protected by the First Amendment, the Supreme Court has held that police must obtain a search warrant prior to searches and seizures of such materials. *Roaden v. Kentucky,* 413 U.S. 496, 93 S. Ct. 2796, 37 L.Ed.2d 757 (1973). The Court has explained, however, that the Fourth Amendment does not prohibit undercover police officers from purchasing allegedly obscene materials because such a purchase would not constitute a "seizure." *Maryland v. Macon,* 472 U.S. 463, 105 S. Ct. 2778, 86 L.Ed.2d 370 (1985).

Likewise, courts are constantly being called upon to interpret the application of obscenity laws. In 1977, in *State v. Anonymous,* 377 A.2d 1342 (Conn. Super. 1977), the court considered a case of a high-school boy who, while riding on a school bus, extended his middle finger toward a highway trooper. He was charged under a statute making it an offense for a person to make an obscene gesture in a public place "with intent to cause inconvenience, annoyance or alarm or recklessly creating a risk thereof." 377 A.2d at 1343. The court found

---

CASE IN POINT

OBSCENITY

In the first federal appeals court decision applying the *Miller v. California* obscenity test to a musical composition, the Eleventh Circuit Court of Appeals ruled that the recording "As Nasty as They Wanna Be" by 2 Live Crew was not obscene. The Eleventh Circuit ruled that, even assuming the work was "patently offensive" and appealed to a "prurient interest," the trial judge erred in concluding, simply on the basis of his own listening to a tape recording, that the work lacked "serious artistic value."

Luke Records, Inc. v. Navarro, 960 F.2d 134 (11th Cir. 1992).

---

that the student was not guilty of violating the statute. To be obscene, the court said, an expression "must be in a significant way erotic." 377 A.2d at 1343 (citing *Cohen v. California*, 403 U.S. 15, 91 S. Ct. 1780, 29 L.Ed.2d 284 (1971)).

Profanity

Many states and local communities have statutes and ordinances making it an offense to use loud and profane language in public places. In recent years there have been challenges to the constitutionality of these measures. In some cases courts have struck down such laws for vagueness. In other instances courts have upheld their validity but ruled that such laws can be applied only where the defendant's language consisted of "fighting words" or the defendant's conduct threatened a breach of the peace (see Chapter 11).

GAMBLING

Traditionally, to gamble has meant to risk money on an event, chance, or contingency in the hope of realizing a gain. See *State v. Stripling*, 21 So. 409 (Ala. 1897). The common law did not regard gambling as an offense. *Bowden v. Nugent*, 226 P. 549 (Ariz. 1924). However, many of the new American states, either by constitution or statute, made all or certain forms of gambling illegal. Today federal laws and a variety of state statutes and local ordinances prohibit gambling. Laws regulating gambling come under the "police power" of the state, and the United States Supreme Court has recognized that there is no constitutional right to gamble. *Lewis v. United States*, 348 U.S. 419, 75 S.Ct. 415, 99 L.Ed. 475 (1955).

Bingo, craps, baccarat, poker, raffles, bookmaking, and slot machines are just a few common forms of gambling. Gambling also includes betting on sports events and card games. Many forms of gambling are legal; therefore, when considering gambling, we must separate the legal from the illegal. For example, those who pay something of value, that is, "a legal consideration," to take a chance to win a prize in a lottery are gambling. In many jurisdictions this is a criminal offense. Yet in several states lotteries are not only legal, they are an important source of public revenue. In effect, it is unregulated gambling that is illegal. A common form of unregulated gambling is "numbers." To play, you place a bet on a number with the hope that it will correspond to a preselected number. The "numbers racket" is widespread and, along with prostitution, is a major source of income for organized crime.

What Constitutes Gambling?

Retail stores conduct a variety of promotional schemes; local carnivals and fairs offer opportunities to play a variety of games for prizes. When are they gambling and when are they games of skill? And if games of skill, are they exempt from laws prohibiting gambling? Some statutes regulating gambling provide the answer. In other instances, courts may be called on to determine whether a particular activity offends a statutory prohibition against gambling. It is generally agreed that to constitute gambling, the activity must include these three elements: (1) a consideration, (2) a prize, and (3) a chance.

Most statutes prohibiting gambling are interpreted to exclude athletics or other contests in which participants pit their physical or mental skills against one another for a prize. Courts tend to be practical in their interpretations. For example, an Ohio appellate court found that a pinball machine that allowed the outcome of its operation to be determined largely by the skill of the user was not "a game of chance," and the pinball operators were not in violation of the Ohio gambling statute. *Progress Vending, Inc. v. Department of Liquor Control*, 394 N.E.2d 324 (Ohio App. 1978).

Statutory Regulation of Gambling

A federal statute called the Travel Act, 18 U.S.C.A. § 1952, prohibits interstate travel in aid of gambling. The act is not aimed at local criminal activity; its purpose is rather to attack crime that has a definite interstate aspect. *United States v. O'Dell*, 671 F.2d 191 (6th Cir. 1982).

Many states proscribe gambling broadly much the same as Florida law, which provides:

> Whoever plays or engages in any game at cards, keno, roulette, faro or other game of chance, at any place, by any device whatever, for money or other thing of value, shall be guilty of a misdemeanor of the second degree. West's Fla. Stat. Ann. § 849.08.

Typically, the Florida law creates exceptions for retail merchandising promotions. West's Fla. Stat. Ann. § 849.09. It also permits charitable, nonprofit, and veterans' organizations to conduct "bingo," a game in which players pay for the use of one or more bingo cards, numbers are drawn by chance, and prizes are awarded. West's Fla. Stat. Ann. §§ 849.093 and 849.0935. Where gambling is prohibited, states customarily make it unlawful to possess gambling devices and provide for their confiscation. See, for example, West's Fla. Stat. Ann. §§ 849.231, 849.232.

TABLE 8.2 LEGALIZED GAMBLING BY STATE

State	Gambling Allowed
Alabama	Pari-mutuel betting, bingo, tribal gaming
Alaska	Bingo only
Arizona	Pari-mutuel betting, lottery, bingo, tribal gaming
Arkansas	Pari-mutuel betting only
California	Pari-mutuel betting, lottery, card rooms, bingo, tribal gaming
Colorado	Pari-mutuel betting, lottery, casinos, bingo, tribal gaming
Connecticut	Pari-mutuel betting, lottery, bingo, tribal gaming, jai alai
Delaware	Pari-mutuel betting, lottery, bingo
District of Columbia	Lottery, bingo
Florida	Pari-mutuel betting, lottery, bingo, tribal gaming, jai alai
Georgia	Bingo
Hawaii	None
Idaho	Pari-mutuel betting, lottery, tribal gaming
Illinois	Pari-mutuel betting, lottery, bingo, riverboat casinos
Indiana	Lottery, bingo
Iowa	Pari-mutuel betting, lottery, riverboat casinos, bingo, tribal gaming
Kansas	Pari-mutuel betting, lottery, bingo, tribal gaming
Kentucky	Pari-mutuel betting, lottery, bingo
Louisiana	Pari-mutuel betting, lottery, bingo, tribal gaming; one casino (New Orleans)
Maine	Pari-mutuel betting, lottery, bingo
Maryland	Pari-mutuel betting, lottery, casinos, bingo
Massachusetts	Pari-mutuel betting, lottery, bingo
Michigan	Pari-mutuel betting, lottery, bingo, tribal gaming
Minnesota	Pari-mutuel betting, lottery, bingo, tribal gaming
Mississippi	Bingo, riverboat casinos
Missouri	Lottery, bingo, tribal gaming
Montana	Lottery, bingo, casinos, pari-mutuel betting, tribal gaming
Nebraska	Lottery, bingo, pari-mutuel betting, jai alai
Nevada	Bingo, casinos, pari-mutuel betting, sports betting
New Hampshire	Lottery, bingo, pari-mutuel betting
New Jersey	Lottery, bingo, pari-mutuel betting, casino gambling (Atlantic City only)
New Mexico	Bingo, pari-mutuel betting, tribal gaming
New York	Lottery, bingo, pari-mutuel betting, tribal gaming
North Carolina	Bingo, jai alai
North Dakota	Bingo, pari-mutuel betting, tribal gaming
Ohio	Lottery, bingo, pari-mutuel betting
Oklahoma	Bingo, pari-mutuel betting, tribal gaming
Oregon	Lottery, bingo, pari-mutuel betting, jai alai, tribal gaming
Pennsylvania	Lottery, bingo, pari-mutuel betting
Rhode Island	Lottery, bingo, pari-mutuel betting
South Carolina	Bingo, jai alai
South Dakota	Lottery, bingo, pari-mutuel betting, tribal gaming
Tennessee	Pari-mutuel betting
Texas	Bingo, pari-mutuel betting
Utah	None
Vermont	Lottery, bingo, pari-mutuel betting
Virginia	Lottery, bingo, pari-mutuel betting
Washington	Lottery, bingo, pari-mutuel betting, tribal gaming
West Virginia	Lottery, bingo, pari-mutuel betting
Wisconsin	Lottery, bingo, pari-mutuel betting, tribal gaming
Wyoming	Bingo, pari-mutuel betting

CASE IN POINT

WHAT CONSTITUTES AN ILLEGAL GAMING MACHINE?

The Michigan Liquor Control Commission imposed a $250 fine on the Sanford Eagles Club for having a "video poker" machine on its premises. The machine had five windows, and when a quarter was deposited, a playing card appeared in each window. Essentially, the contestant played a game of five-card draw against the machine. A "winner" could gain credits entitling the player to free replays based on a random "reshuffling" of the cards. After administrative and judicial hearings, the Court of Appeals held that the machine was not an illegal gaming device, since there was no monetary payoff. The Michigan Supreme Court reversed. The Court based its decision on a provision of the statute addressing gambling devices that exempted mechanical amusement devices that reward a player with replays as long as the device is not allowed to accumulate more than fourteen replays at one time. Because the video poker machine at issue in this case permitted the player to accumulate more than fourteen replays, it did not fall within the statutory exemption.

Automatic Music and Vending Corp. v. Liquor Control Comm., 396 N.W. 204 (Mich. 1986).

Prosecutorial Problems; Defenses

The problems encountered in enforcing prostitution and sexual laws are also obstacles to enforcing gambling statutes. Due to the consensual nature of gambling, apprehension of violators largely depends on the use of informants by police. Procedures for obtaining search and arrest warrants are technical and require close adherence to the Fourth Amendment standards discussed in Chapter 14.

The prosecution, of course, must prove all elements of the offense. In most instances, this requires proof of a consideration, a prize, and a chance; however, some statutes have eliminated the requirement of a consideration. If the statute prohibiting gambling makes intent an element of the offense, the prosecution must prove the defendant's intent; otherwise, it is sufficient merely to prove the act of gambling.

Texas law makes it an offense to bet on results of games, contests, political nominations, or elections or to play games with cards and dice. See Vernon's Tex. Penal Code Ann. § 47.02(a). The state legislature has taken a pragmatic approach by providing that it is a defense to prosecution under that section of the statute if

> (1) the actor engaged in gambling in a private place; (2) no person received any economic benefit other than personal winnings; and (3) except for the advantage of skill or luck, the risks of losing and the chances of winning were the same for all participants. Vernon's Tex. Penal Code Ann. § 47.02(b).

In some instances a defendant charged with gambling may succeed in establishing entrapment, a defense discussed in Chapter 13.

The Paradox of Gambling Laws

The law on gambling seems paradoxical. Some laws authorize nonprofit organizations to conduct certain forms of gambling forbidden to others. In some states people can legally bet at dog tracks and horse tracks, yet may still be prosecuted for betting in their own homes on the World Series or the Kentucky Derby. Many reformers contend that present laws are ineffective to suppress gambling. Instead, they claim these laws actually lend support to the activities of organized crime.

Certain forms of legalized gambling, particularly state lotteries and state-franchised dog and horse tracks, have become increasingly acceptable. Yet unregulated forms of gambling will most likely continue to be prohibited in most instances. In any event, if inroads are to be made in controlling unregulated gambling, enforcement efforts must be directed primarily toward gambling activity that is under control of organized crime syndicates.

CONCLUSION

In addition to defining crimes against persons and property and establishing rules necessary to preserve public order, the law proscribes certain forms of conduct simply because they offend societal morality. Chief among these prohibitions are the laws prohibiting certain forms of sexual activity, public indecency, obscenity, profanity, and gambling. Offenses involving the use of alcohol and drugs, while sometimes categorized as offenses against public morality, also may be seen as threats to the public order, safety, and peace. They are therefore dealt with in a separate chapter.

Most offenses against morality, it should be remembered, are ecclesiastical in origin. Many now question whether the criminal law ought to be a vehicle for enforcing moral standards that originated from religious sources. However, the courts have not rejected morality as a proper basis for the criminal law. Clearly, the fact that a form of conduct was or is proscribed by one or more religious traditions is not a sufficient basis for criminalizing that activity. But if an act violates societal consensus, even if that consensus derives from religious traditions, it may be legitimately prohibited by the criminal law. As societal consensus changes, as it surely has with respect to sexual activities, pornography, and gambling, the prohibitions of the criminal law must, and do, change as well. Thus the offenses against public morality constitute a particularly dynamic area of the criminal law.

QUESTIONS FOR THOUGHT AND DISCUSSION

1. Is there a rational basis for the law to extend the crime of incest to prohibit intermarriage between persons related by affinity?

2. Should it be a defense to a charge of bigamy that both persons in the alleged bigamous union are adherents to a religious faith that sanctions polygamy?

3. Can the criminalization of sexual conduct such as prostitution and sodomy be reconciled with the constitutional right of privacy discussed in Chapter 3?

4. Would prostitution be more or less inimical to the public health, welfare, and morality if it were legalized and regulated?

5. Tanya Thong has been convicted of indecent exposure stemming from an incident in which she appeared topless on a public beach. On appeal, Thong argues that the indecent exposure statute amounts to unconstitutional sex discrimination because it prohibits women, but not men, from baring their breasts in public. Does Thong have a good argument?

6. Is it more desirable to regulate obscenity by criminalizing it or by using zoning to restrict its dissemination to certain locations?

7. How are laws proscribing obscenity susceptible to overbreadth and vagueness challenges discussed in Chapter 3?

8. What, if any, constitutional objections could be raised against a city ordinance making it a criminal offense "to use profane language in a public place"?

9. What forms of gambling are legal and illegal in your state? Are there any particular games that fall into a grey area between permitted and prohibited activity? Is church bingo legal in your state?

10. Gerald N. runs a video game arcade. One of his most popular games is called "Video Blackjack." Essentially, the game is a computerized form of blackjack in which the contestant plays against the computer. The cost of playing the game is 50 cents. If the contestant wins the game, he or she is issued a token that may used to play any other game in the arcade. Suppose your state gambling statute prohibits all "games involving valuable consideration, chance and a possible prize." If you were the public prosecutor, would you be concerned about the legality of this game?

CASES

BOWERS V. HARDWICK

Supreme Court of the United States, 1986.
478 U.S. 186, 106 S.Ct. 2841, 92 L.Ed.2d 140.

[In this case the Supreme Court considers a challenge to the constitutionality of a Georgia sodomy law as applied to homosexual conduct.]

Justice WHITE delivered the opinion of the Court.

In August 1982, respondent was charged with violating the Georgia statute criminalizing sodomy by committing that act with another adult male in the bedroom of respondent's home. After a preliminary hearing, the District Attorney decided not to present the matter to grand jury unless further evidence developed.

Respondent then brought suit in the Federal District Court, challenging the constitutionality of the statute insofar as it criminalized consensual sodomy. He asserted that he was a practicing homosexual, that the Georgia sodomy statute, as administered by the defendants, placed him in imminent danger of arrest, and that the statute for several reasons violates the Federal Constitution. The District Court granted the defendants' motion to dismiss. . . .

A divided panel of the Court of Appeals for the Eleventh Circuit reversed. . . . Relying on our decisions in *Griswold v. Connecticut* . . . [1965], *Eisenstadt v. Baird* . . . [1972], *Stanley v. Georgia* . . . [1969], and *Roe v. Wade* . . . [1969], the court went on to hold that the Georgia statute violated respondent's fundamental rights because his homosexual activity is a private and intimate association that is beyond the reach of the state regulation by reason of the Ninth Amendment and the Due Process Clause of the Fourteenth Amendment. The case was remanded for trial, at which, to prevail, the State would have to prove that the statute is supported by a compelling interest and is the most narrowly drawn means of achieving that end.

Because other Courts of Appeals have arrived at judgments contrary to that of the Eleventh Circuit in this case, we granted the State's petition for certiorari. . . .

This case does not require a judgment on whether laws against sodomy between consenting adults in general, or between homosexuals in particular, are wise or desirable. It raises no question about the right or propriety of state legislative decisions to repeal their laws that criminalize homosexual sodomy, or of state court decisions invalidating those laws on state constitutional grounds. The issue presented is whether the Federal Constitution confers a fundamental right upon homosexuals to engage in sodomy and hence invalidates the laws of the many States that still make such conduct illegal and have done so for a very long time. . . .

We first register our disagreement with the Court of Appeals . . . that the Court's prior cases have construed the Constitution to confer a right of privacy that extends to homosexual sodomy and for all intents and purposes have decided this case. . . .

Accepting the decisions in these cases and the above description of them, we think it evident that none of the rights announced in those cases bears any resemblance to the claimed constitutional right of homosexuals to engage in acts of sodomy, that is asserted in this case. No connection between family, marriage, or procreation on the one hand and homosexual activity on the other has been demonstrated, either by the Court of Appeals or by respondent. Moreover, any claim that these cases nevertheless stand for the proposition that any kind of private sexual conduct between consenting adults is constitutionally insulated from state proscription is insupportable. . . .

Precedent aside, however, respondent would have us announce, as the Court of Appeals did, a fundamental right to engage in homosexual sodomy. This we are quite unwilling to do. . . .

. . . Sodomy was a criminal offense at common law and was forbidden by the laws of the original thirteen States when they ratified the Bill of Rights. In 1868, when the Fourteenth Amendment was ratified, all but 5 of the 37 States in the Union had criminal sodomy laws. In fact, until 1961, all States outlawed sodomy, and today, 24 States and the District of Columbia continue to provide criminal penalties for sodomy performed in private and between consenting adults.... Against this background, to claim that a right to engage in such conduct is "deeply rooted in this Nation's history and tradition" or "implicit in the concept of ordered liberty" is, at best, facetious....

Nor are we inclined to take a more expansive view of our authority to discover new fundamental rights imbedded in the Due Process Clause. The Court is most vulnerable and comes nearest to illegitimacy when it deals with judge-made constitutional law having little or no recognizable roots in the language or design of the Constitution....

Respondent, however, asserts that the result should be different where the homosexual conduct occurs in the privacy of the home.... Plainly enough, otherwise illegal conduct is not always immunized whenever it occurs in the home. Victimless crimes, such as the possession and use of illegal drugs, do not escape the law where they are committed at home.... And if respondent's submission is limited to the voluntary sexual conduct between consenting adults, it would be difficult, except by fiat, to limit the claimed right to homosexual conduct while leaving exposed to prosecution adultery, incest, and other sexual crimes even though they are committed in the home. We are unwilling to start down that road.

Even if the conduct at issue here is not a fundamental right, respondent asserts that there must be a rational basis for the law and there is none in this case other than the presumed belief of a majority of the electorate in Georgia that homosexual sodomy is immoral and unacceptable. This is said to be an inadequate rationale to support the law. The law, however, is constantly based on notions of morality; and if all laws representing essentially moral choices are to be invalidated under the Due Process Clause, the courts will be very busy indeed. Even respondent makes no such claim, but insists that majority sentiments about the morality of homosexuality should be declared inadequate. We do not agree, and are unpersuaded that the sodomy laws of some 25 States should be invalidated on this basis....

Accordingly, the judgment of the Court of Appeals is reversed.

Chief Justice BURGER, concurring.

I join the Court's opinion, but I write separately to underscore my view that in constitutional terms there is no such thing as a fundamental right to commit homosexual sodomy.

As the Court notes, ... the proscriptions against sodomy have very "ancient roots." Decisions of individuals relating to homosexual conduct have been subject to state intervention throughout the history of Western Civilization. Condemnation of those practices is firmly rooted in Judeao-Christian moral and ethical standards. Homosexual sodomy was a capital crime under Roman law.... During the English Reformation when powers of the ecclesiastical courts were transferred to the King's Courts, the first English statute criminalizing sodomy was passed.... Blackstone described "the infamous crime against nature" as an offense of "deeper malignity" than rape, an heinous act "the very mention of which is a disgrace to human nature," and "a crime not fit to be named."... The common law of England, including its prohibition of sodomy, became the received law of Georgia and the other Colonies. In 1816 the Georgia Legislature passed the statute at issue here, and that statute has been continuously in force in one form or another since that time. To hold that the act of homosexual sodomy is somehow protected as a fundamental right would be to cast aside millennia of moral teaching....

Justice POWELL, concurring....

Justice BLACKMUN, with whom Justice BRENNAN, Justice MARSHALL, and Justice STEVENS join, dissenting.

... The Court concludes today that none of our prior cases dealing with various decisions that individuals are entitled to make free of governmental interference "bears any resemblance to the claimed constitutional right of homosexuals to engage in acts of sodomy that is asserted in this case."... We protect ... rights not because they contribute, in some direct and material way, to the general public welfare, but because they form so central a part of an individual's life. "[T]he concept of privacy embodies the 'moral fact that a person belongs to himself and not others nor to society as a whole.'"...

The behavior for which Hardwick faces prosecution occurred in his own home, a place to which the Fourth Amendment attaches special significance. The Court's treatment of this aspect of this case is symptomatic of its overall refusal to consider the broad principles that have informed our treatment of privacy in specific cases. Just as the right to privacy is more than the mere aggregation of a number of entitlements to engage in specific behavior, so too, protecting the physical integrity of the home is more than merely a means of protecting specific activities that often take place there. . . . [T]he essence of a Fourth Amendment violation is "not the breaking of [a person's] doors, and the

rummaging of his drawers," but rather is "the invasion of his indefeasible right of personal security, personal liberty and private property.". . .

. . . [T]he right of an individual to conduct intimate relationships in the intimacy of his or her own home seems to me to be the heart of the Constitution's protection of privacy. . . .

Justice STEVENS, with whom Justice BRENNAN and Justice MARSHALL join, dissenting. . . .

AUSTIN V. STATE
Court of Appeals of Texas, 1990.
794 S.W.2d 408.

[In this case, a Texas appellate court determines whether there was sufficient evidence to support the appellant's conviction for prostitution.]

JOHN F. ONION, Jr., Assigned Justice.
This is an appeal from a conviction for prostitution. Tex. Pen. Code Ann. § 43.02(a)(1) (1989). At the conclusion of the bench trial, the trial court assessed appellant's punishment at sixty (60) days confinement in the county jail, and at a fine of $200.00. The imposition of the sentence was suspended, and the appellant was placed on probation of 180 days subject to certain conditions of probation. . . .

. . . [A]ppellant contends the evidence was insufficient to support her conviction. The elements of the offense under § 43.03(a)(1) are:

(1) A·person
(2) knowingly
(3) offers or agrees to engage in sexual conduct
(4) in return for a fee payable to the actor. . . .

The complaint and information in the instant case alleged in pertinent part that the appellant on or about April 30, 1988, "did then and there knowingly agree to engage in sexual conduct for a fee, to wit: the said Kimberli Austin agreed to have sexual intercourse with J. Hutto for a fee."

Thus, the State had the burden to prove beyond a reasonable doubt that (1) Kimberli Austin (2) did knowingly (3) agree to engage in sexual conduct, to wit: sexual intercourse with J. Hutto (4) for a fee.

In the instant bench trial there was only one witness—Officer John Hutto of the Austin Police Department. He related that on April 20, 1988, he and other officers were in the process of investigating massage parlors and modeling studios; that on that date he went to the Satin Spa in Travis County. Hutto entered a living room area where there was a male and two females. The male told Hutto to select one of the females, and Hutto selected the appellant Austin. She led him down a hall to a room where there was a sign or signs as to the prices for "Basic Body Rub" and "Swedish Deep Muscle Rub." The appellant informed Hutto the "Basic Rub" was a "fingertip" massage, and the "Swedish Deep Muscle Rub" was a "more thorough and stimulating rub." The highest cost of the former was $60.00 for 60 minutes, and the highest cost of the latter was $130.00 for 60 minutes. Hutto, a veteran of several years with the Austin Police Department, had experience with the terminology and understood that "Swedish Deep Muscle Rub" was "a catch phrase" or "key words" for prostitution. Hutto gave appellant $140.00 for the highest price "Swedish" rub. Appellant left the room and returned with his change of $10.00. They both then disrobed. The nude appellant laid face down on the bed and asked Hutto to massage her back, which he did for ten minutes. Then the appellant gave Hutto massage on his back, legs, and buttocks for ten minutes. Appellant then asked Hutto if he would "like to end the session." He pretended not to understand, protesting that he had only been there twenty minutes, and had paid for an hour. Appellant repeated her inquiry. Hutto then asked if they ended the session could he "get more than just a rub." Appellant said "yes," and Hutto inquired whether he needed to pay her more money or give her a tip. Appellant replied "no, it's all taken care of."

The record then reflects on redirect examination:

A. And after she said it was taken care of I asked her what I could get. And she asked me what did I want. And I told her a blow job or maybe a f____k. And she said "Choose one. It's one or the other."
Q. Was that—was either the blow job or the f____k included in the $130.00?
A. That was my understanding. Because she said that it was taken care of when I asked her if I needed to pay more. . . .
A. Well, we agreed on sexual intercourse and she—she—I asked her if she had some protection I could use, and she said "Yes" and got a condom out of her purse.
Q. Did the defendant agree to engage in sexual conduct with you for a fee?
A. Yes.
Q. And specifically what was that sexual conduct?
A. Sexual intercourse.

The trial judge in a bench trial is the sole trier of the facts, the credibility of the witnesses and the weight to be given to their testimony, and may accept any part of or all the testimony given by the witnesses. . . .

Reconciliation of conflicts and inconsistent testimony is for the trier of fact. . . . The trier of fact may believe or disbelieve all or any part of a witness' testimony, and may accept one part of a witness' testimony and reject the remainder. . . . Conflicts will not call for reversal if there is enough credible testimony to support the conviction. . . .

And certainly the credibility of a witness is a matter for the trier of fact rather than for the Court of Appeals. . . .

The standard for review of the sufficiency of evidence is where, viewing the evidence in the light most favorable to the judgment of the court (in a bench trial), any rational trier of fact could have found the essential elements of the crime charged beyond a reasonable doubt. . . . The standard remains the same for direct and circumstantial evidence cases. . . .

Appellant agrees that the prosecution established all the elements of the offense except one. Appellant acknowledges the proof showed she agreed to engage in sexual intercourse, but argues the evidence does not show that she did so "for a fee." She contends the $130.00 "session" ended before she agreed to the sexual intercourse, that she "was no longer being compensated for her personal services, and that she made no effort to obtain compensation for any sexual activity." The State counters that the evidence showed that Hutto agreed to end the 20-minute "session" only after he determined from the appellant that he could get "more than a rub" and that it was "all taken care of," and that the parties agreed to sexual intercourse. There was certainly evidence to this effect, and the trial court was the trier of the facts.". . .

The judgment is affirmed.

POWERS, Justice, dissenting.
 . . . I believe the evidence insufficient to establish . . . that Austin "knowingly" agreed to sexual intercourse for a fee. . . .

In the present case, there was no initial agreement for conduct on Austin's part that was explicitly sexual. Instead, the officer paid $130 for a "massage" described as a "Swedish Deep Muscle Rub." If that meant sexual conduct, it was only by innuendo or suspicion. "Swedish Deep Muscle Rub" was ambiguous at best as to what it meant; nominally at least it was a "massage." Thus, the evidence does not show, *without more,* a link between the fee paid by the officer and Austin's subsequent agreement for sexual relations, reached *after* the the fee was paid and the massage begun. . . .

BARNES V. GLEN THEATRE, INC.

Supreme Court of the United States, 1991.
501 U.S. ___ , 111 S.Ct. 2456, 115 L.Ed.2d 504.

[Two South Bend, Indiana, establishments that featured all-nude dancing brought suit in the United States District Court for the Northern District of Indiana, seeking an injunction against enforcement of an Indiana statute prohibiting complete nudity in public places. The District Court dismissed the case, concluding that "the type of dancing these plaintiffs wish to perform is not expressive activity protected by the Constitution of the United States." On appeal, the Seventh Circuit reversed, holding that the nude dancing at issue was "expressive conduct protected by the First Amendment." The Supreme Court granted certiorari.]

Chief Justice REHNQUIST . . . [announced the judgment of the Court].

. . . The Kitty Kat Lounge, Inc. (Kitty Kat) is located in the city of South Bend. It sells alcoholic beverages and presents "go-go dancing." Its proprietor desires to present "totally nude dancing," but an applicable Indiana statute regulating public nudity requires that the dancers wear "pasties" and a "G-string" when they dance. . . .

Respondent Glen Theatre, Inc. is an Indiana corporation with a place of business in South Bend. Its primary business is supplying so-called adult entertainment through written and printed materials, movie showings, and live entertainment at the "bookstore" consists of nude and seminude performances and showings of the female body through glass panels. Customers sit in a booth and insert coins into a timing mechanism that permits them to observe the live nude and seminude dancers for a period of time. . . .

Several of our cases contain language suggesting that nude dancing of the kind involved here is expressive conduct protected by the First Amendment. . . .

Indiana, of course, has not banned nude dancing as such, but has proscribed public nudity across the board. The Supreme Court of Indiana has construed the Indiana statute to preclude nudity in what are essentially places of public accommodation such as the Glen Theatre and the Kitty Kat Lounge. In such places, respondents point out, minors are excluded and there are no non-consenting viewers. Respondents contend that while the state may license establishments such as the ones involved here, and limit the geographical area in which they do business, it may not in any way limit the performance of the dances within them without violating the First Amendment. The petitioner contends, on the other hand, that Indiana's restriction on nude dancing is a valid "time, place or manner" restriction. . . .

The "time, place, or manner" test was developed for evaluating restriction on expression taking place on the public property which had been dedicated as a "public forum," . . . although we have on at least one occasion applied it to conduct occurring on private property. . . . . . . [T]his test has been interpreted to embody much the same standards as those set forth in *United States v. O'Brien* . . . (1968), and we turn, therefore, to the rule enunciated in *O'Brien.* . . .

. . . [W]hen 'speech' and 'nonspeech' elements are combined in the same course of conduct, a sufficiently important governmental interest in regulating the nonspeech element can justify incidental limitation on First Amendment freedoms. . . . [W]e think it clear that a government regulation is sufficiently justified if it is within the constitutional power of the Government; if it furthers an important or substantial governmental interest; if the governmental interest is unrelated to the suppression of free expression; and if the incidental restriction on alleged First Amendment freedoms is no greater than essential to the furtherance of that interest. . . .

Applying the . . . test enunciated above, we find that Indiana's public indecency statute is justified despite its incidental limitations on some expressive activity. The public indecency statute is clearly within the constitutional power of the State and furthers substantial governmental interests. It is impossible to discern, other than from the test of the statute, exactly what governmental interest the Indiana legislators had in mind when they enacted this statute, for Indiana does not record legislative history, and the state's highest court has not shed additional light on the statute's purpose. Nonetheless, the statute's purpose of protecting societal order and morality is clear from its text and history. Public indecency statutes of this sort are of ancient origin, and presently exist in at least 47 States. Public indecency, including nudity, was a criminal offense at common law, and this Court recognized the common-law roots of the offense of "gross and open indecency" in *Winters v. New York* . . . (1948). Public nudity was considered an act *malum en se*. . . .

This public indecency statute follows a long line of earlier Indiana statutes banning all public nudity. The history of Indiana's public indecency statute shows that it predates barroom nude dancing and was enacted as a general prohibition. . . .

This and other public indecency statutes were designed to protect morals and public order. The traditional police power of the States is defined as the authority to provide for the public health, safety, and morals, and we have upheld such a basis for legislation. . . .

Thus, the public indecency statute furthers a substantial government interest in protecting order and morality. This interest is unrelated to the suppression of free expression. Some may view restricting nudity on moral grounds as necessarily related to expression. We disagree. It can be argued, of course, that almost limitless types of conduct—including appearing in the nude in public—are "expressive," and in one sense of the word this is true. People who go about in the nude in public may be expressing something about themselves by so doing. But the court rejected this expansive notion of "expressive conduct" in *O'Brien*, saying

> We cannot accept the view that an apparently limitless variety of conduct can be labeled 'speech' whenever the person engaging in the conduct intends thereby to express an idea. . . .

Respondents contend that even though prohibiting nudity in public generally may not be related to suppressing expression, prohibiting the performance of nude dancing is related to expression because the state seeks to prevent its erotic message. Therefore, they reason that the application of the Indiana statute to the nude dancing in this case violates the First Amendment, because it fails the third part of the *O'Brien* test, viz: the governmental interest must be unrelated to the suppression of free expression.

But we do not think that when Indiana applies its statute to the nude dancing in these nightclubs it is proscribing nudity because of the erotic message conveyed by the dancers. Presumably numerous other erotic performances are presented at these establishments and similar clubs without any interference from the state, so long as the performers wore a scant amount of clothing. Likewise the requirement that the dancers don pasties and a G-string does not deprive the dance of whatever erotic message it conveys; it simply makes the message slightly less graphic. The perceived evil that Indiana seeks to address is not erotic dancing, but public nudity. The appearance of people of all shapes, sizes and ages in the nude at a beach, for example, would convey little if any erotic message, yet the state still seeks to prevent it. Public nudity is the evil the state seeks to prevent, whether or not it is combined with expressive activity. . . .

The fourth part of the *O'Brien* test requires that the incidental restriction on First Amendment freedom be no greater than is essential to the furtherance of the governmental interest. As indicated in the discussion above, the governmental interest served by the text of the prohibition is societal disapproval of nudity in public places and among strangers. The statutory prohibition is not a means to some greater end, but and end in itself. It is without cavil that the public indecency statute is "narrowly tailored"; Indiana's requirement that the dancers wear at least pasties and a G-string is modest, and the bare minimum necessary to achieve the state's purpose.

The judgment of the Court of Appeals accordingly is . . . reversed.

Justice SCALIA, concurring in the judgment. . . .

Justice SOUTER, concurring in the judgment. . . .

Justice WHITE, with whom Justice MARSHALL, Justice BLACKMUN, and Justice STEVENS join, dissenting.

. . . The purpose of forbidding people from appearing nude in parks, beaches, hot dog stands, and like public places is to protect others from offense. But that could not possibly be the purpose of preventing nude dancing in theaters and barrooms since the viewers are exclusively consenting adults who pay money to see these dances. The purpose of the proscription in these contexts is to protect the viewers from what the State believes is the harmful message that nude dancing communicates. . . .

That the performances in the Kitty Kat Lounge may not be high art, to say the least, and may not appeal to the Court, is hardly an excuse for distorting and ignoring settled doctrine. The Court's assessment of the artistic merits of nude dancing performances should not be the determining factor in deciding this case. In the words of Justice Harlan,

"it is largely because governmental officials cannot make principled decisions in this area that the Constitution leaves matters of taste and style so largely to the individual.". . . "[W]hile the entertainment afforded by a nude ballet at Lincoln Center to those who can pay the price may differ vastly in content (as viewed by judges) or in quality (as viewed by critics), it may not differ in substance from the dance viewed by the person who . . . wants some 'entertainment' with his beer or shot of rye.". . .

. . . Accordingly, I would affirm the judgment of the Court of Appeals, and dissent from this Court's judgment.

RADEY V. STATE

Court of Appeals of Ohio, 1989.
54 Ohio App. 3d 18, 560 N.E. 2d 247.

[In this case, an Ohio appellate court discusses the operational definition of obscenity. The appellant was charged with pandering obscenity in violation of Ohio law. He was tried before a jury and convicted.]

REECE, Judge.

Defendant-appellant, Richard A. Radey, was arrested by members of the Medina Police Department after he had sold ten greeting cards to two Medina police officers. . . . All of the cards have photographic depictions that are either sexually suggestive or explicit. . . . The photographs often show nude male or female figures and in most cases show one or the other's genitals. In none of the cards is penetration, however slight, depicted. Nor is there a showing of contact between a mouth or tongue and a penis, vagina or anus. . . .

This court is obligated to make an independent, *de novo* judgment as to whether the material involved is constitutionally protected. . . .

In *Miller [v. California* (1973)], the Supreme Court set forth the current test for determining whether challenged materials are obscene. *Miller* stated the test for judging whether material is obscene as follows:

"The basic guidelines for the trier of fact must be: (a) whether 'the average person, applying contemporary community standards' would find that the work, taken as a whole, appeals to the prurient interest . . . , (b) whether the work depicts or describes, in a patently offensive way, sexual conduct specifically defined by the applicable state law; and (c) whether the work, taken as a whole, lacks serious literary, artistic, political, or scientific value. . . .

In *Pope v. Illinois* . . . (1987), the Supreme Court reiterated that parts (a) and (b) of the *Miller* tripartite test should be determined with reference to contemporary community standards. The court held that the proper inquiry for part (c) is whether a reasonable person would find value in the material taken as a whole.

The Supreme Court has characterized the second part of the *Miller* test as a two-step inquiry. . . . The threshold or substantive question is whether the materials depicted "hard core" sexual conduct. The second part of the test is whether, as a matter of fact, the materials were patently offensive under contemporary community standards. Moreover, *Miller* requires that this court review the jury finding under part (c). . . .

Radey was charged with pandering obscenity under R.C. 2907.32(A)(2), which stated (134 Ohio Laws, Part II, 1866, 1915):

"(A) No person, with knowledge of the character of the material or performance involved, shall do any of the following: "(2) Exhibit or advertise for sale or dissemination, or sell or publicly disseminate or display any obscene material[.]"

"Obscene" is defined in R.C. 2907.01(F):

"(F) When considered as a whole, and judged with reference to ordinary adults or, if it is designed for sexual deviates or other specially susceptible group, judged with reference to that group, any material or performance is 'obscene' if any of the following apply:
"(1) Its dominant appeal is to prurient interests:
"(2) Its dominant tendency is to arouse lust by displaying or depicting sexual activity, masturbation, sexual excitement, or nudity in a way that tends to represent human beings as mere objects of sexual appetite;
"(3) Its dominant tendency is to arouse lust by displaying or depicting bestiality or extreme or bizarre violence, cruelty, or brutality;
"(4) Its dominant tendency is to appeal to scatological interest by displaying or depicting human bodily functions of elimination in a way that inspires disgust or revulsion in persons with ordinary sensibilities, without serving any genuine scientific, educational, sociological, moral, or artistic purpose;
"(5) It contains a series of displays or descriptions

of sexual activity, masturbation, sexual excitement, nudity, bestiality, extreme or bizarre violence, cruelty, or brutality, or human bodily functions of elimination, the cumulative effect of which is a dominant tendency to appeal to prurient or scatological interest, when the appeal to such an interest is primarily for its own sake or for commercial exploitation, rather than primarily for a genuine scientific, educational, sociological, moral, or artistic purpose."

The Supreme Court of Ohio has found R.C. 2907.01(f) to be constitutional when read *in pari materia* with the *Miller* guidelines. . . . Therefore, the *Miller* test for defining obscenity was incorporated into the statute by an authoritative state court construction specifically sanctioned by *Miller*. . . . Therefore, when the Ohio statutes are read to incorporate the guidelines prescribed in *Miller*, the material:

(a) must depict conduct which is expressly set forth by the definition of "sexual conduct" in R.C. 2907.01(A); and (b) the sexual conduct depicted must be "obscene," as defined in R.C. 2907.01(F)(1) to (5); and (c) the material must meet the three guidelines of *Miller*.

In this case, the purchased articles are not obscene as a matter of law. The items do not, in and of themselves, describe or depict "hard core sexual conduct" as defined in the Ohio statutes and as required by *Miller*. . . .

Accordingly, . . . the judgment of conviction is reversed and appellant is discharged.

UNITED STATES v. PINELLI
United States Court of Appeals, Tenth Circuit, 1989.
890 F.2d 1461.

[In this case, the U.S. Court of Appeals for the Tenth Circuit reviews the sufficiency of the evidence against seven defendants convicted of several federal offenses related to gambling activities.]

PHILLIPS, District Judge, sitting by designation.
This gambling prosecution stems from a thirty-five (35) count indictment returned by a federal grand jury sitting in Colorado on February 5, 1986. The

indictment charged fourteen defendants, including the seven appellants here, with violating several federal criminal statutes. The pertinent statutes on appeal are 18 U.S.C. § 1955 (operating an illegal gambling business in violation of the laws of Colorado, involving five or more persons, with gross wagers in excess of $2,000 on any single day), 18 U.S.C. § 1952 (interstate use of a telephone to facilitate the gambling business); 26 U.S.C. § 7201 (income tax evasion), 26 U.S.C. § 7262 (failure to pay gambling occupation tax), and 26 U.S.C. § 7203 (failure to file requisite tax forms).

Four defendants entered pleas of guilty prior to trial. Three defendants were acquitted on all charges by the jury. The remaining seven defendants, appellants here, suffered convictions on the counts. . . .

Appellants have raised numerous issues on appeal. . . . We find that there was abundant evidence from which a reasonable jury could find the defendants guilty of the offense for which they were convicted, and further find no reversible error in the record of this case. Accordingly, we affirm the convictions of all seven appellants. . . .

In a challenge based upon the sufficiency of the evidence, we must affirm the judgment of conviction if there is record evidence which would allow a rational trier-of-fact to find the appellants guilty of the crimes charged in the indictment. . . . Moreover, this Court must view the evidence in the light most favorable to the government. . . . Viewed in that light, we conclude that the evidence, both direct and circumstantial, satisfies the test.

The government's evidence at trial focused on appellant's gambling activities from September through December, 1984. The evidence consisted of the testimony of thirty-six (36) witnesses, including numerous bettor witnesses, the introduction of several hundred tape recordings of telephone conversations intercepted pursuant to court-authorized electronic surveillance, documentary evidence seized pursuant to search warrants executed on December 9, 1984 after the termination of the wiretap, and expert testimony by an FBI agent on the roles played by the various defendants in the gambling operation.

The electronic surveillance in this case was active for approximately twenty-four days in November and December, 1984. The government's wiretap evidence and seized records in this case indicated the gambling business in question accepted wagers in excess of $2,300,000 in November and December, 1984. . . .

Special Agent William Holmes of the Federal Bureau of Investigation testified as an expert witness for the government as to the roles of each of the participants in the gambling activity in question. His opinions were based on review of the electronic surveillance and search evidence. . . . He did not rely on and was not privy to the testimony of the bettor witnesses. . . . At the outset of his testimony, Holmes explained some basic gambling terminology which will be helpful in explaining the roles of each of the appellants.

Holmes described the "point spread" or "line" as having the purpose of attracting equal amounts of betting on each side of a contest. Bookmakers change the line on a particular game to attract betting on the other team. A line of "Denver minus six" means Denver is favored by six points and to win a bet on Denver, Denver must win by seven or more points. The term "vig" or "vigorish" represents a ten percent commission charged to losing bets, which compensates the bookmaker for the privilege of placing bets. In other words, a $100 losing bet would require payment of $110, which payment includes a $10 "vig." According to Holmes, a bookmaker theoretically strives to accept the same amount of bets on each side of a contest, or balance his books, and take the "vig" as profit.

Agent Holmes explained the concept of "lay-off wagering" as that which allows a bookmaker "to get rid of wagers that he feels he is not financially able to handle and reduce the risk of great financial loss by having to pay off on large sums of money.". . . The following example of lay-off wagering was provided by Holmes during his testimony: Suppose Bookmaker X has wagers of $1,500 on team A and $1,000 on team B. Bookmaker X would lay-off the $500 excess on team A with Bookmaker Y. If team A wins, Bookmaker X would collect $1,000 from those who bet on team B, plus the 10% vig for a total of $1,100. Bookmaker X would collect his $500 lay-off wager from Bookmaker Y, which would make the total amount collected $1,600. From this amount, he would have to pay his bettors who had bet $1,500 on team A. Bookmaker X would thus make a profit of $100 without risking any of his own money. If Bookmaker X had not laid-off his excess wagers and team A had won, then he would have collected $1,100 from the losers ($1,100 + 10% vig) and had to pay out $1,500 to the winners for a net loss of $400.... As will be shown, the concept of lay-off wagering played a central role in the successful prosecution of appellants.

Viewing the evidence in the light most favorable to the government, as we must, a brief summary of the evidence pertaining to each appellant is set forth below.... [The Court summarizes the evidence against all seven appellants. Only the summaries pertaining to Phil Pinelli and David Pinelli are retained here.]

... The evidence introduced by the government established that defendant Phil Pinelli was in the business of accepting wagers on sporting events. Specifically, the evidence indicated that Phil Pinelli accepted over $800,000 in wagers during November and December, 1984....

Evidence consisted of taped conversations between Phil Pinelli and his brother David Pinelli demonstrated a mutuality of risk between the two brothers in their wagering activities, ... and indicated the brothers had mutual financial interests.... Further, wiretapped telephone conversations demonstrated that Phil Pinelli accepted wagers from, and placed wagers with, other bookmakers.

For instance, from taped conversations introduced by the government it was evident that Phil Pinelli accepted wagers from another bookmaker, Aaron Mosko, and placed bets by telephone with Ralph Lackey.... In particular, the government introduced a taped conversation between Aaron Mosko and Phil Pinelli in which Mosko told Pinelli that he "needed" certain amounts on various games.... In another telephone conversation introduced by the government between Pinelli and a person identified as "Doc," Pinelli told Doc that he had "about five or six bookmakers and they unload their, like Aaron and them guys, they load all their shit on me."

The evidence introduced by the government also indicated that Phil Pinelli kept his gambling records in such a way as to obfuscate their true meaning. For instance, a review of seized records indicates that none of his accounts were identified by recognizable names, but rather by entries such as "K" and "PB.".... Moreover, the government introduced a taped conversation between Pinelli and Aaron Mosko in which Pinelli explained to Mosko that he kept his books in a certain manner so "if they ever pick up my book, they'll say twenty to twenty, you know, they can't say what they are.".... Phil Pinelli received line formation for his gambling activities by placing telephone calls to Las Vegas....

FBI Agent Holmes testified that in his opinion Phil Pinelli was in the business of accepting sports wagering activity and David Pinelli was his partner and assisted Phil in accepting wagers, setting line, and deciding lay-off policy...

Tape recorded conversations between the two brothers demonstrated the mutuality of financial interests between the two.... For instance, in one conversation the Pinellis discussed what they collectively had on Denver and how much they wanted to "lay-off.".... In another conversation David and Phil Pinelli went over the day's wagering activity....

Agent Holmes described David Pinelli as a partner of Phil Pinelli in his gambling business who assisted Phil in accepting wagers, setting line, and deciding lay-off policy....

Central to appellants' challenge to the sufficiency of the evidence is their claim that the government did not prove the jurisdictional elements of 18 U.S.C. § 1955. Section 1955 makes it a crime to operate an illegal gambling business in violation of the laws of the State of Colorado involving five or more persons which was in substantially continuous operation in excess of thirty days, or which had gross wagers in excess of $2,000 on any single day. Here, the multiple telephone calls on particular days, as well as the coordination among appellants which was evident in many conversations, together with the generated revenues, which were substantially in excess of $2,000 per day, amply provide a basis for the jury's findings.

The remaining charges may be briefly summarized. Title 18 U.S.C. § 1952 prohibits interstate telephone calls which facilitate a gambling business. Title 26 U.S. § 7203 makes it a misdemeanor for willful attempts to evade the 2% excise tax on wagers accepted. Title 26 U.S.C. § 7203 makes it a misdemeanor for willful failure to file a tax return, while 26 U.S.C. § 7262 is a misdemeanor offense arising out of the failure to pay the gambling occupation tax.

We are convinced that the evidence collectively, both direct and circumstantial, when viewed in the light most favorable to the government, satisfies each of the essential elements of Section 1955 and the other counts of conviction, and demonstrates appellants' participation in a substantial and continuous bookmaking business conducted by multiple bookmakers and others linked through lay-off wagering, exchange and the use of line formation and ancillary activities.

JUDGMENT AFFIRMED.

CHAPTER 9

DRUG AND ALCOHOL OFFENSES

CHAPTER OUTLINE

Introduction
Drug Offenses
Intoxication Offenses
Conclusion

Cases
Robinson v. California
Embry v. State
Powell v. Texas
People v. Randolph

INTRODUCTION

In this chapter we examine a number of offenses involving the misuse of drugs and alcohol. Because the English common law had little to say about the abuse of alcohol, and nothing to say about illicit drugs, these offenses are based on statutory enactments. These enactments reflect the modern awareness of the adverse social consequences of drug and alcohol abuse. While drug and alcohol offenses may be, and often are, classified as crimes against public morality, they are sufficiently distinctive in character and frequent in their occurrence to warrant separate treatment in a study of criminal law.

DRUG OFFENSES

The misuse of drugs is among the oldest vices in society. Drug abuse not only involves moral questions but also creates dramatic economic, social, and health problems. Illegal trafficking in drugs has led to commission of many violent crimes as well as to instances of official corruption. And many violent crimes are committed by people under the influence of illicit drugs. The Bureau of Justice Statistics reports that "a quarter of jail inmates, a third of State prisoners, and two-fifths of youths in long-term, State-operated facilities admit that they were under the influence of an illegal drug at the time of their offense" (U.S. Department of Justice, Bureau of Justice Statistics, *Drug and Crime Facts,* 1991, p. 3).

In the 1980s, the focus of the drug problem was the widespread use of cocaine and, in particular, "crack," an inexpensive form of cocaine that is ingested through smoking. The prevalence of cocaine and the destructive consequences of its use led political leaders to declare a "war on drugs" in the late 1980s. While the national war on drugs has not been completely successful, there is evidence that it has had a positive impact. In 1985, 13.1 percent of high school seniors reported that they had used cocaine within the last twelve months; by 1990 the figure had declined to 5.3 percent (U.S. Department of Justice, Bureau of Justice Statistics, *Drug and Crime Facts,* 1991, p. 17).

Some commentators, believing that the national "war on drugs" has failed, have argued for the legalization of drugs like marijuana, cocaine, and heroin. These commentators would prefer to see use of these drugs legalized, although highly regulated, with increased efforts directed toward educational and treatment programs. Most people disagree with this perspective, however. A 1990 Gallup Poll found that a substantial majority of Americans believed that legalization would make matters worse, not better (see Table 9.1).

Federal Laws

In the United States, the 1960s saw a resurgence of drug abuse, a problem that had caused great concern in the early twentieth century when it was legal to market products containing opium and cocaine. As attention focused on the illegal use of drugs as a national problem, Congress enacted the Comprehensive Drug Abuse Prevention and Control Act of 1970. 21 U.S.C.A. § 811 *et seq.* The act, commonly referred to as the Controlled Substance Act, establishes schedules listing controlled substances according to their potential for abuse. Penalties for

TABLE 9.1   PUBLIC PERCEPTIONS OF THE LIKELY EFFECTS
OF LEGALIZING DRUGS, 1990

Legalization would increase:	% Agreeing:
Drug use in the public schools	65
The number of drug addicts	67
The number of drug overdoses	63
Drug-related crime	52

Source: Gallup Poll, 1990, reported in Bureau of Justice
Statistics, U.S. Department of Justice, *Drug and Crime
Facts, 1991*, p. 21.

offenses involving the manufacture, sale, distribution, and possession depend on
the substance involved, 21 U.S.C.A. § 841, with provision for registered practitioners to dispense narcotics for approved purposes. 21 U.S.C.A. § 823.

In 1972, the Uniform Controlled Substance Act was drafted by the Commissioners on Uniform Laws. Its purpose was to achieve uniformity among state and
federal laws. The majority of states have now adopted the uniform act, often
with some minor modifications. Like the federal statute, the uniform act
classifies controlled substances according to their potential for abuse. For example, opiates are included in Schedule I because they are unsafe for use even
under medical treatment, while Schedule II includes drugs that have a high
potential for abuse but may be medically acceptable under certain conditions.
The remaining schedules include controlled substances that have lesser potential
for abuse and dependency. The range includes such well-known controlled
substances as cocaine, amphetamines, tranquilizers, and barbiturates.

State Statutes

All states make the *manufacture, sale, and possession* of controlled substances
illegal. Offenses involving drugs that have a high potential for abuse (e.g., heroin
and cocaine) are usually very serious felonies. Although it is constitutionally
permissible to enact such laws, states may not criminalize the mere *status* of
being addicted to such drugs without running afoul of the Cruel and Unusual
Punishments Clause of the Eighth Amendment to the U.S. Constitution. *Robinson
v. California*, 370 U.S. 660, 82 S.Ct. 1417, 8 L.Ed.2d 758 (1962).

The Nebraska statue is fairly typical of state drug laws. It stipulates that:

(1) Except as authorized by the Uniform Controlled Substances Act, it shall be
unlawful for any person knowingly or intentionally: (a) To manufacture, distribute,
deliver, dispense, or possess with intent to manufacture, distribute, deliver, or
dispense a controlled substance. . . .

(2) [omitted]

(3) A person knowingly or intentionally possessing a controlled substance, except
marijuana, unless such substance was obtained directly or pursuant to a valid
prescription or order from a practitioner while acting in the course of his or her
professional practice, or except as otherwise authorized by the act, shall be guilty of
a class IV felony.

Rev. Stat. Neb. § 28–416 (1)(2)(3) (1989).

Offenses involving the mere *possession* of less harmful substances are often classified as lesser-degree felonies or, where a very small quantity of marijuana is involved, are frequently classified as misdmeanors. For example, in Nebraska, possession of more than one ounce but less than one pound of marijuana is a misdemeanor; possession of more than one pound is a felony. Rev. Stat. Neb. § 28–416 (6)(7) (1989).

During the 1970s a number of states decriminalized their antimarijuana laws by removing the threat of a jail sentence for possession offenses. In Nebraska, for example, possession of less than one ounce of marijuana is considered an "infraction" for which a first-time offender may be fined no more than one hundred dollars and made to attend a drug education course. Rev. Stat. Neb. § 28–416 (8)(a) (1989).

The impetus of the drive to decriminalize marijuana has diminished, and from 1978 to the present further attempts at decriminalization have been unsuccessful. Despite the attempts at enforcement, marijuana remains widely available and provides an example of the difficulty in enforcing a law that has less than universal public support. Nevertheless, courts have generally declined to reassess legislative judgments in this area, and statutes making it a criminal offense to possess marijuana have withstood numerous constitutional challenges. See, for example, *State v. Smith*, 610 P.2d 869 (Wash. 1980); *People v. Riddle*, 237 N.W.2d 491 (Mich. App. 1975).

One notable exception to the state courts' general deference to legislative prohibitions of marijuana possession is *Ravin v. State*, 537 P.2d 494 (Alaska 1975), where the Alaska Supreme Court ruled that possession of small quantities of marijuana by an adult for personal use in the home was protected by that state's constitutional right of privacy. This decision was effectively overturned, however, by a 1991 amendment to the state constitution.

Prohibition of Drug Paraphernalia; Forfeiture of Property

Possession of paraphernalia associated with illicit drug use is also commonly a criminal offense. Controlled substances and illegal paraphernalia are declared contraband and are subject to confiscation. Likewise, vehicles and aircraft involved in trafficking of controlled substances may be seized and declared forfeited under various federal and state statutes. See, for example, 21 U.S.C.A. § 881. In addition, in 1984 Congress enacted a law providing for forfeiture of real estate used in illegal drug trafficking. 21 U.S.C.A. § 881(h). However, in *United States v. A Parcel of Land*, 507 U.S. ___ , 113 S.Ct. 1126, 122 L.Ed.2d 469 (1993), the Supreme Court ruled that, although proceeds traceable to an unlawful drug transaction are subject to forfeiture, an owner's lack of knowledge that her home had been purchased with proceeds of illegal drug transactions constitutes a defense to a forfeiture proceeding under federal law. Moreover, the Court has set a theoretical limit on the amount of property that may be seized by government through forfeiture. In *Austin v. United States*, 509 U.S. ___ , 113 S.Ct. ___ , 125 L.Ed.2d 488 (1993), the Court remanded for reconsideration a case where the federal government seized a business and a mobile home from a man who sold two grams of cocaine to an undercover agent. The Court ruled that forfeitures, although they are not technically criminal proceedings, are subject to the Excessive Fines Clause of the Eighth Amendment.

Problems of Enforcement

Federal and state laws on controlled substances mirror one another in many respects. Federal enforcement is usually directed against major interstate or international drug traffickers; states usually concentrate on those who possess or distribute controlled substances. Many drug-trafficking violations of federal law involve prosecution for conspiracy. Unlike many state laws, the federal law on conspiracy to violate the Controlled Substance Act does not require proof of an overt act. 21 U.S.C.A. § 846; *United States v. Wilson*, 657 F.2d 755 (5th Cir. 1981).

Because those involved in narcotics transactions are usually willing participants, enforcement often depends on use of confidential informants by police. Obtaining search warrants and making arrests based on probable cause often present difficult Fourth Amendment problems, some of which are discussed in Chapters 14 and 15.

Prosecutorial Problems

The level of intent that the prosecution must establish in contraband cases can vary according to the particular statutory offense (see Chapter 4). However, courts have generally held that statutes making possession, distribution, or trafficking in contraband unlawful require the prosecution to prove only the defendant's general intent. See, for example, *State v. Williams*, 352 So. 2d 1295 (La. 1977); *State v. Bender*, 579 P.2d 796 (N.M. 1978).

In drug possession cases, a critical problem is proving that the defendant was in possession of a controlled substance. The prosecution may prove either *actual* or *constructive* possession of contraband to satisfy the possession requirement. Proof of actual possession is established upon proof that the contraband was found on the accused's person or that the accused was in exclusive possession of the premises or vehicle where the contraband was discovered. However, where the accused is not in actual possession, or where the accused and another person jointly occupy a dwelling or automobile where contraband is discovered, the prosecution must attempt to prove what the law calls constructive possession.

A person has constructive possession of contraband if he or she has ownership, dominion, or control over the contraband itself, or over the premises in which it is concealed. *United States v. Schubel*, 912 F.2d 952 (8th Cir. 1990). The prosecution usually attempts to establish constructive possession by evidence of incriminating statements and circumstances from which the defendant's ability to control the contraband may be inferred. This can pose a formidable difficulty.

Defenses

Defendants on trial for drug offenses sometimes assert that they were entrapped by the police, a defense discussed in Chapter 13. More frequently, defense counsel attempt to suppress the contraband seized by police on the ground that it was obtained in violation of the Fourth Amendment prohibition against unreasonable searches and seizures (see Chapter 14). In some instances, a

CASE IN POINT

Is Cocaine Possession A Crime of Moral Turpitude?

Jimmy Major was arrested and charged with distribution of crack cocaine. At trial, Major took the stand to testify that he "had nothing to do " with illegal drugs or drug dealing. On cross-examination, the prosecutor asked Major whether he had ever used or possessed crack cocaine, to which Major replied in the negative. To impeach Major's credibility, the prosecutor then introduced evidence of Major's prior conviction for simple possession of cocaine. Major was convicted and appealed. The South Carolina Supreme Court was asked to decide whether evidence of the prior simple possession conviction was properly admitted at trial. Under South Carolina law, the question was whether simple possession of cocaine was a crime of moral turpitude. If so, the prior conviction could be used to impeach the credibility of Major's testimony as to his own good character with respect to involvement with drug dealing.

In 1987 the South Carolina Supreme Court had held that the crime of possession of cocaine was not a crime of moral turpitude since it involved "primarily self-destructive behavior." *State v. Ball*, 354 S.E. 2d 906, 908 (S.C. 1987). In *Ball*, the Court noted that "[i]n determining whether a crime is one involving moral turpitude, the Court focuses primarily on the duty to society and fellow men which is breached by the commission of the crime." 354 S.E. 2d at 908.

In Major's case, the Court reversed its prior holding in *Ball*, saying in part:

> We retain the test articulated in *Ball* for determining whether a crime qualifies as one of "moral turpitude," but we overrule *Ball* because of its holding regarding cocaine possession. The drug "cocaine" has torn at the very fabric of our nation. Families have been ripped apart, minds have been ruined, and lives have been lost. It is common knowledge that the drug is highly addictive and potentially fatal. The addictive nature of the drug, combined with its expense, has caused our prisons to swell with those who have been motivated to support their drug habit through criminal acts. In some areas of the world, entire governments have been undermined by the cocaine industry. As stated by Chief Justice Gregory in his dissent in *Ball*, "[o]ne who possesses this controlled substance, even for his own use, fosters the prosperity of the lucrative and destructive industry of illicit cocaine manufacture and trafficking." *Ball*, 354, S.E.2d at 909. (Gregory, C.J. dissenting). Because of our present "war on drugs," and because any involvement with cocaine contributes to the destruction of ordered society, we hold that mere possession of cocaine is a crime of moral turpitude.

State v. Major, 391 S.E.2d 235 (S.C. 1990).

defendant presents an expert witness to contest the type of contraband introduced in evidence, and frequently defendants challenge the chain of custody of the contraband from the time it was seized until the time it was introduced into evidence. Since the gravity of the offense is often based on the amount of contraband seized, defendants sometimes challenge the weight of the contraband

---

C A S E   I N   P O I N T

CONSTRUCTIVE POSSESSION OF DRUGS

After Minneapolis police obtained a tip that crack cocaine was being sold out of cars parked in front of a certain duplex, an officer observed a blue Cadillac parked in front of the building. A female later identified as the defendant, Nina Knox, made several trips between the car and the duplex. At one point she drove the car from the scene, but returned shortly and sat in the car for a period of time as a number of men approached the car and walked away after brief encounters. The officer, who was experienced in dealing with drug offenses, believed the activities he witnessed to be drug transactions, although he was unable to observe money and drugs being exchanged. Knox was arrested, and a search of the car produced 14.3 grams of crack cocaine and $2,200 in cash. A search of Knox's purse produced a large amount of money and food stamps. Knox was convicted in federal court of possession with intent to distribute a controlled substance.

On appeal, Knox challenged the sufficiency of the evidence, arguing that it failed to establish that she was in physical control of the cocaine and was intending to sell it. The U.S. Court of Appeals rejected Knox's contention, holding that there was sufficient evidence for the trial court to conclude that she was in constructive possession of the cocaine and intended to distribute it. The court concluded that the evidence supported a finding that Knox had exercised "dominion over the premises in which the contraband [was] concealed," since she was observed driving the car, sitting in the car, and entering it on several occasions. The court further concluded that intent to distribute could be inferred from the fact that sizable amounts of cash and cocaine were found at the scene. Knox's conviction was affirmed.

United States v. Knox, 888 F.2d 585 (8th Cir. 1989).

---

being introduced into evidence. Finally, in cases where defendants are charged with possession with intent to deliver drugs within a certain proximity of a school, which is a separate and more serious offense in many states, defendants often challenge the measurement of the distance between the school and the location where the defendant was alleged to be when the offense occurred.

In a number of cases, courts have rejected such defenses as economic coercion and duress (see Chapter 13), and several state courts have refused to allow a defendant to claim that possession or use of illicit substances was a "medical necessity." See, for example, *Spillers v. State*, 245 S.E.2d 54 (Ga. App. 1978). However, in 1991 a Florida appellate court reversed a trial court decision refusing to allow evidence in support of such a defense. In *Jenks v. State*, 582 So.2d 676 (Fla. App. 1991), a husband had contracted acquired immune deficiency syndrome (AIDS) through a blood transfusion; his wife acquired it from him. Both were charged with possession and cultivation of marijuana. They claimed their actions were for their own relief, and they presented medical experts who testified that no other drug treatment was available to effectively eliminate the nausea they suffered from AIDS. Observing that the evil to be avoided was more heinous than the unlawful act perpetrated to avoid it, the appellate court directed the lower court to permit the defendants to assert the defense of medical necessity.

INTOXICATION OFFENSES

By the turn of the twentieth century, alcohol had come to be perceived by a substantial segment of the population as an evil that had to be eradicated. In response to growing, but far from unanimous, public sentiment, Congress enacted the Eighteenth Amendment, which was ratified in 1919. This amendment, widely referred to as "Prohibition," made unlawful the "manufacture, sale, or transportation of intoxicating liquors" within the United States. The national prohibition of alcohol was widely violated and contributed greatly to the development of organized crime syndicates in this country. Ultimately, Prohibition was repealed by the Twenty-First Amendment, ratified in 1933. However, under the Twenty-First Amendment, state and local governments retain the authority to ban or regulate the manufacture, sale, and use of alcohol within their borders. Indeed, while the sale of alcohol is widespread today, there are still a number of so-called dry counties throughout the United States, mainly in the South and Midwest, where the sale of all or some alcoholic beverages is prohibited. While no state has chosen to ban the sale of alcohol altogether, all states regulate alcoholic beverages and retain a number of alcohol-related offenses.

Two offenses of statutory origin in the United States are directed at those who consume excessive amounts of alcoholic beverages. They are public drunkenness and driving while under the influence of intoxicants. These are sometimes regarded as offenses against public morality, but they are primarily designed to protect the safety of the public, as well as of the offender.

Public Drunkenness Laws

Laws and ordinances making public drunkenness an offense have long been enforced by all jurisdictions, with most states and municipalities simply providing that whoever shall become intoxicated from the voluntary use of intoxicating liquors shall be punished. The offense merely involves the accused being found in a public place in a state of intoxication and usually has been classified as a minor misdemeanor. A common police practice has been to take offenders into custody and release them once they have "sobered up." Some have referred to this practice as a "revolving door."

Trends in Public Drunkenness Cases

There is a growing awareness that alcoholism is a disease, and many have urged that the criminal law is an inappropriate mechanism to deal with it. Additionally, some reformers have contended that criminalizing the public presence of an intoxicated person is contrary to the Eighth Amendment's prohibition of cruel and unusual punishments. The Supreme Court, however, has declined to accept such a view. Instead, in *Powell v. Texas*, 392 U.S. 514, 88 S. Ct. 2145, 20 L.Ed.2d

---

C A S E I N P O I N T

SUFFICIENCY OF EVIDENCE TO SUSTAIN DWI CONVICTION

After investigating the scene of a one-vehicle accident in which a driver had evidently lost control of his truck, Deputy Sheriff Michael Redmond went to the hospital where the driver had been taken. The deputy later testified that the driver had no apparent injuries, but that his speech was slurred and there was a strong odor of alcohol about him. The driver was subjected to a blood test that revealed a high level of alcohol in the blood, but the results of this test were barred from trial due to evidentiary problems. The defendant, Paul T. Ryan, was nevertheless convicted of driving while intoxicated. On appeal, Ryan challenged the sufficiency of the evidence presented against him. The appellate court sustained the conviction, however, saying: "A careful review of the record convinces us, without considering the result of the blood test, that there is substantial evidence to sustain appellant's conviction."

Ryan v. State, 786 S.W. 2d 835, 837 (Ark. App. 1990).

1254 (1968), it upheld a public intoxication law. In effect, the Court ruled that the defendant Powell was not being punished for his status as an alcoholic, but rather for his presence in a public place in an inebriated condition.

In recent years some states have enacted statutes directing police officers to take persons found intoxicated in public places to treatment facilities rather than to incarcerate them. Consistent with this approach, many statutes now criminalize only "disorderly intoxication." This newer offense involves the offender being intoxicated in public and endangering the safety of others, not merely being in a state of intoxication in public. See, for example, West's Fla. Stat. Ann. § 856.011.

Driving While under the Influence of Alcohol or Drugs

The carnage on the American highways attests to the urgent need for states to take stern measures to keep drunk drivers off the road, and all states have enacted laws attempting to accomplish this goal. The "classical" offense in this area is driving while intoxicated (DWI), or more accurately, operating a motor vehicle while intoxicated. In the 1960s and 1970s, many jurisdictions expanded the offense to prohibit driving while under the influence of intoxicating liquors or drugs (DUI). DWI and DUI laws sometimes allowed a defendant to avoid conviction due to the ambiguity of his or her subjective behavior. In response to this problem, most states have modified their statutes to prohibit driving with an unlawful blood-alcohol level (DUBAL), which is defined as 0.10 percent or more alcohol in the bloodstream. By 1993, eight states had adopted an even stricter standard, prohibiting a 0.08 percent blood alcohol level. This is illustrated by Section 23152 of the California Vehicle Code, which states:

TABLE 9.2 DWI, DUI, and DUBAL
Arrests in the United States, 1972–1990

Year	Arrests (nearest thousand)
1972	604,000
1973	654,000
1974	617,000
1975	909,000
1976	838,000
1977	1,104,000
1978	1,205,000
1979	1,232,000
1980	1,304,000
1981	1,422,000
1982	1,405,000
1983	1,613,000
1984	1,347,000
1985	1,503,000
1986	1,459,000
1987	1,410,000
1988	1,294,000
1989	1,333,000
1990	1,391,000

Source: Source: U.S. Department of Justice, *Criminal Justice Sourcebook, 1991,* p. 468.

(a) It is unlawful for any person who is under the influence of an alcoholic beverage or any drug, or under the combined influence of an alcoholic beverage and any drug, to drive a vehicle.

(b) It is unlawful for any person who has 0.08 percent or more, by weight, of alcohol in his or her blood to drive a vehicle.

West's Cal. Ann. Vehicle Code § 23152 (a) (b).

The California Supreme Court has upheld this statute against constitutional attack, stating that it is a rational exercise of the state's police power, provides adequate notice of the conduct proscribed, and is not void for vagueness. *Burg v. Municipal Court,* 673 P.2d 732 (Cal. 1983), *cert. denied,* 466 U.S. 967, 104 S. Ct. 2337, 80 L.Ed. 2d 812 (1984). Several other state courts have upheld similar statutes against a variety of constitutional attacks.

Prosecution and Defense of DWI, DUI, and DUBAL Charges

To obtain a conviction for DWI, DUI or DUBAL, the prosecution must first establish that the defendant charged with driving while intoxicated or driving under the influence was operating the vehicle. This may be accomplished by eyewitness or circumstantial evidence. Next the prosecution must establish the intoxication. Statutes, it should be noted, often refer to intoxication occurring as a result of alcohol or from ingestion of contraband substances. Intoxication is often a difficult state to articulate. Therefore, police often use such field sobriety techniques as the touching-finger-to-nose, walking-the-line, counting backwards, and similar tests to corroborate their testimony concerning the defendant's condition at the time of arrest.

In *Berkemer v. McCarty*, 468 U.S. 420, 104 S.Ct. 3138, 82 L.Ed.2d 317 (1984), the U.S. Supreme Court held that an officer's roadside questioning of an administration of a field sobriety test to an individual stopped for irregular driving was not a "custodial interrogation" that required giving the suspect the *Miranda* warnings. The Court cautioned, however, that the *Miranda* warnings apply once the suspect is under arrest (see Chapter 15).

There is evidence that field sobriety tests may be somewhat unreliable, and courts are beginning to scrutinize cases that rely solely on field sobriety tests without supporting chemical testing of the blood, urine, or breath of the suspect. Still, most courts permit persons to be convicted of DUI without chemical tests, especially when multiple sobriety tests have been performed by more than one officer.

Increasingly, police videotape suspects' performance on field sobriety tests and make audio tape recordings of suspects' speech. Many police agencies today have mobile blood-alcohol testing units ("Batmobiles") equipped with breathalyzer testing machines, videotape equipment, and voice recorders. These vans, available at the call of the arresting officer, give the police the opportunity to promptly collect evidence at or near the scene of the arrest.

While generally regarded as superior to field sobriety tests from an evidentiary standpoint, chemical tests are not wholly devoid of problems. When prosecutors rely solely on chemical evidence, defense counsel often challenge the reliability and validity of chemical testing equipment and the operator's level of competence. Ideally, to obtain a conviction, a prosecutor would like to have evidence that the defendant was driving abnormally, that he or she smelled of alcohol, exhibited slurred speech, failed a battery of field sobriety tests administered by several officers, and registered an impermissibly high blood-alcohol level on one or more chemical tests performed by a trained technician. Of course, in the real world of law enforcement, such thorough evidence is seldom obtained.

Implied Consent Statutes

To facilitate chemical testing in DWI, DUI, and DUBAL cases, California and most other jurisdictions have enacted "implied consent" statutes. Under these laws, a person who drives a motor vehicle is deemed to have given consent to a urine test for drugs and to blood, breath, or urine testing to determine blood-alcohol content. The testing is made incident to a lawful arrest of a driver. See, for example, West's Ann. Cal. Vehicle Code § 23157. The Supreme Court has upheld the validity of the Massachusetts Implied Consent law providing for suspension of the driver's license of a person who refuses to take a breathalyzer test. *Mackey v. Montrym*, 443 U.S. 1, 99 S. Ct. 2612, 61 L.Ed.2d 321 (1979).

CONCLUSION

The widespread abuse of drugs and alcohol is a serious social problem with many undesirable consequences. Society has responded to this problem largely through the criminal justice system. There are those, however, who believe that criminalizing drug possession is undesirable public policy. Yet, in the 1990s, the public appears to be strongly committed to maintaining, if not increasing, the criminal sanctions against the manufacture, sale, and possession of drugs. It is equally committed to strengthening criminal penalties and stepping up enforcement with respect to drunk driving. For the foreseeable future, these undesirable behaviors will remain criminal offenses and, accordingly, major problems for police, prosecutors, and prison officials.

QUESTIONS FOR THOUGHT AND DISCUSSION

1. Is it sensible to maintain the criminal prohibitions against illicit drugs, or should these substances be legalized, carefully regulated, and their abuse dealt with through other means?

2. What are the typical difficulties facing prosecutors seeking convictions in drug possession cases?

3. Why, according to the Supreme Court in *Robinson v. California*, may a person not be held criminally liable for being addicted to illicit narcotics?

4. Should chronic alcoholism be a defense to intoxication offenses such as public drunkenness or driving under the influence?

5. Is requiring a person suspected of driving while intoxicated to submit to a blood-alcohol test a violation of the Fifth Amendment prohibition against compulsory self-incrimination?

6. During the late afternoon, police were called to quell a disturbance at a motel where the management had reported some disorderly conduct and apparent drug use. Outside the motel, the police observed Henry Egad standing by a tree. About eighteen inches from Egad's feet, the police discovered a matchbox on the ground. Their examination revealed that the matchbox contained a substance that later proved to be PCP, an illegal drug. Police placed Egad under arrest and charged him with possession of a controlled substance. Based on these facts alone, do you think the prosecutor can establish that Egad was in possession of the PCP?

CASES

ROBINSON V. CALIFORNIA

Supreme Court of the United States, 1962.
370 U.S. 660, 82 S.Ct. 1417, 8 L.Ed. 2d 758.

[Robinson was convicted in a California court of violating a state statute that made it a criminal offense to "be addicted to the use of narcotics." In this appeal to the U.S. Supreme Court, Robinson challenges the constitutionality of that statute, as it had been interpreted by the California courts, as violative of the Cruel and Unusual Punishments Clause of the Eighth Amendment to the U.S. Constitution.]

Mr. Justice STEWART delivered the opinion of the Court.

. . . This statute . . . is not one which punishes a person for the use of narcotics, for their purchase, sale or possession, or for anti-social or disorderly behavior resulting from their administration. It is not a law which even purports to provide or require medical treatment. Rather, we deal with a statute which makes the "status" of narcotic addiction a criminal offense, for which the offender may be prosecuted "at any time before he reforms." California has said that a person can be continuously guilty of this offense, whether or not he has ever used or possessed any narcotics within the state, and whether or not he has been guilty of any anti-social behavior there.

It is unlikely that any state at this moment in history would attempt to make it a criminal offense for a person to be mentally ill, or a leper, or to be afflicted with a venereal disease. A state might determine that the general health and welfare require that the victims of these and other human afflictions be dealt with by compulsory treatment, involving quarantine, confinement, or sequestration. But, in the light of contemporary human knowledge, a law which made a criminal offense of such a disease would doubtless be universally thought to be an infliction of cruel and unusual punishment in violation of the eighth and 14th amendments.

We cannot but consider the statute before us as of the same category. In this Court counsel for the state recognized that narcotic addiction is an illness. Indeed, it is apparently an illness which may be contracted innocently or involuntarily. We hold that a state law which imprisons a person thus afflicted as a criminal, even though he has never touched any narcotic drug within the state or been guilty of any irregular behavior there, inflicts a cruel and unusual punishment in violation of the 14th amendment. To be sure, imprisonment for 90 days is not, in the abstract, a punishment which is either cruel or unusual. But the question cannot be considered in the abstract. Even one day in prison would be a cruel and unusual punishment for the "crime" of having a common cold.

We are not unmindful that the vicious evils of the narcotics traffic have occasioned the grave concern of government. There are, as we have said, countless fronts on which those evils may be legitimately attacked. We deal in this case only within an individual provision of a particularized local law as it has so far been interpreted by the California courts.

Reversed.

Mr. Justice FRANKFURTER took no part in the consideration or decision of this case.

Mr. Justice DOUGLAS, concurring.

. . . [T]he addict is a sick person. He may, of course, be confined for treatment or for the protection of society. Cruel and unusual punishment results not from confinement, but from convicting the addict of a crime. A prosecution for addiction, with its resulting stigma and irreparable damage to the good name of the accused, cannot be justified as a means of protecting society, where a civil commitment would do as well.

Mr. Justice CLARK, dissenting. . . .

Mr. Justice WHITE, dissenting. . . .

EMBRY V. STATE

Supreme Court of Arkansas, 1990.
302 Ark. 608, 792 S.W.2d 318.

[In this case, the Arkansas Supreme Court considers the sufficiency of the evidence to support the convictions of two individuals for possession of illegal drugs with intent to deliver.]

TURNER, Justice.

Sammie Lee Embry and John Wesley Phillips, a.k.a. Ibraheem Shabazz, were each convicted of possession of cocaine with intent to deliver and possession of marijuana with intent to deliver. Embry was sentenced to 20 years on the cocaine charge and five years on the marijuana charge. Phillips was found to be an habitual offender, previously convicted of four or more felonies and was thus sentenced to life imprisonment on the cocaine charge and to 20 years on the marijuana charge. Both defendants appeal the convictions. We find the appeal of Embry to be meritorious and reverse and dismiss his convictions. Phillips's appeal, however, is without merit, and we therefore affirm.

Embry and Patricia Booker had an off-and-on relationship; consequently, Embry spent considerable amounts of time at Booker's residence at 1414 May Avenue in Fort Smith. Embry, who was the father of Booker's child, kept clothing at Booker's house and frequently stayed there.

Law enforcement authorities placed the house under surveillance as a probable outlet for drugs and gave identifiable currency to a confidential informant who was to make a drug buy at that address. When the informant returned, he delivered a quantity of crack cocaine to the authorities. The police obtained a search warrant, and at 2:50 P.M. the officers conducted a search of the Booker residence. They found illicit controlled substances and arrested Booker, Phillips, and others at the scene. Embry was not at the house at the time of the search and arrests. About an hour later, after leaving work, he arrived at the residence and was taken into custody. . . .

It is well established that the state need not prove the accused had actual possession of a controlled substance; constructive possession is sufficient. . . . Constructive possession, which is the control or right to control the contraband, can be implied where the contraband is found in a place immediately and exclusively accessible to the accused and subject to his control. . . .

Where there is joint occupancy of the premises where the contraband is seized, some additional factor must be found to link the accused to the contraband. . . . In such instances, the state must prove that the accused exercised care, control, and management over the contraband and also that the accused knew that the matter possessed was contraband. . . .

The appellant Embry was not present when the house was entered and searched and had no controlled substance on his person at the time of the arrest. He had no ownership interest in the house or furnishings, though he was a frequent (if not full-time) occupant and kept personal clothing there. It cannot be said that he had a superior or an equal right to the control of the house. He made no effort to dispose of any incriminating matter and made no incriminating statement. . . .

. . . [Embry] possessed no contraband, and the state failed to prove that he constructively possessed either the marijuana or cocaine found at the residence. His conviction must therefore be reversed.

Considering next the challenge by the appellant Phillips/Shabazz to the sufficiency of the evidence, the record reveals an entirely different scenario under the same facts. Though Phillips had no possessory interest in the house or furnishings, he had sold marijuana, according to testimony, and another substance thought to be cocaine inside the Booker house and at the front door; he was present at the time of the search and attempted to flee from the officer entering the front door; then, when confronted by officers entering through the back door, he tossed away a cigarette package later determined to contain marijuana cigarettes. During the search, the officers discovered a .25 caliber semi-automatic pistol in a closet which had been brought to the Booker house by Phillips and was later found to belong to Phillips's girlfriend.

All of the recited evidence was sufficient to support the jury's finding of guilt. . . .

POWELL V. TEXAS

Supreme Court of the United States, 1968.
392 U.S. 514, 88 S. Ct. 2145, 20 L.Ed.2d 1254.

[In this case the U.S. Supreme Court considers whether it is cruel and unusual punishment under the Eighth Amendment to convict a person suffering from chronic alcoholism of the crime of public drunkenness.]

Mr. Justice MARSHALL announced the judgment of the Court and delivered an opinion in which The CHIEF JUSTICE, Mr. Justice BLACK, and Mr. Justice HARLAN join.

In late December 1966, appellant [Leroy Powell] was arrested and charged with being found in a state of intoxication in a public place....

...[Powell's] counsel urged that appellant was "afflicted with the disease of chronic alcoholism," that "his appearance in public [while drunk was] not of his own volition," and therefore that to punish him criminally for that conduct would be cruel and unusual, in violation of the Eighth and Fourteenth Amendments to the Untied States Constitution.

The trial judge in the county court, sitting without a jury, made certain findings of fact, but ruled as a matter of law that chronic alcoholism was not a defense to the charge. He found appellant guilty, and fined him $50....

Appellant ... seeks to come within the application of the Cruel and Unusual Punishment Clause announced in *Robinson v. California* ... (1962), which ... held ... that "a state statute which imprisons a person thus afflicted [with narcotic addition] as a criminal, even though he has never touched any narcotic drug within the State or been guilty of any irregular behavior there, inflicts a cruel and unusual punishment." ...

On its face the present case does not fall within that holding, since appellant was convicted, not for being a chronic alcoholic, but for being in public while drunk on a particular occasion. The State of Texas thus has not sought to punish a mere status, as California did in *Robinson*, nor has it attempted to regulate appellant's criminal sanction for public behavior which may create substantial health and safety hazards, both for appellant and for members of the general public, and which offends the moral and aesthetic sensibilities of a large segment of the community. This seems a far cry from convicting one for being an addict, being a chronic alcoholic, being "mentally ill, or a leper." ...

...[T]he most troubling aspects of this case, were *Robinson* to be extended to meet it, would be the scope and content of what could only be a constitutional doctrine of criminal responsibility. In dissent it is urged that the decision could be limited to conduct which is "a characteristic and involuntary part of the pattern of the disease as it afflicts" the particular individual, and that "[i]t is not foreseeable" that it would be applied "in the case of offenses such as driving a car while intoxicated, assault, theft, or robbery." ... That is limitation by fiat. In the first place, nothing in the logic of the dissent would limit its application to chronic alcoholics. If Leroy Powell cannot be convicted of public intoxication, it is difficult to see how a State can convict an individual for murder, if that individual, while exhibiting normal behavior in all other respects, suffers from a "compulsion" to kill, which is an "exceedingly strong influence," but "not completely overpowering." Even if we limit our consideration to chronic alcoholics, it would seem impossible to confine the principle within the arbitrary bounds which the dissent seems to envision.

It is not difficult to imagine a case involving psychiatric testimony to the effect that an individual suffers from some aggressive neurosis which he is able to control when sober; that very little alcohol suffices to remove the inhibitions which normally contain these aggressions, with the result that the individual engages in assaultive behavior without becoming actually intoxicated; and that the individual suffers from a very strong desire to drink, which is an "exceedingly strong influence" but "not completely overpowering." Without being untrue to the rationale of this case, should the principles advanced in dissent be accepted here, the Court could not avoid holding such an individual constitutionally unaccountable for his assaultive behavior.

Traditional common-law concepts of personal accountability and essential considerations of federalism lead us to disagree with appellant. We are unable to conclude, on the state of this record or on the current state of medical knowledge, that chronic alcoholics in general, and Leroy Powell in particular, suffer from such an irresistible compulsion to drink and to get drunk in public that they are utterly unable to control their performance of either or both of these acts and thus cannot be deterred at all from public intoxication. And in any event this Court has never articulated a general constitutional doctrine of *mens rea.*

We cannot cast aside the centuries-long evolution of the collection of interlocking and overlapping concepts which the common law has utilized to assess the moral accountability of an individual for his antisocial deeds. The doctrines of *actus reus, mens rea,* insanity, mistake, justification, and duress have historically provided the tools for a constantly shifting adjustment of the tension between the medical views of the nature of man. This process of adjustment has always been thought to be the province of the States.

Nothing could be less fruitful than for this Court to be impelled into defining some sort of insanity test in constitutional terms. . . . It is simply not yet the time to write into the Constitution formulas cast in terms whose meaning, let alone relevance, is not yet clear either to doctors or to lawyers.

Affirmed.

Mr. Justice BLACK, whom Mr. Justice HARLAN joins, concurring. . . .

Mr. Justice WHITE, concurring in the result.

. . . I cannot say that the chronic alcoholic who proves his disease and a compulsion to drink is shielded from conviction when he has knowingly failed to take feasible precautions against committing a criminal act, here the act of going to or remaining in a public place. On such facts the alcoholic is like a person with smallpox, who could be convicted for being on the street but not for being ill, or, like the epileptic, who would be punished for driving a car but not for his disease. . . .

Mr. Justice FORTAS, with whom Mr. Justice DOUGLAS, Mr. Justice BRENNAN, and Mr. Justice STEWART join, dissenting.

In the present case, appellant is charged with a crime composed of two elements—being intoxicated and being found in a public place while in that condition. The crime, so defined, differs from that in *Robinson.* The statute covers more than a mere status. But the essential constitutional defect here is the same as in *Robinson,* for in both cases the particular defendant was accused of being in a condition which he had no capacity to change or avoid. The trial judge sitting as trier of fact found, upon the medical and other relevant testimony, that Powell is a "chronic alcoholic." He defined appellant's "chronic alcoholism" as "a disease which destroys the afflicted person's will power to resist the constant, excessive consumption of alcohol." He also found that "a chronic alcoholic does not appear in public by his own volition but under a compulsion symptomatic of the disease of chronic alcoholism." I read these findings to mean that appellant was powerless to avoid drinking; that having taken his first drink, he had "an uncontrollable compulsion to drink" to the point of intoxication; and that, once intoxicated, he could not prevent himself from appearing in public places. . . .

The findings in this case . . . compel the conclusion that the infliction upon appellant of a criminal penalty for being intoxicated in a public place would be "cruel and inhuman punishment" within the prohibition of the Eighth Amendment. This conclusion follows because appellant is a "chronic alcoholic" who, according to the trier of fact, cannot resist the "constant excessive consumption of alcohol" and does not appear in public by his own volition but under a "compulsion" which is part of his condition.

I would reverse the judgment below.

PEOPLE V. RANDOLPH

Appellate Department, Superior Court of Ventura County, California, 1989.
262 Cal.Rptr. 378.

[Kerry Don Randolph was charged with violating the California Vehicle Code Section 23152, subdivision (a), driving while under the influence of alcohol, and section 23152, subdivison (b), driving with 0.10 percent or more of alcohol in his blood. He admitted a prior similar conviction. Randolph was convicted by a jury and sentenced to probation. He appealed, challenging the sufficiency of the evidence introduced against him at trial.]

OSBORNE, Judge.

...We have reviewed the detailed 31-page engrossed settled statement on appeal to determine whether it discloses substantial evidence such that any reasonable trier of fact could find appellant guilty beyond a reasonable doubt.

At the trial the witnesses were an experienced traffic officer and an experienced criminalist.

1. *Testimony of the Officer:*

The officer testified to the driving, arrest, and tests. At 11:55 P.M., the officer saw two cars southbound on Victoria Avenue on the Santa Clara River bridge. He later ascertained that appellant was driving the first car. The first car hit its brakes, causing the second to come nearly to a complete stop. Appellant then accelerated, began drifting over the double line, slowed down, and accelerated again. At the next curve, both cars slowed, and the second tried to pass appellant on the right shoulder. Appellant abruptly cut the second car off to the right. There could have been a collision. The second car then tried to pass on the left, and appellant pulled into the oncoming lane and cut off the second car again. The officer stopped both cars.

He approached the first car. Appellant ... began yelling that someone had been tailgating him. After appellant calmed down, he was cooperative. The officer smelled the odor of an alcoholic beverage on his breath, and noted appellant's eyes were bloodshot and glassy.

Appellant said he had two burritos to eat at 6 P.M., and drank from 9 to 10:15 that evening at a party. He said he felt the effects of the alcohol "a little bit."

The officer had appellant perform several field sobriety tests. Appellant's performance on some was unremarkable.

The officer asked appellant to select one leg and stand on it for 15 seconds. Defendant held his leg up one second, put his foot down, lifted it for a second, put it down, stood staring into space, lifted it for two seconds, put it down, then lifted it for about ten seconds while hopping on his foot, eventually losing his balance.

Defendant was instructed to walk heel-to-toe nine steps out and seven steps back. Appellant walked seven steps heel-to-toe, then stated, "Oh, yeah, you wanted me to walk nine." He then took three more steps which were not heel-to-toe, turned and walked back eight steps heel-to-toe.

The officer instructed appellant to write numbers backwards from 99 to 69. He transposed two numbers.

After being arrested, appellant selected a breath test which was administered to him at the Ventura County jail by the officer. The officer used a checklist as he had in administering the test 150 to 200 times before. The tests were taken at 12:31 and 12:33 A.M. the day after appellant was stopped. The results were 0.10 and 0.10 percent.

In the opinion of the officer, appellant was under the influence of alcohol.

2. *Testimony of the Criminalist:*

The criminalist testified to his education and experience, the license held by the laboratory, the operation of the Intoxilyzer, and the training of the officer to operate the Intoxilyzer.

If a subject gives an adequate deep-lung air sample, the Intoxilyzer will record an accurate blood-alcohol percent. If the subject provides an inadequate sample, the result shown on the machine will be lower than the subject's actual blood-alcohol percent. The relationship between blood-alcohol and breath-alcohol is good, that is, usually within 0.01 percent, in a healthy subject in the elimination phase.

As a person's alcohol level increases, the probability of causing an accident increases. Mental factors, including judgment and the ability to gather and process information, are affected. The ability to concentrate on a task and one's attitude toward driving change. Inhibitions are one of the first things affected. If the alcohol level gets high enough, balance and coordination are affected. One can be under the influence of alcohol for driving at 0.05 BAL. All persons are impaired and cannot drive safely at 0.10 BAL. Drunk people have more alcohol in their systems than people who are merely impaired. From 0.15 BAL and up, where the physical impairment is more obvious, you see staggering and slurred speech as opposed to just the mental factors. Given defendant's weight, he explained the relationship between blood-alcohol concentration and how much alcohol he must have drunk. Alcohol is metabolized at a "pretty predictable rate" of 0.015 percent per hour.

The manufacturer of the Intoxilyzer states the machine's accuracy is better than plus or minus 0.01 percent.

Because the statute is expressed in terms of blood-alcohol level, breath-alcohol results must be converted to equivalent blood-alcohol results. The ratio between breath alcohol and blood alcohol varies to some degree among individuals. The state requires breath testing machines, such as the Intoxilyzer, to be constructed to use a specified conversion ratio. He referred to the writings of Dr. DeBowski, an expert whose opinion is that the actual ratio for approximately 85 percent of the population is such that a breath test underestimates the actual blood-alcohol level by 0.01 percent. . . .

The jury had evidence of appellant's driving, his performance on field sobriety tests, his behavior, his breath test results, and the time elapsed from drinking and driving to the breath tests. A reasonable trier of fact could have found beyond a reasonable doubt that appellant drove a vehicle while having a blood-alcohol level of 0.10 percent or more. There was sufficient evidence to sustain the conviction. . . .

Finding no error, the judgment is affirmed.

JONES, P.J., and LANE, J., concur.

CHAPTER

10

OFFENSES AGAINST PUBLIC HEALTH
AND THE ENVIRONMENT

CHAPTER OUTLINE

Case
United States v. Sellers

INTRODUCTION

Although developed judicially, common-law crimes were revised and expanded by legislative bodies to meet the needs of our evolving society. In contrast, crimes against the public health and the environment originated directly from federal and state legislatures in response to the needs of a changing society. Many offenses relating to public health developed during the industrial revolution as a result of the widespread distribution of food, drugs, and cosmetics and the need to control communicable diseases. By the early 1900s municipalities perceived the need for zoning to control nuisances and to regulate land use. Since the middle of this century, pollution of the ground, water, and air has been recognized as a major threat to the health and welfare of the people and, indeed, to the ecological balance of the earth.

Enforcement of regulations in these fields is accomplished largely through regulatory agencies and measures imposing civil liability. Nevertheless, legislatures have found it necessary to impose criminal sanctions to effectively enforce standards and to deter violators. While not faced with the severe environmental problems of our age, the common law did regard wildlife, game, and fish as resources to be preserved. Accordingly, state and federal governments have enacted regulations and imposed criminal sanctions on poachers to protect these resources for the benefit of the public.

In contrast to the typical common-law crimes, many offenses against the public health and environment consist of an offender's neglect to comply with required standards or failure to take action required by law. These offenses are *mala prohibita*, and statutes criminalizing conduct in these areas generally contemplate a lower level of intent, frequently imposing a standard of strict liability. For example, in *State v. Budd Co.*, 425 N.E.2d 935 (Ohio App. 1980), the defendant was convicted under a state law that made it a criminal offense to dispose of garbage or other pollutants in any ditch, pond, stream, or other watercourse. On appeal, the court rejected the appellant's argument that it was necessary for the state to prove his criminal intent. The court observed that the statute did not require proof of intent, and that "the destruction of wildlife through pollution, will occur whenever the waterways are intentionally or accidentally polluted." 425 N.E.2d at 938.

PUBLIC HEALTH REGULATION

The authority of government to enact laws to protect the public health is a basic function of the "police power." Statutes delegating to public health agencies the power to declare quarantines, and later to require inoculations to control communicable diseases, were among the earliest application of this police power. At the turn of the century, the Supreme Court reviewed a defendant's sentence to pay a fine for refusing to be vaccinated for smallpox as required by a Cambridge, Massachusetts ordinance. The defendant argued that a compulsory vaccination law invaded his liberty secured by the Constitution. Rejecting this contention, the Court observed that "persons and property are subjected to all kinds of restraints and burdens in order to secure the general comfort, health, and prosperity of the state." *Jacobson v. Massachusetts*, 197 U.S. 11, 26, 25 S.Ct. 358, 361, 49 L.Ed. 643, 650 (1905).

Today numerous federal, state, and local laws address health concerns, providing criminal penalties for serious violations. Modern statutes address a variety of contemporary problems. For example, the California Health and Safety Code in Section 3198 provides that "any person infected with a venereal disease in an infectious state who knows of such condition and who marries or has sexual intercourse, is guilty of a misdemeanor." In *Reynolds v. McNichols*, 488 F.2d 1378 (10th Cir. 1973), a federal appeals court upheld a Denver, Colorado, "hold and treat" ordinance authorizing detention and treatment, if necessary, of a woman arrested for prostitution who was reasonably suspected of having a venereal disease. Indeed, many states now have statutes providing criminal penalties for health care professionals who fail to report communicable diseases. See, for example, West's Colo. Stat. Ann. §§ 25–4–402–408.

A California appellate court recently held that under a "special needs" doctrine, the state, without individualized suspicion, may require that a person convicted of prostitution be tested for acquired immune deficiency syndrome (AIDS). *Love v. Superior Court*, 276 Cal. Rptr. 660 (Cal. App. 1990). Florida has enacted laws criminalizing intentional sexual transmission of HIV without a partner's consent, and making it a felony for a person who is HIV-positive to donate blood or organs. West's Fla. Stat. Ann. §§ 381.004; 384.24. In Nevada a licensed prostitute who practices with knowledge of a positive HIV test result is guilty of a felony. Nev. Rev. Stat. § 201.358.

Most public health laws that impose criminal penalties frequently do not include any intent requirement. In those instances the government need only prove the defendant violated the statute. Offenses of this type are known as "strict-liability offenses," a concept discussed in Chapter 4.

The Federal Pure Food, Drug, and Cosmetics Act

Congress first enacted legislation to prevent the importation of adulterated drugs and medicines in 1848. Today, numerous federal acts relate to foods and drugs, but the basic Food, Drug, and Cosmetic Act dates back to 1906. It was comprehensively amended in 1938, and subsequently amended many times. 21 U.S.C.A. §§ 301–391. The present law prohibits traffic in food, drugs, and cosmetics being prepared or handled under unsanitary circumstances or under conditions that render them injurious to health. Included in its broad sweep are prohibitions against misbranding and adulteration of food, drugs, and cosmetics, as well as requirements for truthful labeling. The act provides substantial fines and imprisonment for violators. Among other prohibitions, Section 331 proscribes:

> (k) The alteration, mutilation, destruction, obliteration, or removal of the whole or any part of the labeling of, or the doing of any other act with respect to, a food, drug, device, or cosmetic, if such act is done while such article is held for sale (whether or not the first sale) after shipment in interstate commerce and results in such article being adulterated or misbranded.

Section 453 (g) states that a food shall be deemed to be adulterated:

> (3) if it consists in whole or in part of any filthy, putrid, or decomposed substance . . . or [if it is] otherwise unfit for food; [or] (4) if it has been prepared, packed, or held under insanitary conditions whereby it may have become contaminated with filth, or whereby it may have been rendered injurious to health. . . .

Like most public health laws, food and drug laws fall in the category of regulatory offenses. Therefore, unless the statute criminalizing conduct or failure to act requires an intent element, criminal liability can attach without proof of the defendant's intent. *United States v. Park*, 421 U.S. 658, 670, 95 S.Ct. 1903, 1910, 44 L.Ed.2d 489, 500 (1975).

Criminal Liability of "Responsible Corporate Officers"

Food, drugs, and cosmetics are usually produced and distributed by corporate enterprises. To effectively enforce regulatory laws imposing criminal sanctions in these areas, government agencies must be able to affix responsibility on individuals in supervisory positions as well as on corporate entities. The Supreme Court first recognized the concept of a "responsible corporate officer" in *United States v. Dotterweich*, 320 U.S. 277, 64 S.Ct. 134, 88 L.Ed. 48 (1943), but prior to 1975 there were conflicting federal court decisions on whether a corporate officer who failed to take measures to prevent violations of the food and drug laws from occurring could be held criminally liable. Noting a conflict in decisions among the courts of appeal, the Supreme Court addressed the standard of liability of corporate officers under the Pure Food, Drug, and Cosmetic Act in *United States v. Park, supra*. There, a national retail food chain and its president and chief executive officer were charged with causing food shipped in interstate commerce to be held in a building accessible to rodents and exposed to contamination. The food chain pled guilty, but its president contested the charges against him. He contended that while he retained authority over corporate affairs, he delegated "normal operating duties," including sanitation, to lower-level personnel. In rejecting his contention as a basis of nonliability, the Court held that the prosecution establishes a *prima facie* case of the guilt of the accused when it establishes that "the defendant had, by reason of his position in the corporation, responsibility and authority either to prevent in the first instance or promptly to correct, the violation complained of, and that he failed to do so." 421 U.S. at 673, 95 S.Ct. at 1912, 44 L.Ed.2d at 502.

Criticism of "Strict Liability" Public Health Laws

Many legal scholars condemn the imposition of strict liability in regulatory offenses, such as food, drug, and health laws. They contend that it brands as criminals people who are without moral fault. Arguing against making violation of such laws punishable by incarceration, critics suggest decriminalization, liability predicated on a negligence standard rather than on strict liability, or punishment by only a monetary fine. These criticisms notwithstanding, Congress has determined that the interest of society requires a high standard of care and has been unwilling to eliminate either the strict-liability standard or incarceration. As previously noted, the courts hold that a corporate agent who bears a responsible relationship to the operation of the enterprise, and has power to take measures necessary to ensure compliance, can be found guilty of violating such regulatory statutes.

CASE IN POINT

RESPONSIBILITY FOLLOWS AUTHORITY

Dean Starr, secretary-treasurer of Cheney Brothers Food Corporation, was convicted of violating the Federal Food, Drug, and Cosmetic Act, 21 U.S.C.A. §§ 301–391, for allowing contamination of food stored in a company warehouse over which he had operational responsibility. After an inspector from the Food and Drug Administration (FDA) pointed out the problem, the janitor for the warehouse was instructed to make corrections, but no action was taken. A month later, a second inspection by the FDA disclosed that the problem had not been corrected.

On appeal, Starr contended that he was not responsible because the janitor in charge had failed to comply with instructions to clean up the warehouse. The court rejected his argument, noting that Mr. Starr was aware of the problem after the first inspection and had ample time to remedy the situation. In affirming his conviction, the court also observed that supervisory officers have a duty to anticipate the shortcomings of their delegees.

United States v. Starr, 535 F.2d 512 (9th Cir. 1976).

PLANNING AND ZONING ACTIVITIES

Although sometimes used interchangeably, the terms, *zoning* and *planning* are not synonymous. Zoning is concerned primarily with the use and regulation of buildings and structures, whereas planning is a broader term embracing the systematic and orderly development of a community. *State ex rel. Kearns v. Ohio Power Co.,* 127 N.E.2d 394, 399 (Ohio 1955). In *Village of Euclid, Ohio v. Ambler Realty Co.,* 272 U.S. 365, 47 S.Ct. 114, 71 L.Ed. 303 (1926), the Supreme Court first upheld the concept of comprehensive zoning, which allows local governments to divide areas of the community and to designate the permitted and prohibited land uses in the respective districts. Since then zoning has become both widespread and sophisticated. Building codes are generally encompassed within the overall local zoning requirements. Today, comprehensive planning guides the development of a community, and that planning is implemented to a large degree by local zoning ordinances (their enactment usually preceded by studies and recommendations of professional consultants). Additionally, local citizens are enlisted to sit on planning and zoning boards that make recommendations to the governing body. Any comprehensive zoning ordinance must provide for a board of adjustment to act in a quasi-judicial capacity. The board must have the power to grant variances where strict enforcement of an ordinance would cause an undue hardship to property owners. It may also be empowered to approve special exceptions based on the landowner's compliance with specified criteria.

As with other regulatory measures, enforcement of local zoning codes is accomplished administratively in most instances. Failing this, local governments resort to civil court actions, commonly seeking injunctive relief against violators. Most zoning ordinances classify violations as misdemeanors and provide for a fine and a jail term upon conviction. Zoning ordinances, like most health regulations, generally do not include an intent requirement. Prosecution of violators is usually undertaken only as a last resort. But once a state or local government commences prosecution of a defendant for violation of a zoning ordinance, it must meet all burdens placed on the prosecution in criminal proceedings. *People v. St. Agatha Home for Children*, 389 N.E.2d 1098 (N.Y. 1979).

THE SCOPE OF FEDERAL AND STATE ENVIRONMENTAL LAWS

Numerous federal statutes and agencies play a part in regulation and enforcement of the laws affecting our environment. Among the older agencies are the Army Corps of Engineers, the Coast Guard, and the Departments of the Interior, Commerce, Transportation, and Justice. A newer agency, the Environmental Protection Agency (EPA), acts under authority of some twenty-nine major congressional enactments and has significant responsibilities in numerous areas including hazardous wastes, toxic substances, and noise pollution. State environmental agencies became active in the 1970s, and planning and coordinating councils now function at state, regional, and local levels. They play an important part in environmental regulation through establishment of pollution controls, water management programs, waste water, and solid-waste disposal programs.

Environmental regulation at the federal and state levels has become a vast undertaking, but until recently government agencies have relied almost exclusively on civil penalties as an enforcement tool. The concept changed in the 1980s, when criminal enforcement of environmental laws became prominent, particularly in instances of egregious violations involving hazardous waste disposal, water pollution, and air pollution. These enforcement policies were in effect long before the *Exxon Valdez* supertanker spilled millions of gallons of crude oil in Alaskan waters in 1989, destroying wildlife and despoiling beaches.

Some environmental crimes only require proof that the defendant committed a proscribed act or failed to comply with a required standard. In prosecutions of these strict-liability offenses, the government may establish the defendant's guilt in a manner similar to prosecuting many crimes against the public health. Other statutes require the government to establish the defendant's "negligent" conduct or a "willful" or "knowing" violation, and many court decisions in environmental prosecutions turn on whether the evidence is sufficient to meet the required statutory standard.

Major Federal Environmental Legislation Providing Criminal Sanctions

Congress enacted its first major environmental law, the Rivers and Harbors Act, in 1899. 33 U.S.C.A. §§ 401–467. This act makes it a misdemeanor to discharge

---

C A S E I N P O I N T

THE *EXXON VALDEZ* PROSECUTION

In March 1989, the supertanker *Exxon Valdez* ran aground and ruptured, spilling more than 240,000 barrels of oil into Alaska's Prince William Sound and wreaking havoc on the natural environment. Subsequently, the federal government brought criminal charges against the Exxon Shipping Co. and its parent, Exxon Corporation, under the Clean Water Act and several other federal environmental statutes. In October 1991, one week before the case was scheduled to go to trial, Exxon accepted a plea bargain under which it agreed to pay $25 million in federal fines and another $100 million in restitution, split between the federal and state governments. The $125 million fine was the largest environmental criminal fine in U.S. history.

Source: Stephen Raucher, "Raising the Stakes for Environmental Polluters: The Exxon Valdez Criminal Prosecution." *Ecology Law Quarterly* 147 (1993).

---

refuse into the navigable waters of the United States. Notwithstanding the act's provisions for criminal enforcement, the federal government traditionally sought enforcement through the civil courts. In recent years, the following acts of Congress have provided significant means to enforce criminal violations of environmental laws and regulations:

- *Clean Air Amendments of 1970*, 42 U.S.C.A. §§ 7401–7642
- *Federal Water Pollution Control Act of 1972* (Clean Water Act), 33 U.S.C.A. §§ 1251–1387
- *Resource Conservation and Recovery Act of 1976* (RCRA), 42 U.S.C.A. §§ 6901–6992
- *Toxic Substances Control Act of 1976* (TSCA), 15 U.S.C.A. §§ 2601–2671
- *Comprehensive Environmental Response, Compensation and Liability Act of 1980* (CERCLA), 42 U.S.C.A. §§ 9601–9675

The Clean Air Act (CLA)

The Clean Air Act sets federal standards designed to enhance the quality of the air by deterring air polluters. In 1977, Congress passed a series of amendments establishing stricter standards for air quality. As amended, the act provides criminal sanctions for violation of any provisions for which civil penalties apply, and for any person who knowingly makes any false representation in a document filed under the act. Enforcement may be delegated to the states pursuant to the State Implementation Plan (SIP), 42 U.S.C.A. § 7410, but the states are not required to enact minimum criminal provisions to receive EPA approval of their implementation plans. Indeed, while some states track the substantial federal penalties in their own statutes, most provide for lesser penalties and some do not include imprisonment as a sanction. For example, in Oklahoma a violation of its Clean Air Act provides for a fine of $500, imprisonment for a year, or both 63 Okl.

Stats. Ann. § 1–1802(L), whereas a first offender who violates the air pollution laws in Maryland is subject to a fine of $25,000 to $50,000 per day of violation. Code of Md. § 2–609.1(b)(2)(i).

Two reasons have been advanced for the relatively few criminal prosecutions in respect to air pollution as compared to prosecutions for violations of hazardous waste and water pollution laws. First, the cost of criminal enforcement in this area apparently is great, and second, the problems of enforcement are made exceedingly difficult for states because pollution of the air is a less stationary category of pollution.

The Federal Water Pollution Control Act of 1972 (Clean Water Act)

The Federal Water Pollution Control Act of 1972 (Clean Water Act), 33 U.S.C.A. §§ 1251–1270, is designed to control water pollution and regulate industrial and other discharges into navigable waters. Although the Clean Water Act is enforced primarily through civil means, criminal sanctions have been imposed for "willful" or "negligent" violations of certain provisions concerning permits and the making of false statements. Amendments in 1987 eliminated the "willful" requirement and imposed more stringent penalties for negligent violations and even more severe penalties for knowing violations of the act's criminal provisions. 33 U.S.C.A. § 1319(c).

A majority of the states have programs approved by the EPA. While states vary somewhat in their approaches, many provide penalties similar to those in the federal act for either willful or negligent violations of water pollution provisions.

Courts tend to construe the penal provisions of the Clean Water Act broadly, and generally hold supervisory personnel vested with authority to a high standard of compliance. The trend in the federal courts seems to be to hold responsible corporate officers criminally liable in environmental offenses despite their lack of "consciousness of wrongdoing." See, for example, *United States v. Brittain*, 931 F.2d 1413, 1419 (10th Cir. 1991).

The Resource Conservation and Recovery Act (RCRA)

Enactment of RCRA in 1976 was a significant step in environmental control. Its objective is to encourage the states—through grants, technical assistance, and advice—to establish standards and provide for civil and criminal enforcement of state regulations. The EPA sets minimum standards requiring the states to enact criminal penalties against any person who knowingly stores or transports any hazardous waste to an unpermitted facility, or who treats such waste without a permit or makes false representations to secure a permit. All states have enacted criminal statutes pursuant to the criteria specified in RCRA.

RCRA proscribes a comprehensive list of illegal actions and imposes criminal penalties on any person who:

1. knowingly transports or causes to be transported any hazardous waste to an unpermitted facility, 42 U.S.C.A. § 6928(d)(1);

CASE IN POINT

CRIMINAL PROSECUTION UNDER THE CLEAN WATER ACT

David W. Boldt was Chemical Engineering Manager for Astro Circuit Corporation, a Massachusetts company that manufactured circuit boards using an electroplating process. Boldt's duties included supervising the company's pretreatment process, a part of the pollution control system. He was charged with six counts of violating the Clean Water Act. He was convicted on two counts: one for knowingly aiding and abetting the discharge of pollutants into a municipal sewer in 1987, when the copper level in Astro's effluent greatly exceeded the federal standards; another for ordering a subordinate in 1988 to dump 3,100 gallons of partially treated industrial waste water containing excessive metals into the municipal sewer. At trial Boldt asserted the defense of impossibility to the first incident, arguing he was only a mid-level manager who was not responsible for the discharge. Boldt acknowledged responsibility for the second discharge, but pleaded the defense of necessity, arguing it was necessary to authorize the discharge to avoid a worse harm.

In upholding both convictions, the appellate court observed that the evidence showed that pollution control was part of Boldt's area of responsibility and that, as to the 1987 violation, he was aware of the practice of bypassing the pollution control system and had condoned it on the occasion at issue. As to the 1988 incident, the court found the evidence undisputed that Boldt directly ordered his subordinate to dump the copper waste water, a conclusion bolstered by his subordinate's testimony that Boldt attempted to cover up the incident. Finally, the appellate court observed that the record of the trial disclosed that the president of Astro testified that Boldt was authorized to shut down the plant.

United States v. Boldt, 929 F.2d 35 (1st Cir. 1991).

---

2. knowingly treats, stores, or disposes of any hazardous waste without a permit, in knowing violation of any material condition or requirement of the interim status regulations, 42 U.S.C.A. § 6928(d)(2)(A)-(C); or one who
3. knowingly omits material information or makes any false statement or representation in any record or document required to be maintained under the regulations or submitted to the [EPA] or any state which is authorized to run RCRA programs, 42 U.S.C.A. § 6928(d)(3).

In addition, Section 6928(e) makes it a criminal offense to knowingly place another person in imminent danger of death or serious bodily injury in conjunction with the transportation, storage, or disposal of hazardous wastes.

RCRA has become an important tool for enforcement and one prosecutors frequently rely on in prosecuting persons who illegally dispose of hazardous wastes. In *United States v. Johnson & Towers, Inc.*, 741 F.2d 662, 664 (3d Cir. 1984), the court held that the term *person* in RCRA Section 6928(d) includes employees as well as owners and operators, and that proof of the knowledge element required may be inferred as to those individuals holding responsible corporate positions.

In prosecutions under RCRA, did Congress intend that it would be necessary for the government to prove that a defendant knew the waste material being stored or transported was listed as a hazardous waste? In *United States v. Hayes International Corp.*, 786 F.2d 1499, 1503 (11th Cir. 1986), the court affirmed a conviction under Section 6928(d)(1) for unlawfully transporting hazardous waste materials to a nonpermitted facility and ruled that neither a lack of knowledge that paint waste was a hazardous material, nor ignorance of the permit requirement, was a defense. Conviction for the treatment, storage, or disposal of hazardous waste without an RCRA permit has been more problematic. In *United States v. Hoflin*, 880 F.2d 1033, 1038 (9th Cir. 1989), the court held that the government is not required to prove the defendant's knowledge of the lack of a permit in order to secure a conviction in either transport or storage cases, but nevertheless a person who does not know that the waste materials he or she is disposing of is hazardous cannot be guilty of violating Section 6928(d)(2)(a).

One of the most serious cases brought under the RCRA involved Section 6928(e), which makes it a criminal violation to knowingly place employees "in imminent danger of death or serious bodily injury." *United States v. Protex Industries, Inc.*, 874 F.2d 740, 742 (10th Cir. 1989), involved a company that operated a drum recycling facility and in connection with its business purchased drums that previously contained toxic chemicals. The evidence revealed that the company's safety provisions were inadequate to protect its employees and that, as a result, certain company employees suffered from solvent poisoning and exhibited serious maladies. The court upheld a conviction of Protex for placing employees in an industrial environment without sufficient protection against exposure to toxic chemicals.

The Toxic Substances Control Act (TSCA)

The Toxic Substances Control Act of 1976 authorizes the EPA to require testing and to prohibit the manufacture, distribution, or use of certain chemical substances that present an unreasonable risk of injury to health or the environment, and to regulate their disposal. Although the act depends primarily on civil penalties, a person who "knowingly" or "willfully" fails to maintain records or submit reports as required violates the criminal provisions of the act. 15 U.S.C.A. §§ 2614; 2615(b). In 1982, the court upheld the conviction of Robert Earl Ward, Jr., the chairman of the board of Ward Transformer Company, on eight counts of the unlawful disposal of toxic substances (PCB-containing oils from used transformers) and willfully aiding and abetting the unlawful disposal of toxic substances. The evidence at trial revealed that while the defendant himself did not dispose of the toxic substances, the company's employees performed the task while he was kept advised of the progress. *United States v. Ward*, 676 F. 2d 94 (4th Cir. 1982).

The Comprehensive Environmental Response, Compensation, and Liability Act (CERCLA)

In 1980 Congress enacted the Comprehensive Environmental Response, Compensation, and Liability Act (CERCLA), commonly known as the Superfund

Law. Its purpose is to finance cleanup and provide for civil suits by citizens. As revised in 1986, the act requires notice to federal and state agencies of any "release" of a "reportable quantity" of a listed hazardous substance. *Release* is broadly defined, and *reportable quantity* is related to each of the several hundred "hazardous substances." CERCLA also provides for EPA to promulgate regulations for the collection and disposal of solid wastes. The act imposes criminal sanctions against those who fail to report as required, or who destroy or falsify records. 42 U.S.C.A. § 9603(d)(2).

Standard of Liability of Corporate Officers

As previously noted, many of the violations in the public health area are caused by corporate entities; therefore, courts often focus on whether an accused by reason of his or her position in the corporate enterprise had sufficient responsibility and authority to either prevent or correct the violation charged. The same legal doctrine of law is being applied by the courts in respect to environmental crimes. In fact, Congress has adopted the "responsible corporate officer" doctrine in the Clean Air Act, 42 U.S.C.A. § 7413(c)(3) and the Clean Water Act, 33 U.S.C.A. § 1319(c)(3)(6). And the doctrine has been upheld in CERCLA cases by federal appeals courts. For example, in *United States v. Carr*, 880 F.2d 1550 (2d Cir. 1989), the court rejected a maintenance supervisor's argument that he could not be guilty because he was a relatively low-level employee. The court explained that CERCLA imposes criminal responsibility on a person "even of relatively low rank" who acts in a supervisory capacity and is "in a position to detect, prevent, and abate a release of hazardous substances." 880 F.2d at 1554. Thus, it is becoming clear that a responsible corporate officer not only cannot avoid criminal liability by delegating tasks to others but also must remedy any violations that occur. At the state level, corporate executives have been charged with criminally negligent homicide and manslaughter where employees' deaths have resulted from the improper use of hazardous substances. See, for example, *People v. Hegedus*, 443 N.W.2d 127 (Mich. 1989); *State ex rel. Cornellier v. Black*, 425 N.W.2d 21 (Wis. App. 1988).

Environmental Laws Lack Uniformity

Disparate environmental standards, enforcement policies, and sanctions in the areas of water and air pollution and disposal of hazardous wastes can lead to "shopping" by industry to secure locations that will enable them to be more competitive by not having to comply with stringent environmental standards. Significant differences exist among the fifty states in the standards of proof required and in the sanctions imposed for criminal violations of hazardous waste, water pollution, and air pollution laws.

Compare the differences between the statutory language in the Kentucky and Vermont offenses set out in Table 10.1. What level of proof should be required for establishing a defendant's guilt under the "knowingly" standard of the Kentucky laws? Would a different standard of proof be required under Vermont's laws concerning hazardous wastes and air pollution?

TABLE 10.1 KENTUCKY AND VERMONT ENVIRONMENTAL LAWS IMPOSING CRIMINAL PENALTIES CONCERNING HAZARDOUS WASTES, WATER POLLUTION, AND AIR POLLUTION

Kentucky Revised Statutes Annotated

HAZARDOUS WASTES

Unlawful acts: Knowingly engaging in the generation, treatment, storage, transportation, or disposal of hazardous wastes in violation of this chapter, or contrary to a permit, order, or administrative regulation issued or promulgated under the chapter; or knowingly making a false statement, representation, or certification in an application for, or form pertaining to, a permit, or in a notice or report required by the terms and conditions of an issued permit. Ky. Rev. Stat. Ann. § 224.99–010(6).

Penalties: Felony; imprisonment between one and five years or a fine up to $25,000 per day of violation, or both. § 224.99–010(6).

WATER POLLUTION

Unlawful acts: Knowingly, or with criminal negligence, violating any of the following:
§ 224.70–110 (water pollution)
§ 224.73–120 (monitoring and reporting)
§ 244.40–100 (waste disposal)
§ 244.50–545 (oil pollution)
§ 224.40–305 (unpermitted waste disposal facilities)
Any determination, permit, administrative regulation, or order of the Cabinet promulgated pursuant to those sections which have become final; or knowingly providing false information in any document filed or required to be maintained under this chapter; or knowingly rendering inaccurate any monitoring device or method required to be maintained. § 294.99–010(4).

Penalties: Misdemeanor; imprisonment up to one year or a fine between $1,000 and $15,000 per day of violation, or both. § 294.99–010(4).

AIR POLLUTION

Unlawful acts: Knowingly, or with criminal negligence, violating § 224 (monitoring and reporting) or 244.330 (air pollution), or any determination, permit, administrative regulation, or order of the Cabinet promulgated pursuant to those sections which have become final; or knowingly providing false information in any document filed or required to be maintained under this chapter, or knowingly rendering inaccurate any monitoring device or method required to be maintained. § 294.99–010(4).

Penalties: Misdemeanor; imprisonment up to one year or a fine between $1,000 and $15,000 per day of violation, or both. § 294.99–010(4).

Vermont Statutes Annotated

HAZARDOUS WASTES

Unlawful acts: Violating any provision of the waste management chapter (transportation, storage, disposal, or treatment of hazardous waste: permit and manifest requirements), rules promulgated therein, or terms or conditions of any order of certification. Vt. Stat. Ann., Title 10, § 6612(a) (1991).
Penalties: Imprisonment up to six months or a fine up to $25,000 per day of violation, or both. Title 10, § 6612(a).

WATER POLLUTION

Unlawful acts: Violating any provision of the water pollution control subchapter, or failing, neglecting, or refusing to obey or comply with any order or the terms of any permit issued under this subchapter. Title 10, § 1275(a).
Penalties: Imprisonment up to six months or a fine up to $25,000 per day of violation, or both. Title 10, § 1275(a).
Unlawful acts: Knowingly making any false statement, representation, or certification in any document filed or required to be maintained under the water pollution control subchapter, or by any permit, rule, regulation, or order issued thereunder; or falsifying, tampering with, or knowingly rendering inaccurate any monitoring device or method required to be maintained under this subchapter, or by any permit, rule, regulation, or order issued thereunder. Title 10, §1275(b).
Penalties: Imprisonment up to six months or a fine up to $10,000 or both. § 1275(b).

AIR POLLUTION

Unlawful acts: Violating a provision of the air pollution control chapter (discharge of air contaminants without a permit or in violation of pollution standards) except § 563 and § 567 (relating to motor vehicles and confidential records), or any rule issued thereunder. Title 10, § 568. *Penalties:* Fine up to $2,000 per violation. Title 10, § 568.

Unfortunately, fines imposed on violators of environmental laws are too often looked upon as "costs of doing business," because in reality these costs may be passed on to the ultimate consumer. The threat of imprisonment, on the other hand, is one cost that cannot be passed on to a consumer, and it is therefore a powerful deterrent to those who would pollute the environment. As states become more aggressive in the prosecution of environmental crimes, more uniformity of criminal sanctions will undoubtedly develop, much as it has in the more common criminal offenses.

Noise Pollution

Congress enacted the Quiet Communities Act of 1978, 42 U.S.C.A. §§ 4901–4918, to protect the environment against noise pollution, which has come to be perceived as a growing danger to health and welfare of the population. Sections 4909 and 4910 provide criminal penalties for those who "knowingly" or "wilfully" import, manufacture, or distribute products that fail to comply with noise standards specified in the statute. The act recognizes, however, that the primary responsibility for protecting communities against noise pollution lies with state and local governments.

Historically, local governments have adopted ordinances that prohibit excessive noise. In the twentieth century, ordinances have reflected concern over amplified sound equipment. The Ithaca, New York, law is fairly typical:

> No person shall play, operate or use, or cause to be played operated or used, any mechanical instrument, radio or wireless, speaker or horn, or any other instrument, device or thing in the city so as to disturb the peace and quiet of any neighborhood. The Code of Ordinances of the City of Ithaca, N.Y., Art. 16, § 16–12, subdivision (b).

Ordinances of this type may be applied to prohibit the use of loud stereo equipment in an apartment building where residents live in close quarters, or to disband loud late-night parties that are disturbing neighbors. Such an ordinance might be enforced against a person whose car stereo is played so loudly as to be an annoyance or even a safety hazard.

Antismoking Legislation

As society has become more aware of the ill effects of smoking and, in particular, the hazards of "second-hand smoke," governments have moved to restrict smoking in public buildings and places of public accommodation and transportation. Perhaps the best known example is the Federal Aviation Administration regulation prohibiting smoking altogether on domestic passenger airline flights. Most antismoking regulations carry minor civil penalties analogous to parking tickets. However, some jurisdictions have experimented with criminal sanctions. For example, a Minnesota statute provides that "[n]o person shall smoke in a public place or at a public meeting except in designated smoking areas." Minn. S.A. § 144.414. Section 144.417 provides that "[a]ny person who violates section 144.414 is guilty of a petty misdemeanor." As people become more aware of the dangers of "passive smoking," the use of criminal sanctions against smokers is apt to increase.

FISH AND GAME LAWS

Since the early common law, fish and game have been viewed as animals *ferae naturae*, meaning that the state as sovereign owns them in trust for the people. *Bayside Fish Flour Co. v. Gentry*, 297 U.S. 422, 56 S.Ct. 513, 80 L. Ed. 772 (1936). As trustee, the state has the duty to preserve and protect wildlife by regulating fishing in public and private streams and controlling the taking of game. *Shively v. Bowlby*, 152 U.S. 1, 14 S.Ct. 548, 38 L.Ed. 331 (1894). Owners of private property retain a qualified interest, so those seeking to take fish or game from the confines of their property must secure their permission.

While it is generally within the jurisdiction of the states to regulate wildlife, fish, and game, it is settled law that the federal government has jurisdiction to enact statutes to carry out treaties in regard to migratory birds. The jealous regard that the states have over wildlife within their borders led Missouri to challenge the constitutionality of the Migratory Bird Conservation Act, a statute passed by Congress to enforce the provisions of the Migratory Bird Treaty entered into by the United States in 1916. Missouri claimed the federal statute infringed rights reserved to the states by the Tenth Amendment to the United States Constitution. The Supreme Court rejected that challenge, thereby settling the issue of federal control. The Court held that Article II, Section 2 of the Constitution grants the president the power to make treaties, and Article I, Section 8 gives Congress the power to enact legislation to enforce those treaties. *Missouri v. Holland*, 252 U.S. 416, 40 S.Ct. 382, 64 L.Ed. 641 (1920). Of course, the federal government retains jurisdiction to protect all wildlife, game, and fish within national game preserves. *Hunt v. United States*, 278 U.S. 96, 49 S.Ct. 38, 73 L. Ed. 200 (1928). Enforcement of the Migratory Bird Act (MBA), 16 U.S.C.A. §§ 703–712, remains a viable part of the federal environmental enforcement program. Following conflicting court decisions on whether the penal provisions of MBA imposed *strict liability* for both misdemeanor and felony violations, Congress inserted the word *knowingly* into the section of the Act providing criminal sanctions, thus requiring the prosecution to prove the defendant's *mens rea* as well as *actus reus* to establish a violation (see Chapter 4).

Modern efforts of the federal government to preserve the environment through protection of wildlife is illustrated by the Federal Endangered Species Act of 1973, 16 U.S.C.A. §§ 1531–1544. This act is designed to conserve ecosystems by preserving wildlife, fish and plants. And while enforcement is largely through civil penalties, criminal liability is imposed against any person who *knowingly* violates regulations issued under the act. 16 U.S.C.A. § 1540(b). In *United States v. Billie*, 667 F.Supp. 1485 (S.D. Fla. 1987), the defendant was charged with killing a Florida panther, an endangered species. He argued that the prosecution had to prove his specific intent; that is, that he knew the animal he shot was a Florida panther, as opposed to a species of panther not on the list of "endangered species." The U.S. District Court rejected his argument and held that the government "need prove only that the defendant acted with general intent when he shot the animal in question." 667 F.Supp. at 1493. The court discussed the fact that the defendant was charged with violating a regulatory statute enacted to conserve and protect endangered species, and that its purposes would be eviscerated if the government had to prove that a hunter who killed an animal recognized the particular subspecies as being protected under the act. 667 F.Supp. at 1492–93.

Legislatures may make it a strict-liability offense to take or possess fish and game in violation of regulations, *Cummings v. Commonwealth*, 255 S.W. 2d 997 (Ky. 1953). Most states have done so, usually imposing strict liability for taking quantities of game or fish in excess of permitted allowances and for hunting and fishing during closed seasons. But it can be quite difficult to determine whether a given law that imposes a criminal penalty for violating a fishing or game regulation is a strict-liability statute. If a wildlife penal statute includes words incorporating a *mens rea* requirement, it is clear that the prosecution must prove the defendant's intent as well as the *actus reus*. While it is difficult to generalize, if a wildlife penal law does not explicitly require intent by including such words as *willfully* or *knowingly*, only proof of the *actus reus* of the offense is required. The courts have tended to make an exception to this general rule where the offense is of a more serious criminal character (e.g., smuggling and chemical trafficking), or where the offense is designated as a felony or carries a severe punishment.

In *State v. Rice*, 626 P.2d 104 (Alaska 1981), the court considered a game regulation that lacked any requirement for criminal intent. As noted, this type of regulation is generally treated much like a traffic law. The Alaska Supreme Court took a different approach, saying that "strict liability is an exception to the rule which requires criminal intent" and criminal statutes will be "strictly construed to require some degree of *mens rea* absent a clear legislative intent to the contrary." 626 P.2d at 108.

Statutes also commonly make it a strict-liability offense to use improper types of fishing nets, to hunt with artificial lights, and to shoot over baited fields. In addition, they provide for forfeiture of illegal equipment used to hunt or fish in violation of laws. See, for example, *State v. Billiot*, 229 So.2d 72 (La. 1969), where the Louisiana Supreme Court upheld the forfeiture of seines and other devices used in trawling for shrimp during a closed season.

Irrespective of whether a penal statute imposes strict liability or proof of intent, the prosecution is not required to establish that a person accused of fishing in a closed season actually caught fish, *State v. Parker*, 167 A. 854, 855 (Me. 1933), nor is it a defense that a hunter has failed to kill any game. *Key v. State*, 384 S.W.2d 22 (Tenn. 1964).

CONCLUSION

Imposing strict criminal liability on responsible corporate officers has proven to be successful in deterring violations of laws protecting the purity and safety of food and drugs. Moreover, the concept of strict liability is firm in respect to traditional public health statutes. Strict liability is also applied to transgressors of wildlife regulations, although—whenever a violation rises to the level of a felony—courts are inclined to require proof of the defendant's intent before upholding a conviction that visits serious consequences on the offender.

Until recently governmental agencies relied almost exclusively on civil penalties to punish violators of environmental laws, but the regulatory climate is changing. During the 1990s, we will continue to witness an increased reliance by federal and state authorities on criminal sanctions, often with greatly increased penalties. As this trend continues, legislatures (or, in their absence, courts of law) will most likely include a *mens rea* requirement in regulatory statutes that subject violators to severe punishment.

Noise pollution and smoking in public places are being increasingly viewed by society as detrimental. It is reasonable to expect that criminal sanctions—which, after all, mirror societal norms—will be increasingly applied to these problems.

QUESTIONS FOR THOUGHT AND DISCUSSION

1. Are criminal sanctions essential to the effective enforcement of food, drug, and cosmetic laws?

2. Should the term *responsible corporate officer* be explicitly defined by statute, or should courts make this determination on a case-by-case basis?

3. Does your community impose criminal penalties for violations of zoning regulations? If so, are violations treated as strict-liability offenses?

4. Should efforts be made to formulate a model state code of environmental regulations?

5. Should smoking be prohibited in all public places? If so, should violations be treated as civil or criminal infractions?

6. Do you think hunting and fishing violations should be decriminalized and treated as civil infractions in the way that many states treat traffic offenses?

7. Should environmental crimes that carry major penalties be strict-liability offenses, or should prosecutors be required to prove that a defendant "knowingly" or "willfully" committed an offense?

CASE

United States v. Sellers
United States Court of Appeals, Fifth Circuit, 1991.
926 F.2d 410.

[In this case, the U.S. Court of Appeals for the Fifth Circuit reviews a criminal conviction under the Resource Conservation and Recovery Act. The appellant, James Ralph Sellers, was convicted of sixteen counts of knowingly and willfully disposing of a hazardous waste without obtaining a permit, as required by RCRA.]

KING, Circuit Judge:

On March 5, 1989, residents in rural Jones County, Mississippi discovered sixteen 55-gallon drums of hazardous paint waste on an embankment of the Camp Branch Creek, which flows into the Leaf River. These drums were later determined to contain paint waste and methylethylketone (M.E.K.), a paint solvent, and one of the drums was found to be leaking. Sellers was indicted on October 16, 1989 on sixteen counts of violating 42 U.S.C. § 6928(d)(2)(A) for disposing of sixteen drums of hazardous waste without a permit on or about March 4 or 5, 1989. Sellers was tried January 8 through 11, 1990 in front of a jury. On the issue of guilt or innocence, the jury heard testimony from 14 government witnesses and two defense witnesses. The government witnesses testified about the discovery of the drums, the circumstances surrounding the waste's origin in Port Violet, Louisiana, and the fact that Sellers had been paid $45 per drum to dispose of the waste. In addition, the government called James William Ward (Ward), who testified that he had assisted Sellers in loading the 55-gallon drums in Louisiana and transporting them to Jones County, Mississippi where Ward and Sellers unloaded them. Ward testified that Sellers did not tell him what was in the drums, but did tell Ward that it was flammable. Subsequently, Ward voluntarily came forward and told the police about his involvement in dumping the drums. Testimony by other witnesses established that Sellers did not have a permit as required for disposing of hazardous waste, nor did he take the waste to a licensed disposal area. The govern-

ment's last witness in its case in chief, Douglas E. Bourgeois (Bourgeois), was allowed to testify over Seller's objection. Bourgeois testified that he had a conversation with Sellers in late April or sometime in May in which Sellers stated that he had been hauling waste chemicals and discarding them in a rural area outside Petal, Mississippi. During the conversation, Sellers referred to M.E.K, which he knew was a solvent used primarily to clean paint equipment.

The crux of Sellers's defense was that he denied dumping the paint waste in question. He testified that it was Ward alone who had dumped the drums into Camp Branch Creek, although he admitted that his family owned property in Jones County near the site of the dumping.

After deliberation, the jury found Sellers guilty of all sixteen counts of the indictment. On March 14, 1990, Sellers was sentenced to 41 months imprisonment on each count, with the sentences to run concurrently. In addition, Sellers was sentenced to three years of supervised release and was ordered to make restitution to the State of Mississippi of $6,130.70, the amount required to clean up the hazardous waste site. Sellers also received a special assessment of $800. Sellers filed a timely notice of appeal.

II

On appeal, Sellers contends that the district court erred 1) by admitting testimony that he contends is inadmissible under Fed.R.Evid. 403 and 404(b), [and] 2) by failing to give the jury a requested charge regarding the knowledge required to violate § 6928. . . .

A. Admission of Testimony

Sellers first contends that the district court erred by admitting the testimony of Bourgeois. Sellers claims that Bourgeois testified that sometime in late April or May, 1989 Sellers stated that he was, at that time, hauling chemicals and dumping them outside of Petal, Mississippi. Sellers argues that this evidence was inadmissible under Fed.R.Evid. 403 and 404(b).

. . .[T]his testimony is admissible either as an admission, or for the permissible purpose of establishing the extent of Sellers's knowledge of his acts. Thus, Sellers's argument is without merit.

B. Jury Charge

Sellers next contends that the district court erred in refusing to give a jury instruction requested by Sellers. . . .

The district court gave the following instructions:

In order to establish the offenses charged in the indictment, the Government must prove each one of the following elements by proof beyond a reasonable doubt.

First. That the Defendant knowingly disposed of, or commanded and caused others to dispose of, wastes as charged in the indictment.

Second. That the Defendant knew what the wastes were.

Third. That the wastes were listed or identified or characterized by the United States Environmental Protection Agency, known as E.P.A., as a hazardous waste pursuant to the Resource Conservation and Recovery Act.

And Fourth. That the Defendant had not obtained a permit from either the E.P.A. or the State of Mississippi authorizing the disposal under the Resource Conservation and Recovery Act.

Although the Government must prove that the waste disposed of was listed or identified or characterized by the E.P.A. as a hazardous waste, the Government is not required to prove that the Defendant knew that the waste was a hazardous waste within the meaning of the regulations. In other words, the Government need only prove that the Defendant knew what the waste was; that is, paint and paint solvent waste, along with the other essential elements the Court has previously given you.

However, the Government is not required to establish that the waste in question actually entered the environment, was emitted into the air,

or discharged into water. It is sufficient for the Government to prove that the hazardous waste was placed into or on the land in such a manner that it could enter the environment, the air, or water, including ground water.

The term hazardous waste, as used in the R.C.R.A. statute, includes any refuse and other discarded or abandoned material, including solid, liquid or semi-solid material resulting from industrial or commercial operations and community activities, which because of its quantity, concentration, or physical chemical or infectious characteristics may; A, cause or significantly contribute to an increase in serious, irreversible, or incapacitating and reversible illness; or B, pose a substantial presence or potential hazard to human health or the environment if improperly treated, stored, transported, or disposed of, or otherwise managed, and which has been identified or listed as a hazardous waste by the United States Environmental Protection Agency.

In his objections to the district court's proposed jury charge, Sellers requested that the district court give the following instruction:

Second: that the Defendant knew or reasonably should have known that the substance was waste;

Or alternatively:

that the Defendant knew or reasonably should have known that the substance was waste and that the waste could be harmful to persons or the environment if . . . improperly disposed of.

The applicable statute [R.C.R.A.] . . . provides criminal penalties for "[a]ny person who . . . knowingly treats, stores, or disposes of any hazardous waste identified or listed under this subchapter . . . without a permit under this subchapter. . . ."

On appeal, Sellers argues that the jury charge should have required the government to prove that Sellers knew that the paint waste could be hazardous or harmful to persons or the environment. Sellers argues that a "reading of the statute involved . . . leads to the conclusion that Congress intended to punish only knowing violations."

In the Supreme Court case of *United States v. International Minerals & Chem. Corp.* [1971], the defendant corporation challenged its conviction for violating I.C.C. regulations while shipping sulfuric acid in interstate commerce.... It claimed that, because it was unaware of the regulations, it could not have "knowingly" violated them as required under 18 U.S.C. § 834(f). The Supreme Court determined that although Congress required some *mens rea* by its use of the word "knowingly" in the statute, knowledge of the regulation was not part of this *mens rea* requirement. Rather, "knowingly" was intended to apply to mistakes of fact such as if "a person thinking in good faith that he was shipping distilled water" actually shipped dangerous acid.... The Court stated that if "[p]encils, dental floss [and] paper clips] were regulated, knowledge of the regulations would have to be an element of the offense because of substantial due process questions."... However, "where ... dangerous or deleterious devices or products or obnoxious waste materials are involved, the probability of regulation is so great that anyone who is aware that he is in possession of them or dealing with them must be presumed to be aware of the regulation."... Thus, when a person knowingly possesses an instrumentality which by its nature is potentially dangerous, he is imputed with the knowledge that it may be regulated by public health legislation....

There is support for Sellers's argument as it relates to § 6928 in the opinions of several other circuits.... We need not reach this issue, however, because we have concluded that it is being raised for the first time on appeal and we find that the district court's failure to give a more complete instruction was not plain error.

At trial, Sellers requested an instruction that the government must prove that "the Defendant knew or reasonably should have known that the substance was waste." This instruction was not necessary as the district court's instruction explicitly required the government to prove that "the Defendants knew what the wastes were ... paint and paint solvent waste."

In the alternative, Sellers requested that the trial court instruct the jury that "the Defendant knew or reasonably should have known that the substance was waste and that the waste could be harmful to persons or the environment if ... improperly disposed of." Although the district judge did not give his reason for rejecting this instruction, it is clear that this instruction is incorrect. There is no requirement that the defendant must know that the waste would be harmful "if improperly disposed of." Under Seller's construction, arguably he would not be liable if he disposed of the harmful waste in what he considered to be proper containers. Because this alternative instruction suggested by Sellers is legally deficient, the district court was correct in rejecting it.

Focusing only on the first half of this second requested instruction, Sellers argues on appeal that the district court erred by not giving an instruction that the government must prove that the defendant knew that the waste was hazardous or dangerous....

Assuming, *arguendo*, that the district court should have charged the jury that the government was required to prove that the defendant knew that the substance he disposed of was potentially hazardous or dangerous to persons or the environment, in the present case the omission was not plain error. It is clear that paint and paint solvent waste, by its very nature, is potentially dangerous to the environment and to persons. Thus it should have come as no surprise to Sellers that the disposal of that waste is regulated. The evidence presented at trial established that Sellers knew that the waste he was disposing included M.E.K., a paint solvent, and that this substance was extremely flammable. There can be no doubt that Sellers knew that the substance he was disposing of was potentially dangerous to human beings and the environment and that regulations, therefore, would exist governing the manner of its disposal. Under these circumstances, we cannot say that the jury charge as a whole constituted "plain error." Therefore, we find no ground for reversal....

Based on the foregoing, we affirm the conviction and sentence imposed on James Ralph Sellers by the district court.

AFFIRMED.

CHAPTER

11

OFFENSES AGAINST PUBLIC ORDER AND SAFETY

CHAPTER OUTLINE

Introduction
The Common-Law
  Background
Breaches of the Peace
Constitutional Limitations on
  Defining Breaches of the
  Peace
Vagrancy
Traffic Violations
Weapons Offenses
Conclusion

INTRODUCTION

Without question, government has a fundamental obligation to protect the public order and safety, much as it has to protect public health and the environment. The criminal law is one way government performs this function—by criminalizing acts that threaten society's interests in order and safety. This category of offenses includes breaches of the peace such as unlawful assembly, riot, and disorderly conduct. It also includes vagrancy and loitering, which are designed to control persons whose conduct society considers threatening or undesirable. All of the aforementioned crimes are based on English common law.

In this chapter, we also briefly discuss traffic violations and weapons offenses, which, while unknown to the common law, exist by virtue of modern legislation aimed at protecting the public safety.

THE COMMON-LAW BACKGROUND

As with most basic criminal offenses, the crimes against public order and safety are rooted in the common law. The common law recognized the right of the people to assemble peaceably for lawful purposes. Nevertheless, the maintenance of public order was given a high priority. To maintain order, the common law developed three misdemeanors: unlawful assembly, rout, and riot. If three or more persons met together with the intention of cooperating to disturb the public peace through the doing of an unlawful act, their gathering was considered an unlawful assembly. If they took steps to achieve their purpose, it was a rout; and if they actually executed their plans, they committed a riot. *State v. Wooldridge,* 40 S.E.2d 899 (W. Va. 1946). Vagrancy was also an offense at common law originally designed to control the economics of the populace by punishing idleness. *Fenster v. Leary,* 229 N.E.2d 426 (N.Y. 1967).

BREACHES OF THE PEACE

In the United States, the responsibility for maintaining public order and peace rests primarily with state and local governments, although the federal government has a significant role as well. A variety of state statutes and local ordinances prohibit unlawful assemblies, riots, and disorderly conduct. Control of unlawful assemblies and riots is aimed at group behavior, while laws proscribing disorderly conduct are aimed at both group and individual behavior. Through enforcement of laws prohibiting disorderly conduct, state and local governments attempt to prevent such undesirable conduct as violent and tumultuous behavior, offensive language and gestures, actions impeding movement of persons on public sidewalks and roads, and disturbances of lawfully conducted meetings.

Unlawful Assembly and Riot

Most states have enacted statutes proscribing unlawful assemblies and riots. For example, the Indiana Code defines *unlawful assembly* as "an assembly of five or more persons whose common object is to commit an unlawful act, or a lawful act by unlawful means." West's Ann. Ind. Code 35–45–1–1. It further defines *tumultuous conduct* as "conduct that results in, or is likely to result in, serious bodily injury to a person or substantial damage to property." West's Ann. Ind. Code 35–45–1–1. Under the Indiana Code, a person who is a "member of an unlawful assembly who recklessly, knowingly, or intentionally engages in tumultuous conduct commits rioting." Under Indiana law, the offense is punishable as a misdemeanor unless committed while armed with a deadly weapon, in which case it becomes a felony. West's Ann. Ind. Code 35–45–1–2.

Historically federal statutes have made it a crime to riot. However, the controversy over the Vietnam War, racial unrest, poverty, and a host of other social ills during the 1960s became catalysts for riotous behavior beyond proportions experienced for many years. To better cope with riots, Congress enacted the Federal Anti-Riot Act of 1968. The act was designed to punish riotous acts occurring in interstate travel or involving the use of interstate facilities. The act makes it unlawful for:

> Whoever travels in interstate or foreign commerce or uses any facility of interstate or foreign commerce, including, but not limited to, the mail, telegraph, telephone, radio, or television, with intent—
> (A) to incite a riot; or
> (B) to organize, promote, encourage, participate in, or carry on a riot; or
> (C) to commit any act of violence in furtherance of a riot; or
> (D) to aid or abet any person in inciting or participating in or carrying on a riot or committing any act of violence in furtherance of a riot;
> and who either during the course of any such travel or use or thereafter performs or attempts to perform any other overt act for any purpose specified in subparagraph (A), (B), (C), or (D) of this paragraph. 18 U.S.C.A. § 2101(a)(1).

The act comprehensively defines *riot* by stating:

> [T]he term "riot" means a public disturbance involving (1) an act or acts of violence by one or more persons part of an assemblage of three or more persons, which act or acts shall constitute a clear and present danger of, or shall result in, damage or injury to the property of any other person or to the person of any other individual or (2) a threat or threats of the commission of an act or acts of violence by one or more persons part of an assemblage of three or more persons having, individually or collectively, the ability of immediate execution of such threat or threats, where the performance of the threatened act or acts of violence would constitute a clear and present danger of, or would result in, damage or injury to the property of any other person or to the person of any other individual. 18 U.S.C.A. § 2102(a).

It defines *to incite a riot* by explaining:

> [T]he term "to incite a riot," or "to organize, promote, encourage, participate in, or carry on a riot," includes, but is not limited to, urging or instigating other persons to riot, but shall not be deemed to mean the mere oral or written (1) advocacy of ideas

or (2) expression of belief, not involving advocacy of any act or acts of violence or assertion of the rightness of, or the right to commit, any such act or acts. 18 U.S.C.A. § 2102(b).

In 1972 the United States Court of Appeals for the seventh circuit held that the Anti-Riot Act is not unconstitutionally vague or overbroad in relation to the First Amendment. *United States v. Dellinger*, 472 F.2d 340 (7th Cir. 1972), cert. denied, 410 U.S. 970, 93 S.Ct. 1443, 35 L.Ed.2d 706 (1973).

Disorderly Conduct

Closely related to statutes prohibiting unlawful assembly and riot are laws making disorderly conduct an offense. The Indiana Code concisely, yet comprehensively, proscribes disorderly conduct by providing:

> A person who recklessly, knowingly or intentionally: (1) engages in fighting or in tumultuous conduct; (2) makes unreasonable noise and continues to do so after being asked to stop; (3) disrupts a lawful assembly of persons; commits disorderly conduct. . . . West's Ann. Ind. Code § 35–45–1–3.

In *Cavazos v. State*, 455 N.E.2d 618 (Ind. App. 1983), an Indiana appellate court said that the application of the disorderly conduct statute to speech must be limited to unprotected classes of expression (e.g., obscenity, fighting words, public nuisance, and incitement to imminent lawless action). Thus, the court found that a defendant calling a police officer an "asshole" and continuing to debate with him about the arrest of her brother was insufficient to support her conviction for disorderly conduct. The court reasoned that the defendant's words to the police officer did not constitute any of the named unprotected classes of speech. Subsequently, another Indiana Court declared that the words *engages in* in the statute require present, completed conduct likely to injure persons. *Gebhard v. State*, 484 N.E.2d 45 (Ind. App. 1985).

Statutes and ordinances similar to those in Indiana are found in virtually every state. Some state statutes and local ordinances go further and prohibit the use of indecent or profane language. Many laws of this type have met the fate of an ordinance in Baton Rouge, Louisiana, that made it unlawful for any person to use "indecent, vile, profane or blasphemous language on or near the streets, alleys, sidewalks, or other places of public resort." That ordinance was declared unconstitutional as a violation of the First Amendment protection of free speech. *Baton Rouge v. Ewing*, 308 So.2d 776 (La. 1975).

CONSTITUTIONAL LIMITATIONS ON DEFINING BREACHES OF THE PEACE

The United States Supreme Court has rendered a number of opinions with respect to First Amendment limitations on laws proscribing disorderly conduct and other breaches of the peace. In 1942 the Court stated:

> There are certain well-defined and narrowly limited classes of speech, the prevention and punishment of which has never been thought to raise a Constitutional problem.

These include the lewd and obscene, the profane, the libelous, and the insulting or "fighting" words—those which by their very utterance inflict or tend to incite an immediate breach of the peace. *Chaplinsky v. New Hampshire,* 315 U.S. 568, 571–572, 62 S.Ct. 766, 769, 86 L.Ed. 1031, 1035 (1942).

The principles announced in *Chaplinsky* have proven difficult to apply. Some seven years after *Chaplinsky,* the Court overturned a conviction of a priest who was charged with breach of the peace after he gave a speech filled with racial and political epithets. His remarks resulted in a riotous crowd gathering outside the meeting hall where he spoke. At trial, the judge defined breach of the peace to include speech which "stirs the public to anger, invites a dispute, brings about a condition of unrest or creates a disturbance." The Supreme Court reversed, holding that a conviction for breach of the peace for conduct as defined by the trial judge violated the First Amendment. *Terminiello v. City of Chicago,* 337 U.S. 1, 69 S.Ct. 894, 93 L.Ed. 1131 (1949).

As noted earlier, the 1960s was an extremely turbulent decade. In a not uncommon scene, on the morning of March 2, 1961, a large group of black students congregated on the lawn of the statehouse in Columbia, South Carolina, to protest the state's segregation laws. Speeches were made; songs were sung. The students responded by clapping and stamping their feet. A large crowd of onlookers gathered nearby. Nobody among the crowd caused or threatened any trouble, and there was no obstruction of pedestrian or vehicular traffic. A contingent of thirty or more police officers was present to meet any foreseeable possibility of disorder. After refusing to obey a police order to disperse, many of the students were arrested and found guity of breach of the peace. In reversing their convictions, the United States Supreme Court said:

CASE IN POINT

APPLICATION OF A RIOT STATUTE

A young black girl was shot and seriously wounded by a white male who claimed she was picking peaches from his trees. The man was arrested but soon released on bail. After his release, a large crowd from the black community gathered and began demonstrating and demanding the man be jailed. As a result of his participation in the demonstration, defendant Miller was charged with violating a state law proscribing riots, the constitutionality of which had been previously upheld by the state supreme court. Miller was convicted and appealed.

On appeal, Miller admitted that he had exhorted the crowd to "take the Mayor's Million-Dollar-Mall" and that in his exhortations he had used such terms as "killer cops." He argued that his conviction should be overturned because his conduct amounted to no more than constitutionally protected "political hyperbole." The Supreme Court of Delaware rejected his contention and found that his conduct, even accepting his own version of the facts, was an incitement to lawless action that fell outside the category of "political hyperbole."

Miller v. State, 374 A.2d 271 (Del. 1977).

These petitioners were convicted of an offense as to be, in the words of the South Carolina Supreme Court, "not susceptible of exact definition." And they were convicted upon evidence which showed no more than that the opinions which they were peaceably expressing were sufficiently opposed to the views of the majority of the community to attract a crowd and necessitate police protection. . . .

The Fourteenth Amendment does not permit a State to make criminal the peaceful expression of unpopular views. *Edwards v. South Carolina,* 372 U.S. 229, 237, 83 S.Ct. 680, 684, 9 L.Ed.2d 697, 703 (1963).

It is instructive to compare and contrast *Edwards* with a case in the 1970s in which the Supreme Court upheld a conviction for disorderly conduct arising out of a confrontation between a police officer and a student protestor. After conducting a political demonstration, a number of students got into their cars and formed an entourage. A police officer stopped one of the vehicles after noting that its license plate had expired. The other cars in the group also pulled over. One of the students approached the officer to find out what was wrong. After explaining the situation, the officer asked the student to leave. Upon refusing to do so, the student was arrested for violating Section 437.016(1)(f) of the Kentucky Revised Statutes, which provided that a person was guilty of disorderly conduct, "if, with intent to cause public inconvenience, annoyance or alarm, or recklessly creating a risk thereof," he "congregates with other persons in a public place and refuses to comply with a lawful order of the police to disperse." A conviction for disorderly conduct was upheld by the Kentucky Court of Appeals. *Colten v. Commonwealth,* 467 S.W.2d 374 (Ky. 1971). In refusing to set aside the action of the state court, the United States Supreme Court said:

As the Kentucky statute was construed by the state court, . . . a crime is committed only where there is no bona fide intention to exercise a constitutional right—in which event, by definition, the statute infringes no protected speech or conduct—or where the interest so clearly outweighs the collective interest sought to be asserted that the latter must be deemed to be insubstantial. . . . Individuals may not be convicted under the Kentucky statute merely for expressing unpopular or annoying ideas. The statute comes into operation only when the individual's interest in expression, judged in the light of all relevant factors, is "minuscule" compared to a particular public interest in preventing that expression or conduct at that time and place. *Colten v. Kentucky,* 407 U.S. 104, 111, 92 S.Ct. 1953, 1958, 32 L.Ed.2d 584, 590 (1972).

The "Fighting Words" Doctrine

As the Supreme Court observed in *Chaplinsky v. New Hampshire, supra,* the utterance of "fighting words" is beyond protection of the First Amendment. But law enforcement officers and courts encounter difficult problems in determining whether given words in a given context fall within the definition of fighting words. In *Chaplinsky* the Supreme Court said that fighting words are those that: (1) inflict injury; (2) tend to create a breach of the peace; and (3) are not an essential part of the exposition of ideas. Thus, when a defendant is charged with verbal conduct in violating a statute or ordinance making the use of profane or obscene language disorderly conduct, the courts must determine the effects of the defendant's particular words in context of the situations. Some courts take the view that when profanities or obscenities are directed at a police officer that a different standard applies from those directed at the ordinary citizen. These courts reason that a police officer by training is taught not to react violently or to retaliate against persons who use such insulting language, and therefore they often refuse to convict defendants in such circumstances. See, for example, *State v. John W.*, 418 A. 2d 1097 (Me. 1980). Irrespective of the situation, the prosecution must establish that such verbal conduct tended to incite violence.

In analyzing statutes proscribing breaches of the peace, unlawful assemblies, riots, and disorderly conduct, we must keep in mind two essential principles. First, unless a statute contains specific definitions of terms, courts generally rely on common-law definitions to interpret its terms. *Commonwealth v. Duitch*, 67 A. 2d 821 (Pa. Super. 1949). Second, the statute must be interpreted and applied in a manner not to offend the First Amendment guarantees of speech, assembly, and religion.

"Hate Crimes"

In response to a growing trend of occurrences in which extremist groups expressed hatred or bigotry toward minorities, some jurisdictions enacted measures prohibiting "hate crimes." One such law was enacted by the city of St. Paul, Minnesota. The St. Paul Bias-Motivated Crime Ordinance, St. Paul, Minn. Legis. Code § 292.02 (1990), provided:

> Whoever places on public or private property a symbol, object, appellation, characterization or graffiti, including, but not limited to, a burning cross or Nazi swastika, which one knows or has reasonable grounds to know arouses anger, alarm or resentment in others on the basis of race, color, creed, religion or gender commits disorderly conduct and shall be guilty of a misdemeanor.

In construing the ordinance, the Minnesota Supreme Court held that it prohibited only "fighting words," that is, those utterances outside the protections of the First Amendment. *In re Welfare of R.A.V.*, 464 N.W. 2d 507 (Minn. 1991). In a much-publicized 1992 decision, the U.S. Supreme Court declared the ordinance unconstitutional. *R.A.V. v. City of St.Paul*, 505 U.S. ___ , 112 S.Ct. 2538, 120 L.Ed.2d 305 (1992). Writing for the Court, Justice Antonin Scalia stated: "Even assuming, *arguendo*, that all of the expression reached by the ordinance is proscribable under the 'fighting words' doctrine, we nonetheless conclude that the ordinance is facially unconstut.utional in that it prohibits otherwise permitted speech solely on the basis of the subjects the speech addresses." 505 U.S. at 112 S.Ct. at 2542, 120 L.Ed.2d at 316.

The Court's decision in *R.A.V.* raised serious questions as to whether hate crimes legislation can be made to conform with constitutional standards. Remember, however, that states and communities have a number of legal means at their disposal in combating hate crimes. For example, an individual who burns a cross on someone else's front lawn may be charged with criminal trespass and possibly with malicious mischief or vandalism (see Chapter 7).

In contrast to its 1992 decision in *R.A.V.*, the Supreme Court in 1993 upheld a Wisconsin statute that increases the severity of punishment if a crime victim is chosen on the basis of race or other designated characteristics. In *Wisconsin v. Mitchell*, 1993, WL 195271 (U.S. Wis.), 508 U.S. ___ , 113 S.Ct. 2194, 124 L.Ed.2d 436 (1993) the Court ruled unanimously that increasing punishment because the defendant targeted the victim on the basis of his race does not infringe the defendant's freedom of conscience protected by the First Amendment. The Court distinguished the case from *R.A.V.*, noting that the Wisconsin statute was aimed at conduct, while the St. Paul ordinance invalidated in *R.A.V.* was aimed squarely at expression.

VAGRANCY

Elites in feudal England placed great emphasis on able-bodied serfs performing labor and not straying from their assigned tasks. This was motivated by both the need for laborers and the desire to prevent idle persons from becoming public charges. Even with the breakup of feudal estates, England found it necessary to prevent workers from moving from one area to another in search of improved working conditions. Thus, to regulate the economics of the populace, the common law developed the misdemeanor offense of vagrancy. The offense comprised three elements: (1) being without visible means of support; (2) being without employment; and (3) being able to work but refusing to do so. *Fenster v. Leary*, 229 N.E.2d 426 (N.Y. 1967).

Eventually the emphasis shifted from merely punishing idleness toward the prevention of crime as England enacted statutes defining vagrancy. The objective then became to protect the people and their property from persons considered potential criminals or simply regarded as undesirables. Thus, by the time the American colonists settled in their new environment, the concept of punishing vagrants had become firmly implanted, and the colonists found it to be a desirable way to prevent idleness and to outlaw conduct offensive to their social mores.

The American Approach to Vagrancy

During the 1800s virtually all American states and most cities enacted statutes and ordinances punishing a wide variety of conduct as vagrancy. Statutory language was intentionally rather vague, presumably to allow police broad discretion to arrest persons they deemed undesirable to the community. Vagrancy laws not only proscribed such acts as disorderly conduct, begging, and loitering; they also criminalized the condition of being poor, idle, of bad reputation, or simply "wandering around without any lawful purpose." By making a person's status an offense, these laws ran counter to the historic concept that a crime consisted of the commission of an unlawful act or the failure to perform a required act. Frequently, vagrancy laws were directed against persons without the means to contest their validity or to challenge the application of such laws to them. Enforcement of vagrancy laws resulted in numerous persons being taken into custody, although many were released shortly thereafter on the condition that they move on to another area.

While there was considerable criticism of these practices, there was little incentive for lawyers to attack the constitutionality of these laws, since the United States Supreme Court had sanctioned them in 1837 by saying:

We think it [is] as competent and as necessary for a state to provide precautionary measures against the moral pestilence of paupers, vagabonds, and possibly convicts; as it is to guard against . . . physical pestilence. . . . *City of New York v. Miln,* 36 U.S. (11 Pet.) 102, 142, 9 L.Ed. 648, 664 (1837).

In the 1900s arrests and convictions for vagrancy were common, yet comparatively few of the convictions were appealed. During the first half of the century, appellate courts issued opinions upholding convictions in a variety of circumstances. For example, in Minnesota a defendant's conviction was affirmed for wandering about the streets with no place of abode and without giving a good account of himself. *State v. Woods,* 163 N.W. 518 (Minn. 1917). In an instance in Virginia, an appellate court held that a defendant's conduct in consorting with gamblers and idlers constituted the offense of vagrancy. *Morgan v. Commonwealth,* 191 S.E. 791 (Va. 1937). Even a defendant's conduct as part of "a group of 4 or 5 suspicious men" at a saloon was, under the particular circumstances, held to be vagrancy. *State v. Carroll,* 30 A.2d 54 (N.J. 1943), *aff'd,* 33 A.2d 907 (1943).

The wide range of vaguely-proscribed conduct in vagrancy laws made them susceptible of arbitrary enforcement by law enforcement agencies. In their efforts to prevent crime and to control the so-called undesirable, these laws became somewhat of a catch-all of the criminal justice system. Police commonly used them as a basis to arrest a suspect, who was then held pending investigation, or as a method of getting the suspect to confess. Vagrancy laws also furnished a convenient basis for police to justify a search incident to arrest as an exception to the warrant requirement of the Fourth Amendment (see Chapter 14 for a discussion of the concept of search incident to lawful arrest).

By the 1950s the vagrancy laws were being enforced primarily against loafers, alcoholics, derelicts, and tramps when they left the environs of "skid row" and ventured into the more "respectable" neighborhoods, where residents found their presence offensive. By 1960 the constitutionality of the vagrancy laws was frequently being challenged on grounds that they were vague, violated due process of law requirements, and exceeded the police power of the states. Such challenges were rejected by state and federal courts, with the courts generally upholding the right of the legislature to define what constitutes being a vagrant. See, for example, *State v. Finrow,* 405 P.2d 600 (Wash. 1965). During the 1960s, however, a number of statutes defining a vagrant as a person "without visible means of support" or who "wanders around the streets at late hours" or who "fails to give account of himself" were declared unconstitutional. In *Fenster v. Leary,* 229 N.E. 2d 426 (N.Y. 1967), New York's highest court declared a statute that defined as vagrants "persons who, not having visible means to maintain themselves, live without employment" was unconstitutional on due process grounds and constituted an overreaching of police power. The court said that the law "provides punishment for a person's conduct which in no way impinges on the rights of others." 229 N.E.2d at 428.

The Death Knell of Vagrancy Laws

In 1972, the United States Supreme Court issued an opinion that was to have a profound effect on the enforcement of vagrancy laws in the United States. *Papachristou v. City of Jacksonville,* 405 U.S. 156, 92 S.Ct. 839, 31 L.Ed.2d 110 (1972).

C A S E   I N   P O I N T

Search Incident to Arrest
for Vagrancy

At about midnight on February 17, 1968, Lloyd Powell and several companions entered the Bonanza Liquor Store in San Bernadino, California. An altercation developed between Powell and the manager over Powell's alleged attempt to steal a bottle of wine. In the ensuing struggle, Powell shot and killed the manager's wife. Ten hours later, a police officer in Henderson, Nevada, arrested Powell under the local vagrancy ordinance. In a search incident to the arrest, the officer discovered a .38-caliber revolver with six spent cartridges in the cylinder. Laboratory analysis determined that the weapon was used in the murder of the liquor store owner's wife. Powell was convicted of second-degree murder and sentenced to prison. Although the Henderson, Nevada, vagrancy ordinance was later declared unconstitutional by a federal court, the use of the evidence against Powell, and his conviction for murder, were ultimately sustained.

Stone v. Powell, 428 U.S. 465, 96 S.Ct 3037, 49 L.Ed.2d 1067 (1976).

In Jacksonville, Florida, eight defendants were convicted under a municipal ordinance that broadly defined vagrancy and levied criminal penalties of up to 90 days imprisonment, a $500.00 fine, or both on violators. The ordinance included language common to many of the statutes and ordinances extant at the time. It provided:

> Rogues and vagabonds, or dissolute persons who go about begging, common gamblers, persons who use juggling or unlawful games or plays, common drunkards, common night walkers, thieves, pilferers or pickpockets, traders in stolen property, lewd, wanton and lascivious persons, keepers of gambling places, common railers and brawlers, persons wandering or strolling around from place to place without any lawful purpose or object, habitual loafers, disorderly persons, persons neglecting all lawful business and habitually spending their time by frequenting houses of ill fame, gaming houses, or places where alcoholic beverages are sold or served, persons able to work but habitually living upon the earnings of their wives or minor children shall be deemed vagrants. . . . Quoted in *Papachristou*, 405 U.S. at 158–159, n. 1, 92 S.Ct. at 840, 31 L.Ed.2d at 112.

Speaking for a unanimous Supreme Court, Justice William O. Douglas said that the Jacksonville ordinance was void for vagueness, both in the sense that it "fails to give a person of ordinary intelligence fair notice that his contemplated conduct is forbidden by the statute and because it encourages arbitrary and erratic arrests and convictions." 405 U.S. at 162, 92 S.Ct. at 843, 31 L.Ed.2d at 115. On the same date, the Court vacated the convictions of several other defendants who had been convicted of vagrancy in a state court under a Florida Statute (Section

856.02) that defined vagrancy similar to the Jacksonville ordinance. *Smith v. Florida*, 405 U.S. 172, 92 S.Ct. 848, 31 L.Ed.2d 122 (1972).

Loitering

The widespread invalidation of vagrancy laws resulted in legislative bodies enacting new laws to control specifically defined behavior that states and local communities found unacceptable. In lieu of proscribing "wandering around without any apparent purpose" legislatures used language to control such activities as "loitering on school grounds without legitimate reason." And instead of proscribing the status of being a "common gambler," they made it unlawful to "loiter in a public place for the purpose of gambling." Thus, by no longer criminalizing a person's *status* and by specifying the circumstances under which a person would be in violation of the law, the new approach sought to give credence to constitutional principles while still providing the police with the tools they needed to prevent crime.

The new approach to proscribing loitering is exemplified by the New York state law that provides:

A person is guilty of loitering when he:
1. Loiters, remains or wanders about in a public place for the purpose of begging [held unconstitutional on the ground that it violated the First Amendment in *Loper v. N.Y. City Police Dept.*, ___ F.2d ___ (2nd. Cir. 1993)]; or
2. Loiters or remains in a public place for the purpose of gambling with cards, dice or other gambling paraphernalia; or
3. Loiters or remains in a public place for the purpose of engaging, or soliciting another person to engage, in deviate sexual intercourse or other sexual behavior of a deviate nature [invalidated in *People v. Uplinger*, 447 N.E.2d 62 (N.Y. 1983), on the ground that there is no requirement that the proscribed conduct be offensive or annoying to others]; or
4. Being masked or in any manner disguised by unusual attire or facial alteration, loiters, remains or congregates in a public place with other persons so masked or disguised, or knowingly permits or aids persons so masked or disguised to congregate in a public place; except that such conduct is not unlawful when it occurs in connection with a masquerade party or like entertainment if, when such entertainment is held in a city which has promulgated regulations in connection with such affairs, permission is first obtained from the police or other appropriate authorities; or
5. Loiters or remains in or about school grounds, a college or university building or grounds, not having any reason or relationship involving custody of or responsibility for a pupil or student, or any other specific, legitimate reason for being there, and not having written permission from anyone authorized to grant the same; or
6. Loiters or remains in any transportation facility, unless specifically authorized to do so, for the purpose of soliciting or engaging in any business, trade or commercial transactions involving the sale of merchandise or services, or for the purpose of entertaining persons by singing, dancing or playing any musical instrument; or

7. Loiters or remains in any transportation facility, or is found sleeping therein, and is unable to give a satisfactory explanation of his presence [held unconstitutional in *People v. Bright*, 520 N.E.2d 1355 (N.Y. 1988), on the ground that it required the suspect to prove "satisfactory explanation of his presence" to avoid arrest].
McKinney's N.Y. Penal Law § 240.35.

As noted above, several provisions of this statute have been declared unconstitutional. But the statute, in the main, remains operative.

On the other hand, some states and municipalities continued to proscribe vagrancy but in a much narrower manner than did the Jacksonville ordinance invalidated by the Supreme Court. For example, Section 207.030 of the Nevada Revised Statutes enumerates specific acts that constitute vagrancy. These prohibited acts include solicitation or engaging in lewd acts in public, loitering on private property of others in the nighttime or upon the streets, and refusing to identify or account for one's presence when requested by a peace officer if the surrounding circumstances indicate that the public safety demands identification.

In 1976 the Georgia legislature enacted a comprehensive law defining loitering and prowling. It provides:

(a) A person commits the offense of loitering or prowling when he is in a place at a time or in a manner not usual for law-abiding individuals under circumstances that warrant a justifiable and reasonable alarm or immediate concern for the safety of persons or property in the vicinity.

(b) Among the circumstances which may be considered in determining whether alarm is warranted is the fact that the person takes flight upon the appearance of a law enforcement officer, refuses to identify himself, or manifestly endeavors to conceal himself or any object. Unless flight by the person or other circumstances make it impracticable, a law enforcement officer shall, prior to any arrest for an offense under this Code section, afford the person an opportunity to dispel any alarm or immediate concern which would otherwise be warranted by requesting the person to identify himself and explain his presence and conduct. No person shall be convicted of an offense under this Code section if the law enforcement officer failed to comply with the foregoing procedure or if it appears at trial that the explanation given by the person was true and would have dispelled the alarm or immediate concern.

(c) A person committing the offense of loitering or prowling shall be guilty of a misdemeanor.

Official Ga. Code Ann. § 16–11–36.

In *Bell v. State*, 313 S.E.2d 678 (Ga. 1984), a defendant was charged with violating the new Georgia loitering and prowling statute after a police officer observed him and a companion in downtown Atlanta near midnight. The two men were squeezing their bodies between the wall and a locked gate of a parking garage in order to exit the garage. When the officer attempted to question them, the companion ran but defendant Bell remained. After Bell's companion was apprehended and the officer gave them an opportunity to explain their presence, the defendant told the officer he was taking a shortcut through the garage. Knowing that this path did not amount to a shortcut, but instead required far greater effort on the part of the defendant, the officer placed him under arrest. Bell was convicted of violating the new Georgia loitering and prowling law.

On appeal to the Georgia Supreme Court, the defendant relied on a prior state supreme court decision striking down a municipal loitering ordinance that provided no guidelines by which "a citizen who desired to conform his conduct to [the law] would be [able] to discern whether he risked criminal responsibility." *Bullock v. City of Dallas*, 281 S.E.2d 613, 615 (Ga. 1981). The ordinance invalidated in *Bullock* provided that:

> No person shall remain or loiter upon any premises to which the public has access, including but not limited to such places as business and shopping area parking lots, where the person's presence upon such premises is unrelated to the normal activity, use or business for which such premises are made available to the public. Dallas City Ordinance § 5–112(a).

In *Bell* the Georgia Supreme Court found the defendant's reliance on its earlier decision in *Bullock* misplaced. The court concluded that unlike the Dallas ordinance, the new Georgia loitering statute was not void for vagueness, since it applies only where peace and order are threatened or where the safety of persons or property is jeopardized. Moreover, the new law sufficiently advises persons of ordinary intelligence of the conduct that is prohibited. Thus the court affirmed Bell's conviction. It did, however, caution that the legislature intended for trial courts to determine whether the defendant's explanation is true and should reasonably have dispelled the arresting officer's concern for the safety of persons or property in the area.

TRAFFIC VIOLATIONS

States, and often municipalities, have adopted laws defining a wide range of motor vehicle violations. These are generally strict-liability offenses; therefore, there is generally no requirement to prove criminal intent to find a defendant guilty of a traffic violation (see Chapter 4). Among other offenses, these laws proscribe speeding; failing to yield the right-of-way; failing to observe traffic officers, signs and signals; driving without required equipment; etc. During the 1970s and 1980s, states adopted a number of "model" laws, so that traffic offenses are highly uniform across the states. This uniformity is both necessary and desirable given the mobility of today's populace and the volume of traffic on the nation's highways.

When a driver is stopped for a traffic violation, police may observe conduct or evidence that gives rise to probable cause to conduct a search or make an arrest. Frequently drugs, alcohol, and weapons are discovered by police officers stopping automobiles for routine traffic violations.

Decriminalization of Traffic Offenses

Historically, traffic offenders were treated like persons committing other misdemeanors; they were arrested and required to post bond in order to avoid confinement pending the adjudication of their case. Since the 1960s most states and municipalities have decriminalized minor traffic offenses, which means that these offenses are now considered "civil infractions" rather than misdemeanors.

Consequently, offenders are now commonly issued citations or "tickets" instead of being subject to arrest. Offenders may avoid a court appearance by simply paying a fine according to a predetermined schedule of fines. Of course, offenders may elect to contest the charge by appearing in the appropriate court, often a municipal or "traffic court." In addition to fines, most states assess "points" against a driver for traffic violations, and an accumulation of points can lead to suspension or revocation of a driver's license. The decriminalization of routine traffic offenses has proved to be an expeditious and efficient means of maintaining discipline and order on the public thoroughfares. However, under most traffic codes, the more serious motor vehicle offenses, such as driving while intoxicated, eluding a police officer, and reckless driving, are still defined as misdemeanors and offenders are subject to arrest.

WEAPONS OFFENSES

The Second Amendment to the United States Constitution provides that "a well regulated Militia, being necessary to the security of a free state, the right of the people to keep and bear Arms, shall not be infringed." Nevertheless, there are numerous state and federal statutory prohibitions against the manufacture, sale, possession, and use of firearms and other weapons. For example, federal law prohibits the sale, possession, and use of machine guns. The Supreme Court has said that federal gun control laws do not violate the Second Amendment, because the amendment only protects the keeping and bearing of arms in the context of a well-regulated militia. See *United States v. Miller*, 307 U.S. 174, 59 S.Ct. 816, 83 L.Ed. 1206 (1939); *Lewis v. United States*, 445 U.S. 55, 100 S.Ct. 915, 63 L.Ed.2d 198 (1980).

The Illinois weapons statute, see Ill. Rev. Stat. Ann. Ch. 38, § 24, is fairly typical of state laws proscribing the unlawful use of weapons. Section 24–1 prohibits the manufacture, sale, and possession of various types of weapons that have no value either for hunting, archery, or marksmanship; or for the protection of a person's home from intruders. Explosives, gaseous devices, machine guns, and gun silencers are among the particular weapons banned. The law also prohibits carrying a wide variety of weapons, including "stun guns," "dangerous knives," "billy clubs," etc., with the intent of unlawfully using the weapon against another.

The Illinois statute also prohibits the manufacture, sale, transfer, possession, or discharge of metal-piercing bullets or bullets represented to be metal-piercing. §§ 24–2.1, 24–2.2, 24–3.2. In addition, the law proscribes the unlawful sale or delivery of firearms on any school premises, § 24–3.3, carrying concealed weapons, § 24–1.4, or carrying weapons while a person's face is masked or hooded so as to conceal a person's identity. § 24–1.9.

Like most states, Illinois exempts police officers and various other public officials, as well as licensed private investigators and security personnel, from the statutory prohibitions regarding possession and use of firearms. Ill. Rev. Stat. Ann. § 24–2.

Concealed Weapons

States commonly enact statutes making it unlawful to carry a concealed weapon. Most define *concealed* as a weapon being carried on or about a person in such a manner as to conceal it from the ordinary sight of another person. It follows that a defendant was properly convicted of carrying a concealed weapon in her purse when it was disclosed by a metal detector at a courthouse. *Schaaf v. Commonwealth*, 258 S.E.2d 574 (Va. 1979). But more often, litigation involves less than absolute concealment. For example, a Georgia appellate court ruled that even though the handle of a pistol tucked in a defendant's pants was visible to some extent through a slit in his shirt, the weapon was concealed. *Marshall v. State*, 200 S.E.2d 902 (Ga. App. 1973). Similarly, in *People v. Charron*, 220 N.W.2d 216 (Mich. App. 1974), a Michigan appellate court held that a knife slightly protruding from a defendant's rear pocket was a concealed weapon.

Many concealed-weapons statutes also make it an offense to carry a concealed weapon in a vehicle, and in numerous cases courts have been called upon to rule on the application of these laws. For example, in one case a defendant reached into his automobile and withdrew a revolver from a shelf behind the driver's seat. In affirming the defendant's conviction, the Wisconsin Supreme Court said, "[i]f the weapon is hidden from ordinary observation, it is concealed." The court noted that "absolute invisibility to other persons" was not "indispensable to concealment." The question was: "Was [the weapon] carried so as not to be discernible by ordinary observation?" *Mularkey v. State*, 230 N.W. 76, 77 (Wis. 1930). More recently, an Illinois appellate court observed that "[i]t is well settled . . . that a weapon is 'concealed' . . . even though there is some notice of its presence to an alert police officer who can see part of the gun when he approaches the vehicle." *People v. Williams*, 350 N.E. 2d 81, 83 (Ill. App. 1976).

CASE IN POINT

UNLAWFUL POSSESSION OF A FIREARM

South Carolina law provides that it is unlawful for any person to carry a pistol about his or her person, regardless of whether the pistol is concealed. S.C. Code § 16–23–20. The statute provides twelve exceptions to the prohibition. Barry Clarke was convicted of violating the statute after he was stopped for a traffic violation and the police officer noticed a gun in a holster next to the driver's seat. On appeal, Clarke argued that the burden of proof should have been on the prosecution to show that he did not qualify under any of the twelve exceptions to the prohibition. The South Carolina Supreme Court disagreed, saying that "[t]he general rule, when dealing statutory crimes to which there are exceptions, is that the defendant 'has the burden of excusing or justifying his act; and hence the burden may be on him to bring himself within an exception in the statute or to prove the issuance of a license or permit.' "

State v. Clarke, 396 S.E. 2d 827 (S.C. 1990).

CONCLUSION

Offenses against public order and safety present a picture of the dynamic development of the common law in a constitutional democracy. The need to maintain order, protect the public safety, and prevent crime are high-priority items on the agenda of any organized society. Yet, the United States Constitution mandates that government maintain a delicate balance between these interests and the rights of the citizens. Of particular relevance to offenses against public order are the protections of the First Amendment.

In studying offenses against public order and safety, indeed the criminal law generally, we should realize that the law must be viewed from a sociological, political, and philosophical perspective and not merely as a set of objective rules of conduct. The offenses against public order have been shaped to a great extent by social change and political events. They have also been sculpted by the values of freedom of speech and assembly that are held within the broader legal and political culture.

QUESTIONS FOR THOUGHT AND DISCUSSION

1. Why has it been necessary for American courts to interpret laws proscribing breach of peace and vagrancy more strictly than did the English common-law courts?

2. How does the Federal Anti-Riot Act seek to prevent the definition of "to incite a riot" from being applied in such a way as to violate First Amendment guarantees of freedom of expression?

3. Is the language of the Indiana Code that proscribes disorderly conduct sufficiently precise to meet the constitutional standard of giving a person of ordinary intelligence fair notice of what conduct is forbidden?

4. Consider the following hypothetical case: Members of the American Nazi Party announced a demonstration to be held in Pleasant Ridge, a predominantly Jewish suburb of Metropolis. The Pleasant Ridge city council quickly adopted an ordinance requiring groups planning demonstrations to obtain a permit from the police department. Under the ordinance, to hold a demonstration without a permit was a misdemeanor, punishable by a $1,000 fine and 60 days in jail. The Nazis applied for a permit and were denied on the grounds that their presence in Pleasant Ridge constituted a "clear and present danger to the public order." The Nazis held their demonstration anyway. Approximately one hundred demonstrators congregated on the city square. Many were dressed in Nazi uniforms; others carried banners emblazoned with swastikas, and others held signs on which were printed anti-Semitic slogans. Pleasant Ridge police arrived at the scene and asked the demonstrators to disperse. When they refused, police arrested a number of demonstrators; others ran to avoid arrest. The leader of the Nazi group, Eisenfaust, was convicted of a number of offenses, including violation of the new ordinance. On appeal, Eisenfaust is challenging the constitutionality of the ordinance. In your opinion, does he have a case?

5. Why did the English common-law concept of making vagrancy a crime take root in America? What purposes did it serve in the early history of the United States?

6. How did the Jacksonville, Florida, vagrancy ordinance invalidated by the Supreme Court in the *Papachristou* case offend the Constitution of the United States? Have

the reforms in vagrancy laws at the state and local levels sufficiently removed the threat of criminalizing a person's status? Are they now written with the precision necessary to protect citizens from arbitrary enforcement of the law?

7. Why have the courts refused to interpret the Second Amendment protection of the "right to keep and bear arms" to prohibit gun control legislation?

8. Why are most traffic violations strict-liability offenses?

9. Have traffic offenses been decriminalized in your state? To what extent? What procedures are available to contest a traffic ticket?

CASES

STATE V. MAST
Missouri Court of Appeals, 1986.
713 S.W.2d 601.

[This case involves the offenses of unlawful assembly and refusal to disperse.]

DOWD, Judge.

Defendant, Steve Mast, appeals his jury conviction on Count I, unlawful assembly in violation of § 574.040 RSMo (1979), a Class B misdemeanor, and on Count II, refusal to disperse from an unlawful assembly, in violation of Sec. 574.060 RSMo (1979), a Class C misdemeanor. On Count I, defendant was sentenced to a fine of $250.00 plus costs. On count II, defendant was sentenced to two days in jail plus a fine of $100.00 plus costs. The information was filed in Lewis County, and after a change in venue, a jury trial was held in the Knox County Circuit Court. Defendant appeals from these convictions.

On appeal, defendant contends the evidence was insufficient to support the convictions and it was therefore error not to grant his motions for judgments of acquittal.

In testing the sufficiency of the evidence by a motion for judgment of acquittal, the evidence must be viewed in the light most favorable to the state, assuming the evidence of the state and every reasonable inference therefrom to be true, and the evidence and inferences to the contrary are disregarded. . . .

On October 31, 1984, Halloween night, defendant, a student at Northeast Missouri State College in Kirksville, drove to the town of Maywood so that he could participate in the traditional Halloween gathering with his friends. Defendant was aware of Maywood's reputation for "anything goes on Halloween." He had been in Maywood on Halloween in past years, and arrived in Maywood around 5:45 P.M. with a friend, Donnie Martin. Defendant was dressed in his ROTC army fatigues and his face was covered with a black substance. Defendant had a bundle of bottle rockets in his possession and Donnie Martin carried a can of spray paint in his back pocket.

After arriving in Maywood, defendant and Donnie Martin socialized with some friends in front of a general store. Jerry Callow, the deputy sheriff, and Steve Waters, the special deputy appointed for Halloween night, warned defendant and his friends "to keep it down and keep it within reason." At that time, the officers explained to them that seven or more gathered constituted an illegal assembly, but as long as they were not doing anything but having fun, then the officers had no objections. Moreover, Waters informed defendant that it was not illegal to possess bottle rockets, but it was illegal to fire the bottle rockets. Additionally, he confiscated Donnie Martin's can of spray paint because of previous acts of vandalism.

Throughout the course of the night, different unlawful activities transpired such as: bottle rockets were set off in close vicinity to the general store's gas pumps and in the direction of the police car; Mr. Seals' house was egged and a stop sign was placed on his front porch; fire bombs and M-80s were set off; and eggs, bottle rockets, and a beer bottle were all thrown in the direction of the officers and their patrol car. In fact, Officer Callow was struck by an egg.

All of the above occurrences are not attributable to the defendant, but in the course of the evening the officers saw the defendant set off one bottle rocket away from the crowd and the buildings. The officers had difficulty identifying and determining the members of the crowd who were taking part in the unlawful activities. At one point in the evening, Deputy Callow told the crowd that they were getting unruly and committing unlawful acts, and consequently he "asked them to break it up." In response to his request, the crowd divided up into groups of four or five, but these groups did not separate far from each other and proceeded to call the officers names. After the officers departed, the crowd regrouped and continued to set off bottle rockets and fire bombs and throw eggs. Shortly after

10:30 P.M., the two officers turned on the red lights of their patrol car, drove up to the scattering crowd and made some arrests. Waters saw defendant in the middle of the crowd, immediately prior to this time, but he did not see defendant after the arrests.

This is the first appellate attack on the present unlawful assembly statute (§ 574.040 (RSMo 1978). This statute provides in part:

> 1. A person commits the crime of unlawful assembly if he knowingly assembles with six or more other persons and agrees with such persons to violate any of the criminal laws of this state or of the United States with force or violence.

A presumption exists "that the intent of the legislature in enacting a statute is to serve the best interests and welfare of the citizenry at large." . . . This presumption must take into consideration the fact that the legislature did not intend to effect an unreasonable, oppressive or absurd result. . . . Consequently, when interpreting § 574.040, we must determine the legislature's intent from what can be necessarily implied from the language it employed, because the legislature did not expressly state its intention. By identifying the general purposes for enacting a statute and by identifying the problem sought to be remedied, we can ascertain legislative intent. . . .

Since § 574.040 was enacted, no Missouri case has interpreted this statute. However, other jurisdictions have addressed this issue interpreting similar statutes. The court in *Lair v. State*, 316 P.2d 225, 234 (Okla. Crim. App. 1957), defined an unlawful assembly as being an assembly which consists of three or more persons assembled to do an unlawful act or who being assembled, attempt to do a lawful act in a violent or unlawful manner to the terror and the disturbance of the public in general. . . . To constitute the offense of unlawful assembly, the participants must have a common purpose and act in concert. The intent or purpose necessary to render an assembly unlawful need not exist from the onset, but may be formed either before or at the time of the assembly. . . .

An unlawful assembly causes a disturbance of the public order so that it is reasonable for rational, firm and courageous persons in the neighborhood of the assembly to believe the assembly will cause injury to persons or damage to property and will interfere with the rights of others by committing disorderly acts. . . . The intent with which such persons assemble is the very offense of unlawful assembly in that this intent is reflected by the participants' acts, conduct and language. . . . The purpose of unlawful assembly statutes is to discourage assemblies which interfere with the rights of others and endanger the public peace and excite fear and alarm among the people.

Even though a person does not individually commit a violent act which poses a clear and present danger of violence, this individual can be guilty of unlawful assembly. . . . The statutory denunciation applies to the assembly at large. Consequently, each member of an assembly need not individually commit unlawful acts to render the assembly unlawful, but a person can become a member of an unlawful assembly by not disassociating himself from the group assembled and by knowingly joining or remaining with the group assembled after it has become unlawful. . . . Whether a person acted knowingly and whether the necessary intent existed, are both questions of fact for the jury. . . .

> If it were necessary that each member of an unlawful assembly commit an unlawful act, before that member could be convicted then there would be no necessity to make participation in the unlawful assembly a crime. The independent unlawful act would itself be grounds for prosecution. . . . In short every person who is present and cognizant of the unlawful acts being committed by the other members of the assembly can be found guilty of being unlawfully assembled.

When applying the foregoing principles to the facts in this case, we must view the evidence in a manner most favorable to the state. At its inception, the gathering in Maywood on Halloween night was a lawful assembly, however as the night progressed, the participants' purpose in assembling changed. Undoubtedly, the assembly was disturbing the public peace and interfering with the rights of others. The persons in the neighborhood of the assembly had cause to fear the assembly would inflict damage to property and would commit disorderly acts. Throughout the evening, fire bombs, bottle rockets, M-80s, and eggs were being thrown at houses and people. Both Waters and Callow saw defendant fire a bottle rocket which is an unlawful act, according to the deputies. Defendant is no less guilty because he fired only one bottle rocket. Additionally, defendant drove his car across Mr. Seals' lawn.

Moreover, defendant had been in Maywood on previous Halloweens, and so he was aware of the type of activities that take place there on Halloween. Therefore, it is evident that defendant knew the purpose of the gathering on Halloween night. To be convicted of unlawful assembly, defendant did not have to participate or encourage every harmful act which occurred that night. For that matter defendant need not have actually committed an unlawful act. His presence alone in the unlawful assembly was enough for conviction, because he knowingly assembled with the other members, and he was under a duty to disassociate himself from the group after other members of the group committed unlawful acts.

Defendant would have us construe the statutory section in such a manner so as to vitiate the purpose of the statute. We will favor a construction that avoids this unjust and unreasonable result. Defendant contends that no agreement existed between the group members, and consequently, he could not be guilty of participating in an unlawful assembly. Such a narrow reading of the statute would defeat its purpose and create an absurd result by making it almost impossible to satisfy the elements of an unlawful assembly. Even though the group assembled did not expressly, verbally agree, their common unlawful purpose was expressed by their overt acts. Therefore, the members of the assembly intended to and in fact participated in an unlawful assembly. The assembly members' acts, conduct and language indicated their adoption of the unlawful conduct of the other members assembled. Moreover, defendant performed an unlawful act himself so his guilt is not established by his presence alone.

The common law offense of unlawful assembly is defined as follows: To constitute an offense it must appear that there was common intent of persons assembled to attain purpose, ... by commission of acts of intimidation and disorder likely to produce danger to peace of neighborhood, and actually tending to inspire courageous persons with well-grounded fear of serious breaches of public peace. ...

The purpose of an unlawful assembly statute is to penalize the members of assemblies when their conduct causes a disturbance or damage.... The members must meet and form a common purpose to violate any of the criminal laws, but they do not have to actually violate the law.... The state has a strong and legitimate interest in protecting against criminal acts of force or violence in order to preserve public tranquility and other rights belonging to the public in general. "In furtherance of this interest, it must be able to 'nip in the bud' riots and may, therefore, regulate and proscribe unlawful assemblies." ... The gathering in Maywood on Halloween originally was a lawful one, but as the night progressed, the members of the assembly acted with common intent to attain a purpose which interfered with the rights of others by committing disorderly and unlawful acts. Based on the foregoing principles, we hold there was substantial evidence to support the conviction of unlawful assembly. Point one is denied.

Defendant's second point on appeal is that the trial court erred in denying his motion for judgment of acquittal on the charge of refusal to disperse because the evidence was manifestly insufficient to sustain a conviction. Taking the evidence in the light most favorable to the state, the evidence was sufficient to show that on Halloween night an unlawful assembly had gathered in Maywood, and defendant had been lawfully warned to disperse. After hearing the warning, the defendant did as requested, but after a short period of time, he returned to the gathering. This evidence is sufficient to sustain his conviction for failure to disperse. Missouri's refusal to disperse statute states:

1. A person commits the crime of refusal to disperse if, being present at the scene of an unlawful assembly, or at the scene of a riot, he knowingly fails or refuses to obey the lawful command of a law enforcement officer to depart from the scene of such unlawful assembly or riot....

Whether a person knowingly fails or refuses to obey the dispersal order is a question of fact for the jury. To be guilty of the charge of refusal to disperse, a person must be at the scene of an unlawful assembly and know of the command to disperse, and still refuse to obey. The evidence favorable to the state showed that defendant heard Callow order the crowd to disperse by telling it "to break it up." In response to this command, the gathering broke up into groups of four and five and then proceeded to regroup shortly thereafter. By regrouping, defendant in effect refused to obey the lawful command of Callow to depart from the scene of the unlawful assembly.

Defendant alleges that the warning given was inadequate because it did not expressly order the crowd to go home or to leave town. § 574.060 does not require a warning to expressly designate a location where the crowd is to disperse. A person who "knowingly fails or refuses to obey the lawful command of a law enforcement officer to disperse from the scene of the such unlawful assembly," is guilty of this crime.... The warning could be reasonably understood to mean that the crowd was to leave the area. The failure of the warning to describe the area to be vacated has nothing to do with the defendant's

failure to comply. After Callow warned the crowd to break it up, the crowd regrouped, thus suggesting that the crowd would have disregarded the warning in any event.

Words are to be interpreted according to their plain and ordinary meaning which is the commonly accepted dictionary definition. "Break up" is defined as "to disrupt the continuity or flow or to bring to an end." ... A person of reasonable intelligence would understand the words "break it up" to mean that he is supposed to depart from the area. In total disregard and in defiance of the command, defendant remained in the area in question. By his inaction, defendant was not complying with the command to disperse. Defendant's second point on appeal, therefore, is denied.

For the foregoing reasons, the judgment of the trial court is affirmed.

REINHARD and CRIST, JJ., concur.

COMMONWEALTH V. YOUNG
Superior Court of Pennsylvania, 1988.
370 Pa. Super. 42, 535 A.2d 1141.

[This decision examines the offense of disorderly conduct.]

HESTER, Judge.

On September 24, 1986, appellant was found guilty of the summary offense of disorderly conduct by a district justice. On appeal to the Court of Common Pleas of Erie County, he was again found guilty of the same offense following a *de novo* hearing held on December 4, 1986. This appeal followed the January 8, 1987 judgment of sentence of thirty days imprisonment, a fine, and costs. We affirm.

The evidence introduced at trial establishes the following. On August 28, 1986, at approximately 2:45 A.M., appellant and Quincy Barnes were on the campus at Behrend College. They went to Perry Hall, a co-ed dormitory. The women's section of the dormitory consists of two floors on the right side of the building. The two sides are separated by a lobby.

To enter the right side, which is locked, a non-resident must be accompanied by a resident with a key. The first-floor women's restroom, located in the middle of the hall, serves approximately fifty dormitory residents and has six stalls containing toilets, six shower stalls, and sinks.

An unidentified resident admitted appellant and Barnes into the first floor women's section, and accompanied them to the room of a dormitory resident the two men knew. They visited briefly with that resident, and on their way out of the dormitory, the two men walked into the women's restroom. Appellant walked over to the stall, which did not lock, opened the door and said: "Hey baby, what you doing." ... The woman screamed, pulled up her pants and chased the men out of the dormitory. She testified that she was extremely frightened by the incident as she was not sure of the men's intentions when they opened the stall door.

In his defense, appellant testified that while he had gone to Perry Hall and visited with the resident he knew, he did not enter the restroom.

He argues that the evidence was insufficient to support his conviction for disorderly conduct. The test we apply in this situation is as follows:

> In testing the sufficiency of the evidence, we must view the evidence in a light most favorable to the Commonwealth as the verdict winner and draw all reasonable inferences upon which the fact finder could have properly based its verdict. . . . A determination must be made as to whether there exists sufficient evidence to enable the trier of fact to find, beyond a reasonable doubt, every element of the crime for which the appellant has been convicted. . . .

Disorderly conduct is defined in relevant part as follows:

§ 5503. **Disorderly Conduct**

(a) Offense defined.—A person is guilty of disorderly conduct if, with intent to cause public inconvenience, annoyance or alarm, or recklessly creating a risk thereof, he: . . . creates a hazardous or physically offensive condition by any act which serves no legitimate purpose of the actor. . . .

(c) Definition.—As used in this section the word "public" means affecting or likely to affect persons in a place to which the public or a substantial group has access; among the places included are highways, transport facilities, schools, prisons, apartment houses, places of business or amusement, any neighborhood, or any premises which are open to the public.

We reject appellant's argument that since his conduct affected only a single individual, he did not have the *mens rea* to cause "public" inconvenience, annoyance or alarm as defined by the statute. The statute specifically states that "recklessly creating a risk" of public annoyance or alarm is sufficient. The evidence viewed in the light most favorable to the Commonwealth establishes that appellant deliberately entered a women's public restroom without justification.

Under the statutory definition, the restroom was a public place. The term includes a place to which the public *or* a "substantial group" has access. . . . The restroom serves the fifty women who reside in the dormitory. Moreover, any female visitor can freely gain access to the area. Thus, the restroom is accessible to a substantial group. The size of the restroom supports this conclusion: it has six toilet stalls and six shower stalls, which is larger than public restrooms in most department stores and restaurants. There are some limitations on access in that a nonresident must be admitted to the general area by a resident. However, this does not alter the fact that a substantial group has access. Apartment houses, defined by the statute as public, are similarly restricted.

When appellant entered the public restroom, he recklessly created a *risk* of public annoyance or alarm. The fortuitous fact that only one individual was in the area does not vitiate the risk he created. Any number of women, in various states of undress, could have been using the showers, sinks and toilets in the area.

We have held that one who exhibits disorderly behavior in a public place is guilty of disorderly conduct even if that behavior is directed at a single individual. . . .

Appellant did not know the victim and was not searching for her. In this context, she was a member of the general public, and appellant deliberately entered the women's restroom solely to find *anyone* in her position or in a similarly embarrassing situation. He thereby created a risk of public annoyance or alarm, even if only one individual was alarmed and annoyed.

Further, the evidence establishes that appellant's conduct created a physically offensive condition to the victim. She was performing a private bodily function. She feared that appellant and his companion were going to assault her. Any reasonable woman in her situation would have been offended by appellant's actions. . . .

In *Commonwealth v. Greene*, 410 Pa. 111, 115–16, 189 A.2d 141, 144 (1963) which is still authoritative on this subject, Justice Musmanno noted that: "In Pennsylvania the crime of disorderly conduct embraces activity which disturbs the peace and dignity of a community." Justice Musmanno emphasized that the touchstone of disorderly conduct is an activity that does not form "an integral part of the movement of a civilized community." . . . Appellant's behavior fits those descriptions.

Viewing the evidence in the light most favorable to the Commonwealth and drawing all reasonable inferences therefrom, we believe that District Justice Peter Nakoski and Judge Shad Connelly of the Court of Common Pleas of Erie County correctly found appellant guilty of disorderly conduct. We therefore affirm the judgment of sentence.

BECK, J., files a dissenting opinion. . . .

FEINER V. NEW YORK
Supreme Court of the United States, 1951.
340 U.S. 315, 71 S. Ct. 303, 95 L.Ed. 295.

[In this classic case, the U.S. Supreme Court considers the First Amendment implications of a conviction for disorderly conduct.]

Mr. Chief Justice VINSON delivered the opinion of the Court.

Petitioner was convicted of the offense of disorderly conduct, a misdemeanor under the New York penal laws, in the Court of Special Sessions of the City of Syracuse and was sentenced to thirty days in the county penitentiary. The conviction was affirmed by the Onondaga County Court and the New York Court of Appeals. . . . The case is here on certiorari, . . . petitioner having claimed that the conviction is in violation of his right of free speech under the Fourteenth Amendment. . . .

On the evening of March 8, 1949, petitioner Irving Feiner was addressing an open-air meeting at the corner of South McBride and Harrison Streets in the City of Syracuse. At approximately 6:30 P.M., the police received a telephone complaint concerning the meeting, and two officers were detailed to investigate. One of these officers went to the scene immediately, the other arriving some twelve minutes later. They found a crowd of about seventy-five or eighty people, both Negro and white, filling the sidewalk and spreading out into the street. Petitioner, standing on a large wooden box on the sidewalk, was addressing the crowd through a loudspeaker system attached to an automobile. Although the purpose of his speech was to urge his listeners to attend a meeting to be held that night in the Syracuse Hotel, in its course he was making derogatory remarks concerning President Truman, the Ameri-

can Legion, the Mayor of Syracuse, and other local political officials.

The police officers made no effort to interfere with petitioner's speech, but were first concerned with the effect of the crowd on both pedestrian and vehicular traffic. They observed the situation from the opposite side of the street, noting that some pedestrians were forced to walk in the street to avoid the crowd. Since traffic was passing at the time, the officers attempted to get the people listening to petitioner back on the sidewalk. The crowd was restless and there was some pushing, shoving and milling around. One of the officers telephoned the police station from a nearby store, and then both policemen crossed the street and mingled with the crowd without any intention of arresting the speaker.

At this time, petitioner was speaking in a "loud, high-pitched voice." He gave the impression that he was endeavoring to arouse the Negro people against the whites, urging that they rise up in arms and fight for equal rights. The statements before such a mixed audience "stirred up a little excitement." Some of the onlookers made remarks to the police about their inability to handle the crowd and at least one threatened violence if the police did not act. There were others who appeared to be favoring petitioner's arguments. Because of the feeling that existed in the crowd both for and against the speaker, the officers finally "stepped in to prevent it from resulting in a fight." One of the officers approached the petitioner, not for the purpose of arresting him, but to get him to break up the crowd. He asked petitioner to get down off the box, but the latter refused to accede to his request and continued talking. The officer waited for a minute and then demanded that he cease talking. Although the officer had thus twice requested petitioner to stop over the course of several minutes, petitioner not only ignored him but continued talking. During all this time, the crowd was pressing closer around petitioner and the officer. Finally, the officer told petitioner he was under arrest and ordered him to get down from the box, reaching up to grab him. Petitioner stepped down, announcing over the microphone that "the law has arrived, and I suppose they will take over now." In all, the officer had asked petitioner to get down off the box three times over a space of four or five minutes. Petitioner had been speaking for over a half hour.

On these facts, petitioner was specifically charged with . . . [disorderly conduct]. The bill of particulars, demanded by petitioner and furnished by the State, gave in detail the facts upon which the prosecution relied to support the charge of disorderly conduct. Paragraph C is particularly pertinent here: "By ignoring and refusing to heed and obey reasonable police orders issued at the time and place mentioned in the Information to regulate and control said crowd and to prevent a breach or breaches of the peace and to prevent injury to pedestrians attempting to use said walk, and being forced into the highway adjacent to the place in question, and prevent injury to the public generally."

We are not faced here with blind condonation by a state court of arbitrary police action. Petitioner was accorded a full, fair trial. The trial judge heard testimony supporting and contradicting the judgment of the police officers that a clear danger of disorder was threatened. After weighing this contradictory evidence, the trial judge reached the conclusion that the police officers were justified in taking action to prevent a breach of the peace. The exercise of the police officers' proper discretionary power to prevent a breach of the peace was thus approved by the trial court and later by two courts on review. The courts below recognized petitioner's right to hold a street meeting at this locality, to make use of loud-speaking equipment in giving his speech, and to make derogatory remarks concerning public officials and the American Legion. They found that the officers in making the arrest were motivated solely by a proper concern for the preservation of order and protection of the general welfare, and that there was no evidence which could lend color to a claim that the acts of the police were a cover for suppression of petitioner's views and opinions. Petitioner was thus neither arrested nor convicted for the making or the content of his speech. Rather, it was the reaction which it actually engendered.

The language of *Cantwell v. Connecticut* . . . is appropriate here. "The offense known as breach of the peace embraces a great variety of conduct destroying or menacing public order and tranquility. It includes not only violent acts but acts and words likely to produce violence in others. No one would have the hardihood to suggest that the principle of freedom of speech sanctions incitement to riot or that religious liberty connotes the privilege to exhort others to physical attack upon those belonging to another sect. When clear and present danger of riot, disorder, interference with traffic upon the public streets, or other immediate threat to public safety, peace, or order, appears, the power of the State to prevent or punish is obvious." . . . The findings of the New York courts as to the condition of the crowd and the refusal of petitioner to obey the police requests, supported as they are by the record of this case, are persuasive that the conviction of petitioner for violation of public peace, order and authority does not exceed the bounds of proper state police action. This Court respects, as it must, the interest of the community in maintaining peace and order on its streets. . . . We cannot say that the preservation of that interest here encroaches on the constitutional rights of this petitioner.

We are well aware that the ordinary murmurings and objections of a hostile audience cannot be allowed to silence a speaker, and are also mindful of the possible danger of giving overzealous police officials complete discretion to break up otherwise lawful public meetings. "A State may not unduly suppress free communication of views, religious or other, under the guise of conserving desirable conditions." . . .

But we are not faced here with such a situation. It is one thing to say that the police cannot be used as an instrument for the suppression of unpopular views, and another to say that, when as here the speaker passes the bounds of argument or persuasion and undertakes incitement to riot, they are powerless to prevent a breach of the peace. Nor in this case can we condemn the considered judgment of three New York courts approving the means which the police, faced with a crisis, used in the exercise of their power and duty to preserve peace and order. The findings of the state courts as to the existing situation and the imminence of greater disorder coupled with petitioner's deliberate defiance of the police officers convince us that we should not reverse this conviction in the name of free speech.

Affirmed.

Mr. Justice FRANKFURTER concurs in the result.

Mr. Justice BLACK, dissenting. . . .

Mr. Justice DOUGLAS, with whom Mr. Justice MINTON concurs, dissenting.

. . . Public assemblies and public speech occupy an important role in American life. One high function of the police is to protect these lawful gatherings so that the speakers may exercise their constitutional rights. When unpopular causes are sponsored from the public platform, there will commonly be mutterings and unrest and heckling from the crowd. When a speaker mounts a platform it is not unusual to find him resorting to exaggeration, to vilification of ideas and men, to the making of false charges. But those extravagances . . . do not justify penalizing the speaker by depriving him of the platform or by punishing him for his conduct.

A speaker may not, of course, incite a riot any more than he may incite a breach of the peace by the use of "fighting words." . . . But this record shows no such extremes. It shows an unsympathetic audience and the threat of one man to haul the speaker from the stage. It is against that kind of threat that speakers need police protection. If they do not receive it and instead the police throw their weight on the side of those who would break up the meetings, the police become the new censors of speech. Police censorship has all the vices of the censorship from city halls which we have repeatedly struck down. . . .

PAPACHRISTOU V. CITY OF JACKSONVILLE
Supreme Court of the United States, 1972.
405 U.S. 156, 92 S. Ct. 839, 31 L.Ed.2d 110.

[In this seminal case, the U.S. Supreme Court considers the constitutionality of a local vagrancy ordinance.]

Mr. Justice DOUGLAS delivered the opinion of the Court.

This case involves eight defendants who were convicted in a Florida municipal court of violating a Jacksonville, Florida, vagrancy ordinance. Their convictions were affirmed by the Florida Circuit Court in a consolidated appeal, and their petition for certiorari was denied by the District Court of Appeal. . . . The case is here on a petition for certiorari, which we granted. . . . For reasons which will appear, we reverse.

At issue are five consolidated cases. Margaret Papachristou, Betty Calloway, Eugene Eddie Melton, and Leonard Johnson were all arrested early on a Sunday morning, and charged with vagrancy— "prowling by auto."

Jimmy Lee Smith and Milton Henry were charged with vagrancy—"vagabonds."

Henry Edward Heath and a codefendant were arrested for vagrancy—"loitering" and "common thief."

Thomas Owen Campbell was charged with vagrancy—"common thief."

Hugh Brown was charged with vagrancy— "disorderly loitering on street" and "disorderly conduct—resisting arrest with violence."

The facts are stipulated. Papachristou and Calloway are white females. Melton and Johnson are black males. Papachristou was enrolled in a job-training program sponsored by the State Employment Service at Florida Junior College in Jacksonville. Calloway was a typing and shorthand teacher at a state mental institution located near Jacksonville. She was the owner of the automobile in which the four defendants were arrested. Melton was a Vietnam war veteran who had been released from the Navy after nine months in a veterans' hospital. On the date of his arrest he was a part-time computer helper while attending college as a full-time student in Jacksonville. Johnson was a tow-motor operator in a grocery chain warehouse and was a lifelong resident of Jacksonville.

At the time of their arrest the four of them were riding in Calloway's car on the main thoroughfare in Jacksonville. They had left a restaurant owned by Johnson's uncle where they had eaten and were on their way to a nightclub. The arresting officers denied that the racial mixture in the car played any part in the decision to make the arrest. The arrest, they said, was made because the defendants had stopped near a used-car lot which had been broken into several times. There was, however, no evidence of any breaking and entering on the night in question.

Of these four charged with "prowling by auto" none had been previously arrested except Papachristou who had once been convicted of a municipal offense.

Jimmy Lee Smith and Milton Henry (who is not a petitioner) were arrested between 9 and 10 A.M. on a weekday in downtown Jacksonville, while waiting for a friend who was to lend them a car so they could apply for a job at a produce company. Smith was a part-time produce worker and part-time organizer for a Negro political group. He had a common-law wife and three children supported by him and his wife. He had been arrested several times but convicted only once. Smith's companion, Henry, was an 18-year-old high school student with no previous record of arrest.

This morning it was cold, and Smith had no jacket, so they went briefly into a dry cleaning shop to wait, but left when requested to do so. They thereafter walked back and forth two or three times over a two-block stretch looking for their friend. The store owners, who apparently were wary of Smith and his companion, summoned two police officers who searched the men and found neither had a weapon. But they were arrested because the officers said they had no identification and because the officers did not believe their story.

Heath and a codefendant were arrested for "loitering" and for "common thief." Both were residents of Jacksonville, Heath having lived there all his life and being employed at an automobile body shop. Heath had previously been arrested but his codefendant has no arrest record. Heath and his companion were arrested when they drove up to a residence shared by Heath's girl friend and some other girls. Some police officers were already there in the process of arresting another man. When Heath and his companion started backing out of the driveway, the officers signaled to them to stop and asked them to get out of the car, which they did. Thereupon they and the automobile were searched. Although no contraband or incriminating evidence was found, they were both arrested, Heath being charged with being a "common thief" because he was reputed to be a thief. The codefendant was charged with "loitering" because he was standing in the driveway, an act which the officers admitted was done only at their command.

Campbell was arrested as he reached his home very early one morning and was charged with "common thief." He was stopped by officers because he was traveling at a high rate of speed, yet no speeding charge was placed against him.

Brown was arrested when he was observed leaving a downtown Jacksonville hotel by a police officer seated in a cruiser. The police testified he was reputed to be a thief, narcotics pusher, and generally opprobrious character. The officer called Brown over to the car, intending at that time to arrest him unless he had a good explanation for being on the street. Brown walked over to the police cruiser, as commanded, and the officer began to search him, apparently preparatory to placing him in the car. In the process of the search he came on two small packets which were later found to contain heroin. When the officer touched the pocket where the packets were, Brown began to resist. He was charged with "disorderly loitering on street" and "disorderly conduct—resisting arrest with violence." While he was also charged with a narcotics violation, that charge was nolled.

Jacksonville's ordinance and Florida's statute were "derived from early English law," . . . and employ "archaic language" in their definitions of vagrants. . . . The history is an oftentold tale. The breakup of feudal estates in England led to labor shortages which in turn resulted in the Statutes of Laborers, designed to stabilize the labor force by prohibiting increases in wages and prohibiting the movement of workers from their home areas in search of improved conditions. Later vagrancy laws became criminal aspects of the poor laws. The series of laws passed in England on the subject became increasingly severe. But "the theory of the Elizabethan poor laws no longer fits the facts." . . . The conditions which spawned these laws may be gone, but the archaic classifications remain.

This ordinance is void for vagueness, both in the sense that it "fails to give a person of ordinary intelligence fair notice that his contemplated conduct is forbidden by the statute," . . . and because it encourages arbitrary and erratic arrests and convictions. . . .

Living under a rule of law entails various suppositions, one of which is that "[all persons] are entitled to be informed as to what the State commands or forbids." . . .

The poor among us, the minorities, the average householder are . . . not alerted to the regulatory schemes of vagrancy laws; and we assume they would have no understanding of their meaning and impact if they read them. Nor are they protected from being caught in the vagrancy net by the necessity of having a specific intent to commit an unlawful act. . . .

The Jacksonville ordinance makes criminal activities which by modern standards are normally innocent. "Nightwalking" is one. Florida construes the ordinance not to make criminal one night's wandering, . . . only the "habitual" wanderer or, as the ordinance describes it, "common night walkers." We know, however, from experience that sleepless people often walk at night, perhaps hopeful that sleep-inducing relaxation will result.

Luis Munoz-Marin, former Governor of Puerto Rico, commented once that "loafing" was a national virtue in his Commonwealth and that it should be encouraged. It is, however, a crime in Jacksonville.

"[P]ersons able to work but habitually living upon the earnings of their wives or minor children"—like habitually living "without visible means of support"—might implicate unemployed pillars of the community who have married rich wives.

"[P]ersons able to work but habitually living upon the earnings of their wives or minor children"

may also embrace unemployed people out of the labor market, by reason of a recession or disemployed by reason of technological or so-called structural displacements.

Persons "wandering or strolling" from place to place have been extolled by Walt Whitman and Vachel Lindsay. The qualification "without any lawful purpose or object" may be a trap for innocent acts. Persons "neglecting all lawful business and habitually spending their time by frequenting . . . places where alcoholic beverages are sold or served" would literally embrace many members of golf clubs and city clubs.

Walkers and strollers and wanderers may be going to or coming from a burglary. Loafers or loiterers may be "casing" a place for a holdup. Letting one's wife support him is an intra-family matter, and normally of no concern to the police. Yet it may, of course, be the setting for numerous crimes.

The difficulty is that these activities are historically part of the amenities of life as we have known them. They are not mentioned in the Constitution or in the Bill of Rights. These unwritten amenities have been in part responsible for giving our people the feeling of independence and self-confidence, the feeling of creativity. These amenities have dignified the right of dissent and have honored the right to be nonconformists and the right to defy submissiveness. They have encouraged lives of high spirits rather than hushed, suffocating silence. . . .

This aspect of the vagrancy ordinance before us is suggested by what this Court said in 1876 about a broad criminal statute enacted by Congress: "It would certainly be dangerous if the legislature could set a net large enough to catch all possible offenders, and leave it to the courts to step inside and say who could be rightfully detained, and who should be set at large." . . .

Another aspect of the ordinance's vagueness appears when we focus, not on the lack of notice given a potential offender, but on the effect of the unfettered discretion it places in the hands of the Jacksonville police. Caleb Foote, an early student of this subject, has called the vagrancy-type law as offering "punishment by analogy." . . . Such crimes, though long common in Russia, are not compatible with our constitutional system. We allow our police to make arrests only on "probable cause," a Fourth and

Fourteenth Amendment standard applicable to the States as well as to the Federal Government. Arresting a person on suspicion, like arresting a person for investigation, is foreign to our system, even when the arrest is for past criminality. Future criminality, however, is the common justification for the presence of vagrancy statutes. . . . Florida has, indeed, construed her vagrancy statute "as necessary regulations," inter alia, "to deter vagabondage and prevent crimes."

A direction by a legislature to the police to arrest all "suspicious" persons would not pass constitutional muster. A vagrancy prosecution may be merely the cloak for a conviction which could not be obtained on the real but undisclosed grounds for the arrest. . . .

Those generally implicated by the imprecise terms of the ordinance—poor people, nonconformists, dissenters, idlers—may be required to comport themselves according to the lifestyle deemed appropriate by the Jacksonville police and the courts. Where, as here, there are no standards governing the exercise of the discretion granted by the ordinance, the scheme permits and encourages an arbitrary and discriminatory enforcement of the law. It furnishes a convenient tool for "harsh and discriminatory enforcement by local prosecuting officials, against particular groups deemed to merit their displeasure."
. . .

A presumption that people who might walk or loaf or loiter or stroll or frequent houses where liquor is sold or who are supported by their wives or who look suspicious to the police are to become future criminals is too precarious for a rule of law. The implicit presumption in these generalized vagrancy standards—that crime is being nipped in the bud—is too extravagant to deserve extended treatment. Of course, vagrancy statutes are useful to the police. Of course, they are nets making easy the roundup of so called undesirables. But the rule of law implies equality and justice in its application. Vagrancy laws of the Jacksonville type teach that the scales of justice are so tipped even-handed administration of the law is not possible. The rule of law, evenly applied to minorities as well as majorities, to the poor as well as the rich, is the great mucilage that holds society together.

The Jacksonville ordinance cannot be squared with our constitutional standards and is plainly unconstitutional.

Reversed.

Mr. Justice POWELL and Mr. Justice REHNQUIST took no part in the consideration or decision of this case.

STATE v. YOUNG
Court of Appeals of Ohio, 1988.
50 Ohio App. 3d 17, 552 N.E.2d 226.

[Kevin W. Young was convicted of violating Ohio R.C. 4511.44 by failing to yield to approaching traffic. In this appeal to the Ohio Court of Appeals, Young claims the trial judge erred in interpreting the statute under which he was convicted].

McCORMAC, Judge.
. . . On April 10, 1987, defendant was driving southbound on U.S. Route 33 through Nelsonville when he noted a traffic jam caused by an accident. To avoid the traffic jam, Young pulled into a private

driveway leading to the Nelsonville Sewage Treatment Plant and turned around.

At this point, U.S. Route 33 has three lanes—a southbound, a northbound, and a center lane, which is a turning lane only.

Young wanted to turn north onto U.S. 33. He waited in the private driveway until a car in the southbound lane of U.S. 33 motioned for him to go. Young drove across the southbound lane before he turned north. He testified that he looked to see if there was any traffic coming but he could not see anything until he got to the center lane because his vision was blocked by stopped traffic.

Officer Waggoner was traveling southbound on U.S. 33 in the center turn lane going thirty miles an hour. He testified that he was trying to get to a car accident and that he could not travel in the normal lane because it was backed up. Officer Waggoner had on his warning lights, but not his siren. He testified that he was trying to turn on his siren, which is located on the floor. When he looked up, Young's car was across the center lane. The two cars collided.

Defendant argues that the trial court erred in interpreting R.C. 4511.44 to require motorists to yield the right-of-way to illegally operated oncoming traffic.

R.C. 4511.44 specifies that a driver entering or crossing a highway from any place other than another roadway shall "yield the right-of-way to all traffic approaching on the roadway to be entered or crossed." R.C. 4511.01(UU) states that:

> " 'Right of way' means the right of a vehicle . . . to proceed uninterruptedly in a lawful manner in the direction in which it or he is moving in preference to another vehicle . . . approaching from a different direction into its or his path."

This definition of right-of-way must be used in conjunction with R.C. 4511.44. . . . Thus, in order to find a defendant guilty of the criminal violation of R.C. 4511.44, it is necessary to find that defendant failed to yield to a vehicle proceeding uninterrupt-

edly in a lawful manner because those are the elements of the offense. It is not sufficient simply to find that defendant was negligent, careless or at fault, partially or totally, in causing the accident.

The issue then is whether the police officer proceeding in the turn-only lane at thirty miles an hour displaying warning lights, but not using his siren, was proceeding in a lawful manner. That question must be answered in the negative. An operator of a public safety vehicle may drive in a turn-only lane lawfully only if he uses at least one flashing, rotating, or oscillating light visible under normal atmospheric conditions from a condition of five hundred feet from the front of the vehicle and he gives an audible signal by siren, exhaust whistle, or bell. . . . The evidence is clear that the police officer failed to give an audible signal and that, therefore, he lost his preferential status as the driver of an emergency vehicle by operating his vehicle unlawfully. . . . Moreover, there was not due regard for the safety of all persons and property on the highway when the police officer drove thirty miles an hour in a turn-only lane, particularly when he failed to use his siren.

Appellant's assignment of error is sustained. The judgment of the trial court is reversed, and the cause is remanded to the trial court with instructions to enter final judgment for defendant.

Judgment reversed and cause remanded.

GREY, P.J., and STEPHENSON, J., concur.

UNITED STATES V. EVANS
United States Court of Appeals, Ninth Circuit, 1991.
928 F.2d 858.

[In this case, the Ninth Circuit Court of Appeals considers the constitutionality of the federal statute that prohibits possession of unregistered machine guns, 26 U.S.C. Sec. 5861(d) (1982). The appellant, Creed M. Evans, was convicted in U.S. District Court of making false statements to the Bureau of Alcohol, Tobacco, and Firearms. In his appeal, Evans

argues that the mere possession of machine guns is not sufficiently related to interstate commerce to permit Congress to make it a criminal offense.]

WIGGINS, Circuit Judge:
. . . Evans contends that Congress lacks the power to prohibit the mere possession of unregistered ma-

chine guns without requiring proof of a nexus with interstate commerce. The general standard by which a statute that is said to violate the Commerce Clause is to be measured is firmly established. Although we independently review the validity of an act that is said to violate the Commerce Clause, . . . our review is conducted in a highly deferential manner. We consider whether a reasonable Congress could find that the class of activity regulated affects interstate commerce. . . . Congress need not make specific findings of fact to support its conclusion that a class of activity affects interstate commerce. . . . However, if Congress does make such findings, they carry great weight in this court's analysis. . . .

The statutes at issue in this case easily meet this standard. Congress specifically found that at least 750,000 people had been killed in the United States by firearms between the turn of the century and the time of the Act's enactment. It was thus reasonable for Congress to conclude that the possession of firearms affects the national economy, if only through the insurance industry. Since Evans does not contend that any specific Constitutional rights are implicated, this rather tenuous nexus between the activity regulated and interstate commerce is sufficient. . . .

We AFFIRM the judgement of the District Court.

CHAPTER 12

OFFENSES AGAINST JUSTICE AND PUBLIC ADMINISTRATION

CHAPTER OUTLINE

Introduction
The Common-Law
   Background
Bribery
Perjury
Obstruction of Justice
Resisting Arrest
Compounding a Crime
Escape
Criminal Contempt
Conclusion

Cases
State v. Gustafson
United States v. Scott
People v. Gettings
State v. Ring
State v. Blanton

INTRODUCTION

We are shocked to read headlines that tell of public officials convicted of corruption and bribery. Likewise, we question the effectiveness of the judicial process when we learn that perjured testimony has sent an innocent person to prison. And, we are frightened by the television announcement that a dangerous criminal has escaped and is at large. Incidents like this remind us of the fallibility of our criminal justice system. We would like to believe that such events are sensational because they are so unusual. Unfortunately, they are all too common. Yet, we must realize that as our nation has become more densely populated, urbanized, and technological, our relationships have become less personal. These and other factors have resulted in an increased need for the criminal law to serve as a deterrent, and where necessary, as a means to punish those who breach the public trust and those who corrupt the orderly processes of government and the justice system by their actions.

THE COMMON-LAW BACKGROUND

Common-law judges found it essential to create certain offenses to maintain the integrity of the law and the administration of justice. Principally, these offenses were bribery, perjury and subornation of perjury, obstruction of justice, compounding a crime, and escape. At common law, these offenses were misdemeanors. Additionally the common law developed the concept of criminal contempt to enable judges to maintain the dignity and authority of the courts and the respect due judicial officers.

As the administration of justice became more sophisticated, these offenses were codified and, in many instances, classified as felonies by federal and state jurisdictions. Criminal contempt, while not a crime in the technical sense, is now regarded as a crime for virtually all purposes. These traditional common-law offenses have been expanded and augmented by a variety of modern statutes.

BRIBERY

The concept of bribery dates back to biblical times. From early in religious history it was regarded as sinful to attempt to influence the judge with a gift, because the judge represented the divine. Thus, when the common law developed the crime of bribery, it sought to penalize only persons whose actions were designed to improperly influence those identified with the administration of justice. Later, it was considered bribery for anyone to give or receive anything of value or any valuable service or promise with the intent to influence any public officer in the discharge of a legal duty. See *People v. Patillo*, 54 N.E.2d 548 (Ill. 1944).

The Modern Statutory Offense of Bribery

Today, federal statutes proscribe bribery of public officers and witnesses as well as jurors and government employees and functionaries. 18 U.S.C.A. § 201. State statutes generally define bribery in broad terms and frequently address specific situations as well. The trend has been to enlarge the common-law approach by extending the offense to new categories of persons and conduct and by making the punishment more severe. The broad statutory definition of bribery is illustrated by the Florida law that provides:

"Bribery" means corruptly to give, offer, or promise to any public servant, or, if a public servant, corruptly to request, solicit, accept, or agree to accept for himself or another, any pecuniary or other benefit with an intent or purpose to influence the performance of any act or omission which the person believes to be, or the public servant represents as being, within the official discretion of a public servant, in violation of a public duty, or in performance of a public duty. Fla. Stat. Ann. § 838.015(1).

Courts generally construe such terms as *public servant* and *benefit* broadly, to accomplish the intended legislative purpose of statutes defining bribery. The quoted statute makes explicit that the person bribed need not have authority to accomplish the act sought or represented. Irrespective of statutes, courts generally hold that where the act intended to be influenced is connected with a person's public duty, it is immaterial whether the person bribed has the authority to do a specific act. See, for example, *State v. Hendricks*, 186 P.2d 943 (Ariz. 1947).

The Range of Bribery Offenses

Acts sought to be accomplished by bribes cover a wide range of conduct. Common examples include obtaining the release or acquittal of an arrestee, securing an award of a government contract, and even obtaining a favorable vote by a legislator on a pending bill. Although we commonly think of money being offered or requested as a bribe, a variety of other things are offered, sought, or exchanged. These not only include tangible items, but also sometimes extend to price advantages, use of vehicles, vacation homes, and even sexual favors.

The Burden of the Prosecution

The gist of the crime of bribery is the unlawful offer or agreement to do something under color of office. Ordinarily, the prosecution must prove not only the offer or agreement or the request or acceptance of a benefit but also that the defendant had a false or corrupt intent. One of the difficulties encountered in prosecuting a bribery charge is establishing the corrupt intent element. For example, it can be extremely difficult to prove that a person received employment or was granted a contract as a result of a bribe. The difficulty is compounded because not infrequently bribes are disguised as gifts or even as political or charitable contributions.

Offenses Extending the Concept of Bribery

Many states have enacted statutes to extend the offense of bribery to encompass conduct of persons other than public officials and employees. These states have classified certain corrupt business practices as "commercial bribery." The New

---

CASE IN POINT

BRIBERY: WHAT CONSTITUTES A *THING OF VALUE*?

Defendant was convicted of bribery under an Alabama statute that provided that it was bribery for any public official to accept "any gift, gratuity, or other thing of value." On appeal, defendant argued that "sexual intercourse, or the promise of sexual intercourse, or the promise of other sexual favors or relationship" did not meet the test of being a "thing of value" under the bribery statute. The Alabama Court of Criminal Appeals rejected the defendant's contention, saying, "The word 'thing' does not necessarily mean a substance. . . . [I]t includes an act, or action."

McDonald v. State, 329 So.2d 583 (Ala. Crim. App. 1975), *cert. quashed*, 329 So.2d 596 (Ala. 1976), *cert. denied*, 429 U.S. 834, 97 S. Ct. 99, 50 L.Ed.2d 99 (1976).

Jersey law making commercial bribery a crime is comprehensive and, as amended in 1986, provides:

Section 2C:21–10:

a. A person commits a crime if he solicits, accepts or agrees to accept any benefit as consideration for knowingly violating or agreeing to violate a duty of fidelity to which he is subject as:

(1). An agent, partner or employee of another;

(2). A trustee, guardian, or other fiduciary;

(3). A lawyer, physician, accountant, appraiser, or other professional adviser or informant;

(4). An officer, director, manager or other participant in the direction of the affairs of an incorporated or unincorporated association;

(5). A labor official, including any duly appointed representative of a labor organization or any duly appointed trustee or representative of an employee welfare trust fund; or

(6). An arbitrator or other purportedly disinterested adjudicator or referee.

b. A person who holds himself out to the public as being engaged in the business of making disinterested selection, appraisal, or criticism of commodities, real properties or services commits a crime if he solicits, accepts or agrees to accept any benefit to influence his selection, appraisal or criticism.

c. A person commits a crime if he confers, or offers or agrees to confer, any benefit the acceptance of which would be criminal under this section.

N.J. Stat. Ann. § 2C:21–10.

Under the New Jersey statute the benefit offered, conferred, agreed to be conferred, solicited, accepted, or agreed to determines the degree of the crime and the penalty.

Most states now have made it a criminal offense to offer anything of value to a participant or official in an amateur or professional athletic contest to vary his or her performance, or for a participant or official in a sports event to accept a bribe under such circumstances. See, for example, Iowa Code Ann. § 722.3; *State v. Di Paglia*, 71 N.W.2d 601 (Iowa 1955).

Defenses to the Crime of Bribery

Of course, the fact that an offer to bribe is not legally enforceable is no defense. The only recognized defense to a charge of bribery, other than denial, is entrapment. See *State v. Harrington*, 332 So.2d 764 (La. 1976). The defense of entrapment is discussed in Chapter 13.

PERJURY

Like bribery, the crime of perjury has its roots in biblical times. The Mosaic Code included an admonition against the bearing of false witness. At common law perjury came to consist of willfully giving under oath in a judicial proceeding false testimony material to the issue. *Commonwealth v. Hinkle*, 197 S.W. 455 (Ky. 1917). Because of the narrow scope of the offense, it was eventually supplemented by the common-law offense of false swearing, a crime committed when an oath was taken in other than a judicial proceeding.

Elements of the Offense of Perjury

These common-law offenses have been codified by federal law, 18 U.S.C.A. § 1621, that provides:

> Whoever (1) having taken an oath before a competent tribunal, officer, or person, in any case in which a law of the United States authorizes an oath to be administered, that he will testify, declare, depose, or certify truly, or that any written testimony, declaration, deposition, or certificate by him subscribed, is true, willfully and contrary to such oath states or subscribes any material matter which he does not believe to be true; or (2) in any declaration, certificate, verification, or statement under penalty of perjury as permitted under section 1746 of title 28, United States Code, willfully subscribes as true any material matter which he does not believe to be true; is guilty of perjury. . . .

All states have laws making perjury a criminal offense. For example, the California perjury statute provides that a person who has taken an oath to tell the truth and who "wilfully and contrary to such oath, states as true any material matter which he knows to be false" is guilty of perjury. West's Ann. Cal. Penal Code § 118. While Section 118 relates to oaths in administrative and judicial proceedings, Section 118 (a) makes it perjury for a person to give a false affidavit to be used in those proceedings. As in other jurisdictions, additional California statutes make it unlawful for anyone to give a false statement under oath in various applications, certificates, and reports.

The Burden of the Prosecution

To convict a defendant of perjury, the prosecution must establish that the defendant took an oath to tell the truth and knowingly made a false statement of fact. Statutes usually permit anyone with scruples against taking an oath to affirm that a statement is true. In either event, a person cannot be lawfully convicted of perjury unless there is proof that he or she was administered the oath by or made an affirmation before someone with legal authority. *Whitaker v. Commonwealth*, 367 S.W.2d 831 (Ky. 1963). Furthermore, the defendant's statement must have been material. This means that the testimony given by the defendant must have been capable of influencing the tribunal on the issues before it. *United States v. Jackson*, 640 F.2d 614 (8th Cir. 1981), *cert. denied*, 454 U.S. 1057, 102 S. Ct. 605, 70 L.Ed.2d 594 (1981), The vast majority of jurisdictions hold that the question of materiality in a prosecution for perjury is an issue to be decided by the judge. In 1992, the New Jersey Supreme Court disagreed. That court held unconstitutional a portion of the state's perjury statute that directed this issue be determined by the court. The court reasoned that since materiality is an element of the crime of perjury, the Constitution requires that the jury must determine that element of the crime, as others, beyond a reasonable doubt. *State v. Anderson*, 603 A.2d 928 (N.J. 1992).

Some statutes that define perjury require the prosecution to prove that the defendant's statement was made with the "intent to deceive." See, for example, Vernon's Tex. Penal Code Ann. § 37.02(a). Irrespective of statutory requirements, most jurisdictions require the prosecution to prove that the defendant's false statement was made "willfully and corruptly," because at common law perjury was a specific-intent crime. Requiring the prosecution to prove the defendant's specific intent generally eliminates the likelihood of a defendant being convicted for simply having made a careless or offhanded statement.

Perjury is frequently said to be one of the most difficult crimes to prove. The inherent difficulty of convicting a defendant of this offense is exacerbated by the "two witness rule" that prevails in most jurisdictions. Under this rule the prosecution must prove the falsity of a defendant's statements either by two witnesses or by one witness and corroborating documents or circumstances. See, for example, McKinney's N.Y. Penal Law § 210.50.

Perjury by Contradictory Statements

Early American cases followed the common-law principle that a defendant could not be convicted of perjury based on having made two contradictory statements unless the prosecution established which one of the statements was false. *Paytes v. State*, 191 S.W. 975 (Tenn. 1917). This rule of law has now been largely eliminated by statutes that make it unnecessary for the prosecution to establish which of two contradictory statements is false to obtain a conviction. See, for example, McKinney's N.Y. Penal Law § 210.20; West's Fla. Stat. Ann. § 837.021(3).

Subornation of Perjury

At common law subornation of perjury consisted of instigating or procuring another person to commit perjury. *State v. Chambers*, 104 S.E. 670 (N.C. 1920). Subornation of perjury is now generally defined by statutes much as it was at common law. To convict a defendant of the offense, the prosecution must first establish that the defendant induced another to testify falsely and that an actual perjury has been committed. *State v. Devers*, 272 A.2d 794 (Md. 1971), *cert. denied*, 404 U.S. 824, 92 S. Ct. 50, 30 L.Ed.2d 52 (1971). Thus, the Tennessee Supreme Court upheld a subornation of perjury conviction of an attorney for counseling

---

CASE IN POINT

PERJURY: THE TRUTH MUST BE UNEQUIVOCAL

A police officer was convicted of committing perjury on the basis of his denial of having received money from certain persons while in performance of his police duties. On appeal, he argued that his answer, "No sir. Not for my duties," to the prosecutor's question whether he received any money from any persons while on official duty as a Chicago policeman was literally true and therefore formed no basis for his conviction. The United States Court of Appeals, Seventh Circuit, rejected his contention. The court explained his initial response, "No sir," was directly responsive and false, so that his nonresponsive attempted hedge that followed was not effective.

United States v. Nickels, 502 F.2d 1173 (7th Cir. 1974), *cert. denied*, 426 U.S. 911, 96 S. Ct. 2237, 48 L.Ed.2d 837 (1976).

---

four men charged with illegally selling whiskey to commit perjury. The attorney was prosecuted, however, only after his four clients were convicted. *Grant v. State*, 374 S.W.2d 391 (Tenn. 1964).

Defenses to the Crime of Perjury

Truth, of course, is a complete defense to a charge of perjury; therefore, a defendant who while under oath gives an answer that is "literally accurate, technically responsive or legally truthful" cannot lawfully be convicted of perjury. *United States v. Wall*, 371 F.2d 398, 400 (6th Cir. 1967).

After making a false statement under oath, a witness sometimes recants and tells the truth. If this recantation occurs before the original tribunal where the testimony was given, some state courts hold it to be a defense. For example, New York courts have held that recantation is a defense, provided it occurs promptly, before the body conducting the inquiry (e.g., a grand jury) has been deceived or any prejudice has occurred, and before the defendant's perjury has most likely become known to the authorities. *People v. Ezaugi*, 141 N.E.2d 580 (N.Y. 1957). On the other hand, many courts take the position that a subsequent recantation, even on cross-examination, is no defense to a charge that a witness has made a perjurious statement. See, for example, *State v. Phillips*, 259 P.2d 185 (Kan. 1953).

Federal law provides for a recantation defense to a prosecution for perjury if the perjured testimony has not substantially affected the proceedings, or it has not become manifest that such falsity has been or will be exposed. 18 U.S.C.A. § 1623(d). To avail of the defense, a defendant must unequivocally repudiate his or her prior testimony. *United States v. Tobias*, 863 F.2d 685 (9th Cir. 1988).

OBSTRUCTION OF JUSTICE

At common law it was a crime to commit an act obstructing or tending to obstruct public justice. See *Baker v. State*, 178 S.E.2d 278 (Ga. App. 1970), *cert.*

denied, 401 U.S. 1012, 91 S. Ct. 1265, 28 L.Ed.2d 549 (1971). Likewise, the perversion of governmental administration was a common-law offense. *Commonwealth v. McKarski,* 222 A.2d 411 (Pa. Super. 1966).

Modern Statutory Development

Several federal statutes make it unlawful to obstruct federal officials in execution of writs and other court processes; to tamper with or retaliate against witnesses, informants, and victims; or to obstruct criminal investigations. Additional federal statutes proscribe interference with governmental proceedings, court orders, jurors, and court officers. See 18 U.S.C.A. §§ 1501–1515.

Postal laws make it an offense to willfully and knowingly obstruct or retard the passage of the mail. 18 U.S.C.A. § 1701. Thus, in *United States v. Upshaw,* 895 F.2d 109 (3d Cir. 1990), a federal appeals court upheld a defendant's conviction for obstructing mail where a postal truck driver took home a package after he signed out from work.

All jurisdictions have statutes proscribing interference with officers in the performance of their duties. Some statutes define obstruction to embrace many forms of conduct. Common examples include making it unlawful to give false information to an officer with the intent to interfere with the officer's lawful performance of duties; to impersonate an officer; to intimidate a victim or witness; and to tamper with a juror or with physical evidence to be offered in official proceedings. Many states have comprehensive statutes making it an offense to refuse to render assistance to law enforcement officers or to prevent, hinder, or delay the discovery or apprehension of persons sought by law enforcement.

The Citizen's Duty to Assist Law Enforcement Officers

Citizens have a duty to come to the assistance of law enforcement officers upon request. Rather typical of the statutory mandates in this area is the Ohio law that states:

> No person shall negligently fail or refuse to aid a law enforcement officer, when called upon for assistance in preventing or halting the commission of an offense, or in apprehending or detaining an offender, when such aid can be given without a substantial risk of physical harm to the person giving it. Ohio Rev. Code Ann. § 2921.23(a).

RESISTING ARREST

All jurisdictions make it unlawful for a person to resist arrest. The common law did not permit a person to resist a lawful arrest by an authorized officer of the law. It did, however, permit a person to use force to resist an unlawful arrest. *United States v. Heliczer,* 373 F.2d 241 (2d Cir. 1967), *cert. denied,* 388 U.S. 917, 87 S.Ct. 2133, 18 L.Ed.2d 1359 (1967). Until recently this rule of law was applied in most American jurisdictions, but the functioning of the rule in modern society brought about the need to change it. The legality of an arrest may frequently be a close question, and since officers will normally overcome resistance with necessary force, there is a great danger of escalating violence between the officer and the arrestee. Thus, courts have been reexamining this common-law doctrine and holding that there is no longer authority to use physical force to resist an arrest by a police officer, whether such arrest is legal or illegal. See *Miller v. State*, 462 P.2d 421 (Alaska 1969).

Legislatures, too, have reexamined the issue of using physical force in resisting arrest. In 1980, the New York legislature amended its penal law to provide:

> A person may not use physical force to resist an arrest, whether authorized or unauthorized, which is being effected or attempted by a police officer or peace officer when it would reasonably appear that the latter is a police officer or peace officer. McKinney's N.Y. Penal Law § 35.27.

Oregon law provides: "A person commits the crime of resisting arrest if the person intentionally resists a person known by the person to be a peace officer in making an arrest." Or. Rev. Stat. § 162.315(1). In *State v. Wright*, 799 P.2d 642 (Or. 1990), the Oregon Supreme Court held that a person may not lawfully resist arrest, even if the arresting officer lacked the legal authority to make the arrest, provided that the officer was acting under color of official authority. Additionally, the court observed that if a police officer uses excessive force in making an arrest, the arrestee may use only such physical force as is reasonably necessary to defend against such excessive force.

The modern statutory and judicial revisions to the common-law approach make sense. It is not too great a burden today for a person who believes himself or herself unlawfully arrested to submit to the officer and seek legal remedies in court. Unlike the conditions that existed when the common law developed the rule permitting an arrestee to use force, legal counsel is readily available today. Moreover, today's detention facilities do not resemble the crude dungeons where arrestees were incarcerated for lengthy periods prior to arraignment under the English common law. The abandonment of the common-law rule is another example of a rule of law ceasing to exist when the rationale for it has ceased to exist.

COMPOUNDING A CRIME

At common law a person who accepted money or something else of value in exchange for agreeing not to prosecute a felony was guilty of compounding a felony. *State v. Hodge*, 55 S.E. 626 (N.C. 1906). Likewise, the common law considered it a misdemeanor to compound a misdemeanor, if the misdemeanor was an offense against public justice and dangerous to society. *State v. Carver*, 39 A. 973 (N.H. 1898). To conceal a felony was also a common-law offense known as misprision of felony. This latter offense was justified by the person's common-law duty to inform authorities about any felony of which that person had knowledge. *Commonwealth v. Lopes*, 61 N.E.2d 849 (Mass. 1945).

The Modern Statutory Approach

The legal theory underlying making it an offense to compound a crime is that it debases justice to allow an offender to bargain to escape the consequences of his or her crime. Most states have enacted statutes making it a crime to compound a felony, but some have expanded the common-law rule by making it a crime to compound any offense. To illustrate, New Hampshire law provides that a person is guilty of a misdemeanor who:

1. Solicits, accepts, or agrees to accept any benefit as consideration for his refraining from initiating or aiding in a criminal prosecution; or
2. Confers, offers, or agrees to confer any benefit upon another as consideration for such person refraining from initiating or aiding in a criminal prosecution.
3. It is an affirmative defense that the value of the benefit did not exceed an amount which the actor believed to be due as restitution or indemnification for the loss caused, or to be caused by the offense. N.H. Rev. Stat. Ann. § 642:5.

Most states have not made misprision of felony a statutory crime, probably relying on enforcement of statutes making it an offense to become an accessory after the fact to an offense (see Chapter 4). The federal criminal code, however, specifically makes misprision of felony a crime, the gist of the offense being concealment and not merely the failure to report a felony. 18 U.S.C.A. § 4.

A Common Scenario of Compounding a Crime

The offense of compounding a crime often appears where a crime victim whose goods have been stolen agrees with the thief to take back the goods in exchange for not prosecuting. Such an action would ordinarily constitute an offense by the victim. But the New Hampshire statute makes it an affirmative defense that the value of the benefit did not exceed that which the actor believed due as restitution for a loss. In some instances courts will approve dismissal of a prosecution upon an agreement for restitution to the victim, but persons should not reach such an agreement without prior court approval.

ESCAPE

At common law a person who departed from lawful custody committed the crime of escape. Where the prisoner used force, the offense came to be known as prison break. Finally, a person who forcibly freed another from lawful custody was guilty of the offense of rescue. See *State v. Sutton*, 84 N.E. 824 (Ind. 1908).

Modern Statutory Approaches to Escape

Statutes proscribing escape are generally broad enough to embrace all three of the common-law offenses relating to escape. Often the punishment is more severe when force has been used. Federal statutes prohibit a person who has been lawfully arrested or confined from escaping or attempting to escape from custody, 18 U.S.C.A. § 751, or from rescuing or attempting to rescue a federal prisoner, 18 U.S.C.A. § 752. Most state statutes define escape in rather simple terms. For example, Texas law provides that a person commits the offense of escape "if he escapes from custody when he is: (1) under arrest for, charged with, or convicted of an offense; or (2) in custody pursuant to a lawful order of court." Vernon's Tex. Penal Code Ann. § 38.07.

The Elements of the Offense of Escape

The gist of the offense of escape is the prisoner's departure from lawful custody. Lawful custody is generally presumed once the prosecutor establishes that the escapee was confined to an institution specified by law. In other instances it may be essential for the prosecutor to establish proof of lawful custody; however, those who escape from a jail, juvenile detention home, penal institution, or reformatory are usually presumed to have been in lawful custody. Likewise, a person who fails to return to detention following a temporary release or furlough generally falls within the ambit of escape statutes.

Of course, if a statute requires specific intent, the prosecution must establish this before a conviction can be lawfully obtained. Absent an explicit statutory requirement, courts are divided on the issue of whether the prosecution must prove the defendant's specific intent to avoid lawful confinement. The Supreme Court has held that under the federal statute, the government need only prove that the escapee knew that his or her actions would result in leaving confinement without permission. *United States v. Bailey,* 444 U.S. 394, 100 S. Ct. 624, 62 L.Ed.2d 575 (1980).

State appellate courts have split on whether the prosecution must prove that the escapee intended to leave or be absent from lawful custody. Recognizing that a slim majority of jurisdictions hold that intent is not an element of the crime, a Florida appellate court in 1975 held that the state must prove that a defendant intended to leave or be absent from lawful custody, despite the lack of such a statutory requirement in Florida law. In justifying its position the court raised some interesting "horribles" under which a defendant charged with escape could be improperly convicted if the state were not required to establish the escapee's specific intent to avoid lawful confinement. In one scenario the court hypothesized that a road gang member had fallen asleep under a tree and was left behind by a negligent guard. The prisoner awakened only to find the guards and work detail had returned to the prison. Because of such possibilities the court opted for what it considered the better view of requiring the prosecution to establish the defendant's specific intent. *Helton v. State,* 311 So.2d 381 (Fla. App. 1975).

Defenses to the Charge of Escape

It occasionally occurs that an innocent person has been unlawfully confined. Nevertheless, if custody was lawful, the fact that a person was innocent is not generally recognized as a defense to a charge of escape. See *Woods v. Commonwealth,* 152 S.W.2d 997 (Ky. 1941). Of course, a person who escapes can always assert the defense of unlawful confinement or custody. *State v. Dickson,* 288 N.W.2d 48 (Neb. 1980).

In 1980 the United States Supreme Court recognized the defense of necessity as being valid in the context of the crime of escape. To sustain the defense, the Court said a prisoner must demonstrate (1) that because of an imminent threat of harm, escape was the prisoner's only reasonable alternative; and (2) that the prisoner made a bona fide effort to surrender or return to custody as soon as the duress or necessity lost its coercive force. *United States v. Bailey*, 444 U.S. 394, 100 S.Ct. 624, 62 L.Ed.2d 575 (1980).

Legislatures generally respond to public opinion, and improvement of prison conditions is not a high priority for most voters. Since courts tend to focus on issues where the legislative process affords no relief, they will undoubtedly continue to give attention to complaints concerning prison conditions. As they do, prisoners will most likely seek to extend the defense of necessity to justify an escape based on the inadequacy of prison conditions. Some have already argued that the denial of needed medical care should be recognized as a defense to escape. Until now courts have generally refused to accept such a defense. See, for example, *Commonwealth v. Stanley*, 446 A.2d 583 (Pa. 1982).

The guidelines established by the court in *Lovercamp* have been favorably received by other appellate courts. See, for example, *People v. Unger*, 338 N.E.2d 442 (Ill. App. 1975), *aff'd.*, 362 N.E.2d 319 (Ill. 1977); *State v. Alcantaro*, 407 So.2d 922 (Fla. App. 1981), *rev. denied*, 413 So.2d 875 (Fla. 1982).

CRIMINAL CONTEMPT

Early in the history of the common law, judges began to exercise the power to punish persons whose conduct interfered with the orderly functioning of the courts in the administration of justice. Federal and state courts exercise the power to hold an offender—sometimes called a "contemnor"—in either civil or criminal contempt.

Civil contempt is beyond the scope of this text. Suffice it to say it is a sanction imposed to coerce a recalcitrant person to obey a court order. For example, a court may hold someone in civil contempt for failing to pay court-ordered support for dependents.

The power of the federal courts to hold persons in criminal contempt is recognized by statute. 21 U.S.C.A. § 401. However, even in the absence of statutory recognition, the courts are deemed to have broad inherent powers to hold persons in contempt. See, for example, *Martin v. Waters*, 259 S.E.2d 153 (Ga. App. 1979); *United States v. Wendy*, 575 F.2d 1025 (2d Cir. 1978).

The Purpose of Imposing Criminal Contempt

A court imposes criminal contempt to punish an offender whose deliberate conduct is calculated to obstruct or embarrass the court or to degrade a judicial officer in the role of administering justice. Intent is always an element in criminal contempt proceedings.

CASE IN POINT

Escape: a Limited Defense of Duress or Necessity

During the 1970s there was considerable focus on the conditions of our prisons. This is illustrated by a landmark California decision in 1974. Defendant Marsha Lovercamp was attacked by other inmates demanding sex. Prison authorities failed to provide Lovercamp with adequate protection and she escaped. She was found guilty of escape, but an appellate court awarded her a new trial because the trial judge had denied her the opportunity to submit evidence of her plight as a justification for her escape. In reversing Lovercamp's conviction, the appellate court enumerated guidelines for asserting the defense of duress or necessity in these situations. The court opined that a limited defense is available if the following conditions exist:

(1) The prisoner is faced with a specific threat of death, forcible sexual attack or substantial bodily injury in the immediate future;

(2) There is no time for a complaint to the authorities or there exists a history of futile complaints which make any result from such complaints illusory;

(3) There is no time or opportunity to resort to the courts;

(4) There is no evidence of force or violence used toward prison personnel or other "innocent" persons in the escape; and

(5) The prisoner immediately reports to the proper authorities when he has attained a position of safety from the immediate threat.

People v. Lovercamp, 118 Cal. Rptr. 110 (Cal. App. 1974).

Criminal contempt is classified as either direct or indirect. Direct contempt is contemptuous behavior committed in the presence of the court. Disruption of the examination of a witness or an assault on a judge or juror are examples of direct contempt. Indirect contempt, sometimes called constructive contempt, occurs outside the court's presence. An illustration of indirect contempt would be a juror discussing the facts of a case with a news reporter at a lunch break before the trial of a case has been completed.

Is Criminal Contempt a Crime?

Until the 1960s there was considerable division of thinking on this subject. In 1968 the United States Supreme Court in *Bloom v. Illinois*, 391 U.S. 194, 88 S. Ct. 1477, 20 L.Ed.2d 522 (1968), held that criminal contempt is a crime in the ordinary sense and may be punished by fine, imprisonment, or both. A person charged with criminal contempt is presumed innocent and must be afforded the procedural and substantive benefits of due process of law. Consequently, a contemnor must be proven guilty beyond a reasonable doubt before being held in criminal contempt. In some states, criminal contempt has been made a statutory crime. See, for example, McKinney's N.Y. Penal Law § 215.50–51.

Direct and Indirect Criminal Contempt

Direct criminal contempt proceedings are usually handled summarily. The judge must inform the contemnor of the accusation and ask if he or she can show any cause to preclude the court from entering a judgment of contempt. The court then proceeds to enter its judgment accordingly. Courts justify the summary character of these proceedings because the contemptuous act has occurred in the presence of the judge.

The process is more formal in indirect contempt proceedings. The judge is required to issue a written order to the contemnor to show cause as to why he or she should not be held in contempt of court. The order must set forth the essential facts of the charge and allow the contemnor a reasonable time to prepare a defense. The judge tries all issues of law and fact, but the contemnor has the right to counsel, to compulsory process to secure witnesses, and to refuse to testify.

United States Supreme Court decisions have established basic due process rights that must be accorded contemnors in these proceedings. Of course, if there are statutes or court rules in a particular jurisdiction that prescribe the method of processing criminal contempt, the judge must not deviate from those rules to the prejudice of the contemnor's rights. In any contempt proceeding, if the contemnor is to be sentenced to a term of imprisonment for more than six months, he or she is entitled to a jury trial. *Baldwin v. New York,* 399 U.S. 66, 90 S. Ct. 1886, 26 L.Ed.2d 437 (1970).

Legislative Contempt

Legislative bodies also have the power to punish by contempt those persons whose deliberate acts impede legislative activities. Some states have enacted statutes to cover specific instances of criminal contempt in respect to legislative functions. New York, for example, makes it criminal contempt of the legislature for a person who has been subpoenaed to refuse to attend, be sworn, answer proper questions, or produce proper evidence. McKinney's N.Y. Penal Law § 215.60.

C A S E   I N   P O I N T

DIRECT CRIMINAL CONTEMPT

Defendant William Carr was convicted of armed robbery and sentenced to serve from four to eight years in prison. When the judge pronounced the sentence, Carr proceeded to punch the prosecutor in the nose. The trial judge found Carr in direct criminal contempt of court and sentenced him to serve an additional six months in prison. In addition to appealing his conviction, Carr also contested his sentence for contempt. In rejecting his challenge, the Appellate Court of Illinois observed, "[i]t would be frivolous to argue that to punch an assistant state attorney in open court was not direct contempt."

People v. Carr, 278 N.E.2d 839 (Ill. App. 1971).

CASE IN POINT

LEGISLATIVE CONTEMPT

An outstanding example of a legislative body acting on its own to hold a person in contempt was the highly publicized and emotionally charged case involving James E. Groppi, a former priest. In September 1969, Father Groppi attracted national attention when he led a group of protesters who allegedly seized a Wisconsin legislative chamber. Groppi was arrested, held in contempt, and sentenced to jail by the Wisconsin legislature. The resolution holding him in contempt was adopted by the legislature without first giving Groppi any notice or an opportunity to respond by way of a defense or to present any matters in extenuation or mitigation. For these reasons, the United States Supreme Court reversed his conviction.

Groppi v. Leslie, 404 U.S. 496, 92 S. Ct. 582, 30 L.Ed.2d 632 (1972).

Courts have been zealous in assuring that legislative bodies afford contemnors due process of law before adjudging them to be in contempt. See, for example, *Watkins v. United States,* 354 U.S. 178, 77 S. Ct. 1173, 1 L.Ed.2d 1273 (1957). In practice, the Congress and state legislative bodies frequently make citations for contempt and then turn the matter over to the courts to handle.

CONCLUSION

The fair and impartial administration of justice and the orderly processes of democratic government depend on the honesty and integrity of those who occupy positions of authority. Hence, the basic common-law offenses described in this chapter have endured over the centuries. The offense of bribery seeks to avoid corruption of those in positions of trust, while the crime of perjury seeks to maintain the integrity of the judicial system and agencies of government.

To safeguard the security and effectiveness of law enforcement personnel, all jurisdictions make it a crime to resist arrest, even if the arrest is later declared to be unlawful. Since society must assure confinement of those it has chosen to incarcerate, it is essential to maintain the offense of escape. However, with increased awareness of inhumane prison conditions and the rights of prisoners, courts have recognized necessity as a defense to a charge of escape. The abandonment of the common-law principle that allowed a person to forcibly resist an unlawful arrest, and the recognition of the necessity defense in the law of escape, both demonstrate the dynamic nature of the criminal law in response to societal change.

Finally, to maintain the effectiveness and the dignity of the judicial and legislative processes, courts and legislatures must have the authority to hold persons in contempt, although that authority must be exercised with due regard for the constitutional rights of contemnors.

QUESTIONS FOR THOUGHT AND DISCUSSION

1. Why have contemporary legislative bodies expanded the scope of bribery and extended it to cover classes of persons beyond public officials?

2. How does the requirement that the prosecution prove a defendant's specific intent to deceive protect citizens from unwarranted prosecutions for perjury?

3. Contrast the common-law rule allowing a person to resist an unlawful arrest with the modern trend of requiring citizens to submit to unlawful arrests by police officers. Which approach makes more sense in modern society?

4. Is a state statute that makes it a criminal offense "to hinder or delay a law enforcement officer in the performance of his or her duties" likely to be held void for vagueness under the tests outlined in Chapter 3?

5. Would a person who accepts the return of stolen goods from a thief without agreeing to refrain from filing a criminal complaint be guilty of compounding a crime?

6. Despite the wording of most statutes proscribing the offense of escape, courts increasingly require the prosecution to prove the defendant's specific intent to avoid lawful confinement. Are courts justified in imposing such a requirement on the statutory law?

7. Have courts aided society by allowing escapees from prison to defend their actions on the basis of intolerable prison conditions? Are such conditions likely to be remedied by the legislative process?

8. Can you describe some specific acts that a trial judge could justifiably consider to be direct contempts of court?

9. Why does the law require more formal proceedings in cases of indirect contempt than in cases of direct criminal contempt?

CASES

STATE V. GUSTAFSON
Court of Appeals of Minnesota, 1986.
396 N.W.2d 583.

[The appellant, Gustafson, was convicted of bribery and conspiracy to commit perjury.]

FOLEY, Judge.

. . . On October 2, 1984 appellant was on a motorcycle talking to someone in a parked car. After ignoring several requests by a police officer to move the motorcycle, which was obstructing traffic, appellant was given a citation. Appellant was placed in the rear of the squad car after failing to have identification and giving a false name; he was patted down pursuant to police department rules. The police officer felt a hard object inside appellant's leather jacket and pulled out a beeper. Two plastic bags were also seized from the jacket; one containing a white powdery substance, the other containing folded pieces of paper. Money totalling $1,330 was also taken from appellant. The bags were later tested and found to contain cocaine. Appellant was charged with possession of cocaine and was released from jail. Upon his release, he picked up a vest and gloves, part of the property taken the night of the arrest. The leather coat, beeper and money were held for evidence. Appellant never claimed that the leather coat or gloves were not his.

Appellant's cocaine possession trial was scheduled for March 12, 1985. In mid-February 1985, appellant called an acquaintance, Andrew Beggs, and offered to give him a car worth $200 to $300 if Beggs would tell appellant's lawyer, Joe Kaminsky, that Beggs owned the leather jacket. Appellant told Beggs that his brother had done something similar and had gotten away with it.

Appellant later told Beggs that if he [Gustafson] were convicted he would go to jail. Appellant explained the circumstances surrounding his arrest and told Beggs to say that he had won the cocaine in a pool game. Appellant then drove Beggs to a street in North Minneapolis to show him the car he had promised, gave Beggs the keys and assured him that he would provide title to the vehicle "in time."

Appellant further told Beggs that since Beggs had a clean record the most he would get was probation.

A few days later appellant drove Beggs to Kaminsky's office where Beggs told Kaminsky the jacket and cocaine were his. When Kaminsky asked Beggs where the jacket was, he responded that he had it for the past two weeks. Kaminsky then informed Beggs that the police still had the jacket.

Appellant told Beggs that another witness was needed to corroborate the story since Beggs had mistakenly claimed possession of the jacket. Appellant then asked Brian Guyant to claim that he had observed Beggs give appellant the jacket. Guyant agreed and met with Beggs to make their stories consistent. A few days later, Beggs met with appellant, appellant's girlfriend and appellant's mother to discuss the story again. Beggs took notes at the meeting.

Beggs and Guyant went to Kaminsky's office on March 11, 1985. Minneapolis Police Officer Wayne Brademan and Hennepin County Attorney's Office Investigator Paul Stanton were also present at the meeting. Beggs was asked to identify the jacket but had difficulty locating the pocket in which the cocaine was found. Stanton testified that Beggs seemed nervous and confused. Beggs testified that Brademan and Stanton laughed when he could not find the inside pocket and he suspected that they did not believe his story that he had loaned appellant the jacket when appellant was about to test drive a motorcycle he had planned to purchase. Beggs was arrested. A search of his pockets produced a marijuana cigarette and two sheets of paper containing notes relating to the story he had just told.

After Beggs was in jail for three hours, he called Stanton and the next day said that he had lied about the cocaine and ownership of the jacket. Beggs explained that appellant had asked him to take the rap and gave a statement. The investigators then decided to set up a taped conversation between

Beggs and appellant to determine who actually owned the cocaine. Beggs was released from jail and a "body bug" was placed on his back. Beggs was also given a phony complaint which stated that he was charged with possession of cocaine and possession of cocaine with intent to sell.

Beggs met appellant at a North Minneapolis home owned by Beggs' brother. Stanton and another police officer were in the basement during this meeting. In the tape recording, appellant makes numerous incriminating statements.

During the conversation, appellant referred to the cocaine as "my stash." He did not disagree when Beggs referred to their fabricated story nor did he disagree when Beggs said that Kaminsky knew he was lying. Appellant did show concern over the crib sheets found in Beggs' pocket, however, and reassured Beggs that at most he would serve 30 days in the workhouse. Appellant disagreed with the description of the seized cocaine in the phony complaint being in a baggie and said it was in a zip lock bag and also said that he had "two white papers" and "three rocks." When Beggs asked for title to the car, appellant said that he forgot it. Subsequently, appellant's brother and Guyant brought the title card to Beggs who then turned it over to the investigators.

On April 18, 1985 a complaint was filed charging appellant with one count of conspiracy to commit perjury and one count of bribery. Both complaints (cocaine possession and conspiracy to commit perjury/bribery) were set for trial and were severed at appellant's request. At the first trial for cocaine possession, appellant did not testify. He was eventually acquitted.

At the second trial, appellant testified in his own defense, claiming that Beggs gave him the jacket and gloves to wear and denying ownership of the cocaine found in the jacket. Appellant stated that he did not tell anyone earlier that the jacket and cocaine belonged to Beggs because he was not a "snitch." He further testified that he sold the car to Beggs for $100 and that Beggs still owed him $50. Appellant was convicted of bribery and conspiracy to commit perjury and this appeal followed. . . .

We . . . conclude that the evidence was sufficient for the jury to convict appellant of bribery and conspiracy to commit perjury. Beggs' testimony was amply corroborated by evidence that appellant gave Beggs a car, by the crib notes found on Beggs at his arrest and by appellant's statements during the taped conversation. . . .

UNITED STATES V. SCOTT
United States Court of Appeals, Eighth Circuit, 1982.
682 F.2d 695.

[This case deals with perjury by contradictory statements. The appellant, Teresa Ann Scott, was convicted in the U.S. District Court for the Western District of Missouri of three counts of making inconsistent material declarations while under oath.]

MCMILLAN, Circuit Judge.
. . . On July 20, 1980, FBI Agent Robert Callahan went to Scott's residence to question her about the November 1979 robbery of the Blue Valley Federal Savings & Loan (Blue Valley) and the January 1980 robbery of the Rockhill Federal Savings Loan (Rockhill). Scott was not at home so Callahan left a

message for her to contact him. The following Monday, July 14, Scott voluntarily went to the FBI office located in Kansas City, Missouri, and met with Agents Callahan and Parnell Miles. Callahan told Scott that he had a government witness who was going to testify in such a way as to implicate Scott in numerous crimes if she did not cooperate in the FBI's investigation of the robberies. Scott agreed and examined three bank surveillance photographs taken during the two robberies. Scott identified Bobby McNeal, her present boyfriend, and George Brown, a former boyfriend, as the individuals in the Blue Valley photograph and McNeal and Olie

Ealom, her half-brother, as the individuals in the Rockhill photographs.

At some point Scott made statements implicating herself as an accessory to the robberies. An understanding was reached whereby Scott would not be indicted in exchange for her cooperation with the government. On December 30, 1980, Scott was deposed in connection with the government's case against McNeal for the Blue Valley robbery. She was shown the same bank surveillance photographs, exhibits C, D, and E, and again identified the individuals in exhibit C, the Blue Valley robbery, as Brown and McNeal and the individuals in exhibit E, the Rockhill robbery, as Ealom and McNeal. The face of the person identified as McNeal was not identifiable in the photographs. However, Scott stated that the striped coat worn by that person during both robberies belonged to her and that she had lent it to McNeal on the morning of the Blue Valley robbery. In addition, exhibit D was a front shot of that person and showed that he was made up to appear as a woman during the Blue Valley robbery. Scott stated that she had applied McNeal's makeup on the morning of the Blue Valley robbery.

On January 20, 1981, Scott was called to testify at McNeal's trial. On direct examination she was again shown exhibits C, D, and E. However, she testified that she could not identify the striped coat worn by one of the individuals in exhibit C, that she could not identify the individual in exhibit D whom she had previously identified as McNeal, and that she could not identify the individuals in exhibit E whom she had previously identified as McNeal and Ealom. The jury found McNeal not guilty and shortly thereafter the government dismissed its case against McNeal and Ealom for the Rockhill robbery.

The government subsequently charged Scott with three counts of making irreconcilably contradictory declarations under oath in violation of 18 U.S.C. § 1623. At her trial Scott testified that her deposition testimony was false and that she had recanted at McNeal's trial. Scott also testified that the reason she lied during the deposition was Callahan's threat that she could be sent to prison and lose custody of her children if she did not cooperate with the investigation. Scott further testified that before she made the July 20, 1980, statement to Callahan he had told her that he already knew the identities of the individuals in the bank surveillance photographs

and also knew that the striped coat belonged to Scott. On cross-examination Scott admitted that she had visited McNeal at the Wyandotte County Jail on January 14, 1981, signed the deposition on January 15, and visited McNeal again on January 16. The jury found Scott guilty on all three counts.

On appeal Scott first argues that her prosecution was barred by the "recant" provision of 18 U.S.C. § 1623(d) which provides:

> Where, in the same continuous court or grand jury proceeding in which a declaration is made, the person making the declaration admits such declaration to be false, such admission shall bar prosecution under this section if, at the time the admission is made the declaration has not substantially affected the proceeding, or it has not become manifest that such falsity has been or will be exposed.

Alternatively, Scott argues that, in light of this section, there was insufficient evidence to support her conviction. We reject these arguments.

Scott did not raise the recantation argument by pretrial motion. Rather, she attempted to convince the jury that her deposition testimony was false and that she had recanted at McNeal's trial. The recantation section of the statute was included in the jury instructions and referred to in her counsel's closing argument. Because Scott chose to submit the issue to the jury the question before us is whether there is substantial evidence, taking the view most favorable to the government to support the verdict. See *Glasser v. United States*, 315 U.S. 60, 80, 62 S.Ct., 457, 469, 86 L.Ed. 680 (1942). Viewed in this light, the evidence shows that the government agreed not to indict Scott as an accomplice in the robberies in exchange for her testimony at McNeal's trial, that her deposition testimony was consistent with earlier statements made to the FBI and finally, that she was romantically involved with McNeal and visited him the day before and after signing the deposition. The jury could reasonably have found from the evidence that Scott was truthful in the deposition and lied at McNeal's trial.

Scott next argues that neither the indictment nor the jury instruction defining the elements of the offense included all the essential elements of the offense. Specifically, Scott asserts that the ancillary nature of her deposition had to be alleged in the indictment and that the instruction should have required the jury to make a finding that the deposition was an ancillary proceeding. There is no merit to this argument.

Title 18 U.S.C. § 1623 applies to inconsistent declarations made "in any proceeding before or ancillary to any court or grand jury of the United States." The term "ancillary" proceedings has been construed to include depositions and exclude "statements given in less formal contexts than deposi-tions." *Dunn v. United States*, 442 U.S. 100, 111, 99S.Ct. 2190, 2196, 60 L.Ed.2d 743 (1979). Therefore, the terms "deposition" and "ancillary proceeding" are synonymous under the statute and requiring the indictment to specifically allege the ancillary nature of the deposition or requiring the jury to find that a deposition is an ancillary proceeding would be redundant. . . .

The judgment of the district court is affirmed.

PEOPLE V. GETTINGS

Appellate Court of Illinois, Third District, 1983.
116 Ill.App. 3d 657, 72 Ill. Dec. 419, 452 N.E.2d 672.

[The defendant, Jimmy L. Gettings, challenges his conviction and sentence on three counts of perjury which followed his jury trial in the circuit court of Tazewell County, Illinois.]

BARRY, Justice:
. . . This cause had its origin in defendant's failure to pay sheriff's fees for two small claims actions. The State's Attorney of Tazewell County brought suits to recover amounts of $50 and $38, respectively, plus costs, and judgments were obtained against defendant. Thereafter, the State's Attorney filed a Citation to Discover Assets, and on July 24, 1980, at the hearing pursuant to the Citation, defendant stated that he did not own any real estate, that he did not own any vehicles, and that no one owed him any money.

He was later indicted on four counts of perjury, and was tried on the first three counts. The indictment alleged that defendant committed the offense of perjury by stating under oath in a civil proceeding a false statement which he did not believe to be true in that he stated (count I) that he did not own any real estate, (count II) that he did not own a vehicle, and (count III) that no one owed him any money. Defendant was tried before a jury and found guilty on all three counts, but upon appeal, his convictions were set aside and the cause remanded for a new trial because of certain remarks by a witness and by the prosecutor which this court found to be inflammatory and prejudicial. . . .

After introducing evidence establishing that at the July 24, 1980, hearing on the Citation to Discover Assets, defendant had denied ownership of real property, had denied ownership of any vehicles, and had stated that no one owed him any money, the State presented additional evidence showing that on July 24, 1980, defendant had title to 1.5 acres of land in Peoria County, that he had title to a 1971 Ford pickup truck, and that he had written a letter on July 22 notifying a customer that he had filed liens against the customer's property and that he would be charged 1½ per cent interest per month until the $122.25 judgment and costs were paid.

Defendant presented no evidence in his own behalf although he exercised his peremptory jury challenges, cross-examined several witnesses, and made a competent closing argument to the jury. The jury returned verdicts of guilty on all three counts, and after receiving updated presentencing reports, the trial court sentenced defendant to 90 days in jail with credit for time served, a fine of $2,000, and 30 months probation with no credit for time previously served while the appeal was pending. Defendant has again appealed from his conviction and sentence.

Defendant first contends that the indictment was insufficient as a matter of law to state an offense because it did not contain an allegation that defendant had knowledge of the falsity of the statements at the time they were made. . . .

We conclude that the indictment in the case before us was sufficient to state the offense of perjury.

Next, defendant contends that the trial court erred in failing to instruct the jury that an essential element of the crime of perjury is defendant's knowledge of the falsity of the statements he made. Without objection from defendant, the court gave IPI Crim. No. 22.01, which states:

"A person commits the offense of perjury when he, under oath or affirmation, makes a false statement and at the time he makes the statement he believes it is not true."

Thus, the court instructed the jury as to the elements of the crime as defined by the statute, and such instruction is not error. . . .

Defendant also contends that the state's evidence did not prove him guilty beyond a reasonable doubt because the questions which were the basis for the charge asked for conclusions or belief and because the State did not establish that defendant had knowledge of the falsity of his answers. The questions to which defendant answered "no" were: "Do you own any real estate?" "Do you own any vehicles?" "Does anyone owe you any money?"

We cannot say that these questions asked for conclusions or mere opinion; they were straight forward, factual questions. Considering the evidence establishing that defendant did at that time own real estate and a truck, and that he was actively trying to collect a judgment owed to him, the jury could quite properly infer that defendant believed his answers to be false at the time he gave them. We hold, therefore, that defendant was proved guilty beyond a reasonable doubt. . . .

Accordingly, we affirm the judgment of conviction and the sentence imposed by the circuit court of Tazewell County.

Affirmed.

STOUDER, P. J., and ALLOY, J., concur.

STATE V. RING
Supreme Court of Maine, 1978.
387 A.2d 241.

[This case involves the offense of attempted escape.]

PER CURIAM.

Appellants Donald Ring and Ricky Waugh bring this appeal from judgments entered following a jury trial in the Knox County Superior Court. Appellants were tried jointly for attempted escape . . . from the Maine State Prison.

Appellants assert two issues on appeal. They . . . challenge the sufficiency of the evidence to demonstrate that there were the overt acts or intent necessary to constitute the offense of attempted escape. . . .

We deny the appeal.

The record shows that on July 28, 1976, the date of the alleged attempted escape, both appellants were incarcerated in the Maine State Prison where they were serving sentences imposed for prior crimes. They had no official permission to be absent on that day. A prison guard testified at trial that he had seen appellants walking together in the prison yard around 1:00 P.M. One appellant was observed carrying an unconcealed "rope" and a hammer.

When it later appeared that neither appellant had showed up for the 4:00 P.M. cell count, a search of the prison was undertaken. Eventually both appellants were discovered in the "steam cage," a dark, enclosed unused portion of the prison. Subsequent searches revealed the presence of the "rope" and hammer hidden in crevices in the room.

Appellant Ring chose to testify on his own behalf. He basically contended that he and some other inmates had been drinking "homebrew" and had decided to hide in the steam cage so that their intoxication would not be discovered. While this story was corroborated by another inmate, the bag out of which appellants had been drinking was never discovered. Appellant Waugh decided not to testify.

Appellants first contend that the evidence was insufficient to prove that they intended to escape.

They further claim that the evidence demonstrated, at most, mere preparation for an escape, not the requisite overt act.

We disagree.

As appellants contend, intent to "leave[s] official custody" or to "fail[s] to return to official custody following temporary leave" must be proven in order to establish a violation.... Moreover, appellants are correct when they argue that in proving an "attempt," the State must prove more than mere preparation; it must prove "a positive action ... directed towards the execution of the crime."...

Our task in assessing the sufficiency of the evidence on these two points, however, is not to retry the case or to substitute our impressions of the facts for those of the jurors. Our function is merely to ascertain if the jury was warranted in finding for the State.... A witness' credibility is a jury matter....

The jury here was justified in rejecting the testimony that appellants were in the "steam cage" solely to avoid detection of their intoxication. The fact of being hidden and the fact of their possession of "rope" and a hammer would have demonstrated to the jury that appellants had an intent to escape and that they had taken actions "directed toward the execution of the crime." This was a justified finding despite the fact that the actual escape might have been difficult to execute under the facts presented in this case....

The entry must be:

Appeal denied.

Judgments affirmed.

DELAHANTY, J., did not sit.

STATE v. BLANTON

Superior Court of New Jersey, Appellate Division, 1979.
166 N.J. Super. 62, 398 A.2d 1328.

[This case involves the offenses of assault and battery upon a police officer, "atrocious assault and battery," and resisting arrest.]

CONFORD, P. J. A. D., Retired (temporarily assigned).

These are consolidated appeals by defendant Elijah Blanton, Sr. ("Elijah") and his son, John Blanton ("John"). Elijah was convicted of assault and battery upon a police officer and John of atrocious assault and battery and resisting arrest. The events giving rise to the charges resulting in these convictions occurred in the course of a disturbance on May 28, 1976 at a playground near a low-income housing project in Long Branch.

The police were originally dispatched to the playground after Elijah's wife called to report an argument between another of her sons and a third person she thought to be in possession of a gun. No gun was found. However, Elijah was carrying on in a loud manner, yelling at and chasing children and arguing with the purported possessor of the gun.

There was other testimony that Elijah was simply trying to restore peace to the area. The police soon withdrew from the scene.

Within a short time the police returned to the scene on the order of a superior officer to arrest Elijah if he was found to be causing trouble. The return of the police developed into a melee either witnessed or participated in by a large number of people, mostly juveniles. According to the State's evidence, Officers Wettermark and Brown accosted Elijah and informed him he was under arrest. He pulled away from them, and sticks and other objects were thrown at the officers, Officer Wettermark being struck by some of them. Officer Brown embraced Elijah in a full nelson and in return was bitten by Elijah on his arm. This action was the basis of the charge against Elijah of assault and battery against a police officer.

The charges against John arose out of the attempt of Officer DeFillipo to go to the aid of the officers seeking to arrest Elijah. DeFillipo testified that as he approached the officers and Elijah he noticed an individual wearing an orange tee shirt to his right at a distance of between six and ten feet and immediately thereafter sustained a blow to the top of his head. The man in the orange shirt was John. DeFillipo at once turned around and confronted John, the latter looking directly at him, about three feet away. John had a stick or pipe in his hand of a cylindrical shape and about 2 ½ feet long. There were no other people in the immediate area. John turned and ran toward his apartment with DeFillipo and Officer Richards in pursuit, the former yelling, "I want him. He hit me." John ran into one door and out another, whereupon he was tackled by one of the officers. There was testimony that John was resisting the officers' efforts to subdue him, "moving his arms about" and attempting to arise from the ground. DeFillipo was bleeding profusely from his scalp. There was other testimony that prior to the assault on Officer DeFillipo John had run into Officer May and had struck him on the arm with a stick and then continued running. However, he was acquitted of a separate charge of assault on Officer May.

John's testimonial version of the events was that he was in the playground practicing for a state championship relay meet to be held the next day and that he was in possession of a relay baton about 12 inches long. When the police came upon the scene they began spraying mace. John saw his father surrounded by police officers and others and asked the officers to let his father alone. One of the officers angrily reached for his gun and John ran away in fear, alleging, before an objection by the State was sustained, that he recalled a former local incident involving the shooting of a juvenile by police. He did not strike anyone but remembered bumping into someone while running away. No one told him he was under arrest at any time. He was assaulted by the police after he emerged from his home. . . .

Defendant [John Blanton] argues that the trial judge's instructions to the jury with respect to the charge of resisting arrest were defective because they permitted the jury to conclude that John's flight from the pursuing officers constituted guilt of the offense of resisting arrest. The specific portion of the charge to the jury objected to consisted of the instruction that among the elements of the crime required to be proven by the State was one that defendant "did know that he was under arrest or that the officer was attempting to arrest him and . . .

that with that knowledge the defendant John Blanton intentionally sought to avoid or frustrate that arrest."

Our examination of the relevant authorities satisfies us that there was no error in the charge even if the jurors could understand therefrom that flight from a police officer with knowledge by the fugitive that the officer was attempting to arrest him and with the purpose of avoiding or frustrating that arrest, constituted guilt of the common-law offense of resisting arrest.

Resisting arrest is an integral part of the common-law crime of "obstruction of or resistance to a public officer in the performance of his duties." . . . [T]he use of actual force is not always necessary to constitute the offense so long as there is some overt act of obstruction. . . . In many jurisdictions this crime has been codified, and the statutes have generally been construed as permitting a determination of guilt without a finding of the use of force or violence against the officer. . . . The California cases hold that flight from an officer seeking to arrest is sufficient to constitute evidence of a violation of a statute punishing a person who willfully resists, delays or obstructs a public officer in the discharge of any duty of his office. . . .

In formulating § 2C:29–2 of The New Jersey Penal Code . . . the New Jersey Criminal Law Revision Commission stated: "We reject the MPC [Model Penal Code] view that mere nonsubmission should not be an offense, believing an affirmative policy of submission to be appropriate as now seems to be our law." . . . The cited section of the Code, both as proposed and adopted, provides for guilt of resisting arrest if the person "purposely prevents a law enforcement officer from effecting a lawful arrest." Such offenses are divided into two categories, one being a crime of the fourth degree and the other a disorderly persons offense. Guilt of the former arises if the person uses or threatens to use physical force or violence against the officer or another, or uses any other means to create a substantial risk of causing physical injury to the officer or another. It thus appears that while mere flight from an intending arresting officer may, depending upon other circumstances, be regarded under the new statute as only a disorderly persons offense, the general offense of resisting arrest may be found to have been committed short of use of force or risk of causing injury so long as the accused has purposely sought to prevent the police officer from effecting an arrest. Our view of the common law . . . is, accordingly, that flight knowingly intended to prevent a police officer from effecting an arrest of the fugitive constitutes guilt of the common-law crime of resisting arrest.

The circumstances given in evidence clearly permitted the jury to find that John knew the police were seeking to arrest him. Office DeFillipo testified that while pursuing John he yelled out, "I want him.

He hit me." John admitted, in effect, that he was seeking to elude the police, although his explanation of his flight was consistent with innocence of the crime of assault. Nevertheless, knowing that a uniformed police officer was seeking to apprehend him, it was his duty to submit and not resist. . . .

We consequently find no error in the trial judge's instructions to the jury in the respect complained of. . . .

C H A P T E R

13

CRIMINAL RESPONSIBILITY AND DEFENSES

INTRODUCTION

As the English common law developed, the concept of criminal responsibility became a significant consideration. As it did, various defenses to criminal conduct emerged. Incapacity to commit a crime because of infancy or insanity and, under some circumstances, as a result of intoxication, came to be recognized as defenses. Self-defense, defense of others, and defense of habitation and other property were also recognized as defenses. Moreover, the common law allowed a defendant to assert ignorance or mistake of fact that occurred honestly as an excuse for having committed a criminal act. Alibi, necessity, duress, and—under limited circumstances—consent were recognized as defenses.

Essentially these defenses have been recognized in the various jurisdictions in the United States, although they have been modified over the years. The Fifth Amendment to the United States Constitution and corresponding provisions of the state constitutions furnish defendants two additional defenses: immunity and double jeopardy. Legislatures initiated the concept of a statute of limitations on the prosecution of most crimes, and through judicial development, entrapment has become a recognized defense where improper governmental conduct has induced an otherwise innocent person to commit a crime.

In previous chapters, we have mentioned some defenses applicable to specific substantive crimes. We revisit some of those defenses in this chapter, further examining the scope of common-law, constitutional, and statutory defenses to criminal charges.

DEFENSES IN GENERAL

For purposes of analysis and study, defenses to crimes may be conveniently divided into six categories: (1) those asserting lack of capacity (infancy, intoxication, insanity, automatism); (2) those justifying use of force (self-defense, defense of others, defense of property and habitation, and defense of using force to resist an arrest); (3) those alleging a mistake of fact or of law; (4) those assailing governmental conduct (entrapment, selective prosecution); (5) those relying on constitutional or statutory rights (immunity, double jeopardy, statutes of limitation); and (6) those claiming alibi, duress, necessity, and consent.

Defendants who plead not guilty to a criminal charge may not only rely on their general denial, they may offer any defense (sometimes called a negative defense) not required to be specifically pled. A defendant merely has the burden of raising some evidence of a negative defense; however, in some instances the prosecution's own evidence may raise the issue. Once such evidence is produced, the prosecution has the burden to overcome it. For example, Henry Homeowner is charged with manslaughter of a person who forced entry into his home one night after Homeowner had gone to bed. Homeowner claims to have acted in self-defense by using deadly force to defend his homeplace. If any evidence discloses that he acted in self-defense, then to establish that Homeowner is guilty of manslaughter, the prosecution must prove that he did not act reasonably.

A defense that must be specifically pled is classified as an affirmative defense, that is, one that does not negate any element of the crime, but rather consists of new matters relied upon as an excuse or justification for the defendant's otherwise illegal conduct. To illustrate, Larry Boatman is charged with burglary of a vacant beach cottage. He pleads not guilty, raising the affirmative defense of necessity. He argues that while he entered the cottage with the intent to take food from within, it was an act of necessity because he and his starving companions were shipwrecked in a desolate area without other means of obtaining food or drinking water. Ordinarily, a defendant has the burden to prove the matters offered as an affirmative defense. Therefore, it is up to Boatman to prove by the preponderance (greater weight) of the evidence that he acted out of necessity.

The prosecution is always required to prove the defendant guilty beyond any reasonable doubt. Nevertheless, a state may constitutionally place the burden on a defendant to establish an affirmative defense as long as that defense is not one that negates any element of the crime the prosecution must prove to convict the defendant. *Patterson v. New York*, 432 U.S. 197, 97 S.Ct. 2319, 53 L.Ed.2d 281 (1977). Defenses authorized by statute are sometimes styled as affirmative defenses, but merely labeling a defense an affirmative defense is not sufficient. Courts must look to the substance to make certain an affirmative defense is one that excuses or justifies conduct that would otherwise lead to criminal responsibility, and not one that negates any element of the crime.

Defenses Asserting Lack of Capacity To Commit a Crime

There are four defenses asserting the lack of capacity to commit a crime: infancy, intoxication, insanity and automatism.

Infancy

The common law regarded a child under age 7 as incapable of forming criminal intent. This gave rise to a conclusive presumption of incapacity for a child under age 7. This presumption of incapacity was rebuttable regarding a child over 7 but under 14, with the prosecution having the burden to demonstrate that a child under 14 was capable of comprehending the wrongdoing involved in commission of an offense. Children over age 14 were treated as adults. *Commonwealth v. Cavalier*, 131 A. 229 (Pa. 1925).

The rationale for these common-law presumptions was that young children require protection from the harshness of the adversary processes of the law. Some jurisdictions have abolished these presumptions because legislatures have provided that children under certain ages, usually 16 to 18, are subject to the jurisdiction of the juvenile courts, where the procedures are tailored toward less mature offenders. In establishing juvenile courts, the legislatures frequently intend to eliminate the common-law presumption of incapacity of infants. See *People v. Miller*, 334 N.E.2d 421 (Ill. App. 1975), for the court's perception of legislative intent under Illinois law. Under federal law, a juvenile is a person who has not attained age 18 at the time of the commission of an offense, 18 U.S.C.A. § 5031.

Starting with Illinois in 1899, all states developed juvenile court systems. These courts traditionally handled juvenile offenders separately from adults in nonadversarial proceedings. The theory was that the state acted as *parens patriae,* taking a clinical and rehabilitative, rather than an adversarial or punitive, approach to youthful offenders. Nevertheless, the system suffered from many deficiencies such as inadequate staffing and substandard facilities, and the results were disappointing. Many youthful offenders were not rehabilitated, nor were they afforded even the most basic constitutional rights accorded adults in the criminal justice system. In the words of the United States Supreme Court, "the child receives the worst of both worlds: that he gets neither the protections accorded to adults nor the solicitous care and regenerative treatment postulated for children." *Kent v. United States,* 383 U.S. 541, 556, 86 S. Ct. 1045, 1054, 16 L. Ed. 2d 84, 94 (1966). We discuss the subject of juvenile justice in Chapter 20.

Intoxication

Intoxication may result from ingestion of alcohol or drugs. The common law did not excuse a person who voluntarily became intoxicated from responsibility for criminal conduct. *State v. Yarborough,* 18 P. 474 (Kan. 1888). In an early English case, the court approved a death sentence for a homicide committed by an extremely intoxicated defendant. *Reniger v. Fogossa,* 75 Eng. Rep. 1 (1550).

In considering intoxication today, we must first distinguish voluntary from involuntary intoxication. In most jurisdictions, voluntary intoxication may be considered in determining whether a defendant can formulate the *specific* intent required to be established in such crimes as larceny, burglary, and premeditated murder. See, for example, *State v. Brooks,* 436 P.2d 91 (Mont. 1967). A few courts will not even permit a jury to consider voluntary intoxication on the issue of specific intent. See, for example, *State v. Hegwood,* 558 S.W.2d 378 (Mo. App. 1977). All courts have rejected the defense of voluntary intoxication to charges in general-intent crimes. See, for example, *United States v. Hanson,* 618 F.2d 1261 (8th Cir. 1980), *cert. denied,* 449 U.S. 854, 101 S. Ct. 148, 66 L.Ed.2d 67 (1980) (assault on a federal officer); *Commonwealth v. Bridge,* 435 A.2d 151 (Pa. 1981) (voluntary manslaughter); *State v. Keaten,* 390 A.2d 1043 (Me. 1978) (gross sexual misconduct). These decisions are grounded on public policy concerns of not excusing conduct by those who voluntarily impair their own judgment.

Involuntary intoxication rarely occurs, but when it does, it relieves the criminality of an act committed under its influence if, as a result of intoxication, the defendant no longer knows right from wrong. *State v. Mriglot,* 564 P.2d 784 (Wash. 1977). A person may become involuntarily intoxicated by fraudulent contrivance or through trickery or fraud of another person. See, for example, *Johnson v. Commonwealth,* 115 S.E. 673 (Va. 1923), or through inadvertent ingestion of medicine. See *People v. Carlo,* 361 N.Y.S.2d 168 (N.Y. App. Div. 1974). The New Hampshire Supreme Court summarized the law in this area when it declared:

> Generally the defense of involuntary intoxication will only be considered when it is
> shown that the intoxication was the product of external pressures such as fraud,

force, or coercion, or when intoxication resulted from a medical prescription. *State v. Plummer*, 374 A.2d 431, 435 (N.H. 1977).

Intoxication as a defense to criminal liability has been codified in some jurisdictions. Section 939.42 of the Wisconsin Statutes summarizes the general law in stating:

> An intoxicated or a drugged condition of the actor is a defense only if such condition:
> (1) Is involuntarily produced and renders the actor incapable of distinguishing between right and wrong in regard to the alleged criminal act at the time the act is committed; or
> (2) Negatives the existence of a state of mind essential to the crime *except as provided in* § 939.24(3). Wis. Stat. Ann. § 939.42.

The Wisconsin legislature inserted the italicized exception in 1987 to assure that a voluntarily produced intoxicated or drugged condition is not a defense to liability for criminal recklessness.

Wisconsin courts have said that to establish the defense of *involuntary* intoxication, the accused must show the inability to tell right from wrong at time of the offense; to establish *voluntary* intoxication, the defendant must show that the defendant's condition negated the existence of the state of mind necessary to commit the crime. *State v. Repp*, 342 N.W.2d 771 (Wis. App. 1983), *aff'd.* 362 N.W.2d 415 (Wis. 1985).

Insanity

All persons are presumed sane unless previously adjudicated insane. Even a person who has been adjudicated legally insane may still be found guilty of a criminal act if it was committed during a lucid interval. Insanity is a legal concept and is defined differently in various jurisdictions in the United States. A person who meets the requirements of the definition as of the time of commission of an offense may rely upon the defense of insanity as an excuse for a crime. Trial will be either continued or canceled for a defendant whose mental condition renders him or her incapable of understanding the nature of the charges, the range of potential penalties, and the nature of the adversary process. In this section we address insanity at the time of commission of an offense and describe the background of the insanity defense, current standards for asserting the defense, and some contemporary developments in this area.

Few cases have caused as great a concern over the functioning of the criminal justice system as the verdict of "not guilty by reason of insanity" in the federal court trial of John Hinckley for the 1981 shooting of President Ronald Reagan, his press secretary, and two law officers. The defense of insanity has never been popular with the public. It has sometimes been called "a rich man's defense," because defendants who invoke it frequently expend considerable financial resources to present psychiatric testimony. The Hinckley verdict motivated Congress and several state legislatures to review the status of insanity defenses.

The concept of mental responsibility has its historic roots in Anglo-American law, for as pointed out in Chapter 4 the common-law crimes included a mental element, the *mens rea*. Nevertheless, the common law was slow to develop any standard for a mental condition that would excuse a person from criminal responsibility. By the eighteenth century some English courts applied what has sometimes been called a "wild beast" test. For example, one English judge opined that

> a man . . . totally deprived of his understanding and memory, . . . and doth not know what he is doing, no more than an infant, than a brute, or a wild beast . . . is never the object of punishment. *Rex v. Arnold,* 16 Howell's State Trials 695 (Eng. 1724).

The M'Naghten Rule.   Little progress occurred in the development of the defense of insanity until 1843, when an event in England caused even greater consternation than the American reaction to the Hinckley verdict. Suffering from delusions that he was being persecuted by government officials, Daniel M'Naghten decided to kill Sir Robert Peel, the British Home Secretary. (Peel was the founder of the British Police System, hence the term *bobbies* is still applied to British law officers.) From outside Peel's home, M'Naghten saw Peel's secretary, Edward Drummond, leave the house. Believing Drummond to be Peel, M'Naghten shot and killed him.

At trial, M'Naghten's barristers argued that he was insane at the time of the shooting and therefore should be found not guilty. The jury agreed. Enraged by the verdict, Queen Victoria insisted that the law provide a yardstick for the defense of insanity. The House of Lords responded, and the test they developed is still referred to as the *M'Naghten rule*. It provides that

> it must be clearly proved that, at the time of committing the act, the party accused was labouring under such a defect of reason, from disease of the mind, as not to know the nature and quality of the act he was doing; or, if he did know it, that he did not know what he was doing was wrong. *M'Naghten's Case,* 8 Eng. Rep. 718 (1843).

The *M'Naghten* rule became the test for insanity used in both federal and state courts in the United States. As psychology and psychiatry developed new theories of mental capacity, critics attacked the *M'Naghten* rule as being based solely on cognition (i.e., a process of the intellect) and ignoring a person's emotions. In response, some courts accepted the "irresistible impulse" test that stressed volition (i.e., self-control) as a supplement to the *M'Naghten* rule. See *Parsons v. State,* 2 So. 854 (Ala. 1887). This allowed a person who knew an act was wrong but who acted under an uncontrollable desire or the duress of mental disease to be excused from a criminal act.

The Durham Test.   Another test for insanity evolved from *Durham v. United States,* where the United States Court of Appeals for the District of Columbia held that an accused is not criminally responsible if that person's unlawful act was "the product of mental disease or defect." 214 F.2d 862, 876 (D.C. Cir. 1954). The *Durham* standard was applauded by many psychiatrists, but it gained little judicial support outside of the District of Columbia. It was eventually discarded even there. *United States v. Brawner,* 471 F.2d 969 (D.C. Cir. 1972).

The ALI Standard.   In 1962, the American Law Institute (ALI), an association of distinguished lawyers and judges, proposed a new standard combining both cognitive and volitional capacities as a test for insanity. It is sometimes referred to as the *substantial capacity* test and says:

A person is not responsible for criminal conduct if at the time of such conduct, as a result of mental disease or defect, a person lacks substantial capacity either to appreciate the wrongfulness of his conduct or to conform his conduct to the requirements of the law.

The ALI test was adopted by most federal courts and has sometimes been referred to as the *Freeman* rule, stemming from an endorsement of the test by the United States Court of Appeals for the Second Circuit in *United States v. Freeman,* 357 F.2d 606 (2d Cir. 1966). It was this substantial capacity concept that was applied in the Hinckley case.

State courts, however, divided in their approaches to the defense of insanity. Many opted to follow the new ALI test; the remainder adhered to the basic *M'Naghten* "right from wrong" test. Under the ALI criteria a showing of substantial impairment of a person's mental faculties is enough to meet the test of insanity. In contrast, to establish insanity under a strict *M'Naghten* approach, there must be a showing of total incapacity, and evidence that does not tend to prove or disprove the defendant's ability to distinguish right from wrong is irrelevant.

New Federal Standard. Dissatisfied with the ALI test, Congress decided to eliminate the volitional prong in the federal test for insanity and to revert substantially to the *M'Naghten* rule when it enacted the Insanity Defense Reform Act of 1984. This act provides that in federal courts:

> It is an affirmative defense to a prosecution under any Federal statute that, at the time of the commission of the acts constituting the offense, the defendant, as a result of a severe mental disease or defect, was unable to appreciate the nature and quality or the wrongfulness of his acts. Mental disease or defect does not otherwise constitute a defense. 18 U.S.C.A. § 17(a).

Additionally, the act stipulates "The defendant has the burden of proving the defense of insanity by clear and convincing evidence." 18 U.S.C.A. § 17(b). The *clear and convincing* standard is higher than the usual civil evidentiary standard of *preponderance of the evidence* but somewhat lower than the standard of *beyond a reasonable doubt,* which is the evidentiary standard required for criminal convictions. While there has been some controversy concerning the legitimacy of placing the burden of proof of insanity on the defendant, the United States Supreme Court has held that this type of "burden shifting" does not violate the defendant's right of due process of law under the federal Constitution. *Patterson v. New York,* 432 U.S. 197, 97 S. Ct. 2319, 53 L.Ed.2d 281 (1977). Moreover, two federal appellate court decisions in 1986 affirmed the constitutionality of this "burden shifting" under the 1984 federal act. *United States v. Freeman,* 804 F.2d 1574 (11th Cir. 1986); *United States v. Amos,* 803 F.2d 419 (8th Cir. 1986).

Effect of the Insanity Defense Reform Act on Use of Psychiatric Evidence to Negate Specific Intent

Under the Insanity Defense Reform Act, psychiatric evidence of impaired volitional control is inadmissible to support an insanity defense. After passage of the new law, a question arose as to whether Congress also intended to prohibit the use of psychiatric evidence to negate a defendant's specific intent to commit an offense. In 1990, the United States Court of Appeals for the Eleventh Circuit addressed the issue observing that "[b]oth Congress and the courts have recognized the crucial distinction between evidence of psychological impairment that supports an 'affirmative defense,' and psychological evidence that negates an element of the offense charged." The court ruled that the language of the new federal act does not bar the use of psychiatric evidence to negate specific intent where that level of intent is an element of the offense charged by the government. *United States v. Cameron*, 907 F.2d 1051, 1063 (11th Cir. 1990).

Contemporary State Developments. Although Congress has now placed the burden to prove their defense on defendants who plead insanity in federal courts, state courts are divided on who bears the burden of proof. In some states where insanity is classified as an affirmative defense, the defendant bears the burden of proof of insanity, usually by a "preponderance of the evidence." See, for example, *Clark v. State*, 588 P.2d 1027 (Nev. 1979). In other states, when a defendant pleads insanity and introduces some evidence of insanity, the state must then establish the defendant's sanity, usually by proof "beyond a reasonable doubt," the standard required for establishing a defendant's guilt. See, for example, *Parkin v. State*, 238 So.2d 817 (Fla. 1970). When the issue of insanity is raised, courts permit laypersons as well as expert witnesses to testify on the issue of the defendant's insanity.

Unlike a defendant who is simply found not guilty, a defendant who is found not guilty by reason of insanity is exposed to institutionalization and may, in some circumstances, be committed to a mental institution. *Jones v. United States*, 463 U.S. 354, 103 S. Ct. 3043, 77 L.Ed.2d 694 (1983). This is generally accomplished subsequent to the verdict by the trial judge, who determines whether protection of the public requires that the defendant be confined.

Guilty, but . . . . On the premise that a person should not be found not guilty on basis of insanity, some states have recently resorted to verdicts of "guilty but mentally ill" in cases where the defendant's insanity has been established. For example, in *People v. Sorna*, the court explained that this category of verdict deals with situations "where a defendant's mental illness does not deprive him of substantial capacity sufficient to satisfy the insanity test but does warrant treatment in addition to incarceration." 276 N.W.2d 892, 896 (Mich. App. 1979).

Automatism

Older cases treat defendants who claim that their unlawful acts were committed because of an involuntary condition such as somnambulism (i.e., sleepwalking) within the context of the insanity defense. Newer cases tend to classify such involuntary actions as automatism and view them as a basis for an affirmative defense independent from insanity. See, for example, *Fulcher v. State*, 633 P.2d 142 (Wyo. 1981). One reason cited in *Fulcher* for regarding automatism as a separate defense is that there are generally no follow-up consequences such as institutionalization, which usually occurs in an acquittal by reason of insanity.

C A S E   I N   P O I N T

INSANITY DEFENSE

Joy Ann Robey was charged with involuntary manslaughter and child abuse in connection with the death of her 10-month-old daughter, Christina. At trial, Robey admitted to beating the child severely and repeatedly over a two-month period but pleaded not guilty by reason of insanity. The trial court found that the defendant was temporarily insane each time she beat the child, but that she returned to sanity thereafter. Accordingly, the defendant could not be held criminally liable for the beatings but was responsible for her failure to seek medical care for her child. Robey was convicted of involuntary manslaughter and child abuse and sentenced to three concurrent ten-year terms in prison. Her conviction was upheld on appeal over her contention that the trial court erred in holding her criminally responsible after acknowledging that she was insane at the time of the beatings.

Robey v. State, 456 A.2d 953 (Md. App. 1983).

DEFENSES JUSTIFYING THE USE OF FORCE

The use of force may be a defense to a criminal charge that the defendant caused injury or death to another. Therefore, the defense of justifiable use of force may be applicable to the assaultive and homicidal offenses.

As a starting point, the use of "deadly force" (i.e., force likely to cause death or serious bodily injury) must be distinguished from the use of "nondeadly force." In general, the use of deadly force in self-defense requires that the person using such force: (1) be in a place where he or she has a right to be; (2) act without fault; and (3) act in reasonable fear or apprehension of death or great bodily harm. *Lilly v. State*, 506 N.E.2d 23 (Ind. 1987). In evaluating whether the use of deadly force is reasonable, courts consider numerous factors. Among these are the respective size, age, and physical abilities of the parties, whether the attacker is armed, and the attacker's reputation for violence. Ordinarily, a person may use whatever nondeadly force that appears reasonably necessary under the circumstances. *State v. Clay*, 256 S.E.2d 176 (N.C. 1979).

Self-Defense

Defendants frequently admit the commission of acts that constitute an assaultive or homicidal offense, but assert having acted in self-defense. Once a defendant raises the issue of self-defense, it becomes incumbent on the prosecution to prove beyond a reasonable doubt that the defendant did not act in self-defense. *Wash v. State*, 456 N.E.2d 1009 (Ind. 1983). There exist variations in the law on the permitted degree of force that can be used in self-defense, but the test of reasonableness appears common to all views. In determining the lawfulness of force used in self-defense, courts first look to see if the force used by the aggressor was unlawful. If so, the defender must show there was a necessity to use force for self-protection and that the degree of force used by the defender was reasonable considering the parties and circumstances.

At common law a person attacked had a duty "to retreat to the wall" before using deadly force in self-defense. *State v. Sipes,* 209 N.W. 458 (Iowa 1926). In *Scott v. State,* 34 So. 2d 718 (Miss. 1948), the court explained that to justify the slaying of another in self-defense at common law there must have been *actual* danger of loss of life or suffering of great bodily harm, but that the American approach has been that the danger *need not be actual but must be reasonably apparent and imminent.*

A majority of courts reject the common-law doctrine of requiring a person to retreat to the greatest extent possible before meeting force with force. Rather, they say that a person attacked or threatened may stand his or her ground and use any force reasonably necessary to prevent harm. Courts that take this view often state it in positive terms, as did the Oklahoma Court of Criminal Appeals when citing one of its 1912 precedents. It said: "The law in Oklahoma is clear: There is no duty to retreat if one is threatened with bodily harm." *Neal v. State,* 597 P.2d 334, 337 (Okl. Crim. App. 1979).

A substantial minority of courts, however, have adopted the principle that a person who can safely retreat must do so before using deadly force. As the Tennessee Supreme Court has stated:

> The law of excusable homicide requires that the defendant must have employed all means reasonably in his power, consistent with his own safety, to avoid danger and avert the necessity of taking another's life. This requirement includes the duty to retreat if, and, to the extent, that it can be done in safety. *State v. Kennamore,* 604 S.W.2d 856, 860 (Tenn. 1980).

Courts that follow the "retreat" rule have generally adopted the principle that a person does not have to retreat in his or her own dwelling. *State v. Bennett,* 105 N.W. 324 (Iowa 1905).

The Wisconsin Statutes codify the general law on use of force in self-defense by providing:

> A person is privileged to threaten or intentionally use force against another for the purpose of preventing or terminating what he reasonably believes to be an unlawful interference with his person by such other person. The actor may intentionally use only such force or threat thereof as he reasonably believes is necessary to prevent or terminate the interference. He may not intentionally use force which is intended or likely to cause death or great bodily harm unless he reasonably believes that such force is necessary to prevent imminent death or great bodily harm to himself. Wis. Stat. Ann. § 939.48(1).

The use of deadly force presents the greatest issue in self-defense. As noted earlier, deadly force may be used only where it reasonably appears necessary to use such force to prevent death or serious injury. In considering whether a defendant is justified in using deadly force, the law has traditionally applied an *objective* test. See, for example, *State v. Bess,* 247 A.2d 669 (N.J. 1968). Today, however, there is a conflict in the law and some courts apply a *subjective* standard of reasonableness to determine if circumstances are sufficient to induce in the defendant an honest and reasonable belief that force must be used. See, for example, *State v. Wanrow,* 559 P.2d 548 (Wash. 1977). The objective test requires the jury to place itself in the shoes of a hypothetical "reasonable and prudent person," whereas the subjective test permits a jury "to place itself in the defendant's own shoes."

Much of the impetus for courts applying the subjective test to determine whether the use of deadly force is reasonable has resulted from cases where women charged with committing assaultive or homicidal offenses against men have defended their use of force. In the leading case just cited (*State v. Wanrow*), Yvonne Wanrow, a woman on crutches, was convicted of second-degree murder and first-degree assault in her fatal shooting of a large, intoxicated man who refused to leave her home. In reversing her convictions, the Washington Supreme Court held that the trial judge erred by giving instructions to the jury that did not make it clear that Ms. Wanrow's actions were to be judged against her own *subjective* impressions and not those which the jury might determine to be objectively reasonable. The Court added:

> In our society women suffer from a conspicuous lack of access to training in and the means of developing those skills necessary to effectively repel a male assailant without resorting to the use of deadly weapons.

The Battered Woman Syndrome (BWS); the Battered Child Syndrome (BCS): Expanding the Concept of Self-Defense

Beyond the subjective standard of self-defense, in recent years the concept of self-defense by women has been expanded where a woman claims to have been continually battered by a man. The "battered spouse syndrome" soon became the "battered woman syndrome" (BWS). It describes a pattern of psychological and behavioral symptoms of women living with males in a battering relationship. Some jurisdictions now permit a female in that situation who is charged with assaulting or killing a man to show that even though she did not face immediate harm, her plea of self-defense should be recognized because her actions were her response to constant battering by the man with whom she lived.

Relatively little decisional law from the higher courts has developed in this area; however, in 1989 a California appellate court held that when a woman kills her batterer and pleads self-defense, expert testimony about BWS is admissible to explain how her particular experiences as a battered woman affected her perceptions of danger and her honest belief in its imminence. *People v. Aris*, 264 Cal. Rptr. 167 (Cal. App. 1989).

Following the same rationale, if there is evidence that a child has been abused continually over an extended period, there is a movement now to assert the "battered child syndrome" (BCS) in defense of a child accused of assaulting or killing a parent. Texas law now allows such evidence, including expert testimony, in cases involving children who kill their parents. Vernon's Tex. Pen. Code Ann. § 19.03. Many prosecutors claim the use of BCS is undermining the law of self-defense, yet there are experts who claim that a child's perceptions of the need to use force are shaped by his or her experience of constant abuse by a parent. They argue that when juries hear such evidence they may be persuaded that a child acted in self-defense and not out of retribution.

In the state of Washington, a boy who killed his stepfather was convicted of second-degree murder and two counts of second-degree assault. At his trial, the court held that evidence of the battered child syndrome could not, as a matter of law, support a finding of self-defense because there was no "imminent threat" to the defendant. In a much-discussed opinion the appellate court held this was error. "Neither law nor logic suggest any reason to limit to women recognition of the impact a battering relationship may have on the victim's actions or perceptions. . . . the rationale underlying the admissibility of testimony regarding the battered women syndrome is at least as compelling, if not more so, when applied to children." *State v. Janes*, 822 P.2d 1238, 1243 (Wash. App. 1992).

Defense of Others

At common law a defender had the right to use reasonable force to prevent commission of a felony or to protect members of the household who were endangered, a principle that was codified in many jurisdictions. See, for example, *State v. Fair*, 211 A.2d 359 (N.J. 1965). The trend in American jurisdictions is to allow a person "to stand in the shoes of the victim" and to use such reasonable force as is necessary to defend anyone, irrespective of relationship, from harm. As the court noted in *State v. Grier*, "What one may do for himself, he may do for another." 609 S.W.2d 201, 203 (Mo. App. 1980). Today a number of states have statutes that permit a person to assert force on behalf of another. To illustrate, the Wisconsin Statute provides:

> A person is privileged to defend a third person from real or apparent unlawful interference by another under the same conditions and by the same means as those under and by which he is privileged to defend himself from real or apparent unlawful interference, provided that he reasonably believes that the facts are such that the third person would be privileged to act in self-defense and that his intervention is necessary for the protection of the third person. Wis. Stat. Ann. § 939.48(4).

Like the quoted Wisconsin statute, many statutes limit a person's right to defend another individual from harm to those persons who "reasonably believe" that force is necessary to protect another. Some courts take a more restrictive view and hold that an intervenor is justified in using force to defend another only if the party being defended would have been justified in using the same force in self-defense. Of course, under either standard, the right to go to the defense of another does not authorize a person to resort to retaliatory force.

Defense of Property

The right to defend your property is more limited than the right to defend your homeplace or yourself. The common law allowed a person in lawful possession of property to use reasonable, but not deadly, force to protect it. *Russell v. State*, 122 So. 683 (Ala. 1929). Today, the use of force to protect a person's property is often defined by statute. Typically, Iowa law provides that "[a] person is justified in the use of reasonable force to prevent or terminate criminal interference with his or her possession or other right to property." Iowa Code Ann. § 704.4. The quoted statutory language generally represents contemporary decisional law even in absence of a statute.

Some older court decisions hold that a person may oppose force with force, even to the extent of taking a life in defense of his or her person, family, or property against a person attempting to commit a violent felony such as murder, robbery, or rape. These decisions, however, focus on preventing a dangerous felony rather than simply on the protection or recapture of property. The prevailing view of the courts is that, in the absence of the felonious use of force by an aggressor, a person must not inflict deadly harm simply for the protection or recapture of property. *State v. McCombs*, 253 S.E.2d 906 (N.C. 1979). The reason for this is that the law places higher value on preserving the life of the wrongdoer than on protection of someone's property.

One method of defending property has been through the use of a mechanical device commonly known as a "spring gun" that is set to go off when someone trips a wire or opens a door. In the earlier history of the country these devices were used on farms, in unoccupied structures, and sometimes set in a residence at night to wound or kill an intruder. Some early court decisions said that use of a spring gun that resulted in the death of an intruder into a person's home was justified in instances where a homeowner, if present, would have been authorized to use deadly force.

Today, if someone is killed or injured as a result of a spring gun or similar mechanical device, the party who set it (and anyone who caused it to be set) generally will be held criminally responsible for any resulting death or injury. This is true even if the intruder's conduct would ordinarily cause a party to believe that the intrusion threatened death or serious bodily injury, conditions that might justify the use of deadly force. The Model Penal Code takes the position that a device for protection of property may be used only if it "is not designed to cause or known to create a substantial risk of causing death or serious bodily harm." M.P.C. § 3.06(5).

Even courts in jurisdictions that have not adopted the MPC take a harsh view of the use of such mechanical devices, reasoning that to allow persons to

---

C A S E I N P O I N T

THE LAW OF SELF-DEFENSE

Defendant Ernest Young was distributing religious literature on the street when he was approached by George Coleman, who began to harass and swear at him. Later Coleman again accosted Young, this time at a table in a fast-food restaurant. Coleman began swearing at Young and grabbed his arm. Young pulled out a handgun and shot Coleman three times, killing him. Young was charged with and tried for murder. Notwithstanding his plea of self-defense, the jury returned a verdict of guilty of voluntary manslaughter. The appellate court reviewing the conviction said: "The jury heard appellant's story and it determined that he acted in the heat of the moment rather than in self-defense. There is ample evidence to support its verdict." The defendant's conviction was affirmed.

Young v. State, 451 N.E.2d 91 (Ind. App. 1983).

use them can imperil the lives of innocent persons such as firefighters, police officers, and even children at play. Finally, some courts point to another reason: While a deadly mechanical device acts without mercy or discretion, yet there is always the possibility that a human being protecting property would avoid taking a human life or injuring someone. See *People v. Ceballos*, 526 P.2d 241 (Cal. 1974).

Defense of Habitation

The common law placed great emphasis on the security of a person's dwelling and permitted the use of deadly force against an intruder. *Russell v. State*, 122 So. 683 (Ala. 1929). This historical view was chronicled by the Illinois Supreme Court in *People v. Eatman*, when it observed:

> As a matter of history the defense of habitation has been the most favored branch of self-defense from the earliest times. Lord Coke, in his Commentaries, says: "A man's home is his castle—for where shall a man be safe if it be not in his house?" 91 N.E.2d 387, 390 (Ill. 1950).

Referring to a person's defense of habitation, the *Eatman* court opined that "he may use all of the force apparently necessary to repel any invasion of his home." 91 N.E. 2d at 390. This is sometimes referred to as the "castle doctrine." While a householder may, under some circumstances, be justified in using deadly force, the householder would not be justified in taking a life to repel a mere trespass.

In *State v. McCombs, supra*, the North Carolina Supreme Court said that the use of deadly force is generally justified to prevent a forcible entry into the habitation by such circumstances as threats or where the occupant reasonably apprehends death or great bodily harm to self or other occupant or reasonably believes the assailant intends to commit a felony. This general principle is subject to some statutory and decisional variations.

The courts have generally applied the castle doctrine against trespassers, but they have divided on whether this doctrine applies to co-occupants or others legally on the premises. Older cases hold that a person need not retreat when assailed by a co-occupant—see, for example, *People v. Tomlins*, 107 N.E. 496 (N.Y. 1914)—but many newer decisions hold that when an assailant and the victim are both legal occupants of the same home, the castle doctrine does not apply. For example, in *State v. Bobbitt*, 415 So.2d 724 (Fla. 1982), the Florida Supreme Court refused to apply the doctrine where both spouses were legally occupying the same home.

Defense to Being Arrested

At common law a person had the right to use such force as reasonably necessary, short of killing, to resist an unlawful arrest. *Regina v. Tooley*, 92 Eng. Rep. 349 (1710). The common-law rule developed at a time when bail was largely unavailable, arraignments were delayed for months until a royal judge arrived,

---

CASE IN POINT

DEFENSE OF HABITATION

Defendant Raines was charged with murder in connection with the death of Ricky Stinson. Stinson was the passenger in a car driven by James Neese. The evidence showed that Neese had threatened to kill Raines, and that Neese had driven past Raines's trailer and fired some shots out the window of his car. Raines was not home at the time, but when he returned his live-in companion, Sharon Quates, told him what had happened. A few minutes later they heard a car approaching and went outside. Quates identified the car as the same one from which the shots had been fired. As the car drove away, Raines fired five shots from a semiautomatic rifle. Quates testified that Raines said that "he'd just shoot the tire out and stop it and we'd go get the law and find out who it was." However, one of the bullets struck Ricky Stinson in the head, killing him. Despite his plea that he acted in self-defense and defense of his habitation, Raines was convicted of manslaughter.

The conviction was upheld on appeal, the appellate court saying that "although Raines may well have been in fear of danger when the . . . car approached, such fear alone did not justify his firing at the car as it drove down the public road past his trailer." The court further observed: "One assaulted in his house need not flee therefrom. But his house is his castle only for the purposes of defense. It cannot be turned into an arsenal for the purpose of offensive effort against the lives of others."

Raines v. State, 455 So.2d 967, 972–3 (Ala. Crim. App. 1984).

---

and conditions in English jails were deplorable. Until recently most American courts have followed the English view. See, for example, *State v. Small,* 169 N.W. 116 (Iowa 1918). In some states a person may still forcibly resist an unlawful arrest.

As pointed out in Chapter 12, the rationale for the rule has substantially eroded. Increasingly, legislatures and courts recognize that resisting an arrest exposes both the officer and the arrestee to escalating violence. Moreover, defendants are now promptly arraigned, and counsel is generally available to debate the legality of an arrest in court. See *United States v. Ferrone,* 438 F.2d 381 (3d Cir. 1971), *cert. denied,* 402 U.S. 1008, 91 S. Ct. 2188, 29 L.Ed.2d 430 (1971); *State v. Ramsdell,* 285 A.2d 399 (R.I. 1971).

Use of Force by Police

Most states have statutes or police regulations that specify the degree of force that may be used to apprehend violators. Officers are usually permitted to use such force as is reasonably necessary to effect an arrest. In practice, deadly force is seldom used by modern police forces; yet many states have statutes that authorize the use of deadly force by police in apprehending felons.

In 1974 a Memphis, Tennessee, police officer shot and killed an unarmed 15-year-old-boy who fled from the scene of a reported burglary. The officer acted pursuant to a state law that permitted use of deadly force in such an instance. Civil litigation ensued and, in 1985, the United States Supreme Court ruled that the use of deadly force to apprehend a suspect is a seizure governed by the Fourth Amendment requirement of reasonableness. The Court held unconstitutional the statute that permitted an officer to use all necessary means to effect an arrest if the suspect flees or forcibly resists. The decision effectively limits an officer's use of deadly force to instances where it is necessary to prevent the escape of an arrestee who, the officer has probable cause to believe, poses a significant threat of death or serious injury to the officer or others. *Tennessee v. Garner*, 471 U.S. 1, 105 S. Ct. 1694, 85 L.Ed.2d 1 (1985).

A law enforcement officer who injures or kills a person or damages someone's property is sometimes charged with a criminal offense. An officer who kills or injures while in line of duty may assert the defense of having performed a public function. As long as the officer acted reasonably and not in violation of the Fourth Amendment, a statute or valid police regulations, the defense is established.

DEFENSES BASED ON MISTAKE

There are two defenses based on a defendant's mistake: mistake of law and mistake of fact.

Mistake of Law

One of the best-known maxims of the law is that "ignorance of the law is no excuse." It is obvious that the safety and welfare of society demand that persons not be excused from commission of criminal acts on the basis of their claims of not knowing that they committed crimes. See, for example, *Hoover v. State*, 59 Ala. 57 (1877). While this is the generally accepted view, in some instances a defendant's honest, but mistaken, view of the law may be accepted as a defense. One example is where such a mistake negates the specific-intent element of a crime. Thus, a mistake of law may be asserted as a defense in a larceny case where there is a technical question of who has legal title to an asset. *State v. Abbey*, 474 P.2d 62 (Ariz. App. 1970). Likewise, a defendant's good-faith, but mistaken, trust in the validity of a divorce has been held to be a defense to a charge of bigamy. *Long v. State*, 65 A.2d 489 (Del. 1949).

The Illinois Criminal Code lists four exceptions to the general rule that a person's ignorance of the law does not excuse unlawful conduct: It provides:

> A person's reasonable belief that certain conduct does not constitute a criminal offense is a defense if:
> (1) The offense is defined by an administrative regulation which is not known to him and has not been published or otherwise made reasonably available to him, and he could not have acquired such knowledge by the exercise of due diligence pursuant to facts known to him; or
> (2) He acts in reliance upon a statute which later is determined to be invalid; or
> (3) He acts in reliance upon an order or opinion of an Illinois Appellate or Supreme Court, or a United States appellate court later overruled or reversed; or

---

C A S E   I N   P O I N T

WHEN A PENALTY IS IMPOSED FOR FAILURE TO ACT, REASONABLE NOTICE OF A LOCAL ORDINANCE MAY BE REQUIRED

A Los Angeles, California, ordinance made it unlawful for any "convicted persons" to remain in the city for more than five days without registering with the police; or if they lived outside of the city, to enter the city on five or more occasions during a thirty-day period without registering. Virginia Lambert, a convicted felon, was found guilty of failing to register, fined $250, and placed on probation for three years.

On appeal to the United States Supreme Court, Lambert's conviction was reversed. Writing for the Court, Justice Douglas observed: "Enshrined in our concept of due process is the requirement of notice. Notice is sometimes essential so that the citizen has the chance to defend charges. . . . Notice is required in a myriad of situations where a penalty or forfeiture might be suffered from mere failure to act."

Lambert v. California, 355 U.S. 225, 78 S.Ct 240, 2 L.Ed.2d 228 (1957).

---

(4) He acts in reliance upon an official interpretation of the statute, regulation or order defining the offense, made by a public officer or agency legally authorized to interpret such statute. Smith-Hurd Ann. 720 ILCS 5/4-8(b).

Citing the preceding exceptions, the Illinois Supreme Court held that a taxpayer who contended that she reasonably believed that she would be subject only to civil penalties, not to criminal sanctions, for failure to file an occupational tax return, did not present a "mistake of law" defense. *People v. Sevilla*, 547 N.E.2d 117 (Ill. 1989).

In *United States v. Moore*, 627 F.2d 830 (7th Cir. 1980), *cert. denied*, 450 U.S. 916, 101 S. Ct. 1360, 67 L.Ed.2d 342 (1981), the court said, "[T]he mistake of law defense is extremely limited and the mistake must be objectively reasonable." 627 F.2d at 833. Furthermore, courts have long made it clear that a dishonest pretense of ignorance of the law will never be recognized by a court as a defense. *State v. Carroll*, 60 S.W. 1087 (Mo. 1901).

A defendant may always raise the unconstitutionality of a statute as a defense to a prosecution for its violation. But a person who violates a statute thinking it unconstitutional does so at his or her peril; for courts have said that a person's belief that a statute is unconstitutional, even if based on advice of counsel, does not constitute a valid defense for violating the law. *State v. Thorstad*, 261 N.W.2d 899 (N.D. 1978), *cert. denied*, 436 U.S. 906, 98 S. Ct. 2237, 56 L.Ed.2d 404 (1978).

Mistake of Fact

In contrast to the ancient common-law maxim that "ignorance of the law is no excuse," at common law ignorance or mistake of fact, guarded by an honest purpose, afforded a defendant a sufficient excuse for a supposed criminal act. *Farrell v. State*, 32 Ohio St. 456 (1877). American courts have agreed, but have generally said that a mistake of fact will not be recognized as a defense to a general-intent crime unless the mistake is a reasonable one for a person to make under the circumstances. However, even an unreasonable mistake may be asserted as a defense to a crime that requires a specific intent. The decisions in recent years have indicated that a mistake of fact may be a defense as long as it negatives the existence of the mental state essential to the crime charged. See, for example, *State v. Fuentes*, 577 P.2d 452 (N.M. App. 1978), *cert. denied*, 577 P.2d 1256 (N.M. 1978).

Some jurisdictions have codified the mistake-of-fact defense. In Indiana, for example, mistake of fact is an affirmative defense by statute:

> It is a defense that the person who engaged in the prohibited conduct was reasonably mistaken about a matter of fact if the mistake negates the culpability required for commission of the offense. West's Ind. Code Ann. § 35–41–3–7.

In strict-liability offenses, the defense of mistake of fact is unavailing since these offenses are not based on intent (see Chapter 4). In pointing out that this view represents the weight of authority, the Montana Supreme Court held that ignorance or even a *bona fide* belief that a minor was of legal age did not constitute a defense to prosecution for selling intoxicating liquor to a minor, unless expressly made so by the statute. *State v. Parr*, 283 P.2d 1086 (Mont. 1955). Likewise, as pointed out in Chapter 4, since having consensual sexual relations with a minor is generally considered a strict-liability offense, a mistake of fact as to a minor's age is generally not a defense to a charge of statutory rape. Even if a court finds that a statutory rape statute requires proof of a general criminal intent to convict, a defendant's reasonable mistake of fact concerning a female's age is generally not available as a defense. *State v. Stiffler*, 788 P.2d 220 (Idaho 1990). However, in 1964 the California Supreme Court departed from this almost universally accepted rule and held that an accused's good-faith, reasonable belief that a female had reached the age of consent would be a defense to statutory rape. *People v. Hernandez*, 393 P.2d 673 (Cal. 1964).

In the past few years, in cases of statutory rape, some trial courts have heard arguments based on a minor's right to privacy. The contention is that since a minor female can consent to an abortion, she should be able to consent to sexual intercourse. Although this argument has generally fallen on deaf ears, some trial judges have questioned the need to continue to employ a strict-liability standard in consensual sexual relationships where the female is a minor and appears and represents herself as an adult.

DEFENSES BASED ON CONSTITUTIONAL AND STATUTORY AUTHORITY

The guarantees of the Bill of Rights give rise to two constitutional defenses: immunity and double jeopardy. In addition, a defense may be based on a so-called "statute of limitations."

Immunity—A Constitutional Defense

Everyone is familiar with the scenario of the witness who invokes the constitutional privilege against self-incrimination based on the Fifth Amendment to the Constitution that provides that "[N]o person . . . shall be compelled in any criminal case to be a witness against himself." The privilege against self-incrimination is applicable to the states through the Fourteenth Amendment, *Malloy v. Hogan*, 378 U.S. 1, 84 S. Ct. 1489, 12 L.Ed.2d 653 (1964), although states have similar protections in their constitutions.

The privilege against self-incrimination guaranteed by the federal Constitution is a personal one that applies only to natural persons and not corporations. *United States v. White*, 322 U.S. 694, 64 S. Ct. 1248, 88 L.Ed. 1542 (1944). A strict reading of the clause would limit the privilege to testimony given in a criminal trial. The Supreme Court, however, has held that an individual may refuse "to answer official questions put to him in any . . . proceeding, civil or criminal, formal or informal, where the answers might incriminate him in future criminal proceedings." *Lefkowitz v. Turley*, 414 U.S. 70, 77, 94 S. Ct. 316, 322, 38 L.Ed.2d 274, 281 (1973). A classic example is the privilege of suspects in police custody to invoke their *Miranda* rights, a subject we discuss in Chapter 15.

Use Immunity.   Frequently, when a witness invokes the Fifth Amendment and refuses to testify, the court is requested to compel the requested testimony. This may be accomplished by conferring on the witness *immunity*, which is a grant of amnesty to protect the witness from prosecution through the use of compelled testimony. A witness compelled to give incriminating testimony thus receives *use immunity* (i.e., the testimony given cannot be used against the witness). This form of immunity is co-extensive with the scope of the privilege against self-incrimination and meets the demands of the Constitution. *Kastigar v. United States*, 406 U.S. 441, 92 S. Ct. 1653, 32 L.Ed.2d 212 (1972).

Transactional Immunity.   In some states a witness who testifies under a grant of immunity is given *transactional immunity*, a broader protection than required under the federal Constitution. Transactional immunity protects a witness from prosecution for any activity mentioned in the witness's testimony. A recent example of requiring broader protection occurred in 1993 when the Alaska Supreme Court ruled that its state constitution requires that witnesses who are compelled to testify be given the more-protective transactional immunity from prosecution, not just use or derivative immunity as required by the federal constitution. *State v. Gonzalez*, 853 P.2d 526 (Alaska 1993).

As noted in Chapter 16, a defendant may assert the defense of immunity by a pretrial motion. Despite a grant of immunity, a witness may be prosecuted for making material false statements under oath. *United States v. Apfelbaum*, 445 U.S. 115, 100 S. Ct. 948, 63 L.Ed.2d 250 (1980) (see Chapter 12).

Contractual Immunity.   Sometimes a witness is granted *contractual immunity* by a prosecutor with approval of the court. The purpose is to induce a suspect to testify against someone and thereby enable the prosecution to obtain a conviction not otherwise obtainable because of constitutional protection against self-incrimination. This type of immunity is rarely granted if other available evidence will lead to a conviction. The authority to grant immunity in federal courts is vested in the United States Attorney with approval of the Attorney General or certain authorized assistants. 18 U.S.C.A. § 6003. At the state level such authority is generally vested in the chief prosecuting officer (i.e., the district or state attorney).

Diplomatic Immunity. Another form of immunity is called diplomatic immunity. Under international law, a person who has diplomatic status and serves as a part of a diplomatic mission, as well as members of the diplomat's staff and household, is immune from arrest and prosecution.

Double Jeopardy: Another Constitutional Defense

The concept of forbidding retrial of a defendant who has been found not guilty developed from the common law. *Ex parte Lange,* 85 U.S. (18 Wall.) 163, 21 L.Ed. 872 (1873). The Fifth Amendment to the United States Constitution embodied the principle by stating "[N]or shall any person be subject for the same offence to be twice put in jeopardy of life or limb." This language in the Fifth Amendment is referred to as the *double jeopardy* clause. It was made applicable to the states through the Fourteenth Amendment in *Benton v. Maryland,* 395 U.S. 784, 89 S. Ct. 2056, 23 L.Ed.2d 707 (1969). Even before that all states provided essentially the same protection through their constitutions, statutes, or judicial decisions recognizing common-law principles.

Justice Black expressed the rationale underlying the double jeopardy clause when he wrote:

> The underlying idea, one that is deeply ingrained in at least the Anglo-American system of jurisprudence, is that the State with all its resources and power should not be allowed to make repeated attempts to convict an individual for an alleged offense, thereby subjecting him to embarrassment, expense and ordeal and compelling him to live in a continuing state of anxiety and insecurity, as well as enhancing the possibility that even though innocent he may be found guilty. *Green v. United States,* 355 U.S. 184, 187–188, 78 S. Ct. 221, 223, 2 L.Ed.2d 199, 204 (1957).

Jeopardy attaches once the jury is sworn in, *Crist v. Bretz,* 437 U.S. 28, 98 S. Ct. 2156, 57 L.Ed.2d 24 (1978), or when the first witness is sworn in to testify in a nonjury trial. *Serfass v. United States,* 420 U.S. 377, 95 S. Ct. 1055, 43 L.Ed.2d 265 (1975). As we note in Chapter 16, the defense of double jeopardy may be asserted by pretrial motion.

The double jeopardy clause forbids a second prosecution for the same offense after a defendant has been acquitted. *Ball v. United States,* 163 U.S. 662, 16 S. Ct. 1192, 41 L.Ed. 300 (1896). In recent years this principle has been applied even after a conviction. *United States v. Wilson,* 420 U.S. 332, 95 S. Ct. 1013, 43 L.Ed.2d 232 (1975). But, if a defendant appeals a conviction and prevails, it is not double jeopardy for the prosecution to retry the defendant unless the appellate court has ruled that there was insufficient evidence to sustain the conviction. *Burks v. United States,* 437 U.S. 1, 98 S. Ct. 2141, 57 L.Ed.2d 1 (1978). Note the distinction between a conviction reversed by a higher court on basis of *insufficient* evidence and a defendant's conviction being vacated and a new trial ordered based on the *weight* of the evidence. In the latter case, a retrial of the defendant would not constitute double jeopardy. *Tibbs v. Florida,* 457 U.S. 31, 102 S. Ct. 2211, 72 L.Ed.2d 652 (1982). Nor is it double jeopardy to retry a defendant if the trial court, at the defendant's request, has declared a mistrial. *Oregon v. Kennedy,* 456 U.S. 667, 102 S. Ct. 2083, 72 L.Ed.2d 416 (1982). If, however, the government moves for a mistrial and the defendant objects, the prosecution must establish a "manifest necessity" for the mistrial in order for a retrial to be permitted. An example of a manifest necessity might be a highly improper opening statement by the defendant's counsel. *Arizona v. Washington,* 434 U.S. 497, 98 S. Ct. 824, 54 L.Ed.2d 717 (1978).

Some offenses are crimes against both the federal and state governments. The policy, and in some instances state law, forbids a second prosecution once an offender has been prosecuted in a different jurisdiction. Nevertheless, under our federal system the double jeopardy clause does not preclude a prosecution by both the federal and state governments, since separate sovereigns are involved. *Bartkus v. Illinois,* 359 U.S. 121, 79 S. Ct. 676, 3 L.Ed.2d 684 (1959). Yet, this principle does not allow two courts within a state to try an accused for the same offense. Therefore, a person who has been prosecuted in a city or county court cannot be tried again in any court in the state for the same offense. *Waller v. Florida,* 397 U.S. 387, 90 S. Ct. 1184, 25 L.Ed.2d 435 (1970). In addition to protecting against a second prosecution for the same offense after conviction or acquittal, the double jeopardy clause protects against multiple punishments for the same offense. *North Carolina v. Pearce,* 395 U.S. 711, 89 S.Ct. 2072, 23 L.Ed.2d 656 (1969). The Constitution, however, does not define *same offense.* In 1932 the Supreme Court said:

> The applicable rule is that, where the same act or transaction constitutes a violation of two distinct statutory provisions, the test to be applied to determine whether there are two offenses or only one is whether each provision requires proof of an additional fact which the other does not. *Blockburger v. United States,* 284 U.S. 299, 304, 52 S. Ct. 180, 182, 76 L.Ed. 306, 309 (1932).

The *Blockburger* test compares the elements of the crimes in question. It is a tool of interpretation and creates a presumption of legislative intent, but it is not designed to contravene such intent. Rather, the Supreme Court has said that it is the "legislative intent" if clear that determines the scope of what constitutes "same offenses." *Missouri v. Hunter,* 459 U.S. 359, 103 S. Ct. 673, 74 L.Ed.2d 535 (1983); *Albernaz v. United States,* 450 U.S. 333, 101 S. Ct. 1137, 67 L.Ed.2d 275 (1981). In 1980, the Supreme Court reviewed a case where the defendant was first convicted of failing to slow down to avoid an accident with his car and later charged with manslaughter arising from the same incident. After reciting the "elements" test in *Blockburger,* the Court stated that "if in the pending manslaughter prosection Illinois relies on and proves a failure to slow to avoid an accident as the reckless act necessary to prove manslaughter, Vitale [the defendant] would have a substantial claim of double jeopardy under the Fifth and Fourteenth Amendments of the United States Constitution" *Illinois v. Vitale,* 447 U.S. 410, 420, 100 S.Ct. 2260, 2267, 65 L.Ed.2d 228, 238 (1980).

The *Blockburger* test examines the *elements,* not the *facts.* Since the Supreme Court's decision in *Vitale,* not all courts have regarded *Blockburger* as the exclusive method of determining whether successive prosecutions violate the principle of double jeopardy. Indeed, some courts look also to the evidence to be presented to prove those crimes. For example, the Connecticut Supreme Court citing *Vitale* held that prosecution of a defendant for operating a vehicle under the influence of intoxicants after prior acquittal for manslaughter with a motor vehicle while intoxicated was barred by principle of double jeopardy. Even though the offenses were not the same under the *Blockburger* test, the same evidence offered to prove a violation of the offense charged in the first prosecution was to be the sole evidence offered to prove an element of the offense charged in the second prosecution. Thus, the court held the second prosecution barred by the principle of double jeopardy. *State v. Lonergan*, 566 A.2d 677 (Conn. 1989). Other courts continue to determine the issue of double jeopardy by applying the *Blockburger* test. See, for example, *Butler v. State*, 816 S.W.2d 124 (Tex. App. 1991).

In *Grady v. Corbin*, 495 U.S. 508, 110 S.Ct. 2084, 109 L.Ed.2d 548 (1990), the Supreme Court continued to follow the approach in *Illinois v. Vitale, supra,* saying that "if to establish an essential element of an offense charged in that prosecution, the government will prove conduct that constitutes an offense for which the defendant has already been prosecuted," a second prosecution may not be had. 495 U.S. at 510, 110 S.Ct. at 2087, 109 L.Ed.2d at ___. This became known as the "same evidence" test and barred a second prosecution based on the same conduct by the defendant that was at issue in the first prosecution. In June 1993, however, in *United States v. Dixon*, 509 U.S. ___, 113 S.Ct. ___, 125 L.Ed.2d 556 (1993), by a 5-4 margin, the Court overruled *Grady v. Corbin* replacing the "same evidence" test for double jeopardy analysis by a return to the "same elements" test from *Blockburger v. United States*, which bars punishment for offenses that have the same elements, or when one offense includes or is included in another offense. In *Dixon* the Court also ruled that a criminal contempt conviction represents a "jeopardy" that triggers the bar against a second prosecution for the same offense.

In a high-profile case in 1992, four Los Angeles police officers were tried by jury in a California state court on charges arising out of the beating of Rodney King, an African-American motorist stopped by the police for traffic infractions. The event was videotaped by an onlooker and televised nationally. The jury's verdict finding them not guilty was followed by considerable outrage and large-scale destructive rioting in Los Angeles. Despite their acquittal, the federal government brought new charges against the officers for violating King's civil rights. Their pleas that the new federal charges were barred by the double jeopardy clause of the Fifth Amendment were rejected by the United States District Court, and in April 1993 two of the four officers were convicted after a jury trial.

As noted earlier, the dual sovereignty of the federal government and the states allow separate trials of a defendant for the same offense. In the past this has not been a major problem, since it has been governmental policy not to cause duplicate prosecutions. Some deviations from this policy have occurred in recent years. In response to increasing attempts to try defendants in state and federal courts on similar charges, the American Bar Association has announced it is forming a task force to study the double jeopardy issue.

Statutes of Limitation

A statute of limitations is a legislative enactment that places a time limit on the prosecution of a crime. Common law placed no time limits on prosecution, but the federal government and almost all states have prescribed certain time limits for prosecution of most offenses. These statutes seldom place time limits on prosecutions for murder and other very serious offenses.

There are two primary public policy reasons for enacting statutes of limitations on the prosecution of crimes. First, it is generally accepted that a person should not be under threat of prosecution for too long a period. Second, after a prolonged period, proof is either unavailable or, if available, perhaps not credible.

Under most statutes of limitations the period for prosecution begins when a crime is committed, and not when it is discovered. The period ends when an arrest warrant is issued, an indictment is returned, or an information is filed. The period of limitations is interrupted while a perpetrator is a fugitive or conceals one's self from authorities. This cessation of the statute of limitations is often referred to as a "tolling" of the statutory period.

Federal statutes of limitations provide a five-year limitation on prosecution of noncapital crimes. 18 U.S.C.A. § 3282 *et seq.* While limitations periods vary among the states, the Ohio law appears representative. It provides:

> Except as otherwise provided in this section, a prosecution shall be barred unless it is commenced within the following periods after an offense is committed:
>
> (1) For a felony other than aggravated murder or murder, six years;
> (2) For a misdemeanor other than a minor misdemeanor, two years;
> (3) For a minor misdemeanor, six months. Page's Ohio Rev. Code Ann. § 2901.13(A).

There is a conflict among the various jurisdictions as to whether a statute of limitations in a criminal action is an affirmative defense. An affirmative defense that is not pled is deemed waived. Therefore, where courts consider a defendant's assertion that a prosecution is barred by the statute of limitations to be an affirmative defense, the running of the statutory period would not necessarily bar the prosecution. Other courts follow the rule that if the state's information or indictment discloses that the prosecution is initiated beyond the period allowed by the applicable statute of limitations, the prosecution is barred. In this latter instance, a convicted defendant could raise on appeal the issue of the statute of limitations having barred prosecution of the offense.

DEFENSES BASED ON GOVERNMENT CONDUCT

There are two defenses based on improper government conduct: entrapment and selective prosecution. These defenses are grounded in the constitutional requirements of due process and equal protection of the law.

Entrapment

Law enforcement officers may provide an opportunity for a predisposed person to commit a crime, but they are not permitted to "manufacture" crime by implanting criminal ideas into innocent minds. Therefore, a person who has been induced to commit an offense under these latter circumstances may plead the defense of entrapment. The defense of entrapment is often asserted by a defendant who claims entrapment as a result of inducement by an undercover police officer or a confidential police informant. It is not available to a defendant who has been entrapped by a person not associated with the government or police. See *Henderson v. United States*, 237 F.2d 169 (5th Cir. 1956).

Entrapment was not a defense under the common law, but it has long been recognized in federal and state courts in the United States. In 1980, the Tennessee Supreme Court acknowledged that Tennessee was the only state in the Union that did not allow entrapment as a defense and proceeded to remedy the situation by declaring, "From this day forward entrapment is a defense to a Tennessee criminal prosecution." *State v. Jones*, 598 S.W.2d 209, 212 (Tenn. 1980).

In a landmark case arising during prohibition days, the United States Supreme Court held that a federal officer had entrapped a defendant by using improper inducements to cause him to buy illegal liquor for the officer. The Court opined that entrapment occurs when criminal conduct involved is "the product of the creative activity of [law enforcement officers]." *Sorrells v. United States*, 287 U.S. 435, 451, 53 S. Ct. 210, 216, 77 L.Ed. 413, 422 (1932).

In *Sorrells*, the majority of the justices viewed entrapment as whether the defendant's criminal intent originated in the mind of the officer or whether the defendant was predisposed to commit the offense. This focus on the predisposition of the defendant has come to be known as the "subjective test" of entrapment. A minority of justices in *Sorrells* would have applied what is now known as the "objective test." Under this view, the court would simply determine whether the police methods were so improper as likely to induce or ensnare a person into committing a crime. The objective test is obviously designed to prohibit police methods that pose a substantial risk of inducing people to commit crimes.

In the past, the majority of federal and state courts have followed the subjective view, and a person who pled entrapment was held to have admitted commission of the offense. See, for example, *United States v. Sedigh*, 658 F.2d 1010 (5th Cir. 1981), *cert. denied*, 455 U.S. 921, 102 S. Ct. 1279, 71 L.Ed.2d 462 (1982); *State v. Amodei*, 563 P.2d 440 (Kan. 1977). A jury would then determine whether the defendant committed the crime because of predisposition, or whether the defendant was improperly induced to do so by the police. To sustain the defense of entrapment, it is usually sufficient for the defendant to show that the police used methods of persuasion likely to cause a normally law-abiding person to commit the offense. See, for example, *State v. Mullen*, 216 N.W. 2d 375 (Iowa 1974); but see *United States v. Demma*, 523 F.2d 981 (9th Cir. 1975), holding that a defendant may assert entrapment without being required to concede commission of the crime or any element thereof.

Where courts follow the objective view, the judge, not the jury, determines whether the police methods were so improper as to constitute entrapment. See, for example, *People v. D'Angelo*, 257 N.W.2d 655 (Mich. 1977). Some federal courts have simply said that where police conduct is outrageous, it becomes a question of law for the judge to determine if governmental misconduct is so shocking as to be a due process of law violation. See, for example, *United States v. Wylie*, 625 F.2d 1371 (9th Cir. 1980), *cert. denied*, 449 U.S. 1080, 101 S. Ct. 863, 66 L.Ed.2d 804

(1981). In courts that strictly follow the objective view, the defendant's predisposition to commit an offense is irrelevant.

Recent decisions indicate that the subjective and objective tests can coexist. Some state courts now first determine whether a defendant who pleads entrapment has been ensnared by outrageous police methods. If so, the judge dismisses the charges against the ensnared defendant. If not, the court then allows the defendant to attempt to establish the defense of entrapment by proving improper inducement. The prosecution usually counters with evidence showing the defendant's prior criminal activity and ready acquiescence in committing the crime charged. The court then instructs the jury to determine whether the defendant committed the crime because of his or her predisposition or through inducement by the police. At least two states have adopted this general approach. *Cruz v. State,* 465 So.2d 516 (Fla. 1985), *cert. denied,* 473 U.S. 905, 105 S. Ct. 3527, 87 L.Ed.2d 652 (1985); *State v. Talbot,* 364 A.2d 9 (N.J. 1976).

Two principal reasons account for the increased assertion of the defense of entrapment in recent years. First, a large number of violations of narcotics laws have been prosecuted on the basis of undercover police activity and evidence given by confidential police informants. Second, there has been increased attention to prosecuting corruption involving government officials. Perhaps the most highly publicized cases in recent years resulted from the 1980 Abscam operation, in which Federal Bureau of Investigation (FBI) agents posed as wealthy Arab businessmen and attempted to buy influence from members of Congress. Despite their claims of entrapment, several members of Congress were found guilty of offenses involving misuse of office. See, for example, *United States v. Jenrette,* 744 F.2d 817 (D.C. Cir. 1984), *cert. denied,* 471 U.S. 1099, 105 S. Ct. 2321, 85 L.Ed.2d 840 (1985).

In 1987, Keith Jacobson was indicted for violating the Child Protection Act of 1984, 18 U.S.C.A. § 2252(a)(2)(A), which criminalizes the knowing receipt through the mails of a "visual depiction [that] involves the use of a minor engaging in sexually explicit conduct." At trial Jacobson contended the government entrapped him into committing the crime. A jury found him guilty, and his conviction was affirmed by the Court of Appeals. The United States Supreme Court granted review.

In evaluating the evidence at Jacobson's trial, the Supreme Court found that while it was still legal to so, Jacobson ordered some magazines containing photos of nude boys. After Congress enacted the Child Protection Act making this illegal, two government agencies sent mail to Jacobson through fictitious organizations to explore his willingness to break the law. He was literally bombarded with solicitations, which included communications decrying censorship and questioning the legitimacy and constitutionality of the government's efforts to restrict availability of sexually explicit materials. He finally responded to an undercover solicitation to order child pornography and was arrested after a controlled delivery of the explicit sexual materials.

After pointing out that for 26 months the government agents had made Jacobson the target of repeated mailings, the Court held that the prosecution failed, as a matter of law, to produce evidence that Jacobson was predisposed, independent of the government's acts, to violate the law. Adding that government agents may not implant a criminal design in an innocent person's mind and

---

CASE IN POINT

Entrapment as a Matter of Law

Law enforcement officers told a female that she might not be prosecuted for possession of cocaine if she would become a confidential informant. She agreed and met with the defendant, James Banks, a suspected drug dealer, on two nights. The meetings included "kissing and hugging," after which she told defendant James Banks that if he "could get her something [they] would get together for the weekend, fool around and party." Defendant obtained some cocaine for her and as a result he was arrested. The trial judge dismissed the charges because the uncontested facts established that the officers used a method with a substantial risk of persuading or inducing the defendant to commit a criminal offense.

The state appealed the dismissal. The appellate court affirmed, observing: "When law enforcement agencies utilize confidential informants who use sex, or the express or implied promise thereof, to obtain contraband the defendant did not already possess, there is no way for the courts or anyone else to determine whether such inducement served only to uncover an existing propensity or created a new one. This violates the threshold objective test."

State v. Banks, 499 So.2d 894 (Fla. App. 1986).

---

then induce commission of a crime, the Court reversed his conviction, observing that Congress had not intended for government officials to instigate crime by luring persons otherwise innocent to commit offenses. *Jacobson v. United States*, 503 U.S. ___ , 112 S.Ct. 1535, 118 L.Ed.2d 174 (1992).

While the Court's decision is not grounded on constitutional principles, it not only affects federal enforcement activities, it signals state enforcement authorities not to play on the weaknesses of innocent parties and beguile them into committing crimes.

Selective Prosecution

Selective enforcement of the criminal law is not itself a constitutional violation, and therefore, without more, it does not constitute a defense. *Oyler v. Boles*, 368 U.S. 448, 82 S. Ct. 501, 7 L.Ed.2d 446 (1962). There are many cases rejecting the defense of selective prosecution. To prevail, a defendant must ordinarily demonstrate that other similarly situated persons have not been prosecuted for similar conduct, and that the defendant's selection for prosecution was based on some impermissible ground such as race, religion, or exercise of the First Amendment rights of free speech. *United States v. Arias*, 575 F.2d 253 (9th Cir. 1978), *cert. denied*, 439 U.S. 868, 99 S. Ct. 196, 58 L.Ed.2d 179 (1978).

Defenses Based on Alibi, Duress, Necessity, and Consent

Individuals prosecuted for crimes often defend themselves by invoking an alibi—a claim that it was impossible for the defendant to have committed the

---

CASE IN POINT

REJECTING THE DEFENSE OF SELECTIVE PROSECUTION

In 1982, David Alan Wayte was indicted for willfully failing to register under the Military Selective Service Act. Wayte sought dismissal of the indictment on the ground of selective prosecution. He contended that he and the others being prosecuted had been singled out of an estimated 674,000 nonregistrants because they had voiced opposition to the Selective Service requirements. The district court dismissed the indictment on the ground that the government had failed to rebut Wayte's *prima facie* showing of selective prosecution. The case was eventually heard by the United States Supreme Court. The Court held that the government's passive enforcement policy, under which it prosecuted only those nonregistrants who reported themselves or were reported by others, did not violate the First or Fifth Amendments to the Constitution.

Wayte v. United States, 470 U.S. 598, 105 S. Ct. 1524, 84 L.Ed.2d 547 (1985).

---

crime because he or she was somewhere else at the time the crime was committed. Less common, but equally well-established, are defenses based on duress, necessity, and consent.

Alibi

Alibi means "elsewhere," and the defense of alibi may be interposed by a defendant who claims to have been at a place other than where the crime allegedly occurred. A criminal defendant who relies on an alibi as a defense does not deny that a crime was committed. Rather, he or she denies the ability to have perpetrated such crime because of having been elsewhere at the time.

As recently pointed out by the Colorado Supreme Court, most jurisdictions that have addressed the issue have concluded that an alibi is not an affirmative defense. *People v. Huckleberry,* 768 P.2d 1235 (Colo. 1989). A few, however, characterize the defense as an affirmative one requiring proof of alibi by the defendant. Generally, a defendant who asserts an affirmative defense essentially admits the conduct charged and seeks to excuse or justify it. One who claims an alibi does not so admit. Therefore, it seems logical not to classify alibi as an affirmative defense. As explained by the Missouri Supreme Court:

> The theory of alibi is that the fact of defendant's presence elsewhere is essentially inconsistent with his presence at the place where the alleged offense was committed and, therefore, defendant could not have personally participated. Although the defense is not an affirmative one, the fact of defendant's presence elsewhere is an affirmative fact logically operating to negative his presence at the time and place. *State v. Armstead,* 283 S.W.2d 577, 581 (Mo. 1955).

Statutes or court rules commonly require that to assert alibi as a defense, a defendant must notify the prosecution in advance of trial and furnish the names of witnesses the defendant intends to use to support the alibi. The Supreme

Court has said that this requirement does not violate the defendant's right to due process of law. *Williams v. Florida*, 399 U.S. 78, 90 S.Ct. 1893, 26 L.Ed. 2d 446 (1970). However, in 1973 the Court held that when the state requires such information, the prosecution must make similar disclosures to the defendant concerning refutation of the evidence the defendant furnishes. *Wardius v. Oregon*, 412 U.S. 470, 93 S.Ct. 2208, 37 L.Ed.2d 82 (1973). Alibi notice statutes and court rules now commonly require disclosure by both defense and the prosecution.

Duress

The common law recognized that duress can be a defense to criminal charges if the coercion exerted involved the use of threats of harm that were "present, imminent and pending" and "of such nature as to include well grounded apprehensions of death or serious bodily harm if the act was not done." Nevertheless, no form of duress, even the threat of imminent death, was sufficient to excuse the intentional killing of an innocent human being. *State v. Toscano*, 378 A.2d 755 (N.J. 1977). American courts have generally followed this approach, with both federal and state courts having made it clear that threats of future harm are not sufficient to constitute duress. See, for example, *United States v. Agard*, 605 F.2d 665 (2d Cir. 1979); *State v. Clay*, 264 N.W. 77 (Iowa 1935).

The defense of duress, sometimes referred to as coercion, compulsion, or duress, is recognized today either by statute or decisional law. Duress has been asserted most frequently by defendants who have committed robberies and thefts and by prisoners who have escaped from custody. Some courts look upon duress as negating an element of the offense charged and classify it as a negative defense. See *People v. Graham*, 129 Cal. Rptr. 31 (Cal. App. 1976). Other courts classify duress as an affirmative defense and require the defendant to prove the defense by the greater weight of the evidence.

There was a common-law presumption that if a wife committed a felony other than murder or treason in her husband's presence, she did so under coercion of her husband. *Morton v. State*, 209 S.W. 644 (Tenn. 1919). The presumption has little significance in modern America and has been abolished in some jurisdictions either by statute, see, for example, Wis. Stat. Ann. § 939.46(2), or by judicial decision. See *People v. Statley*, 206 P.2d 76 (Cal. App. 1949). Despite these precedents, in November 1992 a California appellate court announced a new development in the law of duress. The court held that evidence of the battered woman syndrome (BWS) is admissible to support a woman's defense that she committed robbery offenses because she was afraid the man she lived with would kill her if she did not do as he demanded. *People v. Romero*, 13 Cal. Rptr. 2d 332 (Cal. App. 1992). The court compared the situation to California decisions allowing evidence of BWS when a woman is accused of killing a man she lives with who batters her. (See previous discussion of self-defense in this chapter).

In *People v. Merhige*, 180 N.W. 418 (Mich. 1920), the defendant, a cab driver, transported passengers to a bank, knowing they planned to commit a robbery. It was established at trial that the passengers held a gun to the defendant's head and that he believed he would be killed if he attempted to escape or render his cab inoperable. On basis of the defendant having acted under duress, the Michigan Supreme Court reversed the cab driver's conviction.

Perhaps one of the most dramatic instances where a defendant claimed to have acted under coercion or duress had its beginning on February 4, 1974. On that date members of a radical group known as the Symbionese Liberation Army (SLA) kidnapped Patricia Hearst, a young woman living in California. After being taken captive, Ms. Hearst became involved in the SLA activities and was charged with participating in an armed robbery and other offenses while in captivity. When finally liberated from her captors, Ms. Hearst was tried in a federal district court in San Francisco, California. Among her defenses, she asserted coercion and duress. The Hearst trial was highlighted by considerable psychiatric evidence of "brainwashing" and compulsion. The judge instructed the jury that duress or coercion may provide a legal excuse, but that a compulsion must be present and immediate, carry a well-founded fear of death or bodily injury, and offer no possible escape from such compulsion. Nevertheless, the jury rejected the defense asserted, and convicted and sentenced Ms. Hearst to prison in March 1976. She was later granted executive clemency by President Jimmy Carter.

Prisoners who escape custody frequently plead duress. As pointed out in Chapter 12, the requirement for establishing duress as a defense to escape requires the defendant to show that a *bona fide* effort was made to surrender or return to custody as soon as the claimed duress has ended or lost its coercive force. See *United States v. Bailey*, 444 U.S. 394, 100 S. Ct. 624, 62 L.Ed.2d 575 (1980).

There is a conflict among jurisdictions whether a threat against persons other than the defendant is a sufficient basis for a defendant to invoke the defense of duress. Kansas allows a person to plead duress as a defense to crimes other than murder where the threat is against one's spouse, parent, brother, or sister. Kansas Stat. Ann. § 21–3209. Some courts have adhered to this view irrespective of statute; others have concluded that threats against other persons are not sufficient to constitute duress. For example, in *Jackson v. State*, 504 S.W.2d 488 (Tex. Crim. App. 1974), the court said that since the statute defining duress did not include threats concerning third parties, the court would not permit threats against members of the defendant's family to be considered as a basis to assert the defense of duress.

CASE IN POINT

REJECTING ECONOMIC DURESS AS A DEFENSE

Defendant was arrested on board a boat in the Gulf of Mexico just off the coast of Florida and was charged with trafficking in cannabis in excess of ten thousand pounds. He pled not guilty and asserted the defense of duress. At trial the defendant and his wife testified that economic reasons forced him to participate in trafficking in cannabis by piloting the boat. The trial judge declined to instruct the jury on duress, and the defendant was convicted. On appeal, the court affirmed the conviction and said that such claim of economic coercion was insufficient to call for a jury instruction on duress.

Corujo v. State, 424 So.2d 43 (Fla. App. 1982), *rev. denied*, 434 So.2d 886 (Fla. 1983).

Necessity

In the defense of duress, the situation has its source in the actions of others. In the defense of necessity, forces beyond the actor's control are said to have required a person's choice of the lesser of two evils. Early common-law cases recognized that "a man may break the words of the law . . . through necessity." *Regina v. Fogossa*, 75 Eng. Rep. 1 (1550). Contemporary American judicial authorities hold that if there is a reasonable legal alternative to violating the law, the defense of necessity fails.

Suppose several people are shipwrecked on a cold night. One person swims to shore, breaks into an unoccupied beach cottage, and takes food and blankets to assist the injured until help can be secured. Prosecution in such an event would be unlikely, but if prosecuted, the defendant would properly plead the defense of necessity.

In recent years a number of defendants have attempted to justify actions involving "civil disobedience" on the ground of necessity in instances where they have forcefully asserted their personal or political beliefs. These attempts to employ the defense of necessity have generally been unsuccessful.

One of the most dramatic acts of civil disobedience occurred in 1980 when a group of antinuclear activists entered a factory in Pennsylvania, damaged components of nuclear bombs, and poured human blood on the premises. An appellate court approved of the defendants entering a defense of necessity; however, the Pennsylvania Supreme Court reversed the decision. *Commonwealth v. Berrigan*, 501 A.2d 226 (Pa. 1985). A number of further attempts to plead the necessity defense by antinuclear activists have also failed.

In most but not all cases, the necessity defense has been unavailing to defendants espousing other social and political causes. In one instance, several defendants were charged with criminal trespass when they refused to leave an abortion clinic in Anchorage, Alaska. They claimed their actions were necessary to avert the imminent peril to human life that would result from abortions being performed. They were convicted, and on appeal they argued the trial court erred in refusing to instruct the jury on their claim of necessity as a defense. In rejecting their contention, the Alaska Supreme Court outlined three requirements that must be met by a person who pleads the defense of necessity:

> 1) The act charged must have been done to prevent a significant evil; 2) there must have been no adequate alternative; 3) the harm caused must not have been disproportionate to the harm avoided. *Cleveland v. Municipality of Anchorage*, 631 P.2d 1073, 1078 (Alaska 1981).

Not all social and political protesters have been unsuccessful in pleading the defense of necessity. It was widely reported in the press in April 1987 that Amy Carter, a 19-year-old college student, and fourteen co-defendants charged with trespassing and disorderly conduct in Northampton, Massachusetts, successfully employed the defense of necessity. The defendants were peace activists who claimed their actions were legitimate protests against misleading recruiting and other allegedly illegal activities by the Central Intelligence Agency (CIA) on college campuses. A jury found the defendants not guilty.

An issue is surfacing as to whether to allow a defense of "medical necessity." You may recall that in Chapter 9 concerning offenses involving drugs and alcohol, we noted that several state courts have refused to allow a defendant charged with possession or use of contraband substances to assert the defense of medical necessity. Nevertheless, in 1991 a Florida court of appeal allowed a husband and wife who contracted acquired immune deficiency syndrome (AIDS) to assert that defense to charges of possession and cultivation of marijuana. *Jenks v. State*, 582 So.2d 676 (Fla. App. 1991).

A Wisconsin statute codifies the defense of necessity by providing:

> Pressure of natural physical forces which causes the actor reasonably to believe that his or her act is the only means of preventing imminent public disaster, or imminent death or great bodily harm to the actor or another and which causes him or her so to act, is a defense to a prosecution for any crime based on that act, except that if the prosecution is for first-degree intentional homicide, the degree of the crime is reduced to second-degree intentional homicide. Wis. Stat. Ann. § 939.47.

Consent

Since a victim may not excuse a criminal act, historically courts have said that consent is not a defense to a criminal prosecution. *State v. West*, 57 S.W. 1071 (Mo. 1900). But there are exceptions to this general statement. For example, where lack of consent is an element of the offense, consent may be a defense. This may be true in a prosecution for rape where competent adults freely consent before having sexual relations. In certain contact sports, such as football and boxing, consent is implied and may be a defense to reasonable instances of physical contact that may otherwise be regarded as batteries. Of course, a valid consent presupposes that it is given by a person legally competent to do so and is not induced by force, duress, or deception.

SOME ATTEMPTED DEFENSES

Although they are rarely successful, defendants sometimes employ novel and innovative defenses. Some of the more interesting recent attempted defenses involve the victim's negligence, religious beliefs and practices, premenstrual syndrome, compulsive gambling, post-traumatic stress disorder, "junk food" defense and television intoxication.

Victim's Negligence

Federal and state courts hold that a victim's negligence, credulity, or wrongdoing are not defenses to a prosecution. *United States v. Kreimer*, 609 F.2d 126 (5th Cir. 1980); *State v. Lunz*, 273 N.W.2d 767 (Wis. 1979). Likewise, since a crime is an offense against society as well as the victim, it follows that a victim's forgiveness or condonation does not relieve an actor of criminal responsibility.

Religious Beliefs and Practices

Contentions by defendants that they have been commanded by God or the Scriptures to commit illegal acts have long been rejected by the courts. See *Hotema v. United States,* 186 U.S. 413, 22 S. Ct. 895, 46 L.Ed. 1225 (1902). Moreover, laws prohibiting religious rites that endanger the lives, health, or safety of the participants or others are customarily upheld by the courts. This is illustrated by the Kentucky Court of Appeals' decision in *Lawson v. Commonwealth,* 164 S.W.2d 972 (Ky. 1942). There, despite the defendants' contentions that their constitutional guarantees of freedom of religion were violated, the court upheld the constitutionality of a statute making it a misdemeanor for anyone to handle snakes or reptiles in connection with any religious service.

Courts have traditionally upheld the right of parents to raise their children by their own religious beliefs, ruling that the state's interest must give way to the parents' religious beliefs that preclude medical treatment when the child's life is not immediately imperiled. *In re Green,* 292 A.2d 387 (Pa. 1972). Nevertheless, the courts have held that where a child's life is imperiled the parents have an affirmative duty to provide medical care that will protect a child's life. Thus, an appellate court upheld a conviction of parents for manslaughter when it found that a child's death was directly caused by the parents' failure to secure needed medical care for their child. *Commonwealth v. Barnhart,* 497 A.2d 616 (Pa. Super. 1985), *appeal denied,* 538 A.2d 874 (Pa. 1988).

In about half of the states, child abuse and criminal neglect statutes permit parents to choose "spiritual means or prayer" as a response to illness without regard to a child's medical condition. Thus, in *State v. McKown,* 461 N.W.2d 720 (Minn. App. 1990), the court upheld dismissal of manslaughter charges against a parent and stepparent who relied on spiritual means and failed to secure medical treatment for an 11-year-old boy who died as a result of serious medical problems resulting from diabetes.

The need to furnish medical care to children poses a problem of balancing the parents' interests in bringing up their offspring in accordance with their religious beliefs against the interest of the state in preservation of life. In January 1988, the press reported that the American Academy of Pediatrics urged repeal of laws allowing parents to reject medical treatment for their children on religious grounds. The academy pointed out that about three-fourths of the states have laws that permit some rejection of medical care on religious or philosophical grounds. The academy noted, however, that courts frequently have intervened to order certain treatments for minors.

Premenstrual Syndrome

Premenstrual syndrome (PMS) refers to certain physiological changes that occur in some women, usually in the days close to onset of menstruation. This results from hormonal imbalance and may cause serious depression and irritability. In some cases medical treatment is required. Some argue that a woman so affected should be allowed to assert PMS as a defense to criminal conduct, since some physicians say that PMS directly affects behavior. Nevertheless, PMS has not been accepted as a defense in the United States. In England it has been recognized as a basis to mitigate punishment.

Compulsive Gambling

Evidence of compulsive gambling is generally not considered as a defense unless it rises to the level of insanity. For example, a defendant was convicted of entering a bank with intent to commit larceny and robbery. On appeal, he argued that the trial court erred in instructing the jury that "as a matter of law pathological gambling disorder is not a disease or defect within the meaning of the American Law Institute test for insanity." The United States Court of Appeals, while still applying the former ALI standard, rejected his contention. *United States v. Gould*, 741 F.2d 45 (4th Cir. 1984).

Post-traumatic Stress Disorder (PTSD)

Post-traumatic stress disorder (PTSD) commonly refers to the unique stresses suffered during combat, often manifesting such symptoms as flashbacks, outbursts of anger, and blocked-out memories. After World War I, these conditions were usually referred to as *shell shock*. Following World War II, the term *combat fatigue* was often used to describe such anxiety disorders. Present generations have heard these conditions described as the "Vietnam veteran stress syndrome." Because of the bizarre type of warfare that service personnel endured in Vietnam, the unpopularity of the war, availability of drugs, and the difficulties encountered in adjusting to civilian life, many veterans suffered severe psychological reactions. Whether the stress of the combat operations in the recent Desert Storm operation will cause any widespread traumatic symptoms remains to be seen.

While not a legal defense in itself, in some instances PTSD may affect a defendant's understanding to the point of allowing a plea of insanity. More frequently, PTSD will be introduced as evidence bearing on a defendant's intent, or offered at a sentencing hearing in an effort to mitigate punishment.

The "Junk Food" Defense

Dan White, a former city supervisor, shot and killed the mayor of San Francisco in 1978. Following this he killed another supervisor who was a leader of the local gay community. In defense to charges of first-degree murder, White's counsel sought to establish that his client was depressed by having gorged himself on junk foods. White was convicted of manslaughter instead of murder, giving some credence to reports that the jury may have accepted White's defense. Since this was jury action, it set no precedent to establish any such defense.

Television Intoxication

A novel defense was presented to a trial court in Miami, Florida, in 1978. An adolescent boy was tried for the first-degree murder of an elderly woman. He attempted to establish insanity on the basis of psychiatric testimony concerning the effects of "involuntary subliminal television intoxication." The trial court rejected his claim. An appellate court, stating that the trial judge correctly limited the evidence to the requirements of the *M'Naghten* rule, found no difficulty in upholding the trial court's decision. *Zamora v. State*, 361 So.2d 776 (Fla. App. 1978), *cert. denied*, 372 So.2d 472 (Fla. 1979).

CONCLUSION

Consistent with the historic common-law concept of *mens rea* as an essential element of a crime, infants and insane persons are not held criminally responsible for their acts. Today, courts still encounter difficulties in affixing the legal responsibility of juveniles. Despite our vastly increased knowledge of genetics and mental capacity, courts and legislatures continue to struggle with the definition of insanity and the problem of how to handle those persons adjudged insane. Likewise, with the rise in the use of alcohol and drugs, the problem of intoxication as a defense plagues the judicial system.

A person's right to use reasonable force in self-defense and defense of property and habitation has always been regarded as basic in Anglo-American jurisprudence; yet in modern society it becomes increasingly difficult to determine the extent of force that may be used in other situations. The use of chokeholds by police and the use of force by parents and by guardians and teachers who serve *in loco parentis* present difficult questions. To what extent should police be permitted to use force in making arrests? When does the legitimate use of disciplinary force cease and child abuse begin? And what about the battered woman who seeks to justify her use of force against a charge of homicide or assault on the man she lives with?

Mistake of fact and mistake of law are merely expository of the common-sense foundation of the criminal law. They are a part of the civilized application of law. So too are the defenses of necessity and duress, but these defenses must be viewed in the context of our ever-changing socioeconomic environment.

A number of defenses have developed because of our constitutional system. Immunity, double jeopardy, and the right to a speedy trial have evolved with the continuing constitutional development of individual rights. The statute of limitations defense emerged from our penchant for definiteness and our distrust of prosecutions resting on stale testimony. Our inherent distaste for "frame-ups" and outrageous conduct by the police have caused entrapment to become a viable defense to admitted criminal conduct.

The concepts of criminal responsibility and of criminal defenses will continue to evolve in response to our increased knowledge of human behavior and society's balance of the rights of the individual against its legitimate demand for protection.

QUESTIONS FOR THOUGHT AND DISCUSSION

1. In general, courts permit intoxication evidence only to the extent that it negates the *mens rea of* a specific-intent crime. Should evidence of voluntary intoxication be allowed for both general-intent and specific-intent crimes? Alternatively, should courts bar such evidence for *both* general intent and specific-intent crimes? What position has been taken by the courts of your state?

2. What is the test for insanity in your state? Who has the burden of proof once the defendant introduces some evidence of insanity? Do you think the test in your state adequately protects (a) the public, and (b) the defendant's rights?

3. While taking his nightly walk, Charley Goodneighbor saw Joe Macho commit a battery on Charlene Loverly, a 14-year-old girl. Goodneighbor came to Charlene's defense and struck Macho so hard it fractured his skull. The police arrested both Macho and Goodneighbor. Goodneighbor explained to the police that he came to Charlene's aid to prevent her from being injured by Macho. What factors will the prosecutor probably consider in determining whether to file charges against Goodneighbor?

4. Harvey Homeowner, a "black belt" in karate, arrives at his home to find an intruder fleeing from the garage. Homeowner pursues the intruder across the front yard and catches him in the street. An exchange of blows renders the intruder unconscious. A medical examination reveals substantial brain damage to the intruder as a result of the blows inflicted by Homeowner. In a prosecution for aggravated battery, can Homeowner successfully assert as a defense his use of force to protect his habitation?

5. Sally Shopper drives a 1992 grey Honda Accord. She parks it in a shopping center lot while she shops. Two hours later, Sally enters a car parked nearby that is almost identical to hers. As she drives away the owner spots her and demands that a nearby police officer stop her. Just as the officer approaches her, Sally realizes that she is in someone else's vehicle. Had she looked at the vehicle more carefully, she would have observed that it had a license tag from a different state and some unique bumper stickers. On complaint of the owner, the officer arrests Sally and charges her with theft. What is Sally likely to assert in her defense?

6. A poor man steals food from a convenience market. When prosecuted for theft, he pleads the defense of necessity. The prosecutor urges the trial judge to strike the defense on the ground that the defendant could have qualified for assistance from local welfare organizations. Should the defendant be allowed to present his defense to the jury? Do you think he has a credible defense? Why or why not?

7. A defendant was found guilty of having forcible sexual intercourse with a 15-year-old female of previous chaste character. He is charged, convicted, and sentenced for violating two statutes: (a) common-law rape involving force and lack of consent, and (b) statutory rape involving intercourse with a minor of previous chaste character. On appeal, the defendant contends that his sentence violates the double jeopardy clause of the Fifth Amendment. What arguments is his counsel likely to present to the appellate court? What should be the appellate court's decision?

8. The police suspect Mary Jane Narky of having sold marijuana at the Sibanac Bar. An undercover agent approaches her and asks her to go out with him. After a movie, the agent says that he would like to buy some marijuana for his close friend. At first Mary Jane makes no response. They make another date and after a very pleasant evening together, the undercover agent pleads with Mary Jane to help him find marijuana for his friend. She agrees, and the next day she delivers a quantity of the contraband to the agent, who gives her $200. As he concludes

his purchase, the undercover agent arrests Mary Jane and chargers her with the sale of contraband. Mary Jane's attorney pleads entrapment at her trial. Do you think her defense will be successful? Why or why not?

9. Why did the United States Supreme Court in *Tennessee v. Garner* (1985) invalidate a state law permitting police officers to use deadly force to apprehend fleeing felons? Under *Garner,* when is a police officer justified in using deadly force? What impact has the *Garner* decision had on law enforcement?

10. Boris Bottlemore has just finished celebrating his new job promotion by consuming ten double shots of bourbon in a bar near his home. He staggers from the bar to his home, which is one of twenty identical row houses on his block. In his inebriated state, Boris mistakes his neighbor's home for his own. Finding the door unlocked, he enters and promptly raids the refrigerator. He then collapses on a couch in the living room and passes out. The next morning, Patty Purebred, who has just moved into the home, is shocked to find a stranger sleeping in her living room and her refrigerator standing open, with food strewn across the kitchen floor. She telephones the police, who arrive and take Bottlemore into custody, charging him with burglary. What defense(s) is (are) available to Bottlemore? How would you assess his chances before a jury?

11. Should the courts recognize battered woman syndrome (BWS) as a defense to assaultive and homicidal crimes by a woman living with a man who continually batters her? What position does your state take on this issue?

CASES

MOON V. STATE

Supreme Court of Indiana, 1981.
275 Ind. 651, 419 N.E.2d 740.

[This case raises the issue of intoxication as a defense to a charge of attempted robbery.]

HUNTER, Justice.

The defendant, James C. Moon, was convicted in a bench trial of attempted robbery, a class A felony, Ind.Code § 35–42–5–1 (Burns 1979 Repl.), and carrying a handgun without a license, a class D felony, Ind.Code § 35–23–4.1–18(c) (Burns 1979 Repl.). He was sentenced to concurrent terms of twenty years for the class A felony and two years for the class D felony. Moon presents the following issues for our review:

1. Whether the evidence was sufficient to sustain his conviction; and
2. Whether the judgment of the trial court was contrary to law.

The evidence indicates that during the evening of November 7, 1979, the defendant and a machete-bearing accomplice entered the Brookside Market at 2129 Brookside Avenue in Indianapolis. The defendant, who was carrying a revolver, fired a shot at the ceiling and demanded money from the cashier. Startled by the shot, a patron near the cash register bolted down an aisle toward the rear of the store. The machete-bearing accomplice gave chase.

Their path carried them toward a window, largely veiled from public view, which connected the owner's living quarters to the store. Through the window the owner had been observing the developments. As the two men neared the window, the owner saw the accomplice raise the machete to swing it at the patron. At that point the owner pushed the window open and fired five shots at the accomplice.

Wounded by the gunfire, the accomplice dropped the machete and, together with the defendant, fled the premises. In the aftermath, it was discovered that one of the bullets fired by the owner had ricocheted and hit the cashier in the leg.

I

Defendant contends that the evidence is insufficient to sustain his conviction for attempted robbery as a class A felony. That contention is predicated on the fact that the "bodily injury" necessary to elevate attempted robbery to a felony of class A status, Ind. Code § 35–42–5–1 (Burns 1979 Repl.) was inflicted by a bullet fired by the owner of the Brookside Market. Since neither he nor his accomplice fired the shot which injured the cashier, defendant maintains there is no evidence to establish his liability for class A attempted robbery.

We disagree. The responsibility for any bodily injury which occurs during the commission or attempted commission of a robbery rests on the perpetrators of the crime, regardless of who inflicts the injury, so long as it is a natural and probable consequence of the events and circumstances surrounding the robbery or attempt. . . . Here, the defendant and his accomplice walked into a grocery store armed with a revolver and machete. They fired a shot into the air, demanded money, and swung a machete at a store patron. The bodily injury which ultimately occurred, albeit caused by the gunfire of the store owner, was a natural consequence of the conduct of the defendant and his accomplice in attempting the robbery. Accordingly, the evidence was sufficient to sustain the defendant's conviction for attempted robbery as a class A felony.

Defendant also argues that the evidence was insufficient to support the conclusion that he was capable of forming the specific intent to attempt the robbery. He predicates his defense of intoxication on his testimony and pretrial statements that he had ingested extensive amounts of drugs prior to the robbery attempt and remembered nothing about it.

Voluntary intoxication is no defense in a criminal proceeding unless it is shown that the defendant was so intoxicated as to be incapable of forming the requisite intent. . . .

Testimony of witness at the robbery scene indicates that the defendant was the person who fired the shot at the ceiling, demanded the cashier turn over the money, and ordered a patron not to interfere in the robbery. The record also reveals that once the store owner began shooting, the defendant had the presence of mind and physical capacity to flee the Brookside Market, drive the getaway car, and flee on foot from police pursuit after abandoning the vehicle. Based on this evidence, the fact-finder could reasonably conclude that the defendant was not so intoxicated that he was incapable of forming the requisite intent.

II

Defendant's contention that the judgment of the trial court is contrary to law is predicated on the argument the court erred in permitting a witness to be questioned about the defendant's prior criminal history. The record reveals, however, that defendant neither objected to the questioning at trial nor challenged it in his motion to correct errors. Consequently, the allegation of error has not been preserved for our review. . . .

For all the foregoing reasons, there was no trial court error and the judgment of the trial court should be affirmed.

Judgment Affirmed.

GIVEN, C. J., and PRENTICE and PIVARNIK, JJ., concur.

DeBRULER, J., concurs in result.

United States v. Freeman
United States Court of Appeals, Eleventh Circuit, 1986.
804 F.2d 1574.

[This case examines the insanity defense and the Insanity Defense Reform Act of 1984.]

HILL, Circuit Judge.
Appellant Dwayne Freeman challenges his conviction of bank robbery under 18 U.S.C. § 2113(b), (d) (1982). At trial, the facts surrounding the robbery and the defendant's guilt were never at issue. Freeman merely contests the trial court's determination that [he] was sane at the time of the offense. Freeman bases his appeal on two grounds. First, he challenges the constitutionality of the Insanity Defense Reform Act of 1984, Pub.L.No. 98–473, § 402, 98 Stat. 1837, 2057 (codified at 18 U.S.C. § 20 (Supp. 1986); Fed.R.Evid. 704(b). Second, Freeman asserts that as a matter of law, he has established his insanity by clear and convincing evidence. We reject both of the defendant's arguments.

The Insanity Defense Reform Act produced three principal changes to the insanity defense in federal courts. First, the definition of insanity was restricted so that a valid defense only exists where the defendant was "unable to appreciate the nature of the wrongfulness of his acts" at the time of the offense. The amendment thus eliminated the volitional prong of the defense; prior to the Act, a defendant could assert a valid defense if he were unable to appreciate the nature of his act *or* unable to conform his conduct to the law. . . . The second change produced by the Act resulted in a shifting of the burden of proof from the government to the defendant. Prior to the Act, the government was required to prove beyond a reasonable doubt that the defendant was sane at the time of the offense. . . . Under the current act, the defendant must prove his insanity by clear and convincing evidence. . . . The third change prohibits experts for either the government or defendant from testifying as to the ultimate issue of the accused's sanity. . . .

The defendant's principal contention concerning the constitutionality of the act pertains to the burden of proof being placed on the defendant. . . . *Davis v. United States,* 160 U.S. 469, 16 S. Ct. 353, 40 L.Ed. 499 (1895), established that the prosecution must prove the defendant's sanity beyond a reasonable doubt in federal cases. The Supreme Court, however, has pointed out that *Davis* is not a constitutional ruling, but an exercise of the Supreme Court's supervisory power over prosecutions in federal court. *Leland v. Oregon,* 343 U.S. 790, 72 S. Ct. 1002, 96 L.Ed. 1302 (1952); *Patterson v. New York,* 432 U.S. 197, 97 S. Ct. 2319, 53 L.Ed.2d 281 (1977).

In *Leland,* the Court held that a state could constitutionally require a defendant to prove insanity beyond a reasonable doubt.... The Supreme court ... has repeatedly reaffirmed the *Leland* holding....

At oral argument, Freeman attempted to distinguish *Leland* by urging this court to adopt stricter constitutional standards for federal courts than that required for state courts under *Leland.* The only suggestion we can find indicating that federal courts may discover stricter constitutional requirements for federal criminal trials than state criminal trials is *United States v. Mitchell,* 725 F.2d 832, 835 n. 5 (2d Cir. 1983). To the extent that *Mitchell* goes beyond observing that the Bill of Rights were only partially incorporated by the fourteenth amendment, we disagree with it. No logical basis exists to distinguish between a state legislature's constitutional power to require a defendant to prove insanity and the United States Congress' power to require defendant to prove insanity. The United States Constitution does not draw meaningless distinctions. Therefore, *Leland* compels a holding that the aspect of the Insanity Reform Act of 1984 requiring a defendant to prove insanity by clear and convincing evidence is constitutional.

Additionally, we hold that the Act's restriction against opinion testimony as to the ultimate issue of insanity does not restrict the defendant in the preparation of his defense in violation of the Fifth Amendment.... The defendant is not prohibited from introducing evidence which would assist the jury in making this determination. Furthermore, the restric-

tion ... is applicable to the government, as well as the defendant. There is no constitutional violation....

Freeman additionally contends that he has established his insanity by clear and convincing evidence. [At trial,] Dwayne Freeman asserted that he was an enthusiastic volunteer for the "Save the Children" campaign to feed starving children in drought-stricken Ethiopia. Freeman's evidence was that he degenerated to the point of obsession. He then became depressed about not raising enough money for the children. On February 26, 1985, Freeman robbed a bank, allegedly to obtain money for the Ethiopia fund.

The district court found that the defendant had failed to prove by clear and convincing evidence that he was unable to appreciate the nature and quality of his acts at the time of the offense....

A psychiatric team from the federal institute at Springfield, Missouri did conclude that Freeman was suffering from severe mental illness and was manic depressive or possibly schizophrenic. Additionally, Freeman presented evidence showing that he had been hearing noises and was experiencing severe depression prior to the robbery. Ample evidence exists, however, indicating that Freeman knew his conduct was wrongful. The evidence shows Freeman changed his clothes after robbing the bank to avoid identification. Freeman employed a mask, handgun and satchel to execute the robbery and avoid apprehension. He informed bank personnel that if the police were called, he would come back and kill everyone. When spotted by the police, Freeman ran to avoid apprehension. Finally, Freeman's probation officer observed Freeman's demeanor as being entirely appropriate following his arrest. The district court's decision was not clearly erroneous.

We therefore AFFIRM the district court's decision.

STATE V. FREEMAN
Supreme Court of Iowa, 1990.
450 N.W.2d 826.

[In this case, the Iowa Supreme Court considers the defense of mistake of fact in the context of a conviction for "delivering a simulated controlled substance."]

MCGIVERIN, Chief Justice.

The facts of this case are not disputed. The defendant, Robert Eric Freeman, agreed to sell a controlled substance, cocaine, to Keith Hatcher. Unfortunately for Freeman, Hatcher was cooperating with the government. Hatcher gave Freeman $200, and Freeman gave Hatcher approximately two grams of what was supposed to be cocaine. To everyone's surprise, the "cocaine" turned out to be acetaminophen. Acetaminophen is not a controlled substance.

Freeman was convicted at a bench trial of delivering a simulated controlled substance with respect to a substance represented to be cocaine, in violation of Iowa Code section 204.410(2)(a) (1987). The sole question presented by Freeman's appeal is whether he can be convicted of delivering a simulated controlled substance when, in fact, he believed he was delivering and intended to deliver cocaine.

Our review is to determine whether any error of law occurred. Iowa R.App.P. 4. Finding no error, we affirm the conviction.

I. The statutory framework.

Iowa Code section 204.410(2) provides, in relevant part:

[I]t is unlawful for a person to create, deliver, or possess with intent to deliver . . . a simulated controlled substance. . . .

The term "simulated controlled substance" is defined by Iowa Code section 204.10(27):

"Simulated controlled substance" means a substance which is not a controlled substance but which is expressly represented to be a controlled substance, or a substance which is not a controlled substance but which is impliedly represented to be a controlled substance and which because of its

nature, packaging, or appearance would lead a reasonable person to believe it to be a controlled substance.

Violation of section 204.401(2) with respect to a simulated controlled substance represented to be cocaine is a class "C" felony. . . .

II. Scienter and the offense of delivery of a simulated controlled substance.

Our cases indicate that knowledge of the nature of the substance delivered is an imputed element of section 204.401(1) offenses. . . . Proof of such knowledge has been required to separate those persons who innocently commit the overt acts of the offense from those persons who commit the overt acts of the offense with scienter, or criminal intent. . . . In general, only the latter are criminally responsible for their acts. . . .

The Iowa Code prohibits delivery of controlled substances and imitation controlled substances, as well as delivery of counterfeit substances, in language nearly identical to that prohibiting delivery of simulated controlled substances. . . . The distinctions between these statutory classifications are not relevant to this case.

Seizing upon the similarity of the statutory prohibitions, Freeman argues that he cannot be convicted of delivering a simulated controlled substance because he mistakenly believed he was delivering and intended to deliver an actual controlled substance.

We disagree. Freeman's construction of section 204.401(2) would convert the offense of delivery of a simulated controlled substance into one requiring knowing misrepresentation of the nature of the substance delivered. The statute clearly does not require knowing misrepresentation of the nature of the substance delivered.

Reading sections 204.401(2) and 204.10(27) together shows that the gist of this offense is knowing representation of a substance to be a controlled substance and delivery of a noncontrolled substance rather than knowing misrepresentation and delivery. As one court explained under similar circumstances, statutes like section 204.401(2) are designed "to discourage anyone from engaging or appearing to engage in the narcotics traffic rather than to define the contractual rights of the pusher and his victim. . . ."

Freeman's mistaken belief regarding the substance he delivered cannot save him from conviction. Mistake of fact is a defense to a crime of scienter or criminal intent only where the mistake precludes the existence of the mental state necessary to commit the crime. . . . In this case, Freeman would not be innocent of wrongdoing had the situation been as he supposed; rather he would be guilty of delivering a

controlled substance. His mistake is no defense. The scienter required to hold him criminally responsible for committing the overt acts of the charged offense is present regardless of the mistake. Freeman knowingly represented to Hatcher that the substance he delivered was cocaine.

In conclusion, we hold that a person who delivers a substance that is not a controlled substance, but who knowingly represents the substance to be a controlled substance, commits the offense of delivery of a simulated controlled substance regardless of whether the person believed that the substance was controlled or not controlled. . . .

Affirmed.

PEOPLE V. GREENE

Appellate Court of Illinois, 1987.
160 Ill. App. 3d 1089, 112 Ill. Dec. 483, 513 N.E.2d 1092.

[This case examines, among other things, self-defense as a defense to a homicide charge.]

Justice MANNING delivered the opinion of the court.

Defendant, James Greene, was charged by indictment with the murder of Rickey Baldwin. Following a bench trial in the circuit court of Cook County, the defendant was found guilty of murder (Ill. Rev.Stat.1985, ch. 38, par. 9–1), and sentenced to 27 years imprisonment. . . . Defendant contends in his appeal that: (1) the trial court erred by restricting cross-examination of one of the State's witnesses; (2) he was not proved guilty of murder beyond a reasonable doubt; (3) the evidence justified at the most a conviction for voluntary manslaughter; and (4) the sentence of 27 years imprisonment was excessive.

Hugh Adams testified that during the early morning hours on July 29, 1983, he was standing outside of the Ida B. Wells housing project at 39th and Langley Avenue when he saw the victims, Rickey Baldwin ("Rickey Dog") and Marcus Thompson ("Morocco") leave the building located at 706 East 39th Street. Baldwin (hereinafter referred to as the victim) was carrying a ten-speed bicycle. He called

out to Adams and Adams walked towards him and Thompson. At this time Adams noticed the defendant standing near the side of the 706 East 39th Street building. He saw the defendant reach into his pants, pull out a gun and fire one shot at the group.

Adams yelled, "break" and they all ran in different directions. After Adams ran across the street, he turned and saw defendant chase the victim. When the victim tripped over a chain and tried to flee, defendant shot him in the back. The defendant then put the gun in the front of his pants, ran towards Adams and proceeded to the housing project.

Marcus Thompson testified that on July 29, 1983, during the early morning hours he was on the eighth floor of the 706 East 39th Street building when the victim left this girlfriend's apartment. Thompson told the victim that he had seen the defendant earlier in the building. The victim pulled a 30-inch chain from his ten-speed bicycle and the two of them walked down the back stairs and left the building together. The victim was a member of the Black P. Stone Rangers gang and defendant was a member of the Gangster Goon Squad, a rival gang.

After they exited the building, the victim called Hugh Adams, who began walking towards them, and it was at this time that the defendant shot at the group. The victim, Adams and Thompson ran in different directions. The defendant chased only the victim. Thompson testified that he heard a second shot fired but he did not actually see the defendant shoot the victim, nor did he see a chain beside the victim after he had been shot.

Thompson heard no verbal exchange between defendant and victim before the former fired the weapon nor did he observe the victim physically threaten defendant with a chain.

The defendant, James Greene, testified that he did not intentionally try to kill the victim. However, when the victim, Adams and Thompson began walking towards him, he was "scared" and "panicked" because of a prior encounter with the victim. Specifically, on September 17, 1982, the victim and some of his friends followed defendant after he left a store at 38th and Cottage Grove. Defendant was shot by someone in the victim's group. The defendant was hospitalized for six months as a result of the gunshot wound. Also, the bullet was never removed because it was too close to his heart. The defendant added that a relative of the victim came to the hospital and told defendant that he "better not say nothing." Although the defendant did not at that time tell the police who had shot him, he had told his brother that "Rickey Dog" shot him.

The defendant further testified that on July 29, 1983, at midnight, he visited his girlfriend on the 8th floor of the 706 East 39th Street building. When he arrived on the eighth floor, the victim and Thompson were there, but defendant did not speak to them. When defendant left his girlfriend's apartment at 1:30 A.M. the victim and Thompson faced the front of the building. Defendant added that he went down the back stairs to avoid them but walked "through the building" and exited from the front entrance.

Defendant proceeded to the corner, turned and heard either the victim or Thompson "drop a bicycle." He observed the victim, who had a "chain wrapped double around his hand," and Thompson approached him. Thompson then called Hugh Adams who was across the street. Thompson, Adams and the victim then walked toward the defendant who pulled out a gun and fired a shot. When the three men fled, defendant pursued the victim, whom defendant shot from a distance of 10 to 15 feet while the victim was running away.

Detective Henry Sigler was assigned to investigate the death of Rickey Baldwin. Defendant was arrested on January 3, 1984, and signed a written confession on January 4, 1984, which stated that after the victim tripped over a small chain fence the defendant shot him in the back. The statement was stipulated to at trial. Additionally, there was a stipulation regarding a report submitted by the Cook County Medical Examiner's Office which performed a postmortem examination on the victim. Dr. Eupil Choi would testify "that Rickey Baldwin died of a bullet wound of the back with penetrations in the aorta and the lung, with internal bleeding."

At the close of all the evidence, the court found the defendant guilty of murder, and sentenced him to 27 years imprisonment. Subsequently, defense counsel filed a written motion for a new trial and a motion to reduce the sentence. Both motions were denied by the trial court and the defendant filed this appeal.

The defendant contends that the trial court erred by barring the defense from cross-examination one of the State's occurrence witnesses concerning that witness' recent arrest for possession of a controlled substance and the factual matrix surrounding the victim's and witness' plea of guilty to a charge of felony theft in May of 1983. . . .

The defendant . . . contends that the weight of the evidence showed that he acted in self-defense when he shot the victim and that his conviction for murder should be reversed. Alternatively, the defendant argues that his murder conviction should be reduced to voluntary manslaughter since he had a reasonable belief that he was acting in self-defense. Whether a homicide is murder or manslaughter, or whether it is justified as self-defense, is a question to be determined by the trier of fact. . . .

The defendant relies upon the following factors to support his contention that he acted in self-defense. The victim was: (1) a convicted felon; (2) a member of a rival gang; (3) armed with a chain; (4) older than the defendant; (5) accompanied by two companions while the defendant was alone; and (6) the victim had accompanied other individuals, one of whom had shot the defendant the previous year.

The general rule regarding justifiable use of force provides:

A person is justified in the use of force against another when and to the extent that he reasonably believes that such conduct is necessary to defend himself or another against such other's imminent use of unlawful force. However, he is justified in the use of force which is intended or likely to cause death or great bodily harm only if he reasonably believes that such force is necessary to prevent imminent death or great bodily harm to himself or another, or the commission of a forceable felony. . . .

The use of force in defense of the person is justified where (1) that force is threatened against the person; (2) the person threatened is not the aggressor; (3) the danger of harm is imminent; (4) the force threatened is unlawful; and (5) the person threatened must actually believe that a danger exists, that the use of force is necessary and that such beliefs are reasonable. . . .

The issue of self-defense is an affirmative defense based upon satisfaction of the above elements. . . . This defense is raised only if the defendant presents some evidence regarding each element. . . . Once the issue is raised, the State must prove beyond a reasonable doubt that the defendant did not act in self-defense. . . .

This issue of self-defense is determined by the trier of fact. If the trier of fact has determined that the State has negated beyond a reasonable doubt any one of the elements justifying the use of force, then the State has carried its burden of proof. . . . The trier of fact's decision on the issue of self-defense will not be disturbed on review unless the decision is so improbable or unsatisfactory as to raise a reasonable doubt of the defendant's guilt. . . .

The State argues that in the instant case there was no evidence to support self-defense. We agree. The defendant became the aggressor when he fired a warning shot at the three individuals approaching him who withdrew when defendant fired the weapon. Defendant then proceeded to chase only the victim and shot him in the back. Therefore, he can not claim that he was in imminent fear of death or great bodily harm. If the defendant is the aggressor, the use of deadly force is justified only if:

(1) Such force is so great that he reasonably believes that he is in imminent danger of death or great bodily harm, and that he has exhausted every reasonable means to escape such danger other than the use of force which is likely to cause death or great bodily harm to the assailant; or (2) In good faith, he withdraws from physical contact with the assailant and indicates clearly to the assailant that he desires to withdraw and terminate the use of force. . . .

The defendant as the aggressor never attempted to escape the danger, if such danger existed. Moreover, he never withdrew nor terminated the use of force. In fact, he accelerated his use of force by pursuing the victim and firing a second shot, although the victim had retreated.

A reading of the record fails to reveal any evidence which tends to show that force was threatened against the defendant. Although it is undisputed that the victim was carrying a 30-inch chain, there is no evidence that the victim used the chain to threaten the defendant. Moreover, by the defendant's own testimony he admitted to shooting the victim in the back from a distance of 10 feet.

Even if the victim had been the initial aggressor, the right of self-defense does not permit the pursuit and killing in retaliation or revenge of an initial aggressor after he retreats. . . .

Clearly, the evidence supports the trial court's decision to reject defendant's claim of self-defense. After a review of the record, we must conclude that the trial court's decision was not so improbable or unsatisfactory as to suggest reasonable doubt of the defendant's guilt.

Alternatively, the defendant contends that the evidence supports a finding of voluntary manslaughter. A person commits voluntary manslaughter if he kills an individual without lawful justification under a sudden and intense passion resulting from serious provocation, or if he intentionally or knowingly kills an individual believing the circumstances would justify or exonerate the killing, but his belief is unreasonable. . . .

The record in the instant case revealed that the defendant did not act under a "sudden and intense passion resulting from serious provocation." Defendant testified that no verbal exchange occurred between the defendant and victim nor did the victim physically threaten him with the chain. The defendant deliberately chased and shot the victim after the latter fell.

In regards to the defendant's unreasonable belief that the circumstances would justify the killing, defendant points out that he was "scared" and "panicked" when Thompson, Adams and the victim began to walk towards him. However, we fail to see how the defendant could have been in fear of harm from these individuals when they ran after the first shot was fired. We believe that the evidence supports a finding that the defendant had no subjective belief that the force he used was necessary, which is consistent with the finding of murder, not voluntary manslaughter.

A person commits murder if he either intends to kill or do great bodily harm to that individual or another or if he knows that such acts create a strong probability of death or great bodily harm. . . . It is not necessary to prove that the defendant had the intent to commit murder, only that he voluntarily and willfully committed an act, the natural consequences of which was to cause death or great bodily harm. . . . Although the defendant asserts that he did not intentionally kill the victim, he knew or should have known that the natural and probable consequences of shooting the victim in the back would cause death or do great bodily harm.

The reviewing court's power to reduce a murder conviction to manslaughter . . . should be cautiously exercised. . . . Based on the facts of this case we will not substitute our judgment for that of the trier of fact. We find no reason to disturb the trial court's finding upon review. . . .

JUDGMENT AFFIRMED.

CAMPBELL and O'CONNOR, JJ., concurring.

CRUZ V. STATE
Supreme Court of Florida, 1985.
465 So.2d 516.

[This case examines the defense of entrapment.]

EHRLICH, Justice.
This case is before us on appeal from a decision of the Second District Court of Appeal, *State v. Cruz*, 426 So.2d 1308 (Fla. 2d DCA 1983). The decision directly and expressly conflicts with *State v. Casper*, 417 So.2d 263 (Fla. 1st DCA), review denied, 418 So.2d 1280 (Fla. 1982). We take jurisdiction pursuant to article V. section 3(b)(3), Florida Constitution. We disapprove the district court's decision.

Tampa police undertook a decoy operation in a high-crime area. An officer posed as an inebriated indigent, smelling of alcohol and pretending to drink wine from a bottle. The officer leaned against a building near an alleyway, his face to the wall. Plainly displayed from a rear pants pocket was $150 in currency, paper-clipped together. Defendant Cruz

and a woman happened upon the scene as passersby some time after 10 P.M. Cruz approached the decoy officer, may have attempted to say something to him, then continued on his way. Ten to fifteen minutes later, the defendant and his companion returned to the scene and Cruz took the money from the decoy's pocket without harming him in any way. Officers then arrested Cruz as he walked from the scene. The decoy situation did not involve the same modus operandi as any of the unsolved crimes which had occurred in the area. Police were not seeking a particular individual, nor were they aware of any prior criminal acts by the defendant.

Cruz was charged by information with grand theft. Pursuant to Florida Rule of Criminal Procedure 3.190(c)(4), Cruz moved to dismiss the information, arguing that the arrest constituted entrapment as a matter of law. The trial court granted the motion to dismiss on the authority of *State v. Casper*. . . . On appeal, the Second District court of appeal reversed, acknowledging its decision was in conflict with Casper.

The entrapment defense arises from a recognition that sometimes police activity will induce an otherwise innocent individual to commit the criminal act the police activity seeks to produce. . . .

The entrapment defense . . . normally focuses on the predisposition of the defendant. We adopted this view in *State v. Dickinson*, 370 So.2d 762 (Fla. 1979). The First District, in *State v. Casper*, . . . focused on predisposition when it found the "drunken bum"decoy at issue here to constitute entrapment as a matter of law. In *Casper*, Jacksonville police set up a decoy situation legally indistinguishable from the scenario in this case. The *Casper* court held that the state must prove the defendant was predisposed to steal from the decoy and that predisposition can be found under four circumstances: (1) the defendant has prior convictions for similar crimes; (2) the defendant has a reputation for committing similar crimes; (3) police have a reasonable suspicion the defendant was engaged in similar crimes; or (4) the defendant showed ready acquiescence to commit the crime suggested by police. . . . The *Casper* court found no evidence of the first two elements in that case. The third element is irrelevant in the type of random expedition at issue here. The question thus boiled down to whether Casper "readily acquiesced" to the criminal scenario. The *Casper* court found that an otherwise unpredisposed passerby who chose to take the money did not acquiesce, but "succumbed to temptation . . . to the lure of the bait." . . . The *Casper* court therefore distinguished between "succumbing to temptation" and "readily acquiescing," and found that this is a question of law: where a trial judge finds the defendant succumbed to temptation, the matter shall not be put to a jury.

The Second District, in the case now before us, rejected this position. The *Cruz* court found that such a judgment is one for the jury to make. "[W]here, as here, a defendant's intent or state of mind (i.e., predisposition) is an issue, that issue should not be decided on a motion to dismiss. . . . Petitioner would have this court hold that where the only evidence of predisposition is the commission of the crime the police scenario was designed to elicit,

there is an insufficient showing of predisposition, as a matter of law. We do not agree.

We agree with the Second District that the question of predisposition will always be a question of fact for the jury. However, we also believe that the First District's concern for entrapment scenarios in which the innocent will succumb to temptation is well founded. To protect against such abuse, we turn to another aspect of entrapment.

Entrapment is a potentially dangerous tool given to police to fight crime. "Society is at war with the criminal classes, and courts have uniformly held that in waging this warfare the forces of prevention and detection may use traps, decoys, and deception to obtain evidence of crime." . . . "The appropriate object of this permitted activity, frequently essential to the enforcement of the law, is to reveal the criminal design; to expose the illicit traffic, the prohibited publication, the fraudulent use of the mails, the illegal conspiracy, or other offenses, and thus to disclose the would-be violators of the law. A different question is presented when the criminal design originates with the officials of the Government, and they implant in the mind of an innocent person the disposition to commit the alleged offense and induce its commission in order that they may prosecute." . . . "Such a gross abuse of authority given for the purpose of detecting and punishing crime, and not for the making of criminals, deserves the severest condemnation, but the question whether it precludes prosecution or affords a ground of defense, and, if so, upon what theory, has given rise to conflicting opinions." . . .

To guide the trial courts, we propound the following threshold test of an entrapment defense: Entrapment has not occurred as a matter of law where police activity (1) has as its end the interruption of a specific ongoing criminal activity; and (2) utilizes means reasonably tailored to apprehend those involved in the ongoing criminal activity.

The first prong of this test addresses the problem of police "virtue testing," that is, police activity seeking to prosecute crime where no such crime exists but for the police activity engendering the crime. As Justice Roberts wrote . . . , "society is at war with the criminal classes." . . . Police must fight this war, not engage in the manufacture of new hostilities.

The second prong of the threshold test addresses the problem of inappropriate techniques. Considerations in deciding whether police activity is permissible under this prong include whether a government agent "induces or encourages another person to engage in conduct constituting such offense by either: (a) making knowingly false representations designed to induce the belief that such conduct is not prohibited: or (b) employing methods of persuasion or inducement which create a substantial risk that such an offense will be committed by persons other than those who are ready to commit it." . . .

Applying this test to the case before us, we find that the drunken bum decoy operation fails. In Cruz's motion to dismiss, one of the undisputed facts was that "none of the unsolved crimes occurring near this location involved the same modus operandi as the simulated situation created by the officers." . . . The record thus implies police were apparently attempting to interrupt some kind of ongoing criminal activity. However, the record does not show what specific activity was targeted. This lack of focus is sufficient for the scenario to fail the first prong of the test. However, even if the police were seeking to catch persons who had been "roll-ing" drunks in the area, the criminal scenario here, with $150 (paper-clipped to ensure more than $100 was taken, making the offense a felony) enticingly protruding from the back pocket of a person seemingly incapable of noticing its removal, carries with it the "substantial risk that such an offense will be committed by persons other than those who are ready to commit it." . . . This sufficiently addresses the *Casper* court's proper recognition that entrapment has occurred where "the decoy simply provided the opportunity to commit a crime to anyone who succumbed to the lure of the bait." . . . This test also recognizes, as the *Cruz* court did, that the considerations inherent in our threshold test are not properly addressed in the context of the predisposition element of the second, subjective test.

For the reasons discussed, we hold that the police activity in the instant case constituted entrapment as a matter of law under the threshold test adopted here. Accordingly, we quash the district court decision.

It is so ordered. . . .

ALDERMAN, Justice, dissenting. . . .

PART III

LAW ENFORCEMENT AND CRIMINAL PROCEDURE

CHAPTER 14

SEARCH AND SEIZURE

CHAPTER OUTLINE

Introduction
The Common-Law
 Background
Adoption of the Fourth
 Amendment
When Does the Fourth
 Amendment Apply?
What Constitutes a "Search"
 or "Seizure" Under the
 Fourth Amendment?
The Warrant Requirement
Exceptions to the Warrant
 Requirement
Technology and the Fourth
 Amendment
Contemporary Fourth
 Amendment Problems
The Exclusionary Rule
Conclusion

Cases

Katz v. United States
Illinois v. Gates
Harris v. United States
United States v. Ross
New Jersey v. T.L.O.
Mapp v. Ohio
United States v. Leon

INTRODUCTION

Although the search for and seizure of evidence of crime are essential to the enforcement of the criminal law, search and seizure often entail serious invasions of privacy and are subject to tremendous abuse. Therefore, the power of law enforcement agencies to conduct searches and seizures is limited by the federal and state constitutions, and by a number of federal and state statutes. Most important among these legal limitations is the Fourth Amendment to the United States Constitution:

> The right of the people to be secure in their persons, houses, papers and effects, against unreasonable searches and seizures, shall not be violated, and no Warrants shall issue but upon probable cause, supported by Oath or affirmation, and particularly describing the place to be searched and the persons or things to be seized.

As a general rule, the Fourth Amendment requires law enforcement officers to obtain warrants before conducting searches and seizures. Although some warrantless searches and seizures are permissible, they must all conform to a standard of reasonableness. Law enforcement officers are not permitted to conduct searches and seizures arbitrarily, or even based on their hunches about criminal activity. For a search to be reasonable under the Fourth Amendment police must have "probable cause," or in certain instances "reasonable suspicion," to believe that a search will produce evidence of crime. Subject to certain exceptions, evidence obtained through unreasonable searches and seizures is not admissible in criminal prosecutions.

THE COMMON-LAW BACKGROUND

Prior to the late seventeenth century, there was very little protection at common law against invasions of citizens' privacy by unreasonable searches and seizures. Although a system of warrants had long been in place to provide legal authority for arrests, searches, and seizures, warrants could be issued by executive as well as judicial authorities. Moreover, there was no requirement that a search warrant specify the location to be searched or the items to be seized. For hundreds of years, English subjects (and, later, American colonists) were subjected to the abuse of the "general warrant," that is, a warrant authorizing searches of unspecified persons and places.

In the wake of the Glorious Revolution of 1688, English courts began to place more stringent and effective limitations on the power of the Crown. The power of search and seizure was one area in which courts moved to delimit royal authority.

By far the most significant English case in the area of search and seizure prior to the American Revolution was *Entick v. Carrington*, 95 Eng.Rep. 807 (1765). John Entick, who edited a newspaper highly critical of the government, was arrested on a charge of seditious libel. A warrant was issued calling for the seizure of all his books, letters, and papers. Entick successfully sued for trespass. On appeal, the judgment was upheld and the practice of general warrants was declared illegal. The opinion in *Entick v. Carrington* proved to be very influential. Addressing the House of Commons in 1766, William Pitt declared:

> The poorest man may, in his cottage, bid defiance to all the forces of the Crown. It may be frail; its roof may shake; the wind may blow through it; the storm may enter; but the King of England may not enter; all his force dares not cross the threshold of the ruined tenement.

In that year, Parliament declared the notorious general warrant invalid.

ADOPTION OF THE FOURTH AMENDMENT

Although the common law provided some protection against general warrants, the framers of the Bill of Rights adopted a more explicit, and more thorough, proscription of unreasonable searches and seizures. To a great extent they were motivated by a distaste for the Writs of Assistance, which gave customs officials in the American colonies unlimited powers to search for smuggled goods. In a famous debate in 1761, James Otis called the Writs of Assistance "the worst instrument of arbitrary power, the most destructive of English liberty and the fundamental principles of law, that ever was found in an English law book." Quoted in *Boyd v. United States,* 116 U.S. 616, 625, 6 S. Ct. 524, 529, 29 L.Ed. 746, 749 (1886). The Fourth Amendment was adopted to ensure that officials of the United States government would never be able to exercise such unlimited powers of search and seizure.

Their distaste for general warrants led the framers of the Bill of Rights to write a particularity requirement into the warrant clause of the Fourth Amendment. In *Maryland v. Garrison,* 480 U.S. 79, 84, 107 S.Ct. 1013, 1016, 94 L.Ed.2d 72, 80 (1987), the Supreme Court emphasized that

> limiting the authorization to search to the specific areas and things for which there is probable cause to search ... ensures that the search will be carefully tailored to its justifications, and will not take on the character of the wide-ranging exploratory searches the Framers intended to prohibit.

Extension of the Fourth Amendment to State Criminal Prosecutions

The Fourth Amendment, like all the protections of the Bill of Rights, was originally conceived as a limitation on the powers of the newly created national government. Under the original conception of the Bill of Rights, citizens seeking legal protection against actions of state and local governments had to look to their state constitutions and state courts for relief. *Barron v. Baltimore,* 32 U.S. (7 Pet.) 243, 8 L.Ed. 672 (1833). However, the protection of the Fourth Amendment, along with most of the protections contained in the Bill of Rights, has been extended to defendants in state criminal prosecutions on the basis of the Fourteenth Amendment's limitations on state action. In 1949 the Supreme Court held that the freedom from unreasonable searches and seizures is "implicit in 'the concept of ordered liberty' and as such enforceable against the States through the Due Process Clause [of the Fourteenth Amendment]." *Wolf v. Colorado*, 338 U.S. 25, 27–28, 69 S. Ct. 1359, 1361, 93 L.Ed. 1782, 1785 (1949). The judicial extension of the Fourth Amendment and other protections of the Bill of Rights to limit the actions of the state and local governments is referred to as the "doctrine of incorporation."

As a result of *Wolf* and subsequent court decisions, the Fourth Amendment limits search and seizure activities by law enforcement agencies at all levels of government, whether federal, state, or local. The application of the Fourth Amendment to state prosecutions ensures a minimal national standard governing search and seizure. Under our system of federalism, state courts are free to provide higher levels of protection for individuals under applicable provisions of their state constitutions than are provided by the Fourth Amendment. But they cannot provide less protection to the individual without running afoul of the Fourteenth Amendment. *Mapp v. Ohio*, 367 U.S. 643, 81 S. Ct. 1684, 6 L.Ed.2d 1081 (1961).

In an attempt to reduce confusion and unnecessary complexity owing to different federal and state standards in the law of search and seizure, at least one state has amended its constitution to render its proscription of unreasonable searches and seizures coextensive with the Fourth Amendment. West's Fla. Const. Art. 1, § 12 (as amended 1982). Interpreting this novel amendment, the Florida Supreme Court has held that, in effect, the Florida constitution incorporates all decisions of the United States Supreme Court interpreting the Fourth Amendment, regardless of when they were rendered. *Bernie v. State*, 524 So.2d 988 (Fla. 1988).

WHEN DOES THE FOURTH AMENDMENT APPLY?

Before reviewing the scope of protection afforded by the Fourth Amendment, we must consider the threshold issue of its applicability. First, it must be recognized that the amendment protects a person's rights against the police and other government agents, but not against searches and seizures performed by private individuals. The Supreme Court has said that the

> origin and history [of the Fourth Amendment] clearly show that it was intended as a restraint upon the activities of sovereign authority, and was not intended to be a limitation upon other than governmental agencies. *Burdeau v. McDowell*, 256 U.S. 465, 475, 41 S. Ct. 574, 576, 65 L.Ed. 1048, 1051 (1921).

More recently, the Court said that the Fourth Amendment

> is wholly inapplicable to a search or seizure, even an unreasonable one, effected by a private individual not acting as an agent of the Government or with the participation or knowledge of any government official. *United States v. Jacobsen*, 466 U.S. 109, 113, 104 S. Ct. 1652, 1656, 80 L.Ed.2d 85, 94 (1984).

Consequently, if law enforcement officers do not exceed the scope of a prior private search, they do not infringe upon any privacy interest, and the governmental action is not a "search" within the meaning of the Fourth Amendment. *United States v. Jacobsen, supra.* The Court recently reiterated its position that the

Fourth Amendment does not apply to a private search or seizure unless the private party acted as an instrument or agent of the government. *Skinner v. Railway Labor Executives' Association,* 489 U.S. 602, 109 S.Ct. 1402, 1411, 103 L.Ed. 2d 639 (1989). Of course, if police suspicions form the impetus for the search, and they overtly involve themselves in and encourage it, the search becomes a public one, even if conducted by a private party. See, for example, *State v. Lieder,* 449 N.W. 2d 485 (Minn. App. 1989).

Second, the Fourth Amendment is not designed to protect property that has been abandoned. Therefore, police may search abandoned premises and seize abandoned property without the necessity of legally justifying their actions. *Abel v. United States,* 362 U.S. 217, 80 S. Ct. 683, 4 L.Ed.2d 668 (1960).

Third, the requirement for a warrant is ordinarily applicable to commercial premises. However, statutes can provide an exception to allow warrantless inspection of pervasively regulated premises (e.g., alcoholic beverage establishments). In the year the Fourth Amendment was ratified (1791), Congress authorized inspection of alcoholic beverage establishments without a warrant. See *Colonnade Catering Corp. v. United States,* 397 U.S. 72, 90 S.Ct. 774, 25 L.Ed.2d 60 (1970).

Finally, as the Supreme Court pointed out in 1990, the purpose of the Fourth Amendment is to restrict searches and seizures conducted in domestic matters, and it is inapplicable to searches and seizures conducted by United States agents of a nonresident's property located in a foreign country. *United States v. Verdugo-Urquidez,* 494 U.S. 259, 110 S.Ct. 1056, 108 L.Ed. 2d 222 (1990).

The Concept of Curtilage and the Open Fields Doctrine

The term *curtilage* refers to the enclosed space of ground surrounding a dwellinghouse. At common law, the concept of curtilage was developed to afford the area immediately surrounding a house the same protection under the law of burglary as was afforded the house itself (see Chapter 7). The Supreme Court has employed the concept of curtilage in defining the applicability of Fourth Amendment protection. The Fourth Amendment provides the same protection to the curtilage as to the house itself. See, for example, *United States v. Van Dyke,* 643 F.2d 992 (4th Cir. 1981). On the other hand, the "open fields" surrounding the house and curtilage are not entitled to Fourth Amendment protection. *Hester v. United States,* 265 U.S. 57, 44 S. Ct. 445, 68 L.Ed. 898 (1924). Writing for the Supreme Court in *Hester,* Justice Oliver Wendell Holmes noted that

> the special protection accorded by the Fourth Amendment to the people in their "persons, houses, papers and effects," is not extended to the open fields. The distinction between the latter and the house is as old as the common law. 265 U.S. at 59, 44 S. Ct. at 446, 68 L.Ed. at 900.

The open fields doctrine has recently been reaffirmed by the Supreme Court. *Oliver v. United States,* 466 U.S. 170, 104 S. Ct. 1735, 80 L.Ed.2d 214 (1984). In *Oliver,* narcotics officers entered the defendant's land by going around a locked gate and ignoring "No Trespassing" signs. They observed a field of marijuana, whereupon they arrested the owner of the property for manufacturing contraband. The Court upheld the warrantless search because it concluded the defendant had no reasonable expectation of privacy in the open fields around his home, despite his attempt to protect it by posting signs.

The New York Court of Appeals has determined that the Supreme Court's opinion in *Oliver* does not adequately protect the rights against unreasonable search and seizure guaranteed under the New York Constitution. In *People v. Scott*, 593 N.E.2d 1328 (N.Y. 1992), the court ruled that where property owners fence or post "No Trespassing" signs on their private property or, by some other means, indicate that entry is not permitted, they have a reasonable expectation of privacy that must be respected. The New York decision illustrates the important point, discussed in Chapter 3, that a state is free to provide greater protection under its state constitution than the U.S. Supreme Court determines is required under the federal constitution.

In *United States v. Dunn*, 480 U.S. 294, 107 S. Ct. 1134, 94 L.Ed.2d 326 (1987), the Supreme Court held that a barn located some sixty yards from a house was not within the curtilage, despite the existence of a perimeter fence designed to corral cattle. The Court said that, notwithstanding any expectation of privacy that the owner may have had in the barn, police were justified in crossing a perimeter fence and peering into the open door of the barn, from where they observed illegal activity. For Fourth Amendment purposes, police were standing in the open fields.

Although the Fourth Amendment refers to "houses," its protections are extended to stores, offices, and places of business. *See v. City of Seattle*, 387 U.S. 541, 87 S. Ct. 1737, 18 L.Ed.2d 943 (1967). However, an exception is made in respect to those areas of commercial properties that carry an implied invitation for the public to enter. *Maryland v. Macon*, 472 U.S. 463, 105 S. Ct. 2778, 86 L.Ed.2d 370 (1985). In *Macon*, a case involving the seizure of allegedly obscene materials, the Supreme Court held that there was no Fourth Amendment protection for a bookseller who sold two pornographic magazines to an undercover police officer. The police officer later returned to arrest the bookseller on an obscenity charge. The Court said that the bookseller did not have a "reasonable expectation of privacy in areas of the store where the public was invited to enter and to transact business." 472 U.S. at 469, 105 S. Ct. at 2781, 86 L.Ed.2d at 376.

WHAT CONSTITUTES A "SEARCH" OR "SEIZURE" UNDER THE FOURTH AMENDMENT?

The Fourth Amendment forbids unreasonable searches and seizures by the police and other government agents. The term *seizure* refers to the taking into custody of physical evidence, property, or even a person. What constitutes a search? Originally, the protection of the Fourth Amendment was limited to physical intrusions on one's person or property. *Olmstead v. United States*, 277 U.S. 438, 48 S. Ct. 564, 72 L.Ed. 944 (1928). Historically, courts looked at whether a trespass had taken place in deciding whether the Fourth Amendment was implicated. Thus surveillance without physical contact with the suspect or the suspect's property was deemed to fall outside the protections of the Fourth Amendment. Accordingly, the Fourth Amendment was not deemed applicable to wiretapping or eavesdropping.

Reasonable Expectations of Privacy

In *Katz v. United States*, 389 U.S. 347, 88 S. Ct. 507, 19 L.Ed.2d 576 (1967), the Supreme Court overruled *Olmstead* and abandoned the trespass doctrine, saying that "the Fourth Amendment protects people, not places." 389 U.S. at 361, 88 S. Ct. at 516, 19 L.Ed.2d at 582. The contemporary approach to determining the scope of protected privacy under the Fourth Amendment is nicely stated in Justice Harlan's concurring opinion in *Katz*:

> My understanding of the rule as it has emerged from prior decisions is that there is a twofold requirement, first that a person have exhibited an actual (subjective) expectation of privacy and, second, that the expectation be one that society is prepared to recognize as "reasonable." 389 U.S. at 361, 88 S. Ct. at 516, 19 L.Ed.2d at 587.

Katz teaches that essentially a search and seizure under the Fourth Amendment covers any official invasion of a person's reasonable expectation of privacy as to his or her person, house, papers, or effects. Specifically, the Court recognized that a suspected bookie who was using a public telephone allegedly in conduct of a gambling business enjoyed a reasonable expectation of privacy, and that a police wiretap of the phone booth was a search within the meaning of the Fourth Amendment. This decision brought wiretapping and other forms of electronic eavesdropping within the limitations of the Fourth Amendment. Currently, any means of invading a person's "reasonable expectation of privacy" is considered a "search" for Fourth Amendment purposes. The critical question that courts must address in reviewing cases where police conduct surveillance or eavesdropping without probable cause or judicial authorization is whether such surveillance intruded on a suspect's reasonable expectation of privacy.

The issue of what constitutes a "reasonable expectation of privacy" has been litigated in hundreds of cases in federal and state courts. Police techniques such as canine sniffs are considered among the least intrusive means of government investigation. Thus, police were allowed to conduct a "sniff test" of a passenger's luggage at an airport without reasonable cause because it did not violate a person's reasonable expectation of privacy. *United States v. Place*, 462 U.S. 696, 106 S.Ct. 2637, 77 L.Ed.2d 110 (1983). However, the uniqueness of individual situations has resulted in disparate views, with police frequently complaining that judicial decisions fail to furnish any "bright line" rules.

In the usual situation, a house guest has a reasonable expectation of privacy in someone else's home. *Minnesota v. Olson*, 495 U.S. 91, 110 S.Ct. 1684, 109 L.Ed.2d 85 (1990). Courts, however, address some rather unique situations encountered by law enforcement officers. Consider the following decisions from state appellate courts. An Ohio court found that a state trooper did not infringe on the defendants' rights when the officer opened the unlocked door of an outhouse at a public rest area and observed them engaging in fellatio. *State v. Johnson*, 536 N.E. 2d 648 (Ohio App. 1987). In another instance, police seized drugs from a bedroom sometimes occupied by the defendant and charged him with dealing in narcotics. The defendant did not live in the house on a regular basis, but merely slept in a room there at times, and control over the bedroom where drugs were found was dependent on the will of the owner, not the defendant. The court ruled the defendant had no reasonable expectation of privacy in the bedroom. *Livingston v. State*, 542 N.E. 2d 192 (Ind. 1989). A similar result was reached in *Commonwealth v. Johnson*, 777 S.W. 2d 876 (Ky. 1989). There, the act of officers shining a flashlight beam into a darkened motel room through a partially opened door and through a window did not violate the defendant's reasonable expectation of privacy.

The lower federal courts have issued hundreds of opinions in this area of the law. Two recent opinions typify the decisional law. In *United States v. Hessling*, 845 F. 2d 617 (6th Cir. 1988), the court ruled that a police officer who used his senses to hear a conversation from a vantage point where he was legally permitted to be did not conduct a search. Note that the officer heard the conversation without the aid of a listening device. In *United States v. Williams*, 902 F.2d 678 (8th Cir. 1990), another federal appellate court rejected Williams' argument that the trial court erred in not suppressing, as the fruit of an unconstitutional search, the results of an ultraviolet light examination. The court upheld the trial court's decision, which compared the use of the light to fingerprinting and voice exemplars, and concluded its use did not constitute a search under the Fourth Amendment.

In *California v. Greenwood*, 486 U.S. 35, 108 S.Ct. 1625, 100 L.Ed. 2d 30 (1988), a police officer requested a trash collector to turn over bags of garbage collected from the Greenwood home in Laguna Beach, California. The officer searched the garbage bags and found evidence indicating illicit drug use. She used this evidence as a basis for obtaining a warrant to search the Greenwood home. During the search, the police discovered cocaine and hashish. As a result the police charged the defendants with possession of contraband, but the trial court dismissed the charges on the ground the warrantless trash search violated the Fourth Amendment. The California appellate court affirmed. The United States Supreme Court reversed on the ground that the defendants, by placing their garbage *outside* the curtilage, had exposed their garbage to the public; and regardless whether they may have had an expectation of privacy in their garbage, it was not an expectation that society is prepared to accept as being objectively reasonable.

THE WARRANT REQUIREMENT

As pointed out, when searches are challenged as being unreasonable, courts must first determine if the Fourth Amendment is applicable. We have seen that it does not apply to open fields or abandoned property. Where it does apply, the Fourth Amendment expresses a decided preference for searches and seizures to be conducted pursuant to a warrant. The warrant requirement is designed to ensure that the impartial judgment of a judge or magistrate is interposed between the citizen and the state. The Supreme Court emphasized this point in *McDonald v. United States*, 335 U.S. 451, 69 S. Ct. 191, 93 L.Ed. 153 (1948), saying that

> The presence of a search warrant serves a high function. Absent some grave emergency, the Fourth Amendment has interposed a magistrate between the citizen and the police. This was done not to shield criminals nor to make the home a safe

haven for illegal activities. It was done so that an objective mind might weigh the need to invade that privacy in order to enforce the law. The right of privacy was deemed too precious to entrust to the discretion of those whose job is the detection of crime and the arrest of criminals. 335 U.S. at 455–456, 69 S. Ct. at 195–96, 93 L.Ed. at 158.

While stressing the importance of the warrant requirement, courts have been willing to allow certain exceptions. Courts have recognized that an absolute warrant requirement would be impractical. Consequently, they have upheld the reasonableness of warrantless searches under so-called exigent circumstances.

A good example of a legitimate warrantless search and seizure is one undertaken to preserve "evanescent evidence," such as a quantity of drugs that a suspect is trying to consume to avoid arrest and seizure of the contraband. This principle is illustrated in a recent case in Iowa where a suspect admitted swallowing some crack cocaine after being told by police to "spit it out!" The Iowa Supreme Court recognized that pumping a person's stomach is a "search and seizure" but the court found that the suspect's ingestion of the cocaine was an "exigent circumstance" that gave the officer probable cause to arrest the suspect and justified a warrantless pump of the suspect's stomach. The court was careful to point out that the procedure was done in accordance with accepted medical standards. *State v. Strong*, 493 N.W. 2d 834 (Iowa 1992). Yet despite a number of exceptions (which we will discussed later in the chapter), the warrant requirement remains a central feature of Fourth Amendment law. Whenever possible, police officers should obtain warrants, because their failure to do so may jeopardize the fruits of a successful search.

CASE IN POINT

REASONABLE EXPECTATIONS OF PRIVACY

In 1986 the Supreme Court refused to recognize a reasonable expectation of privacy to invalidate a search warrant predicated upon aerial observations of a suspect's backyard. Police received a tip that defendant Ciraolo was growing marijuana in his backyard. The backyard was not visible from the street due to a privacy fence that surrounded the property. The police then obtained an aircraft that was flown above the suspect's home at 1,000 feet. From that altitude, they observed marijuana plants visible to the naked eye. Police then obtained a warrant, conducted a search, and seized the contraband. The defendant objected to the search on the grounds that the aerial observation on which it was predicated was an unreasonable invasion of his privacy. The Supreme Court disagreed and upheld the aerial observation, the search warrant, and the seizure of the contraband. The Court concluded that simply because Ciraolo's backyard was within the curtilage did not bar any and all forms of police observation. The Court said: "[W]e readily conclude that [Ciraolo's] expectation that his garden was protected from [aerial] observation is unreasonable and is not an expectation that society is prepared to honor."

California v. Ciraolo, 476 U.S. 207, 106 S. Ct. 1809, 90 L.Ed.2d 210 (1986).

The Probable Cause Requirement

Subject to narrow exceptions, all searches, whether conducted with or without a warrant, must be based on probable cause. Like many legal terms, *probable cause* is not susceptible to precise definition. Probable cause exists when prudent and cautious police officers have trustworthy information leading them to believe that evidence of crime may be obtained through a particular search. See *Brinegar v. United States,* 338 U.S. 160, 69 S. Ct. 1302, 93 L.Ed. 1879 (1949); *Carroll v. United States,* 267 U.S. 132, 45 S. Ct. 280, 69 L.Ed. 543 (1925).

The Supreme Court has set the contemporary approach to determine probable cause by saying that courts should view the issue as a "commonsense, practical question" that must be decided by the issuing magistrate viewing the "totality-of-the-circumstances" on a case-by-case basis. *Illinois v. Gates,* 462 U.S. 213, 230, 103 S.Ct. 2317, 2328, 76 L.Ed. 2d 527, 543 (1983). This approach has been amplified by lower federal courts, which have observed that even though an innocent explanation may be consistent with the facts alleged in an affidavit seeking a search warrant, this does not negate probable cause. See, for example, *United States v. Fama,* 758 F. 2d 834 (2d Cir. 1985).

Although state courts are free to impose a higher standard, most have followed this approach. For example, the Ohio Supreme Court ruled that an affidavit, by a police agent saying that he observed a tall marijuana plant growing in an enclosed backyard, furnished probable cause for a magistrate to conclude there was marijuana or related paraphernalia in the residence. *State v. George,* 544 N.E. 2d 640 (Ohio 1989). Some state courts have declined to follow the *Gates* approach and have opted to provide their citizens more protection than allowed by the federal view. In some instances these state views result from linguistic variations in state constitutional counterparts to the Fourth Amendment. See, for example, *Commonwealth v. Upton,* 476 N.E. 2d 548 (Mass. 1985); *State v. Jacumin,* 778 S.W. 2d 430 (Tenn. 1989).

Issuance of the Search Warrant

Under normal circumstances a police officer with probable cause to believe that evidence of a crime is located in a specific place must submit an application for a search warrant to the appropriate judge or magistrate. Rule 41(a) of the Federal Rules of Criminal Procedure allows a federal agent to obtain a search warrant from a federal magistrate or a judge of a state court of record within the district wherein the property or person sought is located.

In *Coolidge v. New Hampshire,* 403 U.S. 443, 91 S. Ct. 2022, 29 L.Ed.2d 564 (1971), the Supreme Court invalidated a warrant issued by the state attorney general. The Court said that a warrant must be issued by a neutral and detached magistrate and certainly not by an official responsible for criminal prosecutions. Similarly, in *United States v. United States District Court,* 407 U.S. 297, 92 S. Ct. 2125, 32 L.Ed.2d 752 (1972), the Court invalidated a statute that permitted electronic eavesdropping to be authorized solely by the U.S. Attorney General in cases involving national security. Writing for the Court, Justice Powell said that

> those charged with . . . [the] investigative and prosecutorial duty should not be the sole judges of when to utilize constitutionally sensitive means in pursuing their tasks.

ACODC NO. 29

Commonwealth of Massachusetts

Middlesex _____ , ss.

Concord District Court
Court

AFFIDAVIT IN SUPPORT OF APPLICATION FOR SEARCH WARRANT*
G.L. c. 276, ss. 1 to 7; St. 1964, c. 557 As Amended

21 ___ June ___ , 19 80

I, __Sam Buckley_____ , being duly sworn, depose and say:
Name of applicant

1. I am __Police Chief of Concord, Massachusetts_____
(Describe position, assignment, office, etc.)

2. I have information based upon (describe sources, facts indicating reliability of source and nature of information; if based on personal knowledge and belief, so state) (If space is insufficient, attach affidavit or affidavits hereto)

Based on information from a Federal Drug Enforcement Officer, the above has reason to belive at 123 Smith Street, one-story red brick house, with garage, 2 bedrooms, kitchen, living room, and bathroom, there is a small brown suitcase containing a controlled substance believed to be heroin.

*3. Based upon the foregoing reliable information - and upon my personal knowledge and belief - and ~~searched affidavits~~ - there is probable cause to believe that the property hereinafter described - has been stolen - or is being concealed, etc.
and may be found in the possession of __Miss Francine Taggart_____
Name or person or persons

at premises __123 Smith Street, Concord_____
(Identify number, street, place, etc.)

4. The property for which I seek the issuance of a search warrant is the following (here describe the property as particularly as possible).

One small brown suitcase taken from a station locker by Francine Taggart on June 19, 1980, containing heroin.

WHEREFORE, I respectfully request that the court issue a warrant and order of seizure, authorizing the search of (identify premises and the person or persons to be searched)

and directing that if such property or evidence or any part thereof be found that it be seized and brought before the court; together with such other and further relief that the court may deem proper.

Police Chief Sam Buckley
Signature of applicant

Then personally appeared the above named _Chief Buckley_____
and made oath that the foregoing affidavit by him subscribed is true.

Before me this __21__ day of __June__ 19 __80__

J. P. Jones - Special Justice

Justice of Special Justice
Clerk or Assistant Clerk of the   Municipal   District   Court.

* Strike inapplicable clauses

REVISED JULY 1965

APPROVED BY THE CHIEF JUSTICE OF THE DISTRICT COURTS

FIGURE 14.1 Application for a Search Warrant

The historical judgment, which the Fourth Amendment accepts, is that unreviewed executive discretion may yield too readily to pressures to obtain incriminating evidence and overlook potential invasions of privacy.... 407 U.S. at 317, 92 S. Ct. at 2136, 32 L.Ed.2d at 766.

However, in *Shadwick v. City of Tampa*, 407 U.S. 345, 92 S. Ct. 2119, 32 L.Ed.2d 783 (1972), the Court allowed municipal court clerks to issue warrants because they were sufficiently disengaged from the activities of law enforcement. The Court observed that "communities may have sound reasons for delegating the responsibility of issuing warrants to competent personnel other than judges or lawyers." 407 U.S. at 352, 92 S. Ct. at 2123, 32 L.Ed.2d at 790.

The Supporting Affidavit

An affidavit is a signed document attesting under oath to certain facts of which the affiant has knowledge (fig. 14.1). Generally, an affidavit by a law enforcement officer requesting issuance of a search warrant is presented to a judge or magistrate. The manner in which the affidavit is recorded and transmitted may vary. For example, the Idaho Supreme Court, finding that electronically recorded testimony was no less reliable than a sworn, written statement, held that the word *affidavit* under the Idaho constitution was sufficiently broad to include tape recording of oral testimony. *State v. Yoder*, 534 P.2d 771 (Idaho 1975). California law permits police officers to complete affidavits using the telephone in order to expedite the issuance of a warrant. West's Ann. Cal. Pen. Code. § § 1526(b), 1528(b).

Evidentiary Requisites to Obtain a Search Warrant

The officer's affidavit in support of a search warrant must always contain a rather precise description of the place(s) or person(s) to be searched and the things to be seized. Moreover, the affidavit must attest to specific facts that establish probable cause to justify a search.

An affidavit cannot establish probable cause for issuance of a search warrant if it is based merely on the affiant's suspicion or belief without stating the facts and circumstances that belief is based upon. Information upon which an affidavit is based must be sufficiently fresh to ensure that the items to be seized are probably located on the premises to be searched. The issue of when a search warrant becomes invalid because the information the affidavit is based upon is stale has been litigated in many cases, with varying results. No set rule can be formulated. For example, in *State v. Pulgini*, 366 A.2d 1198 (Del. Super. 1976), the court invalidated a search warrant where there was an unexplained delay of twenty-three days between the last alleged fact and the issuance of the warrant. On the other hand, in *United States v. Rosenbarger*, 536 F.2d 715 (6th Cir. 1976), *cert. denied*, 431 U.S. 965, 97 S. Ct. 2920, 53 L.Ed.2d 1060 (1977), a twenty-one-day time lapse between observation of the receipt of stolen property and issuance of the warrant did not invalidate the warrant because the magistrate could determine there was a reasonable probability that the stolen goods were still in the defendant's home.

Tips from Police Informants

A magistrate's finding of probable cause may be based on hearsay evidence. See, for example, Fed. R. Crim. P. 41(c)(2). This permits police to obtain search warrants based on tips from anonymous or confidential informants. Police informants, referred to as "confidential informants" or "CIs," are often persons who have been involved with the police and are seeking favorable consideration in respect to their own offenses. Because their motivation may be suspect, their reliability is checked carefully. For many years the Supreme Court required magistrates to apply a rigorous two-pronged test to determine probable cause. See *Aguilar v. Texas,* 378 U.S. 108, 84 S. Ct. 1509, 12 L.Ed.2d 723 (1964); *Spinelli v. United States,* 393 U.S. 410, 89 S. Ct. 584, 21 L.Ed.2d 637 (1969). The so-called *Aguilar-Spinelli* test required that informants be both credible and reliable, a test that ordinarily precluded the use of anonymous tips. In 1983 the Supreme Court relaxed the test and permitted magistrates to consider the "totality of circumstances" when evaluating applications based on hearsay evidence. *Illinois v. Gates,* 462 U.S. 213, 103 S. Ct. 2317, 76 L.Ed.2d 527 (1983). The following year, the Court held that the standard for determining probable cause announced in the *Gates* decision was to be given a broad interpretation by lower courts. *Massachusetts v. Upton,* 466 U.S. 727, 104 S. Ct. 2085, 80 L.Ed.2d 721 (1984).

Despite the Supreme Court's relaxed standard for determining probable cause based on tips from informants, some states have chosen to follow the stricter standards formerly imposed by the *Aguilar* and *Spinelli* cases. This, of course, is the prerogative of the states. In a comprehensive opinion in *State v. Cordova,* 784 P. 2d 30 (N.M. 1989), the New Mexico Supreme Court reviewed an affidavit for a search warrant that recited that Cordova had brought heroin into town and was selling it at the house in question. The affidavit, however, was devoid of information as to how the informant gathered this information. Further, although the affidavit stated the informant had personal knowledge that "heroin users" had been at the residence in question, there was nothing to indicate the source of the informant's knowledge, and no explanation as to how the informant knew the persons in question were heroin users. Since the affidavit did not meet the two prongs of establishing the informant was both credible and reliable, the court found it did not provide a substantial basis for believing the informant and for concluding the informant gathered the information in a reliable manner. Further, it did not adequately state the informant's basis of knowledge that the defendant was selling heroin. In rejecting the state's appeal, the New Mexico Supreme Court declined to follow the *Gates* "totality of circumstances" rule and found the affidavit did not meet the requirements of the New Mexico Constitution and its rules of criminal procedure.

In 1985, the Connecticut Supreme Court criticized the "totality of the circumstances" test as being "too amorphous" and an inadequate safeguard against unjustified police intrusions. That court has recently held that if the information supplied by a CI fails the *Aguilar-Spinelli* test, probable cause may still be found if the affidavit sets forth other circumstances that bolster any deficiencies. *State v. Barton,* 594 A.2d 917 (Conn. 1991).

When a defendant demands to know the identify of the informant who provided the police with information on which they based their affidavit for a search warrant, courts face a delicate problem. There is a limited privilege to withhold identity of the confidential informant. In determining whether to require disclosure, the court balances the interest of the public in preserving the anonymity of the informant against the defendant's need to have this information to prepare a defense, and where the questioned identity "is relevant and helpful to the defense of an accused, or is essential to a fair determination of a cause, the privilege must give way." *Roviaro v. United States,* 353 U.S. 53, 77 S.Ct. 623, 1 L.Ed.2d 639 (1957).

Required Specificity of a Search Warrant

The Fourth Amendment mandates that "no warrants shall issue" except those "particularly describing the place to be searched and the persons or things to be seized." Thus the scope of a search and seizure is bound by the terms of the warrant (fig. 14.2). For example, a search warrant that described a certain third-floor apartment was insufficient to permit the search of an adjacent apartment, when police mistakenly entered the wrong apartment. *Garrison v. State,* 494 A.2d 193 (Md. 1985). Similarly, a warrant that described property to be seized as "various long play phonographic albums, and miscellaneous vases and glassware" was likewise held insufficient. Nevertheless, the court approved seizure of items described as "a set of antique ceramic book ends in the shape of horses and advertising Rolling Rock Beer." *State v. Noll,* 343 N.W.2d 391, 393 (Wis. 1984).

Courts tend to be less strict when it comes to the description of contraband (such as heroin), since it is illegal per se, but more strict in cases involving First Amendment rights. For example, a federal appeals court invalidated a warrant authorizing the seizure of "a quantity of obscene materials, including books, pamphlets, magazines, newspapers, films and prints." *United States v. Guarino,* 729 F.2d 864, 865 (1st Cir. 1984).

Anticipatory Search Warrants

The dramatic increase in drug trafficking over the last decade has given rise to a countermeasure known as the "anticipatory search warrant." Traditionally,

---

CASE IN POINT

REQUIRED SPECIFICITY OF A SEARCH WARRANT

A police officer was executing a search warrant that specified a particular copyrighted software program and gave its serial number and added "all other computer related software." The officer was unable to find a floppy disk containing the program, but did locate the program on the hard drive of the defendant's computer. In affirming the defendant's conviction for an offense involving intellectual property, the court held that the hard drive was properly seized even though not specifically listed in the warrant.

State v. Tanner, 534 So. 2d 535 (La. App. 1988).

ACODC NO. 30

Commonwealth of Massachusetts

Middlesex _____ , ss.   Concord District _____
                                                                              Court

(Search Warrant)

TO THE SHERIFFS OF OUR SEVERAL COUNTIES, OR THEIR DEPUTIES, ANY STATE POLICE OFFICER, OR ANY CONSTABLE OR POLICE OFFICER OF ANY CITY OR TOWN, WITHIN OUR SAID COMMONWEALTH:

Proof by affidavit having been made this day before __Special Justic J.Q. Jones_____
                                                                    (Name of person issuing warrant)

by _____Police Chief Sam Buckley_____
                              (Name of person or persons signing affidavit)

*that there is probable cause for believing that certain property has been stolen, embezzled, or obtained by false pretences — certain property is intended for use or has been used as the means of committing a crime — certain property has been concealed to prevent a crime from being discovered — certain property is unlawfully possessed or kept or concealed for an unlawful purpose.

    WE THEREFORE COMMAND YOU in the daytime (or at any time of the day or night) to make an immediate search of _____123 Smith Street, Concord_____
                                                              (Identify premises)

(occupied by ____Francine Taggart_____) and of the person of
                              (Name of occupant)

_____ , and of any person present who may
                              (Name of person)

be found to have such property in his possession or under his control or to whom such property may have been delivered, for the following property:

_____
                              (Description of property)

    One small brown suitcase believed to contain heroin.

and if you find any such property or any part therof to bring it and the persons in who possession it is found before the __Concord District Court_____
                              (Name of Court)

at ____Concord, Massachusetts_____
                              (Court location)

in said County and Commonwealth, as soon as it has been served and in any event not later than seven days of issuance thereof. (Officer to make return on reverse side)

Witness _J. Q. Jones_____ , Esquire, Justice, at _Concord_____ ,

_Dist. Court_____

_____ aforesaid, this ___21___ day of ___June_____

in the year of our Lord one thousand nine hundred and ___80___

                                   P.L. Norman

* Strike inapplicable clauses   Justice
                                                  (Clerk)
                                                  Assistant Clerk

G.L. c. 276, ss. 1 to 7; St. 1964, c. 557

          APPROVED BY THE CHIEF JUSTICE OF THE DISTRICT COURTS

FIGURE 14.2 A Typical Search Warrant

police wait until a suspect receives contraband and then prepare an affidavit to obtain a search warrant. If the magistrate finds that probable cause exists at that time, a search warrant is issued. In the case of an anticipatory warrant, probable cause does not have to exist until the warrant is executed and the search conducted.

During the 1980s, several state appellate courts approved anticipatory search warrants. See, for example, *State v. Coker*, 746 S.W.2d 167 (Tenn. 1987). In one of these cases, *Bernie v. State*, 524 So.2d 988 (Fla. 1988), a freight delivery service notified police that a package that broke in transit revealed a suspicious substance that later proved to be cocaine. An anticipatory warrant was issued to search the residence to which the package was addressed. Police were on the scene when the freight company delivered the package. The warrant was served, the cocaine seized, and the defendant taken into custody. On appeal, the search was upheld by the state supreme court, which observed that neither the federal nor the state constitution prohibited issuance of a search warrant to be served at a future date in anticipation of delivery of contraband.

The Alaska Supreme Court has cautioned that a magistrate issuing an anticipatory warrant should make its execution contingent on the occurrence of an event that evidences probable cause that the items to be seized are in the place to be searched, rather than directing that the warrant be executed forthwith. *Johnson v. State*, 617 P.2d 1117 (Alaska 1980).

The United States Supreme Court has not yet addressed the issue of whether a search based on an anticipatory warrant passes muster under the Fourth Amendment. However, some federal and state appellate courts have upheld the basic concept that contraband does not have to be currently located at the place described in a search warrant if there is probable cause to believe it will be there when the warrant is executed. In 1986, the Ninth Circuit Court of Appeals held that an anticipatory search warrant is permissible "where the contraband to be seized is on a sure course to its destination." *United States v. Hale*, 784 F.2d 1465, 1468 (9th Cir. 1986).

The use of anticipatory search warrants is not limited to drug raids, of course. For example, in 1988, the U.S. Court of Appeals for the Fourth Circuit upheld an anticipatory search warrant permitting an inspector to search an apartment for child pornography where the issuing magistrate conditioned the validity of the warrant on the contraband being placed in the mail. Thus, when the mailing was accomplished, the contraband was on a certain course to its destination. *United States v. Dornhofer*, 859 F.2d 1195 (4th Cir. 1988).

Execution of a Search Warrant

The manner and time in which warrants are executed is governed by applicable federal and state laws and rules of criminal procedure. Rule 41(c)(1) of the Federal Rules of Criminal Procedure provides that the warrant

> shall command the officer to search, within a specified period of time not to exceed 10 days, the person or place named for the property specified. The warrant shall be served in the daytime, unless the issuing authority ... authorizes its execution at times other than daytime.

Rule 41(h) defines *daytime* as between 6:00 A.M. and 10:00 P.M. according to local time. States have varying provisions governing when a search warrant may be executed. Texas allows three days, Vernon's Tex. Code Crim. P. art. 18.06(a), while California allows ten. West's Ann. Cal. Penal Code § 1534. Likewise, state laws vary on the hours during which a search warrant may be executed. California law permits a warrant to be executed between the hours of 7:00 A.M. and 10:00 P.M. West's Ann. Cal. Penal Code § 1533. Some states, including Texas, do not impose restrictions on the hours when a warrant may be executed; others allow nighttime searches under special circumstances.

Under federal law an officer is required to knock and announce upon arrival at the place to be searched. 18 U.S.C.A. § 3109. Most states have similar knock-and-announce requirements, but courts have created some exceptions to protect officers and to prevent the destruction of evidence. The purpose of the knock-and-announce requirement is to reduce the potential for violence and protect the right of privacy of the occupants. Courts have generally ruled that there are no rigid limits as to the time that must elapse between the announcement and the officers' entry. A few seconds may even suffice. Moreover, courts frequently excuse compliance when to require it would endanger the lives of the officers or simply provide an occasion for occupants to dispose of evidence. The most common example of disposing of evidence after police have announced their presence is flushing of contraband down a toilet. See, for example, *State v. Stalbert,* 783 P. 2d 1005 (Or. App. 1989).

Officers who conduct a search are generally required to inventory the items seized and leave a receipt. See, for example, Fed. R. Crim. P. 41(d). However, federal and state courts have generally held that the failure of police to comply strictly with such requirements does not necessarily invalidate a search. See, for example, *United States v. Hall,* 505 F.2d 961 (3d Cir. 1974); *Smith v. State,* 566 S.W.2d 553 (Tenn. Crim. App. 1978).

Testing the Sufficiency of the Basis for Issuing a Search Warrant

In *Franks v. Delaware,* 438 U.S. 154, 98 S.Ct. 2674, 57 L.Ed.2d 667 (1978), the Supreme Court was faced with the issue of whether a defendant can challenge the affidavit for a search warrant in a pretrial proceeding. The Delaware Supreme Court had ruled that a defendant could not challenge the veracity of the statements made by the police to obtain their search warrant. The United States Supreme Court granted review and ruled that a defendant may challenge the sufficiency of the basis for a magistrate having issued a search warrant by attacking the veracity of the affidavit supporting its issuance. To obtain a *"Franks* hearing" on the veracity of the affiant, the defendant must first make a substantial, credible showing that the affidavit is "deliberately false or made with reckless disregard for the truth," and that the allegedly false statements were necessary to the finding of probable cause to issue the warrant. *United States v. Curry,* 911 F.2d 72 (8th Cir. 1990).

EXCEPTIONS TO THE WARRANT REQUIREMENT

As noted, there are reasonable exceptions to the warrant requirement. These exceptions involve "exigent circumstances" that justify a relaxation of the warrant requirement. There are nine well-defined exceptions to the warrant requirement:

1. The seizure of evidence in plain view of the police officer
2. A search incident to a lawful arrest
3. A search of a motor vehicle based on probable cause to believe that it contains articles an officer is entitled to seize
4. An inventory search of an impounded vehicle
5. A search conducted with consent
6. A search conducted in "hot pursuit"
7. A search conducted in an emergency situation
8. A search for evanescent evidence
9. A limited "stop-and-frisk" of a suspicious person

Exception 1: Evidence in Plain View

The Supreme Court has said that evidence in plain view of a police officer is not subject to the warrant requirement. *Harris v. United States,* 390 U.S. 234, 88 S. Ct. 992, 19 L.Ed.2d 1067 (1968). Obviously, police officers are not required to close their eyes or wear blinders in the face of evidence of a crime. A police officer may seize evidence that comes to his or her attention inadvertently, provided that (1) the officer has a legal justification to be in a constitutionally protected area when the seizure occurs; (2) the evidence seized is in the plain view of the officer who comes across it; and (3) it is apparent that the object constitutes evidence of a crime. *Coolidge v. New Hampshire,* 403 U.S. 443, 91 S. Ct. 2022, 29 L.Ed.2d 564 (1971).

The "inadvertent" requirement announced in *Coolidge v. New Hampshire* remained extant for more than a decade; however, in *Horton v. California,* 496 U.S. 128, 110 S.Ct. 2301, 110 L.Ed.2d 112 (1990), the Supreme Court noted that the inadvertence requirement was not an essential part of the plurality opinion in *Coolidge v. New Hampshire.* As the Court observed in 1983, "There is no reason [the police officer] should be precluded from observing as an officer what would be entirely visible to him as a private citizen." *Texas v. Brown,* 460 U.S. 730, 740, 103 S.Ct. 1535, 1542, 75 L.Ed. 2d 502 (1983). Notwithstanding, some state courts have continued to insist that the inadvertent requirement is a limitation on the plain-view exception to the warrant requirement.

The plain-view doctrine may apply both where the item seized is in plain view before the commencement of a search, and where it comes into the plain view of an officer conducting an otherwise valid search or entry. For example, in *United States v. Pacelli,* 470 F.2d 67 (2d Cir. 1972), *cert. denied,* 410 U.S. 983, 93 S. Ct. 1501, 36 L.Ed.2d 178 (1973), the court invoked the plain-view doctrine to uphold the seizure of illegal chemicals found during a search based on a warrant to search for heroin. The search warrant gave police officers the right to enter and search the premises; other items of contraband found in plain view during the search were deemed properly seized.

By way of contrast to *Pacelli,* consider the case of *Arizona v. Hicks,* 480 U.S. 321, 107 S. Ct. 1149, 94 L.Ed.2d 347 (1987). There, police who had lawfully entered an apartment to search for weapons noticed stereo equipment that seemed out of

---

> **CASE IN POINT**
>
> ## WHAT CONSTITUTES A MOTOR VEHICLE?
>
> In 1985 the Court upheld a warrantless search of a motor home despite the defendant's contention that it was his place of residence and thus should have been accorded the greater Fourth Amendment protection associated with a home. In the Court's view, the fact that the motor home was "readily mobile" and "licensed to operate on the public streets" rendered it an automobile for the purposes of Fourth Amendment analysis.
>
> *California v. Carney,* 471 U.S. 386, 105 S. Ct. 2066, 85 L.Ed.2d 406 (1985).

---

place, given the squalid condition of the apartment. His suspicion aroused, an officer moved the stereo equipment to locate the serial numbers. A check of the numbers indicated that the equipment was stolen. The Supreme Court disallowed the "search" of the serial numbers, since they were not in plain view when the police entered the apartment.

Exception 2: Search Incident to a Lawful Arrest

It has long been recognized that a search incident to a lawful arrest to seize the fruits or evidence of crime is permissible. *Weeks v. United States,* 232 U.S. 383, 34 S. Ct. 341, 58 L.Ed. 652 (1914). For many years this rule was interpreted quite broadly. For example, in *United States v. Rabinowitz,* 339 U.S. 56, 70 S. Ct. 430, 94 L.Ed. 653 (1950), the Supreme Court upheld a warrantless search of an entire home incident to a lawful arrest that occurred there. In 1969, the Supreme Court narrowed the permissible scope of searches incident to lawful arrests. *Chimel v. California,* 395 U.S. 752, 89 S. Ct. 2034, 23 L.Ed.2d 685 (1969). Under *Chimel,* police may search the body of an arrestee and the area within that person's immediate control. The area of immediate control is often defined as the area within the "grasp" or "lunge" of the arrestee. To conduct a more extensive search, police must generally obtain a search warrant.

Even if a formal arrest is not made until after a search, the search will be upheld as one incident to arrest if there was probable cause for the arrest before the search was begun. *Bailey v. United States,* 389 F.2d 305 (D.C. Cir. 1967). On the other hand, courts will not uphold a search where it is shown that the arrest was a mere pretext to conduct a warrantless search. See, for example, *United States v. Jones,* 452 F.2d 884 (8th Cir. 1971).

There are definite limitations on police conducting a search incident to arrest. Despite the existence of probable cause, absent extraordinary circumstances, the police have no right to search a dwelling when an arrest occurs outside it. As the Supreme Court observed in *Payton v. New York,* 445 U.S. 573, 591, 100 S.Ct. 1371, 1382, 63 L.Ed.2d 639, 653 (1980): "The Fourth Amendment has drawn a firm line at the entrance to the house. Absent exigent circumstances, that threshold may not reasonably be crossed without a warrant." Exigent circumstances would most likely include a situation where, after an arrest, the officers have a reasonable basis to suspect there may be others on the premises who pose a danger to the police or who may destroy evidence. See *Vale v. Louisiana*, 399 U.S. 30, 90 S.Ct. 1969, 26 L.Ed.2d 409 (1970). Thus, police who made an arrest outside a residence, and had knowledge regarding cocaine trafficking taking place inside, were not barred from entering the house to conduct a "protective sweep" for other persons who might pose a threat to their safety. *United States v. Hoyos*, 892 F. 2d 1387 (9th Cir. 1989). Nevertheless, once a person is arrested and in custody, searching that person's car at another location is not a search incident to arrest. *Preston v. United States*, 376 U.S. 364, 84 S.Ct. 881, 11 L.Ed.2d 777 (1964).

Exception 3: Motor Vehicle Searches

The Supreme Court has long recognized the validity of the warrantless automobile search, assuming that the police officer has probable cause to believe the vehicle contains contraband or evidence of crime, on the premise that the mobile character of a motor vehicle creates a practical necessity for an immediate search. *Carroll v. United States*, 267 U.S. 132, 45 S. Ct. 280, 69 L.Ed. 543 (1925). The Court has held that once begun under exigent circumstances, a warrantless search of an automobile may continue after the vehicle has been taken to the police station. *Chambers v. Maroney*, 399 U.S. 42, 90 S. Ct. 1975, 26 L.Ed.2d 419 (1970).

One of the perennial problems associated with warrantless automobile searches is how closed containers, such as suitcases, found inside automobiles should be treated. In 1982 the Court held that a police officer having probable cause to believe that evidence of crime is concealed within an automobile may conduct a search as broad as one that could be authorized by a magistrate issuing a warrant. *United States v. Ross*, 456 U.S. 798, 102 S. Ct. 2157, 72 L.Ed.2d 572 (1982). This ruling effectively allowed police officers to search closed containers found during the course of an automobile search without first having to obtain a warrant. In *United States v. Johns*, 469 U.S. 478, 105 S. Ct. 881, 83 L.Ed.2d 890 (1985), the Court upheld the warrantless search of plastic containers seized during an automobile search, even though the police had waited several days before opening the containers. The Court reasoned that since the containers were legitimately seized by police during the original search of the automobile, no reasonable expectation of privacy could be maintained once the containers came under police control. The search of the containers, which produced a substantial quantity of marijuana, was therefore not unreasonable simply because it was delayed.

Exception 4: Inventory Searches

The inventory search exception to the warrant requirement involves the search of automobiles. Most law enforcement agencies that impound automobiles for parking violations or abandonment, or pursuant to the arrest of a motorist, routinely conduct an inventory of the contents and remove any valuables for safekeeping. If a routine inventory search yields evidence of crime, it may be seized without violating the Fourth Amendment. *South Dakota v. Opperman*, 428 U.S. 364, 96 S. Ct. 3092, 49 L.Ed.2d 1000 (1976). Among the justifications the

Court found for the warrantless inventory search are protection of the owner's property while the vehicle remains in police custody, protection of the police from claims of lost property, and the need to protect the police from potential dangers that might be lurking inside closed automobiles.

Police cannot use an inventory search as a pretext for a criminal investigation. Nevertheless, once the police have legitimately taken a vehicle into custody they are not required to overlook contraband articles discovered during a valid inventory search, and such items may be used as evidence. In *South Dakota v. Opperman*, the Court stated that the police were engaged in a caretaking search of the vehicle involved because the owner was not present to make arrangements for the vehicle and there was no evidence that the standard inventory procedure used by the police was a pretext for an investigatory search. An inventory search must follow local police procedures and cannot be used merely as a pretext for investigation. *Colorado v. Bertine*, 479 U.S. 367, 107 S.Ct. 738, 93 L.Ed.2d 739 (1987). Lower federal and state courts have emphasized the requirement that the search conducted must be in accordance with established inventory procedures. See, for example, *United States v. Velarde*, 903 F. 2d 1163 (7th Cir. 1990); *State v. Williams*, 516 So. 2d 1081 (Fla. App. 1987).

Exception 5: Consent Searches

Constitutional rights may be waived, and Fourth Amendment rights are no exception. Voluntary cooperation with police officers often results in fruitful searches and seizures. The Supreme Court has refused to require law officers to inform a suspect of his or her right to refuse to consent to a search. *Schneckloth v. Bustamonte*, 412 U.S. 218, 93 S. Ct. 2041, 36 L.Ed.2d 854 (1973). The only requirement is that consent must be truly voluntary. If a person actually assists the police in conducting a search, or if he or she consents after having been advised that consent is not required, courts have little difficulty in finding that consent was voluntary. Yet consent has to involve more than mere acquiescence to the authority of the police. Thus in *Bumper v. North Carolina*, 391 U.S. 543, 88 S. Ct. 1788, 20 L.Ed.2d 797 (1968), the Court held that a claim of police authority based on a nonexistent warrant was so coercive as to invalidate the defendant's consent. Similarly, a Georgia appellate court invalidated an automobile search where the defendant and a companion were surprised by six heavily armed law officers, were searched at gunpoint, and were then asked to consent to a search of their automobile. *Love v. State*, 242 S.E.2d 278 (Ga. App. 1978).

A perennial problem in the area of consent searches is that of third-party consent. The problem is especially acute in situations where several persons share a single dwelling, as is common among college students. For example, may an apartment dweller consent to the search of his roommate's bedroom? The Supreme Court has said that the consent of a third party is valid only when there is

> mutual use of the property by persons generally having joint access or control for most purposes so that it is reasonable to recognize that any of the co-inhabitants has the right to permit the inspection in his own right and that the others have assumed the risk that one of their number might permit the common area to be searched. *United States v. Matlock*, 415 U.S. 164, 171 n.7, 94 S.Ct. 988, 993 n.7, 39 L.Ed.2d 242, 250 n.7 (1974).

Matlock stands for the principle that the validity of third-party consent is tested by the degree of dominion and control exercised by the third party over the searched premises, and that a joint occupant may provide valid consent only if the other party is not present.

In many situations a third-party consent is not valid. Tenancy arrangements are a good example. A landlord does not have the implied authority to consent to the search of the tenant's premises. *Chapman v. United States*, 365 U.S. 610, 81 S.Ct. 776, 5 L.Ed.2d 828 (1961). Likewise, a hotel manager or clerk does not have the right to consent to search of a guest's room during the time the guest has a legal right to occupy the room. *Stoner v. California*, 376 U.S. 483, 84 S.Ct. 889, 11 L.Ed.2d 856 (1964). But what about the college student who lives in a dormitory? In *Commonwealth v. McCloskey*, 272 A. 2d 271 (Pa. Super. 1970), the court held that absent exigent circumstances, police entry into a college dormitory room by means of a pass key possessed by the head resident was improper. Even though the university had reserved the right to check the room for damage and use of unauthorized appliances, the court found that the university did not have authority to consent to a governmental search of the student's room.

As previously mentioned, police who have probable cause to search an automobile can lawfully search any container found inside. *United States v. Ross*, 456 U.S. 798, 102 S.Ct. 2157, 72 L.Ed.2d 572 (1982). But the considerations under *Ross* are inconsistent with a warrantless search based on consent; rather, in consent searches the scope of the search is defined by the terms of the consent. *Ledda v. State*, 564 A. 2d 1125 (Del. 1989).

When police seek to conduct a warrantless search, they need not advise a person that he or she has the right to refuse consent to a search. But such a warning, if given, may be taken into account in determining whether the consent is voluntary. *Schneckloth v. Bustamonte*, 412 U.S. 218, 93 S.Ct. 2041, 36 L.Ed.2d 854 (1973).

Some current problems in the area of third-party consent involve parental consent to searches of premises occupied by their adult children and spousal consent to searches of the other spouse's property, such as an automobile.

Exception 6: Hot Pursuit

Officers in "hot pursuit" of a fleeing suspect may pursue the suspect into a protected place, such as a home, without having to abandon their pursuit until a warrant can be obtained. For example, in *United States v. Santana*, 427 U.S. 38, 96 S. Ct. 2406, 49 L.Ed.2d 300 (1976), the Supreme Court upheld the warrantless seizure of heroin where police pursued a suspect into the house into which she had fled.

Exception 7: Emergency Searches

Police frequently must respond to emergencies involving reports of crime or injuries. In other instances they may accompany firefighters to the scene of a fire. While on premises in response to an emergency, police may seize evidence in plain view during the course of their legitimate emergency activities. *Michigan v. Tyler*, 436 U.S. 499, 98 S. Ct. 1942, 56 L.Ed.2d 486 (1978).

CASE IN POINT

HOT PURSUIT

An interesting hot pursuit situation is described in the Supreme Court's opinion in *Warden v. Hayden,* 387 U.S. 294, 87 S. Ct. 1642, 18 L.Ed.2d 782 (1967):

> About 8 A.M. on March 17, 1962, an armed robber entered the business premises of the Diamond Cab Company in Baltimore, Maryland. He took some $363 and ran. Two cab drivers in the vicinity, attracted by shouts of "Holdup," followed the man to 2111 Cocoa Lane. One driver notified the company dispatcher by radio that the man was a Negro about 5'8" tall, wearing a light cap and a dark jacket, and that he had entered the house on Cocoa Lane. The dispatcher relayed the information to the police who were proceeding to the scene of the robbery. Within minutes, police arrived at the house in a number of patrol cars. An officer knocked and announced their presence. Mrs. Hayden answered, and the officers told her they believed that a robber had entered the house, and asked to search the house. She offered no objection.
>
> The officers spread out through the first and second floors and the cellar in search of the robber. Hayden was found in an upstairs bedroom feigning sleep. He was arrested when the officers on the first floor and in the cellar reported that no other man was in the house. Meanwhile an officer was attracted to an adjoining bathroom by the noise of running water, and discovered a shotgun and a pistol in a flush tank; another officer . . . found in a washing machine a jacket and trousers of the type the fleeing man was said to have worn. A clip of ammunition for the pistol and a cap were found under the mattress of Hayden's bed, and ammunition for the shotgun was found in a bureau drawer in Hayden's room. All these items were introduced . . . at trial.

Based on the exigencies of the arrest and search scenario, the Supreme Court upheld the use of the evidence against Mr. Hayden.

Police do not violate the Fourth Amendment if they stop a vehicle when they have adequate grounds to believe the driver is ill or falling asleep. *State v. Pinkham,* 565 A.2d 318 (Me. 1989). Likewise, the protections against unreasonable search and seizure are not violated by police who make warrantless entries and searches when they reasonably believe that a person within is in need of immediate aid. Once inside, the police may justifiably seize evidence in plain view. See *Mincey v. Arizona,* 437 U.S. 385, 392, 98 S.Ct. 2408, 2413, 57 L.Ed.2d 290, 300 (1978). An officer's belief that an emergency exists must be reasonable, however, former Chief Justice (then judge) Burger in *Wayne v. United States,* 318 F.2d 205, 212 (D.C. Cir. 1963), opined that "the need to protect or preserve life or avoid serious injury is justification for what would be otherwise illegal absent an exigency or emergency." In *United States v. Al-Azzawy,* 784 F. 2d 890 (9th Cir. 1985), the court upheld a warantless search where a suspect was believed to be in possession of explosives and in such an agitated state as to create a risk of endangering the lives of others.

Exception 8: Evanescent Evidence

A frequently invoked justification for a warrantless search and seizure is the preservation of evidence that might otherwise be destroyed. Where there is a reasonable belief that loss or destruction of evidence is imminent, a warrantless entry of premises may be justified, *United States v. Elkins,* 732 F. 2d 1280, 1284 (6th Cir. 1984), but a mere possibility of such is insufficient. *United States v. Hayes,* 518 F. 2d 675, 678 (6th Cir. 1975). The leading case in this area is *Schmerber v. California,* 384 U.S. 757, 86 S. Ct. 1826, 16 L.Ed.2d 908 (1966), where the Supreme Court upheld a warrantless blood-alcohol test of a person who appeared to be intoxicated. The Court characterized the forcible blood test as a "minor intrusion" and noted that the test was performed by qualified medical personnel. However, the most significant fact of the case was that the suspect's blood-alcohol level was rapidly diminishing, and the time required for police to obtain a search warrant could well have changed the results of the test.

Exception 9: Stop-and-Frisk

The "stop-and-frisk" is a routine law enforcement technique whereby police officers stop, question, and sometimes search a suspicious person. In *Terry v. Ohio,* 392 U.S. 1, 88 S. Ct. 1868, 20 L.Ed.2d 889 (1968), the Supreme Court upheld the authority of police officers to detain and conduct a limited "pat-down" search of several men who were acting suspiciously. Given the limited intrusiveness of the pat-down, and the compelling need to protect officers in the field, the Court allowed the warrantless search for weapons on a "reasonable suspicion" standard, instead of imposing the traditional probable cause requirement. Subsequently, the Court stressed the narrow scope of the stop-and-frisk exception by saying that "nothing in *Terry* can be understood to allow . . . any search whatever for anything but weapons." *Ybarra v. Illinois,* 444 U.S. 85, 93–94, 100 S. Ct. 338, 343, 62 L.Ed.2d 238, 247 (1979). (More attention is given to the so-called *Terry*-stop in Chapter 15.)

In *Michigan v. Long,* 463 U.S. 1032, 103 S.Ct. 3469, 77 L.Ed.2d 1201 (1983), the Supreme Court held that seizure of contraband other than weapons during a lawfully conducted *Terry* search was justified under the "plain view" doctrine. Going a step further in *Minnesota v. Dickerson,* 508 U.S. ___ , 113 S.Ct. 2130, 124 L.Ed.2d 334 (1993), the Court said that police may seize nonthreatening contraband detected through their sense of touch during a protective patdown search as long as that search stays within the bounds of a *Terry* search. This extension of *Terry* is sometimes referred to as a "plain feel" exception to the warrant requirement of the Fourth Amendment. Nevertheless, in *Dickerson* the Court found the search and seizure of contraband invalid because the officer conducting the search determined the item he seized was contraband only after searching beyond the scope authorized in *Terry*.

Technology and the Fourth Amendment

The drafters of the Fourth Amendment obviously did not contemplate present-day technology. Yet, in framing the Bill of Rights, they used simple, straightforward language that has endured through the centuries—language capable of being adapted to the needs of the people. Today's technology makes possible silent and invisible intrusions on the privacy of the individual, and the courts are responding to these new, innovative means of surveillance, always cognizant that the touchstone of the Fourth Amendment is its prohibition of "unreasonable" searches and seizures. We present a sampling of some of these technological advances in this section.

Electronic Surveillance

Electronic surveillance refers to eavesdropping through the use of wiretaps, highly sensitive microphones, and other electronic devices. When conducted without consent, such surveillance generally infringes the right of privacy and thus implicates the protections of the Fourth Amendment.

Responding to growing concern over electronic eavesdropping, Congress enacted Title III of the Omnibus Crime Control and Safe Streets Act of 1968, 18 U.S.C.A. § § 2510–20. The act prohibits interception of electronic communications without a court order unless one party to the conversation consents. *Interception* is defined as "aural or other acquisition of the contents of any wire, electronic or oral communication through the use of any electronic, mechanical, or other device." 18 U.S.C.A. § 2510(4). In 1986, *wire communications* was broadened to include conversations through "switching stations." 18 U.S.C.A. § 2510(1). Therefore, it appears that the statute now covers cellular telephones.

The act permits issuance of court orders by federal and state courts upon sworn application authorized by the United States Attorney General or specially designated assistant or a state official at a similar level. The act expressly preempts state law. Therefore, to permit the use of electronic surveillance, a state must adopt legislation along the lines of the federal act. Many states have adopted legislation along these lines. See, for example, the New Jersey Wiretapping and Electronic Surveillance Control Act of 1968, N.J. Stat. Ann. 2A:156A–(1), *et seq.*

An application for what is commonly known as a wiretap order must contain considerable detailed information along with an explanation of why less intrusive means of investigation will not suffice. 18 U.S.C.A. § 2518(1)(c). The statute requires that normal investigative procedures be employed first. But it does not require an officer to exhaust all possible investigative methods before applying for a wiretap order. Before a court may issue a wiretap order, it must find probable cause that the subject of the wiretap has committed or is committing one of a series of enumerated crimes for which wiretapping is authorized and that conventional modes of investigation will not suffice. 18 U.S.C.A. § 2518(3). Originally these offenses included narcotics, organized crime, and national security violations. In 1986 the act was amended to include numerous other serious crimes, including interstate transportation of stolen vehicles, mail fraud, and illegal surveillance. 18 U.S.C.A. § 2516(1)(c).

Court orders permit surveillance for a thirty-day period. Upon expiration of the period, the recordings made of intercepted communications must be delivered to the judge who issued the order. They are then sealed under the judge's direction. 18 U.S.C.A. § 2518(8)(a).

Critics of electronic surveillance by police argue that it is too drastic an invasion of individual privacy to be countenanced under any circumstances. Law enforcement officials insist that it is an essential investigative tool where other less intrusive means prove nonproductive. Despite the controversy, it is clear that electronic surveillance will continue to be employed by law enforcement agencies.

Pen Registers

A "pen register" is a device that traces the origin of incoming telephone calls. It allows the police to learn every number dialed from a specifically targeted telephone. Arguments have been advanced that the use of a pen register by the police without a warrant violates the Fourth Amendment. The Supreme Court has rejected such arguments, saying that using a pen register to obtain numbers dialed from a telephone does not constitute a search and therefore does not require a warrant. *Smith v. Maryland*, 442 U.S. 735, 99 S.Ct. 2577, 61 L.Ed. 2d 220 (1979). Would this principle prevail under a state constitution that proscribes the "unreasonable interception of private communications"?

Cordless Telephones

Cordless telephones use radio waves that can be received by many people, and federal and state courts have held that a warrantless police interception of a cordless telephone conversation does not violate a defendant's reasonable expectation of privacy. *Tyler v. Berodt*, 877 F. 2d 705 (8th Cir. 1989); *State v. Delaurier*, 488 A.2d 688 (R.I. 1985). In *United States v. Knotts*, 460 U.S. 276, 103 S.Ct. 1081, 75 L.Ed. 2d 55 (1983), the Supreme Court reviewed the warrantless use of a beeper to trace an automobile to the defendant's property where a search with a warrant then discovered an illegal drug laboratory. The Court referred to a 1927 decision holding that the use of a searchlight or field glasses is not unreasonable, and found that the Fourth Amendment does not prohibit police from augmenting their sensory faculties. The FBI has even used a miniaturized television camera surveillance, and this has been held not to be unreasonable where it involved securing evidence concerning an alleged terrorist. *United States v. Torres*, 751 F. 2d 875 (7th Cir. 1984).

CONTEMPORARY FOURTH AMENDMENT PROBLEMS

Search and seizure is a highly dynamic, constantly evolving area of the law. Some of the more interesting contemporary Fourth Amendment problems include airport searches, school searches, drug testing and strip searches.

Border Searches

Warrantless searches are routine at the border of the United States. Border searches are justified not so much by the existence of compelling exigencies, but on the theory that persons crossing a national border have no reasonable expectation of privacy and are thus not entitled to the protections of the Fourth Amendment.

United States v. Ramsey, 431 U.S. 606, 97 S. Ct. 1972, 52 L.Ed.2d 617 (1977). The border search exemption extends to searches conducted at established stations near the border or other functional equivalents of a border search. An example would be the search of a ship when it first docks after entering the territorial waters of the United States. *United States v. Prince,* 491 F.2d 655 (5th Cir. 1974).

Agents conducting border searches are limited only by a broad statement of reasonableness under the due process clause of the Fifth Amendment. Accordingly, their methods may not be so severe or extreme as to "shock the conscience." *Rochin v. California,* 342 U.S. 165, 72 S. Ct. 205, 96 L.Ed. 183 (1952).

Under the Immigration and Nationality Act, 8 U.S.C.A. § 1357(a)(3), border patrol agents are authorized to search any vehicle believed to be carrying illegal aliens, either at or within a reasonable distance from the border. The Supreme Court has effectively limited the scope of the act by invalidating a search by a roving patrol some twenty-five miles within the border because agents lacked probable cause. *Almeida-Sanchez v. United States,* 413 U.S. 266, 93 S. Ct. 2535, 37 L.Ed.2d 596 (1973).

Airport Searches

With increased concern over airplane hijacking has come increased security at the nation's airports. Passengers attempting to board aircraft are routinely subjected to x-ray scans. Should these scans show the presence of metallic items, physical searches are conducted to determine what the metal objects are. There is little question that such searches are reasonable, given the weight of the safety interests involved and the reduced privacy expectations associated with airline travel.

More controversial are detentions and searches of suspected drug couriers attempting to board airplanes. The Supreme Court has applied the stop-and-frisk standard in permitting brief investigatory detentions of persons at an airport if there is "reasonable and articulable suspicion that the person . . . is engaged in criminal activity." *Reid v. Georgia,* 448 U.S. 438, 440, 100 S. Ct. 2752, 2753, 65 L.Ed.2d 890, 894 (1980).

C A S E I N P O I N T

Airport Searches

A suspected drug courier was held incommunicado in an airport security room for sixteen hours while officers obtained a court order permitting an x-ray and rectal examination. During the examination a plastic balloon containing cocaine was retrieved. Over the next several days, the defendant passed some eighty-eight cocaine-filled balloons. The Supreme Court upheld the protracted detention and search, despite the lack of probable cause. The Court said that in such circumstances the lesser standard of reasonable suspicion was sufficient.

United States v. Montoya de Hernandez, 473 U.S. 531, 105 S. Ct. 3304, 87 L.Ed.2d 381 (1985).

In attempting to identify and to apprehend drug smugglers, law enforcement agencies have developed "drug courier profiles." These profiles are sets of characteristics that typify drug couriers, such as paying for airline tickets in cash, appearing nervous, carrying certain types of luggage, etc. In *Reid v. Georgia*, 448 U.S. 438, 100 S. Ct. 2752, 65 L.Ed.2d 890 (1980), the Supreme Court suggested that fitting a drug courier profile was not in itself sufficient to constitute the reasonable suspicion necessary to allow police to detain a passenger. Therefore, the stopping of an airline passenger on that basis was violative of the Fourth Amendment.

School Searches

In the First Amendment context, the Supreme Court has said that students in public schools do not "shed their constitutional rights . . . at the schoolhouse gate." *Tinker v. Des Moines Independent Community School District*, 393 U.S. 503, 506, 89 S. Ct. 733, 736, 21 L.Ed.2d 731, 737 (1969). Following this premise, the Court has held that the Fourth Amendment protects children in the public schools from unreasonable searches and seizures. However, the Court has said that such searches are to be judged by a reasonableness standard and are not subject to the requirement of probable cause. Moreover, the Court has said that the warrant requirement is particularly unsuited to the unique circumstances of the school environment. *New Jersey v. T.L.O.*, 469 U.S. 325, 105 S. Ct. 733, 83 L.Ed.2d 720 (1985).

Drug Testing

Illicit use of drugs has become a national concern. Because of the paramount interest in ensuring the public safety, courts have recently upheld the constitutionality of regulations permitting supervisory personnel to order urinalysis testing of public safety officers based on reasonable suspicion of drug abuse. See, for example, *Turner v. Fraternal Order of Police*, 500 A.2d 1005 (D.C. App. 1985). In 1989, the United States Supreme Court upheld federal regulations requiring drug and alcohol testing of railroad employees involved in train accidents. *Skinner v. Railway Labor Executives' Association*, 489 U.S. 602, 109 S.Ct. 1402, 103 L.Ed.2d 639 (1989). The Court also has sustained a Customs Service policy requiring drug tests for persons seeking positions as customs inspectors. *National Treasury Employees Union v. Von Raab*, 489 U.S. 656, 109 S.Ct. 1384, 103 L.Ed.2d 685 (1989). As yet, the Supreme Court has not addressed the issue of general, random drug testing of public employees. But some state courts have, and at least one state appellate court has found such a policy to be unconstitutional. *City of Palm Bay v. Bauman*, 475 So.2d 1322 (Fla. App. 1985). Given the scope of the drug problem, and governmental resolve to do something about it, the issue of random drug testing is certain to be litigated for some time to come.

Strip Searches

As previously noted, the Supreme Court has upheld a warrantless blood-alcohol test of a person who appeared to be intoxicated. This type of test has been characterized as a "minor intrusion" where the methods used were reasonable,

---

CASE IN POINT

DRUG TESTING

A union and a union official brought suit in the United States District Court contending that the drug-testing program adopted by the U.S. Customs Service violated the Fourth Amendment. Under the program, the Customs Service advised the employee by letter that his or her final selection for transfer was contingent upon successful completion of drug screening. Employees tentatively selected for transfer were required to submit urine samples for drug testing. Customs employees who tested positive were subject to dismissal. The federal district court enjoined the program on the ground it was overly intrusive; in 1987, the U.S. Court of Appeals vacated the injunction. On review the Supreme Court said: "The Government's compelling interest in preventing the promotion of drug users to positions where they might endanger the integrity of our Nation's borders or the life of the citizenry outweigh the privacy interests of those who seek promotion to these positions, who enjoy a diminished expectation of privacy by virtue of the special and obvious, physical and ethical demands of those positions."

National Treasury Employees Union v. Von Raab, 489 U.S. 656, 109 S.Ct. 1384, 103 L.Ed.2d 685 (1989).

---

there was probable cause to believe that evidence would be discovered, and exigent circumstance made it impracticable to first obtain a search warrant. The degree of intrusiveness is important in determining the validity of any searches that invade the dignity of the human body.

The Supreme Court in *Bell v. Wolfish*, 441 U.S. 520, 99 S. Ct. 1861, 60 L.Ed.2d 447 (1979), upheld strip searches of prison inmates because of the demands for institutional security. But in *Bell*, the Court held that the Fourth Amendment requires a balancing of the need for the particular search against the invasion of personal rights. Thus courts must consider the justification and scope of the intrusion, and the manner and place in which it is conducted. In reviewing cases involving bodily intrusions, courts have generally disapproved of blanket policies that allow strip searches of arrestees, particularly where traffic violators are concerned. Some courts hold that strip searches are violative of Fourth Amendment rights unless there is probable cause to believe the arrestee is concealing weapons or contraband. See, for example, *Mary Beth G. v. Chicago*, 723 F.2d 1263 (7th Cir. 1983). Other courts have permitted such searches where there is a reasonable suspicion that the arrestee is concealing weapons or contraband. See, for example, *Weber v. Dell*, 804 F.2d 796 (2d Cir. 1986).

Strip searches can also have civil consequences. For example, in *Jones v. Edwards*, 770 F.2d 739 (8th Cir. 1985), Marlin E. Jones was arrested and taken into custody for failing to sign a summons and complaint on an animal leash law violation. He was subjected to a visual strip search of his anal and genital area. The court ruled that such a search, under these circumstances, subjected the police and jail personnel to liability for violation of the arrestee's civil rights. The court emphasized that the police had no reason to suspect that Jones was harboring weapons or contraband on his person.

The Exclusionary Rule

The Supreme Court long ago held that evidence obtained through an unlawful search and seizure could not be used to convict a person of a federal crime. *Weeks v. United States,* 232 U.S. 383, 34 S. Ct. 341, 58 L.Ed. 652 (1914). In 1961 this rule was extended to state criminal trials on the basis of the limitations on state action contained in the Fourteenth Amendment. *Mapp v. Ohio,* 367 U.S. 643, 81 S. Ct. 1684, 6 L.Ed.2d 1081 (1961). Previously, in *Wolf v. Colorado,* 338 U.S. 25, 69 S. Ct. 1359, 93 L.Ed. 1782 (1949), the Supreme Court had refused to require states to follow the exclusionary rule, saying that it was not an essential element of Fourth Amendment protection. In *Mapp,* the Court held that there was no other effective means of enforcing the protections of the Fourth Amendment. The Court reasoned that if the Fourth Amendment was applicable to the states under the Fourteenth Amendment, then the exclusionary rule was also, since it was the only effective means of enforcing the Fourth Amendment against overzealous police officers.

In *Wong Sun v. United States,* 371 U.S. 471, 83 S.Ct. 407, 9 L.Ed. 2d 441 (1963), the Supreme Court extended the exclusionary rule to evidence that is the "fruit" of unlawful police conduct. This developed the doctrine of "fruit of the poisonous tree" as a basis for suppressing evidence derived from illegal searches and seizures. The Fourth Amendment, however, does not require evidence to be excluded even if it was initially discovered during an illegal search of private property if that evidence is later discovered during a valid search that is wholly independent of the initial illegal activity. *Murray v. United States,* 487 U.S. 533, 108 S.Ct. 2529, 101 L.Ed.2d 472 (1988). The general rule is that where there has been an illegal seizure of property, such property cannot be introduced into evidence and no testimony may be given in respect to any facts surrounding the seizure.

As crime rates rose dramatically during the 1960s and 1970s, the exclusionary rule came under attack from critics who argued that it exacted too high a price for deterring police from violating the Fourth Amendment. During the 1970s and 1980s, the Supreme Court curtailed the scope of the exclusionary rule in a series of controversial decisions. In *United States v. Calandra,* 414 U.S. 338, 94 S. Ct. 613, 38 L.Ed.2d 561 (1974), the Court held that illegally obtained evidence could be used to obtain grand jury indictments. In *Michigan v. DeFillippo,* 443 U.S. 31, 99 S. Ct. 2627, 61 L.Ed.2d 343 (1979), the Court allowed the use of evidence obtained through a search incident to arrest pursuant to a law that was later ruled unconstitutional.

The Good-Faith Exception to the Exclusionary Rule

In the most significant exclusionary rule cases decided in the 1980s, the Supreme Court held that evidence obtained on the basis of a search warrant that is later held invalid may be admitted in evidence at trial if the police officer who conducted the search relied on the warrant in "good faith." *United States v. Leon,* 468 U.S. 897, 104 S. Ct. 3405, 82 L.Ed.2d 677 (1984); *Massachusetts v. Sheppard,* 468

U.S. 981, 104 S. Ct. 3424, 82 L.Ed.2d 737 (1984). It must be noted that, as of 1989, the good-faith exception to the exclusionary rule applies only in cases where police officers rely on warrants that are later held to be invalid; it does not apply to warrantless searches.

There are four situations in which the good-faith exception to the exclusionary rule does not apply: First, if the magistrate was misled by an affidavit that the affiant knew was false or would have known was false except for reckless disregard for the truth. Second, if the magistrate wholly abandons his or her judicial role. Third, if the affidavit is so lacking in indicia of probable cause as to render belief in its existence unreasonable. Fourth, if the warrant is so facially deficient that the executing officer cannot reasonably presume its validity. *United States v. Leon, supra.*

As previously noted, the Fourth Amendment sets a minimal national standard; state courts are free to provide greater levels of protection under the search and seizure of state constitutions. This latter approach was followed by the New Jersey Supreme Court in *State v. Novembrino,* 519 A.2d 820 (N.J. 1987), where it refused to follow the good-faith exception to the exclusionary rule as a matter of state law. The court observed that the exclusionary rule was firmly embedded in its own jurisprudence and that a good-faith exception would "ultimately reduce respect for and compliance with the probable cause standard." 519 A.2d 854.

Standing to Invoke the Exclusionary Rule

A person who seeks the benefits of the exclusionary rule must have "standing" to invoke the rule. The concept of standing limits the class of defendants who

---

C A S E   I N   P O I N T

The "Good-Faith Exception" Under State Constitutional Law

Acting on the basis of an informant's tip, police obtained a warrant to search a building owned by the defendant. Inside the building they discovered seventeen growing marijuana plants, as well as cultivating equipment. After a suppression hearing, the trial judge determined that the warrant upon which the search was based was defective in that it had not been adequately supported by probable cause. Nevertheless, the judge refused to suppress the evidence, citing the "good-faith exception" to the exclusionary rule created by the U.S. Supreme Court's decision in *United States v. Leon.* On appeal, the Pennsylvania Supreme Court interpreted its state constitution as affording more protection to a defendant against unreasonable searches and seizures than the federal constitution as interpreted in *Leon.* Thus, the court concluded that the Pennsylvania Constitution does not permit a *Leon*-style good-faith exception to the exclusionary rule.

Commonwealth v. Edmunds, 586 A.2d 887 (Pa. 1991).

may challenge an allegedly illegal search and seizure. In *Jones v. United States*, 362 U.S. 257, 80 S. Ct. 725, 4 L.Ed.2d 697 (1960), the Supreme Court granted automatic standing to anyone who was legitimately on the premises searched. However, in *Rakas v. Illinois*, 439 U.S. 128, 99 S. Ct. 421, 58 L.Ed.2d 387 (1978), the Court restricted the *Jones* doctrine by refusing to allow passengers of an automobile to challenge the search of the vehicle in which they were riding.

In *United States v. Salvucci*, 448 U.S. 83, 100 S. Ct. 2547, 65 L.Ed.2d 619 (1980), the Court took the final step in overruling the automatic-standing rule of *Jones v. United States*. Salvucci was charged with possession of stolen mail. The evidence was recovered by police in a search of an apartment that belonged to the mother of Salvucci's accomplice. The federal district court granted Salvucci's motion to suppress the evidence, relying on the automatic-standing doctrine. The Supreme Court reversed, holding that Salvucci was not automatically entitled to challenge the search of another person's apartment. Explaining the Court's more conservative stance on the issue of standing, Justice Rehnquist said:

> We are convinced that the automatic standing rule . . . has outlived its usefulness in this Court's Fourth Amendment jurisprudence. The doctrine now serves only to afford a windfall to defendants whose Fourth Amendment rights have *not* been violated. 448 U.S. at 95, 100 S. Ct. at 2554, 65 L.Ed.2d at 630.

The Court's current approach is to grant standing only to those persons who have a possessory or legitimate privacy interest in the place that was searched. Thus, a casual visitor to an apartment has no legitimate expectation of privacy in an apartment hallway that would grant standing to contest a search of those premises. *United States v. Burnett*, 890 F. 2d 1233 (D.C. Cir. 1989). To successfully invoke the exclusionary rule now, a defendant must show that his or her legitimate expectation of privacy was violated.

Of course, states may still grant automatic standing to challenge seized evidence because "it is an established principle of our federalist system that state constitutions may be a source of 'individual liberties more expansive than those conferred by the Federal Constitution.' " *PruneYard Shopping Center v. Robins*, 447 U.S. 74, 81, 100 S.Ct. 2035, 2040, 64 L.Ed.2d 741, 752 (1980). In *Commonwealth v. Amendola*, 550 N.E. 2d 121 (Mass. 1990), the court rejected the Supreme Court's abandonment of the automatic-standing rule and held:

> When a defendant is charged with a crime in which possession of the seized evidence at the time of the contested search is an essential element of guilt, the defendant shall be deemed to have standing to contest the legality of the search and the seizure of that evidence.

The court observed that courts in Louisiana, Michigan, New Hampshire, New Jersey, Pennsylvania, and Vermont have reached similar conclusions.

CONCLUSION

The constitutional protection against unreasonable searches and seizures is a fundamental right; yet the constitutional law governing search and seizure is extremely complex. Moreover, it is highly dynamic, as courts decide countless cases in this area each year. In a nutshell, the Fourth Amendment protects persons from unreasonable intrusions where they have a reasonable expectation of privacy. To guard against unreasonable intrusions of privacy, police are normally required to obtain a warrant before engaging in a search and seizure. Courts rigorously enforce the Fourth Amendment requirement that search warrants be issued only "upon probable cause, supported by Oath or affirmation," and are specific as to "the place to be searched and the persons or things to be seized," U.S. Const., Amend. 4.

In addition to searches based on consent or conducted incident to a lawful arrest, there are a number of exceptions to the warrant requirement based on the doctrine of exigent circumstances. Hot pursuit, evanescent evidence, and certain emergencies qualify as exigent circumstances allowing warrantless searches.

Normally, police must have probable cause before conducting a search. Here too, there are exceptions—the so-called stop-and-frisk situation, the airport search, and the school search—where police may conduct searches on the basis of a less stringent standard of reasonableness.

One of the most controversial Fourth Amendment issues is how unreasonable searches and seizures are to be remedied. The Supreme Court has fashioned a rule excluding illegally obtained evidence from criminal trials. Here again, there are exceptions to the rule, such as the limited good-faith exception announced in the *Leon* case.

While technological advances have afforded law enforcement new means to ferret out crime, the use of helicopters and such modern devices as infrared sensors, detectaphone microphones, and miniature radio transmitters challenge the traditional right of privacy enjoyed by citizens in a free country.

The Fourth Amendment has applicability beyond the seizure of evidence. Since the arrest of a suspect is considered a "seizure," the Fourth Amendment applies to arrests and various lesser police-citizen encounters, as well as to the use of force by police in making arrests. We examine these issues, along with police interrogation, in the next chapter.

QUESTIONS FOR THOUGHT AND DISCUSSION

1. Today a substantial proportion of security personnel are "private police"; yet, Fourth Amendment protection has been extended only to those searches conducted by government officials. What arguments can be made for and against expanding the prohibitions of the Fourth Amendment to include security personnel?

2. Courts generally hold that it is not an invasion of a person's reasonable expectation of privacy for police to conduct surveillance with binoculars and use their observations as a basis to establish probable cause to obtain a search warrant. What position should the courts take on police intrusion of privacy through miniaturized fiber-optic television surveillance?

3. Does a person using a public restroom in a government office building have a reasonable expectation of privacy?

4. Acting without a search warrant, police arrive at a home after receiving an anonymous tip that a man has been making illegal explosives in his workshop. The officers find that the man is not at home. Can the man's wife consent to a warrantless search of her husband's workshop, or must police wait until the husband returns to obtain his consent?

5. Police observed an automobile travelling at a high rate of speed and swerving on the road. They gave pursuit and stopped the vehicle after a five-minute chase. The driver, later identified as Jerome Johnson, emerged from the car and began to verbally abuse and threaten the officers. Johnson appeared intoxicated, but refused to take any of the standard field sobriety tests. Under state law, a driver must perform a sobriety test or lose his or her driver's license for a period of one year. The law does not authorize police to force suspects to perform any sobriety tests against their will. Johnson was arrested and transported to a local hospital, where he was forcibly restrained and asked to submit to a blood-alcohol test. Johnson refused, saying "I'd rather lose my license than let you stick me with that needle." The test was administered over Johnson's objection, and the results indicated that Johnson's blood-alcohol level was substantially above the legal limit. Johnson was charged with driving under the influence of alcohol. Prior to trial, Johnson's attorney moved to suppress the results of the blood-alcohol test, arguing that it was taken without Johnson's consent, without probable cause, and in violation of the state's implied consent law. If you were the judge in this case, how would you be inclined to rule on the admissability of this evidence? What additional information would you need to render your decision?

6. In *New Jersey v. T.L.O.*, 469 U.S. 325, 105 S. Ct. 733, 83 L.Ed.2d 720 (1985), the Supreme Court adopted a reasonableness standard for school searches. Should this standard be applied to searches of students in public colleges and universities? What about private colleges? Does it make a difference if the search is conducted in a public setting or in the student's dormitory room?

7. What is the rationale for excluding from trial evidence obtained in violation of the Fourth Amendment? Is this a compelling justification for the exclusion of criminal evidence from the trial of a defendant accused of a serious felony such as aggravated battery?

8. What alternatives to the exclusionary rule might be adopted to enforce the protections of the Fourth Amendment? How effective are such alternatives likely to be?

9. The Supreme Court has created a "good-faith" exception to the exclusionary rule where police rely on a search warrant that is later held to be invalid because the magistrate erred in assuming probable cause for a search. Should the good-faith exception be extended to cases where police acting "in good faith" conduct warrantless searches that are later held to be unlawful?

```
┌──────────────────────────────────────────────────────────┐
│                         C A S E S                          │
└──────────────────────────────────────────────────────────┘
```

KATZ v. UNITED STATES

Supreme Court of the United States, 1967.
389 U.S. 347, 88 S. Ct. 507, 19 L.Ed.2d 576.

[In this seminal case, the Supreme Court addresses the scope of protection afforded by the Fourth Amendment.]

Mr. Justice STEWART delivered the opinion of the Court.

The petitioner was convicted in the District Court for the Southern District of California under an eight-count indictment charging him with transmitting wagering information by telephone from Los Angeles to Miami and Boston in violation of a federal statute. At trial the Government was permitted, over the petitioner's objection, to introduce evidence of the petitioner's end of telephone conversations, overheard by FBI agents who had attached an electronic listening and recording device to the outside of the public telephone booth from which he had placed his calls. In affirming his conviction, the Court of Appeals rejected the contention that the recordings had been obtained in violation of the Fourth Amendment, because "[t]here was no physical entrance into the area occupied by [the petitioner]." We granted certiorari in order to consider the constitutional questions thus presented. . . .

The question . . . is whether the search and seizure conducted in this case complied with constitutional standards. In that regard, the Government's position is that its agents acted in an entirely defensible manner: They did not begin their electronic surveillance until investigation of the petitioner's activities had established a strong probability that he was using the telephone in question to transmit gambling information to persons in other States, in violation of federal law. Moreover, the surveillance was limited, both in scope and in duration, to the specific purpose of establishing the contents of the petitioner's unlawful telephonic communications. The agents confined their surveillance to the brief periods during which he used the telephone booth, and they took great care to overhear only the conversations of the petitioner himself.

Accepting this account of the Government's actions as accurate, it is clear that this surveillance was so narrowly circumscribed that a duly authorized magistrate, properly notified of the need for such investigation, specifically informed of the basis on which it was to proceed, and clearly apprised of the precise intrusion it would entail, could constitutionally have authorized, with appropriate safeguards, the very limited search and seizure that the Government asserts in fact took place.

The Government urges that, because its agents . . . did no more here than they might properly have done with prior judicial sanction, we should retroactively validate their conduct. That we cannot do. It is apparent that the agents in this case acted with restraint. Yet the inescapable fact is that this restraint was imposed by the agents themselves, not by a judicial officer. They were not required, before commencing the search, to present their estimate of probable cause for detached scrutiny by a neutral magistrate. They were not compelled, during the conduct of the search itself, to observe precise limits established in advance by a specific court order. Nor were they directed, after the search had been completed, to notify the authorizing magistrate in detail of all that had been seized. In the absence of such safeguards, this Court has never sustained a search upon the sole ground that officers reasonably expected to find evidence of a particular crime and voluntarily confined their activities to the least intrusive means consistent with that end. Searches conducted without warrants have been held unlawful "notwithstanding facts unquestionably showing probable cause," for the Constitution requires "that the deliberate, impartial judgment of a judicial officer . . . be interposed between the citizen and the police. . . ." "Over and again this Court has emphasized that the mandate of the [Fourth] Amendment requires adherence to judicial processes," and that searches conducted outside the judicial process, without prior approval by judge or magistrate, are per se unreasonable under the Fourth Amendment—

subject only to a few specifically established and well-delineated exceptions.

It is difficult to imagine how any of those exceptions could ever apply to the sort of search and seizure involved in this case. Even electronic surveillance substantially contemporaneous with an individual's arrest could hardly be deemed an "incident" of that arrest. Nor could the use of electronic surveillance without prior authorization be justified on grounds of "hot pursuit." And, of course, the very nature of electronic surveillance precludes its use pursuant to the suspect's consent.

The Government does not question these basic principles. Rather, it urges the creation of a new exception to cover this case. It argues that surveillance of a telephone booth should be exempted from the usual requirement of advance authorization by a magistrate upon a showing of probable cause. We cannot agree. Omission of such authorization

> bypasses the safeguards provided by an objective predetermination of probable cause, and substitutes instead the far less reliable procedure of an after-the-event justification for the . . . search, too likely to be subtly influenced by the familiar shortcomings of hindsight judgment. . . .

And bypassing a neutral predetermination of the scope of a search leaves individuals secure from Fourth Amendment violations "only in the discretion of the police." . . .

These considerations do not vanish when the search in question is transferred from the setting of a home, an office, or a hotel room to that of a telephone booth. Wherever a man may be, he is entitled to know that he will remain free from unreasonable searches and seizures. The government agents here ignored "the procedure of antecedent justification . . . that is central to the Fourth Amendment," . . . a procedure that we hold to be a constitutional precondition of the kind of electronic surveillance involved in this case. Because the surveillance here failed to meet that condition, and because it led to the petitioner's conviction, the judgment must be reversed.

Mr. Justice MARSHALL took no part in the consideration or decision of this case.

Mr. Justice DOUGLAS, with whom Mr. Justice BRENNAN joins, concurring. . . .

Mr. Justice HARLAN, concurring.

I join the opinion of the Court, which I read to hold only (a) that an enclosed telephone booth is an area where, like a home, a person has a constitutionally protected reasonable expectation of privacy; (b) that electronic as well as physical intrusion into a place that is in this sense private may constitute a violation of the Fourth Amendment; and (c) that the invasion of a constitutionally protected area by federal authorities is, as the Court has long held, presumptively unreasonable in the absence of a search warrant.

As the Court's opinion states, "the Fourth Amendment protects people, not places." The question, however, is what protection it affords to those people. Generally, as here, the answer to that question requires reference to a "place." My understanding of the rule that has emerged from prior decisions is that there is a twofold requirement, first that a person have exhibited an actual (subjective) expectation of privacy and, second, that the expectation be one that society is prepared to recognize as "reasonable." Thus a man's home is, for most purposes, a place where he expects privacy, but objects, activities, or statements that he exposes to the "plain view" of outsiders are not "protected" because no intention to keep them to himself has been exhibited. On the other hand, conversations in the open would not be protected against being overheard, for the expectation of privacy under the circumstances would be unreasonable.

The critical fact in this case is that "[o]ne who occupies it, [a telephone booth] shuts the door behind him, and pays the toll that permits him to place a call is surely entitled to assume" that his conversation is not being intercepted. The point is not that the booth is "accessible to the public" at other times, but that it is a temporarily private place whose momentary occupants' expectations of freedom from intrusion are recognized as reasonable. . . .

Mr. Justice WHITE, concurring. . . .

Mr. Justice BLACK, dissenting. . . .

ILLINOIS V. GATES
Supreme Court of the United States, 1983.
462 U.S. 213, 103 S. Ct. 2317, 76 L.Ed.2d 527.

[In this case the Supreme Court considers the appropriate standard magistrates should apply in deciding whether there is probable cause to justify the issuance of a search warrant.]

Justice REHNQUIST delivered the opinion of the Court.

Respondents Lance and Susan Gates were indicted for violation of state drug laws after police officers, executing a search warrant, discovered marihuana and other contraband in their automobile and home. Prior to trial the Gates' moved to suppress evidence seized during this search. The Illinois Supreme Court affirmed the decisions of lower state courts granting the motion. It held that the affidavit submitted in support of the State's application for a warrant to search the Gates' property was inadequate under this Court's decisions in *Aguilar v. Texas* ... (1964) and *Spinelli v. United States* ... (1969)....

We now turn to the question presented in the State's original petition for certiorari, which requires us to decide whether respondents' rights under the Fourth and Fourteenth Amendments were violated by the search of their car and house. A chronological statement of events usefully introduces the issues at stake. Bloomingdale, Ill., is a suburb of Chicago located in DuPage County. On May 3, 1978, the Bloomingdale Police Department received by mail an anonymous handwritten letter which read as follows:

This letter is to inform you that you have a couple in your town who strictly make their living on selling drugs. They are Sue and Lance Gates, they live on Greenway, off Bloomingdale Rd. in the condominiums. Most of their buys are done in Florida. Sue, his wife drives their car to Florida, where she leaves it to be loaded up with drugs, then Lance flys down and drives it back. Sue flys back after she drops the car off in Florida. May 3 she is driving down there again and Lance will be flying down in a few days to drive it back. At the time Lance drives the car back he has the trunk loaded with over $100,000.00 in drugs. Presently, they have over $100,000.00 worth of drugs in

their basement. They brag about the fact they never have to work, and make their entire living on pushers.

I guarantee if you watch them carefully you will make a big catch. They are friends with some big drug dealers, who visit their house often....

The letter was referred by the Chief of Police of the Bloomingdale Police Department to Detective Mader, who decided to pursue the tip. Mader learned from the office of the Illinois Secretary of State, that an Illinois driver's license had been issued to one Lance Gates, residing at a stated address in Bloomingdale. He contacted a confidential informant, whose examination of certain financial records revealed a more recent address for the Gateses, and he also learned from a police officer assigned to O'Hare Airport that "L. Gates" had made a reservation on Eastern Airlines flight 245 to West Palm Beach, Fla., scheduled to depart from Chicago on May 5 at 4:15 P.M.

Mader then made arrangements with an agent of the Drug Enforcement Administration for surveillance of the May 5 Eastern Airlines flight. The agent later reported to Mader that Gates had boarded the flight, and that federal agents in Florida had observed him arrive in West Palm Beach and take a taxi to the nearby Holiday Inn. They also reported that Gates went to a room registered to one Susan Gates and that, at 7:00 A.M. the next morning, Gates and an unidentified woman left the motel in a Mercury bearing Illinois license plates and drove northbound on an interstate frequently used by travelers to the Chicago area. In addition, the DEA agent informed Mader that the license plate number on the Mercury was registered to a Hornet station wagon owned by Gates.

Mader signed an affidavit setting forth the foregoing facts, and submitted it to a judge of the Circuit Court of DuPage County, together with a copy of the anonymous letter. The judge of that court thereupon issued a search warrant for the Gates' residence and for their automobile. The judge, in deciding to issue the warrant, could have determined that the modus operandi of the Gateses had been substantially corroborated.

At 5:15 A.M. on March 7th, only 36 hours after he had flown out of Chicago, Lance Gates, and his wife, returned to their home in Bloomingdale, driving the car in which they had left West Palm Beach some 22 hours earlier. The Bloomingdale police were awaiting them, searched the trunk of the Mercury, and uncovered approximately 350 pounds of marijuana. A search of the Gateses' home revealed marijuana, weapons, and other contraband. The Illinois Circuit Court ordered suppression of all these items, on the ground that the affidavit submitted to the Circuit Judge failed to support the necessary determination of probable cause to believe that the Gateses' automobile and home contained the contraband in question. This decision was affirmed in turn by the Illinois Appellate Court and by a divided vote of the Supreme Court of Illinois. . . .

The Illinois Supreme Court concluded—and we are inclined to agree—that, standing alone, the anonymous letter sent to the Bloomingdale Police Department would not provide the basis for a magistrate's determination that there was probable cause to believe contraband would be found in the Gateses' car and home. The letter provides virtually nothing from which one might conclude that its author is either honest or his information reliable; likewise, the letter gives absolutely no indication of the basis for the writer's predictions regarding the Gateses' criminal activities. Something more was required, then, before a magistrate could conclude that there was probable cause to believe that contraband would be found in the Gateses' home and car. . . .

The Illinois Supreme Court also properly recognized that Detective Mader's affidavit might be capable of supplementing the anonymous letter with information sufficient to permit a determination of probable cause. . . . In holding that the affidavit in fact did not contain sufficient additional information to sustain a determination of probable cause, the Illinois court applied a "two-pronged test," derived from our decision in *Spinelli v. United States.* . . . The Illinois Supreme Court, like some others, apparently understood *Spinelli* as requiring that the anonymous letter satisfy each of two independent requirements before it could be relied on. According to this view, the letter, as supplemented by Mader's affidavit, first had to adequately reveal the "basis of knowledge" of the letter writer—the

particular means by which he came by the information given in his report. Second, it had to provide facts sufficiently establishing either the "veracity" of the affiant's informant, or, alternatively, the "reliability" of the informant's report in this particular case.

The Illinois court, alluding to an elaborate set of legal rules that have developed among various lower courts to enforce the "two-pronged test," found that the test had not been satisfied. First, the "veracity" prong was not satisfied because, "there was simply no basis [for] . . . conclud[ing] that the anonymous person [who wrote the letter to the Bloomingdale Police Department] was credible." The court indicated that corroboration by police of details contained in the letter might never satisfy the "veracity" prong, and in any event, could not do so if, as in the present case, only "innocent" details are corroborated. . . . In addition, the letter gave no indication of the basis of the writer's knowledge of the Gates' activities. The Illinois court understood *Spinelli* as permitting the detail contained in a tip to be used to infer that the informant had a reliable basis for his statements, but it thought that the anonymous letter failed to provide sufficient detail to permit such an inference. Thus, it concluded that no showing of probable cause had been made.

We agree with the Illinois Supreme Court that an informant's "veracity," "reliability" and "basis of knowledge" are all highly relevant in determining the value of his report. We do not agree, however, that these elements should be understood as entirely separate and independent requirements to be rigidly exacted in every case, which the opinion of the Supreme Court of Illinois would imply. Rather, as detailed below, they should be understood simply as closely intertwined issues that may usefully illuminate the commonsense, practical question whether there is "probable cause" to believe that contraband or evidence is located in a particular place.

This totality of the circumstances approach is far more consistent with our prior treatment of probable cause than is any rigid demand that specific "tests" be satisfied by every informant's tip. Perhaps the central teaching of our decisions bearing on the probable cause standard is that it is a "practical, nontechnical conception." . . . "In dealing with probable cause, . . . as the very name implies, we deal with probabilities. These are not technical, they are the factual and practical considerations of everyday life on which reasonable and prudent men, not legal technicians, act." . . .

. . . [P]robable cause is a fluid concept—turning on the assessment of probabilities in particular factual contexts—not readily, or even usefully, reduced to a neat set of legal rules. Informants' tips doubtless come in many shapes and sizes from many different types of persons. "Informants' tips, like all other clues and evidence coming to a policeman on the scene, may vary greatly in their value and reliability." Rigid legal rules are ill-suited to an area of such diversity. "One simple rule will not cover every situation." . . .

Moreover, the "two-pronged test" directs analysis into two largely independent channels—the informant's "veracity" or "reliability" and his "basis of knowledge." There are persuasive arguments against according these two elements such independent status. Instead, they are better understood as relevant considerations in the totality of circumstances analysis that traditionally has guided probable cause determinations: a deficiency in one may be compensated for, in determining the overall reliability of a tip, by a strong showing as to the other, or by some other indicia of reliability. . . .

If, for example, a particular informant is known for the unusual reliability of his predictions of certain types of criminal activities in a locality, his failure in a particular case, to thoroughly set forth the basis of his knowledge surely should not serve as an absolute bar to a finding of probable cause based on his tip. . . . Likewise, if an unquestionably honest citizen comes forward with a report of criminal activity—which if fabricated would subject him to criminal liability—we have found rigorous scrutiny of the basis of his knowledge unnecessary. Conversely, even if we entertain some doubt as to an informant's motives, his explicit and detailed description of alleged wrong-doing, along with a statement that the event was observed first-hand, entitles his tip to greater weight than might otherwise be the case. Unlike a totality of circumstances analysis, which permits a balanced assessment of the relative weights of all the various indicia of reliability (and unreliability) attending an informant's tip, the "two-pronged test" has encouraged an excessively technical dissection of informants' tips, with undue attention being focused on isolated issues that cannot sensibly be divorced from the other facts presented to the magistrate. . . .

We also have recognized that affidavits "are normally drafted by nonlawyers in the midst and haste of a criminal investigation. Technical requirements of elaborate specificity once exacted under common law pleading have no proper place in this area." . . . Likewise, search and arrest warrants long have been issued by persons who are neither lawyers nor judges, and who certainly do not remain abreast of each judicial refinement of the nature of "probable cause." . . . The rigorous inquiry into the *Spinelli* prongs and the complex superstructure of evidentiary and analytical rules that some have seen implicit in our *Spinelli* decision, cannot be reconciled with the fact that many warrants are—quite properly, . . . issued on the basis of nontechnical common-sense judgments of laymen applying a standard less demanding than those used in more formal legal proceedings. . . .

Similarly, we have repeatedly said that after-the-fact scrutiny by courts of the sufficiency of an affidavit should not take the form of de novo review. A magistrate's determination of probable cause should be paid great deference by reviewing courts. . . .

If the affidavits submitted by police officers are subjected to the type of scrutiny some courts have deemed appropriate, police might well resort to warrantless searches, with the hope of relying on consent or some other exception to the warrant clause that might develop at the time of the search. In addition, the possession of a warrant by officers conducting an arrest or search greatly reduces the perception of unlawful or intrusive police conduct, by assuring "the individual whose property is searched or seized of the lawful authority of the executing office, his need to search, and the limits of his power to search.". . . . Reflecting this preference for the warrant process, the traditional standard for review of an issuing magistrate's probable cause determination has been that so long as the magistrate had a "substantial basis for . . . conclud[ing]" that a search would uncover evidence of wrongdoing, the Fourth Amendment requires no more. . . . We think reaffirmation of this standard better serves the purpose of encouraging recourse to the warrant procedure and is more consistent with our traditional deference to the probable cause determinations of magistrates than is the "two-pronged test."

Finally, the direction taken by decisions following *Spinelli* poorly serves "the most basic function of any government": "to provide for the security of the individual and of his property." . . . The structures that inevitably accompany the "two-pronged test" cannot avoid seriously impeding the task of law enforcement. . . . Ordinary citizens, like ordinary witnesses, generally do not provide extensive recitations of the basis of their everyday observations. Likewise, as the Illinois Supreme Court observed in this case, the veracity of persons supplying anonymous tips is by hypothesis largely unknown and unknowable. As a result, anonymous tips seldom could survive a rigorous application of either of the *Spinelli* prongs. Yet, such tips, particularly when supplemented by independent police investigation, frequently contribute to the solution of otherwise "perfect crimes." While a conscientious assessment of the basis for crediting such tips is required by the Fourth Amendment, a standard that leaves virtually no place for anonymous citizen informants is not.

For all these reasons, we conclude that it is wiser to abandon the "two-pronged test" established by our decisions in *Aguilar* and *Spinelli*. In its place we reaffirm the totality of the circumstances analysis that traditionally has informed probable cause determinations. . . . We are convinced that this flexible, easily applied standard will better achieve the accommodation of public and private interests that the Fourth Amendment requires than does the approach that has developed from *Aguilar* and *Spinelli*. . . .

Justice WHITE, concurring in the judgment. . . .

Justice BRENNAN, with whom Justice MARSHALL joins, dissenting.

. . . In recognition of the judiciary's role as the only effective guardian of Fourth Amendment rights, this Court has developed over the last half century a set of coherent rules governing a magistrate's consideration of a warrant application and the showings that are necessary to support a finding of probable cause. We start with the proposition that a neutral and detached magistrate, and not the police, should determine whether there is probable cause to support the issuance of a warrant. . . .

In order to emphasize the magistrate's role as an independent arbiter of probable cause and to insure that searches and seizures are not effected on less than probable cause, the Court has insisted that police officers provide magistrates with the underlying facts and circumstances that support the officer's conclusions. . . .

To suggest that anonymous informant's tips are subject to the tests established by *Aguilar* and *Spinelli* is not to suggest that they can never provide a basis for a finding of probable cause. It is conceivable that police corroboration of the details of the tip might establish the reliability of the informant under *Aguilar*'s veracity prong, as refined in *Spinelli,* and that the details in the tip might be sufficient to qualify under the "self-verifying detail" test established by *Spinelli* as a means of satisfying *Aguilar*'s basis of knowledge prong. The *Aguilar* and *Spinelli* tests must be applied to anonymous informants' tips, however, if we are to continue to insure that findings of probable cause, and attendant intrusions, are based on information provided by an honest or credible person who has acquired the information in a reliable way. . . .

In light of the important purposes served by *Aguilar* and *Spinelli,* I would not reject the standards they establish. If anything, I simply would make more clear that *Spinelli,* properly understood, does not depart in any fundamental way from the test established by *Aguilar*. For reasons I shall next state, I do not find persuasive the Court's justifications for rejecting the test established by *Aguilar* and refined by *Spinelli*. . . .

Justice STEVENS, with whom Justice BRENNAN joins, dissenting. . . .

HARRIS v. UNITED STATES

Supreme Court of the United States, 1968.
390 U.S. 234, 88 S. Ct. 992, 19 L.Ed.2d 1067.

[This case deals with the admissibility of evidence obtained by police during an inventory search of an impounded vehicle.]

PER CURIAM.

Petitioner was charged with robbery under the District of Columbia Code. . . . At his trial in the United States District Court for the District of Columbia, petitioner moved to suppress an automobile registration card belonging to the robbery victim, which the Government sought to introduce in evidence. Petitioner was convicted of the crime charged and sentenced to imprisonment for a period of two to seven years. On appeal, a panel of the United States Court of Appeals for the District of Columbia Circuit reversed, holding that the card had been obtained by means of an unlawful search. The Government's petition for rehearing *en banc* was, however, granted, and the full Court of Appeals affirmed petitioner's conviction with two judges dissenting. We granted certiorari to consider the problem presented under the Fourth Amendment. . . .

Petitioner's automobile had been seen leaving the site of the robbery. The car was traced and petitioner was arrested as he was entering it, near his home. After a cursory search of the car, the arresting officer took petitioner to a police station. The police decided to impound the car as evidence, and a crane was called to tow it to the precinct. It reached the precinct about an hour and a quarter after petitioner. At this moment, the windows of the car were open and the door unlocked. It had begun to rain.

A regulation of the Metropolitan Police Department requires the officer who takes an impounded vehicle in charge to search the vehicle thoroughly, to remove all valuables from it, and to attach to the vehicle a property tag listing certain information about the circumstances of the impounding. Pursuant to this regulation, and without a warrant, the arresting officer proceeded to the lot to which petitioner's car had been towed, in order to search the

vehicle, to place a property tag on it, to roll up the windows, and to lock the doors. The officer entered on the driver's side, searched the car, and tied a property tag on the steering wheel. Stepping out of the car, he rolled up an open window on one of the back doors. Proceeding to the front door on the passenger side, the officer opened the door in order to secure the window and he then saw the registration card, which lay face up on the metal stripping over which the door closes. The officer returned to the precinct, brought petitioner to the car, and confronted petitioner with the registration card. Petitioner disclaimed all knowledge of the card. The officer then seized the card and brought it into the precinct. Returning to the car, he searched the trunk, rolled up the windows, and locked the doors.

The sole question for our consideration is whether the officer discovered the registration card by means of an illegal search. We hold that he did not. The admissibility of evidence found as a result of a search under the police regulation is not presented by this case. The precise and detailed findings of the District Court, accepted by the Court of Appeals, were to the effect that the discovery of the card was not the result of a search of the car, but of a measure taken to protect the car while it was in police custody. Nothing in the Fourth Amendment requires the police to obtain a warrant in these narrow circumstances.

Once the door had lawfully been opened, the registration card, with the name of the robbery victim on it, was plainly visible. It has long been settled that objects falling in the plain view of an officer who has a right to be in the position to have that view are subject to seizure and may be introduced in evidence. . . .

Mr. Justice MARSHALL took no part in the consideration or decision of this case.

Mr. Justice DOUGLAS, concurring. . . .

UNITED STATES V. ROSS

Supreme Court of the United States, 1982.
456 U.S. 798, 102 S. Ct. 2157, 72 L.Ed.2d 572.

[In *Carroll v. United States,* 267 U.S. 132 (1925), the Supreme Court upheld a warrantless search of a motor vehicle that was harboring contraband. Thus began the so-called automobile exception to the Fourth Amendment warrant requirement. In the instant case, the Court considers the scope of the automobile exception.]

Justice STEVENS delivered the opinion of the Court. ... In this case, we consider the extent to which police officers—who have legitimately stopped an automobile and who have probable cause to believe that contraband is concealed somewhere within it—may conduct a probing search of compartments and containers within the vehicle whose contents are not in plain view. We hold that they may conduct a search of the vehicle that is as thorough as a magistrate could authorize in a warrant "particularly describing the place to be searched."

In the evening of November 27, 1978, an informant who had previously proved to be reliable telephoned Detective Marcum of the District of Columbia Police Department and told him that an individual known as "Bandit" was selling narcotics kept in the trunk of a car parked at 439 Ridge Street. The informant stated that he had just observed "Bandit" complete a sale and that "Bandit" had told him that additional narcotics were in the trunk. The informant gave Marcum a detailed description of "Bandit" and stated that the car was a "purplish maroon" Chevrolet Malibu with District of Columbia license plates.

Accompanied by Detective Cassidy and Sergeant Gonzales, Marcum immediately drove to the area and found a maroon Malibu parked in front of 439 Ridge Street. A license check disclosed that the car was registered to Albert Ross; a computer check on Ross revealed that he fit the informant's description and used the alias "Bandit." In two passes through the neighborhood the officers did not observe anyone matching the informant's description. To avoid alerting persons on the street, they left the area.

The officers returned five minutes later and observed the maroon Malibu turning off Ridge Street

onto Fourth Street. They pulled alongside the Malibu, noticed that the driver matched the informant's description, and stopped the car. Marcum and Cassidy told the driver—later identified as Albert Ross, the respondent in this action—to get out of the vehicle. While they searched Ross, Sergeant Gonzales discovered a bullet on the car's front seat. He searched the interior of the car and found a pistol in the glove compartment. Ross then was arrested and handcuffed. Detective Cassidy took Ross' keys and opened the trunk, where he found a closed brown paper bag. He opened the bag and discovered a number of glassine bags containing a white powder. Cassidy replaced the bag, closed the trunk, and drove the car to headquarters.

At the police station Cassidy thoroughly searched the car. In addition to the "lunch-type" brown paper bag, Cassidy found in the trunk a zippered red leather pouch. He unzipped the pouch and discovered $3,200 in cash. The police laboratory later determined that the powder in the bag was heroin. No warrant was obtained.

Ross was charged with possession of heroin with intent to distribute. ... Prior to trial, he moved to suppress the heroin found in the paper bag and the currency found in the leather pouch. After an evidentiary hearing, the District Court denied the motion to suppress. The heroin and currency were introduced in evidence at trial and Ross was convicted. ...

[On appeal, Ross' conviction was reversed on the grounds that the warrantless search of the containers in the trunk was unreasonable.]

... [T]he exception to the warrant requirement established in *Carroll [v. United States* (1925)]—the scope of which we consider in this case—applied only to searches of vehicles that are supported by probable cause. In this class of cases, a search is not unreasonable if based on facts that would justify the issuance of a warrant, even though a warrant has not actually been obtained.

The rationale justifying a warrantless search of an automobile that is believed to be transporting contraband arguably applies with equal force to any movable container that is believed to be carrying an illicit substance. . . .

. . . [T]he decision in *Carroll* was based on the Court's appraisal of practical considerations viewed in the perspective of history. It is therefore significant that the practical consequences of the *Carroll* decision would be largely nullified if the permissible scope of a warrantless search of an automobile did not include containers and packages found inside the vehicle. Contraband goods are rarely strewn across the trunk or floor of a car; since by their very nature such goods must be withheld from pubic view, they rarely can be placed in an automobile unless they are enclosed within some form of container. . . .

A lawful search of fixed premises generally extends to the entire area in which the object of the search may be found and is not limited by the possibility that separate acts of entry or opening may be required to complete the search. Thus, a warrant that authorizes an officer to search a home for illegal weapons also provides authority to open closets, chests, drawers, and containers in which the weapon might be found. A warrant to open a footlocker to search for marihuana would also authorize the opening of packages found inside. A warrant to search a vehicle would support a search of every part of the vehicle that might contain the object of the search. When a legitimate search is under way, and when its purpose and its limits have been precisely defined, nice distinctions between closets, drawers and containers, in the case of a home, or between glove compartments, upholstered seats, trunks and wrapped packages, in the case of a vehicle, must give way to the interest in the prompt and efficient completion of the task at hand.

This rule applies equally to all containers, as indeed we believe it must. . . . [A] constitutional distinction between "worthy" and "unworthy" containers would be improper. Even though such a distinction perhaps could evolve in a series of cases in which paper bags, locked trunks, lunch buckets, and orange crates were placed on one side of the line or the other, the central purpose of the Fourth Amendment forecloses such a distinction. For just as the most frail cottage in the kingdom is absolutely entitled to the same protection as the most majestic mansion, so also may a traveler who carries a toothbrush and a few articles of clothing in a paper bag or knotted scarf claim an equal right to conceal his possessions from official inspection as the sophisticated executive with the locked attache case.

The scope of a warrantless search of an automobile thus is not defined by the nature of the container in which the contraband is secreted. Rather, it is defined by the object of the search and the places where there is probable cause to believe it may be found. Just as probable cause to believe that a stolen lawnmower may be found in a garage will not support a warrant to search an upstairs bedroom, probable cause to believe that undocumented aliens are being transported in a van will not justify a warrantless search of a suitcase. Probable cause to believe that a container placed in the trunk of a taxi contains contraband or evidence does not justify search of the entire cab. . . .

The [automobile] exception recognized in *Carroll* is unquestionably one that is "specifically established and well delineated." . . . We hold that the scope of a warrantless search authorized by that exception is no broader and no narrower than a magistrate could legitimately authorize by warrant. If probable cause justifies the search of a lawfully stopped vehicle, it justifies the search of every part of the vehicle that may contain the object of the search.

The judgment of the Court of Appeals is reversed. The case is remanded for further proceedings consistent with this opinion.

It is so ordered.

Justice BLACKMUN, concurring. . . .

Justice POWELL, concurring. . . .

Justice WHITE, dissenting. . . .

Justice MARSHALL, with whom Justice BRENNAN joins, dissenting.

The majority today not only repeals all realistic limits on warrantless automobile searches, it repeals the Fourth Amendment warrant requirement itself. By equating a police officer's estimation of probable cause with a magistrate's, the Court utterly disregards the value of a neutral and detached magistrate. . . .

This case will have profound implications for the privacy of citizens traveling in automobiles.... The Court derives satisfaction from the fact that its rule does not exalt the rights of the wealthy over the rights of the poor. A rule so broad that all citizens lose vital Fourth Amendment protection is no cause for celebration.

NEW JERSEY V. T.L.O.
Supreme Court of the United States, 1985.
469 U.S. 325, 105 S. Ct. 733, 83 L.Ed.2d 720.

[T.L.O. was a 14-year-old female high school student in a New Jersey public school. After being caught smoking in the school restroom, she was taken to the principal's office. The principal searched T.L.O.'s purse and discovered cigarettes and rolling papers. A further search revealed a small quantity of marijuana. T.L.O. was turned over to the police along with the marijuana. After unsuccessfully challenging the search and seizure, T.L.O. was sentenced to one year probation by the juvenile court. The New Jersey Supreme Court reversed and found that T.L.O.'s Fourth Amendment rights had been violated. The state petitioned the U.S. Supreme Court for certiorari.]

Justice WHITE delivered the opinion of the Court.
We granted certiorari in this case to examine the appropriateness of the exclusionary rule as a remedy for searches carried out in violation of the Fourth Amendment by public school authorities. Our consideration of the proper application of the Fourth Amendment to the public schools, however, has led us to conclude that the search that gave rise to the case now before us did not violate the Fourth Amendment. Accordingly, we here address only the questions of the proper standard for assessing the legality of searches conducted by public school officials and the application of that standard to the facts of this case....

II

In determining whether the search at issue in this case violated the Fourth Amendment, we are faced initially with the question whether that Amendment's prohibition on unreasonable searches and seizures applies to searches conducted by public school officials. We hold that it does.

It is now beyond dispute that the Federal Constitution, by virtue of the Fourteenth Amendment, prohibits unreasonable searches and seizures by state officers.... Equally indisputable is the proposition that the Fourteenth Amendment protects the rights of students against encroachment by public school officials....

III

To hold that the Fourth Amendment applies to searches conducted by school authorities is only to begin the inquiry into the standards governing such searches. Although the underlying command of the Fourth Amendment is always that searches and seizures be reasonable, what is reasonable depends on the context within which a search takes place. The determination of the standard of reasonableness governing any specific class of searches requires "balancing the need to search against the invasion which the search entails." ... On the other side of the balance are arrayed the individual's legitimate expectations of privacy and personal security; on the other, the government's need for effective methods to deal with breaches of public order.... A search of a child's person or of a closed purse or other bag carried on her person, no less than a similar search carried out on an adult, is undoubtedly a severe violation of subjective expectations of privacy.

Although this Court may take notice of the difficulty of maintaining discipline in the public schools today, the situation is not so dire that students in the schools may claim no legitimate expectations of privacy.... How, then, should we strike the balance between the schoolchildren's legitimate expectations of privacy and the school's equally legitimate need to maintain an environment in which learning can take place? It is evident that the school setting requires some easing of the restrictions to which searches by public authorities are ordinarily subject. The warrant requirement, in particular, is unsuited to the school environment: requiring a teacher to obtain a warrant before searching a child suspected of an infraction of school rules (or of the criminal law) would unduly interfere with the maintenance of the swift and informal disciplinary procedures needed in the schools. Just as we have in other cases dispensed with the warrant requirement when "the burden of obtaining a warrant is likely to frustrate the governmental purpose behind the search," ... we hold today that school officials need not obtain a warrant before searching a student who is under their authority.

The school setting also requires some modification of the level of suspicion of illicit activity needed to justify a search. Ordinarily, a search—even one that may permissibly be carried out without a warrant— must be based upon "probable cause" to believe that a violation of the law has occurred. However, "probable cause" is not an irreducible requirement of a valid search.... Where a careful balancing of governmental and private interests suggests that the public interest is best served by a Fourth Amendment standard of reasonableness that stops short of probable cause, we have not hesitated to adopt such a standard.

We join the majority of courts that have examined this issue in concluding that the accommodation of the privacy interests of schoolchildren with the substantial need of teachers and administrators for freedom to maintain order in the schools does not require strict adherence to the requirement that searches be based on probable cause to believe that the subject of the search has violated or is violating the law. Rather, the legality of a search of a student should depend simply on the reasonableness, under all the circumstances, of the search. Determining the reasonableness of any search involves a twofold inquiry: first, one must consider whether the ... action was justified at its inception, second, one must determine whether the search actually conducted was reasonably related in scope to the circumstances which justified the interference in the first place. Under ordinary circumstances, a search of a student by a teacher or other school official will be "justified at its inception" when there are reasonable grounds for suspecting that the search will turn up evidence that the student has violated or is violating either the law or the rules of the school. Such a search will be permissible in its scope when the measures adopted are reasonably related to the objectives of the search and not excessively intrusive in light of the age and sex of the student and the nature of the infraction.

This standard will, we trust, neither unduly burden the efforts of school authorities to maintain order in their schools nor authorize unrestrained intrusions upon the privacy of schoolchildren. By focusing attention on the question of reasonableness, the standard will spare teachers and school administrators the necessity of schooling themselves in the niceties of probable cause and permit them to regulate their conduct according to the dictates of reason and common sense. At the same time, the reasonableness standard should ensure that the interests of students will be invaded no more than is necessary to achieve the legitimate end of preserving order in the schools.

IV

There remains the question of the legality of the search in this case. We recognize that the "reasonable grounds" standard applied by the New Jersey Supreme Court in its consideration of this question is not substantially different from the standard that we have adopted today. Nonetheless, we believe that the New Jersey court's application of that standard to strike down the search of T.L.O.'s purse reflects a somewhat crabbed notion of reasonableness. Our review of the facts surrounding the search leads us to conclude that the search was in no sense unreasonable for Fourth Amendment purposes.

The incident that gave rise to this case actually involved two separate searches, with the first—the search for cigarettes—providing the suspicion that gave rise to the second—the search for marihuana. Although it is the fruits of the second search that are at issue here, the validity of the search for marihuana must depend on the reasonableness of the initial search for cigarettes, as there would have been no reason to suspect that T.L.O. possessed marihuana had the first search not taken place. Accordingly, it is to the search for cigarettes that we first turn our attention. . . .

T.L.O. had been accused of smoking, and had denied the accusation in the strongest possible terms when she stated that she did not smoke at all. Surely it cannot be said that under these circumstances, T.L.O.'s possession of cigarettes would be irrelevant to the charges against her or to her response to those charges. T.L.O.'s possession of cigarettes, once it was discovered, would both corroborate the report that she had been smoking and undermine the credibility of her defense to the charge of smoking. To be sure, the discovery of the cigarettes would not prove that T.L.O. had been smoking in the lavatory; nor would it, strictly speaking, necessarily be inconsistent with her claim that she did not smoke at all. But it is universally recognized that evidence, to be relevant to an inquiry, need not conclusively prove the ultimate fact in issue, but only have "any tendency to make the existence of any fact that is of consequence to the determination of the action more probable or less probable than it would be without the evidence." . . . The relevance of T.L.O.'s possession of cigarettes to the question whether she had been smoking and to the credibility of her denial that she smoked supplied the necessary "nexus" between the item searched for and the infraction under investigation. . . . Of course, even if the teacher's report were true, T.L.O. *might* not have had a pack of cigarettes with her; she might have borrowed a cigarette from someone else or have been sharing a cigarette with another student. But the requirement of reasonable suspicion is not a requirement of absolute certainty. . . . Because the hypothesis that T.L.O. was carrying cigarettes in her purse was itself not unreasonable, it is irrelevant that other hypotheses were also consistent with the teacher's accusation. . . .

Our conclusion that [the principal's] decision to open T.L.O.'s purse was reasonable brings us to the question of the further search for marihuana once the pack of cigarettes was located. The suspicion upon which the search for marihuana was founded was provided when [the principal] observed a package of rolling papers in the purse as he removed the pack of cigarettes. Although T.L.O. does not dispute the reasonableness of [the principal's] belief that the rolling papers indicated the presence of marihuana, she does contend that the scope of the search [the principal] conducted exceeded permissible bounds when he seized and read certain letters that implicated T.L.O. in drug dealing. This argument, too, is unpersuasive. The discovery of the rolling papers concededly gave rise to a reasonable suspicion that T.L.O. was carrying marihuana as well as cigarettes in her purse. This suspicion justified further exploration of T.L.O.'s purse, which turned up more evidence of drug-related activities: a pipe, a number of plastic bags of the type commonly used to store marihuana, a small quantity of marihuana, and a fairly substantial amount of money. Under these circumstances, it was not unreasonable to extend the search to a separate zippered compartment of the purse; and when a search of that compartment revealed an index card containing a list of "people who owe me money" as well as two letters, the inference that T.L.O. was involved in marihuana trafficking was substantial enough to justify [the principal] in examining the letters to determine whether they contained any further evidence. In short, we cannot conclude that the search for marihuana was unreasonable in any respect.

Because the search resulting in the discovery of the evidence of marihuana dealing by T.L.O. was reasonable, the New Jersey Supreme Court's decision to exclude that evidence from T.L.O.'s juvenile delinquency proceedings on Fourth Amendment grounds was erroneous. Accordingly, the judgment of the Supreme Court of New Jersey is reversed.

Justice BLACKMUN, concurring in the judgment. . . .

Justice BRENNAN, with whom Justice MARSHALL joins, concurring in part and dissenting in part:

I fully agree with Part [I] of the Court's opinion. Teachers, like all other government officials, must conform their conduct to the Fourth Amendment's protections of personal privacy and personal security. This principle is of particular importance when applied to schoolteachers, for children learn as much by example as by exposition. It would be incongruous and futile to charge teachers with the task of embuing their students with an understanding of our system of constitutional democracy, while at the same time immunizing those same teachers from the need to respect constitutional protections. . . .

I do not, however, otherwise join the Court's opinion. Today's decision sanctions school officials to conduct full-scale searches on a "reasonableness" standard whose only definite content is that it is *not* the same test as the "probable cause" standard found in the text of the Fourth Amendment. In adopting this unclear, unprecedented, and unnecessary departure from generally applicable Fourth Amendment standards, the Court carves out a broad exception to standards that this Court had developed over years of considering Fourth Amendment problems. Its decision is supported neither by precedent nor even by

a fair application of the "balancing test" it proclaims in this very opinion. . . .

In my view, the presence of the word "reasonable" in the text of the Fourth Amendment does not grant a shifting majority of this Court the authority to answer *all* Fourth Amendment questions by consulting its momentary vision of the social good. Full-scale searches unaccompanied by probable cause violate the Fourth Amendment. I do not pretend that our traditional Fourth Amendment doctrine automatically answers all of the difficult legal questions that occasionally arise. I do contend, however, that this Court has an obligation to provide some coherent framework to resolve such questions on the basis of more than a conclusory recitation of the results of a "balancing test." The Fourth Amendment itself supplies that framework and, because the Court today fails to heed its message, I must respectfully dissent.

Justice STEVENS, with whom Justice MARSHALL joins, and with whom Justice BRENNAN joins as to Part I, concurring in part and dissenting in part. . . .

MAPP V. OHIO

Supreme Court of the United States, 1961.
367 U.S. 643, 81 S. Ct. 1684, 6 L.Ed.2d 1081.

[In this landmark decision, the Supreme Court applies the Fourth Amendment exclusionary rule to the state courts by way of the Fourteenth Amendment.]

Mr. Justice CLARK delivered the opinion of the Court.
Appellant stands convicted of knowingly having had in her possession and under her control certain lewd and lascivious books, pictures, and photographs in violation of . . . Ohio's Revised Code. The Supreme Court of Ohio found that her conviction was valid though "based primarily upon the introduction in evidence of lewd and lascivious books and pictures unlawfully seized during an unlawful search of defendant's home." . . .

On May 23, 1957, three Cleveland police officers arrived at appellant's residence in that city pursuant to information that "a person [was] hiding out in the home, who was wanted for questioning in connection with a recent bombing, and that there was a large amount of policy paraphernalia being hidden in the home." Miss Mapp and her daughter by a former marriage lived on the top floor of the two family dwelling. Upon their arrival at that house, the officers knocked on the door and demanded entrance but appellant, after telephoning her attorney, refused to admit them without a search warrant. They advised their headquarters of the situation and undertook a surveillance of the house.

The officers again sought entrance some three hours later when four or more additional officers arrived on the scene. When Miss Mapp did not come to the door immediately at least one of the several doors to the house was forcibly opened and the policemen gained admittance. Meanwhile Miss Mapp's attorney arrived, but the officers, having secured their own entry, and continuing in their defiance of the law, would permit him neither to see Miss Mapp nor to enter the house. It appears that Miss Mapp was halfway down the stairs from the upper floor to the front door when the officers, in this highhanded manner, broke into the hall. She demanded to see the search warrant. A paper, claimed to be a warrant, was held up by one of the officers. She grabbed the "warrant" and placed it in her bosom. A struggle ensued in which the officers recovered the piece of paper and as a result of which they handcuffed appellant because she had been "belligerent" in resisting their official rescue of the "warrant" from her person. Running roughshod over appellant, a policeman "grabbed" her, "twisting" [her] hand, and she "yelled [and] pleaded with him" because "it was hurting." Appellant, in handcuffs, was then forcibly taken upstairs to her bedroom where the officers searched a dresser, a chest of drawers, a closet and some suitcases. They also looked into a photo album and through personal papers belonging to the appellant. The search spread to the rest of the second floor including the child's bedroom, the living room, the kitchen and a dinette. The basement of the building and a trunk found therein were also searched. The obscene materials for possession of which she was ultimately convicted were discovered in the course of that widespread search.

At the trial no search warrant was produced by the prosecution, nor was the failure to produce one explained or accounted for. At best, "There is, in the record, considerable doubt as to whether there ever was any warrant for the search of defendant's home." . . . The Ohio Supreme Court believed a "reasonable argument" could be made that the conviction should be reversed "because the 'methods' employed to obtain the [evidence] . . . were such to 'offend "a sense of justice," ' "but the court found determinative the fact that the evidence had not been taken "from defendant's person by the use of brutal or offensive physical force. . . ." . . .

Since the Fourth Amendment's right of privacy has been declared enforceable against the States through the Due Process Clause of the Fourteenth, it is enforceable against them by the same sanction of exclusion as is used against the Federal Government. Were it otherwise, . . . the assurance against unreasonable federal searches and seizures would be "a form of words," valueless and undeserving of mention in a perpetual charter of inestimable human liberties, so too, without that rule the freedom from state invasion of privacy would be so ephemeral and so nearly severed from its conceptual nexus with the freedom from all brutish means of coercing evidence as not to merit this Court's high regard as a freedom "implicit in the concept of ordered liberty." . . .

Moreover, our holding that the exclusionary rule is an essential part of both the Fourth and Fourteenth Amendments is not only the logical dictate of prior cases, but it also makes very good sense. There is no war between the Constitution and common sense. Presently, a federal prosecutor may make no use of evidence illegally seized, but a State's attorney across the street may, although he supposedly is operating under the enforceable prohibitions of the same Amendment. Thus the State, by admitting evidence unlawfully seized, serves to encourage disobedience to the Federal Constitution which it is bound to uphold. Moreover, . . . "[t]he very essence of a healthy federalism depends upon the avoidance of needless conflict between state and federal courts." . . .

Federal-state cooperation in the solution of crime under constitutional standards will be promoted, if only by recognition of their now mutual obligation to respect the same fundamental criteria in their approaches. "However much in a particular case insistence upon such rules may appear as a technicality that inures to the benefit of a guilty person, the history of the criminal law proves that tolerance of shortcut methods in law enforcement impairs its enduring effectiveness." . . . Denying shortcuts to only one of two cooperating law enforcement agencies tends naturally to breed legitimate suspicion of "working arrangements" whose results are equally tainted.

There are those who say, as did Justice (then Judge) Cardozo, that under our constitutional exclusionary doctrine, "[t]he criminal is to go free because the constable has blundered." . . . In some cases this will undoubtedly be the result. But, ... "There is another consideration—the imperative of judicial integrity." ... The criminal goes free, if he must, but it is the law that sets him free. Nothing can destroy a government more quickly than its failure to observe its own laws, or worse, its disregard of the charter of its own existence. As Mr. Justice Brandeis, dissenting, said in *Olmstead v. United States:* "Our Government is the potent, the omnipresent teacher. For good or for ill, it teaches the whole people by its example.... If the Government becomes a lawbreaker, it breeds contempt for law; it invites every man to become a law unto himself; it invites anarchy." ... Nor can it lightly be assumed that, as a practical matter, adoption of the exclusionary rule fetters law enforcement. Only last year this Court expressly considered that contention and found that "pragmatic evidence of a sort" to the contrary was not wanting.

The federal courts themselves have operated under the exclusionary rule ... for almost half a century; yet it has not been suggested either that the Federal Bureau of Investigation has thereby been rendered ineffective, or that the administration of criminal justice in the federal courts has thereby been disrupted. Moreover, the experience of the states is impressive....

The ignoble shortcut to conviction left open to the State tends to destroy the entire system of constitutional restraints on which the liberties of the people rest. Having once recognized that the right to privacy embodied in the Fourth Amendment is enforceable against the States, and that the right to be secure against rude invasions of privacy by state

officers is, therefore, constitutional in origin, we can no longer permit that right to remain an empty promise. Because it is enforceable in the same manner and to like effect as other basic rights secured by the Due Process Clause, we can no longer permit it to be revocable at the whim of any police officer who, in the name of law enforcement itself, chooses to suspend its enjoyment. Our decision, founded on reason and truth, gives to the individual no more than that which the Constitution guarantees him, to the police officer no less than that to which honest law enforcement is entitled, and, to the courts, that judicial integrity so necessary in the true administration of justice.

The judgment of the Supreme Court of Ohio is reversed and the cause remanded for further proceedings not inconsistent with this opinion.

Mr. Justice BLACK, concurring. . . .

Mr. Justice DOUGLAS, concurring. . . .

Mr. Justice HARLAN, whom Mr. Justice FRANK-FURTER and Mr. Justice WHITTAKER join, dissenting. . . .

Memorandum of Mr. Justice STEWART.

... I express no view as to the merits of the constitutional issue which the Court today decides. I would, however, reverse the judgment in this case, because I am persuaded that the provision of ... the Ohio Revised Code upon which the petitioner's conviction was based is ... not "consistent with the rights of free thought and expression assured against state action by the Fourteenth Amendment." . . .

UNITED STATES V. LEON

Supreme Court of the United States, 1984.
468 U.S. 897, 104 S. Ct. 3405, 82 L.Ed.2d 677.

[Here the Supreme Court considers a limited good-faith exception to the Fourth Amendment exclusionary rule.]

Justice WHITE delivered the opinion of the Court.
... In August 1981, a confidential informant of unproven reliability informed an officer of the Bur-

bank Police Department that two persons known to him as "Armando" and "Patsy" were selling large quantities of cocaine and methaqualone from their residence at 620 Price Drive in Burbank, Cal. The informant also indicated that he had witnessed a sale of methaqualone by "Patsy" at the residence approximately five months earlier and had observed at that time a shoebox containing a large amount of cash that belonged to "Patsy." He further declared that "Armando" and "Patsy" generally kept only small quantities of drugs at their residence and stored the remainder at another location in Burbank.

On the basis of this information, the Burbank police initiated an extensive investigation focusing first on the Price Drive residence and later on two other residences as well. Cars parked at the Price Drive residence were determined to belong to respondents Armando Sanchez, who have previously been arrested for possession of marihuana, and Patsy Stewart, who had no criminal record. During the course of the investigation, officers observed an automobile belonging to respondent Ricardo Del Castillo, who had previously been arrested for possession of 50 pounds of marihuana, arrive at the Price Drive residence. The driver of that car entered the house, exited shortly thereafter carrying a small paper sack, and drove away. A check of Del Castillo's probation records let the officers to respondent Alberto Leon, whose telephone number Del Castillo had listed as his employer's. Leon had been arrested in 1980 on drug charges, and a companion had informed the police at that time that Leon was heavily involved in the importation of drugs into this country. Before the current investigation began, the Burbank officers had learned that an informant had told a Glendale police officer that Leon stored a large quantity of methaqualone at his residence in Glendale. During the course of this investigation, the Burbank officers learned that Leon was living at 716 South Sunset Canyon in Burbank.

Subsequently, the officers observed several persons, at least one of whom had prior drug involvement, arriving at the Price Drive residence and leaving with small packages; observed a variety of other material activity at the two residences as well as at a condominium at 7902 Via Magdalena; and witnessed a variety of relevant activity involving respondents' automobiles. The officers also observed respondents Sanchez and Stewart board separate flights for Miami. The pair later returned to Los Angeles together, consented to a search of their luggage that revealed only a small amount of marihuana, and left the airport. Based on these and other observations summarized in the affidavit, Officer Cyril Rombach of the Burbank Police Department, an experienced and well-trained narcotics investigator, prepared an application for a warrant to search 620 Price Drive, 716 South Sunset Canyon, 7902 Via Magdalena, and automobiles registered to each of the respondents for an extensive list of items believed to be related to respondents' drug-trafficking activities. Officer Rombach's extensive application was reviewed by several Deputy District Attorneys.

A facially valid search warrant was issued in September 1981 by a state superior court judge. The ensuing searches produced large quantities of drugs at the Via Magdalena and Sunset Canyon addresses and a small quantity at the Price Drive residence. Other evidence was discovered at each of the residences and in Stewart's and Del Castillo's automobiles. Respondents were indicted by a [federal] grand jury ... and charged with conspiracy to possess and distribute cocaine and a variety of substantive counts.

The respondents then filed motions to suppress the evidence seized pursuant to the warrant. The District Court ... concluded that the affidavit was insufficient to establish probable cause, but did not suppress all of the evidence as to all of the respondents because none of the respondents had standing to challenge all of the searches. In response to a request from the Government, the court made clear that Officer Rombach had acted in good faith, but it rejected the Government's suggestion that the Fourth Amendment exclusionary rule should not apply where evidence is seized in reasonable, good-faith reliance on a search warrant. ...

[The Court of Appeals held that the evidence was inadmissible because the search warrant was not based on probable cause. The Court of Appeals refused to recognize any "good-faith exception" to the exclusionary rule.]

The Fourth Amendment contains no provision expressly precluding the use of evidence obtained in violation of its commands, and an examination of its origin and purposes makes clear that the use of fruits of a past unlawful search or seizure "work[s] no new Fourth Amendment wrong." ... The wrong condemned by the Amendment is "fully accomplished" by the unlawful search or seizure itself, and the exclusionary rule is neither intended nor able to "cure the invasion of the defendant's rights which he has already suffered." . . . The rule thus operates as "a judicially created remedy designed to safeguard Fourth Amendment rights generally through its deterrent effect, rather than a personal constitutional right of the person aggrieved." . . .

Whether the exclusionary sanction is appropriately imposed in a particular case, our decisions make clear, is "an issue separate from the question whether the Fourth Amendment rights of the party seeking to invoke the rule were violated by police conduct." . . . Only the former question is currently before us, and it must be resolved by weighing the costs and benefits of preventing the use in the prosecution's case-in-chief of inherently trustworthy tangible evidence obtained in reliance on a search warrant issued by a detached and neutral magistrate that ultimately is found to be defective.

The substantial social costs exacted by the exclusionary rule for the vindication of Fourth Amendment rights have long been a source of concern. "Our cases have consistently recognized that unbending application of the exclusionary sanction to enforce ideals of government rectitude would impede unacceptably the truth-finding functions of judge and jury." . . . An objectionable collateral consequence of this interference with the criminal justice system's truth-finding function is that some guilty defendants may go free or receive reduced sentences as a result of favorable plea bargains. Particularly when law enforcement officers have acted in objective good faith or their transgressions have been minor, the magnitude of the benefit conferred on such guilty defendants offends basic concepts of the criminal justice system. Indiscriminate application of the exclusionary rule, therefore, may well "generat[e] disrespect for the law and the administration of justice." . . . Accordingly, "[a]s with any remedial device, the application of the rule has been restricted to those areas where its remedial objectives are thought most efficaciously served." . . .

The Court has, to be sure, not seriously questioned, "in the absence of a more efficacious sanction, the continued application of the rule to suppress evidence from the [prosecution's] case where a Fourth Amendment violation has been substantial and deliberate. . . ." . . . Nevertheless, the balancing approach that has evolved in various contexts—including criminal trials—"forcefully suggest[s] that

the exclusionary rule be more generally modified to permit the introduction of evidence obtained in the reasonable good-faith belief that a search or seizure was in accord with the Fourth Amendment." . . .

As cases considering the use of unlawfully obtained evidence in criminal trials themselves make clear, it does not follow from the emphasis on the exclusionary rule's deterrent value that "anything which deters illegal searches is thereby commanded by the Fourth Amendment." . . . In determining whether persons aggrieved solely by the introduction of damaging evidence unlawfully obtained from their co-conspirators or co-defendants could seek suppression, for example, we found that the additional benefits of such an extension of the exclusionary rule would not outweigh its costs. Standing to invoke the rule has thus been limited to cases in which the prosecution seeks to use the fruits of an illegal search or seizure against the victim of police misconduct. . . .

. . . We have expressed a strong preference for warrants and declared that "in a doubtful or marginal case a search under a warrant may be sustainable where without one it would fail." Reasonable minds frequently may differ on the question whether a particular affidavit establishes probable cause, and we have thus concluded that the preference for warrants is most appropriately effectuated by according "great deference" to a magistrate's determination.

Deference to the magistrate, however, is not boundless. It is clear, first, that the deference accorded to a magistrate's finding of probable cause does not preclude inquiry into the knowing or reckless falsity of the affidavit on which that determination was based. Second, the courts must also insist that the magistrate purport to "perform his 'neutral and detached' function and not serve merely as a rubber stamp for the police." . . .

Third, reviewing courts will not defer to a warrant based on an affidavit that does not "provide the magistrate with a substantial basis for determining the existence of probable cause." . . .

Even if the warrant application was supported by more than a "bare bones" affidavit, a reviewing court may properly conclude that, notwithstanding the deference that magistrates deserve, the warrant was invalid because the magistrate's probable-cause determination reflected an improper analysis of the totality of the circumstances, or because the form of the warrant was improper in some respect.

Only in the first of these three situations, however, has the Court set forth a rationale for suppressing evidence obtained pursuant to a search warrant; in the other areas, it has simply excluded such evidence without considering whether Fourth Amendment interests will be advanced. To the extent that proponents of exclusion rely on its behavioral effects on judges and magistrates in these areas, their reliance is misplaced. First, the exclusionary rule is designed to deter police misconduct rather than to punish the errors of judges and magistrates. Second, there exists no evidence suggesting that judges and magistrates are inclined to ignore or subvert the Fourth Amendment or that lawlessness among those actors requires application of the extreme sanction of exclusion.

Third, and most important, we discern no basis, and are offered none, for believing that exclusion of evidence seized pursuant to a warrant will have a significant deterrent effect on the issuing judge or magistrate. Judges and magistrates are not adjuncts to the law enforcement team; as neutral judicial officers, they have no stake in the outcome of particular criminal prosecutions. The threat of exclusion thus cannot be expected significantly to deter them. Imposition of the exclusionary sanction is not necessary meaningfully to inform judicial officers of their errors, and we cannot conclude that admitting evidence obtained pursuant to a warrant while at the same time declaring that the warrant was somehow defective will in any way reduce judicial officers' professional incentives to comply with the Fourth Amendment, encourage them to repeat their mistakes, or lead to the granting of all colorable warrant requests.

If exclusion of evidence obtained pursuant to a subsequently invalidated warrant is to have any deterrent effect, therefore, it must alter the behavior of individual law enforcement officers or the policies of their departments.

We have frequently questioned whether the exclusionary rule can have any deterrent effect when the offending officers acted in the objectively reasonable belief that their conduct did not violate the Fourth Amendment. "No empirical researcher, proponent or opponent of the rule, has yet been able to estab-lish with any assurance whether the rule has a deterrent effect. . . ." . . . But even assuming that the rule effectively deters some police misconduct and provides incentives for the law enforcement profession as a whole to conduct itself in accord with the Fourth Amendment, it cannot be expected, and should not be applied, to deter objectively reasonable law enforcement activity.

We conclude that the marginal or nonexistent benefits produced by suppressing evidence obtained in objectively reasonable reliance on a subsequently invalidated search warrant cannot justify the substantial costs of exclusion. We do not suggest, however, that exclusion is always inappropriate in cases where an officer has obtained a warrant and abided by its terms. "[S]earches pursuant to a warrant will rarely require any deep inquiry into reasonableness," for "a warrant issued by a magistrate normally suffices to establish" that a law enforcement officer has "acted in good faith in conducting the search." . . . Nevertheless, the officer's reliance on the magistrate's probable-cause determination and on the technical sufficiency of the warrant he issues must be objectively reasonable, and it is clear that in some circumstances the officer will have no reasonable grounds for believing that the warrant was properly issued.

Suppression therefore remains an appropriate remedy if the magistrate or judge in issuing a warrant was misled by information in an affidavit that the affiant knew was false or would have known was false except for his reckless disregard of the truth. The exception we recognize today will also not apply in cases where the issuing magistrate wholly abandoned his judicial role. . . . Nor would an officer manifest objective good faith in relying on a warrant based on an affidavit "so lacking in indicia of probable cause as to render official belief in its existence entirely unreasonable." . . . Finally, depending on the circumstances of the particular case, a warrant may be so facially deficient—i.e., in failing to particularize the place to be searched or the things to be seized—that the executing officers cannot reasonably presume it to be valid. . . .

Nor are we persuaded that application of a good-faith exception to searches conducted pursuant to warrants will preclude review of the constitutionality of the search or seizure, deny needed guidance from the courts, or freeze Fourth Amendment law in its present state.

If the resolution of a particular Fourth Amendment question is necessary to guide future action by law enforcement officers and magistrates, nothing will prevent reviewing courts from deciding that question before turning to the good-faith issue. Indeed, it frequently will be difficult to determine whether the officers acted reasonably without resolving the Fourth Amendment issue. Even if the Fourth Amendment question is not one of broad import, reviewing courts could decide in particular cases that magistrates under their supervision need to be informed of their errors and so evaluate the officers' good faith only after finding a violation. In other circumstances, those courts could reject suppression motions posing no important Fourth Amendment questions by turning immediately to a consideration of the officers' good faith. We have no reason to believe that our Fourth Amendment jurisprudence would suffer by allowing reviewing courts to exercise an informed discretion in making this choice.

When the principles we have enunciated today are applied to the facts of this case, it is apparent that the judgment of the Court of Appeals cannot stand. The Court of Appeals applied the prevailing legal standards to Officer Rombach's warrant application and concluded that the application could not support the magistrate's probable-cause determination. In so doing, the court clearly informed the magistrate that he had erred in issuing the challenged warrant. . . .

Having determined that the warrant should not have issued, the Court of Appeals understandably declined to adopt a modification of the Fourth Amendment exclusionary rule that this Court had not previously sanctioned. Although the modification finds strong support in our previous cases, the Court of Appeals' commendable self-restraint is not to be criticized. We have now re-examined the purposes of the exclusionary rule and the propriety of its application in cases where officers have relied on a subsequently invalidated search warrant. Our conclusion is that the rule's purposes will only rarely be served by applying it in such circumstances. . . .

Accordingly, the judgment of the Court of Appeals is reversed.

Justice BLACKMUN, concurring. . . .

Justice BRENNAN, with whom Justice MARSHALL joins, dissenting.

Ten years ago in *United States v. Calandra* . . . (1974), I expressed the fear that the Court's decision "may signal that a majority of my colleagues have positioned themselves to reopen the door [to evidence secured by official lawlessness] still further and abandon altogether the exclusionary rule in search-and-seizure cases." Since then, in case after case, I have witnessed the Court's gradual but determined strangulation of the rule. It now appears that the Court's victory over the Fourth Amendment is complete. That today's decision represents the piece de resistance of the Court's past efforts cannot be doubted, for today the Court sanctions the use in the prosecution's case-in-chief of illegally obtained evidence against the individual whose rights have been violated—a result that had previously been thought to be foreclosed.

The Court seeks to justify this result on the ground that the "costs" of adhering to the exclusionary rule in cases like those before us exceed the "benefits." But the language of deterrence and of cost/benefit analysis, if used indiscriminately, can have a narcotic effect. It creates an illusion of technical precision and ineluctability. It suggests that not only constitutional principle but also empirical data support the majority's result. When the Court's analysis is examined carefully, however, it is clear that we have not been treated to an honest assessment of the merits of the exclusionary rule, but have instead been drawn into a curious world where the "costs" of excluding illegally obtained evidence loom to exaggerated heights and where the "benefits" of such exclusion are made to disappear with a mere wave of the hand. . . .

At bottom, the Court's decision turns on the proposition that the exclusionary rule is merely a " 'judicially created remedy designed to safeguard Fourth Amendment rights generally through its deterrent effect, rather than a personal constitutional right.' " . . . The essence of this view, as expressed initially in the *Calandra* opinion and as reiterated today, is that the sole "purpose of the Fourth Amendment is to prevent unreasonable governmental intrusions into the privacy of one's person, house, papers, or effects. The wrong condemned is the unjustified governmental invasion of these areas of an individual's life. That wrong . . . is fully accomplished by the original search without probable cause." ... This reading of the Amendment implies that its proscriptions are directed solely at those government agents, who may actually invade an individual's constitutionally protected privacy. The courts are not subject to any direct constitutional duty to exclude illegally obtained evidence, because the question of the admissibility of such evidence is not addressed by the Amendment. This view of the scope of the Amendment relegates the judiciary to the periphery. Because the only constitutionally cognizable injury has already been "fully accomplished" by the police by the time a case comes before the courts, the Constitution is not itself violated if the judge decides to admit the tainted evidence. Indeed, the most the judge can do is wring his hands and hope that perhaps by excluding such evidence he can deter future transgressions by the police. ...

I submit that such a crabbed reading of the Fourth Amendment casts aside the teaching of those Justices who first formulated the exclusionary rule, and rests ultimately on an impoverished understanding of judicial responsibility in our constitutional scheme. For my part, "[t]he right of the people to be secure in their persons, houses, papers and effects, against unreasonable searches and seizures" comprises a personal right to exclude all evidence secured by means of unreasonable searches and seizures. The right to be free from the initial invasion of privacy and the right of exclusion are coordinate components of the central embracing right to be free from unreasonable searches and seizures. ...

Justice STEVENS, dissenting.

... It is of course true that the exclusionary rule exerts a high price—the loss of probative evidence of guilt. But that price is one courts have often been required to pay to serve important social goals. That price is also one the Fourth Amendment requires us to pay, assuming as we must that the Framers intended that its strictures "shall not be violated." For in all such cases, as Justice Stewart has observed, "the same extremely relevant evidence would not have been obtained had the police officer complied with the commands of the Fourth Amendment in the first place." ...

We could, of course, facilitate the process of administering justice to those who violate the criminal laws by ignoring the commands of the Fourth Amendment—indeed, by ignoring the entire Bill of Rights—but it is the very purpose of a Bill of Rights to identify values that may not be sacrificed to expediency. In a just society those who govern, as well as those who are governed, must obey the law. ...

ARREST, INTERROGATION, AND IDENTIFICATION

CHAPTER OUTLINE

Introduction
Arrest
Interrogation and Confessions
Lineups and Other
   Identification Procedures
Conclusion

Cases
Terry v. Ohio
Delaware v. Prouse
Tennessee v. Garner
Miranda v. Arizona
Oregon v. Mathiason
Rhode Island v. Innis
New York v. Quarles

Introduction

The term *arrest* refers to the deprivation of a person's liberty by someone with legal authority. Generally, an arrest occurs when a person suspected of having committed a crime is taken into custody by a police officer, although there are some circumstances in which an arrest can be effected by a private individual.

The term *interrogation* refers to the questioning of a suspect by law enforcement officers, either to elicit a confession or assist them in solving a crime.

Both arrest and interrogation play a crucial role in law enforcement. Equally obvious is that both are serious intrusions into the privacy of the individual. Accordingly, courts have recognized certain constitutional limitations on the power of law enforcement officers to make arrests and conduct interrogations. Because an arrest is, in effect, a "seizure," it is subject to the probable cause and warrant requirements of the Fourth Amendment. Police interrogation of a suspect, on the other hand, carries with it a potential for compulsory self-incrimination; it is thus subject to constitutional attack under the Fifth Amendment.

Arrest

A formal arrest occurs when police take an individual into custody and charge that person with the commission of a crime. Because an arrest is, in effect, a "seizure," it is subject to the Fourth Amendment prohibition of "unreasonable searches and seizures." However, the formal arrest is not the only type of encounter between police and citizens that implicates the Fourth Amendment.

A seizure, for Fourth Amendment purposes, occurs when a police officer, "by means of physical force or show of authority, has in some way restrained the liberty of a citizen." *Terry v. Ohio,* 392 U.S. 1, 19 n. 16, 88 S. Ct. 1868, 1879 n. 16, 20 L.Ed.2d 889, 905 n. 16 (1968). As noted earlier, the traditional full-blown arrest clearly constitutes a seizure. So too does a police officer's fatal shooting of a fleeing suspect. *Tennessee v. Garner,* 471 U.S. 1, 105 S.Ct. 1694, 85 L.Ed 2d 1 (1985). Other instances may not be so clear, however. In 1988 the Supreme Court declined to formulate a "bright-line" rule as to what constitutes a seizure; rather, it asserted that the test requires an assessment of whether in view of all the circumstances surrounding an incident, "a reasonable person would have believed that he was not free to leave." *Michigan v. Chesternut,* 486 U.S. 567, 108 S.Ct. 1975, 100 L.Ed. 2d 565 (1988). The following year, the Court ruled that stopping a motorist at a police roadblock is a seizure for Fourth Amendment purposes. *Brower v. County of Inyo,* 489 U.S. 593, 109 S.Ct. 1378, 103 L.Ed 2d 628 (1989).

More recently, the Supreme Court addressed the issue of whether a seizure takes place when a police officer pursues a fleeing suspect. The California Court of Appeal held that when a defendant saw police officers pursuing him, that constituted a seizure within the meaning of the Fourth Amendment. The United States Supreme Court reversed, saying that:

> The word "seizure" readily bears the meaning of a laying on of hands or application of physical force to restrain movement, even when it is ultimately unsuccessful. . . . It does not remotely apply, however, to the prospect of a policeman yelling, "stop, in the name of the law!" at a fleeing form that continues to flee. *California v. Hodari D.,* 499 U.S. 621, ____, 111 S. Ct. 1547, 1550, 113 L.Ed. 2d 690, 697 (1991).

The same year, the Court reviewed an appeal by a bus passenger who had consented to a search of his luggage when accosted by sheriff's officers in Broward County, Florida. *Florida v. Bostick,* 501 U.S. ____, 111 S.Ct. 2382, 115 L.Ed 2d 389 (1991). The Florida Supreme Court had previously addressed this practice, and had adopted the view that such police activity was unconstitutional under the Fourth Amendment. The United States Supreme Court held that the officers, who were engaged in drug control efforts, did not seize Bostick when they approached him and asked to search his luggage.

As suggested by the previous example, encounters between citizens and police range from the formal arrest to a situation in which police approach an individual and ask questions. In fact, courts have identified four distinct types of police-citizen encounters. Each level of encounter is unique from the standpoint of the Fourth Amendment.

Level 1: The Request for Information or Identification

In level 1, the lowest level of encounter, police officers approach an individual in public and ask questions or ask for identification. The Supreme Court has held that citizens are under no duty to cooperate with police in such situations. State laws that make it a misdemeanor for persons to refuse to identify themselves or otherwise cooperate with police in such situations are presumptively unconstitutional. *Brown v. Texas,* 443 U.S. 47, 99 S. Ct. 2637, 61 L.Ed.2d 357 (1979).

Level 2: Roadblocks and Sobriety Checkpoints

Police sometimes set up roadblocks for apprehending a fleeing suspect or conducting field sobriety tests, or even merely performing safety checks on automobiles. In addition to locating drunk drivers, roadblocks often lead to the discovery of illegal weapons, drugs, and other contraband. In 1979 the Supreme Court indicated its approval of this form of police investigation. In *Delaware v. Prouse,* 440 U.S. 648, 99 S.Ct. 1391, 59 L.Ed.2d 660 (1979), the Supreme Court held that police could not stop a single automobile at random without particular suspicion that the motorist was violating the law. In his majority opinion, Justice White wrote that the Fourth Amendment prohibited police from stopping an automobile "except in those situations in which there is at least articulable and reasonable suspicion that a motorist is unlicensed or that an automobile is not registered, or that either the vehicle or an occupant is otherwise subject to seizure for a violation of the law." 440 U.S. at 663, 99 S.Ct. at 1401, 59 L.Ed.2d at 673. On the other hand, White opined, States are not precluded from "developing" methods for spot checks that involve less intrusion or that do not involve the unconstrained exercise of discretion. 440 U.S. at 663, 99 S.Ct. at 1401, 59 L. ed.2d at 673. He suggested that "questioning of all oncoming traffic at roadblock-type stops is one possible alternative." 440 U.S. at 663, 99 S.Ct. at 1401, 59 L.Ed.2d at 674.

Because roadblocks do constitute a restraint on the liberty of the motorist, courts have held that they are susceptible to challenge under the Fourth Amendment. Police agencies, therefore, must take care that roadblocks are established and operated according to guidelines that minimize the inconvenience to motorists and constrain the exercise of discretion by police officers.

In *Michigan Dept. of State Police v. Sitz,* 496 U.S. 444, 110 S.Ct. 2481, 110 L.Ed.2d 412 (1990), the Supreme Court upheld the use of roadblocks for conducting field sobriety tests. In *Sitz,* the Michigan State Police operated a pilot roadblock program under guidelines drafted by an advisory committee. The roadblocks operated essentially as follows. Checkpoints were established at predetermined points along state highways. All vehicles passing through the checkpoints were stopped, and drivers were briefly observed for signs of intoxication. The average length of the stop was less than thirty seconds, except in cases where drivers appeared to be intoxicated. These drivers were instructed to pull their vehicles over to the side of the road for a license and registration check and, if indicated, a field sobriety test. Those who failed the test were placed under arrest. At one checkpoint, which was in operation for 75 minutes, 126 vehicles were stopped. Two drivers were given field sobriety tests, and one was arrested for driving under the influence of alcohol. One vehicle failed to stop at the roadblock, but was apprehended and its drivers arrested for driving under the influence (DUI).

Level 3: Investigatory Detention

The third level of police encounter involves the so-called stop-and-frisk discussed in Chapter 14. A more descriptive term for this type of encounter is

---

CASE IN POINT

THE USE OF ROADBLOCKS

The Heard County, Georgia, sheriff's department received an anonymous call alleging that a party was going on at a certain address, and that teenagers there were drinking alcohol and using drugs. Similar calls had been received in the past regarding this address. Police immediately set up a roadblock on the road between the house and the state highway. The roadblock was designed to stop vehicles going in either direction. Appellant's van was stopped. Police smelled alcohol on appellant and instructed him to exit the car for a field sobriety test. While the test was being administered, an officer leaned into the car and, according to his later testimony, looked over the driver's seat to look for weapons. On the floor of the van, the officer found a small plastic bag containing a white powder. Appellant was arrested and later convicted for possession of cocaine. On appeal, the Georgia Court of Appeals upheld the conviction against appellant's challenge to the use of the roadblock. In upholding the trial court's finding that the roadblock was founded on a legitimate concern for public safety, the appellate court noted that the roadblock had been ordered and conducted by an experienced senior officer.

Brimer v. State, 411 S.E.2d 128 (Ga. App. 1991).

"investigatory detention." Police are permitted to detain persons temporarily for questioning as long as they have reasonable suspicion that criminal activity is afoot. Police may then perform a limited "pat-down" search of the suspect's outer clothing to ascertain whether the suspect is armed. In conducting the "frisk," police may seize items that plainly feel like contraband. See *Minnesota v. Dickerson*, discussed in Chapter 14.

The Supreme Court has said that investigatory detentions must be brief (unless, that is, they confirm police suspicions of criminal conduct). *Dunaway v. New York*, 442 U.S. 200, 99 S.Ct. 2248, 60 L.Ed. 2d 824 (1979). Nevertheless, the Supreme Court has been disinclined to place an arbitrary time limit on detention. Instead, the Court has considered the purpose of the stop and the reasonableness of the time required for the police to obtain any additional required information. This approach looks at the totality of the circumstances to determine whether there has been an infringement of the suspect's Fourth Amendment rights. In *Florida v. Royer*, 460 U.S. 491, 103 S.Ct. 1319, 75 L.Ed.2d 229 (1983), the Court held that a fifteen-minute detention of a suspect in a police room was unreasonable where the police detained the suspect while they brought his luggage to him. Yet, a twenty-minute detention of a truck driver stopped on suspicion of transporting marijuana was found to be reasonable, since the time was used by police in pursuing a second, related vehicle necessary to the investigation, and the suspect's actions contributed to the delay. *United States v. Sharpe*, 470 U.S. 675, 105 S.Ct. 1568, 84 L.Ed. 2d 605 (1985). Consequently, while detention must be brief in stop-and-frisk situations, the time span must be evaluated in light of the totality of circumstances. In *State v. Merklein*, 388 So. 2d 218 (Fla. App. 1980), the court said it was reasonable for officers to detain suspects for 20 to 40 minutes pending arrival of another officer, witnesses, and the victim of a robbery.

A valid "*Terry*-stop" does not necessarily permit an officer to conduct a frisk. Rather, it is the need for protection of the police that justifies a frisk. Therefore, an officer who undertakes to frisk a suspect must be able to point to specific facts and reasonable inferences to believe the individual is armed. Initially a frisk is limited to a pat-down search of an individual's outer garments. If during the pat-down search the officer feels an object that may be a weapon, the officer may seize it. If it turns out that the object is other than a weapon, it may still be seized if it is contraband. As noted, a stop-and-frisk may be based on reasonable suspicion, but absent probable cause, an officer is not justified in simply searching a suspect for contraband when a pat-down does not reveal any weapon-like objects. *Terry v. Ohio, supra*.

In *Ybarra v. Illinois*, 444 U.S. 85, 100 S.Ct. 338, 62 L.Ed.2d 238 (1979), the Supreme Court ruled that since police could not show any specific facts to support their belief that the suspect was armed and dangerous, they had no grounds for frisking him. The Court has made it amply clear that a frisk must be based on an officer's reasonable suspicion that the suspect is armed, rather than on a desire to locate incriminating evidence. *Sibron v. New York*, 392 U.S. 40, 88 S.Ct. 1889, 20 L.Ed.2d 917 (1968). However, under the doctrine of "plain view" (discussed in Chapter 14), contraband that is discovered during a legitimate pat-down for weapons may be admissible into evidence. For example, if during the course of a lawful frisk, a police officer feels what he suspects is a knife concealed in the suspect's pocket, the officer may retrieve the object. If the object turns out to be a metal smoking pipe wrapped inside a plastic bag containing "crack" cocaine, the crack would most likely be admissible as evidence of crime.

Lower federal and state courts have routinely applied the stop-and-frisk doctrine to stops of vehicles as well as individuals. In many instances, this was stipulated in local statutes codifying the *Terry* standard; otherwise it was based on the *Terry* rationale. Of course, as in the case of the individual on the street, police must have reasonable suspicion that criminal activity is afoot before they can stop a single motor vehicle. *Delaware v. Prouse, supra.*

Normal police practice is for the officer who makes an automobile stop to examine the suspect and his or her vehicle registration and license plate, to scan objects being carried or transported, and to confirm the suspect's identification. If necessary, the officer verifies any explanation the suspect offers, and checks with the station house to find out if there are any outstanding arrest warrants for the suspect.

In 1983 the Supreme Court held that when police stop an automobile based on reasonable suspicion, they may search the passenger compartment for weapons, assuming they have reason to believe—based on specific and articulable factors, together with rational inferences—that a suspect is dangerous. The search, of course, must be limited to those areas in which a weapon may be placed or hidden. *Michigan v. Long,* 463 U.S. 1032, 103 S.Ct. 3469, 77 L.Ed.2d 1201 (1983). In determining whether an officer possessed such a reasonable suspicion, courts look to many factors. Among these are the knowledge, expertise, and experience of the officer; the physical appearance of a person or vehicle as fitting the description of a person or vehicle wanted for a crime, the item and place where the suspect or vehicle is seen, and their nearness to the scene of a crime. Additionally, the suspect's demeanor and any furtive gestures or attempts to flee are relevant considerations.

In recent years police have developed "drug courier profiles" based on typical characteristics and behaviors of drug smugglers. The profiles include such factors as paying cash for airline tickets, taking short trips to drug-source cities, not checking luggage, appearing nervous, etc. Police often use these profiles to identify and detain suspected drug couriers, a controversial practice that has resulted in disparate court decisions. In 1989, the Supreme Court upheld an investigative stop of an air passenger for which a number circumstances, including the use of the profile, furnished the police a reasonable suspicion of criminal activity. While the Court found that any one of the several factors relied on by the police may have been consistent with innocent travel, it observed that the evaluation of the validity of the stop requires a consideration of the "totality of the circumstances." *United States v. Sokolow,* 490 U.S. 1, 109 S.Ct. 1581, 104 L.Ed. 2d 1 (1989).

Although the Supreme Court has upheld the use of profiles in locating suspicious persons, courts must remain on guard against abuse of the practice. In 1990, a Minnesota appellate court reversed a conviction in which the defendant's automobile had been stopped not on the basis of a particular suspicion, but because the driver's behavior loosely fit the police profile of a person looking for prostitutes. In rejecting the use of the profile, the court distinguished the case from *Sokolow, supra,* saying that "the observable facts taken together do not approach the composite bundle available to the DEA in *Sokolow." City of St. Paul v. Uber,* 450 N.W. 2d 623, 626 (Minn. App. 1990). The court concluded that "we cannot sustain what was, in effect, a random stop." 450 N.W.2d at 629.

CASE IN POINT

DRUG COURIER PROFILES

An interesting, but fairly typical, description of the use of a drug courier profile by federal customs agents is found in *United States v. Gomez-Norena*, 908 F.2d 497, 498 (9th Cir. 1990). Quoting from the opinion:

. . . Late in the afternoon of Friday, January 22, 1988, Avianca Airlines Flight Number 80 from Bogota, Colombia touched down at Los Angeles International Airport. Near the passenger arrival gate, and behind a screening podium, stood United States Customs Inspector Sergio Espinoza. As a "rover screener," Espinoza had to evaluate each disembarking passenger according to a "drug courier profile." Espinoza's scanning eyes fixed on Gomez, who walked aimlessly down the concourse with a carry-on bag in his hand and a "dumbfounded" look on his face. After failing to attract Gomez's attention in English, Espinoza used Spanish to hail Gomez over to the podium.

A quick review of Gomez's ticket, passport and customs declaration enabled Espinoza to draw several inferences. First, Gomez had begun his trip from the reputed drug capital, Medellin, Colombia. Second, Gomez paid for his ticket with cash. Third, Gomez had an Australian visa and would be in the United States only for the three hours before his flight to Sydney. Fourth, the 23 year-old Gomez was a newcomer to internation travel. Fifth, Gomez had checked only one piece of baggage.

Consequently, Inspector Espinoza made a coded note of his suspicions on Gomez's customs declaration. He then told Gomez that he would have to visit the Immigration Office on the first level of the airport before he could go on to Sydney. As Gomez hurried away to make his stop, Espinoza called over Senior Customs Inspector Sal Zito, Inspector Harold Little and other members of the customs roving team. He told them to watch out for Mr. Gomez because he fit the drug courier profile.

Inspector Little met Gomez at the second customs inspection station. He searched both Gomez's carry-on bag and suitcase. He found clothing and some papers, including a letter of acceptance from the Australian College of English. Little then asked Gomez if he owned and packed the suitcase. Gomez answered, "Yes." Finding the small suitcase disproportionately heavy, Inspector Little began a "scratch test," rubbing his hands on the inside and the outside of the suitcase at the same time, in an effort to discover a hidden lining. The test confirmed Little's suspicions. He immediately called Senior Inspector Zito over to his work station. After Little related his suspicions, Zito passed the suitcase under a nearby X-ray machine and discovered a double compartment.

At that point, Inspectors Little and Espinoza ushered Gomez to the Customs search room. Espinoza's pat-down search revealed no weapons or contraband. Inspector Little drilled through the side of Gomez's suitcase and discovered two plastic bags containing roughly two kilograms of cocaine.

On appeal, the Court of Appeals upheld the detention, search, and seizure.

Level 4: Arrest

The fourth and highest level of encounter is arrest, where police take a person into custody or make it impossible for a person to leave after a reasonable period of time. Arrest is subject to the probable cause and warrant requirements of the Fourth Amendment, although there are exceptions to the latter. The Supreme Court has said that the legality of arrests by state and local officers is to be judged by the same constitutional standards applicable to federal agents. *Ker v. California*, 374 U.S. 23, 83 S. Ct. 1623, 10 L.Ed.2d 726 (1963).

Probable Cause to Make An Arrest

It is clear that for any arrest or significant deprivation of liberty to occur, police officers must have probable cause. Although not susceptible of precise definition, probable cause in the context of arrest means the same thing as in the context of search and seizure (see Chapter 14). The Supreme Court has said that probable cause exists

> where the facts and circumstances within . . . [the officers'] knowledge, and of which they had reasonably trustworthy information, . . . [are] sufficient in themselves to warrant a man of reasonable caution in the belief . . . [that a particular crime had been or was being committed]. *Carroll v. United States*, 267 U.S. 132, 162, 45 S. Ct. 280, 288, 69 L.Ed. 543, 555 (1925).

Police can establish probable cause without personally observing the commission of a crime as long as they have sufficient information to conclude that the suspect probably committed it. Officers often obtain their information from crime victims, eyewitnesses, official reports, and confidential or even anonymous informants. Such information is placed in an affidavit and submitted to a

---

CASE IN POINT

ARREST AND INTERROGATION

On March 26, 1971, the owner of a pizza parlor in Rochester, New York, was killed during an attempted armed robbery. Acting without a warning, police took Irving Dunaway into custody and interrogated him in connection with the attempted robbery and murder. Dunaway was not told that he was under arrest, but he was interrogated, confessed, and was ultimately convicted. On appeal, the state argued that although the police did not have probable cause to make an arrest, the "stationhouse detention" and interrogation of the suspect could be allowed on the lesser standard of reasonable suspicion. The Supreme Court reversed the conviction, saying that probable cause was necessary to justify a station-house detention and interrogation, irrespective of whether it is termed an "arrest."

Dunaway v. New York, 442 U.S. 200, 99 S. Ct. 2248, 60 L.Ed.2d 824 (1979).

County of _____ . State of _____ .

To any peace officer of said State:
Complaint on oath having this day been laid before me that the crime of _____
(designating it generally) has been committed and accusing _____
(naming defendant) thereof, you are therefore commanded forthwith to arrest the
above named defendant and bring him before me at _____
(naming the place), or in case of my absence or inability to act, before the nearest or
most accessible magistrate in this county.
Dated at _____ (place) this _____ day of _____, 19 ___.

_____

(Signature and full official title of magistrate.)

FIGURE 15.1   The Typical Form of an Arrest Warrant

magistrate who must determine whether the information establishes probable
cause to issue an arrest warrant.

In *Rawlings v. Kentucky,* 448 U.S. 98, 100 S.Ct. 2556, 65 L.Ed.2d 633 (1980), the
Supreme Court upheld a search incident to arrest even though the search briefly
preceded the arrest. The key point is that probable cause to make the arrest must
precede the search; police may not use the search as a means to justify the arrest.

The Warrant Requirement

An arrest warrant is routine in those cases where arrests are to be made based on
a secret investigation of criminal activity (fig. 15.1). In such cases suspects are
often not aware that they are under investigation, and police officers have ample
time to obtain an arrest warrant without fear that suspects will flee. However,
most arrests are not made pursuant to secret investigations but are made by
police officers who observe a criminal act, respond to a complaint filed by a crime
victim, or have probable cause to arrest after completing an investigation. In such
cases it is often unnecessary for police to obtain an arrest warrant, but it is always
essential that they have probable cause to make the arrest.

Warrantless Arrests

At common law, police had the right to make a warrantless arrest if they
observed someone in the commission of a felony or they had probable cause to
believe that a person had committed or was committing a felony. To make a
warrantless arrest for a misdemeanor, an officer had to observe someone in the
commission of the act. Otherwise, to make an arrest, a warrant was required. *In
re Kellam,* 41 P. 960 (Kan. 1895).

Many states adopted common-law rules of arrest in statutes allowing police
officers broad discretion to make warrantless arrests. As with warrantless
searches and seizures, the Supreme Court has approved warrantless arrests:
(1) where crimes are ccmmitted in plain view of police officers; or (2) officers

possess probable cause to make an arrest, but .exigent circumstances prohibit them from obtaining a warrant. Absent plain view or compelling exigencies, the need to obtain an arrest warrant is unclear. As a matter of policy, it makes sense for police officers to obtain arrest warrants when possible. However, given the time it takes to obtain an arrest warrant and the fact that magistrates are not always available around the clock, it is not always feasible for police to obtain warrants prior to arrest.

The Supreme Court has upheld the authority of police officers to make warrantless arrests in public, assuming probable cause to do so. *United States v. Watson,* 423 U.S. 411, 96 S. Ct. 820, 46 L.Ed.2d 598 (1976). More problematic are warrantless arrests involving forcible entry of a dwelling. Here we encounter the classic Fourth Amendment concern for the sanctity of the home. For example, in *Payton v. New York,* 445 U.S. 573, 100 S. Ct. 1371, 63 L.Ed.2d 639 (1980), the Supreme Court held that, absent exigent circumstances, a warrantless, nonconsensual entry into a suspect's home to make a routine felony arrest violates the Fourth Amendment. In a footnote, the Court pointed out that, as of 1980, twenty-three states had laws permitting a warrantless entry into the home for the purpose of making an arrest, even in the absence of exigent circumstances. 445 U.S. at 598, n. 46, 100 S.Ct. at 1386, n. 46, 63 L.Ed.2d at 658, n. 46.

Courts are generally inclined to uphold warrantless entries into homes for the purpose of arrest if the following conditions are met:

- There is probable cause to arrest the suspect.
- The police have good reason to believe the suspect is on the premises.
- There is good reason to believe the suspect is armed and dangerous.
- There is a strong probability that the suspect will escape or evidence will be destroyed if the suspect is not soon apprehended.
- The entry can be effected peaceably.
- The offense under investigation is a serious felony.

It should be noted that where there has been an arrest without warrant, it is the duty of the police officer to promptly take the arrestee before a magistrate. See, for example, West's Ann. Cal. Penal Code § 849(a).

While the Supreme Court has recognized the practical necessity of permitting police to make warrantless arrests, it has stressed the need for immediate *ex post facto* judicial review of detention of a suspect. Writing for the Supreme Court in *Gerstein v. Pugh,* 420 U.S. 103, 95 S.Ct. 854, 43 L.Ed.2d 54 (1975), Justice Stewart observed that "once the suspect is in custody, . . . the reasons that justify dispensing with the magistrate's neutral judgment evaporate." 420 U.S. at 114, 95 S.Ct. at 863, 43 L.Ed.2d at 65. When a suspect is in custody pursuant to a warrantless arrest, "the detached judgment of a neutral magistrate is essential if the Fourth Amendment is to furnish meaningful protection from unfounded interference with liberty." 420 U.S. at 114, 95 S.Ct. at 863, 43 L.Ed.2d at 65. (For further discussion of probable cause hearings, see Chapter 16.)

Use of Force by Police Making Arrests

Since suspects frequently resist attempts to take them into custody, police officers must often use force in making arrests. Sometimes the use of force by police is challenged in civil suits for damages. Typically, in such cases, the courts have said that in making a lawful arrest, police officers may use such force as necessary to effect the arrest and prevent the escape of the suspect. See, for example, *Martyn v. Donlin*, 198 A.2d 700 (Conn. 1964). Generally, a police officer has less discretion to use force in apprehending suspected misdemeanants than suspected felons. See, for example, *City of Mason v. Banks*, 581 S.W.2d 621 (Tenn. 1979). Most states have statutes providing that police officers have the right to require bystanders to assist them in making arrests. See, for example, West's Ann. Cal. Penal Code § 839.

Nearly every state has a law governing the use of force by police attempting to make arrests. The Illinois statute on the use of force by police is typical. It provides that:

> A peace officer, or any person he has summoned or directed to assist him, need not retreat or desist from efforts to make a lawful arrest because of resistance or threatened resistance to the arrest. He is justified in the use of any force which he reasonably believes to be necessary to effect the arrest and of any force which he reasonably believes to be necessary to defend himself or another from bodily harm while making the arrest. However, he is justified in using force likely to cause death or great bodily harm only when he reasonably believes that such force is necessary to prevent death or great bodily harm to himself or other such person, or when he reasonably believes both that:
>
> 1. Such force is necessary to prevent the arrest from being defeated by resistance or escape; and
> 2. The person to be arrested has committed or attempted a forcible felony which involves the infliction or threatened infliction of great bodily harm or is attempting to escape by use of a deadly weapon, or otherwise indicates that he will endanger human life or inflict great bodily harm unless arrested without delay. S.H.A. 720 ILCS 517–5(a).

In *Tennessee v. Garner*, 471 U.S. 1, 105 S. Ct. 1694, 85 L.Ed.2d 1 (1985), the Supreme Court struck down a statute that permitted police to use deadly force against fleeing suspects even when there was no threat to the safety of the officer or the public. This ruling effectively narrowed the discretion of police officers in using force to make arrests and broadened the possibility for civil actions against police for using excessive force.

Concern over police brutality took center stage in 1991, when the nation viewed on television a videotape of what appeared to be the unnecessarily brutal beating of motorist Rodney King by Los Angeles police officers. In response to public outrage, four police officers involved in the incident were prosecuted by state authorities for assault and battery and related crimes. On the motion of the defense, the trial was moved out of Los Angeles to a suburban community. No one can forget the riot that ensued in Los Angeles in April 1992 after the jury returned its verdict of "not guilty." In response to the widespread perception that a miscarriage of justice had occurred, the U.S. Justice Department launched its own investigation of the case. In the summer of 1992, a federal grand jury indicted the four officers for violating Rodney King's Fourth Amendment rights. In April 1993, a trial jury returned verdicts of guilty against two of the officers; the other two were acquitted.

CRIMINAL PROVISIONS OF FEDERAL CIVIL RIGHTS LAWS

As the federal trials of four police officers accused in the Rodney King beating case indicates, police officers who use excessive force or engage in acts of brutality toward suspects are subject to prosecution under Title 18 of the U.S. Code Ann., Sections 241 and 242. These statutes provide:

§ 241. *Conspiracy against rights of citizens*

If two or more persons conspire to injure, oppress, threaten, or intimidate any citizen in the free exercise or enjoyment of any right or privilege secured to him by the Constitution or laws of the United States, or because of his having so exercised the same; or

If two or more persons go in disguise on the highway, or on the premises of another, with intent to prevent or hinder his free exercise or enjoyment of any right or privilege so secured—

They shall be fined not more than $10,000 or imprisoned not more than ten years, or both; and if death results, they shall be subject to imprisonment for any term of years or for life.

§ 242. *Deprivation of rights under color of law*

Whoever, under color of any law, statute, ordinance, regulation, or custom, willfully subjects any inhabitant of any State, Territory, or District to the deprivation of any rights, privileges or immunities secured or protected by the Constitution or laws of the United States, or to different punishments, pains or penalties, on account of such inhabitant being an alien, or by reason of his color, or race, than are prescribed for the punishment of citizens, shall be fined not more than $10,000 or imprisoned not more than one year, or both; and if death results shall be subject to imprisonment for any term of years or for life.

"Citizen's Arrest"

At common law, a private individual could make an arrest without a warrant for a felony or breach of the peace committed in the presence of that individual. See *Malley v. Lane,* 115 A. 674 (Conn. 1921). The common-law rule prevails in some states; in others it has been revised by statute. A California law enacted in 1872 broadens the common law in that it permits a private person to make a warrantless arrest in any of three situations. It states that:

A private person may arrest another:
1. For a public offense committed or attempted in his presence.
2. When the person arrested has committed a felony, although not in his presence.
3. When a felony has been in fact committed, and he has reasonable cause for believing the person arrested to have committed it.

West's Ann. Cal. Penal Code § 837.

Arrests for Minor Traffic Offenses

In most states a police officer may either make an arrest or issue a summons to a person who commits a minor traffic violation. Generally, police exercise their discretion by giving the motorist a "ticket," yet there is little judicial guidance in regard to the proper action to be taken. The Supreme Court has never ruled on the question of whether an arrest for a minor traffic offense violates any constitutional protection. Critics argue that arrests in lieu of citations may often

"You are under arrest. You have the right to remain silent. Anything you say can and will be used against you in a court of law. You are entitled to have an attorney present during questioning. If you cannot afford an attorney, one will be appointed to represent you."

FIGURE 15.2   The *Miranda* Warnings

be pretextual so that police can conduct a search incident to a lawful arrest. See *Gustafson v. Florida*, 414 U.S. 260, 94 S. Ct. 488, 38 L.Ed.2d 456 (1973).

That this area of broad police discretion is subject to abuse was recognized in *State v. Hehman*, 578 P.2d 527 (Wash. 1978), where the Washington Supreme Court ruled that arrests for minor traffic offenses are unjustified if the defendant signs a promise to appear in court as provided by statute. By contrast, an Illinois appellate court upheld the arrest and jailing of a motorist for lacking a front license plate and being unable to produce a driver's license. *People v. Pendleton*, 433 N.E.2d 1076 (Ill. App. 1982).

As an alternative, states can decriminalize certain traffic violations and permit persons cited for such infractions to accept citations and agree to pay a stipulated civil fine or appear in court on schedule. Florida adopted such a statutory scheme in 1974 excepting certain offenses such as leaving the scene of an accident and driving under the influence of drugs or alcohol. West's Fla. Stat. Ann. § 318.14. Further reform could be accomplished by having contested infractions resolved by hearing officers authorized to impose civil fines. On November 8, 1988, voters in Florida approved a constitutional amendment to permit this. These fines could be suspended for violators who complete traffic school training courses.

INTERROGATION AND CONFESSIONS

To safeguard the constitutional rights of suspects, the Supreme Court has held that before interrogating suspects who are in custody, police must warn them of their right to remain silent and their right to have counsel present during questioning. Unless these warnings have been given, no statement made by the suspect may be used in evidence, subject to certain narrow exceptions. *Miranda v. Arizona*, 384 U.S. 436, 86 S. Ct. 1602, 16 L.Ed.2d 694 (1966). The *Miranda* decision was severely criticized by law enforcement interests when it was handed down in 1966. After some twenty years, it has come to be accepted, even supported, by most law enforcement agencies and has been integrated into routine police procedure.

The Public Safety Exception to *Miranda*

Police generally provide the *Miranda* warnings (fig. 15.2) immediately upon arrest or as soon as is practicable, in order to preserve as evidence any statements that the suspect might make. However, in some situations the *Miranda* warnings are delayed because police are preoccupied with apprehending other individuals or taking actions to protect themselves or others on the scene. In *New York v. Quarles,* 467 U.S. 649, 104 S. Ct. 2626, 81 L.Ed.2d 550 (1984), the Supreme Court recognized a public safety exception to the *Miranda* exclusionary rule. Under *Quarles,* police may ask suspects questions designed to locate weapons that might be used to harm the police or other persons before providing the *Miranda* warnings. If this interaction produces incriminating statements or physical evidence, the evidence need not be suppressed.

What Constitutes an Interrogation?

Although interrogation normally occurs at the station house after arrest, it may occur anywhere. For the purpose of determining when the *Miranda* warnings must be given, the Supreme Court has defined interrogation as "express questioning or its functional equivalent," including "any words or actions on the part of the police that the police should know are reasonably likely to elicit an incriminating response from the suspect." *Rhode Island v. Innis,* 446 U.S. 291, 301, 100 S. Ct. 1682, 1693, 64 L.Ed.2d 297, 308 (1980). Before police may engage in such interaction, they must provide the *Miranda* warnings or risk the possibility that useful incriminating statements will be suppressed as illegally obtained evidence.

Waiver of *Miranda* Rights

It is axiomatic that all constitutional rights may be waived. A suspect may elect to waive the right to remain silent and/or the right to have counsel present during questioning as long as he or she does so voluntarily. Courts are apt to strictly scrutinize waivers to make sure they were not the product of some coercion or deception by police. For example, in *United States v. Blocker,* 354 F. Supp. 1195 (D. D.C. 1973), a federal district court observed that a written waiver signed by the accused is not in itself conclusive evidence. "The court must still decide whether, in view of all the circumstances, defendant's subsequent decision to speak was a product of his free will." 354 F. Supp. at 1198 n. 11.

Perhaps no case has tested the Supreme Court's commitment to *Miranda* and its willingness to scrutinize an alleged waiver of rights more than did *Brewer v. Williams,* 430 U.S. 387, 97 S. Ct. 1232, 51 L.Ed.2d 424 (1977). Williams was convicted of having abducted a 10-year-old girl from a YMCA in Des Moines, Iowa, and later murdering her. Upon arrest, he was given the *Miranda* warnings, and he indicated that he wished to consult with counsel before answering questions. Before Williams was able to meet with his attorney, police elicited damaging statements from him, which were later used to obtain a conviction for first-degree murder. The Supreme Court reversed Williams's conviction and granted him a new trial, holding that he had not waived his rights to remain silent and consult with his lawyer before talking to police. In overturning Williams's conviction, the Court said:

> The crime of which Williams was convicted was senseless and brutal, calling for swift and energetic action by the police to apprehend the perpetrator and gather evidence with which he could be convicted. No mission of law enforcement officials is more

important. . . . The pressures on . . . judicial officers charged with the administration of the criminal law are great, especially when the crime is murder and the victim a small child. But it is precisely the predictability of those pressures that makes imperative a resolute loyalty to the guarantees that the Constitution extends to us all. 430 U.S. at 406, 97 S. Ct. at 1243, 51 L.Ed.2d at 441.

At Williams's second trial the jury was not permitted to learn of the incriminating statements he made to the police. He was convicted nevertheless, based largely on evidence derived from the girl's corpse. The body was discovered when Williams, prior to meeting with his attorney, led police to the place where he had dumped it. On subsequent review by an appellate tribunal, Williams argued that evidence of the body was improperly admitted at trial, because its discovery was based on inadmissible statements and thus constituted the "fruit of a poisonous tree." Again the case went all the way to the United States Supreme Court. It held that the evidence of the body was properly admissible at trial because a search party operating in the area where the body was discovered would eventually have located the body, even without assistance from the defendant. *Nix v. Williams*, 467 U.S. 431, 104 S. Ct. 2501, 81 L.Ed.2d 377 (1984).

Although they must honor a suspect's refusal to cooperate, police are under no duty to inform a suspect who is considering whether to cooperate that an attorney has already been arranged for him. In *Moran v. Burbine*, 475 U.S. 412, 106 S. Ct. 1135, 89 L.Ed.2d 410 (1986), police arrested a man on a burglary charge and subsequently linked him to an unsolved murder. The suspect's sister, not aware that a murder charge was about to be filed against her brother, arranged for a lawyer to represent her brother on the burglary charge. The attorney contacted the police to arrange a meeting with her client. The police did not mention the possible murder charge and told the attorney that her client was not going to be questioned until the next day. The police then began to interrogate Burbine, failing to tell him that a lawyer had been arranged for him and had attempted to contact him. Burbine waived his rights and eventually confessed to the murder. The Supreme Court upheld the use of the confession in evidence.

Voluntariness of Confessions

Even where police officers provide the *Miranda* warnings and the suspect agrees to talk to police without having counsel present, a confession elicited from the suspect is inadmissible if it is obtained through coercion, whether physical intimidation or psychological pressure. *United States v. Tingle*, 658 F.2d 1332 (9th Cir. 1981).

Although the courts have always recognized the need for police interrogation of suspects, they have also recognized the potential for violation of an individual's constitutional rights. At early common law, any confession was admissible even if extracted from the accused by torture. As the common law progressed, judges came to insist on proof that a confession was made voluntarily before it could be admitted in evidence. See *Baughman v. Commonwealth*, 267 S.W. 231 (Ky. 1924).

In 1897 the Supreme Court held that to force a suspect to confess violates the Fifth Amendment. *Bram v. United States*, 168 U.S. 532, 18 S. Ct. 183, 42 L.Ed. 568.

CASE IN POINT

Coerced Confessions

As an example of psychological coercion, a confession was ruled involuntary where a defendant was incarcerated and subjected to questioning over a four-day period. The defendant's relatives were denied permission to see him, and he was unable to communicate with anyone outside the jail. At one point during the interrogation, defendant was forced to hold for twenty-five minutes a gory picture of the deceased lying in a pool of blood.

Davis v. State, 308 S.W.2d 880, 882 (Tex. Crim. App. 1957).

In 1936 the Court held that a coerced confession deprived a defendant in a state criminal case due process of law as guaranteed by the Fourteenth Amendment. *Brown v. Mississippi*, 297 U.S. 278, 56 S. Ct. 461, 80 L.Ed. 682. In 1964 the self-incrimination clause was made applicable to state criminal prosecutions. *Malloy v. Hogan*, 378 U.S. 1, 84 S. Ct. 1489, 12 L.Ed.2d 653. As a result, federal and state police are held to the same standards in evaluating the voluntariness of confessions of guilt. In *Malloy*, the Court said that the Fifth Amendment prohibits the extraction of a confession by "exertion of any improper influence." 378 U.S. at 7, 84 S. Ct. at 1493, 12 L.Ed.2d at 659. A confession is voluntary when it is made with knowledge of its nature and consequences and without duress or inducement. *United States v. Carignan*, 342 U.S. 36, 72 S. Ct. 97, 96 L.Ed. 48 (1951).

In the landmark *Miranda* decision, the Supreme Court recognized the inherently coercive atmosphere of police interrogation and imposed the famous *Miranda* warnings as a means of protecting the constitutional rights of suspects. Two years earlier, the Court had recognized the right of suspects to have counsel present during interrogation. *Escobedo v. Illinois*, 378 U.S. 478, 84 S. Ct. 1758, 12 L.Ed.2d 977 (1964). *Miranda* and *Escobedo* were a response to what the Supreme Court perceived to be the inherently coercive environment of custodial interrogation. The Court's opinion in *Miranda* was concerned as much with the psychological means of coercing confessions as with physical coercion.

A classic example of psychological coercion is the so-called Mutt-and-Jeff strategy. Under this tactic, one police officer, the "bad guy," is harsh, rude, and aggressive, while another police officer, the "good guy," is friendly and sympathetic to the suspect. Obviously the objective of the strategy is to get the accused to confess to the "good guy," and there is reason to believe that it is an effective technique. There is controversy over whether the Mutt-and-Jeff tactic is a constitutional means of eliciting a confession from a suspect who has waived his or her *Miranda* rights and agreed to talk to police without the presence of counsel. In *Miranda*, the Supreme Court alluded to the Mutt-and-Jeff routine as a possible example of impermissible psychological coercion. 384 U.S. at 452, 86 S. Ct. at 1614 16 L.Ed.2d at 711. Yet, absent other indications of coercion, courts have generally acquiesced in the practice.

Police Deception

The use of tricks or factual misstatements by police in an effort to induce a defendant to confess does not automatically invalidate a confession. A misstatement by police may affect the voluntariness of a confession, but the effect of any misstatements must be considered in light of the totality of surrounding circumstances. In *Frazier v. Cupp,* 394 U.S. 731, 89 S.Ct. 1420, 22 L.Ed.2d 684 (1969), the Supreme Court reversed a conviction where the police had falsely informed a suspect that his codefendant had confessed. While the Supreme Court found the misstatement relevant to the issue of whether the confession had been given voluntarily, it did not find that the misstatement per se made the confession inadmissible. The Nebraska Supreme Court has held that even deceptive statements referring to nonexistent autopsies of victims will not automatically render a confession involuntary. *State v. Norfolk,* 381 N.W.2d 120 (Neb. 1986).

How far may police go in their use of deception? In 1989, a Florida appellate court, in a case of first impression, affirmed a trial judge's order holding a confession involuntary where police had presented fabricated laboratory reports to the defendant in order to secure a confession. The "reports," which were on stationery of a law enforcement agency and a DNA testing firm, indicated that traces of the defendant's semen had been found on the victim's underwear. Among the factors cited by the appellate court in support the exclusion of the confession were the indefinite life span of manufactured documents, their self-authenticating character, and the ease of duplication. The court expressed concern that false documents could find their way into police files or the courtroom and be accepted as genuine. *State v. Cayward,* 552 So.2d 971 (Fla. App. 1989).

Police deception must be distinguished from cases where the police use or threaten force or promise leniency to elicit a confession. In both instances, courts will suppress confessions obtained. See *Spano v. New York,* 360 U.S. 315, 79 S.Ct. 1202, 3 L.Ed.2d 1265 (1959). Moreover, when the police furnish a suspect an incorrect or incomplete advisory statement of the penalties provided by law for a particular crime, courts will generally suppress the suspect's confession. See, for example, *People v. Lytle,* 704 P.2d 331 (Colo. App. 1985).

Factors Considered by Judges in Evaluating Confessions

Judges consider a number of variables in determining whether a challenged confession was voluntary. These include the duration and methods of the interrogation, the length of the delay between arrest and appearance before a magistrate, the conditions of detention, the attitudes of the police toward the defendant, the defendant's physical and psychological state, and anything else that might bear on the defendant's resistance. *Commonwealth v. Kichline,* 361 A.2d 282, 290 (Pa. 1976). Courts are particularly cautious in receiving confessions by juveniles. See, for example, *Haley v. Ohio,* 332 U.S. 596, 68 S. Ct. 302, 92 L.Ed. 224 (1948).

In a landmark ruling, *Arizona v. Fulminante,* 499 U.S. 279, 111 S.Ct. 1246, 113 L.Ed.2d 302 (1991), the Supreme Court said that the use in evidence of a confession that should have been suppressed does not automatically require reversal of a defendant's conviction. Rather, the appellate court must determine whether the defendant would have been convicted in the absence of the confession. If so, the admission of the confession is deemed to be harmless error, which does not require reversal. See, for example, *People v. Lytle*, 704 P.2d 331 (Colo. App. 1985).

LINEUPS AND OTHER IDENTIFICATION PROCEDURES

The procedures employed by law enforcement agencies to assist in the identification of suspects fall into two basic categories. First, police rely on scientific means to match the physical evidence taken from a suspect with that found at a crime scene. These methods commonly include fingerprint identification, comparison of blood samples, matching of clothing fibers, head and body hair comparisons, identification of semen, and, more recently, DNA tests. When these methods are conducted by qualified persons, the results are usually admissible in evidence.

The three most common nonscientific methods of identification are the "showup," the "photo pack," and the "lineup." In a showup, the police take the victim to the suspect to see if the former can make an identification. While this method has been subject to criticism, when it occurs shortly after the crime has been committed and the showup is conducted near the scene of the crime, it is considered an acceptable method of securing an identification. *People v. Love*, 443 N.E.2d 948 (N.Y. 1982).

A photo pack is simply a set of "mug shots" that are shown individually to the victim or eyewitness in the hope that he or she will be able to identify the perpetrator. To produce a reliable, hence admissible, identification, the presentation of the photo pack should not emphasize one photo over the others. The words and actions of the officers making the presentation must manifest an attitude of disinterest. *State v. Thamer*, 777 P.2d 432 (Utah 1989). In analyzing a defendant's claim that he or she was the victim of an impermissibly suggestive photo pack identification, courts generally apply a two-part test. First, did the photo array present the defendant in an impermissibly suggestive posture? Second, if so, under the totality of circumstances, did the procedure give rise to a substantial likelihood of misidentification? *State v. Bedwell*, 417 N.W.2d 66 (Iowa 1987).

In a lineup, a group of individuals, one of whom is the suspect in custody, appear before a victim or witness, who is usually shielded from the suspect's view. Often, the individuals in the lineup are asked to walk, turn sideways, wear certain items of clothing, or speak to assist the victim or eyewitness in making a positive identification. The Supreme Court has said that the Fifth Amendment

> offers no protection against compulsion to submit to fingerprinting, photography, or measurements, to write or speak for identification, to appear in court, to stand, to assume a stance, to walk, or to make a particular gesture. *Schmerber v. California*, 384 U.S. 757, 764, 86 S. Ct. 1826, 1832, 16 L.Ed.2d 908, 916 (1966).

In the same vein, the Court has held that there is no Fifth Amendment immunity against being placed in a lineup as an identification procedure. *United States v.*

CASE IN POINT

Lineups

The following is the complete memorandum opinion of the New York Supreme Court, Appellate Division, in *People v. Ayala,* 542 N.Y.S.2d 91 (A.D. 1989). Only the citations to the state penal code and previous state court decisions have been deleted. The case is a good example of a fairly routine appeal challenging a police lineup. The case illustrates a lineup that was performed properly, providing the defendant no compelling basis to challenge the use in evidence of the crime victim's identification of him as the perpetrator.

Memorandum:

Defendant appeals from a judgment convicting him, following a jury trial, of three counts of robbery in the first degree, . . . criminal possession of a weapon in the second degree, . . . burglary in the second degree, . . . sodomy in the first degree. . . and assault in the second degree. . . . His principal claim is that evidence of a pretrial identification should have been suppressed and that, without such evidence, there is insufficient evidence to corroborate the testimony of an accomplice.

Defendant and three others, all of whom were armed and wearing ski masks, broke into a closed supermarket. They were unable to open the safe and waited for the store's employees to arrive. During the robbery, one store employee was shot, another pistol whipped, and a female employee was sodomized. A lineup was conducted during which defendant and the other participants wore ski masks. Each participant was asked to walk and speak two sentences. They then left the room, reappeared in different order and each again walked and spoke. The sodomy victim identified defendant as the robber who attacked her.

The defendant may be compelled to conform his appearance at a lineup to his appearance at the time of the crime, . . . and the subject lineup was not unduly suggestive because the participants were masked. The lineup participants were not grossly dissimilar to the defendant in height or weight and each spoke with a Spanish accent. During the course of the robbery, the victim had an opportunity to observe the physical appearance and to hear the voice of her attacker. Defense counsel was present at the lineup, and there is no claim that the police suggested that any person was the perpetrator. We conclude, therefore, that the procedure employed at the pretrial lineup was not unduly suggestive and that the court did not err in denying the motion to suppress. . . . The identification testimony of the witness was properly admitted at trial and constituted sufficient corroborative evidence.

We have reviewed the defendant's remaining claims and find them to lack merit.

Judgment unanimously affirmed.

Wade, 388 U.S. 218, 87 S. Ct. 1926, 18 L.Ed.2d 1149 (1967). Suspects may be asked to wear certain articles of clothing, *Holt v. United States,* 218 U.S. 245, 31 S. Ct. 2, 54 L.Ed. 1021 (1910); may be forced to give handwriting exemplars, *United States v. Mara,* 410 U.S. 19, 93 S.Ct. 774, 35 L.Ed.2d 99 (1973); or have their voices recorded for identification purposes, *United States v. Dionisio,* 410 U.S. 1, 93 S. Ct.

764, 35 L.Ed.2d 67 (1973). However, courts must guard against the possibility that identification procedures, especially lineups, are unfair by suggesting that a victim or witness identify a particular suspect as the perpetrator. See, for example, *Foster v. California,* 394 U.S. 440, 89 S.Ct. 1127, 22 L.Ed.2d 402 (1969). Obviously, if the perpetrator is known to have been black, it is impermissibly suggestive for police to place a black suspect in a lineup with five white individuals. In practice, however, it is the more subtle suggestiveness of lineups that causes problems for the courts. To avoid such problems, police should place several persons with similar physical characteristics in a lineup.

To further protect the rights of the accused, the Supreme Court has said that after formal charges have been made against a defendant, the defendant has the right to have counsel present at a lineup. *Kirby v. Illinois,* 406 U.S. 682, 92 S. Ct. 1877, 32 L.Ed.2d 411 (1972). To assure that police and prosecutors honor that right, the Supreme Court has said that a pretrial identification obtained in violation of the right to counsel is per se inadmissible at trial. *Gilbert v. California,* 388 U.S. 263, 87 S.Ct. 1951, 18 L.Ed.2d 1178 (1967). A per se exclusionary rule was deemed necessary to assure that the police and the prosecution would respect the defendant's right to have counsel present at a lineup. On the other hand, a pretrial identification obtained through impermissibly suggestive identification procedures is not per se inadmissible. Instead, such an identification may be introduced into evidence if the trial judge first finds that the witness' in-court identification is reliable and based on independent recall. In making this determination, the trial judge must consider: (1) the opportunity of the witness to view the accused at the time of the crime, (2) the witness' degree of attention, (3) the accuracy of the witness' prior description of the accused, (4) the level of certainty demonstrated at the confrontation, and (5) the time that elapsed between the crime and the confrontation. *Neil v. Biggers,* 409 U.S. 188, 93 S.Ct. 375, 34 L.Ed.2d 401 (1972); see also *Wethington v. State,* 560 N.E.2d 496 (Ind. 1990).

CONCLUSION

Police are permitted broad discretion in their interactions with the public. There are no legal prerequisites to the many consensual encounters through which police routinely perform their investigative and preventive duties. Nonconsensual encounters are subject to legal requirements. To stop and frisk requires an articulable basis of suspicion; to make an arrest, police must have probable cause to believe that a crime has been committed. When practicable, it is desirable that police obtain an arrest warrant, but this is not always essential to legitimate an arrest based on probable cause.

Even without probable cause, police are permitted to stop and frisk persons where there is reasonable suspicion that a crime is about to take place. Courts are still struggling with the permissible length and scope of such field detentions.

Persons who are detained or arrested by police possess a constitutional right to remain silent. Police may not even compel a suspicious person to identify himself or herself.

When police make an arrest, they must inform the suspect of the constitutional rights to remain silent and consult with counsel. Failure to do so jeopardizes the admissibility of incriminating statements that the suspect might make even voluntarily. It also jeopardizes the use of physical evidence discovered as a result of statements that are later held to be inadmissible. Although the courts are willing to recognize certain exceptional situations, the prudent police officer will "Mirandize" the suspect immediately upon arrest.

There is no constitutional prohibition against police taking fingerprints, voice samples, handwriting exemplars, and the like from suspects. Nor is there any prohibition against forcing suspects to appear in lineups for identification by a witness or victim, as long as police avoid suggesting the person to be identified.

It is fair to say that, despite the increased scrutiny of courts over the last several decades, law enforcement officers retain considerable discretion in making arrests, conducting investigations, and interviewing suspects. As long as certain essential safeguards are observed, police are not seriously hampered in their efforts to ferret out crime.

QUESTIONS FOR THOUGHT AND DISCUSSION

1. Operationally speaking, what is the difference between "probable cause" and "reasonable suspicion"? How long can police detain a suspect based on reasonable suspicion?

2. Police obtained a warrant to search a single-family residence for "illegal amphetamines and equipment used in the manufacture of same." The warrant also authorized the search of the person of Harry Hampton, described in the warrant as a white male, 32 years of age, 6 ft. 2 in., and 225 lbs. When they arrived at the scene, one officer began to search Hampton. When that search yielded contraband, another officer detained a second man sitting on the porch (he was later identified as Jimmy Jaffers). The officer subjected Jaffers to a pat-down search. No weapons were discovered on Jaffers' person, but the officer, having felt a "suspicious lump" in Jaffers' front pants pocket, retrieved a plastic bag of capsules that later proved to be illegal amphetamines. In a pretrial motion, Jaffers' counsel moves to suppress the contraband, arguing that his client was the victim of an unreasonable search. Is Jaffers likely to prevail in this contention?

3. A police officer on night patrol saw a car parked off a dirt road in an area known to be a "lovers' lane." As his cruiser approached the car, he observed a male and a female sitting inside. He noticed the male occupant make a movement that the officer interpreted as an attempt to hide something under the seat. The officer approached the vehicle and directed the occupants to get out. As they did, he observed a marijuana "roach" in the open ashtray. The officer then reached under the front seat and retrieved a small quantity of marijuana. The officer placed both individuals under arrest. In court the officer admitted that he was not concerned for his safety, but simply had a "hunch" that the couple could be "doing drugs." Did the officer make a legal arrest? Why or why not?

4. What are the practical arguments for and against allowing private citizens to make arrests when they observe criminal activity taking place? What is the law in your state governing "citizens' arrests"?

5. Does your state make any distinction between minor and serious traffic offenses in permitting arrests? Is the use of arrest procedures for relatively minor traffic offenses unnecessary? Is it better to give the individual police officer discretion in these matters, or to adopt laws decriminalizing such infractions?

6. In the *Miranda* case, the Supreme Court released a convicted rapist in order to impose a requirement that police advise suspects of their constitutional rights before conducting interrogations. Was the Court's decision a wise one? What has been the impact of the *Miranda* decision on law enforcement?

7. What factors do courts consider in determining whether an individual is "in custody" when a police interrogation takes place?

8. How might police coerce a suspect into waiving his rights to counsel and to remain silent during interrogation? How can courts ensure that cooperation with police was voluntary?

9. Are the courts correct in limiting the scope of the Fifth Amendment self-incrimination clause to verbal statements so that there is no constitutional protection against compulsory police identification procedures? What would be the implications for law enforcement if the courts included physical evidence like fingerprints or handwriting samples within the scope of the Fifth Amendment privilege?

10. Would it be permissible for police to construct a lineup including four visibly overweight persons along with a slim suspect where the victim told police that her assailant was "very thin"?

CASES

TERRY V. OHIO

Supreme Court of the United States, 1968.
392 U.S. 1, 88 S. Ct. 1868, 20 L.Ed.2d 889.

[In this landmark case, the U.S. Supreme Court considers whether police officers may stop and frisk persons based on "reasonable suspicion" that criminal activity is afoot.]

Mr. Chief Justice WARREN delivered the opinion of the Court.

... Petitioner Terry was convicted of carrying a concealed weapon and sentenced to the statutorily prescribed term of one to three years in the penitentiary. Following the denial of a pretrial motion to suppress, the prosecution introduced in evidence two revolvers and a number of bullets seized from Terry and a codefendant, Richard Chilton, by Cleveland police Detective Martin McFadden. At the hearing on the motion to suppress this evidence, Officer McFadden testified that while he was patrolling in plain clothes in downtown Cleveland at approximately 2:30 in the afternoon of October 31, 1963, his attention was attracted by two men, Chilton and Terry, standing on the corner of Huron Road and Euclid Avenue. He had never seen the two men before, and he was unable to say precisely what first drew his eye to them. However, he testified that he had been a policeman for 39 years and a detective for 35 and that he had been assigned to patrol this vicinity of downtown Cleveland for shoplifters and pickpockets for 30 years. He explained that he had developed routine habits of observation over the years and that he would "stand and watch people or walk and watch people at many intervals of the day." He added: "Now, in this case when I looked over they didn't look right to me at the time."

His interest aroused, Officer McFadden took up a post of observation in the entrance to a store 300 to 400 feet away from the two men. "I get more purpose to watch them when I seen their movements," he testified. He saw one of the men leave the other one and walk southwest on Huron Road, past some stores. The man paused for a moment and looked in a store window, then walked on a short distance, turned around and walked back toward the corner, pausing once again to look in the same store window. He rejoined his companion at the corner, and the two conferred briefly. Then the second man went through the same series of motions, strolling down Huron Road, looking in the same window, walking on a short distance, turning back, peering in the store window again, and returning to confer with the first man at the corner. The two men repeated this ritual alternately between five and six times apiece—in all, roughly a dozen trips. At one point, while the two were standing together on the corner, a third man approached them and engaged them briefly in conversation. This man then left the two others and walked west on Euclid Avenue. Chilton and Terry resumed their measured pacing, peering and conferring. After this had gone on for 10 to 12 minutes, the two men walked off together, heading west on Euclid Avenue, following the path taken earlier by the third man.

By this time Officer McFadden had become thoroughly suspicious. He testified that after observing their elaborately casual and oft-repeated reconnaissance of the store window on Huron Road, he suspected the two men of "casing a job, a stick-up," and that he considered it his duty as a police officer to investigate further. He added that he feared "they may have a gun." Thus, Officer McFadden followed Chilton and Terry and saw them stop in front of Zucker's store to talk to the same man who had conferred with them earlier on the street corner. Deciding that the situation was ripe for direct action, Officer McFadden approached the three men, identified himself as a police officer and asked for their names. At this point his knowledge was confined to what he had observed. He was not acquainted with any of the three men by name or by sight, and he had received no information concerning them from any other source. When the men "mumbled something" in response to his inquiries,

Officer McFadden grabbed petitioner Terry, spun him around so that they were facing the other two, with Terry between McFadden and the others, and patted down the outside of his clothing. In the left breast pocket of Terry's overcoat Officer McFadden felt a pistol. He reached inside the overcoat pocket, but was unable to remove the gun. At this point, keeping Terry between himself and the others, the officer ordered all three men to enter Zucker's store. As they went in, he removed Terry's overcoat completely, removed a .38-caliber revolver from the pocket and ordered all three men to face the wall with their hands raised. Officer McFadden proceeded to pat down the outer clothing of Chilton and the third man, Katz. He discovered another revolver in the outer pocket of Chilton's overcoat, but no weapons were found on Katz. The officer testified that he only patted the men down to see whether they had weapons, and that he did not put his hands beneath the outer garments of either Terry or Chilton until he felt his guns. So far as appears from the record, he never placed his hands beneath Katz' other garments. Officer McFadden seized Chilton's gun, asked the proprietor of the store to call a police wagon, and took all three men to the station, where Chilton and Terry were formally charged with carrying concealed weapons. . . .

After the court denied their motion to suppress, Chilton and Terry waived jury trial and pleaded not guilty. The court adjudged them guilty, and the Court of Appeals for the Eighth Judicial District, Cuyahoga County, affirmed. The Supreme Court of Ohio dismissed their appeal. . . . We granted certiorari . . . to determine whether the admission of the revolvers in evidence violated petitioner's rights under the Fourth Amendment. . . . We affirm the conviction. . . .

Our first task is to establish at what point in this encounter the Fourth Amendment becomes relevant. That is, we must decide whether and when Officer McFadden "seized" Terry and whether and when he conducted a "search." There is some suggestion in the use of such terms as "stop" and "frisk" that such police conduct is outside the purview of the Fourth Amendment because neither action rises to the level of a "search" or "seizure" within the meaning of the Constitution. We emphatically reject this notion. It is quite plain that the

Fourth Amendment governs "seizures" of the person which do not eventuate in a trip to the station house and prosecution for crime—"arrests" in traditional terminology. It must be recognized that whenever a police officer accosts an individual and restrains his freedom to walk away, he has "seized" that person. And it is nothing less than sheer torture of the English language to suggest that a careful exploration of the outer surfaces of a person's clothing all over his or her body in an attempt to find weapons is not a "search." Moreover, it is simply fantastic to urge that such a procedure performed in public by a policeman while the citizen stands helpless, perhaps facing a wall with his hands raised, is a "petty indignity." It is a serious intrusion upon the sanctity of the person, which may inflict great indignity and arouse strong resentment, and it is not to be undertaken lightly.

The danger in the logic which proceeds upon distinctions between a "stop" and an "arrest," or "seizure" of the person, and between a "frisk" and a "search" is two-fold. It seeks to isolate from constitutional scrutiny the initial stages of the contact between the policeman and the citizen. And by suggesting a rigid all-or-nothing model of justification and regulation under the Amendment, it obscures the utility of limitations upon the scope, as well as the initiation, of police action as a means of constitutional regulation. This Court has held in the past that a search which is reasonable at its inception may violate the Fourth Amendment by virtue of its intolerable intensity and scope. . . . The scope of the search must be "strictly tied to and justified by" the circumstances which rendered its initiation permissible. . . .

The distinctions of classical "stop-and-frisk" theory thus serve to divert attention from the central inquiry under the Fourth Amendment—the reasonableness in all the circumstances of the particular governmental invasion of a citizen's personal security. "Search" and "seizure" are not talismans. We therefore reject the notions that the Fourth Amendment does not come into play at all as a limitation upon police conduct if the officers stop short of something called a "technical arrest" or a "full-blown search."

In this case there can be no question, then, that Officer McFadden "seized" petitioner and subjected him to a "search" when he took hold of him and patted down the outer surfaces of his clothing. We must decide whether at that point it was reasonable for Officer McFadden to have interfered with petitioner's personal security as he did. And in determining whether the seizure and search were "unreasonable" our inquiry is a dual one—whether the officer's action was justified at its inception, and whether it was reasonably related in scope to the circumstances which justified the interference in the first place. . . .

We must now examine the conduct of Officer McFadden in this case to determine whether his search and seizure of petitioner were reasonable, both at their inception and as conducted. He had observed Terry, together with Chilton and another man, acting in a manner he took to be preface to a "stick-up." We think on the facts and circumstances Officer McFadden detailed before the trial judge a reasonably prudent man would have been warranted in believing petitioner was armed and thus presented a threat to the officer's safety while he was investigating his suspicious behavior. The actions of Terry and Chilton were consistent with McFadden's hypothesis that these men were contemplating a daylight robbery—which, it is reasonable to assume, would be likely to involve the use of weapons—and nothing in their conduct from the time he first noticed them until the time he confronted them and identified himself as a police officer gave him sufficient reason to negate the hypothesis. Although the trio had departed the original scene, there was nothing to indicate abandonment of an intent to commit a robbery at some point. Thus when Officer McFadden approached the three men gathered before the display window at Zucker's store he had observed enough to make it quite reasonable to fear that they were armed; and nothing in their response to his hailing them, identifying himself as a police officer, and asking their names served to dispel that reasonable belief. We cannot say his decision at that point to seize Terry and pat his clothing for weapons was the product of a volatile or inventive imagination, or was undertaken simply as an act of harassment; the record evidences the tempered act of a policeman who in the course of an investigation had to make a quick decision as to how to protect himself and others from possible danger, and took limited steps to do so.

The manner in which the seizure and search were conducted is, of course, as vital a part of the inquiry as whether they were warranted at all. The Fourth Amendment proceeds as much by limitations upon the scope of governmental action as by imposing preconditions upon its initiation. The entire deterrent purpose of the rule excluding evidence seized in violation of the Fourth Amendment rests on the assumption that "limitations upon the fruit to be gathered tend to limit the quest itself." Thus, evidence may not be introduced if it was discovered by means of a seizure and search which were not reasonably related in scope to the justification for their initiation.

We need not develop at length in this case, however, the limitations which the Fourth Amendment places upon a protective seizure and search for weapons. These limitations will have to be developed in the concrete factual circumstances of individual cases. Suffice it to note that such a search, unlike a search without a warrant incident to a lawful arrest, is not justified by any need to prevent the disappearance or destruction of evidence of crime. The sole justification of the search in the present situation is the protection of the police officer and others nearby, and it must therefore be confined in scope to an intrusion reasonably designed to discover guns, knives, clubs, or other hidden instruments for the assault of the police officer.

The scope of the search in this case presents no serious problems in light of these standards. Officer McFadden patted down the outer clothing of petitioner and his two companions. He did not place his hands in their pockets or under the outer surface of their garments until he had felt weapons, and then he merely reached for and removed the guns. He never did invade Katz' person beyond the outer surfaces of his clothes, since he discovered nothing in his pat-down which might have been a weapon. Officer McFadden confined his search strictly to what was minimally necessary to learn whether the men were armed and to disarm them once he discovered the weapons. He did not conduct a general exploratory search for whatever evidence of criminal activity he might find. . . .

We conclude that the revolver seized from Terry was properly admitted in evidence against him. At the time he seized petitioner and searched him for weapons, Officer McFadden had reasonable grounds to believe that petitioner was armed and dangerous, and it was necessary for the protection of himself and others to take swift measures to discover the true facts and neutralize the threat of harm if it materialized. The policeman carefully restricted his search to what was appropriate to the discovery of the particular items which he sought. Each case of this sort will, of course, have to be decided on its own facts. We merely hold today that where a police officer observes unusual conduct which leads him reasonably to conclude in light of his experience that criminal activity may be afoot and that the persons with whom he is dealing may be armed and presently dangerous, where in the course of investigating this behavior he identifieshimself as a policeman and makes reasonable inquiries, and where nothing in the initial stages of the encounter serves to dispel his reasonable fear for his own or others' safety, he is entitled for the protection of himself and others in the area to conduct a carefully limited search of the outer clothing of such persons in an attempt to discover weapons which might be used to assault him. Such a search is a reasonable search under the Fourth Amendment, and any weapons seized may properly be introduced in evidence against the person from whom they were taken. . . .

Mr. Justice BLACK concurs in the judgment.

Mr. Justice HARLAN, concurring. . . .

Mr. Justice WHITE, concurring. . . .

Mr. Justice DOUGLAS, dissenting. . . .

DELAWARE V. PROUSE
Supreme Court of the United States, 1979.
440 U.S. 648, 99 S. Ct. 1391, 59 L.Ed.2d 660.

[Here the U.S. Supreme Court considers whether police may stop an automobile for the purpose of checking the driver's license when they have neither probable cause nor reasonable suspicion to believe that an offense has taken or is taking place.]

Mr. Justice WHITE delivered the opinion of the Court.

. . . At 7:20 P.M. on November 30, 1976, a New Castle County, Del., patrolman in a police cruiser stopped the automobile occupied by respondent. The patrolman smelled marihuana smoke as he was walking toward the stopped vehicle, and he seized marihuana in plain view on the car floor. Respondent was subsequently indicted for illegal possession of a controlled substance. At a hearing on respondent's motion to suppress the marihuana seized . . . , the patrolman testified that prior to stopping the vehicle he had observed neither traffic or equipment violations nor any suspicious activity, and that he made the stop only in order to check the driver's license and registration. The patrolman was not acting pursuant to any standards, guidelines, or procedures pertaining to document spot checks, promulgated by either his department or the State Attorney General. Characterizing the stop as "routine," the patrolman explained, "I saw the car in the area and was not answering any complaints so I decided to pull them off." The trial court granted the motion to suppress, finding the stop and detention to have been wholly capricious and therefore violative of the Fourth Amendment.

The Delaware Supreme Court affirmed. . . .

We have only recently considered the legality of investigative stops of automobiles where the officers making the stop have neither probable cause to believe nor reasonable suspicion that either the automobile or its occupants are subject to seizure under the applicable criminal laws. . . .

Although not dispositive, these decisions undoubtedly provide guidance in balancing the public interest against the individual's Fourth Amendment interests implicated by the practice of spot checks such as occurred in this case. We cannot agree that stopping or detaining a vehicle on an ordinary city street is less intrusive than a roving patrol stop on a major highway and that it bears greater resemblance to a permissible stop and secondary detention at a checkpoint near the border. . . . We cannot assume that the physical and psychological intrusion visited upon the occupants of a vehicle by a random stop to check documents is of any less moment than that occasioned by a stop by border agents on roving patrol. Both of these stops generally entail law-enforcement officers signaling a moving automobile to pull over to the side of the roadway, by means of a possibly unsettling show of authority. Both interfere with freedom of movement, are inconvenient, and consume time. Both may create substantial anxiety. For Fourth Amendment purposes, we also see insufficient resemblance between sporadic and random stops of individual vehicles making their way through city traffic and those stops occasioned by roadblocks where all vehicles are brought to a halt or to a near halt, and all are subjected to a show of the police power of the community. "At traffic checkpoints, the motorist can see that other vehicles are being stopped, he can see visible signs of the officer's authority, and he is much less likely to be frightened or annoyed by the intrusion." . . .

The marginal contribution to roadway safety possibly resulting from a system of spot checks cannot justify subjecting every occupant of every vehicle on the roads to a seizure—limited in magnitude compared to other intrusions but nonetheless constitutionally cognizable—at the unbridled discretion of law-enforcement officials. To insist upon neither an appropriate factual basis for suspicion directed at a particular automobile nor upon some other substantial and objective standard or rule to govern the exercise of discretion "would invite intrusions upon constitutionally guaranteed rights based on nothing more substantial than inarticulate hunches . . . ." . . . By hypothesis, stopping apparently safe drivers is necessary only because the danger presented by some drivers is not observable at the time of the stop. When there is not probable cause to believe that a driver is violating any one of the multitude of applicable traffic and equipment regulations—nor other articulable basis amounting to reasonable suspicion that the driver is unlicensed or his vehicle unregistered—we cannot conceive of any legitimate

basis upon which a patrolman could decide that stopping a particular driver for a spot check would be more productive than stopping any other driver. This kind of standardless and unconstrained discretion is the evil the Court has discerned when in previous cases it has insisted that the discretion of the official in the field be circumscribed, at least to some extent. . . .

. . . An individual operating or travelling in an automobile does not lose all reasonable expectation of privacy simply because the automobile and its use are subject to government regulation. Automobile travel is a basic, pervasive, and often necessary mode of transportation to and from one's home, workplace, and leisure activities. Many people spend more hours each day travelling in cars than walking on the streets. Undoubtedly, many find a greater sense of security and privacy in travelling in an automobile than they do in exposing themselves by pedestrian or other modes of travel. Were the individual subject to unfettered governmental intrusion every time he entered an automobile, the security guaranteed by the Fourth Amendment would be seriously circumscribed. . . .

Accordingly, we hold that except in those situations in which there is at least articulable and reasonable suspicion that a motorist is unlicensed or that an automobile is not registered, or that either the vehicle or an occupant is otherwise subject to seizure for violation of law, stopping an automobile and detaining the driver in order to check his driver's license and the registration of the automobile are unreasonable under the Fourth Amendment. This holding does not preclude the State of Delaware or other States from developing methods for spot checks that involve less intrusion or that do not involve the unconstrained exercise of discretion. Questioning of all oncoming traffic at roadblock-type stops is one possible alternative. We hold only that persons in automobiles on public roadways may not for that reason alone have their travel and privacy interfered with at the unbridled discretion of police officers. The judgment below is affirmed.

So ordered.

Mr. Justice REHNQUIST, dissenting.

The Court holds, in successive sentences, that absent an articulable, reasonable suspicion of unlawful conduct, a motorist may not be subjected to a random license check, but that the States are free to develop "methods for spot checks that . . . do not involve the unconstrained exercise of discretion," such as "questioning . . . all oncoming traffic at roadblock-type stops. . . ." Because motorists, apparently like sheep, are much less likely to be "frightened" or "annoyed" when stopped en masse, a highway patrolman needs neither probable cause nor articulable suspicion to stop all motorists on a particular thoroughfare, but he cannot without articulable suspicion stop less than all motorists. The Court thus elevates the adage "misery loves company" to a novel role in Fourth Amendment jurisprudence. The rule becomes "curiouser and curiouser" as one attempts to follow the Court's explanation for it. . . .

TENNESSEE V. GARNER
Supreme Court of the United States, 1985.
471 U.S. 1, 105 S. Ct. 1694, 85 L.Ed.2d 1.

[In this case, the Supreme Court holds that use of deadly force by police to prevent the escape of an unarmed felony suspect who does not pose a threat of serious harm is an unreasonable seizure under the Fourth Amendment.]

Justice WHITE delivered the opinion of the court.

I

At about 10:45 P.M. on October 3, 1974, Memphis Police Officers Elton Hymon and Leslie Wright were dispatched to answer a "prowler inside call." Upon arriving at the scene they saw a woman standing on her porch and gesturing toward the adjacent house. She told them she had heard glass breaking and that "they" or "someone" was breaking in next door. While Wright radioed the dispatcher to say that they were on the scene, Hymon went behind the house. He heard a door slam and saw someone run across the backyard. The fleeing suspect, . . . Edward Garner, stopped at a 6-feet-high chain link fence at the edge of the yard. With the aid of a flashlight, Hymon was able to see Garner's face and hands. He saw no sign of a weapon, and, though not certain, was "reasonably sure" and "figured" that Garner was unarmed. . . . He thought Garner was 17 or 18 years old and about 5'5" or 5'7" tall. While Garner was crouched at the base of the fence, Hymon called out "police, halt" and took a few steps toward him. Garner then began to climb over the fence. Con-

vinced that if Garner made it over the fence he would elude capture, Hymon shot him. The bullet hit Garner in the back of the head. Garner was taken by ambulance to a hospital, where he died on the operating table. Ten dollars and a purse taken from the house were found on his body.

In using deadly force to prevent the escape, Hymon was acting under the authority of a Tennessee statute and pursuant to Police Department policy. The statute provides that "[i]f, after notice of the intention to arrest the defendant, he either flee or forcibly resist, the officer may use all the necessary means to effect the arrest." Tenn. Code Ann. Sec. 40–7–108 (1982). The Department policy was slightly more restrictive than the statute, but still allowed the use of deadly force in cases of burglary. . . . The incident was reviewed by the Memphis Police Firearm's Review Board and presented to a grand jury. Neither took any action. . . .

Garner's father then brought this action in the Federal District Court for the Western District of Tennessee, seeking damages under 42 USC Sec. 1983 for asserted violations of Garner's constitutional rights. The complaint alleged that the shooting violated the Fourth, Fifth, Sixth, Eighth, and Fourteenth Amendments of the United States Constitution. It named as defendants Officer Hymon, the Police Department, its Director, and the Mayor and city of Memphis. After a 3-day bench trial, the District Court entered judgment for all defendants. It dismissed the claims against the Mayor and the

Director for lack of evidence. It then concluded that Hymon's actions were authorized by the Tennessee statute, which in turn was constitutional. Hymon had employed the only reasonable and practicable means of preventing Garner's escape. Garner had "recklessly and heedlessly attempted to vault over the fence to escape, thereby assuming the risk of being fired upon". . . .

The Court of Appeals reversed and remanded. . . . It reasoned that the killing of a fleeing suspect is a "seizure" under the Fourth Amendment, and is therefore constitutional only if "reasonable." The Tennessee statute failed as applied to this case because it did not adequately limit the use of deadly force by distinguishing between felonies of different magnitudes—"the facts, as found, did not justify the use of deadly force under the Fourth Amendment." . . . Officers cannot resort to deadly force unless they "have probable cause . . . to believe that the suspect [has committed a felony and] poses a threat to the safety of the officers or a danger to the community if left at large." . . .

The State of Tennessee, which had intervened to defend the statute . . . appealed to this Court. The city filed a petition for certiorari. We noted probable jurisdiction in the appeal and granted the petition. . . .

II

Whenever an officer restrains the freedom of a person to walk away, he has seized that person. . . . While it is not always clear just when minimal police interference becomes a seizure, . . . there can be no question that apprehension by the use of deadly force is a seizure subject to the reasonableness requirement of the Fourth Amendment.

A

A police officer may arrest a person if he has probable cause to believe that person committed a crime. . . . Petitioners and appellant argue that if this requirement is satisfied the Fourth Amendment has nothing to say about how that seizure is made. This submission ignores, the many cases in which this Court, by balancing the extent of the intrusion against the need for it, has examined the reasonable-

ness of the manner in which a search or seizure is conducted. To determine the constitutionality of a seizure "[w]e must balance the nature and quality of the intrusion on the individual's Fourth Amendment interests against the importance of the governmental interests alleged to justify the intrusion." . . . We have described "the balancing of competing interests" as "the key principle of the Fourth Amendment." . . . Because one of the factors is the extent of the intrusion, it is plain that reasonableness depends on not only when a seizure is made, but also how it is carried out. . . .

B

[N]otwithstanding probable cause to seize a suspect, an officer may not always do so by killing him. The intrusiveness of a seizure by means of deadly force is unmatched. The suspect's fundamental interest in his own life need not be elaborated upon. The use of deadly force also frustrates the interest of the individual, and of society, in judicial determination of guilt and punishment. Against these interests are ranged governmental interests in effective law enforcement. It is argued that overall violence will be reduced by encouraging the peaceful submission of suspects who know that they may be shot if they flee. Effectiveness in making arrests requires the resort to deadly force, or at least the meaningful threat thereof. "Being able to arrest such individuals is a condition precedent to the state's entire system of law enforcement." . . .

Without in any way disparaging the importance of these goals, we are not convinced that the use of deadly force is a sufficiently productive means of accomplishing them to justify the killing of nonviolent suspects. . . . The use of deadly force is a self-defeating way of apprehending a suspect and so setting the criminal justice mechanism in motion. If successful, it guarantees that the mechanism will not be set in motion. And while the meaningful threat of deadly force might be thought to lead to the arrest of more live suspects by discouraging escape attempts, the presently available evidence does not support this thesis. The fact is that a majority of police departments in this country have forbidden the use of deadly force against nonviolent suspects. . . . If those charged with the enforcement of the criminal law have abjured the use of deadly force in arresting non-dangerous felons, there is a substantial basis for doubting that the use of such force is an essential attribute of the arrest power in all felony cases. . . . Petitioners and appellant have not persuaded us that shooting nondangerous fleeing suspects is so vital as to outweigh the suspect's interest in his own life.

The use of deadly force to prevent the escape of all felony suspects, whatever the circumstances, is constitutionally unreasonable. It is not better that all felony suspects die than that they escape. Where the suspect poses no immediate threat to the officer and no threat to others, the harm resulting from failing to apprehend him does not justify the use of deadly force to do so. It is no doubt unfortunate when a suspect who is in sight escapes, but the fact that the police arrive a little late or are a little slower afoot does not always justify killing the suspect. A police officer may not seize an unarmed, nondangerous suspect by shooting him dead. The Tennessee statute is unconstitutional insofar as it authorizes the use of deadly force against such fleeing suspects.

It is not, however, unconstitutional on its face. Where the officer has probable cause to believe that the suspect poses a threat of serious physical harm, either to the officer or to others, it is not constitutionally unreasonable to prevent escape by using deadly force. Thus, if the suspect threatens the officer with a weapon or there is probable cause to believe that he has committed a crime involving the infliction or threatened infliction of serious physical harm, deadly force may be used if necessary to prevent escape, and if, where feasible, some warning has been given. As applied in such circumstances, the Tennessee statute would pass constitutional muster.

III

[omitted]

IV

The District Court concluded that Hymon was justified in shooting Garner because state law allows, and the Federal Constitution does not forbid, the use of deadly force to prevent the escape of a fleeing felony suspect if no alternative means of apprehen-

sion is available. . . . This conclusion made a determination of Garner's apparent dangerousness unnecessary. The court did find, however, that Garner appeared to be unarmed, though Hymon could not be certain that was the case. . . . Restated in Fourth Amendment terms, this means Hymon had no articulable basis to think Garner was armed.

In reversing, the Court of Appeals accepted the District Court's factual conclusions and held that "the facts, as found, did not justify the use of deadly force." . . . We agree. Officer Hymon could not reasonably have believed that Garner—young, slight, and unarmed—posed any threat. Indeed, Hymon never attempted to justify his actions on any basis other than the need to prevent an escape. The District Court stated in passing that "[t]he facts of this case did not indicate to Officer Hymon that Garner was 'non-dangerous.'" . . . This conclusion is not explained, and seems to be based solely on the fact that Garner had broken into a house at night. However, the fact that Garner was a suspected burglar could not, without regard to the other circumstances, automatically justify the use of deadly force. Hymon did not have probable cause to believe that Garner, whom he correctly believed to be unarmed, posed any physical danger to himself or others.

The dissent argues that the shooting was justified by the fact that Officer Hymon had probable cause to believe that Garner had committed a nighttime burglary. . . . While we agree that burglary is a serious crime, we cannot agree that it is so dangerous as automatically to justify the use of deadly force. The FBI classifies burglary as a "property" rather than a "violent" crime. . . . Although the armed burglar would present a different situation, the fact that an unarmed suspect has broken into a dwelling at night does not automatically mean he is physically dangerous. This case demonstrates as much. . . . In fact, the available statistics demonstrate that burglaries only rarely involve physical violence. During the 10-year period from 1973–1982, only 3.8% of all burglaries involved violent crime. . . .

V

We hold that the statute is invalid insofar as it purported to give Hymon the authority to act as he did. As for the policy of the Police Department, the absence of any discussion of this issue by the courts below, and the uncertain state of the record, preclude any consideration of its validity. The judgment of the Court of Appeals is affirmed, and the case is remanded for further proceedings consistent with this opinion.

So ordered.

Justice O'CONNOR, with whom The CHIEF JUSTICE and Justice REHNQUIST join, dissenting.

The Court today holds that the Fourth Amendment prohibits a police officer from using deadly force as a last resort to apprehend a criminal suspect who refuses to halt when fleeing the scene of a nighttime burglary. This conclusion rests on the majority's balancing of the interests of the suspect and the public interest in effective law enforcement. . . . Notwithstanding the venerable common-law rule authorizing the use of deadly force if necessary to apprehend a fleeing felon, and continued acceptance

of this rule by nearly half the States,. . . the majority concludes that Tennessee's statute is unconstitutional inasmuch as it allows the use of such force to apprehend a burglary suspect who is not obviously armed or otherwise dangerous. Although the circumstances of this case are unquestionably tragic and unfortunate, our constitutional holdings must be sensitive both to the history of the Fourth Amendment and to the general implications of the Court's reasoning. By disregarding the serious and dangerous nature of residential burglaries and the longstanding practice of many States, the Court effectively creates a Fourth Amendment right allowing a burglary suspect to flee unimpeded from a police officer who has probable cause to arrest, who has ordered the suspect to halt, and who has no means short of firing his weapon to prevent escape. I do not believe that the Fourth Amendment supports such a right, and I accordingly dissent. . . .

MIRANDA V. ARIZONA
Supreme Court of the United States, 1966.
384 U.S. 436, 86 S. Ct. 1602, 16 L.Ed.2d 694.

[In this landmark decision, the Supreme Court declares that the police must inform suspects of their constitutional rights before commencing custodial interrogation.]

Mr. Chief Justice WARREN delivered the opinion of the Court.

The cases before us raise questions which go to the roots of our concepts of American criminal jurisprudence: the restraints society must observe consistent with the Federal Constitution in prosecuting individuals for crime. More specifically, we deal with the admissibility of statements obtained from an individual who is subjected to custodial police interrogation and the necessity for procedures which assure that the individual is accorded his privilege under the Fifth Amendment to the Constitution not to be compelled to incriminate himself.

We dealt with certain phases of this problem recently in *Escobedo v. Illinois* . . . (1964).

We start here, as we did in *Escobedo*, with the premise that our holding is not an innovation in our jurisprudence, but is an application of principles long recognized and applied in other settings. We have undertaken a thorough reexamination of the *Escobedo* decision and the principles it announced, and we reaffirm it. That case was but an explication of basic rights that are enshrined in our Constitution—that "No person . . . shall be compelled in any criminal case to be a witness against himself," and that "the accused shall . . . have the Assistance of Counsel"—rights which were put in jeopardy in that case through official overbearing. These precious rights were fixed in our Constitution only after centuries of persecution and struggle. And in the words of Chief Justice Marshall, they were secured "for ages to come, and . . . designed to approach immortality as nearly as human institutions can approach it." . . .

Our holding will be spelled out with some specificity in the pages which follow but briefly stated it is this: the prosecution may not use statements, whether exculpatory or inculpatory, stemming from custodial interrogation of the defendant unless it demonstrates the use of procedural safeguards effective to secure the privilege against self-incrimination. By custodial interrogation, we mean questioning initiated by law enforcement officers after a person has been taken into custody or otherwise deprived of his freedom of action in any significant way. As for the procedural safeguards to be employed, unless other fully effective means are devised to inform accused persons of their right of silence and to assure a continuous opportunity to exercise it, the following measures are required. Prior to any questioning, the person must be warned that he has a right to remain silent, that any statement he does make may be used as evidence against him, and that he has a right to the presence of an attorney, either retained or appointed. The defendant may waive effectuation of these rights, provided the waiver is made voluntarily, knowingly and intelligently. If, however, he indicates in any manner and at any stage of the process that he wishes to consult with an attorney before speaking there can be no questioning. Likewise, if the individual is alone and indicates in any manner that he does not wish to be interrogated, the police may not question him. The mere fact that he may have answered some questions or volunteered some statements on his own does not deprive him of the right to refrain from answering any further inquiries until he has consulted with an attorney and thereafter consents to be questioned.

The constitutional issue we decide ... is the admissibility of statements obtained from a defendant questioned while in custody or otherwise deprived of his freedom of action in any significant way. In each, the defendant was questioned by police officers, detectives, or a prosecuting attorney in a room in which he was cut off from the outside world. In none of these cases was the defendant given a full and effective warning of his rights at the outset of the interrogation process. In all the cases, the questioning elicited oral admissions, and in three of them, signed statements as well which were admitted at their trials. They all thus share salient features—incommunicado interrogation of individuals in a police-dominated atmosphere, resulting in self-incriminating statements without full warnings of constitutional rights.

An understanding of the nature and setting of this in-custody interrogation is essential to our decisions today. The difficulty in depicting what transpires at such interrogations stems from the fact that in this country they have largely taken place incommunicado. From extensive factual studies undertaken in the early 1930's, including the famous Wickersham Report to Congress by a Presidential Commission, it is clear that police violence and the "third degree" flourished at that time. In a series of cases decided by this Court long after these studies, the police resorted to physical brutality—beating, hanging, slapping—and to sustained and protracted questioning incommunicado in order to extort confessions. The Commission on Civil Rights in 1961 found much evidence to indicate that "some policemen still resort to physical force to obtain confessions." The use of physical brutality and violence is not, unfortunately, relegated to the past or to any part of the country. Only recently in Kings County, New York, the police brutally beat, kicked and placed lighted cigarette butts on the back of a potential witness under interrogation for the purpose of securing a statement incriminating a third party. ...

The examples given above are undoubtedly the exception now, but they are sufficiently widespread to be the object of concern. Unless a proper limitation upon custodial interrogation is achieved—such as these decisions will advance—there can be no assurance that practices of this nature will be eradicated in the foreseeable future.

Again we stress that the modern practice of in-custody interrogation is psychologically rather than physically oriented. Interrogation still takes place in privacy. Privacy results in secrecy and this in turn results in a gap in our knowledge as to what in fact goes on in the interrogation rooms. A valuable source of information about present police practices, however, may be found in various police manuals and texts which document procedures employed with success in the past, and which recommended various other effective tactics. These texts are used by law enforcement agencies themselves as guides. It should be noted that these texts professedly present the most enlightened and effective means presently used to obtain statements through custodial interrogation. By considering these texts and other data, it is possible to describe procedures observed and noted around the country. . . .

Even without employing brutality, the "third degree" or the specific strategems described above, the very fact of custodial interrogation exacts a heavy toll on individual liberty and trades on the weakness of individuals.

In the cases before us today, given this background, we concern ourselves primarily with this interrogation atmosphere and the evils it can bring.

In these cases, we might not find the defendants' statements to have been involuntary in traditional terms. Our concern for adequate safeguards to protect precious Fifth Amendment rights is, of course, not lessened in the slightest. In each of the cases, the defendant was thrust into an unfamiliar atmosphere and run through menacing police interrogation procedures. The potentiality for compulsion is forcefully apparent, for example, in *Miranda,* when the indigent Mexican defendant was a seriously disturbed individual with pronounced sexual fantasies. . . .

It is obvious that such an interrogation environment is created for no purpose other than to subjugate the individual to the will of his examiner. This atmosphere carries its own badge of intimidation. . . . The current practice of incommunicado interrogation is at odds with one of our Nation's most cherished principles— that the individual may not be compelled to incriminate himself. Unless adequate protective devices are employed to dispel the compulsion inherent in custodial surroundings, no statement obtained from the defendant can truly be the product of his free choice.

From the foregoing, we can readily perceive an intimate connection between the privilege against self-incrimination and police custodial questioning. It is fitting to turn to history and precedent underlying the Self-Incrimination Clause to determine its applicability in this situation.

We sometimes forget how long it has taken to establish the privilege against self-incrimination, the sources from which it came and the fervor with which it was defended. Its roots go back into ancient times.

As a "noble principle often transcends its origins," the privilege has come rightfully to be recognized in part as an individual's substantive right, a "right to a private enclave where he may lead a private life. That right is the hallmark of our democracy." . . . We have recently noted that the privilege against self-incrimination—the essential mainstay of our adversary system—is founded on a complex of values. . . . All these policies point to one overriding thought: the constitutional foundation underlying the privilege is the respect a government—state or federal—must accord to the dignity and integrity of its citizens.

We are satisfied that all the principles embodied in the privilege apply to informal compulsion exerted by law-enforcement officers during in-custody questioning. An individual swept from familiar surroundings into police custody, surrounded by antagonistic forces, and subjected to the techniques of persuasion described above cannot be otherwise than under compulsion to speak. As a practical matter, the compulsion to speak in the isolated setting of the police station may well be greater than in courts or other official investigations, where there are often impartial observers to guard against intimidation or trickery.

The presence of counsel, in all the cases before us today, would be the adequate protective device necessary to make the process of police interrogation conform to the dictates of the privilege. His presence would insure that statements made in the government-established atmosphere are not the product of compulsion.

It is impossible for us to foresee the potential alternatives for protecting the privilege which might be devised by Congress or the States in the exercise of their creative rulemaking capacities. Therefore we cannot say that the Constitution necessarily requires adherence to any particular solution for the inherent compulsions of the interrogation process as it is presently conducted. Our decision in no way creates a constitutional straitjacket which will handicap sound efforts at reform, nor is it intended to have this effect. We encourage Congress and the States to continue their laudable search for increasingly effective ways of protecting the rights of the individual while promoting efficient enforcement of our criminal laws.

A recurrent argument made in these cases is that society's need for interrogation outweighs the privilege. This argument is not unfamiliar to this Court. . . .

In announcing these principles, we are not unmindful of the burdens which law enforcement officials must bear, often under trying circumstances. We also fully recognize the obligation of all citizens to aid in enforcing the criminal laws. This Court, while protecting individual rights, has always given ample latitude to law enforcement agencies in the legitimate exercise of their duties. The limits we have placed on the interrogation process should not constitute an undue interference with a proper system of law enforcement. As we have noted, our decision does not in any way preclude police from carrying out their traditional investigatory functions. Although confessions may play an important role in some convictions, the cases before us present graphic examples of the overstatement of the "need" for confessions.

Therefore, in accordance with the foregoing, the judgments of the Supreme Court of Arizona . . . [are] reversed. . . .

Mr. Justice HARLAN, whom Mr. Justice STEWART and Mr. Justice WHITE join, dissenting. . . .

Mr. Justice WHITE, with whom Mr. Justice HARLAN and Mr. Justice STEWART join, dissenting.
. . . The obvious underpinning of the Court's decision is a deep-seated distrust of all confessions. As the Court declares that the accused may not be interrogated without counsel present, absent a waiver of the right to counsel, and as the Court all but admonishes the lawyer to advise the accused to remain silent, the result adds up to a judicial judgment that evidence from the accused should not be used against him in any way, whether compelled or not. This is the not so subtle overtone of the opinion—that it is inherently wrong for the police to gather evidence from the accused himself. And this is precisely the nub of this dissent. I see nothing wrong or immoral, and certainly nothing unconstitutional, in the police's asking a suspect whom they have reasonable cause to arrest whether or not he killed his wife or in confronting him with the evidence on which the arrest was based, at least where he has been plainly advised that he may remain completely silent. . . .

The most basic function of any government is to provide for the security of the individual and of his property. These ends of society are served by the criminal laws which for the most part are aimed at the prevention of crime. Without the reasonably effective performance of the task of preventing private violence and retaliation, it is idle to talk about human dignity and civilized values.

The rule announced today will measurably weaken the ability of the criminal law to perform these tasks. It is a deliberate calculus to prevent interrogations, to reduce the incidence of confessions and pleas of guilty and to increase the number of trials.

There is, in my view, every reason to believe that a good many criminal defendants who otherwise would have been convicted on what this Court has previously thought to be the most satisfactory kind of evidence will now, under this new version of the Fifth Amendment, either not be tried at all or will be acquitted if the State's evidence, minus the confession, is put to the test of litigation.

I have no desire whatsoever to share the responsibility for any such impact on the present criminal process.

In some unknown number of cases the Court's rule will return a killer, a rapist or other criminal to the streets and to the environment which produced him, to repeat his crime whenever it pleases him. As a consequence, there will not be a gain, but a loss, in human dignity. The real concern is not the unfortunate consequences of this new decision on the criminal law as an abstract, disembodied series of authoritative proscriptions, but the impact on those who rely on the public authority for protection and who without it can only engage in violent self-help with guns, knives and the help of their neighbors similarly inclined. There is, of course, a saving factor: the next victims are uncertain, unnamed and unrepresented in this case.

Nor can this decision do other than have a corrosive effect on the criminal law as an effective device to prevent crime. A major component in its effectiveness in this regard is its swift and sure enforcement. The easier it is to get away with rape and murder, the less the deterrent effect on those who are inclined to attempt it. This is still good common sense. If it were not, we should posthaste liquidate the whole law enforcement establishment as a useless, misguided effort to control human conduct.

And what about the accused who has confessed or would confess in response to simple, noncoercive questioning and whose guilt could not otherwise be proved? Is it so clear that release is the best thing for him in every case? Has it so unquestionably been resolved that in each and every case it would be better for him not to confess and to return to his environment with no attempt whatsoever to help him? I think not. It may well be that in many cases it will be no less than a callous disregard for his own welfare as well as for the interests of his next victim.

Much of the trouble with the Court's new rule is that it will operate indiscriminately in all criminal cases, regardless of the severity of the crime or the circumstances involved. It applies to every defendant, whether the professional criminal or one committing a crime of momentary passion who is not part and parcel of organized crime. It will slow down the investigation and the apprehension of confederates in those cases where time is of the essence, such as kidnapping, those involving the national security, and some of those involving organized crime. In the latter context the lawyer who arrives may also be the lawyer for the defendant's colleagues and can be relied upon to insure that no breach of the organization's security takes place even though the accused may feel that the best thing he can do is to cooperate. . . .

OREGON V. MATHIASON
Supreme Court of the United States, 1977.
492 U.S. 492, 97 S. Ct. 711, 50 L.Ed.2d 714.

[In this case the Supreme Court limits the *Miranda* rule to those situations in which a suspect is taken into custody or significantly deprived of his freedom.]

PER CURIAM.
Respondent Carl Mathiason was convicted of first-degree burglary after a bench trial in which his confession was critical to the State's case. At trial he moved to suppress the confession as the fruit of questioning by the police not preceded by the warnings required in *Miranda v. Arizona*. . . . The trial court refused to exclude the confession because it found that Mathiason was not in custody at the time of the confession.

The Oregon Court of Appeals affirmed respondent's conviction, but on his petition for review in the Supreme Court of Oregon that court by a divided vote reversed the conviction. It found that although Mathiason had not been arrested or otherwise formally detained, "the interrogation took place in a 'coercive environment'" of the sort to which *Miranda* was intended to apply . . . . We think that the court has read *Miranda* too broadly, and we therefore reverse its judgment.

The Supreme Court of Oregon described the factual situation surrounding the confession as follows:

An officer of the State Police investigated a theft at a residence near Pendleton. He asked the lady of the house which had been burglarized if she suspected anyone. She replied that the defendant was the only one she could think of. The defendant was a parolee and a "close associate" of her son. The officer tried to contact defendant on three or four occasions with no success. Finally, about 25 days after the burglary, the officer left his card at defendant's apartment with a note asking him to call because "I'd like to discuss something with you." The next afternoon the defendant did call. The officer asked where it would be convenient to meet. The defendant had no preference; so the officer asked if the defendant could meet him at the state patrol office in about an hour and a half, about 5:00 P.M. The patrol office was about two blocks from defendant's apartment. The building housed several state agencies.

The officer met defendant in the hallway, shook hands and took him into an office. The defendant was not told that he was under arrest. The door was closed. The two sat across a desk. The police radio in another room could be heard. The officer told defendant he wanted to talk to him about a burglary and that his truthfulness would possibly be considered by the district attorney or judge. The officer further advised that the police believed defendant was involved in the burglary and [falsely stated that] defendant's fingerprints were found at the scene. The defendant sat for a few minutes and then said he had taken the property. This occurred within five minutes after the defendant had come to the office. The officer then advised defendant of his *Miranda* rights and took a taped confession.

At the end of the taped conversation the officer told defendant he was not arresting him at this time; he was released to go about his job and return to his family. The officer said he was referring the case to the district attorney for him to determine whether criminal charges would be brought. It was 5:30 P.M. when the defendant left the office.

The officer gave all the testimony relevant to this issue. The defendant did not take the stand either at the hearing on the motion to suppress or at the trial. . . .

The Supreme Court of Oregon reasoned from these facts that:

We hold that the interrogation took place in a "coercive environment." The parties were in the offices of the State Police; they were alone behind closed doors; the officer informed the defendant he was a suspect in a theft and the authorities had evidence incriminating him in the crime; and that the defendant was a parolee under supervision. We are of the opinion that this evidence is not overcome by the evidence that the defendant came to the office in response to a request and was told he was not under arrest. . . .

Our decision in *Miranda* set forth rules of police procedure applicable to "custodial interrogation." "By custodial interrogation, we mean questioning initiated by law enforcement officers after a person has been taken into custody or otherwise deprived of his freedom of action in any significant way." . . .

Subsequently we have found the *Miranda* principle applicable to questioning which takes place in a prison setting during a suspect's term of imprisonment on a separate offense, . . . and to questioning taking place in a suspect's home, after he has been arrested and is no longer free to go. . . .

In the present case, however, there is no indication that the questioning took place in a context where respondent's freedom to depart was restricted in any way. He came voluntarily to the police station, where he was immediately informed that he was not under arrest. At the close of a ½-hour interview, respondent did in fact leave the police station without hindrance. It is clear from these facts that Mathiason was not in custody "or otherwise deprived of his freedom of action in any significant way."

Such a noncustodial situation is not converted to one in which *Miranda* applies simply because a reviewing court concludes that . . . the questioning took place in a "coercive environment." Any interview of one suspected of a crime will have coercive aspects to it, simply by virtue of the fact that the police officer is part of a law enforcement system which may ultimately cause the suspect to be charged with a crime. But police are not required to administer *Miranda* warnings to everyone they question. Nor is the requirement of warnings to be imposed simply because the questioning takes place within the station house, or because the questioned person is one whom the police suspect. *Miranda* warnings are required only when there has been such a restriction on a person's freedom as to render him "in custody." It was that sort of coercive environment to which *Miranda* by its terms was made applicable, and to which it is limited.

The officer's false statement about having discovered Mathiason's fingerprints at the scene was found by the Supreme Court of Oregon to be another circumstance contributing to the coercive environment which makes the *Miranda* rationale applicable. Whatever relevance this fact may have to other issues in the case, it has nothing to do with whether respondent was in custody for purposes of the *Miranda* rule. . . .

[Justices BRENNAN, MARSHALL, and STEVENS dissented from the decision of the Court.]

RHODE ISLAND V. INNIS

Supreme Court of the United States, 1980.
446 U.S. 291, 100 S. Ct. 1682, 64 L.Ed.2d 297.

[Here the Supreme Court considers whether the defendant was "interrogated" in violation of the standards announced in *Miranda v. Arizona*.]

Mr. Justice STEWART delivered the opinion of the Court.

. . . On the night of January 12, 1975, John Mulvaney, a Providence, R.I., taxicab driver, disappeared after being dispatched to pick up a customer. His body was discovered four days later buried in a shallow grave in Coventry, R.I. He had died from a shotgun blast aimed at the back of his head.

On January 17, 1975, shortly after midnight, the Providence police received a telephone call from Gerald Aubin, also a taxicab driver, who reported that he had just been robbed by a man wielding a sawed-off shotgun. Aubin further reported that he had dropped off his assailant near Rhode Island College in a section of Providence known as Mount Pleasant. While at the Providence police station waiting to give a statement, Aubin noticed a picture of his assailant on a bulletin board. Aubin so informed one of the police officers present. The officer prepared a photo array, and again Aubin identified a picture of the same person. That person was the respondent. Shortly thereafter, the Providence police began a search of the Mount Pleasant area.

At approximately 4:30 A.M. on the same date, Patrolman Lovell, while cruising the streets of Mount Pleasant in a patrol car, spotted the respondent standing in the street facing him. Patrolman Lovell did not converse with the respondent other than to respond to the latter's request for a cigarette.

Within minutes, Sergeant Sears arrived at the scene of the arrest, and he also gave the respondent the *Miranda* warnings. Immediately thereafter, Captain Leyden and other police officers arrived. Captain Leyden advised the respondent of his *Miranda* rights. The respondent stated that he understood those rights and wanted to speak with a lawyer. Captain Leyden then directed that the respondent be placed in a "caged wagon," a four-door police car with a wire screen mesh between the front and rear seats, and be driven to the central police station. Three officers, Patrolmen Gleckman, Williams, and McKenna, were assigned to accompany the respondent to the central station. They placed the respondent in the vehicle and shut the doors. Captain Leyden then instructed the officers not to question the respondent or intimidate or coerce him in any way. The three officers then entered the vehicle, and it departed.

While en route to the central station, Patrolman Gleckman initiated a conversation with Patrolman McKenna concerning the missing shotgun. As Patrolman Gleckman later testified:

A. At this point, I was talking back and forth with Patrolman McKenna stating that I frequent this area while on patrol and [that because a school for handicapped children is located nearby,] there's a lot of handicapped children running around in this area, and God forbid one of them might find a weapon with shells and they might hurt themselves. . . .

Patrolman McKenna apparently shared his fellow officer's concern:

A. I more or less concurred with him [Gleckman] that this was a safety factor and that we should, you know, continue to search for the weapon and try to find it. . . .

While Patrolman Williams said nothing, he overheard the conversation between the two officers:

A. He [Gleckman] said it would be too bad if the little—I believe he said a girl—would pick up the gun, maybe kill herself. . .

The respondent then interrupted the conversation, stating that the officers should turn the car around so he could show them where the gun was located. At this point, Patrolman McKenna radioed back to Captain Leyden that they were returning to the scene of the arrest, and that the respondent would inform them of the location of the gun. At the time the respondent indicated that the officers should turn back, they had traveled no more than a mile, a trip encompassing only a few minutes.

The police vehicle then returned to the scene of the arrest where a search for the shotgun was in progress. There, Captain Leyden again advised the respondent of his *Miranda* rights. The respondent replied that he understood those rights but that he "wanted to get the gun out of the way because of the kids in the area in the school." The respondent then led the police to a nearby field, where he pointed out the shotgun under some rocks by the side of the road.

On March 20, 1975, a grand jury returned an indictment charging the respondent with the kidnaping, robbery, and murder of John Mulvaney. Before trial, the respondent moved to suppress the shotgun and the statements he had made to the police regarding it. After an evidentiary hearing at which the respondent elected not to testify, the trial judge found that the respondent had been "repeatedly and completely advised of his *Miranda* rights." He further found that it was "entirely understandable that [the officers in the police vehicle] would voice their concern [for the safety of the handicapped children] to each other." The judge then concluded that the respondent's decision to inform the police of the location of the shotgun was "a waiver, clearly, and on the basis of the evidence that I have heard, and [*sic*] intelligent waiver, of his [*Miranda*] right to remain silent." Thus, without passing on whether the police officers had in fact "interrogated" the respondent, the trial court sustained the admissibility of the shotgun and testimony related to its discovery. That evidence was later introduced at the respondent's trial, and the jury returned a verdict of guilty on all counts.

. . . In the present case, the parties are in agreement that the respondent was fully informed of his *Miranda* rights and that he invoked his *Miranda* right to counsel when he told Captain Leyden that he wished to consult with a lawyer. It is also uncontested that the respondent was "in custody" while being transported to the police station.

The issue, therefore, is whether the respondent was "interrogated" by the police officers in violation of the respondent's undisputed right under *Miranda* to remain silent until he had consulted with a lawyer. In resolving the issue, we first define the term "interrogation" under *Miranda* before turning to a consideration of the facts of this case.

The starting point for defining "interrogation" in this context is, of course, the Court's *Miranda* opinion. There the Court observed that "[b]y custodial interrogation, we mean *questioning* initiated by law enforcement officers after a person had been taken into custody or otherwise deprived of his freedom of action in any significant way." . . . This passage and other references throughout the opinion to "questioning" might suggest that the *Miranda* rules were to apply only to those police interrogation practices that involve express questioning of a defendant while in custody.

We do not, however, construe the *Miranda* opinion so narrowly. The concern of the Court in *Miranda* was that the "interrogation environment" created by interplay of interrogation and custody would "subjugate the individual to the will of his examiner" and thereby undermine the privilege against compulsory self-incrimination. . . . The police practices that evoked this concern included several that did not involve express questioning. For example, one of the practices discussed in *Miranda* was the use of lineups in which a coached witness would pick the defendant as the perpetrator. This was designed to establish that the defendant was in fact guilty as a predicate for further interrogation. . . . A variation on this theme discussed in *Miranda* was the so-called "reverse line-up" in which a defendant would be identified by coached witnesses as the perpetrator of a fictitious crime, with the object of inducing him to confess to the actual crime of which he was suspected in order to escape the false prosecution. . . . The Court in *Miranda* also included in its survey of interrogation practices the use of psychological ploys, such as to "posi[t]" "the guilt of the subject," to "minimize the moral seriousness of the offense," and "to cast blame on the victim or on society." . . . It is clear that these techniques of persuasion, no less than express questioning, were thought, in a custodial setting, to amount to interrogation.

. . . We conclude that the *Miranda* safeguards come into play whenever a person in custody is subjected to either express questioning or its functional equivalent. That is to say, the term "interrogation" under *Miranda* refers not only to express questioning, but also to any words or actions on the part of the police (other than those normally attendant to arrest and custody) that the police should know are reasonably likely to elicit an incriminating response from the suspect. The latter portion of this definition focuses primarily upon the perceptions of the suspect, rather than the intent of the police. This focus reflects the fact that the *Miranda* safeguards were designed to vest a suspect in custody with an added measure of protection against coercive police practices, without regard to objective proof of the underlying intent of the police. A practice that the police should know is reasonably likely to evoke an incriminating response from a suspect thus amounts to interrogation. But, since the police surely cannot be held accountable for the unforeseeable results of their words or actions, the definition of interrogation can extend only to words or actions on the part of police officers that they *should have known* were reasonably likely to elicit an incriminating response.

Turning to the facts of the present case, we conclude that the respondent was not "interrogated" within the meaning of *Miranda*. It is undisputed that the first prong of the definition of "interrogation" was not satisfied, for the conversation between Patrolman Gleckman and McKenna included no express questioning of the respondent. Rather, that conversation was, at least in form, nothing more than a dialogue between the two officers to which no response from the respondent was invited.

Moreover, it cannot be fairly concluded that the respondent was subjected to the "functional equivalent" of questioning. It cannot be said, in short, that Patrolman Gleckman and McKenna should have known that their conversation was reasonably likely to elicit an incriminating response from the respondent. There is nothing in the record to suggest that the officers were aware that the respondent was peculiarly susceptible to an appeal to his conscience concerning the safety of handicapped children. Nor is there anything in the record to suggest that the police knew that the respondent was unusually disoriented or upset at the time of his arrest.

The case thus boils down to whether, in the context of a brief conversation, the officers should have known that the respondent would suddenly be moved to make a self-incriminating response. Given the fact that the entire conversation appears to have consisted of no more than a few offhand remarks, we cannot say that the officers should have known that it was reasonably likely that Innis would so respond. This is not a case where the police carried on a lengthy harangue in the presence of the suspect. Nor does the record support the respondent's contention that, under the circumstances, the officers' comments were particularly "evocative." It is our view, therefore that the respondent was not subjected by the police to words or actions that the police should have known were reasonably likely to elicit an incriminating response from him.

For the reasons stated, the judgment of the Supreme Court of Rhode Island is vacated, and the case is remanded to the court for further proceedings not inconsistent with this opinion.

It is so ordered.

Mr. Justice WHITE, concurring. . . .

Mr. Chief Justice BURGER, concurring in the judgment. . . .

Mr. Justice MARSHALL, with whom Mr. Justice BRENNAN joins, dissenting.

I am substantially in agreement with the Court's definition of "interrogation" within the meaning of *Miranda v. Arizona* . . . (1966). In my view, the *Miranda* safeguards apply whenever police conduct is intended or likely to produce a response from a suspect in custody. As I read the Court's opinion, its definition of "interrogation" for *Miranda* purposes is equivalent, for practical purposes, to my formulation, since it contemplates that "where a police practice is designed to elicit an incriminating response from the accused, it is unlikely that the practice will not also be one which the police should have known was reasonably likely to have that effect. . . . Thus, the Court requires an objective inquiry into the likely effect the police conduct on a typical individual, taking into account any special susceptibility of the suspect to certain kinds of pressure of which the police know or have reason to know.

I am utterly at a loss, however, to understand how this objective standard as applied to the facts before us can rationally lead to the conclusion that there was no interrogation. Innis was arrested at 4:30 A.M., handcuffed, searched, advised of his rights, and placed in the back seat of a patrol car. Within a short time he had been twice more advised of his rights and driven away in a four-door sedan with three police officers. Two officers sat in the front seat and one sat beside Innis in the back seat. Since the car traveled no more than a mile before Innis agreed to point out the location of the murder weapon, Officer Gleckman must have begun almost immediately to talk about the search for the shotgun.

The Court attempts to characterize Gleckman's statements as "no more than a few offhand remarks" which could not reasonably have been expected to elicit a response.... If the statements had been addressed to respondent, it would be impossible to draw such a conclusion. The simple message of the "talking back and forth" between Gleckman and McKenna was that they had to find the shotgun to avert a child's death.

One can scarcely imagine a stronger appeal to the conscience of a suspect—*any* suspect—than the assertion that if the weapon is not found an innocent person will be hurt or killed. An not just any innocent person, but an innocent child—a little girl—a helpless, handicapped little girl on her way to school. The notion that such an appeal could not be expected to have any effect unless the suspect were known to have some special interest in handicapped children verges on the ludicrous. As a matter of fact, the appeal to a suspect to confess for the sake of others, to "display some evidence of decency and honor," is a classic interrogation technique....

Gleckman's remark would obviously have constituted interrogation if they had been explicitly directed to respondent, and the result should not be different because they were nominally addressed to McKenna. This is not a case where police officers speaking among themselves are accidentally overheard by a suspect. These officers were "talking back and forth" in close quarters with the handcuffed suspect, traveling past the very place where they believed the weapon was located. They knew respondent would hear and attend to their conversation, and they are chargeable with knowledge of and responsibility for the pressures to speak which they created.

I firmly believe that this case is simply an aberration, and that in future cases the Court will apply the standard adopted today in accordance with its plain meaning.

Mr. Justice STEVENS, dissenting....

NEW YORK V. QUARLES
Supreme Court of the United States, 1984.
467 U.S. 649, 104 S. Ct. 2626, 81 L.Ed.2d 550.

[In this case, the Supreme Court declares the "public safety exception" to the requirements of *Miranda v. Arizona.*]

Justice REHNQUIST delivered the opinion of the Court.

Respondent Benjamin Quarles was charged in New York trial court with criminal possession of a weapon. The trial court suppressed the gun in question, and a statement made by respondent, because the statement was obtained by police before they read respondent his "*Miranda* rights." That ruling was affirmed on appeal through the New York Court of Appeals. We granted certiorari, ... and we now reverse. We conclude that under the circumstances involved in this case, overriding considerations of public safety justify the officer's fail-ure to provide Miranda warnings before he asked questions devoted to locating the abandoned weapon.

On September 11, 1980, at approximately 12:30 A.M., Officer Frank Kraft and Officer Sal Scarring were on road patrol in Queens, New York, when a young woman approached their car. She told them that she had just been raped by a black male, approximately six feet tall, who was wearing a black jacket with the name "Big Ben" printed in yellow letters on the back. She told the officers that the man had just entered the A & P supermarket located nearby and that the man was carrying a gun.

The officers drove the woman to the supermarket, and Officer Kraft entered the store while Officer Scarring radioed for assistance. Officer Kraft quickly spotted respondent, who matched the description given by the woman, approaching a check out counter. Apparently upon seeing the officer, respondent turned and ran toward the rear of the store, and Officer Kraft pursued him with a drawn gun. When respondent turned the corner at the end of an aisle, Officer Kraft lost sight of him for several seconds, and upon regaining sight of respondent, ordered him to stop and put his hands over his head.

Although more than three officers had arrived on the scene by that time, Officer Kraft was the first to reach respondent. He frisked him and discovered that he was wearing a shoulder holster which was then empty. After handcuffing him, Officer Kraft asked him where the gun was. Respondent nodded in the direction of some empty cartons and responded, "the gun is over there." Officer Kraft thereafter retrieved a loaded .38 caliber revolver from one of the cartons, formally placed respondent under arrest, and read him his *Miranda* rights from a printed card. Respondent indicated that he would be willing to answer questions without an attorney present. Officer Kraft then asked respondent if he owned the gun and where he had purchased it. Respondent answered that he did own it and that he had purchased it in Miami, Florida.

In the subsequent prosecution of respondent for criminal possession of a weapon, the judge excluded the statement, "the gun is over there," because the officer had not given respondent the warnings required by our decision in *Miranda v. Arizona*, ... before asking him where the gun was located. The judge excluded the other statements about respondent's ownership of the gun and the place of purchase, as evidence tainted by the prior *Miranda* violation. The Appellate Division of the Supreme Court of New York affirmed without opinion.

The Court of Appeals ... concluded that respondent was in "custody" within the meaning of *Miranda* during all questioning and rejected the state's argument that the exigencies of the situation justified Officer Kraft's failure to read respondent his *Miranda* rights until after he had located the gun. The court declined to recognize an exigency exception to the usual requirements of *Miranda* because it found no indication from Officer Kraft's testimony at the suppression hearing that his subjective motivation in asking the question was to protect his own safety or the safety of the public. ... For the reasons which follow, we believe that this case presents a situation where concern for public safety must be paramount to adherence to the literal language of the prophylactic rules enunciated in *Miranda*. ...

In this case we have before us no claim that respondent's statements were actually compelled by police conduct which overcame his will to resist. ... Thus the only issue before us is whether Officer Kraft was justified in failing to make available to respondent the procedural safeguards associated with the privilege against compulsory self-incrimination since *Miranda*.

The New York Court of Appeals was undoubtedly correct in deciding that the facts of this case came within the ambit of the *Miranda* decision as we have subsequently interpreted it. We agree that respondent was in police custody because we have noted that "the ultimate inquiry is simply whether there is a 'formal arrest or restraint on freedom of movement' of the degree associated with a formal arrest." ... Here Quarles was surrounded by at least four police officers and was handcuffed when the questioning at issue took place. As the New York Court of Appeals observed, there was nothing to suggest that any of the officers were any longer concerned for their own safety. The New York Court of Appeals' majority declined to express an opinion as to whether there might be an exception to the *Miranda* rule if the police had been acting to protect the public, because the lower courts in New York had made no factual determination that the police had acted with that motive. ...

We hold that on these facts there is a "public safety" exception to the requirement that *Miranda* warnings be given before a suspect's answers may be admitted into evidence, and the availability of that exception does not depend upon the motivation of the individual officers involved. In a kaleidoscopic situation such as the one confronting these officers, where spontaneity rather than adherence to a police manual is necessarily the order of the day, the application of the exception which we recognize today should not be made to depend on post hoc findings at a suppression hearing concerning the subjective motivation of the arresting officer. Undoubtedly most police officers, if placed in Officer Kraft's position, would act out of a host of different, instinctive, and largely unverifiable motives—their own safety, the safety of others, and perhaps as well the desire to obtain incriminating evidence from the suspect.

Whatever the motivation of individual officers in such a situation, we do not believe that the doctrinal underpinnings of *Miranda* required that it be applied in all its rigor to a situation in which police officers ask questions reasonably prompted by a concern for the public safety. The *Miranda* decision was based in large part on this Court's view that the warnings which it required police to give to suspects in custody would reduce the likelihood that the suspects would fall victim to constitutionally impermissible practices of police interrogation in the presumptively coercive environment of the station house. . . . The dissenters warned that the requirement of *Miranda* warnings would have the effect of decreasing the number of suspects who respond to police questioning. . . . The *Miranda* majority, however, apparently felt that whatever the cost to society in terms of fewer convictions of guilty suspects, that cost would simply have to be borne in the interest of enlarged protection for the Fifth Amendment privilege.

The police in this case, in the very act of apprehending a suspect, were confronted with the necessity of ascertaining the whereabouts of a gun which they had every reason to believe the suspect had just removed from his empty holster and discarded in the supermarket. So long as the gun was concealed somewhere in the supermarket, with its actual whereabouts unknown, it obviously posed more than one danger to the public safety: an accomplice might make use of it, a customer or employee might later come upon it.

In such a situation, if the police are required to recite the familiar *Miranda* warnings before asking the whereabouts of the gun, suspects in Quarles' position might well be deterred from responding. Procedural safeguards which deter a suspect from responding were deemed acceptable in *Miranda* in order to protect the Fifth Amendment privilege; when the primary social cost of those added protections is the possibility of fewer convictions, the *Miranda* majority was willing to bear that cost. Here, had *Miranda* warnings deterred Quarles from responding to Officer Kraft's question about the whereabouts of the gun, the cost would have been something more than merely the failure to obtain evidence useful in convicting Quarles. Officer Kraft needed an answer to his question not simply to make his case against Quarles but to insure that

further danger to the public did not result from the concealment of the gun in a public area.

We conclude that the need for answers to questions in a situation posing a threat to the public safety outweighs the need for the prophylactic rule protecting the Fifth Amendment's privilege against self-incrimination. We decline to place officers such as Officer Kraft in the untenable position of having to consider, often in a matter of seconds, whether it best serves society for them to ask the necessary questions without the *Miranda* warnings and render whatever probative evidence they uncover inadmissible, or for them to give the warnings in order to preserve the admissibility of evidence they might uncover but possibly damage or destroy their ability to obtain that evidence and neutralize the volatile situation confronting them.

In recognizing a narrow exception to the *Miranda* rule in this case, we acknowledge that to some degree we lessen the desirable clarity of that rule. At least in part in order to preserve its clarity, we have over the years refused to sanction attempts to expand our *Miranda* holding. . . . But as we have pointed out, we believe that the exception which we recognize today lessens the necessity of that on-the-scene balancing process. The exception will not be difficult for police officers to apply because in each case it will be circumscribed by the exigency which justifies it. We think police officers can and will distinguish almost instinctively between questions necessary to secure their own safety or the safety of the public and questions designed solely to elicit testimonial evidence from a suspect.

The facts of this case clearly demonstrate that distinction and an officer's ability to recognize it. Officer Kraft asked only the question necessary to locate the missing gun before advising respondent of his rights. It was only after securing the loaded revolver and giving the warnings that he continued with investigatory questions about the ownership and place of purchase of the gun. The exception which we recognize today, far from complicating the thought processes and the on-the-scene judgments of police officers, will simply free them to follow their legitimate instincts when confronting situations presenting a danger to the public safety.

We hold that the Court of Appeals in this case erred in excluding the statement, "the gun is over there," and the gun because of the officer's failure to read respondent his *Miranda* rights before attempting to locate the weapon. Accordingly we hold that it also erred in excluding the subsequent statements as illegal fruits of a *Miranda* violation. We therefore reverse and remand for further proceedings not inconsistent with this opinion.

It is so ordered.

Justice O'CONNOR, concurring in part in the judgment and dissenting in part. . . .

Justice MARSHALL, with whom Justice BRENNAN and Justice STEVENS join, dissenting.

The police in this case arrested a man suspected of possessing a firearm in violation of New York law. Once the suspect was in custody and found to be unarmed, the arresting officer initiated an interrogation. Without being advised of his right not to respond, the suspect incriminated himself by locating the gun. The majority concludes that the State may rely on this incriminating statement to convict the suspect of possessing a weapon. I disagree. The arresting officers had no legitimate reason to interrogate the suspect without advising him of his rights to remain silent and to obtain assistance of counsel. By finding on these facts justification for unconsented interrogation, the majority abandons the clear guidelines enunciated in *Miranda v. Arizona* . . . and condemns the American judiciary to a new era of post hoc inquiry into the propriety of custodial interrogations. More significantly and in direct conflict with this Court's longstanding interpretation of the Fifth Amendment, the majority has endorsed the introduction of coerced self-incriminating statements in criminal prosecutions. I dissent. . . .

C H A P T E R

16

THE PRETRIAL PROCESS

CHAPTER OUTLINE

Introduction
The Right to Counsel
Availability of Compulsory
   Process
Stages in the Pretrial Process
The Right to a Speedy Trial
Conclusion

Cases

INTRODUCTION

The United States Constitution and the constitutions of all fifty states guarantee due process of law to all persons accused of criminal wrongdoing. Due process requires that persons accused of crimes be given fair notice of criminal charges and an adequate opportunity to contest them. The Supreme Court has said:

> No principle of procedural due process is more clearly established than that notice of the specific charge, and a chance to be heard in a trial of the issues raised by that charge, if desired, are among the constitutional rights of every accused in a criminal proceeding, in all courts, state or federal. *Cole v. Arkansas,* 333 U.S. 196, 201, 68 S. Ct. 514, 517, 92 L.Ed. 644, 647 (1948).

In the case of petty offenses (minor misdemeanors), due process may require no more than the opportunity for the accused to contest the charge before a magistrate in a single, summary proceeding. In the case of more serious crimes (treason, felonies, and major misdemeanors), the federal and state constitutions impose more elaborate procedural requirements.

As a practical matter, judicial decisions interpreting the generalities of the federal and state constitutions have greatly expanded the procedural rights that must be observed in criminal prosecutions. One result of this judicial activity is that the area of law known as criminal procedure has developed substantially over the past several decades.

Although many people equate the term *criminal procedure* with the criminal trial, the term is actually much broader. It includes search and seizure, arrest and interrogation (see Chapters 14 and 15), as well as a variety of other procedures that must occur before a trial can take place. The importance of these pretrial procedures is underscored by the fact that the overwhelming majority of criminal cases never make it to trial. A number of cases are dropped or dismissed for lack of sufficient evidence; many others result in convictions pursuant to guilty pleas. A substantial proportion of these guilty pleas results from negotiations between prosecutors and defense counsel. In such cases, trials are unnecessary. Where a defendant pleads guilty or "no contest" to an offense, and there is a factual basis for the plea, and the court is satisfied that the plea has been entered voluntarily, guilt is pronounced and the process moves along to the sentencing stage. Given the relative infrequency of trials, pretrial procedures take on greater importance in the day-to-day operation of the criminal justice system.

The main components of the pretrial process are the initial appearance before a magistrate, the preliminary hearing, the grand jury proceeding, and the arraignment. In addition, judges consider various motions made by the defense and prosecution at pretrial hearings. These pretrial procedures are designed to eliminate from the system those cases for which there is insufficient evidence of criminal wrongdoing, and to set the stage for a fair and orderly resolution of cases for which the evidence is sufficiently strong to proceed to trial.

THE RIGHT TO COUNSEL

Before undertaking a detailed examination of pretrial procedures, it is helpful to consider the contours of the right to counsel, which is widely regarded as essential to preserving the fundamental fairness of pretrial procedures. The defense attorney not only represents the accused in pretrial court proceedings but also advises on strategy and often serves as the negotiator between the defendant and the prosecutor. Thus the attorney for the defense plays an essential role in the criminal process. Indeed, in our adversarial legal system, the right to counsel may be the single most important right possessed by persons accused of serious crimes. As the Supreme Court has observed, "the right of one charged with crime to counsel may not be deemed fundamental and essential in some countries, but it is in ours." *Gideon v. Wainwright,* 372 U.S. 335, 344, 83 S. Ct. 792, 796, 9 L.Ed.2d 799, 805 (1963).

Common-Law Background of the Right to Counsel

Under the early English common law, there was no right to counsel for persons accused of treason or felonies. Somewhat ironically, by modern standards, the common law did recognize a right to counsel in misdemeanor cases. *Argersinger v. Hamlin,* 407 U.S. 25, 92 S. Ct. 2006, 32 L.Ed.2d 530 (1972). In 1698 Parliament enacted a law recognizing a right to counsel in cases of treason. 7 & 8 Will. 3, ch. 3, sec. 1. By the late eighteenth century, the common law came to recognize a limited right to counsel in felony cases, and in 1836 Parliament passed legislation recognizing the right to counsel for all criminal defendants. 6 & 7 Will. 4, ch. 114, sec. 1. Under the common law and the aforementioned acts of Parliament, the right to counsel meant the right to hire a barrister (a lawyer admitted to trial practice) at a person's own expense. It was not until 1903 that Parliament passed the Poor Prisoner's Defense Act, 3 Edw. 7, ch. 38, sec. 1, requiring that indigent defendants be provided counsel at public expense.

The Modern American Approach

In the United States, the right to counsel has likewise evolved through both judicial decisions and legislation. The Sixth Amendment to the United States Constitution provides:

> In all criminal prosecutions, the accused shall enjoy the right ... to have the Assistance of Counsel for his defense.

The Sixth Amendment has been consistently interpreted to allow defendants to employ counsel in all federal prosecutions, including treason, felony, and misdemeanor cases. Similar provisions in the constitutions of the fifty states have been interpreted to allow defendants to retain counsel in state criminal prosecutions. Irrespective of state constitutional protection, the accused is protected by the federal Constitution. In 1963 the Supreme Court held that the Sixth Amendment right to counsel applies to prosecutions in the state courts by way of the due process clause of the Fourteenth Amendment. *Gideon v. Wainwright,* 372

U.S. 335, 83 S. Ct. 792, 9 L.Ed.2d 799 (1963). Today, there is no question that criminal defendants have the right to retain attorneys to represent them in all types of criminal prosecutions, whether in state court, federal court, or before military tribunals.

Indigency and the Right to Counsel

While there has never been any serious question whether defendants have the right to employ attorneys to represent them, in fact many defendants have been too poor to afford private counsel. To what extent does the law mandate that they be provided counsel at public expense?

In 1790, Congress first addressed the issue of indigency in the context of federal criminal prosecutions for capital crimes. The Judiciary Act of 1790 required federal judges to assign counsel to indigent defendants in capital cases, at least where defendants requested representation. 1 Stat. 118, § 29 (1790). Some states emulated the act of Congress by providing for appointed counsel in capital cases, but most did not.

The Scottsboro Case. In a highly publicized case in the early 1930s, the Supreme Court held that the Fourteenth Amendment required states to observe the requirement long since imposed on federal courts by Congress. *Powell v. Alabama,* 287 U.S. 45, 53 S. Ct. 55, 77. L.Ed. 158 (1932). In the "Scottsboro case," as it has come to be known, several black youths were charged with raping two white women. Within a week of being arrested, the defendants were tried, convicted, and sentenced to death, all without meaningful assistance of counsel. In reversing their convictions, the Supreme Court said:

> In light of the . . . ignorance and illiteracy of the defendants, their youth, the circumstances of public hostility, the imprisonment and the close surveillance of the defendants by the military forces, the fact that their friends and families were all in other states and communication with them necessarily difficult, and above all that they stood in deadly peril of their lives . . . we think that . . . the failure of the trial court to make an effective appointment of counsel was . . . a denial of due process within the meaning of the Fourteenth Amendment. 287 U.S. at 71, 53 S. Ct. at 65, 77 L.Ed. at 171 (1932).

Relying heavily on its reasoning in *Powell v. Alabama,* the Supreme Court held four years later that the Sixth Amendment requires federal courts to appoint counsel for indigent defendants in all felony cases. *Johnson v. Zerbst,* 304 U.S. 458, 58 S. Ct. 1019, 82 L.Ed. 1461 (1938). Subsequently, Congress enacted the Criminal Justice Act of 1964, 18 U.S.C.A. § 3006A, that provided that all indigent defendants in federal criminal cases are entitled to appointed counsel.

In the wake of *Powell v. Alabama,* many states adopted laws creating a right to counsel at state expense, at least in capital cases. Some states went further by providing counsel for all indigent defendants in felony prosecutions. In states where appointed counsel was not a legal requirement, it was not uncommon for trial judges to appoint new members of the bar to represent indigent felony defendants *pro bono.* In so doing these judges anticipated a landmark court decision that was to have a tremendous impact on the criminal justice system.

The **Gideon** *Decision.*   In 1963, the Supreme Court decided that the Fourteenth Amendment requires states to provide counsel to indigent defendants in all felony cases, observing that "any person haled into court, who is too poor to hire a lawyer, cannot be assured a fair trial unless counsel is provided for him." *Gideon v. Wainwright*, 372 U.S. 335, 344, 83 S. Ct. 792, 796, 9 L.Ed.2d 799, 805 (1963). The impact of the *Gideon* decision was amplified by the fact that it was made retroactive. In Florida, where the *Gideon* case originated, the state was forced to release or retry hundreds of convicted criminals. Other states experienced similar problems. Today, the *Gideon* decision has come to be widely accepted by state officials who recognize that representation by counsel is essential to the fair and effective functioning of the adversary system of justice.

In 1972 the Supreme Court extended the *Gideon* decision to encompass defendants who were sentenced to jail terms for misdemeanors. *Argersinger v. Hamlin*, 407 U.S. 25, 92 S. Ct. 2006, 32 L.Ed.2d 530 (1972). The Court's decision, however, left unresolved the question whether counsel had to be provided to misdemeanor defendants who face *possible* jail terms, as distinct from those who are actually sentenced to jail. In 1979, the Court opted for the *actual imprisonment* standard. *Scott v. Illinois*, 440 U.S. 367, 99 S. Ct. 1158, 59 L.Ed.2d 383 (1979). The actual imprisonment standard poses a problem for magistrates; for if an indigent defendant to a misdemeanor charge is denied counsel and is subsequently found guilty, the magistrate is barred from imposing a jail term. To do so would be a constitutional violation, likely to result in a reversal of the defendant's conviction. This places the magistrate in the anomalous position of having to consider the sentence before determining the guilt of the accused. As a result, a number of states have gone beyond the federal constitutional requirement announced in *Scott v. Illinois* by providing counsel to indigent defendants in all misdemeanor cases where defendants face *possible* jail terms.

The Right to Representation at Pretrial Proceedings

Most people think of the right to counsel in terms of a defendant being represented at trial. While this may be the most important stage of the criminal process for a defendant who pleads not guilty, most criminal cases do not go to trial. For the defendant who elects to plead guilty, the pretrial procedures are critically important. The right of indigent persons to be provided counsel extends to many pretrial procedures. The United States Supreme Court has specifically identified a number of critical stages where the right of counsel attaches. Such critical pretrial stages include preliminary hearings, *White v. Maryland*, 373 U.S. 59, 83 S. Ct. 1050, 10 L.Ed.2d 193 (1963); lineups after charges have been filed against the accused, *United States v. Wade*, 388 U.S. 218, 87 S. Ct. 1926, 18 L.Ed.2d 1149 (1967); post-indictment interrogations, *Massiah v. United States*, 377 U.S. 201, 84 S. Ct. 1199, 12 L.Ed.2d 246 (1964); and arraignments, *Hamilton v. Alabama*, 368 U.S. 52, 82 S. Ct. 157, 7 L.Ed.2d 114 (1961).

Alternative Means of Providing Counsel to Indigent Persons

The representation provided to indigent defendants may take the form of a public defender or an attorney appointed ad hoc by the court. Many states have established successful public defender systems. In most states that use this system, the public defender is an elected official provided with funds to hire a staff of lawyers, much like the public prosecutor. In other states indigent defendants still depend largely on ad hoc appointment of counsel. Very often the attorneys appointed to represent indigent defendants are new members of the bar, with little trial experience. Remuneration for appointed counsel tends to be modest.

There remains considerable controversy over which method of providing counsel is more cost effective and which method more effectively meets the state's constitutional responsibilities. Proponents of the pubic defender systems note that public defenders are full-time specialists in criminal law, whereas appointed counsel may be relatively inexperienced in the field. Critics of the public defender system express concern about the constant contact between public defenders and prosecutors. They argue that this undermines the adversary system, resulting in a routinization of the criminal process, in which the interests of the accused become subordinated to a bureaucratic effort to maximize efficiency in the processing of cases.

Sometimes the public defender's office has a conflict in which codefendants want to pursue inconsistent defenses. In such instances an outside attorney should be appointed. If trial counsel representing multiple defendants brings a conflict of interest to the judge's attention, separate counsel must be appointed unless the judge determines that the risk of conflict is remote. *Holloway v. Arkansas,* 435 U.S. 475, 98 S. Ct. 1173, 55 L.Ed.2d 426 (1978). Most states have statutes providing for the appointment of private counsel in instances where public defenders have conflicts, but even in the absence of such statutes courts generally, to take the position that they have inherent authority to make such appointments.

Determining Who Is Indigent

Federal law leaves the determination of indigency to the discretion of the courts. This is also the case in most states. See, for example, Vernon's Ann. Tex. Code Crim. P. art. 26.04(a). Courts tend to be liberal in this regard, refusing to equate indigency with destitution. Courts are generally inclined to appoint counsel if the cost of hiring a lawyer would prevent the defendant from making bail.

After arrest, the accused is asked to complete a form to elicit information about employment, income, assets, and liabilities. Before the defendant's first appearance in court, staff persons will attempt to verify the accuracy of the defendant's statement. This information is then passed along to assist the magistrate in determining whether the defendant is entitled to appointed counsel. In most jurisdictions, more than 75 percent of felony defendants are classified as indigent. Some states provide for an assessment of an attorney's fee against a defendant who is represented by the public defender's office. See, for example, *State v. Williams,* 343 So.2d 35 (Fla. 1977). An indigent defendant may be assessed the costs of appointed counsel and these costs may be collected at some later time if the defendant becomes solvent. See *Fuller v. Oregon,* 417 U.S. 40, 94 S.Ct. 2116, 40 L.Ed.2d 642 (1974).

Self-Representation

The Supreme Court has held that there is a constitutional right to represent yourself in a criminal prosecution. *Faretta v. California*, 422 U.S. 806, 95 S. Ct. 2525, 45 L.Ed.2d 562 (1975). In *Faretta*, the Court said that the defendant's legal knowledge or skill has no bearing on the right to self-representation. However, the Court stressed that the defendant who waives the right to counsel and proceeds *pro se* must do so "knowingly and intelligently." Critics of the *Faretta* decision believe that criminal law and procedure have become too complex and technical to permit the nonlawyer defendant to engage in effective self-representation. They argue that due process requires that defendants be represented by trained counsel, lest fundamental fairness be denied. As the Supreme Court recognized in *Powell v. Alabama:*

> Even the intelligent and educated layman has small and sometimes no skill in the science of the law. If charged with a crime, he is incapable, generally, of determining for himself whether the indictment is good or bad. He is unfamiliar with the rules of evidence. Left without the aid of counsel he may be put on trial without a proper charge, and convicted upon incompetent evidence, or evidence irrelevant to the issue or otherwise inadmissible. He lacks both the skill and knowledge adequately to prepare his defense, even though he may have a perfect one. He requires the guiding hand of counsel at every step in the proceedings against him. Without it, though he be not guilty, he faces a danger of conviction because he does not know how to establish his innocence. 287 U.S. 45, 69, 53 S. Ct. 55, 64, 77 L.Ed. 158, 170 (1932).

Despite the potential dangers of the *pro se* defense, the Supreme Court held in *Faretta* that the Constitution places the defendant's "free choice" above the need for effective representation in a criminal trial. The constitutional issue aside, many lawyers have said that "the defendant who chooses to represent himself has a fool for a client!"

In 1984 the Supreme Court ruled that a defendant "does not have a constitutional right to receive personal instruction from the trial judge on courtroom procedure. Nor does the Constitution require the judge to take over chores for a *pro se* defendant that would normally be attended to by trained counsel as a matter of course." *McKaskle v. Wiggins*, 465 U.S. 168, 183–184, 104 S. Ct. 944, 954, 79 L.Ed.2d 122, 136–137 (1984). Moreover, the constitutional right to self-representation does not imply a right to obstruct the workings of the criminal process. A trial judge may terminate self-representation by a defendant who engages in obstructionist conduct. *Illinois v. Allen*, 397 U.S. 337, 90 S. Ct. 1057, 25 L.Ed.2d 353 (1970).

Judges sometimes appoint standby counsel to assist defendants who choose self-representation. There are two principal advantages: (1) standby counsel can be available to answer questions by a *pro se* defendant; and (2) if it is necessary to terminate the *pro se* defense because of misconduct or incompetence, standby counsel is available to complete the case.

Although a defendant has the right to self-representation, he or she may not be represented by another person who is not a member of the bar. Nor may a defendant force an unwilling attorney to represent him or her. *Wheat v. United States*, 486 U.S. 153, 108 S.Ct. 1692, 100 L.Ed.2d 140 (1988).

AVAILABILITY OF COMPULSORY PROCESS

The Sixth Amendment to the Constitution guarantees a defendant in a criminal case the right to "have the compulsory process of the law to obtain witnesses in his favor." The "compulsory process" clause was applied to the states in *Washington v. Texas*, 388 U.S. 14, 87 S.Ct. 1920, 18 L.Ed.2d 1019 (1967), although the right previously existed in state constitutions and laws anyway. The method of securing this right is through use of a subpoena, a formal written demand, available in all federal and state jurisdictions. Subpoenas are available to both the prosecution and defense.

Rule 17 of the Federal Rules of Criminal Procedure implements this right at the federal level by allowing a defendant to have the court issue a subpoena for witnesses, documents, and objects and providing for services of such subpoenas. Court clerks, and sometimes judges, issue subpoenas. They are usually served by a marshal in the federal system or a sheriff in the state system. There are costs associated with subpoenas, but the federal rule provides for issuance without cost when a defendant is financially unable to pay costs as long as the witness is "necessary to an adequate defense." States generally have statutes or court rules roughly paralleling the federal rule.

In the pretrial stages, challenges may be made to the right to subpoena a witness, document, or object. Challenges are usually based on the contention that such witness or items are not material to issues in the case. Judges have considerable discretion in ruling on these challenges.

STAGES IN THE PRETRIAL PROCESS

All jurisdictions require the prompt appearance of an arrestee before a court of law. After arrest and booking, suspects are brought before a magistrate, usually within twenty-four hours of arrest. See, for example, West's Fla. R. Crim. P. Rule 3.130 (a). The purpose of the appearance is to initiate the formal charging process. Essentially, the magistrate must perform three important functions at the initial appearance: (1) the charges must be read so that the accused knows exactly what he or she is being charged with; (2) the accused must be informed of relevant constitutional rights, including the right to remain silent and the right to counsel; and (3) a determination must be made of whether the accused should be released pending trial or remanded to custody to await the disposition of the case.

As noted, most jurisdictions require a suspect to be brought before a magistrate for an initial appearance within twenty-four hours after arrest. Nevertheless, in a controversial 5–4 decision, the Supreme Court held in 1991 that a suspect could be detained for as long as forty-eight hours before being taken before a magistrate. *County of Riverside v. McLaughlin*, 500 U.S. ___ , 111 S.Ct. 1661, 114 L.Ed.2d 49 (1991).

Disposition of Petty Offenses

In minor misdemeanor cases such as many violations of the motor vehicle code, the first appearance before a magistrate is likely to be the only court appearance the accused will have. Such petty offenses are often disposed through summary justice. In such cases, the accused enters a plea ("not guilty," "guilty," or "no contest"), evidence is taken, and a verdict is rendered by the magistrate. If the defendant is found guilty, sentence is generally pronounced immediately. Although defendants clearly have a right to hire attorneys to represent them in minor misdemeanor cases, few exercise this right. Most people would rather go it alone before the magistrate. If they lose, which is highly probable, they typically pay a fine, which tends to be substantially cheaper than hiring an attorney. As noted earlier, the Supreme Court has said that there is no constitutional right for indigent persons to have counsel appointed in such minor cases, except where defendants are *actually sentenced* to jail terms. *Scott v. Illinois*, 440 U.S. 367, 99 S. Ct. 1158, 59 L.Ed.2d 383 (1979).

Pretrial Release

The most important thing to a person who has been arrested and confined to jail is to secure release as soon as possible. Beyond the obvious desirability of freedom, an accused who remains at liberty can be of considerable assistance to defense counsel in locating witnesses and by being able to confer with counsel outside the jail setting. In addition, a person who remains at liberty can usually pursue gainful employment and discharge family responsibilities pending the disposition of the criminal charges.

Granting an accused pretrial release is commonly referred to as granting bail. The authority to grant a defendant bail is of common-law origin. *State v. Konigsberg*, 164 A.2d 740 (N.J. 1960). Today the authority is commonly granted by statutes or court rules. In determining whether a defendant is entitled to pretrial release, the court usually considers the accused's prior convictions (if any), character, employment history, and ties to family and the community, as well as the nature and scope of the current charges.

Pretrial release may take one of several forms. The four most common are release on personal recognizance; release to the custody of another; posting an individual bond; and posting a surety bond.

- *Personal recognizance.* A recognizance is a person's promise to appear in court as required. The defendant signs a guarantee to appear at all required proceedings and, in some cases, acknowledges certain restrictions on his or her activities.
- *Release to the custody of another.* The magistrate may release the defendant to the custody of some responsible person, often the defendant's attorney, who agrees to exercise custodial supervision and to assume responsibility for the defendant's required court appearances.
- *Posting an individual bond.* The defendant posts a bond agreeing to appear in court as required. The defendant may or may not be required to post an amount of cash or other security to guarantee the undertaking.
- *Posting a surety bond.* This is the historic bail-bond method of securing pretrial release. The magistrate sets the amount of a bond for the particular offense. Often this is based on a schedule of bonds set by the judge of the court having jurisdiction over the offense. The defendant signs the bond,

agreeing to appear as required. The bond is guaranteed by the defendant's surety, which means that should the defendant default, the surety, usually an insurance company, is bound to pay the court the amount of the bond (called the "penal sum"). A defendant usually pays a premium of about 10 percent of the amount of the bond and in most instances provides the surety with collateral to induce the surety to sign the bond. Sureties bonding a defendant are responsible for assuring the defendant's appearance; therefore, they are commonly given the statutory authority to arrest an absconding defendant. To this end, sureties often employ "skip tracers" who are, in effect, modern bounty hunters who seek out and return an absconding defendant. When a surety promptly produces a defendant, it can usually recover any money forfeited to the court because of the defendant's failure to appear.

The Issue of Excessive Bail

Recognizing the common-law practice of allowing pretrial release on bail, the Eighth Amendment to the federal Constitution states that "excessive bail shall not be required." The Supreme Court has made it clear that the purpose of bail is to ensure the appearance of the accused in court, not to inflict punishment. "Bail set at a figure higher than an amount reasonably calculated to fulfill this purpose is 'excessive' under the Eighth Amendment." *Stack v. Boyle*, 342 U.S. 1, 5, 72 S. Ct. 1, 3, 96 L.Ed. 3, 6 (1951). However, the Supreme Court has never held that the excessive bail clause of the Eighth Amendment is enforceable against the states via the Fourteenth Amendment, leaving the matter of excessive bail in state criminal cases to the state constitutions, state legislatures, and state courts.

The Illinois Code of Criminal Procedure provides that "the amount of bail shall be: (1) Sufficient to assure compliance with the conditions set forth in the bail bond; (2) Not oppressive; (3) Considerate of the financial ability of the accused." Ill. S.H.A. 725 ILCS 5/110–5. Similarly, the Texas Code of Criminal Procedure states that "the power to require bail is not to be so used as to make it an instrument of oppression." Vernon's Ann. Tex. Code Crim. P. art. 17.15(2).

Pretrial Detention

The constitutional prohibition of "excessive bail" is vague regarding the existence of a constitutional right to pretrial release. However, the Supreme Court has ruled that there is no right to bail under the Eighth Amendment. *United States v. Salerno*, 481 U.S. 739, 107 S. Ct. 2095, 95 L.Ed.2d 697 (1987). The Federal Bail Reform Act of 1984, 18 U.S.C.A. § 3141 *et seq.*, allows federal courts to detain arrestees without bail on the ground of the arrestee's dangerousness to the community, as well as the need to ensure future court appearances.

First, the court must determine whether the government has established "by a preponderance of the evidence that the defendant either has been charged with one of the crimes enumerated in Section 3142(f)(1) or that the defendant presents a risk of flight or obstruction of justice." *United States v. Friedman*, 837 F.2d 48 (2d Cir. 1988). If the government satisfies that burden, the court must determine if there are "conditions or a combination of conditions which reasonably will assure the presence of the defendant at trial." *United States v. Shakur*, 817 F.2d 189 (2d Cir. 1987). Congress has set forth various factors a court must consider in weighing the appropriateness of pretrial detention. Among these are the nature of the offense, the weight of the evidence against the suspect, the history and character of the person charged, and the nature and seriousness of the risk to the community. 18 U.S.C.A. § 3142(g). The statute provides for an adversary hearing on the issue of detention. The government must show by "clear and convincing evidence" that pretrial release will not "reasonably assure the appearance of the person as required and the safety of any other person and the community." The judge or magistrate who denies bail must prepare a written statement justifying the decision to detain the accused. Finally, the law provides for immediate appellate review of the detention decision. In upholding the Bail Reform Act of 1984 against an Eighth Amendment challenge, the Supreme Court said in *United States v. Salerno* that

> when Congress has mandated detention on the basis of a compelling interest other than prevention of flight, as it has here, the Eighth Amendment does not require release on bail. 481 U.S. at 754–755, 107 S. Ct. at 2105, 95 L.Ed.2d at 713–714.

The *Salerno* decision, although technically limited to the constitutionality of federal pretrial detention, suggests the validity of state laws or court decisions that deny bail to persons accused of violent crimes, especially where arrestees have a record of violent crime.

In many states a defendant is ineligible for pretrial release if charged with a crime punishable by death or life imprisonment if the "proof is evident or the presumption [of guilt] is great." See, for example, *State v. Arthur*, 390 So.2d 717, 718 (Fla. 1980). In the majority of these states, before denying pretrial release courts must determine whether the facts, viewed in the light most favorable to the state, are legally sufficient to sustain a verdict of guilty. See *Fountaine v. Mullen*, 366 A.2d 1138 (R.I. 1976).

The Prosecutor's Decision to Charge

Along with judges and defense counsel, prosecutors are the most important actors in the determination of criminal cases. The prosecutor decides whether to proceed with a criminal case and whether to negotiate charges with the defense, and must, at various stages of the process, demonstrate the veracity of the government's case to the satisfaction of the court. The prosecutor causes the court to issue subpoenas to compel the attendance of witnesses to testify, to bring in documents, and to provide nontestimonial physical evidences such as handwriting specimens, *United States v. Mara*, 410 U.S. 19, 93 S.Ct. 774, 35 L.Ed.2d 99 (1973), and voice exemplars, *United States v. Dionisio*, 410 U.S. 1, 93 S.Ct. 764, 35 L.Ed.2d 67 (1973).

State and federal prosecutors have broad discretion in deciding whether to proceed with criminal charges initiated by a complainant or the police. The prosecutor may decide to drop a case for a variety of reasons, ranging from insufficient evidence to a judgment that the criminal sanction is inappropriate in a given situation. Alternatively, the prosecutor may decide to proceed on a lesser charge.

The American Bar Association's *Standards Relating to the Prosecution and Defense Function* offers prosecutors guidelines for the exercise of their discretion in making the decision to charge. The standards admonish prosecutors not to be influenced by personal or political motivations and not to bring more charges, in number or degree, than can reasonably be supported at trial.

The broad discretion vested in public prosecutors facilitates the widespread yet controversial practice of plea bargaining, which we discuss later in the chapter. Although very broad, prosecutorial discretion is not altogether unlimited, the equal protection clause of the Fourteenth Amendment imposes certain limitations on selective prosecution. Prosecutors may not single out defendants for prosecution on the basis of race, religion, or other impermissible classifications. *Oyler v. Boles,* 368 U.S. 448, 82 S. Ct. 501, 7 L.Ed.2d 446 (1962).

Courts have not only cloaked prosecutors with broad discretion in determining whether to prosecute, but they have also long held prosecutors immune from civil actions for malicious prosecution, as long as they are acting within the scope of their offices. *Griffith v. Slinkard,* 44 N.E. 1001 (Ind. 1896). More recently, the United States Supreme Court has ruled that the same considerations that underlie prosecutorial immunity in tort actions require that prosecutors be immune from damages for deprivation of defendants' constitutional rights under 42 U.S.C.A. § 1983. See *Imbler v. Pachtman,* 424 U.S. 409, 96 S. Ct. 984, 47 L.Ed.2d 128 (1976).

Determining the Sufficiency of the Government's Case

Assuming the prosecutor decides to proceed with criminal charges, an examination of the sufficiency of the evidence generally follows. The purpose of this procedure is to ensure that there is probable cause for trial. This determination is made by a magistrate or a grand jury or both. In some jurisdictions, the prosecutor files a document called an *information* in the appropriate court of law.

CASE IN POINT

LIMITATIONS ON PROSECUTORIAL CONDUCT

E. J. Reagan was charged with torturing a child and assault with intent to do great bodily harm. The prosecutor agreed to drop the charges if Reagan could pass a lie detector test. The defendant agreed and passed the test. Pursuant to the agreement, the prosecutor filed a *nolle prosequi* and the charges were dismissed. Subsequently, the prosecutor became convinced that the polygraph examination was flawed. He then filed a new complaint on the same charges. The defendant was tried and convicted. The Michigan Supreme Court reversed the conviction and discharged the defendant. The court said that "a pledge of public faith in this instance gave force to an unwise agreement."

People v. Reagan, 235 N.W.2d 581, 587 (Mich. 1975).

An information is a formal accusatorial document detailing the specific charges against a defendant. After the filing of the information, a hearing may be requested to determine the sufficiency of the evidence in support of the information. In other jurisdictions, the prosecutor must obtain an *indictment* from a grand jury. Some jurisdictions employ a combination of both mechanisms. In Tennessee, for example, a person accused of a felony must be indicted by a grand jury; a preliminary examination prior to the grand jury proceeding is available at the option of the accused. Tenn. R. Crim. P., Rule 5.1.

The Preliminary Hearing

In a preliminary hearing (not to be confused with the initial appearance), a magistrate examines the state's case to determine whether there is probable cause to bind the accused over to the grand jury or (in the absence of a grand jury requirement) hold the accused for trial. The Supreme Court has said that a preliminary hearing is constitutionally required in the absence of grand jury review to determine the sufficiency of an information, where an arrest is made without a warrant. *Gerstein v. Pugh*, 420 U.S. 103, 95 S. Ct. 854, 43 L.Ed.2d 54 (1975). However, *Gerstein* does not require preliminary hearings to be full-blown adversarial proceedings. Nevertheless, most states do provide for open hearings with both parties represented. See, for example, New Jersey Rules of Criminal Practice 3:4–3(a).

Typically in a preliminary hearing the defense has the privilege of cross-examining witnesses for the prosecution and is able to learn the details and strengths of the state's case. The state is able to preserve testimony of witnesses who may balk at testifying at the trial. Thus the preliminary hearing serves the interests of both the prosecution and the defense by providing an inquiry into probable cause for arrest and detention, a screening device for prosecutors, as well as an opportunity for defense counsel to discover the prosecutor's case.

The Grand Jury

In many jurisdictions, prosecutors must obtain an indictment or "true bill" from the grand jury in addition to, or instead of, the preliminary hearing. The Fifth Amendment to the United States Constitution states that

> No person shall be held to answer for a capital, or otherwise infamous crime, unless on a presentment or indictment of a grand jury.

The Supreme Court has held that states are not bound by the Fourteenth Amendment to abide by the grand jury requirement imposed on the federal courts by the Fifth Amendment. *Hurtado v. California*, 110 U.S. 516, 4 S. Ct. 111, 28 L.Ed. 232 (1884). Nevertheless, about half the states have constitutional provisions or statutes requiring the use of grand juries in certain types of criminal cases. Other states use the grand jury primarily in an investigatory or supervisory capacity.

Like bail, the grand jury is an ancient common-law institution, preceding the Magna Charta of 1215. At common law, the grand jury comprised twenty-three persons, at least twelve of whom had to agree in order to hand down an indictment. See *State v. Hartley*, 40 P. 372 (Nev. 1895). Today, federal grand juries comprise sixteen to twenty-three persons, Fed. R. Crim. P. 6(a), but the "12-votes for indictment" rule applies in every case. Fed. R. Crim. P. 6(f). States vary in regard to the size of grand juries, but in every state at least a majority of grand jurors must agree that there is probable cause for trial in order to hand down an indictment against the accused. In Texas, for example, the grand jury consists of twelve jurors, at least nine of whom must agree in order to indict. Vernon's Ann. Tex. Code Crim. P. art. 20.19.

Historically the grand jury acted as a shield to prevent unfounded charges and arbitrary and overzealous prosecution. Today grand juries seldom refuse to hand down indictments sought by prosecutors, causing some critics to question the utility of the institution as a safeguard for the rights of the accused. Perhaps it is this perception that has led a number of states to adopt the information/preliminary hearing mechanism in lieu of the grand jury. In most of the midwestern and western states, the grand jury is seldom used to charge persons with crimes.

The grand jury, like the magistrate presiding over the preliminary hearing, examines the evidence and testimony the prosecution has collected against the accused. Unlike the preliminary hearing, the grand jury proceeding is normally closed: The defendant is generally not represented by counsel or even present at the proceeding. Testimony before the grand jury is not always transcribed, and if it is, access to transcripts is either limited or nonexistent. While controversial, grand jury secrecy encourages uninhibited testimony by witnesses and prevents the circulation of derogatory statements about persons who are ultimately not indicted. *Pittsburgh Plate Glass Co. v. United States*, 360 U.S. 395, 79 S. Ct. 1237, 3 L.Ed.2d 1323 (1959). As noted in *United States v. Procter & Gamble Co.*, 356 U.S. 677, 78 S. Ct. 983, 2 L.Ed.2d 1077 (1958), grand jury secrecy also protects grand jurors from intimidation and possible reprisals.

After the prosecutor has presented testimony and physical evidence, the members of the grand jury vote whether to hand down an indictment. There is some variation among jurisdictions in the rules that determine grand jury indictments, but in no case can a grand jury return a true bill unless a majority of grand jurors votes to indict.

Grand Jury Powers. Grand juries possess the authority to compel the appearance of witnesses, to subpoena documents, to hold individuals in contempt, and to grant immunity from prosecution in exchange for testimony. Immunity is of two kinds. Transactional immunity bars any further prosecution of the witness in regard to the specific transaction he or she testified to. Use immunity is more limited, barring only the use of the witness's testimony against him or her in a subsequent prosecution. Federal grand juries are authorized to grant use immunity. 18 U.S.C.A. § 6002. Many states follow the federal statute; some states go further and permit grand juries to grant transactional immunity. The federal statutory bar against the use of immunized testimony applies equally to federal and state proceedings. *In re Grand Jury Proceedings*, 860 F.2d 11 (2d Cir. 1988).

Rights of Witnesses and Suspects.   The Supreme Court has held that grand jury witnesses retain their Fifth Amendment privileges against compulsory self-incrimination. *Lefkowitz v. Turley,* 414 U.S. 70, 94 S. Ct. 316, 38 L.Ed.2d 274 (1973). Nevertheless, through a limited grant of immunity, a grand jury can override a witness's refusal to answer questions on Fifth Amendment grounds. The Supreme Court has held that a grand jury's grant of immunity must be coextensive with the privilege against self-incrimination. Use immunity satisfies this requirement; transactional immunity is not required by the Constitution. *Kastigar v. United States,* 406 U.S. 441, 92 S. Ct. 1653, 32 L.Ed.2d 212 (1972).

Witnesses testifying before grand juries have no right to be represented by counsel, *In re Groban's Petition,* 352 U.S. 330, 77 S. Ct. 510, 1 L.Ed.2d 376 (1957), although a number of jurisdictions allow witnesses to consult with counsel outside the grand jury room. An attorney's appearance before grand jury on behalf of a witness is generally thought to cause unnecessary delays and violate the secrecy of the proceeding.

A suspect is not afforded the same degree of legal protection against the grand jury as in a criminal trial. In only a few states does the defendant have a right to appear before the grand jury to confront his or her accusers. As in the case of witnesses, a defendant has no federal constitutional right to be represented by counsel inside the grand jury room. *United States v. Mandujano,* 425 U.S. 564, 96 S. Ct. 1768, 48 L.Ed.2d 212 (1976).

Evidence before the Grand Jury.   Many of the rules of evidence that apply to the criminal trial do not apply to the grand jury. *Costello v. United States,* 350 U.S. 359, 76 S. Ct. 406, 100 L.Ed. 397 (1956), *rehearing denied,* 351 U.S. 904, 76 S.Ct. 692, 100 L.Ed. 1440 (1956). For example, hearsay evidence is generally admissible, whereas at trial, it is not admitted over the defendant's objection. Moreover, evidence excluded from trial on Fourth or Fifth Amendment grounds is admissible before the grand jury. *United States v. Calandra,* 414 U.S. 338, 94 S. Ct. 613, 38 L.Ed.2d 561 (1974). The theory is, of course, that the grand jury is an investigative body and that any infringement of the rights of the accused can be corrected in subsequent adversary court proceedings. Notwithstanding the fact that a grand jury may consider evidence that is inadmissible at trial, it may not violate a valid privilege, whether established by the Constitution, statutes, or the common law. *Branzburg v. Hayes,* 408 U.S. 665, 92 S. Ct. 2646, 33 L.Ed.2d 626 (1972).

Selection of Grand Jurors.   An additional limitation on grand jury proceedings concerns the selection of grand jurors. Their selection, like the selection of trial jurors, must not systematically exclude certain groups in the community. For example, in *Castaneda v. Partida,* 430 U.S. 482, 97 S. Ct. 1272, 51 L.Ed.2d 498 (1977), the Supreme Court reversed a conviction after finding that Mexican Americans had been grossly underrepresented on a grand jury that indicted a Mexican American defendant.

The grand jury is a common-law institution deeply rooted in our history. For detailed discussion, see *Costello v. United States,* 350 U.S. 359, 362, 76 S.Ct. 406, 408, 100 L.Ed. 397, 401 (1956).

Right to a Prompt Indictment

Both federal and state courts have ruled that constitutional due process standards require dismissal of an indictment, even if it is brought within the applicable statute of limitations period, if the defendant can prove that the prosecution's delay in bringing the indictment was a deliberate device to gain an advantage over the defendant and that it caused the defendant actual prejudice in presenting a defense. See, for example, *United States v. Rein*, 848 F.2d 777 (7th Cir. 1988); *State v. Smith*, 699 P.2d 711 (Utah 1985).

Extradition

Extradition is the surrender, upon demand, of an individual accused or convicted of an offense within the territorial jurisdiction of the demanding government and outside the territory of the ceding government. See *Terlinden v. Ames*, 184 U.S. 270, 22 S. Ct. 484, 46 L.Ed. 534 (1902). The objective is to prevent escape of persons who stand accused or convicted of crimes and to secure their return to the jurisdiction from which they fled.

In a mobile society such as ours, it is not uncommon for persons accused of crimes to flee across state lines in order to avoid prosecution. Anticipating this problem, Article 4, Section 2 of the Constitution provides that:

> A Person charged in any State with Treason, Felony or any other crime, who shall flee from Justice, and be found in another state, shall on demand of the executive Authority of the State from which he fled, be delivered up, to be removed to the State having Jurisdiction of the crime.

To effectuate the constitutional provision, Congress has enacted statutes governing interstate extradition. 18 U.S.C.A. § 3182. Interstate extradition is a summary executive proceeding designed to enable each state to bring offenders to trial swiftly in the state where the alleged crime was committed. *Michigan v. Doran*, 439 U.S. 282, 99 S.Ct. 530, 58 L.Ed.2d 521 (1978). Every offense punishable by law of a jurisdiction where committed can be subject to extradition, but extradition is usually sought only in serious offenses. Frequently it is used to regain custody of parole violators, prison escapees, or those persons who have "jumped bail."

Most states have adopted the Uniform Criminal Extradition Law that sets out procedural rules for handling interstate extradition. The governor of the "demanding" state issues a requisition warrant seeking return of the fugitive. This is presented to the governor of the "asylum" state (i.e., the state in which the fugitive is located). After investigation, the governor of the asylum state issues a warrant for the fugitive's arrest. An opportunity exists for the person sought as a fugitive to contest the extradition in a court of law in the asylum state. Often this challenge takes the form of a petition for a writ of *habeas corpus* challenging whether the petitioner is in fact the person charged or attacking the regularity of the proceedings. See, for example, N.J. Stat. Ann. § 2A:160–18. Such proceedings seek release of the prisoner who is to be extradited but do not focus on the issue of the prisoner's guilt or innocence.

Jurisdiction and Venue

Before it may hear and adjudicate a case, a court must possess jurisdiction over the subject matter and the parties to the case. State courts have jurisdiction only over persons who commit crimes in their particular states. Of course, it is necessary for a court to acquire jurisdiction over a person in order to try that individual for an offense. This is generally accomplished by arresting the person or by executing process, sometimes called a *capias,* issued by a court following an indictment or information. As previously noted, in some instances a state must resort to extradition proceedings to acquire jurisdiction over an individual who has fled the state after committing an offense.

The term *venue* is sometimes confused with the concept of jurisdiction; however, it is a distinct concept. Venue refers to the place of the trial, and its importance is underscored by the fact that it is twice mentioned in the U.S. Constitution. Article III, Section 2 provides, in part:

> Trial shall be held in the State where the said crimes shall have been committed; but when not committed within the State, the Trial shall be at such Place or Places as the Congress may by law have directed.

The Sixth Amendment provides that:

> In all criminal prosecutions, the accused shall enjoy the right to a . . . public trial, by an impartial jury of the State and district wherein the crime shall have been committed.

The Sixth Amendment applies to state criminal trials via the Fourteenth Amendment. *Duncan v. Louisana,* 391 U.S. 145, 88 S. Ct. 1444, 20 L.Ed.2d 491 (1968). State constitutions, statutes, or court rules usually mirror the provisions of the Sixth Amendment.

Federal courts sit in all fifty states, as well as in federal territories. In some states, federal court jurisdiction is divided into two or more districts. State courts are usually organized by districts of one or more counties. A federal offense is normally tried in the particular federal district where the crime was committed. Likewise, a state criminal case is tried in the particular state district (county, circuit, etc.) where the offense was committed.

While venue lies in the district where the offense was committed, there are unique situations in which the nature of the crime makes it difficult to determine in which of two districts the crime occurred. For example, consider the situation where a person fires a rifle across a county or state line, killing a victim in the adjoining county or state. A more probable scenario is a kidnapping in which the perpetrator takes the victim across county or state lines. Courts must resolve these jurisdictional quandaries according to the relevant statutes and precedents.

It is not uncommon for a defendant to seek a change of venue if he or she believes it is impossible to obtain a fair trial in the venue in which the crime occurred. Rule 21(a) of the Federal Rules of Criminal Procedure stipulates:

> The court upon motion of the defendant shall transfer the proceeding as to that defendant to another district . . . if the court is satisfied that there exists in the district where the prosecution is pending so great a prejudice against the defendant that the

defendant cannot obtain a fair and impartial trial at any place fixed for holding court in that district.

State statutes and court rules generally contain similar provisions. In determining whether to grant a change of venue, courts consider a variety of factors, including (1) the nature of the pretrial publicity and the degree to which it has circulated in the community; (2) the connection of government officials with the release of the publicity; (3) the length of time elapsing between the dissemination of the publicity and the trial; (4) the severity and notoriety of the offense; (5) the area from which the jury is to be drawn; (6) other events occurring in the community that either affect or reflect the attitude of the community or individual jurors toward the defendants; and (7) any factor likely to affect the candor and veracity of the prospective jurors. See, for example, *State v. Bell*, 315 So.2d 307 (La. 1975).

A defendant seeking a change of venue bears the burden of showing the necessity for the change. Changing venue may offend the community sense of justice in not having a trial take place within the community. Additionally, it may create hardships and inefficiencies due to the need to transport witnesses and court personnel to sometimes distant locations. Because a decision to change venue may depend on many factors that can best be determined by the local judge, trial courts are accorded considerable discretion in determining whether to grant a motion to change venue in a criminal case.

Joinder of Offenses

Very often, a defendant stands accused of several distinct offenses arising out of one set of related facts. Conceivably, each offense could be prosecuted separately. It would be more efficient, in most instances, to prosecute such offenses jointly.

Most state rules of criminal procedure follow the federal rule on joinder of offenses, which provides

> Two or more offenses may be charged in the same indictment or information in a separate count for each offense if the offenses charged, whether felonies or misdemeanors or both, are of the same or similar character or are based on the same act or transaction or on two or more acts or transactions connected together or constituting parts of a common scheme or plan. Fed. R. Crim. Proc. 8(a).

In determining whether to proceed on multiple criminal charges jointly or separately, a prosecutor must consider the double jeopardy clause of the Fifth Amendment. This clause bars successive prosecutions for the "same offense." A particular set of actions by the defendant may constitute distinct violations of criminal law and yet be considered part of the same offense under the double jeopardy clause. For example, in *Harris v. Oklahoma*, 433 U.S. 682, 97 S. Ct. 2912, 53 L.Ed.2d 1054 (1977), the Supreme Court held that a defendant could not be prosecuted for armed robbery after being convicted of felony murder for a homicide committed during an armed robbery.

The basic test laid down by the Supreme Court for determining whether there are two separate offenses is "whether each provision [of the criminal law] requires proof of an additional fact that the other does not." *Blockburger v. United*

States, 284 U.S. 299, 304, 52 S. Ct. 180, 182, 76 L.Ed. 306, 309 (1932). Separate statutory crimes need not be identical—either in constituent elements or in actual proof—in order to be the "same offense" within the meaning of the double jeopardy clause of the Fifth Amendment. Thus a defendant cannot be convicted of an offense *and* a lesser included offense. *Brown v. Ohio,* 432 U.S. 161, 97 S. Ct. 2221, 53 L.Ed.2d 187 (1977). State courts have held that a person cannot be convicted of two separate homicide charges where there is only one victim. *Houser v. State,* 474 So.2d 1193 (Fla. 1985). (The defense of double jeopardy is discussed more fully in Chapter 13.)

Severance

Where two or more related offenses are charged in a single indictment or information, the trial judge ordinarily grants a severance of the charges on the motion of either the defense or prosecution, if it is necessary to achieve a fair determination of the defendant's guilt or innocence on each offense. Trial judges have considerable discretion in this area, but there are certain situations in which severance would appear mandatory. For example, a defendant charged with two offenses may want to testify in one case but decline to testify in the other. Again, a defendant may be charged in one case with possession of a firearm by a convicted felon, and in another case with robbery. To sustain the charge in the firearm case, the prosecution would have to show the defendant's prior conviction of a felony. Such a showing would obviously be prejudicial to defense of the robbery charge being heard by the same jury.

Joinder and Severance of Parties

As in the case of multiple offenses, prosecutors generally have broad discretion in deciding whether to prosecute multiple defendants separately or jointly. However, here too there are constitutional considerations. For example, it has been held that separate trials are required where the prosecution plans to use evidence against one defendant that has no relevance to the other defendants. *Kotteakos v. United States,* 328 U.S. 750, 66 S. Ct. 1239, 90 L.Ed. 1557 (1946).

Rule 8(b) of the Federal Rules of Criminal Procedure authorizes joinder of two or more defendants in the same indictment "if they are alleged to have participated in the same act or transaction or the same series of acts or transactions constituting an offense or offenses." Rule 14, however, states that the court "may grant" a severance "if it appears that a defendant or the government is prejudiced by a joinder of offenses or of defendants." Thus federal judges look to determine whether the failure to sever prevents the moving party from getting a fair trial. Denial of a motion for severance is generally held to be an abuse of discretion if the defendants present conflicting and irreconcilable defenses, and there is a danger that the jury will infer that such conflict demonstrates that both are guilty. *United States v. Tarantino,* 846 F.2d 1384 (D.C. Cir. 1988).

The right of severance of parties is usually spelled out in the rules of criminal procedure in each jurisdiction. The purpose of such rules is to ensure that where two or more persons are charged jointly, each will receive a fair determination of guilt or innocence. The Tennessee Rules of Criminal Procedure are fairly typical in this respect:

> The Court, on motion of the State or on motion of the defendant . . . shall grant a severance of defendants if:
>
> I. before trial, it is deemed necessary to protect a defendant's right to a speedy trial or it is deemed appropriate to promote a fair determination of the guilt or innocence of one or more defendants; or
>
> II. during trial, with the consent of the defendant to be severed, it is deemed necessary to promote a fair determination of the guilt or innocence of one or more defendants. Tenn. R. Crim. Proc., Rule 14(c)(2).

Severance of defendants is almost always granted where defendants charged jointly pursue inconsistent defenses or their interests are otherwise antagonistic, or where one defendant chooses to testify and the other does not. If a severance is not granted, a critical problem can arise in a joint trial where a defendant's confession refers to a codefendant's participation. If the defendant who confessed refuses to testify, there are technical problems in using the confession. See *Bruton v. United States*, 391 U.S. 123, 88 S. Ct. 1620, 20 L.Ed.2d 476 (1968).

Lower federal courts have generally taken the position that Rule 14 entitles defendants to separate trials if their defenses are mutually contradictory. See, for example, *United States v. Tarantino*, 846 F.2d 1384 (D.C. Cir. 1988). In 1993 the U.S. Supreme Court addressed the issue. Writing for the Court, Justice O'Connor made it clear that severance of defendants is not required, as a matter of law, when defendants present mutually antagonistic defenses. Rather severance is required only if the trial court finds a serious risk that a joint trial would compromise a specific trial right of a properly joined defendant or prevent the jury from making a reliable judgment about guilt or innocence. Circumstances that may require a severance include a case in which joinder results in the admission of evidence the jury could consider against one defendant but not another, or a case in which evidence exculpating one defendant would have to be excluded at a joint trial. But in federal courts reliance simply upon antagonistic defenses without articulating any specific prejudice is not sufficient to require a trial court to sever the trial of a codefendant. *Zafiro v. United States*, 506 U.S. ___, 113 S.Ct. ___, 122 L.Ed.2d 317 (1993).

Pretrial Motions

Pretrial motions are written requests to the court on behalf of the government or the defendant. They are the means by which defense counsel and prosecutors seek to attain certain objectives before trial. Typically, many motions are available to both the defense and prosecution during the pretrial phase of a criminal case. One common set of motions deals with joinder and severance of offenses and defendants, as previously discussed. Other common pretrial motions include:

1. **Motion to dismiss.** Frequently the defense files a motion to dismiss the indictment or information, alleging (a) that the government's allegations, assuming the truth thereof, do not allege a crime, or that the accusatorial document is not correct in form; or (b) that the undisputed facts do not establish a case of *prima facie* guilt against the defendant. In the former case, the court reaches a determination after receiving written memoranda

or hearing oral argument from both counsel. In the latter case, the motion is usually denied simply on the basis of the prosecution's denial of the defendant's factual allegations. Often the court's determination on a motion to dismiss is not final, as the government may be given an opportunity to amend its documentation. Additionally, a defendant may file a motion to dismiss on grounds of double jeopardy or having been granted immunity, defenses discussed in Chapter 13.

2. **Motion to determine the competency of the accused to stand trial.** In cases where the defendant is mentally disturbed, he or she may be declared incompetent to stand trial on the motion of the defense. In federal cases the trial judge must determine whether the defendant has (1) a rational and factual understanding of the proceedings against him or her; and (2) the ability to consult with his or her lawyer with a reasonable degree of rational understanding. *Dusky v. United States*, 362 U.S. 402, 80 S.Ct. 788, 4 L.Ed.2d 824 (1960). State courts use varying standards to determine whether an accused person is competent to stand trial. The differences are largely semantic. Some state courts apply the federal standard with the additional requirement that the accused must understand the range of penalties that would attend conviction and be able to perceive the adversarial nature of the trial process. A person declared incompetent to stand trial is often institutionalized pursuant to a separate civil proceeding initiated by the government. Such a person remains institutionalized by the court until restored to competency on the basis of medical evidence. If restored to legal competency, he or she may then be tried for the criminal offense originally charged.

3. **Motion to suppress evidence obtained through unlawful search or seizure.** As discussed in Chapter 14, evidence obtained in violation of a defendant's Fourth Amendment rights cannot be used against him or her in a criminal trial. *Weeks v. United States*, 232 U.S. 383, 34 S. Ct. 341, 58 L.Ed. 652 (1914); *Mapp v. Ohio*, 367 U.S. 643, 81 S. Ct. 1684, 6 L.Ed.2d 1081 (1961). When the defense moves to suppress evidence on Fourth Amendment grounds, the court generally holds an evidentiary hearing. At this hearing, testimony is taken regarding the procedures used to obtain the challenged evidence. Where the evidence was obtained through a warrantless search or seizure, the government has the burden to establish that it was lawful. Where a search or seizure is conducted pursuant to a warrant, the defendant usually has the burden to establish the invalidity of the search. In the latter case, the defense generally attacks the legal sufficiency of the warrant. If the defense is successful in causing the suppression of evidence, it may undermine the government's case, leading to a favorable ruling on a subsequent defense motion to dismiss.

4. **Motion to suppress confessions, admissions, or other statements made to the police.** A defendant is constitutionally entitled to a determination by the court whether a confession is voluntary prior to the confession being made known to the jury. *Jackson v. Denno*, 378 U.S. 368, 84 S. Ct. 1774, 12 L.Ed.2d 908 (1964). The motion to suppress the confession is the means of bringing this issue before the court. The motion can bring into play a number of related inquiries, such as whether the confession was obtained in violation of the *Miranda* rules (see Chapter 15). Generally,

before ruling on a motion to suppress a confession, the court holds an evidentiary hearing. Again, the disposition of such a motion may have a significant impact on the prosecution of a criminal case. If the confession is crucial to the prosecution's case, a favorable ruling on the motion to suppress may lead to a dismissal of the charges.

5. **Motion to suppress pretrial identification of the accused.** This motion is designed to determine whether the pretrial identification procedures employed by the police in having an eyewitness identify an accused violated the due process standards outlined in *Neil v. Biggers,* 409 U.S. 188, 93 S. Ct. 375, 34 L.Ed.2d 401 (1972). The court's inquiry here focuses on whether the identification procedures were impermissibly suggestive to the witness (see Chapter 15).

6. **Motion to require the prosecution to disclose the identity of a confidential informant.** The prosecution is not ordinarily required to disclose the identity of a confidential informant who merely furnishes the probable cause on which an arrest or search is predicated. Nevertheless, if the informant was an "active participant" in the offense, the prosecution may be required to disclose the informant's identity. The test calls for balancing the public interest in protecting the free flow of information to the police against the individual's right to prepare a defense. See *Roviaro v. United States,* 353 U.S. 53, 77 S. Ct. 623, 1 L.Ed.2d 639 (1957). Trial judges have considerable discretion in ruling on this motion.

7. **Motion for change of venue.** The defendant, and in some instances the government, may move for a change of venue (i.e., place of trial) on the ground that a fair and impartial trial cannot be had where the case is pending. In recent years, heightened media coverage of crime and criminal prosecutions has generated tremendous concern over the ability of defendants to receive a fair trial. The concern usually focuses on the difficulty of selecting an impartial jury where potential jurors have been exposed to intensive newspaper, radio, and television coverage of a crime. The Supreme Court, in *Sheppard v. Maxwell,* 384 U.S. 333, 86 S. Ct. 1507, 16 L.Ed.2d 600 (1966), set out some guidelines for dealing with the effects of pretrial publicity (see Chapter 17). Since then an increasing number of defendants have filed motions seeking a change of venue.

8. **Motion for a continuance.** Either the government or the defendant may seek a continuance, or postponement, of the trial. A variety of grounds may be asserted, including illness or emergency that makes it difficult or impossible for the defendant, prosecutor, defense counsel, or an important witness to be present as scheduled; the unavailability of a significant witness or piece of documentary evidence; or the lack of adequate time to prepare for trial. The "bottom line" of the request is the contention that the movant cannot receive a fair trial if required to proceed as scheduled. In considering motions for continuances, trial judges are vested with considerable discretion, and appellate courts consistently hold that there is no abuse of discretion unless a party can show that specific prejudice has resulted to the defendant as a result of the denial of the requested continuance.

9. **Other pretrial motions.** Other common pretrial motions include motions to take a deposition to preserve the testimony of an infirm witness or one

who may not be available for trial; inspect the minutes of the grand jury proceeding; compel the prosecutor to disclose evidence that may be favorable to the accused; and disqualify the trial judge on grounds of bias, close relationship to parties, or that the judge will be a material witness.

Arraignment

The arraignment is the accused's first appearance before a court of law with the authority to conduct a criminal trial. At this stage of the process, the accused must enter a plea to the charges contained in the indictment or information. There are several options. The accused may choose to plead *not guilty*, in which case the plea is noted and a trial date is set. He or she may plead *guilty*, in which case no trial is necessary. Instead, guilt is simply pronounced and sentencing follows, either immediately or at some future court appearance, after a presentence investigation has been completed (see Chapter 18). A plea of guilty containing a protestation of innocence, sometimes called an "*Alford* plea," can be made when a defendant intelligently concludes that his or her interests require entry of a guilty plea. *North Carolina v. Alford*, 400 U.S. 25, 91 S.Ct. 160, 27 L.Ed.2d 162 (1970). In some jurisdictions, the accused has the option of pleading *nolo contendere* (no contest). This plea, although functionally equivalent to a guilty plea in a criminal trial, provides the accused the advantage that it generally cannot be construed as an admission of guilt in a related civil suit.

Since a plea of guilty or *nolo contendere* represents a waiver of constitutional rights, it is essential that the plea be made knowingly and voluntarily. The Federal Rules of Criminal Procedure preclude trial judges from accepting such a plea unless the court determines the plea is "voluntary and not the result of force or threats or of promises apart from a plea agreement." Fed. R. Crim. P. 11(d). In addition to determining voluntariness, a judge must decide whether a factual basis exists for a plea of guilty or *nolo contendere*. A factual basis is necessary to assure that the accused does not admit to an offense where his or her conduct does not fall within the bounds of the government's accusations. See, for example, *United States v. Montoya-Camacho*, 644 F.2d 480 (5th Cir. 1981).

Most states have adopted similar rules of procedure to assure that pleas are voluntary and comply with constitutional requirements. For example, Rule 3.170(j) of the Florida Rules of Criminal Procedure specifies: "No plea of guilty or nolo contendere shall be accepted by a court without first determining . . . that the circumstances surrounding the plea reflect . . . its voluntariness and that there is a factual basis for the plea."

Rules concerning voluntariness and factual basis generally do not specify any precise method to be followed by the court. Judges employ various methods to determine voluntariness. Often these methods include interrogation of the defendant by the judge, and sometimes by the prosecutor and defense counsel. The extent of questioning often depends on the defendant's educational level and maturity. Frequently, judges ask indigent defendants about their satisfaction with court-appointed counsel. The objective is to establish that no improper inducements have been made to secure a plea, that the defendant understands the basic constitutional rights incident to a trial, that these rights are being waived, and that he or she comprehends the consequences of the plea. *Boykin v. Alabama*, 395 U.S. 238, 89 S. Ct. 1709, 23 L.Ed.2d 274 (1969).

In determining that a factual basis exists for the defendant's plea, judges often have the prosecutor briefly outline available proof to establish a *prima facie* case of the defendant's guilt. A more extensive inquiry may be in order for specific-intent crimes. The thoroughness of the court's determination of voluntariness and factual basis comes into play if a defendant later moves to withdraw a plea and enter a plea of not guilty.

Plea Bargaining

Probably more than 90 percent of felony suspects arraigned plead guilty or no contest. Very often the guilty plea is the result of a bargain struck between the defense and the prosecution. In a plea bargain, the accused agrees to plead guilty in exchange for a reduction in the number and/or severity of charges or a promise by the prosecutor not to seek the maximum penalty allowed by law. Plea negotiations are subject to the approval of the trial court. In most instances the bargain is arrived at between experienced and knowledgeable counsel on both sides and is readily approved by the court. If, however, the court is unwilling to approve the plea bargain, the defendant must choose between withdrawing the guilty plea (and thus going to trial), and accepting the plea bargain with such modifications as the judge may approve. Once the court has accepted a guilty plea pursuant to a plea bargain, the court cannot unilaterally alter it without permitting the defendant the opportunity to withdraw the plea.

In some jurisdictions, judges participate directly in plea-bargaining discussions. The justification for this practice is that a judge can guide the parties to an equitable and expeditious resolution of the case. On the other hand, some courts disfavor the participation of a trial judge in plea-bargaining discussions on the basis that the power and position of the judge may improperly influence the defendant to enter a guilty plea. See, for example, *Perkins v. Court of Appeals*, 738 S.W.2d 276, 282 (Tex. Crim. App. 1987).

Plea bargaining has been sharply criticized by observers with different perspectives on the criminal process. Some critics fault plea bargaining for reducing the severity of criminal penalties. Others view plea bargaining as an unconstitutional effort to deprive defendants of their right to a fair trial. Plea bargaining has never been popular, but few stop to consider the tremendous costs and delays that would result if the numerous cases currently resolved through plea bargaining were to go to trial.

In addition to permitting a substantial conservation of prosecutorial and judicial resources, plea bargaining provides a means by which, through mutual concession, the parties may obtain a prompt resolution of criminal proceedings with the benefits that flow from final disposition of a case. The plea bargain, or negotiated sentence, enables the parties to avoid the delay and uncertainties of trial and appeal and permits swift and certain punishment of law violators with a sentence tailored to the circumstances of the case at hand.

Despite constitutional attacks, the Supreme Court has upheld the practice of plea bargaining. In *Brady v. United States*, 397 U.S. 742, 90 S. Ct. 1463, 1471, 25

L.Ed.2d 747, 759 (1970), the Court said that "we cannot hold that it is unconstitutional for the State to extend a benefit to a defendant who in turn extends a substantial benefit to the State." In a subsequent case, the Court was even more sanguine about plea bargaining:

> The disposition of criminal charges by agreement between the prosecutor and the accused, sometimes loosely called "plea bargaining," is an essential component of the administration of justice. Properly administered, it is to be encouraged. *Santobello v. New York,* 404 U.S. 257, 260, 92 S. Ct. 495, 498, 30 L.Ed.2d 427, 432 (1971).

Since the plea bargain necessarily entails a waiver of the constitutional right to trial, it must be examined by the trial court to determine whether the accused has knowingly waived his/her rights and agreed to plead guilty without coercion by the state. *Boykin v. Alabama,* 395 U.S. 238, 89 S. Ct. 1709, 23 L.Ed.2d 274 (1969). Despite such procedural protections, cases still arise challenging the fundamental fairness of certain plea-bargaining tactics. See, for example, *Bordenkircher v. Hayes,* 434 U.S. 357, 98 S. Ct. 663, 54 L.Ed.2d 604 (1978), where a prosecutor threatened a defendant with a more serious indictment in order to induce him to plead guilty to an indictment already pending against him.

Pretrial Discovery

The courts have long recognized a prosecutorial duty to disclose exculpatory information (i.e., information that tends to vindicate the accused) to the defense. This is based on the fundamental concept of our system of justice that individuals accused of crimes must be treated fairly. The Supreme Court has stated that

> the suppression by the prosecution of evidence favorable to the accused upon request violates due process where the evidence is material either to guilt or punishment, irrespective of the good faith or bad faith of the prosecution. *Brady v. Maryland,* 373 U.S. 83, 87, 83 S. Ct. 1194, 1996, 10 L.Ed.2d 215, 218 (1963).

CASE IN POINT

PLEA BARGAINING

Defendant Paul LaVallee was charged in a New Hampshire court with the crime of aggravated assault. He elected to plead not guilty, was convicted at trial, and was sentenced to ten to thirty years in prison. LaVallee brought a *habeas corpus* action challenging his sentence, arguing that it was disproportionate to the sentences given defendants who agreed to plead guilty. He claimed that it was impermissible for the courts to give harsher sentences to defendants who insist on their constitutional right to a trial. The state supreme court rejected LaVallee's challenge. *LaVallee v. Perrin,* 466 A.2d 932 (N.H. 1983). The court said that the defendant's argument ignored "the realities of the plea bargaining process." 466 A.2d at 935. Further, it noted that "In this state, we have rejected the notion that it is impermissible to compensate one who pleads guilty by extending him a proper degree of leniency." 466 A.2d at 935.

The Supreme Court has held that, in addition to substantive exculpatory evidence, evidence tending to impeach the credibility of prosecution witnesses falls within *Brady's* definition of evidence "favorable" to an accused. Therefore, under *Brady*, a defendant is entitled to disclosure of information that might be used to impeach government witnesses. See *United States v. Bagley*, 473 U.S. 667, 105 S.Ct. 3375, 87 L.Ed.2d 481 (1985).

Generally, the defense must request the disclosure of the exculpatory evidence. However, if the defense is unaware of the existence of the evidence, such a request is impossible. The Supreme Court has held that failure to request disclosure is not necessarily fatal to a later challenge based on *Brady v. Maryland*, but it may significantly affect the standard for determining materiality. *United States v. Agurs*, 427 U.S. 97, 96 S. Ct. 2392, 49 L.Ed.2d 342 (1976).

In a similar vein, it has been held to be a denial of due process if a prosecutor knowingly allows perjured testimony to be used against the accused. *Mooney v. Holohan*, 294 U.S. 103, 55 S. Ct. 340, 79 L.Ed. 791 (1935); *Alcorta v. Texas*, 355 U.S. 28, 78 S. Ct. 103, 2 L.Ed.2d 9 (1957).

In 1993 a question arose as to whether the *Brady* principle would allow a defendant to challenge the truthfulness of statements made in an affidavit for a search warrant. In *United States v. Barton*, 995 F.2d 931 (9th Cir. 1993), the police obtained a warrant to search the defendant's home based on an officer's affidavit that he had smelled marijuana during a consensual entry of the home. At a pretrial suppression hearing, the defendant claimed that the officer could not have smelled the marijuana plants that were seized because they had no odor. But by the time of the suppression hearing, the plants had rotted because the police had not ventilated the bag in which they stashed the plants. The court recognized that the destruction by the government of evidence that tends to impeach allegations in an affidavit demonstrating probable cause for a search warrant may violate due process principles. Nevertheless, the defendant did not prevail. Rather, the *Barton* court relied upon the principle declared by the U.S. Supreme Court in *Arizona v. Youngblood*, 488 U.S. 51, 109 S.Ct. 333, 102 L.Ed. 2d 281 (1988). There the Court held that the failure of law enforcement officers through mere negligence and not in bad faith to preserve evidence which might have been helpful to the defendant does not violate a defendant's right to due process of law.

Most states have now adopted liberal rules pertaining to pretrial discovery, rules designed to avoid unfairness to the defense resulting from abdications of prosecutorial duty. Using appropriate pretrial motions, the defense and prosecution can gain access to the evidence possessed by the opposing party. Pretrial discovery thus not only enhances the fairness of the criminal process but also militates against surprises at trial.

Under statutory authority, Ill. S.H.A. 725 ILCS 5/114-3, the Illinois Supreme Court has promulgated rules governing discovery procedures in criminal cases. In part, those rules are

Supreme Court Rule 412. Disclosure to Accused

(a) Except as is otherwise provided in these rules . . . , the State shall, upon written motion of defense counsel, disclose . . . the following information or material within its possession or control:

(i) the names and last known addresses of persons whom the State intends to call as witnesses, together with their relevant written or recorded statements. . . ;

(ii) any written or recorded statements and the substance of any oral statements made by the accused or by a codefendant, and a list of witnesses to the making and acknowledgment of such statements;

(iii) a transcript of those portions of grand jury minutes containing testimony of the accused and relevant testimony of persons whom the prosecuting attorney intends to call as witnesses at the hearing or trial;

(iv) any reports or statements of experts, made in connection with the particular case, including results of physical or mental examinations and of scientific tests, experiments, or comparisons, and a statement of the qualifications of the expert;

(v) any books, papers, documents, photographs or tangible objects which the prosecuting attorney intends to use in the hearing or trial or which were obtained from or belong to the accused; and

(vi) any record of prior criminal convictions, which may be used for impeachment, of persons whom the State intends to call as witnesses at the hearing or trial. . . .

Supreme Court Rule 413. Disclosure to Prosecution

(a) **The person of the accused.** Notwithstanding the initiation of judicial proceedings, and subject to constitutional limitations, a judicial officer may require the accused, among other things, to:

(i) appear in a line-up;

(ii) speak for identification by witnesses to an offense;

(iii) be fingerprinted;

(iv) pose for photographs not involving reenactment of a scene;

(v) try on articles of clothing;

(vi) permit the taking of specimens material under his fingernails;

(vii) permit the taking of samples of his blood, hair and other materials of his body which involve no unreasonable intrusion thereof;

(viii) provide a sample of his handwriting; and

(ix) submit to a reasonable physical or medical inspection of his body.

(b) [provision for appearance of accused and counsel at foregoing]

(c) **Medical and scientific reports.** . . .

(d) **Defenses.** Subject to constitutional limitations and within reasonable time after the filing of a written motion by the State, defense counsel shall inform the State of any defenses which he intends to make at a hearing or trial and shall furnish the state with the following material and information within his possession or control:

(i) the names and last known addresses of persons he intends to call as witnesses together with their relevant written or recorded statements. . . .

(ii) any books, papers, documents, photographs, or tangible objects he intends to use as evidence or for impeachment at a hearing or trial;

(iii) and if the defendant intends to prove an alibi, specific information as to the place where he maintains he was at the time of the alleged offense.

(e) **Additional disclosure.** Upon a showing of materiality, and if the request is reasonable, the court in its discretion may require disclosure to the State of relevant material and information not covered by this rule.

Discovery in the Federal Courts

Discovery in a criminal case is somewhat more limited in federal than in state courts. Under the provisions of 18 U.S.C.A. § 3500, a federal criminal defendant is not entitled to inspect a statement or report prepared by a government witness "until said witness has testified on direct examination in the trial of the case." After a witness testifies, the government, upon proper request of the defense, must then produce that portion of any statement or report that relates to the subject matter as to which the witness has testified. The federal statute is commonly referred to as the "Jencks Act" because its effect was first recognized in *Jencks v. United States*, 353 U.S. 657, 77 S.Ct. 1007, 1 L.Ed.2d 1103 (1957). In *Jencks,* a defendant was allowed to obtain for impeachment purposes previous statements made to government agents by prosecution witnesses.

Courts have indicated that the principal purpose of the Jencks Act is to facilitate a defendant's right to cross-examination. In some instances the trial judge must make an *in camera* inspection of documents where the government asserts that the documents contain statements not relevant to the subject matter to which the witness has testified.

THE RIGHT TO A SPEEDY TRIAL

The Sixth Amendment to the federal Constitution guarantees the defendant the right to a speedy trial. In *Barker v. Wingo*, 407 U.S. 514, 92 S. Ct. 2182, 33 L.Ed.2d 101 (1972), the Supreme Court refused to mandate a specific time limit between the filing of charges and the commencement of trial, but adopted a balancing test to determine whether a defendant was denied the right to a speedy trial. Under this test, courts must consider (1) the length of the delay; (2) the reasons for the delay; (3) the defendant's assertion of the right; and (4) prejudice to the defendant.

In response to the Court's decision in *Barker v. Wingo*, Congress enacted the Speedy Trial Act of 1974, 18 U.S.C.A. § 3161. The act provides specific time limits for pretrial and trial procedures in the federal courts. For example, an indictment must be filed within thirty days of arrest; arraignment must be held within ten days of indictment; and trial must commence within seventy days after indictment. Violations of the time limitations are remedied by dismissal of charges. However, there are a number of exceptions to the time limits, especially where delays are caused by defendants' motions.

Under federal law, the indictment of the accused activates the clock governing the right to a speedy trial. *United States v. Marion*, 404 U.S. 307, 92 S.Ct. 455, 30 L.Ed.2d 468 (1971). Apart from the right to a speedy trial, a defendant who can establish that the prosecutor intentionally delayed indicting him or her in order to gain a tactical advantage *and* that the defendant incurred actual prejudice as a result of the delay can assert a claim of denial of due process. *United States v. Lovasco*, 431 U.S. 783, 97 S.Ct. 2044, 52 L.Ed.2d 752 (1977); *United States v. Amuny*, 767 F.2d 1113, 1119 (5th Cir. 1985).

The speedy trial clause of the Sixth Amendment is made applicable to the states through the Fourteenth Amendment. *Klopfer v. North Carolina*, 386 U.S. 213, 87 S.Ct. 988, 18 L.Ed.2d 1 (1967). Most states have adopted legislation or court rules along the lines of the federal speedy trial law. See, for example, Ill. S.H.A. § 725 ILCS 5/103–5. State laws frequently provide that the right to a speedy trial is activated on either the date of the filing of an indictment, information, or other formal accusatorial document; or on the date the accused is taken into custody.

CONCLUSION

The rights afforded by the Fourth, Fifth, Sixth, and Eighth Amendments to the United States Constitution (and similar provisions in the state constitutions) vitally affect the procedures used in criminal cases. Many of these rights were redefined or enlarged by the courts during the 1960s and 1970s, and come into frequent play long before a criminal prosecution reaches the trial stage.

Indeed, most criminal cases never reach the trial stage. It is therefore essential that the student of criminal justice have a good grasp of the various pretrial procedures that often influence and frequently determine the outcome of a criminal case. It is equally important to understand the substantial discretion vested in key actors in the pretrial process, especially in the prosecutor. The prosecutor's discretion is manifested not only in the charging process, but also in the pervasive but highly controversial practice of plea bargaining. When the exercise of prosecutorial discretion fails to achieve a negotiated guilty plea, then a trial must be held. In the next chapter, we discuss the procedures specific to the criminal trial.

QUESTIONS FOR THOUGHT AND DISCUSSION

1. Compare the Supreme Court's decisions in *Gideon v. Wainwright* and *Faretta v. California*. Are there any inconsistencies between the two decisions? Are any such inconsistencies reconcilable?

2. In your opinion, does the Eighth Amendment guarantee the right to pretrial release on bail in a felony case? What about a misdemeanor case? Did the Supreme Court decide the *Salerno* case correctly? How does a magistrate determine how much bail is appropriate and how much is "excessive"? What alternatives, if any, do you see to the traditional bail-bond system to ensure the appearance of the defendant in court?

3. Can you imagine a situation in which a prosecutor would run afoul of the federal Constitution by engaging in selective prosecution? In your state, can a prosecutor be sued for malicious prosecution? How is this proved?

4. What tactical advantage does the defendant gain by pleading *nolo contendere* rather than guilty? Does your state permit the *nolo contendere* plea? Under what circumstances?

5. How might a prosecutor persuade a defendant to plead guilty to a criminal charge without running afoul of due process? What prosecutorial tactics are likely to be viewed as fundamentally unfair?

6. Compare the advantages and disadvantages to the defendant of insisting on the right to a speedy trial.

7. Why do you think the United States Supreme Court has never held that the Fifth Amendment requirement of indictment by a grand jury applies to the states as well as to the federal government? Does the grand jury still play a viable role in the criminal justice system? Are the criticisms of the grand jury valid? Why or why not?

8. Should plea bargaining be abolished? If not, are any modifications necessary to protect (a) the defendant and (b) the public?

CASES

SCOTT V. ILLINOIS
Supreme Court of the Unites States, 1979.
440 U.S. 367, 99 S. Ct. 1158, 59 L.Ed.2d 383.

[In *Gideon v. Wainwright* (1963), the Supreme Court held that indigent defendants facing felony charges in state court are entitled to court-appointed counsel at public expense. In 1972, in *Argersinger v. Hamlin*, the Court extended the *Gideon* decision to encompass misdemeanors punishable by jail terms. Left unsettled, however, was the question whether the right to appointed counsel applies in a case where an indigent defendant is accused of a misdemeanor that, although *punishable* by incarceration, is *actually punished* only by a fine. In the instant case, the Court addresses this issue.]

Mr. Justice REHNQUIST delivered the opinion of the Court.

. . . Petitioner Scott was convicted of theft and fined $50 after a bench trial in the Circuit Court of Cook County, Ill. His conviction was affirmed by the state intermediate appellate court and then by the Supreme Court of Illinois, over Scott's contention that the Sixth and Fourteenth Amendments to the United States Constitution required that Illinois provide trial counsel to him at its expense.

Petitioner Scott was convicted of shoplifting merchandise valued at less than $150. The applicable Illinois statute set the maximum penalty for such an offense at a $500 fine or one year in jail, or both. The petitioner argues that a line of this Court's cases culminating in *Argersinger v. Hamlin*, . . . requires State provision of counsel whenever imprisonment is an authorized penalty.

The Supreme Court of Illinois rejected this contention. . . .

The Supreme Court of Illinois went on to state that it was "not inclined to extend *Argersinger*" to the case where a defendant is charged with a statutory offense for which imprisonment upon conviction is authorized but not actually imposed upon the defendant. We agree with the Supreme Court of Illinois that the Federal Constitution does not require a state trial court to appoint counsel for a criminal defendant such as petitioner, and we therefore affirm its judgment. . . .

There is considerable doubt that the Sixth Amendment itself, as originally drafted by the Framers of the Bill of Rights, contemplated any guarantee other than the right of an accused in a criminal prosecution in a federal court to employ a lawyer to assist in his defense. In *Powell v. Alabama*, 287 U.S. 45, 53 S. Ct. 55, 77 L.Ed. 158 (1932), the Court held that Alabama was obligated to appoint counsel for the Scottsboro defendants, phrasing the inquiry as "whether the defendants were in substance denied the right of counsel, and if so, whether such denial infringes the due process clause of the Fourteenth Amendment."

Betts v. Brady, 316 U.S. 455, 62 S. Ct. 1252, 86 L.Ed. 1595 (1942), held that not every indigent defendant accused in a state criminal prosecution was entitled to appointment of counsel. A determination had to be made in each individual case whether failure to appoint counsel was a denial of fundamental fairness. *Betts* was in turn overruled in *Gideon v. Wainwright*, 372 U.S. 335, 83 S. Ct. 792, 9 L.Ed.2d 799 (1963). . . . In *Gideon*, *Betts* was described as holding "that a refusal to appoint counsel for an indigent defendant charged with a felony did not necessarily violate the Due Process Clause of the Fourteenth Amendment. . . ."

Several Terms later the Court held in *Duncan v. Louisiana*, 391 U.S. 145, 88 S. Ct. 1444, 20 L.Ed.2d 491 (1968), that the right to jury trial in federal court guaranteed by the Sixth Amendment was applicable to the States by virtue of the Fourteenth Amendment. The Court held, however: "It is doubtless true that there is a category of petty crimes or offenses which is not subject to the Sixth Amendment jury trial provision and should not be subject to the Fourteenth Amendment jury trial requirement here applied to the States. Crimes carrying possible penalties up to six months do not require a jury trial if they otherwise qualify as petty offenses. . . ." In

Baldwin v. New York, 399 U.S. 66, 69, 26 L.Ed.2d 437, 90 S. Ct. 1886 (1970), the controlling opinion of Mr. Justice White concluded that "no offense can be deemed 'petty' for purposes of the right to trial by jury where imprisonment for more than six months is authorized."

In *Argersinger* the State of Florida urged that a similar dichotomy be employed in the right-to-counsel area: Any offense punishable by less than six months in jail should not require appointment of counsel for an indigent defendant. The *Argersinger* Court rejected this analogy, however, observing that "the right to trial by jury has a different genealogy and is brigaded with a system of trial to a judge alone."

The number of separate opinions in *Gideon, Duncan, Baldwin,* and *Argersinger,* suggests that constitutional line drawing becomes more difficult as the reach of the Constitution is extended further, and as efforts are made to transpose lines from one area of Sixth Amendment jurisprudence to another. The process of incorporation creates special difficulties, for the state and federal contexts are often different and application of the same principle may have ramifications distinct in degree and kind. The range of human conduct regulated by state criminal laws is much broader than that of the federal criminal laws, particularly on the "petty" offense part of the spectrum. As a matter of constitutional adjudication, we are, therefore, less willing to extrapolate an already extended line when, although the general nature of the principle sought to be applied is clear, its precise limits and their ramifications become less so. We have now in our decided cases departed from the literal meaning of the Sixth Amendment. And we cannot fall back on the common law as it existed prior to the enactment of that Amendment, since it perversely gave less in the way of right to counsel to accused felons than to those accused of misdemeanors.

In *Argersinger* the Court rejected arguments that social cost or a lack of available lawyers militated against its holding, in some part because it thought these arguments were factually incorrect. But they were rejected in much larger part because of the Court's conclusion that incarceration was so severe a sanction that it should not be imposed as a result of a criminal trial unless an indigent defendant had been offered appointed counsel to assist in his defense, regardless of the cost to the States implicit in such a rule. The Court in its opinion repeatedly referred to trials "where an accused is deprived of his liberty," and to "a case that actually leads to imprisonment even for a brief period." The Chief Justice in his opinion concurring in the result also observed that "any deprivation of liberty is a serious matter."

Although the intentions of the *Argersinger* Court are not unmistakably clear from its opinion, we conclude today that *Argersinger* did indeed delimit the constitutional right to appointed counsel in state criminal proceedings. Even were the matter res nova, we believe that the central premise of *Argersinger*—that actual imprisonment is a penalty different in kind from fines or the mere threat of imprisonment—is eminently sound and warrants adoption of actual imprisonment as the line defining the constitutional right to appointment of counsel. *Argersinger* has proved reasonably workable, whereas any extension would create confusion and impose unpredictable, but necessarily substantial, costs on 50 quite diverse States. We therefore hold that the Sixth and Fourteenth Amendments to the United States Constitution require only that no indigent criminal defendant be sentenced to a term of imprisonment unless the State has afforded him the right to assistance of appointed counsel in his defense. The judgment of the Supreme Court of Illinois is accordingly affirmed.

Mr. Justice POWELL concurring. . . .

Mr. Justice BRENNAN, with whom Mr. Justice MARSHALL and Mr. Justice STEVENS join, dissenting.

. . . The Court in an opinion that at best ignores the basic principles of prior decisions, affirms Scott's conviction without counsel because he was sentenced only to pay a fine. In my view, the plain wording of the Sixth Amendment and the Court's precedents compel the conclusion that Scott's uncounseled conviction violated the Sixth Amendment and Fourteenth Amendments and should be reversed. . . .

The apparent reason for the Court's adoption of the "actual imprisonment" standard for all misdemeanors is concern for the economic burden that an "authorized imprisonment" standard might place on the States. But, with all respect, that concern is both irrelevant and speculative.

The Court's opinion turns the reasoning of *Argersinger* on its head. It restricts the right to counsel, perhaps the most fundamental Sixth Amendment right, more narrowly than the admittedly less fundamental right to jury trial. The abstract pretext that "constitutional line drawing becomes more difficult as the reach of the Constitution is extended further, and as efforts are made to transpose lines from one area of Sixth Amendment jurisprudence to another,"

cannot camouflage the anomalous result the Court reaches. Today's decision reminds one of Mr. Justice Black's description of *Betts v. Brady:* "an anachronism when handed down" that "ma[kes] an abrupt break with its own well-considered precedents."

Mr. Justice BLACKMUN, dissenting. . . .

FARETTA V. CALIFORNIA
Supreme Court of the United States, 1975.
422 U.S. 806, 95 S. Ct. 2525, 45 L.Ed.2d 562.

[Faretta was charged with grand theft and a public defender was appointed to represent him. Faretta was denied permission to represent himself or even to serve as co-counsel in his own defense. He was convicted after trial and his conviction was affirmed by the state appellate courts. The Supreme Court granted Faretta's petition for certiorari.]

Mr. Justice STEWART delivered the opinion of the Court.
. . . The question before us now is whether a defendant in a state criminal trial has a constitutional right to proceed without counsel when he voluntarily and intelligently elects to do so. Stated another way, the question is whether a State may constitutionally hale a person into its criminal courts and there force a lawyer upon him, even when he insists that he wants to conduct his own defense. It is not an easy question, but we have concluded that a State may not constitutionally do so.

. . . The Sixth Amendment does not provide merely that a defense shall be made for the accused; it grants to the accused personally the right to make his defense. It is the accused, not counsel, who must be "informed of the nature and cause of the accusation," who must be "confronted with witnesses against him," and who must be accorded "compulsory process for obtaining witnesses in his favor." Although not stated in the Amendment in so many words, the right to self-representation—to make one's own defense personally—is thus necessarily implied by the structure of the Amendment. The right to defend is given directly to the accused;

for it is he who suffers the consequences if the defense fails.

The counsel provision supplements this design. It speaks of the "assistance" of counsel, and an assistant, however expert, is still an assistant. The language and spirit of the Sixth Amendment contemplate that counsel, like the other defense tools guaranteed by the Amendment, shall be an aid to a willing defendant—not an organ of the State interposed between an unwilling defendant and his right to defend himself personally. To thrust counsel upon the accused, against his considered wish, thus violates the logic of the Amendment. In such a case, counsel is not an assistant, but a master; and the right to make a defense is stripped of the personal character upon which the Amendment insists. . . .

[Here Justice Stewart reviews the right to counsel under English common law.]

. . . [T]here is no evidence that the colonists and the Framers ever doubted the right of self-representation, or imagined that this right might be considered inferior to the right of assistance of counsel. To the contrary, the colonists and the Framers, as well as their English ancestors, always conceived of the right to counsel as an "assistance" for the accused, to be used at his option, in defending himself. The Framers selected in the Sixth Amendment a form of words that necessarily implies the right of self-representation. That conclusion is supported by centuries of consistent history.

There can be no blinking the fact that the right of an accused to conduct his own defense seems to cut against the grain of this Court's decisions holding that the Constitution requires that no accused can be convicted and imprisoned unless he has been accorded the right to the assistance of counsel. . . .

But it is one thing to hold that every defendant, rich or poor, has the right to the assistance of counsel, and quite another to say that a State may compel a defendant to accept a lawyer he does not want. The value of state-appointed counsel was not unappreciated by the Founders, yet the notion of compulsory counsel was utterly foreign to them. And whatever else may be said of those who wrote the Bill of Rights, surely there can be no doubt that they understood the inestimable worth of free choice.

It is undeniable that in most criminal prosecutions defendants could better defend with counsel's guidance than by their unskilled efforts. But where the defendant will not voluntarily accept representation by counsel, the potential advantage of a lawyer's training and experience can be realized, if at all, only imperfectly. To force a lawyer on a defendant can only lead him to believe that the law contrives against him. Moreover, it is not inconceivable that in some rare instances, the defendant might in fact present his case more effectively by conducting his own defense. Personal liberties are not rooted in the law of averages. The right to defend is personal. The defendant, and not his lawyer or the State, will bear the personal consequences of a conviction. It is the defendant, therefore, who must be free personally to decide whether in his particular case counsel is to his advantage. And although he may conduct his own defense ultimately to his own detriment, his choice must be honored out of "that respect for the individual which is the lifeblood of the law." . . .

In forcing Faretta, under these circumstances, to accept against his will a state-appointed public defender, the California courts deprived him of his constitutional right to conduct his own defense. Accordingly, the judgment before us is vacated, and the case is remanded for further proceedings not inconsistent with this opinion.

Mr. Chief Justice BURGER, with whom Mr. Justice BLACKMUN and Mr. Justice REHNQUIST join, dissenting.

. . . [B]oth the "spirit and the logic" of the Sixth Amendment are that every person accused of crime shall receive the fullest possible defense; in the vast majority of cases this command can be honored only by means of the expressly guaranteed right to counsel, and the trial judge is in the best position to determine whether the accused is capable of conducting his defense. True freedom of choice and society's interest in seeing that justice is achieved can be vindicated only if the trial court retains discretion to reject any attempted waiver of counsel and insist that the accused be tried according to the Constitution. This discretion is as critical an element of basic fairness as a trial judge's discretion to decline to accept a plea of guilty. . . .

The Court's attempt to support its result by collecting dicta from prior decisions is no more persuasive than its analysis of the Sixth Amendment. Considered in context, the cases upon which the Court relies to "beat its path" either lead it nowhere or point in precisely the opposite direction. . . .

In short, what the Court represents as a well-traveled road is in reality a constitutional trail which it is blazing for the first time today, one that has not even been hinted at in our previous decisions. Far from an interpretation of the Sixth Amendment, it is a perversion of the provision to which we gave full meaning in *Gideon v. Wainwright* and *Argersinger v. Hamlin.* . . .

It hardly needs repeating that courts at all levels are already handicapped by the unsupplied demand for competent advocates, with the result that it often takes far longer to complete a given case than experienced counsel would require. If we were to assume that there will be widespread exercise of the newly discovered constitutional right to self-representation, it would almost certainly follow that there will be added congestion in the courts and that the quality of justice will suffer. Moreover, the Court blandly assumes that once an accused has elected to defend himself he will be bound by his choice and not be heard to complain of it later. . . . This assumption ignores the role of appellate review, for the reported cases are replete with instances of a convicted defendant being relieved of a deliberate decision even when made with the advice of counsel. . . . It is totally unrealistic, therefore, to suggest that an accused will always be held to the consequences of a decision to conduct his own defense. Unless, as may be the case, most persons accused of crime have more wit than to insist upon the dubious benefit that the Court confers today, we can expect that many expensive and good-faith prosecutions will be

nullified on appeal for reasons that trial courts are now deprived of the power to prevent.

STACK V. BOYLE
Supreme Court of the United States, 1951.
342 U.S. 1, 72 S. Ct. 1, 96 L.Ed. 3.

[In this federal case, the Supreme Court considers the question of "excessive bail" under the Eighth Amendment.]

Mr. Chief Justice VINSON delivered the opinion of the Court.

Indictments have been returned in the Southern District of California charging the twelve petitioners with conspiring to violate the Smith Act. . . . Upon their arrest, bail was fixed for each petitioner in the widely varying amounts of $2,500, $7,500, $75,000 and $100,000. On motion of petitioner Schneiderman following arrest in the Southern District of New York, his bail was reduced to $50,000 before his removal to California. On motion of the Government to increase bail in the case of other petitioners, and after several intermediate procedural steps not material to the issues presented here, bail was fixed in the District Court for the Southern District of California in the uniform amount of $50,000 for each petitioner.

Petitioners moved to reduce bail on the ground that bail as fixed was excessive under the Eighth Amendment. In support of their motion, petitioners submitted statements as to their financial resources, family relationships, health, prior criminal records, and other information. The only evidence offered by the Government was a certified record showing that four persons previously convicted under the Smith Act in the Southern District of New York had forfeited bail. No evidence was produced relating those four persons to the petitioners in this case. At a hearing on the motion, petitioners were examined by the District Judge and cross-examined by an attorney for the Government. Petitioners' factual statements stand uncontroverted.

After their motion to reduce bail was denied, petitioners filed applications for habeas corpus in the same District Court. Upon consideration of the record on the motion to reduce bail, the writs were denied. The Court of Appeals for the Ninth Circuit affirmed. . . . Prior to filing their petition for certiorari in this Court, petitioners filed with Mr. Justice Douglas an application for bail and an alternative application for habeas corpus seeking interim relief. Both applications were referred to the Court and the matter was set down for argument on specific questions covering the issues raised by this case.

Relief in this type of case must be speedy if it is to be effective. The petition for certiorari and the full record are now before the Court and, since the questions presented by the petition have been fully briefed and argued, we consider it appropriate to dispose of the petition for certiorari at this time. Accordingly, the petition for certiorari is granted for review of questions important to the administration of criminal justice.

First. From the passage of the Judiciary Act of 1789, 1 Stat. 73, 91, to the present Federal Rules of Criminal Procedure, Rule 46 (a) (1), federal law has unequivocally provided that a person arrested for a non-capital offense shall be admitted to bail. This traditional right to freedom before conviction permits the unhampered preparation of a defense, and serves to prevent the infliction of punishment prior to conviction. . . . Unless this right to bail before trial is preserved, the presumption of innocence, secured only after centuries for struggle, would lose its meaning.

The right to release before trial is conditioned upon the accused's giving adequate assurance that he will stand trial and submit to sentence if found guilty.... Like the ancient practice of securing the oaths of responsible persons to stand as sureties for the accused, the modern practice of requiring a bail bond or the deposit of a sum of money subject to forfeiture serves as additional assurance of the presence of an accused. Bail set at a figure higher than an amount reasonably calculated to fulfill this purpose is "excessive" under the Eighth Amendment....

Since the function of bail is limited, the fixing of bail for any individual defendant must be based upon standards relevant to the purpose of assuring the presence of that defendant. The traditional standards as expressed in the Federal Rules of Criminal Procedure are to be applied in each case to each defendant. In this case petitioners are charged with offenses under the Smith Act and, if found guilty, their convictions are subject to review with the scrupulous care demanded by our Constitution.... Upon final judgment of conviction, petitioners face imprisonment of not more than five years and a fine of not more than $10,000. It is not denied that bail for each petitioner has been fixed in a sum much higher than that usually imposed for offenses with like penalties and yet there has been no factual showing to justify such action in this case. The Government asks the courts to depart from the norm by assuming, without the introduction of evidence, that each petitioner is a pawn in a conspiracy and will, in obedience to a superior, flee the jurisdiction. To infer from the fact of indictment alone a need for bail in an unusually high amount is an arbitrary act. Such conduct would inject into our own system of government the very principles of totalitarianism which Congress was seeking to guard against in passing the statute under which petitioners have been indicted.

If bail in an amount greater than that usually fixed for serious charges of crimes is required in the case of any of the petitioners, that is a matter to which evidence should be directed in a hearing so that the constitutional rights of each petitioner may be preserved. In the absence of such a showing, we are of the opinion that the fixing of bail before trial in these cases cannot be squared with the statutory and constitutional standards for admission to bail....

The Court concludes that bail has not been fixed by proper methods in this case and that petitioners' remedy is by motion to reduce bail, with right of appeal to the Court of Appeals. Accordingly, the judgment of the Court of Appeals is vacated and the case is remanded to the District Court with directions to vacate its order denying petitioners' applications for writs of habeas corpus and to dismiss the application without prejudice. Petitioners may move for reduction of bail in the criminal proceeding so that a hearing may be held for the purpose of fixing reasonable bail for each petitioner.

It is so ordered.

UNITED STATES V. SALERNO
Supreme Court of the United States, 1987.
481 U.S. 739, 107 S. Ct. 2095, 95 L.Ed.2d 697.

[This case stems from the prosecution of two alleged organized crime figures under the federal Racketeer Influenced and Corrupt Organizations (RICO) Act. Here the Supreme Court upholds the constitutionality of a federal statute permitting denial of bail in cases where pretrial release of a defendant threatens the safety of other persons and/or the community.]

Chief Justice REHNQUIST delivered the opinion of the Court.

The Bail Reform Act of 1984 allows a federal court to detain an arrestee pending trial if the government demonstrates by clear and convincing evidence after an adversary hearing that no release conditions "will reasonably assure ... the safety of any other person and the community." The United States Court of Appeals for the Second Circuit struck down this provision of the Act as facially unconstitutional, because, in that court's words, this type of pretrial detention violates "substantive due process." We granted certiorari because of a conflict among the Courts of Appeals regarding the validity of the Act.... We hold that, as against the facial attack mounted by these respondents, the Act fully comports with constitutional requirements. We therefore reverse.

Responding to "the alarming problem of crimes committed by persons on release," ... Congress formulated the Bail Reform Act of 1984 ... as the solution to a bail crisis in the federal courts. The Act represents the National Legislature's considered response to numerous perceived deficiencies in the federal bail process. By providing for sweeping changes in both the way federal courts consider bail applications and the circumstances under which bail is granted, Congress hoped to "give the courts adequate authority to make release decisions that give appropriate recognition to the danger a person may pose to others if released." ...

To this end, Sec. 314(a) of the Act requires a judicial officer to determine whether an arrestee shall be detained. Section 3142(e) provides that "[i]f, after a hearing pursuant to the provisions of subsection (f), the judicial officer finds that no condition or combination of conditions will reasonably assure the appearance of the person as required and the safety of any other person and the community, he shall order the detention of the person prior to trial." Section 3142(f) provides the arrestee with a number of procedural safeguards. He may request the presence of counsel at the detention hearing, he may testify and present witnesses in his behalf, as well as proffer evidence, and he may cross-examine other witnesses appearing at the hearing. If the judicial officer finds that no conditions of pretrial release can reasonably assure the safety of other persons and the community, he must state his findings of fact in writing, 3142(i), and support his conclusion with "clear and convincing evidence." 3142(f).

The judicial officer is not given unbridled discretion in making the detention determination. Congress has specified the considerations relevant to

that decision. These factors include the nature and seriousness of the charges, the substantiality of the government's evidence against the arrestee, the arrestee's background and characteristics, and the nature and seriousness of the danger posed by the suspect's release. 3142(g). Should a judicial officer order detention, the detainee is entitled to expedited appellate review of the detention order. 3145(b), (c).

Respondents Anthony Salerno and Vincent Cafaro were arrested on March 21, 1986, after being charged in a 29-count indictment alleging various Racketeer Influenced and Corrupt Organizations Act (RICO) violations, mail and wire fraud offenses, extortion, and various criminal gambling violations. The RICO counts alleged 35 acts of racketeering activity, including fraud, extortion, gambling, and conspiracy to commit murder. At respondents' arraignment, the Government moved to have Salerno and Cafaro detained pursuant to 3142(e), on the ground that no condition of release would assure the safety of the community or any person. The District Court held a hearing at which the Government made a detailed proffer of evidence. The Government's case showed that Salerno was the "boss" of the Genovese Crime Family of La Cosa Nostra and that Cafaro was a "captain" in the Genovese Family. Accordingly, to the Government's proffer, based in large part on conversations intercepted by a court-ordered wiretap, the two respondents had participated in wide-ranging conspiracies to aid their illegitimate enterprises through violent means. The Government also offered the testimony of two of its trial witnesses, who would assert that Salerno personally participated in two murder conspiracies. Salerno opposed the motion for detention, challenging the credibility of the Government's witnesses. He offered the testimony of several character witnesses as well as a letter from his doctor stating that he was suffering from a serious medical condition. Cafaro presented no evidence at the hearing, but instead characterized the wiretap conversations as merely "tough talk."

The District Court granted the Government's detention motion, concluding that the Government had established by clear and convincing evidence that no condition or combination of conditions of release would ensure the safety of the community or any person.

Respondents appealed, contending that to the extent that the Bail Reform Act permits pretrial detention on the ground that the arrestee is likely to commit future crimes, it is unconstitutional on its face. Over a dissent, the United States Court of Appeals for the Second Circuit agreed. . . .

Respondents . . . contend that the Bail Reform Act violates the Excessive Bail Clause of the Eighth Amendment. The Court of Appeals did not address this issue because it found that the Act violates the Due Process Clause. We think that the Act survives a challenge founded upon the Eighth Amendment.

The Eighth Amendment addresses pretrial release by providing merely that "Excessive bail shall not be required." The Clause, of course, says nothing about whether bail shall be available at all. Respondents nevertheless contend that this Clause grants them a right to bail calculated solely upon considerations of flight. They rely on *Stack v. Boyle* . . . (1951), in which the Court stated that "bail set at a figure higher than an amount reasonably calculated [to ensure the defendant's presence at trial] is 'excessive' under the Eighth Amendment." In respondent's view, since the Bail Reform Act allows a court essentially to set bail at an infinite amount for reasons not related to the risk of flight, it violates the Excessive Bail Clause. Respondents concede that the right to bail they have discovered in the Eighth Amendment is not absolute. A court may, for example, refuse bail in capital cases. And, as the Court of Appeals noted and respondents admit, a court may refuse bail when the defendant presents a threat to the judicial process by intimidating witnesses. . . . Respondents characterize these exceptions as consistent with what they claim to be the sole purpose of bail—to ensure integrity of the judicial process.

While we agree that a primary function of bail is to safeguard the courts' role in adjudicating the guilt or innocence of defendants, we reject the proposition that the Eighth Amendment categorically prohibits the government from pursuing other admittedly compelling interests through regulation of pretrial release. The above-quoted dicta in *Stack v. Boyle* is far too slender a reed on which to rest this argument. The Court in *Stack* had no occasion to consider whether the Excessive Bail Clause requires courts to admit all defendants to bail, because the statute before the Court in that case in fact allowed the defendants to be bailed. Thus, the Court had to determine only whether bail, admittedly available in that case, was excessive if set at a sum greater than that necessary to ensure the arrestees' presence at trial. . . .

In our society liberty is the norm, and detention prior to trial or without trial is the carefully limited exception. We hold that the provisions for pretrial detention in the Bail Reform Act of 1984 fall within that carefully limited exception. The Act authorizes the detention prior to trial of arrestees charged with serious felonies who are found after an adversary hearing to pose a threat to the safety of individuals or to the community which no condition of release can dispel. The numerous procedural safeguards detailed above must attend this adversary hearing. We are unwilling to say that this congressional determination, based as it is upon the primary concern of every government—a concern for the safety and indeed the lives of its citizens—on its face violates . . . the Excessive Bail Clause of the Eighth Amendment.

The judgment of the Court of Appeals is therefore reversed.

Justice MARSHALL, with whom Justice BRENNAN joins, dissenting.

This case brings before the Court for the first time a statute in which Congress declares that a person innocent of any crime may be jailed indefinitely, pending the trial of allegations which are legally presumed to be untrue, if the Government shows to the satisfaction of a judge that the accused is likely to commit crimes, unrelated to the pending charges, at any time in the future. Such statutes, consistent with the usages of tyranny and the excesses of what bitter experience teaches us to call the police state, have long been thought incompatible with the fundamental human rights protected by our Constitution. Today a majority of this Court holds otherwise. Its decision disregards basic principles of justice established centuries ago and enshrined beyond the reach of governmental interference in the Bill of Rights. . . .

Throughout the world today there are men, women, and children interned indefinitely, awaiting trials which may never come or which may be a mockery of the word, because their governments believe them to be "dangerous." Our Constitution, whose construction began two centuries ago, can shelter us forever from the evils of such unchecked power. Over two hundred years it has slowly, through our efforts, grown more durable, more expansive, and more just. But it cannot protect us if we lack the courage, and the self-restraint, to protect ourselves. Today a majority of the Court applies itself to an ominous exercise in demolition. Theirs is truly a decision which will go forth without authority, and come back without respect.

I dissent.

Justice STEVENS, dissenting. . . .

UNITED STATES V. CALANDRA

Supreme Court of the United States, 1974.
414 U.S. 338, 94 S. Ct. 613, 38 L.Ed.2d 561.

[In the first paragraph of the majority opinion, Justice Powell concisely explains the precise issue before the Supreme Court in this case. In his opinion, Powell discusses the historic role and function of the grand jury in the criminal justice system.]

Mr. Justice POWELL delivered the opinion of the court.

This case presents the question whether a witness summoned to appear and testify before a grand jury may refuse to answer questions on the ground that they are based on evidence obtained from an unlawful search and seizure. The issue is of considerable importance to the administration of criminal justice.

I

On December 11, 1970, federal agents obtained a warrant authorizing a search of respondent John Calandra's place of business, the Royal Machine & Tool Co. in Cleveland, Ohio. The warrant was issued in connection with an extensive investigation of suspected illegal gambling operations. . . .

Although the agents found no gambling paraphernalia, one discovered, among certain promissory notes, a card indicating that Dr. Walter Loveland had been making periodic payments to Calandra. The agent stated in an affidavit that he was aware that the United States Attorney's office for the Northern District of Ohio was investigating possible violations of . . . [federal law] . . . dealing with extortionate credit transactions, and that Dr.

Loveland had been the victim of a "loansharking" enterprise then under investigation. The agent concluded that the card bearing Dr. Loveland's name was a loansharking record and therefore had it seized along with various other items, including books and records of the company, stock certificates, and address books.

On March 1, 1971, a special grand jury was convened in the Northern District of Ohio to investigate possible loansharking activities in violation of federal laws. The grand jury subpoenaed Calandra in order to ask him questions based on the evidence seized during the search of his place of business on December 15, 1970. Calandra appeared before the grand jury on August 17, 1971, but refused to testify, invoking his Fifth Amendment privilege against self-incrimination. The Government then requested the District Court to grant Calandra transactional immunity. . . . Calandra requested and received a postponement of the hearing on the Government's application for the immunity order so that he could prepare a motion to suppress the evidence seized in the search.

Calandra later moved pursuant to Fed. Rule Crim. Proc. 41(e) for suppression and return of the seized evidence on the grounds that the affidavit supporting the warrant was insufficient and that the search exceeded the scope of the warrant. On August 27, the District Court held a hearing at which Calandra stipulated that he would refuse to answer questions based on the seized materials. On October 1, the District Court entered its judgment ordering the evidence suppressed and returned to Calandra and further ordering that Calandra need not answer any of the grand jury's questions based on the suppressed evidence. . . .

The Court of Appeals for the Sixth Circuit affirmed. . . .

We granted the Government's petition for certiorari. . . . We now reverse.

II

The institution of the grand jury is deeply rooted in Anglo-American history. In England, the grand jury served for centuries both as a body of accusers sworn to discover and present for trial persons suspected of criminal wrongdoing and as a protector of citizens against arbitrary and oppressive governmental action. In this country the Founders thought the grand jury so essential to basic liberties that they provided in the Fifth Amendment that federal prosecution for serious crimes can only be instituted by "a presentment or indictment of a Grand Jury." . . . The grand jury's historic functions survive to this day. Its responsibilities continue to include both the determination whether there is probable cause to believe a crime has been committed and the protection of citizens against unfounded criminal prosecutions. . . .

Traditionally the grand jury has been accorded wide latitude to inquire into violations of criminal law. No judge presides to monitor its proceedings. It deliberates in secret and may determine alone the course of its inquiry. The grand jury may compel the production of evidence or the testimony of witnesses as it considers appropriate, and its operation generally is unrestrained by the technical procedural and evidentiary rules governing the conduct of criminal trials. "It is a grand inquest, a body with powers of investigation and inquisition, the scope of whose inquiries is not to be limited narrowly by questions of propriety or forecasts of the probable result of the investigation, or by doubts whether any particular individual will be found properly subject to an accusation of crime." . . .

The scope of the grand jury's powers reflects its special role in insuring fair and effective law enforcement. A grand jury proceeding is not an adversary hearing in which the guilt or innocence of the accused is adjudicated. Rather, it is an ex parte investigation to determine whether a crime has been committed and whether criminal proceedings should be instituted against any person. The grand jury's investigative power must be broad if its public responsibility is adequately to be discharged. . . .

The grand jury's sources of information are widely drawn, and the validity of an indictment is not affected by the character of the evidence considered. Thus, an indictment valid on its face is not subject to challenge on the ground that the grand jury acted on the basis of inadequate or incompetent evidence, . . . or even on the basis of information obtained in violation of a defendant's Fifth Amendment privilege against self-incrimination. . . .

The power of a federal court to compel persons to appear and testify before a grand jury is also firmly established. . . . The duty to testify has long been recognized as a basic obligation that every citizen owes his Government. . . . The duty to testify may on occasion be burdensome and even embarrassing. It may cause injury to a witness' social and economic status. Yet the duty to testify has been regarded as "so necessary to the administration of justice" that the witness' personal interest in privacy must yield to the public's overriding interest in full disclosure. . . . Furthermore, a witness may not interfere with the course of the grand jury's inquiry. He "is not entitled to urge objections of incompetency or irrelevancy, such as a party might raise, for this is no concern of his." . . . Nor is he entitled "to challenge the authority of the court or of the grand jury" or "to set limits to the investigation that the grand jury may conduct." . . .

Of course, the grand jury's subpoena power is not unlimited. It may consider incompetent evidence, but it may not itself violate a valid privilege, whether established by the Constitution, statutes, or the common law. . . . Although, for example, an indictment based on evidence obtained in violation of a defendant's Fifth Amendment privilege is nevertheless valid, . . . the grand jury may not force a witness to answer questions in violation of that constitutional guarantee. Rather, the grand jury may override a Fifth Amendment claim only if the witness is granted immunity co-extensive with the privilege against self-incrimination. . . . Similarly, a grand jury may not compel a person to produce books and papers that would incriminate him. . . .

The grand jury is also without power to invade a legitimate privacy interest protected by the Fourth Amendment. A grand jury's subpoena duces tecum will be disallowed if it is "far too sweeping in its terms to be regarded as reasonable" under the Fourth Amendment. . . . Judicial supervision is properly exercised in such cases to prevent the wrong before it occurs.

III

In the instant case, the Court of Appeals held that the exclusionary rule of the Fourth Amendment limits the grand jury's power to compel a witness to answer questions based on evidence obtained from a prior unlawful search and seizure. The exclusionary rule was adopted to effectuate the Fourth Amendment right of all citizens "to be secure in their persons, houses, papers, and effects, against unreasonable searches and seizures. . . ." Under this rule, evidence obtained in violation of the Fourth Amendment cannot be used in a criminal proceeding against the victim of the illegal search and seizure. . . . This prohibition applies as well to the fruits of the illegally seized evidence. . . .

The purpose of the exclusionary rule is not to redress the injury to the privacy of the search victim. . . . Instead, the rule's prime purpose is to deter future unlawful police conduct and thereby effectuate the guarantee of the Fourth Amendment against unreasonable search and seizures. . . . In sum, the rule is a judicially created remedy designed to safeguard Fourth Amendment rights generally through its deterrent effect, rather than a personal constitutional right of the party aggrieved.

Despite its broad deterrent purpose, the exclusionary rule has never been interpreted to proscribe the use of illegally seized evidence in all proceedings or against all persons. As with any remedial device, the application of the rule has been restricted to those areas where its remedial objectives are thought most efficaciously served. . . .

IV

In deciding whether to extend the exclusionary rule to grand jury proceedings, we must weigh the potential injury to the historic role and functions of the grand jury against the potential benefits of the rule as applied in this context. It is evident that this extension of the exclusionary rule would seriously impede the grand jury. Because the grand jury does not finally adjudicate guilt or innocence, it has traditionally been allowed to pursue its investigative and accusatorial functions unimpeded by the evidentiary and procedural restrictions applicable to a criminal trial. Permitting witnesses to invoke the exclusionary rule before a grand jury would precipitate adjudication of issues hitherto reserved for the trial on the merits and would delay and disrupt grand jury proceedings. Suppression hearings would halt the orderly progress of an investigation and might necessitate extended litigation of issues only tangentially related to the grand jury's primary objective. The probable result would be "protracted interruption of grand jury proceedings," . . . effectively transforming them into preliminary trials on the merits. In some cases the delay might be fatal to the enforcement of the criminal law. . . . [W]e believe that allowing a grand jury witness to invoke the exclusionary rule would unduly interfere with the effective and expeditious discharge of the grand jury's duties.

Against this potential damage to the role and functions of the grand jury, we must weigh the benefits to be derived from this proposed extension of the exclusionary rule. Suppression of the use of illegally seized evidence against the search victim in a criminal trial is thought to be an important method of effectuating the Fourth Amendment. But it does not follow that the Fourth Amendment requires adoption of every proposal that might deter police misconduct. . . .

Any incremental deterrent effect which might be achieved by extending the rule to grand jury proceedings is uncertain at best. Whatever deterrence of police misconduct may result from the exclusion of illegally seized evidence from criminal trials, it is unrealistic to assume that application of the rule to grand jury proceedings would significantly further that goal. Such an extension would deter only police investigation consciously directed toward the discovery of evidence solely for use in a grand jury investigation. The incentive to disregard the requirement of the Fourth Amendment solely to obtain an indictment from a grand jury is substantially negated by the inadmissibility of the illegally seized evidence in a subsequent criminal prosecution of the search victim. For the most part, a prosecutor would be unlikely to request an indictment where a conviction could not be obtained. We therefore decline to embrace a view that would achieve a speculative and undoubtedly minimal advance in the deterrence of police misconduct at the expense of substantially impeding the role of the grand jury. . . .

The judgment of the Court of Appeals is Reversed.

Mr. Justice BRENNAN, with whom Mr. Justice DOUGLAS and Mr. Justice MARSHALL join, dissenting.

The Court holds that the exclusionary rule in search-and-seizure cases does not apply to grand jury proceedings because the principal objective of the rule is "to deter future unlawful police conduct" . . . and "it is unrealistic to assume that application of the rule to grand jury proceedings would significantly further that goal." . . .

This downgrading of the exclusionary rule to a determination whether its application in a particular type of proceeding furthers deterrence of future police misconduct reflects a startling misconception, unless it is a purposeful rejection, of the historical objective and purpose of the rule.

The commands of the Fourth Amendment are, of course, directed solely to public officials. Necessarily, therefore, only official violations of those commands could have created the evil that threatened to make the Amendment a dead letter. But curtailment of the evil, if a consideration at all, was at best only a hoped-for effect of the exclusionary rule, not its ultimate objective. Indeed, there is no evidence that the possible deterrent effect of the rule was given any attention by the judges chiefly responsible for its formulation. Their concern as guardians of the Bill of Rights was to fashion an enforcement tool to give content and meaning to the Fourth Amendment's guarantees. . . . Since, however, those judges were without power to direct or control the conduct of law enforcement officers, the enforcement tool had necessarily to be one capable of administration by judges. The exclusionary rule, if not perfect, accomplished the twin goals of enabling the judiciary to avoid the taint of partnership in official lawlessness and of assuring the people—all potential victims of unlawful government conduct—that the government would not profit from its lawless behavior, thus minimizing the risk of seriously undermining popular trust in government. . . .

I dissent and would affirm the judgment of the Court of Appeals.

BOYKIN V. ALABAMA
Supreme Court of the United States, 1969.
395 U.S. 238, 89 S. Ct. 1709, 23 L.Ed.2d 274.

[Here the Supreme Court holds that, because a plea of guilty constitutes a waiver of the right to trial, the trial judge must determine that a defendant's guilty plea is being entered knowingly and intelligently before accepting the plea.]

Mr. Justice DOUGLAS delivered the opinion of the Court.
In the spring of 1966, within the period of a fortnight, a series of armed robberies occurred in Mobile, Alabama. The victims, in each case, were local shopkeepers open at night who were forced by a

gunman to hand over money. While robbing one grocery store, the assailant fired his gun once, sending a bullet through a door into the ceiling. A few days earlier in a drugstore, the robber had allowed his gun to discharge in such a way that the bullet, on ricochet from the floor, struck a customer in the leg. Shortly thereafter a local grand jury returned five indictments against petitioner, a 27-year-old Negro, for common-law robbery—an offense punishable in Alabama by death.

Before the matter came to trial, the court determined that petitioner was indigent and appointed counsel to represent him. Three days later, at his arraignment, petitioner pleaded guilty to all five indictments. So far as the record shows, the judge asked no questions of petitioner concerning his plea, and petitioner did not address the court.

Trial strategy may of course make a plea of guilty seem the desirable course. But the record is wholly silent on that point and throws no light on it.

Alabama provides that when a defendant pleads guilty, "the court must cause the punishment to be determined by a jury" (except where it is required to be fixed by the court) and may "cause witnesses to be examined, to ascertain the character of the offense." ... In the present case a trial of that dimension was held, the prosecution presenting its case largely through eyewitness testimony. Although counsel for petitioner engaged in cursory cross-examination, petitioner neither testified himself nor presented testimony concerning his character and background. There was nothing to indicate that he had a prior criminal record.

In instructing the jury, the judge stressed that petitioner had pleaded guilty in five cases of robbery, defined as "the felonious taking of money ... from another against his will ... by violence or by putting him in fear ... [carrying] from ten years minimum in the penitentiary to the supreme penalty of death by electrocution." The jury upon deliberation, found petitioner guilty and sentenced him severally to die on each of the five indictments.

Taking an automatic appeal to the Alabama Supreme Court, petitioner argued that a sentence of death for common-law robbery was cruel and unusual punishment within the meaning of the Federal Constitution, a suggestion which that court unanimously rejected. ... On their own motion, however, four of the seven justices discussed the constitutionality of the process by which the trial judge had accepted petitioner's guilty plea. From the order affirming the trial court, three justices dissented on the ground that the record was inadequate to show that petitioner had intelligently and knowingly pleaded guilty. The fourth member concurred separately, conceding that "a trial judge should not accept a guilty plea unless he had determined that such a plea was voluntarily and knowingly entered by the defendant, "but refusing "[f]or

aught appearing" "to presume that the trial judge failed to do his duty." ... We granted certiorari. ...

Respondent does not suggest that we lack jurisdiction to review the voluntary character of petitioner's guilty plea because he failed to raise that federal question below and the state court failed to pass upon it. But the question was raised on oral argument and we conclude that it is properly presented. The very Alabama statute ... that provides automatic appeal in capital cases also requires the reviewing court to comb the record for "any error prejudicial to the appellant, even though not called to our attention in brief of counsel." ... The automatic appeal statute "is the only provision under the Plain Error doctrine of which we are aware in Alabama criminal appellate review." ... In the words of the Alabama Supreme Court:

"Perhaps it is well to note that in reviewing a death case under the automatic appeal statute, ... we may consider any testimony that was seriously prejudicial to the rights of the appellant and may reverse thereon, even though no lawful objection or exception was made thereto.... Our review is not limited to the matters brought to our attention in brief of counsel." ... It was error, plain on the face of the record, for the trial judge to accept petitioner's guilty plea without an affirmative showing that it was intelligent and voluntary. That error, under Alabama procedure, was properly before the court below and considered explicitly by a majority of the justices and is properly before us on review.

A plea of guilty is more than a confession which admits that the accused did various acts; it is itself a conviction; nothing remains but to give judgment and determine punishment.... Admissibility of a confession must be based on a "reliable determination on the voluntariness issue which satisfies the constitutional rights of the defendant." ... The requirement that the prosecution spread on the record the prerequisites of a valid waiver is no constitutional innovation. In *Carnley v. Cochran* ... we dealt with a problem of waiver of the right to counsel, a Sixth Amendment right. We held: "Presuming waiver from a silent record is impermissible. The record must show, or there must be an allegation and evidence which show, that an accused was offered counsel but intelligently and understandingly rejected the offer. Anything less is not waiver."

We think that the same standard must be applied to determining whether a guilty plea is voluntarily made. For, as we have said, a plea of guilty is more than an admission of conduct; it is a conviction. Ignorance, incomprehension, coercion, terror, inducements, subtle or blatant threats might be a perfect cover-up of unconstitutionality. The question of an effective waiver of a federal constitutional right in a proceeding is of course governed by federal standards. . . .

Several federal constitutional rights are involved in a waiver that takes place when a plea of guilty is entered in a state criminal trial. First, is the privilege against compulsory self-incrimination guaranteed by the Fifth Amendment and applicable to the States by reason of the Fourteenth. . . . Second, is the right to trial by jury. . . . Third, is the right to confront one's accusers. . . . We cannot presume a waiver of these three important federal rights from a silent record.

What is at stake for an accused facing death or imprisonment demands the utmost solicitude of which courts are capable in canvassing the matter with the accused to make sure he has a full understanding of what the plea connotes and of its consequence. When the judge discharges that function, he leaves a record adequate for any review that may be later sought . . . and forestalls the spin-off of collateral proceedings that seek to probe murky memories.

The three dissenting justices in the Alabama Supreme Court stated the law accurately when they concluded that there was reversible error "because the record does not disclose that the defendant voluntarily and understandingly entered his pleas of guilty." . . .

Reversed.

Mr. Justice HARLAN, whom Mr. Justice BLACK joins, dissenting. . . .

BORDENKIRCHER V. HAYES
Supreme Court of the United States, 1978.
434 U.S. 357, 98 S. Ct. 663, 54 L.Ed.2d 604.

[In this case, the Supreme Court evaluates a particular exercise of prosecutorial discretion associated with the plea-bargaining process.]

Mr. Justice STEWART delivered the opinion of the Court.

The question in this case is whether the Due Process Clause of the Fourteenth Amendment is violated when a state prosecutor carries out a threat made during plea negotiations to reindict the accused on more serious charges if he does not plead guilty to the offense with which he was originally charged.

The respondent, Paul Lewis Hayes, was indicted by a Fayette County, Ky., grand jury on a charge of uttering a forged instrument in the amount of $88.30, an offense then punishable by a term of two to 10 years in prison. After arraignment, Hayes, his retained counsel, and the Commonwealth's attorney met in the presence of the clerk of the court to discuss a possible plea agreement. During these conferences the prosecutor offered to recommend a sentence of five years in prison if Hayes would plead guilty to the indictment. He also said that if Hayes did not plead guilty and "save the court the inconvenience of a trial," he would return to the grand jury to seek an indictment under the Kentucky Habitual Criminal Act, which would subject Hayes to a mandatory sentence of life imprisonment by reason of his two prior felony convictions. Hayes chose not to plead guilty, and the prosecutor did obtain an indictment charging him under the Habitual Criminal Act. It is not disputed that the recidivist charge was fully justified by the evidence, that the prosecutor was in possession of this evidence at the time of the original indictment, and that Hayes' refusal to plead guilty to the original charge was what led to his indictment under the habitual criminal statute.

A jury found Hayes guilty on the principal charge of uttering a forged instrument and, in a separate proceeding, further found that he had twice before been convicted of felonies. As required by the habitual offender statute, he was sentenced to a life term in the penitentiary. The Kentucky Court of Appeals rejected Hayes' constitutional objections to the enhanced sentence, holding in an unpublished opinion that imprisonment for life with the possibility of parole was constitutionally permissible in light of the previous felonies of which Hayes had been convicted, and that the prosecutor's decision to indict him as an habitual offender was a legitimate use of available leverage in the plea bargaining process.

On Hayes' petition for a federal writ of habeas corpus, the United States District Court for the Eastern District of Kentucky agreed that there had been no constitutional violation in the sentence or the indictment procedure, and denied the writ. The Court of Appeals for the Sixth Circuit reversed the District Court's judgment. While recognizing "that plea bargaining now plays an important role in our criminal justice system," the appellate court thought that the prosecutor's conduct during the bargaining negotiations had violated the principles ... which "protect[ed] defendants from the vindictive exercise of a prosecutor's discretion." ... We granted certiorari to consider a constitutional question of importance in the administration of criminal justice.

It may be helpful to clarify at the outset the nature of the issue in this case. While the prosecutor did not actually obtain the recidivist indictment until after the plea conferences had ended, his intention to do so was clearly put forth at the outset of the plea negotiations. Hayes was thus fully informed of the true terms of the offer when he made his decision to plead not guilty. This is not a situation, therefore, where the prosecutor without notice brought an additional and more serious charge after plea negotiations relating only to the original indictment had ended with the defendant's insistence on pleading not guilty. As a practical matter, in short, this case would be no different if the grand jury had indicted Hayes as a recidivist from the outset, and the prosecutor had offered to drop that charge as part of the plea bargain.

We have recently had occasion to observe that "whatever might be the situation in an ideal world, the fact is that the guilty plea and the often concomitant plea bargain are important components of this country's criminal justice system. Properly administered, they can benefit all concerned." The open acknowledgment of this previously clandestine practice has led this Court to recognize the importance of counsel during plea negotiations, *Brady v. United States*, 397 U.S. 742, 758, the need for a public record indicating that a plea was knowingly and voluntarily made, *Boykin v. Alabama*, 395 U.S. 238, 242, and the requirement that a prosecutor's plea bargaining promise must be kept, *Santobello v. New York*, 404 U.S. 257, 262. . . .

To punish a person because he has done what the law plainly allows him to do is a due process violation of the most basic sort, . . . and for an agent of the State to pursue a course of action whose objective is to penalize a person's reliance on his legal rights is "patently unconstitutional. . . ." But in the "give-and-take" of plea bargaining, there is no such element of punishment or retaliation so long as the accused is free to accept or reject the prosecution's offer.

Plea bargaining flows from "the mutuality of advantage" to defendants and prosecutors, each with his own reasons for wanting to avoid trial. . . . Defendants advised by competent counsel and protected by other procedural safeguards are presumptively capable of intelligent choice in response to prosecutorial persuasion, and unlikely to be driven to false self-condemnation. Indeed, acceptance of the basic legitimacy of plea bargaining necessarily implies rejection of any notion that a guilty plea is involuntary in a constitutional sense simply because it is the end result of the bargaining process. By hypothesis, the plea may have been induced by promises of a recommendation of a lenient sentence or a reduction of charges, and thus by fear of the possibility of a greater penalty upon conviction after a trial.

While confronting a defendant with the risk of more severe punishment clearly may have a "discouraging effect on the defendant's assertion of his trial rights, the imposition of these difficult choices [is] an inevitable"—and permissible—"attribute of any legitimate system which tolerates and encourages the negotiation of pleas." . . . It follows that, by tolerating and encouraging the negotiation of pleas, this Court has necessarily accepted as constitutionally legitimate the simple reality that the prosecutor's interest at the bargaining table is to persuade the defendant to forego his right to plead not guilty.

It is not disputed here that Hayes was properly chargeable under the recidivist statute, since he had in fact been convicted of two previous felonies. In our system, so long as the prosecutor has probable cause to believe that the accused committed an offense defined by statute, the decision whether or not to prosecute, and what charge to file or bring before a grand jury, generally rests entirely in his discretion. Within the limits set by the legislature's constitutionally valid definition of chargeable offenses, "the conscious exercise of some selectivity in enforcement is not in itself a federal constitutional violation" so long as "the selection was [not] deliberately based upon an unjustifiable standard such as race, religion, or other arbitrary classification. . . ." To hold that the prosecutor's desire to induce a guilty plea is an "unjustifiable standard," which, like race or religion, may play no part in his charging decision, would contradict the very premises that underlie the concept of plea bargaining itself. Moreover, a rigid constitutional rule that would prohibit a prosecutor from acting forthrightly in his dealings with the defense could only invite unhealthy subterfuge that would drive the practice of plea bargaining back into the shadows from which it has so recently emerged.

There is no doubt that the breadth of discretion that our country's legal system vests in prosecuting attorneys carries with it the potential for both individual and institutional abuse. And broad though that discretion may be, there are undoubtedly constitutional limits upon its exercise. We hold only that the course of conduct engaged in by the prosecutor in this case, which no more than openly presented the defendant with the unpleasant alternatives of foregoing trial or facing charges on which he was plainly subject to prosecution, did not violate the Due Process Clause of the Fourteenth Amendment.

Accordingly, the judgment of the Court of Appeals is reversed.

Mr. Justice POWELL, dissenting.

Although I agree with much of the Court's opinion, I am not satisfied that the result in this case is just or that the conduct of the plea bargaining met the requirements of due process. . . .

There may be situations in which a prosecutor would be fully justified in seeking a fresh indictment for a more serious offense. The most plausible justification might be that it would have been reasonable and in the public interest initially to have charged the defendant with the greater offense. In most cases a court could not know why the harsher indictment was sought, and an inquiry into the prosecutor's motive would neither be indicated nor likely to be fruitful. In those cases, I would agree with the majority that the situation would not differ materially from one in which the higher charge was brought at the outset.

But this is not such a case. Here, any inquiry into the prosecutor's purpose is made unnecessary by his candid acknowledgment that he threatened to procure and in fact procured the habitual criminal indictment because of respondent's insistence on exercising his constitutional rights. . . .

The plea-bargaining process, as recognized by this Court, is essential to the functioning of the criminal-justice system. It normally affords genuine benefits to defendants as well as to society. And if the system is to work effectively, prosecutors must be accorded the widest discretion, within constitutional limits, in conducting bargaining. . . . This is especially true when a defendant is represented by counsel and presumably is fully advised of his rights. Only in the most exceptional case should a court conclude that the scales of the bargaining are so unevenly balanced as to arouse suspicion. In this case, the prosecutor's actions denied respondent due process because their admitted purpose was to discourage and then to penalize with unique severity his exercise of constitutional rights. Implementation of a strategy calculated solely to deter the exercise of constitutional rights is not a constitutionally permissible exercise of discretion. I would affirm the opinion of the Court of Appeals on the facts of this case.

[Justices BLACKMUN, BRENNAN and MARSHALL also dissented.]

C H A P T E R

17

THE CRIMINAL TRIAL

CHAPTER OUTLINE

Introduction
The Common-Law
  Background
The Right to a Jury Trial
The Right to Counsel and the
  Right of Self-Representation
Selection of the Jury
Free Press vs. Fair Trial
The Trial Proper
Conclusion

Cases
Williams v. Florida
Batson v. Kentucky
Sheppard v. Maxwell
Jackson v. State
Harris v. New York
United States v. North

INTRODUCTION

More than 90 percent of felony charges and an even higher percentage of misdemeanor offenses are disposed of before trial. Nevertheless, the criminal trial has become the centerpiece of the criminal justice system for several reasons. First, trials are generally held before juries drawn from the community. Second, they are the most visible aspect of the justice system and often attract widespread media coverage. Finally, cases disposed of by trial often have an important impact on the administration of the criminal law.

THE COMMON-LAW BACKGROUND

Prior to the arrival of William the Conqueror in England in 1066, criminal trials took the forms of compurgation or ordeal. In a trial by compurgation, a defendant who had denied guilt under oath attempted to recruit a body of men to attest to the defendant's honor. If a group would swear to the defendant's innocence, the law considered the defendant to be innocent. In a trial by ordeal, the defendant was tortured by fire or water. If a defendant survived the ordeal, God had intervened to prove the defendant's innocence before the law.

Jury trials as we know them today originated with the Magna Charta that the English nobles forced King John to sign at Runnymede in 1215. The Magna Charta granted freemen the right of trial by their peers. Early juries comprised persons who had knowledge of the facts of a case—it was centuries before trial juries were to function in the role they now perform.

Despite the somewhat crude status of the common-law jury, the principle of trial by jury was important to the American colonists. It was firmly written into the United States Constitution in Article 3, Section 2, that trial of all crimes, except in cases of impeachment, shall be by jury. Subsequently the Sixth Amendment was adopted guaranteeing that "In all criminal prosecutions, the accused shall enjoy the right to a speedy and public trial, by an impartial jury." The constitutional mandate leaves unanswered questions concerning the qualifications of jurors, the method of their selection, and the requirements for a jury to convict a person accused of a crime.

THE RIGHT TO A JURY TRIAL

An accused may waive the right to a jury trial. Indeed, many persons who plead not guilty to misdemeanor charges elect a bench trial. On the other hand, most defendants who plead not guilty to felony charges choose to be tried by jury. The United States Supreme Court has ruled that the constitutional right to a jury trial extends to the class of cases for which an accused was entitled to a jury trial when the Constitution was adopted. This did not include juvenile cases, hence there is no right to a jury trial for juveniles under the federal Constitution. *McKeiver v. Pennsylvania*, 403 U.S. 528, 91 S. Ct. 1976, 29 L.Ed.2d 647 (1971). Furthermore, the right to trial by jury is not applicable to military tribunals. *Ex parte Quirin*, 317 U.S. 1, 63 S. Ct. 1, 87 L.Ed. 3 (1942).

As now interpreted, the Sixth Amendment guarantees an accused the right to a jury trial in criminal cases where a penalty of more than six months imprisonment can be imposed. *Codispoti v. Pennsylvania*, 418 U.S. 506, 94 S. Ct. 2687, 41 L.Ed.2d 912 (1974). Offenses that carry a possible penalty of no more than six months imprisonment are generally termed "petty offenses," and a jury trial is not required under the United States Constitution. *Baldwin v. New York*, 399 U.S. 66, 90 S. Ct. 1886, 26 L.Ed.2d 437 (1970). Nevertheless, in some states, under the state constitution or statutory law, an accused has the right to a jury trial for certain offenses even though they may be classified as "petty offenses" from a federal constitutional standpoint. In Florida, for example, a defendant is entitled to a jury trial under the state constitution for any offense that was a *malum in se* and indictable at common law even though the maximum punishment is less than six months. *Reed v. State*, 470 So.2d 1382 (Fla. 1985).

The constitutional requirement of a jury trial applies to the states, thereby guaranteeing a defendant a right to a jury trial in a state criminal prosecution if such a right would exist in a federal prosecution *Duncan v. Louisiana*, 391 U.S. 145, 88 S. Ct. 1444, 20 L.Ed.2d 491 (1968). Interestingly, the Sixth Amendment right to a jury trial does not afford a defendant the corresponding right to be tried before a judge without a jury. *Singer v. United States*, 380 U.S. 24, 85 S. Ct. 783, 13 L.Ed.2d 630 (1965).

The Right to a Public Trial

The Sixth Amendment also guarantees that "in all criminal prosecutions, the accused shall enjoy the right to a speedy and public trial by an impartial jury of the State and district wherein the crime shall have been committed." While the right to an open public trial is central to our system of justice, that right is not absolute. After pointing out that a public trial is for the benefit of the accused and to ensure the judge and prosecutor carry out their duties responsibly, the Supreme Court in *Waller v. Georgia*, 467 U.S. 39, 45, 104 S.Ct. 2210, 2215, 81 L.Ed.2d 31, 38 (1984) explained that

> the right to an open trial may give way in certain cases to other rights or interests, such as the defendant's right to a fair trial or the government's interest in inhibiting disclosure of sensitive information. Such circumstances will be rare, however, and the balance of interest must be struck with special care.

The Supreme Court has ruled that the requirement for openness extends to all phases of the trial. Consequently, in 1982 it declared invalid a statute requiring closure of the courtroom during the testimony of victims of sexual offenses. The Court said the issue of closure is a matter that must be left to the discretion of the court in specific cases where the court finds that closure is necessary to protect the interests of a minor who is testifying. *Globe Newspaper Company v. Superior Court*, 457 U.S. 596, 102 S.Ct. 2613, 73 L.Ed.2d 248 (1982). Two years later, the Court held that *voir dire* proceedings (see later topic in this chapter) in criminal trials can be closed only by overcoming the presumption of openness. Accordingly, before a trial court orders closure of court proceedings, it must make specific findings that closure is essential and explain why available alternatives are inadequate. *Press-Enterprise Company v. Superior Court of California*, 464 U.S. 501, 104 S.Ct. 819, 78 L.Ed.2d 629 (1984).

Among the reasons frequently cited by courts for limiting public access to criminal proceedings are the need to protect rape victims or children who have been molested and the need to protect witnesses and jurors from embarrassment, trauma, or intimidation.

The Defendant's Right to Compulsory Process

The Sixth Amendment to the United States Constitution is the basis of many trial rights for defendants. The Sixth Amendment is made applicable to state criminal trials by the Fourteenth Amendment. *Pointer v. Texas,* 380 U.S. 400, 85 S.Ct. 1065, 13 L.Ed.2d 923 (1965). It guarantees a defendant the right "to have compulsory process for obtaining witnesses in his favor." This affords the defendant the right to obtain court process (a subpoena) to compel witnesses to appear in court. There are some restrictions (e.g., a defendant cannot cause numerous witnesses to be subpoenaed simply to give cumulative testimony), but courts allow defendants a fair degree of liberality in causing witnesses to be subpoenaed. Of course, the prosecution also has access to process to compel the attendance of witnesses.

Composition of the Trial Jury

At common law a jury consisted of twelve men. Rule 23(b), Federal Rules of Criminal Procedure, requires a twelve-member jury in criminal cases in federal courts unless the defendant stipulates to fewer in writing. All states require twelve-member juries in capital cases. Most require the same number for all felony prosecutions. Many, however, now use less than twelve jurors in misdemeanor cases. Florida uses six-person juries for all but capital felonies. Fla. R. Crim. P. 3.270. In *Williams v. Florida,* 399 U.S. 78, 90 S. Ct. 1893, 26 L.Ed.2d 446 (1970), the Supreme Court upheld the use of six-person juries in the trial of felony offenses in Florida. Subsequently, in *Ballew v. Georgia,* 435 U.S. 223, 98 S. Ct. 1029, 55 L.Ed.2d 234 (1978), the Court held that a jury of only five persons was not acceptable under the Sixth Amendment.

In federal courts and in the great majority of state courts, a jury verdict in a criminal trial must be unanimous. A few states, however, accept less than unanimous verdicts. The Supreme Court has approved a less-than-unanimous verdict of twelve-person juries—*Johnson v. Louisiana,* 406 U.S. 356, 92 S. Ct. 1620, 32 L.Ed. 2d 152 (1972); *Apodaca v. Oregon,* 406 U.S. 404, 92 S. Ct. 1628, 32 L.Ed.2d 184 (1972)—but has ruled that a verdict by a six-person jury, even in a nonpetty offense, must be unanimous. *Burch v. Louisiana,* 441 U.S. 130, 99 S. Ct. 1623, 60 L.Ed.2d 96 (1979).

THE RIGHT TO COUNSEL AND THE RIGHT OF SELF-REPRESENTATION

As discussed in Chapter 16, the Sixth Amendment right to counsel at a criminal trial is well established. *Gideon v. Wainwright,* 372 U.S. 335, 83 S. Ct. 792, 9 L.Ed.2d

---

C A S E   I N   P O I N T

WHERE TWELVE JURORS ARE REQUIRED, CAN LESS THAN TWELVE RENDER A VERDICT?

Fred Mills was convicted of aggravated robbery in Dallas County, Texas. After exhausting his state appellate remedies, he petitioned the United States District Court for *habeas corpus* relief, claiming his Sixth Amendment rights were violated when his trial proceeded with only eleven jurors. That court denied relief, and Mills appealed to the United States Court of Appeals for the Fifth Circuit.

The record of the lower court proceedings revealed that on the morning of Mills' trial, one of the jurors empaneled to hear the case requested permission to attend a memorial service for his grandfather, who had died the previous evening. The trial judge found the juror was "emotionally disabled" and would not be able to concentrate if not allowed to attend the memorial service. Attempts to postpone the trial disclosed conflicts for other jurors and schedules for other docketed cases, so over Mills' objection, the judge proceeded with the trial with the remaining eleven jurors.

The Court of Appeals noted that Article 36.29 of the Texas Code of Criminal Procedure specifies a norm of twelve jurors in felony cases, yet it provides that if one juror becomes "disabled," the remaining eleven can render a verdict. Citing *Williams v. Florida*, 399 U.S. 78, 90 S.Ct. 1893, 26 L.Ed.2d 446 (1970), in which the U.S. Supreme Court upheld the use of six-person juries in state criminal trials, the court denied Mills' petition. The court observed that "since Texas provided Mills with a jury possessing the fundamental attributes of the jury guaranteed by the Sixth and Fourteenth Amendments, Mills has no claim for relief."

Mills v. Collins, 924 F.2d 89 (5th Cir. 1991).

---

799 (1963); *Argersinger v. Hamlin*, 407 U.S. 25, 92 S. Ct. 2006, 32 L.Ed.2d 530 (1972). This right is generally exercised by the defendant after counsel has been appointed at the early pretrial stages. But a defendant also has a constitutional right of self-representation, and at times the defendant does not exercise that right until the trial. If the defendant does choose self-representation, then the trial judge must determine whether the defendant has made a voluntary and intelligent decision. If a careful inquiry by the judge indicates that the defendant's election is voluntary and intelligent, then it is incumbent on the court to allow self-representation. Any such waiver of counsel must be carefully documented in the court records, and the court, at its option, may appoint "standby counsel" to assist the defendant. *Faretta v. California*, 422 U.S. 806, 95 S. Ct. 2525, 45 L. Ed.2d 562 (1975).

At trial a defense counsel who represents multiple defendants may discover a possible conflict in his or her representation of the defendants. In such an instance it is the trial court's duty "either to appoint separate counsel or to take adequate steps to ascertain whether the risk was too remote to warrant separate counsel." *Holloway v. Arkansas*, 435 U.S. 475, 484, 98 S. Ct. 1173, 1178, 55 L.Ed.2d 426, 434 (1978).

In 1976, the Supreme Court ruled that it is a violation of a defendant's Sixth Amendment right to counsel for a trial judge to bar the defendant from conferring with defense counsel during an overnight recess of a trial. *Geders v. United States*, 425 U.S. 80, 96 S.Ct. 1330, 47 L.Ed. 2d 592 (1976). More than a decade later, the Court held it was not a denial of the right to counsel for a trial judge to bar a defendant from conferring with counsel during a brief trial recess that occurred after the defendant testified on direct examination, but before cross-examination by the prosecutor. *Perry v. Leeke*, 488 U.S. 272, 109 S.Ct. 594, 102 L.Ed.2d 624 (1989). The Court's holdings acknowledge the importance of a close relationship between attorney and client during a trial, but also recognize that because the pursuit of truth is the purpose of the in-court examination of witnesses, there are valid reasons not to allow any witness to confer with counsel between the direct and the cross-examination.

Selection of the Jury

State and federal laws prescribe certain basic qualifications for jurors. Statutes commonly require that jurors be at least eighteen years of age and registered voters in the state or district from which they are to be selected. In contrast to past practices, it has become clear that laws prescribing qualifications cannot discriminate to prevent women as a class from serving as jurors. *Taylor v. Louisiana*, 419 U.S. 522, 95 S. Ct. 692, 42 L.Ed.2d 690 (1975). Convicted felons whose civil rights have not been restored are usually excluded from serving on juries. Beyond this, statutes frequently carve out exemptions for expectant mothers and mothers with young children, persons over seventy years of age, and for physicians, dentists, attorneys, judges, teachers, elected officials, police, fire, and emergency personnel.

The goal is to select prospective jurors at random from lists of persons representative of the community. The Jury Selection and Service Act of 1968 was enacted to assure that jury panels in federal courts are selected at random from a fair cross-section of the community. 28 U.S.C.A. § 1861. States also have statutes prescribing the process of selection. Local officials compile a list of persons qualified to serve as jurors, generally from the rolls of registered voters, driver's license lists, or some combination thereof. From this list prospective jurors are randomly selected and summoned to court. Compensation paid to trial jurors ranges from meager to modest amounts for their travel and per diem expenses.

The body of persons summoned to be jurors are referred to as the "venire." After outlining the case to be tried and reciting the names of those expected to participate, the judge may excuse those whose physical disabilities or obvious conflicts of interest based on family relationships or business connections disqualify them from serving. After excusing those who do not qualify, the judge swears in the remaining members of the venire to answer correctly questions put to them by the court and counsel, and six or twelve of these prospective jurors are called at random to take their seats in the jury box.

CASE IN POINT

DISQUALIFICATION OF PROSPECTIVE JURORS

Does knowledge about a defendant's previous convictions disqualify a prospective juror from serving as a juror on that defendant's case? The U.S. Supreme Court has given an answer in a case involving a defendant known to the media as "Murph the Surf," a state prisoner in Florida who achieved notoriety for his involvement in the 1964 theft of the Star of India sapphire from a New York museum. When this defendant was tried for being involved in a robbery in Miami Beach, he claimed that the jurors in his case were biased because they knew about his previous convictions. The Supreme Court rejected his contention and observed that juror exposure to information about a defendant's prior convictions or to new accounts of the crime do not alone presumptively deprive the defendant of due process of law.

Murphy v. Florida, 421 U.S. 794, 95 S.Ct. 2031, 44 L.Ed.2d 589 (1975).

The *Voir Dire*

Lawyers for the prosecution and the defense are permitted to challenge prospective jurors either *for cause* or *peremptorily.* A challenge is a request that a juror be excused from serving. Challenges are customarily asserted at a stage called the *voir dire.* The words *voir dire* come from the French language and mean "to tell the truth." The function of the *voir dire* is to enable the court and counsel to obtain the information necessary to assure selection of a fair and impartial jury. In some courts this examination is conducted by the trial judge, who may invite the lawyers to suggest questions to ask the prospective jurors. In others the *voir dire* is conducted by lawyers for each side. In either event, the presiding judge exercises broad discretion to keep the questioning within proper bounds.

Challenges for cause may be directed to the panel of jurors on basis of the panel having been improperly selected. An example would be where the defense counsel contends that the selection procedures exclude minority members. More commonly, challenges for cause are directed to a prospective juror individually alleging some fact that would disqualify him or her from serving on the particular case. Among the more common reasons for disqualification are having a close relationship with counsel, being significantly involved in the case as a witness or in some other capacity, or having formed a definite opinion in the case. However, it is not expected that the jurors be totally ignorant of the facts and issues involved in the case. More than a quarter-century ago Justice Clark, writing for the Supreme Court, observed:

> In these days of swift, widespread and diverse methods of communication, an important case can be expected to arouse the interest of the public in the vicinity, and scarcely any of those best qualified to serve as jurors will not have formed some

---

CASE IN POINT

SHOULD A JUROR BE EXCUSED FOR CAUSE?

The defendant was tried by jury for rape, sodomy, and some weapons offenses. Prospective jurors were not asked during the *voir dire* if they had ever been raped or had a family member or friend who had been raped. After the jury had been selected, a female juror suggested to the court that she should be excused because her daughter had been raped five years earlier. After being closely questioned by the judge and defense lawyer, she expressed convincingly that she and her daughter had effectively recovered from the trauma of the rape and that she could be a fair and impartial juror. The court refused to excuse her from the jury panel. The defendant was convicted and appealed.

The Georgia Court of Appeals affirmed the defendant's conviction. *Jamison v. State*, 295 S.E.2d 203 (Ga. App. 1982). In rejecting the defendant's argument that the trial court erred in not excusing the juror for cause, the court said: "Because the court had an ample basis upon which to believe the juror would perform her duty justly, we do not find the court's refusal to strike from the jury for cause to be an abuse of discretion." 295 S.E.2d at 204-205.

---

impression or opinion as to the merits of the case. *Irvin v. Dowd,* 366 U.S. 717, 722, 81 S. Ct. 1639, 1642, 6 L.Ed.2d 751, 756 (1961).

With widespread access to television, Justice Clark's observation is even more compelling today than in 1961. Nevertheless, prospective jurors who acknowledge that they have formed an opinion on the merits of the case and cannot disregard it may be excused for cause. Absent unusual circumstances concerning the parties involved in a case, a person would not be excused for cause because of religious or political affiliations.

The Problem of "Death-Qualified" Juries

In 1970 the Supreme Court expressed concern about some courts automatically excluding from juries trying capital cases persons who oppose or who have conscientious scruples against capital punishment. The Court held that opponents of capital punishment could not be excluded from juries empaneled to hear cases where the death penalty could be imposed unless the prospective jurors indicated that they could not make an impartial decision on the issue of guilt or could never vote to impose the death penalty. *Witherspoon v. Illinois*, 391 U.S. 510, 88 S. Ct. 1770, 20 L.Ed.2d 776 (1968).

A decade later in *Adams v. Texas*, the Court said:

[A] juror may not be challenged for cause based on his views about capital punishment unless those views would prevent or substantially impair the performance of his duties as a juror in accordance with his instructions and oath. 448 U.S. 38, 45, 100 S. Ct. 2521, 2526, 65 L.Ed.2d 581, 589 (1980).

In 1985 the Supreme Court revisited the problem in a case where Johnny Paul Witt had been convicted of first-degree murder and sentenced to death. After Witt exhausted his appeals in the state court and after a federal district judge denied his petition for *habeas corpus,* the United States Court of Appeals for the Eleventh Circuit reversed his conviction, finding that a prospective juror who had expressed opposition to capital punishment during *voir dire* had been improperly excused for cause. In *Wainwright v. Witt,* 469 U.S. 412, 105 S. Ct. 844, 83 L.Ed.2d 841 (1985), the Supreme Court noted that the following exchange had occurred between the prosecutor (P) and the prospective juror (J):

(P) Do you have religious beliefs or personal beliefs against the death penalty?

(J) I am afraid of being a little personal, but definitely not religious.

(P) Now, would that interfere with you sitting as a juror in this case?

(J) I'm afraid it would.

(P) You are afraid it would?

(J) Yes, Sir.

(P) Would it interfere with judging the guilt or innocence of the defendant in this case?

(J) I think so.

469 U.S. at 416, 105 S. Ct. at 848, 83 L.Ed.2d at 846.

The Supreme Court reversed the court of appeals and reiterated its view from *Adams v. Texas* that the proper standard for determining when a prospective juror may be excluded for cause because of views on capital punishment is whether the juror's views would "prevent or substantially impair the performance of his duties as a juror in accordance with his instructions and oath." *Wainwright v. Witt,* 469 U.S. 412, 424, 105 S. Ct. 844, 852, 83 L.Ed.2d 841, 851-852 (1985) (quoting *Adams v. Texas*). Justice Brennan, with whom Justice Marshall joined in dissent, observed that "basic justice demands that juries with the power to decide whether a capital defendant lives or dies not be poisoned against the defendant." 469 U.S. at 439, 105 S. Ct. at 860, 83 L.Ed.2d at 861.

In capital cases it has become common for the jury first to hear the evidence bearing on the defendant's guilt or innocence and then to receive evidence on whether the death penalty should be imposed. This practice is referred to as a "bifurcated trial." The Supreme Court has said that "death qualification" of a jury (i.e., the exclusion of prospective jurors who will not under any circumstances vote for imposition of the death penalty) is designed to obtain a jury that can properly and impartially apply the law to the facts at both the guilt and sentencing phases of a capital trial. On this rationale, the Court held that removal before the guilt phase in a capital trial of prospective jurors whose opposition to the death penalty would impair or prevent performance of their duties at the sentencing phase is not unconstitutional. *Lockhart v. McCree,* 476 U.S. 162, 106 S.Ct. 1758, 90 L.Ed.2d 137 (1986).

Peremptory Challenges of Jurors

It is not always possible to articulate a basis for dismissing a juror who may appear to be biased. Therefore, each side in a criminal trial is also allowed a limited number of peremptory challenges that may be exercised on *voir dire* to excuse prospective jurors without stating any reason. The number of peremptory challenges is usually provided by statute or court rules. Rather typical is Article 35.15 of the Vernon's Ann. Texas Code of Criminal Procedure, which allows the state and defendant fifteen peremptory challenges in capital cases and ten in noncapital felony cases. In misdemeanor cases, each side is allowed either three or five peremptory challenges, depending on the level of court where the defendant is tried.

The objective of the *voir dire* examination is to select jurors who can render a verdict fairly and impartially. It would be naive, however, to expect that the prosecutor and defense counsel are both striving to seat a wholly objective panel of jurors. Obviously, each trial lawyer wants jurors who may be sympathetic to the cause he or she advocates. To accomplish this, trial lawyers must be well versed in the facts of the case and the relevant law. They must also display ingenuity in questioning the prospective jurors to determine whether to exercise their peremptory challenges. Lawyers must be conversant with local court practices, since judges have broad discretion in conducting the *voir dire*. Trial lawyers have their own peculiar theories on how to conduct a *voir dire* examination, but most would agree that a practical knowledge of psychology is helpful. In recent years some have even retained social scientists for advice and assistance in the jury selection process.

If the court anticipates that a trial may be protracted, it may have one or more alternate jurors selected to serve should any juror become ill or have to respond to an emergency. After selection of the jury is complete, it is sworn as a body by the judge or the clerk of the court to carry out its duties and is advised not to discuss the case until instructed by the court to deliberate.

To eliminate vestiges of racial discrimination that may subtly occur in the exercise of peremptory challenges, courts have recently reassessed the historic freedom accorded counsel in exercising peremptory challenges.

In 1965, in *Swain v. Alabama*, 380 U.S. 202, 85 S. Ct. 824, 13 L.Ed.2d 759, the Supreme Court said that it was a violation of the equal protection clause of the Fifth Amendment to systematically exclude someone from serving on a jury because of the person's race. To make a *prima facie* case of purposeful discrimination, the defendant faced the formidable task of proving that the peremptory challenge system as a whole was being perverted. There was considerable criticism of the Court's ruling in *Swain v. Alabama*, and the Court again addressed the problem in *Batson v. Kentucky*, 476 U.S. 79, 106 S. Ct. 1712, 90 L.Ed.2d 69 (1986).

In *Batson*, the Supreme Court held that a prosecutor's peremptory challenges to exclude African Americans from a jury trying African American defendants was ground for a defendant to claim discrimination under the equal protection clause of the Fourteenth Amendment to the Constitution. *Batson* became the basis for trial courts to deny the prosecution's use of a peremptory challenge for exclusion of an African American juror from a trial of a person of that race, if the court was persuaded the challenge was racially motivated. In 1991, the Supreme Court broadened the rule so that racial motivation of the prosecutor became subject to challenge irrespective of the defendant and prospective juror being of the same race. *Powers v. Ohio*, 499 U.S. ____, 111 S.Ct. 1364, 113 L.Ed.2d 411 (1991).

In its 1986 decision in *Batson*, the Supreme Court reserved the issue of whether the rule it made applicable to the prosecution should apply equally to the discriminatory use of peremptory challenges by defendants. In 1992, the Court revisited this area of the law and extended the rule by holding that a defendant's exercise of peremptory challenges was state action, and that the Equal Protection Clause also prohibits defendants from engaging in purposeful discrimination on the ground of race. *Georgia v. McCollum*, 505 U.S. ___, 112 S.Ct. 2348, 120 L.Ed.2d 33 (1992). In dissenting from the ruling, Justice O'Connor pointed out that while *Batson* was properly decided, criminal defendants and their lawyers are not government actors when they perform trial functions. She expressed the view that the Constitution affords no similar protection to that afforded defendants against racially motivated challenges by the prosecutor. Justice Scalia also dissented, lamenting the destruction of the right of criminal defendants to exercise peremptory challenges to secure a jury they consider to be fair.

The views of the dissenters notwithstanding, if the prosecution can now demonstrate a *prima facie* case of racial discrimination by a defendant, the defense must articulate a racially neutral explanation for the peremptory challenge. As a result of the pronouncements in *Batson, Powers,* and *McCollum,* federal and state courts have reevaluated their views on the exercise of peremptory challenges. In general, trial judges are still vested with broad discretion in determining whether peremptory challenges are racially intended, but many trial lawyers have expressed great concern that peremptory challenges may become relics in our system of jurisprudence. They question whether courts will further restrict the use of peremptory challenges by prohibiting their exercise of such challenges based on gender or against members of cognizable economic, social, religious, and political groups. Indeed, the United States Court of Appeals for the Ninth Circuit recently prohibited criminal defendants from exercising peremptory challenges on the basis of gender. *United States v. De Gross*, 960 F.2d 1433 (9th Cir. 1992). In 1993 the Fifth Circuit disagreed, pointing out that gender discrimination is very different from racial discrimination and should not be governed by the *Batson* rationale. *United States v. Broussard*, 61 L.W. 2599.

FREE PRESS VS. FAIR TRIAL

First Amendment guarantees of freedom of the press may collide with a defendant's right to a fair trial before an impartial jury. This is particularly true when heightened public interest results in mass media coverage of a trial, with potential prejudicial effects on witnesses and jurors. When this occurs the trial court must protect the defendant's right to a fair trial by taking steps to prevent these influences from affecting the rights of a defendant. Failure to do so can result in a verdict of guilty being overturned by an appellate tribunal.

In *Sheppard v. Maxwell,* 384 U.S. 333, 86 S. Ct. 1507, 16 L.Ed.2d 600 (1966), the Supreme Court reversed Dr. Sam Sheppard's murder conviction because the jurors were constantly exposed to intense media coverage until the time of their deliberations. Noting that the "newsmen took over practically the entire courtroom," *Sheppard,* 384 U.S. at 355, 86 S. Ct. at 1518, 16 L.Ed.2d at 616, the Court found that the highly prejudicial publicity contributed to the denial of due process of law to the defendant. Acknowledging that nothing proscribes the press from reporting events that go on in the courtroom, the Court in *Sheppard* suggested that courts can combat the problem through such measures as (1) proscribing out-of-court statements by lawyers, parties, witnesses, or court officials concerning matters that could be prejudicial to the accused, and (2) insulating the witnesses and sequestering the jury to prevent exposure to reports by the media.

Although the media cannot "take over" the courtroom, it is equally clear that because of First Amendment rights, the public and the press cannot ordinarily be excluded from criminal trials. In 1980 Chief Justice Burger, writing for the Supreme Court, traced the history of criminal trials in Anglo-American jurisprudence and concluded that public access is an indispensable element of criminal trials. Therefore, the Court concluded that trials may not be closed without findings sufficient to overcome the presumption of openness. *Richmond Newspapers, Inc. v. Virginia*, 448 U.S. 555, 100 S. Ct. 2814, 65 L.Ed.2d 973 (1980).

Cameras in the Courtroom

In 1965, in a five-to-four decision, the Supreme Court held that the defendant, Billy Sol Estes, was denied due process of law where the proceedings of his criminal trial were televised over his objection. *Estes v. Texas*, 381 U.S. 532, 85 S. Ct. 1628, 14 L.Ed.2d 543 (1965). This was consistent with the longtime ban that courts had imposed on allowing cameras in the courtroom. During the 1970s many state courts began to allow radio, television, and still-camera coverage of court proceedings subject to limitations necessary to preserve the essential dignity of a trial (for example, equipment must be noiseless, and strong lights are not permitted). Also, judges may limit coverage by requiring pooling of media equipment. Nevertheless, Rule 53 of the Federal Rules of Criminal Procedure still prohibits the taking of photographs in the courtroom during the progress of judicial proceedings in federal courts.

Florida is among the states that began permitting televising of trials in the late 1970s. *In re Post-Newsweek Stations, Florida, Inc.*, 370 So.2d 764 (Fla. 1979). Thereafter, Noel Chandler and another defendant, who were charged with several offenses, requested the trial court to exclude live television coverage from their jury trial. The court denied their request and they were found guilty. A state appellate court affirmed their convictions. *Chandler v. State*, 366 So.2d 64 (Fla. App. 1978), *cert. denied*, 376 So.2d 1157 (Fla. 1979), *aff'd.*, 449 U.S. 560, 101 S. Ct. 802, 66 L.Ed.2d 740 (1981).

The Supreme Court granted review. At the outset, the Court acknowledged that it had no supervisory jurisdiction over state courts. Therefore it confined its review to evaluating the constitutionality of Florida's program permitting radio, television, and photographic coverage of criminal proceedings over an accused's objection. The Court declined to prohibit television cameras from state courts, but said that defendants have a right to show that their use prejudiced them in obtaining a fair trial. Finding that Chandler and his codefendant had not shown they were prejudiced in any way by the televising of their trials, the Court denied them any relief. *Chandler v. Florida,* 449 U.S. 560, 101 S. Ct. 802, 66 L.Ed.2d 740 (1981).

By 1993 cameras were allowed in the courtrooms of almost all state courts. Nevertheless, the Supreme Court has allowed cameras in only a few federal courts on an experimental basis. The federal ban came into focus in March and April 1993, when four police officers, previously acquitted of criminal charges in a state court trial, were tried in a federal district court in Los Angeles on charges of violating the Fourth Amendment rights of Rodney King (see Chapter 15). Since this trial attracted widespread interest, the media voiced displeasure at their inability to bring to the public live camera coverage.

Security in the Courtroom

In 1970 Justice Black, writing for the Supreme Court, observed:

> It is essential to the proper administration of criminal justice that dignity, order, and decorum be the hallmarks of all court proceedings in our country. The flagrant disregard in the courtroom of elementary standards of proper conduct should not and cannot be tolerated. *Illinois v. Allen,* 397 U.S. 337, 343, 90 S. Ct. 1057, 1061, 25 L.Ed.2d 353, 359 (1970).

Occasionally a trial judge is confronted with a defendant or others in attendance at a trial whose disruptive behavior impedes the court from conducting a trial in a proper judicial atmosphere. The problem is more likely encountered in a so-called political trial, where there may be support for the cause the defendant claims to represent. One such highly publicized instance of courtroom disruption occurred in the 1969–70 "Chicago Seven" conspiracy trial in federal court in Chicago, Illinois. The seven defendants, including antiwar activist David T. Dellinger, were prosecuted under the Federal Anti-Riot Statute (18 U.S.C.A. §§ 2101–2102) for their actions at the August 1968 Democratic National Convention in Chicago. An eighth defendant, Black Panther party leader Bobby G. Seale, was tried separately on similar charges. Considerable antagonism developed between the trial judge and the defendants and their counsel. As a result of their actions during their trials, all defendants and two of their attorneys were found guilty of contempt of court. However, despite the number of unruly and disrespectful actions that took place, the contempt convictions were reversed because of procedural irregularities. *United States v. Seale,* 461 F.2d 345 (7th Cir. 1972); *In re Dellinger,* 461 F.2d 389 (7th Cir. 1972). Subsequently the defendants' convictions were also reversed by the same federal court of appeals on basis of judicial error. In this latter opinion the appellate court criticized the trial judge for his own antagonistic behavior during the trial. *United States v. Dellinger,* 472 F.2d 340 (7th Cir. 1972), *cert. denied,* 410 U.S. 970, 93 S. Ct. 1443, 35 L.Ed.2d 706 (1973).

It is not too difficult for judges to exercise control over members of the public who attend court trials. The problem that confronts judges is when a defendant becomes unruly. In most instances judges control disruption and defiance by defendants and others through exercise of the power of contempt (see Chapter

12). Yet in recent years some courts have had to go further. In *Illinois v. Allen,*
supra, the Supreme Court recognized that there is no one formula for maintaining the appropriate courtroom atmosphere, but indicated

> there are at least three constitutionally permissible ways for a trial judge to handle an
> obstreperous defendant. . .: (1) bind and gag him, thereby keeping him present;
> (2) cite him for contempt; (3) take him out of the courtroom until he promises to
> conduct himself properly. 397 U.S. at 343–344, 90 S. Ct. at 1061, 25 L.Ed.2d at 359.

The Sixth Amendment protects the defendant's right to be present at every
critical stage of criminal proceedings. *Snyder v. Massachusetts,* 291 U.S. 97, 54 S.Ct.
330, 78 L.Ed. 674 (1934). The right to be present at trial is fundamental; however,
it may be forfeited if the defendant is disruptive or fails to comply with
reasonable standards of the court. For example, in New York a defendant
repeatedly insisted on appearing in court while wearing only his underwear
covered by a sheet. After being warned of the consequences of not wearing
proper attire to court, the trial court allowed the trial to proceed in the
defendant's absence. On appeal, the trial court's action was affirmed. *People v.*
Hinton, 550 N.Y.S.2d 438 (N.Y. App. Div. 1990).

Courts insist that a defendant not disrupt courtroom proceedings, thus if
there is a real threat of serious disruption by a defendant, or where threats of
escape or danger to those in and around the courtroom exist, a defendant may be
shackled. Nevertheless, federal and state courts are reluctant to shackle a
defendant unless it becomes imperative, for in addition to concerns over
appearance of the defendant, shackling may have a prejudicial effect on a
defendant's decision to testify at trial. *People v. Duran,* 545 P.2d 1322 (Cal. 1976).
Moreover, in some cases such restraints "may . . . impair [the defendant's] ability
to confer with counsel, and significantly affect the trial strategy he chooses to
follow." *Zygadlo v. Wainwright,* 720 F.2d 1221, 1223 (11th Cir. 1983).

THE TRIAL PROPER

A trial is the centerpiece of the criminal justice system, and in American courts
the trial judge is the person most responsible for assuring the system operates in
a fair, efficient, and impartial manner. Trial judges come into office through
election or appointment. Ideally, they are selected because of their scholarship
and integrity and the patience and compassion the public associates with the fair
and impartial administration of justice. To those appearing before the court, and
to the jurors and court personnel, the black-robed judge stands as a symbol of
justice. In previous chapters, we have pointed out that judges perform numerous
functions in the pretrial phases of the criminal justice system, but the most
visible aspects of the judge's work are presiding at a trial, and where a conviction
results, setting punishment.

During a trial the judge serves as an umpire by ruling on the questions that
may be asked of potential jurors, determining whether witnesses are competent
to testify, controlling the scope of interrogation of lay and expert witnesses,
instructing the jury on the law applicable to the particular case, and in general
ruling on all important judicial and administrative matters concerning the trial.

Trial judges are held accountable by appellate courts sitting to review judgments and sentences and to correct harmful errors. Yet, in numerous administrative and procedural areas (e.g., whether to grant a postponement of a trial or to limit the number of expert witnesses), a judge's actions are discretionary, and the standard of appellate review in such areas is one of determining whether the trial judge abused that discretion.

Trial judges must be very cautious of being critical of attorneys, especially in a jury trial, because jurors place great importance on the judge's attitudes. The area is especially delicate in respect to defense counsel. A trial judge who is critical of a defendant's attorney may hold that attorney up to ridicule in the eyes of the jury and thereby impede the fairness of the trial. *People v. Kelley*, 449 N.W.2d 109 (Mich. App. 1989).

Witnesses are interrogated by counsel in the adversary system of American justice; however it is the right, and sometimes becomes the duty, of a judge to interrogate a witness. This is another delicate area, and appellate courts have emphasized that questioning from the bench should not show bias or feeling and should not be unduly protracted. *Commonwealth v. Hammer*, 494 A.2d 1054, 1060 (Pa. 1985).

Usually either or both sides in a criminal trial request the court to invoke the traditional "rule" that requires all witnesses except the defendant to remain outside the courtroom except when testifying. The purpose of "putting witnesses under the rule," as it is commonly referred to by lawyers, is to prevent them from matching narratives. Whether witnesses should be excluded from the courtroom is a matter within the sound discretion of the trial court, *Witt v. United States*, 196 F.2d 285 (9th Cir. 1952), *cert. denied*, 344 U.S. 827, 73 S. Ct. 28, 97 L.Ed. 644 (1952); however, the request is generally granted.

The Opening Statements

Once the jury is in place, the trial is ready to begin. The prosecution and the defense are each allowed to make an opening statement outlining their respective theories of the case and the evidence to be presented. These opening statements must not be argumentative; nor may counsel make disparaging remarks against one another. Often a defense lawyer defers making an opening statement until the prosecution rests its case. Opening statements are designed to orient the jury; therefore, if the defendant elects a bench trial, they are frequently waived. If not waived, opening statements of counsel are usually very brief in bench trials. After the opening statements have been presented, the prosecution calls its first witness to take the stand.

The Case for the Prosecution

Prosecutors are ever mindful that when a defendant pleads not guilty the government must establish the defendant's guilt beyond any reasonable doubt, a standard given constitutional status in *In re Winship*, 397 U.S. 358, 90 S. Ct. 1068, 25 L.Ed.2d 368 (1970).

In presenting the government's case, the prosecuting attorney usually calls as witnesses police officers, the victim, and any other available witnesses whose testimony can support the charge against the defendant. The government's witnesses may also include experts. For example, in a homicide prosecution the prosecutor usually calls a physician; in a drug trafficking case, a chemist; in a forgery prosecution, a handwriting expert—and so it goes.

The Rights to Confrontation and Cross-Examination

The Sixth Amendment to the Constitution guarantees the defendant the right to be confronted with the witnesses who offer evidence against the defendant. This means that the defendant has the right to be present at trial, *Illinois v. Allen*, 397 U.S. 337, 90 S. Ct. 1057, 25 L. Ed.2d 353 (1970), and to cross-examine each witness. As explained in *California v. Green*, this right of confrontation:

1. insures that the witness will give his statements under oath . . .
2. forces the witness to submit to cross examination, the "greatest legal engine ever invented for the discovery of truth" [and]
3. permits the jury . . . to observe the demeanor of the witness . . . thus aiding the jury in assessing his credibility. 399 U.S. 149, 158, 90 S. Ct. 1930, 1935, 26 L.Ed.2d 489, 497 (1970).

The right of cross-examination of an adversary's witness is absolute. *Alford v. United States*, 282 U.S. 687, 51 S. Ct. 218, 75 L.Ed. 624 (1931). However, the permissible scope of cross-examination varies somewhat in different jurisdictions and is a matter largely within the discretion of the trial court. *Smith v. Illinois*, 390 U.S. 129, 88 S. Ct. 748, 19 L.Ed.2d 956 (1968). Courts generally agree that the right of cross-examination is limited to (1) questioning the witness about matters he or she testified to on direct examination; and (2) asking any questions that may tend to impeach the witness's credibility or demonstrate any bias, interest, or hostility on the part of the witness.

The right of cross-examination is available to both the prosecutor and the defense counsel and is extremely valuable in the trial of criminal cases. Although in most instances it is objectionable for a lawyer who is examining a witness to ask leading questions on direct examination, the rules of evidence permit a cross-examiner to ask leading questions. When skillfully employed, cross-examination often develops facts favorable to the cross-examiner's side of the case. Frequently, a cross-examiner is successful in bringing out inconsistencies and contradictions and any bias or hostility of the witness. A witness may also be "impeached," that is, his or her credibility attacked, on cross-examination. A witness's credibility may be attacked by, for example, demonstrating that the witness has made conflicting statements on an important point, showing the witness has been convicted of a crime, or establishing that the witness bears a bad reputation for truth in the community.

In 1988, the Supreme Court held that a defendant's Sixth Amendment right to confront witnesses was violated in a sexual abuse case in which the trial judge, pursuant to an Iowa law, allowed a screen to be erected between the defendant and the two thirteen-year-old girls that Coy was accused of assaulting. The two children were situated so they could not see the defendant during their testimony. *Coy v. Iowa*, 487 U.S. 1012, 108 S. Ct. 2798, 101 L.Ed.2d 857 (1988). The

Court left open the question of whether a procedure that shields a child sex abuse victim may be constitutionally acceptable if there is an individualized finding that the witness is need of such protection.

Since the Supreme Court's decision in *Coy*, several states have refined their "child shield" statutes affecting children who are victims of sexual abuse. These revised statutes have met with varying reactions from state appellate courts, but one thing seems clear: To avoid the constitutional requirements of the confrontation clause, the prosecution must show and the trial judge must make particularized findings that a child victim of sexual abuse would suffer unreasonable and unnecessary mental or emotional harm if the child were to testify in the presence of the defendant.

It must be remembered that all evidence, whether from the prosecution or defense, must comport with the rules of evidence. When the prosecution rests its case, the next move is up to the defense. Before discussing this stage, it may be helpful briefly to review some basic rules of evidence.

The Rules of Evidence

In our adversary system, the purpose of a trial is to search for the truth. Guilt or innocence is determined based on the evidence produced at a trial. Evidence consists of verbal statements, writings, documents, photographs, and tangible items that tend to prove or disprove some fact in issue. Certain rules govern the introduction of evidence in a court of law. Sometimes judges tend to relax these rules in a nonjury trial because the judge is trained to "sort out" the probative evidence from the nonprobative. However, in a jury trial in a criminal case, the rules of evidence are strictly enforced.

The subject of evidence is complex. The rules of evidence prescribed by Congress for use in federal courts are known as Federal Rules of Evidence and are found in Title 28 of the United States Code Annotated. Some states have legislatively or judicially adopted codes of evidence; in other states the rules of evidence must be gleaned from a study of the decisional law of the state. Volumes have been written on the subject, and thousands of court decisions address its various aspects and refinements of general rules. From a basic text on criminal law and procedure, the reader can only expect to gain a very basic grasp of the principles involved.

Judicial Notice.   Facts commonly known are accepted by courts without formal proof, a process known as the court taking "judicial notice" of certain established facts. Usually there is a request by counsel; however, in some instances courts take judicial notice without request. The rationale for the doctrine of judicial notice is that courts should not exclude consideration of matters of general knowledge that are well known to informed members of the public. See *State v. Finch*, 280 P. 910 (Kan. 1929). To illustrate: Courts take judicial notice of who is president of the United States, that a particular date in a given month was on a certain day of the week, or that whiskey is an intoxicating liquor. In some instances it may be necessary to bring such commonly accepted facts to the court's attention by presentation of a calendar or almanac. Courts in a particular area may be asked to take judicial notice of certain facts within the geographic area of the court's jurisdiction. Judicial notice of a fact, however, must never be used as a substitute for proof of an essential element of a crime. *State v. Welch,* 363 A.2d 1356 (R.I. 1976). Taking judicial notice is not conclusive, because a party can always offer proof to the contrary.

Courts also take judicial notice of the law. All courts take judicial notice of the United States Constitution, and federal courts take judicial notice of the federal law. State courts take judicial notice of their own state constitution and state laws. Municipal ordinances and laws of other states generally must be established by formal proof; however, counsel frequently stipulate as to the text of these laws.

Evidentiary Presumptions. In Chapter 13 we noted that at common law, a child under seven years of age was conclusively presumed to be incapable of committing a crime. A legal presumption of this type is called an irrebuttable presumption. In other words, no evidence can be introduced in court to overcome it. In criminal law, an irrebuttable presumption that provides that based on proof of one fact, the fact finder (judge or jury) must conclusively find the existence of another fact is troublesome because it encroaches upon a defendant's due process right to have the prosecution prove the defendant guilty beyond a reasonable doubt.

Historically the requirement for proof "beyond any reasonable doubt" has required proof whereby the fact finder would have "an abiding conviction, to a moral certainty, of the truth of the charge." *Commonwealth v. Webster,* 59 Mass. (5 Cush.) 295, 320 (1850). In a more sophisticated definition, the Supreme Court has said that a reasonable doubt exists when jurors lack "a subjective state of near certitude of the guilt of the accused." *Jackson v. Virginia,* 443 U.S. 307, 315, 99 S.Ct. 2781, 2787, 61 L.Ed.2d 560, 571 (1979). This standard of requiring proof beyond a reasonable doubt is central to judicial consideration of the validity of presumptions. Today most presumptions in criminal law are permissive. These are evidentiary devices designed to aid a party who has the burden of proof. For example, under this type of presumption, once evidence establishes a fact, the jury may infer something else is true, provided there is a rational connection between the basic fact and the presumed fact.

In *County Court of Ulster County, New York v. Allen,* 442 U.S. 140, 99 S.Ct. 2213, 60 L.Ed.2d 777 (1979), the Supreme Court upheld the application of a New York statutory presumption that occupants of a car in which firearms were present were in illegal possession of them as applied to a case in which three adults and a juvenile were tried for illegal possession of handguns. When the police stopped the vehicle they were riding in, they saw the handguns located crosswise in an open handbag. The juvenile admitted ownership of the bag. At the conclusion of the trial, the judge instructed the jury, in part, "you may infer and draw a conclusion that such prohibited weapon was possessed by each of the defendants who occupied the automobile at the time when such instruments were found. The presumption or presumptions is effective only so long as there is no substantial evidence contradicting the conclusion flowing from the presumption, and the presumption is said to disappear when such contradictory evidence is adduced." The Supreme Court pointed out that "the presumption was merely a part of the prosecution's case, that it gave rise to a permissive inference available only in certain circumstances, rather than a mandatory conclusion of possession, and that it could be ignored by the jury even if there was no affirmative proof offered by defendants in rebuttal." 442 U.S. at 160–161, 99 S.Ct. at 2213, 60 L.Ed.2d at 794.

Shortly thereafter in *Sandstrom v. Montana,* 442 U.S. 510, 99 S.Ct. 2450, 61 L.Ed.2d 39 (1979), the Court reviewed a case in which the State of Montana charged the defendant, David Sandstrom, with a homicidal crime where intent was a necessary element of the offense. The trial court instructed the jury that "the law presumes that a person intends the ordinary consequences of his voluntary act." Although historically many trial courts commonly instructed juries substantially as quoted, the Supreme Court noted that since the jury was not told that the presumption could be rebutted, it may have interpreted the presumption as being conclusive or as shifting to the defendant the burden of persuasion on the element of intent. Thus, the Court viewed the issue to be whether such an instruction relieved the state of its burden to prove the defendant guilty beyond any reasonable doubt. The court found that such an instruction mandated a conclusive presumption that removed the need to prove the essential element of intent and ruled that such a presumption violated the defendant's due process rights.

A decade later, the Illinois Supreme Court held that instructing a jury that it "may presume" that a defendant was under the influence of intoxicating liquors if the defendant's blood-alcohol level was .10 merely created a permissive presumption that did not violate the defendant's due process rights. *People v. Hester,* 544 N.E.2d 797 (Ill. 1989).

Expert Witnesses.   Today forensic experts in nearly every field make a speciality of testifying in court. To qualify as an expert, a witness must present proper credentials and be received by the trial court as an expert. A court may call experts on its own motion, but usually experts are produced by the prosecution or defense. After one side offers a witness as an expert, opposing counsel may cross-examine the prospective witness about his or her qualifications. For example, a physician who is to give evidence as to the cause of death of someone is first asked to relate his or her educational background and experience in the specialized area of medical practice in question. In many cases attorneys for the prosecution and defense will stipulate that a particular witness is an expert in the field concerning which the witness will testify. The trial judge has considerable discretion in determining whether a witness is to be received as an expert.

Unlike lay witnesses, a witness once received as an expert by the court may respond to hypothetical questions and may express opinions within the realm of his or her expertise. Fingerprint identification, ballistics tests, handwriting exemplars, and medical tests have been prominent among areas where expert evidence is commonly received in criminal cases. More recently evidence of speed detection devices, Intoximeters, and other devices to test blood-alcohol content have become commonplace in the courts. Judges and jurors are not necessarily scientists. Indeed, it is unlikely that many have more than a basic knowledge of scientific principles. Yet courts must make rational judgments in the field of new scientific advances to determine their admissibility in court. To accomplish this, courts must depend on experts in the field.

An expert who has knowledge from personal observation may testify on that basis. For example, a psychiatrist who has examined the accused may offer an opinion as to the accused's sanity. If the expert is not acquainted with the person or subject from personal observation, the expert's opinion can be based upon hypothetical questions that assume the existence of facts the evidence tends to establish. Medical experts and handwriting experts frequently are asked hypothetical questions in court, and experts on the subject of accident reconstruction frequently offer testimony as to speed, braking, and other factors relevant to determining fault in cases involving auto accidents.

Classifications of Evidence

There are several classifications of evidence. First, evidence may be real or testimonial. Real evidence consists of maps, blood samples, x-rays, photographs, stolen goods, fingerprints, knives, guns, and other tangible items. Testimonial evidence consists of sworn statements of witnesses. Watching a television drama might give you the impression that a criminal trial consists largely of real evidence, but the great majority of evidence presented in criminal trials comes from the mouths of the witnesses, both lay and expert.

Next, evidence may be direct or indirect. Direct evidence includes eyewitness testimony, while indirect evidence usually consists of circumstantial evidence (i.e., attendant facts from which inferences can be drawn to establish other facts in issue at the trial). To illustrate: A person who testifies to having seen the defendant enter the victim's house is giving direct evidence. Testimony that reveals that the defendant's fingerprints were found on a window pane of that house shortly after it was broken into is circumstantial evidence from which, depending on the circumstances, it may be inferred that the defendant entered the house through that window. The admissibility of circumstantial evidence in criminal trials is well established in American law. *Tot v. United States*, 319 U.S. 463, 63 S. Ct. 1241, 87 L.Ed. 1519 (1943).

The same evidence may be direct in regard to one fact and circumstantial in regard to another. The witness who testifies that the defendant had a pistol in his or her possession is giving direct evidence of that fact. Depending on other circumstances, it may be inferable from proof of that fact that the defendant attacked the victim.

In fact, there is no real difference in the weight given circumstantial as opposed to real evidence. Because of very early history, circumstantial evidence may have been suspect, yet lawyers and judges can point to many instances where circumstantial evidence has proven to be more reliable than testimonial evidence. As the Supreme Court has observed,

> circumstantial evidence may in some cases point to a wholly incorrect result. Yet this is equally true of testimonial evidence. In both instances, a jury is asked to weigh the chances that the evidence correctly points to guilt against the possibility of inaccuracy or ambiguous inference. In both the jury must use its experience with people and events in weighing the probabilities. *Holland v. United States*, 348 U.S. 121, 140, 75 S.Ct. 127, 137-138, 99 L.Ed. 150, 166-167 (1954).

Scientific Evidence in the Courtroom

Evidence obtained through scientific and technological innovations can be both relevant and probative in a criminal case. Yet care must be taken to ensure that a new principle or technique is well supported by research and is generally accepted by the scientific community. The traditional test for determining the admissibility of emerging scientific techniques was outlined over a half- century ago in the seminal decision in *Frye v. United States*, 293 F. 1013 (D.C.Cir. 1923) In *Frye*, the court said:

> Just when a scientific principle or discovery crosses the line between the experimental and demonstrable stages is difficult to define. Somewhere in this twilight zone the evidential force of the principle must be recognized, and while courts will go a long way in admitting expert testimony deduced from a well-recognized scientific principle or discovery, the thing from which the deduction is made must be sufficiently established to have gained general acceptance in the particular field in which it belongs. 293 F. at 1014.

The *Frye* test is commonly applied in federal and most state courts faced with the issue of whether new scientific tests should be admitted into evidence in criminal trials.

Hypnotically Induced Testimony.   One controversial area of expert testimony concerns whether hypnotically enhanced testimony is admissible in a criminal trial. After examining extensive scientific literature, research, and testimony on the reliability of hypnotically refreshed memory, and determining that the scientific community was divided on the subject, the California Supreme Court determined that hypnotically refreshed memory should not be admitted in judicial proceedings. *People v. Shirley*, 723 P.2d 1354 (Cal. 1982), cert. denied, 459 U.S. 860, 103 S.Ct. 133, 74 L.Ed.2d 114 (1982). In earlier years some courts tended to admit such evidence—see, for example, *Harding v. State*, 246 A.2d 302 (Md. App. 1968)—however, the trend seems to have moved in the direction of not allowing such evidence. The majority of courts that have considered the issue in the last decade have held that it has not been established that hypnotically enhanced testimony is reliable. Therefore, it is not admissible. In *State v. Tuttle*, 780 P.2d 1203 (Utah 1989), the Utah Supreme Court published an exhaustive opinion analyzing the status of the law in this area and held that hypnotically enhanced testimony, as well as testimony regarding anything first recalled from time of a hypnotic session forward, is inadmissible as evidence.

In *Rock v. Arkansas*, 483 U.S. 44, 107 S.Ct. 2704, 97 L.Ed.2d 37 (1987), the United States Supreme Court held that excluding hypnotically enhanced testimony, when applied to prevent an accused from testifying to her own posthypnotic recall, violated her constitutional right to testify on her own behalf. Accordingly, the position of the majority of courts to exclude all hypnotically induced testimony should not prevent an accused from testifying to his or her own posthypnotic recall.

Polygraph Evidence.   A polygraph is a device that records the subject's physiological activities, such as blood pressure and heartbeat, as the subject is questioned by an examiner. The examiner poses certain questions and records the subject's responses. The use of a polygraph is controversial. Polygraph operators argue that a properly administered polygraph test is effective in detecting deception, and they cite impressive figures attesting to the accuracy of results.

Some critics argue that an individual can so control his or her responses as to distort the findings.

Historically, federal and state courts have declined to admit polygraph evidence. As late as 1989, the Minnesota Supreme Court held that results of polygraph tests, as well as any direct or indirect references to taking of or refusal to take such tests, are inadmissible. *State v. Fenney,* 448 N.W.2d 54 (Minn. 1989). Most state courts agree and hold that the reliability of polygraph testing has not been scientifically demonstrated to such a degree of certainty as to permit its use in evidence. However, some courts allow results of polygraph testing to be admitted in court on stipulation of the prosecution and the defense. See, for example, *State v. Valdez,* 371 P.2d 894 (Ariz. 1962).

The prognosis for use of polygraph evidence remains uncertain. Advocates of polygraph evidence were heartened in 1989 when the Eleventh Circuit Court of Appeals observed that polygraph testing has gained increasingly widespread acceptance as a useful and reliable scientific tool. "We agree," said the court "with those courts which have found that a *per se* rule disallowing polygraph evidence is no longer warranted." *United States v. Piccinonna,* 885 F.2d 1529, 1535 (11th Cir. 1989).

Battered Woman Syndrome. As we explained in Chapter 13, expert testimony concerning the battered woman syndrome has gained substantial scientific acceptance, and in the past several years has been received in many courts in cases where women claim to have acted in self-defense. In 1989, the Ohio Supreme Court receded from its 1981 decision declaring such evidence inadmissible. The court took a fresh look at the literature published in this area since 1981 and said that "expert testimony on the battered woman syndrome would help dispel the ordinary lay person's perception that a woman in a battering relationship is free to leave at any time. Popular misconceptions about battered women should be put to rest, including beliefs that the women are masochistic." *State v. Koss,* 551 N.E.2d 970, 971 (Ohio 1990).

DNA Evidence. A new scientific procedure that has proved to be of value to law enforcement in identifying those who perpetrate homicidal and sexual assault offenses is called "DNA Printing." DNA is an abbreviation of deoxyribonucleic acid, the chemical that carries an individual's genetic information, and is extracted from a biological specimen (e.g., white blood cells, semen, body hair, and tissue). Through sophisticated testing results, "DNA printing tests" compare DNA molecules extracted from a suspect's specimen with DNA molecules extracted from specimens found at a crime scene to determine whether the samples match. Scientists and law enforcement attempt to develop what a layperson may call "genetic fingerprints." Evidence of the reliability of DNA typing analysis is now generally accepted when such a test is properly conducted by qualified personnel. *State v. Woodall,* 385 S.E.2d 253 (W.Va. 1989).

Shortly after being introduced judicially in 1987, DNA profiling was widely heralded by many courts. One federal court referred to the reliability and accuracy of DNA profiling as justifying "an aura of amazement." See *United States v. Jakobetz,* 747 F. Supp. 250, 258 (D.Vt. 1990). More recently, however, false positive and false negative entries by DNA laboratories have been documented, leading some courts to express skepticism about the use of DNA results.

Requirements of Admissibility

A defendant has certain constitutional protections concerning the prosecution's use of forced admissions and confessions and other evidence that has been illegally obtained. In addition, before evidence may be admitted in court, whether real or testimonial and whether direct or circumstantial, it must meet certain legal requirements. First, all evidence must be relevant (i.e., it must tend to prove or disprove a material fact in issue). For example, where the defendant is charged with armed robbery it would be relevant to show where the defendant and victim were located when the offense occurred, the money or other articles stolen, the force applied by the victim's assailant, details of any weapon used, the victim's resistance, and the defendant's fingerprints. Flight by the defendant when the police sought to make an arrest and, of course, any admissions or confessions of the defendant material to the crime would also be relevant. But offenses committed by the defendant completely unrelated to the crime of robbery would be irrelevant, as would be the defendant's individual likes, dislikes, and life-style.

"Similar Fact" Evidence.   So-called similar fact evidence is evidence of facts similar to the crime charged. Such evidence may reveal the commission of a collateral crime. The test of admissibility is whether such evidence is relevant and has a probative value in establishing a material issue. Thus, under some limited circumstances, evidence of other crimes or conduct similar to that charged against the defendant may be admitted in evidence in a criminal prosecution. While such evidence cannot be admitted to prove the defendant's bad character or propensity to commit a crime, in some instances it may be admitted to show motive, identity, or absence of mistake or accident. See, for example, *Williams v. State,* 110 So.2d 654 (Fla. 1959), *cert. denied,* 361 U.S. 847, 80 S. Ct. 102, 4 L.Ed.2d 86 (1959). This is a very technical area of the law of evidence.

There has been a trend to admit "similar fact" evidence in cases involving prosecutions for sexual abuse of children, where it often becomes important to establish opportunity, motive, intent, identity, or the absence of a mistake or accident, or even when a child's credibility as a witness is attacked by the defendant. This last point is illustrated by *Gezzi v. State,* 780 P.2d 972 (Wyo. 1989). There, the Wyoming Supreme Court reviewed a defendant's conviction of two counts of committing indecent acts with the younger of his two daughters. During the defendant's trial, the older sister testified to a course of sexual misconduct occurring between herself and the defendant similar to the molestation occurring between the defendant and the younger sister. Admission of this testimony was upheld, since the younger sister's credibility was attacked and the evidence admitted at trial was inconclusive as to the cause of the younger sister's physical symptoms. In affirming the defendant's conviction, the court included an exhaustive footnote showing that about half of the state courts now liberally recognize the admissibility of prior bad acts (similar acts) as evidence in sexual offenses for various purposes.

The Requirement of Competency.   To be admissible in court, evidence must also be competent. In determining whether a witness is competent to testify, the trial judge must consider the ability of the witness to receive and recollect impressions, understand questions, and have the ability to appreciate the moral duty to tell the truth. A very young child may or may not be competent to testify. This depends on the court's finding regarding the child's ability to understand the meaning of telling the truth. No precise rule can be set forth about when a young child may be competent to testify. Rather, it is a matter for determination in the sound discretion of the trial judge, and considerations include the child's age, intelligence, and capacity to appreciate the requirement to tell the truth. See *Wheeler v. United States,* 159 U.S. 523, 16 S. Ct. 93, 40 L.Ed. 244 (1895). Persons of unsound mind may not be competent to testify; but again, a judge must determine this. The presiding judge and members of the jury would not be competent to testify at a trial where they serve.

"Your Honor, I Object"

Anyone who has observed a criminal trial, or even a television drama depicting one, is familiar with the advocates frequently addressing the court, "Your honor, I object. . ." To this, the objecting lawyer may add "on the ground that the testimony is irrelevant." This is called a "general objection." Or, the lawyer may be more specific and add "because the testimony sought would be hearsay," or "because the answer calls for an opinion of the witness which the witness is not qualified to give," or the lawyer may advance another specific reason. This form of objection is called a "specific objection."

Beyond the general objection as to relevancy and competency, here are three of the most common reasons for a lawyer to make a specific objection to testimony during a criminal trial:

- **On the ground of hearsay.** Hearsay evidence refers to an oral or written statement by a person, other than the one testifying in court, offered to prove the truth of the matter asserted. A witness who testifies, "I know the defendant was home on the night of the offense because my sister told me so" would be giving hearsay testimony. The hearsay rule has many exceptions. By the very definition just given, you can see that sometimes a hearsay statement is admissible to prove something other than the truth of the statement itself. Spontaneous or excited utterances, a person's dying declaration, evidence of a person's reputation, matters contained in old family records, and certain business and public records are among the most common exceptions recognized by courts. Likewise, a defendant's out-of-court statement may be used if it is an admission, confession, or some other statement against the defendant's interest.
- **On the ground of the best evidence rule.** Ordinarily, the best evidence of a transaction must be offered in court. This rule applies to writings and means that an original document must be offered unless the party who offers a copy can present a plausible explanation of why the original is not available. For example, the original check allegedly forged by the defendant should be produced and not a photocopy of it.
- **On the ground that the question calls for an opinion of the witness.** A lay witness is supposed to testify regarding facts of which he or she has personal knowledge. In addition, lay witnesses are generally permitted to

testify about such matters as speed of a vehicle, sizes, distances, or appearance of a person. They cannot give opinions on matters beyond the common experience and understanding of laypersons. To illustrate: A driver can give an estimate of the speed of a vehicle he or she observed traveling on the street, but a witness must be qualified as an expert to be permitted to testify as to the speed of a car based on observation of the car's skid marks on the pavement. Such an opinion must generally be based on facts perceived by the witness and not on hearsay statements. Rule 701 of the Federal Rules of Evidence limits lay witnesses to testifying to those opinions rationally based on the perception of the witness and helpful to an understanding of the testimony or determination of a fact in issue. A trial judge has considerable discretion in determining whether to admit opinion evidence from a lay witness. While it is difficult to formulate precise rules, two illustrations shed light on the views of appellate courts. In *State v. Anderson*, 390 So.2d 878 (La. 1980), the Louisiana Supreme Court held it was error for the trial court to have allowed a police detective to give his opinion regarding the reasons why he received an anonymous call in a homicide case; however, the court found the error harmless under the circumstances of the case. In *State v. Lagasse*, 410 A.2d 537 (Me. 1980), the court held that a lay witness's opinion testimony that a girl "looked like she had been slapped" was admissible.

Privileged Communications

The rules of evidence also recognize certain privileges that limit testifying. In addition to the privilege against self-incrimination previously discussed, the most common privileges are

- **Attorney-client privilege.** This privilege can be claimed either by the client or by the attorney on behalf of the client in regard to communications between them in the course of the attorney's legal representation. The privilege belongs to the client, and if the client waives that privilege, the attorney can be required to disclose the communication. *Hunt v. Blackburn*, 128 U.S. 464, 9 S. Ct. 125, 32 L.Ed. 488 (1888).
- **Husband and wife privilege.** Confidential communications between married persons are generally privileged from disclosure. Therefore, married persons generally have the privilege not to testify against one another. The marital privilege emanates from the common law and was based on the policy of promoting and preserving domestic harmony and the repugnance against convicting one person through the testimony of another who shares intimate secrets of domestic life. The temptation to perjure was another consideration. See *State v. Gyngard*, 333 S.W.2d 73 (Mo. 1960). Some courts have held that even after divorce a spouse has the privilege not to testify against his or her former spouse concerning confidential communications made between them during their marriage. See, for example, *Shepherd v. State*, 277 N.E.2d 165 (Ind. 1971); *State v. Richards*, 391 S.E.2d 354 (W.Va. 1990).

CASE IN POINT

THE HEARSAY RULE: THREE COMMON EXCEPTIONS

Lawyers can cite a dozen or more exceptions to the rule that excludes the use of hearsay evidence in a criminal trial over a defendant's objection. The following cases illustrate three of the more common exceptions:

The Excited or Spontaneous Statement:

Five minutes after she was raped and while still crying and saying that she had lost her virginity and that the defendant and "Louie the Rat" had engaged in intercourse with her, a female victim verbally identified the defendant as one of her attackers. Over the defendant's objection, the court permitted a witness who overheard the victim's statement to testify to it at trial. On appeal, the West Virginia Supreme Court held that even though hearsay, the statement was properly admitted into evidence since it was spontaneously made just after the event occurred and thereby an exception to the hearsay rule. *State v. Mahramus,* 200 S.E.2d 357 (W.Va. 1973).

The Business Records Exception:

The defendant was prosecuted for theft of gasoline. A computer printout verifying that the missing gasoline was dispensed by means of a key card was held admissible under the business records exception to the hearsay rule since the printout was made in the usual course of business. *Hutchinson v. State,* 642 S.W.2d 537 (Tex. App. 1982).

The Dying Declaration Exception:

Defendant Connor was convicted of second-degree murder as a result of having run over his former wife with an automobile. A statement made by the victim that "it was no accident" was admitted at trial. On appeal the court noted that the statement was made when the victim was aware of her impending death and just after she said, "get a priest." The court ruled that the victim's statement was admissible in evidence as a dying declaration, an exception to the hearsay rule. *Connor v. State,* 171 A.2d 699 (Md. 1961).

- **Clergy-penitent privilege.** Generally priests, ministers, and rabbis are prohibited from testifying about matters related to them by the penitent in confidence. The member of the clergy, like the attorney, can assert the privilege on behalf of the penitent.
- **Other privileges.** Some jurisdictions also recognize testimonial privileges between a physician and patient, between a psychotherapist and a patient, and between an accountant and client. These expand the common-law concept of testimonial privilege, so the statutes and judicial decisions of a particular jurisdiction must be consulted.

The Defense Strategy in Moving for a Judgment of Acquittal

At the close of the prosecution's evidence, the defense counsel will frequently move the court to grant a "directed verdict" or, as it is called in federal courts and many state courts, a "judgment of acquittal." The purpose of such a motion is to have the trial judge determine whether the evidence presented by the prosecution is legally sufficient to support a verdict of guilty. For the purpose of ruling on the motion, the trial judge must view the prosecution's evidence in the light most favorable to the government. The trial judge's authority to direct a verdict has long been recognized. *France v. United States,* 164 U.S. 676, 17 S. Ct. 219, 41 L.Ed. 595 (1897).

Should the motion be granted, the defendant is discharged. If, as in most cases, the motion is denied, defense counsel proceeds with the case on behalf of the defendant, and if additional evidence is offered, defense counsel may renew the motion at the close of the evidence. Federal appellate courts will not review the sufficiency of the evidence to support a verdict unless a motion for a judgment of acquittal was made at the close of all the evidence in the trial court. See, for example, *Corbin v. United States,* 253 F.2d 646 (10th Cir. 1958). This principle also prevails in many state appellate courts.

The Defense Case—Will the Defendant Take the Stand?

Under the Fifth Amendment, the defendant does not have to testify in a criminal case and may choose to rely simply on cross-examination of the government's witnesses to obtain an acquittal. Or, the defendant may present witnesses in support of an alibi, or to establish an affirmative defense (see Chapter 13).

Perhaps the major tactical decision a defendant and defense counsel must make at trial is whether the defendant will take the stand and testify in his or her behalf. The Fifth Amendment privilege against self-incrimination that applies to the states through the Fourteenth Amendment, *Malloy v. Hogan,* 378 U.S. 1, 84 S. Ct. 1489, 12 L.Ed.2d 653 (1964), protects the defendant from being required to testify, absent a grant of immunity. Moreover, it also forbids any direct or indirect comment by the prosecution on the accused's failure to testify. *Griffin v. California,* 380 U.S. 609, 85 S. Ct. 1229, 14 L.Ed.2d 106 (1965).

When an accused voluntarily chooses to testify in his or her own behalf, the prosecution may cross-examine the accused in respect to his or her testimony with the same latitude as with any other witness. *Fitzpatrick v. United States,* 178 U.S. 304, 20 S. Ct. 944, 44 L.Ed. 1078 (1900). Moreover, even though illegally obtained evidence cannot be used to prove the government's case, in recent years it has been held that there is no federal constitutional prohibition that prevents the prosecution from using such evidence to impeach statements made by the defendant on cross-examination. *United States v. Havens,* 446 U.S. 620, 100 S. Ct. 1912, 64 L.Ed.2d 559 (1980); *Harris v. New York,* 401 U.S. 222, 91 S. Ct. 643, 28 L.Ed.2d 1 (1971).

These realities must weigh heavily in a defendant's decision whether to testify since the threat of contradiction and impeachment always exists in cross-examination. Regardless of whether the defendant testifies, any witnesses presented by the defendant are subject to cross-examination by the prosecution.

The Rebuttals

At the conclusion of the defendant's case, the prosecution is entitled to present rebuttal witnesses to dispute the testimony of the defendant's witnesses. After examination by the prosecution and cross-examination by the defense counsel, the defense may then present its rebuttal witnesses. They, in turn, are subject to examination by the defense counsel and to cross-examination by the prosecutor. This usually concludes the evidentiary phase of the trial.

Conduct of the Jury During the Trial

The traditional role of the juror has been to attentively listen to the evidence as presented by the prosecution and defense, to avoid any outside influences, and to withhold judgment until all the evidence has been presented and the jury retires to deliberate. In recent years many trial judges have allowed jurors to take notes. But is a juror privileged to ask questions of a witness? In *United States v. Land*, 877 F.2d 17, 19 (8th Cir. 1989), the court noted that the practice is "fraught with dangers which can undermine the orderly progress of the trial to verdict." Some courts have suggested that the trial judge should require jurors to submit questions in writing, whereupon the court may pose the question in its original or restated form. Nevertheless, trial judges have substantial latitude in overseeing the conduct of the jury, and appellate courts are not prone to reverse their decisions on allowing questions from a juror where the evidence is clearly sufficient to support the jury's verdict. See, for example, *United States v. Gray*, 897 F.2d 1428 (8th Cir. 1990).

The Jury Instructions Conference

At the close of all evidence in a jury trial, it is customary for the trial judge to confer with counsel outside the presence of the jury concerning the instructions on the law the judge will give to the jury. The prosecutor and defense counsel may be asked to present proposed instructions for the court to consider. More commonly, the trial judge announces that the court will give certain standard instructions and offers to supplement them with specific instructions to be chosen from those submitted by counsel. A defendant is entitled to have the jury instructed on the law applicable to any legitimate theory of defense that is supported by the evidence presented. See *United States v. Creamer*, 555 F.2d 612 (7th Cir. 1977), *cert. denied*, 434 U.S. 833, 98 S. Ct. 118, 54 L.Ed.2d 93 (1977). Jury instructions are settled in advance of closing arguments by counsel so that the prosecutor and defense counsel can present their arguments with assurance of how the judge will instruct the jury.

The Closing Arguments of Counsel

The Sixth Amendment guarantee of the right to assistance of counsel has been interpreted to include the right to present closing arguments in a criminal case, whether the case is tried before a jury or before the judge. *Herring v. New York*, 422 U.S. 853, 95 S.Ct. 2550, 45 L.Ed.2d 593 (1975). A defendant represented by counsel has no right to share the closing argument with his or her counsel, but if the defendant is *pro se*, that is, representing self, the court must allow the defendant to make a closing argument. *State v. Plaskonka*, 577 A.2d 729 (Conn.

App. 1990). While the constitutional guarantee accords the right of closing argument to the defendant, by statute or rules of court, the government and the defendant each are accorded the right for counsel to make closing arguments. The order of the arguments may be set by statute or court rule, but the trial judge retains control of the extent of the argument. The prosecutor usually argues first, followed by the defense counsel, with the prosecutor having an opportunity for a brief rebuttal.

Closing arguments are designed to assist the jury in recalling and evaluating the evidence and in drawing inferences therefrom. Many lawyers begin by recapitulating the evidence in the light most favorable to their client. After that the arguments frequently become emotional, with each side entreating the jury to "do its duty" by either convicting or acquitting the defendant.

In closing arguments counsel may comment on the weight of the evidence and the credibility of the witnesses, but it is improper for either the prosecutor or defense counsel to state a personal belief about the guilt or innocence of the accused. Likewise, it is improper for counsel to refer to any matters—other than those of common, everyday knowledge—that have not been introduced in evidence. Because a judge is trained in evaluating evidence, counsel in nonjury cases frequently waive their right to make closing arguments; otherwise, the arguments are generally quite brief.

While prosecutors may use every legitimate method to obtain a conviction, a legion of appellate court opinions admonishes them to be fair and objective in their presentations to a jury. Characteristically, the Wisconsin Supreme Court observed that the prosecutor's role should be

> to analyze the evidence and present facts with a reasonable interpretation to aid the jury in calmly and reasonably drawing just inferences and arriving at a just conclusion . . . . *State v. Genova*, 8 N.W.2d 260, 263 (Wis. 1943).

Prosecutors are prohibited from making inflammatory remarks to the jury. If a prosecutor does make inflammatory remarks or statements that have no basis in the evidence or that can be interpreted as a comment on the defendant's failure to testify, the judge may admonish the prosecutor. Usually this is followed by a cautionary instruction directing the jury to disregard such remarks. If the defendant objects and the trial judge fails to take appropriate action, or if the prosecutor's remarks are so prejudicial that they cannot be erased from the minds of the jurors, the defendant may be able to obtain a mistrial or, if convicted, win a new trial from an appellate court.

Perhaps because the government cannot ordinarily appeal on basis of improper comments by a defense counsel, the law seems to indulge a defendant in a somewhat wider latitude in jury arguments. Nevertheless, there are restraints, and sanctions for violations may take the form of an admonition by the trial judge or even disciplinary action where a defense lawyer's performance is egregious. Despite the fact that counsel must strive for acquittal of a client in our adversary system of justice, courts frequently remind defense lawyers that they, too, are officers of the court who must aid in the administration of justice and whose primary duty is to see that the lawful rights and privileges of the defendant are not violated. See, for example, *State v. Leaks*, 10 A.2d 281 (N.J. 1940).

CASE IN POINT

IMPROPER ARGUMENT BY A PROSECUTOR

Defendant, Larry Witted, was charged with attempted murder and armed robbery. At his jury trial, the chief issue was whether the victim had correctly identified the defendant as the person who robbed him. While the victim's testimony was positive, it was uncorroborated by any other evidence. During closing argument, the defense counsel argued that the process used to identify the defendant as the perpetrator was unduly suggestive. In rebuttal, the prosecutor implied that witnesses for the defense had perjured themselves at the request of defense counsel, and that the defendant had a criminal background that the defense was hiding from the jury. Since the prosecutor's remarks were made during his closing argument, the defense had no opportunity to challenge the inferences that were made. Witted was convicted, but the Illinois Court of Appeals awarded him a new trial.

People v. Witted, 398 N.E.2d 68 (Ill. App. 1979).

The Judge Instructs the Jury

Typically, at the conclusion of the closing arguments the judge either reads the indictment or information or explains the charges against the defendant to the jury. This is followed by an admonition that the defendant is presumed innocent unless and until the government proves the defendant guilty beyond a reasonable doubt of each element of the crime. The judge defines the elements of any crime charged and explains any technical legal terms. Where the jury may convict the defendant of a lesser offense, the judge must go further than merely defining the crime charged. For example, if the defendant is charged with first-degree murder, the judge must describe the lesser degrees of murder as well as manslaughter and excusable and justifiable homicide. Again, in a grand theft prosecution, the judge must generally define petit theft as well.

These instructions on the crimes may be followed by an explanation of any defenses pled by the defendant and the burden of proof, if any, on the defendant to sustain such defenses. Upon request of the defendant, a judge usually informs the jury that it should not consider any inference of guilt because the defendant exercised the right not to testify. However, many defense lawyers prefer not to have the judge give this instruction.

The trial judge always explains to the jury that its role is to be the sole judge of the facts and advises the jury on some of the things it should consider in evaluating the credibility of the evidence presented. If expert witnesses have testified, the judge explains their role and informs the jury that it is free to accept or reject their opinions. In America, in contrast to the English practice, the trial judge generally is not permitted to sum up the evidence or express an opinion on the weight of that evidence or the credibility of the witnesses.

The judge's instructions are given orally, and in some instances the jury is given a copy of the instructions. The clerk furnishes the jury forms of verdicts so they may find the defendant not guilty, guilty as charged, or guilty of some degree of the offense charged or of a lesser included offense. In federal criminal trials and in most state courts, the judge explains the requirement for a unanimous verdict. In some states the judge is required to inform the jury of the penalties that can be imposed for the offense charged. Finally, the jury is directed to retire, select one of its members as foreperson, and deliberate on its verdict. Usually a jury is allowed to take with it to the jury room all exhibits received in evidence.

Rule 31(c) of the Federal Rules of Criminal Procedure provides that "a defendant may be found guilty of an offense necessarily included in the offense charged." This means that a defendant is entitled to have the jury instructed on any lesser included offense whenever: (1) the elements of the lesser offense are a subset of elements of the charged offense; and (2) the evidence at trial is such that a jury could rationally find the defendant guilty of the lesser offense, yet acquit the defendant of the greater offense. *Schmuck v. United States*, 489 U.S. 705, 109 S.Ct. 1443, 103 L.Ed.2d 734 (1989).

Practices in state courts vary as to the extent to which the trial judge must instruct a jury on offenses that are lesser than the offense charged against a defendant. Some courts distinguish between those offenses that are necessarily included in the offense charged and those that may be included based on the allegations of the offense charged and the evidence presented at trial. In state courts, a defendant is generally entitled to an instruction of an offense of a less serious nature than the one charged if the elements of the charged offense can constitute the lesser crime. However, if the evidence is such that no rational jury could conclude the lesser offense was proper, then the trial court's refusal to give the lesser offense instruction is not necessarily considered reversible error by most appellate courts. See, for example, *People v. Tucker*, 542 N.E.2d 804 (Ill. App. 1989).

In a few states juries determine sentences (see Chapter 18). In these jurisdictions the judge must also instruct the jury on the range of sentences permitted. In most states that have the death penalty, a jury trial in a capital case is bifurcated, with the jury first determining guilt or innocence. If the jury finds the defendant guilty, a second phase ensues, during which the jury hears evidence of aggravating and mitigating circumstances and determines whether the death penalty should be imposed (see Chapter 18).

The Jury Deliberates and Returns its Verdict

When directed to deliberate, the jurors are escorted to their quarters by a court bailiff. In some cases the judge orders the jury sequestered, which means the jury must remain together until it reaches its verdict. This often requires the bailiff to escort the jurors to a hotel and to be present with them during meals to assure that no outside influences are brought to bear on their judgment.

Until directed to retire to deliberate, the jurors have been listeners, for in our system they are usually discouraged from asking any questions during the trial. They are always prohibited from discussing the case until they begin deliberations. Once in the jury room, their first order of business is to elect a foreperson. Then they are ready to commence their deliberations.

Since jury deliberations are secret, we can only speculate about the reasoning processes of jurors. We do know, however, that juries usually take a preliminary vote shortly after electing a foreperson. In most cases the jury probably arrives at its verdict without much discussion. In other instances jurors may deliberate for hours or days and many votes may be taken.

Often juries become "hung," that is, they cannot agree on a verdict. This was illustrated in March 1988, when a young man named Robert Chambers was tried in New York City for allegedly strangling a young woman in Central Park. The so-called yuppie murder drew national attention, partly because the testimony revealed that the victim's death grew out of "a rough sexual encounter" between the defendant and the victim. After a twelve-week trial, a panel of eight men and four women deliberated for nine days. They then sent a note to the judge saying they had reached an impasse. At that point, in a desire to conclude the proceedings—and perhaps rather than risk another trial—the defendant entered a negotiated plea of guilty to manslaughter, a lesser offense than that charged.

The Deadlocked Jury

If a jury reports that it is deadlocked, the trial judge can either declare a mistrial or urge the jury to make further attempts to arrive at a verdict. One tool that both federal and state trial judges sometimes employ is to give the jury a supplemental instruction called an "*Allen* charge." The instruction takes its name from an opinion issued by the Supreme Court at the turn of the century, *Allen v. United States*, 164 U.S. 492, 17 S. Ct. 154, 41 L.Ed. 528 (1896). A number of modifications have been made to the original *Allen* charge, but the basic thrust remains to urge

> that if much the larger number were for conviction, a dissenting juror should consider whether his doubt was a reasonable one. . . . If, upon the other hand, the majority were for acquittal, the minority ought to ask themselves whether they might not reasonably doubt the correctness of a judgment which was not concurred in by the majority. 164 U.S. at 501, 17 S. Ct. at 157, 41 L.Ed. at 531.

In Colorado it is called "the third-degree instruction" and the New Mexico courts have referred to it as the "shotgun instruction." *Leech v. People*, 146 P.2d 346, 347 (Colo. 1944); *State v. Nelson*, 321 P.2d 202, 204 (N.M. 1958). The use of the *Allen* charge in its original or in its many modified forms has been criticized for having a coercive effect, for implying that the majority view is the correct one, and for importuning the minority to change their views. In a few states (e.g., Montana) the state supreme court has banned its use. See *State v. Randall*, 353 P.2d 1054 (Mont. 1960). Nevertheless, federal and most state courts have generally approved the use of some version of the instruction when it has been cautiously given. See, for example, *Benscoter v. United States*, 376 F.2d 49 (10th Cir. 1967).

Jury Pardons

At times juries disregard the judge's instructions on the law and acquit a defendant or convict the defendant for a lesser offense than charged. This is referred to as "jury nullification" or as granting the defendant a "jury pardon."

CASE IN POINT

FACTORS CONSIDERED IN APPROVING TRIAL COURT'S USE OF *ALLEN* CHARGE WHERE JURY IS DEADLOCKED

Defendants Lindell and others were charged in the United States District Court with 35 counts of various crimes stemming from a marijuana importation scheme. They were convicted on several counts and appealed. Among their points on appeal, the defendants contended that when the jury sent notes that they were hopelessly deadlocked, the trial court should have declared a mistrial instead of giving an *Allen* charge to the jury. In rejecting the defendants' challenge, the United States Court of Appeals for the Fifth Circuit first noted that the language in the judge's charge to the jury comported with the modified *Allen* charge language repeatedly approved. Then the court pointed out that the trial lasted for three weeks, the verdict was a discriminating one returning both guilty and not guilty verdicts on the various counts, that in giving the *Allen* charge the judge did not set a deadline on deliberations, and that the verdict was not returned until two days after the *Allen* charge was given. Considering these factors, the court found no abuse of discretion in the trial judge having given the charge, and after rejecting other points raised by the defendants, the court of appeals affirmed the defendants' convictions.

United States v. Lindell, 881 F.2d 1313 (5th Cir. 1989).

Jurors, of course, take an oath to follow the law as charged by the judge and are expected to do so. *United States v. Powell*, 469 U.S. 57, 105 S. Ct. 471, 83 L.Ed.2d 461 (1984). But it is also recognized that a jury has the prerogative to exercise its judgment and bring in a verdict of not guilty or guilty of a lesser offense.

In death penalty cases there has been explicit recognition of the principle. For instance, in *Beck v. Alabama*, 447 U.S. 625, 100 S. Ct. 2382, 65 L.Ed.2d 392 (1980), the Supreme Court held that the death penalty may not be imposed if the jury is not permitted to consider a verdict of guilt of a lesser included noncapital offense when the evidence would have supported such a verdict. The Court explained:

> While we have never held that a defendant is entitled to a lesser included offense instruction as a matter of due process, the nearly universal acceptance of the rule in state and federal courts establishes the value to the defendant of this procedural safeguard. 447 U.S. at 637, 100 S. Ct. at 2389, 65 L.Ed.2d at 402.

In trials for other than capital offenses the reality of jury nullification exists, but there is no requirement for a judge to inform the jury of that power. See, for example, *United States v. Dougherty*, 473 F.2d 1113 (D.C. Cir. 1972). Since acquittals by juries are not subject to appeal, it is difficult to know when jury nullification occurs, but undoubtedly some defendants are acquitted or convicted of lesser offenses as a result of a "jury pardon." In *United States v. Dougherty*, the court in footnote 33 cites a number of examples taken from a study undertaken at the

University of Chicago Law School of the types of cases in which a jury voted to acquit because of its empathy with the defendant. The examples mentioned include statutory rape of an unchaste female, sale of liquor to a minor who is a member of the armed forces, and violence erupting after domestic strife.

The Verdict

The Sixth Amendment to the United States Constitution requires a unanimous verdict in federal cases. *Andres v. United States,* 333 U.S. 740, 68 S. Ct. 880, 92 L.Ed. 1055 (1948); see also, Fed. R. Crim. P. 31(a). A few states permit less than a unanimous verdict in criminal cases. State constitutional and statutory provisions that authorize a less than unanimous verdict by a twelve-person jury have been held not to violate the federal Constitution, *Johnson v. Louisiana,* 406 U.S. 356, 92 S. Ct. 1620, 32 L.Ed.2d 152 (1972), although verdicts by six-person juries must be unanimous. *Burch v. Louisiana,* 441 U.S. 130, 99 S. Ct. 1623, 60 L.Ed.2d 96 (1979).

When a jury has concluded its deliberations, it returns to the courtroom and delivers its written verdict. The verdict is usually first handed to the judge, who reviews it to determine whether it is in proper form. If it is, the judge hands the verdict to the clerk or jury foreperson to be read aloud in open court. A defendant who is acquitted by a jury is immediately discharged. If a jury finds the defendant guilty, the defendant is generally taken into custody to await sentencing. In some instances the defendant may be continued on bail, pending application for a new trial or an appeal. We discuss sentencing and appellate procedures in Chapters 18 and 19.

Polling the Jury

After a verdict has been read, the court or any party may have the jury polled individually. The clerk or judge asks each juror, "Is this your verdict?" or words to that effect. In most cases each juror responds affirmatively and the jury is discharged. If, on the other hand, a juror expresses dissent from the verdict, the trial judge may either direct the jury to retire for further deliberation or discharge the jury. See *People v. Kellogg,* 397 N.E.2d 835 (Ill. 1979).

Posttrial Motions

A convicted defendant may file a motion for a new trial, alleging that errors were committed at trial. This type of motion affords the trial judge an opportunity to rectify errors by awarding the defendant a new trial. In most instances, however, it is a pro forma prelude to an appeal and is denied by the trial court. A defendant may also seek bail pending appeal (see Chapter 19). When the trial court disposes of these motions, the defendant is sentenced (see Chapter 18).

CONCLUSION

Despite the relatively small percentage of criminal cases that go to trial, a criminal trial is a vital part of the criminal justice system. Adjudications at trial set the overall tone for the administration of the criminal law in the community. Jury verdicts become "weather vanes" of the public's attitude on the enforcement of the law.

Criminal trials also have an important bearing on the reshaping of both the statutory and decisional law in light of contemporary community values. With counsel now readily available to indigent defendants for handling their appeals as well as for representation at trial, appellate courts have the opportunity to update precedents and refine their procedures in light of the present constitutional standards.

Courts are slow to change, but change will occur. Scientific evidence now plays a more important role in criminal trials, especially in sexual assault, homicide offenses, and offenses involving intoxication. Increasingly, evidence at trials will be presented by videotapes and other photographic means. With the increased emphasis on efficiency, legislative bodies may soon find it advisable to reexamine the need for a jury of twelve persons. The decriminalization of most traffic offenses should soon be a reality, and pretrial diversionary programs should increase in popularity for first offenders charged with misdemeanor offenses.

Despite changes, the basic function of the criminal trial by a jury of one's peers will remain. It must because it is not only the citizen's protection against overzealous law enforcement and prosecutions; it also assures the public that no defendant will gain preferred status by virtue of prominence or be dealt with unfairly because of lowly status.

QUESTIONS FOR THOUGHT AND DISCUSSION

1. Jurors are generally selected from among those citizens who have registered to vote. Does this method of selection produce jurors drawn from a "representative cross-section of the community"? Can you suggest a better way for selecting jurors?

2. In England the *voir dire* process is conducted by the trial judge and is extremely limited. Do you think the American system of criminal justice would have more credibility if *voir dire* was conducted exclusively by the judge with only challenges for cause permitted?

3. What factors do you think a defense attorney considers in deciding whether to advise a client to testify in his or her own behalf at trial?

4. In *Estes v. Texas*, Justice Clark, writing for the Supreme Court, observed:

   Trial by television is, therefore, foreign to our system. Furthermore, telecasting may also deprive an accused of effective counsel. The distractions, intrusions into confidential attorney-client relationships and the temptation offered by television to play to the public audience might often have a direct effect not only upon the lawyers, but the judge, the jury and witnesses. 381 U.S. 532, 549, 85 S. Ct. 1628, 1636, 14 L.Ed.2d 543, 554 (1965).

   Evaluate Justice Clark's statement in light of the development in communications technology since 1965.

5. Many of the rules of evidence applied in jury trials are derived from the early common law, when jurors were largely uneducated. These rules were

designed to prevent jurors from hearing evidence that might prejudice their judgment in the case. In light of the educational standards in the United States, should these rules be made less restrictive in regard to evidence that can be presented in courts? What constitutional problems would arise by allowing hearsay evidence to be presented against a defendant?

6. A defendant is being tried for first-degree murder. The prosecutor presents an eyewitness to the victim's being shot. After asking the witness some preliminary questions, the prosecutor asks, "When the defendant shot and killed the victim . . . ." Would the defense attorney pose an objection to this question? On what ground?

7. What testimonial privileges are available to witnesses in your state? What is the rationale for each?

8. Do you think a trial judge should be allowed to sum up the evidence for the benefit of the jury before it retires to deliberate? What advantages and disadvantages can you see in such a practice? Would it be constitutional?

9. In some jurisdictions judges instruct a jury in regard to its general duties and responsibilities at the beginning of the trial rather than waiting until the evidence has been presented. Do you favor this approach? Why or why not?

10. As pointed out in this chapter, since 1923 federal courts and most state courts have applied the test articulated in *Frye v. United States* in determining whether evidence of emerging scientific principles and discoveries should be admissible. This test requires proof that the principle or discovery has gained "general acceptance" in the relevant scientific community. In June 1993, in *Daubert v. Merrell Dow Pharmaceuticals, Inc.,* 61 L. W. 4805, the U.S. Supreme Court rules that the "general acceptance" standard is superseded by the Federal Rules of Evidence; that henceforth federal courts should look to the "methods and procedures" used by scientific experts. The Court said that the trial judge must be responsible to limit a jury's consideration to evidence that is "not only relevant, but reliable." Do you think that state courts should continue to follow the *Frye* test or adopt the view now current in the federal courts? Can you suggest an alternative test for state courts to follow?

11. The Supreme Court has said that state criminal trial juries need not observe the unanimity principle that obtains in the federal courts. Could it not be argued that the reasonable doubt standard necessarily entails the unanimity principle, since the doubt of one juror is sufficient to suggest a reasonable doubt about the guilt of the accused?

C A S E S

WILLIAMS V. FLORIDA

Supreme Court of the United States, 1970.
399 U.S. 78, 90 S. Ct. 1893, 26 L.Ed.2d 446.

[In this case the U.S. Supreme Court considers whether six-person juries may be used in noncapital felony trials.]

Mr. Justice WHITE delivered the opinion of the Court.

... [Williams] filed a pretrial motion to impanel a 12-man jury instead of the six-man jury provided by Florida law in all but capital cases. That motion ... was denied. Petitioner was convicted [of robbery] as charged and was sentenced to life imprisonment. The District Court of Appeal affirmed, rejecting petitioner's claims that his Fifth and Sixth Amendment rights had been violated. We granted certiorari. ...

In *Duncan v. Louisiana*, 391 U.S. 145, 88 S. Ct. 1444, 20 L.Ed.2d 491 (1968), we held that the Fourteenth Amendment guarantees a right to trial by jury in all criminal cases that—were they to be tried in a federal court—would come within the Sixth Amendment's guarantee. Petitioner's trial for robbery on July 3, 1968, clearly falls within the scope of that holding. ... The question in this case then is whether the constitutional guarantee of a trial by "jury" necessarily requires trial by exactly 12 persons, rather than some lesser number—in this case six. We hold that the 12-man panel is not a necessary ingredient of "trial by jury," and that respondent's refusal to impanel more than the six members provided for by Florida law did not violate petitioner's Sixth Amendment rights as applied to the States through the Fourteenth.

We had occasion in *Duncan v. Louisiana* ... to review briefly the oft-told history of the development of trial by jury in criminal cases. That history revealed a long tradition attached great importance to the concept of relying on a body of one's peers to determine guilt or innocence as a safeguard against arbitrary law enforcement. That same history, however, affords little insight into the considerations that gradually led the size of that body to be

generally fixed at 12. Some have suggested that the number 12 was fixed upon simply because that was the number of the presentment jury from the hundred, from which the petit jury developed. Other, less circular but more fanciful reasons for the number 12 have been given, "but they were all brought forward after the number was fixed," and rest on little more than mystical or superstitious insights into the significance of "12." Lord Coke's explanation that the "number of twelve is much respected in holy writ, as 12 apostles, 12 stones, 12 tribes, etc.," is typical. In short, while sometime in the 14th century the size of the jury at common law came to be fixed generally at 12, that particular feature of the jury system appears to have been a historical accident, unrelated to the great purposes which gave rise to the jury in the first place. The question before us is whether this accidental feature of the jury has been immutably codified into our Constitution. ...

While "the intent of the Framers" is often an elusive quarry, the relevant constitutional history casts considerable doubt on the easy assumption in our past decisions that if a given feature existed in jury at common law in 1789, then it was necessarily preserved in the Constitution. Provisions for jury trial were first placed in the Constitution in Article III's provision that "the Trial of all Crimes ... shall be by Jury; and such Trial shall be held in the State where the said Crimes shall have been committed." The "very scanty history [of this provision] in the records of the Constitution Convention" sheds little light either way on the intended correlation between Article III's "jury" and the features of the jury at common law. ...

We do not pretend to be able to divine precisely what the word "jury" imported to the Framers, the First Congress, or the States in 1789. It may well be that the usual expectation was the jury would consist of 12, and that hence, the most likely conclusion to be drawn is simply that little thought was actually given to the specific question we face today. But there is absolutely no indication in "the intent of the Framers" of an explicit decision to equate the constitutional and common-law characteristics of the jury. Nothing in this history suggests, then, that we do violence to the letter of the Constitution by turning to other than purely historical considerations to determine which features of the jury system, as it existed at common law, were preserved in the Constitution. The relevant inquiry, as we see it, must be the function that the particular feature performs and its relation to the purposes of the jury trial. Measured by this standard, the 12-man requirement cannot be regarded as an indispensable component of the Sixth Amendment.

The purpose of the jury trial, as we noted in *Duncan,* is to prevent oppression by the Government. "Providing an accused with the right to be tried by a jury of his peers gave him an inestimable safeguard against the corrupt or overzealous prosecutor and against the compliant, biased, or eccentric judge." . . . Given this purpose, the essential feature of a jury obviously lies in the interposition between the accused and his accuser of the commonsense judgment of a group of laymen, and in the community participation and shared responsibility that results from that group's determination of guilt or innocence. The performance of this role is not a function of the particular number of the body that makes up the jury. To be sure, the number should probably be large enough to promote group deliberation, free from outside attempts at intimidation, and to provide a fair possibility for obtaining a representative cross-section of the community. But we find little reason to think that these goals are in any meaningful sense less likely to be achieved when the jury numbers six, than when it numbers 12—particularly if the requirement of unanimity is retained. And, certainly the reliability of the jury as a factfinder hardly seems likely to be a function of its size.

It might be suggested that the 12-man jury gives a defendant a greater advantage since he has more "chances" of finding a juror who will insist on acquittal and thus prevent conviction. But the advantage might just as easily belong to the State, which also needs only one juror out of twelve insisting on guilt to prevent acquittal. What few experiments have occurred—usually in the civil area—indicate that there is no discernible difference between the results reached by the two different-sized juries. In short, neither currently available evidence nor theory suggests that the 12-man jury is necessarily more advantageous to the defendant than a jury composed of fewer members.

Similarly, while in theory the number of viewpoints represented on a randomly selected jury ought to increase as the size of the jury increases, in practice the difference between the 12-man and the six-man jury in terms of the cross-section of the community represented seems likely to be negligible. Even the 12-man jury cannot insure representation of every distinct voice in the community, particularly given the use of the peremptory challenge. As long as arbitrary exclusions of a particular class from the jury rolls are forbidden, . . . the concern that the cross-section will be significantly diminished if the jury is decreased in size from 12 to six seems an unrealistic one.

We conclude, in short, as we began: the fact that the jury at common law was composed of precisely 12 is a historical accident, unnecessary to effect the purposes of the jury system and wholly without significance "except to mystics." . . . To read the Sixth Amendment as forever codifying a feature so incidental to the real purpose of the Amendment is to ascribe a blind formalism to the Framers which would require considerably more evidence than we have been able to discover in the history and language of the Constitution or in the reasoning of our past decisions. We do not mean to intimate that legislatures can never have good reasons for concluding that the 12-man jury is preferable to the smaller jury, or that such conclusions—reflected in the provisions of most States and in our federal system—are in any sense unwise. Legislatures may well have their own views about the relative value of the larger and smaller juries, and may conclude that, wholly apart from the jury's primary function, it is desirable to spread the collective responsibility for the determination of guilt among the larger group. In capital cases, for example, it appears that no State provides for less than 12 jurors—a fact that suggests implicit recognition of the value of the larger body as a means of legitimating society's decision to impose the death penalty. Our holding does no more than leave these considerations to Congress and the States, unrestrained by an interpretation of the Sixth Amendment that would forever dictate the precise number than can constitute a jury. Consistent with this holding, we conclude that petitioner's Sixth Amendment rights, as applied to the States through the Fourteenth Amendment, were not violated by Florida's decision to provide a six-man rather than a 12-man jury. The judgment of the Florida District Court of Appeal is Affirmed.

Mr. Justice BLACKMUN took no part in the consideration or decision of this case.

Mr. Chief Justice BURGER, concurring. . . .

Mr. Justice BLACK, with whom Mr. Justice DOUGLAS joins, concurring in part and dissenting in part. . . .

Mr. Justice MARSHALL, dissenting in part. . . .

BATSON V. KENTUCKY

Supreme Court of the United States, 1986.
476 U.S. 79, 106 S. Ct. 1712, 90 L.Ed.2d 69.

[In this case the Supreme Court considers the use of peremptory challenges to exclude persons of the defendant's race from the trial jury.]

Justice POWELL delivered the opinion of the Court. This case requires us to reexamine that portion of *Swain v. Alabama*, 380 U.S. 202, 13 L.Ed.2d 759, 85 S. Ct. 824 (1965), concerning the evidentiary burden placed on a criminal defendant who claims that he has been denied equal protection through the State's use of peremptory challenges to exclude members of his race from the petit jury.

Petitioner, a black man, was indicted in Kentucky on charges of second-degree burglary and receipt of stolen goods. On the first day of trial in Jefferson Circuit Court, the judge conducted voir dire examination of the venire, excused certain jurors for cause, and permitted the parties to exercise peremptory challenges. The prosecutor used his peremptory challenges to strike all four black persons on the venire, and a jury composed only of white persons was selected. Defense counsel moved to discharge the jury before it was sworn on the ground that the prosecutor's removal of the black veniremen violated petitioner's rights under the Sixth and Fourteenth Amendments to a jury drawn from a cross-section of the community, and under the Fourteenth Amendment to equal protection of the laws. Counsel requested a hearing on his motion. Without expressly ruling on the request for a hearing, the trial judge observed that the parties were entitled to

use their peremptory challenges to "strike anybody they want to." The judge then denied petitioner's motion, reasoning that the cross-section requirement applies only to selection of the venire and not to selection of the petit jury itself.

The jury convicted petitioner on both counts. . . .

The Supreme Court of Kentucky affirmed. . . . We granted certiorari . . . and now reverse.

In *Swain v. Alabama*, this Court recognized that a "State's purposeful or deliberate denial to Negroes on account of race of participation as jurors in the administration of justice violates the Equal Protection Clause." . . . This principle has been "consistently and repeatedly" reaffirmed, . . . in numerous decisions of this Court both preceding and following Swain. We reaffirm the principle today.

More than a century ago, the Court decided that the State denies a black defendant equal protection of the laws when it puts him on trial before a jury from which members of his race have been purposefully excluded. *Strauder v. West Virginia*, 100 U.S. 303, 25 L.Ed. 664 (1880). That decision laid the foundation for the Court's unceasing efforts to eradicate racial discrimination in the procedures used to select the venire from which individual jurors are drawn. In *Strauder*, the Court explained that the central concern of the recently ratified Fourteenth Amendment was to put an end to governmental discrimination on account of race. . . . Exclusion of black citizens from service as jurors constitutes a primary example of the evil the Fourteenth Amendment was designed to cure.

In holding that racial discrimination in jury selection offends the Equal Protection Clause, the Court in *Strauder* recognized, however, that a defendant has no right to a "petit jury composed in whole or in part of persons of his own race." . . . "The number of our races and nationalities stands in the way of evolution of such a conception" of the demand of equal protection. . . . But the defendant does have the right to be tried by a jury whose members are selected pursuant to nondiscriminatory criteria. . . . The Equal Protection Clause guarantees the defendant that the State will not exclude members of his race from the jury venire on account of race, . . . or on the false assumption that members of his race as a group are not qualified to serve as jurors. . . .

Purposeful racial discrimination in selection of the venire violates a defendant's right to equal protection because it denies him the protection that a trial by jury is intended to secure. "The very idea of a jury is a body . . . composed of the peers or equals of the person whose rights it is selected or summoned to determine; that is, of his neighbors, fellows, associates, persons having the same legal status in society as that which he holds." . . . The petit jury has occupied a central position in our system of justice by safeguarding a person accused of crime against the arbitrary exercise of power by prosecutor or judge. . . . Those on the venire must be "indifferently chosen" to secure the defendant's right under the Fourteenth Amendment to "protection of life and liberty against race or color prejudice." . . .

Racial discrimination in selection of jurors harms not only the accused whose life or liberty they are summoned to try. Competence to serve as a juror ultimately depends on an assessment of individual qualifications and ability impartially to consider evidence presented at a trial. . . . A person's race simply "is unrelated to his fitness as a juror." . . . As long ago as *Strauder*, therefore, the Court recognized that by denying a person participation in jury service on account of his race, the State unconstitutionally discriminated against the excluded juror. . . .

The harm from discriminatory jury selection extends beyond that inflicted on the defendant and the excluded juror to touch the entire community. Selection procedures that purposefully exclude black persons from juries undermine public confidence in the fairness of our system of justice. . . . Discrimination within the judicial system is most pernicious because it is "a stimulant to that race prejudice which is an impediment to securing to [black citizens] that equal justice which the law aims to secure to all others." . . .

As in any equal protection case, the "burden is, of course," on the defendant who alleges discriminatory selection of the venire "to prove the existence of purposeful discrimination." . . . In deciding if the defendant has carried his burden of persuasion, a court must undertake "a sensitive inquiry into such circumstantial and direct evidence of intent as may be available." . . . Circumstantial evidence of invidious intent may include proof of disproportionate impact. . . . We have observed that under some circumstances proof of discriminatory impact "may for all practical purposes demonstrate unconstitutionality because in various circumstances the discrimination is very difficult to explain on nonracial grounds." . . . For example, "total or seriously disproportionate exclusion of Negroes from jury venires is itself such an 'unequal application of the law . . . as to show intentional discrimination.' " . . .

Moreover, since *Swain*, we have recognized that a black defendant alleging that members of his race have been impermissibly excluded from the venire may make out a prima facie case of purposeful discrimination by showing that the totality of the relevant facts gives rise to an inference of discriminatory purpose. . . . Once the defendant makes the requisite showing, the burden shifts to the State to explain adequately the racial exclusion. . . . The State cannot meet this burden on mere general assertions that its officials did not discriminate or that they properly performed their official duties. . . . Rather, the State must demonstrate that "permissible racially neutral selection criteria and procedures have produced the monochromatic result." . . .

The showing necessary to establish a prima facie case of purposeful discrimination in selection of the venire may be discerned in this Court's decisions. . . . The defendant initially must show that he is a member of a racial group capable of being singled out for differential treatment. . . . In combination with the evidence, a defendant may then make a prima facie case by proving that in the particular jurisdiction members of his race have not been summoned for jury service over an extended period of time. . . . Proof of systematic exclusion from the venire raises an inference of purposeful discrimination because the "result bespeaks discrimination." . . .

Since the ultimate issue is whether the State has discriminated in selecting the defendant's venire, however, the defendant may establish a prima facie case "in other ways than by evidence of long-continued unexplained absence" of members of his race "from many panels." . . . In cases involving the venire, this Court has found a prima facie case on proof that members of the defendant's race were substantially underrepresented on the venire from which his jury was drawn, and that the venire was selected under a practice providing "the opportunity for discrimination." . . . This combination of factors raises the necessary inference of purposeful discrimination because the Court has declined to attribute to chance the absence of black citizens on a particular jury array where the selection mechanism is subject to abuse. When circumstances suggest the need, the trial court must undertake a "factual inquiry" that "takes into account all possible explanatory factors" in the particular case. . . .

Thus, since the decision in *Swain*, this Court has recognized that a defendant may make a prima facie showing of purposeful racial discrimination in selection of the venire by relying solely on the facts concerning its selection *in his case*. These decisions are in accordance with the proposition . . . that "a consistent pattern of official racial discrimination" is not "a necessary predicate to a violation of the Equal Protection Clause. A single invidiously discriminatory governmental act" is not "immunized by the absence of such discrimination in the making of the comparable decisions." . . . For evidentiary requirements to dictate that "several must suffer discrimination" before one could object, . . . would be inconsistent with the promise of equal protection to all.

The standards for assessing a prima facie case in the context of discriminatory selection of the venire have been fully articulated since *Swain*. . . . These principles support our conclusion that a defendant may establish a prima facie case of purposeful discrimination in selection of the petit jury solely on evidence concerning the prosecutor's exercise of peremptory challenges at the defendant's trial. To establish such a case, the defendant first must show that he is a member of a cognizable racial group, . . . and that the prosecutor has exercised peremptory challenges to remove from the venire members of the defendant's race. Second, the defendant is entitled to rely on the fact, as to which there can be no dispute, that peremptory challenges constitute a jury selection practice that permits "those to discriminate who are of a mind to discriminate." . . . Finally, the defendant must show that these facts and any other relevant circumstances raise an inference that the prosecutor used that practice to exclude the veniremen from the petit jury on account of their race. This combination of factors in the empanelling of the petit jury, as in the selection of the venire, raises the necessary inference of purposeful discrimination.

In deciding whether the defendant has made the requisite showing, the trial court should consider all relevant circumstances. For example, a "pattern" of strikes against black jurors included in the particular venire might give rise to an inference of discrimination. Similarly, the prosecutor's questions and statements during voir dire examination and in exercising his challenges may support or refute an inference of discriminatory purpose. These examples are merely illustrative. We have confidence that trial judges, experienced in supervising voir dire, will be able to decide if the circumstances concerning the prosecutor's use of peremptory challenges creates a prima facie case of discrimination against black jurors.

Once the defendant makes a prima facie showing, the burden shifts to the State to come forward with a neutral explanation for challenging black jurors. Though this requirement imposes a limitation in some cases on the full peremptory character of the historic challenge, we emphasize that the prosecutor's explanation need not rise to the level justifying exercise of a challenge for cause. But the prosecutor may not rebut the defendant's prima facie case of discrimination by stating merely that he challenged jurors of the defendant's race on the assumption—or his intuitive judgment—that they would be partial to the defendant because of their shared race. . . . Just as the Equal Protection Clause forbids the States to exclude black persons from the venire on the assumption that blacks as a group are unqualified to serve as jurors, ... so it forbids the States to strike black veniremen on the assumption that they will be biased in a particular case simply because the defendant is black. The core guarantee of equal protection, ensuring citizens that their State will not discriminate on account of race, would be meaningless were we to approve the exclusion of jurors on the basis of such assumptions, which arise solely from the jurors' race. Nor may the prosecutor rebut the defendant's case merely by denying that he had a discriminatory motive or "affirming his good faith in individual selections." ... If these general assertions were accepted as rebutting a defendant's prima facie case, the Equal Protection Clause "would be but a vain and illusory requirement." ... The prosecutor therefore must articulate a neutral explanation related to the particular case to be tried. The trial court then will have the duty to determine if the defendant has established purposeful discrimination.

The State contends that our holding will eviscerate the fair trial values served by the peremptory challenge. Conceding that the Constitution does not guarantee a right to peremptory challenges and that *Swain* did state that their use ultimately is subject to the strictures of equal protection, the State argues that the privilege of unfettered exercise of the challenge is of vital importance to the criminal justice system.

While we recognize, of course, that the peremptory challenge occupies an important position in our trial procedures, we do not agree that our decision today will undermine the contribution the challenge generally makes to the administration of justice. The reality of practice, amply reflected in many state and federal court opinions, shows that the challenge may be, and unfortunately at times has been, used to discriminate against black jurors. By requiring trial courts to be sensitive to the racially discriminatory use of peremptory challenges, our decision enforces the mandate of equal protection and furthers the ends of justice. In view of the heterogeneous population of our nation, public respect for our criminal justice system and the rule of law will be strengthened if we ensure that no citizen is disqualified from jury service because of his race.

Nor are we persuaded by the State's suggestion that our holding will create serious administrative difficulties. In those states applying a version of the evidentiary standard we recognize today, courts have not experienced serious administrative burdens, and the peremptory challenge system has survived. We decline, however, to formulate particular procedures to be followed upon a defendant's timely objection to a prosecutor's challenges.

In this case, petitioner made a timely objection to the prosecutor's removal of all black persons on the venire. Because the trial court flatly rejected the objection without requiring the prosecutor to give an explanation for his action, we remand this case for further proceedings. If the trial court decides that the facts establish, prima facie, purposeful discrimination and the prosecutor does not come forward with a neutral explanation for his action, our precedents require that petitioner's conviction be reversed. ...

It is so ordered.

Justice WHITE, concurring. ...

Justice MARSHALL, concurring. ...

Justice STEVENS, with whom Justice BRENNAN joins, concurring. ...

Justice REHNQUIST, with whom The CHIEF JUSTICE joins, dissenting.

... I cannot subscribe to the Court's unprecedented use of the Equal Protection Clause to restrict the historic scope of the peremptory challenge, which has been described as "a necessary part of trial by jury." ... In my view, there is simply nothing "unequal" about the State using its peremptory challenges to strike blacks from the jury in cases involving black defendants, so long as such challenges are also used to exclude whites in cases involving white defendants, Hispanics in cases involving Hispanic defendants, Asians in cases involving Asian defendants, and so on. This case-specific use of peremptory challenges by the State does not single out blacks, or members of any other race for that matter, for discriminatory treatment. Such use of peremptories is at best based upon seat-of-the-pants instincts, which are undoubtedly crudely stereotypical and may in many cases be hopelessly mistaken. But as long as they are applied across the board to jurors of all races and nationalities, I do not see—and the Court most certainly has not explained—how their use violates the Equal Protection Clause. . . .

SHEPPARD V. MAXWELL
Supreme Court of the United States, 1966.
384 U.S. 333, 86 S. Ct. 1507, 16 L.Ed.2d 600.

[In this classic case, the Supreme Court reviews a murder conviction rendered in an atmosphere of intense media activity.]

Mr. Justice CLARK delivered the opinion of the Court.

This federal habeas corpus application involves the question whether Sheppard was deprived of a fair trial in his state conviction for the second-degree murder of his wife because of the trial judge's failure to protect Sheppard sufficiently from the massive, pervasive and prejudicial publicity that attended his prosecution. The United States District Court held that he was not afforded a fair trial and granted the writ subject to the State's right to put Sheppard to trial again. . . . The Court of Appeals for the Sixth Circuit reversed by a divided vote. . . . We have concluded that Sheppard did not receive a fair trial consistent with the Due Process Clause of the Fourteenth Amendment and, therefore, reverse the judgment.

Marilyn Sheppard, petitioner's pregnant wife, was bludgeoned to death in the upstairs bedroom of their lakeshore home in Bay Village, Ohio, a suburb of Cleveland. On the day of the tragedy, July 4, 1954, Sheppard pieced together for several local officials the following story: He and his wife had entertained neighborhood friends, the Aherns, on the previous evening at their home. After dinner they watched television in the living room. Sheppard became drowsy and dozed off to sleep on a couch. Later, Marilyn partially awoke him saying that she was going to bed. The next thing he remembered was hearing his wife cry out in the early morning hours. He hurried upstairs and in the dim light from the hall saw a "form" standing next to his wife's bed. As he struggled with the "form" he was struck on the back of the neck and rendered unconscious. On regaining his senses he found himself on the floor next to his wife's bed. He rose, looked at her, took her pulse and "felt that she was gone." He then went to his son's room and found him unmolested. Hearing a noise he hurried downstairs. He saw a "form" running out the door and pursued it to the lake shore. He grappled with it on the beach and again lost consciousness. Upon his recovery he was lying face down with the lower portion of his body in the water. He returned to his home, checked the pulse on his wife's neck, and "determined or thought that she was gone." He then went downstairs and called a neighbor, Mayor Houk of Bay Village. The Mayor and his wife came over at once, found Sheppard slumped in an easy chair downstairs and asked, "What happened?" Sheppard replied: "I don't know but somebody ought to try to do something for Marilyn." Mrs. Houk immediately went up to the bedroom. The Mayor told Sheppard, "Get hold of yourself. Can you tell me what happened?" Sheppard then related the above-outlined events. After Mrs. Houk discovered the body, the Mayor called the local police, Dr. Richard Sheppard, petitioner's brother, and the Aherns. The local police were the first to arrive. They in turn notified the Coroner and Cleveland police. Richard Sheppard then arrived, determined that Marilyn was dead, examined his brother's injuries, and removed him to the nearby clinic operated by the Sheppard family. When the Coroner, the Cleveland police and other officials arrived, the house and surrounding area were thoroughly searched, the rooms of the house were photographed, and many persons, including the Houks and the Aherns, were interrogated. The Sheppard home and premises were taken into "protective custody" and remained so until after the trial.

From the outset officials focused suspicion on Sheppard. After a search of the house and premises on the morning of the tragedy, Dr. Gerber, the Coroner, is reported—and it is undenied—to have told his men, "Well, it is evident the doctor did this, so let's go get the confession out of him." He proceeded to interrogate and examine Sheppard while the latter was under sedation in his hospital room. On the same occasion, the Coroner was given the clothes Sheppard wore at the time of the tragedy together with the personal items in them. Later that afternoon Chief Eaton and two Cleveland police officers interrogated Sheppard at some length, confronting him with evidence and demanding explanations. Asked by Officer Shotke to take a lie detector test, Sheppard said he would if it were reliable. Shotke replied that it was "infallible" and "you might as well tell us all about it now." At the end of the interrogation Shotke told Sheppard: "I think you killed your wife." Still later in the same afternoon a physician sent by the Coroner was permitted to make a detailed examination of Sheppard. Until the Coroner's inquest on July 22, at which time he was subpoenaed, Sheppard made himself available for frequent and extended questioning without the presence of an attorney.

On July 7, the day of Marilyn Sheppard's funeral, a newspaper story appeared in which Assistant County Attorney Mahon—later the chief prosecutor of Sheppard—sharply criticized the refusal of the Sheppard family to permit his immediate questioning. From there on headline stories repeatedly stressed Sheppard's lack of cooperation with the police and other officials. Under the headline "Testify Now In Death, Bay Doctor Is Ordered," one story described a visit by Coroner Gerber and four police officers to the hospital on July 8. When Sheppard insisted that his lawyer be present, the Coroner wrote out a subpoena and served it on him. Sheppard then agreed to submit to questioning without counsel and the subpoena was torn up. The officers questioned him for several hours. On July 9, Sheppard, at the request of the Coroner, reenacted

the tragedy at his home before the Coroner, police officers, and a group of newsmen, who apparently were invited by the Coroner. The home was locked so that Sheppard was obliged to wait outside until the Coroner arrived. Sheppard's performance was reported in detail by the news media along with photographs. The newspapers also played up Sheppard's refusal to take a lie detector test and "the protective ring" thrown up by his family. Front-page newspaper headlines announced on the same day that "Doctor Balks at Lie Test; Retells Story." A column opposite that story contained an "exclusive" interview with Sheppard headlined: " 'Loved My wife, She Loved Me,' Sheppard Tells News Reports." The next day, another headline story disclosed that Sheppard had "again late yesterday refused to take a lie detector test" and quoted an Assistant County Attorney as saying that "at the end of a nine-hour questioning of Dr. Sheppard, I felt he was now ruling [a test] out completely." But subsequent newspaper articles reported that the Coroner was still pushing Sheppard for a lie detector test. More stories appeared when Sheppard would not allow authorities to inject him with "truth serum."

On the 20th, the "editorial artillery" opened fire with a front-page charge that somebody is "getting away with murder." The editorial attributed the ineptness of the investigation to "friendships, relationships, hired lawyers, a husband who ought to have been subjected instantly to the same third-degree to which any other person under similar circumstances is subjected . . . ." The following day, July 21, another page-one editorial was headed: "Why No Inquest? Do It Now, Dr. Gerber." The Coroner called an inquest the same day and subpoenaed Sheppard. It was staged the next day in a school gymnasium; the Coroner presided with the County Prosecutor as his advisor and two detectives as bailiffs. In the front of the room was a long table occupied by reporters, television and radio personnel, and broadcasting equipment. The hearing was broadcast with live microphones placed at the Coroner's seat and the witness stand. A swarm of reporters and photographers attended. Sheppard was brought into the room by police who searched him in full view of several hundred spectators. Sheppard's counsel were present during the three-day inquest but were not permitted to participate. When

Sheppard's chief counsel attempted to place some documents in the record, he was forcibly ejected from the room by the Coroner, who received cheers, hugs, and kisses from ladies in the audience. Sheppard was questioned for five and one-half hours about his actions on the night of the murder, his married life, and a love affair with Susan Hayes. At the end of the hearing the Coroner announced that he "could" order Sheppard held for the grand jury, but did not do so.

Throughout this period the newspapers emphasized evidence that tended to incriminate Sheppard and pointed out discrepancies in his statements to authorities. At the same time, Sheppard made many public statements to the press and wrote feature articles asserting his innocence. During the inquest on July 26, a headline in large type stated: "Kerr [Captain of the Cleveland Police] Urges Sheppard's Arrest." In the story, Detective McArthur "disclosed that scientific tests at the Sheppard home have definitely established that the killer washed off a trail of blood from the murder bedroom to the downstairs section," a circumstance casting doubt on Sheppard's accounts of the murder. No such evidence was produced at trial. The newspapers also delved into Sheppard's personal life. Articles stressed his extramarital love affairs as a motive for the crime. The newspapers portrayed Sheppard as a Lothario, fully explored his relationship with Susan Hayes, and named a number of other women who were allegedly involved with him. The testimony at trial never showed that Sheppard had any illicit relationships besides the one with Susan Hayes.

On July 28, an editorial entitled "Why Don't Police Quiz Top Suspect" demanded that Sheppard be taken to police headquarters. It described him in the following language:

Now proved under oath to be a liar, still free to go about his business, shielded by his family, protected by a smart lawyer who had made monkeys of the police and authorities, carrying a gun part of the time, left free to do whatever he pleases. . . .

A front-page editorial on July 30 asked: "Why Isn't Sam Sheppard in Jail?" It was later titled "Quit Stalling—Bring Him In." After calling Sheppard "the most unusual murder suspect ever seen around these parts" the article said that "[e]xcept for some

superficial questioning during Coroner Sam Gerber's inquest he has been scot-free of any official grilling . . . ." It asserted that he was "surrounded by an iron curtain of protection [and] concealment."

That night at 10 o'clock Sheppard was arrested at his father's home on a charge of murder. He was taken to the Bay Village City Hall where hundreds of people, newscasters, photographers and reporters were awaiting his arrival. He was immediately arraigned—having been denied a temporary delay to secure the presence of counsel—and bound over to the grand jury.

The publicity then grew in intensity until his indictment on August 17. Typical of the coverage during this period is a front-page interview entitled: "DR. SAM: 'I Wish There Was Something I Could Get Off My Chest—but There Isn't.' " Unfavorable publicity included items such as a cartoon of the body of a sphinx with Sheppard's head and the legend below: " 'I Will Do Everything In My Power to Help Solve This Terrible Murder.'—Dr. Sam Sheppard." Headlines announced, inter alia, that: "Doctor Evidence is Ready for Jury," "Corrigan Tactics Stall Quizzing," "Sheppard 'Gay Set' Is Revealed By Houk," "Blood Is Found In Garage," "New Murder Evidence Is Found, Police Claim," "Dr. Sam Faces Quiz At Jail On Marilyn's Fear Of Him." On August 18, an article appeared under the headline "Dr. Sam Writes His Own Story." And reproduced across the entire front page was a portion of the typed statement signed by Sheppard: "I am not guilty of the murder of my wife, Marilyn. How could I, who have been trained to help people and devoted my life to saving life, commit such a terrible and revolting crime?" We do not detail the coverage further. There are five volumes filled with similar clippings from each of the three Cleveland newspapers covering the period from the murder until Sheppard's conviction in December 1954. The record includes no excerpts from newscasts on radio and television but since space was reserved in the courtroom for these media we assume that their coverage was equally large.

With this background the case came on for trial two weeks before the November general election at which the chief prosecutor was a candidate for common pleas judge and the trial judge, Judge Blythin, was a candidate to succeed himself.

Twenty-five days before the case was set, 75 veniremen were called as prospective jurors. All three Cleveland newspapers published the names and addresses of the veniremen. As a consequence, anonymous letters and telephone calls, as well as calls from friends, regarding the impending prosecution were received by all of the prospective jurors. The selection of the jury began on October 18, 1954.

The courtroom in which the trial was held measured 26 by 48 feet. A long temporary table was set up inside the bar, in back of the single counsel table. It ran the width of the courtroom, parallel to the bar railing, with one end less than three feet from the jury box. Approximately 20 representatives of newspapers and wire services were assigned seats at this table by the court. Behind the bar railing there were four rows of benches. These seats were likewise assigned by the court for the entire trial. The first row was occupied by representatives of television and radio stations, and the second and third rows by reporters from out-of-town newspapers and magazines. One side of the last row, which accommodated 14 people, was assigned to Sheppard's family and the other to Marilyn's. The public was permitted to fill vacancies in this row on special passes only. Representatives of the news media also used all the rooms on the courtroom floor, including the room where cases were ordinarily called and assigned for trial. Private telephone lines and telegraphic equipment were installed in these rooms so that reports from the trial could be speeded to the papers. Station WSRS was permitted to set up broadcasting facilities on the third floor of the courthouse next door to the jury room, where the jury rested during recesses in the trial and deliberated. Newscasts were made from this room throughout the trial, and while the jury reached its verdict.

On the sidewalk and steps in front of the courthouse, television and newsreel cameras were occasionally used to take motion pictures of the participants in the trial, including the jury and the judge. Indeed, one television broadcast carried a staged interview of the judge as he entered the courthouse. . . .

We now reach the conduct of the trial. While the intense publicity continued unabated, it is sufficient to relate only the more flagrant episodes:

1. On October 9,. 1954, nine days before the case went to trial, an editorial in one of the newspapers criticized defense counsel's random poll of people on the streets as to their opinion of Sheppard's guilt or innocence in an effort to use the resulting statistics to show the necessity for change of venue. The article said the survey "smacks of mass jury tampering," called on defense counsel to drop it, and stated that the bar association should do something about it. It characterized the poll as "non-judicial, non-legal, and nonsense." The article was called to the attention of the court but no action was taken.

2. On the second day of *voir dire* examination a debate was staged and broadcast live over WHK radio. The participants, newspaper reporters, accused Sheppard's counsel of throwing roadblocks in the way of the prosecution and asserted that Sheppard conceded his guilt by hiring a prominent criminal lawyer. Sheppard's counsel objected to this broadcast and requested a continuance, but the judge denied the motion. When counsel asked the court to give some protection from such events, the judge replied that "WHK doesn't have much coverage," and that "[a]fter all, we are not trying this case by radio or in newspapers or any other means. We confine ourselves seriously to it in this courtroom and do the very best we can."

3. While the jury was being selected, a two-inch headline asked: "But Who Will Speak for Marilyn?" . . .

4. As has been mentioned, the jury viewed the scene of the murder on the first day of the trial. Hundreds of reporters, cameramen and onlookers were there, and one representative of the news media was permitted to accompany the jury while it inspected the Sheppard home. The time of the jury's visit was revealed so far in advance that one of the newspapers was able to rent a helicopter and fly over the house taking pictures of the jurors on their tour.

5. On November 19, a Cleveland police officer gave testimony that tended to contradict details in the written statement Sheppard made to the Cleveland police. Two days later, in a broadcast heard over Station WHK in Cleveland, Robert Considine likened Sheppard to a perjurer and

compared the episode to Alger Hiss' confrontation with Whittaker Chambers. Though defense counsel asked the judge to question the jury to ascertain how many heard the broadcast, the court refused to do so. The judge also overruled the motion for continuance based on the same ground, saying: "Well, I don't know, we can't stop people, in any event, listening to it. It is a matter of free speech, and the court can't control everybody. . . . We are not going to harass the jury every morning . . . . It is getting to the point where if we do it every morning, we are suspecting the jury. I have confidence in this jury . . . ."

6. On November 24, a story appeared under an eight-column headline: "Sam Called a 'Jekyll-Hyde' By Marilyn, Cousin To Testify." It related that Marilyn had recently told friends that Sheppard was a "Dr. Jekyll and Mr. Hyde" character. No such testimony was ever produced at the trial. The story went on to announce: "The prosecution has a 'bombshell witness' on tap who will testify to Dr. Sam's display of fiery temper—countering the defense claim that the defendant is a gentle physician with an even disposition." Defense counsel made motions for change of venue, continuance and mistrial, but they were denied. No action was taken by the court.

7. When the trial was in its seventh week, Walter Winchell broadcast over WXEL television and WJW radio that Carole Beasley, who was under arrest in New York City for robbery, had stated that, as Sheppard's mistress, she had borne him a child. The defense asked that the jury be queried on the broadcast. Two jurors admitted in open court that they had heard it. The judge asked each: "Would that have any effect upon your judgment?" Both replied, "No." This was accepted by the judge as sufficient; he merely asked the jury to "pay no attention whatever to that type of scavenging. . . . Let's confine ourselves to this courtroom if you please."

8. On December 9, while Sheppard was on the witness stand he testified that he had been mistreated by Cleveland detectives after his arrest. Although he was not at the trial, Captain Kerr of the Homicide Bureau issued a press statement denying Sheppard's allegations which appeared under the headline: " 'Bare-faced Liar,' Kerr Says

of Sam." Captain Kerr never appeared as a witness at the trial.

9. After the case was submitted to the jury, it was sequestered for its deliberations, which took five days and four nights. After the verdict, defense counsel ascertained that the jurors had been allowed to make telephone calls to their homes every day while they were sequestered at the hotel. Although the telephones had been removed from the jurors' rooms, the jurors were permitted to use the phones in the bailiffs' rooms. The calls were placed by the jurors themselves; no record was kept of the jurors who made calls, the telephone numbers or the parties called. The bailiffs sat in the room where they could hear only the jurors' end of the conversation. The court had not instructed the bailiffs to prevent such calls. By a subsequent motion, defense counsel urged that this ground alone warranted a new trial, but the motion was overruled and no evidence was taken on the question.

. . . Due process requires that the accused receive a trial by an impartial jury free from outside influences. Given the pervasiveness of modern communications and the difficulty of effacing prejudicial publicity from the minds of the jurors, the trial courts must take strong measures to ensure that the balance is never weighed against the accused. And appellate tribunals have the duty to make an independent evaluation of the circumstances. Of course, there is nothing that proscribes the press from reporting events that transpire in the courtroom. But where there is a reasonable likelihood that prejudicial news prior to trial will prevent a fair trial, the judge should continue the case until the threat abates, or transfer it to another county not so permeated with publicity. In addition, sequestration of the jury was something the judge should have raised . . . with counsel. If publicity during the proceedings threatens the fairness of the trial, a new trial should be ordered. But we must remember that reversals are but palliatives; the cure lies in those remedial measures that will prevent the prejudice at its inception. The courts must take such steps by rule and regulation that will protect their processes from prejudicial outside interferences. Neither prosecutors, counsel for defense, the accused, witnesses, court staff nor enforcement officers coming under the jurisdiction of the court should be permitted to frustrate its function. Collaboration between counsel and the press as to information affecting the fairness of a criminal trial is not only subject to regulation, but is highly censurable and worthy of disciplinary measures.

Since the state trial judge did not fulfill his duty to protect Sheppard from the inherently prejudicial publicity which saturated the community and to control disruptive influences in the courtroom, we must reverse the denial of the habeas petition. The case is remanded to the District Court with instructions to issue the writ and order that Sheppard be released from custody unless the State puts him to its charges again within a reasonable time.

Mr. Justice BLACK dissents.

JACKSON V. STATE
District Court of Appeal of Florida, 1987.
511 So.2d 1047.

[Here a Florida appellate court considers whether the trial judge erred in denying the defendant's motion for a directed verdict of acquittal.]

SCHEB, Acting Chief Judge.
The state charged John William Jackson with first degree murder and armed burglary. Jackson was tried by jury and found guilty of both offenses. The trial court sentenced him to life imprisonment with a minimum mandatory term of twenty-five years. In this appeal we focus on the one meritorious point presented by Jackson that the trial court erred in denying his motion for judgment of acquittal.

At Jackson's trial, the state's evidence revealed that on December 19, 1983, around 4:30 A.M. Marie Felver Porter was raped and stabbed in her house trailer on Drawdy Road, Plant City. She went to a neighbor's door for help and told him that "an orange picker, Michigan tag" had done it. She died shortly thereafter from multiple stab wounds to her neck. An autopsy revealed a bruise on her right wrist which was later determined to be a bite mark. At approximately 7:30 A.M. on the day of the crime the police arrived at the scene, where they obtained blood, semen and saliva stains, fingerprints, and hair samples.

Jackson, a 31-year-old, Caucasian male, had lived in the vicinity of the victim's trailer from approximately July 1983 until a few days before the crime, when he moved a few miles away. He lived in the yards of various neighbors, either in a tent or in his car.

On January 13, 1984, Jackson was questioned by the police. He appeared voluntarily and denied knowing the victim or her husband. He told the police he had spent the night of the murder at a rest area on Interstate 4, some fifteen to twenty miles from Marie Porter's trailer. He said that on December 19, 1983, at around 5:15 A.M. he went to the Minute Man Labor Pool in Tampa, where he remembered seeing a Mr. Abe Abdu. The Minute Man Labor Pool records did not reveal that he had worked on that day. Mr. Abdu did not see Jackson at the labor pool in the early morning; he saw him only at the time he was leaving. With Jackson's consent he was fingerprinted. Also with his consent, the police took impressions of his teeth and collected samples of his pubic and head hair and his blood.

On January 31, 1984, Jackson had a conversation with Charles and Patricia Fuller, on whose property he had lived during the latter part of 1983. Jackson told them that when the police had interrogated him he learned that the victim had been raped, stabbed and bitten. This was before the police had released the information that the victim had been bitten. Mrs. Fuller acknowledged that Jackson had told her that he had been picking oranges. She also stated that she had seen the defendant carrying a knife.

Mr. Fuller testified that during the time he knew him, the defendant had worked as a heavy equipment operator out of a labor pool in Tampa.

The state presented a number of expert witnesses. Dr. Richard Souviron, a forensic odontologist, concluded that the bite mark on the victim's wrist was consistent with Jackson's teeth impressions. FBI Agent Michael Malone, an expert in hair and fibers analysis, identified two head hairs found on the victim's pajama top as being indistinguishable from Jackson's hair sample. These hairs on the victim's pajamas were identified as having been forcibly removed. Negroid hairs found in a window screen and a Negroid pubic hair found in the combed pubic hair of the victim plus several other strands of Caucasian hair, were not identified.

At the conclusion of the state's case, Jackson moved for a judgment of acquittal under Florida Rule of Criminal Procedure 3.380. He argued that the state's case was based entirely on circumstantial evidence and did not exclude any reasonable hypothesis consistent with innocence. The trial court denied his motion. The defendant then introduced evidence on his own behalf, none of which tended to incriminate him. At the conclusion of all evidence, the defendant again moved for judgement of acquittal. Again, the trial court denied the motion.

When, as here, the state's evidence against the defendant is circumstantial, this court's role is to determine whether the jury might have reasonably concluded that the evidence excluded every reasonable hypothesis but that of guilt. ... The weight of the evidence is a matter for the trier of fact, and a jury verdict should not be reversed when there is substantial, competent evidence to support it. ... Nevertheless, in criminal convictions based solely on circumstantial evidence, it is our duty to reverse the conviction when that evidence, although strongly suggesting guilt, fails to eliminate any reasonable hypothesis of innocence. ... Here, we conclude that the state did not present substantial, competent evidence to support the jury's verdict; hence, we must vacate the defendant's convictions.

There were three items of crucial evidence presented by the state: first, the consistent bite mark; second, Jackson's statement to the Fullers that the victim had been bitten; and the third, the strands of hair found on the victim matching Jackson's hair. We now examine the probative effect of each of these items of evidence.

Dr. Souviron was qualified as an expert in forensic odontology and bite-mark analysis. He testified that the bite mark on the victim's wrist was made through clothing. In his own words, it was a tough bite: "It's tough because it's a bite through the cloth ... a difficult bite to diagnose." Dr. Souviron matched the impressions of Jackson's teeth to pictures of the bite and found similarities such as a left tooth sticking out, space between front teeth, and unique characteristics of the curvature of the arch. However, Dr. Souviron stated that "this was not a positive bite ... and said "I certainly hope he [Detective Baker] didn't arrest John Jackson on this bite." Moreover, testimony for the defense of another forensic odontologist cast considerable doubt on the reliability of Dr. Souviron's conclusions.

In *Bradford v. State*, 460 So.2d 926 (Fla. 2d DCA 1984), ... this court affirmed the defendant's conviction of murder where bite-mark evidence was introduced by the state. In *Bradford*, Dr. Souviron, again the state's expert witness, testified that, to a reasonable degree of dental certainty or probability, the two abrasion patterns on the index finger of the appellant had been made by the victim's teeth. However, in *Bradford*, the state presented substantial evidence that the defendant had been in the victim's apartment at or about the time the crime had been committed. It also introduced other circumstantial evidence tending to show the defendant's guilt.

The fact that Jackson knew that the victim had been bitten is not probative of his guilt. Prior to defendant's conversation with the Fullers, the police had taken impressions of his teeth. This would certainly be a strong indication to anyone that a bite mark was involved.

The only other significant evidence presented against Jackson was Agent Malone's testimony that two strands of hair found on the victim's pajamas matched the defendant's hair samples. Agent Malone explained that he was trained to recognize the unique microscopic characteristics of hair. He testified that he has to come up with at least fifteen matching characteristics before he can say that two hair samples are consistent with having originated from the same person. Malone identified twenty characteristics present in Jackson's hair samples and in the hair found on the victim's pajamas. He concluded that the hairs were indistinguishable. Despite his conclusion, Agent Malone testified that "hair will never get unique enough to be like a fingerprint." He also agreed that hair comparisons do not constitute a basis for positive personal identification and stated that "it's not a fingerprint, no. I cannot say that hair came from John Jackson and nobody else."

Given the quality of the state's evidence, it is clear that Jackson's conviction hinges on two hairs found on the victim's clothing which match his hair sample. Hair comparison testimony, while admissible, does not result in identifications of absolute certainty. . . . There was no evidence placing the defendant at the scene of the crime, no indication of a relationship of any kind between the defendant and the victim, or that they even knew each other. The victim's dying words pointed to an "orange picker, Michigan tag." Jackson's car, however, had a Florida tag. None of the fingerprints found at the scene of the crime matched Jackson's. This, plus the presence of Negroid pubic hair in the victim's pubic hair combings, adds support to a reasonable hypothesis that someone else committed the crime.

Even if the hair evidence were as positive as a fingerprint, the state would have to show that the hair could only have been placed on the victim's pajamas during the commission of the crime. . . . This the state failed to show. Furthermore, although a defendant's motive is not an element of a crime, where, as here, the evidence is entirely circumstantial, the lack of any motive on the part of the defendant becomes a significant consideration. . . .

The Supreme Court of Florida has repeatedly said that "[w]here the only proof of guilt is circumstantial, no matter how strongly the evidence may suggest guilt a conviction cannot be sustained unless the evidence is inconsistent with any reasonable hypothesis of innocence." . . .

Viewing all the evidence presented in a light most favorable to the state, as we must do on appellate review, we find that the state failed to present substantial, competent evidence sufficient to enable the jury to exclude every reasonable hypothesis of defendant's innocence.

Accordingly, we reverse the trial court's denial of the defendant's motion for a judgment of acquittal and vacate the defendant's convictions and sentence.

CAMPBELL and SCHOONOVER, JJ., concur.

HARRIS V. NEW YORK
Supreme Court of the United States, 1971.
401 U.S. 222, 91 S. Ct. 643, 28 L.Ed.2d 1.

[In this case, the U.S. Supreme Court considers whether evidence obtained in violation of *Miranda v. Arizona* may be admitted at trial to impeach the credibility of a defendant who testifies in his own behalf.]

Mr. Chief Justice BURGER delivered the opinion of the Court.

We granted the writ in this case to consider petitioner's claim that a statement made by him to police under circumstances rendering it inadmissible to establish the prosecution's case in chief under *Miranda v. Arizona* . . . may not be used to impeach his credibility.

The State of New York charged petitioner in a two-count indictment with twice selling heroin to an undercover police officer. At a subsequent jury trial the officer was the State's chief witness, and he testified as to details of the two sales. A second officer verified collateral details of the sales, and a third offered testimony about the chemical analysis of the heroin.

Petitioner took the stand in his own defense. He admitted knowing the undercover police officer but denied a sale on January 4, 1966. He admitted making a sale of contents of a glassine bag to the officer on January 6 but claimed it was baking power and part of a scheme to defraud the purchaser.

On cross-examination petitioner was asked seriatim whether he had made specified statements to the police immediately following his arrest on January 7—statements that partially contradicted petitioner's direct testimony at trial. In response to the cross-examination, petitioner testified that he could not remember virtually any of the questions or answers recited by the prosecutor. At the request of petitioner's counsel the written statement from which the prosecutor had read questions and answers in his impeaching process was placed in the record for possible use on appeal; the statement was not shown to the jury.

The trial judge instructed the jury that the statements attributed to petitioner by the prosecution could be considered only in passing on petitioner's credibility and not as evidence of guilt. In closing summations both counsel argued the substance of the impeaching statements. The jury then found petitioner guilty on the second count of the indictment. The New York Court of Appeals affirmed in a *per curiam* opinion. . . .

At trial the prosecution made no effort in its case in chief to use the statements allegedly made by petitioner, conceding that they were inadmissible under *Miranda v. Arizona*. . . . The transcript of the interrogation used in the impeachment, but not given to the jury, shows that no warning of right to appointed counsel was given before questions were put to petitioner when he was taken into custody. Petitioner makes no claim that the statements made to the police were coerced or involuntary.

Some comments in the *Miranda* opinion can indeed be read as indicating a bar to use of an uncounseled statement for any purpose, but discussion of that issue was not at all necessary to the Court's holding and cannot be regarded as controlling. *Miranda* barred the prosecution from making its case with statements of an accused made while in custody prior to having or effectively waiving counsel. It does not follow from *Miranda* that evidence inadmissible against an accused in the prosecution's case in chief is barred for all purposes, providing of course that the trustworthiness of the evidence satisfies legal standards.

. . . Every criminal defendant is privileged to testify in his own defense, or to refuse to do so. But that privilege cannot be construed to include the right to commit perjury. . . . Having voluntarily taken the stand, petitioner was under an obligation to speak truthfully and accurately, and the prosecution here did no more than utilize the traditional truth-testing devices of the adversary process. Had inconsistent statements been made by the accused to some third person, it could hardly be contended that the conflict could not be laid before the jury by way of cross-examination and impeachment.

The shield provided by *Miranda* cannot be perverted into a license to use perjury by way of a defense, free from the risk of confrontation with prior inconsistent utterances. We hold, therefore, that petitioner's credibility was appropriately impeached by use of his earlier conflicting statements.

Affirmed.

Mr. Justice BLACK dissents.

Mr. Justice BRENNAN, with whom Mr. Justice DOUGLAS and Mr. Justice MARSHALL join, dissenting.

It is conceded that the question-and-answer statement used to impeach petitioner's direct testimony was, under *Miranda v. Arizona*, . . . constitutionally inadmissible as part of the State's direct case against petitioner. I think that the Constitution also denied the State the use of the statement on cross-examination to impeach the credibility of petitioner's testimony given in his own defense. . . .

. . . The objective of deterring improper police conduct is only part of the larger objective of safeguarding the integrity of our adversary system. The "essential mainstay" of the system . . . is the privilege against self-incrimination, which for that reason has occupied a central place in our jurisprudence since before the Nation's birth. Moreover, "we may view the historical development of the privilege as one which groped for the proper scope of governmental power over the citizen. . . . All these policies point to one overriding thought: the constitutional foundation underlying the privilege is the respect a government . . . must accord to the dignity and integrity of its citizens." . . . These values are plainly jeopardized if an exception against admission of tainted statements is made for those used for impeachment purposes. Moreover, it is monstrous that courts should aid or abet the law-breaking police officer. It is abiding truth that "[n]othing can destroy a government more quickly than its failure to observe its own laws, or worse, its disregard of the charter of its own existence." . . . Thus, even to the extent that *Miranda* was aimed at deterring police practices in disregard of the Constitution, I fear that today's holding will seriously undermine the achievement of the objective. The Court today tells the police that they may freely interrogate an accused incommunicado and without counsel and know that although any statement they obtain in violation of *Miranda* cannot be used on the State's direct case, it may be introduced if the defendant has the temerity to testify in his own defense. This goes far toward undoing much of the progress made in conforming police methods to the Constitution. I dissent.

UNITED STATES v. NORTH

United States Court of Appeals, District of Columbia Circuit, 1990.
910 F.2d 843.

[Lt. Col. Oliver North was convicted of a number of offenses stemming from his role in the Iran-Contra Affair and his related testimony before a Congressional committee investigating the scandal. On appeal, North raised a number of issues, including the contention that the Independent Counsel who prosecuted the case had made improper comments to the jury during closing argument. Although North did not prevail on this particular issue, he did win reversal of his convictions on other grounds.]

Before WALD, Chief Judge, SILBERMAN and SENTELLE, Circuit Judges.
PER CURIAM.

. . . In particular, North complains about the IC's [Independent Counsel's] comparison of his conduct to Adolf Hitler's, and about the IC's statement that Richard Secord and Albert Hakim made a "killing" from arms sales to Iran and the Contras, despite the absence of any evidence in the record concerning the amount of their profits. Although both of the prosecutor's remarks were clearly improper, we find that neither was sufficiently prejudicial to North as to warrant the reversal of any or all of his convictions.

A. Legal Standard

A prosecutor may not make "statements calculated to arouse the passions or prejudices of the jury," *United States v. Monaghan*, 741 F.2d 1434, 1440 (D.C.Cir. 1984), *cert. denied*, 470 U.S. 1085, 105 S. Ct. 1847, 85 L.Ed.2d 146 (1985), or "statements of fact to the jury not supported by proper evidence introduced during trial," *United States v. Perholtz*, 842 F.2d 343, 360 (D.C. Cir.). When an objection is timely made, such remarks, while improper, are cause for reversal only if they "sufficiently prejudiced" the defendant. *United States v. Fowler*, 608 F.2d 2, 12 (D.C. Cir. 1979). We have generally looked to three factors in determining whether improper remarks by the prosecutor sufficiently prejudiced a defendant: "the closeness of the case, the centrality of the issue affected by the error, and the steps taken to mitigate the effects of the error." . . . We have also framed the test for prejudice in terms of the severity of the prosecutor's misconduct, the measures adopted to cure the misconduct, and the certainty of conviction absent the improper remarks. . . . "[I]n assessing the effect a prosecutor's remark would have had on a jury," however, we seek to avoid an overly mechanistic application of these criteria by according "due respect" to "the jurors' common sense and discrimination." . . .

B. Application

1. Reference to Hitler

The IC stated during closing argument that:

So far in this drama in August and September of 1985, North and McFarlane are following Adolf Hitler's old strategy. He was the one who said, the victor will never be asked if he told the truth. And the idea here was if the lies work, Congress will stop asking questions. . . .

Unquestionably inflammatory, the reference to Hitler reflected remarkably poor judgment by the IC. Nonetheless, in response to North's timely motion for a mistrial, the District Court pointed out that "defendant's . . . counsel took full advantage of the reference in his effective response before the jury." . . . Clearly, the District Judge is better situated than we are to assess the impact of both sides' hyperbole upon the jury. In light of defense counsel's forceful reply to the IC's ill-chosen remark, we have no reason to disagree with the District Court's perception that the IC's statement caused no substantial prejudice to North. To suspect that the reference to Hitler swayed the jury on a close and critical issue would underestimate the common sense that we properly attribute to the jury. We therefore decline to reverse any of North's convictions on this ground.

2. Reference to Secord's and Hakim's "Killing"

During the course of the trial, the IC elicited testimony from Willard Zucker that Zucker had distributed "profits" from certain bank accounts to Albert Hakim and Richard Secord. . . . The IC also sought to introduce evidence that would have established the amount of profits Secord and Hakim had made from arms sales to Iran. North objected, claiming that the amount of profits was immaterial to the charges against him. . . . In an ensuing bench conference, the IC explained that the evidence was crucial to establishing North's motive in accepting a security fence from Secord in return for official acts, as charged in Count 10. By showing that Secord had made large profits through the business channeled to him by North, the IC apparently hoped to persuade the jury that North accepted the fence as an illegal gratuity, rather than as a gift from a solicitous friend seeking to protect North's family. . . . As the IC told the trial judge, "[t]he amount [of profits] certainly gives a powerful motive on both sides". . . .

The District Judge initially suggested that "the way to deal with it is to simply say were those amounts substantial or something of that kind and go on." . . . North's counsel objected to that pro-posal, intimating that if the IC introduced any evidence about the amount of profits, North would be entitled to respond by explaining Secord's and Hakim's businesses in detail. The District Judge agreed and told the IC that "if you want to put some figure in terms of small or large profits, if you want to call it profits," then North would be permitted to explore "[a]ll the other businesses that [Secord and Hakim] do." . . . Faced with that prospect, the prosecutor said, "We don't want to do that." . . . He then added, "I think we'll leave it alone." . . . Nevertheless, the IC did raise the issue of the amount of Secord's and Hakim's profits in the closing argument. He stated:

> To understand the security fence charge I think you need to consider the testimony about North's relationship with Secord and Hakim. Secord and Hakim were making a killing, a killing. Millions in Contra arms sales, millions coming in from the Iranian arms sales. All from the business that Oliver North, the government official, the action officer of the NSC, the person who could say this is the White House calling, all from the business that he brought to them. . . . [North knew] that Secord and Hakim were taking a fair and reasonable profit but he didn't know what they considered a fair and reasonable profit. Would you send ten million or 20 million or 14 million or five million or even $5 to somebody who is going to take a fair and reasonable profit without talking to them about what a fair and reasonable profit was? Secord and Hakim were making a killing. . . .

Although North moved for a mistrial on the basis of that statement, the District Judge denied the motion on the grounds that "the use of the word 'killing' was mere characterization." . . .

In light of the prosecutor's agreement not to introduce evidence of the size of Secord's and Hakim's profits, his description of their profits as a "killing" or as "millions" was improper. Whether or not those references were slips of the tongue in the heat of oral argument, they amounted to "statements of fact . . . not supported by proper evidence introduced during trial." . . . We must therefore determine whether the remarks sufficiently prejudiced North to require reversal of his conviction on count 10—the only conviction count implicated by the prosecutor's misstatement. As we consider the various factors that this Court has identified as relevant to the prejudicial effect of prosecutorial misconduct, ... we focus on three criteria: the magnitude of the potential prejudice, the magnitude of the prosecutor's error, and the curative measures adopted by the trial judge.

a. Magnitude of Potential Prejudice. To convict North under Count 10, the jury had to find only that he accepted the security system "for or because of" an official act. ... The evidence that North channeled a substantial amount of arms business to Secord and Hakim is undisputed; North himself testified that he knew Secord sold the Contras approximately $11 million worth of weapons and made a sufficient profit on those transactions so as to receive "fair and just" and "reasonable" compensation. ... Even absent evidence as to the size of Secord's and Hakim's profits, the jury had ample grounds to infer that Secord gave North the security fence as a gratuity in exchange for referring to him millions of dollars of arms business. As this inference provided sufficient basis for conviction, the jury's decision to convict could not have turned critically on the prosecutor's improper description of the size of Secord's and Hakim's profits. In light of the record evidence of the substantial links between North and Secord and Hakim, the reference to the size of the profits could have had only limited corroborative effect on the jury's perception of North's motive in accepting the fence. The prosecutor's comments, therefore, were at worst minimally prejudicial.

b. Magnitude of Prosecutorial Misconduct. Like other courts of appeal, we have traditionally been chary of reversing convictions solely on the grounds of a misstatement in a closing argument. ... Without other compelling factors, a single misstatement confined to a closing argument rarely amounts to severe misconduct. The Supreme Court has approved this approach, holding that absent "consistent repeated misrepresentation" to influence a jury, "[i]solated passages of a prosecutor's argument, billed in advance to the jury as a matter of opinion not of evidence, do not reach the same proportions." ... By contrast, tainted closing arguments that follow on the heels of improper and indecorous prosecutorial conduct during trial are more likely to amount to the type of severe misconduct that justifies reversing a conviction. ...

c. Curative Measures. Our unwillingness to reverse a conviction has been particularly pronounced when the trial judge issues curative instructions. ... Indeed, a former member of this Court declared that "it is the law, pure and simple, that jury instructions can sufficiently protect a defendant's interest in being free from undue prejudice." ... Here, Judge Gesell expressly addressed the role that closing arguments should play in the jury's deliberations, and explicitly reminded the jurors that "the statements, opinion, and arguments of counsel are not evidence." ... He stressed repeatedly that the jurors' "recollection alone" is controlling as to "all aspects of the evidence." ... The District Judge could not have more directly communicated to the jury the limited evidentiary value of closing arguments.

C. Conclusion

North does not make out any of the components of substantial prejudice resulting from the prosecutor's closing argument. The District Court found that the reference to Hitler plainly was not prejudicial, and we have no reason to disagree. Furthermore, while a verdict of not guilty on Count 10 would not have been irrational, in light of North's own testimony about the scope of Secord's and Hakim's arms dealings, it appears virtually certain that the jury would have convicted North on this Count in the absence of the prosecutor's reference to the size of their profits. Finally, the prosecutor's misconduct was at most marginal, limited to a few lines in a closing statement; and the trial judge offered clear curative instructions.

This Court reverses a conviction on the grounds of a prosecutor's summation in only the rarest and most prejudicial circumstances. ... We have not reversed a conviction in over twenty years on the grounds of a prosecutor's reference during closing argument to facts outside the record. Reversing North's conviction for a single inappropriate remark of this nature in the prosecutor's closing argument is not only inconsistent with our past application of the substantial prejudice standard but would set a precedent requiring us to overturn virtually every conviction even marginally tainted by such a prosecutorial miscue. We therefore deny North's appeal for reversal on this ground. ...

SENTENCING AND PUNISHMENT

CHAPTER OUTLINE

Cases

INTRODUCTION

When a defendant has been convicted of a crime, it remains for the trial court to impose sentence. The sentence is an official pronouncement of criminal punishment. Judges are primarily responsible for sentencing, although some jurisdictions allow juries to recommend sentences, and a few even provide for jury sentencing in some cases. Where defendants are convicted of capital crimes and the government seeks the death penalty, juries typically play a more prominent role in determining whether defendants are sentenced to death.

The concept of criminal punishment is of ancient origin. Yet it remains the most intensely controversial aspect of the modern American system of criminal justice. Today the criminal law provides for a variety of criminal punishments including probation, community service, monetary fines, incarceration, and even death. While most people agree on the propriety of punishing criminal behavior, they disagree about the legality, morality, and efficacy of specific modes of criminal punishment. The death penalty in particular remains a hotly debated issue.

There are procedural as well as substantive issues in the area of sentencing and punishment. Sharp disagreements exist regarding the roles that legislatures, judges, and corrections officials should play in determining punishments. Generally, judges are required to impose sentences that fall within parameters of appropriate punishment specified by statute; yet within these parameters, courts exercise substantial discretion. Recent concern over sentencing disparities has resulted in a variety of measures aimed at reducing the range of judicial discretion in sentencing.

Just as judges' sentencing decisions are constrained by statutes, statutory penalties must comport with substantive and procedural requirements imposed by the federal and state constitutions. Specifically, criminal punishment is limited by the Eighth Amendment prohibition of "cruel and unusual punishments," the due process clauses of the Fifth and Fourteenth amendments, and by similar provisions in all fifty state constitutions. Recent judicial activity in the areas of sentencing and punishment has focused on the need for procedural regularity in sentencing and proportionality in punishment.

LEGAL JUSTIFICATIONS FOR CRIMINAL PUNISHMENT

Most people agree that criminals should be punished, but there are a number of different theories explaining how and why such punishment should be imposed. The variety of criminal punishments extant in the United States reflects an underlying diversity in the philosophical justifications for criminal punishment.

Retribution

Retribution is the oldest and most tenacious justification for criminal punishment. The classic statement of the doctrine of retribution is found in Leviticus 24:17–20:

When one man strikes another and kills him, he shall be put to death. Whoever strikes a beast and kills it shall make restitution, life for life. When one man injures and disfigures his fellow-countryman, it shall be done to him as he has done, eye for eye, tooth for tooth; the injury and disfigurement that he has inflicted upon another shall in turn be inflicted upon him.

Many regard the notion of retribution to be little more than legalized vengeance. Yet it must be remembered that the concept of retribution mandated by the Old Testament was a great leap forward in the evolution of criminal punishment. It replaced the personal or familial (and often excessive) acts of vengeance that frequently followed injuries to persons or property. Moreover, it carried with it a sense of proportionality, which continues to have relevance in criminal sentencing today. If gouging an eye for an eye seems barbaric, it is much less so than slaughtering an entire family because one of its members committed an act of robbery. It has been observed that:

> The instinct for retribution is part of the nature of man, and channeling that instinct in the administration of criminal justice serves an important purpose in promoting the stability of a society governed by law. When people begin to believe that organized society is unwilling or unable to impose upon criminal offenders the punishment they "deserve," then are sown the seeds of anarchy—of self-help, vigilante justice and lynch law. *Furman v. Georgia*, 408 U.S. 238, 308, 92 S. Ct. 2726, 2761, 33 L.Ed.2d 346, 389 (1972) (Stewart, J., concurring).

Retribution, with its emphasis on proportionality, remains widely accepted in society. Thus, while society no longer prescribes mutilation for those who commit mayhem, it clings to the idea that people who commit crimes deserve to be punished in equal measure to their wrongs. Generally, society attempts to measure appropriate punishment in terms of time in prison or monetary fines. Yet most people still subscribe to the classical view that a just punishment is one that fits the crime.

General Deterrence

Jeremy Bentham and the other Utilitarian reformers of the late eighteenth and early nineteenth centuries were highly critical of the concept of retribution. For the Utilitarians, the only rational basis for punishing criminals was to deter others from committing crimes. The goal of general deterrence might require some deviation from the classical concept of retribution, depending on what was required to impress upon society at large the consequences of criminal behavior.

Today it is generally assumed that deterrence plays a role in the scheme of criminal punishment, and that criminal sanctions do in fact deter most people from violating the law. These assumptions are seldom subjected to critical scrutiny, so we really do not know the extent of the deterrent effect of the criminal law. Nor do we know the extent of punishment necessary to deter criminal conduct. Clearly, if everyone convicted for speeding were executed or even forbidden from driving, the rate of this "crime" would drop precipitously. Yet such penalties are unthinkable for many reasons, not the least of which is that they would violate the collective sense of justice. The question then becomes one of adjusting penalties up and down around some norm of proportionality. Whether such "fine tuning" of criminal penalties has any deterrent value is questionable. A strong argument can be made that the swiftness and certainty of punishment, even if the punishment is minimal, is of greater deterrent value than the *degree* of punishments imposed by the law. Whereas in colonial America, the emphasis of the criminal law was on swift and certain punishments, today it is on due process. In a society committed to procedural fairness, it is virtually impossible to achieve swift and certain punishment.

Rehabilitation

In the nineteenth and twentieth centuries, the academic community focused considerable attention on the phenomenon of crime, developing numerous theories of crime causation and control. Many of these theories stressed psychological and sociological causes. Reformers argued that to the extent that such factors could be understood and manipulated, society could rehabilitate criminals. Numerous forms of psychological, sociopsychological, and behavioral therapies have been utilized in efforts at rehabilitation. The results to date have generally been disappointing. It may be that the theoretical underpinnings of rehabilitation are weak. Alternatively, it may be unrealistic to expect any effort at rehabilitation to be effective in the setting of the prison, where most rehabilitation programs have been located. Finally, the efficacy of certain rehabilitation programs may have been diminished by insufficient funding. Whatever the cause of its failures, the general public has become disillusioned with the concept of rehabilitation, particularly in respect to serious offenders. Nevertheless, among professionals in the field, it remains one of the frequently cited goals of the corrections system. Rehabilitation remains the primary theory underlying the juvenile justice system.

Incapacitation

Perhaps the most pragmatic justification for criminal punishment is the incapacitation of the offender. Incapacitation refers to punishments that prevent offenders from committing further criminal acts. In ancient societies, banishment was used to protect the community from those whose presence was regarded as unduly threatening. Contemporary American society resorts to imprisonment or, in rare cases, execution to rid itself of seriously threatening behavior. While nearly everyone favors incapacitation of violent offenders, in practice incapacitation extends beyond the execution or incarceration of violent criminals. For instance, when someone convicted of driving while intoxicated has his or her driver's license revoked, the purpose is primarily incapacitation. Similarly, some states have laws offering convicted rapists the option of taking a drug to render them incapable of committing rape. Other forms of incapacitation can be extremely controversial. For example, may a judge order a convicted child abuser to refrain from having any more children in order to prevent future child abuse?

Those who favor incapacitation to the exclusion of the other purposes of punishment are likely to favor harsh sentences, even for relatively minor crimes. They prefer to "lock 'em up and throw away the key." Again, we must consider the issue of proportionality: Crime control is not the only goal of the criminal justice system—dispensing justice is equally important.

ALTERNATIVE FORMS OF CRIMINAL PUNISHMENT

In the early nineteenth century, corporal punishment was still in wide use in America for a variety of crimes, including many misdemeanors. Flogging was the most common method of corporal punishment. The convicted criminal was taken into the public square, bound to the whipping post, and administered as many lashes as were prescribed by law for the offense. In 1963, the Delaware Supreme Court considered a challenge to a state statute that allowed judges to order whipping as punishment for certain crimes. The court refused to invalidate the law as a form of "cruel and unusual punishment." It concluded that, since whipping had been used since 1719 while other forms of punishment (for example, burning at the stake) had been abolished, the people of Delaware did not consider whipping to be cruel and unusual punishment. *State v. Cannon*, 190 A.2d 514 (Del. 1963). Nonetheless, the state legislature abolished public whipping in 1973.

In 1968 a federal court declared whipping of prisoners unconstitutional under the Eighth Amendment's cruel and unusual punishments clause. In striking down Arkansas' long-standing practice of flogging prison inmates for disciplinary purposes, the court said that

> the strap's use, irrespective of any precautionary conditions which may be imposed, offends contemporary concepts of decency and human dignity and precepts of civilization which we profess to possess; . . . it also violates those standards of good conscience and fundamental fairness enunciated by this court. . . . *Jackson v. Bishop*, 404 F.2d 571, 579 (8th Cir. 1968).

As a criminal penalty, corporal punishment is apparently a thing of the past, although there are those who would like to see it resurrected. Today, the spectrum of criminal punishment includes incarceration, probation, community control, monetary fines, community service, restitution, or some combination of these. The death penalty remains available in most jurisdictions to punish the most heinous homicides.

The Death Penalty

The death penalty remains the single most controversial issue in the realm of criminal punishment. Although the death penalty has deep roots in religious and legal traditions, in the twentieth century we have witnessed widespread abolition of capital punishment. At present, the United States is the only Western democracy that retains the death penalty. Federal law allows the death penalty as punishment for air piracy that results in loss of life. 49 U.S.C.A. § 1472(i)(1)(B). Thirty-seven states currently authorize capital punishment for first-degree murder or other types of aggravated homicide.

At common law the death penalty was prescribed for most felonies. The Massachusetts Code of 1648 mandated capital punishment in cases of idolatry, witchcraft, blasphemy, sodomy, adultery, and "man stealing," in addition to the common-law capital crimes. A reform movement in the nineteenth century succeeded in limiting public executions and reducing the range of capital offenses. The movement to eliminate the death penalty achieved its first victory in 1847 when Michigan abolished capital punishment. This movement grew steadily throughout the twentieth century. By the 1960s, it appeared that the death penalty was on the way out. Public opinion no longer favored it; many states abolished it. In those that did not, the courts began to impose restrictions on its use. In 1967, two persons were executed in the United States. Ten years passed before another person was put to death in America. When the Supreme Court declared Georgia's death penalty law unconstitutional in *Furman v. Georgia,* 408 U.S. 238, 92 S. Ct. 2726, 33 L.Ed.2d 346 (1972), many observers thought it signaled the demise of the death penalty.

The Supreme Court's 1972 decision striking the Georgia death penalty concentrated on the virtually unlimited discretion the state placed in trial juries empowered to impose death sentences. According to Justice Stewart's concurring opinion in *Furman,* Georgia's administration of the death penalty was unpredictable to the point of being "freakishly imposed." 408 U.S. 238, 310, 92 S. Ct. 2726, 2763, 33 L.Ed.2d 346, 390 (1972). In the wake of the *Furman* decision, Georgia and most other states revised their death penalty laws to address the concerns raised by the Court.

Under the revised Georgia statute, there is a "bifurcated trial" in cases where the state seeks the death penalty. In the first stage, guilt is determined according to the usual procedures, rules of evidence, and standard of proof. If the jury finds the defendant guilty, the same jury considers the appropriateness of the death sentence in a separate proceeding where additional evidence is received in aggravation or mitigation of the punishment. In order to impose the death penalty, the jury must find at least one "aggravating circumstance" specified in the statute. See, generally, Official Ga. Code Ann. § 17–10–30. The purpose of requiring aggravating factors before imposing the death penalty is to narrow the cases and persons eligible for capital punishment and make the imposition of the death penalty more predictable.

In *Gregg v. Georgia,* 428 U.S. 153, 96 S. Ct. 2909, 49 L.Ed.2d 859 (1976), the Supreme Court upheld Georgia's revised death penalty statute by a vote of seven to two. Apparently the Court was satisfied that this scheme had sufficiently addressed the evils identified in *Furman.* More than thirty-five states now have death penalty statutes modeled along the lines of the law upheld in *Gregg.*

Shortly after the death penalty was effectively reinstated by the Supreme Court's *Gregg* decision, executions in the United States began anew. On January 17, 1977, the state of Utah executed convicted murderer Gary Gilmore by firing squad. Between the date of the Gilmore execution and May 1, 1993, 200 prisoners were executed in the United States. As of May 1993 there were 2,676 individuals under sentence of death in thirty-five jurisdictions.

Whether the Court achieved the even-handedness in the administration of capital punishment it sought through its decisions in *Furman* and *Gregg* is questionable. Evidence indicates that the death penalty remains racially discriminatory, as regards both the race of the offender and the race of the murder victim. Criminologist David Baldus collected data on more than one thousand murder cases in Georgia during the 1970s and found significant disparities in the imposition of the death penalty, based primarily on the race of the murder victims and, to a lesser extent, on the race of the defendants. The data reveal that blacks who killed whites were more than seven times more likely to receive the death sentence than were whites who killed blacks.

In April 1987, the Supreme Court reviewed the death sentence of a black man convicted of killing a white police officer in Georgia. The Court refused to accept statistical evidence derived from the Baldus study as a basis for reversing the death sentence in this case. In the Court's view, even if there is statistical evidence of race discrimination, a defendant sentenced to death cannot prevail on appeal unless the defendant can show that he or she received the death sentence due to race discrimination. *McCleskey v. Kemp*, 481 U.S. 279, 107 S. Ct. 1756, 95 L.Ed.2d 262 (1987). Obviously, this would be difficult, although perhaps not impossible, for a defendant to demonstrate.

Supporters of the death penalty place great stress on retribution. Many would argue, perhaps ironically, that the value of human life is underscored by imposing the severest of sanctions on those who commit murder. Certainly the death penalty is proportionate to the crime of murder. Indeed, the Supreme Court has made it clear that murder is the only crime for which the death penalty is permissible. *Coker v. Georgia*, 433 U.S. 584, 97 S. Ct. 2861, 53 L.Ed.2d 982 (1977). Advocates of capital punishment also stress the incapacitation of the offender, and it is difficult to argue that death is not a complete incapacitator. But are retribution and incapacitation sufficient justifications for the death penalty?

One of the most intense battles among academicians in the field of criminal justice has been waged over the alleged deterrent value of the death penalty. At this point, the evidence appears to be mixed, making firm conclusions impossible. Obviously, the death penalty has no value as a means of rehabilitation, unless it helps to rehabilitate other convicted murderers who have not been sentenced to death. Therefore, if the death penalty is to be justified, it must be primarily on grounds of retribution and incapacitation.

When Can a Juvenile Be Executed?

One very difficult issue that the Supreme Court faced during the 1980s was whether, and under what circumstances, a juvenile may be executed when convicted of a capital crime. The Court responded in three decisions. In *Eddings v. Oklahoma*, 455 U.S. 104, 102 S.Ct. 869, 71 L.Ed.2d 1 (1982), the Court voted 5–4 to vacate a death sentence of a sixteen-year-old boy. In *Thompson v. Oklahoma*, 487 U.S. 815, 108 S.Ct. 2687, 101 L.Ed. 2d 702 (1988), in a 6–3 decision the Court ruled that the Constitution forbids executing a juvenile who was fifteen years of age or younger at the time of commission of a capital crime. The following year, in *Stanford v. Kentucky*, 492 U.S. 361, 109 S.Ct. 2969, 106 L.Ed.2d 306 (1989), in another 5–4 decision the Court held that a juvenile sixteen or older at the time of the crime may be sentenced to death. Concurring in *Stanford*, Justice O'Connor commented that "it is sufficiently clear that no national consensus forbids the imposition of capital punishment on 16- or 17-year-old capital murderers." 492

U.S. at 381, 109 S.Ct. at 2981, 106 L.Ed.2d at 325. In both *Thompson* and *Stanford*, the Court referred to "evolving standards of decency" as the proper test for judging the constitutionality of whether a juvenile may be executed. Given this standard and with the sharp disagreement on the Supreme Court, the present judicial consensus may change with changing membership on the United States Supreme Court. (For further discussion, see Chapter 20.)

Fines

By far the most common form of criminal punishment today is the monetary fine. Most misdemeanors carry monetary fines, especially for first offenses. Indeed, some courts of limited jurisdiction continue to be funded primarily by the collection of fines from convicted misdemeanants.

A number of felonies, especially serious economic crimes defined by federal law, carry heavy monetary fines as penalties. Offenses against federal banking laws and securities and exchange laws, for example, are punishable by fines reaching into the millions of dollars. Increasingly, drug trafficking offenders are being punished by the imposition of large fines.

In many states a court may sentence a defendant to pay a fine in addition to a sentence of imprisonment or probation (see Table 18.1). In New Jersey, for example, such fines may range from $500 to $100,000, depending on the nature and degree of the offense. N.J. Stat. Ann. 2C:43–3.

Fines may be appropriate devices of retribution and deterrence for economic crimes, but they hardly seem suitable as punishments for criminal acts of violence. And many have questioned the fairness of established minimum and maximum fines that do not take into account the economic circumstances of individual defendants.

Incarceration

Confinement is generally regarded as the only way to deal with the serious problem of violent crime. By November 1993, there were more than 900,000 inmates in federal and state penal institutions. Yet prisons are a fairly recent invention, dating only from the late eighteenth century. Before that, punishments tended to be capital or corporal. Thus, the modern prison was seen as a great stride in the civilizing of criminal punishment. Its Quaker inventors viewed prison as a place where criminals would be isolated, to reflect on their crimes and eventually repent; hence, the term *penitentiary*. Today, many question the efficacy of the prison, regarding it as little more than a factory for producing future criminals. The overcrowding in many prisons has led in some cases to judicial intervention; yet society appears reluctant to provide additional resources to expand prison capacity. Undoubtedly imprisonment is expensive, currently costing taxpayers about $16 billion per year.

As criminologists have become increasingly dissatisfied with the effects of the prison system, judges have responded by imposing limits on prison populations and scrutinizing the conditions of confinement. Meanwhile, fiscal pressures

---

CASE IN POINT

DOES THE EIGHTH AMENDMENT PROHIBIT THE EXECUTION OF A PRISONER WHO HAS BECOME INSANE?

In 1974 Alvin Ford was convicted of murder and sentenced to death by a Florida court. There was no indication that he was mentally incompetent at the time of the trial. However, while in prison awaiting execution, Ford began to exhibit profound changes in behavior and experience bizarre delusions. In 1983, a prison psychiatrist diagnosed Ford as suffering from a severe and uncontrollable mental disease closely resembling paranoid schizophrenia. Ford's attorney then invoked procedures under Florida law governing the determination of competency of a condemned prisoner. A panel of psychiatrists examined Ford and, although they differed in their specific diagnoses, all agreed that Ford was not insane under Florida law.

On April 30, 1984, Governor Bob Graham signed Alvin Ford's death warrant. Ford's attorney then filed a petition for *habeas corpus* in the United States District Court, seeking an evidentiary hearing on his client's sanity. The district court denied relief, and the court of appeals affirmed. The United States Supreme Court agreed to review the case to resolve the issue of whether the Eighth Amendment prohibits the execution of a person who is insane. On June 26, 1986, the Supreme Court announced its decision in *Ford v. Wainwright*, 477 U.S. 399, 106 S. Ct. 2595, 91 L.Ed.2d 335 (1986). The Court held that the Eighth Amendment bars the execution of a person who is insane. Writing for a plurality of justices, Justice Thurgood Marshall declared that "It is no less abhorrent today than it has been for centuries to exact in penance the life of one whose mental illness prevents him from comprehending the reasons for the penalty or its implications." 477 U.S. at 417, 106 S. Ct. at 2606, 91 L.Ed.2d at 351.

---

prevent legislatures from appropriating the funds necessary to construct more prisons. Accordingly, attention has shifted to alternatives to incarceration. One of the most serious criticisms of all such alternatives emphasizes the difficulty of determining who should be eligible for an alternative form of punishment. In an age of overcrowded prisons, alternative punishments carry the real possibility that truly dangerous offenders will not be sufficiently controlled.

The Boot Camp: An Alternative to Prison?

In recent years, one alternative to the traditional prison setting has been the boot camp, a program designed to employ a system of discipline much like the military uses to instill discipline in its recruits. In early 1993, the American Correctional Association counted 65 adult boot camps in 27 states and 19 juvenile camps in eight states. The inmates are generally young, nonviolent offenders who have committed theft, burglary, forgery, and other nonviolent offenses, often brought about by their drug abuse. In lieu of a prison sentence, they elect

TABLE 18.1   A Sample of Crimes and Punishments under Texas Law

Classification *FELONIES*	Punishment	Examples of Offenses
Capital	Death or life imprisonment	Capital murder
First degree	Life imprisonment or 5–99 years and max. fine $10,000	Felony murder Aggravated sexual assault Armed robbery Arson (injury or death)
Second degree	Two–twenty years and max. fine $10,000	Voluntary manslaughter Aggravated kidnapping Aggravated assault Theft ($20,000 or more) Robbery
Third degree	Two–ten years and max. fine $10,000	Involuntary manslaughter Kidnapping Theft (under $20,000) Tampering with a witness Aggravated perjury
MISDEMEANORS		
Class A	Max. jail term one year and/or max. fine $2,000	Theft (under $750) Resisting arrest Perjury Cruelty to animals
Class B	Max. jail term 180 days and/or max. fine $1,000	Theft (under $200) Prostitution Evading arrest False report to police
Class C	No jail term and/or max. fine $200	Theft (under $20) Public intoxication Gambling Reckless destruction of property

Source: Vernon's Texas Penal Code Annotated §§ 12.01–12.34.

to undergo three to six months of training that often includes drug rehabilitation and repairing roads and other public facilities. Ideally, their stint in boot camp is followed by a period of supervised probation. In addition to being less costly than traditional methods of incarceration, communities gain from the labor performed by the inmates, and their early release conserves financial resources essential to operate regular prisons.

Probation

Of the various alternatives to incarceration, probation is by far the most common. Probation is the conditional release of a convicted offender by a trial court. If

---

CASE IN POINT

CONDITIONS OF PROBATION

In 1990, the Supreme Court of Ohio reviewed the conviction of a defendant on a charge of contributing to the delinquency of a child by furnishing alcohol to three young boys. The court focused on a single point: whether the trial court abused its discretion in imposing a condition of probation stipulating that the defendant "have no association or communication, direct or indirect, with anyone under the age of 18 years not a member of his immediate family." The court noted that while a trial judge is granted broad discretion in setting conditions of probation, that discretion is not limitless, and courts must guard against overly broad conditions that impinge upon the probationer's liberty. Nevertheless, the court found the restriction imposed against the defendant "reasonably related to rehabilitating [the defendant] without being unduly restrictive." Citing various state and federal authorities, the court said that in setting conditions of probation, trial judges should consider whether a condition to be imposed (1) is reasonably related to rehabilitating the offender, (2) has some relationship to the crime for which the offender was convicted, and (3) relates to conduct that is criminal or reasonably related to future criminality.

State v. Jones, 550 N.E.2d 469 (Ohio 1990).

---

prisons are little more than factories for producing future criminals, then probation seems to be a reasonable response to many first offenses punishable by prison terms. The offender is released under the supervision of a probation officer who is responsible for making sure that the offender abides by the conditions of probation.

Probation is usually granted on the conditions that the probationer will not commit further crimes, will avoid certain persons and/or places, will maintain gainful employment and support any dependents, will not travel without permission of the court or probation officer, etc. Typically, courts have broad discretion in imposing conditions of probation. Thus, constitutional rights may be limited by conditions that are related to the goal of rehabilitation. Even the highly protected First Amendment rights of free speech and association may be severely restricted by probation conditions. *Malone v. United States,* 502 F.2d 554 (9th Cir. 1974), *cert. denied,* 419 U.S. 1124, 95 S. Ct. 809, 42 L.Ed.2d 824 (1975); *Porth v. Templar,* 453 F.2d 330 (10th Cir. 1971).

Nevertheless, there are limits to probation conditions. For example, a Florida appellate court held that a condition prohibiting custody of children had a clear relationship to the crime of child abuse and was valid, but that conditions prohibiting marriage and pregnancy added nothing to decrease the possibility of further child abuse and were accordingly invalid. *Rodriguez v. State,* 378 So.2d 7 (Fla. App. 1979). Three years later, the same court struck down a condition of probation that required that the defendant "must not father any children during [the] probation period." *Burchell v. State,* 419 So.2d 358 (Fla. App. 1982).

Community Service

Of the several alternatives to incarceration, community service seems to be growing in popularity. Community service refers to sentences whereby offenders are required to perform a specified number of hours of service to the community, doing specified tasks. Often, community service is required as one of several conditions of probation.

Community service has the virtues of keeping the offender out of the undesirable prison environment and exacting a penalty that is useful to the community. Ideally, it seems like an excellent way to instill a sense of responsibility to the community for having committed criminal actions, but community service also has its drawbacks. It is difficult for the community to reap any real benefit without providing a degree of training and supervision of the offender. Training and supervision can be costly and may, in many instances, exceed the value of the community service to be performed.

Community Control

Another alternative to incarceration is community control, a neologism for an ancient practice known as house arrest. Under this alternative, an offender is allowed to leave home only for employment and approved community service activities. Community control is generally employed when incarceration is not warranted, but probation is not considered sufficiently restrictive. Community control requires intensive surveillance and supervision and may not be practical in many cases. For example, consider the case of a convicted rapist whose occupation is plumbing. To allow this offender to carry on his trade may pose a significant risk to householders. Comparable risks often militate against placing offenders under community control.

Creative Alternatives to Confinement

Judges seeking alternatives to jail or prison have been increasingly creative of late. In some cities billboards have been erected bearing the names of persons convicted for driving while under the influence of intoxicating substances. One county judge in Sarasota, Florida, made national news in 1986 by requiring that DWI offenders—as a condition of probation—place bumper stickers on their cars to alert the driving public to their convictions! On appeal, the practice was upheld against an Eighth Amendment attack. The court said, "The mere requirement that a defendant display a 'scarlet letter' as part of his punishment is not necessarily offensive to the Constitution." *Goldschmitt v. State*, 490 So.2d 123, 125 (Fla. App. 1986), *review denied*, 496 So.2d 142 (Fla. 1986).

In October 1987, a convicted child molester was sentenced by an Oregon court to five years' probation on the condition that he display on his front door and automobile a warning sign: "Dangerous Sex Offender: No Children Allowed." While the unusual sentence drew praise from prosecutors and many citizens' groups, civil libertarians objected, likening the sign to branding or the "scarlet letter" of seventeenth-century Massachusetts.

THE SENTENCING STAGE OF THE CRIMINAL PROCESS

Every jurisdiction requires that criminal sentences for adults be imposed in open court, although in many instances juvenile offenders may be sentenced *in camera.* In misdemeanor cases, sentencing usually occurs immediately upon conviction. In felony cases, where penalties are greater, sentencing may be postponed to allow the court to conduct a presentence investigation.

Rule 32(c)(1) of the Federal Rules of Criminal Procedure requires that a presentence investigation be conducted and a report made to the court "unless the court finds that there is in the record information sufficient to enable the meaningful exercise of sentencing authority . . . and the court explains this finding on the record." Rule 32(c)(3) now requires that the report be disclosed to the defendant, counsel for the defendant, and attorney for the government at least ten days before the sentencing hearing. It authorizes the court to exempt from disclosure: (1) diagnostic opinions that, if disclosed, might seriously disrupt a program of rehabilitation; (2) sources of information obtained upon a promise of confidentiality; and (3) any other information that, if disclosed, might result in harm, physical or otherwise, to the defendant or other persons.

In some states the court is required to order a presentence report where the offender to be sentenced is a first offender, or under a certain age. In other state jurisdictions the sentencing judge is accorded discretion in this area. For example, Rule 1403 of the Pennsylvania Rules of Criminal Procedure provides:

A. Presentence Investigation Report.

1. The sentencing judge may, in his discretion, order a presentence investigation report in any case.
2. The sentencing judge shall place on the record his reasons for dispensing with the presentence investigation report if the court fails to order a presentence report in any of the following instances;
   (a) where incarceration for one year or more is a possible disposition under the applicable sentencing statutes; or
   (b) where the defendant is less than twenty-one years old at the time of conviction or entry of a plea of guilty; or
   (c) where a defendant is a first offender in that he has not heretofore been sentenced as an adult.

Rule 1404 makes the reports confidential and available only to the sentencing judge or counsel for the state and the defense.

In some states, statutes, court rules, or judicial interpretations mandate that courts release a presentence report to the defendant or defendant's counsel, usually allowing some exemptions for sensitive material. In other states, courts have ruled that this is a matter within the discretion of the sentencing judge. In some instances courts will reveal factual material such as police reports, but decline to disclose statements made in confidence to investigators. Often the judicial interpretation depends on the language of the statute or court rule. Of course, as illustrated by the Case In Point on page 603, the Supreme Court requires release of presentence reports to defendants who may be sentenced to death.

The presentence report sets forth the defendant's history of delinquency or criminality, medical history, family background, economic status, education, employment history, etc. Much of this information is obtained by probation officers who interview defendants' families, friends, employers, and so on. Additionally, most jurisdictions allow courts to order physical and/or mental examinations of defendants. This information can be very useful to a judge who must determine a sentence that is at once fair, humane, and meaningful.

The Sentencing Hearing

After the presentence report is completed, a sentencing hearing is held. At this hearing, the court considers the evidence received at trial, the presentence report, any evidence offered by either party in aggravation or mitigation of sentence, and any statement the defendant wishes to make. Additionally, most jurisdictions require judges to hear arguments concerning various sentencing alternatives. Sentencing is a critical stage of the criminal process, and counsel must be supplied to indigent defendants. *Mempa v. Rhay*, 389 U.S. 128, 88 S. Ct. 254, 19 L.Ed.2d 336 (1967).

Types of Sentences

After affording the defendant the opportunity to be heard and hearing arguments of counsel, the trial judge pronounces sentence. As noted, trial judges have considerable discretion in imposing sentences, yet the mode and parameters of sentences are established by Congress and state legislatures.

Concurrent and Consecutive Sentences.   A defendant who is convicted of multiple crimes must be given separate sentences for each offense. These sentences may run consecutively or concurrently, usually at the discretion of the sentencing judge. See, for example, Pa. R. Crim. P. 1406.

Suspended Sentences.   In most instances where defendants are convicted of noncapital crimes, courts are authorized to suspend imposition of sentence and place defendants on probation or under community control. See, for example, Vernon's Ann. Tex. Code Crim. P. art. 42.12.

Indeterminate Sentencing.   For much of the twentieth century, legislatures commonly allowed judges to sentence criminals to imprisonment for indeterminate periods. This was designed to assist corrections officials in the process of rehabilitating offenders. Officials were permitted to hold the criminal in custody until they determined that he or she was rehabilitated. Abuses of the system, combined with the decline of popular support for rehabilitation, have led most jurisdictions to abandon the concept of indeterminate sentencing.

Notwithstanding the trend away from indeterminate sentencing, a number of state laws retain indeterminate sentencing for youthful offenders. For example, New Jersey law specifies that:

Any person who, at time of sentencing, is less than 26 years of age and who has been convicted of a crime may be sentenced to an indeterminate term at the Youth

Correctional Institution Complex, . . . in the case of men, and to the Correctional Institute for Women, . . . in the case of women, instead of the sentences otherwise authorized by the code. N.J. Stat. Ann. 2C:43–5.

Definite and Determinate Sentencing.   At the opposite extreme from indeterminate sentencing is definite or flat sentencing. The concept here is to eliminate discretion and ensure that offenders who commit the same crimes are punished equally. The definite sentence is set by the legislature with no leeway for judges or corrections officials to individualize punishment. In variation of the definite sentence, sometimes called determinate sentencing, the judge sets a fixed term of years within statutory parameters and the offender is required to serve that term without the possibility of early release.

Indefinite Sentencing.   Under a scheme of indefinite sentencing, there is judicial discretion to impose sentences within a range of prescribed minimum and maximum penalties for specific offenses. What distinguishes indefinite from determinate sentencing is that the law allows early release from prison on parole. An example of a statute that permits indefinite sentencing can be drawn from the New Jersey Code:

> Except as otherwise provided, a person who has been convicted of a crime may be sentenced to imprisonment, as follows: (1) In the case of a crime of the first degree, for a specific term of years which shall be fixed by the court and shall be between 10 years and 20 years; (2) In the case of a crime of the second degree, for a specific term of years which shall be fixed by the court and shall be between 5 years and 10 years; (3) In the case of a crime of the third degree, for a specific term of years which shall be fixed by the court and shall be between 3 years and 5 years; (4) In the case of a crime of the fourth degree, for a specific term which shall be fixed by the court and shall not exceed 18 months. N.J. Stat. Ann. 2C:43–6(a).

Under the New Jersey sentencing scheme, a judge retains discretion to impose probation, a fine, or some other alternative to incarceration. N.J. Stat. Ann.

C A S E   I N   P O I N T

PRESENCE REPORTS

Daniel Gardner was found guilty of first-degree murder and the jury recommended a sentence of life imprisonment. The jury's recommendation was based on its finding that mitigating factors outweighed the aggravating circumstances of the crime. The trial judge, however, sentenced Gardner to death, relying on a confidential portion of a presentence report that had not been made available to the defense. The United States Supreme Court vacated the sentence and directed the trial court to conduct another sentencing proceeding in which the defendant would have an opportunity to deny or explain the contents of the presentence report.

Gardner v. Florida, 430 U.S. 349, 97 S. Ct. 1197, 51 L.Ed.2d 393 (1977).

2C:43–2. If the judge opts for imprisonment, the judge's discretion is channeled as indicated earlier. The New Jersey scheme qualifies as indefinite sentencing because in most cases the law allows offenders to be released on parole before the completion of their prison terms.

Mandatory Sentencing.   Mandatory sentences result from legislative mandates that offenders who commit certain crimes must be sentenced to prison terms for minimum periods. Under mandatory sentencing, there is no option for judges to place offenders on probation. Most often, mandatory sentences are required for violent crimes, especially those involving the use of firearms. For example, Iowa law mandates that persons who use firearms in the commission of "forcible felonies" must be sentenced to five-year minimum prison terms, with no possibility of parole. Iowa Code Ann. § 902.7.

Enhanced Sentences for Defendants who Choose Victims on the Basis of Protected Status.   In Chapter 11 we pointed out that the U.S. Supreme Court's 1992 decision in *R.A.V. v. City of St. Paul*, 505 U.S. ___ , 112 S.Ct. 2538, 120 L.Ed.2d 305, declared unconstitutional a St. Paul ordinance prohibiting "hate speech." Thereafter, in June 1993, the Court upheld a Wisconsin statute that provided extra punishment for defendants who choose their victims on basis of race, religion, or other protected status. The Wisconsin Law is similar to sentencing enhancement statutes in about half of the states. In a unanimous opinion, the Court said that such statutes do not violate the First Amendment. The Court distinguished the Wisconsin statute from the ordinance struck down in *R.A.V.* by saying the Minnesota ordinance "was explicitly directed at expression," while the Wisconsin statute is aimed at "conduct unprotected by the First Amendment." *Wisconsin v. Mitchell*, 508 U.S. ___ , 113 S.Ct. ___ , 124 L.Ed.2d 436.

Habitual Offender Statutes.   In an effort to incapacitate habitual criminal offenders, the laws of many states require automatic increased penalties for persons convicted of repeated felonies. For example, Iowa law states that

> An habitual offender is any person convicted of a class "C" or a class "D" felony, who has twice before been convicted of a felony in a court of this or any other state, or of the United States. An offense is a felony if, by the law under which the person was convicted, it is so classified at the time of his or her conviction. A person sentenced as an habitual offender shall not be eligible for parole until he or she has served the minimum sentence of confinement of three years. Iowa Code Ann. § 902.8.

Most courts hold that habitual offender status is not established if a defendant committed the present offense before having been convicted of a prior offense. Courts have struggled with the issue of whether multiple convictions entered on one day are to be treated as separate or as one conviction, but usually treat these multiple convictions as one irrespective of whether they arise from one or multiple criminal transactions.

In *Rummel v. Estelle*, 445 U.S. 263, 100 S. Ct. 1133, 63 L.Ed.2d 382 (1980), the United States Supreme Court upheld a life sentence imposed under the Texas habitual offender statute mandating life terms for persons convicted of three felonies. Rummel was convicted of obtaining $120.75 under false pretenses after previously being convicted of the fraudulent use of a credit card to obtain $80 worth of goods and passing a forged check for $28.36. Upon his third felony conviction, Rummel was sentenced to life imprisonment.

In *Solem v. Helm,* 463 U.S. 277, 103 S. Ct. 3001, 77 L.Ed.2d 637 (1983), the Court vacated a life sentence without parole under a South Dakota habitual offender statute. Because the defendant's convictions involved nonviolent felonies, the Court found the life sentence to be "significantly disproportionate" and thus invalid under the Eighth Amendment.

Sentencing Guidelines

In the face of considerable criticism of the exercise of judicial discretion, which often resulted in great disparities in sentences, Congress and a number of state legislatures adopted "sentencing guidelines." Some states have adopted voluntary guidelines; others have mandated that sentencing conform to guidelines absent a compelling reason for departing from them.

The federal guidelines came into being with the enactment of the Sentencing Reform Act of 1984, now codified at 18 U.S.C.A. §§ 3551–3586, 28 U.S.C.A. §§ 9991–9998. The new act applies to all crimes committed after November 1, 1987. The stated purpose of the act was "to establish sentencing policies and practices for the federal criminal justice system that will assure the ends of justice by promulgating detailed guidelines prescribing the appropriate sentences for offenders convicted of federal crimes." To accomplish this, the act created the United States Sentencing Commission to promulgate sentencing guidelines. The Commission promulgated guidelines that drastically reduced the discretion of federal judges by establishing a narrow sentencing range with the requirement that judges who depart from these ranges state in writing their reasons for doing so. In addition, the new act provides for appellate review for sentences and abolishes the United States Parole Commission.

In *United States v. Scroggins,* 880 F.2d 1204 (11th Cir. 1989), the Eleventh Circuit Court of Appeals discussed the mechanics of sentencing under the new federal guidelines. It explained that

> the district court begins the guidelines sentencing process by determining the circumstances of the defendant's offense conduct, the defendant's criminal history, and any other facts deemed relevant by the guidelines. The court then proceeds to assess the severity of the defendant's offense by applying the guidelines to the facts and circumstances of the defendant's offense conduct.... This process yields a numeric "total offense level" that consists of three elements: a "base offense level," which reflects the seriousness of the average offense sentenced under that particular guideline; "specific offense characteristics," which increase or decrease the base offense level in light of various factors considered relevant to the defendant's offense conduct; and "adjustments," which increase or decrease the offense level in light of certain factors considered generally relevant for sentencing purposes. The resulting total offense level can range from 1 (least serious) to 43 (most serious).

Having determined the total offense level, the court next surveys the criminal history of the offender. . . . This inquiry places the defendant within a "criminal history category" that evaluates the need to increase his sentence incrementally to deter him from further criminal activity. By correlating the offense level with the offender's criminal history category on the sentencing table developed by the Sentencing Commission, the court then identifies the "guideline range" for the offender's sentence." . . . In general, the district court must sentence the offender within this range.

The sentence prescribed by the guidelines is not absolute. The sentencing court may depart from the guidelines if it "finds that there exists an aggravating or mitigating circumstance of a kind, or to a degree, not adequately taken into consideration . . . in formulating the guidelines that should result in a sentence different from that described." *United States v. Aguilar-Pena,* 887 F.2d 347, 349 (1st Cir. 1989). Of course, it is impermissible to depart from the guidelines on the basis of the defendant's race, sex, national origin, religion, or socioeconomic status. *United States v. Burch,* 873 F.2d 765 (5th Cir. 1989). Other factors not ordinarily deemed relevant in determining whether to depart include the defendant's age, education, mental and physical condition, employment history, and family and community ties. *United States v. Lira-Barraza,* 897 F.2d 981 (9th Cir. 1990), n. 5.

Sentencing in Capital Cases

In those cases where the prosecution is permitted by law to seek the death penalty, the sentencing procedure is considerably more complex. As noted previously in the discussion of the death penalty, a bifurcated trial is employed. Following conviction of a defendant for a capital crime, the jury hears testimony in aggravation and/or mitigation of the sentence. For the jury to hand down the death penalty, it must find that the aggravating factors outweigh the mitigating ones.

Under Georgia law, the specific aggravating factors to be considered by the jury are whether

1. The offense . . . was committed by a person with a prior record of conviction for a capital felony;
2. The offense . . . was committed while the offender was engaged in . . . another capital felony or aggravated battery, or the offense of murder was committed while the offender was engaged in the commission of burglary or arson in the first degree;
3. The offender by his act of murder . . . knowingly created a great risk of death to more than one person in a public place by means of a weapon or device which would normally be hazardous to the lives of more than one person;
4. The offender committed the offense of murder for himself or another for the purpose of receiving money or any other thing of monetary value;
5. The murder of a judicial officer, former judicial officer, district attorney or solicitor or former district attorney or solicitor was committed during or because of the exercise of his official duty;

6. The offender caused or directed another to commit murder or committed murder as an agent or employee of another person;

7. The offense . . . was outrageously or wantonly vile, horrible or inhuman in that it involved torture, depravity of mind or an aggravated battery to the victim;

8. The offense of murder was committed against any peace officer, corrections employee, or fireman while engaged in the performance of his official duties;

9. The offense of murder was committed by a person in, or who has escaped from, the lawful custody of a peace officer or place of lawful confinement; or

10. The murder was committed for the purpose of avoiding, interfering with, or preventing a lawful arrest or custody in a place of lawful confinement, of himself or another. Official Ga. Code Ann. § 17–10–30(b).

In order to hand down a death sentence, the jury must find that at least one of the aforementioned aggravating circumstances was present. Should the jury make this finding and opt for the death penalty, the statute provides for automatic appeal to the state supreme court. That court is required to consider

1. Whether the sentence of death was imposed under the influence of passion, prejudice or any other arbitrary factor; and

2. Whether . . . the evidence supports the jury's or judge's finding of a statutory aggravating circumstance. . . , and

3. Whether the sentence of death is excessive or disproportionate to the penalty imposed in similar cases, considering both the crime and the defendant. Official Code Ga. Ann. § 17–10–35(c).

Under the capital sentencing procedures in Georgia, where a statutory aggravating circumstance is found and a recommendation of death is made, the trial judge must sentence the defendant to death. Official Ga. Code Ann. § 17–10–31. In other states a different method is employed. For example, in Florida it remains for the trial court to decide whether to accept a jury's recommendation of death or life imprisonment. See *Spaziano v. Florida*, 468 U.S. 447, 104 S.Ct. 3154, 82 L.Ed.2d 340 (1984). Where a jury recommends life imprisonment and the trial court overrides that recommendation and imposes the death penalty, the decision is carefully scrutinized by the Florida Supreme Court. For the trial court's override to be sustained, the life imprisonment recommendation by the jury must have been unreasonable. If the supreme court's review finds there was a reasonable basis for the jury's recommendation, it reverses the court's imposition of the death penalty and remands the case for a sentence as recommended by the jury. *Buford v. State*, 570 So. 2d 923 (Fla. 1990).

Granting Probation

Probation is a sentencing option in the federal courts and in most state courts. Under federal law a defendant who has been found guilty of an offense may be sentenced to a term of probation unless: (1) the offense is a felony where the maximum term of imprisonment authorized is twenty-five years or more, life imprisonment, or death; or (2) the offense is one for which probation has been expressly precluded; or (3) the defendant is sentenced at the same time to a term

---

CASE IN POINT

FOUR RECENT U.S. SUPREME COURT RULINGS ON AGGRAVATING AND MITIGATING CIRCUMSTANCES IN DEATH PENALTY LITIGATION

In the past decade, litigation in federal and state courts involving the death penalty has been prolific. The Supreme Court has made a series of rulings considering the aggravating and mitigating circumstances that now guide the trial courts in states where the death penalty is extant.

Under Oklahoma law, one statutory aggravating circumstance was whether the murder was "especially heinous, atrocious, or cruel." The Supreme Court said this language was unconstitutionally vague under the Eighth Amendment. *Maynard v. Cartwright*, 486 U.S. 356, 108 S.Ct. 1853, 100 L.Ed.2d 372 (1988).

A Florida jury was instructed to consider the statutory mitigating circumstances only in deciding whether to recommend the death penalty. The Supreme Court ruled that consideration of mitigating circumstances could not be limited to those contained in a statute, but that relevant nonstatutory mitigating circumstances must also be considered. *Hitchcock v. Dugger*, 481 U.S. 393, 107 S.Ct. 1821, 95 L.Ed.2d 347 (1987).

A Texas death penalty statute provided that the jury was to be instructed to answer three "special issues": (1) whether the defendant acted deliberately or with reasonable expectation that death would result; (2) whether the defendant would be a continuing violent threat to society; and (3) if applicable, whether the killing was an unreasonable response to any provocation by the deceased. If the jury answered all three questions in the affirmative, the judge was required to enter a death sentence. The Supreme Court found that although the application of the Texas statute permitted the jury to consider evidence of the defendant's mental retardation and abuse as a child as mitigation, the special issues prevented the jury from giving effect to that evidence. *Penry v. Lynaugh*, 492 U.S. 302, 109 S.Ct. 2934, 106 L.Ed.2d 256 (1989).

The U.S. Supreme Court said that the Mississippi Supreme Court could uphold a death sentence based in part on an invalid or improperly defined aggravating circumstance by reweighing the aggravating and mitigating circumstances or by conducting a harmless-error analysis. *Clemons v. Mississippi*, 494 U.S. 738, 110 S.Ct. 1441, 108 L.Ed.2d 725 (1990).

---

of imprisonment for the same or a different offense. Probation terms for a felony must not be less than one nor more than five years. 18 U.S.C.A. § 3561. Certain conditions of probation are mandatory and others are discretionary with the federal judge who imposes probation. 18 U.S.C.A. § 3563.

In state courts, the term of probation is limited to the maximum statutory term of confinement for the particular offense. As previously noted, probation is granted on the condition that the defendant abide by various stipulations. In some instances mandatory conditions are imposed by statute, but the trial court may impose additional conditions. In many instances probation is combined with a fine, a short term of incarceration to give the probationer "a taste of jail," and restitution to the victim. Because the procedures in state courts vary widely, it is difficult to generalize; however, it is important for the probationer to receive a written order incorporating the terms of probation and outlining his or her responsibilities to the probation officer and the court. Courts must guard against imposing vague conditions of probation or delegating overly broad authorities to probation officers.

Revocation of Probation

In every jurisdiction, the commission of a felony while on probation is grounds for revocation. In many jurisdictions, certain misdemeanors qualify as grounds for revocation. The violation of any substantive condition of probation is grounds for revocation. Typically, a probation officer is vested with broad discretion in determining when to seek revocation of probation. As in the case of parole revocation, a probationer facing the loss of freedom is entitled to a fair hearing. At this hearing the probationer has the right to call favorable witnesses, to confront hostile witnesses, and has a right to be represented by counsel. *Gagnon v. Scarpelli*, 411 U.S. 778, 93 S. Ct. 1756, 36 L.Ed.2d 656 (1973). In *Gagnon*, the Court said that indigent probationers may have a constitutional right to have counsel appointed at revocation hearings, depending on the complexity of the issues involved, and that if counsel is not provided, the judge must state the reason. In practice, counsel is usually provided. There is a statutory right to appointment of counsel for those financially unable to obtain counsel in federal probation revocation proceedings. 18 U.S.C.A. § 3006A.

The Federal Rules of Criminal Procedure require a two-step process before probation can be revoked:

1. **Preliminary Hearing.** Whenever a person is held in custody on the ground that the person has violated a condition of probation, . . . the person shall be afforded a prompt hearing . . . in order to determine whether there is probable cause to hold the person for a revocation hearing. The person shall be given

   (A) notice of the preliminary hearing and of its purpose and of the alleged violation. . . ;

   (B) an opportunity to appear at the hearing and present evidence in the person's own behalf;

   (C) upon request, the opportunity to question witnesses against the person unless, for good cause, the federal magistrate decides that justice does not require the appearance of the witness; and

   (D) notice of the person's right to be represented by counsel.

   The proceedings shall be recorded stenographically or by an electronic recording device. If probable cause is found to exist, the person shall be held for a revocation hearing. . . .

2. **Revocation Hearing.** The revocation hearing, unless waived by the person, shall be held within a reasonable time in the district of . . . [the] jurisdiction. The person shall be given

(A) written notice of the alleged violation...;

(B) disclosure of the evidence against the person;

(C) an opportunity to appear and to present evidence in the person's own behalf;

(D) the opportunity to question adverse witnesses; and

(E) notice of the person's right to be represented by counsel. Fed. R. Crim. Proc. 32.1(a).

The rules of evidence applicable at criminal trials are relaxed at probation revocation hearings. For example, hearsay evidence may be received over a probationer's objection, since a probation revocation hearing is not a criminal trial. *United States v. Miller*, 514 F.2d 41 (9th Cir. 1975). However, a legion of appellate court decisions holds that probation cannot be revoked solely on the basis of hearsay evidence. *Turner v. State*, 293 So.2d 771 (Fla. App. 1974). Courts have frequently articulated that the standard to be applied at revocation hearings is not "reasonable doubt" or "preponderance of evidence," but whether from the evidence presented the court is reasonably satisfied of the probationer's viola-tion. Nor is there any requirement that a probationer be granted a jury trial in revocation proceedings, even when those proceedings are predicated on a violation of a criminal law. *United States v. Czajak*, 909 F.2d 20 (1st Cir. 1990). Generally a court may modify rather than revoke a defendant's probation, but if the court does revoke probation, statutory and decisional law generally permit it to sentence the defendant to any term that would have been appropriate for the underlying offense. And while a probationer may not be sentenced on revocation for the conduct that constituted the probation violation, it is proper for the trial court to consider the probationer's conduct while on probation to assess a potential for rehabilitation. See, for example, *People v. Vilces*, 542 N.E.2d 1269 (Ill. App. 1989).

CASE IN POINT

SENTENCING IN CAPITAL CASES

Defendant Bobby Caldwell was charged with fatally shooting the owner of a grocery store while committing a robbery. After a jury trial, he was convicted of capital murder and sentenced to death. On appeal, the Mississippi Supreme Court unanimously upheld Caldwell's conviction, but divided 4–4 in affirming his death sentence. The four dissenting justices argued that the death sentence was invalid because the prosecutor had made an improper argument to the jury by suggesting that the responsibility for deciding the appropriateness of the death penalty lay not with them, but with the appellate courts. On *certiorari*, the United States Supreme Court vacated Caldwell's death sentence, saying that "This Court has always premised its capital punishment decisions on the assumption that a capital sentencing jury recognizes the gravity of its task and proceeds with an awareness of its 'truly awesome responsibility.' "

Caldwell v. Mississippi, 472 U.S. 320, 341, 105 S. Ct. 2633, 2646, 86 L.Ed.2d 231, 247 (1985).

> ### CASE IN POINT
>
> ## REVOCATION OF PROBATION REQUIRES A WILLFUL VIOLATION OF CONDITIONS IMPOSED BY COURT
>
> Danny Bearden pled guilty to charges of burglary and theft. Pursuant to Georgia's First Offenders Act, Official Code Ga. Ann. § 27-2727 et seq., current version at § 42–8–60, he was placed on three years' probation. As a condition of his probation, Bearden was required to pay a $500 fine and make restitution of $250, according to a court-imposed payment schedule. After making some payments, Bearden was laid off from work and became unable to continue making payments. As a result, the trial court revoked his probation and sentenced him to serve the remaining portion of his term of probation in prison. The United States Supreme Court reversed the revocation of probation because the trial court had made no finding that Bearden was responsible for his failure to make the required payments. Nevertheless, the Court said, "If the probationer willfully refused to pay or failed to make sufficient bona fide efforts legally to acquire the resources to pay, the court may revoke probation."
>
> *Bearden v. Georgia*, 461 U.S. 660, 672, 103 S. Ct. 2064, 2073, 76 L.Ed.2d 221, 233 (1983).

THE RIGHTS OF PRISONERS

Contrary to popular mythology, America's prisons are not country clubs. While it is true that some minimum security facilities (like the military base where the Watergate conspirators were confined) are reasonably comfortable, maximum security prisons are another story. They are sometimes unsanitary; they are almost all overcrowded. All are violent, dangerous places to live.

The federal courts have made it clear that the Eighth Amendment's prohibition of "cruel and unusual punishments" imposes obligations on prison administrators to maintain certain standards of confinement. A sizable number of state prison systems have been or are currently under court orders to improve conditions of confinement or reduce overcrowding. In recent years some state courts have begun to focus their attention on the deplorable conditions existing in many city and county jails.

Traditionally, courts were quite unreceptive to claims brought by prisoners. They essentially adopted a "hands-off" policy, allowing prison officials free rein. In the late 1960s that began to change, as federal and state tribunals came to examine prison conditions and policies. As the courts signaled their willingness to scrutinize the prisons, litigation in this area mushroomed.

In one dramatic case involving prison conditions, Federal District Judge Frank M. Johnson, Jr., found that the conditions of confinement in the Alabama system were barbarous and inhumane, thus violating the Eighth Amendment. Judge Johnson issued a detailed set of requirements to remedy the situation and appointed a special committee to oversee implementation of the order. Moreover, he threatened to close down the prison system unless his requirements were met. *Pugh v. Locke,* 406 F. Supp. 318 (M.D. Ala. 1976), *aff'd sub nom Newman v. Alabama,* 559 F.2d 283 (5th Cir. 1977), *cert. denied,* 438 U.S. 915, 98 S. Ct. 3144, 57 L.Ed.2d 1160 (1978).

Perhaps the most notorious story of prison conditions is that of the Arkansas prison system, which came under scrutiny in a series of federal lawsuits beginning in 1969. *Holt v. Sarver,* 309 F. Supp. 362 (E.D. Ark. 1970), *aff'd.,* 442 F.2d 304 (8th Cir. 1971). The most egregious conditions occurred at prison farms run largely by "trusties," senior prisoners entrusted with the job of controlling their fellow inmates. It should be noted that the trusty system is widely condemned by penologists. Under the Arkansas system, trusties smuggled in weapons, liquor, and drugs and sold them to the other inmates. Trusties hoarded food purchased with taxpayers' money and forced the other inmates to pay for their meals. Violence and even torture were commonly used by the trusties in maintaining their grip over the other prisoners. Medical care was almost totally lacking, and conditions of sanitation were miserable. Some prisoners were held in punitive isolation cells for months at a time. Overall, the penal farms were characterized by pervasive filth, disease, and violence.

In a series of decisions handed down during the 1970s, the federal district court issued detailed orders aimed at remedying the conditions in the Arkansas prison system. Especially controversial was an order placing a maximum limit of thirty days on the use of punitive isolation. However, the Supreme Court had little difficulty upholding this measure on appeal. *Hutto v. Finney,* 437 U.S. 678, 98 S. Ct. 2565, 57 L.Ed.2d 522 (1978).

As currently interpreted, the Eighth Amendment requires that prisoners must be provided with reasonably adequate food, clothing, shelter, medical care, and sanitation and that there must be a reasonable assurance of their personal safety. It does not require that prisoners must be provided every amenity they deem essential to their physical or psychological well-being. *Newman v. Alabama,* 559 F.2d 283 (5th Cir. 1977), *cert. denied,* 438 U.S. 915, 98 S. Ct. 3144, 57 L.Ed.2d 1160 (1978).

Much of the current litigation challenging conditions of criminal confinement focuses on the problem of prison overcrowding. Rising crime rates and an increasingly punitive posture adopted by legislatures and courts, combined with fiscal stress, have led to an overcrowding crisis in many state prison systems. As mandatory sentence laws and sentencing guidelines have required judges to imprison larger numbers of convicted criminals, the number of prisoners has far outstripped the capacity of prisons in the United States. In 1990, federal and state prisons housed 698,570 prisoners, the average prison housing 674 inmates. Federal prisons designed to accommodate 38,794 prisoners housed 56,821, accounting for about 8 percent of prisoners in the nation. By 1990, state prisons had increased their designed capacity to 541,568; however, these prisons housed 658,828 prisoners. Moreover, in 1990, federal prisons were housing an average of 2.01 inmates per housing unit while state prisons housed 2.16 per housing unit. (U.S. Department of Justice, Bureau of Justice Statistics, *National Update,* July 1992).

Trends of Prison Litigation in the 1980s and 1990s

During the 1980s the prison population in the United States nearly doubled. Throughout that decade, litigation in the federal courts by prisoners increased dramatically, yet the Supreme Court continued to follow a policy of restraint in its review of prison polices and the rights of inmates. Declaring that "the Constitution does not mandate comfortable prisons" in *Rhodes v. Chapman*, 452 U.S. 337, 101 S.Ct. 2392, 69 L.Ed.2d 59 (1981), the Court concluded that although prisoners were double-bunked, the totality of conditions did not constitute cruel and unusual punishment under the Eighth Amendment.

In 1983, the Court held that an inmate has no justifiable expectation of imprisonment in any particular state, therefore transfer of a prisoner to a prison in another state does not deprive the prisoner of any liberty interest protected by the constitutional requirement of due process of law. *Olim v. Wakinekona*, 461 U.S. 238, 103 S.Ct. 1741, 75 L.Ed.2d 813 (1983). In 1986, the Court ruled that negligent acts of prison officials in failing to protect an inmate from an attack by another inmate do not violate the due process clause of the federal constitution. *Davidson v. Cannon*, 474 U.S. 344, 106 S.Ct.. 668, 88 L.Ed.2d 677 (1986).

In 1987, a group of prisoners brought a class action challenging regulations promulgated by the Missouri Division of Corrections dealing with inmate-to-inmate correspondence and inmate marriages. The correspondence regulation limited written communication to immediate family members, where it concerned legal matters, or as otherwise approved by the officials. The marriage regulation permitted an inmate to marry only with permission of prison authorities. The federal district court found the regulations unconstitutional, and the court of appeals affirmed. On review, the Supreme Court was unanimous in striking down the regulation prohibiting marriage. Dividing 5–4, the Court reversed the district court as to the correspondence regulation, finding it reasonably related to valid corrections goals of security and safety. *Turner v. Safley*, 482 U.S. 78, 107 S.Ct. 2254, 96 L.Ed.2d 64 (1987). In the same year, the Court reviewed a case in which Muslim prisoners alleged that New Jersey Department of Corrections polices of prohibiting prison work details from returning to the main building during the work day prevented them from attending certain religious services held in the main building at midday on Fridays. Again, by a 5–4 decision, the Court overturned a court of appeals decision that required the federal district court to consider methods of requiring corrections officials to accommodate the religious practices of the prisoners. For the majority of the Court, Chief Justice Rehnquist wrote, "the approach articulated by the Court of Appeals fails to reflect the respect and deference that the United States Constitution allows for the judgment of prison administrators." *O'Lone v. Estate of Shabazz*, 482 U.S. 342, 107 S.Ct. 2400, 96 L.Ed.2d 282 (1987).

In 1989, the Supreme Court decided two cases affecting the rights of prisoners. In *Thornburgh v. Abbott*, 490 U.S. 401, 109 S.Ct. 1874, 104 L.Ed.2d 459 (1989), the Court reversed a court of appeals ruling that required a federal district court to make an individualized determination of the validity of a regulation that excluded 46 publications that prison officials had found detrimental to institutional security. The Supreme Court held that regulations limiting the publications that inmates can receive are valid if related to legitimate penological interests. On the same date, in *Kentucky Department of Corrections v. Thompson*, 490 U.S. 454, 109 S.Ct. 1904, 104 L.Ed.2d 506 (1989), the Court reviewed a federal class action challenging conditions of confinement in the Kentucky State Penitentiary. The litigation focused on denial of visitation privileges for a limited time of relatives and friends who allegedly were bringing contraband into the prison facility. A federal district court directed prison officials to develop minimal due process procedures for reviewing decisions to exclude a visitor. The court of appeals affirmed, but in a 6–3 decision, the Supreme Court reversed. Writing for the majority, Justice Blackmun said: "The denial of prison access to a particular visitor is 'well within the terms of confinement ordinarily contemplated by a prison sentence,' . . . and therefore is not independently protected by the Due Process Clause." 490 U.S. at 461, 109 S.Ct. at 1909, 104 L.Ed.2d at 515.

In *Washington v. Harper,* 494 U.S. 210, 110 S.Ct. 1028, 108 L.Ed.2d 178 (1990), the Supreme Court ruled that due process of law does not require a judicial hearing before the state may treat mentally ill prison inmates with antipsychotic drugs against their will. Justice Kennedy said that state's interest in prison safety and security is sufficient to justify subordinating the inmate's liberty interest in order to prevent a prisoner with a serious mental disorder from harming himself or others. The Court found the involuntary medication policy to be a rational means of accomplishing that objective.

In the 1990s there is some indication that the Supreme Court is taking a more solicitous attitude toward prisoners. In 1992, the Court held that a prisoner who is beaten maliciously by guards may bring a civil action for damages based on a claim of cruel and unusual punishment, even if the prisoner does not suffer "significant injuries." The Court's newest member, Justice Clarence Thomas, along with Justice Scalia, dissented. They expressed the view that nonserious injury to a prisoner does not rise to the level of cruel and unusual punishment. *Hudson v. McMillian,* 503 U.S. ____, 112 S.Ct. 995, 1004, 117 L.Ed.2d 156, ____ (1992).

During the 1990s prisoners have begun litigating the question of whether being subjected to environmental tobacco smoke (ETS) amounts to a violation of a prisoner's rights to due process of law and to protection from a deliberate indifference to the prisoner's health (in violation of the Eighth Amendment's prohibition against cruel and unusual punishment). Lower federal courts have recognized that the state has a duty to provide a safe environment for those incarcerated in its institutions. Recently, one United States court of appeals held that exposing a prisoner to ETS in a small cell by involuntary double-celling with smokers raises an issue of fact as to whether such exposure creates an unreasonable risk to the prisoner's health. *Clemmons v. Bohannon,* 918 F.2d 858 (10th Cir. 1990). Litigation of this type in the lower federal courts may lead to revisions in prison policies to protect the nonsmokers from ETS in instances where inmates are closely confined. The prospect of relief in this area has been enhanced by a Supreme Court ruling in June 1993. In context of a civil suit, the Court ruled that involuntary exposure of prisoners to second-hand tobacco smoke is grounds for them to sue their custodians on basis of an Eighth Amendment violation. *Helling v. McKinney,* 509 U.S. ____, 113 S.Ct. ____, 125 L.Ed.2d 22 (1993).

Other Rights of Prisoners

In addition to Eighth Amendment challenges to prison conditions, numerous lawsuits have sought to persuade the courts to recognize other constitutional rights of prison inmates. Traditionally, convicted felons were viewed as having forfeited most, if not all, of their constitutional rights. Thus, even reform-minded judges have been cautious in this area. For the most part they have deferred to prison officials, stressing the traditional view that "lawful incarceration brings about the necessary withdrawal or limitation of many privileges and rights, a retraction justified by the considerations underlying our penal system." *Price v. Johnston*, 334 U.S. 266, 285, 68 S. Ct. 1049, 92 L.Ed. 1356, 1369 (1948). Nevertheless, certain constitutional rights have been recognized. The Supreme Court has held that a prison inmate retains those First Amendment rights "that are not inconsistent with his status as a prisoner or with the legitimate penological objectives of the corrections system." *Pell v. Procunier*, 417 U.S. 817, 822, 94 S. Ct. 2800, 2804, 41 L.Ed.2d 495, 501 (1974).

For example, consider rights arising under the free exercise of religion clause of the First Amendment. Courts are generally receptive to prisoners' rights to possess bibles, prayer books, and other religious materials, as well as inmates' rights to be visited by the clergy. On the other hand, courts have generally upheld restrictions on religious exercises if they disrupt prison order or routine. However, if prison officials allow inmates who belong to mainstream religious denominations to attend worship services, then members of other religious sects must be given a reasonable opportunity to exercise their religious beliefs as well. *Cruz v. Beto*, 405 U.S. 319, 92 S. Ct. 1079, 31 L.Ed.2d 263 (1972).

One of the most firmly established rights of prisoners is the right of access to the courts. The Supreme Court made it clear decades ago that prison officials may not deny inmates access to the courts, nor penalize them for utilizing that access. *Ex parte Hull*, 312 U.S. 546, 61 S. Ct. 640, 85 L.Ed. 1034 (1941). Similarly, courts have held that indigent inmates must be furnished writing materials and notarial services to assist them in filing petitions and seeking writs from courts. Courts have generally upheld the right of prisoners to meet with counsel in privacy and, in the absence of other forms of legal assistance, to have access to law libraries. See *Bounds v. Smith*, 430 U.S. 817, 97 S. Ct. 1491, 52 L.Ed.2d 72 (1977).

The courts have also recognized that prisoners are entitled to limited rights of expression. For example, prisoners retain a limited right to communicate with the outside world via the mails, although prison officials may limit and censor the mail prisoners send and receive, provided there is no interference with attorney-client relationships. *Lee v. Tahash*, 352 F.2d 970 (8th Cir. 1965).

On the other hand, prison regulations impinging on inmates' interests in free assembly and association have been consistently upheld. See, for example, *Jones v. North Carolina Prisoners' Labor Union, Inc.*, 433 U.S. 119, 97 S. Ct. 2532, 53 L.Ed.2d 629 (1977), where the Supreme Court refused to extend First Amendment protection to an effort to organize a labor union among prisoners.

Prison Disciplinary Hearings

The federal courts have imposed limits on prison disciplinary measures such as corporal punishment and the extended use of isolation cells. Today, prison discipline is largely accomplished by the granting and removal of "good-time credit," that is, early release for good behavior. If officials pursue this policy, then due process demands that certain procedural requirements be observed before good time is removed for disciplinary purposes. Specifically, there must be written notice of the disciplinary action, and the inmate has the right to an administrative hearing with a written record. The inmate must be accorded the right to produce evidence refuting the charges of misconduct and may even call witnesses on his or her behalf. *Wolff v. McDonnell,* 418 U.S. 539, 94 S. Ct. 2963, 41 L.Ed.2d 935 (1974). These rights have not been extended to allow an inmate to have counsel present at such a hearing. *Baxter v. Palmigiano,* 425 U.S. 308, 96 S. Ct. 1551, 47 L.Ed.2d 810 (1976).

Parole and its Revocation

Many states provide for early release from prison on parole for those inmates who can demonstrate to the satisfaction of a parole board their willingness to conform their conduct to the requirements of the law. Naturally, there are also provisions by which parole can be revoked if the offender violates the conditions of release. However, as in the case of internal prison disciplinary actions, the revocation of parole is affected by due process considerations. Essentially, before parole can be revoked, the parolee has the right to a hearing within a reasonable time after being retaken into custody. *Morrissey v. Brewer,* 408 U.S. 471, 92 S. Ct. 2593, 33 L.Ed.2d 484 (1972). The Supreme Court has stressed the informality of this hearing, however, saying that "the process should be flexible enough to consider evidence including letters, affidavits, and other material that would not be admissible in an adversary criminal trial." 408 U.S. at 489, 92 S. Ct. at 2604, 33 L.Ed.2d at 499. In practice, courts generally admit any relevant evidence not privileged, but generally do not allow revocation based solely on hearsay evidence. See, for example, *Grello v. Commonwealth,* 477 A.2d 45 (Pa. Cmwlth. 1984).

A year after its decision in *Morrissey v. Brewer,* the Supreme Court held that the right to counsel may apply to parole revocation hearings, depending on the complexity of the issues involved. *Gagnon v. Scarpelli,* 411 U.S. 778, 93 S. Ct. 1756, 36 L.Ed.2d 656 (1973). There is a statutory right to appointment of counsel for those financially unable to obtain counsel in federal parole revocation hearings. 18 U.S.C.A. § 3006A; *Baldwin v. Benson,* 584 F.2d 953 (10th Cir. 1978).

THE RIGHTS OF CRIME VICTIMS

Although crime is by definition an injury against society as a whole, we must not forget that most serious crimes injure individual victims, often quite severely. The injury may transcend physical or economic injury to include emotional hardship. If during the 1960s the dominant concern of the criminal law was for the rights of the accused, in the 1990s the trend has been to recognize the rights of crime victims. A number of states—including Arizona, California, Florida, Michigan, New Jersey, Rhode Island, Texas, and Washington—have adopted constitutional amendments specifically recognizing victims' rights. Other states have adopted statutes along these lines.

The Uniform Victims of Crime Act

The Uniform Victims of Crime Act (UVCA) is an attempt to lend uniformity to the patchwork of victims' rights laws that now exists at the state level. The

UVCA was developed by the Uniform Law Commission, a voluntary association representing the legal profession. Like the Model Penal Code developed by the American Law Institute, the UVCA has no status as law unless and until it is adopted by a state legislature.

Under the UVCA, prosecutors or court personnel must notify victims of their rights under the act, as well as the times of any court proceedings involving the person or persons who allegedly victimized them. A crime victim has a right to be present at any court proceeding that the defendant has a right to attend. If the defendant is convicted, the victim has the right to make an impact statement during the sentencing hearing and assert an opinion as to the proper sentence. Finally, the UVCA provides for victims to be compensated by the state, up to $25,000, for any physical or emotional injuries suffered as the result of the victimization. However, this amount may be denied or reduced if the victim receives compensation through insurance or restitution from the defendant.

Restitution

Restitution is a time-honored means of protecting the interests of crime victims. Restitution refers to "the return of a sum of money, an object, or the value of an object which the defendant wrongfully obtained in the course of committing the crime." *State v. Stalheim*, 552 P.2d 829, 832 (Or. 1976). Although restitution was practiced under the early common law, it was eventually abandoned as a remedy in criminal cases in favor of fines payable to the Crown. In modern America, however, restitution is making a comeback in the criminal law. A number of states have enacted laws allowing trial courts to require restitution as a condition of probation, in lieu of sentencing offenders to prison. In states that have adopted restitution laws, courts have held that (1) restitution is not necessarily incompatible with incarceration, *State v. Murray*, 621 P.2d 334 (Hawaii 1980); (2) restitution may be ordered for damages caused by the defendant during a criminal episode, irrespective of whether the loss is directly related to a specific conviction, *People v. Gallagher*, 223 N.W.2d 92 (Mich. App. 1974); and (3) a defendant may be ordered to pay restitution to a party other than the victim, *Shenah v. Henderson*, 476 P.2d 854 (Ariz. 1970).

Restitution is not practical in many criminal cases. Many offenders are not suited to probation and, even among those who are, there is no guarantee that they will be able to make payments to the victim. Recognizing this problem, a number of states have established victims' compensation commissions. For example, the Florida Crimes Compensation Act of 1977 makes victims and certain relatives eligible for compensation by a state commission where a crime results in injuries and is reported within 72 hours. Awards are limited to meeting the actual needs of victims. West's Fla. Stat. Ann. § 960.001–960.28.

Victim Impact Statements

Another recent attempt to recognize the interests of crime victims involves the presentation of a "victim impact statement" at the sentencing hearing. The statement addresses the impact of the crime on the victim and the victim's family, including the physical, economic, and psychological effects of the crime.

In 1987, the United States Supreme Court struck down a Maryland statute requiring that victim impact statements be considered during the penalty phase of capital cases. *Booth v. Maryland,* 482 U.S. 496, 107 S. Ct. 2529, 96 L.Ed.2d 440 (1987). The Court said that such statements raised the real possibility that death sentences would be based on irrelevant considerations. However, four years later, in *Payne v. Tennessee,* 501 U.S. ___ , 111 S.Ct. 2597, 115 L.Ed.2d 720 (1991), the Court overruled its decision in *Booth.* According to Chief Justice Rehnquist, who wrote the majority opinion in *Payne,* the *Booth* decision "deprives the State of the full moral force of its evidence and may prevent the jury from having before it all the information necessary to determine the proper punishment for a first-degree murder." 501 U.S. at ___ , 111 S.Ct. at 2608, 115 L.Ed.2d at 735. Notwithstanding the Supreme Court's decision in *Payne v. Tennessee,* appellate courts may still find that a particular victim impact statement has impermissibly injected too much emotionalism into the jury's sentencing deliberations.

CONCLUSION

The various forms of punishment meted out to convicted criminals rest on differing assumptions about crime and human nature. These assumptions lead to differing philosophies of punishment that stress retribution, deterrence, incapacitation, or rehabilitation. A great debate continues regarding both the propriety of these goals and the efficacy of the measures designed to achieve them. In particular, the deterrent value of the death penalty and the rehabilitative value of incarceration have been questioned.

Courts of law tend to avoid the philosophical, theoretical, and empirical questions that surround the various forms of criminal punishment. Rather, they focus on the substantive and procedural limitations that the federal and state constitutions impose on the criminal justice system. In so doing they tend to reflect the dominant values of the society. Thus, courts have not hesitated to invalidate torture and flogging as cruel and unusual punishments forbidden by the Eighth Amendment, yet they have been extremely reluctant to reach similar conclusions regarding the death penalty.

One of the current issues in criminal justice is the problem of sentencing disparity. The death penalty has been challenged, albeit unsuccessfully, as being racially discriminatory. But the allegations of disparity extend well beyond the death penalty to encompass the entire regime of criminal punishment. One approach to reducing sentencing disparity is to limit judicial discretion through more determinate sentencing. Another is the development of sentencing guidelines.

Over the last several decades, courts have become more active in the area of prisoners' rights. Decisions have been handed down protecting inmates' access to counsel and the courts, invalidating extreme conditions of confinement, and recognizing limited First Amendment freedoms. Courts have imposed minimal due process requirements on prison disciplinary proceedings, and on parole and probation revocation decisions as well. On the other hand, they have tended to defer to corrections officials on most substantive restrictions on inmate behavior.

There is profound dissatisfaction with the nation's prison system. Little evidence exists that prisons provide any sort of meaningful rehabilitation. Yet, few have proposed viable alternatives for dealing with violent criminals. As crime rates soared over the last three decades, the public began to demand stiffer sentences, especially for repeat offenders. The result is a prison system that is grossly overcrowded. In truth, the correctional system of the nation is in a state of crisis. As the crisis worsens, policymakers face three choices: (1) change the criminal laws to make sentencing more lenient; (2) appropriate more revenues to construct new prison facilities; or (3) develop effective alternatives to confinement. Since society appears reluctant to follow either of the first two courses, exploration of meaningful alternatives to incarceration is essential.

QUESTIONS FOR THOUGHT AND DISCUSSION

1. Why have the courts generally viewed corporal punishment as "cruel and unusual," yet been unwilling to take the same view of capital punishment?

2. How could a prisoner on "death row" establish that his death sentence was the result of racial discrimination?

3. Does your state impose the death penalty? If so, what does the state law provide with respect to juries considering aggravating and mitigating factors? Do you think your state's law governing the death penalty should be amended? If so, in what respect?

4. What alternatives to imprisonment exist to deal with violent criminals who are repeat offenders? What alternatives, if any, would you propose? What legal problems are implicit in these alternatives to incarceration?

5. Suppose you were a probation officer and a judge asked you to recommend probation conditions for a first-time offender convicted of sale and possession of cocaine. What specific conditions would you propose?

6. Should a defendant always be permitted to view the contents of a presentence report? What are the arguments pro and con?

7. What is the rationale for granting only minimal due process rights to parolees and probationers and to prisoners in disciplinary proceedings?

8. How have the legal rights of prisoners been expanded since the 1960s? Have the courts been unduly solicitous in entertaining lawsuits brought by prison inmates?

9. Which of the four theories of criminal punishment do you find most compelling: retribution, deterrence, incapacitation, or rehabilitation? Why? Are there other compelling justifications for criminal punishment?

10. Do you think that the introduction of a "victim impact statement" during the sentencing phase of a capital trial is appropriate, or do you think it injects too much emotionalism into the process?

CASES

FURMAN v. GEORGIA

Supreme Court of the United States, 1972.
408 U.S. 238, 92 S. Ct. 2726, 33 L.Ed.2d 346.

[In this landmark decision, the U.S. Supreme Court invalidates Georgia's death penalty statute.]

PER CURIAM.

The Court holds that the imposition and carrying out of the death penalty in these cases constitutes cruel and unusual punishment in violation of the Eighth and Fourteenth Amendments. The judgment in each case is therefore reversed insofar as it leaves undisturbed the death sentence imposed, and the cases are remanded for further proceedings.

Mr. Justice Douglas, Mr. Justice Brennan, Mr. Justice Stewart, Mr. Justice White, and Mr. Justice Marshall have filed separate opinions in support of the judgments. The Chief Justice, Mr. Justice Blackmun, Mr. Justice Powell, and Mr. Justice Rehnquist have filed separate dissenting opinions.

Mr. Justice DOUGLAS concurring.

In these three cases the death penalty was imposed, one of them for murder, and two for rape. In each the determination of whether the penalty should be death or a lighter punishment was left by the State to the discretion of the judge or of the jury. In each of the three cases the trial was to a jury. They are here on petitions for certiorari which we granted limited to the question whether the imposition and execution of the death penalty constitutes "cruel and unusual punishment" within the meaning of the Eighth Amendment as applied to the States by the Fourteenth. I vote to vacate each judgment, believing that the exaction of the death penalty does violate the Eighth and Fourteenth Amendments. . . .

The words "cruel and unusual" certainly include penalties that are barbaric. But the words, at least when read in light of the English proscription against selective and irregular use of penalties, suggest that it is "cruel and unusual" to apply the death penalty—or any other penalty selectively to minorities whose numbers are few, who are outcasts of society, and who are unpopular, but whom society is willing to see suffer though it would not countenance general application of the same penalty across the board.

Jackson, a black, convicted of the rape of a white woman, was 21 years old. A court-appointed psychiatrist said that Jackson was of average education and average intelligence, that he was not an imbecile, or schizophrenic, or psychotic, that his traits were the product of environmental influences, and that he was competent to stand trial. Jackson had entered the house after the husband left for work. He held scissors against the neck of the wife, demanding money. She could find none and a struggle ensued for the scissors, a battle which she lost; and she was then raped, Jackson keeping the scissors pressed against her neck. While there did not appear to be any long-term traumatic impact on the victim, she was bruised and abrased in the struggle but was not hospitalized. Jackson was a convict who had escaped from a work gang in the area, a result of a three-year sentence for auto theft. He was at large for three days and during that time had committed several other offenses—burglary, auto theft and assault and battery.

Furman, a black, killed a householder while seeking to enter the home at night. Furman shot the deceased through a closed door. He was 26 years old and had finished the sixth grade in school. Pending trial he was committed to the Georgia Central State Hospital for a psychiatric examination on his plea of insanity tendered by court-appointed counsel. The superintendent reported that a unanimous staff diagnostic conference on the same date had concluded "that this patient should retain his present diagnosis of Mental Deficiency, Mild to Moderate, with Psychotic Episodes associated with Convulsive Disorder." The physicians agreed that "at present the patient is not psychotic, but he is not capable of cooperating with his counsel in the preparation of his defense"; and the staff believed "that he is in need of further psychiatric hospitalization and treatment."

Later the superintendent reported that the staff diagnosis was Mental Deficiency, Mild to Moderate, with Psychotic Episodes associated with Convulsive Disorder. He concluded, however, that Furman was "not psychotic at present, knows right from wrong and is able to cooperate with his counsel in preparing his defense."

Branch, a black, entered the rural home of a 65-year-old widow, a white, while she slept and raped her, holding his arm against her throat. Thereupon he demanded money and for 30 minutes or more the widow searched for money, finding little. As he left, Jackson said if the widow told anyone what happened, he would return to kill her. The record is barren of any medical or psychiatric evidence showing injury to her as a result of Branch's attack.

He had previously been convicted of felony theft and found to be a borderline mentally deficient and well below the average IQ of Texas prison inmates. He had the equivalent of five and a half years of grade school education. He had a "dull intelligence" and was in the lowest fourth percentile of his class.

We cannot say from facts disclosed in these records that these defendants were sentenced to death because they were black. Yet our task is not restricted to an effort to define what motives impelled these death penalties. Rather, we deal with a system of law and of justice that leaves to the uncontrolled discretion of judges or juries the determination whether defendants committing these crimes should die or be imprisoned. Under these laws no standards govern the selection of the penalty. People live or die, dependent on the whim of one man or of 12.

In a Nation committed to equal protection of the laws there is no permissible "caste" aspect of law enforcement. Yet we know that the discretion of judges and juries in imposing the death penalty enables the penalty to be selectively applied, feeding prejudices against the accused if he is poor and despised, lacking political clout, or if he is a member of a suspect or unpopular minority, and saving those who by social position may be in a more protected position. . . .

The high service rendered by the "cruel and unusual" punishment clause of the Eighth Amendment is to require legislatures to write penal laws that are evenhanded, nonselective, and nonarbitrary, and to require judges to see to it that general laws are not applied sparsely, selectively, and spottily to unpopular groups.

A law that stated that anyone making more than $50,000 would be exempt from the death penalty would plainly fall, as would a law that in terms said that blacks, those who never went beyond the fifth grade in school, those who made less than $3,000 a year, or those who were unpopular or unstable should be the only people executed. A law which in the overall view reaches that result in practice has no more sanctity than a law which in terms provides the same.

Thus, these discretionary statutes are unconstitutional in their operation. They are pregnant with discrimination and discrimination is an ingredient not compatible with the idea of equal protection of the laws that is implicit in the ban on "cruel and unusual" punishments.

Mr. Justice BRENNAN, concurring.

Ours would indeed be a simple task were we required merely to measure a challenged punishment against those that history has long condemned. That narrow and unwarranted view of the Clause, however, was left behind with the 19th century. Our task today is more complex. We know "that the words of the [Clause] are not precise and that their scope is not static." We know, therefore, that the Clause "must draw its meaning from the evolving standards of decency that mark the progress of a maturing society." That knowledge, of course, is but the beginning of the inquiry.

. . . [T]he question is whether [a] penalty subjects the individual to a fate forbidden by the principle of civilized treatment guaranteed by the [Clause]." It was also said that a challenged punishment must be examined "in light of the basic prohibition against inhuman treatment" embodied in the Clause.

. . . "The basic concept underlying the [Clause] is nothing less than the dignity of man. While the State has the power to punish, the [Clause] stands to assure that this power be exercised within the limits of civilized standards." At bottom, then, the Cruel and Unusual Punishment Clause prohibits the infliction of uncivilized and inhuman punishments. The State, even as it punishes, must treat its members with respect for their intrinsic worth as human beings. A punishment is "cruel and unusual," therefore, if it does not comport with human dignity.

This formulation, of course, does not of itself yield principles for assessing the constitutional validity of particular punishments. Nevertheless, even though "[t]his Court has had little occasion to give precise content to the [Clause]," there are principles recognized in our cases and inherent in the Clause sufficient to permit a judicial determination whether a challenged punishment comports with human dignity.

In sum, the punishment of death is inconsistent with all four principles: Death is an unusually severe and degrading punishment; there is a strong probability that it is inflicted arbitrarily; its rejection by contemporary society is virtually total; and there is no reason to believe that it serves any penal purpose more effectively than the less severe punishment of imprisonment. The function of these principles is to enable a court to determine whether a punishment comports with human dignity. Death, quite simply, does not. . . .

Mr. Justice STEWART, concurring.

The penalty of death differs from all other forms of criminal punishment, not in degree but in kind. It is unique in its total irrevocability. It is unique in its rejection of rehabilitation of the convict as a basic purpose of criminal justice. And it is unique, finally in its absolute renunciation of all that is embodied in our concept of humanity.

For these and other reasons, at least two of my Brothers have concluded that the infliction of the death penalty is constitutionally impermissible in all circumstances under the Eighth and Fourteenth Amendments. Their case is a strong one. But I find it unnecessary to reach the ultimate question they would decide. . . .

Legislatures—state and federal—have sometimes specified that the penalty of death shall be the mandatory punishment for every person convicted of engaging in certain designated criminal conduct.

If we were reviewing death sentences imposed under these or similar laws, we would be faced with the need to decide whether capital punishment is

unconstitutional for all crimes and under all circumstances. We would need to decide whether a legislature—state or federal—could constitutionally determine that certain criminal conduct is so atrocious that society's interest in deterrence and retribution wholly outweighs any considerations of reform or rehabilitation of the perpetrator, and that, despite the inconclusive empirical evidence, only the automatic penalty of death will provide maximum deterrence.

On that score I would say only that I cannot agree that retribution is a constitutionally impermissible ingredient in the imposition of punishment. The instinct for retribution is part of the nature of man, and channeling that instinct in the administration of criminal justice serves an important purpose in promoting the stability of a society governed by law. When people begin to believe that organized society is unwilling or unable to impose upon criminal offenders the punishment they "deserve," then there are sown the seeds of anarchy—of self-help, vigilante justice and lynch law.

The constitutionality of capital punishment in the abstract is not, however, before us in these cases. For the Georgia and Texas Legislatures have not provided that the death penalty shall be imposed upon all those who are found guilty of forcible rape. And the Georgia Legislature has not ordained that death shall be the automatic punishment for murder.

Instead, the death sentences now before us are the product of a legal system that brings them, I believe, within the very core of the Eighth Amendment's guarantee against cruel and unusual punishments, a guarantee applicable against the States through the Fourteenth Amendment. In the first place, it is clear that these sentences are "cruel" in the sense that they excessively go beyond, not in degree but in kind, the punishments that the state legislatures have determined to be necessary. In the second place, it is equally clear that these sentences are "unusual" in the sense that the penalty of death is infrequently imposed for murder, and that its imposition for rape is extraordinarily rare. But I do not rest my conclusion upon these two propositions alone.

These death sentences are cruel and unusual in the same way that being struck by lightning is cruel and unusual. For, of all the people convicted of rapes and murders in 1967 and 1968, many just as reprehensible as these, the petitioners are among a capriciously selected random handful upon whom the sentence of death has in fact been imposed. My concurring Brothers have demonstrated that, if any basis can be discerned for the selection of these few to be sentenced to die, it is the constitutionally impermissible basis of race. But racial discrimination has not been proved, and I put it to one side. I simply conclude that the Eighth and Fourteenth Amendments cannot tolerate the infliction of a sentence of death under legal systems that permit this unique penalty to be so wantonly and so freakishly imposed.

Mr. Justice WHITE, concurring.

The facial constitutionality of statutes requiring the imposition of the death penalty for first-degree murder, for more narrowly defined categories of murder, or for rape would present quite different issues under the Eighth Amendment than are posed by the cases before us. In joining the Court's judgments, therefore, I do not at all intimate that the death penalty is unconstitutional per se or that there is no system of capital punishment that would comport with the Eighth Amendment. That question, ably argued by several of my Brethren, is not presented by these cases and need not be decided.

The narrow question to which I address myself concerns the constitutionality of capital punishment statutes under which (1) the legislature authorizes the imposition of the death penalty for murder or rape; (2) the legislature does not itself mandate the penalty in any particular class or kind of case (that is, legislative will is not frustrated if the penalty is never imposed), but delegates to judges or juries the decisions as to those cases, if any, in which the penalty will be utilized; and (3) judges and juries have ordered the death penalty with such infrequency that the odds are now very much against imposition and execution of the penalty with respect to any convicted murderer or rapist. It is in this context that we must consider whether the execution of these petitioners would violate the Eighth Amendment.

. . . [L]ike my Brethren, I must arrive at judgment; and I can do no more than state a conclusion based on 10 years of almost daily exposure to the facts and circumstances of hundreds and hundreds of federal and state criminal cases involving crimes for which

death is the authorized penalty. That conclusion, as I have said, is that the death penalty is exacted with great infrequency even for the most atrocious crimes and that there is no meaningful basis for distinguishing the few cases in which it is imposed from the many cases in which it is not. The short of it is that the policy of vesting sentencing authority primarily in juries—a decision largely motivated by the desire to mitigate the harshness of the law and to bring community judgment to bear on the sentence as well as guilt or innocence—has so effectively achieved its aims that capital punishment within the confines of the statutes now before us has for all practical purposes run its course. . . .

Mr. Justice MARSHALL, concurring.

The criminal acts with which we are confronted are ugly, vicious, reprehensible acts. Their sheer brutality cannot and should not be minimized. But, we are not called upon to condone the penalized conduct; we are asked only to examine the penalty imposed on each of the petitioners and to determine whether or not it violates the Eighth Amendment. The question then is not whether we condone rape or murder, for surely we do not; it is whether capital punishment is "a punishment no longer consistent with our own self-respect" and therefore, violative of the Eighth Amendment.

Perhaps the most important principle in analyzing "cruel and unusual" punishment questions is one that is reiterated again and again in the prior opinions of the Court: i.e., the cruel and unusual language "must draw its meaning from the evolving standards of decency that mark the progress of a maturing society." Thus, a penalty that was permissible at one time in our Nation's history is not necessarily permissible today. . . .

In judging whether or not a given penalty is morally acceptable, most courts have said that the punishment is valid unless "it shocks the conscience and sense of justice of the people."

While a public opinion poll obviously is of some assistance in indicating public acceptance or rejection of a specific penalty, its utility cannot be very great. This is because whether or not a punishment is cruel and unusual depends, not on whether its mere mention "shocks the conscience and sense of justice of the people," but on whether people who were fully informed as to the purposes of the penalty and its liabilities would find the penalty shocking, unjust, and unacceptable.

In other words, the question with which we must deal is not whether a substantial proportion of American citizens would today, if polled, opine that capital punishment is barbarously cruel, but whether they would find it to be so in the light of all information presently available.

This information would almost surely convince the average citizen that the penalty was unwise, but a problem arises as to whether, it would convince him that the penalty was morally reprehensible. This problem arises from the fact that the public's desire for retribution, even though this is a goal that the legislature cannot constitutionally pursue as its sole justification for capital punishment, might influence the citizenry's view of the morality of capital punishment. The solution to the problem lies in the fact that no one has ever seriously advanced retribution as a legitimate goal of our society. Defenses of capital punishment are always mounted on deterrent or other similar theories. This should not be surprising. It is the people of this country who have urged in the past that prisons rehabilitate as well as isolate offenders, and it is the people who have injected a sense of purpose into our penology. I cannot believe that at this stage in our history, the American people would ever knowingly support purposeless vengeance. Thus, I believe that the great mass of citizens would conclude on the basis of the material already considered that the death penalty is immoral therefore unconstitutional.

In striking down capital punishment, this Court does not malign our system of government. On the contrary, it pays homage to it. Only in a free society could right triumph in difficult times, and could civilization record its magnificent advancement. In recognizing the humanity of our fellow beings, we pay ourselves the highest tribute. We achieve "a major milestone in the long road up from barbarism" and join the approximately 70 other jurisdictions in the world which celebrate their regard for civilization and humanity by shunning capital punishment.

Mr. Chief Justice BURGER, with whom Mr. Justice BLACKMUN, and Mr. Justice REHNQUIST, join, dissenting.

... If we were possessed of legislative power, I would either join with Mr. Justice Brennan and Mr. Justice Marshall or, at the very least, restrict the use of capital punishment to a small category of the most heinous crimes. Our constitutional inquiry, however, must be divorced from personal feelings as to the morality and efficacy of the death penalty, and be confined to the meaning and applicability of the uncertain language of the Eighth Amendment. There is no novelty in being called upon to interpret a constitutional provision that is less than self-defining, but, of all our fundamental guarantees, the ban on "cruel and unusual punishments" is one of the most difficult to translate into judicially manageable terms. The widely divergent views of the Amendment expressed in today's opinions reveals the haze that surrounds this constitutional command. Yet it is essential to our role as a court that we not seize upon the enigmatic character of the guarantee as an invitation to enact our personal predilections into law.

Although the Eighth Amendment literally reads as prohibiting only those punishments that are both "cruel" and "unusual," history compels the conclusion that the Constitution prohibits all punishments of extreme and barbarous cruelty, regardless of how frequently or infrequently imposed.

But where, as here, we consider a punishment well known to history, and clearly authorized by legislative enactment, it disregards the history of the Eighth Amendment and all the judicial comment that has followed to rely on the term "unusual" as affecting the outcome of these cases. Instead, I view these cases as turning on the single question whether capital punishment is "cruel" in the constitutional sense. The term "unusual" cannot be read as limiting the ban on "cruel" punishments or as somehow expanding the meaning of the term "cruel." For this reason I am unpersuaded by the facile argument that since capital punishment has always been cruel in the everyday sense of the word, and has become unusual due to decreased use, it is, therefore, now "cruel and unusual." ...

Mr. Justice BLACKMUN, dissenting.

I join the respective opinions of The Chief Justice, Mr. Justice Powell, and Mr. Justice Rehnquist, and add only the following, somewhat personal, comments.

Cases such as these provide for me an excruciating agony of the spirit. I yield to no one in the depth of my distaste, antipathy, and, indeed, abhorrence, for the death penalty, with all its aspects of physical distress and fear and of moral judgment exercised by finite minds. That distaste is buttressed by a belief that capital punishment serves no useful purpose that can be demonstrated. For me, it violates childhood's training and life's experiences, and is not compatible with the philosophical convictions I have been able to develop. It is antagonistic to any sense of "reverence for life." Were I a legislator, I would vote against the death penalty for the policy reasons argued by counsel for the respective petitioners and expressed and adopted in the several opinions filed by the Justices who vote to reverse these convictions.

Although personally I may rejoice at the Court's result, I find it difficult to accept or to justify as a matter of history, of law, or of constitutional pronouncement. I fear the Court has overstepped. It has sought and has achieved an end.

Mr. Justice POWELL, with whom The CHIEF JUSTICE, Mr. Justice BLACKMUN, and Mr. Justice REHNQUIST join, dissenting.

The Court granted certiorari in these cases to consider whether the death penalty is any longer a permissible form of punishment. It is the judgment of five Justices that the death penalty, as customarily prescribed and implemented in this country today, offends the constitutional prohibition against cruel and unusual punishments. The reasons for that judgment are stated in five separate opinions, expressing as many separate rationales. In my view, none of these opinions provides a constitutionally adequate foundation for the Court's decision. . . .

Mr. Justice REHNQUIST, with whom The Chief Justice, Mr. Justice BLACKMUN, and Mr. Justice POWELL join, dissenting.

Whatever its precise rationale, today's holding necessarily brings into sharp relief the fundamental question of the role of judicial review in a democratic society. How can government by the elected representatives of the people co-exist with the power of the federal judiciary, whose members are constitutionally insulated from responsiveness to the popular will, to declare invalid laws duly enacted by the popular branches of government?

Sovereignty resides ultimately in the people as a whole and, by adopting through their States a written Constitution for the Nation and subsequently adding amendments to that instrument, they have both granted certain powers to the National Government, and denied other powers to the National and the State Governments. Courts are exercising no more than the judicial function conferred upon them by Art. III of the Constitution when they assess, in a case before them, whether or not a particular legislative enactment is within the authority granted by the Constitution to the enacting body, and whether it runs afoul of some limitation placed by the Constitution on the authority of that body. For the theory is that the people themselves have spoken in the Constitution, and therefore its commands are superior to the commands of the legislature, which is merely an agent of the people.

The Founding Fathers thus wisely sought to have the best of both worlds, the undeniable benefits of both democratic self-government and individual rights protected against possible excesses of that form of government.

The very nature of judicial review, as pointed out by Justice Stone in his dissent in the *Butler* case, makes the courts the least subject to Madisonian check in the event that they shall, for the best of motives, expand judicial authority beyond the limits contemplated by the Framers. It is for this reason that judicial self-restraint is surely an implied, if not an expressed, condition of the grant of authority of judicial review. The Court's holding in these cases has been reached, I believe, in complete disregard of that implied condition.

GREGG V. GEORGIA

Supreme Court of the United States, 1976.
428 U.S. 153, 96 S. Ct. 2909, 49 L.Ed.2d 859.

[Here the Supreme Court effectively reinstates the death penalty by sustaining a revised Georgia death penalty law.]

Judgment of the Court, and opinion of Mr. Justice STEWART, Mr. Justice POWELL, and Mr. Justice STEVENS, announced by Mr. Justice STEWART.

The issue in this case is whether the imposition of the sentence of death for the crime of murder under the law of Georgia violates the Eighth and Fourteenth Amendments.

The petitioner, Troy Gregg, was charged with committing armed robbery and murder. In accordance with Georgia procedure in capital cases, the trial was in two stages, a guilt stage and a sentencing stage. The evidence at the guilt trial established that on November 21, 1973, the petitioner and a traveling companion, Floyd Allen, while hitchhiking north in Florida were picked up by Fred Simmons and Bob Moore. Their car broke down, but they continued north after Simmons purchased another vehicle with some of the cash he was carrying. While still in Florida, they picked up another hitchhiker, Dennis Weaver, who rode with them to Atlanta, where he was let out about 11 P.M. A short time later the four men interrupted their journey for a rest stop along the highway. The next morning the bodies of Simmons and Moore were discovered in a ditch nearby.

On November 23, after reading about the shootings in an Atlanta newspaper, Weaver communicated with the Gwinnett County police and related information concerning the journey with the victims, including a description of the car. The next afternoon, the petitioner and Allen, while in Simmons' car, were arrested in Asheville, N.C. In the search incident to the arrest a .25-caliber pistol, later shown to be used to kill Simmons and Moore, was found in the petitioner's pocket. After receiving the warnings required by *Miranda v. Arizona*, and signing a written waiver of his rights, the petitioner signed a statement in which he admitted shooting, then robbing Simmons and Moore. He justified the slayings on grounds of self-defense. The next day, while being transferred to Lawrenceville, Ga., the petitioner and Allen were taken to the scene of the shootings. Upon arriving there, Allen recounted the events leading to the slayings. His version of these events was as follows: After Simmons and Moore left the car, the petitioner stated that he intended to rob them. The petitioner then took his pistol in hand and positioned himself on the car to improve his aim. As Simmons and Moore came up an embankment toward the car, the petitioner fired three shots and the two men fell near a ditch. The petitioner, at close range, then fired a shot into the head of each. He robbed them of valuables and drove away with Allen.

A medical examiner testified that Simmons died from a bullet wound in the eye and that Moore died from bullet wounds in the cheek and in the back of the head. He further testified that both men had several bruises and abrasions about the face and head which probably were sustained either from the fall into the ditch or from being dragged or pushed along the embankment. Although Allen did not testify, a police detective recounted the substance of Allen's statements about the slayings and indicated that directly after Allen had made these statements the petitioner had admitted that Allen's account was accurate. The petitioner testified in his own defense. He confirmed that Allen had made the statements described by the detective, but denied their truth or ever having admitted to their accuracy. He indicated that he had shot Simmons and Moore because of fear and in self-defense, testifying they had attacked Allen and him, one wielding a pipe and the other a knife. The trial judge submitted the murder charges to the jury on both felony-murder and nonfelony-murder theories. He also instructed on the issue of self-defense but declined to instruct on manslaughter. He submitted the robbery case to the jury on both an armed-robbery theory and on the lesser included offense of robbery by intimidation. The jury found the petitioner guilty of two counts of armed robbery and two counts of murder.

At the penalty stage, which took place before the same jury, neither the prosecutor nor the petitioner's lawyer offered any additional evidence. Both counsel, however, made lengthy arguments dealing generally with the propriety of capital punishment under the circumstances and with the weight of the evidence of guilt. The trial judge instructed the jury that it could recommend either a death sentence or a life prison sentence on each count. The judge further charged the jury that in determining what sentence was appropriate the jury was free to consider the facts and circumstances, if any, presented by the parties in mitigation or aggravation.

Finally, the judge instructed the jury that it "would not be authorized to consider [imposing] the penalty of death" unless it first found beyond a reasonable doubt one of these aggravating circumstances:

One—That the offense of murder was committed while the offender was engaged in the commission of two other capital felonies, to-wit the armed robbery of [Simmons and Moore].

Two—That the offender committed the offense of murder for the purpose of receiving money and the automobile described in the indictment.

Three—The offense of murder was outrageously and wantonly vile, horrible and inhuman, in that they [sic] involved the depravity of [the] mind of the defendant.

Finding the first and second of these circumstances, the jury returned verdicts of death on each count.

The Supreme Court of Georgia affirmed the convictions and the imposition of the death sentences for murder. After reviewing the trial transcript and the record, including the evidence, and comparing the evidence and sentence in similar cases in accordance with the requirements of Georgia law, the court concluded that, considering the nature of the crime and the defendant, the sentences of death had not resulted from prejudice or any other arbitrary factor and were not excessive or disproportionate to the penalty applied in similar cases.

We granted the petitioner's application for a writ of certiorari limited to his challenge to the imposition of the death sentences in this case as "cruel and unusual" punishment in violation of the Eighth and the Fourteenth Amendments.

Before considering the issues presented it is necessary to understand the Georgia statutory scheme for the imposition of the death penalty. The Georgia statute, as amended after our decision in *Furman v.*

Georgia, retains the death penalty for six categories of crime: murder, kidnapping for ransom or where the victim is harmed, armed robbery, rape, treason, and aircraft hijacking. The capital defendant's guilt or innocence is determined in the traditional manner, either by a trial judge or a jury, in the first stage of a bifurcated trial.

If trial is by jury, the trial judge is required to charge lesser included offenses when they are supported by any view of the evidence. After a verdict, finding, or plea of guilty to a capital crime, a presentence hearing is conducted before whoever made the determination of guilt. The sentencing procedures are essentially the same in both bench and jury trials. At the hearing:

> [T]he judge [or jury] shall hear additional evidence in extenuation, mitigation, and aggravation of punishment, including the record of any prior criminal convictions and pleas of guilty or pleas of nolo contendere of the defendant, or the absence of any prior conviction and pleas: Provided, however, that only such evidence in aggravation as the State has made known to the defendant prior to his trial shall be admissible. The judge [or jury] shall also hear argument by the defendant or his counsel and the prosecuting attorney . . . regarding the punishment to be imposed.

The defendant is accorded substantial latitude as to the types of evidence that he may introduce. Evidence considered during the guilt stage may be considered during the sentencing stage without being resubmitted.

In the assessment of the appropriate sentence to be imposed the judge is also required to consider or to include in his instructions to the jury "any mitigating circumstances or aggravating circumstances otherwise authorized by law and any of [10] statutory aggravating circumstances which may be supported by the evidence . . . ." The scope of the non-statutory aggravating or mitigating circumstances is not delineated in the statute. Before a convicted defendant may be sentenced to death, however, except in cases of treason or aircraft hijacking, the jury, or the trial judge in cases tried without a jury, must find beyond a reasonable doubt one of the 10 aggravating circumstances specified in the statute. If the verdict is death the jury or judge must specify the aggravating circumstance(s) found. In jury cases, the trial judge is bound by the jury's recommended sentence.

In addition to the conventional appellate process available in all criminal cases, provision is made for special expedited direct review by the Supreme Court of Georgia of the appropriateness of imposing the sentence of death in the particular case. The court is directed to consider "the punishment as well as any errors enumerated by way of appeal," and to determine:

1. Whether the sentence of death was imposed under the influence of passion, prejudice, or any other arbitrary factor, and
2. Whether, in cases other than treason or aircraft hijacking, the evidence supports the jury's or judge's finding of a statutory aggravating circumstance . . . .
3. Whether the sentence of death is excessive or disproportionate to the penalty imposed in similar cases, considering both the crime and the defendant.

If the court affirms a death sentence, it is required to include in its decision reference to similar cases that it has taken into consideration.

A transcript and complete record of the trial, as well as a separate report by the trial judge, are transmitted to the court for its use in reviewing the sentence. The report is in the form of a 6 1/2-page questionnaire, designed to elicit information about the defendant, the crime, and the circumstances of the trial. It requires the trial judge to characterize the trial in several ways designed to test for arbitrariness and disproportionality of sentence. Included in the report are responses to detailed questions concerning the quality of the defendant's representation, whether race played a role in the trial, and, whether, in the trial court's judgment, there was any doubt about the defendant's guilt or the appropriateness of the sentence. A copy of the report is served upon defense counsel. Under its special review authority, the court may either affirm the death sentence or remand the case for resentencing. In cases in which the death sentence is affirmed there remains the possibility of executive clemency.

We address initially the basic contention that the punishment of death for the crime of murder is, under all circumstances, "cruel and unusual" in violation of the Eighth and Fourteenth Amendments of the Constitution. . . . We will consider the sentence of death imposed under the Georgia statutes at issue in this case.

The Court on a number of occasions has both assumed and asserted the constitutionality of capital punishment. In several cases that assumption provided a necessary foundation for the decision, as the Court was asked to decide whether a particular method of carrying out a capital sentence would be allowed to stand under the Eighth Amendment. But until *Furman v. Georgia,* the Court never confronted squarely the fundamental claim that the punishment of death always, regardless of the enormity of the offense or the procedure followed in imposing the sentence, is cruel and unusual punishment in violation of the Constitution. Although this issue was presented and addressed in *Furman,* it was not resolved by the Court. Four Justices would have held that capital punishment is not unconstitutional per se; two Justices would have reached the opposite conclusion; and three Justices, while agreeing that the statutes then before the Court were invalid as applied, left open the question whether such punishment may ever be imposed. We now hold that the punishment of death does not invariably violate the Constitution. . . .

The petitioners in the capital cases before the Court today renew the "standards of decency" argument, but developments during the four years since *Furman* have undercut substantially the assumptions upon which their argument rested. Despite the continuing debate, dating back to the 19th century, over the morality and utility of capital punishment, it is now evident that a large proportion of American society continues to regard it as an appropriate and necessary criminal sanction.

The most marked indication of society's endorsement of the death penalty for murder is the legislative response to *Furman.* The legislatures of at least 35 States have enacted new statutes that provide for the death penalty for at least some crimes that result in the death of another person. And the Congress of the United States, in 1974, enacted a statute providing the death penalty for aircraft piracy that results in death. These recently adopted statutes have attempted to address the concerns expressed by the Court in *Furman* primarily (i) by specifying the factors to be weighed and the procedures to be followed in deciding when to impose a capital sentence, or (ii) by making the death penalty mandatory for specified crimes. But all of the post-*Furman* statutes make clear that capital punishment itself has not been rejected by the elected representatives of the people.

In the only statewide referendum occurring since *Furman* and brought to our attention, the people of California adopted a constitutional amendment that authorized capital punishment, in effect negating a prior ruling by the Supreme Court of California that the death penalty violated the California Constitution.

The jury also is a significant and reliable objective index of contemporary values because it is so directly involved. The Court has said that "one of the most important functions any jury can perform in making . . . a selection [between life imprisonment and death for a defendant convicted in a capital case] is to maintain a link between contemporary community values and the penal system." It may be true that evolving standards have influenced juries in recent decades to be more discriminating in imposing the sentence of death. But the relative infrequency of jury verdicts imposing the death sentence does not indicate rejection of capital punishment per se. Rather, the reluctance of juries in many cases to impose the sentence may well reflect the humane feeling that this most irrevocable of sanctions should be reserved for a small number of extreme cases.

Indeed, the actions of juries in many States since *Furman* is fully compatible with the legislative judgments, reflected in the new statutes, as to the continued utility and necessity of capital punishment in appropriate cases. At the close of 1974 at least 254 persons had been sentenced to death since *Furman,* and by the end of March 1976, more than 460 persons were subject to death sentences.

As we have seen, however, the Eighth Amendment demands more than that a challenged punishment be acceptable to contemporary society. The Court also must ask whether it comports with the basic concept of human dignity at the core of the Amendment. Although we cannot "invalidate a category of penalties because we deem less severe penalties adequate to serve the ends of penology,"

the sanction imposed cannot be so totally without penological justification that it results in the gratuitous infliction of suffering.

The death penalty is said to serve two principal social purposes: retribution and deterrence of capital crimes by prospective offenders.

In part, capital punishment is an expression of society's moral outrage at particularly offensive conduct. This function may be unappealing to many, but it is essential in an ordered society that asks its citizens to rely on legal processes rather than self-help to vindicate their wrongs. "Retribution is no longer the dominant objective of the criminal law," but neither is it a forbidden objective nor one inconsistent with our respect for the dignity of men. Indeed, the decision that capital punishment may be the appropriate sanction in extreme cases is an expression of the community's belief that certain crimes are themselves so grievous an affront to humanity that the only adequate response may be the penalty of death.

Statistical attempts to evaluate the worth of the death penalty as a deterrent to crimes by potential offenders have occasioned a great deal of debate. The results simply have been inconclusive.

Although some of the studies suggest that the death penalty may not function as a significantly greater deterrent than lesser penalties, there is no convincing empirical evidence either supporting or refuting this view. We may nevertheless assume safely that there are murderers, such as those who act in passion, for whom the threat of death has little or no deterrent effect. But for many others, the death penalty undoubtedly is a significant deterrent. There are carefully contemplated murders, such as murder for hire, where the possible penalty of death may well enter into the cold calculus that precedes the decision to act. And there are some categories of murder, such as murder by a life prisoner, where other sanctions may not be adequate.

The value of capital punishment as a deterrent of crime is a complex factual issue the resolution of which properly rests with the legislatures, which can evaluate the results of statistical studies in terms of their own local conditions and with a flexibility of approach that is not available to the courts. Indeed, many of the post-*Furman* statutes reflect just such a responsible effort to define those crimes and those criminals for which capital punishment is most probably an effective deterrent.

In sum, we cannot say that the judgment of the Georgia legislature that capital punishment may be necessary in some cases is clearly wrong. Considerations of federalism, as well as respect for the ability of a legislature to evaluate, in terms of its particular state the moral consensus concerning the death penalty and its social utility as a sanction, require us to conclude, in the absence of more convincing evidence, that the infliction of death as a punishment for murder is not without justification and thus is not unconstitutionally severe.

Finally, we must consider whether the punishment of death is disproportionate in relation to the crime for which it is imposed. There is no question that death as a punishment is unique in its severity and irrevocability. When defendant's life is at stake, the Court has been particularly sensitive to insure that every safeguard is observed. But we are concerned here only with the imposition of capital punishment for the crime of murder, and when a life has been taken deliberately by the offender, we cannot say that the punishment is invariably disproportionate to the crime. It is an extreme sanction, suitable to the most extreme of crimes.

We hold that the death penalty is not a form of punishment that may never be imposed, regardless of the circumstances of the offense, regardless of the character of the offender, and regardless of the procedure followed in reaching the decision to impose it.

We now turn to consideration of the constitutionality of Georgia's capital-sentencing procedures. In the wake of *Furman*, Georgia amended its capital punishment statute, but chose not to narrow the scope of its murder provisions. Thus, now as before *Furman*, in Georgia "[a] person commits murder when he unlawfully and with malice aforethought, either express or implied, causes the death of another human being." All persons convicted of murder "shall be punished by death or by imprisonment for life."

Georgia did act, however, to narrow the class of murderers subject to capital punishment by specifying 10 statutory aggravating circumstances, one of which must be found by the jury to exist beyond a reasonable doubt before a death sentence can ever be imposed. In addition, the jury is authorized to consider any other appropriate aggravating or miti-

gating circumstances. The jury is not required to find any mitigating circumstance in order to make a recommendation of mercy that is binding on the trial court, but it must find a statutory aggravating circumstance before recommending a sentence of death.

These procedures require the jury to consider the circumstances of the crime and the criminal before it recommends sentence. No longer can a Georgia jury do as *Furman's* jury did: reach a finding of the defendant's guilt and then, without guidance or direction, decide whether he should live or die. Instead, the jury's attention is directed to the specific circumstances of the crime: Was it committed in the course of another capital felony? Was it committed for money? Was it committed upon a peace officer or judicial officer? Was it committed in a particularly heinous way or in a manner that endangered the lives of many persons? In addition, the jury's attention is focused on the characteristics of the person who committed the crime: Does he have a record of prior convictions for capital offenses? Are there any special facts about this defendant that mitigate against imposing capital punishment (e.g., his youth, the extent of his cooperation with the police, his emotional state at the time of the crime). As a result, while some jury discretion still exists, "the discretion to be exercised is controlled by clear and objective standards so as to produce nondiscriminatory application."

As an important additional safeguard against arbitrariness and caprice, the Georgia statutory scheme provides for automatic appeal of all death sentences to the State's Supreme Court. That court is required by statute to review each sentence of death and determine whether it was imposed under the influence of passion or prejudice, whether the evidence supports the jury's finding of a statutory aggravating circumstance, and whether the sentence is disproportionate compared to those sentences imposed in similar cases.

In short, Georgia's new sentencing procedures require as a prerequisite to the imposition of the death penalty, specific jury findings as to the circumstances of the crime or the character of the defendant. Moreover to guard further against a situation comparable to that presented in *Furman*, the Supreme Court of Georgia compares each death sentence with the sentences imposed on similarly situated defendants to ensure that the sentence of death in a particular case is not disproportionate. On their face these procedures seem to satisfy the concerns of *Furman*. No longer should there be "no meaningful basis for distinguishing the few cases in which [the death penalty] is imposed from the many cases in which it is not."

The basic concern of *Furman* centered on those defendants who were being condemned to death capriciously and arbitrarily. Under the procedures before the Court in that case, sentencing authorities were not directed to give attention to the nature or circumstances of the crime committed or to the character or record of the defendant. Left unguided, juries imposed the death sentence in a way that could only be called freakish. The new Georgia sentencing procedures, by contrast, focus the jury's attention on the particularized nature of the crime and the particularized characteristics of the individual defendant. While the jury is permitted to consider any aggravating or mitigating circumstances, it must find and identify at least one statutory aggravating factor before it may impose a penalty of death. In this way the jury's discretion is channeled. No longer can a jury wantonly and freakishly impose the death sentence; it is always circumscribed by the legislative guidelines. In addition, the review function of the Supreme Court of Georgia affords additional assurance that the concerns that prompted our decision in *Furman* are not present to any significant degree in the Georgia procedure applied here.

Mr. Justice WHITE, with whom The CHIEF JUSTICE and Mr. Justice REHNQUIST join, concurring in the judgment. . . .

Mr. Justice BLACKMUN, concurring in the judgment. . . .

Mr. Justice MARSHALL, dissenting.

In *Furman v. Georgia*, I set forth at some length my views on the basic issue presented to the Court in these cases. The death penalty, I concluded, is a cruel and unusual punishment prohibited by the Eighth and Fourteenth Amendments. That continues to be my view.

In *Furman* I concluded that the death penalty is constitutionally invalid for two reasons. First, the death penalty is excessive. And second, the American people, fully informed as to the purposes of the death penalty and its liabilities, would in my view reject it as morally unacceptable. . . .

The mere fact that the community demands the murderer's life in return for the evil he has done cannot sustain the death penalty, for as the plurality reminds us, "the Eighth Amendment demands more than that a challenged punishment be acceptable to contemporary society." To be sustained under the Eighth Amendment, the death penalty must "[comport] with the basic concept of human dignity at the core of the Amendment." . . . Under these standards, the taking of life "because the wrongdoer deserves it" surely must fall, for such a punishment has as its very basis the total denial of the wrongdoer's dignity and worth.

The death penalty, unnecessary to promote the goal of deterrence or to further any legitimate notion of retribution, is an excessive penalty forbidden by the Eighth and Fourteenth Amendments. I respectfully dissent from the Court's judgment upholding the sentences of death imposed upon the petitioners in these cases.

Mr. Justice BRENNAN, dissenting. . . .

Solem v. Helm
Supreme Court of the United States, 1983.
463 U.S. 277, 103 S. Ct. 3001, 77 L.Ed.2d 637.

[In this case the Supreme Court considers the constitutionality of a South Dakota habitual offender statute.]

Justice POWELL delivered the opinion of the Court. The issue presented is whether the Eighth Amendment proscribes a life sentence without possibility of parole for a seventh nonviolent felony.

I

By 1975 the State of South Dakota had convicted respondent Jerry Helm of six nonviolent felonies. In 1964, 1966, and 1969 Helm was convicted of third-degree burglary. In 1972 he was convicted of obtaining money under false pretenses. In 1973 he was convicted of grand larceny. And in 1975 he was convicted of third-offense driving while intoxicated. The record contains no details about the circumstances of any of these offenses, except that they were all nonviolent, none was a crime against a person, and alcohol was a contributing factor in each case.

In 1979 Helm was charged with [and convicted of] uttering a "no account" check for $100. . . .

Ordinarily the maximum punishment for uttering a "no account" check would have been five years imprisonment in the state penitentiary and a $5,000 fine. . . . As a result of his criminal record, however, Helm was subject to South Dakota's recidivist statute:

> When a defendant has been convicted of at least three prior convictions [sic] in addition to the principal felony, the sentence for the principal felony shall be enhanced to the sentence for a Class 1 felony. S.D. Codified Laws Sec. 22–7–8 (1979) (amended 1981).

The maximum penalty for a "Class 1 felony" was life imprisonment in the state penitentiary and a $25,000 fine. . . . Moreover, South Dakota law explicitly provides that parole is unavailable: "A person sentenced to life imprisonment is not eligible for parole by the board of pardons and paroles." . . . The Governor is authorized to pardon prisoners, or to commute their sentences but no other relief from sentence is available even to a rehabilitated prisoner.

Immediately after accepting Helm's guilty plea, the South Dakota Circuit Court sentenced Helm to life imprisonment. . . . The South Dakota Supreme Court, in a 3–2 decision, affirmed the sentence despite Helm's argument that it violated the Eighth Amendment. . . .

After Helm had served two years in the state penitentiary, he requested the Governor to commute his sentence to a fixed term of years. Such a commutation would have had the effect of making Helm eligible to be considered for parole when he had served three-fourths of his new sentence. . . . The Governor denied Helm's request in May 1981. . . .

In November 1981, Helm sought habeas relief in the United States District Court for the District of South Dakota. . . . [The Court] denied the writ. The United States Court of Appeals for the Eighth Circuit reversed. . . .

We granted certiorari to consider the Eighth Amendment question presented by this case. . . . We now affirm.

II

The Eighth Amendment declares: "Excessive bail shall not be required, nor excessive fines imposed, nor cruel and unusual punishments inflicted." The final clause prohibits not only barbaric punishments, but also sentences that are disproportionate to the crime committed. . . .

In sum, we hold as a matter of principle that a criminal sentence must be proportionate to the crime for which the defendant has been convicted. Reviewing courts, of course, should grant substantial deference to the broad authority that legislatures necessarily possess in determining the types and limits of punishments for crimes, as well as to the discretion that trial courts possess in sentencing convicted criminals. But no penalty is per se constitutional. As the Court noted in *Robinson v. California*, . . . a single day in prison may be unconstitutional in some circumstances.

III

[omitted]

IV

It remains to apply the analytical framework established by our prior decisions to the case before us. We first consider the relevant criteria, viewing Helm's sentence as life imprisonment without possibility of parole. We then consider the state's argument that the possibility of commutation is sufficient to save an otherwise unconstitutional sentence.

A

Helm's crime was "one of the most passive felonies a person could commit." ... It involved neither violence nor threat of violence to any person. The $100 face value of Helm's "no-account" check was not trivial, but neither was it a large amount. One hundred dollars was less than half the amount South Dakota required for a felonious theft. It is easy to see why such a crime is viewed by society as among the less serious offenses. ...

Helm, of course, was not charged simply with uttering a "no-account" check, but also with being an habitual offender. And a State is justified in punishing a recidivist more severely than it punishes a first offender. Helm's status, however, cannot be considered in the abstract. His prior offenses, although classified as felonies, were all relatively minor. All were non-violent and none was crime against a person. Indeed, there was no minimum amount in either the burglary or the false pretenses statutes ... and the minimum amount covered by the grand larceny statute was fairly small. ...

Helm's present sentence is life imprisonment without possibility of parole. ... Helm's sentence is the most severe punishment that the State could have imposed on any criminal for any crime. ... Only capital punishment, a penalty not authorized in South Dakota when Helm was sentenced, exceeds it.

We next consider the sentences that could be imposed on other criminals in the same jurisdiction. When Helm was sentenced, a South Dakota court was required to impose a life sentence for murder, ... and was authorized to impose a life sentence for treason, ... first degree manslaughter, ... first degree arson, ... and kidnapping .... No other crime was punishable so severely on the first offense. Attempted murder, ... placing an explosive device on an aircraft, ... and first degree rape, ... were only Class 2 felonies. Aggravated riot was only a Class 3 felony. ... Distribution of heroin, ... and aggravated assault, ... were only Class 4 felonies.

Helm's habitual offender status complicates our analysis, but relevant comparisons are still possible. Under [South Dakota law] the penalty for a second or third felony is increased by one class. Thus a life sentence was mandatory when a second or third conviction was for treason, first degree manslaugh-

ter, first degree arson, or kidnapping, and a life sentence was mandatory when a second or third conviction was for such crimes as attempted murder, placing an explosive device on an aircraft, or first degree rape. Finally, [the law] under which Helm was sentenced, authorized life imprisonment after three prior convictions, regardless of the crimes.

In sum, there were a handful of crimes that were necessarily punished by life imprisonment: murder, and, on a second or third offense, treason, first degree manslaughter, first degree arson, and kidnapping. There was a larger group for which life imprisonment was authorized in the discretion of the sentencing judge, including: treason, first degree manslaughter, first degree arson, and kidnapping; attempted murder, placing an explosive device on an aircraft, and first degree rape on a second or third offense; and any felony after three prior offenses. Finally, there was a large group of very serious offenses for which life imprisonment was not authorized, including a third offense of heroin dealing or aggravated assault.

Criminals committing any of these offenses ordinarily would be thought more deserving of punishment than one uttering a "no account" check—even when the bad-check writer had already committed six minor felonies. Moreover, there is no indication in the record that any habitual offender other than Helm has ever been given the maximum sentence on the basis of comparable crimes. It is more likely that the possibility of life imprisonment ... generally is reserved for criminals such as fourth-time heroin dealers, while habitual bad-check writers receive more lenient treatment. In any event, Helm has been treated in the same manner as, or more severely than, criminals who have committed far more serious crimes.

Finally, we compare the sentences imposed for commission of the same crime in other jurisdictions. The Court of Appeals found that "Helm could have received a life sentence without parole for his offense in only one other state, Nevada," ... and we have no reason to doubt this finding. ... At the very least, therefore, it is clear that Helm could not have received such a severe sentence in 48 of the 50 States. But even under Nevada law, a life sentence without possibility of parole is merely authorized in these circumstances. . . . We are not advised that any defendant such as Helm, whose prior offenses were so minor, actually has received the maximum penalty in Nevada. It appears that Helm was treated more severely than he would have been in any other States. . . .

V

The Constitution requires us to examine Helm's sentence to determine if it is proportionate to his crime. Applying objective criteria, we find that Helm has received that penultimate sentence for relatively minor criminal conduct. He has been treated more harshly than other criminals in the State who have committed more serious crimes. He has been treated more harshly than he would have been in any other jurisdiction, with the possible exception of a single State. We conclude that his sentence is significantly disproportionate to his crime, and is therefore prohibited by the Eighth Amendment. The judgment of the Court of Appeals is accordingly Affirmed.

Chief Justice BURGER, with whom Justice WHITE, Justice REHNQUIST, and Justice O'CONNOR join, dissenting.

The controlling law governing this case is crystal clear, but today the Court blithely discards any concept of stare decisis, trespasses gravely on the authority of the States, and distorts the concept of proportionality of punishment by tearing it from its moorings in capital cases. Only two Terms ago, we held in *Rummel v. Estelle*, 445 U.S. 263, 100 S.Ct. 1133, 63 L.Ed.2d 382 (1980), that a life sentence imposed after only a third nonviolent felony conviction did not constitute cruel and unusual punishment under the Eighth Amendment. Today, the Court ignores its recent precedent and holds that a life sentence imposed after a seventh felony conviction constitutes cruel and unusual punishment under the Eighth Amendment. Moreover, I reject the fiction that all Helm's crimes were innocuous or nonviolent. Among his felonies were three burglaries and a third conviction for drunk driving. By comparison Rummel was a relatively "model citizen." Although today's holding cannot rationally be reconciled with *Rummel*, the Court does not purport to overrule *Rummel*. I therefore dissent. . . .

HUTTO V. FINNEY

Supreme Court of the United States, 1978.
437 U.S. 678, 98 S. Ct. 2565, 57 L.Ed.2d 522.

[In this decision, the Supreme Court upholds a federal district court order stemming from litigation challenging prison conditions in Arkansas.]

Mr. Justice STEVENS delivered the opinion of the Court.
After finding that conditions in the Arkansas penal system constituted cruel and unusual punishment, the District Court entered a series of detailed remedial orders. On appeal to the United States Court of Appeals for the Eighth Circuit, petitioners challenged . . . an order placing a maximum limit of 30 days on confinement in punitive isolation. . . .

The Court of Appeals affirmed. . . . We granted certiorari . . . and now affirm.

This litigation began in 1969; it is a sequel to two earlier cases holding that conditions in the Arkansas prison system violated the Eighth and Fourteenth Amendments. Only a brief summary of the facts is necessary to explain the basis for the remedial order.

The routine conditions that the ordinary Arkansas convict had to endure were characterized by the District Court as a "dark and evil world completely alien to the free world." ... That characterization was amply supported by the evidence.[#]

The inmates slept together in large, 100-man barracks and some convicts, known as "creepers," would slip from their beds to crawl along the floor, stalking their sleeping enemies. In one 18-month period, there were 17 stabbings, all but one occurring in the barracks. Homosexual rape was so common and uncontrolled that some potential victims dared not sleep; instead they would leave their beds and spend the night clinging to the bars nearest the guards' station. The punishments for misconduct not serious enough to result in punitive isolation were cruel,[$] unusual,[a] and unpredictable.[&] It is the

discipline known as "punitive isolation" that is most relevant for present purposes.

Confinement in punitive isolation was for an indeterminate period of time. An average of four, and sometimes as many as 10 or 11, prisoners were crowded into windowless 8' × 10' cells containing no furniture other than a source of water and a toilet that could only be flushed from outside the cell. At night the prisoners were given mattresses to spread on the floor. Although some prisoners suffered from infectious diseases such as hepatitis and venereal disease, mattresses were removed and jumbled together each morning, then returned to the cells at random in the evening. Prisoners in isolation received fewer than 1,000 calories a day; their meals consisted primarily of 4-inch squares of "grue," a substance created by mashing meat, potatoes, oleo, syrup, vegetables, eggs, and seasoning into a paste and baking the mixture in a pan.

After finding the conditions of confinement unconstitutional, the District Court did not immediately impose a detailed remedy of its own. Instead, it directed the Department of Correction to "make a substantial start" on improving conditions and to file reports on its progress.... When the Department's progress proved unsatisfactory, a second hearing was held. The District Court found some improvements, but concluded that prison conditions remained unconstitutional.... Again the court offered prison administrators an opportunity to devise a plan of their own for remedying the constitutional violations, but this time the court issued guidelines, identifying four areas of change that would cure the worst evils: improving conditions in the isolation cells, increasing inmate safety, eliminating the barracks sleeping arrangements, and putting an end to the trusty system.... The Department was ordered to move as rapidly as funds became available....

After this order was affirmed on appeal.... more hearings were held in 1972 and 1973 to review the Department's progress. Finding substantial improvements, the court concluded that continuing supervision was no longer necessary. The court held, however, that its prior decrees would remain in effect and noted that sanctions, as well as an award of costs and attorney's fees, would be imposed if violations occurred....

[#]The administrators of Arkansas's prison system evidently tried to operate their prisons at a profit. Cummins Farm, the institution at the center of this litigation, required its 1,000 inmates to work in the fields ten hours a day, six days a week, using mule-drawn tools and tending crops by hand. The inmates were sometimes required to run to and from the fields, with a guard in an automobile or on horseback driving them on. They worked in all sorts of weather, so long as the temperature was above freezing, sometimes in unsuitable light clothing or without shoes.

[$]Inmates were lashed with a wooden-handled leather strap five feet long and four inches wide. Although it was not official policy to do so, some inmates were apparently whipped for minor offenses until their skin was bloody and bruised.

[a]The "Tucker telepone," a hand-cranked device, was used to administer electrical shocks to various sensitive parts of an inmate's body.

[&]Most of the guards were simply inmates who had been issued guns. Although it had 1,000 prisoners, Cummins employed only eight guards who were not themselves convicts. Only two nonconvict guards kept watch over the 1,000 men at night. While the "trusties" maintained an appearance of order, they took a high toll from the other prisoners. Inmates could obtain access to medical treatment only if they bribed the trusty in charge of sick call. As the district court found, it was "within the power of a trusty guard to murder another inmate with practical impunity," because trusties with weapons were authorized to use deadly force against escapees. "Accidental shootings" also occurred, and one trusty fired his shotgun into a crowded barracks because the inmates would not turn off their TV. Another trusty beat an inmate so badly the victim required partial dentures.

The Court of Appeals reversed the District Court's decision to withdraw its supervisory jurisdiction, . . . and the District Court held a fourth set of hearings. . . . It found that, in some respects, conditions had seriously deteriorated since 1973, when the court had withdrawn its supervisory jurisdiction. Cummins Farm, which the court had condemned as overcrowded in 1970 because it housed 1,000 inmates, now had a population of about 1,500. . . . The situation in the punitive isolation cells was particularly disturbing. The court concluded that either it had misjudged conditions in these cells in 1973 or conditions had become much worse since then. . . . There were still twice as many prisoners as beds in some cells. And because inmates in punitive isolation are often violently antisocial, overcrowding led to persecution of the weaker prisoners. The "grue" diet was still in use, and practically all inmates were losing weight on it. The cells had been vandalized to a "very substantial" extent. . . . Because of their inadequate numbers, guards assigned to the punitive isolation cells frequently resorted to physical violence, using nightsticks and Mace in their efforts to maintain order. Prisoners were sometimes left in isolation for months, their release depending on "their attitudes as appraised by prison personnel."

The court concluded that the constitutional violations identified earlier had not been cured. It entered an order that placed limits on the number of men that could be confined in one cell, required that each have a bunk, discontinued the "grue" diet, and set 30 days as the maximum isolation sentence. The District Court gave detailed consideration to the matter of fees and expenses, made an express finding that petitioners had acted in bad faith, and awarded counsel "a fee of $20,000.00 to be paid out of [the] Department of Correction funds." . . . The Court of Appeals affirmed and assessed an additional $2,500 to cover fees and expenses on appeal. . . .

. . . The Eighth Amendment's ban on inflicting cruel and unusual punishments, made applicable to the States by the Fourteenth Amendment, "proscribes more than physically barbarous punishments." . . . It prohibits penalties that are grossly disproportionate to the offense, . . . as well as those that transgress today's broad and idealistic concepts of dignity, civilized standards, humanity, and decency." . . . Confinement in a prison or in an isolation cell is a form of punishment subject to scrutiny under Eighth Amendment standards. Petitioners do not challenge this proposition; nor do they disagree with the District Court's original conclusion that Arkansas prisons, including its punitive isolation cells, constituted cruel and unusual punishment. Rather, petitioners single out that portion of the District Court's most recent order that forbids the Department to sentence inmates to more than 30 days in punitive isolation. Petitioners assume that the District Court held that indeterminate sentences to punitive isolation always constitute cruel and unusual punishments. This assumption misreads the District Court's holding.

Read in its entirety, the District Court's opinion makes it abundantly clear that the length of isolation sentences was not considered in a vacuum. In the court's words, punitive isolation "is not necessarily unconstitutional, but it may be, depending on the duration of the confinement and the conditions thereof." . . . It is perfectly obvious that every decision to remove a particular inmate from general prison population for an indeterminate period could not be characterized as cruel and unusual. If new conditions of confinement are not materially different from those affecting other prisoners, a transfer for the duration of a prisoner's sentence might be completely unobjectionable and well within the authority of the prison administrator. . . . It is equally plain, however, that the length of confinement cannot be ignored in deciding whether the confinement meets constitutional standards. A filthy, overcrowded cell and a diet of "grue" might be tolerated for a few days and be intolerably cruel for weeks or months.

The question before the trial court was whether past constitutional violations had been remedied. The court was entitled to consider the severity of those violations in assessing the constitutionality of conditions in the isolation cells. The court took note of the inmates' diet, the continued overcrowding, the rampant violence, the vandalized cells, and the "lack of professionalism and good judgment on the part of maximum security personnel." . . . The length of time each inmate spent in isolation was simply one consideration among many. We find no error in the court's conclusion that, taken as a whole, conditions in the isolation cells continued to violate the prohibition against cruel and unusual punishment.

The judgment of the Court of Appeals is accordingly affirmed.

Mr. Justice POWELL, with whom the CHIEF JUSTICE joins, concurring in part and dissenting in part. . . .

Mr. Justice REHNQUIST, dissenting.

. . . No person of ordinary feeling could fail to be moved by the Court's recitation of the conditions formerly prevailing in the Arkansas prison system. Yet I fear the Court has allowed itself to be moved beyond the well-established bounds limiting the exercise of remedial authority by the federal district courts. . . .

The District Court's order limiting the maximum period of punitive isolation to 30 days in no way related to any condition found offensive to the Constitution. It is, when stripped of descriptive verbiage, a prophylactic rule, doubtless well designed to assure a more humane prison system in Arkansas, but not complying with [the limitations on district court remedies]. . . .

Certainly the provision is not remedial in the sense that it "restore[s] the victims of discriminatory conduct to the position they would have occupied in the absence of such conduct." . . . The sole effect of the provision is to grant future offenders against prison discipline greater benefits than the Constitution requires; it does nothing to remedy the plight of past victims of conditions which may well have been unconstitutional. . . .

PAYNE V. TENNESSEE
Supreme Court of the United States, 1991.
501 U.S. ___ , 111 S.Ct. 2597, 115 L.Ed.2d 720.

[In this case the Supreme Court overturns its decisions in *Booth v. Maryland*, 482 U.S. 496, 107 S.Ct. 2529, 96 L.Ed.2d 440 (1987), and *South Carolina v. Gathers*, 490 U.S. 805, 109 S.Ct. 2207, 104 L.Ed.2d 876 (1989), barring the admission of victim impact evidence during the sentencing phase of a capital trial.]

Chief Justice REHNQUIST delivered the opinion of the Court.

. . . The petitioner, Pervis Tyrone Payne, was convicted by a jury on two counts of first-degree murder and one count of assault with intent to commit murder in the first degree. He was sentenced to death for each of the murders, and to 30 years in prison for the assault.

The victims of Payne's offenses were 28-year-old Charisse Christopher, her 2-year-old daughter Lacie, and her 3-year-old son Nicholas. The three lived together in an apartment in Millington, Tennessee, across the hall from Payne's girlfriend, Bobbie Thomas. On Saturday, June 27, 1987, Payne visited Tho-

mas' apartment several times in expectation of her return from her mother's house in Arkansas, but found no one at home. On one visit, he left his overnight bag, containing clothes and other items for his weekend stay, in the hallway outside Thomas' apartment. With the bag were three cans of malt liquor.

Payne passed the morning and early afternoon injecting cocaine and drinking beer. Later, he drove around the town with a friend in the friend's car, each of them taking turns reading a pornographic magazine. Sometime around 3 P.M., Payne returned to the apartment complex, entered the Christophers' apartment, and began making sexual advances towards Charisse. Charisse resisted and Payne became violent. A neighbor who resided in the apartment directly beneath the Christophers, heard Charisse screaming, " 'Get out, get out' as if she were telling the children to leave." The noise briefly subsided and then began " 'horribly loud.' " The neighbor called the police after she heard a "blood curdling scream" from the Christopher apartment. . . .

When the first police officer arrived at the scene, he immediately encountered Payne who was leaving the apartment building, so covered with blood that he appeared to be " 'sweating blood.' " The officer confronted Payne, who responded, " 'I'm the complainant.' " . . . When the officer asked, " 'What's going on up there?' " Payne struck the officer with the overnight bag, dropped his tennis shoes, and fled.

Inside the apartment, the police encountered a horrifying scene. Blood covered the walls and floor throughout the unit. Charisse and her children were lying on the floor in the kitchen. Nicholas, despite several wounds inflicted by a butcher knife that completely penetrated through his body from front to back, was still breathing. Miraculously, he survived, but not until after undergoing seven hours of surgery and a transfusion of 1700 cc's of blood—400 to 500 cc's more than his estimated normal blood volume. Charisse and Lacie were dead.

Charisse's body was found on the kitchen floor on her back, her legs fully extended. She had sustained 42 direct knife wounds and 42 defensive wounds on her arms and hands. The wounds were caused by 41 separate thrusts of a butcher knife. None of the 84 wounds inflicted by Payne were individually fatal; rather, the cause of death was most likely bleeding from all of the wounds.

Lacie's body was on the kitchen floor near her mother. She had suffered stab wounds to the chest, abdomen, back, and head. The murder weapon, a butcher knife, was found at her feet. Payne's baseball cap was snapped on her arm near her elbow. Three cans of malt liquor bearing Payne's fingerprints were found on a table near her body, and a fourth empty one was on the landing outside the apartment door.

Payne was apprehended later that day hiding in the attic of the home of a former girlfriend. As he descended the stairs of the attic, he stated to the arresting officers, "Man, I ain't killed no woman." According to one of the officers, Payne had "a wild look about him. His pupils were contracted. He was foaming at the mouth, saliva. He appeared to be very nervous. He was breathing real rapid." He had blood on his body and clothes and several scratches across his chest. It was later determined that the

blood stains matched the victims' blood types. A search of his pockets revealed a packet containing cocaine residue, a hypodermic syringe wrapper, and a cap from a hypodermic syringe. His overnight bag, containing a bloody white shirt, was found in a nearby dumpster.

At trial, Payne took the stand and, despite the overwhelming and relatively uncontroverted evidence against him, testified that he had not harmed any of the Christophers. Rather, he asserted that another man had raced by him as he was walking up the stairs to the floor where the Christophers lived. He stated that he had gotten blood on himself when, after hearing moans from the Christopher's apartment, he had tried to help the victims. According to his testimony, he panicked and fled when he heard police sirens and noticed the blood on his clothes. The jury returned guilty verdicts against Payne on all counts.

During the sentencing phase of the trial, Payne presented the testimony of four witnesses: his mother and father, Bobbie Thomas, and Dr. John T. Huston, a clinical psychologist specializing in criminal court evaluation work. Bobbie Thomas testified that she met Payne at church, during a time when she was being abused by her husband. She stated that Payne was a very caring person, and that he devoted much time and attention to her three children, who were being affected by her marital difficulties. She said that the children had come to love him very much and would miss him and that he "behaved just like a father that loved his kids." She asserted that he did not drink, nor did he use drugs, and that it was generally inconsistent with Payne's character to have committed these crimes.

Dr. Huston testified that based on Payne's low score on an IQ test, Payne was "mentally handicapped." Huston also said that Payne was neither psychotic nor schizophrenic, and that Payne was the most polite prisoner he had ever met. Payne's parents testified that their son had no prior criminal record and had never been arrested. They also stated that Payne had no history of alcohol or drug abuse, he worked with his father as a painter, he was good with children, and that he was a good son.

The State presented the testimony of Charisse's mother, Mary Zvolanek. When asked how Nicholas had been affected by the murders of his mother and sister, she responded:

"He cries for his mom. He doesn't seem to understand why she doesn't come home. And he cries for his sister Lacie. He comes to me many times during the week and asks me, Grandmama, do you miss my Lacie. And I tell him yes. He says, I'm worried about my Lacie." . . .

In arguing for the death penalty during closing argument, the prosecutor commented on the continuing effects of Nicholas' experience, stating:

"But we do know that Nicholas was alive. And Nicholas was in the same room. Nicholas was still conscious. His eyes were open. He responded to the paramedics. He was able to follow their directions. He was able to hold his intestines in as he was carried to the ambulance. So he knew what happened to his mother and baby sister." . . .

"There is nothing you can do to ease the pain of any of the families involved in this case. There is nothing you can do to ease the pain of Bernice or Carl Payne, and that's a tragedy. There is nothing you can do basically to ease the pain of Mr. and Mrs. Zvolanek, and that's a tragedy. They will have to live with it the rest of their lives. There is obviously nothing you can do for Charisse and Lacie Jo. But there is something that you can do for Nicholas.

"Somewhere down the road Nicholas is going to grow up, hopefully. He's going to want to know what happened. And he is going to know what happened to his baby sister and his mother. He is going to want to know what type of justice was done. He is going to want to know what happened. With your verdict, you will provide the answer." . . .

In the rebuttal to Payne's closing argument, the prosecutor stated:

"You saw the videotape this morning. You saw what Nicholas Christopher will carry in his mind forever. When you talk about cruel, when you talk about atrocious, and when you talk about heinous, that picture will always come into your mind, probably throughout the rest of your lives.

". . . No one will ever know about Lacie Jo because she never had the chance to grow up. Her life was taken from her at the age of two years old. So, no, there won't be a high school-principal to talk about Lacie Jo Christopher, and there won't be anybody to take her to her high school prom. And there won't be anybody there—there won't be her mother there or Nicholas' mother there to kiss him at night. His mother will never kiss him good night or pat him as he goes off to bed, or hold him and sing him a lullaby.

"[Petitioner's attorney] wants you to think about a good reputation, people who love the defendant and things about him. He doesn't want you to think about the people who love Charisse Christopher, her mother and daddy who loved her. The people who loved little Lacie Jo, the grandparents who are still here. The brother who mourns for her every single day and wants to know where his best little playmate is. He doesn't have anybody to watch cartoons with him, a little one. These are the things that go into why it is especially cruel, heinous, and atrocious, the burden that that child will carry forever." . . .

The jury sentenced Payne to death on each of the murder counts.

The Supreme Court of Tennessee affirmed the convictions and sentence. The court rejected Payne's contention that the admission of the grandmother's testimony and the State's closing argument constituted prejudicial violations of his rights under the Eighth Amendment. . . . but concluded that it "did not create a constitutionally unacceptable risk of an arbitrary imposition of the death penalty and was harmless beyond a reasonable doubt." . . .

The court determined that the prosecutor's comments during closing argument were "relevant to [Payne's] personal responsibility and moral guilt." The court explained that "[w]hen a person deliberately picks a butcher knife out of a kitchen drawer and proceeds to stab to death a twenty-eight-year-old mother, her two and one-half year old daughter and her three and one-half year old son, in the same room the physical and mental condition of the boy he left for dead is surely relevant in determining his 'blameworthiness.'" The court concluded that any violations of Payne's rights under *Booth [v. Maryland]* and *[South Carolina v.] Gathers* "was harmless beyond a reasonable doubt." . . .

We granted certiorari . . . to reconsider our holdings in *Booth* and *Gathers*. . . .

We are now of the view that a State may properly conclude that for the jury to assess meaningfully the defendant's moral culpability and blameworthiness, it should have before it at the sentencing phase evidence of the specific harm caused by the defendant. "[T]he State has a legitimate interest in counteracting the mitigating evidence which the defendant is entitled to put in, by reminding the sentencer that just as the murderer should be considered as an individual, so too the victim is an individual whose death represents a unique loss to society and in particular to his family." . . . *Booth* deprives the State of the full moral force of its evidence and may prevent the jury from having before it all the information necessary to determine the proper punishment for a first-degree murder.

The present case is an example of the potential for such unfairness. The capital sentencing jury heard testimony from Payne's girlfriend that they met at church, that he was affectionate, caring, kind to her children, that he was not an abuser of drugs or alcohol, and that it was inconsistent with his character to have committed the murder. Payne's parents testified that he was a good son, and a clinical psychologist testified that Payne was an extremely polite prisoner and suffered from a low IQ. None of this testimony was related to the circumstances of Payne's brutal crimes. In contrast, the only evidence of the impact of Payne's offenses during the sentencing phase was Nicholas' grandmother's description—in response to a single question—that the child misses his mother and baby sister. Payne argues that the Eighth Amendment commands that the jury's death sentence must be set aside because the jury heard this testimony. But the testimony illustrated quite poignantly some of the harm that Payne's killing had caused; there is nothing unfair about allowing the jury to bear in mind that harm at the same time as it considers the mitigating evidence introduced by the defendant. The Supreme Court of Tennessee in this case obviously felt the unfairness of the rule pronounced by *Booth* when it said "[i]t is an affront to the civilized members of the human race to say that at sentencing in a capital case, a parade of witnesses may praise the background, character and good deeds of Defendant (as was done in this case) without limitation as to relevancy, but nothing may be said that bears upon the character of, or the harm imposed, upon the victims." . . .

We thus hold that if the State chooses to permit the admission of victim impact evidence and prosecutorial argument on that subject, the Eighth Amendment erects no *per se* bar. A State may legitimately conclude that evidence about the victim and about the impact of the murder on the victim's family is relevant to the jury's decision as to whether or not the death penalty should be imposed. There is no reason to treat such evidence differently than other relevant evidence is treated. . . . Reconsidering these decisions now, we conclude for the reasons heretofore stated, that they were wrongly decided and should be, and now are, overruled. We accordingly affirm the judgment of the Supreme Court of Tennessee.

Justice O'CONNOR, with whom Justice WHITE and Justice KENNEDY join, concurring. . . .

Justice SCALIA, with whom Justice O'CONNOR and Justice KENNEDY join [in part], concurring. . . .

Justice SOUTER, with whom Justice KENNEDY joins, concurring. . . .

Justice MARSHALL, with whom Justice BLACKMUN joins, dissenting. . . .

Justice STEVENS, with whom Justice BLACKMUN joins, dissenting.

. . . Until today our capital punishment jurisprudence has required that any decision to impose the death penalty be based solely on evidence that tends to inform the jury about the character of the offense and the character of the defendant. Evidence that serves no purpose other than to appeal to the sympathies or emotions of the jurors has never been considered admissible. Thus, if a defendant, who had murdered a convenience store clerk in cold blood in the course of an armed robbery, offered evidence unknown to him at the time of the crime about the immoral character of his victim, all would recognize immediately that the evidence was irrelevant and inadmissible. Even-handed justice requires that the same constraint be imposed on the advocate of the death penalty. . . .

CHAPTER **19**

APPEAL AND POSTCONVICTION RELIEF

CHAPTER OUTLINE

Introduction
The Common-Law
  Background
Criminal Appeals in the
  United States
The Appellate Process
Postconviction Relief
Criticism of the Appeals
  Process

Nonjudicial Remedies
  Available to Persons
  Convicted of Crimes
Conclusion

Cases
Douglas v. California
Fay v. Noia
Stone v. Powell
Darden v. Wainwright
McCleskey v. Zant
Keeney v. Tamayo-Reyes

INTRODUCTION

S ociety's commitment to standards of fairness and procedural regularity is reflected in the opportunities that exist for defendants in criminal cases to seek higher judicial review of adverse court decisions. These opportunities have greatly increased since the 1960s, largely as a consequence of the courts' expansion of the rights of the accused.

Forms of review in criminal cases include *trial de novo, appeal by right, discretionary review* (certiorari), and *postconviction relief.* Each of these mechanisms plays an important part in the determination of cases that move beyond the trial stage of the criminal process. In addition to performing the function of correcting errors made by lower courts, appeals allow higher courts to refine and standardize both the substantive and procedural law.

THE COMMON-LAW BACKGROUND

Prior to the eighteenth century, there was no common-law right to appeal from a criminal conviction. On rare occasions the Crown issued a "writ of error" to require a new trial, but there was no "appeal" in the modern sense. Indeed, the term *appeal* at common law had a very different usage from ours. At common law, appeal referred to an effort by a person convicted of treason to obtain a pardon from the Crown by accusing others of being accomplices to the treasonable act.

In a landmark decision, the Court of King's Bench ruled in 1705 that a writ of error had to be issued where a person convicted of a misdemeanor made proper application for the writ. *Paty's Case,* 91 Eng. Rep. 431 (K.B. 1705). In cases of felony and treason, the writ of error continued to be discretionary, although after 1700 the courts became more liberal in their issuance of the writ. The writ of error was finally abolished when Parliament enacted the Criminal Appeal Act of 1907, affording defendants the right to appeal their convictions.

CRIMINAL APPEALS IN THE UNITED STATES

The federal Constitution makes no mention of the right to appeal from a criminal conviction, although some might argue that the right to appeal is implicit in the due process clauses of the Fifth and Fourteenth Amendments. In 1894, the United States Supreme Court held that the federal Constitution affords no right to appeal from a criminal conviction. *McKane v. Durston,* 153 U.S. 684, 14 S. Ct. 913, 38 L.Ed. 867 (1894). Given the recent expansion of the concept of due process, it is likely that the Court would reconsider this holding, but for the fact that federal and state statutes allow criminal defendants to appeal their convictions and seek other forms of postconviction relief. Defendants convicted after entering a plea of not guilty are entitled under federal and state law to one appeal as a matter of right. A defendant whose conviction is affirmed on appeal may seek further review by higher courts through *certiorari.* Finally, a defendant confined to prison may seek further review of his or her conviction or sentence by applying for a writ of *habeas corpus.*

Appeals by right in federal criminal cases are heard by United States Courts of Appeal (circuit courts). State criminal appeals are heard by state supreme courts, intermediate appellate courts, and in four states (Alabama, Oklahoma, Tennessee, and Texas), by specialized courts that hear only criminal appeals. Beyond these appeals by right, opportunities exist for defendants to have their cases reviewed by the highest state courts and the United States Supreme Court, which may review convictions by issuing writs of *certiorari.* Many states provide for automatic appeal of death sentences to their highest court (see Chapter 18).

A party who takes an appeal by right is called the appellant; the party against whom the appeal is taken is the appellee. A party who seeks further review is referred to as the petitioner; the other party is designated the respondent.

What Defendants May Challenge on Appeal

In a direct appeal from a criminal conviction, a defendant may challenge any act of the trial court objected to by the defendant during the pretrial, trial, or posttrial phases of the defendant's case. Irrespective of whether an objection was made in the trial court, a defendant may challenge the trial court's jurisdiction and those trial court actions or rulings considered to be "fundamental errors." Appellate courts take different approaches to how serious an error must be to be classified as fundamental. Courts are more liberal in reviewing errors first challenged at the appellate stage where the defendant has been convicted of a capital crime. Indeed, the United States Supreme Court has said that those fundamental errors not specifically challenged by the appellant should be corrected when a person's life is at stake. *Fisher v. United States,* 328 U.S. 463, 66 S. Ct. 1318, 90 L.Ed. 1382 (1946).

In practice a defendant usually raises from one to six major points on appeal as a basis for reversal of the trial court's judgment and/or sentence. The most common points raised by defendants on direct appeal are claims that the trial court erred in rulings in one or more of the following areas:

1. Pretrial violations of the defendant's rights, particularly those rights guaranteed by the Fourth, Fifth, and Sixth Amendments to the federal Constitution
2. Procedural matters, especially trial court rulings admitting or excluding evidence
3. Irregularities in the empaneling or conduct of the jury
4. Interpretations of statutes or ordinances
5. Prosecutorial misconduct such as improper remarks or arguments
6. Sufficiency of the evidence to support a finding of the defendant's guilt beyond a reasonable doubt
7. Failure to give jury instructions requested by the defendant or the giving of instructions objected to by the defendant
8. The legality and, in some jurisdictions, the reasonableness of the sentence imposed
9. Jury selection, deliberation, and misconduct
10. The voluntariness of a guilty plea

TABLE 19.1   Distribution of Outcomes in Five Appellate Courts*

Appeal Outcomes	Percent of all Appeals	Percent of Nonaffirmances
Affirmed	79.4	—
Reversed	20.6	100.0
Acquitted	1.9	9.4
New trial	6.6	31.9
Resentencing	7.3	35.3
Other	4.8	23.4

Source: Reprinted, with permission, from Joy A. Chapper and Roger A. Hanson, "Understanding Reversible Error in Criminal Appeals," Final Report Submitted to the State Justice Institute, National Center for State Courts, October 1989, p. 5.
*Based on a survey of criminal appeals in five courts: the California Court of Appeal, 3rd District; the Colorado Court of Appeals; the Appellate Court of Illinois, 4th District; the Maryland Court of Special Appeals; and the Rhode Island Supreme Court.

TABLE 19.2   Reversible Error by Issue; Success Rate for Selected Issues*

Issue	Percentage of All Error Associated with Issue	Success Rate
Admission/exclusion of evidence	20.6%	7.7%
Instructions	13.5	9.7
Procedural or discretionary ruling	13.1	7.8
Sufficiency of the evidence	12.0	5.8
Merger of offenses	10.5	51.9
Suppression of evidence, statements, or identification	10.5	8.4
Ineffective assistance/waiver of counsel	6.0	12.9
Other constitutional claims (double jeopardy, speedy trial)	4.9	11.5
Jury selection or deliberation	3.4	8.8
Statutory interpretation or application	2.2	19.4
Plea voluntariness	2.2	15.0
Prosecutoral misconduct	1.1	1.9

Source: Reprinted with permission, from Joy A. Chapper and Roger A. Hanson, "Understanding Reversible Error in Criminal Appeals," Final Report Submitted to the State Justice Institute, National Center for State Courts, October 1989, p. 41.
*Based on a survey of criminal appeals in five courts: the California Court of Appeal, 3rd District; the Colorado Court of Appeals; the Appellate Court of Illinois, 4th District; the Maryland Court of Special Appeals; and the Rhode Island Supreme Court.

Table 19.1 shows the distribution of outcomes in five representative appellate courts. It indicates that nearly 80 percent of all judgments were affirmed in these courts during the period under study. Of the reversals, the most frequent outcome was remand for resentencing. In less than 10 percent of these reversals did defendants win acquittal outright. Table 19.2 indicates that the most frequent claims of error in criminal appeals in these five appellate courts involved the admissibility of challenged evidence. Yet less than 8 percent of these claims resulted in reversals. The second-most commonly raised issue involved the trial judge's instructions to the jury. Roughly 10 percent of these claims resulted in reversals.

The Doctrine of Harmless Error

Although appellate review is designed to correct errors that occur during or before trial, not all errors necessitate reversal. To obtain reversal of a judgment, the appellant must show that some prejudice resulted from the error and that the outcome of the trial would probably have been different in the absence of the error. Although specific standards vary among jurisdictions, all appellate courts operate on the principle that reversal is required only when substantial, as distinct from merely technical, errors are found in the record. This approach is illustrated by a provision of the California Constitution that permits reversal on appeal only to prevent a "miscarriage of justice." The California Supreme Court has interpreted this standard as follows:

> [A] "miscarriage of justice" should be declared only when the court, after an examination of the entire cause, including the evidence, is of the opinion that it is reasonably probable that a result more favorable to the appealing party would have been reached in the absence of the error. *People v. Watson,* 299 P.2d 243, 254 (Cal. 1956), *cert. denied,* 355 U.S. 846, 78 S. Ct. 70, 2 L.Ed.2d 55 (1957).

Appellate courts frequently find that technical errors cited by appellants are harmless and do not merit a reversal; however, the United States Supreme Court has imposed a strict standard on the finding of harmless error. Where an error at trial involves provisions of the federal Constitution, the Supreme Court has said that appellate courts must find beyond a reasonable doubt that the error was harmless in order to affirm the trial court. *Chapman v. California,* 386 U.S. 18, 87 S. Ct. 824, 17 L.Ed.2d 705 (1967).

The doctrine of harmless error is subject to certain qualifications. For example, appellate courts generally do not consider each error at trial in isolation. Rather, they often consider the cumulative effect of a series of errors. Thus, an appellant may secure reversal of a conviction where the trial was replete with error, even though each particular error might be considered harmless by itself.

When an Appeal May Be Taken by a Defendant

Generally, only a defendant who has pled not guilty has the right to appeal, and that appeal must wait until the defendant has been convicted and sentenced. There are, however, some instances in which courts permit other appeals by defendants. For example, an order modifying or revoking probation is usually appealable.

A defendant who pleads guilty may raise on appeal only those issues relating to trial court jurisdiction, voluntariness of the guilty plea, and the legality of the sentence imposed. See, for example, *State v. Saylors,* 422 P.2d 477 (Wash. 1966). Even then an appellate court may refuse to review these aspects of a case unless the trial court has refused the defendant's request to withdraw the plea of guilty. *Counts v. State,* 376 So.2d 59 (Fla. App. 1979).

Some jurisdictions permit a defendant to plead *nolo contendere* and reserve the right to appeal a specific ruling of the trial court. See, for example, *Cooksey v. State,* 524 P.2d 1251 (Alaska 1974). Defendants who unsuccessfully urge a constitutional defense frequently rely on this procedure. For instance, a defendant may file a pretrial motion to suppress certain evidence on the ground that it was obtained in violation of the Fourth Amendment. If the trial judge denies the motion, the defendant can plead *nolo contendere,* reserving the right to appeal that specific point of law.

Appeals by the Prosecution

Early rulings by American state courts uniformly denied state governments the right to appeal from acquittals of criminal defendants. The United States Supreme Court adopted this position in 1892 when it ruled that the federal government had no right to appeal from an acquittal. *United States v. Sanges,* 144 U.S. 310, 12 S. Ct. 609, 36 L.Ed. 445 (1892). This prohibition is sensible inasmuch as the double jeopardy clause of the Fifth Amendment (applicable to the states through the Fourteenth Amendment) provides that a defendant who has been acquitted may not be tried again for the same offense (see Chapter 13).

Notwithstanding the general prohibition on appeals by the prosecution, there are limited opportunities provided by statute for the prosecution to appeal from certain trial court decisions before acquittal, such as unfavorable rulings on pretrial motions. For example, Virginia law provides:

> An appeal may be taken by the Commonwealth only in felony cases, before a jury is impaneled and sworn in a jury trial, or before the court begins to hear or receive evidence or the first witness is sworn, whichever occurs first, in a nonjury trial. The appeal may be taken from:
>
> 1. An order of a circuit court dismissing a warrant, information or indictment, or any count or charge thereof on the ground that a statute upon which it was based is unconstitutional; or
> 2. An order of a circuit [trial] court proscribing the use of certain evidence at trial on the grounds that such evidence was obtained in violation of the provisions of the Fourth, Fifth, or Sixth Amendments to the Constitution of the United States or Article I, Sections 8, 10, or 11 of the Constitution of Virginia proscribing illegal searches and seizures and protecting rights against self-incrimination, provided that the Commonwealth certifies the evidence is essential to the prosecution. Va. Code Ann. § 19.2–398.

Similarly, 18 U.S.C.A. § 3731 permits the federal government to appeal from an order of a federal district court (a) dismissing an indictment; (b) granting a new trial after judgment or verdict; (c) releasing a defendant before trial or after conviction; or (d) suppressing evidence prior to the time that the defendant is put in jeopardy.

The constitutional proscription of double jeopardy does not prevent appeals by the prosecutor of pretrial orders, since jeopardy does not attach prior to the empaneling of a jury or taking of evidence in a nonjury trial. *Crist v. Bretz,* 437 U.S. 28, 98 S. Ct. 2156, 57 L.Ed.2d 24 (1978); *Serfass v. United States,* 420 U.S. 377, 95 S. Ct. 1055; 43 L.Ed.2d 265 (1975).

Trial de Novo in Minor Misdemeanor Cases

Most criminal appeals are heard "on the record." This means that the appellate court is asked to scrutinize the official record of the trial for procedural errors that would require reversal of the judgment. Many misdemeanor cases are tried in local courts that are not courts of record, and therefore no record of the proceedings is available for review. Most of these involve "summary justice." Trial is before a judge or magistrate without a jury, in what is commonly called a bench trial. Counsel are rarely present and frequently no witnesses are called to testify. Yet, persons convicted of misdemeanors are generally entitled to an appeal by law. Where no record has been made of the proceedings, a *trial de novo* (literally, a "new trial") is held in a trial court of superior jurisdiction. In some instances, persons convicted at *trial de novo* may take an appeal to a higher court, but further review of such cases is generally discretionary.

Error Correction and Lawmaking Functions of Appellate Courts

Appellate courts perform dual functions in the criminal process. Most criminal appeals are reviewed by intermediate federal or state appellate courts, although in the less populous states routine appeals are handled by the highest court of the state. In these routine appeals, the primary function of appellate courts is error correction. Appellate review is designed to assure that substantive justice has been accomplished under constitutional standards of due process of law. Because of gaps in the statutory law and the inevitable need to interpret both statutory and constitutional provisions, appellate courts also perform a lawmaking function. This latter function is more characteristic of the highest levels of courts than of intermediate appellate tribunals.

THE APPELLATE PROCESS

To the layperson, the jurisdictional requisites and procedures of appellate courts appear complex. While these procedures vary in detail, they essentially follow the same basic path. In some instances the defendant must first file a motion for a new trial before taking an appeal. This is often a *pro forma* measure, but it affords the trial judge an opportunity to review the defendant's claim of error and award a new trial if necessary.

Release of Defendant on Bail Pending Appeal

Federal and state statutes and rules of court usually specify criteria for release of a convicted defendant pending appeal. Admission to bail after conviction is not a matter of right but rests in the discretion of the trial court. A defendant wishing to appeal is not aided by a presumption in favor of release on bail. Principally the trial judge attempts to determine whether an appeal is taken in good faith, and whether it presents a debatable point of law for appellate review. An appeal must not be frivolous or taken for the purpose of delay. *Birge v. State*, 230 S.E.2d 895 (Ga. 1976).

Trial judges typically consider a number of factors in exercising their discretion to grant or deny an application for bail pending appeal. Among those factors are the defendant's habits and respect for the law, family and community ties, and the severity of punishment imposed. If the term of imprisonment

TRIAL AND APPELLATE JURISDICTION OF FLORIDA COURTS

Florida has a relatively simple, streamlined judicial system (see fig. 19.1). This simplicity is due to reform efforts during the 1970s that consolidated multiple, specialized tribunals into courts of general jurisdiction. As a result, the Florida court system contrasts sharply with many state judicial systems that remain extremely (and unnecessarily) complicated.

In Florida, the county court is the principal trial court for misdemeanors and violations of city and county ordinances. Because it is a court of record, appeals from county court convictions are heard on the record by the circuit court. Except in large metropolitan areas of the state, a circuit court usually has jurisdiction over several counties. In addition to hearing appeals from the county courts, the circuit court is the court of original jurisdiction in felony cases and for trial of misdemeanors arising out of the circumstances of a felony. Convictions in circuit court may be appealed as a matter of right to a district (i.e., regional) court of appeal. In cases where the death penalty has been imposed, state law provides for direct appeal to the Florida Supreme Court. There are five district courts of appeal within the state of Florida. Each consists of a number of judges who ordinarily sit in panels of three. Decisions made by these appellate tribunals are final in the great majority of appeals from the circuit courts. In most cases, an appellant whose conviction is affirmed by the district court has no right of appeal to the state supreme court. However, when the district courts disagree on legal issues, the state supreme court may use its power of discretionary review to resolve these conflicts.

In addition, the district courts of appeal may, and often do, certify issues of great public importance to the supreme court for its resolution. The supreme court usually answers these certified questions, thereby affording an additional avenue of review in a few criminal cases. The supreme court also hears appeals from district court decisions on constitutional issues. The supreme court and the district courts of appeal may issue extraordinary writs where necessary. Examples of these writs in the criminal area are writs of prohibition (prohibiting lower courts from acting beyond their jurisdiction) and writs of *habeas corpus*.

---

imposed is relatively short, the court may also consider whether the denial of bail would render the defendant's right to appeal meaningless. Rules of criminal procedure generally provide for prompt appellate review of a decision denying bail to a convicted defendant or setting that bail unreasonably high.

Under the Federal Bail Reform Act of 1966 (repealed in 1984), the defendant in a federal court was entitled to bail unless there was "reason to believe that no one or more conditions of release will reasonably assure that the person will not flee, or pose a danger to any other person or any other community." The Bail Reform Act of 1984, 18 U.S.C.A. §§ 3141–3150, reversed that presumption of entitlement. Under the 1984 act, the defendant now has the burden of proving an entitlement to bail based on criteria specified in the law. Before granting bail pending appeal, the court must find

1. that the defendant is not likely to flee or pose a danger to the safety of any other person or the community if released;
2. that the appeal is not for the purpose of delay;
3. that the appeal raises a substantial question of law or fact; and
4. that if that substantial question is determined favorably to defendant on appeal, that decision is likely to result in reversal or an order for a new trial of all counts on which imprisonment has been imposed. *United States v. Miller*, 753 F.2d 19, 24 (3d Cir. 1985).

FIGURE 19.1   Criminal Appeals in the Florida Court system

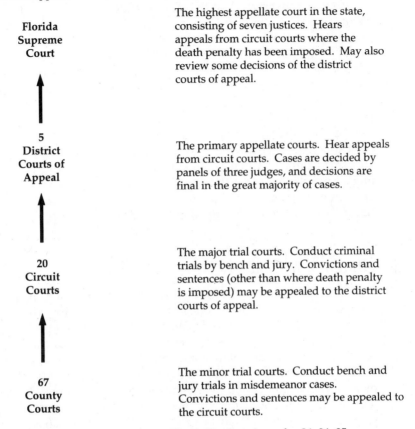

Florida
Supreme
Court

The highest appellate court in the state, consisting of seven justices. Hears appeals from circuit courts where the death penalty has been imposed. May also review some decisions of the district courts of appeal.

5
District
Courts of
Appeal

The primary appellate courts. Hear appeals from circuit courts. Cases are decided by panels of three judges, and decisions are final in the great majority of cases.

20
Circuit
Courts

The major trial courts. Conduct criminal trials by bench and jury. Convictions and sentences (other than where death penalty is imposed) may be appealed to the district courts of appeal.

67
County
Courts

The minor trial courts. Conduct bench and jury trials in misdemeanor cases. Convictions and sentences may be appealed to the circuit courts.

Sources: West's Fla. Stat. Ann. Const. art. V, §§ 1–6; West's Fla. Stat. Ann. chs. 26, 34, 35.

If the government takes an appeal it is common for the defendant to be released on personal recognizance until the appeal is determined. In Illinois, "a defendant shall not be held in jail or to bail during the pendency of an appeal by the State ... unless there are compelling reasons for his continued detention or being held to bail." Ill. Sup. Ct. Rule 604(a) (3).

The Right to Counsel on Appeal

We have seen that the United States Supreme Court has interpreted the federal Constitution to require that indigent defendants be furnished assistance of counsel in criminal prosecutions (see Chapter 16). To what extent does the Constitution require appointment of counsel for indigent defendants who appeal their convictions to higher courts? In *Douglas v. California*, 372 U.S. 353, 83 S. Ct. 814, 9 L.Ed.2d 811 (1963), the Supreme Court said that counsel should be provided by the states where indigent persons convicted of felonies have a statutory right to appeal. However, in *Ross v. Moffitt*, 417 U.S. 600, 94 S. Ct. 2437, 41 L.Ed.2d 341 (1974), the Supreme Court held that a state's failure to provide counsel to an indigent defendant seeking discretionary review in the state and federal supreme courts did not violate due process or equal protection. Thus, government must provide counsel as a matter of course when defendants have a statutory right to be heard in an appellate court; at later stages of the appeals process, there is no such requirement.

The Supreme Court's decision in *Douglas v. California* produced a tremendous increase in appellate case loads. Many appeals were frivolous (i.e., lacking in any arguable basis for reversal). In such cases appointed counsel will often attempt to withdraw. In *Anders v. California*, 386 U.S. 738, 87 S. Ct. 1396, 18 L.Ed.2d 493 (1967), the Supreme Court invalidated a state rule that allowed appointed counsel to withdraw by stating that an appeal had no merit. Reasoning that the right to counsel meant the right to have an effective advocate on appeal, the Supreme Court held that appointed counsel could withdraw only after submitting a brief claiming that the appeal was wholly frivolous. With the proliferation of criminal appeals by indigent defendants, the *Anders* brief has become a commonplace element of appellate procedure.

Filing the Appeal

Once the appellant has determined the correct forum for an appeal or a petition for discretionary review, a series of steps follows. First, the appeal or petition must be filed in the appropriate court within a specified period of time. The time requirement tends to be strictly enforced because it is this notice that confers jurisdiction for the appellate court to act on the case.

Rule 4 of the Federal Rules of Appellate Procedure provides that an appeal by a defendant from a judgment and sentence in a federal district court must be filed within ten days after the entry of the judgment. Under certain circumstances the time period may be extended, not to exceed an additional thirty days. When an appeal by the government is authorized by statute, the notice of appeal must be filed within thirty days after the entry of judgment.

Rule 13 of the Rules of the United States Supreme Court states that

> A petition for a writ of certiorari . . . shall be in time when it is filed . . . within 90 days after the entry of the judgment.

In deciding whether to exercise its discretion to grant *certiorari*, the United States Supreme Court looks to whether there is a substantial federal question involved. If so, the Court is then interested in whether the petitioner has exhausted all other remedies available. In deciding whether to grant *certiorari*, the Court follows the *rule of four*, meaning that at least four of the nine justices must vote to place a case on the docket.

In state courts an aggrieved party usually has thirty days after entry of judgment and sentence to file an appeal. For example, Maryland requires that the notice of appeal must be filed within thirty days after the trial court has entered its judgment. Md. R. 8–202.

The filing of a notice of appeal must be accompanied by the payment of a required filing fee. Indigent defendants may move to proceed *in forma pauperis* to avoid filing fees and other costs associated with the appeal. (Figure 19.2 details the procedures associated with appeals in South Carolina.)

FIGURE 19.2 Major Steps in Processing an Appeal in South Carolina
This chart shows the major steps in processing an appeal under the South Carolina Appellate
Court Rules, and is intended to provide an overview of the appeals process. . . .

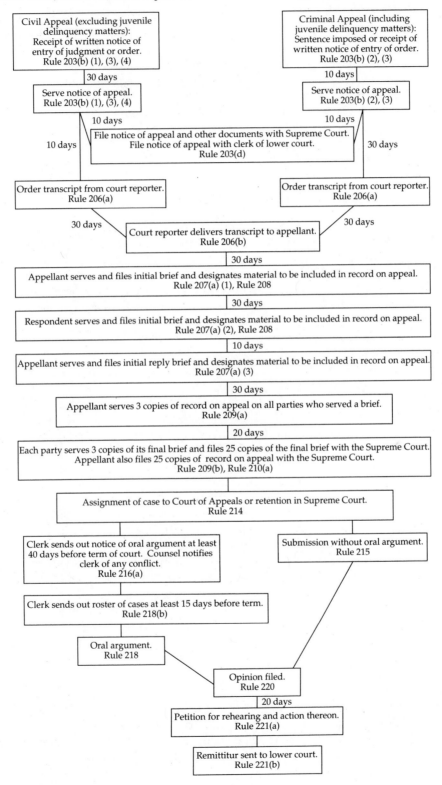

Source: Court Rules, Supreme Court of South Carolina, West's *Southeastern Reporter* August 30, 1990, pages CXXI–CXXII.

Motions

During the early stages of the appellate process, counsel for both parties frequently file motions in the appellate court. Counsel use motions to draw the court's immediate attention to procedural matters outside the routine of the appellate process. For example, counsel may request additional time to meet deadlines for filing petitions and briefs. Occasionally counsel will move for expedited consideration of an appeal. By appropriate motions, separate appeals may be consolidated; multiple appeals may be severed. Upon a showing of good cause, an appellate court may stay a judgment or sentence of a lower court pending resolution of the appeal.

Filing of Briefs

After a notice of appeal or a petition for discretionary review has been filed, a series of procedural steps are set in motion. It is incumbent on the appellant or petitioner to have the clerk of the trial court forward to the appellate tribunal certified copies of pertinent records and transcripts of testimony relevant to the issues to be raised on appeal. Beyond this, procedures vary somewhat depending largely on whether the appeal is one by right or whether the defendant is seeking discretionary relief.

In an appeal by right, the appellant files a brief summarizing the legal posture and the factual background of the case in the lower tribunal. Briefs are the principal instruments used to persuade the appellate court to reverse, affirm, or modify the decision being appealed. They are usually heavily laden with citations to constitutional provisions, statutes, and court decisions regarded as determinative by the advocates. The extent of background information contained in the briefs depends on the points to be presented to the appellate court. The appellee is permitted to respond by filing an answer brief, and the appellant is usually permitted a reply brief. The whole process resembles the order of a classroom debate where the affirmative presents its case, followed by the negative and a rebuttal by the affirmative.

Where a petitioner seeks discretionary review, the appellate court must first decide whether to accept or deny the request to take jurisdiction. If the court determines to proceed on the petition, it will order all affected parties to furnish the court a written response. As in an appeal by right, often the petitioner is permitted to file a reply to that response. The petition and response may be supplemented by such briefs as the court requires.

The format and submission of briefs must adhere closely to the requirements of the particular jurisdiction. Counsel must always furnish copies of briefs and other materials to their adversaries.

Oral Argument

After briefs have been submitted and reviewed by the appellate court, frequently an oral argument is held where counsel for both parties appear. Counsel make oral presentations summarizing their positions and are then subjected to questions from the bench. Fairly typical is the Texas Rule of Appellate Procedure, which provides that "each side may be allowed thirty minutes in the argument at the bar, with fifteen minutes more in conclusion by the appellant." Tex. R. App. Proc. 423(d). Increasingly oral arguments are punctuated by questions from the bench. Indeed, some oral arguments are taking the form of a dialogue rather than that of a structured presentation.

The Judicial Conference

It is customary for appellate judges to confer on disposition of appeals. This function is regarded as part of the collegial process that distinguishes the appellate role from that of the trial court. If there has been oral argument, it is common for the panel of judges who heard the case to confer shortly thereafter. At that time the panel frequently attempts to determine the disposition of the appeal but, in some instances, may find it necessary to further canvass the record or call upon counsel or the court's own staff lawyers for additional legal research. Where there has been no oral argument, the panel of judges assigned to the case usually confers after each judge has had the opportunity to review the briefs and pertinent records and the results of any research assignments given to the court's legal staff.

Preparation of Opinions

After an appellate court has arrived at a decision, it remains for the court to issue an opinion announcing its decision. Some opinions simply announce the court's decision; others are quite lengthy in considering the arguments of counsel and articulating the reasons for the court's decision.

Opinions are generally prepared by an individual judge or justice. If responsibility for preparation of an opinion has not been previously given to one judge, that responsibility is usually assigned at conference by the senior judge or the senior judge voting with the majority of the panel.

Types of Appellate Opinions. There are two basic types of appellate court opinions: *per curiam* and signed. A *per curiam* opinion represents the appellate court as a whole; it is not attributed to any individual judge or group of judges on the court. More commonly the decision of the appellate court is announced in an opinion signed by one judge and joined by other judges comprising a majority. Judges who disagree with the decision of the court may render dissenting opinions. Judges who agree with the court's decision but wish to address or emphasize certain arguments not addressed or emphasized in the opinion of the court may write separate concurring opinions. Sometimes, these separate opinions are listed as "concurring in the judgment only," meaning that they support the decision of the court, but for reasons other than those articulated in the court's opinion.

Publication of Appellate Decisions. Most decisions of appellate courts in America are published in books known as reporters. Access to published opinions is discussed in some detail in Appendix B. The publication of appellate decisions plays an important role in the development of the law, since judges and lawyers regularly consult the case reporters for guidance in pending cases.

CASE IN POINT

TYPES OF ISSUES RAISED ON APPEAL
AND POSTCONVICTION RELIEF

Warren McCleskey was convicted of murder and sentenced to death by a Georgia court in 1978. He then initiated a series of appeals and petitions for *habeas corpus,* the litigation of which spanned more than a decade. The following is an appendix to the majority opinion in *McCleskey v. Zant,* 499 U.S. 467, 111 S.Ct. 1454, 113 L.Ed.2d 517 (1991), in which the Supreme Court held that McCleskey had abused the writ of *habeas corpus.* (Excerpts from the majority opinion and dissent in *McCleskey* are reprinted at the end of the chapter.)

APPENDIX—Petitioner's Claims for Relief at Various Stages of the Litigation

1. Direct Appeal. On direct appeal, McCleskey raised the following claims: (1) the death penalty was administered in a discriminatory fashion because of prosecutorial discretion, (2) the prosecutor conducted an illegal postindictment lineup, (3) the trial court erred in admitting at trial the statement McCleskey made to the police, (4) the trial court erred in allowing Evans to testify about McCleskey's jail-house confession, (5) the prosecutor failed to disclose certain impeachment evidence; and (6) the trial court erred in admitting evidence of McCleskey's prior criminal acts. . . .

2. First State Habeas Corpus Petition. McCleskey's first state habeas petition alleged the following constitutional violations: (1) the Georgia death penalty is administered arbitrarily, capriciously, and whimsically; (2) Georgia officials imposed McCleskey's capital sentence pursuant to a pattern and practice of discrimination on the basis of race, sex, and poverty; (3) the death penalty lacks theoretical or factual justification and fails to serve any rational interest; (4) McCleskey's death sentence is cruel and unusual punishment in light of all mitigating factors; (5) McCleskey received inadequate notice and opportunity to be heard; (6) the jury did not constitute a fair cross section of the community; (7) the jury was biased in favor of the prosecution; (8) the trial court improperly excused two jurors who were opposed to the death penalty; (9) McCleskey's postarrest statement should have been excluded because it was obtained after an allegedly illegal arrest; (10) the postarrest statement was extracted involuntarily; (11) the State failed to disclose an "arrangement" with one of its key witnesses, Evans; (12) the State deliberately withheld a statement made by McCleskey to Evans; (13) the trial court erred in failing to grant McCleskey funds to employ experts in aid of his defense; (14) three witnesses for the State witnessed a highly suggestive lineup involving McCleskey prior to trial; (15) the trial court's jury instructions concerning intent impermissibly shifted the burden of persuasion to McCleskey; (16) the prosecution impermissibly referred to the appellate process during the sentencing phase; (17) the trial court improperly admitted evidence of other crimes for which McCleskey had not been convicted; (18) the trial court's instructions concerning evidence of McCleskey's other bad acts was overbroad; (19) the appellate review procedures of Georgia denied McCleskey effective assistance of counsel, a fair hearing, and the basic tools of an adequate defense; (20) the means by which the death penalty is administered inflicts wanton and unnecessary torture; (21) McCleskey was denied effective assistance of counsel in numerous con-

(continued)

CASE IN POINT

texts; (22) introduction of statements petitioner made to Evans were elicited in a situation created to induce McCleskey to make incriminating statements; and (23) the evidence was insufficient to convict McCleskey of capital murder. . . .

3. First Federal Habeas Corpus Petition. McCleskey raised the following claims in his first federal habeas petition: (1) the Georgia death penalty discriminated on the basis of race; (2) the State failed to disclose an "understanding" with Evans; (3) the trial court's instructions to the jury impermissibly shifted the burden to McCleskey; (4) the prosecutor improperly referred to the appellate process at the sentencing phase; (5) the trial court impermissibly refused to grant McCleskey funds to employ experts in aid of his defense; (6) the trial court's instructions concerning evidence of McCleskey's other bad acts was overbroad; (7) the trial court's instructions gave the jury too much discretion to consider nonstatutory aggravating circumstances; (8) the trial court improperly admitted evidence of other crimes for which McCleskey had not been convicted; (9) three witnesses for the State witnessed a highly suggestive lineup involving McCleskey prior to trial; (10) McCleskey's postarrest statement should have been excluded because it was extracted involuntarily; (11) the trial court impermissibly excluded two jurors who were opposed to the death penalty; (12) the death penalty lacks theoretical or factual justification and fails to serve any rational interest; (13) the State deliberately withheld a statement made by McCleskey to Evans; (14) the evidence was insufficient to convict McCleskey of capital murder; (15) McCleskey's counsel failed to investigate the State's evidence adequately; (16) McCleskey's counsel failed to raise certain objections or make certain motions at trial; (17) McCleskey's counsel failed to undertake an independent investigation of possible mitigating circumstances prior to trial; and (18) after trial, McCleskey's counsel failed to review and correct the judge's sentence report. . . .

4. Second State Habeas Corpus Petition. In his second state habeas petition, McCleskey alleged the following claims: (1) the prosecutor systematically excluded blacks from the jury; (2) the State of Georgia imposed the death penalty against McCleskey in a racially discriminatory manner; (3) the State failed to disclose its agreement with Evans; (4) the trial court impermissibly refused to grant McCleskey funds to employ experts in aid of his defense; and (5) the prosecutor improperly referred to the appellate process at the sentencing phase. . . .

5. Second Federal Habeas Corpus Petition. In his second federal habeas petition, McCleskey alleged the following claims: (1) Evans' testimony concerning his conversation with McCleskey was inadmissible because Evans acted as a state informant in a situation created to induce McCleskey to make incriminating statements; (2) the State failed to correct the misleading testimony of Evans; (3) the State failed to disclose "an arrangement" with Evans; (4) the prosecutor improperly referred to the appellate process at the sentencing phase; (5) the State systematically excluded blacks from McCleskey's jury; (6) the death penalty was imposed on McCleskey pursuant to a pattern and practice of racial discrimination by Georgia officials against black defendants; and (7) the trial court impermissibly refused to grant McCleskey funds to employ experts in aid of his defense. . . .

Motions for Rehearing

Rules of appellate procedure uniformly permit the filing of a motion asking the appellate court to reconsider its decision in a given case. A motion for rehearing is designed to address some misstatement of material fact or to direct the court's attention to an overlooked or misapprehended proposition of law. In the United States Courts of Appeals, and in many state appellate courts, where cases are decided by panels of judges, a party may request that all judges of the court participate in what is called an *en banc* rehearing. Appellate courts view many motions for rehearing as little more than attempts by dissatisfied parties to have another chance to persuade the court of their position. Accordingly, motions for rehearing are seldom granted.

POSTCONVICTION RELIEF

Normally, an appeal of a lower court decision must be made in a timely manner, usually within thirty days. Petitions for *certiorari* (or other forms of discretionary review) are also subject to time limits. Yet there exists a mechanism whereby incarcerated criminals may seek review of their convictions long after their rights to appeal have been exhausted or expired. This mechanism is known as the writ of *habeas corpus*. It is available in the federal courts and in all fifty state judicial systems.

Habeas corpus is a Latin term meaning "you have the body." In law, it refers to a writ issued by a court to a person who is holding another in custody, requiring that the former show cause for holding the latter. *Habeas corpus* has roots deep in the common law. Blackstone called it "the most celebrated writ in the English law." 3 W. Blackstone, Commentaries 129.

The framers of the American Constitution explicitly recognized *habeas corpus* as a fundamental right of citizens by declaring that "[t]he Privilege of the Writ of Habeas Corpus shall not be suspended unless when in Cases of Rebellion or Invasion the public Safety may require it." U.S. Const., Art. 1, Sec. 9. Only once in our history, during the Civil War, was the writ of *habeas corpus* suspended throughout the federal courts. This thoroughgoing suspension was subsequently declared unconstitutional. *Ex parte Milligan*, 71 U.S. (4 Wall.) 2, 18 L.Ed. 281 (1866).

Challenging State Court Convictions in Federal Court

The United States Supreme Court can review only a minute proportion of the appeals and petitions for *certiorari* where persons convicted in state courts seek to challenge their convictions on federal constitutional grounds. The writ of *habeas corpus* is another means of obtaining federal judicial review of state court convictions.

The Federal Judiciary Act of 1789, 1 Stat. 82 (1789), recognized the power of federal courts to issue writs of *habeas corpus* only in respect to federal prisoners. In 1867, federal law was amended, 14 Stat. 385, 386, to allow federal courts to entertain *habeas* petitions from state prisoners who allege that their incarceration violates provisions of the U.S. Constitution or federal statutes or treaties. The federal law on *habeas corpus* currently provides:

The Supreme Court, a Justice thereof, a circuit judge, or a district court shall entertain an application for a writ of habeas corpus in behalf of a person in custody pursuant to the judgment of a State court only on the ground that he is in custody in violation of the Constitution or laws or treaties of the United States. 28 U.S.C.A. § 2254.

Prior to the twentieth century, the federal *habeas corpus* jurisdiction was seldom used to review state criminal convictions. When *habeas corpus* was granted, it was merely to ascertain that the state trial court had jurisdiction over the person being tried. In *Frank v. Mangum*, 237 U.S. 309, 35 S. Ct. 582, 59 L.Ed. 969 (1915), the Supreme Court broadened federal *habeas corpus* review to ensure that states supplied some "corrective process" whereby criminal defendants could seek to vindicate their federal constitutional rights. In 1953, the Court held that federal courts could use *habeas corpus* review to readjudicate federal constitutional issues that had been addressed in state court proceedings. *Brown v. Allen*, 344 U.S. 443, 73 S. Ct. 397, 97 L.Ed. 469 (1953).

Federal law had long provided that federal *habeas corpus* relief was available only to state prisoners who had exhausted all available remedies in the state courts. In 1963 the Supreme Court held that a state prisoner did not have to take a direct appeal to the state supreme court in order to seek federal *habeas corpus* review. Nor was the prisoner barred from raising constitutional issues in federal court merely because he had not raised them on direct appeal. *Fay v. Noia*, 372 U.S. 391, 83 S. Ct. 822, 9 L.Ed.2d 837 (1963).

The Supreme Court's efforts to broaden the availability of federal *habeas corpus* review coincided with its expansion of the constitutional rights of the accused. No doubt the Court was initially reluctant to depend on state courts to implement these expanded rights, so it broadened the power of the federal district courts to review state criminal convictions. This resulted in numerous state convictions being overturned by the federal courts, often on Fourth or Fifth Amendment grounds. Indeed, many observers came to see state criminal trials merely as precursors to inevitable federal intervention.

A growing criticism of federal court intervention, coupled with the increasing professionalism of the state judiciaries, persuaded the Supreme Court to restrict access to federal *habeas corpus* relief. During the 1970s a more conservative Supreme Court began to narrow access to federal *habeas corpus* relief. In a seminal case, *Stone v. Powell*, 428 U.S. 465, 96 S.Ct. 3037, 49 L.Ed.2d 1067 (1976), the Court held that state prisoners could not use federal *habeas corpus* hearings to challenge searches and seizures where they had been provided an opportunity for full and fair litigation of a Fourth Amendment claim in the state courts.

Despite *Stone v. Powell*, federal *habeas corpus* review remains available to state prisoners seeking to challenge their convictions on a variety of constitutional grounds. For instance, the Supreme Court has said that federal *habeas corpus* review must remain available to state prisoners alleging racial discrimination in their indictments or convictions, regardless of their opportunity to raise such objections in the state courts. *Rose v. Mitchell*, 443 U.S. 545, 99 S. Ct. 2993, 61 L.Ed.2d 739 (1979). In another significant decision in 1979, *Jackson v. Virginia*, 443 U.S. 307, 99 S. Ct. 2781, 61 L.Ed.2d 560 (1979), it held that a federal court reviewing a state conviction on *habeas corpus* must consider whether any reasonable trier of fact could have found a defendant guilty beyond a reasonable

CASE IN POINT

FEDERAL *HABEAS CORPUS* JURISDICTION

In 1975 defendant Lincoln Isaac was convicted in an Ohio court of the crime of aggravated assault. The charge stemmed from an incident in which Isaac had severely beaten his former wife's boyfriend. At trial Isaac claimed that the boyfriend had struck him first and that he acted in self-defense. The trial judge instructed the jury that the defendant carried the burden of proving self-defense by a preponderance of evidence. Isaac did not object to the judge's instruction to the jury at that time. He was convicted and sentenced to prison.

The year after Isaac's conviction, the Ohio Supreme Court ruled in another case that once a defendant produces some evidence of self-defense, the burden is on the prosecutor to disprove self-defense beyond a reasonable doubt. *State v. Robinson,* 351 N.E.2d 88 (Ohio 1976).

Relying on *State v. Robinson,* Isaac appealed to an intermediate state appellate court. That court rejected his challenge because he had failed to object to the jury instruction at the time it was given. The Ohio Supreme Court dismissed Isaac's appeal for lack of a substantial constitutional question.

Isaac subsequently filed a petition for a writ of *habeas corpus* in federal district court. That court denied relief, holding that Isaac had waived any constitutional claims by failing to present them to the Ohio trial court. The Court of Appeals for the Sixth Circuit reversed, holding that the jury instructions violated the due process clause of the Fourteenth Amendment.

Isaac's appellate odyssey culminated in 1982 in a decision by the United States Supreme Court. The high court reversed the court of appeals, saying that Isaac's failure to raise a constitutional claim at trial precluded litigation of this claim on federal *habeas corpus* review.

Engle v. Isaac, 456 U.S. 107, 102 S. Ct. 1558, 71 L.Ed.2d 783 (1982).

doubt. Prior to *Jackson,* federal courts would not reverse state convictions for insufficient evidence if there was "any evidence" of the defendant's guilt.

In *Engle v. Isaac,* 456 U.S. 107, 102 S.Ct. 1558, 71 L.Ed.2d 783 (1982), the Supreme Court refused to allow a state prisoner to use federal *habeas corpus* to challenge a questionable jury instruction to which he failed to object during trial. Other decisions of the Court during the 1980s chipped away at Court's earlier expansive interpretations of federal *habeas corpus* relief. See, for example, *Kuhlmann v. Wilson,* 477 U.S. 436, 106 S.Ct. 2616, 91 L.Ed.2d 364 (1986); *Straight v. Wainwright,* 476 U.S. 1132, 106 S.Ct. 2004, 90 L.Ed.2d 683 (1986).

During the early 1990s the Supreme Court continued the trend ·toward limiting access to federal *habeas corpus.* In 1991, the Court barred Warren McCleskey, a prisoner on "death row" in Georgia, from filing a second federal *habeas corpus* petition, holding that he had "abused the writ." *McCleskey v. Zant,* 499 U.S. 467, 111 S.Ct. 1454, 113 L.Ed.2d 517 (1991). In the *McCleskey* case, the Court held that a state need not prove that a petitioner deliberately abandoned a constitutional claim in his or her first *habeas corpus* petition for the petitioner to be barred from raising the claim in a subsequent petition. The Court thus moved away from the "deliberate abandonment" standard it had previously articulated in *Sanders v. United States,* 373 U.S. 1, 83 S.Ct. 1068, 10 L.Ed.2d 148 (1963).

Similarly, in *Keeney v. Tamayo-Reyes,* 504 U.S. ___ , 112 S.Ct. 1715, 118 L.Ed.2d 318 (1992), the Court overruled another earlier *habeas corpus* decision, *Townsend v. Sain,* 372 U.S. 293, 83 S.Ct. 745, 9 L.Ed.2d 770 (1963). In *Townsend,* the Court had held that a petitioner could challenge a state conviction despite a failure to develop a material fact in state proceedings unless it was determined that he or she deliberately bypassed the opportunity to develop the fact in the state courts. In *Keeney v. Tamayo-Reyes,* the Court held that a petitioner's failure to develop a claim in state-court proceedings should be excused only if he or she can show that a fundamental miscarriage of justice would result from failure to hold a federal evidentiary hearing.

The Supreme Court's decisions in *McCleskey v. Zant* and *Keeney v. Tamayo-Reyes* came at a time when many in Congress were calling for legislative restrictions on federal *habeas corpus.* Both the Supreme Court and Congress were responding to a widespread perception that state prisoners were being afforded excessive opportunities to challenge their convictions in federal courts. Indeed, some conservative commentators questioned the need for federal postconviction review of state criminal cases altogether. While federal *habeas corpus* has been subject to abuse by state prisoners, eliminating this aspect of federal jurisdiction altogether would remove some of the pressure that has led to an increased awareness of and appreciation for defendants' rights in the state courts. Indeed, in the *McCleskey* case the Supreme Court expressed a commitment to the continued efficacy of *habeas corpus* to prevent miscarriages of justice in the state courts.

Collateral Attack in State Court

The constitutional rights of criminal defendants were greatly expanded as a result of the "nationalizing" of the criminal law during the 1960s. During those years the states began to review the efficacy of the writ of *habeas corpus* as a basis for permitting challenges to judgments and sentences subsequent to conclusion of a direct appeal. As a result most states adopted statutes or court rules that permit a postappeal challenge to an illegal conviction or sentence. These procedures, known as collateral attack or collateral relief, provide a mechanism to permit review of judgments and sentences imposed in violation of the federal or state constitutions. For example, under Rule 3:22–2 of the New Jersey Rules Governing Criminal Practice, a person may seek postconviction relief on any of the following grounds:

a. Substantial denial in the conviction proceedings of defendant's rights under the Constitution of the United States or the Constitution or laws of the state of New Jersey;

b. Lack of jurisdiction of the court to impose the judgment rendered upon defendant's conviction;

c. Imposition of sentence in excess of or otherwise not in accordance with the sentence authorized by law;

d. Any ground heretofore available as a basis for collateral attack upon a conviction by *habeas corpus* or any other common-law or statutory remedy.

C A S E   I N   P O I N T

Ineffective Counsel as a Basis for Relief on Appeal or Collateral Attack

Here are several examples of cases from the 1980s in which appellate or postconviction relief was afforded to defendants who received ineffective representation:

Ex parte Duffy, 607 S.W.2d 507 (Tex. Crim. App. 1980). In a capital murder case, counsel failed to (1) contact or confer with potentially valuable defense witnesses or witnesses for the state; (2) confer with the defendant in a manner deemed consistent with the gravity of a capital case; (3) visit the crime scene; and (4) attempt the defense of insanity despite good reasons for doing so.

State v. McBride, 296 N.W.2d 551 (S.D. 1980). Defense counsel's entire handling of the case was so casual it was deemed to have infected the defense with "adversarial mediocrity."

State v. Schoelerman, 315 N.W.2d 67 (Iowa 1982). Counsel permitted his client to plead guilty to a felony carrying a maximum sentence of ten years in prison instead of pointing out that the defendant might have been guilty of a lesser crime carrying a maximum penalty of thirty days in jail.

Arthur v. Bordenkircher, 715 F.2d 118 (4th Cir. 1983). Counsel failed to object to the judge's jury instruction that stated that the defendant had been previously convicted on the same murder charge but had won a new trial on procedural grounds.

People v. Wagner, 479 N.Y.S.2d 66 (App. Div. 1984). Counsel's opening statement was incoherent and failed to state the nature of the defense. Additionally, counsel failed to (1) move for inspection of grand jury minutes; (2) request a hearing on the admissibility of key evidence despite a factual basis for doing so; (3) challenge prospective jurors, resulting in a jury where nine jurors had friends or relatives in law enforcement; and (4) attempt to impeach the credibility of the state's witnesses where there was inconsistency between their trial testimony and their pretrial testimony.

Thomas v. Lockhart, 738 F.2d 304 (8th Cir. 1984). Counsel failed to investigate the defendant's history of mental problems as a possible basis for an insanity plea; failed to investigate a case that the prosecution relied on in recommending a thirty-year sentence; and indicated to the defendant that he would "feel funny" about representing a black man accused of raping a white woman.

Commonwealth v. Graham, 528 A.2d 620 (Pa. Super 1987). Counsel failed to object to the prosecutor's statements made during closing argument to the effect that the jury should disregard the "unbelievable" testimony of the defendant.

Rule 3:22–3 stipulates, however, that such a motion for relief is not "a substitute for appeal from conviction" and may not be filed "while such appellate review . . . is available." Furthermore, under Rule 3:22–4, a petitioner is barred from raising grounds for relief not raised in prior appellate proceedings unless "(a) that the ground for relief not previously asserted could not have reasonably been raised in any prior proceeding; or (b) that enforcement of the bar would result in fundamental injustice; or (c) that denial of relief would be contrary to the Constitution of the United States or the State of New Jersey."

Among the most common grounds assigned by defendants in seeking collateral relief in post-appeal challenges are:

- The discovery of new evidence that was not available to the defendant during trial but may be determinative of the defendant's innocence
- The applicability of a retroactive decision from the United States Supreme Court or the highest court of a state where the defendant was tried
- Whether the defendant's plea was involuntarily induced or the defendant was incompetent at the time the plea was entered
- Whether the defendant's counsel was ineffective in representing the defendant

Ineffective Counsel as a Basis for Postconviction Relief

The Supreme Court has recognized that the right to counsel means little unless counsel provide defendants with effective representation. *McMann v. Richardson*, 397 U.S. 759, 90 S. Ct. 1441, 25 L.Ed.2d 763 (1970). Failure of counsel, whether appointed or retained, to be an effective advocate for the defendant constitutes a basis to award a defendant a new trial. *Cuyler v. Sullivan*, 446 U.S. 335, 100 S. Ct. 1708, 64 L.Ed.2d 333 (1980). Some examples of ineffective representation where relief might well be afforded include failure of counsel to present evidence favorable to the accused, failure to challenge the admissibility of evidence presented by the prosecution, and failure to challenge prosecutorial misconduct.

It is likely that the requirement to furnish counsel to indigent defendants has contributed to a rise in claims of ineffective assistance of counsel. Indigent defendants are sometimes distrustful of public defenders and other appointed counsel. If convicted, these defendants may be more likely to feel that the representation they were provided was ineffective compared to the representation of privately retained attorneys. The issue of ineffective counsel is rarely, if ever, raised on direct appeal since it is not a matter that would ordinarily be challenged in the trial court. Understandably, this issue is one of the most common grounds today for challenging a conviction in a post-appeal collateral attack.

Until recently, most courts followed the "mockery of justice" standard in addressing claims of ineffective assistance. To prevail under such a standard, the defendant had to show that counsel's efforts were so incompetent as to constitute a "farce or mockery of justice." See, for example, *Edwards v. United States*, 256 F.2d 707 (D.C. Cir. 1958), *cert. denied*, 358 U.S. 847, 79 S. Ct. 74, 3 L.Ed.2d 82 (1958). In the 1960s and 1970s, state and federal courts began to adopt standards more favorable to the defendant. However, in the absence of guidance from the U.S. Supreme Court, there was tremendous variance in the standards that courts were following in determining ineffective assistance of counsel. In *Strickland v. Washington*, 466 U.S. 668, 104 S. Ct. 2052, 80 L.Ed.2d 674 (1984), the Supreme Court articulated a uniform constitutional standard. Specifically, the Court held:

> First, the defendant must show that counsel's performance was deficient. This requires showing that counsel made errors so serious that counsel was not functioning as the "counsel" guaranteed the defendant by the Sixth Amendment. Second, the defendant must show that the deficient performance prejudiced the defense. This requires showing that counsel's errors were so serious as to deprive the defendant of a fair trial, a trial whose result is reliable. Unless a defendant makes both showings, it cannot be said that the conviction ... resulted from a breakdown in the adversary process that renders the result unreliable. 466 U.S. at 687, 104 S. Ct. at 2063, 80 L.Ed.2d at 693.

CRITICISM OF THE APPEALS PROCESS

Recently there has been much criticism of the seemingly inexhaustible routes of appellate review. Some would argue that the numerous opportunities for defendants to obtain review of their convictions by higher courts result in unnecessary delays in dispensing justice. On the premise that "justice is due the accuser as well as the accused," critics would cite the old aphorism that "justice delayed is justice denied."

Certainly there is an abundance of cases to support the criticism. Many involve the controversial issue of capital punishment. Such cases attract the attention of the media and arouse the righteous indignation of the public. There is an unfortunate tendency to assume that such cases are typical and that the appellate process is incapable of moving expeditiously. The public is generally unaware of the thousands of appeals that are resolved in a timely manner for every one that becomes a case study in delay.

NONJUDICIAL REMEDIES AVAILABLE TO PERSONS CONVICTED OF CRIMES

Under the English common law, appeal to the Crown predated appeal to higher courts as the remedy for an unjust conviction or unreasonable sentence. Additionally, since a crime was viewed as an offense against the Crown, the monarch possessed the authority to forgive the wrongdoer or grant "clemency." In contemporary America, the appeal to executive authority remains as a carryover from the common law and a supplement to judicial review.

Article 2, Section 2, Clause 1 of the United States Constitution states that the president "shall have Power to grant Reprieves and Pardons for Offences against the United States, except in Cases of Impeachment." This broad power includes the right to commute sentences, remit fines and penalties, and even grant conditional pardons. Indeed, the presidential pardon may be issued prior to conviction, as was amply demonstrated in 1974 when President Gerald Ford pardoned former President Richard Nixon for his role in the Watergate scandal. It was demonstrated again in December 1992 when President George Bush granted a pardon to Caspar Weinberger, the former Secretary of Defense, and five others who allegedly were involved in the much-publicized controversy concerning the trading of arms for hostages. The Supreme Court has said that

> The plain purpose of the broad power conferred . . . was to allow . . . the President to "forgive" the convicted person in part or entirely, to reduce a penalty in terms of a specified number of years, or to alter it with conditions which are in themselves constitutionally unobjectionable. *Schick v. Reed,* 419 U.S. 256, 266, 95 S. Ct. 379, 385, 42 L.Ed.2d 430, 438-439 (1974).

A full presidential pardon totally restores any civil rights the recipient may have lost as a result of conviction. In effect, the full pardon makes an individual as innocent as if the crime had never been committed. *Ex parte Garland,* 71 U.S. (4 Wall.) 333, 18 L.Ed. 366 (1866).

CASE IN POINT

THE APPELLATE ODYSSEY OF ROBERT ALTON HARRIS

In a protracted series of appeals spanning some fourteen years, federal and state courts wrangled with a variety of legal issues surrounding the death sentence imposed on Robert Alton Harris, who was convicted of murdering two teenage boys in San Diego, California, in 1978. In trying to escape the death sentence, Harris filed nine petitions for *habeas corpus* in California state courts and four federal *habeas corpus* petitions. Harris' appellate odyssey provides a case study in the complex appeals process that often occurs in death penalty cases.

March 6, 1979: Harris convicted and sentenced to die in California's gas chamber.

February 11, 1981: On appeal, the California Supreme Court upholds Harris' conviction and death sentence.

October 5, 1981: The U.S. Supreme Court denies Harris' petition for certiorari.

November 1981: Harris files three *habeas corpus* petitions in California state courts; all are denied.

March 5, 1982: Harris files the first of several *habeas corpus* petitions in United States District Court for the Southern District of California.

March 12, 1982: The federal district court denies Harris' first *habeas* petition.

August 13, 1982: Harris files his second federal *habeas corpus* petition in District Court for Southern California.

October 1984: After fine points have been resolved by the U.S. Supreme Court and the Ninth Circuit Court of Appeals, the district court denies Harris' second petition for *habeas corpus*.

July 8, 1988: Ninth Circuit Court of Appeals affirms district court's denial of *habeas corpus* relief.

September 28, 1989: Ninth Circuit denies petition for *en banc* rehearing.

January 5, 1990: Harris files fourth state *habeas* petition in California court.

January 16, 1990: U.S. Supreme Court declines Harris' petition for review of district court's denial of federal *habeas corpus*.

February 5, 1990: State judge in San Diego schedules Harris' execution for April 3.

March 16, 1990: California Supreme Court rejects Harris' fourth state *habeas* petition.

March 26, 1990: Harris files third federal *habeas* petition.

March 29, 1990: Federal district court denies third *habeas* petition.

March 30, 1990: Judge on Ninth Circuit Court of Appeals issues stay of execution.

April 2, 1990: U.S. Supreme Court rejects state of California's request to vacate stay of execution.

August 29, 1990: Ninth Circuit rejects claims raised in Harris' third federal *habeas corpus* petition.

November 30, 1990: Harris petitions federal district court for new hearing on third *habeas corpus* petition.

March 22, 1991: Ninth Circuit orders district court to consider request for rehearing.

May 15, 1991: Federal district court denies petition for rehearing.

(continued)

```
┌─────────────────────────────────────────────────────────────┐
│                    C A S E   I N   P O I N T                 │
├─────────────────────────────────────────────────────────────┤
```

(continued)

August 21, 1991: Ninth Circuit upholds district court's denial of petition for rehearing.

November 8, 1991: Ninth Circuit denies petition for *en banc* rehearing on its decision upholding district court's denial of rehearing.

March 2, 1992: U.S. Supreme Court rejects Harris' petition for review of lower court rulings on third federal *habeas corpus* petition.

March 13, 1992: State court in San Diego sets April 21 as execution date.

April 16, 1992: Harris files ninth *habeas corpus* petition in California courts.

April 17, 1992: California Supreme Court rejects Harris' ninth state *habeas* petition.

April 18, 1992: Harris files fourth *habeas corpus* petition in U.S. District Court for Southern California; it is summarily denied.

April 18, 1992: Judge on U.S. District Court for the Northern District of California issues order prohibiting state of California from executing anyone by means of the gas chamber.

April 19, 1992: Ninth Circuit vacates District Court order prohibiting use of gas chamber.

April 21, 1992: In the early morning hours, four separate stays of execution were issued by different judges on the Ninth Circuit Court of Appeals. Each of these stays was immediately vacated by the U.S. Supreme Court. The fourth of these stays came at 3:51 A.M., after Harris had been strapped into the chair in the gas chamber. At 5:45 Pacific time, the Supreme Court issued an order prohibiting lower federal courts from issuing any additional stays of execution. The vote on the high court was 7–2, with Justices Blackmun and Stevens dissenting. This final action by the Supreme Court cleared the way for Harris' execution, which began at 6:10 A.M. Pacific time. Harris' final words to the prison warden were, "You can be a king or a street sweeper, but everybody dances with the Grim Reaper." Harris was pronounced dead at 6:21 A.M.

Source: Reprinted, with permission, from Otis H. Stephens, Jr., and John M. Scheb, II, *American Constitutional Law* (St. Paul: West Publishing Co., 1993), pp. 849–50.

```
└─────────────────────────────────────────────────────────────┘
```

Either by constitutional or statutory provisions, executive authorities in all fifty states are likewise granted broad powers to pardon and commute sentences of persons convicted of violations of state criminal law. In many states, the pardoning power is vested exclusively in the governor. In a few states, the governor is limited to granting pardons approved by a state commission. In some states, the pardoning power is vested entirely in a state commission. A recent high profile case of clemency was that of Jean Harris, former headmistress of a girls' school who was convicted in 1980 of killing Dr. Herman Tarnower, author of the "Scarsdale Diet." After serving about twelve years of a fifteen years-to-life sentence, in December 1992, Ms. Harris was granted clemency by Governor Mario Cuomo of New York.

CONCLUSION

Under the early English common law, the right to appeal was nonexistent. Eventually, through court decisions and statutes, defendants gained the right to appeal from criminal convictions.

In America, statutes and judicial decisions have created numerous opportunities for appeal in criminal cases. Federal and state statutes guarantee at least one appeal by right to defendants who are convicted after entering a plea of not guilty. Beyond these appeals by right, defendants may seek review from higher courts by filing petitions for *certiorari* or discretionary review. Finally, the historic writ of *habeas corpus* provides an avenue of postconviction relief in state and federal tribunals. In many states postconviction relief has become structured under criteria specified by statute or rules of court.

Recently there has been considerable criticism of the delays that can result from a protracted process of appellate review. Perhaps as a response to such criticism, the United States Supreme Court has narrowed the access of state prisoners to federal postconviction relief. Yet substantial opportunities remain for persons to have criminal convictions reviewed by state and federal tribunals. One of the most common issues raised on postconviction review is whether defendants received effective assistance of counsel at trial.

While it must be conceded that the appellate process does often delay the imposition of criminal punishments, such delay must be weighed against our society's deep and historic commitment to fundamental fairness. In America, criminal law and procedure are guided by due process values as well as by the societal need for crime control.

QUESTIONS FOR THOUGHT AND DISCUSSION

1. What court(s) in your state has (have) jurisdiction to hear appeals from felony convictions? What changes, if any, would you propose for your state's system of appellate courts?

2. Is the right to appeal a necessary concomitant of due process of law? In the absence of statutory rights to appeal, would the current Supreme Court find a Constitutional right to appeal implicit in the due process and equal protection clauses of the Constitution?

3. What new or revised procedures would expedite the resolution of criminal appeals? Would such procedures detract from the fair and deliberative review essential to determine whether the decision of the trial court in a criminal case was arrived at fairly and accurately?

4. In addition to determining whether a sentence imposed on a convicted defendant is within the statutory bounds, do you think an appellate court is an appropriate forum to reconsider the reasonableness of the sentence imposed by the trial court?

5. How has the "nationalization" of the criminal law that occurred through decisions of the United States Supreme Court during the 1960s and 1970s affected the appellate process?

6. Why did the Supreme Court in *Stone v. Powell* (1976) restrict access to federal *habeas corpus* review for state prisoners raising Fourth Amendment claims? Could the Court's rationale apply equally to Fifth and Sixth Amendment issues?

7. The U.S. Supreme Court has recognized a constitutional right to represent yourself in a criminal trial. Could a person who insisted on self-representation at trial later challenge his or her conviction by claiming ineffective assistance of counsel?

8. Where a defendant has had an opportunity for a full and fair review of his trial through an appeal, what justifies the availability of additional avenues of review through collateral attack?

CASES

DOUGLAS V. CALIFORNIA
Supreme Court of the United States, 1963.
372 U.S. 353, 83 S. Ct. 814, 9 L.Ed.2d 811.

[This case deals with the right of an indigent defendant to have appointed counsel to assist in an appeal.]

Mr. Justice DOUGLAS delivered the opinion of the Court.

Petitioners, Bennie Will Meyes and William Douglas, were jointly tried and convicted in a California court on an information charging them with thirteen felonies. A single public defender was appointed to represent them. At the commencement of the trial, the defender moved for a continuance, stating that the case was very complicated, that he was not as prepared as he felt he should be because he was handling a different defense every day, and that there was a conflict of interest between the petitioners requiring the appointment of separate counsel for each of them. This motion was denied. Thereafter, petitioners dismissed the defender, claiming he was unprepared, and again renewed motions for separate counsel and for a continuance. These motions also were denied, and petitioners were ultimately convicted by a jury of all 13 felonies, which included robbery, assault with a deadly weapon, and assault with intent to commit murder. Both were given prison terms. Both appealed as of right to the California District Court of Appeal. That court affirmed their convictions. Both Meyes and Douglas then petitioned for further discretionary review in the California Supreme Court, but their petitions were denied without a hearing.

Although several questions are presented in the petition for certiorari, we addressed ourselves to only one of them. The record shows that petitioners requested, and were denied, the assistance of counsel on appeal, even though it plainly appeared they were indigents. In denying petitioners' requests, the California District Court of Appeal stated that it had "gone through" the record and had come to the conclusion that "no good whatever could be served

by appointment of counsel." . . . The District Court of Appeal was acting in accordance with a California rule of criminal procedure which provides that state appellate courts, upon the request of an indigent for counsel, may make "an independent investigation of the record and determine whether it would be of advantage to the defendant or helpful to the appellate court to have counsel appointed. . . . After such investigation, appellate courts should appoint counsel if in their opinion it would be helpful to the defendant or the court, and should deny the appointment of counsel only if in their judgment such appointment would be of no value to either the defendant or the court."

. . . [U]nder [California's] present practice the type of an appeal a person is afforded in the District Court of Appeal hinges upon whether or not he can pay for the assistance of counsel. If he can, the appellate court passes on the merits of his case only after having the full benefit of written briefs and oral argument by counsel. If he cannot, the appellate court is forced to prejudge the merits before it can even determine whether counsel should be provided. At this stage in the proceedings only the barren record speaks for the indigent, and, unless the printed pages show that an injustice has been committed, he is forced to go without a champion on appeal. Any real chance he may have had of showing that his appeal has hidden merit is deprived him when the court decides on an ex parte examination of the record that the assistance of counsel is not required.

We are not here concerned with problems that might arise from the denial of counsel for the preparation of a petition for discretionary or mandatory review beyond the stage in the appellate process at which the claims have once been presented by a lawyer and passed upon by an appellate court. We are dealing only with the *first appeal*, granted as a matter of right to rich and poor alike . . . from a criminal conviction. We need not now decide whether California would have to provide counsel for an indigent seeking a discretionary hearing from the California Supreme Court after the District Court of Appeal had sustained his conviction . . . or whether counsel must be appointed for an indigent seeking review of an appellate affirmance of his conviction in this Court by appeal as of right or by petition for a writ of certiorari which lies within the Court's discretion. But it is appropriate to observe that a State can, consistently with the Fourteenth Amendment, provide for differences so long as the result does not amount to a denial of due process or an "invidious discrimination." . . . Absolute equality is not required; lines can be and are drawn and we often sustain them. . . . But where the merits of the one and only appeal an indigent has as of right are decided without benefit of counsel, we think an unconstitutional line has been drawn between rich and poor.

When an indigent is forced to run this gauntlet of a preliminary showing of merit, the right to appeal does not comport with fair procedure. In the federal courts, on the other hand, an indigent must be afforded counsel on appeal whenever he challenges a certification that the appeal is not taken in good faith. . . . The federal courts must honor his request for counsel regardless of what they think the merits of the case may be; and "representation in the role of an advocate is required." . . . In California, however, once the court has "gone through" the record and denied counsel, the indigent has no recourse but to prosecute his appeal on his own, as best he can, no matter how meritorious his case may turn out to be. The present case, where counsel was denied petitioners on appeal, shows that the discrimination is not between "possibly good and obviously bad cases," but between cases where the rich man can require the court to listen to argument of counsel before deciding on the merits, but a poor man cannot. There is lacking that equality demanded by the Fourteenth Amendment where the rich man,

who appeals as of right, enjoys the benefit of counsel's examination into the record, research of the law, and marshalling of arguments on his behalf, while the indigent, already burdened by a preliminary determination that his case is without merit, is forced to shift for himself. The indigent, where the record is unclear or the errors are hidden, has only the right to a meaningless ritual, while the rich man has a meaningful appeal.

We vacate the judgment of the District Court of appeal and remand the case to that court for further proceedings not inconsistent with this opinion. It is so ordered. . . .

Mr. Justice CLARK, dissenting.

. . . With this new fetish for indigency the Court piles an intolerable burden on the State's judicial machinery. Indeed, if the Court is correct it may be that we should first clean up our own house. We have afforded indigent litigants much less protection that has California. Last Term we received over 1,200 in *forma pauperis* applications in none of which had we appointed attorneys or required a record. Some were appeals of right. Still we denied the petitions or dismissed the appeals on the moving papers alone. At the same time we had hundreds of paid cases in which we permitted petitions or appeals to be filed with not only records but briefs by counsel, after which they were disposed of in due course. On the other hand, California furnishes the indigent a complete record and if counsel is requested requires its appellate courts either to (1) appoint counsel or (2) make an independent investigation of that record and determine whether it would be of advantage to the defendant or helpful to the court to have counsel appointed. . . .

There is an old adage which my good Mother used to quote to me, i.e., "People who live in glass houses had best not throw stones." I dissent.

Mr. Justice HARLAN, whom Mr. Justice STEWART joins, dissenting. . . .

FAY V. NOIA

Supreme Court of the United States, 1963.
372 U.S. 391, 83 S. Ct. 822, 9 L.Ed.2d 837.

[This case deals with the scope of federal *habeas corpus* review of state convictions.]

Mr. Justice BRENNAN delivered the opinion of the Court.

This case presents important questions touching the federal habeas corpus jurisdiction ... in its relation to state criminal justice. The narrow question is whether the respondent Noia may be granted federal habeas corpus relief from imprisonment under a New York conviction now admitted by the State to rest upon a confession obtained from him in violation of the Fourteenth Amendment, after he was denied state post-conviction relief because the coerced confession claim had been decided against him at the trial and Noia had allowed the time for a direct appeal to lapse without seeking review by a state appellate court.

Noia was convicted in 1942 with Santo Caminito and Frank Bonino in the County Court of Kings County, New York, of a felony murder in the shooting and killing of one Hammeroff during the commission of a robbery.

The sole evidence against each defendant was his signed confession. Caminito and Bonino, but not Noia, appealed their convictions to the Appellate Division of the New York Supreme Court. These appeals were unsuccessful, but subsequent legal proceedings resulted in the releases of Caminito and Bonino on findings that their confessions had been coerced and their convictions therefore procured in violation of the Fourteenth Amendment. Although it has been stipulated that the coercive nature of Noia's confession was also established, the United States District Court for the Southern District of New York held in Noia's federal habeas corpus proceeding that because of his failure to appeal he must be denied relief under the provision of 28 U.S.C. § 2254 whereby "An application for a writ of habeas corpus in behalf of a person in custody pursuant to the judgment of a State court shall not be granted unless it appears that the applicant has exhausted the remedies available in the courts of the State ... ." The Court of Appeals for the Second Circuit reversed, one judge dissenting, and ordered that Noia's conviction be set aside and that he be discharged from custody unless given a new trial forthwith.... The Court of Appeals questioned whether § 2254 barred relief on federal habeas corpus where the applicant had failed to exhaust state remedies no longer available to him at the time the habeas proceedings was commenced (here a direct appeal from the conviction), but held that in any event exceptional circumstances were present which excused compliance with the section. The court also rejected other arguments advanced in support of the proposition that the federal remedy was unavailable to Noia. The first was that the denial of state post-conviction coram nobis relief on the ground of Noia's failure to appeal barred habeas relief because such failure constituted an adequate and independent state ground of decision, such that this Court on direct review of the state coram nobis proceedings would have declined to adjudicate the federal questions presented. In rejecting this argument, the court ... held that the exceptional circumstances excusing compliance with § 2254 also established that Noia's failure to appeal was not a state procedural ground adequate to bar the federal habeas remedy.... The second argument was that Noia's failure to appeal was to be deemed a waiver of his claim that he had been unconstitutionally convicted. The Court of Appeals rejected this argument on the ground that no waiver could be inferred in the circumstances....

We granted certiorari.... We affirm the judgment of the Court of Appeals but reach that court's result by a different course of reasoning. We hold: (1) Federal courts have power under the federal habeas statute to grant relief despite the applicant's failure to have pursued a state remedy not available to him at the time he applies; the doctrine under which state procedural defaults are held to constitute an adequate and independent state law ground barring direct Supreme Court review is not to be extended to limit the power granted the federal courts under the federal habeas statute. (2) Noia's failure to appeal was not a failure to exhaust "the remedies available in the courts of the State" as required by § 2254; that requirement refers only to a failure to exhaust state remedies still open to the applicant at the time he files his application for habeas corpus in the federal court. (3) Noia's failure to appeal cannot under the circumstances be deemed an intelligent and understanding waiver of his right to appeal such as to justify the withholding of federal habeas corpus relief. . . .

Although we hold that the jurisdiction of the federal courts on habeas corpus is not affected by procedural defaults incurred by the applicant during the state court proceedings, we recognize a limited discretion in the federal judge to deny relief to an applicant under certain circumstances. Discretion is implicit in the statutory command that the judge, after granting the writ and holding a hearing of appropriate scope, "dispose of the matter as law and justice require," 28 U.S.C. § 2243; and discretion was the flexible concept employed by the federal courts in developing the exhaustion rule. Furthermore, habeas corpus has traditionally been regarded as governed by equitable principles. . . . Among them is the principle that a suitor's conduct in relation to the matter at hand may disentitle him to the relief he seeks. Narrowly circumscribed, in conformity to the historical role of the writ of habeas corpus as an effective and imperative remedy for detentions contrary to fundamental law, the principle is unexceptionable. We therefore hold that the federal habeas judge may in his discretion deny relief to an applicant who has deliberately by-passed the orderly procedure of the state courts and in so doing has forfeited his state court remedies.

But we wish to make very clear that this grant of discretion is not to be interpreted as a permission to introduce legal fictions into federal habeas corpus. The classic definition of waive enunciated in *Johnson v. Zerbst*, 304 U.S. 458, 464, 58 S. Ct. 1019, 1023, 82 L.Ed. 1461—"an intentional relinquishment or abandonment of a known right or privilege"—furnishes the controlling standard. If a habeas applicant, after consultation with competent counsel or otherwise, understandingly and knowingly forewent the privilege of seeking to vindicate his federal claims in the state courts, whether for strategic, tactical, or any other reasons that can fairly be described as the deliberate by-passing of state procedures, then it is open

to the federal court on habeas to deny him all relief if the state courts refused to entertain his federal claims on the merits—though of course only after the federal court has satisfied itself, by holding a hearing or by some other means, of the facts bearing upon the applicant's default. . . . At all events we wish it clearly understood that the standard put forth here depends on the considered choice of the petitioner. . . . A choice made by counsel not participated in by the petitioner does not automatically bar relief. Nor does a state court's finding of waiver bar independent determination of the question by the federal courts on habeas, for waiver affecting federal rights is a federal question. . . .

The application of the standard we have adumbrated to the facts of the instant case is not difficult. Under no reasonable view can the State's version of Noia's reason for not appealing support an inference of deliberate by-passing of the state court system. For Noia to have appealed in 1942 would have been to run a substantial risk of electrocution. His was the grisly choice whether to sit content with life imprisonment or to travel the uncertain avenue of appeal which, if successful, might well have led to a retrial and death sentence. . . . He declined to play Russian roulette in this fashion. This was a choice by Noia not to appeal, but under the circumstances it cannot realistically be deemed a merely tactical or strategic litigation step, or in any way a deliberate circumvention of state procedures. This is not to say that in every case where a heavier penalty, even the death penalty, is a risk incurred by taking an appeal or otherwise foregoing a procedural right, waiver as we have defined it cannot be found. Each case must stand on its facts. In the instant case, the language of the judge in sentencing Noia, . . . made the risk that Noia, if reconvicted, would be sentenced to death, palpable and indeed unusually acute.

It should be unnecessary to repeat what so often has been said and what so plainly is the case: that the availability of the Great Writ of habeas corpus in the federal courts for persons in the custody of the States offends no legitimate state interest in the enforcement of criminal justice or procedure. Our decision today swings open no prison gates. Today as always few indeed is the number of state prisoners who eventually win their freedom by means of federal habeas corpus. Those few who are ultimately successful are persons whom society has grievously wronged and for whom belated liberation is little enough compensation. Surely no fair-minded person would contend that those who have been deprived of their liberty without due process of law ought nevertheless to languish in prison. Noia, no less than his codefendants Caminito and Bonino, is conceded to have been the victim of unconstitutional state action. Noia's case stands on its own; but surely no just and humane legal system can tolerate a result whereby a Caminito and a Bonino are at liberty because their confessions were found to have been coerced yet a Noia, whose confession was also coerced, remains in jail for life. For such anomalies, such affronts to the conscience of a civilized society, habeas corpus is predestined by its historical role in the struggle for personal liberty to be the ultimate remedy. If the States withhold effective remedy, the federal courts have the power and the duty to provide it. Habeas corpus is one of the precious heritages of Anglo-American civilization. We do no more today than confirm its continuing efficacy.

Affirmed.

Mr. Justice CLARK, dissenting.

. . . Beyond question the federal courts until today have had no power to release a prisoner in respondent Noia's predicament, there being no basis for such power in either the Constitution or the statute. But the Court today in releasing Noia makes an "abrupt break" not only with the Constitution and the statute but also with its past decisions, disrupting the delicate balance of federalism so foremost in the minds of the Founding Fathers and so uniquely important in the field of law enforcement. The short of it is that Noia's incarceration rests entirely on an adequate and independent state ground—namely, that he knowingly failed to perfect any appeal from his conviction of murder. While it may be that the Court's "decision today swings open no prison gates," the Court must admit in all candor that it effectively swings closed the doors of justice in the face of the State, since it certainly cannot prove its case 20 years after the fact. In view of this unfortunate turn of events, it appears important that we canvass the consequences of today's action on state law enforcement. . . .

Mr. Justice HARLAN, whom Mr. Justice CLARK and Mr. Justice STEWART join, dissenting. . . .

STONE V. POWELL
Supreme Court of the United States, 1976.
428 U.S. 465, 96 S. Ct. 3037, 49 L.Ed.2d 1067.

[In this decision, the Supreme Court restricts federal *habeas corpus* review of state convictions where Fourth Amendment issues are involved.]

Mr. Justice POWELL delivered the opinion of the Court.

Respondents in these cases were convicted of criminal offenses in state courts, and their convictions were affirmed on appeal. The prosecution in each case relied upon evidence obtained by searches and seizures alleged by respondents to have been unlawful. Each respondent subsequently sought relief in a Federal District Court by filing a petition for a writ of federal habeas corpus. . . . The question presented

is whether a federal court should consider, in ruling on a petition for habeas corpus relief filed by a state prisoner, a claim that evidence obtained by an unconstitutional search or seizure was introduced at his trial, when he has previously been afforded an opportunity for full and fair litigation of his claim in the state courts. The issue is of considerable importance to the administration of criminal justice. . . .

Respondent Lloyd Powell was convicted of murder in June 1968 after trial in a California state court. At about midnight on February 17, 1968, he and three companions entered the Bonanza Liquor Store in San Bernardino, Cal., where Powell became involved in an altercation with Gerald Parsons, the store manager, over the theft of a bottle of wine. In the scuffling that followed Powell shot and killed Parsons' wife. Ten hours later an officer of the Henderson, Nev., Police Department arrested Powell for violation of the Henderson vagrancy ordinance, and in the search incident to the arrest discovered a .38-caliber revolver with six expended cartridges in the cylinder.

Powell was extradited to California and convicted of second-degree murder in the Superior Court of San Bernardino County. Parsons and Powell's accomplices at the liquor store testified against him. A criminologist testified that the revolver found on Powell was the gun that killed Parsons' wife. The trial court rejected Powell's contention that testimony by the Henderson police officer as to the search and the discovery of the revolver should have been excluded because the vagrancy ordinance was unconstitutional. In October 1969, the conviction was affirmed by a California District Court of Appeal. Although the issue was duly presented, that court found it unnecessary to pass upon the legality of the arrest and search because it concluded that the error, if any, in admitting the testimony of the Henderson officer was harmless beyond a reasonable doubt under *Chapman v. California*, 386 U.S. 18, 17 L.Ed.2d 705, 87 S. Ct. 824, 24 ALR3d 1065 (1967). The Supreme Court of California denied Powell's petition for habeas corpus relief.

In August 1971 Powell filed an amended petition for a writ of federal habeas corpus . . . in the United States District Court for the Northern District of California, contending that the testimony concerning the .38-caliber revolver should have been excluded as the fruit of an illegal search. He argued that his arrest had been unlawful because the Henderson vagrancy ordinance was unconstitutionally vague, and that the arresting officer lacked probable cause to believe that he was violating it. The District Court concluded that the arresting officer had probable cause and held that even if the vagrancy ordinance was unconstitutional, the deterrent purpose of the exclusionary rule does not require that it be applied to bar admission of the fruits of a search incident to an otherwise valid arrest. In the alternative, that court agreed with the California District Court of Appeal that the admission of the evidence concerning Powell's arrest, if error, was harmless beyond a reasonable doubt.

In December 1974, the Court of Appeals for the Ninth Circuit reversed. . . . The court concluded that the vagrancy ordinance was unconstitutionally vague, that Powell's arrest was therefore illegal, and that although exclusion of the evidence would serve no deterrent purpose with regard to police officers who were enforcing statutes in good faith, exclusion would serve the public interest by deterring legislators from enacting unconstitutional statutes. After an independent review of the evidence the court concluded that the admission of the evidence was not harmless error since it supported the testimony of Parsons and Powell's accomplices. . . .

The primary justification for the exclusionary rule then is the deterrence of police conduct that violates Fourth Amendment rights. Post-*Mapp* decisions have established that the rule is not a personal constitutional right. It is not calculated to redress the injury to the privacy of the victim of the search or seizure, for any "[r]eparation comes too late." Instead, "the rule is a judicially created remedy designed to safeguard Fourth Amendment rights generally through its deterrent effect . . . ."

Respondents allege violations of Fourth Amendment rights guaranteed them through the Fourteenth Amendment. The question is whether state prisoners—who have been afforded the opportunity for full and fair consideration of their reliance upon the exclusionary rule with respect to seized evidence by the state courts at trial and on direct review—may invoke their claim again on federal habeas corpus review. The answer is to be found by weighing the utility of the exclusionary rule against the costs of extending it to collateral review of Fourth Amendment claims.

The costs of applying the exclusionary rule even at trial and on direct review are well known: the focus of the trial, and the attention of the participants therein, are diverted from the ultimate question of guilt or innocence that should be the central concern in a criminal proceeding. Moreover, the physical evidence sought to be excluded is typically reliable and often the most probative information bearing on the guilt or innocence of the defendant. . . . Application of the rule thus deflects the truthfinding process and often frees the guilty. The disparity in particular cases between the error committed by the police officer and the windfall afforded a guilty defendant by application of the rule is contrary to the idea of proportionality that is essential to the concept of justice. Thus, although the rule is thought to deter unlawful police activity in part through the nurturing of respect for Fourth Amendment values, if applied indiscriminately it may well have the opposite effect of generating disrespect for the law and administration of justice. These long-recognized costs of the rule persist when a criminal conviction is sought to be overturned on collateral review on the ground that a search-and-seizure claim was erroneously rejected by two or more tiers of state courts.

Evidence obtained by police officers in violation of the Fourth Amendment is excluded at trial in the hope that the frequency of future violations will decrease. Despite the absence of supportive empirical evidence, we have assumed that the immediate effect of exclusion will be to discourage law enforcement officials from violating the Fourth Amendment by removing the incentive to disregard it. More importantly, over the long term, this demonstration that our society attaches serious consequences to violation of constitutional rights is thought to encourage those who formulate law enforcement policies, and the officers who implement them, to incorporate Fourth Amendment ideals into their value system.

We adhere to the view that these considerations support the implementation of the exclusionary rule at trial and its enforcement on direct appeal of state-court convictions. But the additional contribution, if any, of the consideration of search-and-seizure claims of state prisoners on collateral review is small in relation to the costs. To be sure, each case in which such claim is considered may add marginally to an awareness of the values protected by the Fourth Amendment. There is no reason to believe, however, that the overall educative effect of the exclusionary rule would be appreciably diminished if search-seizure claims could not be raised in federal habeas corpus review of state convictions. Nor is there reason to assume that any specific disincentive already created by the risk of exclusion of evidence at trial or the reversal of convictions on direct review would be enhanced if there were the further risk that a conviction obtained in state court and affirmed on direct review might be overturned in collateral proceedings often occurring years after the incarceration of the defendant. The view that the deterrence of Fourth Amendment violations would be furthered rests on the dubious assumption that law enforcement authorities would fear that federal habeas review might reveal flaws in a search or seizure that went undetected at trial and on appeal. Even if one rationally could assume that some additional incremental deterrent effect would be present in isolated cases, the resulting advance of the legitimate goal of furthering Fourth Amendment rights would be outweighed by the acknowledged costs to other values vital to a rational system of criminal justice.

In sum, we conclude that where the State has provided an opportunity for full and fair litigation of a Fourth Amendment claim, a state prisoner may not be granted federal habeas corpus relief on the ground that evidence obtained in an unconstitutional search or seizure was introduced at his trial. In this context the contribution of the exclusionary rule, if any, to the effectuation of the Fourth Amendment is minimal and the substantial societal costs of application of the rule persist with special force.

Accordingly, the judgments of the Court of Appeals are reversed.

Mr. Chief Justice BURGER, concurring....

Mr. Justice BRENNAN, with whom Mr. Justice MARSHALL concurs, dissenting.

... In summary, while unlike the Court I consider that the exclusionary rule is a constitutional ingredient of the Fourth Amendment, any modification of that rule should at least be accomplished with some modicum of logic and justification not provided today. The Court does not disturb the holding of *Mapp v. Ohio* that, as a matter of federal constitutional law, illegally obtained evidence must be excluded from the trial of a criminal defendant whose rights were transgressed during the search that resulted in acquisition of the evidence. In light of that constitutional rule it is a matter for Congress, not this Court, to prescribe what federal courts are to review state prisoners' claims of constitutional error committed by state courts. Until this decision, our cases have never departed from the construction of the habeas statutes as embodying a congressional intent that, however substantive constitutional rights are delineated or expanded, those rights may be asserted as a procedural matter under federal habeas jurisdiction. Employing the transparent tactic that today's is a decision construing the Constitution, the Court usurps the authority—vested by the Constitution in the Congress—to reassign federal judicial responsibility for reviewing state prisoners' claims of failure of state courts to redress violations of their Fourth Amendment rights. Our jurisdiction is eminently unsuited for that task, and as a practical matter the only result of today's holding will be that denials by the state courts of claims by state prisoners of violations of their Fourth Amendment rights will go unreviewed by a federal tribunal. I fear that the same treatment ultimately will be accorded state prisoners' claims of violations of other constitutional rights; thus the potential ramifications of this case for federal habeas

jurisdiction generally are ominous. The Court, no longer content just to restrict forthrightly the constitutional rights of the citizenry, has embarked on a campaign to water down even such constitutional rights as it purports to acknowledge by the device of foreclosing resort to the federal habeas remedy for their redress.

I would affirm the judgments of the Courts of Appeals.

Mr. Justice WHITE, dissenting.

. . . I cannot agree that the writ of habeas corpus should be any less available to those convicted of state crimes where they allege Fourth Amendment violations than where other constitutional issues are presented to the federal court. . . .

DARDEN V. WAINWRIGHT
Supreme Court of the United States, 1986.
477 U.S. 168, 106 S. Ct. 2464, 91 L.Ed.2d 144.

[This case demonstrates the potentially protracted character of the appeals process and the kinds of issues often raised by defendants seeking postconviction relief.]

Justice POWELL delivered the opinion of the Court. This case presents three questions concerning the validity of petitioner's criminal conviction and death sentence: (i) whether the exclusion for cause of a member of the venire violated the principles announced in *Wainwright v. Witt*, 469 U.S. 412, 83 L.Ed.2d 841, 105 S. Ct. 844 (1985); (ii) whether the prosecution's closing argument during the guilt phase of a bifurcated trial rendered the trial fundamentally unfair and deprived the sentencing determination of the reliability required by the Eighth Amendment; and (iii) whether petitioner was denied effective assistance of counsel at the sentencing phase of this trial.

Petitioner was tried and found guilty of murder, robbery, and assault with intent to kill in the Circuit Court for Citrus County, Florida, in January 1974. Pursuant to Florida's capital sentencing statute, the

same jury that convicted petitioner heard further testimony and argument in order to make a nonbinding recommendation as to whether a death sentence should be imposed. The jury recommended a death sentence, and the trial judge followed that recommendation. On direct appeal, the Florida Supreme Court affirmed the conviction and the sentence. Petitioner made several of the same arguments in that appeal that he makes here. With respect to the prosecutorial misconduct claim, the court disapproved of the closing argument, but reasoned that the law required a new trial "only in those cases in which it is reasonably evident that the remarks might have influenced the jury to reach a more severe verdict of guilt . . . or in which the comment is unfair." . . . It concluded that the comments had not rendered petitioner's trial unfair. Petitioner's challenge to the juror exclusion was rejected without comment. Petitioner did not at that time raise his claim of ineffective assistance of counsel. This Court granted certiorari, . . . limited the grant to the claim of prosecutorial misconduct, . . . heard oral argument, and dismissed the writ as improvidently granted. . . .

Petitioner then sought federal habeas corpus relief, raising the same claims he raises here. The District Court denied the petition.... A divided panel of Court of Appeals for the Eleventh Circuit affirmed.... The Court of Appeals granted rehearing en banc, and affirmed the District Court by an equally divided court.... Following a second rehearing en banc the Court of Appeals reversed on the claim of improper excusal of a member of the venire.... This Court granted the State's petition for certiorari on the claim, vacated the Court of Appeals' judgment and remanded for reconsideration in light of *Wainwright v. Witt*, 469 U.S. 412, 83 L.Ed.2d 841, 105 S. Ct. 844 (1985). On remand, the en banc court denied relief.... Petitioner filed an application for a stay of his execution that this Court treated as a petition for certiorari and granted, at the same time staying his execution.... We now affirm....

As petitioner's arguments all relate to incidents in the course of his trial, they will be taken up, together with the relevant facts, in chronological order.

Petitioner contends that one member of the venire, Mr. Murphy, was excluded improperly under the test enunciated in *Wainwright v. Witt*.... That case modified this Court's opinion in *Witherspoon v. Illinois*, 391 U.S. 510, 20 L.Ed.2d 776, 88 S. Ct. 1770 (1968). *Witherspoon* had held that potential jurors may be excused for cause when their opposition to the death penalty is such that they automatically would vote against a sentence of death or would be impaired in the task of determining defendant's guilt. *Witt* held that the proper test is whether the juror's views on capital punishment would "prevent or substantially impair the performance of his duties as a juror in accordance with his instructions and his oath."... *Witt* also made clear that the trial judge's determination that a potential juror is impermissibly biased is a factual finding entitled to a presumption of correctness....

Petitioner's argument on this issue relies solely on the wording of a question the trial court asked Murphy before excluding him. The court asked, "Do you have any moral or religious, conscientious moral or religious principles in opposition to the death penalty so strong that you would be unable without violating your own principles to vote to

recommend a death penalty regardless of the facts?"... Petitioner argues that this question does not correctly state the relevant legal standard. As *Witt* makes clear, however, our inquiry does not end with a mechanical recitation of a single question and answer.... We therefore examine the context surrounding Murphy's exclusion to determine whether the trial court's decision that Murphy's beliefs would "substantially impair the performance of his duties as a juror" was fairly supported by the record.

During voir dire, but prior to individual questioning on this point, the trial court spoke to the entire venire, including Murphy, saying:

> Now I am going to ask each of you individually the same question so listen to me carefully. I want to know if any of you have such strong religious, moral, or conscientious principles in opposition to the death penalty that you would be unwilling to vote to return an advisory sentence recommending the death sentence even though the facts presented to you should be such as under the law would require that recommendation. Do you understand my question?

The court then proceeded to question the members of the venire individually, but did so while the entire venire was present in the courtroom. Thus, throughout the individual questioning, all the veniremen could hear the questions and answers. In fact, the prosecution frequently incorporated prior questioning of the veniremen by reference, each time with the assurance from the individual being questioned that he or she had heard and understood the previous questions....

The court repeatedly stated the correct standard when questioning individual members of the venire. Murphy was present and heard the court ask the proper *Witherspoon* question over and over again. After many instances of such questioning, Murphy was seated in the jury box. The court first asked Murphy his occupation, and learned that he was retired, but had spent the eight years before retirement working in the administration office of St. Pios Seminary. The court then asked, "Do you have any moral or religious, conscientious moral or religious principles in opposition to the death penalty so strong that you would be unable without violating your own principles to vote to recommend a death penalty regardless of the facts." After Murphy responded, "Yes, I have" he was excused.

The precise wording of the question asked of Murphy, and the answer he gave, do not by themselves compel the conclusion that he could not under any circumstance recommend the death penalty. But *Witt* recognized that "determinations of juror bias cannot be reduced to question-and-answer sessions which obtain results in the manner of a catechism." ... The trial court, "aided as it undoubtedly was by its assessment of [the potential juror's] demeanor," ... was under the obligation to determine whether Murphy's views "would prevent or substantially impair the performance of his duties as a juror." ... In making this determination, the trial court could take account of the fact that Murphy was present throughout an entire series of questions that made the purpose and meaning of the *Witt* inquiry absolutely clear. No specific objection was made to the excusal of Murphy by defense counsel. Nor did the court perceive, as it had previously, any need to question further. Viewing the record of voir dire in its entirety, we agree with the reasoning of the Court of Appeals that the trial court's decision to exclude this juror was proper. ...

Petitioner next contends that the prosecution's closing argument at the guilt-innocence stage of the trial rendered his conviction fundamentally unfair and deprived the sentencing determination of the reliability that the Eighth Amendment requires.

It is helpful as an initial matter to place these remarks in context. Closing argument came at the end of several days of trial. Because of a state procedural rule petitioner's counsel had the opportunity to present the initial summation as well as a rebuttal to the prosecutors' closing arguments. The prosecutors' comment must be evaluated in light of the defense argument that preceded it, which blamed the Polk County Sheriff's Office for a lack of evidence, alluded to the death penalty, characterized the perpetrator of the crimes as an "animal," and contained counsel's personal opinion of the strength of the state's evidence.

The prosecutors then made their closing argument. That argument deserves the condemnation it has received from every court to review it, although no court has held that the argument rendered the

trial unfair. Several comments attempted to place some of the blame for the crime on the Division of Corrections, because Darden was on weekend furlough from a prison sentence when the crime occurred. Some comments implied that the death penalty would be the only guarantee against a future similar act. Others incorporated the defense's use of the word "animal." Prosecutor McDaniel made several offensive comments reflecting an emotional reaction to the case. These comments undoubtedly were improper. But as both the District Court and the original panel of the Court of Appeals (whose opinion on this issue still stands) recognized, it "is not enough that the prosecutor's remarks were undesirable or even universally condemned." ... The relevant question is whether the prosecutor's comments "so infected the trial with unfairness as to make the resulting conviction a denial of due process." ... Moreover, the appropriate standard of review for such a claim on writ of habeas corpus is "the narrow one of due process, and not the broad exercise of supervisory power." ...

Under this standard of review, we agree with the reasoning of every court to consider these comments that they did not deprive petitioner of a fair trial. The prosecutor's argument did not manipulate or misstate the evidence, nor did it implicate other specific rights of the accused such as the right to counsel or the right to remain silent. ... Much of the objectionable content was invited by or was responsive to the opening summation of the defense. ... The trial court instructed the jurors several times that their decision was to be made on the basis of the evidence alone, and that the arguments of counsel were not evidence. The weight of the evidence against petitioner was heavy; the "overwhelming eyewitness and circumstantial evidence to support a finding of guilt on all charges" ... reduced the likelihood that the jury's decision was influenced by argument. Finally, defense counsel made the tactical decision not to present any witness other than petitioner. This decision not only permitted them to give their summation prior to the prosecution's closing argument, but also gave them the opportunity to make a final rebuttal argument. Defense counsel were able to use the opportunity for rebuttal very effectively, turning much of the prosecutor's comments and actions in a light that was more likely to engender strong disapproval than result in inflamed passions against petitioner. For these reasons, we agree with the District Court below that "Darden's trial was not perfect—few are—but neither was it fundamentally unfair." . . .

Petitioner contends that he was denied effective assistance of counsel at the sentencing phase of trial. That claim must be evaluated against the two-part test announced in *Strickland v. Washington*, 466 U.S. 668, 80 L.Ed.2d 674, 104 S. Ct. 2052 (1984). First, petitioner must show that "counsel's representation fell below an objective standard of reasonableness." . . . Second, petitioner must show that "there is a reasonable probability that, but for counsel's unprofessional errors, the result of the proceeding would have been different." . . . Petitioner argues that his trial counsel did not delve sufficiently into his background, and as a result were unprepared to present mitigating evidence at the sentencing hearing.

As an initial matter, petitioner contends that trial counsel devoted only the time between the close of the guilt phase of trial and the start of the penalty phase—approximately one-half hour—to preparing the case in mitigation. That argument is without merit. Defense counsel engaged in extensive preparation prior to trial, in a manner that included preparation for sentencing. Mr. Jack Johnson, head of the Public Defender's Office at the time, stated to the habeas court that "I would say we have expended more man hours on this case than on any case to my knowledge." . . . Mr. Goodwill, an experienced criminal trial lawyer, testified he "spent more time on this case than I spent on . . . any capital case I have been involved in, probably more time than any case I've ever been involved in." . . . That included time investigating petitioner's alibi, and driving petitioner around the scene of events to establish each point of his story. Counsel obtained a psychiatric report on petitioner, with an eye toward using it in mitigation during sentencing. Counsel also learned in pre-trial preparation that Mrs. Turman was opposed to the death penalty, and considered the possibility of putting her on the stand at the sentencing phase. The record clearly indicates that a great deal of time and effort went into the defense of this case; a significant portion of that time was devoted to preparation for sentencing.

Petitioner also claims that his trial counsel interpreted Fla. Stat. 921.141(7), a statutory list of mitigating factors, as an exclusive list. He contends that their failure to introduce any evidence in mitigation was the result of this interpretation of the statute, and that he was thereby deprived of effective assistance of counsel. We express no view about the reasonableness of that interpretation of Florida law, because in this case, the trial court specifically informed petitioner and his counsel just prior to the sentencing phase of trial that they could "go into any other factors that might really be pertinent to full consideration of your case and the analysis of you and your family situation, your causes, or anything else that might be pertinent to what is the appropriate sentence." . . . At that point, even if counsel previously believed the list to be exclusive, they knew they were free to offer nonstatutory mitigating evidence, and chose not to do so.

As we recognized in *Strickland*, "[j]udicial scrutiny of counsel's performance must be highly deferential. . . . A fair assessment of attorney performance requires that every effort be made to eliminate the distorting effects of hindsight, to reconstruct the circumstances of counsel's perspective at the time." . . . In particular, "a court must indulge a strong presumption that counsel's conduct falls within the wide range of reasonable professional assistance; that is, the defendant must overcome the presumption that, under the circumstances, the challenged action might be considered sound trial strategy." . . . In this case, there are several reasons why counsel reasonably could have chosen to rely on a simple plea for mercy from petitioner himself. Any attempt to portray petitioner as a non-violent man would have opened the door for the State to rebut with evidence of petitioner's prior convictions. This evidence had not previously been admitted in evidence, and trial counsel reasonably could have viewed it as particularly damaging. The head of the Public Defender's Office testified at the habeas corpus hearing that petitioner "had been in and out of jails and prisons for most of his adult life . . . ." . . . Petitioner had, for example, previously been convicted of assault with intent to commit rape. . . . In addition, if defense counsel had attempted to offer testimony that petitioner was incapable of committing the crimes at issue here, the State could have responded with a psychiatric report that indicated that petitioner "very well could have committed the crime; that he was, as I recall his [the psychiatrist's] term, a sociopathic type personality; that he would act entirely on impulse with no premeditation from the standpoint of planning. But that when a situation arose, the decision would be made simultaneously to commit the act." . . . For that reason, after consultation with petitioner, defense counsel rejected use of the psychiatric testimony. . . . Similarly, if defense counsel had attempted to put on evidence the petitioner was a family man, they would have been faced with his admission at trial that, although still married, he was spending the weekend furlough with a girlfriend. In sum, petitioner has not "overcome the presumption that, under the circumstances, the challenged action might be considered sound trial strategy." . . . Petitioner has failed to satisfy the first part of the Strickland test, that his trial counsels' performance fell below an objective standard of reasonableness. We agree with both the District Court and the Court of Appeals that petitioner was not deprived of the effective assistance of counsel. . . .

Chief Justice BURGER, concurring. . . .

Justice BRENNAN, dissenting. . . .

Justice BLACKMUN, with whom Justice BRENNAN, Justice MARSHALL, and Justice STEVENS join, dissenting.

Although the Constitution guarantees a criminal defendant only "a fair trial [and] not a perfect one," . . . this Court has stressed repeatedly in the decade since *Gregg v. Georgia*, 428 U.S. 153, 49 L.Ed.2d 859, 96 S. Ct. 2909 (1976), that the Eighth Amendment requires a heightened degree of reliability in any case where a State seeks to take the defendant's life. Today's opinion, however, reveals a Court willing to tolerate not only imperfection but a level of fairness and reliability so low it should make conscientious prosecutors cringe. . . .

McCleskey v. Zant

Supreme Court of the United States, 1991.
499 U.S. 467, 11 S.Ct. 1454, 113 L.Ed.2d 517.

[Warren McCleskey was involved in an armed robbery of a Georgia furniture store in 1978. In the course of the robbery, one of the perpetrators shot and killed an off-duty police officer. McCleskey confessed to the shooting, but at trial renounced his confession after taking the stand with an alibi denying his involvement in the robbery. To refute McCleskey's testimony, the prosecution called Offie Evans, who had occupied a jail cell next to McCleskey's. Evans testified that McCleskey admitted shooting the officer during the robbery. After hearing this and other evidence, the jury found McCleskey guilty of felony-murder and sentenced him to death. On appeal, the Georgia Supreme Court affirmed his conviction and sentence.

In January 1981, McCleskey sought a writ of *habeas corpus* in state court, raising twenty-three challenges to his murder conviction and death sentence. Included in his contentions was the allegation that the admission of Evans' testimony violated his Sixth Amendment right to counsel as construed in *Massiah v. United States*, 377 U.S. 201, 84 S.Ct. 1199, 12 L.Ed.2d 246 (1964). After a hearing, the state court denied relief, and the Georgia Supreme Court denied review.

In December 1981, McCleskey filed a petition for *habeas corpus* in the U.S. District Court for the Northern District of Georgia. McCleskey asserted eighteen grounds for relief, but with no mention of the alleged *Massiah* violation. After extensive hearings, the District Court granted relief, but the Court of Appeals for the Eleventh Circuit reversed. On certiorari, the U.S. Supreme Court affirmed the Court of Appeals reversal of the District Court decision granting relief.

McCleskey filed a second state *habeas corpus* petition in 1987, alleging five grounds, including reference to Evans' testimony. Again, the state courts denied relief.

In July 1987, McCleskey filed a second federal *habeas* petition, asserting, among other things, a *Massiah* violation, to wit, that a relationship between the prosecution and Evans, the inmate witness, existed but had not been disclosed at the time of trial. After evidentiary hearings, the District Court in December 1987 granted relief based on its finding that the state had violated the Sixth Amendment as construed in *Massiah.* The U.S. Court of Appeals for the Eleventh Circuit reversed, holding that the District Court erred by failing to dismiss McCleskey's *Massiah* claim as an abuse of the writ of *habeas corpus.*]

Justice KENNEDY delivered the opinion of the Court.

... McCleskey petitioned this Court for a writ of certiorari, alleging numerous errors in the Eleventh Circuit's abuse of the writ analysis. In our order granting the petition, we requested the parties to address the following additional question: "Must the State demonstrate that a claim was deliberately abandoned in an earlier petition for a writ of habeas corpus in order to establish that inclusion of that claim in a subsequent habeas petition constitutes abuse of the writ?" ...

Our discussion demonstrates that the doctrine of abuse of the writ refers to a complex and evolving body of equitable principles informed and controlled by historical usage, statutory developments, and judicial decisions. Because of historical changes and the complexity of the subject, the Court has not "always followed an unwavering line in its conclusions as to the availability of the Great Writ." ... Today we attempt to define the doctrine of abuse of the writ with more precision.

Although our decisions on the subject do not all admit of ready synthesis, one point emerges with clarity: Abuse of the writ is not confined to instances of deliberate abandonment. Our recent decisions confirm that a petitioner can abuse the writ by raising a claim in a subsequent petition that he could have raised in his first, regardless of whether the failure to raise it earlier stemmed from a deliberate choice.

The inexcusable neglect standard demands more from a petitioner than the standard of deliberate abandonment. But we have not given the former term the content necessary to guide district courts in the ordered consideration of allegedly abusive habeas corpus petitions. For reasons we explain below,

a review of our habeas corpus precedents leads us to decide that the same standard used to determine whether to excuse state procedural defaults should govern the determination of inexcusable neglect in the abuse of the writ context.

The prohibition against adjudication in federal habeas corpus of claims defaulted in state court is similar in purpose and design to the abuse of the writ doctrine, which in general prohibits subsequent habeas consideration of claims not raised, and thus defaulted, in the first federal habeas proceeding. The terms "abuse of the writ" and "inexcusable neglect," on the one hand, and "procedural default," on the other, imply a background norm of procedural regularity binding on the petitioner. This explains the presumption against habeas adjudication both of claims defaulted in state court and of claims defaulted in the first round of federal habeas. ...

... One of the law's very objects is the finality of its judgments. Neither innocence nor just punishment can be vindicated until the final judgment is known. "Without finality, the criminal law is deprived of much of its deterrent effect." ... And when a habeas petitioner succeeds in obtaining a new trial, the " 'erosion of memory' and 'dispersion of witnesses' that occur with the passage of time," ... prejudice the government and diminish the chances of a reliable criminal adjudication. Though *Fay v. Noia* ... may have cast doubt upon these propositions, since *Fay* we have taken care in our habeas corpus decisions to reconfirm the importance of finality. ...

Finality has special importance in the context of a federal attack on a state conviction. ... Reexamination of state convictions on federal habeas "frustrate[s] ... 'both the States' sovereign power to punish offenders and their good-faith attempts to honor constitutional rights.' " ... Our federal system recognizes the independent power of a State to articulate societal norms through criminal law; but the power of a State to pass laws means little if the State cannot enforce them.

Habeas review extracts further costs. Federal collateral litigation places a heavy burden on scarce federal judicial resources, and threatens the capacity of the system to resolve primary disputes. ... Finally, habeas corpus review may give litigants incentives to withhold claims for manipulative purposes and may establish disincentives to present claims when evidence is fresh. ...

Far more severe are the disruptions when a claim is presented for the first time in a second or subsequent federal habeas petition. If "[c]ollateral review of a conviction extends the ordeal of trial for both society and the accused," ... the ordeal worsens during subsequent collateral proceedings. Perpetual disrespect for the finality of convictions disparages the entire criminal justice system.... If re-examination of a conviction in the first round of federal habeas stretches resources, examination of new claims raised in a second or subsequent petition spreads them thinner still. These later petitions deplete the resources needed for federal litigants in the first instance, including litigants commencing their first federal habeas action. The phenomenon calls to mind [the] admonition that "[i]t must prejudice the occasional meritorious application to be buried in a flood of worthless ones." ... And if re-examination of convictions in the first round of habeas offends federalism and comity, the offense increases when a State must defend its conviction in a second or subsequent habeas proceeding on grounds not even raised in the first petition.

The federal writ of habeas corpus overrides all these considerations, essential as they are to the rule of law, when a petitioner raises a meritorious constitutional claim in a proper manner in a habeas petition. Our procedural default jurisprudence and abuse of the writ jurisprudence help define this dimension of procedural regularity. Both doctrines impose on petitioners a burden of reasonable compliance with procedures designed to discourage baseless claims and to keep the system open for valid ones; both recognize the law's interest in finality; and both invoke equitable principles to define the court's discretion to excuse pleading and procedural requirements for petitioners who could not comply with them in the exercise of reasonable care and diligence....

We conclude from the unity of structure and purpose in the jurisprudence of state procedural defaults and abuse of the writ that the standard for excusing a failure to raise a claim at the appropriate time should be the same in both contexts. We have held that a procedural default will be excused upon a showing of cause and prejudice.... We now hold that the same standard applies to determine if there has been an abuse of the writ through inexcusable neglect.

Considerations of certainty and stability in our discharge of the judicial function support adoption of the cause and prejudice standard in the abuse of the writ context. Well defined in the case law, the standard will be familiar to federal courts. Its application clarifies the imprecise contours of the term "inexcusable neglect." The standard is an objective one, and can be applied in a manner that comports with the threshold nature of the abuse of the writ inquiry.... Finally, the standard provides "a sound and workable means of channeling the discretion of federal habeas courts." ... "[I]t is important, in order to preclude individualized enforcement of the Constitution in different parts of the Nation, to lay down as specifically as the nature of the problem permits the standards or directions that should govern the District Judges in the disposition of applications for habeas corpus by prisoners under sentence of State Courts." ...

The cause and prejudice standard should curtail the abusive petitions that in recent years have threatened to undermine the integrity of the habeas corpus process. "Federal courts should not continue to tolerate—even in capital cases—this type of abuse of the writ of habeas corpus." ... The writ of habeas corpus is one of the centerpieces of our liberties. "But the writ has potentialities for evil as well as for good. Abuse of the writ may undermine the orderly administration of justice and therefore weaken the forces of authority that are essential for civilization." ... Adoption of the cause and prejudice standard acknowledges the historic purpose and function of the writ in our constitutional system, and, by preventing its abuse, assures its continued efficacy....

The history of the proceedings in this case, and the burden upon the State in defending against allegations made for the first time in federal court some 9 years after the trial, reveal the necessity for the abuse of the writ doctrine. The cause and prejudice standard we adopt today leaves ample room for consideration of constitutional errors in a first federal habeas petition and in a later petition under appropriate circumstances. Petitioner has not satisfied this standard for excusing the omission of the *Massiah* claim from his first petition. The judgment of the Court of Appeals is affirmed.

Justice MARSHALL, with whom Justice
BLACKMUN and Justice STEVENS join,
dissenting.

Today's decision departs drastically from the
norms that inform the proper judicial function.
Without even the most casual admission that it is
discarding longstanding legal principles, the Court
radically redefines the content of the "abuse of the
writ" doctrine, substituting the strict-liability "cause
and prejudice" standard ... for the good-faith
"deliberate abandonment" standard.... This doctrinal innovation, which repudiates a line of judicial
decisions codified by Congress in the governing
statute and procedural rules, was by no means

foreseeable when the petitioner in this case filed his
first federal habeas application. Indeed, the new
rule announced and applied today was not even
requested by respondent at any point in this
litigation. Finally, rather than remand this case for
reconsideration in light of its new standard, the
majority performs an independent reconstruction of
the record, disregarding the factual findings of the
District Court and applying its new rule in a
manner that encourages state officials to conceal
evidence that would likely prompt a petitioner to
raise a particular claim on habeas. Because I cannot
acquiesce in this unjustifiable assault on the Great
Writ, I dissent....

KEENEY V. TAMAYO-REYES
Supreme Court of the United States, 1992.
504 U.S. ___ , 112 S. Ct. 1715, 118 L Ed 2d 318.

[In this case, the U.S. Supreme Court further restricts the availability of federal *habeas corpus* review
to state prisoners who have exhausted appellate
remedies in the state courts.]

Justice WHITE delivered the opinion of the Court.
Respondent is a Cuban immigrant with little education and almost no knowledge of English. In 1984,
he was charged with murder arising from the stabbing death of a man who had allegedly attempted to
intervene in a confrontation between respondent
and his girlfriend in a bar.

Respondent was provided with a defense attorney
and interpreter. The attorney recommended to respondent that he plead *nolo contendere* to first-degree
manslaughter.... Respondent signed a plea form
that explained in English the rights he was waiving
by entering the plea. The state court held a plea
hearing, at which petitioner was represented by
counsel and his interpreter. The judge asked the-
attorney and interpreter if they had explained to
respondent the rights in the plea form and the
consequences of his plea; they responded in the
affirmative. The judge then explained to respondent,
in English, the rights he would waive by his plea,

and asked the interpreter to translate. Respondent
indicated that he understood his rights and still
wished to plead *nolo contendere.* The judge accepted
his plea.

Later, respondent brought a collateral attack on
the plea in a state-court proceeding. He alleged his
plea had not been knowing and intelligent and
therefore was invalid because his translater had not
translated accurately and completely for him the
mens rea element of manslaughter. He also contended that he did not understand the purposes of
the plea form or the plea hearing. He contended that
he did not know he was pleading no contest to
manslaughter, but rather that he thought he was
agreeing to be tried for manslaughter.

After a hearing, the state court dismissed respondent's petition, finding that respondent was properly served by his trial interpreter and that the
interpreter correctly, fully, and accurately translated
the communications between respondent and his
attorney. The state court of appeals affirmed, and
the state supreme court denied review.

Respondent then entered Federal District Court
seeking a writ of habeas corpus. Respondent contended that the material facts concerning the trans-

lation were not adequately developed at the state-court hearing, implicating the fifth circumstance of *Townsend v. Sain*, 372 U.S. 293, 313, 9 L.Ed.2d 770, 83 S.Ct. 745 (1963), and sought a federal evidentiary hearing on whether his *nolo contendere* plea was unconstitutional. The District Court found that the failure to develop the critical facts relevant to his federal claim was attributable to inexcusable neglect and that no evidentiary hearing was required. . . . Respondent appealed.

The Court of Appeals for the Ninth Circuit recognized that the alleged failure to translate the *mens rea* element of first-degree manslaughter, if proved, would be a basis for overturning respondent's plea, . . . and determined that material facts had not been adequately developed in the state postconviction court, . . . apparently due to the negligence of post-conviction counsel. The court held that *Townsend v. Sain, supra,* and *Fay v. Noia,* 372 U.S. 391, 438, 9 L.Ed.2d 837, 83 S.Ct 822 (1963), required an evidentiary hearing in the District Court unless respondent had deliberately bypassed the orderly procedure of the state courts. Because counsel's negligent failure to develop the facts did not constitute a deliberate bypass, the Court of Appeals ruled that respondent was entitled to an evidentiary hearing on the question whether the *mens rea* element of first-degree manslaughter was properly explained to him. . . .

We granted certiorari to decide whether the deliberate bypass standard is the correct standard for excusing a habeas petitioner's failure to develop a material fact in state-court proceedings. . . .

Because the holding of *Townsend v. Sain* that *Fay v. Noia's* deliberate bypass standard is applicable in a case like this had not been reversed, it is quite understandable that the Court of Appeals applied that standard in this case. However, in light of more recent decisions of this Court, *Townsend's* holding in this respect must be overruled. *Fay v. Noia* was itself a case where the habeas petitioner had not taken advantage of state remedies by failing to appeal—a procedural default case. Since that time, however, this Court has rejected the deliberate bypass standard in state procedural default cases and has applied instead a standard of cause and prejudice. . . .

Applying the cause-and-prejudice standard in cases like this will obviously contribute to the finality of convictions, for requiring a federal evidentiary hearing solely on the basis of a habeas petitioner's negligent failure to develop facts in state-court proceedings dramatically increases the opportunities to relitigate a conviction. . . .

Respondent Tamayo-Reyes is entitled to an evidentiary hearing if he can show cause for his failure to develop the facts in state-court proceedings and actual prejudice resulting from that failure. We also adopt the narrow exception to cause-and-prejudice requirement: A habeas petitioner's failure to develop a claim in state-court proceedings will be excused and a hearing mandated if he can show that a fundamental miscarriage of justice would result from failure to hold a federal evidentiary hearing. . . .

The State concedes that a remand to the District Court is appropriate in order to afford respondent the opportunity to bring forward evidence establishing cause and prejudice . . . and we agree that the respondent should have that opportunity. Accordingly, the decision of the Court of Appeals is reversed, and the cause is remanded to the District Court for further proceedings consistent with this opinion.

So ordered.

Justice O'CONNOR, with whom Justice BLACKMUN, Justice STEVENS, and Justice KENNEDY join, dissenting.

Jose Tamayo-Reyes' habeas petition stated that because he does not speak English he pleaded *nolo contendere* to manslaughter without any understanding of what "manslaughter" means. If this assertion is true, his conviction was unconstitutionally obtained, . . . and Tamayo-Reyes would be entitled to a writ of habeas corpus. Despite the Court's attempt to characterize his allegation as a technical quibble—"his translator had not translated accurately and completely for him the *mens rea* element of manslaughter," . . . this much is not in dispute. Tamayo-Reyes has alleged a fact that, if true, would entitle him to the relief he seeks. . . .

Jose Tamayo-Reyes alleges that he pleaded *nolo contendere* to a crime he did not understand. He has exhausted state remedies, has committed no procedural default, has properly presented his claim to a federal district court in his first petition for a writ of habeas corpus, and would be entitled to a hearing under the standard set forth in *Townsend*. Given that his claim is properly before the district court, I would not cut off his right to prove his claim at a hearing. I respectfully dissent.

Justice KENNEDY, dissenting.

By definition, the cases within the ambit of the Court's holding are confined to those in which the factual record developed in the state-court proceedings is inadequate to resolve the legal question. I should think those cases will be few in number. *Townsend v. Sain* ... has been the law for almost 30 years and there is no clear evidence that this particular classification of habeas proceedings has burdened the dockets of the federal courts. And in my view, the concept of factual inadequacy comprehends only those petitions with respect to which there is a realistic possibility than an evidentiary hearing will make a difference in the outcome. This serves to narrow the number of cases in a further respect and to insure that they are the ones, as Justice O'Connor points out, in which we have valid concerns with constitutional error.

Our recent decisions in *Coleman v. Thompson*, 501 U.S. ___, 111 S.Ct. 2546, 115 L.Ed. 2d 640 (1991), *McCleskey v. Zant*, 499 U.S. 467, 111 S.Ct. 1454, 113 L.Ed.2d 517 (1991), and *Teague v. Lane*, 489 U.S. 288, 109 S.Ct. 1060, 103 L.Ed.2d 334 (1989), serve to protect the integrity of the writ, curbing its abuse and insuring that the legal questions presented are ones which, if resolved against the State, can invalidate a final judgment. So we consider today only those habeas actions which present questions federal courts are bound to decide in order to protect constitutional rights. We ought not to take steps which diminish the likelihood that those courts will base their legal decision on an accurate assessment of the facts. For these reasons and all those set forth by Justice O'Connor, I dissent from the opinion and judgment of the Court.

PART IV

SPECIALIZED TOPICS IN CRIMINAL LAW AND PROCEDURE

C H A P T E R

20

JUVENILE JUSTICE

CHAPTER OUTLINE

INTRODUCTION

The juvenile justice system includes specialized courts, law enforcement agencies, social services agencies, and corrections facilities designed to address problems of juvenile delinquency as well as child neglect and abuse. In addition to being charged with delinquency, young people may be subjected to the jurisdiction of a juvenile court for engaging in conduct that would not be considered criminal if committed by adults. These behaviors, which include truancy (chronic absence from school) and incorrigibility, are often called "status offenses," because they are peculiar to the status of children. Because this book is concerned with criminal law and procedure, in this chapter we are concerned primarily with explaining how the juvenile justice system deals with instances of juvenile misconduct that would be classified as crimes if committed by adults.

Of the nearly two million juveniles arrested every year, more than half are dealt with by specialized juvenile courts. Of course, some juveniles are charged with very serious crimes, such as murder, rape, aggravated battery, and armed robbery. Indeed, in the state of Florida in 1991, one-half of the car thefts, one-third of the burglaries, one-fourth of all larcenies and robberies, and one-fifth of the sex offenses were committed by persons under eighteen. These grave offenses, especially when committed by older juveniles with prior arrest records, are often adjudicated by the regular criminal courts. Accordingly, in this chapter we also explain the concept of "waiver of juvenile court jurisdiction," which permits juveniles to be prosecuted as adults. Finally, we examine disposition of juvenile cases, which includes sentencing and punishment, both by the specialized juvenile courts and by the regular criminal courts.

THE COMMON-LAW BACKGROUND

Although the English common law did not recognize specific protections for juveniles, it created an irrebuttable presumption that children under the age of seven were incapable of *mens rea,* and therefore immune to criminal responsibility. Children between the ages of seven and fourteen were also presumed not to be responsible for criminal acts, but the presumption was rebuttable. Thus, for example, if evidence could be adduced to show that a ten-year-old boy knew that his conduct in taking the life of another was wrongful, he could be held liable for a homicidal offense. The common law treated all persons above the age of fourteen as adults (for further discussion of "infancy" as it relates to criminal responsibility, see Chapter 13).

Because the American legal system was based on English common law, American courts followed the common-law rules for the treatment of juveniles. Young teenagers were treated essentially as adults for the purposes of criminal justice. During the colonial period of American history, it was not uncommon for teenagers to be hanged, flogged, or placed in the public pillory as punishment for their crimes. Later, as state penitentiaries were established, it was not unusual for 20 percent of prison populations to be juveniles.

Establishment of the Juvenile Justice System

In the late nineteenth century, public outcry against treating juveniles like adults led to the establishment of a separate justice system for juveniles. The first state to act was Illinois, which in 1899 enacted "An Act to Regulate the Treatment and Control of Dependent, Neglected, and Delinquent Children." The city of Denver and the state of Rhode Island created specialized juvenile courts that same year. By the 1920s, many states had followed suit, and by 1945 juvenile court legislation had been enacted by Congress and all state legislatures.

Specialized juvenile courts were created to deal with young offenders not as hardened criminals, but as misguided youth in need of special care. In its landmark decision, *In re Gault*, 387 U.S. 1, 87 S.Ct. 1428, 18 L.Ed.2d 527 (1967), the Supreme Court discussed the philosophy that led to creation of the juvenile justice system:

> The early reformers were appalled by adult procedures and penalties and by the fact that children could be given long prison sentences and mixed in jails with hardened criminals. They were profoundly convinced that society's duty to the child could not be confined by the concept of justice alone. They believed that society's role was not to ascertain whether the child was "guilty" or "innocent," but "What is he, how has he become what he is, and what had best be done in his interest and in the interest of the state to save him from a downward career." The child—essentially good, as they saw it—was to be made "to feel that he is the object of [the state's] care and solicitude," not that he was under arrest or on trial. The rules of criminal procedure were therefore altogether inapplicable. The apparent rigidities, technicalities, and harshness which they observed in both substantive and procedural criminal law were therefore to be discarded. The idea of crime and punishment was to be abandoned. The child was to be "treated" and "rehabilitated" and the procedures, from apprehension through institutionalization, were to be "clinical" rather than punitive. 387 U.S. at 15, 87 S.Ct. at 1437, 18 L.Ed.2d at 539.

This special treatment was justified legally by the concept of *parens patriae*, "the power of the state to act *in loco parentis* [in the place of the parents] for the purpose of protecting the property interests and the person of the child." *In re Gault, supra*, 387 U.S. at 16, 87 S.Ct. at 1438, 18 L.Ed.2d at 540.

The New Juvenile Courts

The newly created juvenile courts were usually separate from the regular tribunals; often the judges or referees presiding over these courts did not have formal legal training. The proceedings were generally nonadversarial, and there was little in the way of procedural regularity or even the opportunity for the juvenile offender to confront his or her accusers. In fact, juvenile delinquency proceedings were conceived as civil, as opposed to criminal, proceedings. Dispositions of cases were usually nonpunitive in character; therefore, accused juvenile offenders were not afforded most of the rights of criminal defendants. As the Supreme Court recognized in *Gault*,

> [t]he right of the state, as *parens patriae*, to deny to the child procedural rights available to his elders was elaborated by the assertion that a child, unlike an adult,

has a right "not to liberty but to custody." He can be made to attorn to his parents, to go to school, etc. If his parents default in effectively performing their custodial functions—that is, if the child is "delinquent"—the state may intervene. In doing so, it does not deprive the child of any rights, because he has none. It merely provides the "custody" to which the child is entitled. On this basis, proceedings involving juveniles were described as "civil" not "criminal" and therefore not subject to the requirements which restrict the state when it seeks to deprive a person of his liberty. 387 U.S. at 17, 87 S.Ct. at 1438, 18 L.Ed.2d at 540.

Because the juvenile justice system emphasized rehabilitation (rather than retribution, incapacitation, or deterrence), juveniles who were found delinquent were often placed in reformatories for indeterminate periods, sometimes until they reached the age of majority. Juvenile courts often suffered from lack of trained staff and adequate facilities, and by the 1960s, a system that was conceived by reformers was itself under attack by a new generation of reformers.

The *Gault* Decision and Subsequent Developments

The abuses that came to be associated with juvenile courts were addressed by the Supreme Court in the landmark case of *In re Gault, supra*. In *Gault*, the Court essentially required that juvenile courts adhere to standards of due process, applying most of the basic procedural safeguards enjoyed by adults accused of crimes. Moreover, *Gault* held that juvenile courts must respect the right to counsel, the freedom from compulsory self-incrimination, and the right to confront (cross-examine) hostile witnesses. Writing for a nearly unanimous bench, Justice Fortas observed that "under our Constitution, the condition of being a boy does not justify a kangaroo court." 387 U.S. at 28, 87 S.Ct. at 1444, 18 L.Ed.2d at 546.

In *McKeiver v. Pennsylvania*, 403 U.S. 528, 91 S.Ct. 1976, 29 L.Ed.2d 647 (1971), however, the Court refused to extend the right to trial by jury to juvenile proceedings. Writing for a plurality, Justice Blackmun concluded that juries are not indispensable to fair and equitable juvenile proceedings. Thirteen years later, in *Schall v. Martin*, 467 U.S. 253, 104 S.Ct. 2403, 81 L.Ed.2d 207 (1984), the Court upheld a pretrial detention program for juveniles that might well have been found violative of due process had it applied to adults. Writing for the Court, Justice Rehnquist stressed that "the Constitution does not mandate elimination of all differences in the treatment of juveniles." 467 U.S. at 263, 104 S.Ct. at 2409, 81 L.Ed.2d at 216. While it is likely that the Supreme Court will maintain the requirements imposed in *Gault* and subsequent cases, at this time further expansion of juvenile due process seems unlikely.

ARREST AND INTERROGATION OF JUVENILES

Juveniles may be arrested by police who observe them in the commission of a crime, or otherwise have probable cause to believe that they have committed a crime. However, arrests of juveniles are more often made in response to complaints from victims of juvenile misconduct or parents who cannot control their children. In most states, arrests of juveniles may be effected by a broad category of law enforcement officials. In Texas, for example, it includes agents of the Liquor Control Board and privates in the Texas Rangers, as well as "private persons specially appointed to execute criminal process." Vernon's Ann. Tex. Fam. Code § 51.02(8). In some states, probation officers are authorized to make arrests. See, for example, *In re S.E.B.*, 514 S.W.2d 948 (Tex. Civ. App. 1974).

A juvenile taken into custody by agents of the state is entitled to all the legal protections afforded adults. Agents must have probable cause, although not necessarily a warrant, to effectuate an arrest. After being taken into brief custody, most juveniles are released to the custody of their parents or legal guardians, who assume responsibility to ensure that their dependents appear in court as may be required. In the case of more serious offenses, or where parents or guardians cannot be located, police may opt for detention. Most state statutes require a hearing before a judge or magistrate to determine whether continued custody is warranted. See, for example, W.Va. Code Ann. § 49–5–8(d). Most state courts have held that juveniles held in custody have no right to pretrial release on bail, however.

Interrogation and Confessions

The courts have extended to juveniles all the protections afforded adult suspects facing custodial interrogation by the police. Most courts that have considered the question have held that juveniles must be given the so-called *Miranda* warnings before they are subjected to custodial interrogation by the police or other agents of the state. See, for example, *State v. Whatley*, 320 So.2d 123 (La. 1975). Because juveniles are considered to be more susceptible to the coercive pressures inherent in the custodial environment, some states have enacted laws enhancing the legal protection of juveniles facing interrogation by police. See, for example, W.Va. Code Ann. § 49–5–8. Some state courts have gone so far as to hold that *Miranda* warnings are valid only if provided to parents or legal guardians *in addition* to juvenile suspects. See, for example, *Hall v. State*, 346 N.E.2d 584 (Ind. 1976).

In the landmark *Gault* decision of 1967, the U.S. Supreme Court recognized the right of juveniles to have counsel present during custodial interrogation, although it has not made this an absolute requirement. Writing for the Court in *Gault*, Justice Fortas declared:

> The participation of counsel will, of course, assist the police, Juvenile Courts and appellate tribunals in administering the privilege [against compulsory self-incrimination]. If counsel was not present for some permissible reason when an admission was obtained, the greatest care must be taken to assure that the admission was voluntary, in the sense not only that it was not coerced or suggested, but also that it was not the product of ignorance of rights or of adolescent fantasy, fright or despair. 387 U.S. at 55, 87 S.Ct. at 1458, 18 L.Ed.2d at 561.

Implementing the Supreme Court's *Gault* holding, the North Dakota legislature, for example, has mandated that at all stages of any proceedings under the Juvenile Code, including custodial interrogation, counsel must be provided for a child who is not represented by his parent, guardian, or custodian. Interpreting the law, the North Dakota Supreme Court has said that "this right to counsel

---

CASE IN POINT

ARREST AND INTERROGATION OF JUVENILES

One morning in 1987, police discovered the dead body of a seventy-three-year-old woman in her home in Fayette County, West Virginia. The woman's throat had been cut, and she had been sexually assaulted. Police obtained information that Elbert Wayne Giles, a seventeen-year-old juvenile, had been seen near the decedent's home around 10 P.M. the previous evening. Police also obtained a knife, which they believed to be the murder weapon, that Giles had allegedly given to a friend the morning after the homicide. Police located Giles at a friend's home and took him into custody. At the station house, police read Giles his *Miranda* warnings and permitted him to make a telephone call. Giles indicated that he was willing to answer questions and was interrogated for about an hour and a half before confessing to the crime. Giles' case was transferred from juvenile to adult jurisdiction. He was tried before a jury, convicted, and sentenced to life imprisonment, the confession having been admitted into evidence against him. On appeal, the West Virginia Supreme Court reversed, holding that Giles' confession should have been suppressed. The Court noted a prior case in which it had held that "[u]nder W.Va. Code, 49–5–8(d), when a juvenile is taken into custody, he must immediately be taken before a referee, circuit judge, or magistrate. If there is a failure to do so, any confession obtained as a result of the delay will be invalid where it appears that the primary purpose of the delay was to obtain a confession from the juvenile." *State v. Ellsworth (J.R.)*, 331 S.E.2d 503, 508 (W.Va. 1985). In the instant case, the Supreme Court said that Giles "was illegally detained for the purpose of investigatory questioning" and that his confession was "the product of the exploitation of this illegal arrest."

State v. Giles, 395 S.E.2d 481, 488 (W.Va. 1990).

---

cannot be waived by a child who is not represented by his parent, guardian or custodian" *In Interest of D.S.*, 263 N.W.2d 114, 120 (N.D. 1978).

Like adult suspects, juveniles may challenge the voluntariness of a confession or admission, irrespective of whether *Miranda* warnings were provided before—or counsel was present during—questioning. *Fare v. Michael C.*, 442 U.S. 707, 99 S.Ct. 2560, 61 L.Ed.2d 197 (1979). Of course, there is a stronger presumption that a juvenile's confession was made voluntarily if he or she was "Mirandized" and counsel was present when the confession was given.

Special concerns are raised when a juvenile challenges the voluntariness of a confession. The Supreme Court has said that courts must consider "the juvenile's age, experience, education, background, and intelligence, and . . . whether he has the capacity to understand the warnings given him, the nature of his Fifth Amendment rights, and the consequences of waiving those rights." *Fare v. Michael C.*, 442 U.S. at 725, 99 S.Ct. at 2572, 61 L.Ed.2d at 212 (1979).

Detention

Once a petition for delinquency has been filed, it must be determined whether the juvenile is to be detained pending a disposition of the case. In some instances the decision to detain may be based on whether a parent or guardian is willing and able to guarantee that the juvenile will appear in court when required to do so. In other instances a juvenile may be detained for his or her own protection or, particularly in the case of serious charges, to prevent the juvenile from committing additional offenses pending an adjudicatory hearing. Often the decision to detain is made by a social welfare agency after it has been determined that the juvenile should not be released to parental control. Sometimes the decision is made by court order, but in any event it is the juvenile court that has ultimate authority over the question of detention. Unlike adults accused of crimes, alleged juvenile delinquents have no statutory right to bail. However, an unreasonable or unwarranted detention may be attacked through a petition for *habeas corpus*.

In *Schall v. Martin, supra,* the U.S. Supreme Court upheld a statute that permitted detention of a juvenile found to pose a serious threat to the community. Indicating a more conservative trend in its approach to juvenile cases, the Court observed that any attempt to structure juvenile rights "must be qualified by the recognition that juveniles, unlike adults, are always in some form of custody." 467 U.S. at 265, 104 S.Ct. at 2410, 81 L.Ed.2d at 217.

Diversionary Programs

Before a delinquency petition is filed, often there is a discussion of either formal or informal diversion programs. Such programs are diversionary in that they attempt to divert the juvenile from the juvenile justice system. They are often employed in cases of first offenses, especially where the offense is of a less serious nature. Diversion, sometimes termed "judicial nonintervention," may result in no delinquency petition being filed, with the understanding that the juvenile promises to abide by certain rules of conduct or to complete a program of counseling or treatment. In other instances, the case may be held on an "open file" basis, pending the juvenile's timely completion of a program. Diversionary programs are quite varied and often include one or more of the following elements: community service, restitution, family or institutional counseling, and educational or vocational programs.

ADJUDICATION OF JUVENILE OFFENSES

Despite *In re Gault* and efforts to make the juvenile courts conform to due process requirements, juvenile courts retain their distinctive character. Juvenile delinquency proceedings are still, strictly speaking, civil matters, although they now possess many of the accoutrements of criminal cases.

Filing of the Delinquency Petition

The delinquency petition is the juvenile justice counterpart to a grand jury indictment or an information filed by a prosecutor. It is a formal document charging that one or more delinquent acts have been committed by a particular juvenile and requesting that he or she be subjected to the court's disciplinary authority. Petitions are usually filed by law enforcement or social welfare agencies. Where the juvenile is not in custody, the petition is often accompanied by a request for an order to take the juvenile into custody.

The Adjudicatory Hearing

Since there is no arraignment *per se*, the first stage of a juvenile delinquency hearing is the juvenile's answer to the delinquency petition. The juvenile has two options; he or she may admit to or deny the charges. These terms, which are functionally equivalent to pleas of "guilty" and "not guilty," are used to distinguish the juvenile justice system from the adult criminal process. A juvenile who "stands mute" (i.e., refuses to answer) is assumed to have denied the charges. If the juvenile admits to the charges, the juvenile court judge usually adjudicates the juvenile to be delinquent; the only question remaining is that of appropriate treatment or punishment. If, on the other hand, the juvenile denies the charges, then a hearing must be held to determine their validity.

Traditionally, juvenile delinquency hearings were informal proceedings characterized by a high degree of discretion on the part of the judge and a low degree of constitutional protection for the accused juvenile. The juvenile was typically not represented by counsel. Juveniles often had little opportunity to prepare a defense, obtain favorable witnesses, or even confront adverse witnesses. Because juvenile courts usually were not courts of record, rarely were delinquency proceedings transcribed. The Supreme Court's landmark 1967 decision in *In re Gault, supra,* changed forever the character of these proceedings. The *Gault* decision recognized that juvenile delinquency hearings threatened the loss of liberty, and were thus susceptible to the requirements of due process. Specifically, the Court held that juveniles charged with delinquency must be provided fair notice of the charges and an opportunity to prepare a defense; the right to be represented by counsel; the right to subpoena favorable witnesses and cross-examine hostile ones; and the right to be free from compulsory self-incrimination.

In *In re Winship,* 397 U.S. 358, 90 S.Ct. 1068, 25 L.Ed.2d 368 (1970), the Supreme Court continued down the path it had blazed in *Gault* by holding that the reasonable doubt standard characteristic of adult criminal trials is a constitutional requisite in juvenile delinquency proceedings. Note, however, that the reasonable doubt standard applies only to delinquency proceedings where juveniles are charged with acts that would be criminal if committed by adults. It does not apply to the adjudication of cases involving children who are merely "in need of supervision." *Winship, supra,* 397 U.S. at 359, n. 1, 90 S.Ct. at 1070, 25 L.Ed.2d at 372. Although the Court's footnote is somewhat vague, this exception presumably applies to the so-called status offenses, such as truancy and incorrigibility.

The *Gault* and *Winship* decisions transformed in particular the role of the juvenile court judge. Traditionally, juvenile judges (or "referees," as they were often called) had little or no formal training in the law. Generally unconcerned with procedural regularity or strict rules of evidence, juvenile judges often assumed the role of benign patriarch. In the wake of *Gault* and *Winship*, a number of states revised their juvenile codes to reflect the requirements of those decisions and, moreover, to increase the qualifications of persons serving as juvenile judges and to transform juvenile courts into courts of record. Today it is common for the juvenile court to simply be a division of a court of general jurisdiction, such as a circuit or a superior court.

DISPOSITION OF JUVENILE DELINQUENCY CASES

The typical statute governing disposition of juvenile delinquency cases provides the following dispositional alternatives: dismissal of the petition; suspended judgment; probation; placement in a treatment program; and, finally, commitment to a juvenile correctional institution. As a general rule, dispositions in juvenile cases tend to be more lenient and place more emphasis on rehabilitation than do sentences imposed on adults convicted of crimes. The U.S. Supreme Court has held that a juvenile offender may not be incarcerated for a term exceeding that which would be imposed on an adult convicted of the same offense. Moreover, the Court ruled in the same case that federal sentencing guidelines must be applied in federal juvenile proceedings where juvenile offenses are comparable to adult crimes governed by the guidelines. *United States v. R.L.C.*, 503 U.S. ___ , 112 S.Ct.1329, 117 L.Ed.2d 559 (1992).

A Right to Treatment?

The U.S. Supreme Court has not decided whether a juvenile who is confined for an offense has a constitutional right to rehabilitative treatment. However, in holding that juveniles placed in a state training school must be given appropriate individualized care and treatment, a federal appeals court has stated: "When a state assumes the place of the juvenile's parents, it assumes as well the parental duties, and its treatment of juveniles should, so far as can be reasonably required, be what proper parental care would provide." *Nelson v. Heyne*, 491 F.2d 352, 360 (7th Cir. 1974). Although not a criminal proceeding, in *Nelson* the court ruled that beating a juvenile with a "fraternity paddle" that caused painful injuries violated the Eighth Amendment's prohibition against "cruel and unusual punishments."

In 1983, in the context of a civil suit, another federal court addressed a juvenile's right to rehabilitative treatment and training. Although it recognized that a number of lower federal courts have said that states have an obligation to provide such treatment, the U.S. Court of Appeals for the First Circuit concluded that juveniles in custody have no constitutional right to rehabilitative treatment. *Santana v. Collazo*, 714 F.2d 1172 (1st Cir. 1983). Of course, like adult prisoners, juveniles in custody have the right to be assured of a reasonably safe and sanitary environment, as well as adequate health care. Thus far, the issue of a confined juvenile's right to rehabilitative treatment has surfaced principally in litigation involving claims for damages. Future cases will undoubtedly bring to the forefront the question of whether a confined juvenile must be afforded rehabilitative treatment.

Restitution and Other Community-Based Alternatives

Increasingly, states are providing for restitution as one of a number of community-based alternatives to incarceration. For example, Florida law permits the court to order the child or parent to make restitution in money or in kind for the damage or loss caused by the child's offense in a reasonable amount or manner to be determined by the court. West's Fla. Stat. Ann. § 39.054 (1)(f). While the law permits parents to be held liable to make restitution for their childrens' offenses, it provides that

> the liability of a parent under this paragraph shall not exceed $2,500 for any one criminal episode. A finding by the court, after a hearing, that the parent has made diligent good faith efforts to prevent the child from engaging in delinquent acts shall absolve the parent of liability for restitution under this paragraph. West's Fla. Stat. Ann. § 39.054(1)(f).

POST-DISPOSITIONAL REMEDIES

In the *Gault* case, the Supreme Court noted that the Arizona law under scrutiny did not provide any right to appeal. Yet the Court stopped short of holding that juveniles have a constitutional right to appeal, or that due process required that juveniles be afforded the same appellate remedies available to adults convicted of crimes. Some states do provide a right of appeal in juvenile delinquency cases, either by statute, court rule, or judicial decision. Others permit a *de novo* hearing in a higher trial court. All states make available the writ of *habeas corpus*, by which a juvenile who believes that he or she is being wrongfully held in custody may challenge the custody in court. Availability of these remedies permits juveniles adjudicated delinquent an opportunity to have their cases reviewed by higher courts. (For discussion of the appellate process generally, see Chapter 19.)

TRIAL AND PUNISHMENT OF JUVENILE OFFENDERS AS ADULTS

As noted earlier, older juveniles accused of serious offenses are sometimes tried as adults. This entails a waiver of the jurisdiction of the juvenile court. The U.S. Supreme Court has held that, before it can waive its jurisdiction and transfer the juvenile to the criminal court, the juvenile court must conduct a hearing. Although this hearing may be informal, the juvenile must be represented by counsel, and the records of social services agencies that have dealt with the juvenile must be made available to counsel. *Kent v. United States*, 383 U.S. 541, 86 S.Ct. 1045, 16 L.Ed.2d 84 (1966). As a consequence of this decision, waiver hearings are now commonly held throughout the United States.

The Pennsylvania Juvenile Act, 42 Pa.C.S.A. § 6355, is a fairly typical example of a state statute permitting waiver of juvenile court jurisdiction. It provides that a juvenile, age fourteen years or older, may be tried as an adult, the burden being on the Commonwealth to prove that the juvenile should be tried as an adult. *Commonwealth v. Rush*, 562 A.2d 285 (Pa. 1989). In *Commonwealth v. McDonald*, 582 A.2d 328, 331 (Pa.Super. 1990), a Pennsylvania Superior Court explained the circumstances under which waiver of juvenile court jurisdiction is appropriate:

> The certifying court must determine if the evidence demonstrates:
> (i)   that there is a *prima facie* case that the child committed the delinquent act alleged;
> (ii) that the delinquent act would be considered a felony if committed by an adult; and

(iii) that there are reasonable grounds to believe all of the following:

   (A) That the child is not amenable to treatment, supervision or rehabilitation as a juvenile through available facilities, even though there may not have been a prior adjudication of delinquency. In determining this the court shall consider the following factors:

      Age.

      Mental capacity.

      The degree of criminal sophistication shown by the child.

      Previous records, if any.

      The nature and extent of any prior delinquent history. . . .

      Whether the child can be rehabilitated prior to the expiration of the Juvenile Court jurisdiction.

      Probation or institutional reports, if any.

      The nature and circumstances of the acts for which the transfer is sought.

      Any other relevant factors.

   (B) That the child is not committable to an institution for the mentally retarded or mentally ill.

   (C) That the interests of the community require that the child be placed under legal restraint or discipline or that the offense is one which would carry a sentence of more than three years if committed by an adult.

The Death Penalty

One of the most difficult issues in the area of juvenile justice is whether, and under what circumstances, persons below the age of legal majority (but who are tried as adults in regular criminal courts) should face the death penalty when convicted of capital crimes. Mitigating factors are always considered before the death penalty is imposed; some unique mitigating circumstances may be present when a juvenile is facing the death penalty. Peer pressure and criminal involvement with an adult (particularly one who has a familial or custodial relationship to the juvenile), as well as the juvenile's level of maturity, often become important considerations.

During the past decade, the U.S. Supreme Court has decided a number of cases involving the imposition of the death penalty on juvenile offenders tried and convicted as adults. In *Eddings v. Oklahoma*, 455 U.S. 104, 102 S.Ct. 869, 71 L.Ed.2d 1 (1982), the Supreme Court voted 5–4 to vacate the death sentence of a sixteen-year-old boy. In 1988, the Court divided 6–3 in ruling that the Constitution forbids execution of juveniles who are fifteen or younger at the time they committed their capital crimes. *Thompson v. Oklahoma*, 487 U.S. 815, 108 S.Ct. 2687, 101 L.Ed.2d 702 (1988). One year later, in *Stanford v. Kentucky*, 492 U.S. 361, 109 S.Ct. 2969, 106 L.Ed.2d 306 (1989), the Court split 5–4 in deciding that juveniles sixteen and older at the time of their crimes may be sentenced to death. In her concurring opinion in *Stanford*, Justice O'Connor observed that "it is sufficiently clear that no national consensus forbids the imposition of capital punishment on 16- or 17-year-old capital murderers." 492 U.S. at 381, 109 S.Ct. at 2981, 106 L.Ed.2d at 325. As suggested by the quotation from Justice O'Connor's opinion, the focus in *Stanford* was whether the juvenile's sentence comported with the standards of contemporary society. This approach permits the law

---

CASE IN POINT

TRIAL OF A JUVENILE OFFENDER AS AN ADULT

Gerald N., a seventeen-year-old Native American residing on a reservation in Arizona, was charged with assault with intent to commit rape and assault with a deadly weapon with intent to do bodily harm after allegedly attacking an eighty-year-old blind woman. The federal district court granted the government's motion to proceed against Gerald N. as an adult. Gerald N. filed an immediate appeal. The Ninth Circuit upheld the district court's determination, saying in part:

> . . .The district judge here made specific findings that Appellant was seventeen years and ten months of age at the time the offense was alleged to have been committed and that his social background was one of a low to moderate education with certain problems associated with alcohol and drug abuse; that the nature of the offense . . . was very serious; that according to Appellant's tribal arrest record he had an extensive six-year history of delinquency; that according to an examination by a certified psychologist there was insufficient reason to conclude that Appellant was either incompetent or unable to understand the proceedings brought against him and further that he was intellectually mature; that there was insufficient basis to conclude one way or the other that Appellant had been exposed to past treatment efforts and that he had failed to respond; and that because of a change in the Youth Corrections Act there were better rehabilitative programs available for adults than juveniles in the State of Arizona. None of these factual determinations is clearly erroneous. . . . Each of the district judge's findings is fully supported either by the witness's testimony or by exhibits properly admitted into evidence.

United States v. Gerald N., 900 F.2d 189, 191 (9th Cir. 1990).

---

governing application of capital punishment to juveniles to evolve, but in the immediate future, juveniles who were at least sixteen years old at the time of their crimes may be subjected to the death penalty without offending the Supreme Court's sense of the Eighth Amendment.

CONCLUSION

By the mid-twentieth century, administration of juvenile justice in the United States had moved from a strict disciplinary system to an informal, but often arbitrary, one. Since the *Gault* decision in 1967, the system has moved to one that recognizes juveniles' constitutional rights but continues to provide a "soft glove" treatment to provide guidance and rehabilitation and seeks to avoid bringing the child into the harsh realities of the adult criminal justice system. Although different terminology is employed, the functional counterparts between the juvenile justice system and adult criminal justice system are easily recognizable. Custody, delinquency petitions, adjudicatory and dispositional hearings, and treatment all have their parallels in arrest, indictments and informations, trials, and sentences. The primary goal of the juvenile justice system continues to be rehabilitation rather than incapacitation, retribution, or deterrence. Consequently, and despite procedural reforms, the juvenile system remains more flexible and less formal than the adult criminal process, particularly in its dispositional phases.

The continuing rise in violent crimes committed by teenagers is prompting many people to rethink the juvenile justice system. Some argue that older juveniles, those charged with violent offenses, and those with previous offenses should be treated as adults. Some would lower the age definition of "juvenile" to fifteen or sixteen years. To some extent, recent statutes and court decisions reflect this reconsideration of juvenile justice. Recent enactments and rulings have tended to facilitate treating the more hardened and mature juvenile offenders as adults. Assuming that alarming trends in juvenile crime continue unabated, the growing tendency to treat juvenile offenders more punitively will probably continue.

QUESTIONS FOR THOUGHT AND DISCUSSION

1. David D., a sixth-grader at a public school, was suspected by his teacher of stealing $50 from her purse while she was out of the classroom and before the other students had returned from lunch break. On the following day, the teacher questioned David after school hours, but he denied taking the money. The teacher referred the matter to the principal, who detained David in her office for 90 minutes without notifying David's parents. David asked to leave on several occasions, but his requests were denied. Finally, David confessed to stealing the money and was permitted to leave the premises. The principal referred the matter to the juvenile authorities, who initiated a delinquency petition. At the delinquency hearing, David's counsel objected to the use of the confession made to the principal on the ground that David had not been advised of his constitutional right to remain silent. How do you think the juvenile court judge should rule?

2. In your opinion, should plea bargaining be permitted in juvenile delinquency cases? If so, should any special requirements apply?

3. Since juveniles facing delinquency charges are now afforded most of the rights the Constitution provides for persons accused of crimes, is it rational that they should be denied the right to trial by jury?

4. After adjudicating a fourteen-year-old boy delinquent for having committed a series of theft offenses, the judge ordered the juvenile placed under "community control," a program similar to adult probation. In your opinion, what restraints on the juvenile's liberty would be appropriate?

5. If a sixteen-year-old boy is convicted of first-degree murder in an adult criminal court, would he be exempt from the death penalty under your state statutes?

CASES

IN RE GAULT

Supreme Court of the United States, 1967.
387 U.S. 1, 87 S.Ct. 1428, 18 L.Ed.2d 527.

[In this landmark case, the U.S. Supreme Court holds that juveniles facing delinquency proceedings must be afforded certain basic constitutional rights.]

Mr. Justice FORTAS delivered the opinion of the Court.

... On Monday, June 8, 1965, at about 10 A.M., Gerald Francis Gault and a friend, Ronald Lewis, were taken into custody by the Sheriff of Gila County. Gerald was then still subject to a six months' probation order which had been entered on February 25, 1964, as a result of his having been in the company of another boy who had stolen a wallet from a lady's purse. The police action on June 8 was taken as the result of a verbal complaint by a neighbor of the boys, Mrs. Cook, about a telephone call made to her in which the caller or callers made lewd or indecent remarks. . . .

At the time Gerald was picked up, his mother and father were both at work. No notice that Gerald was being taken into custody was left at the home. No other steps were taken to advise them that their son had, in effect, been arrested. Gerald was taken to the Children's Detention Home. When his mother arrived home at about 6 o'clock, Gerald was not there. Gerald's older brother was sent to look for him at the trailer home of the Lewis family. He apparently learned then that Gerald was in custody; He so informed his mother. The two of them went to the Detention Home. The deputy probation officer, Flagg, who was also superintendent of the Detention Home, told Mrs. Gault "why Jerry was there" and said that a hearing would be held in Juvenile Court at 3 o'clock the following day, June 9.

Officer Flagg filed a petition with the court on the hearing day, June 9, 1964. It was not served on the Gaults. Indeed, none of them saw this petition until the habeas corpus hearing on August 17, 1964. The petition was entirely formal. It made no reference to any factual basis for the judicial action which it initiated. It recited only that "said minor is under the age of eighteen years and is in need of the protection of this Honorable court; [and that] said minor is a delinquent minor," It prayed for a hearing and an order regarding "the care and custody of said minor." Officer Flagg executed a formal affidavit in support of the petition.

On June 9, Gerald, his mother, his older brother, and Probation Officers Flagg and Henderson appeared before the Juvenile Judge in chambers. Gerald's father was not there. He was at work out of the city. Mrs. Cook, the complainant, was not there. No one was sworn at this hearing. No transcript or recording was made. No memorandum or record of the substance of the proceedings was prepared. Our information about the proceedings and the subsequent hearing on June 15, derives entirely from the testimony of the Juvenile Court Judge, Mr. and Mrs. Gault, and Officer Flagg at the habeas corpus proceeding conducted two months later. From this, it appears that at the June 9 hearing Gerald was questioned by the judge about the telephone call. There was conflict as to what he said. His mother recalled that Gerald said he only dialed Mrs. Cook's number and handed the telephone to his friend, Ronald. Officer Flagg recalled that Gerald had admitted making the lewd remarks. Judge McGhee testified that Gerald "admitted making one of these [lewd] statements." At the conclusion of the hearing, the judge said he would "think about it." Gerald was taken back to the Detention Home. He was not sent to his own home with his parents. On June 11 or 12, after having been detained since June 8, Gerald was released and driven home. There is no explanation in the record as to why he was kept in the Detention Home or why he was released. At 5 P.M. on the day of Gerald's release, Mrs. Gault received a note signed by Officer Flagg. It was on plain paper, not letterhead. Its entire text was as follows:

Mrs. Gault:

Judge McGhee has set Monday, June 15, 1964 at 11:00 A.M. as the date and time for further Hearings on Gerald's delinquency.

/s/Flagg

At the appointed time on Monday, June 15, Gerald, his father and mother, Ronald Lewis and his father, and Officers Flagg and Henderson were present before Judge McGhee. Witnesses at the habeas corpus proceeding differed in their recollections of Gerald's testimony at the June 15 hearing. Mr. and Mrs. Gault recalled that Gerald again testified that he had only dialed the number and that the other boy had made the remarks. Officer Flagg agreed that at this hearing Gerald did not admit making the lewd remarks. But Judge McGhee recalled that "there was some admission again of some of the lewd statements. He—he didn't admit any of the more serious lewd statements." Again, the complainant, Mrs. Cook, was not present. Mrs. Gault asked that Mrs. Cook be present "so she could see which boy that done the talking, the dirty talking over the phone." The Juvenile Judge said "she didn't have to be present at that hearing." The judge did not speak to Mrs. Cook or communicate with her at any time. Probation Officer Flagg had talked to her once—over the telephone on June 9.

At this June 15 hearing a "referral report" made by the probation officers was filed with the court, although not disclosed to Gerald or his parents. This listed the charge as "Lewd Phone Calls." At the conclusion of the hearing, the judge committed Gerald as a juvenile delinquent to the State Industrial School "for the period of his minority [that is, until 21] unless sooner discharged by due process of law." ...

No appeal is permitted by Arizona law in juvenile cases. On August 3, 1964, a petition for a writ of habeas corpus was filed with the Supreme Court of Arizona and referred by it to the Superior Court for hearing.

At the habeas corpus hearing on August 17, Judge McGhee was vigorously cross-examined as to the basis for his actions. He testified that he had taken into account the fact that Gerald was on probation. He was asked "under what section of ... the code you found the boy delinquent."

His answer is set forth in the margin. In substance, he concluded that Gerald came within ARS 8–201–6(a), which specifies that a "delinquent child" includes one "who has violated a law of the state or an ordinance or regulation of a political subdivision thereof." The law which Gerald was found to have violated ... provides that a person who "in the presence of hearing of any woman or child ... uses vulgar, abusive or obscene language, is guilty of a misdemeanor. ..." The penalty specified in the Criminal Code, which would apply to an adult, is $5 to $50, or imprisonment for not more than two months. The judge also testified that he acted under ARS 8–201–6(d) which includes in the definition of a "delinquent child" one who, as the judge phrased it, is "habitually involved in immoral matters."

Asked about this basis for his conclusion that Gerald was "habitually involved in immoral matters," the judge testified, somewhat vaguely, that two years earlier, on July 2, 1962, a "referral" was made concerning Gerald, "where the boy had stolen a baseball glove from another boy and lied to the Police Department about it." The judge said there was "no hearing," and "no accusation" relating to this incident, "because of lack of material foundation." But it seems to have remained in his mind as a relevant factor. The judge also testified that Gerald had admitted making other nuisance phone calls in the past which, as the judge recalled the boy's testimony, were "silly calls, or funny calls, or something like that."

The Superior Court dismissed the writ, and appellants sought review in the Arizona Supreme Court. ... The Supreme Court handed down an elaborate and wide-ranging opinion affirming dismissal of the writ and stated the court's conclusions as to the issues raised by appellants and other aspects of the juvenile process.

...[A]ppellants ... urge that we hold the Juvenile Code of Arizona invalid on its face or as applied in this case because, contrary to the Due Process Clause of the Fourteenth Amendment, the juvenile is taken from the custody of his parents and committed to a state institution pursuant to proceedings in which the Juvenile Court has virtually unlimited discretion, and in which ... basic rights are denied. ...

... [T]he highest motives and most enlightened impulses led to a peculiar system for juveniles, unknown to our law in any comparable context. The constitutional and theoretical basis for this peculiar system is—to say the least—debatable. And in practice, ... the results have not been entirely satisfactory. Juvenile Court history has again demonstrated that unbridled discretion, however benevolently motivated, is frequently a poor substitute for principle and procedure....

It is claimed that juveniles obtain benefits from the special procedures applicable to them which more than offset the disadvantages of denial of the substance of normal due process. As we shall discuss, the observance of due process standards, intelligently and not ruthlessly administered, will not compel the States to abandon or displace any of the substantive benefits of the juvenile process. But it is important, we think, that the claimed benefits of the juvenile process should be candidly appraised....

Further, it is urged that the juvenile benefits from informal proceedings in the court. The early conception of the Juvenile Court proceeding was one in which a fatherly judge touched the heart and conscience of the erring youth by talking over his problems, by paternal advice and admonition, and in which, in extreme situations, benevolent and wise institutions of the State provided guidance and help "to save him from a downward career." ... Then, as now, goodwill and compassion were admirably prevalent. But recent studies have, with surprising unanimity, entered sharp dissent as to the validity of this gentle conception. They suggest that the appearance as well as the actuality of fairness, impartiality and orderliness—in short, the essentials of due process—may be a more impressive and more therapeutic attitude so far as the juvenile is concerned....

Ultimately, however, we confront the reality of that portion of the Juvenile Court process with which we deal in this case. A boy is charged with misconduct. The boy is committed to an institution where he may be restrained of liberty for years. It is of no constitutional consequence—and of limited practical meaning—that the institution to which he is committed is called an Industrial School. The fact of the matter is that, however euphemistic the title, a "receiving home" or an "industrial school" for juveniles is an institution of confinement in which the child is incarcerated for a greater or lesser time. His world becomes "a building with whitewashed walls, regimented routine and institutional hours...." ... Instead of mother and father and sisters and brothers and friends and classmates, his world is peopled by guards, custodians, state employees, and "delinquents" confined with him for anything from waywardness to rape and homicide.

In view of this, it would be extraordinary if our Constitution did not require the procedural regularity and the exercise of care implied in the phrase "due process." Under our Constitution, the condition of being a boy does not justify a kangaroo court. The traditional ideas of Juvenile Court procedure, indeed, contemplated that time would be available and care would be used to establish precisely what the juvenile did and why he did it—was it a prank of adolescence or a brutal act threatening serious consequences to himself or society unless corrected? Under traditional notions, one would assume that in a case like that of Gerald Gault, where the juvenile appears to have a home, a working mother and father, and an older brother, the Juvenile Judge would have made a careful inquiry and judgment as to the possibility that the boy could be disciplined and dealt with at home, despite his previous transgressions. Indeed, so far as appears in the record before us ... the points to which the judge directed his attention were little different from those that would be involved in determining any charge of violation of a penal statute. The essential difference between Gerald's case and a normal criminal case is that safeguards available to adults were discarded in Gerald's case. The summary procedure as well as the long commitment was possible because Gerald was 15 years of age instead of over 18....

Appellants allege that the Arizona Juvenile Code is unconstitutional or alternatively that the proceedings before the Juvenile Court were constitutionally defective because of failure to provide adequate notice of the hearings....

... Notice, to comply with due process requirements, must be given sufficiently in advance of scheduled court proceedings so that reasonable opportunity to prepare will be afforded, and it must "set forth the alleged misconduct with particularity." It is obvious that no purpose of shielding the child from the public stigma of knowledge of his having been taken into custody and scheduled for hearing is served by the procedure approved by the court below. The "initial hearing" in the present case was a hearing on the merits. Notice at that time is not timely; and even if there were a conceivable purpose served by the deferral proposed by the court below, it would have to yield to the requirements that the child and his parents or guardian be notified, in writing, of the specific charge or factual allegations to be considered at the hearing, and that such written notice be given at the earliest practicable time, and in any event sufficiently in advance of the hearing to permit preparation. . . .

Appellants charge that the Juvenile Court proceedings were fatally defective because the court did not advise Gerald or his parents of their right to counsel, and proceeded with the hearing, the adjudication of delinquency and the order of commitment in the absence of counsel for the child and his parents or an express waiver of the right thereto. . . . A proceeding where the issue is whether the child will be found to be "delinquent" and subjected to the loss of his liberty for years is comparable in seriousness to a felony prosecution. The juvenile needs the assistance of counsel to cope with problems of law, to make skilled inquiry into the facts, to insist upon regularity of the proceedings, and to ascertain whether he has a defense and to prepare and submit it. The child "requires the guiding hand of counsel at every step in the proceedings against him." . . .

We conclude that the Due Process Clause of the Fourteenth Amendment requires that in respect of proceedings to determine delinquency which may result in commitment to an institution in which the juvenile's freedom is curtailed, the child and his parents must be notified of the child's right to be represented by counsel retained by them, or if they are unable to afford counsel, that counsel will be appointed to represent the child. . . .

It would indeed be surprising if the privilege against self-incrimination were available to hardened criminals but not to children. The language of the Fifth Amendment, applicable to the States by operation of the Fourteenth Amendment, is unequivocal and without exception. And the scope of the privilege is comprehensive. . . .

Against the application to juveniles of the right to silence, it is argued that juvenile proceedings are "civil" and not "criminal," and therefore the privilege should not apply. It is true that the statement of the privilege in the Fifth Amendment, which is applicable to the States by reason of the Fourteenth Amendment, is that no person "shall be compelled in any criminal case to be a witness against himself." However, it is also clear that the availability of the privilege does not turn upon the type of proceeding in which its protection is invoked, but upon the nature of the statement or admission and the exposure which it invites. The privilege may, for example, be claimed in a civil or administrative proceeding, if the statement is or may be inculpatory.

It would be entirely unrealistic to carve out of the Fifth Amendment all statements by juveniles on the grounds that these cannot lead to "criminal" involvement. In the first place, juvenile proceedings to determine "delinquency," which may lead to commitment to a state institution, must be regarded as "criminal" for purposes of the privilege against self-incrimination. To hold otherwise would be to disregard substance because of the feeble enticement of the "civil" label-of-convenience which has been attached to juvenile proceedings. . . .

We conclude that the constitutional privilege against self-incrimination is applicable in the case of juveniles as it is with respect to adults. We appreciate that special problems may arise with respect to waiver of the privilege by or on behalf of children, and that there may well be some differences in technique—but not in principle—depending upon the age of the child and the presence and competence of parents. The participation of counsel will, of course, assist the police, Juvenile Courts and appellate tribunals in administering the privilege. If counsel was not present for some permissible reason when an admission was obtained, the greatest care must be taken to assure that the admission was voluntary, in the sense not only that it was not coerced or suggested, but also that it was not the product of ignorance of rights or of adolescent fantasy, fright or despair. . . .

Absent a valid confession adequate to support the determination of the Juvenile Court, confrontation and sworn testimony by witnesses available for cross-examination were not essential for a finding of "delinquency. . . ."

. . . We now hold that, absent a valid confession, a determination of delinquency and an order of commitment to a state institution cannot be sustained in the absence of sworn testimony subjected to the opportunity for cross-examination in accordance with our law and constitutional requirements. . . .

For the reasons stated, the judgment of the Supreme Court of Arizona is reversed and the cause remanded for further proceedings not inconsistent with this opinion.

It is so ordered.

Mr. Justice BLACK, concurring. . . .

Mr. Justice WHITE, concurring. . . .

Mr. Justice HARLAN, concurring in part and dissenting in part. . . .

Mr. Justice STEWART, dissenting. . . .

SCHALL V. MARTIN

Supreme Court of the United States, 1984.
467 U.S. 253, 104 S.Ct. 2403, 81 L.Ed.2d 207.

[In this case, the Supreme Court rules on the constitutionality of a preventive detention policy for juveniles facing delinquency charges.]

Justice REHNQUIST delivered the opinion of the Court.

. . . [T]he New York Family Court Act authorizes pretrial detention of an accused juvenile delinquent based on a finding that there is a "serious risk" that the child "may before the return date commit an act which if committed by an adult would constitute a crime." Appellees brought suit on behalf of a class of all juveniles detained pursuant to that provision. The district court struck down . . . [the provision] . . . as permitting detention without due process of law and ordered the immediate release of all class members. The Court of Appeals for the Second Circuit affirmed. . . .

Appellee Gregory Martin was arrested on December 13, 1977, and charged with first-degree robbery, second-degree assault, and criminal possession of a weapon based on an incident in which he, with two others, allegedly hit a youth on the head with a loaded gun and stole his jacket and sneakers. Martin had possession of the gun when he was arrested. He was 14 years old at the time and, therefore, came within the jurisdiction of New York's Family Court. The incident occurred at 11:30 at night, and Martin lied to the police about where and with whom he lived. He was consequently detained overnight.

A petition of delinquency was filed, and Martin made his "initial appearance" in Family Court. . . . The Family Court judge, citing the possession of the loaded weapon, the false address given to the police, and the lateness of the hour, as evidencing a lack of supervision, ordered Martin detained. . . . A . . . hearing was held five days later . . . and probable cause was found to exist for all the crimes charged. At the fact-finding hearing . . . Martin was found guilty on the robbery and criminal possession charges. He was adjudicated a delinquent and placed on two years' probation. He had been detained . . . between the initial appearance and the completion of the fact-finding hearing, for a total of fifteen days. . . . [W]hile still in preventive detention pending his fact-finding hearing, Gregory Martin instituted a habeas corpus class action. . . .

The statutory provision at issue in this case . . . permits a brief pretrial detention based on a finding of a "serious risk" that an arrested juvenile may commit a crime before his return date. The question before us is whether preventive detention of juveniles . . . is compatible with the "fundamental fairness" required by due process. Two separate inquiries are necessary to answer this question. First, does preventive detention under the New York statute serve a legitimate state objective? And, second, are the procedural safeguards contained in the Family Court Act adequate to authorize the pretrial detention of at least some juveniles charged with crimes?

Preventive detention under the Family Court Act is purportedly designed to protect the child and society from the potential consequences of his criminal acts. When making any detention decision, the Family Court judge is specifically directed to consider the needs and best interests of the juvenile as well as the need for the protection of the community. . . . We must decide whether, in the context of the juvenile system, the combined interest in protecting both the community and the juvenile himself from the consequence of future criminal conduct is sufficient to justify such detention.

. . . The harm suffered by the victim of a crime is not dependent upon the age of the perpetrator. And the harm to society generally may even be greater in this context given the high rate of recidivism among juveniles.

The juvenile's countervailing interest in freedom from institutional restraints, even for the brief time involved here, is undoubtedly substantial as well. But that interest must be qualified by the recognition that juveniles, unlike adults, are always in some form of custody. Children, by definition, are not assumed to have the capacity to take care of themselves. They are assumed to be subject to the control of their parents, and if parental control falters, the State must play its part as *parens patriae*. . . . In this respect, the juvenile's liberty interest may, in appropriate circumstances, be subordinated to the State's "*parens patriae* interest in preserving and promoting the welfare of the child." . . .

There is no indication in the statute itself that preventive detention is used or intended as a punishment. First of all, the detention is strictly limited in time. If a juvenile is detained at his initial appearance and has denied the charges against him, he is entitled to a probable cause hearing to be held not more than three days after the conclusion of the initial appearance or four days after the filing of the petition, whichever is sooner. If the Family Court judge finds probable cause, he must also determine whether continued detention is necessary. . . .

Detained juveniles are also entitled to an expedited fact-finding hearing. If the juvenile is charged with one of a limited number of designated felonies, the fact-finding hearing must be scheduled to commence not more than fourteen days after the conclusion of the initial appearance. If the juvenile is charged with a lesser offense, then the fact-finding hearing must be held not more than three days after the initial appearance. . . .

Thus, the maximum possible detention . . . of a youth accused of a serious crime, assuming a three-day extension of the fact-finding hearing for good cause shown, is seventeen days. The maximum detention for less serious crimes, again assuming a three-day extension for good cause shown, is six days. These time-frames seem suited to the limited purpose of providing the youth with a controlled environment and separating him from improper influences pending the speedy disposition of his case.

The conditions of confinement also appear to reflect the regulatory purposes relied upon by the State. When a juvenile is remanded after his initial appearance, he cannot, absent exceptional circumstances, be sent to a prison or lockup where he would be exposed to adult criminals. Instead, the child is screened by an "assessment unit" of the Department of Juvenile Justice. . . .

The judgment of the Court of Appeals is reversed.

Justice MARSHALL, with whom Justice BRENNAN and Justice STEVENS join, dissenting.

. . . The majority acknowledges—indeed, founds much of its argument upon—the principle that a State has both the power and the responsibility to protect the interests of the children within its jurisdiction. . . . Yet the majority today upholds a statute whose net impact on the juveniles who come within its purview is overwhelmingly detrimental. Most persons detained under the provision reap no benefit and suffer serious injuries thereby. The welfare of only a minority of the detainees is even arguably enhanced. The inequity of this regime, combined with the arbitrariness with which it is administered, are bound to disillusion its victims regarding the virtues of our system of criminal justice. I can see—and the majority has pointed to—no public purpose advanced by the statute sufficient to justify the harm it works. . . .

COMMONWEALTH V. MCDONALD

Superior Court of Pennsylvania, 1990.
399 Pa. Super. 250, 582 A.2d 328.

[In this case, a Philadelphia Superior Court must determine whether the Court of Common Pleas erred in permitting a juvenile to be tried as an adult. The Superior Court distinguishes the instant case from a case in which the Pennsylvania Supreme Court found that a juvenile had been improperly certified for trial as an adult.]

KELLY, Judge:

... On July 4, 1988, John Sanders, age 20, was squirting the fifteen year old appellant and a friend, Paul James Oliver, with a squirt gun in the stairwell of a public housing building where he and appellant lived. Both Paul Oliver and appellant insisted that he stop squirting them. When Paul saw appellant draw a real gun from his waist band, however, Paul pleaded with appellant not to play around with the gun because it might be loaded and go off. Apparently enraged at being squirted with water, appellant aimed the gun at John Sanders, and stated coldly, "watch this." He then shot John Sanders in the neck from a distance of six feet, which sent John Sanders tumbling down the stairwell with a bullet in his neck.

John Sanders was taken to the hospital for emergency treatment. His bleeding was controlled, but the bullet was lodged too close to the spinal cord to be surgically removed. After five days in the hospital, John Sanders was sent home with a bullet still in his neck. The bullet had not been removed by the time of the trial in this case; rather, it had actually migrated even closer to John Sander's spinal cord.

A delinquency petition was initially filed against appellant charging him with aggravated assault and related offenses. A preliminary hearing was held on the petition, and a *prima facie* case was found to have been established. Subsequently, an amenability hearing was held on August 5, 1988. Appellant was certified to be tried as an adult.

On May 2, 1989, following a jury trial, appellant was convicted of aggravated assault and a firearms offense. ... Appellant was sentenced to the mandatory minimum term of five to ten years imprisonment. This timely appeal follows.

The sole issue raised on appeal is whether the trial court erred or abused its discretion in certifying appellant for trial as an adult. ...

I. Adequacy of the Statement of Reasons for Certification

Appellant contends that the juvenile court failed to provide a sufficient statement of its reasons for certifying appellant to be tried as an adult. Appellant relies upon various cases which have held that a specific statement of grounds for certification must be provided. ... We find no merit in the contention. ...

II. Sufficiency of the Reasons for Certification

In a related argument, appellant contends that the trial court improperly focused solely on the seriousness of the crime involved in deciding to certify appellant to be tried as an adult. In support of this argument appellant quotes the juvenile court's statement of reasons for certification ... and cites *Commonwealth v. Greiner*, 479 Pa. 364, 388 A.2d 698 (1978). Again, we find no merit in the contention.

In *Commonwealth v. Greiner, supra,* our Supreme Court addressed two critical and inter-related issues: who had the burden of proof and production in juvenile certification hearings, and was the evidence sufficient to support certification of the juvenile to be tried as an adult in that case. Our Supreme Court ruled in Greiner's favor on both issues.

In finding that the evidence was insufficient to support certification, our Supreme Court noted that appellant had been a co-conspirator in a botched attempted rape turned aggravated assault, at age 15 with an *older* brother and an *adult*. The aggravated assault victim was the father of the intended rape victim, whose bedroom the trio of co-conspirators had broken into in error. Our Supreme Court had noted that the victim had fully recovered from his stab wounds (which were not further described), and was silent as to who had actually stabbed the victim. Appellant had *no* prior record. He was an *above* average student. He enjoyed a *stable* home life and had *no* prior disciplinary problems at home or at school.... Finally, our Supreme Court emphasized that the county probation officer who intervewed Greiner had repeatedly recommended that Greiner be treated as a juvenile, rather than as an adult.... It was in this context that our Supreme Court had held that the seriousness of the offense *alone,* could not provide the basis for certification....

Here, the seriousness of the offense and the callousness of appellant as demonstrated by the manner in which the offense was committed, were unquestionably proper considerations for the juvenile court which strongly favored certification. We note that, the offense in this case is distinguishable from that in *Greiner* in several respects. The seriousness of the threat of the victim's life in this case was clear in this case, but not in *Greiner* where our Supreme Court merely noted that the victim had fully recovered from undescribed stab wounds. Here, appellant acted individually and with extreme callousness, rather than as the junior member of a conspiracy led by an adult and an older brother. Indeed, the juvenile in *Greiner* may or may not have been involved in the actual stabbing of the intended victim's father, making *Greiner* all the more distinguishable. While not by themselves dispositive, we find no error in the juvenile court's consideration of the callousness of appellant's excessive retaliation for being squirted with water, or in its consideration of how few inches this case had been from automatic certification (i.e., had the shot killed John Sanders). These were plainly strong factors favoring certification of appellant to be tried as an adult.

What dispositively distinguishes this case from *Greiner,* however, is the presence of additional factors in favor of certification of appellant to be tried as an adult, and the absence of compelling factors against certification. Factors favoring certification included: appellant's outstanding prior arrests for dealing a large quantity of cocaine and for trying with two others to steal a car; his chronic truancy; his poor school performance; and his identified need for a "secure, well-structured placement." . . .

The factors weighing against certification hardly rose to the compelling level of those cited in *Greiner.* Appellant had never been committed to a juvenile facility, and so there was no prior failure to rehabilitate. Neither had there been a prior commitment.... Moreover, this factor would seem to involve more the absence of an aggravating factor (i.e., a failed rehabilitative attempt) than the presence of a mitigating one (e.g., a demonstration of an actual potential for rehabilitation.)

Similarly, appellant's alleged lack of school disciplinary problems during a period of chronic truancy is hardly a compelling mitigating circumstance. Indeed, chronic truancy may be considered a serious school disciplinary problem, by itself.

Finally, there is appellant's age, fifteen and a half. While an appropriate mitigating consideration, perhaps, it is far from being a compelling mitigating factor considering the strong counterveilling factors supporting certification.

In the end, certification depends on a complex balancing of numerous factors, not the least of which is the general demeanor of the juvenile as observed by the juvenile court during the certification hearing, a factor which this Court is ill-equipped to evaluate on appeal.... [O]ur focus on review must be limited to whether the record as a whole reveals an abuse of discretion.... We find no abuse of discretion here....

Conclusion

Finding no error in the decision to certify appellant to be tried as an adult, we Affirm Judgment of Sentence.

Stanford v. Kentucky and Wilkins v. Missouri

Supreme Court of the United States, 1989.
492 U.S. 361, 109 S.Ct. 2969, 106 L.Ed.2d 306.

[In separate cases that were consolidated for the purpose of this decision, the Supreme Court considers whether the imposition of the death penalty on an individual for a crime committed at age sixteen or seventeen constitutes a violation of the Eighth Amendment Cruel and Unusual Punishments Clause. Kevin Stanford, age seventeen years, four months at the time of his crime, was convicted of robbing, raping, sodomizing, and murdering a female gas station attendant. Heath Wilkins, sixteen years and six months old at the time of his crime, was convicted of first-degree murder, armed criminal action, and possession of a concealed weapon stemming from an incident in which he and an accomplice robbed a convenience store, stabbed the store operator, and left her to die.]

Justice SCALIA [joined by Chief Justice REHNQUIST, Justice WHITE, and Justice KENNEDY] announced the judgment of the Court. . . .

. . . The thrust of both Wilkins' and Stanford's arguments is that imposition of the death penalty on those who were juveniles when they committed their crimes falls within the Eighth Amendment's prohibition against "cruel and unusual punishments." Wilkins would have us define juveniles as individuals 16 years of age and under; Stanford would draw the line at 17.

Neither petitioner asserts that his sentence constitutes one of "those modes or acts of punishments that had been considered cruel and unusual at the time that the Bill of Rights was adopted." . . . Nor could they support such a contention. . . .

Thus petitioners are left to argue that their punishment is contrary to the "evolving standards of decency that mark the progress of a maturing society." . . . They are correct in asserting that this Court has "not confined the prohibition embodied in the Eighth Amendment to 'barbarous' methods that were generally outlawed in the 18th century," but instead has interpreted the Amendment "in a flexible and dynamic manner." . . . In determining what standards have "evolved," however, we have looked not to our own conceptions of decency, but to those of modern American society as a whole. . . . This

approach is dictated both by the language of the Amendment—which proscribes only those punishments that are both "cruel and unusual"—and by the "deference we owe to the decisions of the state legislatures under our federal system." . . .

Of the 37 States whose laws permit capital punishment, 15 decline to impose it upon 16-year-old offenders and 12 decline to impose it on 17-year-old offenders. This does not establish the degree of national consensus this Court has previously thought sufficient to label a particular punishment cruel and unusual. . . .

. . . [A] majority of the States that permit capital punishment authorize it for crimes committed at age 16 or above. . . . [T]he number is 15 [states] for offenders under 17, and 12 [states] for offenders under 18. . . .

Petitioners make much of the recently enacted federal statute [the Anti-Drug Abuse Act of 1988] providing capital punishment for certain drug-related offenses, but limiting that punishment to offenders 18 and over. . . . That reliance is entirely misplaced. To begin with, the statute in question does not embody a judgment by the Federal Legislature that no murder is heinous enough to warrant the execution of such a youthful offender, but merely that the narrow class of offense it defines is not. The congressional judgment on the broader question, if apparent at all, is to be found in the law that permits 16- and 17-year-olds (after appropriate findings) to be tried and punished as adults for all federal offenses, including those bearing a capital penalty that is not limited to 18-year-olds.

Wilkins and Stanford argue, however, that even if the laws themselves do not establish a settled consensus, the application of the laws does. That contemporary society views capital punishment of 16- and 17-year-old offenders as inappropriate is demonstrated, they say, by the reluctance of juries to impose, and prosecutors to seek, such sentences. Petitioners are quite correct that a far smaller number of offenders under 18 than over 18 have been sentenced to death in this country. From 1982 through 1988, for example, out of 2,106 total death sentences, only 15 were imposed on individuals who were 16 or under when they committed their crimes, and only 30 on individuals who were 17 at the time of the crime. . . . These statistics, however, carry little significance. Given the undisputed fact that a far smaller percentage of capital crimes is committed by persons under 18 than over age 18, the discrepancy in treatment is much less than might seem. Granted, however, that a substantial discrepancy exists, that does not establish the requisite proposition that the death sentence for offenders under 18 is categorically unacceptable to prosecutors and juries. To the contrary, it is not only possible but overwhelmingly probable that the very considerations which induce petitioners and their supporters to believe that death should never be imposed on offenders under 18 cause prosecutors and juries to believe that it should rarely be imposed.

This last point suggests why there is also no relevance to the laws . . . which set 18 or more as the legal age for engaging in various activities, ranging from driving to drinking alcoholic beverages to voting. It is, to begin with, absurd to think that one must be mature enough to drive carefully, to drink responsibly, or to vote intelligently, in order to be mature enough to understand that murdering another human being is profoundly wrong, and to conform one's conduct to that most minimal of all civilized standards. . . .

Having failed to establish a consensus against capital punishment for 16- and 17-year-old offenders through state and federal statutes and the behavior of prosecutors and juries, petitioners seek to demonstrate it through other indicia, including public opinion polls, the views of interest groups and the positions adopted by various professional associations. We decline the invitation to rest constitutional law upon such uncertain foundations. . . .

We discern neither a historical nor a modern societal consensus forbidding the imposition of capital punishment on any person who murders at 16 or 17 years of age. Accordingly, we conclude that such punishment does not offend the Eighth Amendment's prohibition against cruel and unusual punishment.

The judgments of the Supreme Court of Kentucky and the Supreme Court of Missouri are therefore Affirmed.

Justice O'CONNOR, concurring in the judgment.

Last term, in *Thompson v. Oklahoma,* . . . I expressed the view that a criminal defendant who would have been tried as a juvenile under state law, but for the granting of a petition waiving juvenile court jurisdiction, may only be executed for a capital offense if the State's capital punishment statute specifies a minimum age at which the commission of a capital crime can lead to an offender's execution and the defendant had reached that minimum age at the time the crime was committed. As a threshold matter, I indicated that such specificity is not necessary to avoid constitutional problems if it is clear that no national consensus forbids the imposition of capital punishment for crimes committed at such an age. Applying this two-part standard in *Thompson,* I concluded that Oklahoma's imposition of a death sentence on an individual who was 15 years old at the time he committed a capital offense should be set aside. Applying the same standard today, I conclude that the death sentences for capital murder imposed by Missouri and Kentucky on petitioners Wilkins and Stanford respectively should not be set aside because it is sufficiently clear that no national consensus forbids the imposition of capital punishment on 16 or 17-year-old capital murderers. . . .

Justice BRENNAN, with whom Justice MARSHALL, Justice BLACKMUN, and Justice STEVENS join, dissenting. . . .

C H A P T E R

21

THE MILITARY JUSTICE SYSTEM

INTRODUCTION

Since the 1940s, millions of men and women have served in the armed forces of the United States. Despite the ending of the cold war, it is certain that in the foreseeable future our nation will continue to maintain strong defense forces at home, on the high seas, and abroad. The Desert Storm operation of 1991 illustrates the nation's dependence on its armed forces to meet its worldwide commitments. To maintain the discipline essential to the mission of the armed forces, and yet assure service personnel the benefits of a system of laws that protects their individual rights, Congress established a separate system of criminal law and procedure. It is known as the military justice system, and its definition of crimes and the procedures for investigation, apprehension, trial, review, and punishment vary in many ways from the criminal justice system in the civilian community. Because the armed forces are an integral part of our society, it is desirable for the student of criminal law and procedure to have a basic grasp of the military justice system.

The Need for a Separate System of Criminal Law and Procedure

Although there are similarities between the requirements for civilian and military justice, there are three principal reasons for the armed forces to have a separate system of criminal law and procedure. First, some conduct that would not constitute a crime in civilian society must be defined as a crime under military law, for example, insubordination, being absent without leave (AWOL), and desertion. Second, the need for discipline in the armed forces requires that the system operate promptly and with uniformity throughout the military services. Finally, the armed forces must have a system of justice capable of functioning on a worldwide basis in times of war and peace, sometimes in unfriendly nations.

Sources of Military Law

The ultimate source of military law is the United States Constitution, which delegates to Congress the power "to make rules for government and regulation of the land and naval forces." U.S. Const. Art. I, Sec. 8. The president is designated as commander in chief of the armed forces. U.S. Const. Art. II, Sec. 2. Additionally, the Fifth Amendment, which requires a presentment or indictment before a person is held to answer for capital or otherwise infamous crimes, contains an exception "in cases arising in the land or naval forces, or in the Militia when in actual service in time of war or public danger." From time to time Congress has enacted legislation to provide a system of military justice for the armed forces, just as states have enacted criminal laws to meet their particular needs.

BACKGROUND OF THE MILITARY JUSTICE SYSTEM

The Continental Congress first adopted Articles of War in 1775, a draft soon replaced by the Second Continental Congress in 1776. Not surprisingly, the

Articles of War were patterned after the then-existing British Articles of War, which evolved from rules for discipline of the army, and not from the English common law. Congress made major changes in 1806, specifically prohibiting cruel and unusual punishment and adopting 101 articles that remained in effect until 1874, when it consolidated the 1806 Act, subsequent amendments, and court decisions.

With some modernization, Congress adopted revised Articles of War in 1916. Within a year, the United States entered World War I. As a result of considerable controversy over the way justice was administered during that war, Congress again revised the Articles of War in 1920 to afford more protection to accused members of the armed forces. Essentially these represented the state of military justice in 1941, when the United States entered World War II.

Reforms Following World War II

During World War II more than 16 million men and women served in the armed forces of the United States. While a nation is engaged in war it is difficult to focus on reforms in its system of military justice, but at the end of World War II many service personnel came home leveling complaints against the military justice system. They expressed dissatisfaction concerning arbitrary procedures, lack of availability of qualified counsel, and the severity of sentences. Much of the criticism focused on commanders exercising too much control over court-martial procedures from their inception through review.

By 1948 the armed services were unified under a secretary of defense, who appointed a committee of prominent civilian and military lawyers to draft a revised system of military justice to apply uniformly to all branches of the service. Upon their recommendation and after considerable debate, Congress—on May 5, 1950—enacted the Uniform Code of Military Justice (UCMJ), 10 U.S.C.A. §§ 801–940. The new UCMJ modified and consolidated the Army Articles of War, the Articles for Government of the Navy, and the Disciplinary Laws of the Coast Guard. Adoption of the UCMJ accomplished sweeping changes, the most dramatic being the establishment of a three-judge civilian court, the Court of Military Appeals (COMA), now composed of five such judges and designated as the United States Court of Military Appeals. It also authorized the president to implement the new act, and on February 8, 1951, President Harry Truman issued an executive order promulgating the *Manual for Courts-Martial (MCM)*, 1951, binding on all persons subject to the UCMJ, thereby achieving the greatest reform in the history of military justice. Later executive orders brought about revisions.

The Continuing Reforms in Military Justice

The wars in Korea and Vietnam produced additional demands to modernize the military justice system. In 1968, Congress responded by enacting further reforms designed to eliminate command influence over court-martial proceedings, provide for military judges, increase the availability of qualified defense counsel, and provide additional safeguards for the accused. Those convicted by courts-martial during the Vietnam conflict were demanding new mechanisms to enable them to seek postconviction relief, and Congress responded by creating new remedies for those convicted. The *Manual for Courts-Martial* was revised in 1969 to incorporate these reforms.

In the Military Justice Act of 1983, Congress streamlined much of the pretrial and posttrial procedures, and President Ronald Reagan issued an executive order adopting the *Manual for Courts-Martial, 1984*. This present manual reflects court interpretations and modifications in the rules of evidence and court procedures, and its format is more readable for lawyers and nonlawyers alike. The manual provides Rules for Courts-Martial (commonly designated by number as RCMs) and Military Rules of Evidence (also designated by number as MREs).

Resolution of Constitutional Issues

Historically, military courts exercised jurisdiction over all offenses committed by military personnel, as well as over civilian dependents and employees accompanying service personnel. Despite statutory provisions granting the military services court-martial jurisdiction over civilians in certain instances, in modern times the Supreme Court has generally invalidated such areas of jurisdiction over civilians and former members of the military services.

In *United States ex rel. Toth v. Quarles*, 350 U.S. 11, 76 S.Ct. 1, 100 L.Ed. 8 (1955), the Supreme Court held that a former member of the armed forces was no longer subject to court-martial jurisdiction for offenses committed while in service. Following this, in *Reid v. Covert*, 354 U.S. 1, 77 S.Ct. 1222, 1 L.Ed.2d 1148 (1957), the Court ruled that military tribunals have no jurisdiction to try a civilian for a capital offense in time of peace. This decision was followed by *Kinsella v. United States ex rel. Singleton*, 361 U.S. 234, 80 S.Ct. 297, 4 L.Ed.2d 268 (1960), prohibiting military jurisdiction over all civilians for any offenses during time of peace. The Court of Military Appeals has since ruled that for a civilian to be triable by court-martial in "time of war," there must be a war formally declared by Congress. Thus, in *United States v. Averette*, 19 USCMA 363, 41 C.M.R. 363 (1970), the Court of Military Appeals ordered charges dismissed against a civilian employee of an Army contractor in Vietnam who was convicted of conspiracy to commit larceny and attempted larceny of government-owned batteries.

In 1969, the Supreme Court held that the military courts did not have jurisdiction over a soldier who was charged with an assault and attempted rape that occurred while the soldier was on leave. *O'Callahan v. Parker*, 395 U.S. 258, 89 S.Ct. 1683, 23 L.Ed.2d 291 (1969). Thereafter, the military services had to find a "service connection" before trying one of their members for an offense. The Court's decision in *O'Callahan v. Parker* gave little guidance for determining what constituted a service connection, and considerable litigation resulted. The Supreme Court revisited the issue in *Solorio v. United States*, 483 U.S. 435, 107 S.Ct. 2924, 97 L.Ed.2d 364 (1987), and overruled *O'Callahan v. Parker*. Now there is no requirement that an offense be service-connected to fall within jurisdiction of a court-martial. In abandoning the service connection test, Chief Justice Rehnquist explained that "the notion that civil courts are 'ill-equipped' to establish policies regarding matters of military concern is substantiated by experience under the service-connection approach." 483 U.S. at 448, 107 S.Ct. at 2931, 97 L.Ed.2d at 3786. Nevertheless, military regulations, Status of Forces Agreements, and even local policies limit the prosecution of military personnel who have been tried by civilian courts for off-the-base offenses.

Constitutional Rights of Service Personnel

Historically, members of the armed forces were viewed as sacrificing most of their individual rights upon entry into service. Courts did not recognize that the Bill of Rights to the United States Constitution was applicable to service. As late as 1953, the Supreme Court recognized that "the rights of men in the armed forces must perforce be conditioned to meet certain overriding demands of discipline and duty." *Burns v. Wilson*, 346 U.S. 137, 140, 73 S.Ct 1045, 1048, 97 L.Ed. 1508, 1514 (1953). However, in *United States v. Jacoby*, 11 USCMA 428, 430, 29 C.M.R. 244, 246 (1960), the Court of Military Appeals said, "it is apparent that the protections in the Bill of Rights, except those which are expressly or by necessary implication inapplicable, are available to members of our armed forces." Since the decision in *United States v. Tempia*, 16 USCMA 629, 37 C.M.R. 249 (1967), a military counterpart to the Supreme Court's 1966 *Miranda* decision implementing Fifth Amendment rights, courts have made it clear that such rights are applicable to military personnel "except those which are expressly or by necessary implication inapplicable." The Court of Military Appeals has issued a number of decisions to provide a clearer understanding of the constitutional rights of service personnel. See, for example, *United States v. Middleton*, 10 M.J. 123 (CMA 1981).

First Amendment Rights. As previously mentioned, the only protection of the Bill of Rights *expressly* inapplicable to military personnel is the Fifth Amendment requirement for grand jury indictments. Nevertheless, it has always been understood that the constitutional power of Congress "to make rules for the government of the land and naval forces" at least *by necessary implication* allows restriction of certain First Amendment rights of freedom of speech and assembly. For example, a federal statute prohibits military members from forming unions, staging protests, and publishing papers urging disobedience to orders. 10 U.S.C.A. § 976. The military services have a history of tolerance for religious freedom of their personnel; however, the First Amendment does not require the military services to accommodate all religious practices to the extent they may be followed in the civilian community.

Fourth Amendment Rights. As we explained in Chapter 14, the Fourth Amendment protects persons from unreasonable searches and seizures where there is "a reasonable expectation of privacy." While service personnel do not forfeit their Fourth Amendment rights, military exigencies require some limitations not present in civilian society. For example, military commanders may authorize searches of military quarters, and vehicles entering military installations may be searched without a warrant. See, for example, *United States v. Grisby*, 335 F. 2d 652 (4th Cir. 1964).

Fifth Amendment Rights. As previously noted, the Fifth Amendment, which requires prosecutors to obtain presentments or indictments before an accused is tried in federal court, is not applicable to "cases arising in the land or naval

---

CASE IN POINT

RELIGIOUS PRACTICES MUST YIELD TO MILITARY DRESS REGULATIONS

Simcha Goldman, an Orthodox Jew and ordained rabbi, was a commissioned officer on duty with the U.S. Air Force as a clinical psychologist. He was ordered not to wear a yarmulke (skullcap) while on duty. When he refused to comply, he was informed that he was in violation of an Air Force regulation that states "[h]eadgear will not be worn . . . [w]hile indoors except by armed security police in the performance of their duties." After being warned that his failure to obey could subject him to a court-martial, Goldman filed suit in Federal District Court, claiming the regulation infringed upon his First Amendment freedom to exercise his religious beliefs. The District Court enjoined the Air Force from enforcing the regulation, and after the U.S. Court of Appeals reversed, the Supreme Court granted Goldman's petition for review. The Supreme Court affirmed the Court of Appeals, saying, "The First Amendment does not require the military to accommodate such practices in the face of its view that they would detract from the uniformity sought by the dress regulations. . . . The First Amendment therefore does not prohibit them from being applied to [Goldman] even though their effect is to restrict the wearing of the headgear required by his religious beliefs."

Goldman v. Weinberger, 475 U.S. 503, 509, 106 S.Ct. 1310, 1314, 89 L.Ed.2d 478, 485 (1986).

---

forces." Notwithstanding, Article 32 of the UCMJ requires that before referring charges to a general court-martial, a commander must appoint an officer to conduct an investigation of the facts. In contrast to a grand jury proceeding in the civilian community, the accused may be present, represented by counsel, and allowed to call witnesses during the investigation. Many lawyers and scholars regard this as a distinct improvement over the grand jury system that exists in federal and many state jurisdictions. While military personnel are afforded all the protections against self-incrimination under the *Miranda* decision, it is interesting to note that Article 31 of the UCMJ, which predated the *Miranda* decision by sixteen years, codified most of the elements subsequently required by *Miranda.* Moreover, Article 31 requires that warnings be given before *any* questioning of a suspect, whereas in the civilian community the requirements apply only when a suspect is in custody.

UNIFORM CODE OF MILITARY JUSTICE (UCMJ)

In addition to outlining procedural and evidentiary requirements, the UCMJ defines substantive criminal offenses punishable under certain provisions referred to as the "punitive articles." Articles 77 through 134 of the UCMJ outline the military law concerning principals and accessories, attempts, conspiracy, and solicitation; and they define other conduct commonly proscribed in the civilian community (e.g., assault, arson, burglary, murder, robbery, and rape). In addition, these punitive articles proscribe certain conduct peculiarly applicable to the military community (e.g., disrespect toward a superior officer, desertion, insubordination, and giving intelligence to the enemy). The more controversial provisions are Article 133, which proscribes "conduct unbecoming to an officer," and Article 134 (titled "General Article"), which covers offenses not expressly made punishable by specific articles of the UCMJ. This latter article categorizes offenses as "disorders and neglects to the prejudice of good order and discipline" and "conduct of a nature to bring discredit upon the armed forces."

The Doctrine of Vagueness as Applied in Military Law

During the 1960s and the early 1970s, considerable controversy developed concerning the constitutionality of Articles 133 and 134. In 1974, the Supreme Court reviewed a case involving Captain Levy, an army physician who was convicted of violating these articles by making statements promoting disloyalty among the troops. Levy was convicted by a general court-martial and challenged his conviction in the U.S. Supreme Court. In rejecting Levy's argument that both Articles 133 and 134 were "void for vagueness," the Supreme Court noted the significant differences between the civilian and the military communities. It also emphasized that the articles involved had been given prior judicial construction that gave members of the armed forces "fair notice" of the conduct proscribed by their general language. *Parker v. Levy*, 417 U.S. 733, 94 S.Ct. 2547, 41 L.Ed.2d 439 (1974).

Jurisdiction for Court-Martial Purposes

Service personnel become subject to jurisdiction of the military justice system upon enlistment or induction, and jurisdiction generally terminates upon discharge. Members of reserve components are subject to military jurisdiction while on active duty. Jurisdiction depends on the status of the accused and the offense charged. As previously noted, a person who commits an offense during the term of an enlistment generally cannot be tried in a succeeding enlistment, but there are exceptions. For example, a person who secures an early discharge and immediately reenlists, or a person who fraudulently obtains a discharge, remains subject to military jurisdiction. A service member who commits a serious offense near the end of an enlistment period can be retained in certain instances pending court-martial action. In *United States v. Poole*, 30 M.J. 149 (CMA 1990), the Court of Military Appeals held that jurisdiction to try a service member continues to exist until discharge, despite a delay in effecting discharge of the accused. However, the court cautioned that an unreasonable delay might constitute a defense to some military offenses relating to performance of duties.

In recent years there has been litigation concerning "recruiter malpractice," in which persons not qualified to serve in the armed forces have been enlisted and have later claimed not to be subject to military jurisdiction. The many technical aspects of jurisdiction are beyond the scope of this text.

Nonjudicial Punishment

An important element of the military justice system that distinguishes it from the civilian criminal justice system is the ability of a commander to impose nonjudicial punishment under Article 15 of the UCMJ for minor offenses and breaches of discipline. Nonjudicial punishment may be imposed on officers and enlisted personnel within the commander's unit who have committed an offense in violation of the UCMJ. These proceedings are conducted in a rather summary manner, with the commander's authority limited to certain authorized punishments (e.g., reprimands, arrest in quarters for a limited time, restrictions, extra duties, etc.).

A service person always has the option of refusing punishment under Article 15 and requesting a trial by a court-martial. Before deciding whether to accept nonjudicial punishment, the service member must be advised of his or her rights against self-incrimination, right to consult counsel, and right to an informal hearing. Acceptance of nonjudicial punishment does not constitute an acknowledgment of guilt, and it does not prevent the accused from raising defenses to the accusation in a subsequent hearing. In practice, service personnel usually opt for the informality of nonjudicial punishment rather than risk the consequences of an adverse judgment from a court-martial. Note that conviction by a court-martial is a federal criminal conviction that may have extremely serious consequences for a defendant.

Pretrial Proceedings

An accused must be brought to trial within 120 days after notice to the accused of preferral of charges, or the imposition of restraint, whichever is earlier. If the accused is in confinement, the period is 90 days. RCM 707(a). Absent delays occasioned by the defense, a violation of the right to a speedy trial is presumed if a service member is confined for more than 90 days before trial. Military and civilian defendants enjoy the right to a public trial, and those seeking to close a trial to the public must advance some "overriding interest" such as national security interests.

Appointment of Counsel. To qualify for appointed counsel in a civilian court, an accused must be indigent. In contrast, all service personnel are assured of representation by a qualified military lawyer at no cost. Of course, a military member may be represented by private counsel at his or her own expense.

Pretrial Confinement. While there is no right to bail in the military justice system, the UCMJ calls for pretrial confinement only as a last resort. RCM 305(h)(2)(B)(iii)(b). In any event, the military services have a reputation for conducting prompt trials. A service person is ordered into pretrial confinement only if the commander has probable cause to believe that the accused has committed an offense and that it is necessary to confine the accused to ensure that he or she will appear at trial, or that it is foreseeable that the accused will engage in serious misconduct, and that less severe forms of restraint would be inadequate.

Discovery Proceedings. An accused service member enjoys a somewhat broader right to discover the prosecution's evidence than defendants in most civilian criminal justice systems. Disclosure by the prosecution includes the various documents that accompany the charges and statements in possession of the prosecutor relevant to any offense charged. RCM 701(a)(1). Previously mentioned was the Article 32 investigation, which must be conducted before a service member may be tried by a general court-martial. In addition to the roles mentioned, this investigation provides a defendant with pretrial discovery of evidence and is a military substitute for a grand jury investigation as well as a preliminary hearing (see Chapter 16).

Guilty Pleas. In the civilian system of criminal justice, a properly advised defendant may plead guilty "for his or her best interest" while still maintaining innocence. *North Carolina v. Alford,* 400 U.S. 25, 91 S.Ct. 160, 27 L.Ed.2d 162 (1970). However, in the military an accused who pleads guilty must expressly admit guilt in open court. RCM 910(c). Therefore, military judges conduct a rather protracted hearing to determine that a factual basis exists for a plea of guilty, and that the plea is freely and voluntarily entered.

Court-Martial Proceedings

Court-martial proceedings are convened by commanders of various military units under the authority of Articles 22, 23, and 24 of the UCMJ. The UCMJ defines the authorities of the commanders at various levels. Commanders are referred to as "convening authorities" and are assisted by competent military lawyers designated as staff judge advocates. Charges against a service person may be "preferred" by anyone subject to the UCMJ, but in practice charges are preferred by the individual's commander, then "referred" by the convening authority to the military court once convened.

There are three classes of courts-martial: summary, special, and general. The summary court-martial is somewhat analogous to trial by a civilian justice of the peace. The special and general courts-martial are more analogous to civilian criminal courts of record under the judge and jury system. The objective of courts-martial, as of all courts, is to achieve justice. As in civilian criminal courts, courts-martial are adversary proceedings in which lawyers representing the government and the accused present facts, law, and arguments in conformity with the evidence and rules of procedure. The trial counsel is the prosecutor, and is responsible for witnesses, documents, and arrangements relating to the trial. The defense counsel has the role of civilian defense lawyer and is professionally obliged to present the best defense available and to act solely in the accused's interests. With a few variations, military courts apply the same rules of evidence as prevail in the federal courts.

Summary Court-Martial. A summary court-martial is authorized by Article 20 of the UCMJ. It is composed of only one officer (usually a mature, experienced one), has jurisdiction over enlisted personnel, and has limited authority to impose punishments. The maximum period of confinement that can result from a summary court-martial is one month. The 1968 amendments to the UCMJ allow a service person to reject trial by a summary court-martial. In fact, in recent years this type of proceeding has been used infrequently and has been limited to considering minor breaches of military discipline. Some recent decisions from the Court of Military Appeals have likened these proceedings to disciplinary hearings similar to those concerning nonjudicial punishment.

Special Court-Martial. Article 16 of the UCMJ now provides that a special court-martial must be composed of three or more members and a military judge, or a military judge alone, if requested by the accused. It can impose more serious punishments on both officers and enlisted personnel; however, an officer cannot be confined or dismissed by a special court-martial. In some instances a special court-martial is authorized by the convening authority to adjudge a bad-conduct discharge as part of its maximum sentence.

General Court-Martial. A general court-martial tries the most serious offenses. It may be convened only by commanders of higher rank (usually a general or an admiral), and it must consist of five or more members and a military judge (or a military judge alone, if requested by the accused). Before a general court-martial can be convened, there must be a full pretrial investigation and a written pretrial advisory memorandum from a staff judge advocate of the service concerned. A general court-martial may try any offense made punishable by the UCMJ and may impose any punishment authorized by law, including death for a capital offense. Art. 16, UCMJ. Trial by a military judge alone is not permitted in capital cases. RCM 201(f)(1)(C).

Procedures. Procedures before a special court-martial and a general court-martial and the rules of evidence are similar to those in federal district courts. In all instances the accused is furnished legal counsel at expense of the government; however, an accused may elect to employ civilian counsel at his or her expense. Where court members sit with the military judge, their function is now similar to a civilian jury (i.e., to hear the evidence, make findings, and apply the law as given them by the judge). But there are no "hung juries," because a unanimous verdict is not required. If two-thirds of the court members find the accused guilty, a conviction results; otherwise, the accused is acquitted.

Punishments

Punishments imposed by a summary court martial are limited to thirty days' confinement and/or forfeiture of pay. Special courts-martial have greater authority, and general courts-martial may impose punishments ranging from forfeiture of pay and loss of rank to confinement—and in some instances, release from the service with a bad-conduct or dishonorable discharge. The UCMJ expressly forbids any "cruel or unusual punishment," including some historically associated with military forces, such as placing a soldier in stocks or flogging.

In sentencing, courts-martial hold open-court hearings and a defendant is permitted to have witnesses made available at government expense to testify to his or her character, record, etc. The court or military judge considers the nature of the offense, the personal history of the accused, his or her performance in the

---

CASE IN POINT

UNLAWFUL COMMAND INFLUENCE IN SELECTING MEMBERS OF COURT-MARTIAL

Private Jay M. Hilow of the U.S. Army was convicted by general court-martial of two specifications of wrongful use of marijuana and sentenced to a bad-conduct discharge, four months confinement, forfeitures of pay, and reduction of pay grade. After the convening authority and the Court of Military Review approved his sentence, the United States Court of Military Appeals granted review to resolve whether the convening authority had improperly orchestrated the selection of court members who would be impermissibly severe to sit on Hilow's court-martial. The CMA found that the actions of the convening authority's subordinate in selecting only commanders and supporters of command policy of hard discipline resulted in a deliberate stacking of the pool of potential members detailed to sit on Hilow's court-martial. The court found this to be in violation of Article 37(a) of the Uniform Code of Military Justice (UCMJ), which prohibits use of means designed to influence the action of a court-martial; and Article 25(d) (UCMJ), which requires a convening authority to detail as members to sit on courts-martial of those who are best qualified for the duty by reason of age, education, training, experience, length of service, and judicial temperament. Since Hilow had pled guilty to the charges for which he was convicted, the CMA ordered a rehearing on his sentence before a court-martial whose members would be selected by the convening authority of a different command.

United States v. Hilow, 32 M.J. 439 (CMA 1991).

---

service, and other factors relevant to determine the sentence to be imposed. A sentence is not effective until approved by the convening authority.

Appellate Review

Historically, military justice has been regarded as rather summary; however, Articles 65, 66, 67, 69, and 70 of the UCMJ now provide an elaborate system of review and appeals. The authority who convenes a court-martial must review the record of each trial for legal sufficiency and appropriateness of the sentence and has broad authority to revise the findings and sentence. The convening authority, however, cannot change a finding of "not guilty" and cannot increase the severity of punishment imposed. In practice this form of review is accomplished with the assistance of qualified legal counsel, designated as judge advocates.

The judge advocate general of each military service must establish a Court of Military Review (CMR) composed of at least three appellate military judges. 10 U.S.C.A. § 864. Once the findings and sentence of a general or special court-martial are approved, a CMR reviews those proceedings and has very broad authority to make revisions. For example, a CMR can find a military accused guilty of a lesser included offense notwithstanding the court-martial was not instructed as to lesser included offenses. *United States v. LaFontant*, 16 M.J. 236 (CMA 1983). Appellate review can never increase the severity of a sentence or change an acquittal to a conviction.

The United States Court of Military Appeals

One of the most significant reforms enacted into law by the UCMJ was establishment of the United States Court of Military Appeals, which now consists of five civilian judges appointed by the president for terms of fifteen years, with advice and consent of the Senate. This court reviews all cases in which a sentence affects a general or flag officer or extends to death and all cases in which the judge advocate general of the service involved orders the case up for review. In addition, once the CMR has completed its action, the Court of Military Appeals may grant a petition for review by an accused if he or she can show good cause for review beyond that which the CMR has accomplished.

EVALUATION OF THE MILITARY JUSTICE SYSTEM

Old practices of requiring saluting in military courts ceased long ago. Trial counsel and defense counsel appear in uniform, but the military judge wears a traditional robe. Investigative practices and the accused's right of discovery are often superior to that available in a civilian court. Unlike many civilian judges, the military judge cannot suspend a sentence; however, a convening authority can suspend a sentence but may not increase it.

Unless an accused elects trial before a military judge alone, it is the convening authority, usually a high-ranking officer, who appoints those who are to sit as a "jury" in judgment of the accused. Perhaps the greatest criticism of military courts is that, unlike a civilian jury, these members are not randomly selected. Accordingly, there is concern that the influence of the convening authority may become injected into the proceedings. And, although an enlisted service member may demand that one-third of the court be composed of enlisted personnel, this prerogative has been of limited value to an accused because commanders generally appoint senior noncommissioned officers who are prone to strictly enforce military discipline.

Since 1983, however, the convening authority has been divested of the power to designate a trial judge for a particular case. These judges are now detailed to assignments by judge advocates, who are not under supervision of the commander who convenes the court-martial. Increasingly, military members opt for trial by a military judge rather than a military "jury." This option is not available in a capital offense. Nevertheless, it is a reality that enlisted personnel often consider the military court as an instrument of the commander, because its members are not randomly selected and may tend to reflect the influence of the convening authority. As society has become more sensitive to individual civil rights and liberties, Congress and the military services have taken many commendable steps to remove the specter of "command influence." This area of military justice is likely to be addressed further in future years.

The military justice system affords convicted defendants significant opportunities for taking appeals from judgments of military courts. If a defendant has been sentenced to more than six months' confinement, or if the defendant is given a punitive discharge, he or she is entitled to a free transcript of the proceedings and a military lawyer to handle an appeal. All sentences involving death or confinement for a year or more, or a punitive discharge, are reviewed by a Court of Military Review. RCM 1201(i).

CONCLUSION

In his book, *Military Justice Is to Justice as Military Music Is to Music* (New York: Harper & Row, 1970), Robert Sherrill criticized "military necessity" for absolute discipline, order, and conformity in the armed forces. In contrast, the late Senator Sam Ervin, a noted authority on constitutional law, more recently observed that "military justice has attained virtual parity with civilian criminal justice." These widely divergent views typify attitudes toward military justice. Many Americans who served in World War II, Korea, and Vietnam tend to view the system as it was when they served. Today's system of military justice varies greatly from that of World War II, and has been further reformed since the nation's experiences in later conflicts. Historically, military justice has come into the public eye only after a war, but given the vast numbers of Americans actively serving in the armed forces as well as the large numbers in various reserve components, military justice can and should be subjected to continued scrutiny in peacetime. The goal should be to balance the need for discipline and authority against the need to protect the basic rights of individual members of the armed forces and to provide a fair adjudication of those accused of transgressions.

QUESTIONS FOR THOUGHT AND DISCUSSION

1. Do you agree that it is necessary for the armed forces to have a separate system of criminal justice for prosecution of crimes that occur within the United States?

2. What arguments support the requirement that there must be a "service connection" for a military court to have jurisdiction over an offense committed by a service member? Why did the Supreme Court reject the service-connection doctrine in *Solorio v. United States?*

3. Do you think the method used by the military services to determine whether to charge someone with a major crime is superior to the use of a grand jury or prosecutor's information in the civilian criminal justice system? Why or why not?

4. Is the military practice of administering nonjudicial punishment for minor offenses adaptable to the juvenile justice system in the civilian community? What disadvantages do you see in such a practice?

5. Do you think the courts would consider that a member of the armed forces is seized under Fourth Amendment standards if the service member is ordered to

proceed to an investigative office on the base for the purpose of being finger-printed?

6. A male drill sergeant with authority over a young female recruit orders her to report to him in a private location on the base. While discussing the seriousness of the recruit's infractions of certain regulations, he demands a sexual favor from her. Although no force is displayed, the recruit claims she permitted the sergeant to have sexual relations with her because of his dominant position and the coercive atmosphere of the meeting. Do you think these facts would be sufficient as a basis to charge the drill sergeant with rape of the recruit?

7. To find a service member guilty of an offense other than spying, at least two-thirds of the members of a military court must concur, whereas in most civilian criminal courts the verdict must be unanimous. Do you think the military system is better than the common civilian practice? Why?

8. Do you think it would feasible for the military services to randomly select military court members (jurors) rather than having such members appointed by the commander who convenes a court-martial?

9. What, if any, additional measures should the armed forces take to eliminate the possibility of "command influence" in court-martial proceedings?

CASES

SOLORIO V. UNITED STATES
Supreme Court of the United States, 1987.
483 U.S. 435, 107 S.Ct. 2924, 97 L.Ed.2d 364.

[In this case, the United States Supreme Court considers whether the jurisdiction of a court-martial to try a member of the Armed Forces depends on the "service connection" of the offense charged.]

Chief Justice REHNQUIST delivered the opinion of the Court.

... While Petitioner Richard Solorio was on active duty in the Seventeenth Coast Guard District in Juneau, Alaska, he sexually abused two young daughters of fellow coast guardsmen.

Petitioner engaged in this abuse over a 2-year period until he was transferred by the Coast Guard to Governors Island, New York. Coast Guard authorities learned of the Alaska crimes only after petitioner's transfer, and investigation revealed that he had later committed similar sexual abuse offenses while stationed in New York. The Governors Island commander convened a general court-martial to try petitioner for crimes alleged to have occurred in Alaska and New York.

There is no "base" or "post" where Coast Guard personnel live and work in Juneau. Consequently, nearly all Coast Guard military personnel reside in the civilian community. Petitioner's Alaska offenses were committed in his privately owned home, and the fathers of the 10- to 12-year old victims in Alaska were active duty members of the Coast Guard assigned to the same command as petitioner. Petitioner's New York offenses also involved daughters of fellow coast guardsmen, but were committed in Government quarters on the Governors Island base.

After the general court-martial was convened in New York, petitioner moved to dismiss the charges for crimes committed in Alaska on the ground that the court lacked jurisdiction under this Court's decisions in *O'Callahan v. Parker* [1969] and *Relford v. Commandant, U.S. Disciplinary Barracks* ... (1971). Ruling that the Alaska offenses were not sufficiently "service connected" to be tried in the military criminal justice system, the court-martial judge granted

the motion to dismiss. The government appealed the dismissal of the charges to the United States Coast Guard Court of Military Review, which reversed the trial judge's order and reinstated the charges. ...

The United States Court of Military Appeals affirmed the Court of Military Review, concluding that the Alaska offenses were service connected within the meaning of *O'Callahan and Relford.* ... Stating that "not every off-base offense against a servicemember's dependent is service-connected," the court reasoned that "sex offenses against young children ... have a continuing effect on the victims and their families and ultimately on the morale of any military unit or organization to which the family member is assigned." ... In reaching its holding, the court also weighed a number of other factors, including: the interest of Alaska civilian officials in prosecuting petitioner; the hardship on the victims, who had moved from Alaska, that would result if they were called to testify both at a civilian trial in Alaska and at the military proceeding in New York; and the benefits to petitioner and the Coast Guard from trying the Alaska and New York offenses together. This Court subsequently granted certiorari. ...

The Constitution grants to Congress the power "[t]o make Rules for the Government and Regulation of the land and naval Forces." ... Exercising this authority, Congress has empowered courts-martial to try servicemen for the crimes proscribed by the UCMJ [Uniform Code of Military Justice]. ... The Alaska offenses with which petitioner was charged are each described in the UCMJ. Thus it is not disputed that the court-martial convened in New York possessed the statutory authority to try petitioner on the Alaska child abuse specifications.

In an unbroken line of decisions from 1866 to 1960, this Court interpreted the Constitution as conditioning the proper exercise of court-martial jurisdiction over an offense on one factor: the military status of the accused. ...

In 1969, the Court in *O'Callahan v. Parker* departed from the military status test and announced the "new constitutional principle" that a military tribunal may not try a serviceman charged with a crime that has no service connection.... Applying this principle, the *O'Callahan* Court held that a serviceman's off-base sexual assault on a civilian with no connection with the military could not be tried by court-martial. On reexamination of *O'Callahan*, we have decided that the service connection test announced in that decision should be abandoned.

The constitutional grant of power to Congress to regulate the Armed Forces, Art I, § 8, cl 14, appears in the same section as do the provisions granting Congress authority, inter alia, to regulate commerce among the several States, to coin money, and to declare war. On its face there is no indication that the grant of power in Clause 14 was any less plenary than the grants of other authority to Congress in the same section. Whatever doubts there might be about the extent of Congress' power under Clause 14 to make rules for the "Government and Regulation of the land and naval Forces," that power surely embraces the authority to regulate the conduct of persons who are actually members of the armed services....

The notion that civil courts are "ill-equipped" to establish policies regarding matters of military concern is substantiated by experience under the service connection approach.... In his *O'Callahan* dissent, Justice Harlan forecasted that "the infinite permutations of possibly relevant factors are bound to create confusion and proliferate litigation over the [court-martial] jurisdiction issue." ... In fact, within two years after *O'Callahan*, this Court found it necessary to expound on the meaning of the decision, enumerating a myriad of factors for courts to weigh in determining whether an offense is service connected. Yet the service connection approach, even as elucidated in *Relford*, has proven confusing and difficult for military courts to apply.

Since *O'Callahan* and *Relford*, military courts have identified numerous categories of offenses requiring specialized analysis of the service connection requirement. For example, the courts have highlighted subtle distinctions among offenses committed on a military base, offenses committed off-base, offenses arising from events occurring both on and off a base, and offenses committed on or near the boundaries of a base. Much time and energy has also been expended in litigation over other jurisdictional factors, such as the status of the victim of the crime, and the results are difficult to reconcile. The confusion created by the complexity of the service connection requirement, however, is perhaps best illustrated in the area of off-base drug offenses. Soon after *O'Callahan*, the Court of Military Appeals held that drug offenses were of such "special military significance" that their trial by court-martial was unaffected by the decision.... Nevertheless, the court has changed its position on the issue no less than two times since [1969], each time basing its decision on *O'Callahan* and *Relford*.

When considered together with the doubtful foundations of *O'Callahan*, the confusion wrought by the decision leads us to conclude that we should read Clause 14 in accord with the plain meaning of its language as we did in the many years before *O'Callahan* was decided. That case's novel approach to court-martial jurisdiction must bow "to the lessons of experience and the force of better reasoning." ... We therefore hold that the requirements of the Constitution are not violated where, as here, a court-martial is convened to try a serviceman who was a member of the armed services at the time of the offense charged.

The judgment of the Court of Military Appeals is affirmed.

Justice STEVENS, concurring in the judgment....

Justice MARSHALL ... [joined by Justices BRENNAN and BLACKMUN], dissenting.

O'Callahan v. Parker remains correct and workable today. The Court nonetheless insists on reopening a question which was finally and properly resolved in 1969. In doing so, it shows a blatant disregard for principles of stare decisis, and makes more dubious the presumption "that bedrock principles are founded in the law rather than in the proclivities of individuals." ... This in turn undermines "the integrity of our constitutional system of government, both in appearance and in fact." ...

... Today's decision deprives our military personnel of procedural protections that are constitutionally mandated in trials for purely civilian offenses. The Court's action today reflects contempt, both for the members of our Armed Forces and for the constitutional safeguards intended to protect us all. I dissent.

UNITED STATES V. TEMPIA

United States Court of Military Appeals, 1967.
16 U.S.C.M.A.629, 37, C.M.R. 249.

[In this case, U.S. Court of Military Appeals is asked to decide whether the Supreme Court's decision in *Miranda v. Arizona* (1966) applies to military interrogations of criminal suspects.]

FERGUSON, Judge:

. . . The accused was tried by general court-martial at Dover Air Force Base, Delaware, and convicted of taking indecent liberties with females under the age of sixteen, in violation of Uniform Code of Military Justice, Article 134, 10 USC § 934. He was sentenced to bad-conduct discharge, forfeiture of all pay and allowances, confinement at hard labor for six months, and reduction. Intermediate appellate authorities affirmed. . . .

The accused's trial commenced on June 14, 1966, one day after the effective date of applying the principles set forth in *Miranda*. . . . The testimony of the witnesses therein disclosed the following evidence.

On May 1, 1966, accused accompanied an Airman Keitel to the base library. Upon request, Keitel pointed out the location of the latrine. Accused left Keitel in the reading room and returned in five or six minutes.

From other testimony, it appears he went to the ladies' rest room, stood in its partially opened door, and made obscene proposals to three young girls. The victims left the library, returned with one of their parents and the Air Police, and pointed accused out in the reading room. Accused was asked "to come back to the office" by one of the policemen. He did so.

At the Air Police office, accused was advised by Agent Blessing that he was suspected of taking indecent liberties with children; of his rights under Code, *supra*, Article 31, 10 USC § 831; and "that you may consult with legal counsel if you desire." Agent McQuary assisted Agent Blessing in the interview. It was immediately terminated, as Tempia stated "he wanted counsel." He was released from custody.

On May 3, 1966, Tempia was again called to the "OSI Office" where he was once more advised by Blessing, in the presence of Agent Feczer, of his rights and entitlement to consult with counsel. Accused "stated he had not yet received legal counsel." Blessing thereupon called Major Norman K. Hogue, Base Staff Judge Advocate, and made an appointment for Tempia.

Blessing's interview with Tempia terminated at 8:50 A.M., and the latter proceeded to Major Hogue's office. Hogue informed him he was the Staff Judge Advocate and "that I could not accept an attorney-client relationship with him because if I did, it would disqualify me from acting in my capacity as Staff Judge Advocate." He further stated to Tempia that he would nevertheless "advise him of his legal rights and explained to him that this was different than acting as his defense counsel in that I did not want to hear any of his story, but I would answer any legal questions he had after I explained some rights to him."

Major Hogue also told accused he could not make a military lawyer available to him "as his defense counsel during that OSI investigation," but that he had the right to employ civilian counsel; would be given a reasonable time to do so; that civilian counsel would be entitled to appear with him at the investigation. In addition, Hogue advised him of his rights under Code, *supra*, Article 31, and explained those rights to him, but:

> . . . As I say, I told him no military lawyer would be appointed to represent him during the OSI investigation or any investigation by the law enforcement agents on this base. I told him that if charges are preferred—in his case, referred to trial by special court-martial or general court-martial, where it's referred to an investigation under Article 32b, he would be furnished a military lawyer at that time, one certified under Article 27b of the Uniform Code of Military Justice.

In addition, accused filled out a written form in which it was indicated he had been advised:

a. That he had the right to retain civilian counsel at his own expense;

b. That no military lawyer would be appointed to represent him while under investigation by law enforcement agents;

c. That he would be furnished military counsel if charges were preferred and referred to trial or a pre-trial investigation convened;

d. Of his rights under Code, *supra*, Article 31;

e. Of the maximum punishment involved; and,

f. That he had not discussed his guilt or innocence or any of the facts involved with Major Hogue.

Following his session with Major Hogue, Tempia returned to the Office of Special Investigations, at 9:24 A.M. He "was then called in . . . readvised of his rights, readvised of the nature of the investigation and of his rights to seek legal counsel the second time." He stated he had consulted with Major Hogue, and did not desire further counsel as they could not help him. . . . He said, "They didn't do me no good." Thereafter, he was interrogated by Blessing and Feczer, to whom he began to dictate his confession.

At the trial, defense counsel sought exclusion of the statement on the basis of the Supreme Court decision in *Miranda,* as he had found it reported in the press. The law officer overruled his timely objection and admitted Tempia's confession in evidence.

The Judge Advocate General, United States Navy, has filed a brief *amicus curiae* in which it is urged that military law is in nowise affected by constitutional limitations and, in consequence, that the principles enunciated in *Miranda v. Arizona* do not apply to the situation herein presented. The Government, however, takes a different tack. Conceding the application of the Constitution, it urges the Supreme Court has no supervisory power over military tribunals. Construing *Miranda v. Arizona* as announcing only procedural devices designed to enforce a Constitutional right in the exercise of the Supreme Court's supervisory power, it contends this Court is neither required to follow *Miranda,* nor are its stringent formulae necessary or desirable in the administration of military justice. . . .

The time is long since past . . . when this Court will lend an attentive ear to the argument that members of the armed services are, by reason of their status, *ipso facto* deprived of all protections of the Bill of Rights.

Military jurisprudence is and has always been separated from the ordinary Federal and State judicial systems in this country. Such is the meaning of

Mr. Chief Justice Vinson's language in *Burns v. Wilson* . . . (1953):

> Military law, like state law, is a jurisprudence which exists separate and apart from the law which governs in our federal judicial establishment. This Court has played no role in its development; we have exerted no supervisory power over the courts which enforce it; the rights of men in the armed forces must perforce be conditioned to meet certain overriding demands of discipline and duty, and the civil courts are not the agencies which must determine the precise balance to be struck in this adjustment. The Framers expressly entrusted that task to Congress.

That military law exists and has developed separately from other Federal law does not mean that persons subject thereto are denied their constitutional rights. To the contrary, the very issue before the Supreme Court in *Burns v. Wilson, supra,* was whether such a denial had occurred. The Chief Justice . . . pointed out: "The federal civil courts have jurisdiction over such applications." He then went on to state the duty of this Court and that of every other judicial body inferior to it:

> The military courts, like the state courts, have the same responsibilities as do the federal courts to protect a person from a violation of his constitutional rights.

. . . The impact of *Burns v. Wilson,* then, is of an unequivocal holding by the Supreme Court that the protections of the Constitution are available to servicemen in military trials. . . . We likewise have not been remiss in stating our obligation to protect a serviceman's rights under the Constitution. In *United States v. Jacoby,* . . . we expressly said:

> . . . [I]t is apparent that the protections in the Bill of Rights, except those which are expressly or by necessary implication inapplicable, are available to members of our armed forces.

. . . Thus, it will be seen that both the Supreme Court and this Court itself are satisfied as to the applicability of constitutional safeguards to military trials, except insofar as they are made inapplicable either expressly or by necessary implication. . . .

The point need not, however, be belabored. Sufficient has been said to establish our firm and unshakable conviction that Tempia, as any other member of the armed services so situated, was entitled to the protection of the Bill of Rights, insofar as we are herein concerned with it. We pass, therefore, to the Government's contention that *Miranda, supra,* involves a decision in the area of the Supreme Court's supervisory authority rather than constitutional principles.

At the outset, we must note that the Government's contention misapprehends the extent of the Supreme Court's supervisory authority over the administration of criminal justice. It goes no further than the bounds of the Federal judicial system. *Miranda, supra,* was a State case, prosecuted in the courts of Arizona, as were two of its companion cases. The Court sought not, directly at least, to supervise criminal trials in those States, but to determine whether the utilization of confessions in those hearings violated the privilege of the Fifth Amendment which, in *Malloy v. Hogan* . . . (1964), "we squarely held . . . applicable to the States, and held that the substantive standards underlying the privilege applied with full force to state court proceedings." . . .

. . . [W]e cannot accept the Government's ingenious argument that *Miranda* does not deal with constitutional principles and, hence, may be rejected by this Court, in light of the safeguards with which a military accused has heretofore been protected. . . .

We turn, therefore, to the merits of the controversy before us. *Miranda v. Arizona* explicitly and at length lays down concrete rules which are to govern all criminal interrogations by Federal or State authorities, military or civilian, if resulting statements are to be used in trials commencing on and after June 13, 1966. We commend a reading of that opinion to all involved in the administration of military criminal law as well as the undertaking of educative measures to see that its precepts are not violated in pretrial interrogations.

We now proceed to examine the facts presented in this record, in light of the foregoing requirements.

A. Custodial Interrogation

The Government urges upon us the proposition that the accused was not in custody, and, hence, the need

for appropriate advice and assistance did not arise. We may at once dispose of this contention. The accused was apprehended on May 1, 1966; freed to seek counsel; recalled for interrogation on May 3, 1966; an appointment was made for him with Major Hogue, following which, he immediately returned to the Office of Special Investigations, where his interrogation was successfully completed. The test to be applied is not whether the accused, technically, has been taken into custody, but, absent that, whether he has been "otherwise deprived of his freedom of action in any significant way." Here, the accused was clearly summoned for interrogation. Had he not obeyed, he would have undoubtedly subjected himself to being penalized for a failure to repair. In the military, unlike civil life, a suspect may be required to report and submit to questioning quite without regard to warrants or other legal process. It ignores the realities of that situation to say that one ordered to appear for interrogation has not been significantly deprived of his freedom of action. Hence, we conclude there was "custodial interrogation" in this case.

B. The Warning

The accused was fully advised of his rights under Code, *supra,* Article 31, and of his right to consult with counsel. On indicating a desire to speak with counsel, he was initially freed and, ultimately, on May 3, was referred to Major Hogue for further advice concerning his rights. But that officer went no further than to emphasize to the accused that he could not form an attorney-client relationship with him; to advise him again of his rights under Code, *supra,* Article 31; and to inform him he could retain civilian counsel at his own expense, who could appear at his interrogation. He specifically told accused no military lawyer would be appointed "to represent him during the OSI investigation or any investigation by the law enforcement agents on this base."

Miranda squarely points out "the person must be warned that he has a right to remain silent, that any statement he does make may be used as evidence against him, and that he has a right to the presence of an attorney, either retained or appointed." . . . In addition, if the accused "indicates in any manner and at any stage of the process that he wishes to consult with an attorney before speaking there can be no questioning. Likewise, if the individual is alone and indicates in any manner that he does not wish to be interrogated, the police may not question him." . . .

Undoubtedly, the advice given Tempia under Code, *supra,* Article 31, sufficed to inform him both of his right to remain silent and the purpose for which any statement he might make could be used. The advice as to counsel, however, was deficient.

First, accused was only warned by the agents that he was entitled to consult with counsel. When Major Hogue elaborated on this proposition, he limited the availability of counsel to private attorneys employed by the accused at his own expense. He specifically told accused no attorney would be appointed to represent him in any law enforcement investigation. This is exactly contrary to the information which, under *Miranda* must be preliminarily communicated to the accused.

As accused was informed no counsel would be appointed for him, it follows that the statement thereafter taken from him was inadmissable in evidence.

C. Waiver

The Government suggests that accused knowingly and intelligently waived his rights against self-incrimination by making his statement after being repeatedly warned under Code, *supra,* Article 31, and subjecting himself to further interrogation following his conference with Major Hogue. In connection with the latter circumstance, it invites our attention to testimony that, on returning from Hogue's office, accused stated he did not desire further counsel, "that they could not help him. . . . 'They didn't do me no good.' "

Aside from the fact that accused was improperly advised as to his entitlement to appointed counsel, we point out that he, in fact, received no legal advice, as Major Hogue specifically declined to act as his attorney. The testimony, taken as a whole, indicates not that accused did not desire a lawyer's services but that he had been frustrated in obtaining advice on whether to exercise his rights—hence, his comment: " 'They didn't do me no good.' " There should be small wonder at his feelings, when he had just been refused the opportunity to discuss the case

with Hogue, relate any of the facts to him, or to obtain any information as to a desirable course of action. If the interrogation continues without the presence of an attorney and a statement is taken, a heavy burden rests on the government to demonstrate that the defendant knowingly and intelligently waived his privilege against self-incrimination and his right to retained or appointed counsel.

Quite apart from the insufficiency of the warning as to accused's right to counsel, here the Government did not carry its burden, and no waiver is made out. To the contrary, it merely shows accused's entitlement to consult with counsel was frustrated by the Staff Judge Advocate's well-meant but legally improper statements.

. . . Indeed, the impact of *Miranda* upon the administration of military justice should be far less than that in comparable civilian jurisdictions. The armed services are already provided with a complete, functioning system of appointed counsel, one which, in *Miranda,* merited the approbation of our highest court. In most cases, defense counsel will eventually have to be appointed for the trial. All that will now be required is that the date of appointment be moved back. And should the investigation result in no trial, we daresay that the consequent savings will more than repay any costs involved in the earlier intervention of an appointed counsel.

Be that as it may, we point out another matter overlooked in the Government's claim of lack of authority to furnish counsel on this earlier occasion. *Miranda, supra,* does not specifically require such procedures or their equivalent to be followed. It merely prohibits the receipt in evidence of any statement taken, unless there is compliance with these constitutional standards. If the Government cannot comply with them, it need only abandon its reliance in criminal cases on the accused's statements as evidence. That is the essence of the *Miranda* holding, and it is the choice of the Government whether to pay this price for withholding counsel at the critical moment of police interrogation.

. . . It is well to remember that we, "like the state courts, have the same responsibilities as do the federal courts to protect a person from a violation of his constitutional rights." . . . We necessarily must effectuate that mandate by holding *Miranda v. Arizona* applicable in military prosecutions.

The decision of the board of review is reversed, and the record of trial is returned to the Judge Advocate General of the Air Force. A rehearing may be ordered.

KILDAY, Judge (concurring). . . .

QUINN, Chief Judge (dissenting). . . .

UNITED STATES V. JOHNSON
Court of Military Appeals, 1990.
30 M.J. 53.

[Air Force sergeant Nathaniel Johnson, who was infected with the HIV virus, was convicted under the Uniform Code of Military Justice (UCMJ) of attempted sodomy, and assault with means likely to produce death or grievous bodily harm. In reviewing Johnson's conviction, the Court of Military Appeals considers two basic issues: (1) whether a charge alleging aggravated assault with a means likely to cause death or grievous bodily harm, specifically, the HIV virus, alleges an offense under the UCMJ; and (2) the sufficiency of the evidence to sustain the conviction.]

COX, Judge.

Appellant was tried by general court-martial before a military judge alone for knowingly exposing a 17-year-old male to the Human Immunodeficiency Virus (HIV). . . . After mixed pleas, he was found guilty of attempted consensual sodomy, consensual sodomy, and assault with a means likely to produce death or grievous bodily harm, to wit: attempted anal intercourse while knowingly infected with HIV, in violation of Articles 80, 125, and 128, Uniform Code of Military Justice. . . . He was sentenced to confinement for 10 years, total forfeitures, reduction to E–1, and dishonorable discharge. The convening authority approved the sentence as adjudged. The Court of Military Review approved the findings, but reduced the confinement to 6 years. . . .

In September 1987, while attached to McChord Air Force Base, Washington, appellant learned that he had tested positive for HIV. . . .

On the evening of December 13th, while driving in downtown Tacoma, Washington, appellant met JPH, a 17-year-old male, and offered him a ride home. During the drive, appellant and JPH agreed to buy beer and return to appellant's barracks room at the base.

Once in appellant's room JPH drank several beers as well as a number of mixed drinks made with bourbon. Appellant and JPH engaged in petting and kissing, and appellant eventually performed consensual fellatio on JPH. Appellant then attempted to insert his finger into JPH's anus, but JPH objected; appellant stopped. At that point, JPH was very intoxicated, so much so that he vomited three times. Appellant then laid on top of and beside JPH, and he "just laid . . . [his penis] around" JPH's anus. Appellant admitted that it was his original intent to have anal intercourse with JPH, but he claimed he never attempted to do so. In appellant's own words, after JPH vomited, appellant "lost interest." JPH agreed that appellant never actually tried to penetrate his anus with his penis. JPH testified that appellant was not wearing a condom, but appellant claimed he was. Appellant and JPH apparently left the barracks room on amicable terms, although JPH reported the episode to authorities the next day. JPH testified that if he had known appellant was infected with HIV, he never would have consented to any contact with him.

Lieutenant Colonel Richard E. Winn, U.S. Air Force Medical Corps, testified extensively as a medical expert for the Government. Dr. Winn described in detail how the Human Immunodeficiency Virus is transmitted. According to Dr. Winn, there is up to a 35 percent probability that an individual who tests positive for HIV will develop AIDS. In turn, the mortality rate for those testing positive for AIDS is presently 50 percent. Dr. Winn also stated that the most dangerous transmission of HIV occurs through intravenous drug use and unprotected sexual intercourse, both heterosexual and homosexual. He indicated that the risk of transmission is increased "if one participates in anal intercourse" or if either of the partners "have genital ulcers or ulcerations, or tears." Dr. Winn did testify that physical contact such as actually occurred in this case is "unlikely" to cause transmission of the AIDS virus.

Based upon this evidence, the military judge found that appellant had committed an assault with means likely to produce death or grievous bodily harm. Through special findings pertinent to Charge III and its specification, the military judge stated:

> [S]pecifically ... the accused attempted to have anal intercourse with ... [JPH]. The accused was infected with the Human Immunodeficiency Virus at the time of the attempt ...; and he knew that he was so infected. I [the military judge] did not believe the accused's testimony that he used a condom.
>
> [T]he accused attempted with unlawful force or violence to do bodily harm to ... [JPH] with the specific intent to do bodily harm. The accused's acts in lying naked on the back of ... [JPH] with his penis at or near the anus ... amounted to more than mere preparation and were done with the apparent present ability to do bodily harm....
>
> [U]nlawful force or violence ... exist in this case because there is no legal justification or excuse for the acts. Further, there can be no lawful consent by a victim to this type of assault....
>
> [T]he specific intent involved here is a specific intent to do bodily harm.... Bodily harm means any physical injury to or offensive touching of another person, however slight.... [A]ny rational person would find it offensive to be touched by the Human Immunodeficiency Virus.
>
> [T]he natural and probable consequence of the acts attempted by the accused would be the touching of ... [JPH's body] by the Human Immunodeficiency Virus. I have considered the testimony that not every act of unprotected anal intercourse results in transmission of ... [HIV], and I have considered the testimony that not everyone who is infected with the virus dies or suffers grievous bodily harm. However, given the available medical testimony, I conclude that the ... [HIV] is a means which is likely to produce death or grievous bodily harm....

I

With respect to Issue I, it is now beyond cavil that it is permissible under the Code to charge aggravated assault, where the means alleged as likely to produce death or grievous bodily harm is HIV.... An offense so charged is not void for vagueness. Appellant was provided adequate notice that he could be held criminally liable for consensual sodomy with another person, military or civilian, male or female.... It is well-recognized that the military services and society at large have a compelling interest to ensure that those who defend the nation remain healthy and capable of performing their duty.... Further, sodomy, consensual or otherwise, is not constitutionally protected conduct within the military. Lastly, appellant's claim that he was denied fair notice that his semen or blood contained the means to inflict death or grievous bodily harm would leave any jurist incredulous. Once appellant tested positive for HIV, medical personnel made him overtly aware of the dangers of transmitting the virus should he have unprotected sexual contact with another person. This was substantiated by Dr. Winn and by appellant's own testimony. We are satisfied that alleging aggravated assault under these circumstances does state an offense and that it is constitutionally permissible to charge such an offense under the Uniform Code....

II

Turning to the second issue, we note that Article 128 sets out four elements for the offense of assault with a means likely to produce death or grievous bodily harm. The Manual for Courts-Martial identifies these elements as follows:

(i) That the accused attempted to do, offered to do, or did bodily harm to a certain person;
(ii) That the accused did so with a certain weapon, means, or force;
(iii) That the attempt, offer, or bodily harm was done with unlawful force or violence; and
(iv) That the weapon, means, or force was used in a manner likely to produce death or grievous bodily harm....

The first element of aggravated assault can be satisfied by a mere attempt, i.e., "[t]hat the accused attempted to do ... bodily harm to" a person. Although appellant testified that he did not attempt to penetrate JPH's anus with his penis, it is difficult to imagine how much further appellant would have had to go to commit an overt act constituting an attempt.... Indeed, the military judge specifically found appellant guilty, beyond a reasonable doubt, of the offense of attempted anal sodomy.... Moreover, the military judge expressly stated his disbelief of appellant's claim that he wore a condom (which would have protected JPH from transmission of the virus). The judge heard the evidence and observed the demeanor of the witnesses. As this Court is limited ... "to matters of law," we are precluded from setting aside the military judge's findings of fact in light of the substantial evidence of record supporting those conclusions. ...

The *actus reus* of the crime, however, also requires conduct which goes beyond a simple offer of bodily harm.... It is not necessary that such conduct actually cause death or grievous bodily harm so long as the means employed is "used in a manner likely to produce ... [such] harm." Evidence of record sufficiently demonstrates that appellant's semen containing HIV was certainly a means capable of transmitting a deadly disease, thus producing death or grievous bodily harm. Moreover, the evidenceshows that, in this era of heightened awareness and concern regarding the dangers of transmitting HIV,

both the military and civilian communities recognize that, under many circumstances, AIDS is "the natural and probable consequence" of exposure to HIV. ...

There was some competent evidence, therefore, upon which the military judge could find beyond a reasonable doubt that appellant attempted to do bodily harm to JPH, i.e., engage in unprotected anal intercourse which would have been likely to transmit a disease which can ultimately result in death. ...

The decision of the United States Air Force Court of Military Review affirming the findings and sentence as to sodomy and aggravated assault is affirmed.

Judge SULLIVAN concurs.

EVERETT, Chief Judge (concurring):

Appellant was found guilty of attempted anal sodomy and aggravated assault; but the Air Force Court of Military Review set aside the attempt conviction on grounds of multiplicity. Although this was a legally permissible option, I believe that, in a case like this, it would have been preferable for the Court below to have affirmed the finding of attempted sodomy, considered appellant's HIV infection as a factor in aggravation of that offense, and vacated the conviction of aggravated assault as multiplicious.

APPENDICES

APPENDIX A

RICO: AN ASSAULT ON ORGANIZED CRIME

After the ratification in 1919 of the Eighteenth Amendment outlawing the manufacture, sale, and distribution of alcoholic beverages, organized crime gained a strong foothold in the United States. During the Prohibition Era, organizations operating outside the law trafficked in liquor and were involved in prostitution. Despite the repeal of that amendment in 1933, these crime syndicates continued their activities and expanded into loansharking, gambling, narcotics, and extortion. They infiltrated legitimate businesses and conducted widespread illegal operations through complex business structures.

As discussed in the text, the common-law development of crime definitions focused on particular acts of individual wrongdoing and on inchoate activities. Congress and the state legislatures generally followed this "transactional" approach in defining statutory crimes, but these crime definitions did not cover ongoing criminal activity by organized groups. In addition, traditional methods of law enforcement and criminal prosecution proved ineffective to cope with the activities of organized crime.

In 1967, the President's Commission on Law Enforcement and the Administration of Justice issued a comprehensive report on the dimensions of crime in the United States. This led to congressional findings that organized crime had weakened the stability of the nation's economy through infiltration of legitimate businesses and labor unions and threatened to subvert and corrupt our democratic processes. In response, Congress enacted the Organized Crime Control Act of 1970, Title 9 of which was entitled "Racketeer Influenced and Corrupt Organizations." The act is commonly referred to by the acronym "RICO." In congressional debates Senator McClelland, who conducted investigations leading to passage of the new act, pointed out that Title 9 "[p]rohibits infiltration of legitimate organizations by racketeers . . . where interstate commerce is affected." 116 Cong. Rec. 585 (1970).

RICO created new crimes and a new approach to criminal prosecution. First, it makes it a crime for any person "who has received any income derived, directly or indirectly, from a pattern of racketeering activity or through collection of an unlawful debt . . . to use or invest [in] any enterprise which is engaged in interstate or foreign commerce." 18 U.S.C.A. § 1962(a). Second, it makes it unlawful for any such person to participate, directly or indirectly, in the conduct of the enterprise's affairs through a "pattern of racketeering." 18 U.S.C.A. § 1962(b). Third, it makes it criminal for any person "employed by or associated with any enterprise engaged in, or the activities of which affect, interstate or foreign commerce, to conduct or participate, directly or indirectly, in the conduct of such enterprise's affairs through a pattern of racketeering activity or collection of unlawful debt." 18 U.S.C.A. § 1962(c). Finally, it prohibits conspiracies to violate any of these proscriptions. 18 U.S.C.A. § 1962(d).

In addition to substantial fines, imprisonment for not more than twenty years, or both, the act provides for forfeiture to the United States of any interest acquired or maintained in violation of Section 1962. 18 U.S.C.A. § 1963(a). Recognizing that law enforcement agencies cannot handle the task completely, the act provides for an award of treble damages plus costs and attorney fees in civil actions instituted by persons who suffer losses as a result of RICO violations. 18 U.S.C.A. § 1964(c). Since RICO does not contain its own statute of limitations, the general five-year statute of limitations for noncapital federal offenses applies. *United States v. Bethea*, 672 F.2d 407 (5th Cir. 1982).

The scope of the act is expansive. It broadly defines *racketeering activity* to include a variety of federal offenses and nine state crimes that are characteristically felonies. 18 U.S.C.A. § 1961(1). To establish a "pattern of racketeering activity" requires proof of at least two of these acts of racketeering having occurred within a period of ten years, excluding any period of imprisonment. 18 U.S.C.A. § 1961(5). These acts are frequently referred to by the courts as "predicate acts" and any combination of two or more can constitute a pattern of racketeering. To obtain a conviction under RICO, the government must establish the defendant's involvement in a "pattern of racketeering or collection of an unlawful debt." See, for example, *United States v. Dozier*, 672 F.2d 531 (5th Cir.), *cert. denied*, 459 U.S. 943, 103 S. Ct. 256, 74 L.Ed.2d 200 (1982). The fact that there is but one objective underlying separate acts of racketeering does not diminish the applicability of RICO to those actions. *United States v. Starnes*, 644 F.2d 673 (7th Cir.), *cert. denied*, 454 U.S. 826, 102 S. Ct. 116, 70 L.Ed.2d 101 (1981). There is no requirement that a state conviction be obtained before a state offense can be used as a predicate act of the racketeering activity charged. *United States v. Malatesta*, 583 F.2d 748 (5th Cir. 1978), *cert. denied*, 440 U.S. 962, 99 S. Ct. 1508, 59 L.Ed.2d 777 (1979).

RICO also defines *enterprise* broadly to include "any individual, partnership, corporation, association, or other legal entity, and any union or group of individuals associated in fact although not a legal entity." 18 U.S.C.A. § 1961(4). The Supreme Court has said that the term encompasses both legitimate and illegitimate enterprises. *United States v. Turkette*, 452 U.S. 576, 101 S. Ct. 2524, 69 L.Ed.2d 246 (1981). Lower federal courts have held the term includes both private and public entities such as corporations, banks, and decedents' estates, as well as state agencies, police departments, traffic courts, and prostitution rings.

RICO does not criminalize the status of a person for being a racketeer—it criminalizes a person's conduct of an enterprise through a pattern of racketeering. *United States v. Phillips*, 664 F.2d 971 (5th Cir. 1981), *cert. denied*, 457 U.S. 1136, 102 S. Ct. 2965, 73 L.Ed.2d 1354 (1982). Therefore, when a jury finds that a defendant has committed the predicate acts, it must still find that these acts were committed in connection with a pattern of racketeering or collection of an unlawful debt. A RICO violation involves a separate criminal proceeding. Therefore, the Double Jeopardy Clause of the United States Constitution does not prohibit the government from prosecuting a defendant for a RICO charge where the defendant has been previously prosecuted for a substantive offense used as one of the predicate crimes. *United States. v. Smith,* 574 F.2d 308 (5th Cir.), *cert. denied,* 439 U.S. 931, 99 S. Ct. 321, 58 L.Ed.2d 325 (1978).

The following three cases illustrate some RICO prosecutions:

- Former police officers were charged with violating RICO by accepting bribes to protect individuals involved in gambling and vice. *United States v. Brown,* 555 F.2d 407 (5th Cir. 1977), *cert. denied,* 435 U.S. 904, 98 S. Ct. 1448, 55 L.Ed.2d 494 (1978).
- Defendants were convicted of operating an illegal gambling business and conspiring to obstruct state law enforcement. *United States v. Zemek,* 634 F.2d 1159 (9th Cir. 1980).
- Several members of the Outlaws Motorcycle Club were prosecuted for a RICO violation based on narcotics and prostitution offenses. *United States v. Watchmaker,* 761 F.2d 1459 (11th Cir. 1985), *cert. denied,* 474 U.S. 1100, 106 S. Ct. 879, 88 L.Ed.2d 917 (1986).

Some RICO prosecutions have involved well-known political figures. For example, Maryland governor Marvin Mandel was prosecuted on charges of mail fraud and four other RICO counts. *United States v. Mandel,* 415 F. Supp. 997 (D. Md. 1976).

RICO was conceived as a weapon for prosecution of organized crime. Prosecutors have long experienced difficulty in securing convictions of organized crime leaders for violating specific criminal statutes. In part this occurs because the evidence of a specific statutory violation may be unconvincing to a judge or jury. The reaction of a judge or jury is likely to be different when the prosecution parades before the court evidence of a series of violations that reveals a pattern of criminal behavior.

RICO can be an effective tool in the hands of prosecutors in their fight against crime syndicates. Yet membership in organized crime is not a necessary element for a conviction under RICO. Unlike criminal statutes that historically have been narrowly construed, Congress provided that RICO is to be liberally interpreted to effectuate its remedial purposes. The liberal construction of the enterprise requirement and the fact that the pattern requirement of racketeering activity is cast in numerical terms has caused some critics to contend that RICO is a "catch-all" statute that gives prosecutors too much discretion to expand the range of indictable offenses.

RICO has been extended beyond its original purpose to target such nonorganized crime as the white-collar criminal and the corrupt government official. Thus, through RICO a prosecutor can circumvent statutes of limitation and inflict multiple punishments for the same offenses. Despite criticism, RICO is firmly established as a weapon in the arsenal available to federal prosecutors to combat racketeering and corruption, both private and public, whether organized or not.

RICO has become available to many state prosecutors as most of the states have adopted RICO-type statutes. Some closely parallel the federal act; others have varying provisions concerning prohibited acts, sanctions, forfeitures of property, and the procedures involved.

Because it departs from the traditional transactional approach to criminal law, RICO is a controversial concept. Yet, given RICO's obvious utility in combatting organized crime, white-collar crime, and political corruption, theoretical reservations about RICO are not apt to find a sympathetic ear among legislators and judges.

C A S E

UNITED STATES V. GAMBINO
United States Court of Appeals, Second Circuit, 1977.
566 F.2d 414,

[The appellants, Gambino and Conti, were convicted of a number of offenses including violations of the federal RICO statute.]

GURFEIN, Circuit Judge.

. . . The appellants contend that there was insufficient evidence to prove a conspiracy to acquire and maintain control of the private sanitation industry in the Coop City area of the Bronx through a pattern of racketeering activity. They argue that there was insufficient evidence to warrant a conviction under Count Four, which charged that Gambino and Conti used threats and violence in order to collect an extension of credit for Peter Darminio. Specifically, they point to an alleged lack of corroboration of Darminio's testimony.

The general outline of the case indicates that Gambino and Conti had controlled certain stops for private garbage collection in the Bronx but were unable to get a carting license from the City. They arranged for Terminal Sanitation, a licensed private sanitation firm, owned by Peter and Anthony Darminio, to collect at all of the stops which Gambino had previously acquired in the Bronx. The Darminios were required to kick back to Gambino one-third of all the moneys they received from servicing the stops.

[The trial court] . . . found that Gambino and Conti maintained control of garbage collection in Coop City and other areas of the Bronx by threatening to kill competitors and by administering beatings. This activity included an assault on an undercover agent of the FBI who was posing as a cart man and who had solicited a stop in Coop City. [The trial court] also found that Gambino engaged in extensive loansharking activities, lending a total of $90,000 to Peter and Anthony Darminio in 1970 and 1971 and $75,000 to Peter in 1972. These loans were collected by Gambino and Conti through the use of threats and violence.

The court carefully reviewed the evidence. Ralph Torres, an employee of Gambino and Conti, was found to be a credible witness by . . . [the trial court]. Although the credibility of Peter Darminio was in question, his testimony concerning the defendant's extortionate extensions of credit was corroborated by an exhibit in evidence bearing Gambino's handwriting, headed with the word "Peter" and containing a column of figures and certain calculations. [The trial court] . . . further found that Conti, who was collecting the payments, threatened and beat Darminio from time to time when he was late in making payments.

In July of 1973 one Bernard Ettinger, who had sold Terminal to the Darminios in 1968 and who had not been paid in full in connection with the sale, complained in writing to the New York City Department of Consumer Affairs, requesting that the Department see to it that the Darminios fulfilled their obligations to him before the department approved any sale of stops registered to Terminal. Shortly thereafter, Conti visited Ettinger at his office, slapped Mr. Ettinger on the face, and told him that he had better not complain to the department.

On an earlier occasion when Ettinger had threatened to foreclose on Anthony Darminio's home, on which he held a mortgage, Mr. and Mrs. Darminio had asked Mr. Gambino for assistance, and Gambino replied, "Don't worry about it. I'll send Carlo Conti to straighten it out." In 1974, Ettinger pressed Darminio for payment, which was then a balance of $90,000. A meeting was arranged. Gambino came with Darminio. Gambino said that if Ettinger would settle, Darminio could sell some stops and there would be some stops left over so that Peter Darminio could continue his route. Ettinger agreed to settle for $40,000. One Joseph Perillo, who was also present at the meeting, indicated that he was prepared to purchase some stops from Terminal but did not have money with him for a down payment.

Gambino gave Perillo $5,000, which Perillo, in turn, gave to Ettinger. The court found Ettinger to be a highly credible witness.

In November 1975, Terminal entered into a contract with P & S Sanitation, a newly organized company, to take over Terminal's stops. The court found that Gambino was active in P & S.

In the Fall of 1976, the FBI incorporated American Automated Refuse & Waste Removal, Inc., and set up an office in the Bronx. They bought trucks and a winch, the winch being shipped from Texas, and arranged to dump the garbage in New Jersey. They then began soliciting garbage collection accounts, including Harry's Service Station which they knew was being serviced by P & S Sanitation. On December 1, 1976, Harry's entered into an agreement with American Automated, the Government company. American Automated arranged to drop off a container at Harry's to store garbage which would be collected by Automated. Shortly thereafter, Conti telephoned American Automated and came to the office. He threatened to kill the person seated at the desk, who called himself Wayne Dacon but who was in fact an agent of the FBI named Walter Wayne Orrell. Conti's statement to Orrell included a threat to throw the agent out of the window. This conversation was tape-recorded and the tape was received in evidence. Conti indicated that anything new that opened up in Coop City was his. There were two places on the tape where a crunching sound was audible. Agent Orrell testified that Conti punched him. The evidence established that Conti acted frequently at the behest of Gambino, that both men conspired to acquire and maintain control of the private sanitation industry in Coop City and other areas of the Bronx through a pattern of racketeering activity and they in fact carried out the purpose of the conspiracy, that both men obstructed commerce by extorting payments from Terminal Sanitation and its principals, and that Conti attempted to obstruct commerce by assaulting and threatening to kill persons associated with American Automated, Inc.

These findings ... cannot lightly be set aside. Nor do we see any reason for so doing. We hold that there was sufficient evidence to sustain the conviction. ...

The judgment of conviction of each appellant is affirmed in respects. ...

APPENDIX B

ACCESS TO THE LAW THROUGH LEGAL RESEARCH

THE NATURE OF LEGAL RESEARCH

Successful legal research requires a systematic method of finding the law applicable to a particular problem or set of facts. Before beginning research it is helpful, if not essential, for the criminal justice professional or student to have a basic understanding of the law and the legal system.

After assembling the relevant facts and completing a preliminary analysis of the problem, the researcher must find the applicable constitutional and statutory materials and then search for authoritative interpretations of the law. Interpretations are usually found in appellate court decisions construing the particular constitutional provision or statute in analogous situations. These judicial decisions are referred to as "cases in point." Legislative and judicial sources of the law are referred to as "primary sources" because they are authoritative.

A variety of other legal materials, called "secondary sources," are available to the researcher. These consist of legal encyclopedias, textbooks by scholars and practitioners, law reviews published by law schools and journals, and periodicals published by various legal organizations. These secondary sources are extremely helpful to the researcher, especially to one unfamiliar with the law in a given area.

PRIMARY LEGAL SOURCES

Federal and state constitutions are often the beginning points in legal research in the criminal justice area, since they provide the framework for our government and guarantee certain basic rights to the accused. As explained in this text, the rights of an accused are protected by several provisions of the federal Constitution and the Bill of Rights. Most state constitutions afford criminal defendants similar protections. For instance, a person concerned about the legality of an arrest, search, or seizure would examine the relevant constitutional provisions and then seek to determine how the courts have construed the law in analogous situations.

Federal offenses are defined in statutes enacted by the United States Congress, and state offenses are defined in statutes enacted by state legislatures. Federal statutes (in sequence of their adoption) are published annually in the *United States Statutes at Large*. Most states have similar volumes, called session laws, that incorporate the laws enacted during a given session of the legislature. These federal and state laws are initially compiled in sequence of their adoption. Later they are merged into legal codes that systematically arrange the statutes by subject and provide an index. Of far greater assistance to the criminal justice researcher are commercially prepared codes that classify all federal and state laws of a general and permanent nature by subject and include reference materials and exhaustive indexes. These volumes are kept current by periodic supplements and revised volumes.

The United States Code Annotated

One popular compilation of the federal law widely used by lawyers, judges, and criminal justice professionals is the *United States Code Annotated*. "U.S.C.A.," as it is known, is published by West Publishing Company of St. Paul, Minnesota (the publisher of this text). The U.S.C.A. consists of fifty separate titles that conform to the text of the Official Code of the Laws of the United States. Title 18, for instance, is entitled "Crimes and Criminal Procedure" and is of particular interest to the criminal justice researcher. Each section of statutory law in U.S.C.A. is followed by a series of annotations consisting of court decisions interpreting the particular statute along with historical notes, cross-references, and other editorial features. If the researcher knows only the popular name of a federal statute, the corresponding U.S. Code title and section number can be found in the Popular Name Table. A sample page from the U.S.C.A. is included as Exhibit 1. A sample page from the Popular Name Table is included as Exhibit 2.

Annotated State Codes

Most states have annotated statutes published by either the state or a private publisher. For example, *West's Annotated California Codes* follows the same general format as the United States Code Annotated. A sample page is included as Exhibit 3. Annotated statutes are popular aids to legal research and can save the researcher valuable time in locating cases in point. They are especially effective tools for locating interpretations of criminal statutes.

The National Reporter System

Volumes containing appellate court decisions are referred to as "reporters." The National Reporter System® includes decisions from the United States Supreme Court, the lower federal courts, and the state appellate courts. Back reporters are now available both in West's Ultra Fiche and in bound-volumes editions.

Decisions of the United States Supreme Court are officially published in the United States Reports (abbreviated U.S.). Two private organizations also report these decisions in hard-cover volumes. The *Supreme Court Reporter* (abbreviated S. Ct.) is published by West, and *Lawyers Edition*, now in its second series (abbreviated L.Ed.2d), is published by the Lawyers Cooperative Publishing Company. References to judicial decisions found in the reporters are called "citations." United States Supreme Court decisions are often cited to all three publications: for example, *Miranda v. Arizona*, 384 U.S. 436, 86 S. Ct. 1602, 16 L.Ed.2d 694 (1966). A sample page from West's *Supreme Court Reporter* is included as Exhibit 4.

CHAPTER 87—PRISONS

Sec.
1791. Traffic in contraband articles.
1792. Mutiny, riot, dangerous instrumentalities prohibited.

Cross References

Escape and rescue, see section 751 et seq. of this title.

§ 1791. Traffic in contraband articles

Whoever, contrary to any rule or regulation promulgated by the Attorney General, introduces or attempts to introduce into or upon the grounds of any Federal penal or correctional institution or takes or attempts to take or send therefrom anything whatsoever, shall be imprisoned not more than ten years.

(June 25, 1948, c. 645, 62 Stat. 786.)

Historical and Revision Notes

Reviser's Note. Based on Title 18, U.S.C., 1940 ed., §§ 753j, 908 (May 14, 1930, c. 274, § 11, 46 Stat. 327; May 27, 1930, c. 339, § 8, 46 Stat. 390).

Section consolidates sections 753j and 908 of Title 18, U.S.C., 1940 ed. The section was broadened to include the taking or sending out of contraband from the institution. This was suggested by representatives of the Federal Bureau of Prisons and the Criminal Division of the Department of Justice. In other respects the section was rewritten without change of substance.

The words "narcotic", "drug", "weapon" and "contraband" were omitted, since the insertion of the words "contrary to any rule or regulation promulgated by the attorney general" preserves the intent of the original statutes.

Words "guilty of a felony" were deleted as unnecessary in view of definitive section 1 of this title. (See also reviser's note under section 550 of this title.)

Minor verbal changes also were made.

Cross References

Bureau of Prisons employees, power to arrest without warrant for violations of this section, see section 3050 of this title.

West's Federal Forms

Sentence and fine, see § 7531 et seq.

Code of Federal Regulations

Federal penal and correctional institutions, traffic in contraband articles, see 28 CFR 6.1.

Library References

Prisons ⚞17½.
C.J.S. Prisons § 22.

Notes of Decisions

Aiding and abetting 7
Admissibility of evidence 13

Articles prohibited 3
Assistance of counsel 11

585

EXHIBIT 1 United States Code Annotated Source: Reprinted with permission from 18 U.S.C.A. § 1791, Copyright © 1984 By West Publishing Co., 1-800-328-9352.

Crimes and Criminal Procedure—Continued
Oct. 28, 1992, Pub.L. 102–550, Title XIII, Subtitle A, § 1353, Title XV, Subtitle A, §§ 1504(c), 1512(a), (c), 1522(a), 1523(a), 1524, 1525(c)(1), 1526, 1527, 1528, 1530, 1531, 1533, 1534, 1536, Subtitle D, § 1543, Subtitle E, §§ 1552, 1553, 1554, 106 Stat. 3970, 4055, 4057, 4063, 4064, 4065, 4066, 4067, 4069, 4070, 4071 (Title 18, §§ 474, 474A, 504, 981, 982, 984, 986, 1510, 1905, 1956, 1957, 1960, 6001)

Oct. 28, 1992, Pub.L. 102–561, 106 Stat. 4233 (Title 18, § 2319)

Oct. 29, 1992, Pub.L. 102–572, Title I, § 103, Title VII, §§ 701, 703, 106 Stat. 4507, 4514, 4515 (Title 18, §§ 3143, 3154, 3401, 3603)

Criminal Appeals Act
Mar. 2, 1907, ch. 2564, 34 Stat. 1246 (See Title 18, § 3731)

Criminal Code
Mar. 4, 1909, ch. 321, 35 Stat. 1088 (See Title 18, chapters 1–15)
June 25, 1910, ch. 431, § 6, 36 Stat. 857 (See Title 18, §§ 1853, 1856)
Mar. 4, 1921, ch. 172, 41 Stat. 1444 (See Title 18, §§ 831–835)
Mar. 28, 1940, ch. 73, 54 Stat. 80 (See Title 18, § 1382)
Apr. 30, 1940, ch. 164, 54 Stat. 171 (See Title 18, § 1024)
June 6, 1940, ch. 241, 54 Stat. 234 (See Title 18, § 13)
June 11, 1940, ch. 323, 54 Stat. 304 (See Title 18, § 7)
Apr. 1, 1944, ch. 151, 58 Stat. 149 (See Title 18, § 491)
Sept. 27, 1944, ch. 425, 58 Stat. 752 (See Title 18, § 371)
June 8, 1945, ch. 178, 59 Stat. 234 (See Title 18, §§ 371, 1503, 1505)

Criminal Fine Enforcement Act of 1984
Pub.L. 98–596, Oct. 30, 1984, 98 Stat. 3134 (Title 18, §§ 1, 1 note, 3565, 3565 note, 3569, 3579, 3591 to 3599, 3611 note, 3621 to 3624, 3651, 3655, 4209, 4214; Title 18, F.R.Crim.Proc. Rules 12.2, 12.2 note)

Criminal Fine Improvements Act of 1987
Pub.L. 100–185, Dec. 11, 1987, 101 Stat. 1279 (Title 18, §§ 1 note, 18, 19, 3013, 3559, 3571, 3572, 3573, 3611 note, 3612, 3663; Title 28, § 604)

Criminal Justice Act Revision of 1984
Pub.L. 98–473, Title II, § 1901, Oct. 12, 1984, 98 Stat. 2185 (Title 18, § 3006A)

Criminal Justice Act Revision of 1986
Pub.L. 99–651, Title I, Nov. 14, 1986, 100 Stat. 3642 (Title 18, § 3006A)

Criminal Justice Act of 1964
Pub. L. 88–455, Aug. 20, 1964, 78 Stat. 552 (Title 18, § 3006A)

Criminal Law and Procedure Technical Amendments Act of 1986
Pub.L. 99–646, Nov. 10, 1986, 100 Stat. 3592 (Title 18, §§ 1 note, 3, 17, 18, 113, 115, 201, 201 note, 203, 203 note, 209, 219, 351, 373, 513, 524, 666, 1028, 1029, 1111, 1153, 1201, 1366, 1512, 1515, 1791, 1791 note, 1793, 1961, 1963, 2031, 2032, 2113, 2232, 2241, 2241 notes, 2242, 2243, 2244, 2245, 2315, 2320, 3050, 3076, 3141, 3142, 3143, 3143 note, 3144, 3146, 3147, 3148, 3150a, 3156, 3156 note, 3185, 3522, 3551 note, 3552, 3552 note, 3553, 3553 notes, 3556, 3561, 3561 note, 3563, 3563 notes, 3579, 3579 notes, 3583, 3583 note, 3603, 3603 note, 3624, 3624 note, 3671, 3671 note, 3672, 3672 note, 3673, 3673 note, 3681, 3682, 3731, 3742, 4044, 4045, 4082, 4203, 4204, 4208, 4209, 4210, 4214, 4217, 5003, 5037, 5037 note; Title 18, F.R.Crim.Proc. Rules 12.2, 29, 29 note, 32, 32 note, 32.1, 32.1 note; Title 21, §§ 802, 812, 845a, 875, 878, 881; Title 28, §§ 546, 992, 993, 994, 1921, 1921 note; Title 42, §§ 257, 300w–3, 300w–4, 9511, 10601, 10603, 10604)

Pub.L. 100–185, § 4(c), Dec. 11, 1987, 101 Stat. 1279 (Title 18, § 18)

Pub.L. 100–690, Title VII, §§ 7012 to 7014, Nov. 18, 1988, 102 Stat. 4395 (Title 18, §§ 18, 1961, 4217)

Criminal Victims Protection Act of 1990
Pub.L. 101–581, Nov. 15, 1990, 104 Stat. 2865 (Title 11, §§ 101 note, 523, 523 note, 1328)

Pub.L. 101–647, Title XXXI, Nov. 29, 1990, 104 Stat. 4916 (Title 11, §§ 101 note, 523, 523 note, 1328)

Critical Agricultural Materials Act
Pub.L. 95–592, Nov. 4, 1978, 92 Stat. 2529 (Title 7, §§ 178, 178a to 178n, 1314f); Pub.L. 98–284, May 16, 1984, 98 Stat. 184 (Title 7, §§ 178, 178 note, 178a to 178i, 178k to 178n)

Pub.L. 99–198, Title XIV, § 1439, Dec. 23, 1985, 99 Stat. 1559 (Title 7, § 178c)

Pub.L. 101–624, Title XVI, § 1601(e), Nov. 28, 1990, 104 Stat. 3704 (Title 7, § 178n)

EXHIBIT 2 Popular Name Table (from U.S.C.A) Source: Reprinted with permission from U.S.C.A. Popular Name Table, Copyright © 1992 By West Publishing Co., 1-800-328-9352.

Title 12   **SEARCH WARRANTS**   **§ 1524**

warrant. People v. Golden (1971) 97 Cal.Rptr. 476, 20 C.A.3d 211.

4. Affidavits

"Oral" procedure is permitted only as to affidavit in support of search and warrant itself must be in writing. Bowyer v. Superior Court of Santa Cruz County (1974) 111 Cal.Rptr. 628, 37 C.A.3d 151, rehearing denied 112 Cal.Rptr. 266, 37 C. A.3d 151.

For an affidavit based on informant's hearsay statement to be legally sufficient to support issuance of a search warrant, two requirements must be met: (1) affidavit must allege the informant's statement in language that is factual rather than conclusionary and must establish that informant spoke with personal knowledge of the matters contained in such statement, and (2) the affidavit must contain some underlying factual information from which magistrate issuing the warrant can reasonably conclude that informant was credible or his information reliable. People v. Hamilton (1969) 77 Cal.Rptr. 785, 454 P.2d 681, 71 C.2d 176.

5. Arrest

An arrest without a warrant may not be made on a belief, founded on information received from a third person, that a misdemeanor is being committed. Ware v. Dunn (1947) 183 P.2d 128, 80 C.A.2d 936.

Arrest under warrant issued by justice of peace directed to any sheriff "in the state," where proper sheriff did receive warrant and executed it, and person arrested was not prejudiced, and was not ground for complaint by person arrested, notwithstanding under statutes warrant should have been directed to any sheriff "in the county". Elliott v. Haskins (1937) 67 P.2d 698, 20 C.A.2d 591.

6. Unreasonable searches

Alleged action of city police on specified occasions in blocking off designated portions of city and stopping all persons and automobiles entering or leaving the blocked off area and searching them with-out first obtaining a search warrant and without having probable cause for believing the searched individuals to have violated some law or that automobiles were carrying contraband, would be unconstitutional as being "unreasonable searches and seizures". Wirin v. Horrall (1948) 193 P.2d 470, 85 C.A.2d 497.

7. Admissibility of evidence

Rule excluding in criminal prosecutions evidence obtained through unlawful searches and seizures by police and governmental officers does not apply to evidence obtained by a private person, not employed by nor associated with a governmental unit. People v. Johnson (1957) 315 P.2d 468, 153 C.A.2d 870.

Evidence obtained in violation of constitutional guarantees against unreasonable searches and seizures is inadmissible. People v. Cahan (1955) 282 P.2d 905, 44 C.2d 434, 50 A.L.R.2d 513.

In a prosecution for burglary in the second degree, the fact that articles claimed to have been taken were seized from the person of accused without warrant in violation of Const.Art. 1, § 19 (repealed; see, now, Const.Art. 1, § 13) did not render their introduction in evidence error, although the court overruled the motion of accused to have the articles returned to him. People v. Watson (1922) 206 P. 648, 57 C.A. 85.

8. Federal and state warrants distinguished

Although a California municipal court judge is a "judge of a court of record" and thus authorized to issue federal warrants, the search warrant in question was clearly issued under state, not federal, authority, where it was issued by a California municipal judge on a California form, on the application of a California narcotics agent, and where there was no attempt to comply with the requirements of Fed. Rules of Cr.Proc. rule 41, 18 U.S.C. A. U. S. v. Radlick (C.A.1978) 581 F.2d 225.

§ 1524.   Issuance; grounds; special master

(a) A search warrant may be issued upon any of the following grounds:

(1) When the property was stolen or embezzled.

(2) When the property or things were used as the means of committing a felony.

(3) When the property or things are in the possession of any person with the intent to use it as a means of committing a public of-

EXHIBIT 3   West's Annotated California Code Source: Reprinted with permission from *West's Annotated California Codes,* Vol. 51A, § 1524. Copyright © 1982 By West Publishing Co., 1-800-328-9352.

Since 1889 the decisions of the United States Courts of Appeals have been published in West's *Federal Reporter,* now in its second series (abbreviated F.2d). Decisions of federal district (trial) courts are published in *West's Federal Supplement* (abbreviated F. Supp.). A citation to a case in *Federal Reporter* will read, for example, *Newman v. United States,* 817 F.2d 635 (10th Cir. 1987). This refers to a 1987 case reported in volume 817, page 635 of the *Federal Reporter,* second series, decided by the United States Court of Appeals for the 10th Circuit. A citation to *United States v. Klopfenstine,* 673 F. Supp. 356 (W.D. Mo. 1987), refers to a 1987 federal district court decision from the western district of Missouri reported in volume 673, page 356 of the *Federal Supplement.*

Additional federal reporters publish the decisions from other federal courts (e.g., bankruptcy and military appeals), but the federal reporters referred to earlier are those most frequently used by criminal justice professionals.

The Regional Reporters

The decisions of the highest state courts (usually but not always called supreme courts) and the decisions of other state appellate courts (usually referred to as intermediate appellate courts) are found in seven regional reporters, West's *California Reporter,* and the *New York Supplement.* Regional reporters, with their abbreviation in parentheses, include decisions from the following states:

Atlantic Reporter: (A. and A.2d)	Maine, Vermont, New Hampshire, Connecticut, Rhode Island, Pennsylvania, New Jersey, Maryland, Delaware, and the District of Columbia
North Eastern Reporter: (N.E. and N.E.2d)	Illinois, Indiana, Massachusetts, New York (court of last resort only), and Ohio
North Western Reporter: (N.W. and N.W.2d)	North Dakota, South Dakota, Nebraska, Minnesota, Iowa, Michigan, and Wisconsin
Pacific Reporter: (P. and P.2d)	Washington, Oregon, California, Montana, Idaho, Nevada, Utah, Arizona, Wyoming, Colorado, New Mexico, Kansas, Oklahoma, Alaska, and Hawaii
Southern Reporter: (So. and So.2d)	Florida, Alabama, Mississippi, and Louisiana
South Eastern Reporter: (S.E. and S.E.2d)	Virginia, West Virginia, North Carolina, South Carolina, and Georgia
South Western Reporter: (S.W. and S.W.2d)	Texas, Missouri, Arkansas, Kentucky, and Tennessee

For many states (in addition to New York and California), West publishes separate volumes reporting the decisions as they appear in the regional reporters. *Pennsylvania Reporter* and *Texas Cases* are examples of this.

1602   **86 SUPREME COURT REPORTER**   **384 U.S. 436**

384 U.S. 436
Ernesto A. MIRANDA, Petitioner,

v.

STATE OF ARIZONA.

Michael VIGNERA, Petitioner,

v.

STATE OF NEW YORK.

Carl Calvin WESTOVER, Petitioner,

v.

UNITED STATES.

STATE OF CALIFORNIA, Petitioner,

v.

Roy Allen STEWART.

Nos. 759–761, 584.

Argued Feb. 28, March 1 and 2, 1966.

Decided June 13, 1966.

Rehearing Denied No. 584
Oct. 10, 1966.

See 87 S.Ct. 11.

Criminal prosecutions. The Superior Court, Maricopa County, Arizona, rendered judgment, and the Supreme Court of Arizona, 98 Ariz. 18, 401 P.2d 721, affirmed. The Supreme Court, Kings County, New York, rendered judgment, and the Supreme Court, Appellate Division, Second Department, 21 A.D.2d 752, 252 N.Y.S.2d 19, affirmed, as did the Court of Appeals of the State of New York at 15 N.Y.2d 970, 259 N.Y.S.2d 857, 207 N.E.2d 527. The United States District Court for the Northern District of California, Northern Division, rendered judgment, and the United States Court of Appeals for the Ninth Circuit, 342 F.2d 684, affirmed. The Superior Court, Los Angeles County, California, rendered judgment and the Supreme Court of California, 62 Cal.2d 571, 43 Cal. Rptr. 201, 400 P.2d 97, reversed. In the first three cases, defendants obtained certiorari, and the State of California obtained certiorari in the fourth case. The Supreme Court, Mr. Chief Justice Warren, held that statements obtained from defendants during incommunicado interrogation in police-dominated atmosphere, without full warning of constitu-

tional rights, were inadmissible as having been obtained in violation of Fifth Amendment privilege against self-incrimination.

Judgments in first three cases reversed and judgment in fourth case affirmed.

Mr. Justice Harlan, Mr. Justice Stewart, and Mr. Justice White dissented; Mr. Justice Clark dissented in part.

1. Courts ☞397½
Certiorari was granted in cases involving admissibility of defendants' statements to police to explore some facets of problems of applying privilege against self-incrimination to in-custody interrogation and to give concrete constitutional guidelines for law enforcement agencies and courts to follow.

2. Criminal Law ☞393(1), 641.1
Constitutional rights to assistance of counsel and protection against self-incrimination were secured for ages to come and designed to approach immortality as nearly as human institutions can approach it. U.S.C.A.Const. Amends. 5, 6.

3. Criminal Law ☞412.1(4)
Prosecution may not use statements, whether exculpatory or inculpatory, stemming from custodial interrogation of defendant unless it demonstrates use of procedural safeguards effective to secure privilege against self-incrimination. U.S.C.A.Const. Amend. 5.

4. Criminal Law ☞412.1(4)
"Custodial interrogation", within rule limiting admissibility of statements stemming from such interrogation, means questioning initiated by law enforcement officers after person has been taken into custody or otherwise deprived of his freedom of action in any significant way. U.S.C.A.Const. Amend. 5.

See publication Words and Phrases
for other judicial constructions and
definitions.

The following examples of citation forms appear in some of the regional reporters:

- *State v. Hogan,* 480 So.2d 288 (La. 1985). This refers to a 1985 decision of the Louisiana Supreme Court found in volume 480, page 288 of the *Southern Reporter,* second series.
- *State v. Nungesser,* 269 N.W.2d 449 (Iowa 1978). This refers to a 1978 decision of the Iowa Supreme Court found in volume 269, page 449 of the *North Western Reporter,* second series.
- *Henry v. State,* 567 S.W.2d 7 (Tex. Cr. App. 1978). This refers to a 1978 decision of the Texas Court of Criminal appeals found in volume 567, page 7 of the *South Western Reporter,* second series.

A sample page from *Southern Reporter,* second series, is included as Exhibit 5.

SYLLABI, HEADNOTES, AND KEY NUMBERS

The National Reporter System and the regional reporters contain not only the official text of each reported decision but also a brief summary of the decision, called the "syllabus," and one or more topically indexed "headnotes." These headnotes briefly describe the principles of law expounded by the court and are indexed by a series of topic "key numbers." West assigns these key numbers to specific points of decisional law. For instance, decisions dealing with first-degree murder are classified under the topic "homicide" and assigned a key number for each particular aspect of that crime. Thus a homicide case dealing with the intent requirement in first-degree murder may be classified as: "Homicide 🔑 9—Intent and design to effect death." Using this key number system, a researcher can locate headnotes of various appellate decisions on this aspect of homicide and is, in turn, led to relevant decisional law. In addition, each of these volumes contains a table of statutes construed in the cases reported in that volume, with reference to the American Bar Association's Standards for Criminal Justice.

United States Law Week

United States Law Week, published by the Bureau of National Affairs, Inc., Washington, D.C., presents a weekly survey of American law. *Law Week* includes all the latest decisions from the United States Supreme Court as well as significant current decisions from other federal and state courts.

Criminal Law Reporter

Published by the Bureau of National Affairs, Inc., Washington, D.C., the weekly *Criminal Law Reporter* reviews contemporary developments in the criminal law. It is an excellent source of commentaries on current state and federal court decisions in the criminal law area.

288 La.　　　**480 SOUTHERN REPORTER, 2d SERIES**

imprisonment. It is indeed unlikely that the enactment of art. 893.1 was designed to punish more severely those who commit negligent homicide than perpetrators of second degree murder, manslaughter, aggravated battery, etc.

In summary, therefore, we find as regards defendant's second assignment of error that the art. 893.1 enhancement is not constitutionally infirm as cruel, unusual and excessive punishment; that the absence of art. 894.1 sentence articulation in this case was harmless, there existing in this record sufficient factors to support this penalty which is well within the statutory range; that the two year penalty imposed in this case under § 14:95.2 is illegal; that art. 893.1 is applicable to all felonies, including those specially enumerated in § 14:95.2 and that therefore the art. 893.1 enhancement in this case is valid.

Decree

Accordingly, defendant's conviction is affirmed; his sentence is reversed and the case remanded for resentencing in accordance with the views expressed herein and according to law.

CONVICTION AFFIRMED; SENTENCE REVERSED; CASE REMANDED.

DIXON, C.J., and DENNIS, J., concur.

WATSON, J., dissents as to requiring notice.

STATE of Louisiana

v.

Patrick HOGAN.

No. 84–K–1847.

Supreme Court of Louisiana.

Dec. 2, 1985.

Defendant was convicted in the First Judicial District Court, Parish of Caddo, Charles R. Lindsay, J., of aggravated battery, and he appealed. The Court of Appeal, 454 So.2d 1235, affirmed, and defendant's petition for writ of review was granted. The Supreme Court, Calogero, J., held that: (1) sentence enhancement by reason of use of a firearm in commission of a felony was not constitutionally infirm as cruel, unusual and excessive; (2) existence of some mitigating factors did not preclude enhancement; (3) imposition of an additional two-year penalty for use of a gun while attempting commission of a specified felony was impermissible when not preceded by an appropriate notice; and (4) enhancement was not invalid, however, since minimum sentence mandated by use of firearm was applicable to all felonies.

Conviction affirmed, sentence reversed, and case remanded.

Dennis, J., concurred.

Watson, J., dissented as to requiring notice.

1. Criminal Law ⟳1206.1(1), 1213.2(1)

General sentencing enhancement statute [LSA-R.S. 14:34, 14:95; LSA-C.Cr.P. art. 893.1] applicable when a firearm is used in commission of a felony, does not impose cruel, unusual, and excessive punishment and is not constitutionally infirm on its face or as applied. U.S.C.A. Const. Amend. 8.

2. Criminal Law ⟳1213.8(7)

Imposition of mandatory minimum sentence under enhancement statute [LSA-R.S. 14:34, 14:95; LSA-C.Cr.P. art. 893.1]

The Digests

West also publishes Decennial Digests that topically index all the appellate court decisions from the state and federal courts. Digests are tools that enable the researcher to locate cases in point through topics and key numbers. Ten Decennial Digests have been published as of 1991, the most recent being the *Tenth Decennial Digest* (Part 1) that embraces federal and state appellate decisions from 1986–1991. A series of federal digests contains key number headnotes for decisions of the federal courts. The current series published by West is *Federal Practice Digest* 4th. In addition, separate digests are published for most states as well as for the Atlantic, North Western, Pacific, and South Eastern reporters. The index at the beginning of each topic identifies the various points of law by numerically arranged key numbers. In addition to the basic topic of criminal law, many topics in the field of criminal law are listed by specific crimes (e.g., homicide, forgery, bribery). Procedural topics such as arrest and search and seizure are also included. The digests contain a descriptive word index and a table of cases sorted by name, listing the key numbers corresponding to the decisions. Thus the researcher may find, by key number, reference topics that relate to the principles set out in the headnotes prepared for each judicial decision. A researcher who locates a topic and key number has access to all reported decisions on this point of law. Through use of these volumes, a researcher familiar with a case by name may use it to find a direct reference to a point of law. A sample page from the *Texas Digest*, second series, is reprinted as Exhibit 6.

Shepard's Citations

Shepard's Citations is a series published by Shepard's/McGraw-Hill, Inc., of Colorado Springs, Colorado. It provides the judicial history of cases by reference to the volume and page number of the cases in the particular reporters. By using the symbols explained in this work, the researcher can determine whether a particular decision has been affirmed, followed, distinguished, modified, or reversed by subsequent court decisions. Most attorneys "Shepardize" the cases they cite in their law briefs to support various principles of law. There is a separate set of *Shepard's Citations* for the United States Supreme Court reports, the federal appellate and district courts, for each regional reporter, and for each state that has an official reporter.

SECONDARY LEGAL SOURCES

Legal authorities other than constitutions, statutes, ordinances, regulations, and court decisions are called "secondary sources," yet they are essential tools in legal research. A basic necessity for any legal researcher's work is a good law dictionary. Several are published, and *Black's Law Dictionary*® (6th ed.) is one of the best known. *Black's* is available both in print and computer disk media. Beyond dictionaries, the most common secondary legal authorities are legal

For references to other topics, see Descriptive-Word Index

was observed in act of smoking a marihuana cigarette, for violation of narcotics laws, was legal. Code Cr.Proc.Tex.1925, arts. 212, 215; 26 U.S.C.A. §§ 2557(b) (1), 2593(a).

Rent v. U. S., 209 F.2d 893.

D.C.Tex. 1975. Arrest and subsequent detention of husband plaintiff by deputies without warrant was not unlawful where husband plaintiff appeared to be intoxicated in public place. 28 U.S.C.A. § 1343; 42 U.S.C.A. §§ 1983, 1985; U.S.C.A.Const. Amend. 4; Vernon's Ann.Tex.C.C.P. art. 14.01.

Lamb v. Cartwright, 393 F.Supp. 1081, affirmed 524 F.2d 238.

D.C.Tex. 1972. The "presence" of the officer, under Texas statute providing that a police officer may arrest an offender without a warrant for any offense committed in his "presence" or within his view, is satisfied if the violation occurs within reach of the officer's senses. Vernon's Ann.Tex.C.C.P. art. 14.01(b).

Taylor v. McDonald, 346 F.Supp. 390.

D.C.Tex. 1967. It is not the case that officer may arrest person committing felony in his presence irrespective of whose privacy officer must violate in order to place commission of felony in his presence.

Gonzales v. Beto, 266 F.Supp. 751, affirmed State of Tex. v. Gonzales, 388 F.2d 145.

Tex.Cr.App. 1981. Observation by police officer of the exchange of money between defendant and another person for tinfoil bindles coupled with officer's knowledge that heroin is normally packaged in tinfoil bindles was sufficient to provide probable cause to believe that an offense had been committed and, thus, defendant's warrantless arrest was valid under statute which allows peace officer to arrest an offender without a warrant "for any offense committed in his presence or within his view." Vernon's Ann.C.C.P. art. 14.01(b).

Boyd v. State, 621 S.W.2d 616.

Tex.Cr.App. 1981. Where defendant was observed in supermarket placing a steak and bottle of bath oil in her purse and observed leaving the store without paying for such items and was apprehended and placed in custody of city police officer who had been summoned by the manager, defendant's arrest was lawful. Vernon's Ann.C.C.P. art. 18.16.

Stewart v. State, 611 S.W.2d 434.

Tex.Cr.App. 1980. Peace officer need not determine whether material in question is in fact obscene in order to make a valid arrest for offense of commercially distributing obscene material; warrantless arrest is proper if there is probable cause to believe the publication commercially distributed in officer's pres-

ence or within his view was obscene. Vernon's Ann.C.C.P. art. 14.01(b); V.T.C.A., Penal Code § 43.21(1).

Carlock v. State, 609 S.W.2d 787.

Tex.Cr.App. 1980. Fact that defendants were in possession of a stolen gun several hours prior to their arrest was not a sufficient basis for the officers' conclusion that defendants were committing an offense within their presence so as to justify a warrantless arrest.

Green v. State, 594 S.W.2d 72.

Tex.Cr.App. 1979. Defendant had no reasonable expectation of privacy while sitting in a restaurant, so that, upon observing drug transaction in plain view from public vantage point outside the restaurant and recognizing it as offense, officers were authorized to make warrantless arrest. Vernon's Ann.C.C.P. art. 14.01.

Hamilton v. State, 590 S.W.2d 503.

Tex.Cr.App. 1979. Where defendants' vehicle was not stopped by any overt action on the part of off-duty police officers, who simply turned around and began to follow defendants' vehicle after spotting it traveling in the opposite direction and noting that defendants appeared to be smoking a marihuana cigarette, where it was only after defendants stopped at a traffic light that one officer was able to approach the vehicle and then noticed the odor of marihuana, and where it was at that point that the officer directed defendants to pull over to the side of the street and get out of their car, the arrest and subsequent search were reasonable under the circumstances. Vernon's Ann.C.C.P. art. 14.01(b).

Isam v. State, 582 S.W.2d 441.

Tex.Cr.App. 1979. Although detective did not view any of the reading matter of the magazine before making warrantless arrest of seller, the magazine's front and back covers, depicting an act of fellatio on a nude male and an act of cunnilingus on a nude female, gave the officer sufficient probable cause to reasonably believe that a violation of the obscenity statute had occurred in his presence and within his view justifying a warrantless arrest. V.T.C.A., Penal Code § 43.21(1); Vernon's Ann.C.C.P. art. 14.01(b).

Price v. State, 579 S.W.2d 492.

Tex.Cr.App. 1979. Though the scope of an investigation cannot exceed the purposes which justify initiating the investigation, if, while questioning a motorist regarding the operation of his vehicle, an officer sees evidence of a criminal violation in open view or in some other manner acquires probable cause with respect to a more serious charge, the officer may arrest for that offense and, incident thereto, conduct an additional search for physical evidence. Vernon's Ann.Civ.St. art.

see Vernon's Annotated Texas Statutes

EXHIBIT 6 Texas Digest 2d Source: Reprinted with permission from West's Texas Digest 2d, Vol. 6, Page 155. Copyright © 1982 By West Publishing Co., 1-800-328-9352.

encyclopedias. These are arranged alphabetically by subject and are used much like any standard encyclopedia.

There are two principal national encyclopedias of the law: *Corpus Juris Secundum* (C.J.S.), published by West, and *American Jurisprudence,* second edition (Am.Jur.2d), published by Lawyers Cooperative Publishing Company of Rochester, New York. A sample page from C.J.S. appears as Exhibit 7. Appellate courts frequently document propositions of law contained in their opinions by citations to these encyclopedias, as well as to cases in the reporters. Each of these encyclopedias is an excellent set of reference books; one significant difference is that the West publication cites more court decisions, while the Lawyers Cooperative publication limits its footnote references to the leading cases pertinent to the principles of law in the text. *Corpus Juris Secundum* includes valuable cross-references to West topic key numbers and other secondary sources, including forms. *American Jurisprudence 2d* includes valuable footnote references to another of the company's publications, *American Law Reports,* now in its fourth series. These volumes (cited as A.L.R.) include annotations to the decisional law on selected topics. For example, a 1987 annotation from A.L.R. entitled "Snowmobile Operation as D.W.I. or D.U.I." appears in 56 A.L.R. 4th 1092.

Both *Corpus Juris Secundum* and *American Jurisprudence 2d* are supplemented annually by cumulative pocket parts and are exceptionally well indexed. They serve as an excellent starting point for a researcher, because they provide a general overview of topics. For example, a person researching the defenses available to a defendant charged with forgery would find a good discussion of the law in this area in either of these encyclopedias. A citation to the text on defenses to forgery found in *Corpus Juris Secundum* would read: 37 C.J.S. Forgery § 41; in *American Jurisprudence 2d* it would read: 36 Am. Jur. 2d Forgery § 42.

In addition to these major national encyclopedias, some states have encyclopedias for the jurisprudence of their state, for example, *Pennsylvania Law Encyclopedia* and *Texas Jurisprudence.* Like the volumes of *Corpus Juris Secundum* and *American Jurisprudence 2d,* most encyclopedias of state law are annually supplemented with cumulative pocket parts.

Textbooks and other treatises on legal subjects often read much like encyclopedias. However, most address specific subjects in great depth. Two of the better known textbooks on law are Wharton's *Criminal Evidence,* published by Lawyers Cooperative; and LaFave and Scott, *Substantive Criminal Law,* published by West.

In addition, many leading law schools publish law reviews that contain articles, commentaries, and notes by academics, judges, lawyers, and law students who exhaustively research topics. A recent law review article in the criminal justice field, "Running Rampant: The Imposition of Sanctions and the Use of Force Against Fleeing Criminal Suspects," 80 Geo. L.J. 2175 (August 1992), refers to a scholarly article published in volume 80 at page 2175 of the Georgetown Law Journal.

An example of a professional publication is the *Criminal Law Bulletin,* published bimonthly by Warren, Gorham and Lamont, Inc. of Boston, Massachusetts. It contains many valuable articles of contemporary interest. For instance, "Stop and Frisk: The Triumph of Law Enforcement Over Private Rights" was published in the January–February 1988 issue. The American Bar Association and most state bar associations publish numerous professional articles in their religious beliefs.[38] The burden falls on prison officials to prove that the food available to a religious inmate is consistent with his dietary laws and provides adequate nourishment.[39] Thus, a prisoner who strictly adheres to Jewish dietary laws may be entitled to prepare his own meals during the Passover holiday,[40] and Muslim inmates may be entitled to a diet that provides them with adequate nourishment without requiring them to eat pork.[41]

However, where Muslim inmates are able to practice their religion conscientiously and still receive a sufficiently nutritious diet, the prison is not obligated to provide them with a special diet.[42]

Prison authorities are not required to supply a prisoner with a special religious diet where the prisoner's beliefs are not religious in nature.[43]

§ 95. Religious Names

Although under some authorities prisoners lose the right to change their names for religious purposes, other authorities generally preclude a categorical refusal to accord legal recognition to religious names adopted by incarcerated persons.

Library References

Prisons ☞4(14).

Although it has been held that a common-law name change, even for religious purposes, is among the rights that inmates lose as inconsistent with their status as prisoners,[44] it has also been held that a state's categorical refusal to accord legal recognition to religious names adopted by incarcerated persons is not reasonably and substantially justified by considerations of prison discipline and order.[45]

Thus, the inmates' free exercise of religion may be burdened by prison officials who continue for all purposes to use the names under which the inmates were committed,[46] and it may be unlawful for the state to refuse to deliver mail addressed to the prisoner under his legal religious name.[47]

On the other hand, inmates are not entitled to have prison officials use their new names for all purposes.[48] For example, correctional authorities generally do not have to reorganize institutional records to reflect prisoners' legally adopted religious names.[49]

E. COMMUNICATIONS AND VISITING RIGHTS AND RESTRICTIONS

§ 96. Communications in General

Prison inmates have a right to communicate with people living in free society, but this right is not unfettered and may be limited by prison officials in order to promote legitimate institutional interests.

Library References

Prisons ☞4(5, 6).

Prison inmates have a constitutional right to communicate with people living in free society.[50] However, this right is not absolute, and is subject

---

38. U.S.—Prushinowski v. Hambrick, D.C.N.C., 570 F.Supp. 863.

39. U.S.—Prushinowski v. Hambrick, D.C.N.C., 570 F.Supp. 863.

40. U.S.—Schlesinger v. Carlson, D.C.Pa., 489 F.Supp. 612.

41. U.S.—Masjid Muhammad-D.C.C. v. Keve, D.C.Del., 479 F.Supp. 1311.

42. U.S.—Masjid Muhammad-D.C.C. v. Keve, D.C.Del., 479 F.Supp. 1311.

43. U.S.—Africa v. Commonwealth of Pennsylvania, C.A.Pa., 662 F.2d 1025, certiorari denied 102 S.Ct. 1756, 456 U.S. 908, 72 L.Ed.2d 165.

44. U.S.—Salahuddin v. Coughlin, D.C.N.Y., 591 F.Supp. 353.

45. U.S.—Barrett v. Commonwealth of Virginia, C.A.Va., 689 F.2d 498.

46. U.S.—Masjid Muhammad-D.C.C. v. Keve, D.C.Del., 479 F.Supp. 1311.

47. U.S.—Barrett v. Commonwealth of Virginia, C.A.Va., 689 F.2d 498.

Masjid Muhammad-D.C.C. v. Keve, D.C.Del., 479 F.Supp. 1311.

48. U.S.—Azeez v. Fairman, D.C.Ill., 604 F.Supp. 357—Masjid Muhammad-D.C.C. v. Keve, D.C.Del., 479 F.Supp. 1311.

49. U.S.—Barrett v. Commonwealth of Virginia, C.A.Va., 689 F.2d 498.

Azeez v. Fairman, D.C.Ill., 604 F.Supp. 357.

Failure to follow statutory mechanism

Inmates' constitutional rights were not violated by failure of prison officials to recognize their use of Muslim names in records of department of correctional services, where inmates had not followed statutory mechanism for name change.

U.S.—Salahuddin v. Coughlin, D.C.N.Y., 591 F.Supp. 353.

50. U.S.—Pell v. Procunier, Cal., 94 S.Ct. 2800, 417 U.S. 817, 41 L.Ed.2d 495.

Inmates of Allegheny County Jail v. Wecht, D.C.Pa., 565 F.Supp. 1278.

Friends and relatives

U.S.—Hutchings v. Corum, D.C.Mo., 501 F.Supp. 1276.

501

EXHIBIT 7 Corpus Juris Secundum Source: Reprinted with permission from Corpus Juris Secundum, Vol. 72, Prisons § 96, Pg. 501. Copyright © 1987 By West Publishing Co., 1-800-328-9352.

journals and reports. Some of these present contemporary views on the administration of justice.

The *Index to Legal Periodicals,* published by H. W. Wilson Company of the Bronx, New York, indexes articles from leading legal publications by subject and author. This valuable research tool is found in many law libraries and is kept current by periodic supplements.

Words and Phrases, another West publication, consists of numerous volumes alphabetically arranged in dictionary form. Hundreds of thousands of legal terms are defined with citations to appellate court decisions. The volumes are kept current by annual pocket part supplements. A sample page from *Words and Phrases* is reprinted as Exhibit 8.

Periodicals published by law schools, bar associations, and other professional organizations may be of considerable value both in doing research and in gaining a perspective on many contemporary problems in the criminal justice field. The federal government also publishes numerous studies of value to the criminal justice professional and student.

Computerized Legal Research

WESTLAW® is a computerized legal retrieval system that operates from a central computer system at the West headquarters in St. Paul, Minnesota. Stored there are the data bases for state and federal statutes, appellate decisions, attorney general opinions, and certain legal periodicals. For example, the law review article referred to earlier, "Running Rampant: The Imposition of Sanctions and the Use of Force Against Fleeing Criminal Suspects," 80 Geo. L.J. 2175 (August 1992), is available on WESTLAW in the GEOLJ database, and can be retrieved using the query **ci(80 +5 2175)**. WESTLAW can be accessed through a wide variety of computer equipment, including mainframe terminals, personal computers, and word processors. Subscribers have terminals and printers in their offices and enter queries into the system to begin research. A properly formulated query pinpoints the legal issue to be researched and instructs WESTLAW to retrieve all data relevant to the query.

WESTLAW has available a searching method that uses natural language, called WIN™, that allows queries to be entered in plain English. The statutes, cases, and other research results found on WESTLAW can be printed out on paper or downloaded onto computer disks, allowing the material to be incorporated into word processing documents. Computer-assisted legal research (CALR) is an increasingly useful supplement to traditional methods of legal research.

HOW TO RESEARCH A SPECIFIC POINT OF LAW

The following example demonstrates how a legal researcher might employ the research tools discussed earlier to find the law applicable to a given set of facts. Consider this hypothetical scenario: Mary Jones, a student at a Florida college, filed a complaint accusing Jay Grabbo of taking her purse while she was walking across campus. In her statement to the police, Jones was somewhat vague on whether Grabbo had used any force in taking the purse and whether she had

RESISTANCE

RESISTANCE—Cont'd

Where a contract for the purchase of defendant's stock in plaintiff corporation provided that defendant should not concern himself in the manufacture or sale of resistance or steel armature binding wire, sheet, or strip, such manufactures must be understood as some alloy of copper used in the manufacture of electric apparatus which does not conduct electricity as freely as pure copper, which is the best conductor, and hence is called "resistance, wire, sheet, or strip." Driver-Harris Wire Co. v. Driver, 62 A. 461, 463, 70 N.J.Eq. 34.

Breaking of glass bottles on roadway over which pneumatic-tired trucks, which were loaded with goods being removed from building by United States Marshal under writ of replevin, were required to pass, held criminal contempt of court, since "resistance" as used in contempt statute includes willful purpose and intent to prevent execution of process of court. Russell v. United States, C.C.A.Minn., 86 F.2d 389, 394, 109 A.L.R. 297.

RESIST HORSES, CATTLE AND LIVE STOCK

Under the statute which requires railroad companies to maintain fences sufficient to "resist horses, cattle and live stock," an instruction that a company was required to maintain one sufficient to "turn stock" was not improper; the quoted terms being synonmous. Deal v. St. Louis, I. M. & S. Ry. Co., 129 S.W. 50, 52, 144 Mo.App. 684.

Under Rev.St.1899, § 1105, Mo.St.Ann. § 4761, p. 2144, requiring a railroad company to construct and maintain fences sufficient to prevent stock getting on the track, an instruction in an action under such section for injuries to stock, which defined a lawful fence as one sufficient "to resist horses, cattle, swine, and like stock," was not erroneous for using the phrase "to resist"; such phrase not being as strong as the phrase "to prevent" in the statute. Hax v. Quincy, O. & K. C. R. Co., 100 S.W. 693, 695, 123 Mo.App. 172.

RESISTING AN OFFICER

To constitute the offense of "resisting an officer," under Act March 8, 1831, § 9, it is not necessary that the officer should be assaulted, beaten, or bruised. Woodworth v. State, 26 Ohio St. 196, 200.

RESISTING AN OFFICER—Cont'd

A justice of the peace being a conservator of the peace, under Const. art. 7, § 40, and being, under Crawford & Moses' Dig. § 2906, without authority to make an arrest himself, act of one in resisting an arrest by a justice does not constitute offense of "resisting an officer," in violation of section 2585 et seq. Herdison v. State, 265 S.W. 84, 86, 166 Ark. 33.

"Resist," as used in Code, § 4476, providing for the punishment of any person who shall knowingly and willfully obstruct, resist, or oppose any officer or other person duly authorized in serving or executing any lawful process, imports force. The words "obstruct," "resist," or "oppose" mean the same thing, and the word "oppose" would cover the meaning of the word "resist" or "obstruct." It does not mean to oppose or impede the process with which the officer is armed, or to defeat its execution, but that the officer himself shall be obstructed. Davis v. State, 76 Ga. 721, 722.

RESISTING AN OFFICER IN DISCHARGE OF HIS DUTY

Where police officers investigated defendant's premises to determine whether he was killing sheep or cattle in alleged violation of an ordinance and after failing to discover indications of such killing one of officers informed defendant that he was under arrest and attempted to put upon his hand a wrist chain and defendant resisted such action for three or four minutes and then submitted quietly, defendant's actions did not constitute "resisting an officer in discharge of his duty" since officers had no right to arrest defendant. City of Chicago v. Delich, 1st Dist. No. 20,686, 193 Ill.App. 72.

Where police officers investigated defendant's premises to determine whether he was killing sheep or cattle in alleged violation of an ordinance and after failing to discover indications of such killing one of officers informed defendant that he was under arrest and attempted to put upon his hand a wrist chain and defendant resisted such action for three or four minutes and then submitted quietly, action of wife who took some part in the altercation with the officers did not constitute "resisting an officer in discharge of his duty," since officers had no right to arrest defendant. City of Chicago v. Delich, 1st Dist., No. 20,687, 193 Ill. App. 74.

EXHIBIT 8 Words and Phrases Source: Reprinted with permission from Words and Phrases, Vol. 37, Pg. 612. Copyright © 1992 By West Publishing Co., 1-800-328-9352.

offered any resistance. She stated that she had recently purchased the purse for $59, and that it contained $42 in cash plus a few personal articles of little value. Further inquiry by the police revealed that Grabbo was unarmed and that Jones did try to hold on to the purse, but that Grabbo had yanked it from her.

Under Florida law, theft of Jones's purse would be petit theft if the total value was less than $300. West's Fla. Stat. Ann. § 812.014. This offense is a misdemeanor for which the maximum penalty is sixty days in jail and a $500 fine. West's Fla. Stats. Ann. § 775.082 and § 775.083. Unarmed robbery, on the other hand, is a second-degree felony that subjects the offender to a maximum fifteen years imprisonment and a fine of $10,000. West's Fla. Stats. Ann. § 812.13; § 775.082 & § 775.083. It is therefore very important to determine whether Grabbo should be charged with petit theft or robbery.

A researcher who needs to gain a general background on the offense of robbery and how it differs from theft may profitably consult one of the legal encyclopedias mentioned earlier. Someone with a general knowledge of criminal offenses may still need to review the offense of robbery from the standpoint of state law. If so, *Florida Jurisprudence 2d* or some similar text should be consulted.

Given a general knowledge of the crimes of theft and robbery, a likely starting point would be the state statutes. In this instance reference could be made to the official Florida Statutes. From a research standpoint it might be more productive to locate the statute proscribing robbery in the index to West's *Florida Statutes Annotated* and review the statute and the pertinent annotations in both the principal volume and the pocket part. The researcher would quickly find the offense of robbery defined in Section 812.13 and would then proceed to references noted under the topics of "force" and "resistance" following the text of the statute. These topics would identify pertinent Florida appellate decisions on these points. For example, the researcher would find a headnote to *Mims v. State*, 342 So.2d 116 (Fla. App. 1977), indicating that purse snatching is not robbery if no more force is used than is necessary to physically remove the property from a person who does not resist. If the victim does resist and that resistance is overcome by the force of the perpetrator, however, the crime of robbery is complete. Another reference points the researcher to *Goldsmith v. State*, 573 So.2d 445 (Fla. App. 1991), which held that the slight force used in snatching a $10 bill from a person's hand without touching the person was insufficient to constitute the crime of robbery, and instead constituted the crime of petit theft. Additional decisions refer to these and related points of law.

After locating these and other pertinent references, the researcher should go to the *Southern Reporter 2d* and read the located cases. After concluding the search, the researcher should "Shepardize" the decisions to determine if they have been subsequently commented on, distinguished, or even reversed.

The steps outlined here are basic and are designed to illustrate only the most rudimentary principles of gaining access to the criminal law on a particular subject. As previously indicated, another method may involve the use of digests with the key number system of research. Moreover, there will often be issues of interest still undecided by courts in a particular state. If so, then research into the statutes and court decisions of other states may be undertaken. Often the methodology and level of research pursued depend on the researcher's objective, knowledge of the subject and experience in conducting legal research.

Conclusion

An understanding of how to gain access to the primary and secondary sources of the criminal law is tremendously important. Nevertheless, familiarity with these resources and the basic methodology of legal research does not equate with the professional skill of the lawyer. Unlike the hypothetical scenario given earlier, many legal problems involve extremely complex factual and legal situations. Only persons professionally trained in the law can analyze the facts, discern the key issues, locate the relevant authorities, and make the critical legal judgments routinely called for in the administration of the criminal justice system.

THE CONSTITUTION OF THE UNITED STATES OF AMERICA

We the People of the United States, in Order to form a more perfect Union, establish Justice, insure domestic Tranquility, provide for the common defence, promote the general Welfare, and secure the Blessings of Liberty to ourselves and our Posterity, do ordain and establish this Constitution for the United States of America.

ARTICLE I

Section 1 All legislative Powers herein granted shall be vested in a Congress of the United States, which shall consist of a Senate and House of Representatives.
Section 2 (1) The House of Representatives shall be composed of Members chosen every second Year by the People of the several States, and the Electors in each State shall have the Qualifications requisite for Electors of the most numerous Branch of the State Legislature.

(2) No Person shall be a Representative who shall not have attained to the age of twenty-five Years, and been seven Years a Citizen of the United States, and who shall not, when elected, be an Inhabitant of that State in which he shall be chosen.

(3) Representatives and direct Taxes shall be apportioned among the several States which may be included within this Union, according to their respective Numbers, which shall be determined by adding to the whole Number of free Persons, including those bound to Service for a Term of Years, and excluding Indians not taxed, three fifths of all other Persons. The actual Enumeration shall be made within three Years after the first Meeting of the Congress of the United States, and within every subsequent Term of ten Years, in such Manner as they shall by Law direct. The Number of Representatives shall not exceed one for every thirty Thousand, but each State shall have at Least one Representative; and until such enumeration shall be made, the State of New Hampshire shall be entitled to chuse three, Massachusetts eight, Rhode Island and Providence Plantations one, Connecticut five, New York six, New Jersey four, Pennsylvania eight, Delaware one, Maryland six, Virginia ten, North Carolina five, South Carolina five, and Georgia three.

(4) When vacancies happen in the Representation from any State, the Executive Authority thereof shall issue Writs of Election to fill such Vacancies.

(5) The House of Representatives shall chuse their Speaker and other Officers; and shall have the sole Power of Impeachment.

Section 3 (1) The Senate of the United States shall be composed of two Senators from each State, chosen by the Legislature thereof, for six Years; and each Senator shall have one Vote.

(2) Immediately after they shall be assembled in Consequence of the first Election, they shall be divided as equally as may be into three Classes. The Seats of the Senators of the first Class shall be vacated at the Expiration of the second Year, of the second Class at the Expiration of the fourth Year, and of the third Class at the Expiration of the sixth Year, so that one third may be chosen every second Year; and if Vacancies happen by Resignation, or otherwise, during the Recess of the Legislature of any State, the Executive thereof may make temporary Appointments until the next Meeting of the Legislature, which shall then fill such Vacancies.

(3) No Person shall be a Senator who shall not have attained, to the Age of thirty Years, and been nine Years a Citizen of the United States, and who shall not, when elected, be an Inhabitant of that State for which he shall be chosen.

(4) The Vice President of the United States shall be President of the Senate, but shall have no Vote, unless they be equally divided.

(5) The Senate shall chuse their other Officers, and also a President pro tempore, in the Absence of the Vice President, or when he shall exercise the Office of the President of the United States.

(6) The Senate shall have the sole Power to try all Impeachments. When sitting for that Purpose, they shall be on Oath or Affirmation. When the President of the United States is tried, the Chief Justice shall preside: And no Person shall be convicted without the Concurrence of two thirds of the Members present.

(7) Judgment in Cases of Impeachment shall not extend further than to removal from Office, and disqualification to hold and enjoy any Office of honor, Trust or Profit under the United States: but the Party convicted shall nevertheless be liable and subject to Indictment, Trial, Judgment and Punishment, according to Law.

Section 4 (1) The Times, Places and Manner of holding Elections for Senators and Representatives, shall be prescribed in each State by the Legislature thereof; but the Congress may at any time by Law make or alter such Regulations, except as to the Places of chusing Senators.

(2) The Congress shall assemble at least once in every Year, and such Meeting shall be on the first Monday in December, unless they shall by Law appoint a different Day.

Section 5 (1) Each House shall be the Judge of the Elections, Returns and Qualifications of its own Members, and a Majority of each shall constitute a Quorum to do Business; but a smaller Number may adjourn from day to day, and may be authorized to compel the Attendance of absent Members, in such Manner, and under such Penalties as each House may provide.

(2) Each House may determine the Rules of its Proceedings, punish its Members for disorderly Behaviour, and, with the Concurrence of two thirds, expel a Member.

(3) Each House shall keep a Journal of its Proceedings, and from time to time publish the same, excepting such Parts as may in their Judgment require Secrecy; and the Yeas and Nays of the Members of either House on any question shall, at the Desire of one fifth of those Present, be entered on the Journal.

(4) Neither House, during the Session of Congress, shall, without the Consent of the other, adjourn for more than three days, nor to any other Place than that in which the two Houses shall be sitting.

Section 6 (1) The Senators and Representatives shall receive a Compensation for their Services, to be ascertained by Law, and paid out of the Treasury of the United States. They shall in all Cases, except Treason, Felony and Breach of the Peace, be privileged from Arrest during their Attendance at the Session of their respective Houses, and in going to and returning from the same; and for any Speech or Debate in either House, they shall not be questioned in any other Place.

(2) No Senator or Representative shall, during the Time for which he was elected, be appointed to any civil Office under the Authority of the United States, which shall have been created, or the Emoluments whereof shall have been increased during such time; and no Person holding any Office under the United States, shall be a Member of either House during his Continuance in Office.

Section 7 (1) All Bills for raising Revenue shall originate in the House of Representatives; but the Senate may propose or concur with Amendments as on other Bills.

(2) Every Bill which shall have passed the House of Representatives and the Senate, shall, before it become a Law, be presented to the President of the United States; If he approve he shall sign it, but if not he shall return it, with his Objections to that House in which it shall have originated, who shall enter the Objections at large on their Journal, and proceed to reconsider it. If after such Reconsideration two thirds of that House shall agree to pass the Bill, it shall be sent, together with the Objections, to the other House, by which it shall likewise be reconsidered, and if approved by two thirds of that House, it shall become a Law. But in all such Cases the Votes of both Houses shall be determined by Yeas and Nays, and the Names of the Persons voting for and against the Bill shall be entered on the Journal of each House respectively. If any Bill shall not be returned by the President within ten Days (Sunday excepted) after it shall have been presented to him, the Same shall be a Law, in like Manner as if he had signed it, unless the Congress by their Adjournment prevent its Return, in which Case it shall not be a Law.

(3) Every Order, Resolution, or Vote to which the Concurrence of the Senate and House of Representatives may be necessary (except on a question of Adjournment) shall be presented to the President of the United States; and before the Same shall take Effect, shall be approved by him, or being disapproved by him, shall be repassed by two thirds of the Senate and House of Representatives, according to the Rules and Limitations prescribed in the Case of a Bill.

Section 8 (1) The Congress shall have Power To lay and collect Taxes, Duties, Imposts and Excises, to pay the Debts and provide for the common Defence and general Welfare of the United States; but all Duties, Imposts and Excises shall be uniform throughout the United States;

(2) To borrow Money on the credit of the United States;

(3) To regulate Commerce with foreign Nations, and among the several States, and with the Indian Tribes;

(4) To establish an uniform Rule of Naturalization, and uniform Laws on the subject of Bankruptcies throughout the United States;

(5) To coin Money, regulate the Value thereof, and of foreign Coin, and to fix the Standard of Weights and Measures;

(6) To provide for the Punishment of counterfeiting the Securities and current Coin of the United States;

(7) To establish Post Offices and post Roads;

(8) To promote the Progress of Science and useful Arts, by securing for limited Times to Authors and Inventors the exclusive Right to their respective Writings and Discoveries;

(9) To constitute Tribunals inferior to the supreme Court;

(10) To define and punish Piracies and Felonies committed on the high Seas, and Offenses against the Law of Nations;

(11) To declare War, grant Letters of Marque and Reprisal, and make Rules concerning Captures on Land and Water;

(12) To raise and support Armies, but no Appropriation of Money to that Use shall be for a longer Term than two Years;

(13) To provide and maintain a Navy;

(14) To make Rules for the Government and Regulation of the land and naval Forces;

(15) To provide for calling forth the Militia to execute the Laws of the Union, suppress Insurrections and repel Invasions;

(16) To provide for organizing, arming, and disciplining, the Militia, and for governing such Part of them as may be employed in the Service of the United States, reserving to the States respectively, the Appointment of the Officers, and the Authority of training the Militia according to the discipline prescribed by Congress;

(17) To exercise exclusive Legislation in all Cases whatsoever, over such District (not exceeding ten Miles square) as may, by Cession of particular States, and the Acceptance of Congress, become the Seat of the Government of the United States, and to exercise like Authority over all Places purchased by the Consent of the Legislature of the State in which the Same shall be, for the Erection of Forts, Magazines, Arsenals, dock-Yards, and other needful Buildings;—And

(18) To make all Laws which shall be necessary and proper for carrying into Execution the foregoing Powers, and all other Powers vested by this Constitution in the Government of the United States, or in any Department or Officer thereof.

Section 9 (1) The Migration or Importation of such Persons as any of the States now existing shall think proper to admit, shall not be prohibited by the Congress prior to the Year one thousand eight hundred and eight, but a Tax or Duty may be imposed on such Importation, not exceeding ten dollars for each Person.

(2) The Privilege of the Writ of Habeas Corpus shall not be suspended unless when in Cases of Rebellion or Invasion the public Safety may require it.

(3) No Bill of Attainder or ex post facto Law shall be passed.

(4) No Capitation, or other direct, Tax shall be laid, unless in Proportion to the Census or Enumeration herein before directed to be taken.

(5) No Tax or Duty shall be laid on Articles exported from any State.

(6) No Preference shall be given by any Regulation of Commerce or Revenue to the Ports of one State over those of another; nor shall Vessels bound to, or from, one State, be obliged to enter, clear or pay Duties in another.

(7) No Money shall be drawn from the Treasury, but in Consequence of Appropriations made by Law; and a regular Statement and Account of the Receipts and Expenditures of all public Money shall be published from time to time.

(8) No Title of Nobility shall be granted by the United States: And no Person holding any Office of Profit or Trust under them, shall, without the Consent of the Congress, accept of any present, Emolument, Office, or Title, of any kind whatever, from any King, Prince or foreign State.

Section 10 (1) No State shall enter into any Treaty, Alliance, or Confederation; grant Letters of Marque and Reprisal; coin Money; emit Bills of Credit; make any Thing but gold and silver Coin a Tender in Payment of Debts; pass any Bill of Attainder, ex post facto Law, or Law impairing the Obligation of Contracts, or grant any Title of Nobility.

(2) No State shall, without the Consent of Congress, lay any Imposts or Duties on Imports or Exports, except what may be absolutely necessary for executing its inspection Laws: and the net Produce of all Duties and Imposts, laid by any State on Imports or Exports, shall be for the Use of the Treasury of the United States; and all such Laws shall be subject to the Revision and Control of the Congress.

(3) No State shall, without the Consent of Congress, lay any Duty of Tonnage, keep Troops, or Ships of War in time of Peace, enter into any Agreement or Compact with another State, or with a foreign Power, or engage in War, unless actually invaded, or in such imminent Danger as will not admit of Delay.

ARTICLE II

Section 1 (1) The executive Power shall be vested in a President of the United States of America. He shall hold his Office during the Term of four Years, and, together with the Vice President, chosen for the same Term, be elected, as follows:

(2) Each State shall appoint, in such Manner as the Legislature thereof may direct, a Number of Electors, equal to the whole Number of Senators and Representatives to which the State may be entitled in the Congress: but no Senator or Representative, or Person holding an Office of Trust or Profit under the United States, shall be appointed an Elector.

The Electors shall meet in their respective States, and vote by Ballot for two Persons, of whom one at least shall not be an Inhabitant of the same State with themselves. And they shall make a List of all the Persons voted for, and of the Number of Votes for each; which List they shall sign and certify, and transmit sealed to the Seat of the Government of the United States, directed to the President of the Senate. The President of the Senate shall, in the presence of the Senate and House of Representatives, open all the Certificates, and the Votes shall then be counted. The Person having the greatest Number of Votes shall be the President, if such Number be a Majority of the whole Number of Electors appointed; and if there be more than one who have such Majority, and have an equal Number of Votes, then the House of Representatives shall immediately chuse by Ballot one of them for President; and if no Person have a Majority, then from the five highest on the List the said House shall in like Manner chuse the

President. But in chusing the President, the Votes shall be taken by States, the Representation from each State having one Vote; a quorum for this Purpose shall consist of a Member or Members from two thirds of the States, and a Majority of all the States shall be necessary to a Choice. In every Case, after the Choice of the President, the Person having the greatest Number of Votes of the Electors shall be the Vice President. But if there should remain two or more who have equal Votes, the Senate shall chuse from them by Ballot the Vice President.

(3) The Congress may determine the Time of chusing the Electors, and the Day on which they shall give their Votes; which Day shall be the same throughout the United States.

(4) No Person except a natural born Citizen, or a Citizen of the United States, at the time of the Adoption of this Constitution, shall be eligible to the Office of President; neither shall any Person be eligible to that Office who shall not have attained to the Age of thirty five Years, and been fourteen Years a Resident within the United States.

(5) In Case of the Removal of the President from Office, or of his Death, Resignation, or Inability to discharge the Powers and Duties of the said Office, the Same shall devolve on the Vice President, and the Congress may by Law provide for the Case of Removal, Death, Resignation or Inability, both of the President and Vice President, declaring what Officer shall then act as President, and such Officer shall act accordingly, until the Disability be removed, or a President shall be elected.

(6) The President shall, at stated Times, receive for his Services, a Compensation, which shall neither be increased nor diminished during the Period for which he shall have been elected, and he shall not receive within that Period any other Emolument from the United States, or any of them.

(7) Before he enter on the Execution of his Office, he shall take the following Oath or Affirmation:—"I do solemnly swear (or affirm) that I will faithfully execute the Office of President of the United States, and will to the best of my Ability, preserve, protect and defend the Constitution of the United States."

Section 2 (1) The President shall be Commander in Chief of the Army and Navy of the United States, and of the Militia of the several States, when called into the actual Service of the United States; he may require the Opinion, in writing, of the principal Officer in each of the executive Departments, upon any Subject relating to the Duties of their respective Offices, and he shall have Power to grant Reprieves and Pardons for Offenses against the United States, except in Cases of Impeachment.

(2) He shall have Power, by and with the Advice and Consent of the Senate, to make Treaties, provided two thirds of the Senators present concur; and he shall nominate, and by and with the Advice and Consent of the Senate, shall appoint Ambassadors, other public Ministers and Consuls, Judges of the supreme Court, and all other Officers of the United States, whose Appointments are not herein otherwise provided for, and which shall be established by Law: but the Congress may by Law vest the Appointment of such inferior Officers, as they think proper, in the President alone, in the Courts of Law, or in the Heads of Departments.

(3) The President shall have Power to fill up all Vacancies that may happen during the Recess of the Senate, by granting Commissions which shall expire at the End of their next Session.

Section 3 He shall from time to time give to the Congress Information of the State of the Union, and recommend to their Consideration such Measures as he shall judge necessary and expedient; he may, on extraordinary Occasions, convene both Houses, or either of them, and in Case of Disagreement between them, with Respect to the Time of Adjournment, he may adjourn them to such Time as he shall think proper; he shall receive Ambassadors and other public Ministers; he shall take Care that the Laws be faithfully executed, and shall Commission all the Officers of the United States.

Section 4 The President, Vice President and all Civil Officers of the United States, shall be removed from Office on Impeachment for, and Conviction of, Treason, Bribery, or other high Crimes and Misdemeanors.

ARTICLE III

Section 1 The judicial Power of the United States, shall be vested in one supreme Court, and in such inferior Courts as the Congress may from time to time ordain and establish. The Judges, both of the supreme and inferior Courts, shall hold their Offices during good Behaviour, and shall, at stated Times, receive for their Services, a Compensation, which shall not be diminished during their Continuance in Office.

Section 2 (1) The judicial Power shall extend to all Cases, in Law and Equity, arising under this Constitution, the Laws of the United States, and Treaties made, or which shall be made, under their Authority;—to all Cases affecting Ambassadors, other public Ministers and Consuls;—to all Cases of admiralty and maritime Jurisdiction;—to Controversies to which the United States shall be a party;—to Controversies between two or more States;—between a State and Citizens of another State;—between Citizens of different States;—between Citizens of the same State claiming Lands under Grants of different States, and between a State, or the Citizens thereof, and foreign States, Citizens or Subjects.

(2) In all Cases affecting Ambassadors, other public Ministers and Consuls, and those in which a State shall be Party, the supreme Court shall have original Jurisdiction. In all the other Cases before mentioned, the supreme Court shall have appellate Jurisdiction, both as to Law and Fact, with such Exceptions, and under such Regulations as the Congress shall make.

(3) The Trial of all Crimes, except in Cases of Impeachment, shall be by Jury; and such Trial shall be held in the State where the said Crimes shall have been committed; but when not committed within any State, the Trial shall be at such Place or Places as the Congress may by Law have directed.

Section 3 (1) Treason against the United States, shall consist only in levying War against them, or in adhering to their Enemies, giving them Aid and Comfort. No Person shall be convicted of Treason unless on the Testimony of two Witnesses to the same overt Act, or on Confession in open Court.

(2) The Congress shall have Power to declare the Punishment of Treason, but no Attainder of Treason shall work Corruption of Blood, or Forfeiture except during the Life of the Person attainted.

ARTICLE IV

Section 1 Full Faith and Credit shall be given in each State to the public Acts, Records, and judicial Proceedings of every other State. And the Congress may by general Laws prescribe the Manner in which such Acts, Records and Proceedings shall be proved, and the Effect thereof.

Section 2 (1) The Citizens of each State shall be entitled to all privileges and Immunities of Citizens in the several States.

(2) A Person charged in any State with Treason, Felony, or other Crime, who shall flee from Justice, and be found in another State, shall on Demand of the executive Authority of the State from which he fled, be delivered up, to be removed to the State having Jurisdiction of the Crime.

(3) No Person held to Service of Labour in one State, under the Laws thereof, escaping into another, shall, in Consequence of any Law or Regulation therein, be discharged from such Service or Labour, but shall be delivered up on Claim of the Party to whom such Service or Labour may be due.

Section 3 (1) New States may be admitted by the Congress into this Union; but no new State shall be formed or erected within the Jurisdiction of any other State; nor any State be formed by the Junction of two or more States, or Parts of States, without the Consent of the Legislatures of the States concerned as well as of the Congress.

(2) The Congress shall have power to dispose of and make all needful Rules and Regulations respecting the Territory or other Property belonging to the United States; and nothing in this Constitution shall be so construed as to Prejudice any Claims of the United States, or of any particular State.

Section 4 The United States shall guarantee to every State in this Union a Republican Form of Government, and shall protect each of them against Invasion; and on Application of the Legislature, or of the Executive (when the Legislature cannot be convened) against domestic Violence.

ARTICLE V

The Congress, whenever two thirds of both Houses shall deem it necessary, shall propose Amendments to this Constitution, or, on the Application of the Legislatures of two thirds of the several States, shall call a Convention for proposing Amendments, which, in either Case, shall be valid to all Intents and Purposes, as Part of this Constitution, when ratified by the Legislatures of three fourths of the several States, or by Conventions in three fourths thereof, as the one or the other Mode of Ratification may be proposed by the Congress; Provided that no Amendment which may be made prior to the Year One thousand eight hundred and eight shall in any Manner affect the first and fourth Clauses in the Ninth Section of the first Article; and that no State, without its Consent, shall be deprived of its equal Suffrage in the Senate.

ARTICLE VI

(1) All Debts contracted and Engagements entered into, before the Adoption of this Constitution, shall be as valid against the United States under this Constitution, as under the Confederation.

(2) This Constitution, and the Laws of the United States which shall be made in Pursuance thereof; and all Treaties made, or which shall be made, under the Authority of the United States, shall be the supreme Law of the Land; and the Judges in every State shall be bound thereby, any Thing in the Constitution or Laws of any State to the Contrary notwithstanding.

(3) The Senators and Representatives before mentioned, and the Members of the several State Legislatures, and all executive and judicial Officers, both of the United States and of the several States, shall be bound by Oath or Affirmation, to support this Constitution; but no religious Test shall ever be required as a Qualification to any Office or public Trust under the United States.

ARTICLE VII

The Ratification of the Conventions of nine States, shall be sufficient for the Establishment of this Constitution between the States so ratifying the Same.

ARTICLES IN ADDITION TO, AND AMENDMENT OF, THE CONSTITUTION OF THE UNITED STATES OF AMERICA, PROPOSED BY CONGRESS, AND RATIFIED BY THE SEVERAL STATES, PURSUANT TO THE FIFTH ARTICLE OF THE ORIGINAL CONSTITUTION

AMENDMENT I (1791)

Congress shall make no law respecting an establishment of religion, or prohibiting the free exercise thereof; or abridging the freedom of speech, or of the press; or the right of the people peaceably to assemble, and to petition the Government for a redress of grievances.

AMENDMENT II (1791)

A well regulated Militia, being necessary to the security of a free state, the right of the people to keep and bear Arms, shall not be infringed.

AMENDMENT III (1791)

No Soldier shall, in time of peace be quartered in any house, without the consent of the Owner, nor in time of war, but in a manner to be prescribed by law.

AMENDMENT IV (1791)

The right of the people to be secure in their persons, houses, papers, and effects, against unreasonable searches and seizures, shall not be violated, and no Warrants shall issue, but upon probable cause, supported by Oath or affirmation, and particularly describing the place to be searched, and the persons or things to be seized.

AMENDMENT V (1791)

No person shall be held to answer for a capital, or otherwise infamous crime, unless on a presentment or indictment of a Grand Jury, except in cases arising in the land or naval forces, or in the Militia, when in actual service in time of War or public danger; nor shall any person be subject for the same offence to be twice put in jeopardy of life or limb; nor shall be compelled in any criminal case to be a witness against himself, nor be deprived of life, liberty, or property, without due process of law; nor shall private property be taken for public use, without just compensation.

AMENDMENT VI (1791)

In all criminal prosecutions, the accused shall enjoy the right to a speedy and public trial, by an impartial jury of the State and district wherein the crime shall have been committed, which district shall have been previously ascertained by law, and to be informed of the nature and cause of the accusation; to be confronted with the witnesses against him; to have compulsory process for obtaining witnesses in his favor, and to have the Assistance of Counsel for his defence.

AMENDMENT VII (1791)

In Suits at common law, where the value in controversy shall exceed twenty dollars, the right of trial by jury shall be preserved, and no fact tried by a jury, shall be otherwise re-examined in any Court of the United States, than according to the rules of the common law.

AMENDMENT VIII (1791)

Excessive bail shall not be required, nor excessive fines imposed, nor cruel and unusual punishments inflicted.

AMENDMENT IX (1791)

The enumeration in the Constitution, of certain rights, shall not be construed to deny or disparage others retained by the people.

AMENDMENT X (1791)

The powers not delegated to the United States by the Constitution, nor prohibited by it to the States, are reserved to the States respectively, or to the people.

AMENDMENT XI (1798)

The Judicial power of the United States shall not be construed to extend to any suit in law or equity, commenced or prosecuted against one of the United States by Citizens of another State, or by Citizens or Subjects of any Foreign State.

AMENDMENT XII (1804)

The Electors shall meet in their respective states and vote by ballot for President and Vice-President, one of whom, at least, shall not be an inhabitant of the same state with themselves; they shall name in their ballots the person voted for as President, and in distinct ballots the person voted for as Vice-President, and they shall make distinct lists of all persons voted for as President, and of all persons voted for as Vice-President, and of the number of votes for each, which lists they shall sign and certify, and transmit sealed to the seat of the government of the United States, directed to the President of the Senate;—The President of the Senate shall, in the presence of the Senate and House of Representatives, open all the certificates and the votes shall then be counted;—The person having the greatest number of votes for President, shall be the President, if such number be a majority of the whole number of Electors appointed; and if no person have such majority, then from the persons having the highest numbers not exceeding three on the list of those voted for as President, the House of Representatives shall choose immediately, by ballot, the President. But in choosing the President, the votes shall be taken by states, the representation from each state having one vote; a quorum for this purpose shall consist of a member or members from two-thirds of the states, and a majority of all the states shall be necessary to a choice. And if the House of Representatives shall not choose a President whenever the right of choice shall devolve upon them, before the fourth day of March next following, then the Vice-President shall act as President, as in the case of the death or other constitutional disability of the President—The person having the greatest number of votes as Vice-President, shall be the Vice-President, if such number be a majority of the whole number of Electors appointed, and if no person have a majority, then from the two highest numbers on the list, the Senate shall choose the Vice-President; A quorum for the purpose shall consist of two-thirds of the whole number of Senators, and a majority of the whole number shall be necessary to a choice. But no person constitutionally ineligible to the office of President shall be eligible to that of Vice-President of the United States.

AMENDMENT XIII (1865)

Section 1 Neither slavery nor involuntary servitude, except as a punishment for crime whereof the party shall have been duly convicted, shall exist within the United States, or any place subject to their jurisdiction.
Section 2 Congress shall have power to enforce this article by appropriate legislation.

AMENDMENT XIV (1868)

Section 1 All persons born or naturalized in the United States and subject to the jurisdiction thereof, are citizens of the United States and of the State wherein they reside. No State shall make or enforce any law which shall abridge the privileges or immunities of citizens of the United States; nor shall any State deprive any person of life, liberty, or property, without due process of law; nor deny to any person within its jurisdiction the equal protection of the laws.
Section 2 Representatives shall be apportioned among the several States according to their respective numbers, counting the whole number of persons in each State, excluding Indians not taxed. But when the right to vote at any election for the choice of electors for President and Vice-President of the United States, Representatives in Congress, the Executive and Judicial officers of a State, or the

members of the Legislature thereof, is denied to any of the male inhabitants of such State, being twenty-one years of age, and citizens of the United States, or in any way abridged, except for participation in rebellion, or other crime, the basis of representation therein shall be reduced in the proportion which the number of such male citizens shall bear to the whole number of male citizens twenty-one years of age in such State.

Section 3 No person shall be a Senator or Representative in Congress, or elector of President and Vice-President, or hold any office, civil or military, under the United States, or under any State, who, having previously taken an oath, as a member of Congress, or as an officer of the United States, or as a member of any State legislature, or as an executive or judicial officer of any State, to support the Constitution of the United States, shall have engaged in insurrection or rebellion against the same, or given aid or comfort to the enemies thereof. But Congress may by a vote of two-thirds of each House, remove such disability.

Section 4 The validity of the public debt of the United States, authorized by law, including debts incurred for payment of pensions and bounties for services in suppressing insurrection or rebellion, shall not be questioned. But neither the United States nor any State shall assume or pay any debt or obligation incurred in aid of insurrection or rebellion against the United States, or any claim for the loss or emancipation of any slave; but all such debts, obligations and claims shall be held illegal and void.

Section 5 The Congress shall have power to enforce, by appropriate legislation, the provisions of this article.

AMENDMENT XV (1870)

Section 1 The right of citizens of the United States to vote shall not be denied or abridged by the United States or by any State on account of race, color, or previous condition of servitude.

Section 2 The Congress shall have power to enforce this article by appropriate legislation.

AMENDMENT XVI (1913)

The Congress shall have power to lay and collect taxes on incomes, from whatever source derived, without apportionment among the several States, and without regard to any census or enumeration.

AMENDMENT XVII (1913)

The Senate of the United States shall be composed of two Senators from each State, elected by the people thereof, for six years; and each Senator shall have one vote. The electors in each State shall have the qualifications requisite for electors of the most numerous branch of the State legislatures.

When vacancies happen in the representation of any State in the Senate, the executive authority of such State shall issue writs of election to fill such vacancies: *Provided,* That the legislature of any State may empower the executive thereof to make temporary appointments until the people fill the vacancies by election as the legislature may direct.

This amendment shall not be so construed as to affect the election or term of any Senator chosen before it becomes valid as part of the Constitution.

AMENDMENT XVIII (1919)

Section 1 After one year from the ratification of this article the manufacture, sale, or transportation of intoxicating liquors within, the importation thereof into, or the exportation thereof from the United States and all territory subject to the jurisdiction thereof for beverage purposes is hereby prohibited.

Section 2 The Congress and the several States shall have concurrent power to enforce this article by appropriate legislation.

Section 3 This article shall be inoperative unless it shall have been ratified as an amendment to the Constitution by the legislatures of the several States, as provided in the Constitution, within seven years from the date of the submission hereof to the States by the Congress.

AMENDMENT XIX (1920)

The right of citizens of the United States to vote shall not be denied or abridged by the United States or by any State on account of sex.

Congress shall have power to enforce this article by appropriate legislation.

AMENDMENT XX (1933)

Section 1 The terms of the President and Vice President shall end at noon on the 20th day of January, and the terms of Senators and Representatives at noon on the 3d day of January, of the years in which such terms would have ended if this article had not been ratified; and the terms of their successors shall then begin.

Section 2 The Congress shall assemble at least once in every year, and such meeting shall begin at noon on the 3d day of January, unless they shall by law appoint a different day.

Section 3 If, at the time fixed for the beginning of the term of the President, the President elect shall have died, the Vice President elect shall become President. If a President shall not have been chosen before the time fixed for the beginning of his term, or if the President elect shall have failed to qualify, then the Vice President elect shall act as President until a President shall have qualified; and the Congress may by law provide for the case wherein neither a President elect nor a Vice President elect shall have qualified, declaring who shall then act as President, or the manner in which one who is to act shall be selected, and such person shall act accordingly until a President or Vice President shall have qualified.

Section 4 The Congress may by law provide for the case of the death of any of the persons from whom the House of Representatives may choose a President whenever the right of choice shall have devolved upon them, and for the case of the death of any of the persons from whom the Senate may choose a Vice President whenever the right of choice shall have devolved upon them.

Section 5 Sections 1 and 2 shall take effect on the 15th day of October following the ratification of this article.

Section 6 This article shall be inoperative unless it shall have been ratified as an amendment to the Constitution by the legislatures of three-fourths of the several States within seven years from the date of its submission.

AMENDMENT XXI (1933)

Section 1 The eighteenth article of amendment to the Constitution of the United States is hereby repealed.

Section 2 The transportation or importation into any State, Territory or possession of the United States for delivery or use therein of intoxicating liquors, in violation of the laws thereof, is hereby prohibited.

Section 3 This article shall be inoperative unless it shall have been ratified as an amendment to the Constitution by conventions in the several States, as provided in the Constitution, within seven years from the date of the submission hereof to the States by the Congress.

AMENDMENT XXII (1951)

Section 1 No person shall be elected to the office of the President more than twice, and no person who has held the office of President, or acted as President, for more than two years of a term to which some other person was elected President shall be elected to the office of the President more than once. But this Article shall not apply to any person holding the office of President when this Article was proposed by the Congress, and shall not prevent any person who may be holding the office of President, or acting as President, during the term within which this Article becomes operative from holding the office of President or acting as President during the remainder of such term.

Section 2 This Article shall be inoperative unless it shall have been ratified as an amendment to the Constitution by the legislatures of three-fourths of the several States within seven years from the date of its submission to the States by the Congress.

AMENDMENT XXIII (1961)

Section 1 The District constituting the seat of Government of the United States shall appoint in such manner as the Congress may direct:

A number of electors of President and Vice President equal to the whole number of Senators and Representatives in Congress to which the District would be entitled if it were a State, but in no event more than the least populous State; they shall be in addition to those appointed by the States, but they shall be considered, for the purposes of the election of President and Vice President, to be electors appointed by a State; and they shall meet in the District and perform such duties as provided by the twelfth article of amendment.

Section 2 The Congress shall have power to enforce this article by appropriate legislation.

AMENDMENT XXIV (1964)

Section 1 The right of citizens of the United States to vote in any primary or other election for President or Vice President, for electors for President or Vice

President, or for Senator or Representative in Congress, shall not be denied or abridged by the United States or any State by reason of failure to pay any poll tax or other tax.

Section 2 The Congress shall have power to enforce this article by appropriate legislation.

AMENDMENT XXV (1967)

Section 1 In case of the removal of the President from office or of his death or resignation, the Vice President shall become President.

Section 2 Whenever there is a vacancy in the office of the Vice President, the President shall nominate a Vice President who shall take office upon confirmation by a majority vote of both Houses of Congress.

Section 3 Whenever the President transmits to the President pro tempore of the Senate and the Speaker of the House of Representatives his written declaration that he is unable to discharge the powers and duties of his office, and until he transmits to them a written declaration to the contrary, such powers and duties shall be discharged by the Vice President as Acting President.

Section 4 Whenever the Vice President and a majority of either the principal officers of the executive departments or of such other body as Congress may by law provide, transmit to the President pro tempore of the Senate and the Speaker of the House of Representatives their written declaration that the President is unable to discharge the powers and duties of his office, the Vice President shall immediately assume the powers and duties of the office as Acting President.

Thereafter, when the President transmits to the President pro tempore of the Senate and the Speaker of the House of Representatives his written declaration that no inability exists, he shall resume the powers and duties of his office unless the Vice President and a majority of either the principal officers of the executive department or of such other body as Congress may by law provide, transmit within four days to the President pro tempore of the Senate and the Speaker of the House of Representatives their written declaration that the President is unable to discharge the powers and duties of his office. Thereupon Congress shall decide the issue, assembling within forty-eight hours for that purpose if not in session. If the Congress, within twenty-one days after receipt of the latter written declaration, or, if Congress is not in session, within twenty-one days after Congress is required to assemble, determines by two-thirds vote of both Houses that the President is unable to discharge the powers and duties of his office, the Vice President shall continue to discharge the same as Acting President; otherwise, the President shall resume the powers and duties of his office.

AMENDMENT XXVI (1971)

Section 1 The right of citizens of the United States, who are eighteen years of age or older, to vote shall not be denied or abridged by the United States or by any State on account of age.

Section 2 The Congress shall have power to enforce this article by appropriate legislation.

GLOSSARY

abrogate To annul, destroy, or cancel.

accessory A person who aids in the commission of a crime.

accusatorial system A system of criminal justice where the prosecution bears the burden of proving the guilt of the accused.

actus reus A "wrongful act" that, combined with other necessary elements of crime, constitutes criminal liability.

adjudication The formal decision of a court in a given case.

adultery Voluntary sexual intercourse where at least one of the parties is married to someone other than the sexual partner.

adversary system A system of justice involving conflicting parties where the role of the judge is to remain neutral.

affiant A person who makes an affidavit.

affidavit A written document attesting to specific facts of which the affiant has knowledge, and sworn to by the affiant.

affirm To uphold, ratify, or approve.

affirmative defense Defense to a criminal charge where defendant bears the burden of proof. Examples include automatism, intoxication, coercion, and duress.

aggravating circumstances Factors attending the commission of a crime that make the crime or its consequences worse.

aiding and abetting Assisting in or otherwise facilitating the commission of a crime.

alibi Defense to a criminal charge that places the defendant at some other place than the scene of the crime at the time the crime occurred.

allegation Assertion or claim made by a party to a legal action.

amendment A modification, addition, or deletion.

animus furundi Intent to steal or otherwise deprive an owner of property.

appeal Review by a higher court of a lower court decision.

appellant A person who takes an appeal to a higher court.

appellate jurisdiction The authority of a court to hear appeals from decisions of lower courts.

appellee A person against whom an appeal is taken.

arraignment An appearance before a court of law for the purpose of pleading to a criminal charge.

arrest To take someone into custody or otherwise deprive that person of freedom of movement.

arrestee A person who is arrested.

arson The crime of intentionally burning someone else's house or building—now commonly extended to other property as well.

asportation The carrying away of something: in kidnapping, the carrying away of the victim; in larceny, the carrying away of the victim's property.

assault The attempt or threat to inflict bodily injury upon another person.

asylum Sanctuary; a place of refuge.

attempt An intent to commit a crime coupled with an act taken toward committing the offense.

automatism A set of actions taken during a state of unconsciousness.

bail The conditional release of a person charged with a crime.

battery The unlawful use of force against another person that entails some injury or offensive touching.

bench trial A trial held before a judge without a jury present.

bench warrant An arrest warrant issued by a judge.

best evidence rule To prove the content of a writing, the original document or best facsimile must be produced.

bifurcated trial A capital trial with separate phases for determining guilt and punishment.

bigamy The crime of being married to more than one spouse at the same time.

bill of attainder A legislative act imposing punishment without trial upon persons deemed guilty of treason or felonies. (Prohibited by the U. S. Constitution.)

bona fide "In good faith"; without the attempt to defraud or deceive.

bounty hunter A person paid a fee or commission to capture a defendant who had fled a jurisdiction to escape punishment.

breach of the peace The crime of disturbing the public tranquility and order. A generic term encompassing disorderly conduct, riot, etc.

breaking Forceful, unlawful entry into a building or conveyance.

bribery The crime of offering, giving, requesting, solicitings or receiving something of value to influence a decision of a public official.

brief A document filed by a party to a lawsuit to convince the court of the merits of that party's case.

burden of proof The requirement to introduce evidence to prove an alleged fact or set of facts.

burglary At common law, the crime of breaking and entering a house with the intent to commit a felony therein. Under modern statutes, burglary frequently consists of breaking and entering a structure with the intent to commit any offense therein.

canonical Pertaining to the canons or laws of a church.

capias "That you take." A general term for various court orders requiring that some named person be taken into custody.

capital crime A crime for which death is a permissible punishment.

caption At common law, a taking or seizure.

carnal knowledge Sexual intercourse.

case law Law derived from judicial decisions.

castle doctrine "A man's home is his castle." At common law, the right to use whatever force is necessary to protect one's dwelling and its inhabitants from an unlawful entry or attack.

caveat emptor "Let the buyer beware." Common-law maxim requiring the consumer to judge the quality of a product before making a purchase.

certiorari Writ issued by an appellate court to grant discretionary review of a case decided by a lower court.

challenge for cause Objection to a prospective juror on some specified ground (e.g., a close relationship to a party to the case).

chilling effect A law or policy that discourages persons from exercising their rights.

circumstantial evidence Indirect evidence from which the existence of certain facts may be inferred.

civil action A lawsuit brought to enforce private rights and to remedy violations thereof.

clear and present danger doctrine In constitutional law, the doctrine that the First Amendment does not protect those forms of expression that pose a clear and present danger of bringing about some substantive evil that government has a right to prevent.

clemency A grant of mercy by an executive official commuting a sentence or pardoning a criminal.

code A systematic collection of laws.

collateral attack The attempt to defeat the outcome of a judicial proceeding by challenging it in a different proceeding or court.

common law A body of law that develops through judicial decisions, as distinct from legislative enactments. Originally developed by English courts of law.

community control A sentence imposed on a person found guilty of a crime that requires that the offender be placed in an individualized program of noninstitutional confinement.

community service A sentence requiring that the criminal perform some specific service to the community for some specified period of time.

commutation A form of clemency that lessens the punishment for a person convicted of a crime.

competency The state of being legally fit to give testimony or stand trial.

compounding a crime The crime of receiving something of value in exchange for an agreement not to file a criminal complaint.

compurgation A method of trial used before the thirteenth century whereby a person charged with a crime could be absolved by swearing to innocence and producing a number of other persons willing to swear that they believed the accused's declaration of innocence.

concurring opinion Opinion handed down by a judge that supports the judgment of the court but often based on different reasoning.

confidential informant (C.I.) An informant known to the police but whose identity is held in confidence.

consanguinity Kinship; the state of being related by blood.

consent Voluntarily yielding to the will or desire of another person.

conspiracy The crime of two or more persons agreeing or planning to commit a crime. The crime of conspiracy is distinct from the crime contemplated by the conspirators (the "target crime").

construction Interpretation

constructive breaking Where the law implies a breaking. For example, a person who gains entry into someone's house through fraud or deception may be said to have made a constructive breaking.

constructive possession Being in the position to effectively control something, even if it is not actually in one's possession.

contemnor A person found to be in contempt of court.

contempt of court Any action that embarrasses, hinders, obstructs, or is calculated to lessen the dignity of a court of law.

continuance Delay of a judicial proceeding on the motion of one of the parties.

contraband Any property that is inherently illegal to produce or possess.

controlled substance A drug designated by law as contraband.

conversion The unlawful assumption of the rights of ownership to someone else's property.

corporal punishment Punishment that inflicts pain or injury to a person's body.

corpus delicti "The body of the crime." The material thing upon which a crime has been committed (e.g., a burned-out building in a case of arson).

corroboration Evidence that strengthens evidence already given.

counsel A lawyer who represents a party.

counterfeiting The crime of producing or passing imitations, usually false money or other evidence of value (e.g., stamps or securities).

criminal Pertaining to crime; a person convicted of a crime.

criminal intent A necessary element of a crime—the evil intent associated with the commission of a crime.

criminal negligence A failure to exercise the degree of caution or care necessary to avoid being charged with a crime.

criminal procedure The rules of law governing the procedures by which crimes are investigated, prosecuted, adjudicated, and punished.

criminal syndicalism The crime of advocating violence as a means to accomplish political change.

criminology The study of the nature of, causes of, and means of dealing with crime.

culpability Guilt.

curtilage At common law, the enclosed space surrounding a dwelling house; in modern codes, this space has been extended to encompass other buildings.

deadly force The degree of force that may result in the death of the person against whom the force is applied.

death-qualified jury A trial jury composed of persons who do not entertain scruples against imposing a death sentence.

de facto "In fact"; as a matter of fact.

defendant A person charged with a crime or against whom a civil action has been initiated.

defense A defendant's stated reasons of law or fact as to why thed prosecution or plaintiff should not prevail.

definite sentence Criminal penalty set by law with no discretion for the judge or correctional officials to individualize punishment.

de jure "In law"; as a matter of law.

de minimis "Minimal."

demurrer A document challenging the legal sufficiency of a complaint or indictment.

deposition The recorded sworn testimony of a witness; not given in open court.

depraved mind A serious moral deficiency; the highest level of malice.

detention Holding someone in custody.

determinate sentence Variation on definite sentencing whereby a judge fixes the term of incarceration within statutory limits.

deterrence Prevention of criminal activity by punishing criminals so that others will not engage in such activity.

dicta Statements contained in a judicial opinion that are not essential to the resolution of the case and do not become legal precedents.

discretion The power of public officials to act in certain situations according to their own judgment rather than relying on set rules or procedures.

discretionary review Form of appellate court review of lower court decisions that is not mandatory but occurs at the discretion of the appellate court. *See also* certiorari.

dismissal A judicial order terminating a case.

disorderly conduct Illegal behavior that disturbs the public peace or order.

disposition The final settlement of a case.

dissenting opinion An opinion rendered by a judge disavowing or attacking the decision of a collegial court.

docket The set of cases pending before a court of law.

double jeopardy The condition of being tried twice for the same criminal offense.

drug courier profile A set of characteristics thought to typify persons engaged in drug smuggling.

DUBAL Driving with an unlawful blood alcohol level.

due process Procedural and substantive rights of citizens against government actions that threaten the denial of life, liberty, or property.

DUI The crime of driving under the influence of alcohol or drugs.

duress The use of illegal confinement or threats of harm to coerce someone to do something he or she would not do otherwise.

Durham test A test for determining insanity developed by the United States Court of Appeals for the District of Columbia Circuit in the case of Durham v. United States (1954). Under this test, a person is not criminally responsible for an unlawful act if it was the product of a mental disease or defect.

duty An obligation that a person has by law or contract.

DWI The crime of driving while intoxicated.

ecclesiastical Pertaining to religious laws or institutions.

embezzlement The crime of using a position of trust or authority to transfer or convert the money or property of another to oneself.

en banc "In the bench." Refers to a session of a court, usually an appellate court, in which all judges assigned to the court participate.

entrapment The act of government agents in inducing someone to commit a crime that the person otherwise would not be disposed to commit.

escape Unlawfully fleeing to avoid arrest or confinement.

evidence Testimony, writings, or material objects offered in proof of an alleged fact or proposition.

evidentiary Pertaining to the rules of evidence or the evidence in a particular case.

exclusionary rule Judicial doctrine forbidding the use of evidence in a criminal trial where the evidence was obtained in violation of the defendant's constitutional rights.

exculpatory Tending to exonerate a person of allegations of wrongdoing.

exigent circumstances Situations that demand unusual or immediate action.

ex parte Refers to a proceeding in which only one party is involved or represented.

expert witness A witness called to testify to knowledge of technical matters based on particular training.

ex post facto **law** A retroactive law that criminalizes actions that were innocent at the time they were taken or increases punishment for a criminal act after it was committed.

extortion The crime of obtaining money or property by threats of force or the inducement of fear.

extradition The surrender of a person by one jurisdiction to another for the purpose of criminal prosecution.

false arrest The tort or crime of unlawfully restraining a person.

false imprisonment *See* false arrest.

false pretenses The crime of obtaining money or property through misrepresentation.

felony A serious crime for which a person may be imprisoned for more than one year.

felony murder A homicide committed during the course of committing another felony (e.g., armed robbery).

"fighting words" doctrine The First Amendment doctrine that holds that certain utterances are not constitutionally protected as free speech if they are inherently likely to provoke a violent response from the audience.

flogging Whipping with a lash as a form of corporal punishment.

forfeiture Sacrifice of ownership or some right (usually property) as a penalty.

forgery The crime of making a false written instrument or materially altering a written instrument (e.g., a check, promissory note, or college transcript) with the intent to defraud.

fornication Sexual intercourse between unmarried persons; an offense in some jurisdictions.

fraud Intentional deception or distortion in order to gain something of value.

fundamental error In a judicial proceeding, an error that affects the substantial rights of the accused or is an affront to the integrity of the court.

gambling Operating or playing a game for money in the hope of gaining more than the amount played.

general intent The state of mind to do something prohibited by law without necessarily intending to accomplish the harm that results from the illegal act.

general warrant A search or arrest warrant that is not particular as to the person to be arrested or the property to be seized.

good-time credit Credit toward early release from prison based on good behavior during confinement (often referred to as "gain time").

graft Fraudulent acquisition of public funds for personal gain by a public official.

grand jury A group of citizens convened either to conduct an investigation or to determine if there is sufficient evidence to warrant prosecution of an accused.

habeas corpus "You have the body." A judicial writ requiring that a party be brought before a court. The primary function of *habeas corpus* is to release a person from unlawful confinement.

habitation Residence or dwelling place.

habitual offender statute A law that imposes an additional punishment on a criminal who has previously been convicted of crimes.

harmless error doctrine The doctrine that minor or harmless errors during a trial do not require reversal of the judgment by an appellate court.

hearing A proceeding, usually less formal than a trial, held to determine definite issues of fact or law.

hearsay evidence Statements made by someone other than a witness offered in evidence at a trial or hearing to prove the truth of the matter asserted. Normally inadmissible as evidence, but this is subject to exceptions.

holding The legal principle drawn from a judicial decision.

homicide The killing of a human being.

hot pursuit The right of police to cross jurisdictional lines to apprehend a suspect or criminal; also refers to Fourth Amendment doctrine allowing warrantless searches and arrests where police pursue a fleeing suspect into a protected area.

"hung jury" A trial jury unable to reach a verdict.

hypothetical question A question based on an assumed set of facts. Hypothetical questions may be asked of expert witnesses in criminal trials.

illegitimacy Condition of a child being born out of wedlock.

immunity Exemption from civil suit or prosecution. *See also* use immunity and transactional immunity.

impeachment A legislative act bringing a charge against a public official that, if proven in a legislative trial, will cause his or her removal from public office; impugning the credibility of a witness by introducing contradictory evidence or proving his or her bad character.

in camera In a judge's chambers.

incapacitation Making it impossible for someone to do something.

incapacity An inability, legal or actual, to act.

incarceration Imprisonment.

incest Sexual intercourse with a close blood relative or, in some cases, a person related by affinity.

inchoate offenses Offenses preparatory to committing other crimes. Inchoate offenses include attempt, conspiracy, and solicitation.

incite To provoke or set in motion.

inciting a riot The crime of instigating or provoking a riot.

inculpatory Tending to incriminate.

indefinite sentence Form of criminal sentencing whereby a judge imposes a term of incarceration within statutory parameters, and corrections offi-cials determine actual time served through parole or other means.

indeterminate sentence Form of criminal sentencing where criminals are sentenced to prison for indeterminate periods until corrections officials determine that rehabilitation has been accomplished.

index crimes Offenses included in the F.B.I. Uniform Crime Reports: willful homicide, forcible rape, robbery, burglary, aggravated assault, grand larceny, and motor vehicle theft.

indictment A formal document handed down by a grand jury accusing one or more persons of the commission of a crime or crimes.

indigent Poor; unable to afford legal representation.

infancy The condition of being below the age of legal majority.

in forma pauperis "In the manner of a pauper." Waiver of filing costs and other fees associated with judicial proceedings to allow an indigent person to proceed.

information A document filed by a prosecutor charging one or more persons with commission of crime.

infra "Below."

initial appearance After arrest, the first appearance of the accused before a judge or magistrate.

injunction A court order prohibiting someone from doing some specified act or commanding someone to undo some wrong or injury.

in loco parentis "In the place of the parents."

inmate One who is confined in a jail or prison.

in re "In the matter of."

insanity A degree of mental illness that negates the legal capacity or responsibility of the affected person.

insanity defense A defense that seeks to exonerate the accused by showing that he or she was insane and thus not legally responsible.

intangible property Property with no tangible value, such as bonds, promissory notes, and stock certificates.

intent A state of mind in which a person seeks to accomplish a given result through a course of action.

inter alia "Among other things."

interrogation Questioning of a suspect by police or questioning of a witness by counsel.

interrogatories Written questions put to a witness.

intoxication Condition in which a person has impaired physical and/or mental capacities due to ingestion of drugs or alcohol.

invalidate Annul, negate, set aside.

ipso facto "By the mere fact"; by the fact itself.

irresistible impulse A desire that cannot be resisted due to impairment of the will by mental disease.

joinder   Coupling two or more criminal prosecutions.

joyriding   The temporary taking of an automobile without intent to permanently deprive the owner of same.

judgment   The final and official decision of a court of law in a given case.

judicial review   The power of courts of law to review governmental acts and declare them null and void if they are found to be unconstitutional.

jurisdiction   The authority of a court to hear and decide certain categories of legal disputes. Jurisdiction relates to the authority of a court over the person, subject matter, and geographical area.

jurist   A person who is skilled or well versed in the law; term often applied to lawyers and judges.

jury   A group of citizens convened for the purpose of deciding factual questions relevant to a civil or criminal case.

justifiable homicide   Killing another in self-defense or defense of others when there is serious danger of death or great bodily harm to self or others, or when authorized by law.

juvenile   A person who has not yet attained the age of legal majority.

juvenile delinquency   Condition of a juvenile who has violated criminal laws.

kidnapping   The forcible abduction and carrying away of a person against that person's will.

kinship   Relationship by blood.

larceny   The unlawful taking of property with the intent of permanently depriving the owner of same.

legislation   Law enacted by a lawmaking body.

legislature   A lawmaking body such as the Congress of the United States or a state assembly.

lex non scripta   "The unwritten law" or common law.

libel   The tort of defamation through published writing or pictures.

loitering   Standing around idly, "hanging around."

magistrate   A judge with minor or limited authority.

Magna Charta   The "Great Charter" signed by King John in 1215 guaranteeing the legal rights of English subjects. Generally considered the foundation of Anglo-American constitutionalism.

mala in se   "Evil in itself." Refers to crimes like murder that are universally condemned.

mala prohibita   "Prohibited evil." Refers to crimes that are wrong primarily because the law declares them to be wrong.

malice aforethought   The mental predetermination to commit an illegal act.

malicious mischief   The crime of willful destruction of the personal property of another.

mandate   A command or order.

manslaughter   The crime of unlawful killing of another person without malice.

material   Important, relevant, necessary.

mayhem   At common law, the crime of injuring someone so as to render that person less able to fight.

mens rea   "Guilty mind," criminal intent.

Miranda **warning**   Based on the Supreme Court's decision in *Miranda v. Arizona* (1967), this warning is given by police to individuals who are taken into custody before they are interrogated. The warning informs persons in custody that they have the right to remain silent and to have a lawyer present during questioning, and that anything they say can and will be used against them in a court of law.

miscarriage of justice   Decision of a court that is inconsistent with the substantial rights of a party to the case.

misdemeanor   A minor offense usually punishable by fine or imprisonment for less than one year.

misprision of felony   The crime of concealing a felony committed by another.

misrepresentation   An untrue statement of fact made to deceive or mislead.

mistake of fact   Unconscious ignorance of a fact or belief in the existence of something that does not exist.

mistake of law   An erroneous opinion of legal principles applied to a set of facts.

mitigation   Reduction or alleviation, usually of punishment.

M'Naghten Rule   A classic test of criminal responsibility. Under this test, a person is not criminally responsible for an act if at the time of commission he or she was laboring under such a defect of reason or disease of the mind so as not to know the nature of the act or, if he or she did know the nature of the act, did not know it was wrong.

monogamy   Having only one spouse, as distinct from bigamy or polygamy.

moot   A point that no longer has any practical significance; academic.

motion   An application to a court of law for the purpose of obtaining some particular order or ruling.

murder   The unlawful killing of a person by another, with malice aforethought or premeditation.

necessity   A condition that compels or requires a certain course of action.

negligence The failure to exercise ordinary care or caution.

nolo contendere "I will not contest it." A plea to a criminal charge that, although it is not an admission of guilt, generally has the same effect as a plea of guilty.

notary public A person empowered by law to administer oaths, to certify things as true, and to perform various minor official acts.

nuisance An unlawful or unreasonable use of a person's property that results in an injury to another or to the public.

nullen crimen, nulla poena, sine lege "There is no crime, there is no punishment, without law."

obiter dicta *See* dicta.

obscenity Sexually oriented material that is patently offensive, appeals to a prurient or unnatural interest in sex, and lacks serious scientific, artistic, or literary content.

obstruction of justice The crime of impeding or preventing law enforcement or the administration of justice.

omission The failure to do what the law requires a person to do.

opinion of the court The opinion summarizing the views of the majority of judges participating in a judicial decision.

oral argument Verbal presentation made to an appellate court in an attempt to persuade the court to affirm, reverse, or modify a lower court decision.

ordinance An enactment of a local governing body such as a city council or commission.

organized crime Syndicates involved in racketeering and other criminal activities.

original jurisdiction The authority of a court of law to hear a case in the first instance.

overbreadth doctrine First Amendment doctrine that holds that a law is invalid if it can be applied to punish people for engaging in constitutionally protected expression.

overrule To reverse or annul by subsequent action.

panel A set of jurors or judges assigned to hear a case.

pardon An executive action that mitigates or sets aside punishment for a crime.

parens patriae "The parent of the country." Refers to the role of the state as guardian of minors or other legally disabled persons.

parole Conditional release from jail or prison of a person who has served part of his or her sentence.

penal Of or pertaining to punishment.

penitentiary A prison.

penology The study or practice of prison management.

per curiam "By the court." A phrase used to distinguish an opinion rendered by the whole court rather than by an individual judge.

perjury The crime of lying under oath, as in a court of law.

per se "By itself"; in itself.

petition A formal written request addressed to a court of law.

petitioner A person who brings a petition before a court of law.

petit jury A trial jury, usually composed of either six or twelve persons.

petty (petit) offenses Minor crimes for which fines or short jail terms are the only prescribed modes of punishment.

Pinkerton **Rule** Rule enunciated by the Supreme Court in *Pinkerton v. United States* (1946) holding that a member of a conspiracy is liable for all offenses committed in furtherance of the conspiracy.

PKPA The Parental Kidnapping Prevention Act, designed to prevent "child snatching" by noncustodial parents.

plaintiff A person who initiates a civil suit.

plea bargain An agreement between a defendant and a prosecutor whereby the defendant agrees to plead guilty in exchange for some concession (e.g., a reduction in the number of charges brought).

plurality opinion An opinion of an appellate court that is joined by more judges than have joined any concurring opinion, although not by a majority of judges in the court.

PMS Premenstrual syndrome.

police power The power of government to legislate to protect public health, safety, welfare, and morality.

polygamy Plural marriage; having more than one spouse.

pornography Material that appeals to the sexual impulse or appetite.

postconviction relief Term applied to various mechanisms a defendant may use to challenge a conviction after other routes of appeal have been exhausted.

precedent A judicial decision cited as authority controlling or influencing the outcome of a similar case.

prejudicial error An error at trial that substantially affects the interests of the accused.

preliminary hearing A hearing held to determine whether there is sufficient evidence to hold an accused for trial.

premeditation Deliberate decision or plan to commit a crime.

preponderance of evidence Evidence that has greater weight than countervailing evidence.

presentence investigation An investigation held before sentencing a convicted criminal to aid the court in determining the appropriate punishment.

presentence report A report containing the results of a presentence investigation.

presumption An assumption of a fact not yet proven.

presumption of innocence In a criminal trial, the accused is presumed innocent until proven guilty.

presumption of validity In constitutional law, a statute is generally presumed to be valid until it is demonstrated otherwise.

pretrial motion A request for a ruling or order before the commencement of a trial.

preventive detention Holding a suspect in custody before trial to prevent escape or other wrongdoing.

prima facie "On its face"; at first glance.

principal A perpetrator of, or aider and abettor in, the commission of a crime (as distinguished from an accessory).

probable cause A reasonable ground for belief in certain alleged facts.

probation Conditional release of a convicted criminal in lieu of incarceration.

probative Tending to prove the truth or falsehood of a proposition.

pro bono "For the good." Performing service without compensation.

procedural due process Set of procedures designed to ensure fairness in a judicial or administrative proceeding.

procedural law The law regulating governmental procedure (e.g., rules of criminal procedure).

profanity Irreverence toward sacred things.

proscribe To forbid; prohibit.

pro se On one's own behalf.

prosecution Initiation and conduct of a criminal case.

prosecutor Official empowered to initiate and conduct criminal charges.

prosecutrix A female prosecutor; a female victim who makes a criminal complaint.

pro se **defense** Representing oneself in a criminal case.

prostitution The act of selling sexual favors.

proximate cause The cause that is nearest a given effect in a causal relationship.

prurient interest An excessive or unnatural interest in sex.

public defender An official responsible for defending indigent persons charged with crimes.

public law General classification of law consisting of constitutional law, administrative law, international law, and criminal law.

quash To vacate or annul.

rape shield law A law that protects the identity of a rape victim or prevents disclosure of a victim's sexual history.

real property Land and buildings permanently attached thereto.

reasonable doubt The doubt that a reasonable person might entertain in regard to the veracity of a proposition after hearing the evidence.

reasonable suspicion A reasonable person's suspicion that criminal activity is afoot.

recidivism Repeating criminal activity.

recognizance An obligation to appear in a court of law at a given time.

recusal A decision of a judge to withdraw from a given case, usually because of bias or personal interest.

regulation A rule or order prescribed by controlling authority.

rehabilitation Restoring someone or something to its former status.

relevant evidence Evidence tending to prove or disprove an alleged fact.

remand To send back.

remedy The means by which a right is enforced or a wrong is redressed.

repeal A legislative act removing a law from the statute books.

resisting arrest The crime of obstructing or opposing a police officer making an arrest.

res judicata "Things judged." Matters already decided by courts, not subject to relitigation.

respondent A person asked to respond to a lawsuit or writ.

restitution The act of compensating someone for losses suffered.

retribution Something demanded as payment.

retroactive Referring to things past.

reverse To set aside a decision on appeal.

revocation The withdrawal of some right or power (e.g., the revocation of parole).

riot A public disturbance involving acts of violence, usually by three or more persons.

robbery The crime of taking money or property from a person against that person's will by means of force.

rout At common law, disturbance of the peace similar to riot but without carrying out the intended purpose.

rule of four   U.S. Supreme Court rule whereby the Court grants *certiorari* only on the agreement of at least four justices.

sanction   Penalty or other mechanism of enforcement.

seduction   The common-law crime of inducing a woman of previously chaste character to have sexual intercourse outside of wedlock on the promise of marriage.

self-defense   The protection of one's person against an attack.

self-representation   *See* pro se defense.

sentence   The official pronouncement of punishment in a criminal case.

severance   Separation of cases so that they can be tried separately.

sexual assault   *See* sexual battery.

sexual battery   In modern statutes, the unlawful oral, anal, or vaginal penetration by or union with the sexual organ of another.

sheriff   The chief law enforcement officer of the county.

skip tracer   A person who tracks down alleged offenders who have fled to avoid prosecution.

slander   The tort of defaming someone's character through verbal statements.

sodomy   Oral or anal sex between persons, or sex between a person and an animal (the latter commonly referred to as bestiality).

solicitation   The inchoate offense of requesting or encouraging someone to engage in illegal conduct.

specific intent   The mental purpose to accomplish a specific act prohibited by law.

stare decisis   The doctrine of deciding cases based on precedent.

statute   A law enacted by a legislature.

statute of limitations   A law proscribing prosecutions for specific crimes after specified periods of time.

stay   A court order suspending proceedings or the enforcement of an order.

stay of execution   A court order suspending the enforcement of a judgment of a lower court.

stop-and-frisk   An encounter between a police officer and a suspect during which the latter is temporarily detained and subjected to a "pat-down" search for weapons.

strict liability   A category of offenses that do not require the proof of criminal intent to obtain a conviction.

subornation of perjury   The crime of procuring someone to lie under oath.

subpoena   A judicial order to appear at a certain place and time to give testimony.

substantive due process   Doctrine that due process clauses of the Fifth and Fourteenth Amendments to the United States Constitution require legislation to be fair and reasonable in content as well as application.

substantive law   That part of the law that creates rights and proscribes wrongs.

suicide   The intentional taking of a person's own life.

summary justice   Trial held by court of limited jurisdiction without benefit of a jury.

suppression doctrine   *See* exclusionary rule.

supra   "Above."

surety bond   A sum of money or property that is posted or guaranteed by a party to ensure the future court appearance of another person.

sustain   To uphold.

tangible property   Property that has physical form and substance and value in itself.

Terry-stop   *See* stop-and-frisk.

testimony   Evidence given by a witness who has been sworn to tell the truth.

time, place, and manner doctrine   First Amendment doctrine holding that government may impose reasonable limitations on the time, place, and manner of expressive activities.

tort   A wrong or injury other than a breach of contract for which the remedy is a civil suit for damages.

transactional immunity   A grant of immunity applying to offenses that a witness's testimony relates to.

transcript   A written record of a trial or hearing.

transferred intent   Doctrine holding that if A intends to injure B but instead injures C, then A's intent to injure B supplies the requisite intent to injure C.

treason   The crime of attempting by overt acts to overthrow the government, or of betraying the government to a foreign power.

trespass   An unlawful interference with one's person or property.

trial   A judicial proceeding held for the purpose of making factual and legal determinations.

trial *de novo*   "A new trial." Refers to trial court review of convictions for minor offenses by courts of limited jurisdiction by conducting a new trial instead of merely reviewing the record of the initial trial.

tribunal   A court of law.

true bill   An indictment handed down by a grand jury.

trustee   A person entrusted to handle the affairs of another.

"trusty"   A prisoner entrusted with authority to supervise other prisoners in exchange for certain privileges and status.

UCMJ   The Uniform Code of Military Justice, adopted by the U.S. Congress.

UCR   The Uniform Crime Reports, compiled by the Federal Bureau of Investigation.

ultra vires   Beyond the scope of a prescribed authority.

use immunity   A grant of immunity that forbids prosecutors from using immunized testimony as evidence in criminal prosecutions.

uttering a forged instrument   The crime of passing a false or worthless instrument, such as a check, with the intent to defraud or injure the recipient.

vacate   To annul, set aside, or rescind.

vagrancy   The offense of going about without any visible means of support.

vandalism   The willful destruction of the property of another person.

vehicular homicide   Homicide resulting from the unlawful and negligent operation of a motor vehicle.

venire   The group of citizens from whom a jury is chosen in a given case.

venue   The location of a trial or hearing.

verdict   The formal decision rendered by a jury in a civil or criminal trial.

vice   Crimes of immoral conduct, such as prostitution, gambling, and the use of narcotics.

victim   A person who is the object of a crime or tort.

victim impact statement   Statement read into the record during the sentencing phase of a criminal trial to inform the court about the impact of the crime on the victim or victim's family.

victimless crimes   Crimes in which no particular person appears or claims to be injured, such as prostitution or gambling.

void-for-vagueness doctrine   Doctrine of constitutional law holding unconstitutional (as a violation of due process) legislation that fails to clearly inform the person what is required or proscribed.

voir dire   "To speak the truth." The process by which prospective jurors are questioned by counsel and/or the court before being selected to serve on a jury.

waiver   The intentional and voluntary relinquishment of a right, or conduct from which such relinquishment may be inferred.

Wharton's Rule   Named after Francis Wharton, a well-known commentator on criminal law, this rule holds that two people cannot conspire to commit a crime such as adultery, incest, or bigamy inasmuch as these offenses involve only two participants.

writ   An order issued by a court of law requiring the performance of some specific art.

writ of certiorari   *See* certiorari.

writ of error   A writ issued by an appellate court for the purpose of correcting an error revealed in the record of a lower court proceeding.

writ of habeas corpus   *See* habeas corpus.

writ of prohibition   An appellate court order that prevents a lower court from exercising its jurisdiction in a particular case.

writs of assistance   Ancient writs issuing from the Court of Exchequer ordering sheriffs to assist in collecting debts owed the Crown. Prior to the American Revolution, the writs of assistance gave agents of the Crown in the American colonies the unlimited right to search for smuggled goods. In modern practice, judicial orders to put someone in possession of property.

TABLE OF CASES

The principle cases are in *italic* type. Cases cited or discussed are in roman type. References are to pages.

INDEX